CLARIN

Digital Linguistics

Edited by
Andreas Witt

Volume 1

CLARIN

The Infrastructure for Language Resources

Edited by
Darja Fišer and Andreas Witt

DE GRUYTER

ISBN 978-3-11-076734-6
e-ISBN (PDF) 978-3-11-076737-7
e-ISBN (EPUB) 978-3-11-076740-7
ISSN 2751-1278
DOI https://doi.org/10.1515/9783110767377

Library of Congress Control Number: 2022940325

Bibliographic information published by the Deutsche Nationalbibliothek
The Deutsche Nationalbibliothek lists this publication in the Deutsche Nationalbibliografie; detailed bibliographic data are available on the internet at http://dnb.dnb.de.

Cover image: piranka/E+/Getty Images
Typesetting: Integra Software Services Pvt. Ltd.
Printing and binding: CPI books GmbH, Leck

www.degruyter.com

Preface

During the first decade of its existence, the CLARIN research infrastructure for language resources and technology has made great strides in creating and maintaining an infrastructure to support the sharing, use and sustainability of language data and tools for research in the humanities and social sciences. It has grown into a network of 25 member and observer third-party countries with 70 CLARIN centres, over 900,000 records in its repositories and an immeasurable number of contributors, users, and trainers. As CLARIN transitions from the phase of conception and development to the phase of stable growth, CLARIN's explicit and implicit institutional memory is invaluable not only for all types of the current and future members of CLARIN's network but also for the educational institutions, funding bodies, policy makers, and fellow research infrastructures. While CLARIN's achievements have been individually documented in numerous workshop, conference and journal articles, they have never been collected and presented in a comprehensive, single volume, which was the main motivation behind the call for contributions for this book.

Our primary aim was to offer a volume that will be useful for researchers and lecturers in various fields of humanities and social science, such as linguistics, digital humanities, literary studies, history, media studies, communication studies, and political science. Moreover, as CLARIN is one of the first ERICs set up by the European Commission, we also wanted to make it relevant for everyone interested in EU Research and Development policy. In November 2020 we published a call for contributions documenting CLARIN's organization and its members, its goals and its functioning, the tools and resources hosted by the CLARIN infrastructure as well as prominent use cases and success stories. The response has far exceeded our expectations, with 31 submissions by 109 authors from all corners of the CLARIN network, which were then carefully reviewed by the editors. The process, which was completed in September 2022, resulted in an impressive volume of ca. 800 pages that is organized into 4 parts: Introduction to CLARIN, CLARIN Technical infrastructure, CLARIN Knowledge infrastructure and Research driven by CLARIN. We are especially proud that we are able to present a rich body of work that not only describes how CLARIN is built and what it offers but also hear directly from the researchers with highly diverse profiles and research interests whose work has benefitted from the infrastructure.

The editors would like to thank everyone who has contributed to the success of this volume, which, because of the Covid-19 pandemic, required extra flexibility and dedication: the authors of the chapters for their inspiring contributions, the technical editors for copyediting and CLARIN ERIC for their support

https://doi.org/10.1515/9783110767377-202

with making the book openly accessible. In particular, the editors would like to thank Paweł Kamocki for his support throughout the editing process, and Jennifer Ecker, whose role in handling the communication with the authors and with the publisher cannot be overestimated. The editors accept full responsibility for all mistakes and shortcomings in this volume.

Darja Fišer & Andreas Witt

Contents

Part I: **CLARIN: An Introduction of the ERIC**

Steven Krauwer and Bente Maegaard

CLARIN – How It Started

Abstract: This chapter describes the genesis of CLARIN, from the point of departure in the growing understanding of language resources as important building blocks, through the European political agreement that research infrastructures are essential for the European Research Area, and finally focussing on the actual creation of CLARIN as a language research infrastructure, serving communities that deal with language data.

Keywords: CLARIN, research infrastructure, ESFRI Roadmap, language resources, humanities, social sciences

1 Introduction

In this chapter we give a brief overview of the history of the CLARIN infrastructure. When looking back on the start of CLARIN we noted the degree to which CLARIN was born out of a consensus on the importance of language in the communication age, not least due to the fast development of technology. The European Commission (EC) faced a vast task with regard to the technology required for producing texts and translations between the official languages, so it is not surprising that they proved visionary by asking a small specialist group to propose a policy for this area. The Danzin report *Towards a European Language Infrastructure* (Danzin 1992) is in many ways the starting point in Europe for politically acknowledging language resources as important, and even for using the term *infrastructure*.

Ten years later ESFRI was established, and this led to a call for proposals that resulted in the creation of CLARIN, which was not always an easy process as ideas emerging from several communities had to be aligned. When agreement was found on making a joint proposal, CLARIN succeeded in being part of the first ESFRI Roadmap in 2006. This was the starting point of CLARIN as we know it, and in the following years the basic structure and the basic elements of the CLARIN infrastructure were developed, as described in Section 4 (the CLARIN Preparatory Phase) and Section 5 (the transition to CLARIN ERIC).

Steven Krauwer, Utrecht Institute of Linguistics UiL OTS, Utrecht University, Utrecht, the Netherlands, e-mail: s.krauwer@uu.nl
Bente Maegaard, Centre for Language Technology, Department of Nordic Languages and Linguistics, University of Copenhagen, Copenhagen, Denmark, e-mail: bmaegaard@hum.ku.dk

https://doi.org/10.1515/9783110767377-001

It should be noted that the description that follows is our personal account of the events, concentrating on the parts where the authors, Steven Krauwer and Bente Maegaard, had special responsibilities.

2 Language resources as a concept

Almost as long as computers have existed, they have been used for language matters – machine translation was one of the first applications envisaged. Very early on corpus building was developed as a discipline. The Brown Corpus (Francis and Kucera 1967) and its successors were meant to provide a description of a language; at that time they were not seen as resources for building applications, and they were also quite small compared to corpora being created these days.

Through the development of computers and computers' ability to treat language, the interest in building corpora, lexica, grammars, and so on has grown. Lexica, taggers, and grammars were used for the analysis of language (at that time rule-based). However, with the continued development of computer power and storage, a growing need for larger collections of language data emerged towards the end of the 1980s and the beginning of the 1990s. The terms *linguistic resources* and *language resources* for these collections started to be used. At the EACL 1991 conference Antonio Zampolli (Università degli Studi di Pisa) gave an invited paper titled *Towards reusable linguistic resources* (Zampolli 1991). Through the intensified development and use of language/linguistic resources there also grew a clearly defined focus on the importance of reusability, standards, and so on. It became evident that language resources were a treasure, needed not only for research, but also for the up-and-coming language industry, and for Europe as a whole.

In this section we briefly describe the efforts of the European Commission as shown by the commissioning of the Danzin report and in general through the LRE (Linguistic Research and Engineering) programme 1990–1994, as well as parallel activities emerging from DARPA in the USA.

2.1 Activities at the European Commission

In 1991 the European Commission asked André Danzin and a small specialist group to examine the handling of Community languages in the fast-developing communication age. We quote here from the summary:

> For many years now the Commission has been carrying out work on the languages used in the Community. In September 1991 it commissioned a Study Group of outside experts to prepare a review of the current position regarding the automatic handling of mother tongues and to suggest a policy for the future.

In the report, *Towards a European Language Infrastructure*, also called the Danzin report, the authors point to three forces that are changing the use of languages: (1) the transition from a locally-focused industrial age to an age of communication, knowledge and intelligence, (2) the impact of the new concepts and products spawned by technological advance amounting to millions of new words, (3) the impact of the new information technologies. Therefore, the authors strongly recommend that the European Commission invest in languages by funding general tools and investigations, and leaving the actual development of language resources for the European languages to the members themselves.

The European Commission was running the LRE (Linguistic Research and Engineering) programme[1] during these years (1990–1994) with support for many projects, for example, the project RELATOR[2] (1993–1995) coordinated by Antonio Zampolli was supported (Zampolli, Calzolari, and Palmer 1994). The objectives of RELATOR were as follows:

> The language industries of the future will rely heavily on the availability of large-scale language resources e.g., corpora, speech databases, dictionaries, linguistic descriptions – together with appropriate standards and methodologies. Ready access to harmonised databases of language data and rules would not only provide a direct benefit to research and development efforts across a wide range of private and public organisations, but would also foster fruitful academic and industrial co-operation. The project aims to define a broad organisational framework for the creation of the language resources for both written and spoken language engineering (LRs in short) which are necessary for the development of an adequate language technology and industry in Europe, and to determine the feasibility of creating a co-ordinated European network of repositories which would perform the function of storing, disseminating and maintaining such resources. This activity is intended to contribute towards the long-term goal of making large scale LRs widely available to European organisations involved in R&D and educational activities.

The RELATOR project had as its goal to investigate the possibilities for creating an organisation for the collaboration on the creation, storage, dissemination, and maintenance, that is, it was a clear preparation for establishing the European Language Resources Association.

1 https://cordis.europa.eu/programme/id/FP3-LRE
2 https://cordis.europa.eu/project/id/LRE62056

2.2 The Linguistic Data Consortium and the European Language Resources Association

The Linguistic Data Consortium (LDC)[3] at University of Pennsylvania was established in 1992. The LDC website records that

> 1992: The University of Pennsylvania is chosen as the host site for LDC in response to a call for proposals issued by DARPA; the mission of the new consortium is to operate as a specialized data publisher and archive guaranteeing widespread, long-term availability of language resources. DARPA provides seed money with the stipulation that LDC become self-sustaining within five years.

In their call for proposals, DARPA asked for "linguistic data", not yet using the term "language resources", but the aim was obvious. And LDC was self-sustaining in less than five years.

The European Language Resources Association (ELRA)[4] was established in 1995. ELRA is a non-profit organisation whose main mission is making Language Resources (LRs) for Human Language Technologies (HLT) available to the community at large. Here "the community at large" refers to research as well as industry, that is, the same audience as LDC. Both associations work as brokers for distribution of language resources for a fee.

As we can see, both ELRA and LDC were created based on the need for language resources. This necessity came from the market, as well as from the development in society as described by the Danzin report.

Just after the RELATOR project, the TELRI[5] (Trans European Language Resources Infrastructure, 1995–2000) projects were funded by the EC. TELRI's goals were not too different from those of ELRA, and a few project partners were the same, but TELRI had a special focus on the Central and Eastern European (CEE) countries and in particular CEE countries that were not members of the EU at the time. The funding came from the COPERNICUS programme, whose aim was precisely to reach out to CEE countries. In addition, projects like PAROLE (on textual and lexical resources and tools, 1994–1997) (Zampolli 1997; Calzolari and Zampolli 1999) and many more were supported by the EC.

All these projects and activities meant that there was a very active community in Europe, whose members wanted to contribute to the building of a language infrastructure as suggested by the Danzin report. The concept of language

3 https://www.ldc.upenn.edu/

4 http://www.elra.info/en/

5 http://telri.nytud.hu/

resources was a well-known concept, and the infrastructure concept was mentioned, for example, by RELATOR.

3 Creation of the European Strategy Forum on Research Infrastructures (ESFRI)

The European Strategy Forum on Research Infrastructures[6] was established in 2002, with the purpose of supporting a coherent approach to policymaking on research infrastructures in Europe. Research infrastructures were becoming important instruments to support research in all areas, and there was an obvious need for European countries to collaborate on the construction and further development of research infrastructures, as well as to agree on which research infrastructures would be important for European (and international) research. Consequently, the task for ESFRI would be to monitor the development and needs of research, to prepare a strategy, and to follow it up. ESFRI Delegates represent ministers responsible for research in their country.

3.1 The ESFRI Roadmap

In 2004, ESFRI was asked to develop "a European roadmap for the construction of the next generation of large-scale Research Infrastructures" in close collaboration with the European Commission. The roadmap was published in 2006 (ESFRI 2006b), and contained 35 accepted proposals for research infrastructures, six of which in the field of humanities and social sciences.

The ESFRI Forum decides which proposals for research infrastructures will enter the roadmap, based on a scientific evaluation and on individual countries' political and financial support. As a consequence, consortia are formed by countries, not by institutions, in the ESFRI approach. The driving forces are still researchers and companies in need of, for example, language resources and tools, but the governments have to be convinced of the importance and sustainability of the ideas and the construction (cf. also the Danzin report). For CLARIN, the vision was the ubiquitous availability of language resources, and the driving force was the trust in language resources and tools as being of high and sustainable value,

6 https://www.esfri.eu/

as well as the trust in the technology as the glue that holds the infrastructure together as well as the mechanism that makes it function.

3.2 Getting on the ESFRI Roadmap

From Section 2, it is clearly seen that European collaboration in the area of language resources and tools was already in the air. The ESFRI Roadmap served as a catalyst to make it happen.

Over 2004, ESFRI created the Social Sciences and Humanities Working Group, which sent out questionnaires with a view to mapping potential new or upgraded pan-European Research Infrastructures for ESFRI consideration within the social sciences and humanities domain, with a deadline of 10 November 2005. Two expert groups were established to review the proposals contained in the responses: ECH EG (European Cultural Heritage Expert Group) for the humanities, and EROHS EG (European Research Observatory for the Humanities and Social Sciences Expert Group) for the social sciences. Three of the proposals for the mapping were relevant for the genesis of CLARIN:

- EARL (European Archive for Language Resources), submitted by Peter Wittenburg (Max Planck Institute for Psycholinguistics (MPI), Nijmegen), together with Laurent Romary (LORIA, Nancy), Nicoletta Calzolari (Istituto di Linguistica Computazionale (ILC), Pisa) and Lou Boves (Radboud University, Nijmegen);
- LangWeb (Towards a common access and exploitation infrastructure for distributed language resources), submitted by Martin Everaert and co-authored by Steven Krauwer (both Utrecht University);
- TELRI (Trans-European Language Resources Infrastructure), submitted by Tomaž Erjavec (Jožef Stefan Institute, Ljubljana), in collaboration with Tamás Váradi (Hungarian Academy of Sciences, Budapest).

There were many commonalities between the three proposals:

- All three built on a large number of existing language resources infrastructures operated by individual institutions or emerging from EU funded projects.
- All three built on an existing large community of experts (creators of data and tools) and users.
- Both LangWeb and EARL took their inspiration from an earlier Integrated Infrastructure Initiative proposal (which was also called LangWeb) that was submitted to the EC's 7th Framework Programme in 2004 with MPI and Utrecht University as the leading institutions. Unfortunately this proposal was not successful.

There were also differences:
- EARL had a strong focus on the technical infrastructure as such, and built on a number of EU projects that – in hindsight – could be seen as pilot projects for CLARIN.
- LangWeb was primarily driven by the needs of linguists and other potential parties interested in language, and aimed at interconnecting existing data and tool collections, making them interoperable and accessible to the research community across national and language borders.
- TELRI was rooted in a series of projects that started from the objective to create a counterpart of ELRA, with special focus on Central and Eastern Europe and the so-called Newly Independent States, after the dissolution of the Soviet Union.

In the first evaluation round by ECH EG five of the submitted questionnaires were judged to display maturity and scientific excellence: EURICA (European Research Infrastructure for Conservation and Analysis), DISH (Data Infrastructure for the Humanities and Social Sciences – the starting point for DARIAH), and EARL, LangWeb, and TELRI (which would together become the starting point for CLARIN). As EARL, LangWeb, and TELRI were all about the creation of a research infrastructure centred around language resources and tools, they were invited by ECH EG to investigate whether they could come up with a joint proposal for a single research infrastructure, to be presented for the ECH EG at a meeting in Brussels on 8 March 2006, as a candidate for inclusion in the ESFRI roadmap.

On 6–7 February 2006 the EARL team organised a meeting in Paris to discuss the establishment of a European Research Infrastructure for Language Resources, as an implementation of the ideas presented in the EARL questionnaire. In the brainstorming note for this meeting it was said that

> this group of persons now takes the initiative to establish a formal association or network that will take care of all relevant aspects of forming and establishing EARL. In particular, it has to
> - start and control a Europe wide formation process that includes the relevant centres and archives in the different European member states,
> - organize initiatives at the national level that can be solid building blocks in a European landscape of centres and archives,
> - establish close relations with national centres that are established for the humanities, since all humanities disciplines are potential users of advanced language resource services.

Some of the characteristics of what would later become CLARIN transpire here already: a bottom-up formation process, Europe-wide, but building on initiatives at the national level, and with close relationships with the humanities communities as potential users of our services.

According to the brainstorming note a number of persons from different European countries and from different initiatives (including ELRA, LangWeb and TELRI) had been invited, in order to have a good mix of experts of several sub-domains and a suitable initial geographic and organisational distribution. This first meeting was productive but inconclusive, in that no common view between the three proposals emerged. A second attempt was made at a meeting in Budapest on 27 February between a small group of representatives of the three initiatives: Tamás Váradi for TELRI, Peter Wittenburg for EARL, and Steven Krauwer for LangWeb.

This meeting was successful as it helped to identify both commonalities and differences, and to find a common direction. It was at this meeting that the name CLARIN (Common Language Resources and Technology Infrastructure) was adopted, at first as a temporary working title, however, since it was different enough from the names of the three original proposals, and since a name was already needed for the presentation in Brussels on 8 March, it was never changed to anything else. In the period from 28 February till 8 March, the members of the initial CLARIN team (Váradi, Wittenburg, Everaert and Krauwer) started working on the documents for the Brussels presentation.

The production of the document for the Brussels meeting brought to light a number of issues on which the three proposals had to come to an agreement. The most important one was what the main objective of the future infrastructure should be. Would the main objective of CLARIN be the creation of language technology and tools, and collecting and using language resources to enable this, or would the main objective be to use and create language technology and tools to facilitate research in the humanities and social sciences? In the former view the focus would be on the technology and the resources, and the humanities-oriented ESFRI call for proposals should be seen an opportunity to get this started. In the latter view the main focus of CLARIN would be in line with the ESFRI call, and the emphasis would remain on the humanities and social sciences.

After some discussion, it was agreed that the ESFRI call would determine the future direction of CLARIN and that CLARIN would target the humanities and social sciences at large, as well as other disciplines where language played a role, and that language resources would not just be a means to develop technology, but also objects of study. This would, of course, by no means exclude those whose main interest was the development of language and speech technology and resources, as the availability of such technologies is crucial for the capabilities of the infrastructure to offer advanced services to the user community.

At the March meeting the joint document titled, "Research Infrastructure for Language Resources and Technology", was presented to ECH EG and was well-received, and at following meetings of the ECH EG and the Social Sciences and Humanities Working Group in April 2006 the CLARIN proposal was accepted for inclusion in the ESFRI 2006 Roadmap.

In parallel with the preparation of the documents for the Brussels presentation, a formation process was initiated to bring together relevant centres and archives on a European scale, as envisaged in the EARL brainstorming note. Since all three proposals already had significant (partially overlapping) constituencies, this process had a head start. Initially the term "CLARIN Network" was used to refer to this community of organisations, although later on the term *network* had to be used with care, as a research infrastructure (RI) is much more than a network:

> RIs are facilities, resources and services that are used by the research communities to conduct research and foster innovation in their fields. They include: major scientific equipment (or sets of instruments), knowledge-based resources such as collections, archives and scientific data, e-Infrastructures, such as data and computing systems and communication networks and any other tools that are essential to achieve excellence in research and innovation[7].

An initial informal management structure was set up immediately to coordinate the joint efforts of the members of the network towards the implementation of the CLARIN infrastructure. In the meantime, the network kept growing and at its peak it counted 214 member sites in 33 countries, which clearly demonstrated the interest in CLARIN in Europe.

4 The CLARIN Preparatory Phase project

As a consequence of CLARIN being on the ESFRI 2006 Roadmap, CLARIN had the opportunity to respond to an EC call for proposals to support the construction of research infrastructures. While the agreement between the participating parties to submit a unified proposal to the roadmap had already laid the foundations for the CLARIN concept, it was the Preparatory Phase project that defined CLARIN in more detail.

7 https://www.esfri.eu/research-infrastructure-ri

4.1 Responding to the EC call for proposals

On December 22, 2006, the EC issued a closed call for proposals for the preparatory phase for the construction and exploitation of RIs on the 2006 Roadmap. According to the call, the expected outcome would be a complete blueprint of the whole infrastructure, covering legal work, governance and logistical work, strategic work, financial work, and technical work. Much of the technical work had already been addressed in the CLARIN proposal for the ESFRI Roadmap (see ESFRI 2006a), so we knew where to go and we just had to work very hard with many people to develop the proposal in further detail and to start building prototypes. The biggest non-technical challenge formulated in the call (as part of the legal work) was "a draft agreement, in the form of a *signature-ready* document for the actual construction". It was decided by the management of the CLARIN network to form a broad consortium for the project proposal, including as many of the countries already represented in the network as possible. At the moment of submission 31 partners from 22 countries participated, later on increasing to 36 partners from 26 countries. In our communications with the EC the size of the consortium was frowned upon, but with respect to languages we wanted to be as inclusive as possible, irrespective of size or economic potential. As it was anticipated that the eventual construction and operation of the infrastructure would have to be funded by national funding agencies in the participating countries, rather than by the EC, every partner was requested to provide a letter of support signed by the relevant ministry or research council, so that the funding bodies in all participating countries were aware of the efforts towards the creation of the CLARIN infrastructure, and could take them into account when developing their national roadmaps.

The project proposal was submitted on 2 May 2007, and the positive outcome of the evaluation was received on 12 July. The CLARIN Preparatory Phase project started on 1 January 2008 and was concluded on 30 June 2011. In the rest of this chapter we will refer to it as CLARIN-PP. The project was coordinated by Steven Krauwer (Utrecht), in close collaboration with Peter Wittenburg (Nijmegen), Tamás Váradi (Budapest), Erhard Hinrichs (Tübingen), Dan Cristea (Iași), Kimmo Koskenniemi (Helsinki), and Bente Maegaard (Copenhagen) as work package leaders, and Martin Wynne (Oxford) as a liaison between CLARIN and DARIAH management. Together they constituted the Executive Board of the project. The inclusion of a liaison with DARIAH, which started its Preparatory Phase project around the same time, clearly demonstrates our commitment to close collaboration with our sister infrastructure from the very start. The active involvement of the ministries and research councils in the project was ensured by the creation

of two Boards, the members of which (from each country) were appointed by the national funding agency:
- the Scientific Board, consisting of high-level scientists, who would monitor the execution of the programme and ensure its overall scientific soundness, coherence, completeness, consistency and feasibility;
- the Strategic Coordination Board, consisting of representatives of the funding bodies, who would monitor the execution of the programme of work with a view to compliance with national governments' and funding agencies' policies, and who would determine the overall governance and financial strategy for the infrastructure to be built.

4.2 The problem and the mission

The whole CLARIN idea originated from the observation that, on the one hand, a wealth of digital language data was (and still is) present in many formal and informal repositories covering many different languages all over Europe, collected for many different purposes, but that, on the other hand, much of this material was only known to insiders, these archives were mostly unconnected, every archive used its own standards for storage and access, and if the data was accessible online at all it was only for simple retrieval of files, which could be text, audio or video documents, or images.

At the time, with a few exceptions, humanities and social sciences scholars, the main target audience, did not receive any training in the use of language or speech technology as part of their curriculum and were often not aware of the potential benefits of using these technologies in their research; even if some tools were available they were often hard to use for the non-specialist, since a tool that works for data from one archive may not work for data from another archive without significant adaptations by experienced programmers.

The mission CLARIN formulated for itself was to address this issue by the creation of a Europe-wide research infrastructure that would make language resources and technology seamlessly available to scholars in the social sciences and humanities, and in all other disciplines where language plays a role. This should be done by uniting existing digital archives containing language material to produce a federation of connected archives with unified web access, and by providing a wealth of language and speech technology tools as web services that would operate on language data in archives all across Europe.

From the very start, the European dimension was very important. Looking at the European language resources landscape there was a large amount of fragmentation and very little coordination, both across and within countries. Data and tools that existed were largely invisible to any other than the initiated; there was a lack of interoperability and a lack of sustainability, as many valuable collections of data and tools were created in projects, upon the completion of which no one felt responsible for ensuring their longer-term preservation and accessibility for those who wanted to re-use them for other research projects.

Expertise in the creation and use of language resources and the tools to work with them existed in all European countries, but not at the same level of development. There is no reason to assume that one language is easier or more complex to process digitally than other languages, and the question of how much work can be done on a language will mainly depend on the economic situation in the country. At the European level much can be gained by sharing expertise, sharing language independent tools and methods, and porting language-dependent tools to other languages. Most countries may not be able to bear the cost of mobilising enough language and speech technologists to fully equip their language with advanced technological tools, but collaboration, coordination and sharing at a European level can help to compensate this.

In the rest of this section, we describe how we envisioned the creation of the CLARIN infrastructure by means of the CLARIN Preparatory Phase project.

4.3 The five dimensions

The Preparatory Phase project was based on five main dimensions, each addressing one or more of the expected outcomes listed in the call for proposals mentioned above:

a. the funding and governance dimension;
b. the technical dimension;
c. the legal and ethical dimension;
d. the language dimension;
e. the user dimension.

In the following sections we will go through these five dimensions, and show how the work carried out there led to the establishment of CLARIN ERIC on 29 February 2012 and how it is reflected in the CLARIN infrastructure as we know it. We will not go into detail here but, rather, limit ourselves to describing the approach we took. All project deliverables are available online.[8]

8 https://www.clarin.eu/content/deliverables-clarin-preparatory-phase-project-2008-2011

4.3.1 The funding and governance dimension: Organisational and legal framework

Activities under this heading were completely dedicated to the preparation of an agreement between the funding agencies in the participating countries about the construction and exploitation phase of the CLARIN infrastructure. Key questions to be addressed included: who is going to pay for the construction and operation of the infrastructure? How will it be managed? How will it be coordinated with national policies?

This involved the investigation of possible legal, financial, and organisational models, including the specification of the requirements along the major dimensions. It should be noted that, at least conceptually, the dream was to shape CLARIN as a federation of centres, bringing together in each participating country the strongest language infrastructure activities at the national level, and uniting them to form a pan-European infrastructure. In Section 4.4 below we describe in more detail how this would be implemented in terms of finance and governance.

4.3.2 The technical dimension

From the very start, the backbone of CLARIN was envisaged as a technical infrastructure based on a federation of data and service centres (see Wittenburg et al. 2010 for a panoramic overview), rather than just the network of institutions that we started from, although it should be noted that these institutions and the people populating them are also a crucial part of CLARIN, without which it could not function. The data and service centres were (and still are) the main building bricks of the infrastructure, although, as we will see below, during the execution of the project it became clear that a technical infrastructure can only serve its purpose optimally when it is accompanied by a knowledge infrastructure that facilitates not only sharing of data and tools, but also of the knowledge and expertise needed to use them.

The primary task in the technical dimension was the full technical specification of the infrastructure, followed by the construction of a prototype according to the specifications. During the execution of the project the prototype had to be validated on the basis of a rich variety of languages, resources and resource types, and services for the users. See Odijk (2017) for how this laid the foundations for CLARIN's current technical infrastructure.

Given the background of the initiatives that led to the creation of CLARIN we did not have to start from scratch, and could build on a federation of existing archives, providing existing collections of resources, tools, and services. The creation of new resources and tools was not the main objective of the project.

In order to make everything fit together a strong emphasis was laid on interoperability standards, conversion of existing resources to standards (if necessary), and encapsulation of existing successful tools in order to make them function in environments other than the ones they were originally designed for. See Bański and Hedeland (2022) for how standards and thinking about standards have evolved since then.

Even if at the time of the project no one had heard of the FAIR principles (Wilkinson et al. 2016) it was obvious that findability of data was crucial for the success of the infrastructure, and as a consequence much effort was put into the design of metadata schemes and into the curation of metadata (see Windhouwer and Goosen 2022). During the period of the project it turned out that in this respect, CLARIN was far ahead of many other data communities.

The vision of CLARIN as a federation of repositories and service centres with single sign-on access required a strong framework based on authentication and authorisation, and trust between archives (Odijk 2017).

4.3.3 The legal and ethical dimension

Legal and ethical issues are of key importance to the viability of the CLARIN infrastructure. CLARIN is committed to open access. However, the language resources domain includes material which can only be made available subject to a variety of legal and ethical restrictions. This required building the necessary legal and ethical agreement patterns in CLARIN. Agreements and licenses were needed for successful cooperation among the various actors and users of CLARIN, and for achieving and maintaining sufficient levels of trust. A network of agreements, licences and auditing was needed to relate the actors to each other and to avoid or reduce risks incurred in possible violations of intellectual property rights (IPR) or basic ethical rules. Kamocki, Kelli, and Lindén (2022) describes the current state of the legal and ethical framework that emerged from the Preparatory Phase project, and which was further enhanced and extended after the establishment of CLARIN ERIC.

4.3.4 The language dimension

One very important feature of CLARIN is that it wants to cover all languages spoken or studied in the participating countries, and preferably beyond. In this respect it is very different from many of the EU's funding programmes addressing language and speech technology, where the requirement to involve industry in project consortia inevitably means that the focus is on languages with an economic interest. All languages are equally dear to CLARIN. As a consequence, representational and descriptive standards should be adequate and validated for all languages. The same minimal coverage of basic resources and tools should be achieved for all languages, and the BLARK (Basic Language Resources Toolkit; see Krauwer 2003) should be defined as part of the CLARIN-PP project with a recommendation to implement it for all languages, although for this latter point – the implementation – unfortunately – CLARIN-PP would have to rely on nationally funded contributions.

The wish to serve as many languages as possible also explains the size of the consortium: it covered 24 national and many additional local languages. Activities included surveys of available resources and tools, including encoding and annotation data, as well as quality indicators, the development of common taxonomies and ontologies, and agreement on common standards. In all this, the focus was on integration of tools, interoperability, collection of usage scenarios, the creation of missing essential resources, and the validation of infrastructure specifications and prototype.

4.3.5 The user dimension

The target audiences of CLARIN were and still are scholars in the humanities and social sciences in a very broad sense, including linguists, language teachers, translation experts, literary scholars, historians, and philosophers, and more generally, all researchers and professionals in disciplines where language plays a role as instrument or object of study. In many of these disciplines the use of digital data and tools does not have a long tradition. CLARIN started out as a bottom-up initiative, where the majority of the partners in the project had strong backgrounds in linguistics, computational linguistics, language and speech technology (the latter to a lesser extent), and computer science. As a consequence, the consortium had, at least at the beginning of the project, no complete picture of the needs of the other disciplines CLARIN wanted to serve. In order to remedy this, a number of special activities were included in the programme of work: an analysis of past and ongoing humanities and social sciences projects, user consultation (although users not familiar with digital methods could find it hard to formulate their requirements), the launch of typical example projects to get a better understanding of the needs and of the potential impact, the creation of centres of expertise, and various other awareness actions, organised by the project and/or in collaboration with emerging national CLARIN projects.

The possibility for users alone to gain access to more data and tools is not sufficient to advance research and to integrate research efforts on a European scale. First of all, as already remarked above, the use of digital methods in the humanities and social sciences was (and still is) not yet as wide-spread and well-developed as in other research areas, which means that a major education and awareness effort is needed to equip a whole new generation of researchers with the skills and methods to integrate digital methods in their day-to-day research activities. Secondly, the vast amount of experience and expertise that is available in many different places in Europe can only be mobilised and exploited on a European scale through coordinated efforts. This means that in order to have a real impact CLARIN could not rely on simply providing and coordinating a technical infrastructure; this technical infrastructure would need to be accompanied by a knowledge infrastructure, covering the whole spectrum from basic training and education to the creation of real and virtual centres of expertise, where cutting-edge research could be conducted and expertise and results could be shared. These centres of expertise were named K(nowledge)-centres. The areas of expertise could be languages, technologies, or any other topic of interest for the CLARIN user community. Van den Heuvel et al. (2022) and Ljubešić et al. (2022) show how two (out of now 25) K-centres have shaped their activities. With respect to the developments in the fields of training and education, Wissik, Wessels, and Fischer (2022) describe the Digital Humanities Course Registry, which is a joint activity with DARIAH, and Hennelly et al. (2022) describe training in a new CLARIN country – South Africa.

4.4 The organisational and legal framework for CLARIN

As mentioned above, one of the important tasks of the preparatory phase was the preparation of a ready-to-sign agreement between the participating countries whereby they commit themselves to the joint construction and exploitation of the CLARIN Infrastructure. Such an agreement had to cover governance and management issues, financial issues, and transnational collaboration issues. Consequently, this task covered requirements analysis, investigation of existing organisational frameworks (such as AISBL, Foundation, etc.), cost estimations and financial plans, requirements for transnational coordination and collaboration with third parties, and finally the proposal for a governance and financial structure.

However, CLARIN was not the only RI in need of an organisational framework, and it quickly became clear that the existing legal frameworks were not fully adequate for this purpose. Therefore, in parallel with the CLARIN investigations, the European Commission was investigating the same problem area, and we participated in many teleconferences and some workshops to discuss the Commission's considerations and proposals. The Commission proposal for the ERIC Regulation was adopted May 2009.

This way, the ERIC Regulation became the framework for the CLARIN statutes. Many meetings were held with the stakeholders (the Strategic Coordination Board, ministry representatives), in order to learn about best practice from the various countries, to take into account wishes of various countries as far as possible, to discuss the financial framework – central costs vs. national costs, contribution of the countries to the central costs, and so on.

These discussions about central and local (national) costs led to the distinction of two layers in the financial framework: (1) the layer coordinated by the CLARIN ERIC, (2) the layer coordinated at the national level. As can be seen, this is very much the same structure as we have now. During the discussions with the stakeholders, it was also agreed that the members' annual financial contribution to CLARIN ERIC should cover the first layer, whereas the funding needed for the national contribution would stay at the national level and under the control of the national authorities. The basic principles for distribution of the costs of the central layers were decided and they have not changed much since. The CLARIN ERIC statutes (European Commission 2012) provide the principles in detail. Here we would just like to mention the very important principle that all languages are equally important for CLARIN, but that countries have different size and economic capacity, so the distribution of the costs basically built on the countries' GDP (gross domestic product) as a percentage of the EU's GDP in a specific year, and was kept stable for a period of five years (with a 2% annual increase to compensate for inflation).

One of the other important discussions was the regulation of types of membership. CLARIN does not have affiliates and other types of less committed membership. Countries can decide to join as members, and if a country is not totally ready for this commitment, it can apply to be an observer for a limited period, allowing the country to sort out the details that are needed for membership. Finally, the statutes contain the possibility for CLARIN to enter into agreements with third parties, that is, institutions or regions that are not covered by CLARIN membership or observership, for example, an institution in a country that is not member of CLARIN.

Already towards the end of 2010, the members of the Strategic Coordination Board, consisting of representatives of ministries and research councils, had agreed to prepare a Memorandum of Understanding (MoU) for the establishment of an ERIC for CLARIN, and to set up a Steering Committee consisting of those representatives whose country would sign the MoU. The role of the committee would be to prepare the ERIC application. In the committee it was agreed that the Netherlands would host the ERIC. One consideration was that CLARIN-PP was coordinated from the Netherlands, and another was that in the same period the Netherlands was already preparing the application to establish and host SHARE ERIC, the first ERIC in history.

The first submission of the proposed statutes and technical description for CLARIN ERIC was made in May 2011, just before the end of the CLARIN-PP project, by the parties who signed the MoU: Austria, Croatia, Czech Republic, Denmark, the Dutch Language Union,[9] Estonia, Finland, France, Germany, Greece, Latvia, Lithuania, the Netherlands, Norway, and Poland.

4.5 CLARIN in the RI landscape

CLARIN was one out of (originally) 35 selected ESFRI RI Preparatory Phase proposals. As many of them were confronted with the same or similar problems, a number of initiatives were taken to bring the RIs together and to discuss issues of common interest. This is especially true for the five projects in the humanities and social sciences: CLARIN, DARIAH, CESSDA, ESS, and SHARE. A first joint meeting was organised in London in 2009 and throughout the execution of these projects they remained in close contact with each other and organised joint activities.

As mentioned, liaison with the DARIAH research infrastructure was institutionalised at the start of the project by the arrangement for the University of Oxford to act as the official liaison partner, participating in both the CLARIN Preparatory Phase project and its counterpart, Preparing DARIAH. Communications between the two projects were good, and numerous joint activities and projects resulted. In 2009 and 2010 CLARIN and DARIAH, in collaboration with EU funded e-Infrastructure projects, organised two NEERI workshops (Networking Event for Research Infrastructures) in Helsinki and Vienna, addressing the technical, architectural, and social challenges of building the infrastructure. The most significant joint events within the work plans of the projects were the Supporting the Digital Humanities conferences (SDH), the first held in Vienna in October 2010, with a follow-up in 2011 in Copenhagen, just after completion of both projects.

9 An intergovernmental body between the Dutch and the Flemish government.

At the national level, in many countries where both CLARIN and DARIAH had a presence they worked closely together to build carefully coordinated or joint national research infrastructures, thus ensuring that DARIAH and CLARIN would work together in complementary activities, with maximal synergies, maximum value for money, and a minimum of overlap. Furthermore, the DASISH and EUDAT RI cluster projects involved both infrastructures.

CLARIN has actively participated in the creation and the activities of an informal committee of coordinators of Preparatory Phase projects, called the European Preparatory Phase Project Coordination Committee (ePPCC), in order to exchange and share experiences, problems, and solutions. This committee worked in close collaboration with the EC, and it had regular meetings (mostly virtual, in those days as teleconferences), sent out questionnaires, and organised a number of internal workshops and contributed to workshops organised by the EC. This was continued under the auspices of the CoPoRI project, which could be seen as a predecessor of the present ERIC Forum project.

4.6 Broadening the basis

Participation in the CLARIN-PP project was not limited to the 36 consortium partners. The CLARIN network of interested institutions, which was already initiated before the project had started, grew from 120 member institutions to over 200, covering 33 countries. The original plan to fully integrate CLARIN activities at the national level into the CLARIN-PP project had to be abandoned. The main obstacles were (i) the absence of national funding in some countries; (ii) the fact that different countries had widely different approaches to the creation of the national roadmap and to the time schedule for this process; and (iii) the fact that in most of those countries where funding for CLARIN was made available, the funding was granted on a project basis, after competitive calls for proposals. This latter situation had two serious consequences: (i) some strong players in the CLARIN-PP project did not succeed in the national funding application during the CLARIN-PP project; and (ii) even in successful cases the national projects did not always have sufficient flexibility in their programmes to accommodate tasks following from the CLARIN project. As a consequence, even though the activities undertaken as part of national CLARIN projects constituted without exception valuable contributions to the construction and the population of the emerging CLARIN infrastructure most of them did not feed directly into the CLARIN-PP project. The experiences with the relation between nationally funded and CLARIN-PP activities have had a strong impact on the shape of the present CLARIN infrastructure as it emerged from the project (see 4.4 above).

5 Shaping the ERIC

When the CLARIN-PP project ended on 30 June 2011, the funding from this project ended as well, but fortunately the core governance structure of the project could be kept alive on an interim basis, thanks to the support from the participating institutions, the emerging national consortia, and volunteers. This made it possible to maintain the momentum in the period between the end of the project and the establishment of CLARIN ERIC in February 2012.

5.1 The approval process

When CLARIN-PP ended, the EC's evaluation of the application that had been submitted in May was still underway. The purpose of this evaluation was to check the compliance of the application with the ERIC Regulation. On 1 July the application was presented at a meeting of the ERIC Committee in Brussels. The overall results of the evaluation and the discussions were positive, and work could start on integrating the comments made by the evaluators. Some of the comments were requests for modifications and additions to the proposed statutes in order to ensure compliance, and some were recommendations to improve the clarity of the documents. None of them were controversial and they were all easy to accommodate. In the participating countries, the governments worked hard to take away the last obstacles for joining the ERIC. It turned out that the biggest obstacle of all was the VAT exemption: according to the ERIC Regulation, ERICs do not pay VAT. For infrastructures based on big physical installations this could have a significant impact on the cost of construction (and on the VAT income for the state); however, in the case of CLARIN, where the main expenditure at the ERIC level consists of salaries, the effect of the VAT exemption is negligible, but for some countries this was a matter of principle.

The experts who reviewed the Technical and Scientific Description were very much in support of the proposal, and asked pertinent questions about cross-border and cross-discipline sharing of tools and data, and our embedding in the European landscape of related organisations and activities. The comments and questions could all be taken into account in an updated version of the document prepared for the formal request for the establishment of CLARIN ERIC. On 23 September 2011 the Dutch government submitted to the EC the formal request for setting up CLARIN ERIC, on behalf of Austria, Czech Republic, Croatia, Denmark, the Dutch Language Union, Estonia, Germany, and the Netherlands, that is, 8 out of 15 signatories of the MoU (see Section 4.4). The main reason for MoU countries not to join the request was that their national RI roadmap was not yet in place. During the evaluation of this request the Croatian government had to withdraw: Croatia not (yet) being an EU member, its government had not yet recognised the ERIC as a legal entity, and therefore could not join it. Norway, which had signed the MoU, was confronted with the same problem. In the meantime, the interim Executive Board, led by Steven Krauwer and Bente Maegaard, continued communicating with the countries that had signed the MoU but did not sign the request. As a result of these efforts two more countries – Bulgaria and Poland – were able to join the request and could be included in the list of nine founding members of CLARIN that was submitted to the EC in December.

5.2 Consolidation and continued expansion

One of the main obligations for CLARIN ERIC member countries was (and is) to set up their own national consortium of institutions[10] (repositories, archives, libraries, research institutions, universities, etc.) to coordinate its contribution to the CLARIN infrastructure. In some of the founding countries, national funding to help establishing the national consortium was already available at an early stage and the construction (and in some cases operation) of the infrastructure could make a head-start (see e.g., Hajič et al. 2022, or Odijk and van Hessen 2017).

In many other countries it took considerably more time and effort to reach this stage. As one of the formulated goals for CLARIN was to cover all European countries, the efforts to include more countries did not stop. The enlargement of the member base was one of the important activities after the ERIC was created with nine founding members. However, this turned out to be a very difficult task at the time. Even if in most countries there was a high level of interest from researchers (not least because of the CLARIN-PP project), there were various administrative obstacles: a national roadmap was needed in order to allocate funding, and the teams needed to win a competition for funding in those cases where national roadmaps existed. In some countries, specific bodies (e.g., parliaments) needed to take the decision, which would prolong the process. This meant that, despite considerable efforts, during the first couple of years there were no new accessions to CLARIN, and, apart from Norway, which joined as an observer in 2013, only from 2014 onwards did new members start joining: Lithuania, Sweden, and Portugal joined in 2014, Greece joined in 2015. In March 2018, Croatia joined CLARIN ERIC as the last of the 15 signatories of the MoU that initiated the application process.

10 It should be noted that a national consortium may consist of one institution.

5.3 Some principles

In parallel with the approval process by the EC, we prepared ourselves for the launch of CLARIN ERIC. In this context we formulated a number of principles that should guide us in developing and implementing our strategy:

> (i) Separation of governance and coordination tasks on the one hand, and operational tasks on the other: the construction and operation of the technical infrastructure is the financial and organisational responsibility of the member countries. The rationale is that setting up central services would require new investments at the central level, which would lead to an increase of the annual fees and create an additional flow of cross-border funding. Making central services dependent on CLARIN ERIC funding would also make them more vulnerable from a sustainability point of view.

This principle was abandoned after two years. One important consideration was the assessment of CLARIN by the ESFRI High Level Expert Group, where it was strongly recommended that CLARIN ERIC take more central responsibility for main infrastructure services and facilities (and in fact the CLARIN management had never disagreed); another was that, fortunately, with the increase of the number of members and observers of CLARIN ERIC, it had become financially feasible to make funding available for the operation of central services and facilities, without increasing the annual fees.

> (ii) Keeping the size of the central coordination point small, and delegating tasks to teams in member countries where possible and desirable. Rationale: offices have a tendency to grow, and involvement of member teams in central tasks keeps the distance between central coordination and the work floor small.

The initial number of people working directly for CLARIN ERIC at the end of 2012 was seven, who together represented the equivalent of 2.3 full-time positions, part of which was arranged on a secondment basis with CLARIN sites outside the Netherlands. The temporary secondment approach, where people worked from their home base and where the home institution was reimbursed for the hours worked, proved quite successful, as it not only reduced the distance between central and decentral teams, but also allowed CLARIN to benefit from the vast reservoir of expertise available in the national consortia. Both the members of the Board of Directors and CLARIN Office support staff were employed on a secondment basis.

> (iii) Aiming at making access to and use of the infrastructure free for researchers in member countries. Rationale: contrary to industry, where financial investments in research may eventually result in more profit, in academia the use of research facilities such as CLARIN should pay off in higher productivity or better quality, but not in cash.

Even if each country is responsible for its own language(s), the added value of CLARIN as a pan-European research infrastructure is that its technical infrastructure facilitates the establishment of connections between data and services hosted in different countries, and that its knowledge infrastructure supports cross-border transfer of knowledge as well as porting of tools and methods between languages, so that costly re-invention of wheels can be avoided.

> (iv) Production of digital language data and tools is the primary responsibility of the members and will normally be guided by national research priorities. CLARIN ERIC will not dictate to countries what to do, but will insist on compliance with CLARIN standards and it will offer a platform for (voluntary) coordination of such activities between members so that synergies can be exploited.

Through its strong focus on interoperability and standards, CLARIN aims to facilitate cross-border, cross-language, and cross-disciplinary research and thus to contribute to the development of the European Research Area (see also the CLARIN Value Proposition 2021[11]).

> (v) All data, tools, and services offered through the CLARIN infrastructure will remain the property of the original owners. Depositing data in a CLARIN centre will not change ownership conditions.

This principle was very important to take away the fear on the part of data owners that by depositing resources in a CLARIN repository they would give their data away to CLARIN.

> (vi) CLARIN is open, and participation in centrally organised committees, events, or dissemination activities is by default open to the research community at large unless this would be in conflict with the very nature of the event.

This principle confirms the openness of CLARIN to the research community at large.

> (vii) CLARIN should not duplicate anything that is already done by others or could be done by others.

This principle should help to avoid entering into competitions, and to ensure that we actively look for collaboration opportunities whenever possible.

11 http://hdl.handle.net/11372/DOC-138

5.4 The launch of CLARIN ERIC on 18 April 2012

CLARIN ERIC was officially established by the EC on 29 February 2012, as the second ERIC in history, but it started for real on 18 April 2012, when the General Assembly, consisting of the representatives of the nine founding members, had its first meeting in Den Haag, hosted by the Dutch Ministry of Education, Culture and Research. Representatives of the other countries that had signed the MoU (see Section 4.4) were invited to the meeting as guests.

At this meeting the first President and Vice President were elected: Helge Kahler (DE) and Jacek Gierlinski (PL). Steven Krauwer and Bente Maegaard were appointed as Executive and Vice Executive Director. The Strategic Plan for the Construction and Exploitation Phase, the Work Programme and the Budget for 2012 were all approved by the General Assembly, and this marked the real start of CLARIN ERIC.

6 Conclusion

As this chapter shows, CLARIN came into existence, not as a revolutionary initiative, but as a logical step in an evolution starting from the recognition of the importance of language resources by the research communities dealing with language, followed by the recognition by the European Commission of the central role of language in communication and the opportunities offered by the new information technologies. In parallel, language resources infrastructure initiatives emerged at the national level and, supported by the EC funding programmes, at the European level. The creation of ESFRI served as a catalyst by offering opportunities to bring such initiatives together, leading to the birth of the CLARIN concept and its inclusion in the ESFRI Roadmap in 2006, and the mobilisation of a large community of experts from all over Europe, all willing to contribute to the creation of the CLARIN infrastructure.

The funding opportunities offered by the EC to support the Preparatory Phase projects of RIs on the ESFRI Roadmap made it possible to elaborate and consolidate the foundations of the future infrastructure in the period 2008–2011 through a massive effort. In this chapter we have only focused on a few aspects of the CLARIN Preparatory Phase project, and certainly not done justice to all the efforts made by the participants and their achievements. Interested readers can consult all project deliverables on the CLARIN website.[12]

12 https://www.clarin.eu/content/deliverables-clarin-preparatory-phase-project-2008-2011

The establishment of CLARIN ERIC in 2012 was a major milestone in the history of the CLARIN infrastructure as it was the starting point for creating a new and structured way of collaborating for those countries that were/are members and third parties. These countries are contributing their treasures and expertise to the community.

At the moment of writing, almost on CLARIN ERIC's tenth anniversary, it is a great pleasure to see that the CLARIN infrastructure is thriving, and still gradually expanding in terms of participating countries and in terms of resources and services offered to our users!

Acknowledgements: The CLARIN Preparatory Phase project was supported by the European Union's Seventh Framework Programme (FP7-212230).

Much of what is described in this chapter is derived from or inspired by project reports co-authored with or by many project participants. We would like to thank them all for their contributions to the project and for their efforts to set up a national CLARIN consortium in their own country, both during and after the execution of the project.

We would also like to thank the representatives of ministries and research councils for serving on the project's Strategic Coordination Board, and for helping to prepare the final ERIC application.

We owe special thanks to Richard Derksen (then at the Department for Research and Science Policy of the Dutch Ministry of Education, Culture and Research) and Annika Thies and Harry Tuinder (then legal experts at the Research Infrastructures Unit of the European Commission's Directorate-General for Research and Innovation) for their unwavering support and advice in taking the legal and administrative hurdles we encountered when preparing the application for the establishment of CLARIN ERIC.

Bibliography

Bański, Piotr & Hanna Hedeland. 2022. Standards in CLARIN. In Darja Fišer & Andreas Witt (eds.), *CLARIN. The infrastructure for language resources*. Berlin: De Gruyter.

Calzolari, Nicoletta & Antonio Zampolli. 1999. Harmonised large-scale syntactic/semantic lexicons: A European multilingual infrastructure. In *Proceedings of Machine Translation Summit VII*, 358–366. Singapore.

Danzin, André. 1992. *Towards a European Language Infrastructure*. Commission of the European Communities, DG XIII, Brussels.

ERIC Regulation. 2009. L206 (8 August). *Official Journal of the European Union* 52. 1–20.

ESFRI. 2006a. *Report of the Social Sciences and Humanities Roadmap Working Group*. 58–72. https://www.esfri.eu/sites/default/files/ssh-rwg-roadmap-report-2006_en.pdf
ESFRI. 2006b. *European Roadmap for Research Infrastructures, Report 2006. Luxembourg*, Office for Official Publications of the European Communities. https://www.esfri.eu/sites/default/files/esfri_roadmap_2006_en.pdf
European Commission. 2012. Commission Decision of 29 February 2012: Setting up the Common Language Resources and Technology Infrastructure as a European Research Infrastructure Consortium (CLARIN ERIC). *Official Journal of the European Union*.
Francis, Winthrop Nelson & Henry Kucera. 1969. *Computational analysis of present-day American English*. Providence, RI: Brown University Press.
Hajič, Jan, Eva Hajičová, Barbora Hladká, Jozef Mišutka, Ondřej Košarko & Pavel Straňák. 2022. LINDAT/CLARIAH-CZ: Where we are and where we go. In Darja Fišer & Andreas Witt (eds.), *CLARIN. The infrastructure for language resources*. Berlin: De Gruyter.
Hennelly, Martin, Langa Khumalo, Juan Steyn & Menno van Zaanen. 2022. Training of digital language resources skills in South Africa. In Darja Fišer & Andreas Witt (eds.), *CLARIN. The infrastructure for language resources*. Berlin: De Gruyter.
Heuvel, Henk van den, Nelleke Oostdijk, Caroline Rowland & Paul Trilsbeek. 2022. The CLARIN Knowledge Centre for Atypical Communication Expertise. In Darja Fišer & Andreas Witt (eds.), *CLARIN. The infrastructure for language resources*. Berlin: De Gruyter.
Kamocki, Paweł, Aleksei Kelli & Krister Lindén. 2022. The CLARIN Committee for Legal and Ethical Issues and the Normative Layer of the CLARIN infrastructure. In Darja Fišer & Andreas Witt (eds.), *CLARIN. The infrastructure for language resources*. Berlin: De Gruyter.
Krauwer, Steven. 2003. The basic language resource kit (BLARK) as the first milestone for the language resources roadmap. In *Proceedings of SPECOM 2003*, 8–15. Moscow.
Ljubešić, Nikola, Tomaž Erjavec, Maja Miličević Petrović & Tanja Samardžić. 2022. Together we are stronger: Bootstrapping language technology infrastructure for South Slavic languages with CLARIN.SI. In Darja Fišer & Andreas Witt (eds.), *CLARIN. The infrastructure for language resources*. Berlin: De Gruyter.
Odijk, Jan. 2017. Introduction to the CLARIN Technical Infrastructure. In Jan Odijk & Arjan van Hessen (eds.). *CLARIN in the Low Countries*, 1–9. London: Ubiquity Press. https://doi.org/10.5334/bbi.3
Odijk, Jan & Arjan van Hessen. 2017. *CLARIN in the Low Countries*. London: Ubiquity Press. http://library.oapen.org/handle/20.500.12657/30870
Wilkinson, Mark, Michel Dumontier, IJsbrand Jan Aalbersberg, Gabrielle Appleton, Myles Axton, Arie Baak, Niklas Blomberg, Jan-Willem Boiten, Luiz Bonino da Silva Santos, Philip E. Bourne, Jildau Bouwman, Anthony J. Brookes, Tim Clark, Mercè Crosas, Ingrid Dillo, Olivier Dumon, Scott Edmunds, Chris T. Evelo, Richard Finkers, Alejandra Gonzalez-Beltran, Alasdair J.G. Gray, Paul Groth, Carole Goble, Jeffrey S. Grethe, Jaap Heringa, Peter A.C 't Hoen, Rob Hooft, Tobias Kuhn, Ruben Kok, Joost Kok, Scott J. Lusher, Maryann E. Martone, Albert Mons, Abel L. Packer, Bengt Persson, Philippe Rocca-Serra, Marco Roos, Rene van Schaik, Susanna-Assunta Sansone, Erik Schultes, Thierry Sengstag, Ted Slater, George Strawn, Morris A. Swertz, Mark Thompson, Johan van der Lei, Erik van Mulligen, Jan Velterop, Andra Waagmeester, Peter Wittenburg, Katherine Wolstencroft, Jun Zhao & Barend Mons. 2016. *The FAIR Guiding Principles for scientific data management and stewardship*. *Sci Data* 3. 160018. https://doi.org/10.1038/sdata.2016.18

Windhouwer, Menzo & Twan Goosen. 2022. Component Metadata Infrastructure. In Darja Fišer & Andreas Witt (eds.), *CLARIN. The infrastructure for language resources.* Berlin: De Gruyter.

Wissik, Tanja, Leon Wessels & Frank Fischer. 2022. The DH Course Registry: A piece of the puzzle in CLARIN's Technical and Knowledge Infrastructure. In Darja Fišer & Andreas Witt (eds.), *CLARIN. The infrastructure for language resources*. Berlin: De Gruyter.

Wittenburg, Peter, Nuria Bel, Lars Borin, Gerhard Budin, Nicoletta Calzolari, Eva Hajicova, Kimmo Koskenniemi, Lothar Lemnitzer, Bente Maegaard, Maciej Piasecki, Jean-Marie Pierrel, Stelios Piperidis, Inguna Skadina, Dan Tufis, Remco van Veenendaal, Tamas Váradi & Martin Wynne. 2010. Resource and service centres as the backbone for a sustainable service infrastructure. In *Proceedings of the Seventh International Conference on Language Resources and Evaluation*, 60–63. Valletta, Malta: European Language Resources Association.

Zampolli, Antonio. 1991. Towards reusable linguistic resources. In Jürgen Kunze & Dorothee Reimann (eds.), *Fifth Conference of the European Chapter of the Association for Computational Linguistics 9–11 April 1991, Congress Hall, Alexanderplatz, Berlin*. Morristown, NJ: Association for Computational Linguistics.

Zampolli, Antonio. 1997. The PAROLE project in the general context of the European actions for language resources. In Ruta Marcinkeviciene & Norbert Volz (eds.), *TELRI, Second European Seminar: Language applications for a multilingual Europe, Kaunas, Lithuania, April 17–20, 1997*, 185–210. Mannheim/Kaunas: IDS/VDU.

Zampolli, Antonio, Nicoletta Calzolari & Martha Palmer. 1994. *Current issues in computational linguistics: In honour of Don Walker*. Springer Science & Business Media.

Franciska de Jong, Dieter Van Uytvanck, Francesca Frontini, Antal van den Bosch, Darja Fišer, and Andreas Witt

Language Matters

The European Research Infrastructure CLARIN, Today and Tomorrow

Abstract: CLARIN stands for "Common Language Resources and Technology Infrastructure". In 2012 CLARIN ERIC was established as a legal entity with the mission to create and maintain a digital infrastructure to support the sharing, use, and sustainability of language data (in written, spoken, or multimodal form) available through repositories from all over Europe, in support of research in the humanities and social sciences and beyond. Since 2016 CLARIN has had the status of Landmark research infrastructure and currently it provides easy and sustainable access to digital language data and also offers advanced tools to discover, explore, exploit, annotate, analyse, or combine such datasets, wherever they are located. This is enabled through a networked federation of centres: language data repositories, service centres, and knowledge centres with single sign-on access for all members of the academic community in all participating countries. In addition, CLARIN offers open access facilities for other interested communities of use, both inside and outside of academia. Tools and data from different centres are interoperable, so that data collections can be combined and tools from different sources can be chained to perform operations at different levels of complexity. The strategic agenda adopted by CLARIN and the activities

Acknowledgements: The authors of this chapter are grateful for the input provided by Karina Berger, John Picard, and Leon Wessels. Funding for some of the work underlying the content of this chapter was made available through the grants that CLARIN has received throughout the years. (See for an overview: https://www.clarin.eu/content/clarin-eu-projects.)

Franciska de Jong, CLARIN ERIC's Executive Director, e-mail: f.m.g.dejong@uu.nl
Dieter Van Uytvanck, CLARIN ERIC's Vice Executive Director and Technical Director, e-mail: dieter@clarin.eu
Francesca Frontini, Institute for Computational Linguistics "A. Zampolli", Pisa, Italy, member of the CLARIN ERIC's BoD, e-mail: francesca.frontini@ilc.cnr.it
Antal van den Bosch, Meertens Instituut, Amsterdam, the Netherlands, member of the CLARIN ERIC's BoD, e-mail: antal.van.den.bosch@meertens.knaw.nl
Darja Fišer, Institute of Contemporary History, Ljubljana, Slovenia, member of the CLARIN ERIC's BoD from 2016 to 2020, e-mail: darja.fiser@ff.uni-lj.si
Andreas Witt, Leibniz Institute for the German Language, Mannheim, Germany, member of the CLARIN ERIC's BoD from 2019 to 2022, e-mail: witt@ids-mannheim.de

https://doi.org/10.1515/9783110767377-002

undertaken are rooted in a strong commitment to the Open Science paradigm and the FAIR data principles. This also enables CLARIN to express its added value for the European Research Area and to act as a key driver of innovation and contributor to the increasing number of industry programmes running on data-driven processes and the digitalization of society at large.

Keywords: research infrastructure, language resources, language technology, open science, service interoperability, innovation, SSH

1 Introduction

In this chapter, the CLARIN research infrastructure will be presented from a strategic and organizational perspective. It is authored by some of the current and previous members of the CLARIN Board of Directors (BoD). Krauwer and Maegaard (2022) describe the rationale behind the choice to implement the original ideas for the sharing of language resources in the way that CLARIN is set up – that is, a distributed infrastructure covering a multitude of languages and disciplinary needs – and the provision of a range of tools for the processing of language materials, in alignment with the Open Science agenda. The same chapter also outlines the European interest in structural support for research infrastructures that paved the way for the establishment of the CLARIN consortium as an ERIC[1] in 2012. This chapter will focus on what the intellectual and monetary investments of the past 10 years have produced. The impact of the dynamics in the European ecosystem on the modes of collaboration and the strategic agenda will also be outlined. Additionally, the various types of impact and the sustainability of the uptake, the models of collaboration, the overall service provision and the innovation ambition will be reflected upon. But to start with, the *raison d'être* for CLARIN will be addressed from a philosophical angle.

1.1 The neo-Babylonian paradox

According to a well-known passage from the Hebrew Bible, thousands of years ago, every person on earth spoke the same language. One day, man decided to build a city with a tower that would reach into heaven. But while constructing this tower, the people began to speak different languages. Confused by this sudden emergence

1 ERIC stands for European Infrastructure Consortium, a governance model for cross-country collaboration on research infrastructure.

of multilinguality, the construction of the city with its impressive tower – which was called Babel or Babylon, from the Hebrew word for 'confusion' – was stopped. The story of the Tower of Babel teaches us a contradictory lesson. Language allows humans to communicate. Through language we can tell stories, make agreements, write poetry, plan the construction of skyscrapers, or discuss how to fight global warming. But language also leads to confusion and misunderstanding. Some decades ago, work began on a second Tower of Babel: the internet. Since then, the World Wide Web has connected billions of people across the world. Any device connected to the internet gives access to a wealth of information, ranging from ancient philosophy to tomorrow's weather forecast, and from wildlife documentaries to the quickest route from Vienna to Bangalore. Online discourses affect the outcome of elections and the way people respond to restrictions meant to reduce the impact of pandemics or other global crises. Data has become valuable capital for governments, commercial enterprises, and science. But the internet is not just a goldmine; it is also a junkyard. It is estimated that 80% of all data is unstructured and text-heavy (Sumathy and Chidambaram 2013). It can be written in any of over 7,000 known, actively spoken languages, and may contain fake news, hate speech, and spam. How do we deal with this neo-Babylonian paradox? The CLARIN infrastructure is rooted in the belief that understanding the dynamics of language is key to addressing the challenges of our time. Enabling the use of language materials in scholarly contexts through the sharing of language resources and tools, and strengthening digital literacy, the ability to use and understand language data of any type, are commonly seen by the various communities of researchers and developers involved in CLARIN as key vehicles for the increased understanding of human language in all its forms and facets. Empowering citizens in becoming more versatile and digitally literate in a multilingual world in turn empowers society at large to be more democratic and to more effectively pursue humankind's intellectual and cultural ambitions.

We live in yesterday's future and tomorrow's past. Language has brought humans a great deal. The digital turn in communication as well as the pervasive access to information resources and Artificial Intelligence can help boost the potential impact of language-based service provision, and disentangle the neo-Babylonian paradox. With proper attention for language diversity and by advocating responsible use of the technology on offer, we increase the potential of language as a vehicle that not only allows humans to write history, but also to contribute to development goals for a better future.

1.2 Why language matters

Language is a carrier of socio-cultural content and information. Language also plays a role as the reflection of scientific and societal knowledge, as an instrument for human communication and persuasion, as one of the central aspects of the identity of individuals, groups, cultures, and nations, as an instrument for human cognition and creative expression, and as a formal system. Moreover, language materials form a considerable part of the historical records that are seen as cultural heritage. The faceted nature of language is reinforced by its internal dynamics, which has both synchronic and diachronic dimensions. Recognition of the value of understanding language in all its various facets and the importance of incorporating language data in the spectrum of data types that capture the full range of cultural and social dynamics has inspired the vision underlying the CLARIN initiative.

The CLARIN vision reads: "All digital language resources and tools from all over Europe and beyond are accessible through a single sign-on on-line environment for the support of researchers in the humanities and social sciences". In line with this vision, CLARIN was established as a research infrastructure with the following mission: "Create and maintain an infrastructure to support the sharing, use, and sustainability of language data and tools for research in the humanities and social sciences". The CLARIN infrastructure is thus rooted in the wide acknowledgement of the role of language as social and cultural data and the increased potential for comparative research on cultural and social phenomena across the boundaries of languages.

1.3 For whom CLARIN matters

With its richly faceted nature and its role in determining identity, context, origin, and use, language is a leading data source for researchers in the humanities and social sciences. At the same time, language data has also been recognized as relevant from the perspective of information science, data science, and Artificial Intelligence. CLARIN's aim thus has become to make language resources and tools available and reusable for all disciplines that work with language resources. And while the roots of the CLARIN research infrastructure were mainly in linguistics and language technology, the scholarly communities for which the infrastructure is operated also include fields such as Literary Studies, History, Journalism and Media Studies, Communication Studies, Ethnography and Anthropology, Migration Studies, Political Studies, Culture Studies, Mental Health Studies, Sociology, and Psychology. All in all, the activities taken up, the services developed, and the collaborative links with other RIs have led to a value proposition that, in principle, facilitates researchers working with language materials irrespective of the domain they are rooted in.

To reach out to its diverse potential user base and to stimulate the uptake of the services on offer in the relevant communities of use, in addition to the technical service provision for data sharing and processing through a distributed technical infrastructure, CLARIN has also developed an ecosystem for the exchange of knowledge and information and is investing in a network of experts on topics related to standards (Bański and Hedeland 2022), training (Wissik, Wessels, and Fischer 2022; Hennelly et al. 2022), and legal and ethical issues (Kamocki, Kelli, and Lindén 2022). The value proposition of CLARIN is also addressing the needs of non-academic parties, for example as embodied in the structural cooperation with the GLAM sector (GLAM = Galleries, Libraries, Archives, Museums) and the EU programmes promoting digital cultural heritage. CLARIN acts also as a driver of innovation in the European Research Area (ERA),[2] and the experts in the network provide advice and support on all aspects of the application of language technologies to European industry, both to SMEs developing Artificial Intelligence and Machine Learning applications, as well as in innovation projects set up in the context of the EU Digital Transformation and Recovery Plan across a wide range of industrial sectors.[3]

1.4 Key values: Open access and interoperability

The design, construction, and operation of CLARIN has been strongly inspired by the aim of facilitating the sharing of resources, providing a platform for open access, and stimulating the interoperability of data and services at all levels. The value attributed to open access has been operationalized by working towards a network of certified service centres distributed over all participating countries. The resources hosted by the centre repositories constitute the in-kind contribution from the members of the CLARIN consortium. Via the central services for metadata harvesting and the identity federation that enables login for associated researchers to the central services, access can be granted to the shared resources, irrespective of the centre in which they have been deposited. A crucial precondition for the effectiveness of this model for the sharing of language resources is the interoperability of the services. The harmonization of metadata is a prominent feature of the approach taken by CLARIN, but in addition to this kind of technical

2 See also action 8 in the ERA Policy Agenda: https://ec.europa.eu/info/research-and-innovation/strategy/strategy-2020-2024/our-digital-future/era-en.

3 The CLARIN Value Proposition can be accessed here: https://www.clarin.eu/content/clarin-value-proposition.

interoperability, CLARIN also promotes interoperability along other dimensions, in line with the demands of the Open Science agenda that are addressed in subsection 2.2. (See also de Jong et al. 2020.)

2 CLARIN as part of the European ecosystem of research infrastructures

CLARIN is positioned in the European Strategy Forum on Research Infrastructures (ESFRI) cluster "Social and Cultural Innovation", which largely overlaps with what is commonly referred to as the domain of Social Sciences and Humanities (SSH). Over the past decade, numerous cross-national initiatives supported by the participating countries and the European Commission have contributed to the ecosystem of European Research Infrastructures. The communities that initiated them have taken on the responsibility for enabling the production of new knowledge and innovation in order to help understand and tackle the societal, environmental, and economic challenges facing Europe and the world in the 21st century. Collaboration between the various research strands is often argued to be essential for the promise of advancing the level of excellence in foundational fields of study and the progress towards realizing the potential for impact, especially in research carried out in the context of agendas driven by societal missions. In addition, a crucial role is attributed to the availability of research data and infrastructural services that provide access to data and analysis tools.

2.1 The policy landscape

Partly under the umbrella of the European Strategy Forum on Research Infrastructures (ESFRI), a rich landscape of research infrastructures has emerged. CLARIN is one of the more than twenty ERICs that have been established. It is positioned in the ESFRI cluster "Social and Cultural Innovation", which largely overlaps with what is commonly referred to as the domain of Social Sciences and Humanities (SSH).

The Open Science agenda and in particular open access to data are at the heart of CLARIN's values. The objective of interoperability of data and services has paved the way for large-scale data sharing and growing reuse of language resources, but interoperability has also proven a crucial precondition for the increased support of multidisciplinary collaboration and comparative research agendas. In combination with the inherent multilinguality of Europe and the growing attention paid to language equality, the Open Science agenda is bringing strong incentives for investigations into cultural and societal phenomena across countries and regions. It is CLARIN's ambition to consolidate its role in supporting the emerging research agendas for the SSH domain and to contribute to the innovation potential of the advanced models for interaction between people, data, and machinery (or tools) for data processing. This is facilitated by the strong embedding of the developers of tools and data collections in their local, culturally specific context, and the interoperability paradigm for the model of collaboration between the centres involved.

CLARIN ERIC is one of the infrastructures that have been established under the umbrella of ESFRI. The increasingly rich ESFRI landscape, with a growing recognition of the potential for collaboration for the thematic clusters,[4] collaboration among the established ERICs united in the ERIC Forum,[5] and the emerging European Open Science Cloud (EOSC[6]) are likely to offer interesting opportunities for rearticulating CLARIN's position and the activities aimed at the exchange of knowledge and best practices among research organizations, and to establish CLARIN's profile as a spoke in the more generic knowledge hub for Research Infrastructures (RIs) that is currently being developed.[7]

2.2 Response to the demands of Open Science

The advance of data-driven methods in academia and the promotion of paradigms for open access to research data has increased the need for data registries and data management services to adhere to the guiding principles that make data FAIR: Findable, Accessible, Interoperable, Reusable.[8] In principle, the size of CLARIN's potential user base in Europe could be as big as the entire community of professional SSH researchers, which in Europe alone is estimated to be around 500,000 scholars (=30% of the researchers from all domains).

Since the early days of CLARIN, the values of what has become known as the Open Science agenda have inspired the conception and development of the infra-

4 See the 2020 position paper of the five cluster projects: https://zenodo.org/record/3675081#.Yt71MexBzlw.

5 ERIC Forum aims at advancing the position of the ERICs in the RI landscape. For details, see https://www.eric-forum.eu/.

6 The way in which CLARIN participates in the process of realizing the EOSC is described here: https://www.clarin.eu/eosc.

7 Making Science Happen: ESFRI White Paper 2020, see https://www.esfri.eu/esfri-white-paper.

8 The FAIR Data Principles, Force11, https://www.force11.org/group/fairgroup/fairprinciples.

structure. Providing data in open access and the sharing of language resources in order to allow reuse have been central to the approach adopted. Furthermore, providing open data, open source code, and open standards can help ensure studies based on these open resources are reproducible and replicable, as well as allowing for proper recognition and citation of resources, in alignment with the fundamental principles of academic research. FAIRness of data as a concept did not exist at the time CLARIN was set up, but the CLARIN approach to data curation and integration was FAIR *avant la lettre* (de Jong et al. 2020). Interoperability guidelines have affected integration and collaboration at a range of levels, most prominently in the adoption of a common metadata standard (Monachini et al. 2011; Soria et al. 2014). This has paved the way for the development of a number of technical services that derive their added value in part from the distributed and multilingual nature of the CLARIN data offering: the Virtual Language Observatory (VLO; Windhouwer and Goosen 2022), the Federated Content Search (FCS), and the Language Resource Switchboard (Zinn and Dima 2022). This approach has also enabled the interoperability of data and services across the boundaries of regions, languages, and disciplines, which helped position CLARIN as an initiative that stimulates multidisciplinarity, especially among the various SSH domains.

Putting the principles of Open Science into practice can be an arduous endeavour, as it depends on an interlocked chain of responsibilities and practices. For Open Sciences to succeed, data collectors, curators, data stewards, providers, and researchers need to commit to the adoption of open standards, open data, open source code, and open access. Making language data openly available is particularly challenging. Firstly, for the most part, contemporary language data fall within the ambit of copyright protection, as most linguistic expressions qualify as their author's own intellectual creations. Apart from some rare cases, copyright law grants authors exclusive rights to reproduce their work and communicate them to the public. Secondly, a significant portion of language data relate to identified or identifiable natural persons, and therefore constitute personal data. Providing and processing personal data is restricted by the General Data Protection Regulation (GDPR). Despite these complications, CLARIN is striving to make its data as open and accessible as possible, and only as closed as necessary. This is achieved in part by negotiating contracts with rights-holders which grant as many rights as possible to end users via standardized licenses. Furthermore, a dedicated CLARIN Committee on Legal and Ethical Issues (Kamocki, Kelli, and Lindén 2022) keeps the community informed on new developments in data protection law and practice, with particular attention to solutions that allow sharing of relevant datasets in open access conditions (or as close to these conditions as possible). Finally, alternative approaches are explored, to communicate the results of certain operations on data to the end user, without sharing the underlying data.

2.3 Collaboration with other RIs and platforms

The vision of borderless and seamless interoperability between data and services has recently provided a fertile ground for initiatives such as EOSC and the SSH Open Cluster a model for collaboration between RIs in the SSH domain aimed at sustaining and expanding the results of the cluster project SSHOC (2018-2022). The CLARIN infrastructure has been and will remain closely connected to these upcoming cloud platforms. Similarly, CLARIN has forged active collaborations with consortia and portals that promote language equality and easy access to digital resources, including language resources, such as the European Language Grid (Rehm et al. 2020), Europeana,[9] and the European Open Science marketplaces – the EOSC Portal[10] and the recently launched SSH Open Marketplace.[11] With the reduction of the traditional obstacles for (re)using data from other domains and the sharing of results, it has become clear that the interest in language material as an object of study is shared by quite a range of disciplines. The adoption of the interoperability paradigm has enabled CLARIN to take full advantage of the potential for comparative research based on data from multiple periods, regions, and languages. This insight has led to a number of investments in improved metadata curation and harmonization, carried out in the initiative known as CLARIN Resource Families (Lenardič and Fišer 2022). For a growing number of data types and tools, a continuous and structured effort has been made to increase the diversity of those families in terms of languages and regional background.

The need to foster and encourage an even greater interoperability level within the Resource Families has led CLARIN to launch its flagship project ParlaMint, dedicated to the creation of comparable and uniformly annotated multilingual corpora of parliamentary sessions. ParlaMint is currently available in about 20 languages, and new data and languages are being added for parliaments in Europe and beyond (Erjavec et al. 2021, 2022). The adoption of a common encoding format – TEI ParlaMint – will enable comparative research on topics such as Covid-19 legislations, gender studies, and green transition, among others. The ParlaMint example shows how an infrastructure such as CLARIN can go beyond supporting open data practices and become an actor for the creation of resources that are FAIR by design, and the promotion of agendas for comparable research.

9 See https://pro.europeana.eu/page/clarin

10 See https://eosc-portal.eu/

11 See https://marketplace.sshopencloud.eu/

The increased interoperability of the overall service offering and the growing coverage of the Resource Families is beneficial for a number of the research agendas for which CLARIN aims to provide infrastructural support, in particular in the domains that aim at innovation roadmaps through multidisciplinary collaboration and data-driven methodologies, such as Digital Humanities, Artificial Intelligence (including variants such as human-centered AI), computational social sciences, and political studies.

3 Organizational structure of CLARIN ERIC

A robust and efficient organizational structure is a *conditio sine qua non* for the action lines undertaken to lead to sustainable outcomes. Moreover, a faceted sustainability strategy is crucial for any organization that is dependent on stakeholder support, and trust is necessary for establishing a community within and around the infrastructure. This holds true not only for CLARIN ERIC, but also more generally for any infrastructure or long-term research project. In this section, the model of organization and the rationale behind it will be outlined. The implementation of this model may inspire other infrastructural initiatives and the lessons learned may enable them to benefit from the experience gained during the 10 years of CLARIN's existence.

3.1 CLARIN as ERIC

The organizational structure adopted in CLARIN is, to a large extent, guided by the kind of legal entity that underlies the CLARIN organization. CLARIN is a so-called ERIC: a European Research Infrastructure Consortium. The ERIC model was introduced in 2009 by the European Commission (EC), which defines research infrastructures as facilities that provide resources and services for research communities to conduct research and foster innovation.[12] ERIC status can be granted to research infrastructures that comply with the conditions specified in the ERIC Regulation.[13]

12 See https://ec.europa.eu/info/research-and-innovation/strategy/strategy-2020-2024/our-digital-future/european-research-infrastructures_en.

13 Council Regulation (EC) No 723/2009 of 25 June 2009 on the Community legal framework for a European Research Infrastructure Consortium (ERIC). Available at: https://eur-lex.europa.eu/legal-content/EN/TXT/?uri=CELEX:32009R0723.

3.2 CLARIN ERIC and national consortia

The ERIC model comes with a crucial role for the membership of countries that form the basis of the *C* in the term ERIC: the consortium. Together, the countries form the highest decision-taking body in CLARIN ERIC: the General Assembly. As CLARIN is a distributed digital research infrastructure, which depends heavily on the decentralized service offering and the coordination between these developments, the role of the national consortia is a critical aspect at all other levels in the organizational model, as reflected in the representation of countries in the higher-level committees. The CLARIN website contains a section on its governance structure with an overview of the various bodies and their relationship.[14] The following paragraph describes their role and composition in more detail.

All member and observer countries create their own national consortia, which contribute to the construction and operation of the CLARIN infrastructure, as well as to the outreach to communities of use. For such a joint effort to be successful, coordination is required and, more importantly, collaboration. Each country is represented by a National Coordinator, who acts as the main liaison between CLARIN ERIC and the national consortium. To ensure effective collaboration between CLARIN ERIC's Board of Directors (BoD) and the national consortia, four committees are in place. All National Coordinators participate in the National Coordinators' Forum (NCF), the main tasks of which are to coordinate national activities, exchange ideas and experiences, and advise the BoD. In the monthly NCF meetings, the BoD reports about newly adopted policies and recent activities and solicits input from National Coordinators. The Strategy and Management Board (SAMBA), a subcommittee of the NCF, consists of a balanced delegation of National Coordinators. The SAMBA convenes at least every quarter to discuss matters related to strategic planning, budgeting, and financing with the BoD and to prepare decisions to be taken by the NCF. The CLARIN centre network offers sustainable access to resources, services, and knowledge. The Standing Committee for CLARIN Technical Centres (SCCTC) is responsible for the coordination of the activities of the technical centre network. Each member or observer country has a representative on this committee. The User Involvement Committee (UIC) coordinates the activities aimed at outreach to the relevant communities of use in the national context and to the visibility of their efforts in order to demonstrate the added value of CLARIN. By combining the diversified nature of a distributed infrastructure with a cooperative governance model, CLARIN can work towards its objectives in a truly collaborative manner.

14 Overview of CLARIN governance structure: https://www.clarin.eu/content/governance.

3.3 Central operations

A model has been implemented for collaboration and sharing of responsibilities among the Office team members, who work from a service-oriented mindset that contributes to the overall trust-building among the various national nodes and the central organization. The Office capacity covers topics such as training and education coordination, communication, event organization, technology watch, and collaboration with experts on web design and development. The responsibility for the day-to-day management of the central organization lies with the Board of Directors. On some aspects, the BoD is advised by thematic committees (see Chapters 3.2 and 4.1). The BoD is responsible for the development of multi-annual strategies, annual budget proposals, communication with the Scientific Advisory Board, the acquisition of externally funded projects, the communication with the EC, ESFRI, and other relevant policy bodies and international alliances, the approval of new centres, the models for funding (based on calls for expressions of interest) and grant approval, and as indicated above, collaborating with the various thematic committees and their governance.

3.4 CLARIN and ESFRI

As mentioned already, and as described in detail in this book's chapter on the history of CLARIN and how it all started (Krauwer and Maegaard 2022), CLARIN is one of the infrastructures that have been established under the umbrella of the ESFRI. CLARIN was included in the first ESFRI Roadmap and as of 2016 it was listed by ESFRI as one of its Landmark RIs. In many countries, the national consortia are eligible for infrastructure funding under the condition of ESFRI recognition. Therefore, many of the national CLARIN consortia are dependent on ESFRI recognition. In some countries, the national consortia for CLARIN apply for national funding together with the national DARIAH consortium.[15]

15 In many cases the collaboration has led to the adoption of "CLARIAH" as the common name.

4 Knowledge Infrastructure and Technical Infrastructure: The key pillars

In this section the two main pillars of CLARIN's activities will be introduced and discussed: the Knowledge Infrastructure and the Technical Infrastructure. While the two aspects are presented separately, they are highly intertwined; together they fulfil the overarching objective of bringing language resources and technologies to researchers, students, lecturers, and other users, and enhancing competences for those using them and the potential for impact along a range of dimensions.

4.1 Knowledge Infrastructure

An infrastructure such as CLARIN is built upon the sharing of knowledge, be it factual knowledge (where to find data or tools) or procedural knowledge (workflows, best practices, standards that are used to create, curate, and use language resources). While the technical infrastructure is built to facilitate the discoverability of tools and resources, the CLARIN Knowledge Infrastructure has been developed as the "glue" for the various communities engaged with CLARIN, and as the structure that aims at securing a continuous transfer of knowledge between diverse parties involved in the construction, operation, and use of the infrastructure. The first gateway to the CLARIN Knowledge Infrastructure is the CLARIN website, a channel for disseminating high-quality information aimed at the exchange of knowledge, explaining the organization of the infrastructure and the activities undertaken, and illustrating the function and use of the services. Via the website, researchers and scholars can also access a rich catalogue of video recordings of CLARIN events, many of which originate from the Annual CLARIN conference, which is another pillar of the CLARIN knowledge sharing strategy.

Another crucial element is the network of CLARIN knowledge centres (K-centres) which bring together expertise on specific domains, topics, data modalities, and so on. Currently the K-centres, which can be operated by a single institute/group or arranged as a distributed structure, already cover a large number of research topics, languages, and resource types. However, CLARIN's strategy aims at broadening the range of topics covered by K-centres, incentivizing closer cooperation between them, and promoting their geographic distribution across CLARIN member countries. Knowledge offered by K-centres, the certified technical centres and the national consortia is also promoted by the Tour de CLARIN,[16] an annual publication showcasing resources and competences from CLARIN's distributed network.

The CLARIN Knowledge Infrastructure, together with CLARIN national nodes, is an important source of support and information for researchers who need to comply with the requirements of FAIR and open data in their projects and activities. In particular, the Legal and Ethical Issues Committee (CLIC) offers guidance and expertise on matters of Intellectual Property Rights and licenses, data protection, and privacy, as well as ethical and scientific integrity and responsible data science, while the Standards Committee offers advice on the standards to be supported and adopted within the infrastructure.

The Knowledge Infrastructure also aims to play an important role in training the next generation of scholars in specialized competences and skills, while supporting teachers and trainers throughout the network. The DH Course Registry (Wissik, Wessels, and Fischer 2022) is a joint initiative with DARIAH ERIC, which offers students an overview of the Digital Humanities programmes offered in Europe and beyond; in addition to this, a Teaching with CLARIN[17] section has been added to the website, hosting a selection of training materials shared by members of CLARIN's communities. The recognition of the importance of students, teachers, lecturers, and trainers as users of CLARIN has also led to dedicated support actions, both in terms of funding for the creation of training materials and of dedicated initiatives (such as the Teaching with CLARIN Award).

Finally, CLARIN's Knowledge Infrastructure has recently been strengthened by a network of Ambassadors, that is, recognized researchers in various disciplines, appointed by the central office to reach out to new communities of use. In spring 2020, during the COVID-19 pandemic, the CLARIN ambassadors were instrumental in initiating a series of CLARIN cafés, virtual events which are currently being held on a monthly basis, providing a platform for informal discussion on topics relevant for the infrastructure. The organization of cafés and other virtual events (including two virtual annual conferences) has provided us with a new way to engage with new research communities and to broaden CLARIN's user base, and will become a new element of the Knowledge Infrastructure in the post-Covid era.

16 See https://www.clarin.eu/Tour-de-CLARIN
17 See https://www.clarin.eu/content/teaching-clarin

4.2 Technical Infrastructure

Over the past few years, CLARIN has constructed a sound and robust technical basis to enable the sharing and reuse of language data and tools across institutional, disciplinary, and international borders. By its very nature, technology used for language processing is heterogeneous and country-specific: countries develop technologies that best cater to the needs of their official language. CLARIN's mission is to unify this heterogeneous landscape by building interoperable interfaces and a federated offer of thematic services (i.e., services addressing discipline-specific needs, in contrast to services with domain-independent functionality).

In contrast to many other research infrastructures, especially the single-sited ones operated in the domain of physics, CLARIN was never conceived as an RI that was to be built up from scratch. When CLARIN ERIC was founded in 2012, several of its centres had a long history of archiving, developing, and sharing language resources. Having this experience at hand was beneficial for newcomers to better understand what the result of investing in building up a new centre could look like. A stable repository, well-curated metadata descriptions, persistent identifiers, federated login, interoperable web services: seeing these in action elsewhere is often a better motivator than reading about their merits in a technical report, and having the capability to demonstrate parts of the Technical Infrastructure has always been crucial for reaching out to researchers and policymakers.

In the subsections to follow, the implementation steps and the building blocks of the Technical Infrastructure pillar will be outlined.

4.2.1 From founding principles to centre assessments

With the large interest in establishing technical CLARIN centres, the so-called B-centres, the need to formalize and assess the associated requirements quickly arose. This was a stepwise process, largely inspired by the founding principles that had already been defined in 2009.[18]

- **Principle of Independence**: Every participating centre is independent in its choices of internal organization and set-up as long as it adheres to the agreements that are defined for a smooth interaction within the network.
- **Principle of Service**: Every participating centre needs to make an explicit statement about the services it wants to offer and about the quality characteristics of these services.

18 See D2R-1a, Centres Network Formation, http://hdl.handle.net/11372/DOC-27.

- **Principle of Consistency:** Every participating centre needs to guarantee that the content it provides, when a unique and persistent identifier is used to refer to the content, will not change over time.
- **Principle of Interoperation:** Every participating centre needs to adhere to the set of interaction protocols and agreements defined within CLARIN.
- **Principle of Responsibility:** Every participating centre takes over a responsibility for the coverage of the services it offers.

These principles, balancing the freedom of technical and organizational choices with interoperability and standardization, reflect the philosophy behind CLARIN's infrastructure.

Throughout the preparatory phase of CLARIN that preceded the establishment of the ERIC and ended in 2011 (Krauwer and Maegaard 2022), the operationalization of the principles led to the first versions of the requirements for technical centres.[19] Afterwards this evolved into the B-centre checklist, with some incremental updates.[20] Just like CLARIN ERIC itself, the centre requirements are now 10 years old. Overall, they have not changed drastically: some centre types were scrapped, slightly controversial labels to measure the compliancy (gold, silver, etc.) eventually never saw the light of day. Still, the following interesting evolutions can be spotted, which also apply to other aspects of CLARIN's Technical Infrastructure.

More centres lead to more rules

In the early days, most centres that wanted to achieve B-centre status were actively involved in the drafting of the requirements and fully subscribed to the founding principles. While complying with the rules, later candidates introduced new boundary cases, leading to the introduction of new rules that from that point on applied to all centres, also when applying for re-certification (every three years).

Growth requires more predictability

With more centres queuing for an assessment, it is important that the rules are clear and predictable. Establishing a centre requires careful planning. While the overall construction period differs between individual cases, sudden changes in the rules should not interfere with this process.

---

19 See D2R-1b, Centres Network Formation – Centre types, http://hdl.handle.net/11372/DOC-28.
20 See http://hdl.handle.net/11372/DOC-78

The growing importance of multi-channel communication

To reach more ears at more locations, updates on the assessment procedure need to be broadcast more widely. To achieve this, regular bundled updates on the role of centres in the Technical Infrastructure are distributed under the heading "Centre News".

Overall, the evolution of the centre assessments has been continuously based on the founding principles mentioned above. These have helped to maintain a model that respects the diversity among the centres while maintaining technical compatibility, with changes where needed (e.g., moving from a two-year to a three-year period of validity for a centre's certification to maintain a time window that is in sync with the CoreTrustSeal procedure[21]) and stability where possible.

One principle that was not listed explicitly above was that of mutual trust between CLARIN and its centres. Nevertheless, this has played an important role over time. The proverbial carrot – in the form of recommendations, documentation, and best practices – has been used much more frequently than the stick. This in turn helped to keep up a positive and supportive atmosphere, which is probably at least as crucial as a sound technological framework for a research infrastructure.

4.2.2 Architectural approaches

Now that the technical centre model, and even more importantly the principles behind this model, have been introduced, we can take a look into CLARIN's infrastructural architecture. In this section, after introducing the technical building blocks, an overview of the related balancing acts will be given, concluding with some observations on the role of the people and the teams behind the Technical Infrastructure.

Technical Architecture: The building blocks

Without claiming to be complete, the following subsections will introduce some of the important parts of CLARIN's technical architecture.

---

21 See also https://www.coretrustseal.org/.

Repositories

The repository is the centrepiece of CLARIN's data infrastructure: it is the place that allows access to language resources via the web (HTTP) protocol, gives access to the associated metadata and persistent identifiers, and takes care of authentication and authorization. The repository is the primary access point for machine–machine communication (e.g., metadata harvesting), and most often also for human–machine communication (e.g., manual inspection of a deposited data set).

Each technical centre has a repository, which is subject to assessment. Internally, the assessment committee checks if all technical and CLARIN-internal requirements are fulfilled. Externally, the CoreTrustSeal assessment ensures that the repository is stable, well-maintained, and sustainable. Popular options for repository software are Fedora Commons and DSpace. For the latter, the LINDAT-CLARIAH/CZ team even created a CLARIN-specific version (Hajič et al. 2022), which has proven to be very popular.

An interesting development in the field of CLARIN repositories looks somewhat contradictory. First, there seems to be a growing interest in the adoption of large third-party open source repositories, such as DataVerse and the Zenodo-based InvenioRDM. An important point to note here is that these systems are not fully CLARIN-compliant off the shelf. Here, the need for one or more plug-ins providing this functionality seems obvious. On the other hand, many of the larger CLARIN centres have chosen to implement their repository system themselves, often based on home-made components brought together with a PHP-based frontend.

As always, it is impossible to predict reliably how the future of CLARIN repositories will look. Given the variation in the set-up of centres, however, it might very well be that both models will co-exist.

Metadata

Since the early conception of CLARIN, metadata has always played a key role in the architecture. This is illustrated by the fact that this book contains a full chapter on this subject (Windhouwer and Goosen 2022).

Persistent identifiers

The founding principle of consistency already demands the use of persistent identifiers to ensure reliable references to language resources. This principle was technically translated into the requirement to use the Handle system for persistent identification, based on its proven stability, scalability, and wide adoption. As of 2019, the Handle-based Digital Object Identifier (DOI) scheme is also recognized as valid technology for persistent identifiers. This important step – since

DOIs are an increasingly popular way of citing digital resources – was made possible when it became clear that some key requirements for the technical Centre assessment (the use of content negotiation for CMDI metadata) could be fulfilled by the DOI ecosystem.

Today, CLARIN ERIC is a member of both ePIC[22] (provider of handles) and DataCite[23] (provider of DOIs) and can thus provide access to both persistent identifiers to its centres.

Federated Identity

Language resources sometimes cannot be made openly accessible, due to copyright and privacy-related reasons, while agreements exist with the rights holder that allow the materials to be used for research purposes. In such cases it is important to allow for low-threshold access for researchers who can be granted permission. The use of Federated Identity, sometimes called Single Sign-On or Authentication and Authorization Infrastructure, ensures that a person can reuse institutional credentials (username and password) to access resources that are hosted elsewhere.

More details about CLARIN's implementation of Federated Identity, and some options for future steps in this realm, are described in a report on this topic.[24]

Interoperable web services and applications

Achieving interoperability between different language processing tools has always been an important goal in CLARIN's existence. At the same time, it is also a very ambitious goal that comes with many practical issues that need to be solved. Broadly speaking, there are two levels of interoperability we can distinguish.

Firstly, there is interoperability within the technology stack of a single centre. This level occurs most frequently, since interoperability is a matter of sticking to self-defined standards and the enforcement of these standards is quite easy. The typical case is an NLP pipeline for a single language hosted at one location. Many of these are described in the Tour de CLARIN.

Secondly, there are frameworks to interconnect services that are located at different centres, bringing the potential for a broader palette of tools but requiring more infrastructural efforts to orchestrate the whole. A noteworthy example is WebLicht (Hinrichs, Hinrichs, and Zastrow 2010; Dima et al. 2012), because it has

22 See https://www.pidconsortium.net/.
23 See https://datacite.org.
24 D2.7, SPF full extension, https://office.clarin.eu/v/CE-2017-1014-CLARINPLUS-D2_7.pdf.

also been maintained and developed over a long period and it includes services from many different CLARIN centres.

A simpler level of interoperability can be achieved by passing on a reference to a file and having it processed by the frameworks within a browser. Although limited in functionality and best suited for demonstration purposes, this is the approach chosen for the Language Resource Switchboard.

Finally, it is also worth mentioning that the rise of easy-to-use development libraries for Natural Language Processing (such as NLTK and spaCy) in combination with the popularity of Python and related frameworks (such as Jupyter notebooks) is enabling interoperability in many directions by combining a variety of APIs, including some based on RESTful web services. While requiring more technical skills from the user, these approaches allow by far the most flexibility. This insight is also the reason why CLARIN ERIC has included the topic "CLARIN for programmers" in its multi-year strategy.[25]

Federated Content Search

While it would technically be attractive to apply central indexation to all the corpora available in CLARIN, this is not possible – mostly for legal reasons: centres are not allowed to redistribute resources that are under copyright. Therefore the concept of Federated Content Search was conceived: queries are sent to the centres that host the corpora and the resulting hits are presented in a web application suitably titled "the FCS Aggregator".

This approach requires an enhanced level of infrastructural compatibility, just as it does for the interoperable web services. The initial "low-hanging fruit" approach, based on a simple text search, has been extended with a more powerful multi-layer search protocol,[26] which naturally requires more effort on the side of the implementing endpoints that do the translation for the central aggregator.

The tension between improved functionality and more stringent requirements on the part of the centres is a very apt illustration of some of the recurring infrastructural balancing acts that will be described in the next section.

25 See https://www.clarin.eu/content/vision-and-strategy

26 D2.9, Federated Content Search Engine v2 (software), https://office.clarin.eu/v/CE-2017-1035-CLARINPLUS-D2_9.pdf

4.2.3 Infrastructural balancing acts

In any infrastructure, but especially in a distributed one such as CLARIN, choices need to be made continuously between different organizational and evolutionary models. The options typically do not represent absolute dichotomies, nor do the choices have to be implemented in an absolute manner. Still, it is important to be aware of these options and the consequences of any choices made, as they tend to surface in many of the technological development tracks.

Shop window *versus* deep integration

Showing what CLARIN, as a growing distributed infrastructure, has to offer can be done in many ways. The simplest option is to create a virtual shop window (e.g., a portal or web page) with manually maintained descriptions about and links to the language resources at the centres. This is cost-effective and fast, but not so easy to maintain in the longer term. The other extreme is to create a deeply connected framework in which the resources can be accessed and used together (e.g., via a Virtual Research Environment). While this approach allows for better demonstration of the added value of the research infrastructure, it costs significantly more and requires strict protocols, standards, and policies on all sides to ensure a reasonable service level.

Central *versus* centres

Many parts of the Technical Infrastructure could be implemented and maintained centrally or decentrally. Originally, when CLARIN was initiated, all services were provided by the centres. Some of these offered many technical components and therefore played a crucial role as strongholds of the technology. Later, when the status of some of these centres changed over time, and the ERIC built up a central development team, several services were transferred to the central level.

It is mainly in relation to the technical services that fall outside the scope of language resources that the discussion about where to optimally position a component is raised. Transferring all of these to the central node sounds appealing in terms of efficiency, but misses the importance of decentralized know-how and scalability.

Similar discussions exist regarding the subject of running services in computing centres or networks of computing centres (organized as part of the European Open Science Cloud). Related debates also exist on the usage of commercially provided cloud services (e.g., for helpdesks or monitoring) versus self-hosting of such services.

Stability *versus* flexibility

An infrastructure needs to be stable. A static infrastructure provides optimal stability. On the other hand, staying up to date with upcoming requirements and technology stacks is a prerequisite to avoid obsolescence, and only regular updates provide a shield against huge migration operations with a high failure rate.

Related questions are when to apply the changes, and who can take the risk of being a first mover. CLARIN's history shows that it often makes sense if either the larger centres or the central node can take up these risks and share their experience with the rest of the centre network.

5 Strategy towards impact and sustainability

5.1 Human know-how: The real capital of CLARIN

Notwithstanding all the relevant considerations in the sections above, we should not forget to spotlight the single most important factor behind a successful technical infrastructure: the human know-how. While this aspect was already recognized during the preparatory phase, and has always played an important role up till today, ensuring that the built-up know-how reaches all centres remains challenging, if only because of CLARIN's growth. That is also why the Knowledge Infrastructure (see Section 4.1) is of such paramount importance.

A good example of successful knowledge maintenance and dissemination are the several cases where people who built up experience in designing and implementing the infrastructure passed on their knowledge to another centre as a result of changing jobs. Such scenarios are clearly a mark of success in the effort to maintain and distribute the infrastructural know-how, as is the informal and constructive atmosphere at the expert meetings. After all, it is often during informal discussions and brainstorming sessions that some of the key parts of the infrastructure first emerged.

5.2 The power of the distributed nature of the CLARIN service offering

For a research infrastructure such as CLARIN to offer a sustainable context for the various communities engaged in the development and uptake of the distributed and faceted thematic service provision, a balanced combination of stability and progression is mandatory (Broeder and Odijk 2022). Capitalizing on the federated nature of the infrastructure has proven a critical precondition for remaining at the forefront of technology. Recognition of the contribution from over 170 local nodes that together form the basis for the access to language resources and the exchange of knowledge and expertise is another critical condition for a sustainable service offering.

5.3 Impact

In line with CLARIN's primary mission to enable scientific excellence, over the years a wide range of high-quality and innovative research projects have been realized that were supported by CLARIN tools and resources. A dedicated section on the CLARIN website presents a selection of impact stories that illustrate the variety of disciplines for which the CLARIN infrastructure has proven to be of added value.[27] In view of the number of professional researchers working on SSH agendas it is to be expected that with adequate instruments for enhancing awareness and visibility of the value proposition the scientific and societal impact realized thus far can easily be increased.

The potential for impact that CLARIN and the social sciences and humanities have on societal issues is also illustrated by several of the impact stories; and in addition, this potential is underlined by the next stage of the ParlaMint project, in which the harmonized parliamentary corpora that will have been prepared in around 20 languages will form the basis for studies aiming to capture the public debate on the COVID-19 pandemic from a comparative perspective. Similar investigations of public debate and the corresponding traces of information and opinions on social media channels are vital for studying and developing solutions for the major societal challenges of our time, including worldwide inequality, migration, and climate change.

The aim of fostering the sustainable development of our world is expressed in the Agenda for Sustainable Development adopted by the General Assembly of the United Nations (UN) in 2015. The UN identified 17 Sustainable Development Goals (SDGs). As an international research infrastructure, CLARIN shares these goals and aims to make a contribution towards achieving them. A living web page summarizes these activities.[28]

27 See https://www.clarin.eu/content/clarin-impact-stories.
28 See https://www.clarin.eu/sustainable-development-goals

The CLARIN strategy also specifies action lines aimed at realizing the potential for collaboration with non-academic parties. This is illustrated by the fact that in many countries, institutes from the GLAM-sector, often national libraries and archives, contribute to the work of the national consortia as partners, as they are increasingly adapting to FAIR principles for their language-heavy collections and archives as well.

The existing collaborative links with industrial parties in many regional contexts, for example, for machine translation and speech processing, function as stepping stones for a more systematic innovation strategy that positions CLARIN as a key driver of the digital transformation in society at large. Evidently many CLARIN tools and resources are desirable building blocks in commercial software development; language is an integral part of many AI systems (e.g., chatbots, recommender systems, sentiment mining) and the growing market for AI-powered innovations is likely to lead to a surge in the interest in CLARIN technologies and data.

To ensure that the potential for impact is realized and that the role of CLARIN in the RI ecosystem is sustainable, the uptake of the CLARIN service offering in the various communities of use is a crucial precondition. CLARIN will continue to seek collaboration with other research infrastructures, national infrastructural initiatives, and communities involved in the articulation of disciplinary research agendas that could benefit from the research enabling services offered by CLARIN. Language matters in some way or other in all disciplines and societal domains, but the value proposition will come across only with clear promotion, branding, instruction, illustration, and demonstration.

6 The next decade

Where could CLARIN be in ten years from now? Our future plans focus on:
- reinforced support for multidisciplinary agendas, within and beyond SSH;
- models supporting the use of heterogeneous data/AI;
- responsible use of technology;
- training/capacity development;
- collaboration beyond academia;
- collaboration beyond Europe.

Robustness has been and will continue to be a distinctive quality of CLARIN. In the coming years, CLARIN will sustain, improve, and consolidate both infrastructural pillars, that is, the Knowledge Infrastructure and the Technical Infrastructure. Researchers and developers will be stimulated to integrate (multi)disciplinary research agendas and domain-specific quality requirements in the thematic service offer. Education, training, and capacity-building will be offered and facilitated to enhance the skills of the developers involved, increase the level of data literacy among researchers and citizens, and contribute to the education of new generations of data professionals for whom language data will increasingly demand advanced methods and tools.

Bibliography

Bański, Piotr & Hanna Hedeland. 2022. Standards in CLARIN. In Darja Fišer & Andreas Witt (eds.), *CLARIN. The infrastructure for language resources.* Berlin: De Gruyter.

Broeder, Daan & Jan Odijk. 2022. Sustainability and genericity of CLARIN services in the Netherlands. In Darja Fišer & Andreas Witt (eds.), *CLARIN. The infrastructure for language resources.* Berlin: De Gruyter.

Dima, Emanuel, Erhard Hinrichs, Marie Hinrichs, Alexander Kislev, Thorsten Trippel & Thomas Zastrow. 2012. Integration of WebLicht into the CLARIN infrastructure. In *Proceedings of the joint CLARIN-D/DARIAH workshop "Service-oriented architectures (SOAs) for the humanities: Solutions and impacts" at Digital Humanities Conference 2012*, 17–23.

Erjavec, Tomaž, Maciej Ogrodniczuk, Petya Osenova, Nikola Ljubešić, Kiril Simov, Vladislava Grigorova, Michał Rudolf, Andrej Pančur, Matyáš Kopp, Starkaður Barkar-son, Steinhór Steingrímsson, Henk van der Pol, Griet Depoorter, Jesse de Does, Bart Jongejan, Dorte Haltrup Hansen, Costanza Navarretta, María Calzada Pérez, Luciana D. de Macedo, Ruben van Heusden, Maarten Marx, Çağrı Çöltekin, Matthew Coole, Tommaso Agnoloni, Francesca Frontini, Simonetta Montemagni, Valeria Quochi, Giulia Venturi, Manuela Ruisi, Carlo Marchetti, Roberto Battistoni, Miklós Sebők, Orsolya Ring, Roberts Darģis, Andrius Utka, Mindaugas Petkevičius, Monika Briediene˙, Tomas Krilavičius, Vaidas Morkevičius, Sascha Diwersy, Giancarlo Luxardo & Paul Rayson. 2021. Multilingual comparable corpora of parliamentary debates ParlaMint 2.1. http://hdl.handle.net/11356/1432 (accessed June 14, 2022), Slovenian language resource repository CLARIN.SI.

Erjavec, T., Maciej Ogrodniczuk, Petya N. Osenova, Nikola Ljubesic, Kiril Ivanov Simov, Andrej Pancur, Michal Rudolf, Matyás Kopp, Starkaður Barkarson, Steinþór Steingrímsson, Çagri Çöltekin, Jesse de Does, Katrien Depuydt, Tommaso Agnoloni, Giulia Venturi, María Calzada Pérez, Luciana D. Macedo, Costanza Navarretta, Giancarlo Luxardo, Matthew Coole, Paul Rayson, Vaidas Morkevicius, Tomas Krilavicius, Roberts Dargis, Orsolya Ring, R. van Heusden, Maarten Marx & Darja Fiser. 2022. The ParlaMint corpora of parliamentary proceedings. *Language Resources and Evaluation* 1–34. https://doi.org/https://doi.org/10.1007/s10579-021-09574-0.

Hajič, Jan, Eva Hajičová, Barbora Hladká, Jozef Mišutka, Ondřej Košarko & Pavel Straňák. 2022. LINDAT/CLARIAH-CZ: Where we are and where we go. In Darja Fišer & Andreas Witt (eds.), *CLARIN. The infrastructure for language resources.* Berlin: De Gruyter.

Hennelly, Martin, Langa Khumalo, Juan Steyn & Menno van Zaanen. 2022. Training of digital language resources skills in South Africa. In Darja Fišer & Andreas Witt (eds.), *CLARIN. The infrastructure for language resources.* Berlin: De Gruyter.
Hinrichs, Erhard, Marie Hinrichs & Thomas Zastrow. 2010. WebLicht: Web-based LRT services for German. In Sandra Kübler (ed.), *Proceedings of the 48th Annual Meeting of the Association for Computational Linguistics: System demonstrations*, 25–29. Stroudsberg, PA: Association for Computational Linguistics.
Jong, Franciska de, Bente Maegaard, Darja Fišer, Dieter Van Uytvanck & Andreas Witt. 2020. Interoperability in an infrastructure enabling multidisciplinary research: The case of CLARIN. *International Conference on Language Resources and Evaluation (LREC) 12*, 3406–3413.
Kamocki, Paweł, Aleksei Kelli & Krister Lindén. 2022. The CLARIN Committee for Legal and Ethical Issues and the Normative Layer of the CLARIN infrastructure. In Darja Fišer & Andreas Witt (eds.), *CLARIN. The infrastructure for language resources.* Berlin: De Gruyter.
Krauwer, Steven & Bente Maegaard. 2022. CLARIN – how it started. In Darja Fišer & Andreas Witt (eds.), *CLARIN. The infrastructure for language resources.* Berlin: De Gruyter.
Lenardič, Jakob & Darja Fišer. 2022. The CLARIN Resource and Tool Families. In Darja Fišer & Andreas Witt (eds.), *CLARIN. The infrastructure for language resources.* Berlin: De Gruyter.
Ljubešić, Nikola, Tomaž Erjavec, Maja Miličević Petrović & Tanja Samardžić. 2022. Together we are stronger: Bootstrapping language technology infrastructure for South Slavic languages with CLARIN.SI. In Darja Fišer & Andreas Witt (eds.), *CLARIN. The infrastructure for language resources.* Berlin: De Gruyter.
Monachini, Monica, Valeria Quochi, Nicoletta Calzolari, Núria Bel, Gerhard Budin, P. Caselli, Khalid Choukri, Gil Francopoulou, Erhard Hinrichs, Steven Krauwer, Lothar Lemnitzer, Joseph Mariani, Jan Odijk, Stelios Piperidis, Adam Przepiorkowski, Laurent Romary, Helmut Schmidt, Hans Uszkoreit & Peter Wittenburg. 2011. The standards' landscape towards an interoperability framework: The FLaReNet proposal building on the CLARIN standardisation action plan. http://dspace.library.uu.nl/handle/1874/ 285299.
Rehm, Georg, Maria Berger, Ela Elsholz, Stefanie Hegele, Florian Kintzel, Katrin Marheinecke, Stelios Piperidis, Miltos Deligiannis, Dimitris Galanis, Katerina Gkirtzou, Penny Labropoulou, Kalina Bontcheva, David Jones, Ian Roberts, Jan Hajič, Jana Hamrlová, Lukáš Kačena, Khalid Choukri, Victoria Arranz, Andrejs Vasil,jevs, Orians Anvari, Andis Lagzdin, š, Jūlija Mel,n, ika, Gerhard Backfried, Erinç Dikici, Miroslav Janosik, Katja Prinz, Christoph Prinz, Severin Stampler, Dorothea Thomas-Aniola, José Manuel Gómez-Pérez, Andres Garcia Silva, Christian Berrío, Ulrich Germann, Steve Renals & Ondrej Klejch. 2020. European language grid: An overview. *International Conference on Language Resources and Evaluation (LREC)* 12, 3366–3380.
Soria, Claudia, Nicoletta Calzolari, Monica Monachini, Valeria Quochi, Núria Bel, Khalid Choukri, Joseph Mariani, Jan Odijk & Stelios Piperidis. 2014. The language resource strategic agenda: the FLaReNet synthesis of community recommendations. *Language Resources and Evaluation* 48 (4), 753–775. https://doi.org/10.1007/s10579-014-9279-y
Sumathy, K. L. & M. Chidambaram. 2013. Text mining: Concepts, applications, tools and issues – an overview. *International Journal of Computer Applications* 80 (4), 29–32.
Windhouwer, Menzo & Twan Goosen. 2022. Component Metadata Infrastructure. In Darja Fišer & Andreas Witt (eds.), *CLARIN. The infrastructure for language resources.* Berlin: De Gruyter.

Wissik, Tanja, Leon Wessels & Frank Fischer. 2022. The DH Course Registry: A piece of the puzzle in CLARIN's Technical and Knowledge Infrastructure. In Darja Fišer & Andreas Witt (eds.), *CLARIN. The infrastructure for language resources.* Berlin: De Gruyter.
Zinn, Claus & Emanuel Dima. 2022. The CLARIN Language Resource Switchboard: Current state, impact, and future roadmap. In Darja Fišer & Andreas Witt (eds.), *CLARIN. The infrastructure for language resources.* Berlin: De Gruyter.

Part II: **Technical Infrastructure**

Jan Hajič*, Eva Hajičová, Barbora Hladká, Jozef Mišutka, Ondřej Košarko, and Pavel Straňák

LINDAT/CLARIAH-CZ: Where We Are and Where We Go

Abstract: In this chapter we present the main achievements of the Czech large research infrastructure LINDAT/CLARIAH-CZ. We provide a short description of the infrastructure and its history, and a brief account of its scientific, technological, and infrastructural scope. We focus on the technological innovations already implemented in the repository and in the service offerings, and outline some future plans.

Keywords: infrastructure, repository, web services, natural language processing, linguistics, digital humanities, language resources, software tools

1 LINDAT/CLARIAH-CZ

LINDAT/CLARIAH-CZ is a large research infrastructure serving the national and international research communities in a number of scientific fields in the arts and humanities by providing openly accessible digital resources, technologies, and tools, as well as knowledge, expertise, and help for fully exploiting these resources in users' research.

It forms a virtual networked (distributed) node of the pan-European research infrastructure CLARIN ERIC, being symbolized by one of the rings in the chain of the CLARIN ERIC logo. In fact, its origin dates back to well before when CLARIN ERIC was established in 2012. Figure 1 shows the important dates over a period of 20 years of building this Czech research infrastructure centre.

Acknowledgment: The work described herein, as well as the LINDAT/CLARIAH-CZ Large Research Infrastructure itself, has been supported by the Large Research Infrastructure programme of the Ministry of Education, Youth, and Sports of the Czech Republic (LM2018101) and its predecessors, as well as by the Ministry's Structural Funds (joint EU and national support).

***Corresponding author: Jan Hajič**, Charles University, Faculty of Mathematics and Physics, Institute of Formal and Applied Linguistics, Prague, Czech Republic, e-mail: hajic@ufal.mff.cuni.cz
Eva Hajičová, Charles University, Prague, Czech Republic, e-mail: hajicova@ufal.mff.cuni.cz
Barbora Hladká, Charles University, Prague, Czech Republic, e-mail: hladka@ufal.mff.cuni.cz
Jozef Mišutka, Charles University, Prague, Czech Republic, e-mail: misutka@ufal.mff.cuni.cz
Ondřej Košarko, Charles University, Prague, Czech Republic, e-mail: kosarko@ufal.mff.cuni.cz
Pavel Straňák, Charles University, Prague, Czech Republic, e-mail: stranak@ufal.mff.cuni.cz

https://doi.org/10.1515/9783110767377-003

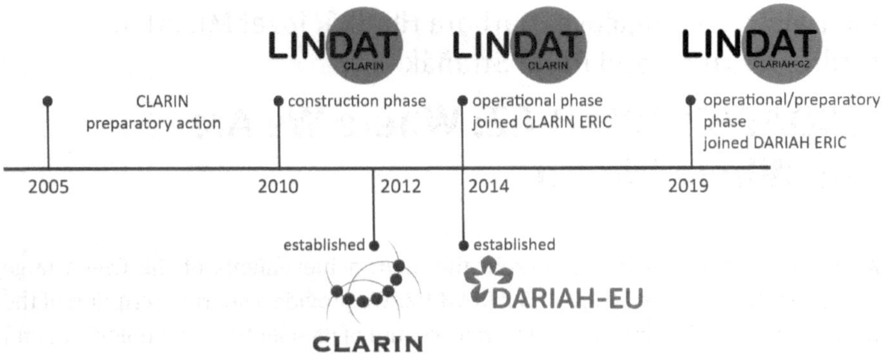

Figure 1: LINDAT timeline.

While this section describes briefly the history, current state, and future plans of LINDAT/CLARIAH-CZ, the next section (Section 2) is devoted to CLARIN-DSpace, the repository solution developed at LINDAT/CLARIAH-CZ, and the final section (Section 3) to the web services architecture provided for running LINDAT/CLARIAH-CZ's tools.

1.1 Where we started

LINDAT/CLARIN, the predecessor of LINDAT/CLARIAH-CZ, was founded as a national project in October 2010 after having participated in the EU-funded CLARIN preparatory action in 2008–2011.[1] These actions aimed at defining the needs of the user community and establishing a structured network of institutions that produce and/or need language resources. Its motivation stemmed from the situation in which language resources and technologies for their processing already existed in European countries, as well as in the USA and Asia. However, the centralized distribution agencies, namely the Linguistic Data Consortium[2] and European Language Resources Association,[3] did not fully suit the requirements for simple, non-bureaucratic and, in particular, free and open access to language resources. This situation led to fragmented, uncoordinated distribution of data with all the associated consequences, such as incompatible formats, different and unclear licensing conditions, the inability to access the data themselves, and

1 EC FP7 project No. 212230; for the creation of CLARIN, the concurrently running FlaReNet project (2008–2011, ECP-2007-LANG-617001) was also important.
2 https://www.ldc.upenn.edu
3 http://www.elra.info/en

the need to use many different search engines to even find them. Therefore the efforts of the various EU-coordinated networks aimed to remove these obstacles and to establish a distributed and uniform way of providing language data and tools. On the other hand, creating (annotated) data and tools was declared to be the responsibility of individual nations. Such activity mostly concerns national languages. This was also the reason why the planned network was designed as a network of national centres.

In the early 2010s, it was widely accepted that statistical methods (both supervised and unsupervised machine learning) give the best results in many Natural Language Processing (NLP) areas, including applications usable in practice. Thus, both annotated and raw language data in large volumes have become the focus of the community, which needed them in order to obtain highly accurate and usable results in, for example systems for grammar checking, basic text analysis tasks like tagging or parsing, machine translation, automatic speech recognition, information extraction, text summarization and many others. For supervised learning, annotated data is needed, which takes a lot of effort to design, collect and produce: it is manual work by highly trained linguists and PhD students of linguistics, most often in interdisciplinary combination(s). Expertise and support is needed in additional areas, including but not limited to statistics, computer science, security and privacy, education, and legal areas, with specific management and organizational support.

In the Czech Republic at that time, data were mainly collected and annotated at three institutions: Charles University in Prague, Masaryk University in Brno, and University of West Bohemia in Pilsen. Together with the Czech Language Institute of the Czech Academy of Sciences which – among other things – digitized and archived old lexical resources, these workplaces became the co-founders of LINDAT/CLARIN. Its mission was to serve as a national centre that (i) makes language data publicly available for straightforward use, free of legal obstacles in the areas of science, research, and education; (ii) makes available both monolingual and multilingual data; (iii) makes already existing software tools, services, and technologies available to users; (iv) annotates, mainly but not exclusively, Czech-language data; (v) provides added value to Czech national activities,especially for connecting them to others on a pan-European scale; (vi) provides important opportunities for innovations; (vii) strengthens the interest in national language as a part of national culture and national heritage; (viii) contributes to the modernization of the educational process.

LINDAT/CLARIN was gradually built during a construction phase that lasted from 2010 to 2013. It reached a number of milestones; here we highlight only some: (1) It has developed a CLARIN-compatible and certified repository based on the open source solution DSpace.[4] (2) It created and opened for community use a number of sizeable, high-quality annotated language resources in Czech and some other languages, most notably the family of Prague Dependency Treebanks. (3) The repository was selected as the official repository for the Universal Dependencies (UD) project, led by University of Uppsala (Sweden), Stanford University (USA), Google's research groups in New York and London, and Charles University, with another 200+ researchers participating.[5] The UD project collects syntactically and morphologically annotated treebanks and unifies their annotation for both linguistic studies and technology development. Two major updates of the UD collection are published every year under the management of LINDAT/CLARIAH-CZ. (4) It established the Center for Visual History Malach as an Access Point for the very large archive of video interviews (testimonies) of Holocaust survivors, owned now by the Visual History Institute at the University of Southern California in Los Angeles, USA, and gradually added further related resources to allow for "one-stop shopping" for oral history research on genocides.[6] (5) The Internet Language Reference Book supported by the Czech Language Institute surpassed 20 million page views.[7]

The Czech Republic joined CLARIN ERIC in January 2014 and LINDAT/CLARIN started its operational phase. The focus shifted slightly from repository building and resource acquisition to services and tools, mainly covering various types of language technologies. Since then, more than 20 open source tools and corresponding services, such as morphological analysers, part-of-speech and feature taggers and lemmatizers, dependency parsers, named-entity recognizers, automatic speech recognizers, spelling corrector tools, and treebank search tools have been implemented, refactored or reused, and integrated.[8] The work on the DSpace extension also continued to fulfil all the requirements of CLARIN ERIC and to improve its features in the areas of open research data and FAIR-compliant[9] storage, long-term preservation, common authentication and authorization infrastructure (AAI), metadata harvesting, content search, distribution, and access. LINDAT/CLARIN has also continued to develop new or updated resources, adding newly established types of linguistic annotation, such as multiword expressions, information structure, named entities, coreference and discourse annotation to its Prague Dependency Treebank "trademark" family of corpora in Czech, English,

4 https://duraspace.org/dspace
5 https://universaldependencies.org
6 https://ufal.mff.cuni.cz/malach
7 https://prirucka.ujc.cas.cz
8 https://lindat.cz/services
9 https://www.go-fair.org

and some additional languages, while enlarging them with new genres.[10] In addition to corpora, several lexicons have been built or extended as well, such as the MorfFlex, PDT-Vallex, EngVallex, CzEngVallex, VALLEX, and SynSemClass morphological, valency, and semantic lexicons.

LINDAT/CLARIN was certified as a K-centre ("knowledge centre"), in a joint venture with the Norwegian node of CLARINO in Bergen, to provide consultations and advice in treebanking activities.

Since 2014, the Ministry of Education, Youth, and Sports performs periodic international panel-based assessments of infrastructures included in the Roadmap of Large Research Infrastructures of the Czech Republic. In 2017, after three years of its operation, LINDAT/CLARIN underwent its first evaluation. In addition, a separate proposal was submitted to create a LINDAT/CLARIN's sister infrastructure, DARIAH-CZ (presumably becoming part of DARIAH ERIC), to enhance and support digitally-enabled research across the arts and humanities, and to facilitate the provision of services and activities for the digital arts and humanities research community. The proposal was accepted and eventually fully merged with LINDAT/CLARIN at the beginning of 2020, which became LINDAT/CLARIAH-CZ, with nine more partner organizations included in the project.[11] The merger was based on the experience of other European countries where CLARIN ERIC and DARIAH ERIC networks were housed under one umbrella project.[12]

1.2 Where we are

Scientific scope of LINDAT/CLARIAH-CZ covers the research fields of language and linguistics, literature, literary and cultural history, history of the arts, general history and historical bibliography, philosophy, film and film history, new media, visual art, musicology and music-related cultural history, ethnology and folklore, archaeology, and Egyptology and interdisciplinary studies.[13]

LINDAT/CLARIAH-CZ provides knowledge and expertise in annotation practices (for illustration see (Hajičová et al. 2022)), data and metadata collection support, data preservation, use of software tools, and application. It is engaged

10 See, e.g., https://ufal.mff.cuni.cz/pdt-c

11 https://lindat.cz/partners

12 See, e.g., CLARIAH-DE, https://www.clariah.de, or the Netherlands CLARIAH project, https://www.clariah.nl.

13 To compare with examples from other countries, please refer to the description of the experience in humanities research being carried out in Austria (Trognitz et al. 2022) and Germany (Draxler et al. 2022).

very strongly in cross-cutting technologies, such as technology for repository access, digital research support, and language and speech technology, including recent Artificial Intelligence techniques, which underpin access to resources in the above fields of science.

Technological scope of LINDAT/CLARIAH-CZ can be divided into four areas: (1) common data and service infrastructure, which serves both humanities (and arts) and technologies; (2) language resources, tools and services intended primarily (but not solely) for the language and linguistic research and language technology community; (3) digital humanities and arts data collections and related tools, primarily but not solely intended for the digital humanities and arts research users; (4) offering education and other types of training at all levels of the university system and providing support to researchers and students using the infrastructure.

The core group at Charles University, the host institution of the research infrastructure LINDAT/CLARIAH-CZ serves its users both inside and outside the LINDAT/CLARIAH-CZ consortium in two essential areas: it provides its repository, which holds all the data and tools (and models and documentation) and makes them openly available, and it provides web services (with a user interface for easy testing and small-scale experiments). These are both described in Sections 2 and 3, which are modified and extended versions of (Straňák et al. 2019).

1.3 Where we go

While continuing to engage in all the activities described earlier in this Section, expanding them as necessary, adding computing facilities to cover increased use, adding language resources and new tools, and improving the existing language tools in terms of accuracy and language coverage, LINDAT/CLARIAH-CZ is looking to expand in novel areas (such as Artificial Intelligence on the technology side and history on the other) to explore the synergies and economies of scale that close integration within one project allows.

To this end, and to expand the offerings of the Center for Visual History Malach with complementary resources and expertise, LINDAT/CLARIAH-CZ is seeking to bring four more institutional partners in the consortium, starting in 2023.[14] These would add documents, written materials, and results of previous research on Holocaust and connect LINDAT/CLARIAH-CZ to the EHRI-CZ network, and through this, to the European EHRI network.

14 Masaryk Institute of the Czech Academy of Sciences, National Archives, Institute of the Terezín Initiative and Terezín Memorial.

2 The repository

When the LINDAT/CLARIN project started, there was no suitable repository system for hosting data and tools at any of the organizations that together form LINDAT/CLARIN. As the Czech CLARIN partner, LINDAT/CLARIN wanted to avoid building a system from scratch; instead, we looked for a repository system that was popular and robust, one that would keep being updated and would allow us to modify it and share the modification. The system would need to have a reasonable frontend that would allow user submissions and offer standalone search functionality directly on the web, not relying solely on CLARIN Virtual Language Observatory (VLO).[15] Ideally, it would be usable straight out of the box while fulfilling CLARIN's requirements.[16] These are namely, to provide (1) support for persistent (permanent) identifiers (PIDs) in the form of handles[17] (this has recently changed so that other PID systems are allowed); (2) support for CMDI metadata[18] harvested via the OAI-PMH protocol[19]; (3) support for federated authentication/authorization via the SAML protocol,[20] and (4) support for handling licenses for the data and tools submitted to the repository.

These requirements resulted in our choice of DSpace: the most popular repository system in the world, which seemed easy to deploy and maintain and could do most of the "heavy lifting" out of the box, while allowing the necessary CLARIN-related modifications.

We first modified DSpace to be compatible with the assignment of Handle PIDs via the EPIC service (Pajas 2010), and later added a simple CMDI metadata schema that was also compatible with the META-SHARE project,[21] based on a prior agreement between CLARIN and META-SHARE to make their repositories compatible. CLARIN-DSpace still uses that original META-SHARE minimal metadata scheme by default. When an option was added to harvest the metadata directly in the CMDI format, the repository became compatible with the CLARIN technical centre guidelines, as they were at the time.

The repository software, which we started calling LINDAT-DSpace when it expanded beyond the original patch for EPIC Handles, was further modified and upgraded in the following years, and it has run continuously at the LINDAT/

15 https://vlo.clarin.eu
16 Most importantly, the requirements for a certification as a CLARIN B-Centre.
17 http://www.handle.net
18 For more details on CMDI see (Windhouwer and Goosen 2022).
19 http://www.openarchives.org/pmh
20 https://www.oasis-open.org/committees/tc_home.php?wg_abbrev=security
21 http://www.meta-share.org

CLARIAH-CZ centre at Charles University since then. The popularity of the service is steadily growing, and over time it has become the repository of choice for many international projects involving language resources, like the Universal Dependencies project, or various Natural Language Processing shared tasks (contests), like some of the Workshop on Machine Translation[22] Shared Tasks or various CoNLL (Computational Natural Language Learning)[23] Shared Tasks, between 2009 and 2020.

At the same time, several other CLARIN centres showed interest in the repository system, which (i) fulfills all the requirements of a CLARIN B-centre, (ii) requires relatively little maintenance, and (iii) is basically a ready-to-use, all-in-one package. The current list of deployments within CLARIN is in Table 1.

Table 1: DSpace deployments within CLARIN as of September 2021.

CLARIN-DK	https://repository.clarin.dk/repository
CLARIN-IS	https://repository.clarin.is/repository
CLARIN-IT ILC4CLARIN	https://dspace-clarin-it.ilc.cnr.it/repository/xmlui
CLARIN-IT ERCC	https://clarin.eurac.edu/repository
CLARIN-LT	http://clarin-lt.lt
CLARIN-PL	https://clarin-pl.eu
CLARIN.SI	https://www.clarin.si/repository/xmlui
CLARINO	https://repo.clarino.uib.no
LINDAT/CLARIAH-CZ	https://lindat.cz/repository
Oxford Text Archive	https://ota.bodleian.ox.ac.uk/repository/xmlui
SWE-CLARIN	https://repo.spraakbanken.gu.se/xmlui

The requirements for changes and improvements were coming from multiple directions. After the initial modification for using the EPIC Handle system, we kept developing the system to best suit the needs of both users and administrators. Some changes were made to fulfil further CLARIN requirements for (what eventually became) B-centres. Some were made to make the administration of the repository more efficient, and yet another set of features was required by our users. Some modifications have been initiated by us as "experiments" because they seemed to offer interesting added value. In addition, we found and shared fixes for several bugs in the system, improved the user interface, and enhanced the federated authentication system.

22 http://www.statmt.org
23 https://conll.org

Currently the repository instance at LINDAT/CLARIAH-CZ hosts 472 data items, 2 TB in total. At the moment, the repository has approximately 1,000 user accounts. While it might seem a small number, accounts are only needed to either submit new datasets or sign licenses for restricted datasets; otherwise, anyone can download most of the resources without even logging in, thanks to their open licences.

2.1 New administrative features

There are two new features that we have successfully merged into the main DSpace: our modified control panel and our health-check system.

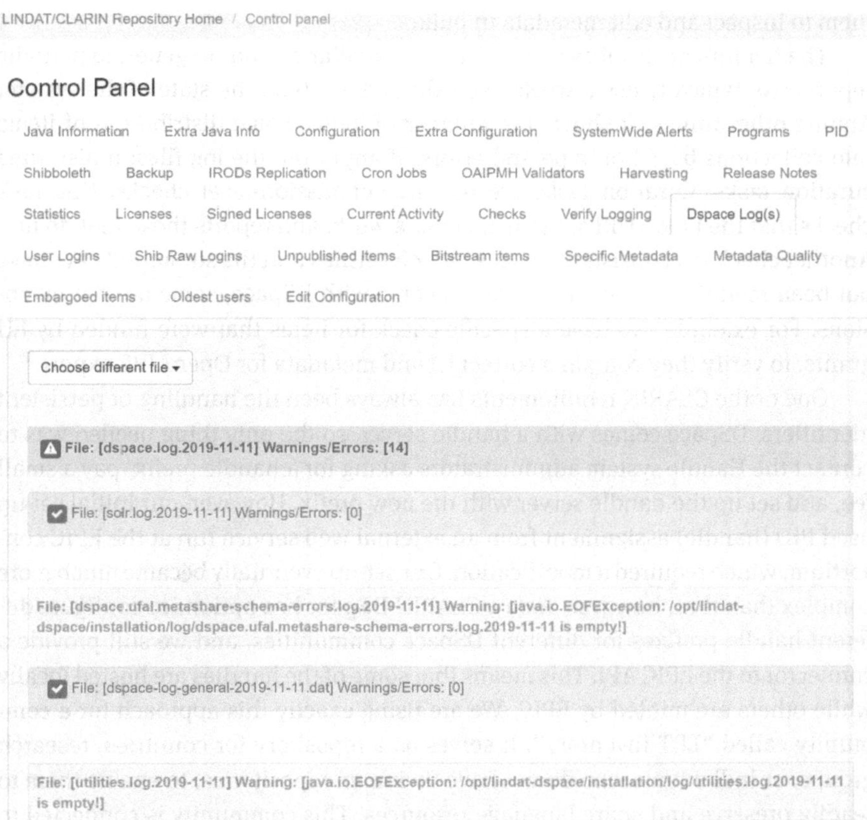

Figure 2: An illustration of control panel with logs tab selected. This provides a brief overview of various log files of the system and allows the user to inspect them without using the command line.

The reason behind those improvements is that the system produces a lot of log messages that were not easy to manage; the whole repository infrastructure comprises not only the DSpace repository software, but also a database server, a web server, the single-sign on federation service provider (Shibboleth service provider),[24] and a handle server (standalone PID system). On the operating system level (or on the virtualization level), there are backups and periodic administrative tasks (performed using cron). To get a good overview of the whole system set-up, and to make this information readily available to repository administrators, we have substantially extended DSpace's control panel (see Figure 2). Originally it only showed basic information like the uptime and some configuration details; with our extensions, it also shows and searches the log files, enables the admins to run some of the occasionally required re-indexing tasks, and allows them to inspect and edit metadata in bulk.

The health-check subsystem exists for a similar reason: to generate periodic reports (we typically use a weekly schedule) describing the state of the system. Among other things, it shows the number of items, some distribution of items into collections based on type and errors (if any) from the log files; it also runs curation tasks. Curation tasks are usually submission-level checks. One task checks that the links (URLs) in the metadata work, and reports those that do not. Another check is a consistency check, which verifies that the submitted data have not been modified. Some of the checks come with DSpace, some are our extensions. For example, we have a specific check for items that were funded by EU grants, to verify they contain a correct ID and metadata for OpenAIRE export.[25]

One of the CLARIN requirements has always been the handling of persistent identifiers. DSpace comes with a handle server, so the only thing needed was to contact the Handle system administrators asking for a handle prefix, pay a small fee, and set up the handle server with the new prefix. However, our initial set-up used PID (handle) assignment from an external web service run at the EPIC consortium, which required a modification. Our set-up eventually became much more complex than that, however. Today, CLARIN-DSpace has options to configure different handle prefixes for different DSpace communities, and we still provide a connector to the EPIC API. This means that some of the handles are hosted locally while others are minted by EPIC. We are using exactly this approach for a community called "LRT Inventory". It serves as a repository for countries, research groups, or individuals who do not have their own repositories, to enable them to readily preserve and share language resources. This community is connected to

24 https://www.shibboleth.net
25 https://www.openaire.eu

CLARIN ERIC, so we are using a handle prefix from EPIC owned by CLARIN ERIC, and CLARIN ERIC's employees serve as editors, checking any new submissions. This gives CLARIN a fundamental level of control over the records.

In 2020, new communities were added to cover the new data types coming from the new LINDAT/CLARIAH-CZ partners. The "original repository", that is the language resources and tools in both the LRT and (the former) LINDAT/CLARIN communities, were moved under a new top-level community called Language Resources. There is another top level community called Digital Humanities which hosts non-linguistic resources. This community has its own handle prefix. The general idea behind that is similar to the CLARIN ERIC's community, that is to be able to move the governance of the data to another entity (e.g., a different LINDAT/CLARIAH-CZ partner) and/or to change the repository software solution. When we see what kind of data we are actually receiving, it might indicate that a smaller, domain-specific repository tailored to the data would be easier to manage (for us) or navigate (for the user). The repository has another community with its own prefix, a community named "NFA" (for the Czech National Film Archive). The long-term plan is that NFA (the institution, a LINDAT/CLARIAH-CZ partner) will eventually run its own publicly available repository and the handle prefix will be transferred; meanwhile, some of their digital collections[26] will be deposited in the LINDAT/CLARIAH-CZ repository.

To be able to manage the handles more efficiently, a new user interface was implemented as part of the CLARIN-DSpace administration interface. One caveat of managing multiple handle prefixes in one repository is that greater care must be taken to submit the right data into the right collection. In the current configuration the handle is assigned when a submission begins, so it is not possible to simply move the resource into a different collection (under a different community) without communicating with the submitter first.

2.2 Licensing

An item (a record) in the repository consists, in general, of two parts: data and metadata. For metadata, our licensing policy is simple: our stance is that metadata is not a "free creative work" within the scope of copyright, thus it does not require any license. In fact, it cannot even be licensed, it is simply in the public

26 https://lindat.cz/repository/xmlui/handle/20.500.12801/2

domain.[27] Data, however, is very often (and language data almost always) creative work that falls within the scope of a copyright law. This means that any handling of such data requires an explicit license. Thus a repository system for language data must have strong licensing support in two respects: the submitters must choose a license for end users, which specifies how they can use the data, but they also must agree to a "deposition license" from the repository. This is an agreement in which the submitters give the repository the right to distribute the data to end users and state explicitly that they have checked the legal situation of the data and have the right to distribute the data under the chosen license and to pass this right onto the repository.

For choosing and attaching a license to an item in the repository, DSpace includes a small module that allows users to specify a Creative Commons (CC) license. This is nice, but not nearly enough even if all the datasets could be licensed under some sort of a public license. Thus CLARIN-DSpace implemented a completely new licensing framework, which allows the repository managers to specify any license in the system and attach it to records. The license definition, in addition to the license text, has several other attributes. The key attributes specify whether the license needs to be signed for each dataset it is attached to or not. Public licenses – which allow redistribution – do not require signatures by their very nature, but many other licenses do. The licensing framework allows all kinds of licenses to be used, thus providing support for datasets that cannot be distributed under the common public licenses. For such restrictive licenses, the system blocks download attempts and redirects users to authentication. After they successfully log in via their academic home institution (or other allowed credentials, using the SAML2 authentication system), the license for the particular dataset can be signed and the data downloaded. The licensing framework logs the information that *this user* signed *this particular license* for *this particular dataset*. While the support for custom licenses and their signing is unique to CLARIN-DSpace, the emphasis is on Open Science. To support users in choosing an optimal license for their data or software, the LINDAT/CLARIAH-CZ project has teamed with expert lawyers (including the CLARIN Committee for Legal and Ethical Issues: see (Kamocki et al. 2022) and created a separate piece of software: the Public License Selector. This small tool presents questions and explanations, and based on the user's answers, guides the user to assign the most open license possible for the given dataset (see Figure 3).

27 However, it will not make any technical difficulty to cover the metadata with the CC0 licence, as some repositories and "legal schools" do, regardless that we disagree with this approach.

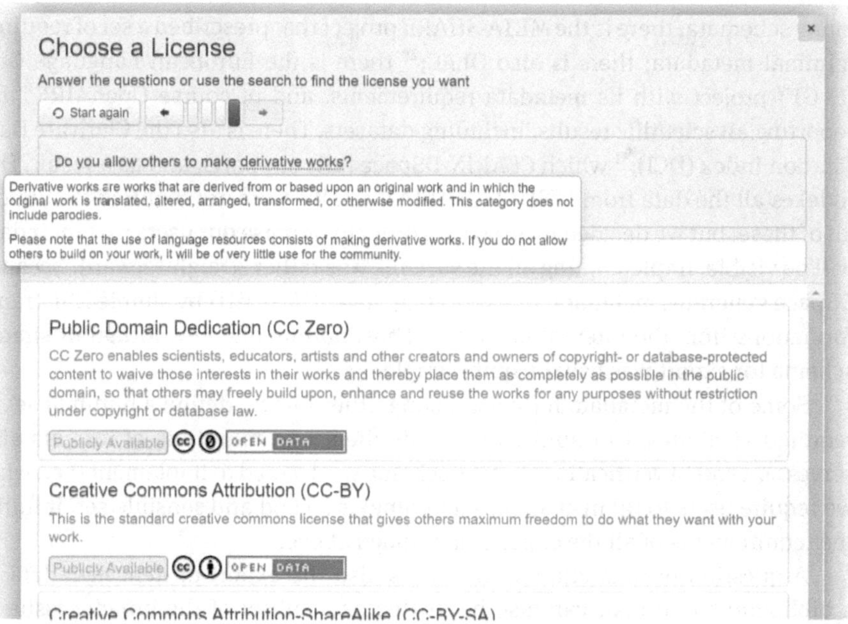

Figure 3: The public license selector asks a series of questions and (based on the answers) filters the suitable licenses. In this particular case we are at question number four, "Do you allow others to make derivative works?" where the phrase "derivative work" is explained in detail as a mouse-over hint.

The selector was integrated directly in the submission workflow of CLARIN-DSpace, so that users who need help with their choice of license can use it directly during their submission.

2.3 Submission workflow and metadata

One of the reasons for choosing DSpace was its customizable submission workflow, which allows us to easily define the metadata fields and to choose, for example, which of them are required and which are optional. Another aspect of metadata handling we could easily support with DSpace was the presentation of the metadata in multiple formats and/or schemata (e.g., during harvesting). In the domain of language resources, there are several schemata and frameworks related to metadata in use. There is the CMDI schema (required by CLARIN), which is in fact not a schema, but rather a framework that lets users create a tailored schema. CMDI also provides means for interoperability in this world of many schemata; there is the META-SHARE project that prescribed a set of required minimal metadata; there is also OLAC;[28] there is the European Language Grid (ELG)[29] project with its metadata requirements, and of course OpenAIRE[30] for reporting all scientific results, including datasets. There is also the Clarivate Data Citation Index (DCI),[31] which CLARIN-DSpace fully supports, and as a result, DCI indexes all the data from LINDAT/CLARIAH-CZ. We were not required to support all of these, but we decided to do so to in order to promise our users that their data will be visible. Implementing all the variants was rather straightforward, because DSpace generates metadata for export (e.g., over OAI-PMH) by simple XSL transformations from the internal metadata. Thus, adding one new format or simple schema for export was usually quite simple.

Some of the metadata formats, among other things, define a minimal set of required attributes. Our ability to provide them in a multitude of formats also serves as a sort of verification that the schema we decided to implement (i.e., what we require users to fill in at submission time) is a good and sensible set. It fulfils the requirements of all the exports mentioned above.

A question of data citation, and thus also the export of item metadata in a bibliographic format, can also be treated as a subset of the broader issue of metadata formats and dissemination. LINDAT/CLARIAH-CZ has the policy of direct data citations as it was pioneered by Force11[32] and implemented a "citation box" feature that is shown prominently on every item landing page. It contains a formatted text citation including the PID, conforming to the Force11 specification and the APA style, and it also contains an option to export the citation in the BibTeX format. This BibTeX support was implemented via XSLT just like all the other metadata exports mentioned before. This means one can also get the BibTeX metadata over OAI-PMH from any CLARIN-DSpace repository.

A positive side-effect of using DSpace is that it integrates well with Google Scholar. While CLARIN-DSpace made some significant changes and is optimized for datasets, not publications, the development team made a conscious effort to keep this integration working. As a result, datasets held in any CLARIN-DSpace instance are indexed by Google Scholar, just like any other scientific publication. When they are cited directly – which we promote, as explained above – the authors of the data get the credit they deserve.

---

28 http://www.language-archives.org
29 https://www.european-language-grid.eu
30 https://www.openaire.eu
31 https://clarivate.com/webofsciencegroup/solutions/webofscience-data-citation-index
32 https://force11.org

2.4 Versioning

One of our policies, stemming from how we view persistent identifiers, is that a handle always resolves to one concrete item (its landing page), that is a concrete dataset. Citing data should always be as precise as possible; vague use would break the principle of reproducibility in science. We analysed how versioning was supported in various repository systems, including DSpace from its early attempts, and we decided to use a different approach. The implementation of versioning in CLARIN-DSpace is very simple. Each version of an item is a separate record with its own handle. The only addition is implemented using the standard Dublin Core attributes "relation.replaces" and "relation.isreplacedby" to chain versions of the same item together. This information is visualized in the UI in two ways: a pop-up list of versions (see Figure 4) on each item that has the relations filled in, and the fact that CLARIN-DSpace by default hides bitstreams of items that have a newer version and showing instead an explanation that this dataset has newer versions (see Figure 5).

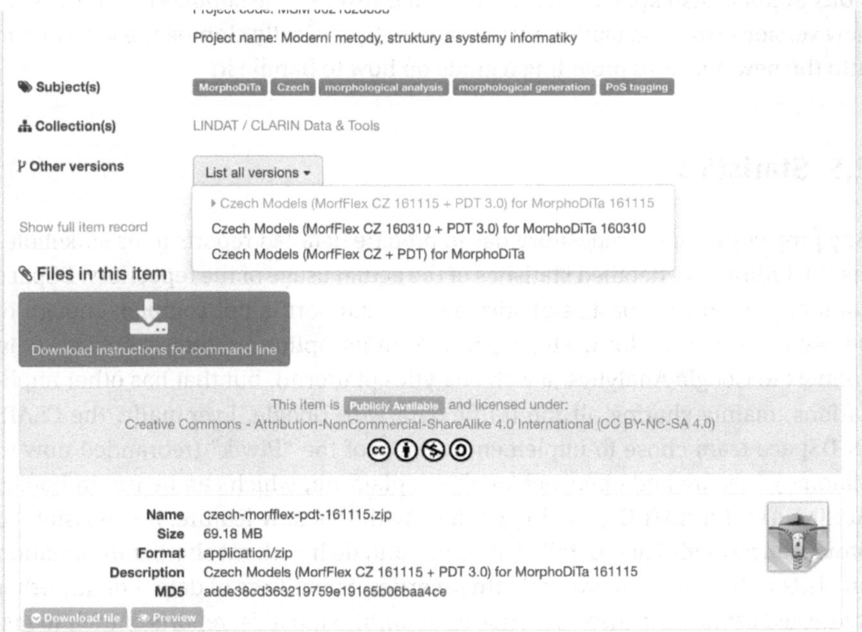

Figure 4: The latest version of a resource (if there are multiple versions) shows both the actual data files and links to all the previous versions.

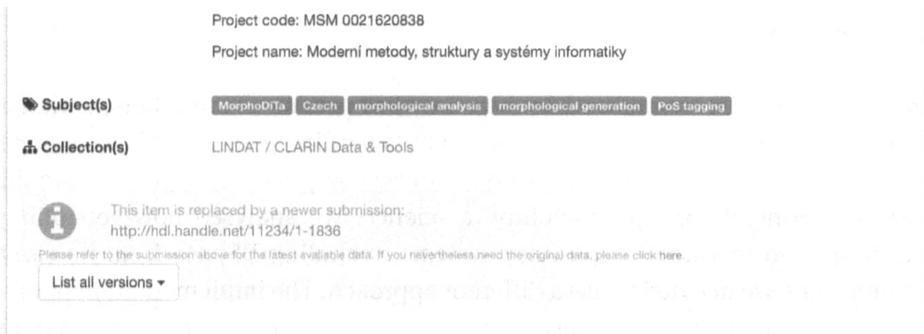

Figure 5: An illustration of what is shown to users when they reach a resource that has a newer version in the system, i.e., a link to the different versions of the resource is shown instead of the files (sometimes multiple links) but the original data can be downloaded as well.

Of course, the bitstreams can still be readily shown and downloaded; it is just a measure of pointing out to users who came to an older record, usually from a PID in a citation, that they can use the latest version if they want. The latest versions of items also appear first in the search results. The submission process for new versions was also made very convenient by basically cloning the last version into the new one, and providing a guide on how to handle it.

2.5 Statistics

Any project running a repository has to prepare detailed reports to its stakeholders, including very detailed statistics of the actual usage of the repository. DSpace contains support for basic statistics but this support is not complex enough to be used as the basis for useful reports. Another option present in DSpace is to connect to Google Analytics (a web analytics platform), but that has other implications, mainly sharing all the traffic data with Google. Eventually, the CLARIN-DSpace team chose to implement support of the "Piwik" (rebranded now to Matomo)[33] secure and open web analytics platform, which can be run in-house. At LINDAT/CLARIAH-CZ, we do just that. With this new feature, it is possible to provide meaningful and detailed statistics and do it without sharing information on visits of individual items with other parties. Submitters of data – or any other interested users – can also subscribe for monthly statistical reports of their items. These reports include the numbers of downloads and views, and graphs showing usage trends.

33 https://piwik.pro

2.6 Working with data

One crucial difference in how CLARIN-DSpace is used compared to regular (publication-only, or plain) DSpace installations is the size of the files (bitstreams) being hosted. Our repository contains files with sizes in tens of gigabyte (at the time of writing, the largest single file is 70 GB). Because a large portion of our users use fast academic or enterprise networks the file size itself is not viewed as a problem. What became a problem, however, was the inefficient and naive implementation of the downloading process by the DSpace stack. It put a lot of stress on the CPU resources, and at the same time was not able to fully exploit the potential of very fast internet connection and storage. A workaround was implemented that allows the web server to handle the file downloads directly when the user is authorized by the repository systems (e.g., the requested item does not require any license signing). With this approach, CLARIN-DSpace added also a new feature – an essential one for a data repository – a support for resuming interrupted downloads.

On the other hand, we are taking a different approach when large files are being submitted to the repository. Uploads of less than 4 GB are available directly through the submission workflow by leveraging the HTTPS protocol, simply by dragging and dropping files onto the browser window. Larger files, however, need the cooperation of the repository staff. There are several reasons for that, one of them being we want to check whether the submitters have considered different ways of splitting the data and whether potential users are able to use big files efficiently. Another reason is to keep a certain level of control. In practice, this is not a problem, because language data are not commonly this large (when compressed), so in practice the load on repository administrators is minimal.

3 Web applications and services

Web applications and web services are now one of the pillars of LINDAT/CLARIAH-CZ's operations, but they started very small. In 2010 we had a few ad hoc web applications running, like an interface with the feature-based tagger (Hajič 2004), but they were not part of the LINDAT infrastructure. They did not provide APIs, were run on old machines, and were generally not intended for serious work, but rather as demos. A consensus at the time was that serious users download, install, and run the software themselves.

In CLARIN, however, we also wanted to make the language technologies accessible to researchers from other fields who are not experts in NLP (see e.g.,

(Gomes et al. 2022) who address the same idea in PORTULAN CLARIN). Web applications seemed like a good idea from the ease-of-use perspective, and when they had APIs, they could also be used in scientific workflows and applied on larger data efficiently.

Even if web applications run slower then a locally downloaded software package, they might still be the effective solution in real-world research workflows. When calling an API from a simple script serving the data is very simple, it can easily offset a little wait for the results. The WebLicht application for chaining REST services into NLP processing chains (Hinrichs et al. 2010) inspired us to start setting up production-ready web applications with REST API.

Our choice of which applications LINDAT should provide has always been a combination of three main criteria: (1) state-of-the-art quality of the NLP processing, (2) clear Open Source licensing, and (3) a responsive and reliable developer willing to install the software, provide both a REST API and a graphical web interface, and support the running service. These guidelines have been made public.[34] LINDAT technical team provides the hardware to run the services, a virtual machine for the service, monitoring, and support in deployment. We also provide a template for the services to use, so that they have a similar basic design.[35] Over the past few years this approach has resulted in a portfolio of about 20 services[36] with steadily increased use. The services provided by LINDAT/CLARIAH-CZ can be grouped as follows: (1) language processing (text and speech), (2) corpus search (corpora and treebanks), and (3) lexical resources (mostly dictionaries). Among the processing services, the most popular are MorphoDiTa (Straková et al. 2014) and UDPipe (Straka et al. 2016) and, since 2020, the high-quality, transformer-based Charles University Machine Translation system CUBBITT (Popel et al. 2020).

MT systems with transformers have been the first services to require GPUs to run at a reasonable speed. Since then, they have been joined by the updated UDPipe 2 and NameTag 2 (Straková et al. 2019) services, with more to follow. Deployments of this new generation of services is more complicated, but it also seems all the more meaningful, because it is no longer true that users can simply download the software and models and run it on their computers, let alone run it on average computers, at speeds faster than the web services run. Except for the most professional deployments, it is more efficient for majority of users, including NLP researchers, to simply use the web services provided by LINDAT/

34 https://github.com/ufal/lindat-common/wiki/Service-Development-Guide
35 https://github.com/ufal/lindat-common/
36 https://lindat.cz/services

CLARIAH-CZ, rather than trying to install the systems themselves. The models are rather large, especially the pre-trained embeddings, the set-up is quite complex with TensorFlow and other libraries and local servers, but most importantly, very large, power-hungry and expensive GPU cards are required, sometimes several of them, to achieve a speed comparable to the web services. The set-up of the GPU-run machine translation service is depicted in Figure 6.

Our search services are represented by three main pillars with distinct but complementary functionality: KonText (Machálek 2020) for search in large corpora, PML-TQ (Pajas and Štěpánek 2009) for treebanks, and TEITOK (Janssen 2018) for the corpora that have rich representation, and also for integration of all of these three approaches together, including lexical resources where possible.

4 Conclusion

Given the limited space available in this chapter, we could not describe all the features of the current LINDAT/CLARIAH-CZ, especially the activities of our long-standing partners as well as new but important consortium partners from various fields and institutions across the Czech Republic. The activities of LINDAT/CLARIAH-CZ also go significantly beyond the technical aspects as described here, e.g., by providing additional resources for many digital humanities and arts fields, educational and training activities (including serving a full master's curriculum in Language Technology worth 120 ECTS credits, in cooperation with the host department and school), being active in providing access to the Oral History archives in the Center for Visual History Malach, serving the public, and so on.

The international cooperation of LINDAT/CLARIAH-CZ goes far beyond CLARIN centres and the CLARIN ERIC – the infrastructure has provided and is currently providing support to many EU-funded projects, such as QT21, HiML, Khresmoi, KConnect, ELITR, Bergamot, ELG, ELE, and several others. It is itself engaged in the EOSC activities and EOSC-related projects, for example, in SSHOC and the CLS Infra network.[37] International cooperation also reaches beyond Europe – LINDAT/CLARIAH-CZ represents CLARIN in the Mellon Foundation project to coordinate interoperability across the Atlantic. We also could not provide full details of the current use. But to give a ballpark figure, we can cite the Internet Language Reference Book with more than 70 million accesses over the past 5 years, over 40,000 accesses monthly (including downloads) of the central repository alone, or a cumulative number of service requests totalling

37 https://lindat.cz/partnership

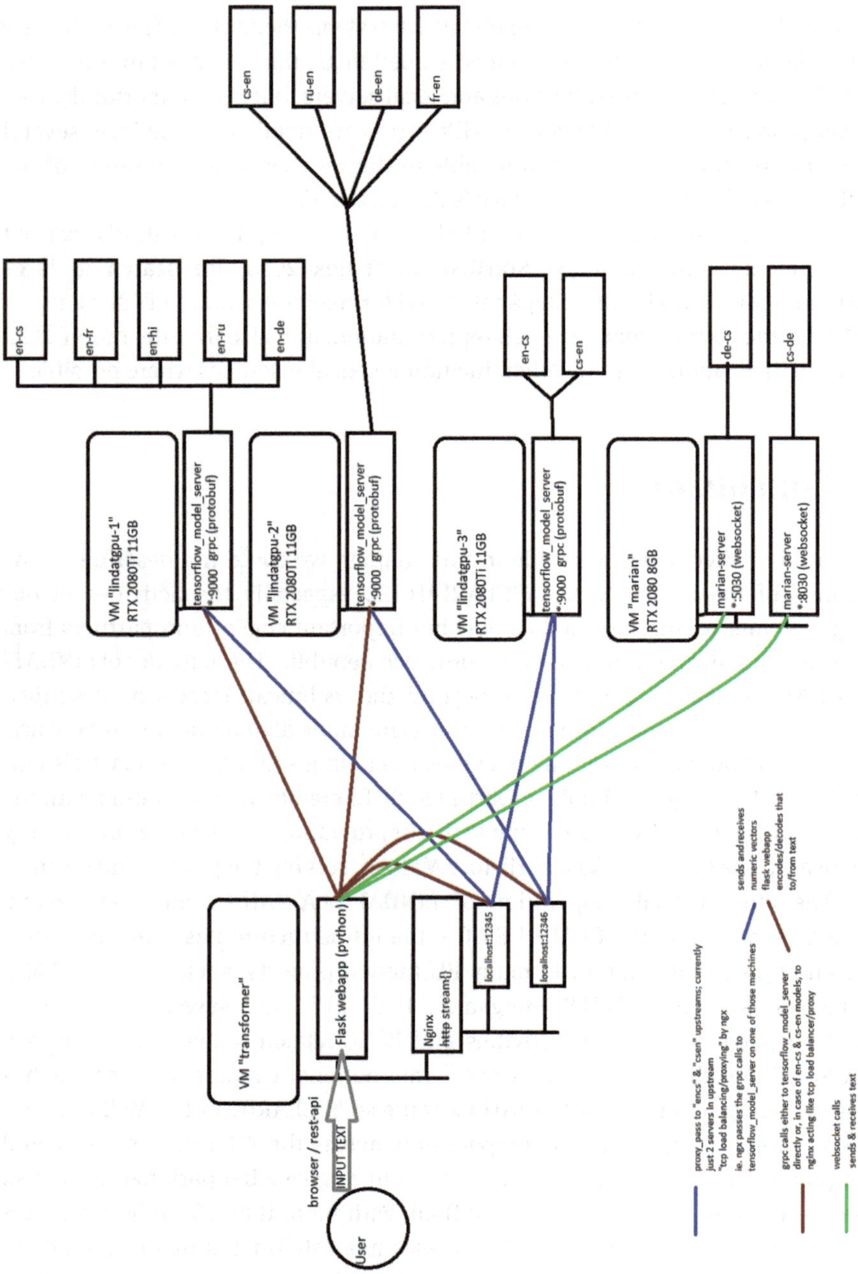

Figure 6: Architecture of the Machine Translation web service with several GPUs containing various translation models and the most-used models in several instances, with load balancing. The application also automatically does pivot translation by sequencing the models as needed.

over 30 million over the whole lifespan of their use. For the future, both near and distant, we are committed to continuing to provide the repository and web services for novel datasets from more and more Digital Humanities fields, while maintaining and expanding our portfolio of language technology services both in terms of coverage and accuracy.

Bibliography

Draxler, Christoph, Alexander Geyken, Erhard Hinrichs, Annette Klosa-Kückelhaus, Elke Teich & Thorsten Trippel. 2022. How to connect Language Resources and Infrastructures, and Communities. In Darja Fišer & Andreas Witt (eds.), *CLARIN. The infrastructure for language resources*. Berlin: De Gruyter.

Gomes, Luís, Ruben Branco, João Silva & António Branco. 2022. Open and Inclusive Language Processing: Language processing services by PORTULAN to meet the widest needs of CLARIN users. In Darja Fišer & Andreas Witt (eds.), *CLARIN. The infrastructure for language resources*. Berlin: De Gruyter.

Hajič, Jan. 2004. *Disambiguation of Rich Inflection (Computational Morphology of Czech)*. Linguistic Data Consortium, University of Pennsylvania.

Hajičová, Eva, Jan Hajič, Barbora Hladká, Jiří Mírovský, Lucie Poláková, Kateřina Rysová, Magdaléna Rysová, Pavel Straňák, Barbora Štěpánková & Šárka Zikánová. 2022. Corpus Annotation as a Feasible and Scientifically Beneficial Task. In Darja Fišer & Andreas Witt (eds.), *CLARIN. The infrastructure for language resources*. Berlin: De Gruyter.

Hinrichs, Erhard, Marie Hinrichs & Thomas Zastrow. 2010. WebLicht: Web-Based LRT Services for German. In *Proceedings of the ACL 2010 System Demonstrations*, 25–29. Uppsala, Sweden: Association for Computational Linguistics.

Janssen, Maarten. 2018. Adding Words to Manuscripts: From PagesXML to TEITOK: 22nd International Conference on Theory and Practice of Digital Libraries, TPDL 2018, Porto, Portugal, September 10–13, 2018, Proceedings. In 152–157.

Kamocki, Paweł, Aleksei Kelli & Krister Lindén. 2022. The CLARIN Committee for Legal and Ethical Issues and the Normative Layer of the CLARIN Infrastructure. In Darja Fišer & Andreas Witt (eds.), *CLARIN. The infrastructure for language resources*. Berlin: De Gruyter.

Machálek, Tomáš. 2020. KonText: Advanced and Flexible Corpus Query Interface. English. In *Proceedings of the 12th Language Resources and Evaluation Conference*, 7003–7008. Marseille, France: European Language Resources Association.

Pajas, Petr. 2010. *DSpace Modifications for Use of EPIC Handles*. LINDAT/CLARIAH-CZ digital library at the Institute of Formal and Applied Linguistics (ÚFAL), Faculty of Mathematics and Physics, Charles University.

Pajas, Petr & Jan Štěpánek. 2009. System for Querying Syntactically Annotated Corpora. In *Proceedings of the ACL-IJCNLP 2009 Software Demonstrations*, 33–36. Suntec, Singapore: Association for Computational Linguistics.

Popel, Martin, Markéta Tomková, Jakub Tomek, Łukasz Kaiser, Jakob Uszkoreit, Ondřej Bojar & Zdeněk Žabokrtský. 2020. Transforming Machine Translation: A Deep Learning System Reaches News Translation Quality Comparable to Human Professionals. In *Nature Communications* 11.4381, 1–15.
Straka, Milan, Jan Hajič & Jana Straková. 2016. UDPipe: Trainable Pipeline for Processing CoNLL-U Files Performing Tokenization, Morphological Analysis, POS Tagging and Parsing. In *Proceedings of the Tenth International Conference on Language Resources and Evaluation (LREC'16)*, 4290–4297. Portorož, Slovenia: European Language Resources Association (ELRA).
Straková, Jana, Milan Straka & Jan Hajič. 2014. Open-Source Tools for Morphology, Lemmatization, POS Tagging and Named Entity Recognition. In *Proceedings of 52nd Annual Meeting of the Association for Computational Linguistics: System Demonstrations*, 13–18. Baltimore, Maryland: Association for Computational Linguistics.
Straková, Jana, Milan Straka & Jan Hajič. 2019. Neural Architectures for Nested NER through Linearization. In *Proceedings of the 57th Annual Meeting of the Association for Computational Linguistics*, 5326–5331. Stroudsburg, PA, USA: Association for Computational Linguistics.
Straňák, Pavel, Ondřej Košarko & Jozef Mišutka. 2019. CLARIN-DSpace Repository at LINDAT/CLARIN. In *Proceedings of the 12th Conference on Grey Literature and Repositories, 2019*, 1–12.
Trognitz, Martina, Matej Ďurčo & Karlheinz Mörth. 2022. Text technology for the digital humanities: Maximising impact in a diverse field of disciplines. In Darja Fišer & Andreas Witt (eds.), *CLARIN. The infrastructure for language resources.* Berlin: De Gruyter.
Windhouwer, Menzo & Twan Goosen. 2022. Component Metadata Infrastructure. In Darja Fišer & Andreas Witt (eds.), *CLARIN. The Infrastructure for Language Resources.* Berlin: De Gruyter.

Claus Zinn* and Emanuel Dima

The CLARIN Language Resource Switchboard

Current State, Impact, and Future Roadmap

Abstract: The CLARIN Language Resource Switchboard helps users to identify and kick-start tools that can process their research data in one way or another. In the last few years, the Switchboard has developed into a central pillar of the CLARIN community. This chapter discusses its central idea, gives an up-to-date summary of its current status and usage, discusses the Switchboard's impact within and beyond the community, and proposes a roadmap for future development.

Keywords: infrastructure, tool brokering, match-making

1 Introduction

The CLARIN infrastructure aims at making available all digital language resources and tools from all over Europe to support researchers in the humanities and social sciences (Hinrichs and Krauwer 2014). For this purpose, the infrastructure has developed and brought into force CMDI, a community-wide metadata standard for the computer-readable description of all resources (Broeder et al. 2010; Windhouwer and Goosen 2022), the Virtual Language Observatory[1] (VLO), where resources can be searched for and accessed (Goosen and Eckart 2014), and the

1 https://vlo.clarin.eu

Acknowledgment: Nationally, our work was funded by the German Federal Ministry of Education and Research (BMBF), the Ministry of Science, Research, and Art of the Federal State of Baden-Württemberg (MWK), and CLARIN-D. Internationally, our work was funded by the European Union's Horizon 2020 research and innovation programme under grant agreement no. 676529 (CLARIN-PLUS), EOSC-hub under grant agreement no. 777536, EUDAT (grant agreement no. 654065), and SSHOC under grant agreement no 823782.

***Corresponding author: Claus Zinn,** Department of General and Computational Linguistics, University of Tübingen, Tübingen, Germany, e-mail: claus.zinn@uni-tuebingen.de
Emanuel Dima, Department of General and Computational Linguistics, University of Tübingen, Tübingen, Germany, e-mail: emanuel.dima@uni-tuebingen.de

https://doi.org/10.1515/9783110767377-004

Language Resource Switchboard[2] where a wide range of tools can be easily found and invoked (Zinn 2016). In this chapter, we present an updated account of the Language Resource Switchboard, which has developed into a central pillar of the CLARIN infrastructure. The chapter builds upon the Switchboard's initial publication (Zinn 2016), a paper that focused on the integration of the Switchboard with EUDAT's B2DROP cloud service (Zinn 2018a), and our paper published as a Squib in *Computational Linguistics* (Zinn 2018b), but extends and updates our accounts significantly.

The central idea of the Switchboard is the following: given a language resource – found while browsing the VLO, or stored on the user's file system or on B2DROP cloud space, or otherwise addressable via a persistent URL handle, or even composed on the fly – enable users to find *and* invoke a tool that can process this resource in one way or another. The Switchboard's design focused on identifying and invoking processing tools with minimal efforts: once the Switchboard has been informed about the resource's whereabouts, it immediately shows all tools that can process it, grouped by the tasks the tools promise to perform. Users can then select and invoke the tool of their interest with a single click. The Switchboard can be described as a broker between users (with their resources and their intention to process them) and developers (with their tools idly waiting to process such resources).

The remainder of this chapter is structured as follows. The Switchboard builds upon simple directory services, some of which are mentioned in the background section of this chapter (see Section 2) but it extends them in several aspects. Section 3 gives a detailed account of the Switchboard, together with an up-to-date description of its current state in terms of the tool space it covers and new developments since 2018. Some of the new developments were shaped by the involvement of Switchboard developers in national and international research projects. Section 4 describes the use and potential of the Switchboard in contributing and shaping those projects. While the idea of the Switchboard is simple and powerful, it also has a good number of side-effects, which have not yet been discussed in great detail. Section 5 describes the impact of the Switchboard within the CLARIN community and across research communities and infrastructures. In Section 6, we discuss future developments and Section 7 concludes.

2 https://switchboard.clarin.eu

2 Background

The Switchboard helps users to find and invoke tools that can process their resources in one way or another. In a sense, the Switchboard can be seen as an intelligent yellow pages server, which not only lists all tools in the CLARIN space of interest, but also allows users to invoke them intelligently.

There have been a number of directory services for language processing software. LT World[3] is one of the older websites on language technology and maintains a classified list of tools, especially for processing written language (Jörg, Uszkoreit, and Burt 2010). The website categorizes its list of tools within the dimensions "Tokenization", "Naming Entities Detection", "Lemmatizer", "Language Guesser" and so on. Most of the information presented at LT World stems from the Natural Language Software Registry (NLSR) formerly hosted by the DFKI at registry.dfki.de, a website that is now defunct. LT World is no longer kept up-to-date, either; many well-known tools are missing, and where tools are listed, their corresponding information is sparse, outdated, or contains broken links.

The Virtual Language Observatory has a few thousand metadata entries for tools and services. To get access to most of them, users will need to do a faceted search on the facet "Resource type" and select each of its values, such as "software" (with 1,672 entries), "Software, multimedia" (1,538), "software, webservice" (829), "web service" (554)", "webservice" (107), "tool service" (75), "Tools" (29), and "web application" (12).[4] Our description shows that the VLO has no systematic classification of the tools it knows about, so it is hard for users to identify tools, say, in terms of their processing task. In large part, this is due to the harvesting nature of the VLO as it gets – and needs to make sense of – metadata records that adhere to many different formats and profiles, and which are of varying quality and expressiveness. While there is post-curation potential in cleaning up the value range of the facet "Resource type" (e.g., by combining "web service" and "webservice"), the blame cannot be simply passed to the metadata providers given that there is no obvious, single metadata vocabulary for the description of tools (and the tasks they achieve) that they can be told to use. Once VLO users have obtained metadata entries for tools and services, they usually get a short description of the tool and sometimes a link ("Landing Page") to the tool's home page, where more information is available such as the tool's download location. Sometimes, however, the link can even point to the endpoint of a web service with little if any readable information on how to use it. In short, the VLO is of

3 https://www.lt-world.org
4 Accessed March 24, 2021. Numbers vary through the days.

limited use for researchers to explore the CLARIN tool space, to find a tool that fits their needs, and to work with the tool without installation and set-up hassle.

Well-curated special-purpose websites fare better. The Institute of Computer Science at the Polish Academy of Sciences has a well organised web page on language tools and resources for Polish.[5] Here, each tool comes with its own web page, often with background information with references to publications, download locations, and installation instructions, and sometimes with a demo page where the tool can be tried online. The LINDAT/CLARIN website is a website that goes beyond a simple yellow paging of tools.[6] While its focus is predominantly on tools for the processing of Czech text files, it allows users to invoke each of the web services via a user interface with a common look and feel across the services. Here, users can define their input, and inspect the output of all REST-based services (Hajič et al. 2022).

The last two examples show what well-curated websites on tools can do: document and provide easy access to tools. WebLicht is a web-based application that goes a step further. WebLicht is a workflow engine that gives users access to a good range of natural language tools that can be arranged in a processing pipeline (Hinrichs and Krauwer 2014). It offers predefined workflows ("easy-chains"), but also an advanced mode, where users can construct their own processing chains. For a tool to be integrated into WebLicht (and hence be part of a processing pipeline), it must be adapted to read and write TCF-compliant data. Each tool in the workflow reads its input from the TCF source, and extends the TCF file with its processing results. WebLicht's tool landscape is dynamic. At regular intervals, it harvests tool metadata from CLARIN repositories; the metadata lists the specific input-output behaviour of the tool, informing the WebLicht orchestrator about permissable workflow constructions.

The transatlantic counterpart of WebLicht is the Language Application Grid (LAPPS Grid[7]), an open, web-based infrastructure that offers a very good range of language-related tools. Similar to WebLicht, the tools can be composed into tool chains using a graphical editor. And as in WebLicht, for tools to become part of the Grid, they need to be adapted so that they can read and write LAPPS Grid formats. Tool developers should be aware of the LAPPS Interchange Format (LIF) and the Web Services Exchange Vocabulary (WSEV). The LAPPS Grid also offers additional features such as visualization and the sharing of various types of data (such as LAPPS interaction histories, workflows, and visualizations).

5 http://clip.ipipan.waw.pl/LRT
6 https://lindat.mff.cuni.cz/en/services
7 https://lappsgrid.org

How does the CLARIN Language Resource Switchboard fit into this spectrum? Like LT World, it gives users a good (but up-to-date) overview of the natural language processing tools. However, the tool space in the Switchboard is restricted to the tools the Switchboard knows about *and* which are – to a large extent – integrated with the Switchboard. It extends directory services like the LINDAT site by helping users to find *applicable* tools for their resources. Applicability of tools is defined by filtering the tool space into dimensions that fit the characteristics of the resource. Once the Switchboard knows about a resource, users can invoke their tool of interest with a single click. Tools integrated with the Switchboard then drive users that came from the Switchboard into a suitable tool state where the tool has been given the resource, and where default parameters for this resource are set. Unlike WebLicht and LAPPS Grid, the Switchboard lacks a tool chaining capability, but offers access to many different predefined WebLicht chains, which can be invoked with a single click.

In the next section, we describe the Switchboard in detail.

3 The Switchboard

The Switchboard's name describes its underlying idea well. Given users' linguistic resource, it helps them in identifying and invoking suitable tools that can process their resource in one way or another. Figure 1 describes this task in more detail.

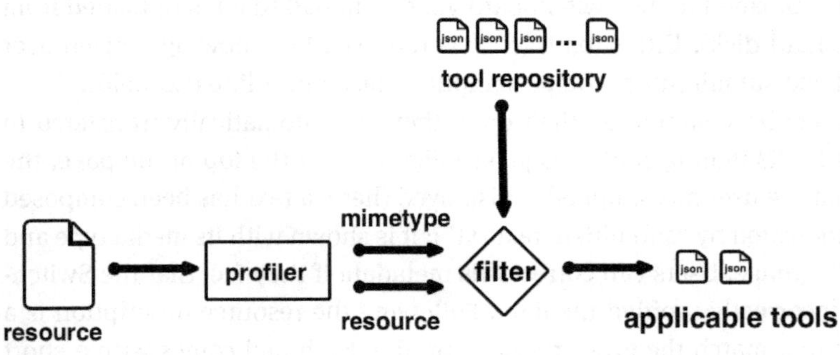

Figure 1: Switchboard – from resources to applicable tools.

The input of the Switchboard is a resource which is characterized by the profiler (based on Apache Tika[8]) in terms of two dimensions: mimetype (aka media

8 https://tika.apache.org

type) and language. For the next stage, the Switchboard makes use of the Switchboard tool repository (see below) that contains a list of JSON files, each of which describes a single tool in some detail. In the filter stage, all tools that cannot process resources of the given mimetype and language are filtered out, with the remaining set of tools becoming the applicable tools. Those are displayed in the "Matching Tools" Page (see Figure 3).

The Switchboard's tool repository is defined as a manually curated Github repository.[9] Each tool is specified by a single JSON file[10] which holds about 20 features, such as the tool's name, short description, task (e.g., "constituency parsing"), the mimetypes it accepts, the languages it can process, and the URL and the parameters that need to be passed to properly invoke the tool.

While the basic idea of the Switchboard is simple, a significant amount of implementation efforts have been carried out, resulting in a tool that aims for high usability, strong visibility, and ease of use.

3.1 Design and implementation

Figure 2 displays the Switchboard's entry page at switchboard.clarin.eu. Users are given two ways to browse the Switchboard's tool space: "Upload" and "Tool Inventory". In the latter, users get an overview of all tools connected with the Switchboard, independently of the data they accept as input. When users go for the "Upload" option, they specifically look for tools that can process their data. Data can be uploaded to the Switchboard via file upload (data is uploaded from the client's hard disk), URL submit (data is retrieved by following a given user link),[11] and text submit (users compose input using a multi-line text field).

Once users have submitted their data, they are automatically transfered to Switchboard's "Matching Tools" page (see Figure 3). At the top of the page, the resource that the user has supplied is displayed (here, a text has been composed on the fly, indicated by "submitted_text.txt"); it is shown with its media type and the data's language. Users can correct this metadata if they feel that the Switchboard has incorrectly profiled the data. Following the resource description is a list of tools that match the given resource profile. Each tool comes with a short description, including its input and output arguments and whether the tool's use

9 https://github.com/clarin-eric/switchboard-tool-registry

10 https://github.com/clarin-eric/switchboard-doc/blob/master/documentation/ToolDescriptionSpec.md

11 The "Submit URL" panel can be used by all users of cloud hosters that offer a "Share Link" functionality, including commercial clouds (e.g., Dropbox) and open-source solutions (e.g., Nextcloud).

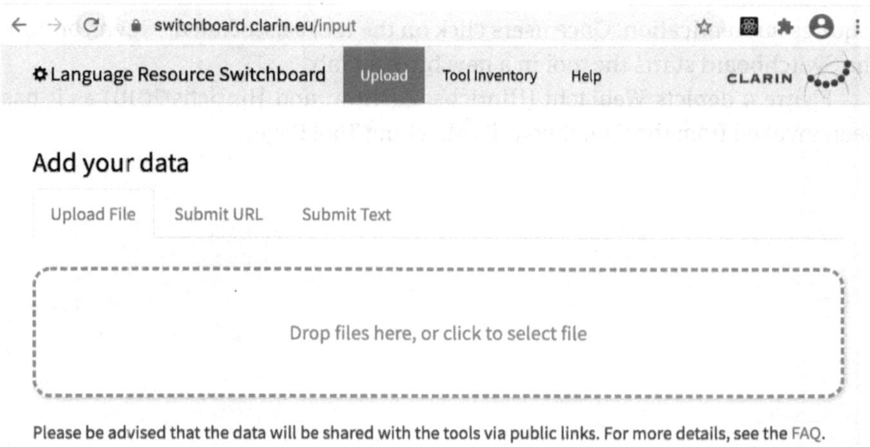

Figure 2: Switchboard's entry page for resource upload.

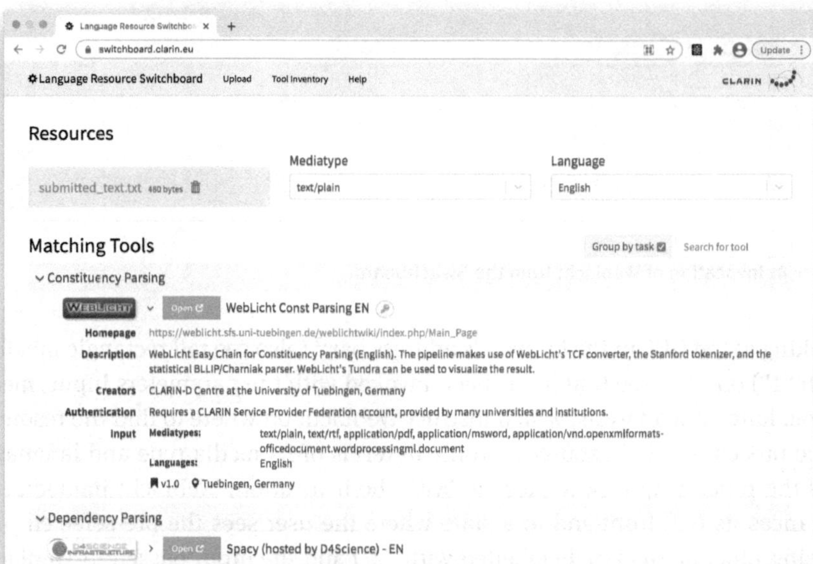

Figure 3: Switchboard's matching tools page for a given resource.

requires authentication. Once users click on the tool's associated "Open" button, the Switchboard starts the tool in a new browser tab.

Figure 4 depicts WebLicht (Hinrichs, Zastrow, and Hinrichs 2010) as it has been invoked from the Switchboard's Matching Tool Page.

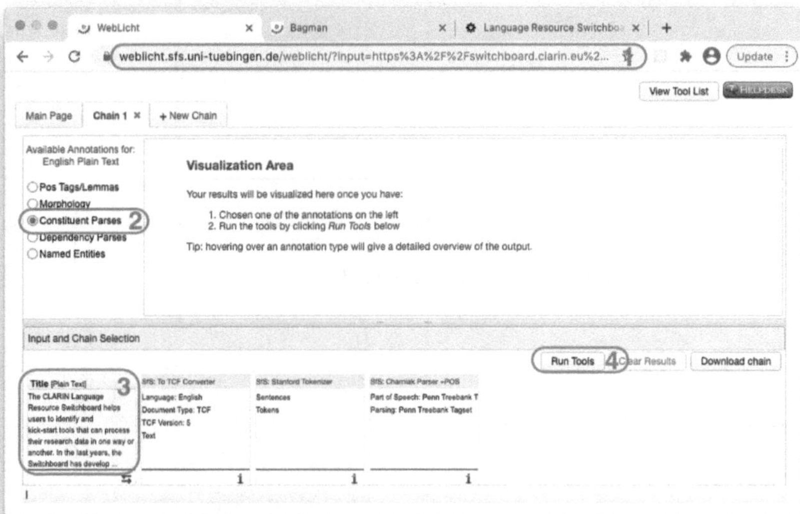

Figure 4: Invocation of WebLicht from the Switchboard.

Looking at the URL in the browser's address bar[12] (also see red rectangle labelled with "1") one can see that it has been invoked with the parameters input, mediatype, lang, and analysis, which instruct WebLicht on where to find the resource to be processed, the resource's profile in terms of its media type and language, and the processing task requested. With the invocation, WebLicht immediately advances its GUI front-end to a state where the user sees the pre-selected processing pipeline (rectangle labelled with "2") and the input passed to WebLicht (rectangle "3"). Users only need to press the "Run Tools" button (rectangle "4") to start the workflow to get a constituent parse for the resource in question.

12 https://weblicht.sfs.uni-tuebingen.de/weblicht/?input=https://switchboard.clarin.eu/api/storage/b1106376-6b3b-4d2d-b7bf-0b94e4ebc474&mediatype=text/plain&lang=en&analysis=const-parsing

Being able to steer users directly towards a GUI state that users intend to see should not be underestimated. Manual navigation through a tool's graphical user interface is time-consuming, and given the vastness of the CLARIN tool space, and the diversity of their GUIs, the Switchboard's help invoking the tool "the right way" is a welcome feature.

3.2 Status

In June 2018, around 60 browser-based applications were connected to the Switchboard. Today, while the number is stable, there have been quite some changes to this tool set. In a move to ensure the high quality and online availability of the tool set, some tools were removed. This consolidation phase was complemented with an extension phase where more tools were added. Established tool providers such as the Polish CLARIN consortium[13] added more of their fine tools to the Switchboard. The integration of new tools also resulted from the Switchboard's use in European projects such as D4Science, SSHOC, and the cooperation of CLARIN with DARIAH (see Section 4).

Figure 5 shows the distribution of tools with regard to the CLARIN consortiums or research groups they originate from. Two thirds of the tools stem from either Polish or German CLARIN consortium members. The last third includes tools from the Polish Academy of Sciences,[14] D4Science,[15] Lindat,[16] and others.

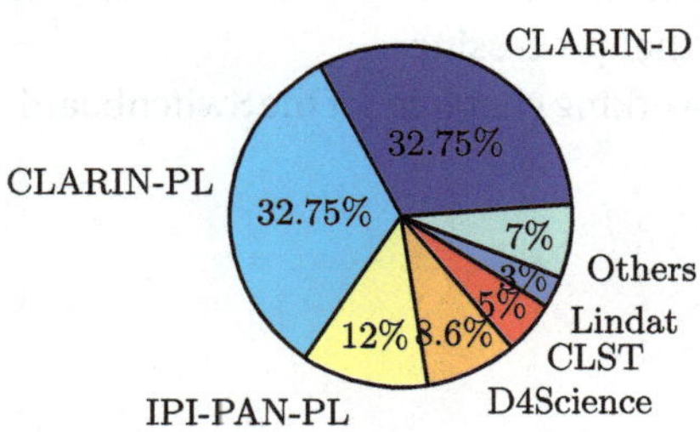

Figure 5: Switchboard's toolset, sorted by consortiums.

13 https://ws.clarin-pl.eu
14 http://clip.ipipan.waw.pl/LRT
15 https://parthenos.d4science.org
16 https://lindat.mff.cuni.cz/en/services

The production version of the Switchboard is accompanied by its beta version,[17] which serves as a playground for new developments, and where new tools are being tested. In the beta version, the tool space is larger. In May 2021, the beta version listed 154 tools, including stand-alone applications which need to be installed on the user's local computer, and also web applications, which are not yet fully integrated (like WebMAUS from the Bavarian Archive of Speech Signals).[18]

The Switchboard currently supports 28 different processing tasks.[19] The vocabulary is purpose-built for our tools and does not use a pre-existing ontology, an issue that is now being addressed in the CLARIAH and SSHOC projects (see below).

3.3 Networking

In addition to the file provision methods (see Figure 2), the Switchboard can also be invoked from the VLO, the Virtual Collection Registry[20] (Elbers 2017), the CMDI Explorer (Arnold et al. 2020), the B2DROP cloud space, and the D4Science platform (both see below).

Figure 6 highlights the networking capabilities of the Switchboard, here a workflow where it is invoked twice. In a first step, the Switchboard is given, or passed on, a CMDI file. The Switchboard then proposes CMDI Explorer as an applicable tool, which is invoked and used to visualize the resources described by the metadata as a hierarchical tree. The user selects a single resource from the tree, and sends it to the Switchboard for further processing.

Future activities will strengthen the networking character of the Switchboard.

17 https://beta-switchboard.clarin.eu

18 http://bas.uni-muenchen.de/Bas/

19 Constituency Parsing, Coreference Resolution, Dependency Parsing, Distant Reading, Extraction of Polish terminology, Inclusion detection, Keyword Extractor, Lemmatization, Machine Translation, Metadata Processing, Morpho-syntactic tagger, Morphological Analysis, Named Entity Recognition, Named Entity Relation Detection, Part-Of-Speech Tagging, Sentiment Analysis, Shallow Parsing, Spatial expression detection, Speech Recognition, Stylometry, TF, IDF, TF-IDF calculation, Text Analytics, Text Enhancement, Text Summarization, Tokenization, Topic Modelling, Visualization of Geographic Data, Word sense disambiguation.

20 https://clarin.eu/vcr

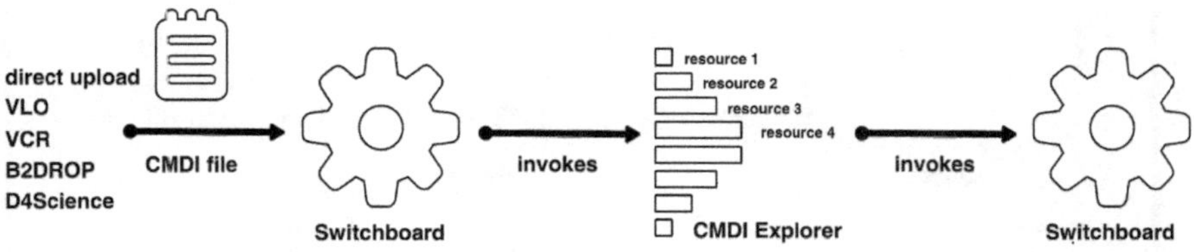

Figure 6: Switchboard invocation example.

4 Outreach activities

The Switchboard team has been participating in a number of national, European, and transatlantic research cooperations, which we would like to report on.

4.1 PARTHENOS

The d4science.org organization offers a data infrastructure that is used by over 10,000 researchers in over 50 countries across a wide range of scientific disciplines. In the Parthenos[21] project, the Switchboard was integrated with the D4Science infrastructure in two ways. Users logged into the D4Science platform can assign a "shared URL" to a datafile of their workspace. To get this file processed with the Switchboard, they copy and paste the shared link to the Switchboard's "Submit URL" panel. As a result, the Switchboard will download the data from the given link, profile it, and propose tools that can process the resource. As an alternative – mirroring the B2DROP approach, see below – Parthenos users can select the Switchboard from the file menu of their workspace (by right-clicking the file) to send the respective resource to the Switchboard (see Figure 7).

The other direction, from the Switchboard to the D4Science platform, is more substantial. Here, a number of tools have been installed *inside* the D4Science processing platform[22] and been registered with the Switchboard with their new D4Science endpoint. As a result, D4Science-based tools are now also available to Switchboard users without the need for such users to have a D4Science user account. The Switchboard hence serves as a bridge between two research infrastructures.

21 https://parthenos.d4science.org

22 Tools integrated: Spacy (for German and English), CSTLemma (English), NER Liner 2 (Polish), NLP Hub (NER for English, German, French, Spanish, Italian).

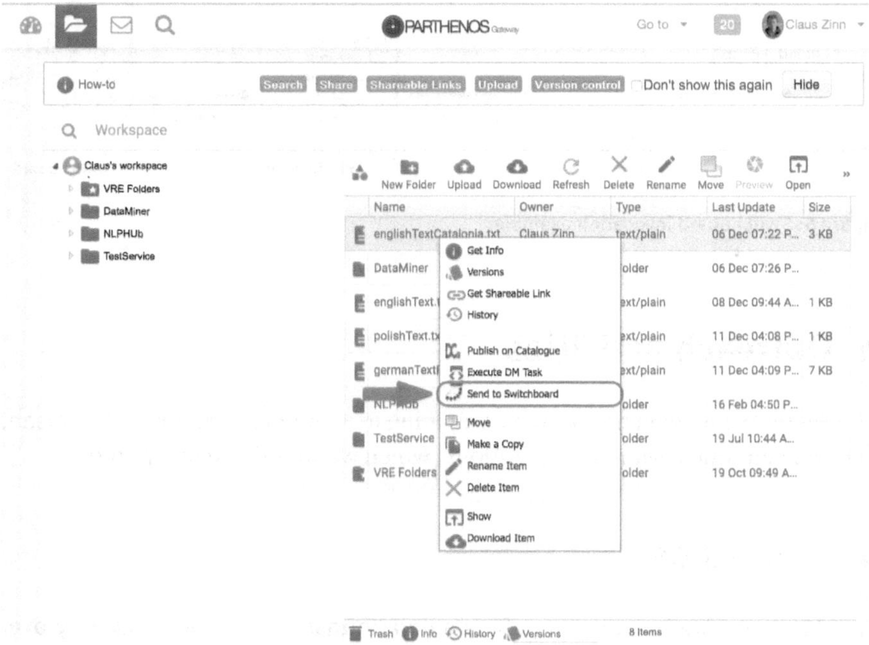

Figure 7: Invocation of the Switchboard from the Parthenos workspace.

4.2 EUDAT and EOSC

B2DROP[23] is one of the main data services offered by the EUDAT Collaborative Data Infrastructure (van de Sanden et al. 2015 (updated 2018)). The service, which is based upon the Nextcloud software (see nextcloud.com), offers 20 GB of cloud storage for research data, cross-platform synchronization support, file versioning, and the ability to share files with other users. B2DROP's added value stems from its embedding in the EUDAT infrastructure. B2DROP is targeted at European researchers and guarantees that all research data stays on European servers.

Figure 8 shows the file menu for a selected file in the B2DROP cloud space. Once the Switchboard option (red rectangle) is selected from the menu, the shared link to the resource (generated by B2DROP) is sent to the Switchboard.

23 https://b2drop.eudat.eu

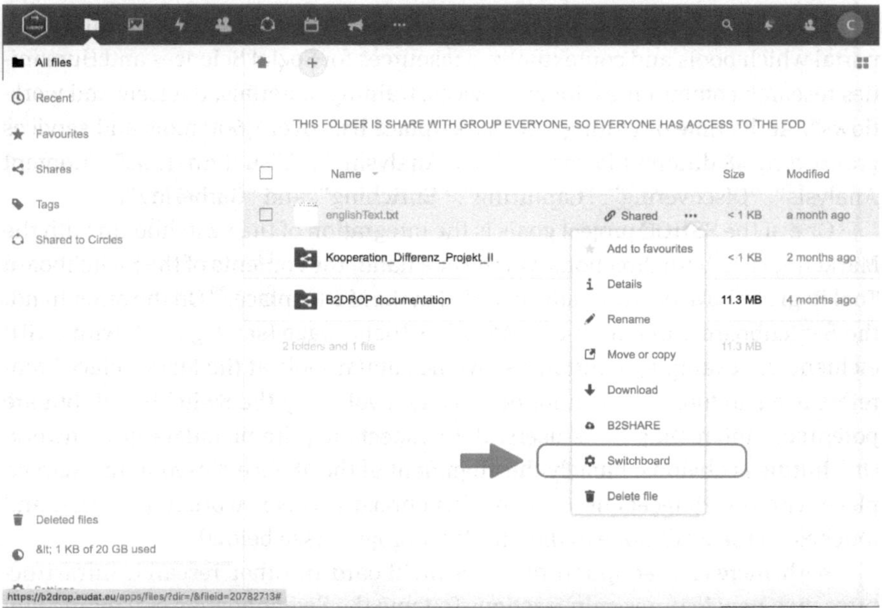

Figure 8: The B2DROP to Switchboard bridge.

B2DROP and its sibling services are continually supported and developed within the European Open Science Cloud project[24] (EOSC), see (Castelli 2020) in which the Switchboard plug-in has officially entered production status. To date, the Switchboard plug-in is the only external tool that B2DROP users can call to process their cloud files. To advertise the plug-in, the B2DROP-Switchboard bridge was recently featured as a community use case.[25]

4.3 SSHOC

The European SSHOC[26] project aims at creating the Social Sciences and Humanities area of the EOSC in order to give researchers access to research data and tools and services to process them. In this project, the CLARIN Switchboard is being extended into the SSHOC Switchboard, taking on board tools from social sciences and humanities.[27]

24 https://sshopencloud.eu
25 https://eosc-portal.eu/language-data-insight-clarin-demonstrator
26 https://eosc-portal.eu
27 https://sshopencloud.eu/sshoc-switchboard

The SSHOC project is hosting the SSH Open Marketplace,[28] a "discovery portal which pools and contextualizes resources for Social Sciences and Humanities research communities: tools, services, training materials, datasets and workflows". At the time of writing, the Marketplace lists over 1,600 tools and services grouped by 48 different facets, such as "Analysing", "Visual Analysis", "Content Analysis", "Discovering", "Capturing", "Enriching", and "Gathering".

One of the SSHOC project goals is the integration of the Switchboard with the Marketplace in both directions. On the one hand, the contents of the Switchboard Tool Registry have been already included in the Marketplace.[29] On the other hand, the Switchboard will enrich its "Matching Tools" page (see Figure 3) with a GUI element, for example, a button "Show me similar tools at the MarketPlace" that refers users to tools that cannot be directly invoked by the Switchboard, but are potentially interesting to its users. Both aspects require metadata groundwork. One hurdle is obvious, namely the alignment of the 48 facets used in the Marketplace with the 28 facets used by the Switchboard. This is work in progress, and touches on the work done in the CLARIAH projects (see below).

With increased adoption of the Switchboard in other research infrastructures, two new features gain traction. To tame the Switchboard's expanding tool space, the two filters "mediatype" and "language" (see Figure 1) will be complemented by a new filter "research domain". Once active, the Switchboard will only show (or rank first) those tools, which stem from a given research domain such as linguistics or social sciences. It is envisioned that the Switchboard will identify the research domain via its invocation path and via user profiles. If the Switchboard is invoked from the VLO, it will show a preference for tools from the CLARIN tool space, whereas an invocation from B2DROP or SSHOC will have the Switchboard favour tools from the social sciences. Moreover, Switchboard users will be encouraged to define a user profile where they can manually set their research domain, but also define other preferences to tailor the list of applicable tools to their needs. Should web services be included, or tools that require authentication, or tools that have not yet reached production status?

Another feature request concerns the local embedding of Switchboard functionality at data repository sites. Here, two possible technical solutions are being investigated: (i) the development of a browser plug-in that provides tool brokering services at the site, or a JAVASCRIPT-based code template that can be embedded in the existing website of a data repository. With such technical embeddings,

28 https://marketplace.sshopencloud.eu

29 Of the 51 tool descriptions harvested from the Switchboard tool inventory, only 31 are described in terms of Marketplace activities such as "Parsing" (12 entries), "Named Entity Recognition" (8), "Tagging" (5), and "Analysing" (3).

it will be possible to get a list of applicable tools directly at the data repository site without a detour to the Switchboard. In the SSHOC project, this is being demonstrated with the Harvard Dataverse,[30] a free data repository software that is widely used across disciplines. In an SSHOC instance of the dataverse,[31] users do not need to leave the archive site to get access to applicable tools for their resources. The Switchboard is displayed inside the dataverse's GUI (technically as an *iframe*) so that applicable tools can be invoked directly from the site hosting the data, which indeed increases the usability (and visibility) of the Switchboard.

4.4 CLARIAH

The CLARIAH infrastructure is the planned result of merging the infrastructures of CLARIN and DARIAH[32] (Edmond et al. 2020); it aims at providing a *unified* set of tools and services for the humanities. The Switchboard provides crucial support for the merging activities as its web-based nature and simple API helps overcome the technical hurdles to establish interoperability between the various CLARIN and DARIAH tools and services. For this, consider Textgrid[33] (Söring, Veentjer, and Funk 2014), a central part of DARIAH. TextgridLab is a desktop-bound application that gives researchers access to tools and services to create, manage, and edit research data. The Textgrid Repository hosts a rich set of XML-based documents, which researchers might want to analyse with external tools. For the Switchboard to offer its broker service, it will need conversion tools that bridge the divide between the format used by the resources in Textgrid Repository, and the formats required by the Switchboard tools (such as plain text for all tools, or e.g., the TCF format used by WebLicht). Here, the Export Tool from Textgrid could be extended to convert files before they are sent to the Switchboard.

The merging of the two toolsets from CLARIN and DARIAH also highlights the need for their common description, a topic already mentioned with regard to the Switchboard's integration with the SSHOC Marketplace. Here, it is envisioned that we will use TaDiRAH,[34] a taxonomy of digital research activities in the humanities.

30 https://dataverse.org
31 https://github.com/SSHOC/dataverse-lrs
32 https://dariah.eu
33 https://textgrid.de
34 http://tadirah.dariah.eu

In a recent development, the German CLARIAH[35] project integrated the *Deutsche Textarchiv* with the Switchboard. All resources of the DTA can now be sent to the Switchboard, and hence can be easily processed with its tool space.

The national Dutch CLARIAH consortium[36] aims at integrating more Dutch applications with the Switchboard. Moreover, and in line with the SSHOC rationale, this project also investigates whether the Switchboard concept could be applied in other CLARIAH core disciplines such as social economic history and media studies. This may require the Switchboard to extend its profiler so it is able to recognize new media types, or differentiate between various XML-based formats. For instance, the integration of DARIAH's Geobrowser requires the Switchboard to recognize the XML-based Keyhole Markup Language.[37]

An important extension of the Switchboard toolset is the inclusion of tools that process audio files. Here, the integration of tools from the Bavarian Archive for Speech Signals[38] is on the agenda. The inclusion of these tools requires the Switchboard to accept resource pairs rather than a single resource. Enabling the Switchboard to accept multiple resources at once will also allow the integration of tools such as the Topics Explorer from the DARIAH project, which requires five inputs in text or XML format.

Within the CLARIAH project, the Switchboard's Tool Inventory will take up DARIAH's Dashboard idea, that is, having the Tool Inventory give a resource-independent overview of tools, including tools that are not integrated with the Switchboard. The Tool Inventory will list tools that do not require inputs at all, such as the ConedaKOR[39] tool that hosts collections of images, or COSMOTool[40] that hosts a database of bibliographical data.

4.5 LAPPS

In the LAPPS project, the transatlantic collaboration between the LAPPS Grid and CLARIN (Hinrichs et al. 2018), one of the main work package objectives is to improve the interoperability between the various tools in these two infrastructures. A central aspect is the use of the Switchboard to make LAPPS tools available to Switchboard users. Similar to the situation in the SSHOC and CLARIAH pro-

35 https://clariah.de
36 https://clariah.nl
37 https://developers.google.com/kml
38 http://bas.uni-muenchen.de/Bas/
39 https://coneda.net
40 https://cosmotool.de.dariah.eu

jects, this requires the Switchboard to allow users to upload multiple resources at once, and to adapt the Switchboard to filter applicable tools given a *set* of resources.

The LAPPS project has access to a large radio archive, where recordings and transcriptions thereof exist. Here, users expect the Switchboard to batch process multiple resources or data items at once, a requirement that is not easy to meet, given the design of the Switchboard. Multilingual content is another challenge for the Switchboard as its profiler must first detect that a resource consists of content in several languages. Once this is detected, a tool is required that splits the resource into its constituent language parts. LAPPS users would also like to see tools integrated with the Switchboard that are able to process spontaneous speech.

These examples show that the Switchboard team is sometimes confronted with use cases it cannot deal with single-handedly. But once tools have been identified to address a use case, the LAPPS project has several options for making a solution available to its users: via a loose integration of tools with the Switchboard, or via a tight integration with workflow tools the Switchboard has experience of interacting with (i.e., WebLicht where tools must be capable of reading and writing TCF), or with LAPPS Grid, where tools must be capable of reading and writing the LAPPS Interchange format.

One aspect not highlighted so far is the use of an authentication and authorization infrastructure (AAI). This is being dealt with in the aforementioned European projects, but must be extended to a transatlantic level. For LAPPS users, it is important to know that their data is sent to the Switchboard securely, and that all tools that access the data can be trusted. However, as yet, there is no certification process that tools integrated with the Switchboard have to pass, an issue that is not easy to resolve.

5 Community impact

The Switchboard impacts on the community and its various stakeholders, see Figure 9.

First, the Switchboard gives tool developers a show-case where their tool is given a "high street" display space, and where their tool can be easily invoked. Tool developers can hence "advertise" their tool via the Switchboard to make their tool more visible to the community. A tool, previously only known to a limited user base, gets immediate access to the entire CLARIN community of users. It suddenly becomes a visible part of the infrastructure. It is this effect that encourages

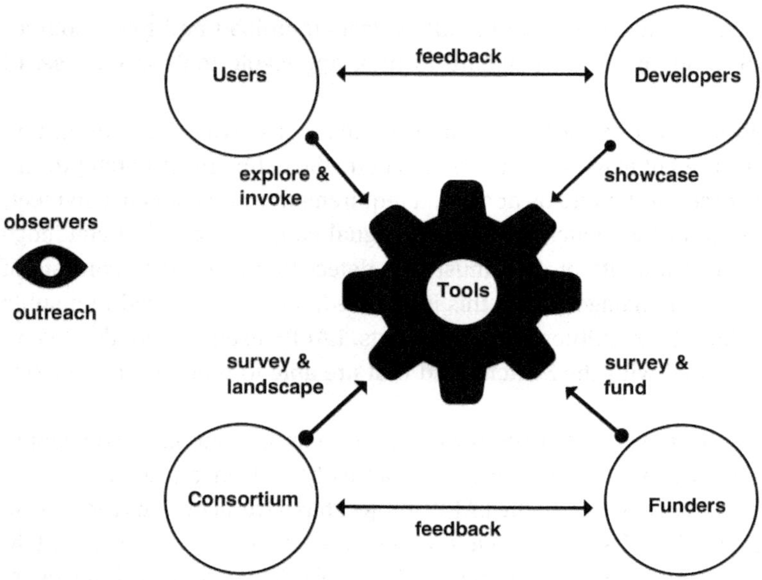

Figure 9: Impact of the Switchboard on stakeholders.

tool developers to have their tool integrated with the Switchboard. While such a tool integration is relatively simple, such a small cooperation between "CLARIN central" and its outposts is not to be underestimated, and often spawns fruitful exchanges between Switchboard developers and tool developers.

Second, the Switchboard gives users a good overview of, and easy access to, the CLARIN tool space. Given a resource, the tool space is filtered into a sub-space of applicable tools, ordered alphabetically or by their processing task. With the Switchboard, it is easy for users to invoke the tool with a single click; often only a second click is needed to start the tool's processing. With the Switchboard's Tool Inventory feature, all tools the Switchboard knows about are listed (even if it cannot invoke them). For newcomers to the field and the community, the Switchboard is valuable as it guides them through an actively maintained tool space. Expert users may – from time to time – find an applicable tool they did not know about, and with the low barrier to tool invocation (i.e., no installation, little if any configuration required), they may be tempted to explore the tool.

Third, the Switchboard gives the CLARIN consortium a good overview of the processing tools in the community. This supports the landscaping of the tool space at a CLARIN global scale: which processing functionality is already available, which parts are still missing, which tool to "water" a little bit more, and which new "trees" to "plant". The Switchboard therefore also serves as a drawing board to strategically guide future tool developments and, lest we forget, to present the current tool space to potential funding organizations. Funders can easily review the state of the CLARIN tool space via the Switchboard to inform their future funding decisions.

The Switchboard hence supports *community building* at varying scales: between tool developers and Switchboard developers but also between tool developers and its widened user base, and between consortium members and funding organizations, or other research infrastructures. As we have seen from the outreach section, the Switchboard can also serve as a bridging device that connects resources and tools from other research infrastructure to the CLARIN world and *vice versa*, with the potential of cross-fertilization between worlds.

6 Roadmap

To a large extent, the Switchboard's roadmap of future developments is prescribed by the aforementioned outreach activities.

A requirement of many projects is to allow the Switchboard to act as a broker for tools that require multiple inputs, which is currently being tested on the beta version of the Switchboard.[41] The implementation is not easy given that the Switchboard is now invocable from many different sites with a *single* resource. Consider, for instance, the bridges from B2DROP, PARTHENOS, or VLO to the Switchboard. Those bridges must be extended so that multiple resources can be selected and their URL-based addresses sent to the Switchboard, a non-trivial UI usability problem yet to be solved.

A big change to the Switchboard is its Tool Inventory, which now also lists tools that the Switchboard cannot invoke. Here, the Switchboard plays the role of a *Virtual Tool Observatory* that gives a complete overview of the tool space it knows about, including desktop-bound tools that users need to install themselves. Having this tool space accessible from the Switchboard is advantageous in several repects. First, it helps users discover tools they do not know about, and second, users (and funders) may succeed in convincing developers to provide a web-based version of their tools, which could eventually be integrated as *applicable* tool in the Switchboard. The new Tool Inventory comes with a few challenges, though. Should the Switchboard harvest, say, the tools from the SSHOC Marketplace and automatically add them to Switchboard Tool Inventory, or should the Switchboard team continue to add tools to the Tool Inventory manually, given

41 https://beta-switchboard.clarin.eu

that the tool and its metadata description satisfies some quality control threshold? It seems that manual labour might be necessary to ensure that the tool space is not cluttered with deficient or badly described tools.

A large tool space puts an additional burden on the user to select the most appropriate tool for their resource. Sometimes, a web-based tool directly invocable from the Switchboard might "shadow" a desktop-bound tool that is better suited to, or more efficient for the task at hand, but requires manual installation. Here, a tool ranking mechanism, integrated within the Switchboard, might prove beneficial. One approach would be to add a "Like" button to each tool in the tool inventory and use this information for ranking. For tools that were invoked by the Switchboard, a feedback loop could be offered. The Switchboard would remember which tools users invoked and ask them later how they would rate their interaction with and the performance of the tool. However, such recommendations are prone to misuse and should be deployed with great care.

There has been some discussion as to whether the Switchboard should be enabled to monitor the state of the tools it knows about (and can invoke itself). Here, the Switchboard should only list a tool as applicable if the tool is live, similar to the CLARIN status page.[42] Tools with a high uptime improve their ranking. The Switchboard could also centrally count the number of tool invocations, something that can easily be recorded with analytics software such as Matomo.[43] Popular tools would then rank higher than unpopular ones. It could also be investigated whether the one-way communication between the Switchboard and its tools shall be extended to a two-way communication, where tools send back statistical data about tool use to the Switchboard (how much CPU and time resources have been consumed, and did the processing succeed?). Tools that were invoked by the Switchboard and that return performance data rank higher than those tools that do not report back. Clearly, such data would be highly useful, but also make tool integration with the Switchboard much harder. It would probably suffice to add a "Report a problem" functionality where users can give natural language feedback on their experience with the Switchboard and the tools they were directed to. In sum, any of the feedback loops could be used to inform a tool ranking and hence improve the usability of the Switchboard. Such feedback would also be forwarded to developers to inform the future development of their tools.

42 https://status.clarin.eu
43 https://matomo.org

The integration of commercial services such as translation services from, say Google[44] or DeepL,[45] is also on the agenda. Here, it has to be investigated whether the CLARIN community is also willing to pay for such services.

There are many other improvements to be made. When using the Switchboard's "Submit URL" functionality, where the URL points to a landing page rather than actual data, can we extend the Switchboard to automatically identify the data that is referred to on the landing page? When users submit images of text, can we extend the Switchboard to automatically perform an OCR pre-processing step, before the result is then processed in the usual way? Once the plug-in/pop-up version of the Switchboard is live on sites that host research data, and the site holds a resource in multiple formats, can it decide to choose a format that maximizes the space of applicable tools? Conversion services also play a central role. Here, standard conversion mechanisms from PDF, RTF, or DOC formats to plain text may soon be hidden under the Switchboard hood.

User adaptation is the most recent trait in the development of the Switchboard. With the Switchboard now used in other infrastructures, users may want to get a view of applicable tools that matches not only a widened set of mimetypes and languages but also their research discipline or features captured in user profiles. Extensions have the danger of decreasing rather than increasing the usability of the Switchboard, which in large part is rooted in its simple idea and design. Special care is needed to ensure that personalized content does indeed improve user satisfaction.

7 Conclusion

The Switchboard has developed into an integral part of the CLARIN infrastructure; its use in many projects demonstrates the integrative effect the Switchboard had and has on CLARIN and other infrastructure projects. Its design serves as a blueprint that other communities and research infrastructures are encouraged to follow. The future of the Switchboard is bright, and we invite tool developers to contact the authors to discuss an integration of their tools with the Switchboard.

44 https://translate.google.de
45 https://deepl.com

Bibliography

Arnold, Denis, Ben Campbell, Thomas Eckart, Bernhard Fisseni, Thorsten Trippel & Claus Zinn. 2020. CMDI explorer. In Costanza Navarretta & Maria Eskevich (eds.), *Selected papers from the CLARIN Annual Conference, Virtual Edition*, (Linköping Electronic Conference Proceedings 180), 8–15. Linköping: Linköping University Electronic Press.

Broeder, Daan, Marc Kemps-Snijders, Dieter Van Uytvanck, Menzo Windhouwer, Peter Withers, Peter Wittenburg & Claus Zinn. 2010. A data category registry- and component-based metadata framework. In *International Conference on Language Resources and Evaluation (LREC) 7*, 43–47.

Castelli, Donatella. 2020. EOSC as a game-changer in the social sciences and humanities research activities. In Daan Broeder, Maria Eskevich & Monica Monachini (eds.), *Proceedings of the Workshop about Language Resources for the SSH Cloud, LR4SSHOC@ LREC 2020, Marseille, France, May 2020*, 37–38. European Language Resources Association. https://aclanthology.org/2020.lr4sshoc-1.7/ (accessed May 5, 2022).

Edmond, Jennifer, Frank Fischer, Laurent Romary & Toma Tasovac. 2020. 9. Springing the floor for a different kind of dance: Building DARIAH as a twenty-first-century research infrastructure for the arts and humanities. In *Digital technology and the practices of humanities research*. Open Book Publishers. https://doi.org/10.11647/OBP.0192.09 (accessed May 5, 2022).

Elbers, Willem. 2017. Virtual collection registry v2. Technical report, CLARIN. https://office.clarin.eu/v/CE-2017-1067-CLARINPLUS-D2_11.pdf (accessed May 5, 2022).

Goosen, Twan & Thomas Eckart. 2014. Virtual language observatory 3.0: What's new? In *CLARIN Annual Conference*. Soesterberg, 23–25 Oktober.

Hajič, Jan, Eva Hajičová, Barbora Hladká, Jozef Mišutka, Ondřej Košarko & Pavel Straňák. 2022. LINDAT/CLARIAH-CZ: Where we are and where we go. In Darja Fišer & Andreas Witt (eds.), *CLARIN. The infrastructure for language resources*. Berlin: De Gruyter.

Hinrichs, Erhard W., Nancy Ide, James Pustejovsky, Jan Hajič, Marie Hinrichs, Mohammad Fazleh Elahi, Keith Suderman, Marc Verhagen, Kyeongmin Rim, Pavel Straňák & Jozef Mišutka. 2018. Bridging the LAPPS Grid and CLARIN. In *International Conference on Language Resources and Evaluation (LREC) 11*, 1294–1302.

Hinrichs, Erhard W. & Steven Krauwer. 2014. The CLARIN research infrastructure: Resources and tools for ehumanities scholars. In *International Conference on Language Resources and Evaluation (LREC) 9*, 1525–1531.

Hinrichs, Marie, Thomas Zastrow & Erhard W. Hinrichs. 2010. Weblicht: Web-based LRT services in a distributed escience infrastructure. In *International Conference on Language Resources and Evaluation (LREC) 7*, 489–493.

Jörg, Brigitte, Hans Uszkoreit & Alastair Burt. 2010. LT world: Ontology and reference information portal. In *International Conference on Language Resources and Evaluation (LREC) 7*, 1002–1006.

Sanden, Marie van de, Christine Staiger, Claudio Cacciari, Roberto Mucci, Carl Johan Hakansson, Adil Hasan, Stephane Coutin, Hannes Thiemann, Benedikt von St. Vieth & Jens Jensen. 2015 (updated 2018). EUDAT D5.3 Final report on EUDAT services. Technical report, EUDAT. http://hdl.handle.net/11304/436879dc-f40a-11e4-ac7e-860aa0063d1f (accessed May 5, 2022).

Söring, Sibylle, Ubbo Veentjer & Stefan E. Funk. 2014. Textgrid: Creating, archiving, publishing and exploring digital editions and other humanistic research data via a Virtual Research Environment. In *9th Annual International Conference of the Alliance of Digital Humanities Organizations, DH 2014, Lausanne, Switzerland, 8–12 July 2014, Conference Abstracts*. Alliance of Digital Humanities Organizations (ADHO). https://textgrid.de/fileadmin/materialien/DH2014_Poster.pdf (accessed May 5 2022).

Windhouwer, Menzo & Twan Goosen. 2022. Component Metadata Infrastructure. In Darja Fišer & Andreas Witt (eds.), *CLARIN. The infrastructure for language resources*. Berlin: De Gruyter.

Zinn, Claus. 2016. The CLARIN Language Resource Switchboard. In *CLARIN Annual Conference*. Aix-en-Provence, France.

Zinn, Claus. 2018a. A bridge from EUDAT's B2DROP cloud service to CLARIN's Language Resource Switchboard. In Maciej Piasecki (ed.), *Selected papers from the CLARIN Annual Conference (Budapest, 18–20 September 2017)*, (Linköping Electronic Conference Proceedings 147), 36–45. Linköping: Linköping University Electronic Press.

Zinn, Claus. 2018b. The Language Resource Switchboard. *Computational Linguistics* 44 (4), 631–639. https://doi.org/10.1162/coli_a_00329 (accessed May 5, 2022).

Luís Gomes*, Ruben Branco, João Silva, and António Branco

Open and Inclusive Language Processing

Language Processing Services by PORTULAN to Meet the Widest Needs of CLARIN users

Abstract: As a research infrastructure for human language, the mission of CLARIN is to serve its users and respond to their research needs, in all their diversity of backgrounds and aims, with the appropriate access level to the functionalities of a wide range of language processing tools. Building on solutions designed, matured, and explored at the Portuguese national node PORTULAN CLARIN, the goal of this chapter is to expand on those solutions and, by providing a detailed description of them, to report on how CLARIN has been undertaking its mission in that respect. Hopefully, this will help to further improve what the infrastructure can do for its users and for the advancement of research in the science and technology of language.

Keywords: research infrastructure, language science, language technology, language processing services, web services, PORTULAN CLARIN

Acknowledgment: The results reported here were partially supported by PORTULAN CLARIN — Research Infrastructure for the Science and Technology of Language, funded by Lisboa2020, Alentejo2020 and FCT — Fundação para a Ciência e Tecnologia under the grant PINFRA/22117/2016.

***Corresponding author: Luís Gomes,** PORTULAN CLARIN and University of Lisbon, Departamento de Informática, Faculdade de Ciências de Lisboa, Lisbon, Portugal, e-mail: luis.gomes@di.fc.ul.pt
Ruben Branco, PORTULAN CLARIN and University of Lisbon, Departamento de Informática, Faculdade de Ciências de Lisboa, Lisbon, Portugal, e-mail: ruben.branco@di.fc.ul.pt
João Silva, PORTULAN CLARIN and University of Lisbon, Departamento de Informática, Faculdade de Ciências de Lisboa, Lisbon, Portugal, e-mail: jsilva@di.fc.ul.pt
António Branco, PORTULAN CLARIN and University of Lisbon, Departamento de Informática, Faculdade de Ciências de Lisboa, Lisbon, Portugal, e-mail: antonio.branco@di.fc.ul.pt

https://doi.org/10.1515/9783110767377-005

1 Introduction

PORTULAN CLARIN Research Infrastructure for the Science and Technology of Language[1] belongs to the Portuguese National Roadmap of Research Infrastructures of Strategic Relevance[2] and is part of the international research infrastructure CLARIN ERIC.[3] Its mission is to support researchers, innovators, citizen scientists, students, language professionals, and general users whose activities draw on research results from the Science and Technology of Language, by distributing scientific resources, supplying technological support, providing consultancy, and fostering scientific dissemination.

In this chapter, we focus in one of these mission lines, namely the provision of technological support, in particular under the form of open and inclusive language processing services. Our goal here is to expand on the solutions designed, matured, and explored at PORTULAN CLARIN and, by providing a detailed description of them, to report on how CLARIN has been undertaking its mission in that respect. We expect that this will help to further improve what the CLARIN infrastructure can do for its users and for the advancement of research in the science and technology of language, specifically in articulation with other chapters in this book, including Hajič et al. (2022), Zinn and Dima (2022), and Kupietz, Diewald, and Margaretha (2022).

Tokenization, part-of-speech tagging, parsing, or concordancing are just a few examples, among many others, of language processing tools that can serve as processing services the users of a research infrastructure for the science and technology of language. In PORTULAN CLARIN, every such web-based language processing service is accessible as an *online service*: users just need to copy the excerpt of interest to be processed from some third-party digital source, paste it into a designed text field, push a button to run the tool, then copy the result that will be displayed, and finally paste it to some digital support. The greatest advantage of this type of user interface is its unsurpassed simplicity, together with the fact that users can see the results of their requests immediately and understand the functionality of the tool at stake. This interface constrains users, however, to work with short inputs only and provides no combinatorial affordance.

In a more evolved user interface, tools are accessible as *file-processing services*. This is the type of interface that has been available through the CLARIN switchboard (Zinn 2018). Users upload files of their choice in a dialog box, push

1 https://portulanclarin.net/
2 https://www.fct.pt/apoios/equipamento/roteiro/index.phtml.en
3 https://www.clarin.eu/content/participating-consortia

the *upload* button below that box, and finally download the returned file with the output. Although they are not provided with any combinatorial affordance here, as in the online services, users are, however, not limited to short inputs, and for most practical purposes most users will not feel limited by the size of the inputs.

In another user interface, language processing tools are available under the modality of a *notebook service*. Notebooks allow users to interleave paragraphs of descriptive text with snippets of code; can be opened in a browser and the code run online by resorting to some non-local server that would otherwise have to be provided locally by the user. As in the file-processing interface, users are no longer limited to short inputs, with the added advantage that now combinatorial affordances are available by adjusting the seed code made available, for which some minimal programming skills are needed.

In yet another user interface that is more demanding in terms of technical skills, a tool can be used as a *web service* through a remote procedure call (RPC) interface. From within a program, written in any programming language of their preference, users can invoke a function to which they pass the input text to be processed and that returns the respective processed output. Like the notebook services, this is also a type of interface that is not yet available through the CLARIN switchboard (see Zinn and Dima 2022). As its greatest advantage, this interface grants users full combinatorial affordance while requiring some minimal programming skills.

This chapter is focused on the workbench with language processing services of PORTULAN CLARIN. For a broader and higher level view of PORTULAN, please refer to Branco et al. (2020).

The remainder of this chapter is organized as follows: In Section 2, we present in more detail the different types of interfaces, mentioned above, as they have been implemented in PORTULAN CLARIN. Then, in Section 3 we will expand on the technical options that were adopted and implemented, and in Section 4 we discuss the current status of the workbench formed by the collection of language processing services made available, before concluding with Section 5.

2 Language processing services for the widest user profiles

2.1 Online services

Every tool in the PORTULAN CLARIN workbench has an *online service* type of interface. This is the central interface for each tool and it serves the following purposes:

1. to allow users to experiment with the tool by changing its input and options and immediately see the effect in the output;
2. to offer one-click usage examples to help users start experimenting with the least amount of effort;
3. to grant access to several forms of documentation;
4. to provide an entry point to the *file-processing* or *web services* interfaces.

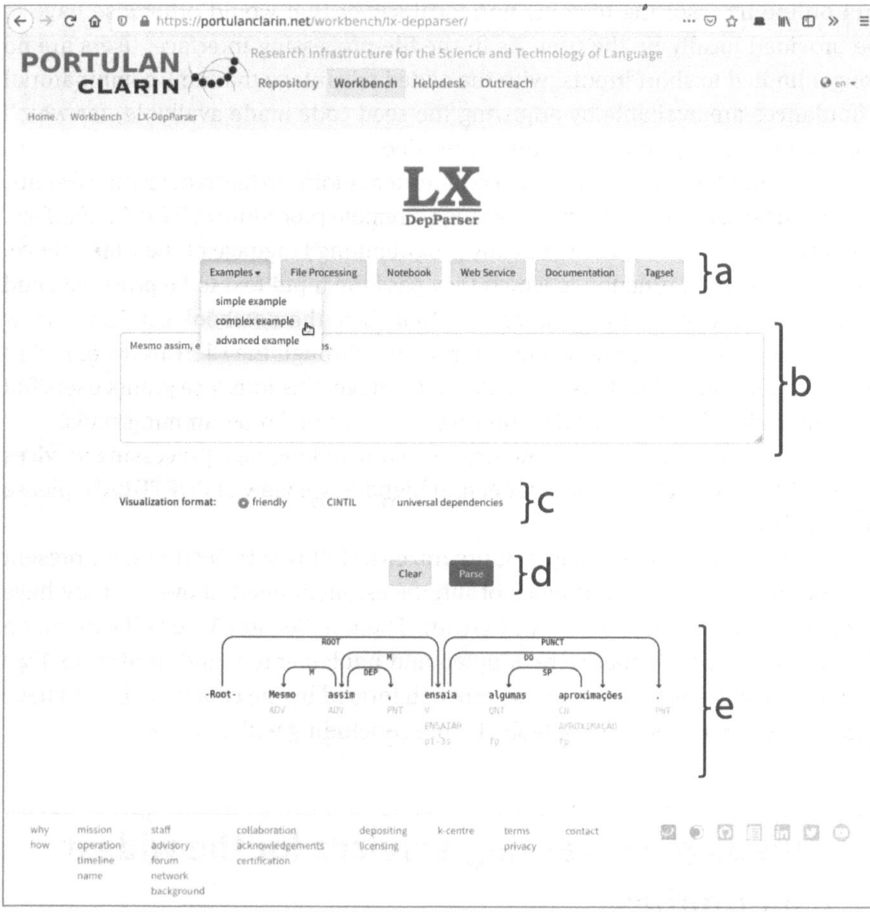

Figure 1: Example of the online service interface. Our guidelines for positioning elements in the interface follows a top-down layout with five groups, (a) to (e), superimposed to this screen shot, and not part of the interface.

As an example, Figure 1 presents the interface of the LX-DepParser tool,[4] which is a prototypical interface for sentence-based text-processing tasks, such as POS tagging, dependency and constituency parsing, or semantic role labelling, etc.

Every online service interface follows the same general layout, which can be sectioned vertically in 5 groups of elements, identified in Figure 1 using letters (a) to (e) for easier reference. In the topmost position, in group (a), we find a row of buttons that give access to examples, the file-processing and web services interfaces, and documentation. The subsequent groups follow the order of user interaction with each of the interface elements: input for the tool is accepted in group (b); options affecting the behaviour and output format of the tool are specified in group (c); processing of current input is started or cleared in group (d); and finally, the results are shown in group (e).

The "Examples" button is the first button on the interface, and thus one of the most prominent, because it provides the best starting point for newly arrived users to start interacting with the tool. Running an example via a simple button click requires no effort from the users, whereas if the common practice of providing examples only as part of the documentation had been followed, users would be required to copy and paste inputs and options from the documentation into the interface. Not only is copying and pasting examples a much more fastidious process than the solution adopted here, but it is also an error-prone one, particularly if the tool has several options affecting its behaviour that need to be changed, which ultimately could hinder the main purpose of examples: to aid users understand what the tool does and how they can use it.

The "File Processing", "Notebook" and "Web Service" buttons each open a dialog interface, which will be described in detail in Sections 2.2, 2.3 and 2.4, respectively.

The documentation button opens a window that will be displayed on top of the online service interface, containing relevant information about the tool, such as:

- a description of the tool, the problem it solves, and the method used;
- the datasets used to train the underlying models, when applicable;
- the tagsets used by the tool, when applicable;
- the input and output formats;
- a user manual or tutorial, where it is justified by the complexity of the tool;
- references to scientific publications describing the tool or its components;
- authorship and contact information;
- acknowledgements;
- licensing terms.

4 https://portulanclarin.net/workbench/lx-depparser/ (based on Branco et al. (2011)).

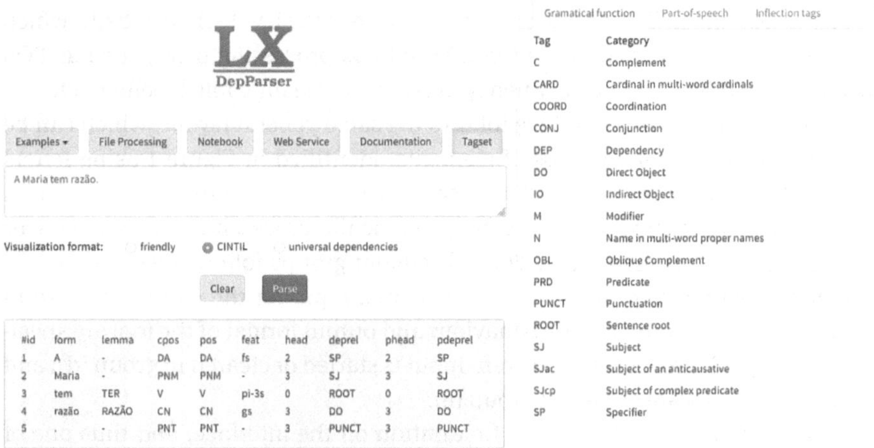

Figure 2: Tagset of LX-DepParser shown side by side with the interface, for user's convenience. Also note that a different output format was selected from the one shown in Figure 1. This interface allows the user to easily compare the output formats available for each tool by looking at the same output encoded in different formats.

The documentation window is presented in a modal form over the tool interface, which means that all page elements not belonging to the documentation window, will appear behind a semi-transparent grey background, allowing users to focus on the documentation without being disturbed by any other elements on the page.

Additionally, because the documentation is often long, a hyperlinked table of contents is automatically inserted at the top of the window, allowing users to jump to any section. A floating button, with an upward-pointing arrow, appears at the top left-hand corner of the screen whenever the document is scrolled down. By clicking this button, users may jump back to the table of contents from any point in the document. These navigation aids are implemented in the interface logic that is shared across all tools in the workbench, contributing to a more uniform and thus less distracting user experience when reading documentation.

Besides being included in the main documentation, tagsets can also be accessed directly by clicking the respective "Tagset" button, the rightmost in group (a) of Figure 1. Once pressed, this button will slightly change its appearance to indicate it has been depressed and a new panel opens on the right-hand side of the interface, sharing half of the horizontal space that was previously fully dedicated to the interface, as shown in Figure 2. Having the tagset shown side by side with the output of the tool is much more convenient to users than having to go back and forth between the documentation view and the interface. To close the tagset panel, users either press the same button that was used to open it, which will revert to its normal appearance, or they press the "close" button, represented by a cross, at the top right-hand corner.

For some tools, instead of a tagset, this side panel may show other types of referencial documentation, such as a cheat sheet for a query syntax, as is the case for the CINTIL Concordancer tool.[5]

Among the output formats of each tool there is usually one termed *friendly*, which is the default and is specifically targeted at human users, as opposed to being suited to further processing by another automatic tool. This friendly format is often graphical in nature, such as the dependency tree output in Figure 1. By contrast, the other formats are generally textual, even if they encode some form of graph structure, and thus harder to interpret for humans; an example is the tabular output shown within the grey rectangle in Figure 2, which encodes a short sentence and its annotated dependency tree graph.

To conclude this section, it is worth mentioning that the layout presented in Figure 1 is a general guideline for organizing components in online service interfaces, which aims at increasing consistency across the interfaces of different tools, but ultimately, these guidelines should always be overridden as needed for the benefit of the interface.

For example, in the LX-Translator[6] online service, shown in Figure 3, which is an interface for a bi-directional machine translation system, there is not one text input box but two, one for each language, displayed side by side. Each of these boxes is used for both input and output, which breaks the guideline of displaying the output on a dedicated area at the bottom of the page. At the beginning, both text boxes are empty and the user may input text in either one, click the "Translate" button below, and the translation will appear in the other box. For providing examples, we have decided to place one "Example" button below each input/output text box, which breaks another guideline – the one that tells us to place the example button prominently in the top row of buttons. However, by breaking this rule, the new placement makes it obvious which text box will be filled with the respective example input text and which will be the translation direction triggered by each of these example buttons.

5 https://portulanclarin.net/workbench/cintil-concordancer/ (based on Barreto et al. (2006)).
6 https://portulanclarin.net/workbench/lx-translator/ (based on Santos et al. (2019)).

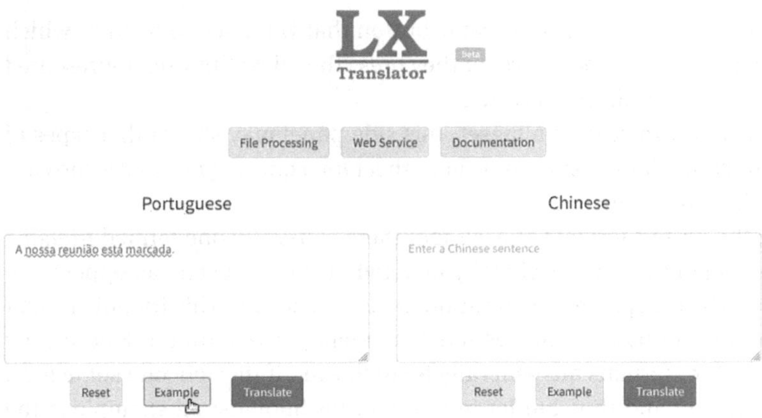

Figure 3: Interface of the LX-Translator online service, illustrating a case where the overall design guidelines may have to be weakened for the benefit of the interface usability, depending on the functionality of the service at stake.

2.2 File-processing services

The file-processing interface, or *fileproc* for short, is a multi-step workflow that is launched by clicking on the “File Processing” button at the top of the online service interface. Figure 4 depicts this workflow, using screenshots of the dialog windows presented to the user at each step.

The first dialog window allows the user to select an input file from their computer to be processed and proceed to upload the file by clicking the “Upload” button. At this point, the workflow takes one of two possible courses, depending on the size of the file that is being uploaded.

Small input files are handled by the path on the left-hand side of Figure 4, and we call these *short* (file-processing) jobs. Large input files are handled by the path on the right-hand side of Figure 4, and we call these *long* jobs. The threshold size, used to determine if a file is to be considered small or large is computed for each tool separately, based on the maximum amount of data that it can process in under two minutes. Further ahead we will discuss the reasoning that led to this specific time threshold.

If the file is small enough that it can be processed in under two minutes, then we consider this to be a short job and processing will start immediately after the file is uploaded. The user is informed of the processing progress through a progress bar, as shown in step 2(a) of Figure 4. As soon as the processing is

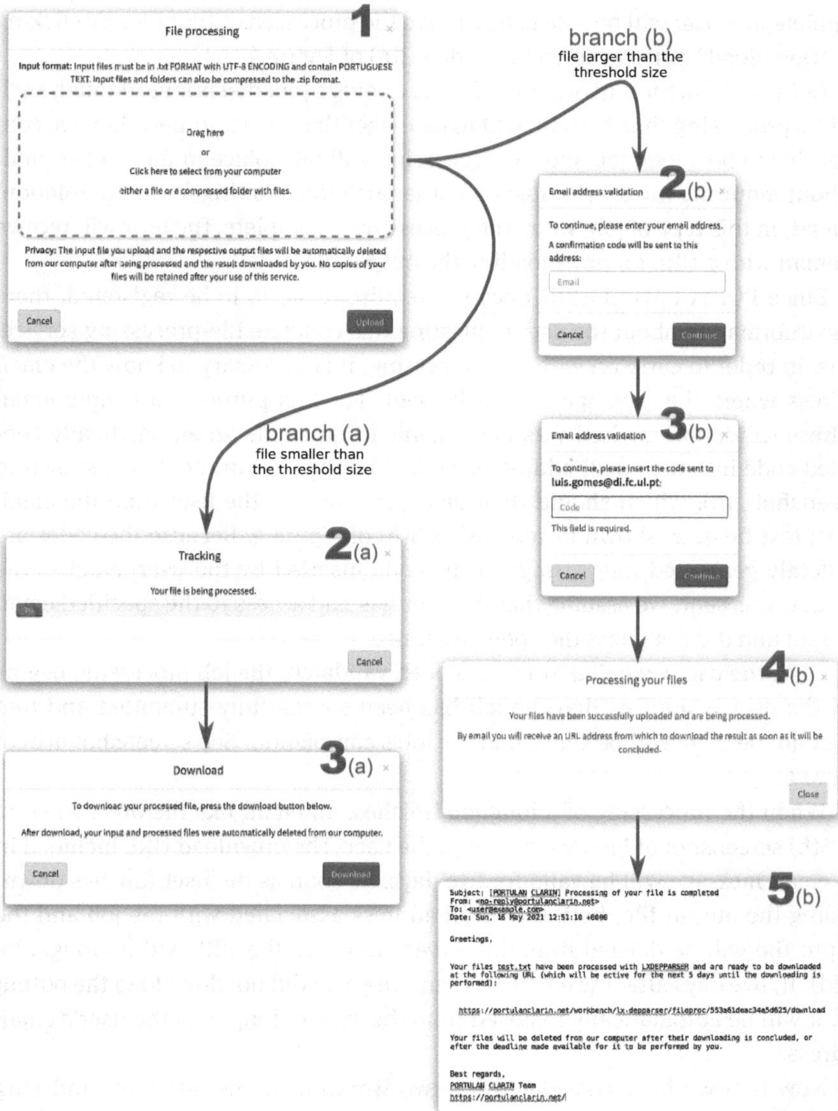

Figure 4: File-processing service interface workflow. Depending on the size of the user supplied input file, the user interaction follows one of two main branches: (a) the file is smaller than a fixed threshold, or (b) otherwise. The threshold size varies from one processing service to another and is determined as the average number of bytes that each specific service can process under two minutes.

complete, the user will be able to download the processed output files by clicking the "Download" button shown in window 3(a) of Figure 4.

Going back to the end of step 1, if the file being uploaded is large enough such that its processing time is estimated to be longer than two minutes, then we consider this to be a long job and the processing will take place in the background, without requiring the user to suspend other activities waiting for its completion. Instead, in this type of job, when the processing is complete, the user will receive an email with a URL for downloading the output file.

Since PORTULAN CLARIN does not require its users to be registered, there is no information about the user requesting this concrete file-processing service. Thus, in order to carry on with the processing, it is necessary to know the email address where the message should be sent. For this purpose, a simple email address validation method was implemented that sends an automatically generated code into the email address specified by the user in the dialog shown in screenshot 2(b), which should then be copied over by the user from the email into a text field, as shown in screenshot 3(b) of Figure 4. Because the codes are randomly generated long strings, if the code inserted by the user matches the one that was sent, we assume that the user has had access to the specified email account and did not guess the code by chance.

Once the user's email address has been validated, the job processing begins and the user is notified that the job has been successfully submitted and that an email message will be sent upon the job's completion. See screenshot 4(b) of Figure 4.

When the processing of a long job finishes, an email like the one shown in the 5(b) screenshot of Figure 4 is sent to the user. The download URL included in the email message will be valid for five days. As soon as the user finishes downloading the output file, both the email address associated with the job and the output file will be deleted from the server (and thus the URL will no longer be valid). If, five days after the email was sent, the user did not download the output file, it will be automatically removed from the server along with the user's email address.

Now that we have considered the two workflow paths, for short and long jobs, let us take a look at the two-minute time threshold which is used to decide whether a file-processing job should be considered short or long. This threshold has been adjusted through experimentation, although in a highly subjective manner because it depends on many factors, including the users themselves. Two minutes is about the point at which we find it is more costly, in terms of inconvenience to users, to require them to go through the extra steps to validate an email address and wait for an email with the URL for downloading the output files, rather than simply wait for the processing to complete.

Compared to the online service interface, presented in detail in the previous section, here in the file-processing mode the user does not have to choose an output format. Instead, we opted to include all output formats in the output file, which will be a zip archive containing one directory for each format. The reasoning for this decision is that the time required by a tool to process the input data largely exceeds the time required to convert the processed output into all available output formats. Thus, not only this is convenient for the users, who do not have to worry about which output format to choose, but it also avoids unnecessary re-processing of the same input data if a user finds out, after a job has been processed into one output format, that a different one is needed.

The accepted formats for the input file will depend on the tool at stake, but in general, the file should be either a UTF-8 encoded plain text file, or a zip archive containing any number of UTF-8 encoded plain text files. In the case of a zip archive, the files may be organized within a directory tree structure, which will be preserved during the processing.

The output file will always be a zip archive, containing several directories, one for each output format. If the input file was a zip archive containing multiple files organized within a directory tree structure, the same structure will be replicated under each output format directory. Otherwise, if a single text file was given as input, then each directory in the output zip archive will contain a single processed output file in the corresponding output format.

2.3 Notebook services

The notebook interface is launched by clicking on the "Notebook" button at the top of the online service interface.

A Jupyter notebook (hereafter *notebook*, for short) is a type of document that contains sections of executable code, called *cells*, interspersed with visualizations of results from the execution of such cells and narrative text with rich formatting (headings, lists, bold, italic, equations, etc.). An example notebook is shown in Figure 5. Notebooks may be written in a tutorial style, embodying the *literate programming* paradigm envisioned by Knuth (1984), which also makes them a valuable tool for teaching. Furthermore, because notebooks may be modified and re-executed interactively, they are also an excellent tool for learning through experimentation.

For several tools in the workbench, the respective notebook service may be explored with only a couple of mouse clicks: a user starts by clicking the "Notebook" button in the tool's online service interface, which brings up a dialog with relevant information and further options to launch the notebook on free supporting servers, such as the Binder offered by Project Jupyter et al. (2018) or Google.

These notebooks are intended to serve as quick and easy starting points for users to start developing their own experiments, and for that purpose, we believe that very short and artificial code examples would not be the most adequate. Instead, we often include code for downloading and cleaning example data to be processed, code for processing the data with a tool from the workbench via its web services interface, and code for some kind of subsequent analysis of the processed data.

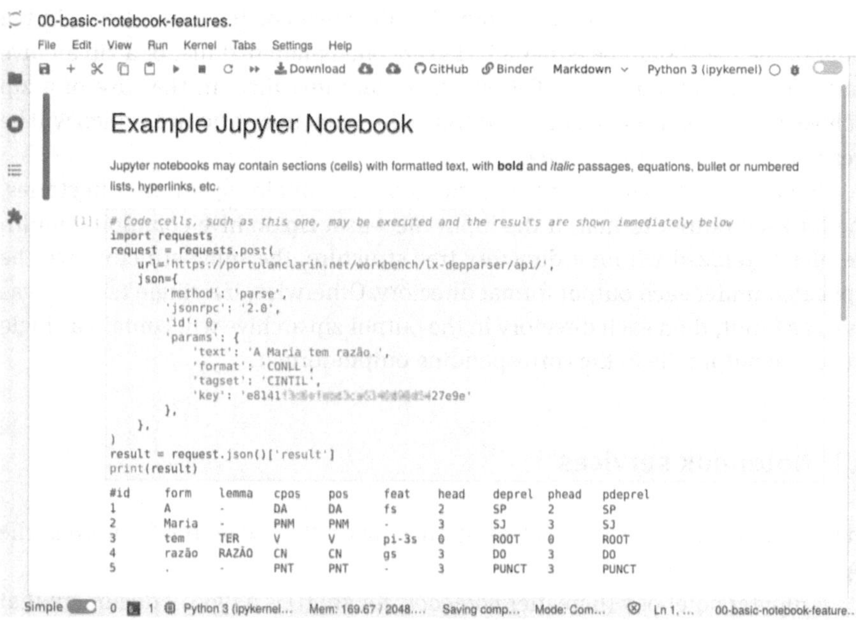

Figure 5: Example notebook illustrating basic features. At the top, there is some text with rich formatting. Within the grey rectangle there is some code. When run, it produces the output that it is displayed in the same page, and which can be input to subsequent code.

With this type of interface with language processing services in PORTULAN workbench, no software needs to be installed on the users' computers: a web browser is all that is needed. By lowering the technical requirements, we believe notebooks will foster users' interest and will help to leverage new research ideas and experimentation.

2.4 Web services

The web services interface is a remote procedure call (RPC) type of interface, through which it is possible to interact with one or several tools in the workbench by means of computer programs. We chose to implement this service using JSON-RPC, which is a lightweight and programming language-agnostic protocol for which implementations are readily available in many programming languages.

The web services interface is available for most tools in the workbench. Exceptions that do not offer this type of interface are, for example, tools that naturally lend themselves more to an interactive usage, through their online service interface, rather than to a data-processing usage scenario. For example, the CINTIL Concordancer[7] and the CINTIL Treebank Searcher[8] are examples of two such tools.

To start using web services, for any given workbench tool that supports them, a user will click the "Web Service" button in the tool's online service interface, which will bring up a dialog as the one shown in Figure 6. This dialog contains detailed information about the requirements that have to be met before this service can be used, as well as a simple and self-contained Python program that can be used as a starting point for users with little programming experience to develop their own programs.

One of the requirements to use a web service is an access key that each user must obtain by clicking the "Request key" button on this dialog. This key is used to implement a basic access control mechanism with the primary goal of preventing any individual user from abusing, either intentionally or inadvertently, the finite computational resources available on PORTULAN CLARIN to serve all its users. By clicking on the "Request key" button, users will go through an email validation process identical to the one required when submitting long file-processing jobs, as described in the previous section. After their email address has been validated, users are sent an email with an access key and information about usage quotas associated with it: the total number of requests allowed, the total number of characters allowed (accumulated over all requests), and the expiry date for the key.

Whenever a user requests a new key using an email address that was used before, if the previous key is still valid (i.e. it has not expired and its usage quotas have not been exhausted), that key is returned in the response email, along with

7 https://portulanclarin.net/workbench/cintil-concordancer/ (based on Barreto et al.(2006)).
8 https://portulanclarin.net/workbench/cintil-treebank-searcher/ (based on Branco et al.(2010)).

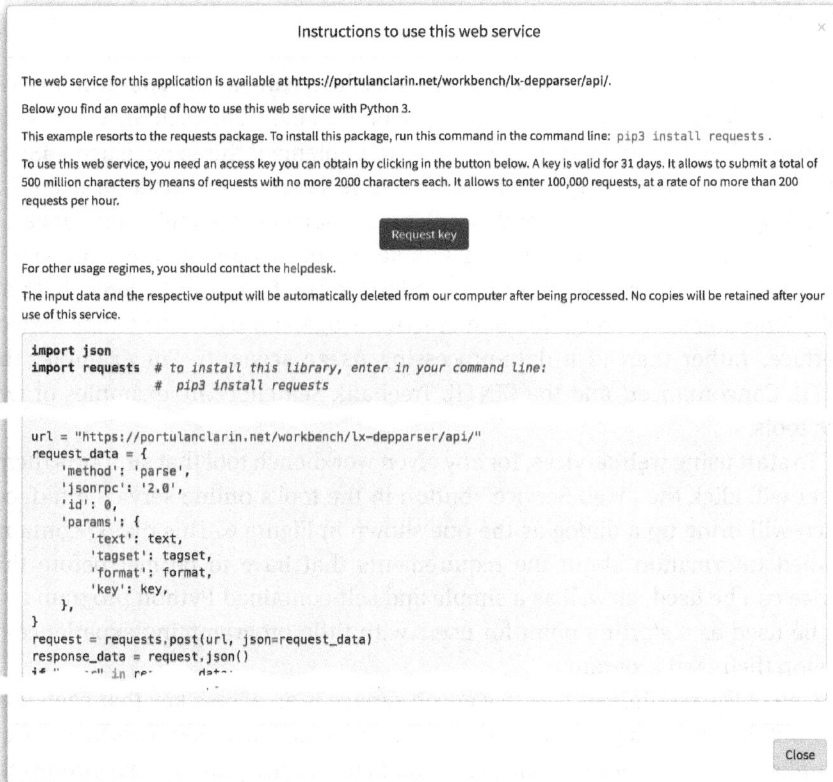

Figure 6: Example web service dialog containing detailed instructions and example Python code (truncated in this screenshot) for using the LX-DepParser web service interface.

the remainder usage quota. Thus, at any point in time, only one valid key is associated with any given email address.

Because any user can have access to several email addresses, this access control mechanism does not prevent a single user from having multiple access keys, each associated with a different address. However, creating new email addresses and requesting access keys requires some effort, which should be enough to discourage fortuitous abuse.

Besides the total number of requests and of characters allowed during the lifespan of a key, there is also a maximum number of requests and characters allowed per hour. If any of these maximum hourly rates are reached, subsequent requests will receive an appropriate error code and message, until enough time has passed since the last successful request such that both hourly rates become lower than their maximum allowed values.

3 Exploring the current stage of technological development

In order to be able to set up a computational infrastructure that seamlessly supports the four different modes of interaction described in the previous sections for dozens of different tools, non-trivial technical options need to be adopted and implemented. These options need to ensure that appropriate levels of factorization can be achieved and that sufficient levels of readability are ensured. We focus here on the design decisions that have the most impact globally.

3.1 HTTP and nginx

The PORTULAN workbench is implemented as a micro-service distributed system with a user-facing HTTP server, a frontend server and several backend servers.

The user-facing HTTP server is the only part of this distributed system that is directly exposed to the internet and it is responsible for negotiating SSL connections with the browser, serving static content such as images, CSS (Cascading Style Sheets) and JavaScript files and acting as a reverse HTTP proxy to the frontend server.

For this HTTP server, we adopted nginx[9] for its clean configuration syntax, low resource usage and excellent performance. SSL certificates are issued by Let's Encrypt,[10] a nonprofit Certificate Authority, and managed through Certbot.[11] From a security perspective, having all HTTP requests served or proxied through a single user-facing HTTP server reduces the attack surface, at least for HTTP protocol-based exploits, and eases security audits.

3.2 Python and Django

We adopted Python as the main programming language, which not only gives one access to an immense array of high-quality libraries and frameworks, and a thriving ecosystem of development tools, but also, since it is an immensely popular and accessible language, ensures that the code base is maintainable, expandable, and accessible by a larger number of people.

---

9 https://www.nginx.com/
10 https://letsencrypt.org/
11 and https://certbot.eff.org/

The frontend server is implemented as a WSGI-compliant[12] application and is served by the gunicorn server.[13] We adopted the WSGI-compliant Django framework,[14] which promotes code factorization and organization, both essential aspects for large-scale projects such as the PORTULAN workbench.

A Django-based server runs a collection of Django applications,[15] and each application holds code and files for a specific part of the the frontend service as a whole. In the context of the PORTULAN CLARIN's workbench, each tool is implemented as a separate Django application. Additionally, some cross-cutting functionalites of the workbench are implemented as Django applications, such as the workbench index page where all tools are listed, email validation, and CAPTCHA validation.

Mirroring this modular organization, workbench tools and cross-cutting functionalities are developed and maintained in independent Git repositories and packaged as separate Python packages. During deployment, these packages are installed and upgraded with the Python package management tool (pip), based on a requirements file which specifies the exact version of each package to be installed.

Thus, during production, whenever a problem occurs and a bug report is filled in our GitLab[16] service, we know exactly what version of each component was installed at the time when the problem occured. This is crucial for reproducing reported errors and pinpointing their exact source within the code, because the latest development versions of packages may no longer exhibit the same error, either because the problem was fixed as part of a refactorization or because it is being masked by some other change.

At its core, a Django application is a set of views, models, and templates.

- **Views** are functions or methods responsible for handling HTTP requests. The core logic of any Django application is either implemented within views or can be traced to calls made from them.
- **Models** are classes that define the properties and structure of data that needs to be persistent in a database. Through inheritance and dynamic method

12 https://www.python.org/dev/peps/pep-3333/

13 https://gunicorn.org/

14 https://www.djangoproject.com/

15 The word *application* has several meanings in the context of web development and thus prone to generate confusion. A *WSGI application* refers to a whole web application. A *Django application* implements a part of the whole web application, which may be composed of many Django applications.

16 GitLab is an open-source development platform that provides web-based interface for managing Git-based code repositories, a ticket system, and much more. PORTULAN CLARIN hosts a private GitLab server, only accessible to staff members.

resolution, Django provides a *Pythonic* interface to its object-relational-mapper (ORM) for querying, retrieving, inserting, updating, and deleting records from a relational database. Model objects are typically instantiated and manipulated from views.
- **Templates** are, in essence, files containing static HTML code[17] enriched with special syntax describing how and where dynamic content will be inserted. The Django template syntax provides basic control flow structures, such as conditionals and loops, an inclusion mechanism that allows templates to be included as part of other templates, and an inheritance mechanism, allowing templates to inherit and extend functionality from other templates. Templates are typically used within views to generate the HTML to be sent to the browser as the body of an HTTP response.

Taking advantage of class and template inheritance, logic that is shared across all tools in the workbench is factored out, such as CAPTCHA validation, email validation, general interface layout, common components, etc. This factorization speeds up the integration of new tools into the workbench by reducing the amount of new code that has to be written for each of them, and ensuring that each bug needs to be fixed only in one place.

3.3 JavaScript, jQuery, VueJS, and Bootstrap

Equally important in building web applications, the JavaScript code running on the web browser is used to manipulate the structure and content of a page after the initial HTML has been transferred from the server.

Furthermore, by making asynchronous HTTP requests from JavaScript code, web applications can be made smoother and more efficient because only small chunks of data need to be transferred from the server, instead of reloading the entire page. For example, when a user submits a snippet of text to be processed through an online service interface, an HTTP request is sent to the server through JavaScript, containing the snippet to be processed. Likewise, through JavaScript, while the HTTP request is ongoing, a visual activity indicator may be displayed next to the button that was clicked to trigger the request, and thus letting the user know that something is happening as a consequence of the click. As soon as the server replies, the processed result will be inserted in the appropriate place

17 In fact, a template may contain any type of textual content, not only HTML, but this is the most common use for templates.

within the page and the visual activity indicator is removed. All of these page content manipulations are made using JavaScript code. Most of the HTML that makes up the page is transferred only once into the browser, when the user navigates into that page.

We have adopted the jQuery[18] library, which introduces a large set of functionalities that simplify manipulation of HTML elements programmatically. Recently, we have also been progressively adopting the VueJS framework,[19] which provides a new, more efficient, and easier-to-use mechanism to manipulate HTML elements in the browser, and enables component-based code organization and reuse.

For the styling of HTML elements, we adopted the Bootstrap[20] framework which provides a comprehensive, well-documented and easy-to-use set of CSS classes that comply with modern web design requirements, such as being able to adapt to the small screens of mobile devices.

3.4 Backend and containers

Let us now turn our attention to the backend services of the PORTULAN infrastructure. Some tools in the workbench have dedicated backend servers that encapsulate the core logic of the tool. Other tools are directly integrated into the frontend server.

Taking into consideration the architecture and inner workings of WSGI servers, for performance and reliability reasons[21] the Django worker processes should have short startup times and moderate memory usage. Thus, the decision as to whether a tool should be integrated in its own backend server depends on the following conditions:

- if it requires a CPU-heavy or long initialization;
- if it requires a large amount of memory;
- if it is multi-threaded, which becomes a problem if any other tool is not thread-safe;
- if it is not thread-safe, which becomes a problem if any other tool is multi-threaded;

18 https://jquery.com/

19 https://vuejs.org/

20 https://getbootstrap.com/

21 The two main reasons are: (1) the WSGI server may dynamically spin up/down Django worker processes depending on the number of concurrent HTTP requests and (2) the WSGI server may restart each Django worker after it serves a pre-configured maximum number of requests.

- if it is implemented in a programming language other than Python and any of the following is true:
  - it does not offer a command line interface;
  - its initialization time is not negligible in comparison to the time it takes to process a typical input unit (e.g. a snippet of text);
- if it is no longer being actively developed or maintained. The reasons underlying this condition are quite different from the previous ones, and will be detailed below, when we discuss the need for containers.

If one or more of the above conditions is true for any given tool, then it should be integrated into a separate backend server that exposes the tool functionality over an appropriate JSON-RPC or XML-RPC interface. We adopted these two standard RPC protocols because they are programming language-agnostic and implementations are readily available for most programming languages.

Other backend services include a Postgres[22] relational database server, a memcache[23] server used for Django session data, and a postfix server for sending emails.

Each server of the PORTULAN CLARIN workbench distributed system, which includes the user-facing nginx server, the Django frontend server, and all the backend services, is deployed in a separate Docker[24] container.

Containers are groups of one or more[25] processes running under a certain level of isolation from other processes on the same host. This isolation is managed by the operating system kernel and extends only as far as controlling access to resources such as files, memory, devices, and CPU time. Thus, all containerized and regular processes are served by the same kernel and can potentially share any resource available on the host.

By contrast, in a virtual machine, a whole new guest kernel is executed within a process running on the host kernel, and then new processes are run and managed by the guest kernel, which incurs a considerable memory and CPU overhead. Processes running within a virtual machine do not have direct access to resources available on the host (such as files, memory, devices, etc.), and vice versa. In order to share resources between the host and guest kernels there are several possible workarounds, but they always incur in yet another memory and CPU overhead.

---

22 https://www.postgresql.org/
23 https://memcached.org/
24 https://www.docker.com/
25 Docker containers usually run a single process.

Containers are the best fit for our needs because they are extremely lightweight, and allow us to run each server in its own tailored environment while sharing files across containers.

As mentioned above, one of the conditions that compels us to segregate a tool into its own backend server is if the tool is no longer being actively developed or maintained. The fundamental reason is because, at some point in the future, the specific versions of libraries and other dependencies of an unmaintained tool will no longer be available for installation in an up-to-date operating system, or even if they are, they may clash with more recent versions required by other tools.

Docker images are standalone executable packages that include everything needed to run a container: code, system tools, system libraries, and settings. Thus, by including all the dependencies of a tool within a dedicated docker image, we create a perfect environment for each tool.

With Docker Swarm,[26] groups of containers are configured and managed as *services*, which communicate with each other through Docker-managed private networks. Service containers can be spread across any number of available swarm *nodes*, that is networked machines that have Docker installed and have been added to the swarm. The swarm also provides some mechanisms for maintaining availability of services: should a container crash, the swarm will restart it; or if one host becomes unavailable, the swarm will relocate containers that were running on it to other available hosts.

4 Current status of the PORTULAN CLARIN workbench

At the time of writing this chapter, dozens of tools have been integrated into the workbench, with more to come.[27]

Tools are spread across the categories listed in Table 1, and new categories will be added as needed to accommodate new tools. As described in Section 3,

26 https://docs.docker.com/engine/swarm/

27 The PORTULAN CLARIN workbench comprises a number of tools that are based on a large body of research work contributed by different authors and teams, which continues to grow and is acknowledged here: Barreto et al. (2006); Branco et al. (2010); Cruz, Rocha, and Cardoso (2018); Veiga, Candeias, and Perdigão (2011); Branco and Henriques (2003); Branco et al. (2011); Branco and Nunes (2012); Silva et al. (2009); Branco et al. (2014); Rodrigues et al. (2016); Branco and Silva (2006); Rodrigues et al. (2020); Costa and Branco (2012); Santos et al. (2019); Miranda et al. (2011).

the workbench provides an automatically generated index with links to individual tools grouped by their category. In its current form, this index is a simple list of categories, with brief descriptions and hyperlinks to the tools available under each category.

This simple design is reminiscent of the initial stages of development of the workbench, when only a handful of categories was involved. Despite its simplicity, this design continues to serve its purpose adequately, even though the number of categories has nearly doubled since that initial development stage. However, as the number of categories continues to grow, albeit at a slower pace, at some point in the future we may have to redesign this index, perhaps by introducing a combination of faceted filtering, free text searching, or another level of categorization.

We bring this up to exemplify how design decisions have been made throughout the development of the workbench: if in doubt, we first try to implement the simplest design that fulfills a given purpose. We defer adding complexity to the interface, until it becomes clear, through usage, that the simpler design is not as effective as it needs to be. And at that point, we will be in a better position to design a good interface, not only because we already have a lean working base design that we can use as starting point, but also because we know its shortcomings.

In order to gather feedback from potential users, the workbench was disseminated among the PORTULAN CLARIN implementation partners and at a number events where the infrastructure has been presented. Feedback was very positive regarding the interface and its usability, even though, during the dissemination events, engaging with the audiences in a productive way may turn out to be a challenge due to the different scientific and technical backgrounds of the participants.

Suggestions that have been submitted for new tools to be incorporated in the workbench have not tended towards novel or complex language technology applications, but towards what is comparatively simple in functionality, such as a concordancer capable of running over any user-submitted corpora.[28] We find such suggestions extremely valuable and will be working towards incorporating them into the workbench.

The workbench gets roughly one-third of the unique page views in PORTULAN CLARIN,[29] with the constituency and dependency parsers being the most

28 The concordancer that is currently available runs over a pre-indexed fixed corpus.

29 The PORTULAN CLARIN repository of language resources (data and software), in turn, is only slightly more popular, with 40% of the unique page views.

popular tools. Following the parsers is LX Semantic Similarity, a tool for measuring the semantic similarity of words.

5 Conclusion

In this chapter we have described the multi-interface approach implemented at PORTULAN, which we believe opens up language processing services to a wider array of users, coming from and carrying the most diverse backgrounds and motivations. We advise against making language processing services available through a single interface, designed with a specific user profile in mind, which would necessarily be too inflexible for some users or too complex for others. Instead, we propose four different interfaces, each one demanding an increased level of technical skill from the user, but empowering the user in return.

Table 1: Tool categories.

Concordancing ...	Retrieval of contexts of occurrence of expressions in annotated texts.
Constituency parsing ...	Analysis of syntactic constituents in sentences.
Dependency parsing ...	Analysis of grammatical functions in sentences.
Grammatical quantitative analysis ...	Occurrence counting of grammatical elements in texts.
Named entity recognition ...	Detection and semantic classification of names in texts.
Nominal inflection ...	Lemmatization and inflection of nominal expressions.
Orthographic normalization ...	Conversion to orthographic standard.
POS tagging ...	Tokenization and morphosyntactic tagging of expressions in texts.
Phonological transcription ...	Conversion of graphemic into phonological representation.
Proficiency classification ...	Quantitative analysis and proficiency level classification of texts.
Semantic role labelling ...	Analysis of semantic roles of syntactic constituents in sentences.
Semantic similarity ...	Semantic similarity between words.
Sentence splitting ...	Segmentation of texts into sentences and paragraphs.
Sentiment analysis ...	Analysis of emotional polarity in texts.
Sub-syntactic analysis ...	Tokenization, lemmatization, inflection analysis, and morphosyntactic tagging of expressions in texts.
Syllabification ...	Syllabification of expressions.

Table 1 (continued)

Temporal analysis . . .	Analysis of events and of temporal information in texts.
Tokenization . . .	Segmentation of texts into lexical tokens.
Transcription . . .	Written representation of speech.
Translation . . .	Translation of a sentence from a source language to a target language.
Treebank searching . . .	Retrieval of syntactic patterns and expressions in annotated sentences.
Verbal conjugation . . .	Conjugation of verbs.
Verbal lemmatization . . .	Lemmatization of verbal expressions.
Wordnet browsing . . .	Browsing of wordnet lexical semantic network.

The most basic type of interface, which we termed *online service*, is designed to be attractive and to invite users to self-guided exploration, for example by providing one-button-click examples. The second type of interface, termed *file processing*, is akin to the CLARIN Switchboard and allows the user to upload a large input file and have it processed with minimal effort. The third type of interface, *Jupyter notebooks*, gives users a starting point for designing and developing their own experiments. Notebooks may be edited and executed through a browser without requiring installation on users' computers. The fourth and most technically demanding, but also the most empowering interface, the *web service*, is a language-agnostic remote procedure call interface to be used from within a computer program written in any programming language.

After expanding on the design and rationale of these four types of interfaces, we shared key aspects of the implementation, which include far-reaching and long lasting decisions such as the choice of a programming language, overall architecture, frameworks, communication protocols, process containerization, code organization, and development and deployment practices.

Lastly, we reported on the current status of the workbench and feedback that we have had from users.

Bibliography

Barreto, Florbela, António Branco, Eduardo Ferreira, Amália Mendes, Maria Fernanda Nascimento, Filipe Nunes & João Silva. 2006. Open resources and tools for the shallow processing of Portuguese: The TagShare project. *Proceedings of the 5th international conference on language resources and evaluation (lrec)*, 1438–1443.

Branco, António, Sérgio Castro, João Silva & Francisco Costa. 2011. CINTIL DepBank handbook: Design options for the representation of grammatical dependencies. Technical Report DI-FCUL-TR-2011-03, University of Lisbon.

Branco, António, Francisco Costa, João Silva, Sara Silveira, Sérgio Castro, Mariana Avelãs, Clara Pinto & João Graça. 2010. Developing a deep linguistic databank supporting a collection of treebanks: the CINTIL DeepGramBank. *Proceedings of the 7th international conference on language resources and evaluation (lrec)*, 1810–1815.

Branco, António, Amália Mendes, Paulo Quaresma, Luís Gomes, João Silva & Andrea Teixeira. 2020. Infrastructure for the science and technology of language PORTULAN CLARIN. *Proceedings of the 1st international workshop on language technology platforms*, 1–7. Marseille, France: European Language Resources Association.

Branco, António & Filipe Nunes. 2012. Verb analysis in a highly inflective language with an MFF algorithm. *Proceedings of the 11th international conference on the computational processing of portuguese (propor)*, Lecture Notes in Artificial Intelligence no. 7243, 1–11. Springer.

Branco, António, João Rodrigues, João Silva, Francisco Costa & Rui Vaz. 2014. Assessing automatic text classification for interactive language learning. *Proceedings of the ieee international conference on information society (isociety)*, 72–80.

Branco, António & João Silva. 2006. A suite of shallow processing tools for Portuguese: LX-Suite. *Proceedings of the 11th conference of the european chapter of the association for computational linguistics (eacl)*, 179–182.

Branco, António & Tiago Henriques. 2003. Aspects of verbal inflection and lemmatization: Generalizations and algorithms. *Proceedings of xviii annual meeting of the portuguese association of linguistics (apl)*, 201–210.

Costa, Francisco & António Branco. 2012. Aspectual type and temporal relation classification. *Proceedings of the 13th conference of the european chapter of the association for computational linguistics*, 266–275.

Cruz, A. F., G. Rocha & H. L. Cardoso. 2018. Exploring spanish corpora for portuguese coreference resolution. *2018 fifth international conference on social networks analysis, management and security (snams)*, 290–295.

Google. Google Colab. https://research.google.com/colaboratory/faq.html (accessed 20 September 2021).

Hajič, Jan, Eva Hajičová, Barbora Hladká, Jozef Mišutka, Ondřej Košarko & Pavel Straňák. 2022. LINDAT/CLARIAH-CZ: Where we are and where we go. In Darja Fišer & Andreas Witt (eds.), *CLARIN. The infrastructure for language resources.* Berlin: De Gruyter.

Project Jupyter, Matthias Bussonnier, Jessica Forde, Jeremy Freeman, Brian Granger, Tim Head, Chris Holdgraf, Kyle Kelley, Gladys Nalvarte, Andrew Osheroff, M Pacer, Yuvi Panda, Fernando Perez, Benjamin Ragan Kelley & Carol Willing. 2018. Binder 2.0 – Reproducible, interactive, sharable environments for science at scale. In Fatih Akici, David Lippa, Dillon Niederhut & M Pacer (eds.), *Proceedings of the 17th Python in Science Conference*, 113–120.

Knuth, Donald Ervin. 1984. Literate programming. *The computer journal* 27 (2): 97–111.

Kupietz, Marc, Nils Diewald & Eliza Margaretha. 2022. Building paths to corpus data: A multi-level least effort and maximum return approach. In Darja Fišer & Andreas Witt (eds.), *CLARIN. The infrastructure for language resources.* Berlin: De Gruyter.

Miranda, Nuno, Ricardo Raminhos, Pedro Seabra, Joao Sequeira, Teresa Gonçalves & Paulo Quaresma. 2011. Named entity recognition using machine learning techniques. *Epia-11, 15th portuguese conference on artificial intelligence*, 818–831.

Rodrigues, João, Francisco Costa, João Silva & António Branco. 2020. Automatic syllabification of portuguese. *Revista da Associação Portuguesa de Linguística*, no. 1.

Rodrigues, João, António Branco, Steven Neale & João Silva. 2016. LX-DSemVectors: Distributional semantics models for the Portuguese language. *Proceedings of the 12th international conference on the computational processing of portuguese (propor'16)*, 259–270.

Santos, Rodrigo, João Silva, António Branco & Deyi Xiong. 2019. The direct path may not be the best: Portuguese-chinese neural machine translation. *Proceedings of the 19th epia conference on artificial intelligence*, 757–768.

Silva, João, António Branco, Sérgio Castro & Ruben Reis. 2009. Out-of-the-box robust parsing of Portuguese. *Proceedings of the 9th international conference on language resources and evaluation (lrec)*, 75–85.

Veiga, Arlindo, Sara Candeias & Fernando Perdigão. 2011. Generating a pronunciation dictionary for European Portuguese using a joint-sequence model with embedded stress assignment. *Proceedings of the 8th Brazilian symposium in information and human language technology*.

Zinn, Claus. 2018. The language resource switchboard. *Computational Linguistics* 44 (4): 631–639.

Zinn, Claus & Emanuel Dima. 2022. The CLARIN Language Resource Switchboard: Current state, impact, and future roadmap. In Darja Fišer & Andreas Witt (eds.), *CLARIN. The infrastructure for language resources*. Berlin: De Gruyter.

Daan Broeder and Jan Odijk

Sustainability and Genericity of CLARIN Services in the Netherlands

Abstract: Based on the ten years that have elapsed since the start of the CLARIN-NL project and its follow-up CLARIAH-NL, this chapter offers an analysis of the sustainability and genericity of services created in the context of CLARIN in the Netherlands. Our focus is on search applications, for which we make a proposal for coming to a more efficient and sustainable approach not only in the Netherlands but also CLARIN-wide. We also offer a number of general recommendations for improving sustainability of infrastructure services.

Keywords: sustainability of software services, genericity of services, specificity of services, research infrastructures, CLARIN, CLARIAH-NL

1 Introduction

In this chapter we analyse the sustainability and (lack of) genericity of services created in the context of CLARIN in the Netherlands. We interpret sustainability as the ability of (a set of) services to endure[1] over time. This goes beyond the sustainability of the service software and importantly also includes the aspects of being able to provide and manage cost-effective hosting and providing funds for the services' maintenance.

By service genericity we mean the aspect of a service being targeted at a broad number of tasks instead of focussing on one specific task only (specificity). Services created for (a limited number) of specific tasks are ideally maximally optimized for those tasks and adhere to the philosophy "do a few specific tasks

1 This is an extension of what is mentioned in Daniel S. Katz's blog on Software Sustainability https://danielskatzblog.wordpress.com/2016/09/13/defining-software-sustainability/.

Acknowledgements: We would like to thank colleagues who commented on parts of earlier versions of this chapter, in particular Katrien Depuydt, Jesse de Does, Jan Niestadt, and Vincent Vandeghinste (all from the Institute for the Dutch Language) as well as anonymous reviewers of an earlier version of this chapter.

Daan Broeder, CLARIN ERIC / Utrecht University, Utrecht, the Netherlands, e-mail: d.g.broeder@uu.nl
Jan Odijk, Utrecht University, Utrecht, the Netherlands, e-mail: j.odijk@uu.nl

https://doi.org/10.1515/9783110767377-006

very well". Although it is not impossible for generic tools to do many tasks very well, in practice this requires significant efforts and is expensive. Finding the optimal compromise between service genericity and specificity certainly is one important aspect of a service's sustainability. More than ten years have passed since the start of CLARIN-NL and the follow-up project CLARIAH-NL and we are now able to analyse and reflect on both issues, which are clearly interrelated. We will argue that a large number of search services developed in these projects are too specific and are better replaced by fewer but more generic search services in order to improve not only their sustainability but also the functionality they offer. All services mentioned offer a reference to extensive descriptions in the CLAPOP portal,[2] which also offers an overview of all NL CLARIN and CLARIAH[3] services via the CLAPOP search service.[4]

This chapter is structured as follows: First we present an overview on how the NL CLARIN infrastructure was populated with tools and services (Section 2). Subsequently, we present an overview of the different types of services thus obtained and an analysis of the different circumstances that determine their sustainability (Section 3). We then focus on the important sub-group of search applications, zooming in on the text search applications, for which we argue that their high specificity or lack of genericity leads to less sustainability and less functionality and propose an approach towards a more sustainable, more efficient way to manage the development and operation of the NL CLARIN search applications (Section 4). At the end of the chapter we conclude with a number of general observations and recommendations to improve overall sustainability of the NL CLARIN / CLARIAH services (Section 5).

2 Populating the NL CLARIN infrastructure

Activities for CLARIN were initiated in the Netherlands via the CLARIN-NL project and continued in the CLARIAH-NL projects.[5] A few projects were initiated centrally to implement basic infrastructural services, but the bulk of the services were user-

2 https://portal.clarin.nl

3 The terms CLARIN-NL and CLARIAH-NL refer to projects, which have created and extended the CLARIN and CLARIAH infrastructures in the Netherlands. For the latter we use the terms NL CLARIN and NL CLARIAH.

4 http://portal.clarin.nl/clariah-tools-fs

5 The CLARIAH-NL projects include the projects CLARIAH-SEED, CLARIAH-CORE and CLARIAH-PLUS.

driven and created in a series of four calls[6] over a period of five years (2011–2016). Invitations to submit proposals for projects for end-user facing services and tools, as well as infrastructural services for the benefit of the community, were issued and resulted in projects by small consortia of partners initially from the domain of Language Resources and Technology. This was followed up by the CLARIAH-NL projects, which have partially continued to support existing services but also added a number of new services to the NL CLARIN infrastructure.

In the original CLARIN-NL calls the strategy was explorative and expansive out of a desire to offer a broad set of organizations (university departments, research institutes, and general research support) the opportunity to get familiar with the initial CLARIN infrastructure components developed during the EU CLARIN preparatory phase by integrating their own data and services into CLARIN. An important reason for this explorative strategy was to investigate the needs of the broader humanities community: although CLARIN originated from the linguistics and computational linguistics communities, it aims to serve all humanities researchers working with language materials. At that time knowledge about the research questions and infrastructural needs of this broader class of humanities researchers was generally insufficient in the community that initiated CLARIN in the Netherlands.

CLARIN-NL tried to bring these two groups together so that humanities research questions could be shared and the potential of natural language processing and general infrastructural facilities for dealing with such research questions could be explored. This could then be translated into concrete plans for infrastructural facilities, and some of these were actually implemented.

As a consequence, many subprojects for CLARIN in the Netherlands were user-driven: we intentionally aimed for the selection of research topics, data, and supporting infrastructure facilities to be made by the researchers themselves. However, this resulted in many pieces of functionality that were highly tuned to a narrow class of specific research questions and often to a single corpus or dataset. We will provide several examples below, and characterize some of them in quite some detail. We do not hold their narrowness against these applications or the projects that developed them, because probably no one had the knowledge and expertise at the time to do it differently. And by encouraging applications from users we ensured a base interest in the topic. But now is a moment to reflect on this and to try to sketch of how they could be incorporated into more generic functionality.

6 http://www.clarin.nl/calls.html

3 Sustainability

The sustainability of services is not easy to ensure. Many factors play a role here, but we focus on the major ones that played a role in CLARIN in the Netherlands.

A first important factor is the organization that hosts the service. In the NL CLARIN context we always stipulated that only CLARIN B-centres should host services, though as will be shown below, we did not always succeed in enforcing this requirement. We also maintained the policy that only institutes with a longer-term mission to make data and services available for research purposes should become CLARIN B-centres in the Netherlands.[7] We discouraged research departments of universities from becoming CLARIN B-centres because their commitment to such a status is highly dependent on specific researchers or the specific research interests of one particular researcher, and therefore not sufficiently stable. Even if the researcher remains interested, there is no reason to expect commitment from the department or university to maintain the required infrastructural facilities (such as servers) for a longer period of time (Broeder et al. 2017). Of course, institutes with a longer-term mission to make data and services available are also not immune to changes and new developments. As shown below, we experienced our fair share of this in the Netherlands. But even then, such institutes are more stable than university research departments as service hosting centres.

A second factor is the degree to which a service is embedded in the hosting centre: if a service has been developed by the centre itself, or is actively used by the centre's employees, the commitment to keeping this service running is higher than for a service that has been developed by external developers or that has an external user base. As will be shown below, it happened regularly that a service developed by external developers and/or with a user base from outside the host had to be hosted by a centre, and this is generally not beneficial to its sustainability.

A third factor is the stability of the developer community. It will be easier to keep a service running if it has a solid and stable developer base. As will be shown below, this has often not been the case, even though measures were taken to improve the stability of the developer base.

Fourth, active use of a service by its targeted users, often leading to requests for new functionality or error reports, is generally beneficial for sustainability. It

7 Examples of such institutes in the Netherlands are the Meertens Institute, the Huygens Institute, the Institute for the Dutch Language, the Max Planck Institute for Psycholinguistics, and DANS.

keeps the maintenance of the service on the agenda and stimulates active search for funding the implementation of new functionality.

Finally, the number of services that must be maintained plays an important role in sustainability: in general, the smaller the number of applications, and the smaller the number of different components (frontend, backend) of such applications, the better it is for sustainability. Of course, a proper balance must be found here, because maintaining just a few extremely complex applications might also hinder sustainability. If one wants to achieve the same functionality with fewer applications, the applications have to be more generic in nature and cannot be too specific. Due to the setup of the initial CLARIN projects in the Netherlands, this has become a very important factor, as will be illustrated below via the case study into text search applications in the CLARIN infrastructure in the Netherlands.

3.1 Background

In order to understand the dynamics that underlie the variety of services, their institutional hosting and (challenges for their) sustainability, it is necessary to describe by which processes they came to be and are funded. Part of this background was already described in (Odijk and van Hessen 2017) and Section 2 "Populating the CLARIN NL Infrastructure".

Only a few technology requirements were imposed in the CLARIN-NL and CLARIAH-NL calls, in particular the requirements for interoperability within the larger CLARIN EU domain. Interoperability with CLARIN requires using CMDI[8] metadata (Broeder et al. 2010, 2011; Windhouwer and Goosen 2022) for describing resources, issuing Persistent Identifiers (PIDs) to identify resources, SAML-based Federated Identity Management (FIM) for authenticating users, and the use of a Server Oriented Architecture (SOA) to permit easy sharing of services by services.

A few of these interoperability requirements had to be relaxed for some partner organizations since they made different technology choices at an earlier stage. An example is the requirement to use the Handle System technology for PIDs, whereas DANS already used URN:NBN, and also waiving, or at least not enforcing, the requirement to use SAML-based FIM for allowing access to CLARIN services from outside of the Netherlands. That last requirement would sometimes require a change to the implemented accepted authentication option, which the service provider considered confusing for existing users. In addition, and

8 For an explanation of acronyms for technical components and standards, see Appendix 5.

especially for smaller software development groups, the required expertise for dealing with SAML-based FIM was lacking.

But these requirements contributed little to sustainability of the services, and no other requirements were imposed by CLARIN in the EU or in the Netherlands to ensure sustainability, in part because sustainability of services was largely uncharted territory. In this respect, we tried to learn from others who were ahead of us (inter alia via workshops with experts from the Software Sustainability Institute[9] and Knowledge Exchange),[10] but this started only as of 2013. However, it was difficult to see how adoption of these best-practices could be captured in requirements for the CLARIN-NL calls.

As stated, initially it was mostly organizations with a language research or language technology focus that responded to the calls, while later the response was broader also including other humanities disciplines and university libraries. The requirement that services must be hosted at a CLARIN B-centre was not only imposed for the stability and sustainability of the services and access to data, but also to foster the relationships of the CLARIN B-centres with their infrastructure specialists and research institutes with their humanities researchers. Unfortunately, we did not always succeed in having the services hosted by a CLARIN B-centre, especially for applications that were originally developed outside of CLARIN and highly interconnected with existing other parts of a research department's computational infrastructure. Examples of such services include PaQu,[11] WAHSP/BILAND,[12] TDS,[13] and WIP,[14] which will be discussed in more detail below.

3.2 Services classification

In this section we will discuss the major services, categorized into three classes: services targeting end users (Section 3.2.1), infrastructural services (Section 3.2.2), and services resulting from special collaborations (Section 3.2.3).

9 https://www.software.ac.uk/
10 https://www.knowledge-exchange.info/event/software-sustainability
11 https://portal.clarin.nl/node/14366
12 https://portal.clarin.nl/node/14383
13 https://portal.clarin.nl/node/14374
14 https://portal.clarin.nl/node/14386

3.2.1 Services and tools targeting end-users

Services and tools targeting end-users constitutes the largest group of services. Most are web applications that enable a user to search and browse through specific existing data-sets or corpora, and that have also a specific user interface for specifying queries and visualization. Most such services support only a fixed dataset, but some (e.g., PaQu, AutoSearch,[15] GRETEL 4[16]) allow the user to upload new data. Linguistic enrichment of new data is sometimes carried out by the search application (PaQu, GRETEL 4) but must be done with other services such as Frog,[17] TICCL,[18] or PICCL[19] outside the application. The resulting enriched data can then be uploaded in the search application (e.g., in AutoSearch). Such services may be essential for specific users and/or be broadly used, but they are not essential for the functioning of the infrastructure as a whole or even for other services, and will therefore not be missed if not used.

3.2.2 Infrastructural services

A second class consists of services that provide infrastructural services not directly seen by end-users. Many of these are currently provided by the CLARIN ERIC infrastructure and some strong B-centres that can afford to develop and host these. Such services require a strong commitment from the developing and hosting organizations in order to avoid long periods of minimal maintenance or even dysfunction,[20] since they are usually not immediately useful within the hosting organization, and receive less attention. Such services in the Netherlands are ISOcat,[21] CCR,[22] CLAVAS,[23] and CMD2RDF[24] (Windhouwer, Indarto, and Broeder 2017). These are basically registries, important for other services but not directly visible for end-users. Another class of infrastructural services are conver-

15 https://portal.clarin.nl/node/14324
16 https://portal.clarin.nl/node/14349
17 https://portal.clarin.nl/node/14344
18 https://portal.clarin.nl/node/1914
19 https://portal.clarin.nl/node/14392
20 Note that when it concerned infrastructure services essential for the operation of the EU wide CLARIN infrastructure, CLARIN ERIC took over their operation when dysfunctioning was imminent.
21 https://portal.clarin.nl/node/14353
22 https://portal.clarin.nl/node/14327
23 https://portal.clarin.nl/node/14330
24 https://portal.clarin.nl/node/14331

sion services such as Openconvert,[25] which also suffered from lack of resources for maintenance.

3.2.3 Special collaborations

Next to the regular calls, some of the services created by the CLARIN-NL projects were the results of projects with an emphasis on the collaborative aspect between partners, for example, TTNWW[26] (Kemps-Snijders et al. 2017), which was a collaboration between the Netherlands and Flanders. It produced a number of NLP workflows for both spoken and written text using existing NLP services. The collaboration aspect heavily influenced choices for architecture, which consisted of workflows of independently implemented NLP services provided as Virtual Machines (VMs), which were not anchored in the normal operations of the partners that provided these VMs. In addition, the VM hosting service provided by SURFsara for TTNWW was not guaranteed. It offered a good opportunity to learn and collaborate with this important Dutch academic IT service provider, but also caused frequent down-times aggravated by the need for specialized knowledge for restarting the TTNWW service.[27] Although this situation proved vulnerable with regard to sustainability of the TTNWW service as a whole (and currently the service is indeed unavailable), TTNWW met its main goals and under different circumstances might have evolved over time into a more stable and larger services framework. Other such special projects, from the CLARIAH-CORE project, are ATHENA,[28] and Amsterdam Time Machine.[29]

3.3 NL CLARIN services status in 2021

This section describes some relevant observations from our list of 85 services and tools that were created in the CLARIN-NL and CLARIAH-NL projects over a period of ten years. We base this on the CLAPOP[30] portal (Odijk 2019), where the results

25 https://portal.clarin.nl/node/14364
26 https://portal.clarin.nl/node/14378
27 Technologies such as docker-compose and Kubernetes, which were unavailable at that point, would have made a considerable difference.
28 https://clariah.nl/en/projects/athena-access-tool-historical-ecology-and-environmental-archeology
29 https://clariah.nl/en/projects/atm-amsterdam-time-machine
30 http://portal.clarin.nl/clariah-tools-fs

of the CLARIN-NL and CLARIAH-NL projects with regard to data provisioning and service building have been registered and from which the actual availability status was (manually) checked.[31] Some of the services listed in CLAPOP are general infrastructural services that are maintained in collaboration with and funded largely by CLARIN ERIC, such as ISOcat and its successor CCR. We exclude them from the sustainability discussion here since their maintenance and availability is steered from outside the NL CLARIN domain. Out of the 85 tracked services a small number must be considered lost, that is they are not on-line anymore and the originally responsible are no longer available or responding to enquiries. This is the case for seven of the listed services. For five other services it was made explicit that these were withdrawn, usually for reasons of technology obsolescence, e.g., Adobe Flash dependency for FESLI[32] and TDS, or dependence on specific environments, e.g., ANNEX, which depended on the obsolete LAT repository software (Kemps-Snijders et al. 2008). For four additional cases, the service was explicitly superseded by a new one, for example TiCClops[33] and COBWWWEB.[34] The manner in which end users are informed about service withdrawal or service succession varies by hosting organization, but almost no service description was complete without the hosting organization being specifically asked to update its service information pages. A large proportion of the tracked services (38) are web applications with functionality for searching in specific corpus content or databases. Some manage several such resources (e.g., the INT hosted dictionaries) but most are dedicated to one resource only. Two general engines were developed for searching through large corpora of linguistic information: MTAS (Brouwer, Brugman, and Kemps-Snijders 2016), and Blacklab (de Does, Niestadt, and Depuydt 2017). These are in use in end user facing services such as AutoSearch and OpenSoNaR[35] (Blacklab) and Nederlab[36] (MTAS). These also require considerable investment and expertise and are vulnerable when experts become unavailable, as happened in the case of MTAS. Although these general search engines would be prime candidates for technology merging, or for concentrating on the development of only one service, it proved very difficult to realize this because of aspects of partner institute autonomy and overlapping ambitions (see also Section 4). Only two services (registries) were true infrastructure services for the CLARIN infrastructure: CLAVAS and CCR. These are not intended for direct

31 This overview of the services will be replaced in 2022 by *ineo*.
32 https://portal.clarin.nl/node/14343
33 https://portal.clarin.nl/node/14376
34 https://portal.clarin.nl/node/14334
35 https://portal.clarin.nl/node/14365
36 https://portal.clarin.nl/node/14362

use by researchers and require special expertise to integrate them with other tools, which is how they should be used. CLAVAS proved not to be so essential since it was off-line for a long period without major problems. The CCR, however, is considered essential for central CLARIN operations and when Meertens was temporarily unable to support it, CLARIN ERIC took over.

3.4 Analysis

In this section we discuss four challenges for sustainability: reorganization of partner institutes that are CLARIN B-centres (Section 3.4.1), changing technologies (Section 3.4.2), the difficulty of maintaining the required expertise (Section 3.4.3), and service hosting (Section 3.4.4).

3.4.1 Reorganizing and restructuring of CLARIN centres

The reorganization and restructuring of partner institutes that were CLARIN B-centres did not only impact the sustainability of their services but rearranged the landscape with regard to the interest and capabilities of partners to continue their participation in the CLARIN commons. Over the past 10 years we have seen three major shifts in CLARIN B-centres in the Netherlands.

The first of these is a reorganization at the Institute for the Dutch Language (INT),[37] one of the NL CLARIN B-centres. For a long period it was unclear in which direction the institute would be heading. This created uncertainty for its employees but also about the role it could play in CLARIN. In the end, this reorganization did not have much impact on the availability of the services, nor on their further maintenance except for a period where the TST data[38] were unavailable. The INT ambitions and the available resources for this work have not changed since their initial participation in the CLARIN projects, which of course supports the sustainability of the services developed and hosted.

On the other hand, the changes at the MPI for Psycholinguistics (MPI-PL), which changed its ambitions in 2014 and decided to be involved only in infrastructure projects that directly were aligned with, and supportive of their immediate research interests, had a large impact. As the major CLARIN B-centre in NL,

37 At the time it was called the Institute for Dutch Lexicology (INL) and it also hosted the so-called 'TST-Centrale' (Language Technology Central).
38 https://ivdnt.org/taalmaterialen/

MPI-PL was very active in providing general infrastructure services (so-called Type A services) and it supported many external researchers. Although MPI-PL faithfully fulfilled its existing obligations, the necessary further software development and the hosting of services beyond direct MPI-PL interests were discontinued. For example, development support for tools such as ARBIL[39] for CMDI metadata editing and the LAT software stack, including a linguistic data repository stack, were terminated. Fortunately, CLARIAH-NL was able to move some services to other organizations and CLARIN ERIC took over responsibility for others. A positive side effect of the above is that, where the opportunity arose, new and better solutions were substituted for the old ones: CLARIN CCR for ISOcat (but with a different hosting organization), and the LAT software stack was replaced by the more modern Islandora-based FLAT repository system.

Thirdly, the clustering of three KNAW institutes (Meertens Institute, Huygens Institute, and the International Institute for Social History) into the Humanities Cluster (HuC), including two NL CLARIN B-centres, is the latest change to have a major impact on the CLARIAH services landscape. These institutes joined forces, inter alia to create a large pool of software developers to improve their working atmosphere, increase the possibilities of education, distribute their knowledge and expertise among multiple persons, and create career opportunities for the developers inside the HuC organization. Ironically enough, this did not prevent the two developers most knowledgeable about MTAS and some other services (TTNWW, PILNAR) from leaving during this reorganization process because they saw no viable future for them after this reorganization. Additionally, the reorganization efforts needed for integrating the three institutes' technical infrastructure (temporarily) took away resources for the planned support for and roll-out of new CLARIN services.

3.4.2 Changing technologies

Over a period of more than 10 years one would expect quite a few services and tools to be withdrawn or to become unusable because of their dependence on technologies no longer developed or having become inadequate, while the cost of upgrading to other technologies would be too steep. This was indeed clearly the case for some of the services depending on the Adobe Flash frontend (e.g., FESLI, PILNAR, TDS). It is notoriously difficult to make safe technology choices for graphical front ends. However, we also note that failing to update services

39 http://portal.clarin.nl/node/14320

with regard to advancing technology might also indicate a lack of interest from both providers and the project management, which should represent the end user and provide resource capacity. A more purposeful, coordinated way of dealing with obsolescence issues would be desirable and is perhaps feasible if more information on applied IT technologies and planned software updates can be tracked, for instance by adding such information separately to central service descriptions such as CLAPOP. Apart from changing technologies there is also the matter of advancing standards, which requires service updates. In our NL context we can think of CMDI as a metadata format and Folia as a linguistic data format. Fortunately the experts and developers involved with such updates are also often involved as implementers of tools using these standards. The tools mostly involved with CMDI, for example CMDI Forms for editing (Zeeman and Windhouwer 2018) and CMD2RDF for CMDI to RDF format conversion, are maintained at the Meertens Institute, which has CMDI experts who are also involved in CMDI standard advancement. With respect to updates of the Folia standard, some interoperability problems have been noticed that stem from insufficient coordination between the maintainers of different services using the Folia format. In situations where many different services depend on a common standard format, the process of updating common standards and adapting services should be coordinated properly, in order to prevent fragmentation in separate, non-interoperable islands.

3.4.3 Scarce expertise

In the CLARIN-NL and CLARIAH-NL projects, the project partners have had to manage challenges with regard to expert staff leaving, especially in times of reorganizations. This was certainly a cause for the withdrawal of some services, but also for the inability to repair or upgrade services when needed. The cost factor for producing academic software is such that it is very difficult to provide proper Service License Agreements (SLAs) and sufficient resources for maintenance and functionality enhancement in comparison with industry.

3.4.4 Service hosting

As already mentioned in the background section (Section 3.1), one of the requirements in the CLARIN-NL calls was the intention to host the resulting service (or data set) at one of the NL CLARIN B-centres, since these were considered to provide better service availability and sustainability. In some cases this led to coincidental collaborations between the organizations responsible for service development and those doing the hosting. It also led to the hosting organization specifying extra requirements with regard to the service's expected environment and resource use, such as the use of a particular type of database or operating system version. This should be considered positive and it contributes to proper service operation and availability, but additional requirements imposed by the B-centres may also have motivated the software developers to (keep) hosting the services themselves. From the services listed on CLAPOP, ten are not hosted by CLARIN B-centres but for instance by university departments from Radboud University Nijmegen or from Groningen University. In addition, there are services hosted properly but outside of the direct CLARIN domain (e.g., at the National Institute for Sound and Vision, NISV). The WIP service, which is no longer available, was initially hosted by a development team at the University of Amsterdam, where the server hosting the service was discarded because it was considered obsolete, but not replaced. This is what one can expect from a research department that has no commitments for providing sustainable services, and this is why CLARIN B-centers, with a focus on sustainable access and stable services should be preferred. Nevertheless, many university departments have done an excellent job keeping services for which they have a specific long-term interest up-to-date and accessible for large groups of users. Therefore, we suggest that if there is no B-centre hosting candidate for a service, it is acceptable to have the service hosted by an organization that has an affinity with the service, even if that organization is not a B-centre. The CLARIN B-centres have not, overall, proven to be more stable than other organizations for services that were created in a small consortium consisting of a researcher and the CLARIN B-centre but that the centre was not interested in. The centres must also be more selective in accepting participation in such consortia.

4 Case study: Specificity and sustainability of search services

As was pointed out above, having a lot of different services is generally not beneficial for sustainability. In this Section we present a case study for one specific class of services: text search services. We argue that each of these services implements a different subset of the desired functionality, and that it is highly desirable to replace them with fewer, more generic services. This will improve sustainability but also the functionality for the user.

Apart from text search services, there are many other search services in CLARIN, but they will not be dealt with here systematically. Among these are services for searching in lexical resources, such as the historical dictionaries of Dutch and Frisian (ONW,[40] VMNW,[41] MNW,[42] WNT, and WFT-GTB[43]) in the historical dictionary portal[44] ANW,[45] DiaMaNT,[46] Cornetto,[47] Duelme,[48] GrNe,[49] and WebCelex.[50] There are also several services that enable search in structured data, for example for literary and historical data. Examples include Arthurian Fiction,[51] BNM-I,[52] COBWWWEB, DSS,[53] and Rembench.[54] There are also services for searching in structured linguistic data, such as TDS[55] and MIMORE[56] (Barbiers et al. 2016).

4.1 Specificity of search services

Many different text search applications have been developed in the CLARIN-NL and CLARIAH-NL projects in the Netherlands. In this section we will consider three subclasses: (1) applications for pure text search; (2) applications for search for text enriched with linguistic annotations at the token level; (3) applications for search in a treebank, that is, a text corpus in which each sentence has been assigned a syntactic structure.

40 http://portal.clarin.nl/node/14363
41 http://portal.clarin.nl/node/14381
42 http://portal.clarin.nl/node/14357
43 http://portal.clarin.nl/node/14385
44 https://gtb.ivdnt.org.
45 http://portal.clarin.nl/node/14319
46 https://diamant.ivdnt.org/diamant-ui/
47 http://portal.clarin.nl/node/14336
48 https://portal.clarin.nl/node/4200
49 http://portal.clarin.nl/node/14350
50 http://portal.clarin.nl/node/14384
51 https://portal.clarin.nl/node/4202
52 http://portal.clarin.nl/node/14326
53 https://portal.clarin.nl/node/4211
54 https://portal.clarin.nl/node/4227
55 https://portal.clarin.nl/node/14374
56 http://portal.clarin.nl/node/14356

4.2 Applications for pure text search

Search applications that are focused on searching purely for text (i.e. without any linguistic annotations) include PILNAR,[57] Polimedia,[58] WAHSP, BILAND,[59] TexCavator,[60] VK[61] and WIP from CLARIN-NL projects, and ePistolarium[62] from the CLARIN and CLARIN-NL supported but independently financed ePistolarium project (Ravenek, van den Heuvel, and Gerritsen 2017). The users who initiated these applications and use them are from humanities disciplines other than linguistics; they are therefore mostly interested in the content of the textual resource and have no specific interest in linguistic properties of these texts.

All applications offer the functionality to search for text using textual queries, often with support for Boolean operators. They also offer the option to narrow down the search to data meeting certain requirements on metadata. The metadata schema differs according to corpus. Most of these applications are highly specific and offer the ability to search in a single corpus – for instance, ePistolarium in correspondence between scholars in the 17th century in the Netherlands, PILNAR in a corpus of pilgrimage narratives, VK in the works of Lou de Jong on the Netherlands in World War II, and WIP in the proceedings of the Netherlands parliament.

Since these were different applications, developed independently of one another, it is not possible to carry out searches across multiple corpora, though that would obviously be useful in several cases. For example, the WIP project aimed to research mentions of World War II in the Dutch Parliament (WIP=War in Parliament), and a combined search in the parliamentary data and in the work of Lou de Jong on World War II as offered by VK would obviously be very useful. Polimedia did enable searching in multiple corpora, even corpora of different modalities: it links the minutes of the debates in the Dutch Parliament (Dutch Hansard) to the databases of historical newspapers and ANP radio bulletins to allow cross-media analysis of coverage in a uniform search interface through a combined search in these resources. WAHSP offered the ability to search in textual data from news media from the period 1863–1940 of the Dutch National Library. WAHSP was further developed into BILAND, which added the textual data from news media of the Staatsbibliothek zu Berlin, enabling bilingual

57 https://portal.clarin.nl/node/4214
58 http://portal.clarin.nl/node/14369
59 http://portal.clarin.nl/node/14383
60 http://portal.clarin.nl/node/14375
61 http://portal.clarin.nl/node/14379
62 http://portal.clarin.nl/node/14329

searching supported by a text translation service. Neither application runs any more, in part because no clear CLARIN-centre was identified for hosting the software, and in part because much of the software used was dependent on software only available on servers of the University of Amsterdam. In order to tackle these problems, the researcher involved had TexCavator developed and maintained by the NL eScience Centre, but it lacked most of the multilingual functionality of BILAND. On the other hand, it gave access to ShiCo (Shifting Concepts) (Martinez and Kenter 2018), developed independently by the NL eScience Center. ShiCo is a tool for visualizing concepts shifting over time, based on word2vec. Later still, the researcher involved transferred ShiCo's maintenance and further development to the Digital Humanities Lab of Utrecht University, which reimplemented it and has made it available as a new search application called iAnalyzer,[63] which offers search in multiple corpora; however, most of the advanced features have disappeared or are available for only a few of the corpora. Furthermore, in this application, one can search in only one corpus at a time. The corpora include several resources that have been licensed by Utrecht University from a commercial publisher and can currently only be used by employees of Utrecht University.

Summarizing, we observe the existence of many different search applications, each with their specific backend engine and own frontend, each developed by a different developer or development group. We also observe, on the one hand, that insufficient functionality is offered by each individual application (one can search only in a single corpus or a limited set of corpora at a time), while on the other hand, there is some duplication in functionality (the National Library newspaper archive can be searched through WAHSP and its successors and through Polimedia).

Many, but not all of the applications offer functionality that goes beyond the text-based search functionality. For example, BILAND offered sentiment mining, TexCavator analysis of shifts in concept over time through ShiCo, as well as some normalization, stemming, and stop word filtering. ePistolarium offers similarity search, and search using topic models. WIP offered the ability to search for text in combination with searching for and analysing metadata on the speaker (e.g., which party the speaker belongs to), which could also be nicely visualized. Many, but not all, offer various visualization options, e.g. word clouds, time lines, heat maps, and the like. But all this additional functionality is useful for all of these applications and for all of the corpora, so it would be much better if there were one generic application which includes all of this functionality for all corpora.

63 https://ianalyzer.hum.uu.nl

With so many different applications, different (small) developer teams and small user bases, it should come as no surprise that several of the applications do not run any more. For WAHSP, BILAND, and TexCavator this is to be expected and normal because they were replaced by iAnalyzer, though with significant loss of functionality and accessibility. For Polimedia it need not come as a surprise either, because its functionality has been integrated into the Media Suite[64] developed in the CLARIAH-CORE project, which is truly a development in the right direction. PILNAR does not run anymore because it used Flash software, which has become obsolete. The development team around PILNAR was small, and some of them left. It seems that the user community was also small and insufficiently influential, otherwise they would have instigated the hosting centre to keep the service running. The hosting institute lacked the means and, apparently, the inherent interest to replace the Flash software with an alternative to keep the service running, and the data have not been integrated in other search applications that are still running at the relevant institute. WIP was never hosted by a CLARIN B-centre, but by the developers at the University of Amsterdam, and does not run any more for the reasons described above.

4.3 Applications for search for linguistic annotations at the token level

Several search applications enable searches in text corpora in which linguistic annotations have been added to tokens ("token-annotated corpora"). These include AutoSearch, CHN',[65] COAVA,[66] Corpus Gysseling,[67] FESLI, NAMESCAPE,[68] Nederlab, OpenSoNaR, and SHEBANQ.[69] See Appendix A for an overview of their properties that are relevant in this context.

All of these search applications share the common functionality of being able to search for words, and word combinations, and, where available, grammatical properties of the tokens such as lemma, word form, part-of-speech tag, and inflectional information. All but COAVA and SHEBANQ use a query language based on the Corpus Query Processing (CQP) language (Evert and The OCWB Development Team 2010). This is, of course, good, but unfortunately each application sup-

64 https://mediasuite.clariah.nl/
65 https://portal.clarin.nl/node/14328
66 http://portal.clarin.nl/node/14333
67 http://portal.clarin.nl/node/14337
68 http://portal.clarin.nl/node/14358
69 https://portal.clarin.nl/node/4210

ports a different subset of CQP. Most allow filtering on the basis of metadata, but usually only before a search starts. Some applications share the same backend system (BlackLab, (de Does, Niestadt, and Depuydt 2017)), but each works with a different instantiation of this backend, thus complicating maintenance. Many also share the basic same front-end, but again each has a different instantiation and each differs from most if not all of the others. Several have options for analysing the search results. By "analysing search results" we mean, grouping, sorting, and/or filtering them, ideally in combination with metadata. This feature is, in our view, crucial for corpora with multiple annotations, especially since these annotations are not guaranteed to be 100% correct. The applications AutoSearch, CHN, and Corpus Gyseling all have more or less (but not exactly) the same system for analysis, which is limited, since one can generally analyse by a single criterion only (e.g., by part of speech, or by lemma, but not by these combined). Only OpenSoNaR allows analysis by multiple criteria, though not combinations of linguistic properties and metadata. One can, for example, create groupings of the data by grammatical properties, and see the relevant individual examples (or a subset thereof) by clicking on the grouping. Similarly, analysis of the search results in combination with metadata is possible but limited. Nederlab has even more limited options for analysing the search results: fewer options for grouping, no option to inspect the actual examples of a grouping. We do not know whether FESLI offered options for analysing the search results, and we can no longer check because it does not run any more, but we suspect that it did not offer this. NAMESCAPE and SHEBANQ do not offer any options for analysing the search results. COAVA enables the user to filter the search results by metadata and selecting nouns only.

As is obvious from this description, there are many different search applications for searches on token-annotated corpora, but each of them has limited options, a limited set of data that can be searched, and limited analysis options, and each implemented this in its own way. At the same time, there is also unnecessary duplication of functionality, for example for searching in the National Library news corpora archive. It is clear that with fewer and less varied applications more functionality can be added, the end user will need to learn less, and sustainability is increased.

There certainly are good developments as well here. As was pointed out above, many search applications are based on the BlackLab backend, and are based on the same basic frontend, and many are based on the same query language. Some search applications have functionality that would be useful in other search applications as well, for example the capability to store queries for reuse later and to share them with others is a helpful feature of SHEBANQ and Nederlab, but this should be a feature for every search application.[70] Similarly, the feature of a combined search in a corpus and a lexicon, as offered by COAVA is functionality that would also be desirable for other search applications, for example to obtain properties of tokens from a search result in a lexicon such as CELEX or Cornetto[71] ("chaining search", (Dekker, Fanee, and de Does 2019; Odijk 2020)). The upload functionality offered by AutoSearch is very important, and it has been used quite extensively over the past five years, for a variety of projects, and also formed the basis for hosting Arabic corpora of Utrecht University developed in a collaboration project between the NL eScience Center and CLARIAH-NL.[72] The upload functionality also requires technology to automatically enrich a text corpus with linguistic annotations if one wants to search for linguistic properties. Such a pipeline was developed in the context of Nederlab, but the experts state that this pipeline is not suited for use by end users. However, one can use the Frog[73] (van den Bosch et al. 2007) web service via its web application interface, download the resulting data and upload them into AutoSearch. For languages other than Dutch one can use the pipelines defined in Weblicht,[74] and upload the results obtained from WebLicht into AutoSearch.[75,76]

The Nederlab project (Brugman et al. 2016), a project independent of CLARIN-NL and CLARIAH-NL but partially funded by them, was actually an attempt to create a single search application for the whole collection of Dutch historical textual data covering the period from 900–1900. This surely was a move in the right direction, because it would create a single search application for a huge amount of data. It was expected that the amount of data in which users could search would become so large that special measures were needed to ensure a reasonable performance of the system. There was close collaboration in the project between multiple partners, in particular Meertens Institute and the Institute for the Dutch Language (INT). INT had earlier developed the BlackLab search engine (de Does, Niestadt, and Depuydt 2017), which was in use for a lot of search applications, both for internal use and

70 The option of storing queries, however, also requires a way of organizing queries in such a way that they can be found back easily, and needs a user-specific store to store queries not shared with others.

71 http://portal.clarin.nl/node/14336

72 http://arabic-dh.hum.uu.nl/corpus-frontend/

73 https://webservices.cls.ru.nl/frog

74 https://weblicht.sfs.uni-tuebingen.de/weblichtwiki

75 It is certainly desirable to have such enrichment as part of the search application (as is possible in PaQu and GrETEL), at least as an option, because that makes enriching one's corpus much easier for the user.

76 See https://surfdrive.surf.nl/files/index.php/s/JkYKlHSNZnj7ysJ for a recorded lecture, a presentation and relevant materials to illustrate this.

for use by external researchers. Meertens did not have a search engine. It would have been natural to start from BlackLab and modify and extend it so that it could deal with the expected volume of data. However, for reasons of autonomy and efficiency, Meertens Institute, which was leading the project, decided to develop a completely new backend from scratch (the MTAS-engine: Multi Tier Annotation Search, (Brouwer, Brugman, and Kemps-Snijders 2016)). This was a risk of course, but defensible since Meertens also has the obligation to build up knowledge and expertise in providing search applications for research purposes. An additional problem, however, was that the MTAS development team was rather small: in essence, two people. As described above, these very two developers left during this reorganization process intended to strengthen sustainability. As a consequence, only limited knowledge of and expertise with MTAS is available now, and we must see how this will develop in the near future. Hopefully, some consolidation of the Blacklab and MTAS efforts can take place.

4.4 Applications for search in treebanks

A treebank is a text corpus in which each sentence has been assigned a syntactic structure. Syntactic structures are often trees, hence the name 'treebank' for such corpora. Examples of applications for search in treebanks are Lassy Search,[77] PaQu, GRETEL 1-4, and Corpus Studio Web.[78]

Lassy Search was originally developed outside of CLARIN-NL though clearly inspired by the desire expressed by CLARIN to make corpus searching easier for non-expert users. It offered the ability to search for grammatical relations between two words in the Lassy-Small Corpus, via a dedicated interface.

This application was not systematically maintained, and when a need for additional functionality arose, a new version, called PaQu, was developed. PaQu offers the ability to search not only for grammatical relations between words via a dedicated interface, but also via Xpath queries. It enables users to search in additional corpora (initially only the Spoken Dutch Corpus, currently several more), and enables a user to upload his/her own corpus. This corpus is automatically parsed by Alpino and the resulting treebank is made available for searching. PaQu also extended the options for (limited) analysis of the search results, and

77 http://www.let.rug.nl/~alfa/lassy/bin/lassy-save
78 http://portal.clarin.nl/node/14338

allows macros to simplify queries and make queries or parts of them reusable (Odijk et al. 2017).[79]

GRETEL (Augustinus et al. 2017) was originally developed by KU Leuven in the context of the cooperation between the Netherlands and Flanders on CLARIN. It originally offered search in the Lassy-Small Corpus and the Spoken Dutch Corpus. Its distinguishing feature is the query by example option: the user can enter an example sentence that illustrates the construction they are interested in and select via a dedicated interface which aspects of this example sentence are crucial for the construction. After that an Xpath query is automatically created by the system and a search is started in the desired corpus. GRETEL also offers the ability to search with Xpath queries.

GRETEL 4 (Odijk, van der Klis, and Spoel 2018) extended the original GRETEL application (which had already gone through three different improved versions) and added two major new functionalities: (1) the option to upload one's own corpus (similar functionality as described for PaQu above), and (2) extensive options for analysing search results in terms of properties of the nodes that match with node descriptions in the Xpath query, in combination with metadata. A user can compose a pivot table in a graphical interface by selecting node properties and metadata in arbitrary combinations of indefinite size and drag them to the table.

Corpus Studio Web (Komen 2017) enables search in treebanks using XQuery and offers a query wizard to make the creation of queries easier. It has a completely independent origin, offers yet another mode of search in treebanks and includes more functionality than search alone.

It is obvious that PaQu and GRETEL 4 have large overlap in terms of the provided functionality. The types of corpora that can be offered for search are similar (and largely overlapping), both offer XPath search, both offer the service for users to upload their own corpora. The crucial difference between the two applications is the dedicated search options they offer: word relation search in PaQu and query by example in GRETEL. But the systems have been implemented differently (e.g., they use different XML-database systems, the programming languages used differ), which also leads to differences in the kind of Xpath queries one can formulate, and there are other differences as well: for example, the options for analysing search results are more limited in PaQu. It is obvious that it would be much preferable to have a single application combining the two distinguishing user interfaces in one application, combining all the corpora offered by

79 PaQu also formed the basis for the SPOD application (van Noord et al. 2020; Hoeksema, de Glopper, and van Noord 2022), but we leave this aside here.

the separate applications, using the best database engine for these systems after an evaluation of the available options, and the search result analysis options of GRETEL because they are more powerful than those of PaQu, the sample selection methods provided by PaQu (but not by GRETEL), the macro options of PaQu since they are better than the ones offered by GRETEL, and so on. There is a long wish list of additional functionality in these applications, which then has to be implemented only once. And it makes sense to investigate whether Corpus Studio Web can be involved in such an integration as well.

The PaQu and GRETEL applications were developed with linguistic research as main intended use. But the syntactic analyses that they offer might be useful for disambiguation purposes in other contexts as well. It is therefore desirable to integrate the treebank search and analysis options in a more generic search application that also offers pure text searching and the ability to search for token-based annotations.

4.5 Sustainability of search services

Since such a large proportion of the NL CLARIN services are in essence specialized search services optimized for specific structured information or data, it should be useful to analyse their existence and evolution in more detail.

As we have seen above, each search application in the NL part of the CLARIN infrastructure offers a different subset of the desired functionality, and each has data- and research goal-specific extensions that are actually useful for other data as well. Each application has its own frontend and backend. In short, we see a highly fragmented situation, which is difficult to maintain over a longer period of time. It is therefore desirable to reduce the number of different applications, backends, and front-ends, and to offer the union of the different functionality subsets in the (reduced number of) applications. This will increase the functionality for the user and increase sustainability.

One might be tempted to suggest that there should be a single instantiation of a single search application in the whole CLARIN infrastructure. That would optimize the prospects for sustainability. However, this is not feasible, for several reasons. First, a single instantiation and a single application imply a single point of failure, so it reduces robustness, which is also a desirable feature of infrastructural facilities. Second, it is not obvious how large the developer community could be, and what the commitment of the individual developers to a central system would be. Third, and most important: the data that are to be searched in are distributed over multiple centres in multiple countries. It is not desirable and not feasible (for legal and technical reasons) to bring all these data together in a central place where the search application runs.

One might consider the option of having one search application per CLARIN member, but this is not in general desirable or feasible. A more natural approach is to have one search application per CLARIN B-centre that makes data available for users to search. After all, most centres want and have the obligation to build up knowledge and expertise to provide data and the capability to search within the data to their clients (researchers). Most CLARIN B-centres are also research institutes, and they offer data and the capability to search within the data to enable their researchers to carry out the institute's research goals. Ideally, each centre combines its obligations to its own researchers and research purposes with the CLARIN requirements. With just a single search application in each institute, the possibilities to reduce the dependence on a single developer or a very small number of developers can be more easily reduced, though this also requires a certain scale (the developing team of the institute must not be too small) and an intentional institute policy to spread the knowledge and expertise among its developers so as to reduce this dependence.

We recommend that CLARIN initiates a description of the desired functionality of a local search application that supports keyword search, lexical and grammatical search and mixed corpus and lexicon search for specific corpora but also for new corpora that a user can submit to the service, supported by linguistic and other enrichment pipelines (POS-tagging, parsing, named entity detection and linking, language detection, etc.), as well as offering a framework for plugging in new advanced services such as topic detection, word-embedding based search, facilities to deal with multilingual corpora, linking to external knowledge sources, etc. The description of the desired functionality must, of course, be regularly updated to reflect new developments. In such a more generic search application, covering multiple corpora, one should keep the metadata associated to the different corpora separate, at least in the first stage of integration. At a later stage one can start integrating the metadata. Of course, there will always be metadata properties that are unique to a corpus, but many of them are shared among all or a significant class of resources. For example, resource properties such as title, publication date, publisher, OCR-confidence, and author properties such as author name, author age, author birthday, author place of birth, author death date, author place of death, and author gender recur in many resources and can probably be relatively easily harmonized. The property genre or category also often recurs, but may be more difficult to harmonize. The search functionality will increase in power to the extent that these metadata have been harmonized.

It should also be clearly defined which data formats and other standards (e.g. for semantic operability) are supported by this search application. Obviously, it should cover most data formats that are actually in use, but a small set might be particularly preferred. Applications such as AutoSearch, PaQu and GRETEL currently already provide such a list of supported formats. Any researcher or data provider can include his/her own data simply by ensuring that it is in one of the supported formats.

With a single application covering a large collection of data, there is of course the danger that a user who is interested in only a single dataset will suffer from the presence of this large collection (most of which he/she is not interested in). It should therefore be easy for a user to restrict search to a subset of the full collection, and to store the selection option so that this option is automatically selected in each next session until the user decides to modify it.

A single application that offers multiple search modes (such as e.g. the simple, extended, advanced, and expert modes of OpenSoNaR) must also ensure that there are multiple interface options, which can be selected depending on the expertise of the user and the character and complexity of the search query.

More generally, it requires careful investigation in each case as to whether search options in a dataset should be offered in a search application that also cover other datasets and/or other search options, or in a separate dedicated application, but for the situation in the Netherlands as sketched above the conclusion is obvious to us. Of course, with one search application per CLARIN B-centre, it is not possible to search across data that resides on servers of different centres. Federated content search (FCS)[80] (Stehouwer, Ďurčo, and Broeder 2012) should make that possible. CLARIN, of course, already worked on FCS, initially for pure text search, at a later stage also for search in token-annotated corpora. But the functionality of FCS should be extended to cover all the options that local search offers, which includes text search, search for grammatical properties, search in treebanks, search for metadata, analysing (grouping, sorting, filtering) search results in combination with metadata, and so forth, and not just the intersection of what all local search applications offer. FCS requires that a FCS endpoint is created for each local search backend and this requires a detailed specification of the character and format of the queries the endpoint must be able to process, and of the character and format of the search and analysis results that it returns to the FCS aggregator. The FCS frontend should offer all the functionality that the frontends of the local search applications offer. The work on developing this specification and its implementation, which has already been started by CLARIN, should therefore be continued, and it may also serve in part as a specification of the functionality that the local search applications should offer. It should be a

80 See https://www.clarin.eu/content/federated-content-search-clarin-fcs

CLARIN policy to commit many central resources to this topic, and to stimulate (or even require) CLARIN members to contribute to FCS via their national projects.

5 General recommendations for improving service sustainability

From our observations and background knowledge on ten years CLARIN service development and funding, we are able to make some recommendations:

1. The need for adequate reliable tracking of service hosting and maintenance history and performance, in addition to public relations and outreach effort and means to measure service uptake in specific domains and organizations: analysing papers and citations, measuring clicks, etc.
2. Such a service registry could be used also for dealing with software obsolescence issues in a coordinated way, maintaining information with regard to applied IT technologies and planned software updates can be helpful to predict and plan for necessary upgrades from a central project level.
3. A service hosting organization should host services that fall within its scope, i.e., align with its own mission and research goals. This is preferably a certified CLARIN B-centre, but it is more important that the hosting organization conforms to interoperability requirements such as, for instance, SAML-based authentication for AAI. Note that technology advancements such as containers make it relatively easy in the case of scalability or computing resource issues to host such services at general academic or commercial hosting providers.
4. Since, compared with the start of the CLARIN-NL project, we now have a sufficiently large consortium of relevant partners involved with creating and using research infrastructure, funding can be more specifically targeted at sustainability aspects, such as making the services part of their own internal research work flows.
5. For selected tasks and application types, specific policies should be agreed to increase efficiency and sustainability:
   (a) For example, for searching in token-annotated corpora there should be as few different search applications as possible,preferably at most one per CLARIN B-centre.
   (b) CLARIN should initiate a description of the desired functionality of a local search application that supports keyword search, lexical and grammatical search, and mixed corpus and lexicon search for specific corpora but also for new corpora that a user can submit to the service (supported

by linguistic and other enrichment pipelines (POS-tagging, parsing, named entity detection and linking, language detection, etc., etc.), as well as offering a framework for plugging in new advanced services such as topic detection, word-embedding based search, facilities to deal with multilingual corpora, linking to external knowledge sources, etc.

Appendix A: Token-Annotated Search applications

App	Data	3	4	5	Backend	Dedicated Interfaces	Search Result Analysis	Languages
AutoSearch	a user's own data	+	+	CQP subset	BlackLab	4	yes	Language independent
CHN	Contemporary Dutch Corpus	+	+	CQP subset	BlackLab	2	yes	Dutch
COAVA	CHILDES	+	–	none	idiosyncratic	yes	no	Dutch
Corpus Gysseling	Corpus Gysseling	+	+	CQP subset	BlackLab	4	yes	13th Century Dutch
FESLI	BISLI CHAT data	+	+	CQP subset	idiosyncratic	no	no	Dutch
Namescape	novels	+	–	none	idiosyncratic	yes	no	Dutch
Nederlab	Dutch texts 900–1900	+	+	CQP subset	MTAS	3	limited	Different historical variants of Dutch
OpenSoNaR	Contemporary Written Dutch Corpus	+	+	CQP subset	BlackLab	4	yes	Dutch
SHEBANQ	Bible texts	+	+	MQL	EMDROS	no	no	Hebrew, Syriac

Column 4 specifies *string search*, column 5 *token search*, and column 5 query language.

Appendix B: Acronyms

Acronym	Expansion	Clarification	URL
CMDI	Component Metadata Infrastructure	Metadata infrastructure required by CLARIN	https://www.clarin.eu/content/component-metadata
FCS	Federated Content Search	Distributed text search infrastructure promoted by CLARIN	https://www.clarin.eu/content/federated-content-search-clarin-fcs
FIM	Federated Identity Management	CLARIN requires SAML based FIM	https://en.wikipedia.org/wiki/Federated_identity#Management
SOA	Server Oriented Architecture		https://en.wikipedia.org/wiki/Service-oriented_architecture
PID	Persistent Identifier		https://en.wikipedia.org/wiki/Persistent_identifier
URN:NBN	Universal Resource Identifier/National Bibliography Number	Publication Identifier system	https://www.ifla.org/files/assets/bibliography/national_bibliography_number.pdf
HS	Handle System	PID technology promoted and required by CLARIN	https://en.wikipedia.org/wiki/Handle_System
SAML	Security Assertion Markup Language	A technology enabling Federated Identity Management and Single Sign-On authentication	https://en.wikipedia.org/wiki/Security_Assertion_Markup_Language
VM	Virtual Machine		https://en.wikipedia.org/wiki/Virtual_machine

Bibliography

Augustinus, Liesbeth, Vincent Vandeghinste, Ineke Schuurman & Frank Van Eynde. 2017. GrETEL: A tool for example-based treebank mining. In Jan Odijk & Arjan van Hessen (eds.), *CLARIN in the low countries*, 269–280. London, UK: Ubiquity. DOI: http://dx.doi.org/10.5334/bbi.22. License: CC-BY 4.0.

Barbiers, Sjef, Marjo van Koppen, Hans Bennis & Norbert Corver. 2016. MIcrocomparative MOrphosyntactic REsearch (MIMORE): Mapping partial grammars of Flemish, Brabantish and Dutch. *Lingua* 178: 5 – 31. Linguistic Research in the CLARIN Infrastructure.

Bosch, Antal van den, G.J. Busser, Walter Daelemans & S. Canisius. 2007. An efficient memory-based morphosyntactic tagger and parser for Dutch. In Frank Van Eynde, Peter Dirix, Ineke Schuurman & Vincent Vandeghinste (eds.), *Selected papers of the 17th computational linguistics in the Netherlands meeting*, 99 – 114. Leuven, Belgium: KU Leuven.

Broeder, D., M. Kemps-Snijders, D. Van Uytvanck, M. Windhouwer, P. Withers, P. Wittenburg & C. Zinn. 2010. A data category registry- and component-based metadata framework. In N. Calzolari, B. Maegaard, J. Mariani, J. Odijk, K. Choukri, S. Piperidis, M. Rosner & D. Tapias (eds.), *Proceedings of the seventh international conference on language resources and evaluation (LREC 2010)*, 43–47. Valetta, Malta: European Language Resources Association (ELRA).

Broeder, Daan, Jan Theo Bakker, Marco van der Laan, Marc Kemps-Snijders, Menzo Windhouwer & Marjan Grootveld. 2017. Building CLARIN infrastructure in the Netherlands. In Jan Odijk & Arjan van Hessen (eds.), *CLARIN in the low countries*, 45–59. London, UK: Ubiquity. DOI: http://dx.doi.org/10.5334/bbi.24. License: CC-BY 4.0.

Broeder, Daan, Oliver Schonefeld, Thorsten Trippel, Dieter Van Uytvanck & Andreas Witt. 2011. A pragmatic approach to XML interoperability – the Component Metadata Infrastructure (CMDI). *Proceedings of balisage: The markup conference 2011*. https://www.balisage.net/Proceedings/vol7/print/Broeder01/BalisageVol7-Broeder01.html.

Brouwer, Matthijs, Hennie Brugman & Marc Kemps-Snijders. 2016. A Solr/Lucene based multi tier annotation search solution. *Selected papers from the CLARIN annual conference 2016, 26–28 October, Aix-en-Provence*, 29–37. Linköping, Sweden: Linköping University Electronic Press.

Brugman, Hennie, Martin Reynaert, Nicoline van der Sijs, René van Stipriaan, Erik Tjong Kim Sang & Antal van den Bosch. 2016. Nederlab: Towards a single portal and research environment for diachronic Dutch text corpora. In Nicoletta Calzolari, Khalid Choukri, Thierry Declerck, Sara Goggi, Marko Grobelnik, Bente Maegaard, Joseph Mariani, Helene Mazo, Asuncion Moreno, Jan Odijk & Stelios Piperidis (eds.), *Proceedings of the tenth international conference on language resources and evaluation (LREC 2016)*. Paris, France: European Language Resources Association (ELRA).

Dekker, Peter, Mathieu Fanee & Jesse de Does. 2019. CLARIAH chaining search: A platform for combined exploitation of multiple linguistic resources. In K. Simov & M. Eskevich (eds.), *Proceedings of CLARIN annual conference 2019*, Theory and Applications of Natural Language Processing, 24–27. CLARIN.

Does, J. de, J. Niestadt & K. Depuydt. 2017. Creating research environments with BlackLab. In Jan Odijk & Arjan van Hessen (eds.), *CLARIN in the low countries*, 245–257. London, UK: Ubiquity. DOI: http://dx.doi.org/10.5334/bbi.20. License: CC-BY 4.0.

Evert, Stefan & The OCWB Development Team. 2010. The IMS Open Corpus Workbench (CWB): CQP Query Language Tutorial. OCWB report, IMS, Stuttgart. http://cwb.sourceforge.net/files/CQP_Tutorial/.

Hoeksema, Jack, Kees de Glopper & Gertjan van Noord. 2022. Syntactic profiles in secondary school writing using PaQu and SPOD. In Darja Fišer & Andreas Witt (eds.), *CLARIN. The infrastructure for language resources*. Berlin: De Gruyter.

Kemps-Snijders, Marc, Alex Klassmann, Claus Zinn, Peter Berck, Albert Russel & Peter Wittenburg. 2008. Exploring and enriching a language resource archive via the web. In Nicoletta Calzolari, Khalid Choukri, Bente Maegaard, Joseph Mariani, Jan Odijk, Stelios Piperidis & Daniel Tapias (eds.), *Proceedings of the sixth international conference on language resources and evaluation (LREC'08)*. Marrakech, Morocco: European Language Resources Association (ELRA). http://www.lrec-conf.org/proceedings/lrec2008/.

Kemps-Snijders, Marc, Ineke Schuurman, Walter Daelemans, Kris Demuynck, Brecht Desplanques, Véronique Hoste, Marijn Huybregts, Jean-Paul Martens, Hans Paulussen, Joris Pelemans, Martin Reynaert, Vincent Vandeghinste. Antal van den Bosch,Henk van

den Heuvel,Maarten van Gompel,Gertjan van Noord &Patrick Wambacq 2017. TTNWW to the rescue: No need to know how to handle tools and resources. In Jan Odijk & Arjan van Hessen (eds.), *CLARIN in the low countries*, 83–93. London, UK: Ubiquity. DOI: http://dx.doi.org/10.5334/bbi.7. License: CC-BY 4.0.
Komen, Erwin. 2017. Beyond counting syntactic hits. In Jan Odijk & Arjan van Hessen (eds.), *CLARIN in the low countries*, 259–268. London, UK: Ubiquity. DOI: http://dx.doi.org/10.5334/bbi.21. License: CC-BY 4.0.
Martinez, Carlos & Tom Kenter. 2018. ShiCo – Exploring Shifting Concepts Through Time. DOI: 10.5281/zenodo.1435021.
Noord, Gertjan van, Jack Hoeksema, Peter Kleiweg & Gosse Bouma. 2020. SPOD: Syntactic profiler of Dutch. *Computational Linguistics in the Netherlands Journal* 10 (Dec.): 129–145.
Odijk, Jan. 2019. Discovering software resources in CLARIN. *Selected papers from the CLARIN annual conference 2018, Pisa, 8–10 October 2018*, Linköping Electronic Conference Proceedings no. 159, 121–132. Linköping University Electronic Press, Linköpings universitet. https://ep.liu.se/en/conference-article.aspx?series=ecp&issue=159 &Article_No=13.
Odijk, Jan. 2020. De verleidingen en gevaren van GrETEL. *Nederlandse Taalkunde* 25 (1): 7–38.
Odijk, Jan & Arjan van Hessen. (eds.) 2017. *CLARIN in the low countries*. London, UK: Ubiquity Press. DOI: http://dx.doi.org/10.5334/bbi. License: CC-BY 4.0.
Odijk, Jan, Martijn van der Klis & Sheean Spoel. 2018. Extensions to the GrETEL treebank query application. *Proceedings of the 16th international workshop on treebanks and linguistic theories (tlt16)*, 46–55. Prague, Czech Republic. http://aclweb.org/anthology/W/W17/W17-7608.pdf.
Odijk, Jan, Gertjan van Noord, Peter Kleiweg & Erik Tjong Kim Sang. 2017. The parse and query (PaQu) application. In Jan Odijk & Arjan van Hessen (eds.), *CLARIN in the low countries*, 281–297. London, UK: Ubiquity. DOI: http://dx.doi.org/10.5334/bbi.23. License: CC-BY 4.0.
Ravenek, Walter, Charles van den Heuvel & Guido Gerritsen. 2017. The ePistolarium: Origins and Techniques. In Jan Odijk & Arjan van Hessen (eds.), *CLARIN in the low countries*, 317–323. London, UK: Ubiquity. DOI: http://dx.doi.org/10.5334/bbi.26. License: CC-BY 4.0.
Stehouwer, Herman, Matej Ďurčo & Daan Broeder. 2012. Federated search: Towards a common search infrastructure. In Nicoletta Calzolari, Khalid Choukri, Thierry Declerck, Mehmet Uğur Doğan, Bente Maegaard, Joseph Mariani, Asunción Moreno, Jan Odijk & Stelios Piperidis (eds.), *Proceedings of the eighth international conference on language resources and evaluation (LREC'12)*. Istanbul, Turkey: European Language Resources Association (ELRA).
Windhouwer, Menzo & Twan Goosen. 2022. Component Metadata Infrastructure. In Darja Fišer & Andreas Witt (eds.), *CLARIN. The infrastructure for language resources.* Berlin: De Gruyter.
Windhouwer, Menzo, Eko Indarto & Daan Broeder. 2017. CMD2RDF: Building a bridge from CLARIN to Linked Open Data. In Jan Odijk & Arjan van Hessen (eds.), *CLARIN in the low countries*, 95–103. London, UK: Ubiquity. DOI: http://dx.doi.org/10.5334/bbi.8. License: CC-BY 4.0.
Zeeman, Rob & Menzo Windhouwer. 2018. Tweak your CMDI Forms to the Max. In Inguna Skadiņa & Maria Eskevich (eds.), *Proceedings of the 2018 CLARIN annual conference*, 95–98. Pisa, Italy. https://office.clarin.eu/v/CE-2018-1292-CLARIN2018_ConferenceProceedings.pdf.

Marc Kupietz, Nils Diewald, and Eliza Margaretha

Building Paths to Corpus Data

A Multi-Level Least Effort and Maximum Return Approach

Abstract: Enabling appropriate access to linguistic research data, both for many researchers and for innovative research applications, is a challenging task. In this chapter, we describe how we address this challenge in the context of the German Reference Corpus DeReKo and the corpus analysis platform KorAP. The core of our approach, which is based on and tightly integrated into the CLARIN infrastructure, is to offer access at different levels. The graduated access levels make it possible to find a low-loss compromise between the possibilities opened up and the costs incurred by users and providers for each individual use case, so that, viewed over many applications, the ratio between effort and results achieved can be effectively optimized. We also report on experiences with the current state of this approach.

Keywords: reusability of research data, research tools, infrastructure technology, sustainability

1 Introduction

A particular characteristic of large repositories of linguistic research data is that it is not easy to make them accessible to a broad research community in the digital humanities. There are two main reasons for this. First, the notorious problem that linguistic research data are affected by intellectual property rights and, in some circumstances, other personal rights of third parties that preclude the making of copies of the data (see also Kamocki, Kelli, and Lindén 2022). Since the rights holders are usually not part of the research community, Open Data models cannot be applied as they are in other disciplines. The second problem is that the data is often too big and too complex in structure to be readily usable by a larger part of the community. The typical approach to solving these problems is to make the data accessible via web-based research tools that provide operations to deal with complex data without the

Marc Kupietz, Leibniz-Institut für Deutsche Sprache, Mannheim, Germany,
e-mail: kupietz@ids-mannheim.de
Nils Diewald, Leibniz-Institut für Deutsche Sprache, Mannheim, Germany,
e-mail: diewald@ids-mannheim.de
Eliza Margaretha, Leibniz-Institut für Deutsche Sprache, Mannheim, Germany,
e-mail: margaretha@ids-mannheim.de

https://doi.org/10.1515/9783110767377-007

need for direct access. Ideally these tools are integrated into large and sustainable infrastructures, to guarantee reliable and reproducible data usage. Through these tools, users can authenticate themselves (e.g., via CLARIN-AAI) and agree to end user licenses. Authorized this way, users are then offered certain operations on the limited data they are allowed to access, such as faceted searches, possibly also on annotations, the display of concordances and, for linguistic applications, possibly collocation analysis options. However, this approach only partially solves the problems mentioned above due to the limited set of operations provided, and can only cover a decreasing share of usage scenarios in the digital humanities and of possibilities offered by large corpora. The functionalities needed here are developing too fast to be satisfied by the provider of the research tool or infrastructure, as they are themselves subject to ever-diversifying research (see also Odijk and Broeder 2022).

With the KorAP analysis platform (Bański et al. 2013; Diewald et al. 2016) which is part of the CLARIN infrastructure and provides access to the German Reference Corpus DeReKo (Kupietz et al. 2010, 2018) at the Leibniz Institute for the German Language (IDS) and the Contemporary Corpus of the Romanian Language CoRoLa (Tufiș et al. 2019), we are trying to solve this problem with an approach that allows researchers to add their own functionalities to the platform on several levels (Kupietz, Diewald, and Fankhauser 2018). In general, it may be said of these functionalities that the higher the level, the lower the effort for users and providers, but the more limited the possibilities. In addition, it should generally be the case that the higher the level, the more users and uses there are, and that a strong interest in certain low-level access options is likely to lead to their rise within the hierarchy. With this approach we try to ensure that (1) as many users as possible are satisfied, (2) a broad spectrum of types of use is possible[1] and (3) the effort for both sides remains low and sustainably manageable – while (4) the legitimate interests of rights holders remain untouched. In this context, we distinguish between the following primary access levels (from high to low):

- **UI level** – the web user interface (level zero)
- **API level** – accessible directly or via client libraries
- **plugin level** – user interface plugins
- **instance level** – independent access by fully customized components
- **open-source level** – introduce new features by corresponding source code contributions
- **corpus level** – direct access to the corpus data (outside the scope of KorAP)

In this chapter, we systematically explore the areas in which our multi-level approach can serve to extend the possibilities for corpus research in a manage-

1 In this respect, our approach is similar to the approach described in Gomes et al. (2022).

able and thus sustainable way. We provide examples to explain which levels are most suitable for extensions for which research questions. We also discuss technical and legal limitations regarding these extensions as well as links to other elements of the CLARIN infrastructure.

2 API level

KorAP provides APIs to directly communicate with its backend system including its authorization system and its search engine. The KorAP web user interface Kalamar uses these APIs for all communications to the backend system.[2] Documentation about the APIs can be accessed on the GitHub wiki of the KorAP user and policy management component Kustvakt.[3]

Beside KorAP's native frontend client Kalamar, other client applications running either within or outside the KorAP server may also communicate with the backend system using these APIs. Client libraries are currently available for R (R Core Team 2021) and Python. With respect to property and personal rights, client application access to corpus data and annotations without user authentication are rather limited. Nevertheless, these applications still have access to large publicly available corpora such as Wikipedia, and all public metadata of any resources including those with restricted contents (Kupietz, Diewald, and Margaretha 2020). Moreover, KorAP supports an authorization mechanism by using the OAuth2 framework (Hardt 2012), allowing users to enable their applications to perform some operations such as searching and retrieving annotations on their behalf. As a result of the authorization, these operations conform to the user agreement for using DeReKo and the data protection declaration of the IDS, and thus are allowed to access the licensed corpora and annotations. Due to restrictions regarding the location of access, however, not all licensed data is necessarily available to third party applications (Kupietz and Lüngen 2014).

2.1 Scope of access

There are several ways that client applications may interact with the KorAP backend and use its APIs accordingly. Applications supporting OAuth2 may use the KorAP authorization APIs to obtain access tokens allowing them to make other API requests

2 See also Section 3.2 for some general remarks on the virtues of providing APIs.
3 See Margaretha et al. 2021, https://github.com/KorAP/Kustvakt/wiki

such as search requests on behalf of users. Applications that do not support OAuth2 may still take advantage of the search and matchInfo APIs to obtain results from public corpora and public metadata of all corpora.

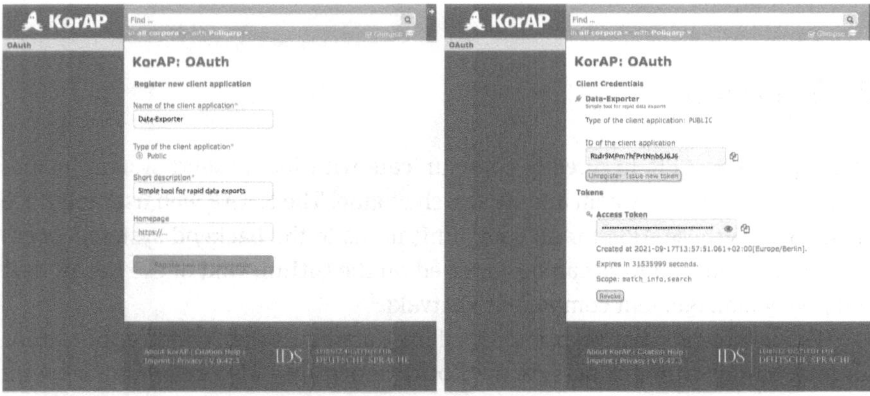

(a) Registration of new OAuth2 clients (b) OAuth2 client and token management

Figure 1: OAuth2 web interface in the Kalamar frontend.

2.1.1 Client registration

To use the authorization APIs, all applications must be registered with the KorAP authorization server by using the client registration APIs. At registration, the authorization server assigns a client id to the applications. Moreover, a client secret may also be assigned to the applications depending on whether it is capable of properly authenticating itself or not. OAuth2 specifies client applications capable of maintaining their credentials as confidential clients, and those not capable of doing so as public clients (Hardt 2012). Since public clients such as mobile and desktop applications are not capable of storing secrets safely, client secrets are not assigned to them. KorAP users can register their applications through the web user interface provided by Kalamar (Figure 1a).

2.1.2 Authorization

Registered client applications may send an authorization request to the authorization server to obtain an authorization code. Within the authorization request, confidential clients must authenticate themselves using the client id and client secret they have received at the registration. Since public clients cannot authenticate themselves properly, they are encouraged to use *Proof Key for Code Exchange* (PKCE) to prevent interception attacks gaining access to the authorization code (Richer et al. 2015). When the KorAP authorization server receives an authorization request, it asks users that have not logged in to KorAP yet to authenticate themselves via the Kalamar web UI. It also asks them if they accept the authorization request with all the requested permissions or not. When users accept an authorization request, the KorAP authorization server sends an authorization code to the redirect URI of the application that has sent the authorization request. The application can then send a token request to exchange the authorization code with an access token and use it for instance within a search request. This whole process is known as *authorization code grant flow* and is illustrated in Figure 2.

KorAP defines super client APIs allowing certain clients to manage access of other clients. For instance, Kalamar as a super client provides a web UI for users to list all their applications and to issue access tokens for them (Figure 1b). This is very useful for non-server-based applications that are not able to provide a redirect URI as required by the authorization procedure for sending an authorization code. In this case, users may feed an access token obtained via Kalamar directly to the applications. Figure 3 illustrates an authorization process for non-server-based applications.

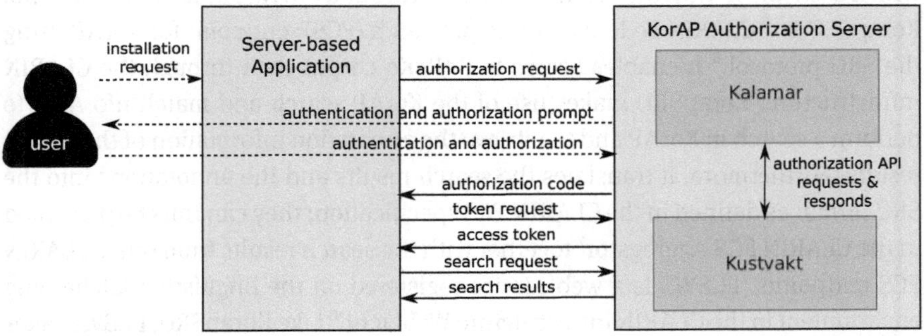

Figure 2: Authorization code grant flow.

2.1.3 Access revocation

It is sometimes necessary for users to revoke application access to their accounts, for instance when they suspect that some application access has been misused or when they do not want to use them any longer. Developers may need to revoke all tokens for their application, for example when they want to delete their appli-

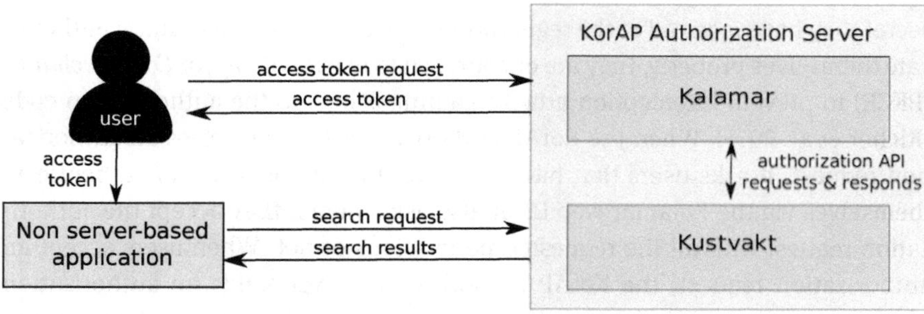

Figure 3: Non server-based authorization.

cations (Parecki 2018). KorAP provides a token revocation API allowing applications to send a token revocation request to the authorization server (Lodderstedt and Scurtescu 2013).

2.2 Scope of usage

2.2.1 Web services

KorAP APIs have been used by two web services, namely KorapSRU[4] and FCSWS, which bind KorAP with the CLARIN infrastructure and provide its access to DeReKo. KorapSRU is a CLARIN Federated Content Search (FCS)[5] endpoint for KorAP using the SRU protocol.[6] It enables access to DeReKo corpus data through the CLARIN infrastructure. KorapSRU makes use of the KorAP search and matchInfo APIs to perform a search in KorAP and to retrieve the annotation information of the search results. Furthermore, it translates the search results and the annotations into the SRU format as defined in the CLARIN FCS specification; they can thus be presented in the CLARIN FCS Aggregator[7] together with the search results from other CLARIN FCS endpoints. FCSWS is a web service registered on the linguistic toolchaining environment in the CLARIN infrastructure WebLicht.[8] Like KorapSRU, FCSWS takes advantage of the KorAP search API to search within DeReKo and to retrieve the search results. It then translates the search results into *Text Corpus Format* (TCF)[9]

4 https://github.com/KorAP/KorapSRU
5 https://www.clarin.eu/content/federated-content-search-clarin-fcs
6 http://www.loc.gov/standards/sru/
7 https://spraakbanken.gu.se/ws/fcs/2.0/aggregator/
8 https://weblicht.sfs.uni-tuebingen.de/weblichtwiki/index.php/Main_Page
9 https://weblicht.sfs.uni-tuebingen.de/weblichtwiki/index.php/The_TCF_Format

which can be used as an input for a linguistic toolchain. Since neither KorapSRU nor FCSWS have supported any authorization mechanism yet, they only have access to public corpora.

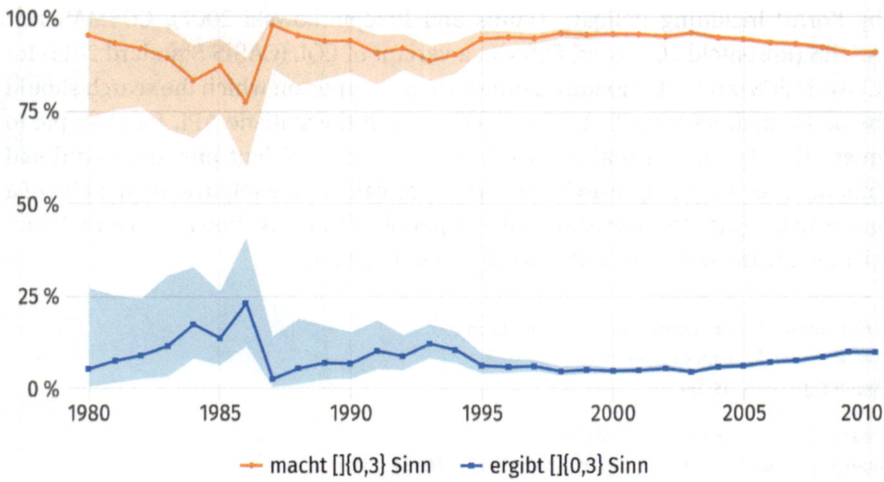

Figure 4: Proportional use of "macht ... Sinn" (lit.: 'makes sense') versus "ergibt ... Sinn" (lit.: 'results in sense') in DeReKo newspaper source (available outside the IDS) between 1980 and 2010.

```
library(RKorAPClient)
query = c("macht []{0,3} Sinn", "ergibt []{0,3} Sinn")
years = c(1980:2010)
as.alternatives = TRUE
vc = "textType = /Zeit.*/ & availability!=QAO-NC-LOC:ids & pubDate in"
new("KorAPConnection", verbose=T) %>%
  frequencyQuery(query, paste(vc, years), as.alternatives = as.alternatives) %>%
  hc_freq_by_year_ci(as.alternatives)
```

Listing 1: Complete R code to generate the plot in Figure 4. The frequencyQuery returns a data frame with one row for each combination of the two queries ("macht ... Sinn", "ergibt ... Sinn") and the 31 virtual corpora (date of publication in 1980–2010).

2.2.2 Client libraries

KorAP can be accessed from R by using RKorAPClient (Kupietz, Diewald, and Margaretha 2020) interacting with KorAP APIs to perform quantitative linguistic analysis on DeReKo corpus data. It supports both authenticated and unauthenticated access to KorAP depending on whether users configure an access token or not. As a non-server-based client, RKorAPClient takes advantage of the authorization procedures described in Figure 3 and Section 2.1. Making the most of the search API, RKorAPClient allows users to perform a search in any query languages supported by KorAP including Poliqarp (Janus and Przepiórkowski 2007), COSMAS II,[10] ANNIS (Rosenfeld 2010) and FCS-QL, a variant of CQL (OASIS Standard 2013) for CLARIN FCS, and to optionally define a virtual corpus on which the search should be performed. RKorAPClient also interacts with the statistic API, for example to query the size of a virtual corpus. Moreover, RKorAPClient provides additional functions for analysing search results such as calculating relative frequencies of a query in a virtual corpus vectorized by a period of time, as shown in Listing 1, and visualizing the results in a plot, as shown in Figure 4.

```
from KorAPClient import KorAPConnection
import plotly.express as px
import pandas as pd

years = list(range(1980, 2011))
query = ["macht []{0,3} Sinn", "ergibt []{0,3} Sinn"]

df = pd.DataFrame({'year': years,
                   'vc': ["textType = /Zeit.*/ & availability!=QAO-NC-LOC:ids" +
                          f"& pubDate in {y}" for y in years]}) \
    .merge(pd.DataFrame(query, columns=["variant"]), how='cross')

results = KorAPConnection() \
    .frequencyQuery(df['variant'], df['vc'], **{"as.alternatives": True})
df = pd.concat([df, results.reset_index(drop=True)], axis=1)
px.line(df, x="year", y="f", color="variant").show()
```

Listing 2: Complete Python code to generate a plot similar to the one in Figure 4 using the KorAPClient Python package, Pandas, and Plotly Express.

PythonKorAPClient[11] is a client library for Python wrapping the RKorAPClient as a Python package, thus providing the same functionality (see Listing 2). It uses rpy2[12] to run R within Python and to convert between R and Python data types, such as between R and Pandas[13] data frames in particular. In addition, the client can be run directly from the command line or shell scripts.

10 https://www2.ids-mannheim.de/cosmas2/web-app/hilfe/suchanfrage/eingabe-zeile/syntax/
11 https://github.com/KorAP/PythonKorAPClient
12 https://rpy2.github.io/
13 https://pandas.pydata.org/

Listings 1 and 2 demonstrate that the client libraries make it quite easy to use the KorAP API and provide at least a small glimpse of the spectrum of possible applications. Accordingly, this offer is aimed, at least in the medium term, at all intensive users of DeReKo or KorAP. First and foremost, this addresses computational linguists, corpus linguists, and digital humanities scholars in particular, as well as projects for which reproducibility or replicability is important.

An important user of the client libraries is, for example, the Council for German Orthography, which benefits from the easy reproducibility on the one hand when observing writing practice, and from the replicability of a large number of queries on new time slices or sub-corpora on the other.

3 Plugin level

The default KorAP user interface Kalamar (Diewald, Barbu Mititelu, and Kupietz 2019) was developed with a special focus on extensibility to allow for a simple and consistent extension of the functional scope of the user interface as the functional demand of the KorAP platform grows. In this context, different functional areas of the user interface were defined, which with the introduction of plugin support can also be used to embed widgets or additional buttons (similar in concept to *OpenSocial* gadgets; see OpenSocial and Gadgets Specification Group 2010). These widgets, realized as *sandboxed iframes*, can be provided by independent web services, which users can integrate individually. A single service may provide multiple widgets or may allow to embed the widget multiple times, even in different areas of the frontend.

Currently, widgets and buttons (which can provide additional functionality even without an embedded widget) can be included in the following functional areas of the user interface: The search input, the definition of virtual corpora, the search results and individual matches. Each area may provide a different context of data to access (see Section 3.1). Further possibilities of integration are planned.

3.1 Scope of access

The communication of these widgets with KorAP can take place in two ways (see Figure 5):

1. by direct communication of the service with the backend (optionally authorized via OAuth2; see Section 2);
2. through a restricted communication protocol with the frontend (via the JavaScript `postMessage` API).

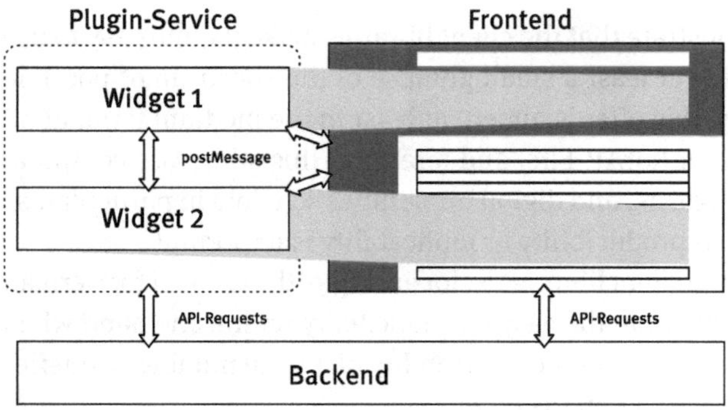

Figure 5: Communication between plugins and KorAP via `postMessage` and API requests.

The backend communication with the KorAP API is only limited by the user's authorization of the plugin service. While widgets of the same plugin service can communicate with each other without any limitations, the communication with the frontend via `postMessage` is very limited. The frontend provides only a small amount of information to the embedded widget that further may be passed to the plugin service. This, for example, can be information on the query issued by the user or the virtual corpus definition. The amount of information available to the embedded widget is also dependent on the context of the widget (i.e., in which functional area of the user interface the widget is embedded). A widget embedded in the area for matches will have access to the identifier and possibly meta information on a specific match, while a widget embedded in the area of the virtual corpus can't provide this information. Using the frontend communication the widget also has limited possibilities to interact with the frontend, for example to communicate the required widget size, or to modify the query string or the virtual corpus definition. Technically the access is limited due to sandboxing. This helps to ensure plugin providers will not be able to add malicious code to be served to the user with the same rights as the embedding frontend.[14] Providing frontend plugins in such a way introduces nonetheless new attack vectors (both on user and corpus data), so our approach is deliberately defensive and functionally limited. Instead of providing maximum access (and with this maximum flexibility) to all plugins, we support a very limited set of actions at this early stage, and will add more functionalities on request and based on reasonable use cases. We also introduced an upper rate boundary for postMessage requests. This way we

14 See LeBlanc (2011) for an overview on security topics regarding that design prior to the establishment of sandboxed iframes.

both try to limit potential misuse of the service and the amount of frontend API methods we have to support.

While the design of the plugin widgets is completely up to the plugin service, Kalamar provides a simple SDK for the frontend communication including CSS rules to layout the widgets following the design of Kalamar (and automatically adopting any changes to it).

3.2 Scope of usage

The support of plugins in the frontend of KorAP offers numerous possibilities for users and developers. Individual plugins allow users to customize the user interface to their own or project-specific needs without overloading the interface for everyone and thus reducing the accessibility. For the developers of KorAP it is possible to provide a rather simple frontend without having to consider and enable all possible use cases. Moreover, the development and maintenance of project-specific plugins can be the responsibility of individual projects and not fall within the scope of responsibility of the KorAP project (with its limited resources). This also opens up the possibility of developing short-lived features for testing or the runtime of a project, without the need to maintain these functions beyond a short period of time. However, this also reveals a disadvantage for the developers of the KorAP system: published plugin interfaces must be supported for a longer period of time and cannot be modified or turned off lightly (similar to the Web-API, see Section 2). Under certain circumstances, this can restrict the flexibility in the design of the frontend. For users, it may be possible that plugins do not work the same way at all times. Changed functionalities in plugins, for example, are not the responsibility of KorAP. And plugins running on separate servers may not be available all the time, fragmenting the availability of the whole system. Further disadvantages for users can arise from the fact that not all project partners have the same plugins installed, which can make it difficult to exchange information about KorAP functionalities.

The field of application for frontend plugins is in principle large – but still limited due to the aforementioned premise regarding API publication. The scope of usage includes, for example:

- implementation of project- or corpus-specific macros that facilitate API access;
- embedding of additional (CLARIN) resources and tools in the KorAP frontend such as lexicons;
- embedding of additional data visualizations;
- support of alternative query mechanisms, e.g., a scratch-like visual query builder.

The first available plugin provides methods to export search results in various formats.[15] The plugin level is not suitable for corpus data access beyond the API level.

4 Instance level

While plugins can significantly increase the usability of the KorAP platform, they are subject to some limitations that can only be solved if a user, a project, or an institution runs their own instance. First and foremost, an advantage of running a dedicated instance is full control over the available corpus data (see Section 6). But it also enables extensive configuration, customization, and replacement of all components of the KorAP platform and thus better integration with other services.

4.1 Scope of access

By configuring or replacing all the components (see Figure 6), it is possible to tailor the services to fit the given server architecture (e.g., regarding processing power and memory), the amount and complexity of provided corpus data and the expected workload. This includes, for example, the specific setting of limits for the maximum number of hits per page, specific timeouts, and the number of desired processes that are to be started for the acceptance of user requests.

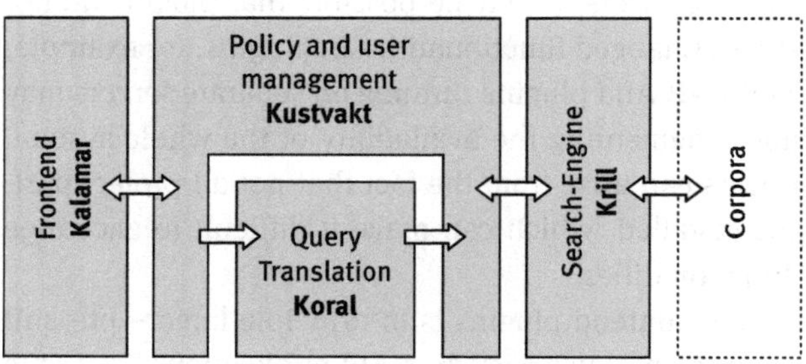

Figure 6: KorAP components forming a single instance.

An instance without any requirement of user management can benefit from replacing the user and policy management component Kustvakt with a simplified yet

15 https://github.com/KorAP/Kalamar-Plugin-Export

officially supported version, called "Kustvakt lite". Without user authentication and authorization as well as user group and virtual corpus management, the simplified Kustvakt serves mainly as an API gateway to the search engine.[16]

Adding server middleware can help maintain the service by introducing IP filtering, intrusion detection and prevention, or API throttling.

The instance level grants more access than the plugin level, but does not add greater accessibility than the API level as long as no further interventions are made at the corpus level.

4.2 Scope of usage

The policy and user management component Kustvakt provides several configurations related to user and policy management; for instance, it is possible to set up the default authorization scopes and the expiration period for authorization codes and access tokens (see Section 2.1). Moreover, default foundries for different annotation levels can be configured, as well as the behaviour of the query rewrite mechanism (Bański et al. 2014) which is fundamental to KorAP.

In addition to extended data access, the user can also be given additional access to information relevant for the specific instance (and thus for the specific corpus) by serving it in the frontend. This includes customized start pages, customized helpers (e.g., for annotations), extended localization, extended documentation or the selection of plugins available by default (see Section 3). Secondary, the default frontend Kalamar is based on the framework Mojolicious[17] and can be extended by further *deployment specific plugins*. By default, the integration of authentication of users via LDAP is supported by such a Mojolicious plugin (not to be confused by plugins as described in Section 3). It is also possible to capture and evaluate requests via the Matomo[18] web analytics platform. Both options are natively supported by the Kustvakt service, too.

16 This variant is also bundled in the official docker image for Kustvakt, enabling users to run KorAP as a single user desktop application; see https://hub.docker.com/r/korap/kustvakt.

17 https://mojolicious.org/

18 https://matomo.org/

5 Open-source level

To extend or modify the data management, search, and analysis capabilities of KorAP beyond the API level, code-based changes are necessary. As research software should always be open source[19] for reproducibility and reusibility purposes (Hasselbring et al. 2020), KorAP is published and actively developed under the BSD 2-Clause license[20] on the platform GitHub;[21] changes to the source code of the individual software components are thus permitted and encouraged. For improved code management and the code review process, the software Gerrit[22] is hosted on the IDS servers. Since KorAP is modular and partially based on the principle of microservices (Diewald et al. 2016), it is not necessary to change and replace all components – it is sufficient to change that component in which the behaviour change is desired. This also reduces the development effort, as new developers do not have to familiarize themselves with all the details of the software, but only with those that are relevant to them. Changes to the core components of KorAP that are included in the official repository should, in principle, be useful to all users and not negatively impact workflows that are already in place. Changes that are only useful for a single instance of KorAP and cannot be made at the plugin or instance level should be handled in separate copies of the corresponding code of the component, in so-called *forks*, and should be developed separately. This allows unrestricted development on a low-level, but also carries the risk that changes may no longer be compatible with future versions of other components of KorAP or the underlying database.

5.1 Scope of access

By modifying the frontend component, the visual experience for the user can be changed beyond the plugin and customization possibilities (see Section 3 and 4). Since the frontend does not have more advanced data access than the API level (see Section 2), this modification does not fundamentally allow increased access to the corpus data (cf. Section 6), but it can, for example, provide extended

---

19 By open source we refer to software that grants users the rights to make copies of the software, redistribute these copies, access the source code, and make improvements to the program (Perens 1999). See Kamocki, Kelli, and Lindén (2022) for the CLARIN perspective on open source licensing.
20 https://opensource.org/licenses/BSD-2-Clause
21 https://github.com/KorAP/
22 https://korap.ids-mannheim.de/gerrit/

possibilities for plugin integration (see Section 3). By modifying the policy and user management component, additional management and monitoring mechanisms for the user and corpus data can be introduced. This includes the management of stored virtual corpora and query references. In addition, the Web API can be extended, provided underlying access capabilities exist. By modifying the query language component, additional query languages can be supported, which translate entered queries into the internal query protocol *KoralQuery* (Bingel and Diewald 2015). KoralQuery itself may also be extended to support query language functions that cannot be represented by the existing specification. By modifying the search engine, additional query constructs can be introduced (if supported by or extended in KoralQuery) or the performance of existing query constructs can be improved. However this may require changes in the design of the underlying database (i.e., the *index*).

The open source level grants all access to the search and analysis capabilities provided by the corpus. The pre-processing pipeline to convert and enrich the corpus data is also open source, so this level is close to the corpus level regarding data accessibility. By changing the code base, users can modify all components of a KorAP instance (see Figure 6). By modifying and extending the pre-processing pipeline, additional annotations can be added to the corpus data, as long as they meet the criteria of the corpus format (see Section 6).

5.2 Scope of usage

Making KorAP components available as open source ensures possible further development of core functionalities independent of the limited capacities of the KorAP development team. This may be of particular interest to project groups that want to switch to KorAP from other corpus research systems, but miss core functionalities that they can only upgrade at this level (since KorAP was designed as a successor platform to COSMAS II, several desired core functionalities are not in central focus). For example, the query language CQP (Christ 1994; Evert and the OCWB Development Team 2010), which is a very common query language, is currently being developed externally and integrated into KorAP in order to provide users who are familiar with CQP-based corpus research systems such as Corpus Workbench or NoSketch Engine. The localization of the frontend has also been extended for Romanian due to the external needs of cooperation partners. Nevertheless, the current support of KorAP development by the open source community is very low, which is probably due to the low demand of specific changes at this level on the one hand and the already small target group on the other hand. Nonetheless, basic groundwork has been laid to enable this level of access if needed. Moreover, we consider the benefits of open source development in the academic field (such as "peer production, shared code, and software as a public good"; Aksulu and Wade 2010: 577) to be undeniable.

6 Corpus level

The possibility of providing access at the level of corpus data can be considered if none of the access options described above prove feasible. The reason why this approach is a last resort is that it requires a large amount of individual staff input for advice and support. Typically, a mix of corpus linguistic methodological and high-level technical expertise is required to find ways to achieve the desired results in a methodologically sound and technically manageable way, using the available data and possibilities.

At an early stage of the KorAP's design phase (Bański et al. 2012: 2906), the intended approach to solve this cost problem was to fully pave the way for Jim Gray's (2003) *put the computation near the data* postulate by providing a mobile code sandbox where users run their own "Kor-App" code with controlled output in order to meet license restrictions (Kupietz et al. 2010). Eventually, however, we refrained from fully implementing this plan (Cosma and Kupietz 2018: 213f). The main reasons were:

- high initial development costs;
- high maintenance costs;
- no improved API-flexibility compared to API- and plugin-level approaches;
- no reduction in methodological expertise for the typically demanding and individual applications.

What we did instead was to split this approach, on the one hand investing more efforts in higher access levels, for example by providing API client libraries, and on the other leaving the way open for a more manual "put the computation near the data" (Kupietz, Diewald, and Fankhauser 2018).

However, due to increasing demand and growing requirements, we largely had to limit this manual corpus level access to genuine collaborations planned in advance over a longer period of time. This slightly changed view – from a purely technical sandbox solution to pre-planned collaborations – also reflects our experience that more sophisticated investigations typically require a high degree of methodological support and experience with the corpus data. One reason for this is that corpus data are often too complex to document their potentially relevant properties with sufficient precision and transparency in general terms for a realistic spectrum of more sophisticated use cases. The complexity starts with the circumstances of the preparation of the corpus data and the heuristics used there, continues with tokenization, and ends with automatic text classifications and linguistic annotations. Which of the properties and circumstances are relevant depends on the use case and its research question.

This should in no way be taken as an excuse for a lack of documentation. The point is that at a potentially relevant level of granularity, the mechanisms are often too complex for their effects to be immediately obvious. An elementary example of this is already the tokenizer used for DeReKo. This is open source and described as transparently as possible by production rules.[23] Nevertheless, the properties of the resulting DFA are not necessarily obvious.

6.1 Scope of usage

Typical application scenarios for the DeReKo corpus level are sophisticated corpus and quantitative linguistic applications and, in general, applications that use specialized language models, such as word embeddings derived from specific virtual corpora or trained with specific parameters.

Typical limiting factors for this approach are computing power, RAM supply, the number of available GPUs and, in particular, the human resources already mentioned above. In the case of DeReKo and KorAP, the corpus data level does, in principle, provide users with access to virtually all the different, sometimes alternative data types and formats generated and used in the production pipelines and internal analysis processes. However, the users do not have access to the data for copyright and contractual reasons. This also applies to IDS staff who are not also members of DeReKo production projects.

The typical organizational workflow therefore looks like this: a DeReKo project member sends legally safe sample data to the user – or rather cooperation partner. The cooperation partner then adapts his/her analysis programs to the DeReKo formats together with the project member in a local git repository. If all tests run satisfactorily, the project member applies the programs to the real data, checks the results again with regard to legal soundness, and sends them back to the cooperation partner (Kupietz and Lüngen 2014).

23 See Kupietz and Diewald 2021, https://github.com/KorAP/KorAP-Tokenizer

Table 1: Data types and representations accessible on the corpus level, and when they are typically used.

Data type	Typical requirements	Tasks / Applications
TEI I5 XML	+ metadata + text structural annotations – linguistic annotations	XML aware applications CMC research communication analysis
KorAP XML	+ multiple annotations + metadata	metadata sensitive ML
KorAP CoNLL-U	+ linguistic annotations – multiple annotations – metadata – structural annotations	text classifiers quantitative linguistics word embeddings count-based models
Metadata DB	+ representativeness of some language domain	(stratified) sampling

As mentioned above, there is access to several partly alternative and partly complementary data and representation formats on the so-called corpus data level. Which data type is typically suitable for which type of application is briefly described in Table 1. The individual data types and formats are described in more detail below.

6.2 Scope of access

6.2.1 TEI-I5 XML data

A well-documented and standardized access to DeReKo is provided by the XML format TEI-I5 (Lüngen and Sperberg-McQueen 2012) which is a customization of the TEI-P5 standard and also the primary corpus encoding format for all DeReKo releases. A DeReKo release currently comprises 3,982 of such I5 documents, with one document typically corresponding to a special corpus, such as the Mannheim Corpus I or a magazine or newspaper volume of a particular year, ranging in file size between 20 KB for some Usenet news corpora (Lüngen and Kupietz 2017) and 30 GB for Wikipedia corpora (Margaretha and Lüngen 2014). These documents contain all metadata and text classifications as well as all existing text structural markup annotated in-line.

Bibliographic metadata include author or editor, title, subtitle if applicable, publisher, and date and place of publication. Among the other bibliographic metadata, the date of first publication and the time of origin should be emphasized, which sometimes deviate from the date of publication (e.g., in the case of literary work editions) and are especially needed for studies of linguistic variation over time. Place of publication metadata also include derived assignments to corresponding countries encoded as ISO 3166-1 alpha-2 two-letter codes.

Non-bibliographic metadata include license information (Kupietz and Lüngen 2014), an assignment of two possible topic domains, according to an automatic domain classification (Weiß 2005), as well as, in part, an assessment of degree of duplicity (Kupietz 2005; Klosa, Kupietz, and Lüngen 2012: 88).

The text-structural markup includes chapter, section, and paragraph structure and the marking of the corresponding headings. Furthermore, lists, tables, citations, URLs, references, and footnotes and the like are marked up, as well as page breaks and page numbers. Book contents are additionally marked up for the areas of the title and appendix. In dramas, plenary debates, chats, and so on, elements appear to mark speakers, utterances, posts, and stage directions. For all types of texts, there are also various elements for the marking of typographically marked text areas. Finally, sentence segmentation is also provided. It must be taken into account that the latter is specified by means of bracketing elements, which are often interrupted in order to maintain the XML well-formedness.

In the case of other text-structural mark-ups, it must be noted that these are only present if they could be reconstructed from the raw data with reasonable effort and sufficient certainty (Kupietz, Schonefeld, and Witt 2010).

6.2.2 KorAP XML data

The KorAP XML format (Bański et al. 2012) is a required intermediate format in the preparation process of DeReKo and other corpora for the indexation with KorAP. It can be generated automatically from various TEI P5 formats.[24] One of the main features of KorAP XML is a consistent and complete implementation of standoff annotations. These are realized by feature structures (Lee et al. 2004) using references to IDs and character offsets of pure text versions of the primary data.

The KorAP XML encoded data are organized in so-called foundries (Bański et al. 2013). A foundry contains all annotation layers of a particular tool family, for instance, part of speech, lemma, dependency, and constituency. Foundries have the property that they are homogeneous in themselves. That means that they can contain multiple interpretations for one item, usually provided with confidence or likelihood ratings, but normally do not contain plain contradictions, for example, in the sense that a word is annotated as verb with 100% certainty on the

24 see https://github.com/KorAP/KorAP-XML-TEI

part of speech level and as head of a noun phrase on a syntactic level. Contradictions among different foundries on the same and on different annotation levels, for instance, between Tree-Tagger and OpenNLP part-of-speech annotations, on the other hand, are frequent and intended as such in order to deal with annotation errors (see Belica et al. 2011; Kupietz et al. 2017).

A special foundry is the *base foundry*. It contains mandatory segmentation information regarding tokenization, sentence boundaries and paragraphs. In addition, it also contains the token segmentation that was generated by KorAP-Tokenizer. With regard to sentence segmentation, it should be noted that this, if available, is mostly taken from the underlying TEI encoded corpora. Due to possible differences between sentence and token segmentations, for instance in the case of abbreviations or due to the necessities of well-formedness mentioned above, the KorAP XML data increasingly also contain sentence boundaries designated by the KorAP-Tokenizer as default.[25]

KorAP XML data consists of many XML documents for each text. However, these are grouped together by year and corpus in a zip archive. For a corpus file in I5 format, for example s20.i5.xml (Der Spiegel 2020), there is a base foundry file s20.zip and several annotation foundry files, such as 20.corenlp.zip, s20.malt.zip, s20.marmot.zip, s20.opennlp.zip s20.spacy.zip, and s20.tree_tagger.zip.

More detailed information about the KorAP XML format can be found along with the documentation of the KorAP-XML-Krill package.[26]

6.2.3 CoNLL-U data

The CoNLL-U[27] column representation is also an essential part of the ingestion pipeline of KorAP. It is needed in order to enable the flexible application of externally developed NLP tools, such as POS taggers and dependency parsers, for which the format has been established as a *de-facto* standard. The *U* variant of the CoNLL convention that was established within the Universal Dependencies (UD) framework is required in this context, as in addition to the typical lines for token and annotation columns, it also provides for comment lines. These are not formally specified in more detail, but are specifically intended to carry application-specific information and to be piped unchanged through tool pipelines. In the case of the KorAP annotation pipeline, they are needed for linking the

25 In the case of DeReKo, the break between the old and new tokenization is not too large, as both rely on the same extensive list of abbreviations.

26 https://github.com/KorAP/KorAP-XML-Krill#about-korap-xml

27 https://universaldependencies.org/format.html

CoNLL-U representation back to their original texts and their metadata, and so on, as exemplified in Listing 3.

```
# foundry = tree_tagger
# filename = S01/JAN/00001/tree_tagger/morpho.xml
# text_id = S01_JAN.00001
# start_offsets =   0 0  4 14 17 21
# end_offsets = 22 3 13 16 21 22
1 Das           die          ART        ART         _   _   _   _   0.962601
2 Universum     Universum    NN         NN          _   _   _   _   1.000000
3 im            in           APPRART    APPRART     _   _   _   _   1.000000
4 Kopf          Kopf         NN         NN          _   _   _   _   0.999975
5 :             :            $.         $.          _   _   _   _   1.000000
```

Listing 3: Example sentence in KorAP's CoNLL-U representaion with Tree-Tagger POS annotations.

KorAP XML and KorAP CoNNL-U data can be automatically converted into each other via the KorAP-XML-CoNNL-U package,[28] which for the conversion to CoNLL-U needs a base foundry KorAP XML zip file and typically, but optionally, one annotation foundry zip file. The base foundry is always needed because, as mentioned above, all annotation layers consistently contain stand-off data, only. The CoNLL-U data contain information on token and sentence segmentation and at most one foundry of lemma, POS, and dependency annotations. They do not contain any metadata or text-structural annotations; these, however, may have to be retrieved by means of the text ID and token-offset information.

Due to its easy processability, the CoNLL-U format also serves as a basis for the generation of various other data types, such as frequency lists or bag-of-words representations, which are used, for example, as input for text classifiers.

6.2.4 DeReKo Metadata database

The DeReKo Metadata DB is a relational database, versioned by DeReKo-releases, containing metadata on all DeReKo texts, sub-corpora and sources. It was first set up in April 2007 for internal use only, as an interim solution to draw stratified random samples from DeReKo based on text metadata, and to provide metadata at different levels of granularity for CLARIN's OAI-PMH (see Windhouwer and Goosen 2022; Hinrichs and Beck 2010). In accordance with its genesis, the DeReKo Metadata DB does not have a perfect design, yet it has not been replaced by a

28 https://github.com/KorAP/KorAP-XML-CoNLL-U

true production system and is updated twice a year with each DeReKo release. Its current version for DeReKo-2022-I contains more than 200 million entries.

```
SELECT sigle FROM textMeta2022I
    WHERE topic1 = “Kultur:Darstellende_Kunst”
    ORDER BY RAND()
    LIMIT 100000;
```

Listing 4: SQL query for the DeReKo-2022-I metadata DB to draw a random sample of 100,000 texts on the subject of fine arts.

Listing 4 shows how the database can be used to draw a sample from DeReKo. The sigles (IDs) returned by the SQL query can easily be used for the definition of a virtual sub-corpus of DeReKo within KorAP or one of its client libraries (see Section 2.2).[29]

At the corpus level, access to the metadata database is rather an exception, as it is limited less for legal reasons than for practical reasons regarding implementation and maintenance efforts and the performance required for a production system. Integrating equivalent functionalities directly into the KorAP search engine and making them available via the API and the user interface is planned as a high priority.

7 Conclusions

We have shown how we enable access to linguistic corpora for many users as well as for demanding applications with limited resources and despite sometimes discipline-specific challenges. The core of our approach is to provide pathways to the data at different levels. As sketched in Figure 7, pathways at a high level enable access with as little effort as possible for many users and frequent applications. Pathways at lower levels, on the other hand, offer more possibilities but also require more effort on the part of the user and sometimes also the corpus provider (in case of different parties).

29 Likewise, in the case of COSMAS II, virtual corpora are in principle defined on the basis of sigle lists. However, since COSMAS II does not provide a user interface or API for the definition of virtual corpora at the sigle level, this requires manual intervention.

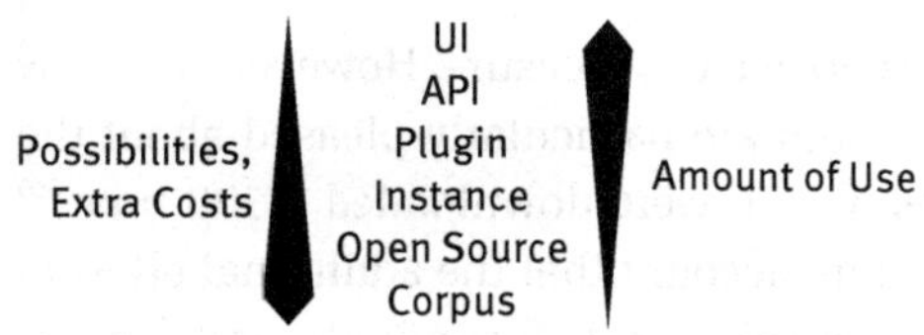

Figure 7: Levels of access and their approximate relations to their possibilities, overall extra costs and typical number of uses.

In the case of KorAP, the user interface level (Diewald, Barbu Mititelu, and Kupietz 2019) allows a very easy entry for all types of users and rarely requires individual support. Also easy to use, thanks to appropriate libraries, but with an admittedly somewhat higher entry threshold, is the API level, which in return offers extended functionalities, especially with regard to quantitative analyses, their visualizations and their reproducibility. The development of additional plugins in particular opens up new possibilities for extending the user interface and can be realized, for example, in projects independent of the core KorAP development. Development costs vary greatly depending on the task of the plugin, but are presumably lower than working directly at the open source level, since developers are free to choose the programming language and development environment, and require little knowledge of the KorAP system. However, additional costs arise due to the operation of the plugin service on its own servers. The instance level represents a special case within the hierarchy, as it extends the access possibilities not to DeReKo, but to corpora provided by the users themselves. The costs incurred there relate in particular to data preparation and the operation of a separate KorAP instance, as well as any support that may be required. Expanding access to corpora through participation in the open source project is certainly one of the most productive paths, as a larger community can benefit from it. Depending on whether it is a bug fix, an additional collocation measure, or a completely new functionality, the spectrum of required efforts is very broad and may range from a few minutes to a scale that can only be achieved by larger initiatives. However, it is important that this possibility exists and that larger projects can include it in their planning. Less productive in terms of its re-usability potential and most expensive in terms of support effort, but also requiring to be planned in advance and sometimes becoming unavoidable, is the approach of conducting collaborative studies directly at the corpus data level – using more or less a manual *put the computation near the data* approach. The most difficult part there is typically the handling of application-specific machine learning tasks, which use, for example, special virtual sub-corpora and annotation layers and therefore have little reusability value and are demanding in terms of expert human and computational resources, disk space, and maintenance effort.

At the intermediate levels, success is not easy to measure. However, we know of some larger running KorAP instances and are particularly pleased about the positive response to the client libraries, which were downloaded 4,500 times[30] in the first year. It should also be taken into account that the additional effort to offer the different access levels is comparatively small. Accordingly, and furthermore, it cannot be emphasized enough that the upper access levels are not in any competition with each other. In particular, for example, the user interface is based entirely on the API, so UI users need not worry about being neglected when API functionalities are opened to the public. It is mainly the corpus level that is affected by a lack of resources and a competitive situation, which is precisely why it is important to create access options at higher levels.

We build these different paths to our corpus data, in order to enable as many users as possible to perform extensive corpus linguistic and related studies with the fewest possible hurdles. In this sense, we follow the paths that the transnational research infrastructure initiative CLARIN has prepared in terms of the use and reuse of language resources and technologies for the social sciences and humanities in general. Within the framework of CLARIN, the necessary foundations were laid in the areas of standards, legal expertise, contractual framework and sustainability, on which we base our efforts. The presented interfaces with the CLARIN infrastructure on all levels show that a joint strategy for the development and promotion of language resources and technologies, as well as for their implementation, maintenance, and use, is essential.

Bibliography

Aksulu, Altay & Michael Wade. 2010. A comprehensive review and synthesis of open source research. *Journal of the Association for Information Systems* 11, 576–656.

Bański, Piotr, Joachim Bingel, Nils Diewald, Elena Frick, Michael Hanl, Marc Kupietz, Piotr Pęzik, Carsten Schnober & Andreas Witt. 2013. KorAP: The new corpus analysis platform at IDS Mannheim. In Zygmunt Vetulani & Hans Uszkoreit (eds.), *Proceedings of the 6th Conference on Language and Technology (LTC-2013)*. Poznań: Uniwersytet im. Adama Mickiewicza w Poznaniu. https://nbn-resolving.org/urn:nbn:de:bsz:mh39-32617

Bański, Piotr, Nils Diewald, Michael Hanl, Marc Kupietz & Andreas Witt. 2014. Access control by query rewriting: The case of KorAP. *International Conference on Language Resources and Evaluation (LREC)* 9, 3817–3822.

30 Adjusted for downloads due to automatic integration tests.

Bański, Piotr, Peter M. Fischer, Elena Frick, Erik Ketzan, Marc Kupietz, Carsten Schnober, Oliver Schonefeld & Andreas Witt. 2012. The new IDS corpus analysis platform: Challenges and prospects. *International Conference on Language Resources and Evaluation (LREC)* 8, 2905–2911.

Belica, Cyril, Marc Kupietz, Harald Lüngen & Andreas Witt. 2011. The morphosyntactic annotation of DeReKo: Interpretation, opportunities and pitfalls. In Marek Konopka, Jacqueline Kubczak, Christian Mair, František Šticha & Ulrich Wassner (eds.), *Selected contributions from the conference Grammar and Corpora 2009*, 451–471. Tübingen: Gunter Narr Verlag.

Bingel, Joachim & Nils Diewald. 2015. KoralQuery – A general corpus query protocol. In Gintare Grigonyte, Simon Clematide, Andrius Utka & Martin Volk (eds.), *Proceedings of the Workshop on Innovative Corpus Query and Visualization Tools at NODALIDA 2015*, 1–5. Linköping: University Electronic Press. https://nbn-resolving.org/urn:nbn:de:bsz:mh39-43102

Christ, Oliver. 1994. A modular and flexible architecture for an integrated corpus query system. In *Proceedings of the 3rd Conference on Computational Lexicography and Text Research (COMPLEX'94)*, 23–32, Budapest, Hungary.

Cosma, Ruxandra & Marc Kupietz. 2018. Von Schienen, Zügen und linguistischen Fragestellungen. In Henning Lobin, Roman Schneider & Andreas Witt (eds.), *Digitale Infrastrukturen für die germanistische Forschung*, 199–218. Berlin [u.a.]: De Gruyter. https://doi.org/10.1515/9783110538663-010

Diewald, Nils, Verginica Barbu Mititelu & Marc Kupietz. 2019. The KorAP user interface. Accessing CoRoLa via KorAP. *Revue Roumaine de Linguistique* 64 (3). https://nbn-resolving.org/urn:nbn:de:bsz:mh39-93866

Diewald, Nils, Michael Hanl, Eliza Margaretha, Joachim Bingel, Marc Kupietz, Piotr Bański & Andreas Witt. 2016. KorAP architecture: Diving in the deep sea of corpus data. *International Conference on Language Resources and Evaluation (LREC)* 10, 3586–3591.

Evert, Stefan & the OCWB Development Team. 2010. CQP query language tutorial. Technical report, The OCWB Development Team. http://cwb.sourceforge.net/files/CQP_Tutorial.pdf (accessed 5 April 2022).

Gomes, Luís, Ruben Branco, João Silva & António Branco. 2022. Open and Inclusive Language Processing: Language processing services by PORTULAN to meet the widest needs of CLARIN users. In Darja Fišer & Andreas Witt (eds.), *CLARIN. The infrastructure for language resources*. Berlin: De Gruyter.

Gray, Jim. 2003. Distributed computing economics. Technical Report MSR-TR-2003-24, Microsoft Research. https://arxiv.org/pdf/cs/0403019.pdf (accessed 5 April 2022).

Hardt, Dick. 2012. The OAuth 2.0 authorization framework. RFC 6749. https://doi.org/10.17487/RFC6749

Hasselbring, Wilhelm, Leslie Carr, Simon Hettrick, Heather Packer & Thanassis Tiropanis. 2020. Open source research software. *Computer* 53 (8), 84–88. https://doi.org/10.1109/MC.2020.2998235

Hinrichs, Erhard & Kathrin Beck. 2010. Documentation of the D-SPIN preparation activities. D-SPIN Report R5.2. https://weblicht.sfs.uni-tuebingen.de/Reports/D-SPIN_R5.2.pdf (accessed 5 April 2022).

Janus, Daniel & Adam Przepiórkowski. 2007. Poliqarp: An open source corpus indexer and search engine with syntactic extensions. In Sophia Ananiadou (ed.), *Proceedings of the 45th annual meeting of the ACL on interactive poster and demonstration sessions*, 85–88, Prague: Association for Computational Linguistics.

Kamocki, Paweł, Aleksei Kelli & Krister Lindén. 2022. The CLARIN Committee for Legal and Ethical Issues and the Normative Layer of the CLARIN Infrastructure. In Darja Fišer & Andreas Witt (eds.), *CLARIN. The infrastructure for language resources*. Berlin: De Gruyter.

Klosa, Annette, Marc Kupietz & Harald Lüngen. 2012. Zum Nutzen von Korpusauszeichnungen für die Lexikographie. *Lexicographica* 28, 71–97.

Kupietz, Marc. 2005. Near-duplicate detection in the IDS corpora of written German. Technical Report kt-2006-01, Institut für Deutsche Sprache. https://www.ids-mannheim.de/fileadmin/kl/misc/ids-kt-2006-01.pdf (accessed 5 April 2022).

Kupietz, Marc, Cyril Belica, Holger Keibel & Andreas Witt. 2010. The German Reference Corpus DeReKo: A primordial sample for linguistic research. *International Conference on Language Resources and Evaluation (LREC)* 7, 1848–1854.

Kupietz, Marc & Nils Diewald. 2021. KorAP/KorAP-Tokenizer. https://doi.org/10.5281/zenodo.5144841

Kupietz, Marc, Nils Diewald & Peter Fankhauser. 2018. How to get the computation near the data: Improving data accessibility to, and reusability of analysis functions in corpus query platforms. In Piotr Bański, Marc Kupietz, Adrien Barbaresi, Hanno Biber, Evelyn Breiteneder, Simon Clematide & Andreas Witt (eds.), *Proceedings of the 6th Workshop on Challenges in the Management of Large Corpora (CMLC-6), LREC'18*, 20–25. Miyazaki & Paris: European Language Resources Association (ELRA). http://lrec-conf.org/workshops/lrec2018/W17/pdf/14_W17.pdf (accessed 5 April 2022).

Kupietz, Marc, Nils Diewald, Michael Hanl & Eliza Margaretha. 2017. Möglichkeiten der Erforschung grammatischer Variation mithilfe von KorAP. In Marek Konopka & Angelika Wöllstein (eds.), *Grammatische Variation. Empirische Zugänge und theoretische Modellierung*, 319–329, 319–329. Berlin [u.a.]: De Gruyter. https://doi.org/10.1515/9783110518214-019

Kupietz, Marc, Nils Diewald & Eliza Margaretha. 2020. RKorAPClient: An R package for accessing the German Reference Corpus DeReKo via KorAP. *International Conference on Language Resources and Evaluation (LREC)* 12, 7015–7021.

Kupietz, Marc & Harald Lüngen. 2014. Recent developments in DeReKo. *International Conference on Language Resources and Evaluation (LREC)* 9, 2378–2385.

Kupietz, Marc, Harald Lüngen, Paweł Kamocki & Andreas Witt. 2018. The German Reference Corpus DeReKo: New Developments – New Opportunities. *International Conference on Language Resources and Evaluation (LREC)* 11, 4353–4360.

Kupietz, Marc, Oliver Schonefeld & Andreas Witt. 2010. The German Reference Corpus: New developments building on almost 50 years of experience. In Victoria Arranz & Laura van Eerten (eds.), *Language resources: From storyboard to sustainability and LR lifecycle management, workshop held at the seventh conference on International Language Resources and Evaluation (LREC)*, 39–43. Valetta & Paris: European Language Resources Association (ELRA). https://nbn-resolving.org/urn:nbn:de:bsz:mh39-45002

LeBlanc, Jonathan. 2011. *Programming Social Applications*. Sebastopol, CA: O'Reilly.

Lee, Kiyong, Lou Burnard, Laurent Romary, Èric Villemonte de la Clergerie, Thierry Declerck, Syd Bauman, Harry Bunt, Lionel Clément, Tomaz Erjavec, Azim Roussanaly & Claude Roux. 2004. Towards an international standard on feature structure representation. *International Conference on Language Resources and Evaluation (LREC)* 4.

Lodderstedt, T. & M. Scurtescu. 2013. OAuth 2.0 Token Revocation. RFC 7009, RFC Editor. https://tools.ietf.org/html/rfc7009 (accessed 5 April 2022).

Lüngen, Harald & Marc Kupietz. 2017. CMC corpora in DeReKo. In Piotr Bański, Marc Kupietz, Harald Lüngen, Paul Rayson, Hanno Biber, Evelyn Breiteneder, Simon Clematide, John Mariani, Mark Stevenson & Theresa Sick (eds.), *Proceedings of the workshop on challenges in the management of large corpora and big data and natural language processing (CMLC-5+BigNLP) 2017*, 20–24. Mannheim: Institut für Deutsche Sprache. https://nbn-resolving.org/urn:nbn:de:bsz:mh39-62592

Lüngen, Harald & C. Michael Sperberg-McQueen. 2012. A TEI P5 Document Grammar for the IDS Text Model. *Journal of the Text Encoding Initiative* 3, 1–18. http://jtei.revues.org/508 (accessed 5 April 2022).

Margaretha, Eliza, Nils Diewald, Michael Hanl, Marc Kupietz & Franck Bodmer. 2021. KorAP/Kustvakt version 0.64. https://doi.org/10.5281/zenodo.5148159

Margaretha, Eliza & Harald Lüngen. 2014. Building linguistic corpora from wikipedia articles and discussions. *Journal of Language Technology and Computational Linguistics* 29 (2), 59–82. https://nbn-resolving.org/urn:nbn:de:bsz:mh39-33306

OASIS Standard. 2013. searchRetrieve: Part 5. CQL: The contextual query language version 1.0. http://docs.oasis-open.org/search-ws/searchRetrieve/v1.0/os/part5-cql/searchRetrieve-v1.0-os-part5-cql.html (accessed 5 April 2022).

Odijk, Jan & Daan Broeder. 2022. Sustainability and genericity of CLARIN services in the Netherlands. In Darja Fišer & Andreas Witt (eds.), *CLARIN. The infrastructure for language resources*. Berlin: De Gruyter.

OpenSocial and Gadgets Specification Group. 2010. OpenSocial specification 2.0 draft. Specification. http://docs.opensocial.org/display/OSD/Specs (accessed 5 April 2022).

Parecki, Aaron. 2018. *OAuth 2.0 Simplified*. Morrisville, NC: Lulu.com.

Perens, Bruce. 1999. The open source definition. In Chris DiBona, Sam Ockman & Mark Stone (eds.), *Open sources: Voices from the open source revolution*, 171–188, 1st edn., 171–188. Sebastopol, CA: O'Reilly.

R Core Team. 2021. *R: A Language and Environment for Statistical Computing*, R Foundation for Statistical Computing, Vienna. https://www.R-project.org/ (accessed 5 April 2022).

Richer, J., M. Jones, J. Bradley, M. Machulak & P. Hunt. 2015. Proof Key for Code Exchange by OAuth Public Clients. RFC 7591, RFC Editor. https://tools.ietf.org/html/rfc7591 (accessed 5 April 2022).

Rosenfeld, Viktor. 2010. An implementation of the Annis 2 query language. Student Thesis, Humboldt-University of Berlin. https://citeseerx.ist.psu.edu/viewdoc/download?doi=10.1.1.403.1104 & rep=rep1&type=pdf (accessed 5 April 2022).

Tufiș, Dan, Verginica Barbu Mititelu, Elena Irimia, Vasile Păiș, Radu Ion, Nils Diewald, Maria Mitrofan & Mihaela Onofrei. 2019. Little strokes fell great oaks. Creating CoRoLa, the reference corpus of contemporary Romanian. *Revue Roumaine de Linguistique* 64 (3). https://nbn-resolving.org/urn:nbn:de:bsz:mh39-93851

Weiß, Christian. 2005. Die thematische Erschließung von Sprachkorpora. *OPAL – Online publizierte Arbeiten zur Linguistik* 1. https://nbn-resolving.org/urn:nbn:de:bsz:mh39-716

Windhouwer, Menzo & Twan Goosen. 2022. Component Metadata Infrastructure. In Darja Fišer & Andreas Witt (eds.), *CLARIN. The infrastructure for language resources*. Berlin: De Gruyter.

Menzo Windhouwer and Twan Goosen

Component Metadata Infrastructure

Abstract: At the start of CLARIN, metadata for language resources faced various problems, for example, different communities using different terminology, which made interoperability difficult. The Component Metadata (CMD) Infrastructure (CMDI) was developed as a solution and is based on specifying reusable components, each of which contains other components and elements. Components are assembled into profiles, the schema for the metadata description of a specific type of language resources. The CMD Infrastructure consists of many interacting parts, including a Component Registry, several semantic registries, a metadata harvester, and a central catalogue (the VLO). It is supported by repository systems and metadata editors developed and maintained by various stakeholders across the CLARIN network. The CMDI landscape has expanded throughout the years, and has remained sustainable by adapting itself, as it will continue to do in the future.

Keywords: metadata, semantic interoperability, search and discovery, curation, FAIR

1 Introduction

Metadata plays a key role in making language resources and tools findable and accessible, which is one of CLARIN's primary objectives. In the world of research data and data processing, metadata is ubiquitous and fulfils many roles. The main value of metadata lies in its ability to facilitate discovery: there are all kinds of possibilities for searching and filtering within and across collections and repositories. Thanks to metadata, discovery can take place on the basis of information beyond the *content* of a resource. The importance of metadata derives from the fact that most resources do not "internally" encode all information that could serve as search terms, filter criteria, or usage guidance to its potential consumer. For instance, a simple monolingual wordlist resource might consist of a single file containing only words and numbers, and no explicit specification of the language it pertains to. This is not helpful to a researcher looking for a word-

Menzo Windhouwer, KNAW Humanities Cluster, CLARIN ERIC,
e-mail: menzo.windhouwer@di.huc.knaw.nl
Twan Goosen, CLARIN ERIC, e-mail: twan@clarin.eu

https://doi.org/10.1515/9783110767377-008

list in a particular language. Therefore, additional information about resources (in other words, data about the data: metadata) has to be provided, managed, distributed, and processed in order to integrate these into a functioning research infrastructure.

In theory, metadata could be provided in "free form" and still fulfil a role in terms of informing potential users, as well as, to some extent, enhancing findability. There are, however, many advantages to making sure that metadata conforms to one or more metadata *standards* and makes use of predefined *vocabularies*. Standards and vocabularies can both prescribe and constrain the manner in which metadata is encoded, as well as the properties and values that are contained in the metadata. Practical reasons for using metadata standards and common vocabularies are to ensure syntactic and semantic uniformity and unambiguousness, and to potentially promote a range of quality aspects such as completeness and correctness. In particular, machine processing of metadata, for instance for discovery purposes and interoperability between metadata processing pipelines, depends strongly on the use of standards and vocabularies that are well defined and carefully followed.

Before CLARIN, several metadata standards were already in use for the description of language resources and tools. As different communities and sub-communities have different needs, conceptual frameworks, technological contexts, etc., different standards were used in parallel, and these standards were generally not mutually interoperable, and in many cases not easily extensible or adaptable to suit the needs of other new or existing communities or platforms. Rather than adopting one of these existing, more or less "opinionated" standards or adding yet another standard, CLARIN's approach to metadata was designed to be much more flexible, modular, and community driven, with a focus on semantic interoperability across different models and syntactic variations. On the foundation of these principles, CLARIN introduced the Component Metadata Infrastructure or CMDI as its metadata framework and one of the cornerstones of its language resources infrastructure.

The remainder of this chapter is structured as follows: we first discuss the context and requirements that motivated the creation of CMDI (Section 2), followed by its core principles and workings (Section 3), its adoption and evolution thus far (Section 4), its practical application from the perspective of the end user (Section 5), the challenges that exist for CLARIN and an outlook on the future (Section 6); finally, conclusions regarding the above-mentioned themes are presented (Section 7).

2 Metadata for language resources pre-CMDI

The preparatory phase of the CLARIN Infrastructure started in 2008 (Váradi et al. 2008). At that time, several metadata standards played a role in the LRT domain (Broeder et al. 2008; Broeder et al. 2010).

In the domain of the library sciences, the Dublin Core Metadata Initiative (DCMI 2021) was established, resulting in the 15 metadata fields of the Dublin Core Metadata Element Set (DCMES) as a generic means of describing all kinds of objects, for instance, *title* ("a name given to the resource"), *creator* ("an entity primarily responsible for making the resource"), *subject* ("the topic of the resource"), and *description* ("an account of the resource"). However, it makes heavy use of library-specific terminology and is a flat list of descriptors, which some feel makes it unsuitable for the description of complex objects.

Still, DCMES was systematically used by the Open Language Archives Community (OLAC) (OLAC 2011) which, starting with the definition of the additional "language identifier" metadata element, became a useful set of qualified metadata elements. This DC application profile combined with the Open Archive Initiative's metadata harvesting protocol (OAI-PMH) is still a metadata exchange paradigm supported by many archives of (endangered) language resources.

In the linguistic domain, metadata also started to be included in headers of resources such as CHAT (MacWhinney 2021) and Text Encoding Initiative (TEI) (TEI Consortium 2021) annotation files. However, the encoding and semantics of the metadata were in these cases often corpus specific and always tightly bound to the file format of the resource itself.

The IMDI metadata scheme (MPI 2020) was designed to describe resources in the linguistic domain. Although IMDI can be used to describe text corpora and lexical resources, its main strength and primary use is the detailed description of bundles of tightly related resources of multimodal corpora. It uses domain-specific terminology and supports complex resources. Furthermore, IMDI supports a limited form of extensibility by key-value pairs in various parts of the schema. Additional metadata schemes were created as community-specific extensions, such as those for the Dutch Spoken Corpus and the Sign Language community.

Like OLAC, many community networks use OAI-PMH to exchange metadata and collect it in one place for disclosure via a central catalogue. OAI-PMH uses XML as its core technology and, although it is open to any XML-based metadata format, makes support for Dublin Core obligatory in its specification (OAI 2015).

The metadata landscape thus clearly showed the tension between the need for sufficiently rich and domain-specific terminology to adequately describe resources and the desire for interoperability, where terms have to be understood by humans (from varying disciplines) and machines alike. This has led to the concurrent use of small sets of descriptors with broad semantics to large sets with highly specific descriptors.

3 CMDI

3.1 Components and Profiles

In their proposal for a “Component-based Flexible Registry for Language Resources and Technology”, Broeder et al. (2008) list a number of major concerns with respect to the prevailing metadata praxis, three of which we can interpret as the original core requirements for CMDI in terms of features available to its users:

1. Users must be able to “create and use their own schema tailored specifically towards the requirements of [their] project”.
2. Users must be able to “use the terminology that the specific (sub-) community is used to”.
3. Users must be able to “mix vocabularies from various initiatives such as to extend IMDI by TEI header elements”.

The essential aim of the initiators of CMDI was to unite the above requirements, which reflect and address the heterogeneous nature of the metadata landscape with a high degree of interoperability and reusability, both *within* and *across* communities. What they proposed was a *Component-based* metadata infrastructure, revolving around a basic meta-model with *Components* and *Profiles* as its main entities, and *concept links* as the key to interoperability. The remainder of this section further describes the Component Metadata (CMD) model.

Strictly speaking, the CMD model itself provides a solution for *metadata modelling*. Its direct users are metadata modellers, not metadata creators or other “end users”. The end result of the metadata modelling process is a Profile. Such a profile acts as a complete blueprint for a *metadata record*, a document that describes one or more aspects of a resource. A record, which is per definition derived from one particular Profile, is often referred to as an *instance* of that Profile. Both the syntax and the semantics of a metadata record are defined in the Profile, which thus provides all necessary information for either creating a “valid” instance, or to interpret and verify the content of an existing CMD metadata record.

Figure 1 presents a high-level overview of this CMD model. It shows that a Profile is essentially defined by its “root Component”, which in turn can be composed of one or more additional levels of Components. These Components can be

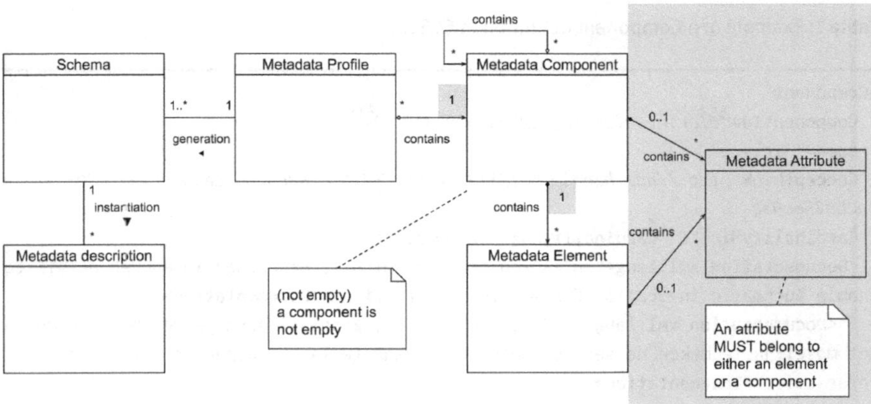

Figure 1: High level overview of the CMD model based on (TC37, Language resource management 2015) and its extension (grey parts) by (CLARIN CMDI Task Force 2014) and (TC37, Language resource management 2019).

considered the reusable "building blocks" of the CMD model. Components can be composed out of other components as well as more atomic, non-reusable constituent parts, namely Elements and Attributes, which will be explained in further detail below. Before that, it is important to point out that Components and Profiles are very similar at a technical level, that is, with regard to how they are defined, stored, and so on. The main differences are that the CMD infrastructure (1) only allows Components to be reused inside Profiles or other Components, and (2) only makes Profiles available to be used as a mechanism for creating and validating metadata records. Both Profiles and Components are published with a small amount of descriptive metadata, at which point they are assigned a unique identifier that makes it possible to reference them and use them according to their intended purpose. Section 3.3 describes how this is currently implemented in the actual infrastructure.

Components are containers that are defined by inner definitions of Components (see Table 1), Elements (see Table 2), or Attributes, or references to separately defined Components. These definitions or references are always specified with associated cardinality information – in other words, the minimum and maximum number of occurrences of the "child object" may occur in an instantiation of that Component inside a metadata record. Elements are the most common value-bearing entities; they represent a standard metadata property and allow for a "primitive" value (string, date, or numerical), or may have an associated value constraint defined by either a regular expression[1] or a closed controlled

1 https://en.wikipedia.org/wiki/Regular_expression

Table 1: Example of a Component definition in CCSL.

```
<Component
  ComponentId="clarin.eu:cr1:c_1320657629631"
  name="Service"
  ConceptLink=http://hdl.handle.net/11459/CCR_C-4159_ca0e6cba-cab5-b51a-f430-fdcb0756c9ac
  CardinalityMin="0" CardinalityMax="unbounded">
  <Documentation xml:lang="en">A web service which is described in enough detail to enable automatic invocation for machine interaction.</Documentation>
    <Documentation xml:lang="nl">Een webservice, gedetailleerd genoeg beschreven om het mogelijk te maken de service automatisch aan te laten roepen voor machine-interactie.</Documentation>
     <AttributeList>
       ...
     </AttributeList>
       ...
</Component>
```

Table 2: Example of an Element definition in CCSL.

```
<Element
  name="Name"
  ConceptLink="http://hdl.handle.net/11459/CCR_C-4160_192be757-0d8f-f4fe-b10b-d3d50de92482"
  CardinalityMin="1" CardinalityMax="1"
  ValueScheme="string"
  Multilingual="false">
    <Documentation>The name of the web service or set of web services.
</Documentation>
</Element>
```

vocabulary. The allowed number of occurrences within its parent Component can be defined freely, ranging from [0:1] to [N:unbounded], where N is any positive integer. It is also possible to associate an external vocabulary with an Element, which provides a non-constraining context for the value of the Element.

A third type of entity that can be associated with both Elements and Components is the Attribute. These entities serve a purpose similar to that of XML attributes (W3C 2008): providing contextual information to the Components or Elements to which they belong. Attributes can be defined as either optional or mandatory and have the same range of value options as Elements (primitive value, constrained by regular expression, or closed vocabulary). However, as is the case with XML attributes but unlike CMD Elements, they can never be repeated within a given context.

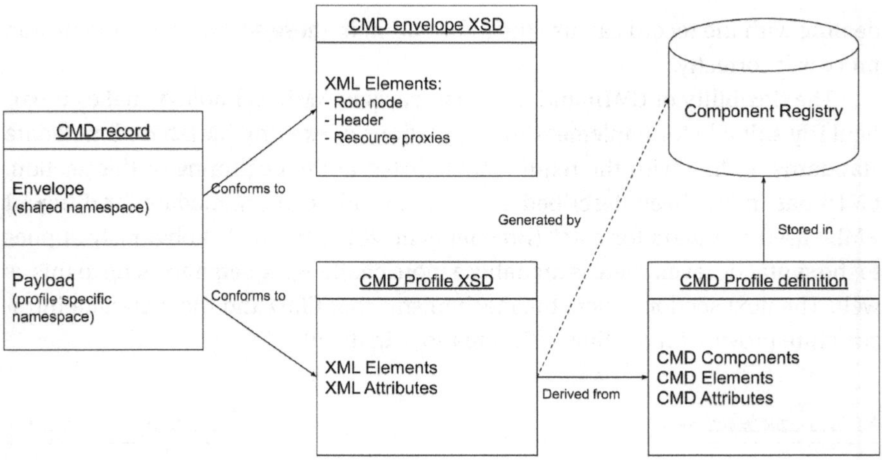

Figure 2: Main relations between a CMD record and the types of entities it depends on.

Now that the conceptual meta-model of CMD has been discussed, to facilitate a full understanding of the overall CMD "architecture" it is important to explain how this relates to the technologies underlying the implementation of CMDI, and how concrete metadata records (Profile instances) can be formed, processed, and validated in practice. Figure 2 shows the main relations between the various types of entities involved. A CMDI record is an XML document that adheres to a number of conventions that are specified in the CMDI specification (Ďurčo and Windhouwer 2013) and implemented in an XML Schema Definition (XSD). The XSD ("schema") for a CMDI record can be used to verify an XML document's compliance with the CMDI specification up to a certain level. This level is referred to as the *CMD envelope* and is uniform across all CMDI records that are based on the same version of CMDI. The envelope definition requires, among other things, the specification of a small amount of basic information about the metadata record itself and defines a standardized structure for referring to the resource(s) to which the record relates. A second level, referred to as the *payload*, is not governed by the generic envelope XSD but rather by a schema that is specific to a particular Profile. This Profile-specific schema is provided by the metadata infrastructure, which generates it automatically based on the Profile's definition – one of the tasks carried out by the Component Registry (see Section 3.3). This schema defines a valid structure of the metadata description "below" the envelope level by specifying XML elements and attributes, and their value constraints, mirroring the definition of the corresponding Profile and the Components, Elements, and Attributes of which it consists. The CMDI record is expected to refer to the generic envelope schema as well as to one profile specific schema, so that any software dealing with the record can use the information in these schemas to validate and process it correctly.

The flexibility of CMDI and its strong basis in XML technology makes it particularly suitable for implementing adaptations of existing XML-based metadata standards, in line with the requirements listed at the beginning of this section. CMDI has in fact been described as a "framework to accommodate for different XML-based metadata formats" (Broeder et al. 2011). While this obviously applies to the syntactic level, there is arguably a more challenging semantic side to this as well. The next section covers the mechanisms that CMD and the metadata infrastructure provide for dealing with semantics in detail.

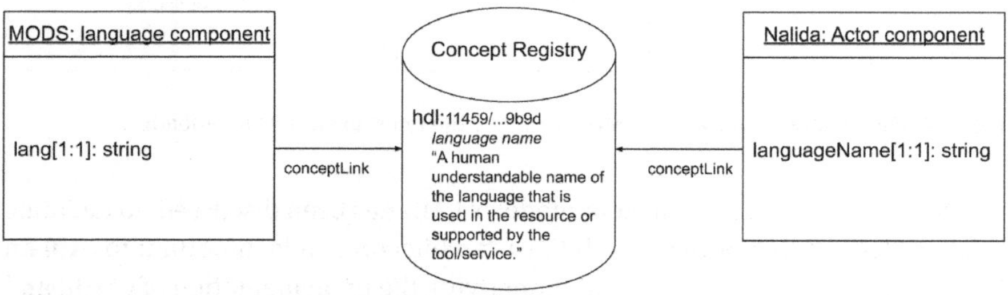

Figure 3: Example of semantic operability in the case of distinct terminology in different components. The *lang* and *languageName* properties both refer to the same, uniquely identified concept *language*.

3.2 Semantic interoperability

Components, Elements, and Attributes, as well as the individual items of a closed vocabulary, can all be annotated with a URI called the *concept link*. This URI should point to a semantic definition in a semantic registry (see Section 3.4) and is the key to CMDI's approach to semantic interoperability. In this approach the concept links allow the use of domain specific terminology for the metadata building blocks, while still sharing common semantics. For example, the concept link "http://hdl.handle.net/11459/CCR_C-2484_669684e7-cb9e-ea96-59cb-a25fe89b9b9d" can be used on both elements or attributes that use abbreviated names like *lang* or full names such as *languageName*, and thus mark them as semantically equivalent. This is illustrated in Figure 3. Through this mechanism, a common semantic overlay for the growing collection of CMD Profiles and Components emerged within several years: the CMD cloud (Ďurčo and Windhouwer 2014). As an illustration, part of this cloud is shown in Figure 4. This semantic layer can be used for harmonized processing and presentation of metadata records from many different sources. The VLO (CLARIN's central catalogue, see Section 5.1) is the primary example of this: for each of its facets, a list of concept links is defined; by using these, the path to the relevant information in a CMD record can be determined and the faceted search index populated without the need to rely on exact names or paths of metadata properties (Van Uytvanck, Stehouwer, and Lampen 2012).

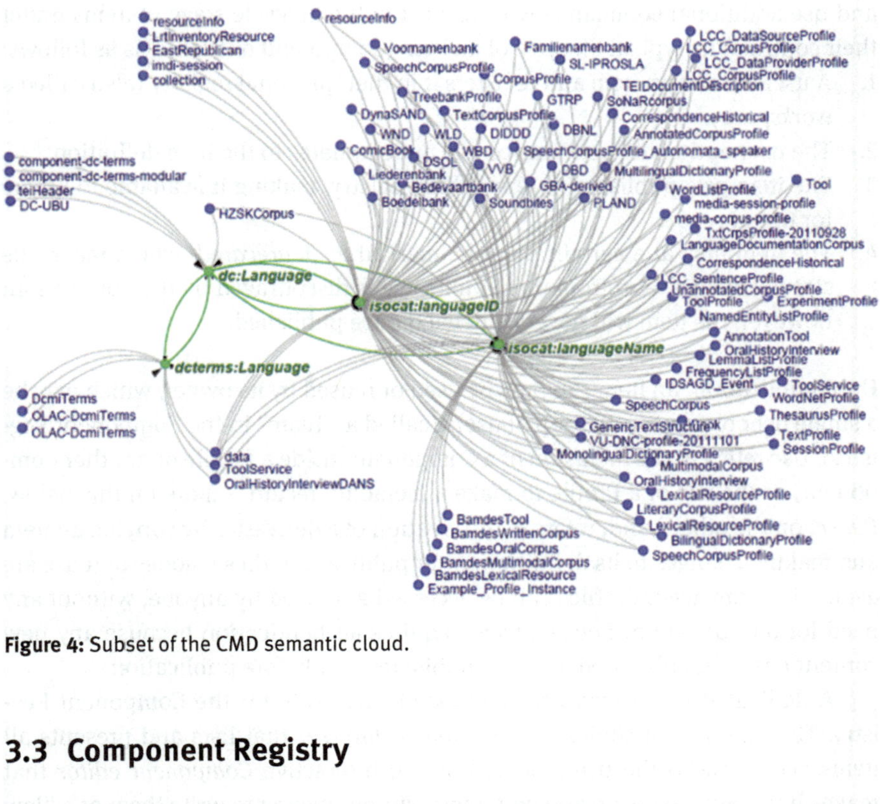

Figure 4: Subset of the CMD semantic cloud.

3.3 Component Registry

The preceding section explained how the CMD model supports flexible definitions of metadata structure and semantics, and how the component-based architecture fosters reuse. For the practical implementation of this model, CLARIN has chosen to put in operation a "nexus" that is responsible for the storage and exchange of the entities that populate the "model level" of the metadata infrastructure – that is, the Component and Profile definitions but not the metadata instances. The service that carries out these tasks is called the CMDI Component Registry, "Component Registry" for short.

The first responsibility of the Component Registry is to ingest and store Component and Profile definitions and make these available for use within the metadata infrastructure. These definitions for Components and Profiles are expressed using the dedicated CMDI Component Specification Language (CCSL). The Component Registry is implemented as a web service that exposes a set of paths that represent various sub-registries based on the common representational state transfer (REST) principles: clients can perform “create”, “read”, “update”, and “delete” operations on individual items – Component and Profile definitions – and use additional commands with respect to the lifecycle stage of items under their control. The typical lifecycle of an item (Component or Profile) is as follows:

1. A user defines an item and registers it in their personal registry (also called a *workspace*).
2. The user optionally performs one or more updates to the item definition.
3. The item gets published in the public registry, making it available to others for use or reuse.
4. The item may at a certain point be marked as *deprecated*, which means its status changes, and from there on its use is discouraged by the application; however, the item will never be deleted once published.

Until publication, an item can only be used or reused by its owner, which may be a single user or a defined group of users (called a “Team” in the Component Registry). *Use* refers to the inclusion of a Component inside a Profile or another Component, or the use of a Profile to make a metadata record – more on this below. *Reuse*, on the other hand, refers to the creation of a derivative by copying an item and making changes to its definition. After publication, these modes of reuse are available to any user. Profiles can be accessed and used by anyone, without any need for authorization. Reuse always requires authentication because any new content has to be submitted to a non-public registry before publication.

A dedicated web-based user interface is available for the Component Registry. This interface includes the *Component browser* that lists and presents all items accessible to the user, as well as the interactive *Component editor* that makes it possible to create and edit items without having to write them at a “low level”, that is, directly in the CCSL. It gives the user control over the lifecycle of individual items and provides basic support for collaboration on (sets of) Components and Profiles.

A final, crucial responsibility of the Component Registry is to serve XSDs for individual profiles. As explained earlier in this chapter, a metadata record contains a profile-specific payload section that can be validated in terms of the definition of the associated profile. In the CMD infrastructure, this validation is made possible by providing an XSD that can be generated from a CCSL profile definition by means of an XML Stylesheet (XSLT) based conversion method. This conversion is carried out by the Component Registry automatically upon request, which any client can make. The Profile specific XSD is enriched with CMD specific annotations. Thus, the XSD can be used transparently by any software that can carry out XML Schema validation to verify the correctness of a CMD record, but also by dedicated software that can use these additional annotations, for instance for semantic interpretation of the metadata in the record. Metadata editors and exploitation software such as the Virtual Language Observatory (see later in this chapter) are examples of such software making use of the enhanced XSDs.

3.4 Semantic registries

At the start of the preparatory phase, CLARIN teamed up with ISO Technical Committee 37 *Language and Terminology* to set up a semantic registry, namely, a Data Category Registry (DCR) (TC37, Terminology and other language and content resources, 2009), named ISOcat (Kemps-Snijders et al. 2009). Data categories are defined as the "result of the specification of a given data field", which means that next to a semantic definition they also contain *representation info* such as a value domain. ISOcat was accompanied by an ISO standardization process to build up a widely accepted base of common semantics. The registry was very open, allowing anyone to register the data categories they needed. This fostered not only uptake but also proliferation. Another source of proliferation was the representation information needed for a data category, for example, a /*noun*/ with a value domain for arbitrary strings was created next to a /*noun*/ that could appear as a value in a closed value domain. Unfortunately, the standardization process, which was envisioned to filter the upcoming semantics and proliferation into a coherent set of thematic profiles, did not take off. This resulted in CLARIN and TC37 deciding to part ways in 2015 (Wright et al. 2014). The data categories relevant to CLARIN were stripped of their data category specific properties (i.e., representation info), and transformed into SKOS concepts and imported into the OpenSKOS-based (Brugman and Lindeman 2012) CLARIN Concept Registry (CCR) (Schuurman, Windhouwer, Ohren, & Zeman, 2015). SKOS stands for Simple Knowledge Organization Scheme and is a recommendation from W3C, which enables the construction of a lightweight knowledge base. A group of CCR coordinators was assembled to manage the content of the CCR. TC37 also reassessed and rearranged ISOcat, resulting in a new Data Category Repository (Warburton and Wright 2020). This decade of work on shared semantics shows that the development of semantic registries is still an ongoing process and has not reached a stable state yet (Chiarcos, Fäth, and Abromeit 2020). The main problematic issues are, however, organizational – that is, channelling the knowledge embedded in the community into widely accepted shared semantics – and are not so much on the technical side.

In parallel to the DCR, a vocabulary registry named CLAVAS was developed (Brugman 2017). Like the CCR it has also been implemented on top of OpenSKOS. In CMDI 1.2 (see Section 4), it became possible to refer to CLAVAS in the specification of an open or closed vocabulary value domain. At time of writing, 2021, both CLAVAS and the CCR are moving to SKOSMOS (Suominen et al. 2015) as an implementation platform. Research and experiments in opening the infrastructure to more vocabulary servers than just CLAVAS are also ongoing.

Another registry that is currently under development is the Relation Registry, which is a new implementation of RELcat (Windhouwer 2012), a companion registry for ISOcat that was never released. In this registry, various views – either individual or community-based – on how concepts or terms relate to each other can be stored. CLAVAS contains, for example, a huge vocabulary of the languages of the world based on ISO 639-3 (SIL 2021). To navigate this vocabulary, one can group the languages in language families; however, there is no single generally agreed upon taxonomy of language families. In the Relation Registry various of these taxonomies can be stored and overlaid over the CLAVAS language vocabulary and be used by metadata creators to browse the vocabulary.

3.5 Harvesting

The process of collecting all the metadata records in the CLARIN infrastructure and beyond is called *metadata harvesting*. For this process, the OAI PMH protocol is used (OAI 2015). CLARIN build a powerful OAI-PMH harvester (Van Uytvanck, Stehouwer, and Lampen, 2012), the key features of which include:

1. Endpoints can be taken from the harvester's configuration, but also dynamically requested from the CLARIN Centre Registry (CLARIN ERIC 2021a), (Dima et al. 2012), the authoritative source of information on centres which are part of the CLARIN network.
2. Easy and flexible configuration of a chain of actions to take on specific types of metadata, including XSL Transformations (W3C 2021) to CMDI from other formats.
3. Technical connection parameters for the harvest can be set globally for all centres as well as being specific to a centre, which over the years has led to a very robust and reliable harvesting process.
4. By using various combinations of OAI PMH API methods, several harvesting scenarios have been implemented that can be optionally tweaked on the level of individual endpoints.

Recently a viewer has been added, which allows centres to inspect their metadata records as they were harvested by CLARIN, and to access log files for the harvest of their endpoints.

Once all metadata is collected and available in the CMDI 1.2 format, which currently is the latest version of the CMDI specification, the output of this process can be processed by the VLO importer. The VLO importer uses the semantic registry, that is, the CCR (see Section 3.4), to fill the faceted index (see Section 5.1). This pipeline is illustrated in Figure 5.

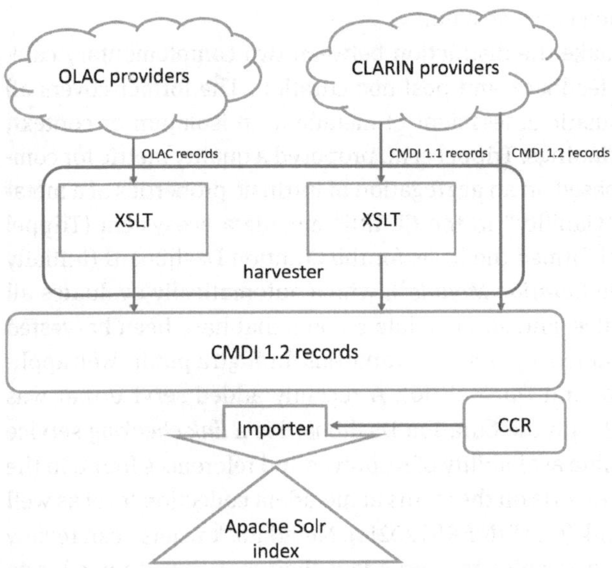

Figure 5: The harvesting and ingesting pipeline.

3.6 Curation solutions

Issues related to metadata quality can, and therefore in practice will exist at many levels; for instance, the correctness, accuracy, or completeness of the information in an individual metadata record may be less than desirable. Or if the information is correct and complete, it may not be encoded in line with community standards. In the context of aggregation, it may become apparent that different community standards may differ and possibly even clash. While metadata quality is hard to define in absolute terms, it is possible to look at the main user tasks that depend on metadata and can therefore be impacted by issues in the metadata: finding resources, identifying resources, selecting resources, and acquiring access to resources (Bruce and Hillmann 2004). In concrete terms, within the CLARIN infrastructure, such issues may play out as a regression in functionality of services such as the VLO (see Section 5.1), the Language Resource Switchboard (Zinn and Dima 2022), and repository, cataloguing or linguistic processing solutions that rely on metadata for their functioning. For this reason, it has long been recognized that an active approach is required to resolve or mitigate metadata quality issues to the extent that an acceptable quality of service can be guaranteed for the (potentially) "vulnerable" services. Here, the umbrella term of *metadata curation* will be used to refer to such types of actions.

In general, we can make the distinction between two complementary categories of action: quality feedback and post-hoc curation. The former covers all forms of manual or automatic assessment of metadata, in isolation or context, and the reporting of any findings. Trippel et al. proposed a quality metric for component metadata that is based on an aggregation of intrinsic properties of a metadata document and its "viability" in the CLARIN metadata ecosystem (Trippel et al. 2014). This proposal formed the basis for the Curation Dashboard (initially deployed under the name *Curation Module*[2]), which automatically evaluates all published metadata profiles, and all metadata records that have been harvested for the VLO, and offers detailed reports of this analysis through a public web application (Ostojic, Sugimoto, and Ďurčo 2016). A recently added service that was designed to be integrated with the Curation Dashboard is a *link checking* service that keeps track of the online availability of resources and references found in the harvested metadata, and reports on the status at metadata collection level as well as that of the individual link (CLARIN ERIC 2021c). Metadata "owners" can review the reports in the Curation Dashboard, and adapt their metadata as needed to increase its potential for discoverability and processing as well as presentation to metadata users in the CLARIN infrastructure.

There also exist more manual types of quality feedback; an expert assuming a *curator* role may evaluate records or entire collections, either as part of curation activities or in response to reports by users or metadata owners themselves, and report issues or suggestions for improvements to the metadata owners. Some tools have been developed over the years that can aid curators in their evaluation tasks by visualizing the metadata space and making it navigable. The SMC browser (Ďurčo and Windhouwer 2013) and an adapted, dedicated curation instance of the VLO, both developed at ACDH-ÖAW, are examples of such tools.

2 The Curation Dashboard is publicly accessible at https://curation.clarin.eu.

The second category of action – i.e., post-hoc curation – depends on analysis by curators, who can be aided by specialized tools in their task as well. It differs from quality feedback in that metadata collections, records, or values are filtered or transformed at a point in the retrieval and processing pipeline, and such alterations have "downstream" effects only. In practice, post-hoc curation takes place in the context of the VLO. The VLO importer is able to apply a set of so-called *value mapping definitions* that are stored and maintained in a shared, publicly accessible location. The curators who maintain these definitions can specify targets for values or patterns in a specific context (i.e., the facet to which the value was mapped). Thus, problematic values can be corrected, removed, or moved to a different context. This type of post-hoc curation through mapping definitions has taken place over the years by members of a dedicated task force of the SCTCC. The programmatic, facet-specific post-processing that takes place in the VLO importer could also be considered a form of post-hoc curation (see Sections 3.6 and 5.1).

4 CLARIN's expanding metadata landscape

As CLARIN's preparatory phase was coming to a close (around 2011), the CMDI "proposition" was in a good position to support wider adoption by metadata end users, and also, at the same time, the enhancement and extension of CMDI based metadata exploitation within the broader CLARIN infrastructure. A CMDI toolkit had been developed to a mature state, and on that basis a set of stable and reliably operated infrastructure components had been implemented. These made it possible to model and author metadata without the need for specialized technical skills with respect to, for instance, XML technologies and APIs. Documentation materials were prepared, and training sessions were being organized by the centres responsible for maintaining the CMDI stack as well as within the national consortia. A metadata exchange (providing/harvesting) pipeline had been put in place, and those centres providing metadata could see their records presented and made discoverable in several catalogues, including an early version of the Virtual Language Observatory. At the national consortia, the metadata providing centres increasingly used repository solutions that had been developed or adapted to support the ingestion, storage, and/or dissemination of CMDI metadata.

The implementation of tailor-made metadata Components and Profiles ensured a workable degree of interoperability with other (existing or newly developed) metadata standards and frameworks. For example, OLAC (Bird & Simons, 2003), IMDI (Broeder and Wittenburg 2006), TEI header (Giordano, 1995) (Hansen, Offersgaard, and Olsen 2014), MODS (Guenther 2003) and the Europeana Data

Model (Doerr et al. 2010; Goosen 2017) are among standards that over the years have been given support within the CMDI ecosystem through the implementation of dedicated profiles and conversion logic, in either one or both directions. In the same period, during which CMDI was growing substantially, other initiatives were also ongoing that had significant relevance to metadata for (among other domains) language resources. Several CLARIN centres are part of the META-SHARE network, which offers the META-SHARE model capable of describing various common types of language resources (Piperidis 2012). From an early stage on, this model was also implemented as a set of CMDI components and profiles, thus offering CMDI interoperability for those building their repository and metadata solution on the META-SHARE platform. The META-SHARE model and parts of its CMDI implementation were also used as a basis for the default profile used in the CLARIN DSpace repository solution (Straňák, Košarko, and Mišutka 2019) which was developed at LINDAT (CLARIAH-CZ) and is currently used by multiple other CLARIN centres (see Section 5.3). Other important standards for metadata that have emerged or gained significant traction within the SSH domain since the introduction of CMDI are CIDOC CRM and its extensions, developed in the Parthenos project (Bruseker, Doerr, and Theodoriou 2017); (Ďurčo, Lorenzini, and Sugimoto 2017), and DDI (Vardigan 2014); and in the broader research data content we can mention the DataCite schema (closely associated with DOIs for data(sets)) (Neumann and Brase 2014), DCAT (Albertoni et al. 2020) and Schema.org (Guha, Brickley, and Macbeth 2016).

As the distribution of CMDI metadata through the conversion of existing records as well as the creation of new metadata "from scratch" took off, the number of harvested records started to increase steadily from this point on. As can be seen in Figure 6, the VLO had about 111,000 records in its index in 2011 and crossed the million-records mark in 2017. A strong increase in the number of components and profiles could be observed in the years 2012 to 2014 (see Figure 7).

While the uptake of CMDI by the CLARIN community can be considered a success, certain risks were also identified – in particular that of *proliferation* of profiles and components in the Component Registry (see, e.g., Goosen et al. 2014). Although CMDI has been specifically designed to cope with a high degree of metadata heterogeneity, in practice certain costs can be expected in terms of maintenance and curation in the exploitation stack in relation to the number of profiles on which actual metadata is based, and the overall degree of heterogeneity. Moreover, the new, community-designed components and profiles turned out not to be of uniformly high quality. Tools and strategies were discussed and implemented to keep a grip on the evolving metadata (component) landscape. An early example of such a tool was the SMC browser (Ďurčo and Windhouwer 2013) which visualizes the existing data categories (later concepts), Components and Profiles

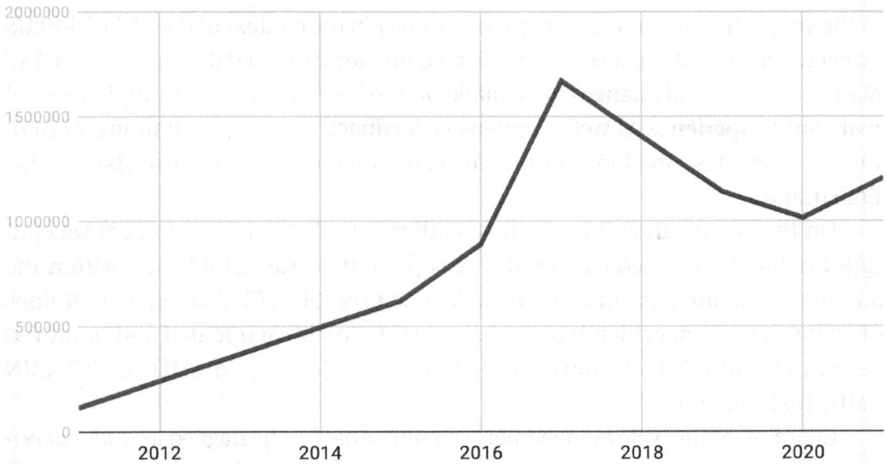

Figure 6: Development of the total number of records in the VLO since 2012.

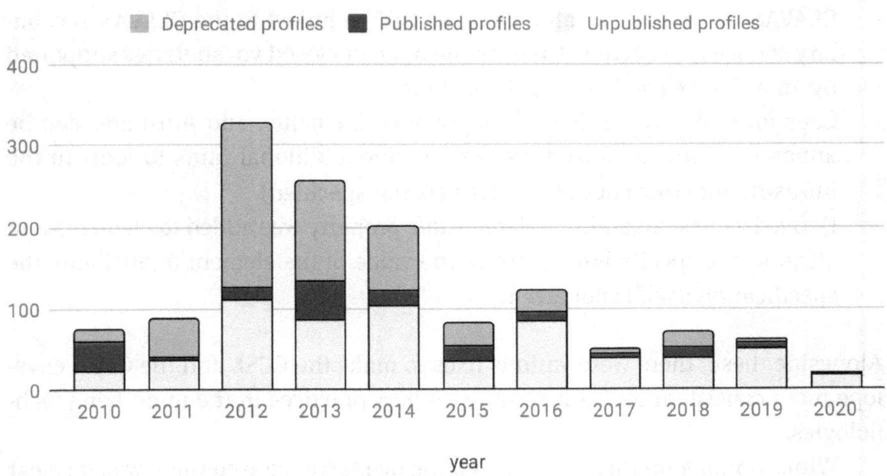

Figure 7: Number of registered profiles by registration year and current (2021) status.

and their relations and allows for interactive navigation and filtering. Section 3.6 covers tooling for monitoring and curation in more detail. Section 6 will further discuss proliferation and related challenges, and how these have been mitigated and may be addressed in the future.

Developments on the "core" of CMDI and the centralized infrastructure components – harvesting, search and discovery, integration with processing solutions in the wider infrastructure, and streamlined curation solutions – picked up pace in the years after the preparatory phase, largely in the context of the CLARIN-PLUS project, which contained several dedicated metadata-related development tasks.[3] Many additions and changes were made on the basis of by then multiple years of real-world experience as well as extensive feedback from the community. Most of the solutions described in Section 5 reached a more or less mature state in this time frame.

On the organizational level, the coordination of CMDI development was put into the hands of a dedicated *CMDI task force* that was established within the *Standing Committee for CLARIN Technical Centres* (SCCTC). Among its first lines of action was the specification and implementation of an updated and improved version of CMDI. This resulted in the following additions in CMDI 1.2 (CLARIN CMDI Task Force 2014):

- Component lifecycle management: components can be flagged as *under development*, *in production* or *deprecated*, and linked to other components with *derived from* or *succeeding* relations.
- Mandatory Attributes: Attributes can be either optional or mandatory.
- CLAVAS vocabularies: value domains can be linked to the CLAVAS vocabulary service (see Section 3.4) to create open or closed vocabularies supported by an API to be used by metadata editors.
- Cues for tools: in the CCSL, Components, Elements, and Attributes can be annotated with *cue* attributes that provide additional hints to tools in the infrastructure (the cues themselves are not specified).
- Derived values: an additional *autovalue* property was added to elements and attributes to specify how to derive the value of the element or attribute, the specification itself is not given.

Alongside these, there were various fixes to make the CCSL and the CMDI envelope more consistent and compliant with best practices in the underlying technologies.

While working on this new version, the taskforce realised there was no clear specification of CMDI. Instead, documentation existed in the form of various distributed web pages, some of which were public, but many only accessible to CLARIN developers. For CMDI 1.2, therefore, an elaborate formal specification was written (CLARIN CMDI Task Force 2016). Care was taken to avoid making the specification CLARIN-specific, but rather use CLARIN specific approaches as illustrative examples – thus making it clear that CMDI is ready to be taken up by

3 For detailed reports regarding the activities in CLARIN-PLUS, see https://www.clarin.eu/content/clarin-plus-deliverables.

other communities (Windhouwer et al. 2016). The CMDI taskforce subsequently teamed up with the Metadata Curation taskforce in documenting these CLARIN best practices in a continuously maintained guide (CLARIN CMDI and Metadata Curation Task Forces 2019).

Parallel to these efforts within CLARIN, work was started to get CMDI standardized (Broeder et al. 2012) within ISO TC37. The work plan was accepted to create a family, ISO 24622, of three related standards:

1. for the component metadata model, which was published in 2015 (TC37, Language resource management, 2015) (see also Figure 1, except for the grey parts);
2. for a possible instantiation of this model, which was based on the CMDI 1.2 specification (CLARIN CMDI Task Force 2016) and published in 2019 (TC37, Language resource management 2019) (see also Figure 1);
3. for a core set of components, which is, at time of writing, still under construction.

In line with this last part of the CMDI standards family, the CMDI task force is, at time of writing, working on a set of core components that will be tagged as recommended in the Component Registry.

5 Component Metadata for the end user

5.1 Virtual Language Observatory

Since its introduction in 2010, the Virtual Language Observatory (VLO) has played a central role in CLARIN's infrastructure as a means of discovering language resources and technology. In their first extensive paper describing the features and workings of the VLO, Van Uytvanck, Stehouwer, and Lampen lay out the need for such a solution:

> In the era of the digital data deluge, a researcher needs efficient ways to navigate to the language resources that really matter, whatever the selection criterion is. A plethora of resource inventories and catalogues has been proposed to address this need. The challenge that comes with [the component metadata approach] is providing a uniform and easy to use interface to search in the resulting meta-data records.
>
> (Van Uytvanck, Stehouwer, and Lampen 2012)

The name of the VLO is a reference to other *virtual observatories* that already existed at the time: "in analogy with the astronomical virtual observatories . . ., [the VLO] tries to give a consistent online overview of the data that is available at a variety of computing centres" (Van Uytvanck et al. 2010). Early versions of the VLO were designed with a primary focus on exploration and visualization of variations among different aspects of the resources. Furthermore, the VLO offered two distinct views: one offering geographic exploration by means of a Google Earth overlay, and one allowing for narrowing down the search space according to the *faceted browsing* paradigm. The former view was later abandoned, while the latter evolved into the version of the VLO that is currently available and actively maintained by CLARIN ERIC.[4]

Faceted browsing or *faceted search* is a means of presenting different categories – referred to as *facets* in this context – within which each individual potential search result item is classified. The values within each of the categories are presented to the user, along with a number indicating the amount of available matches; upon selection of one or more of these facet values by the user, the search results are limited to the records that have been classified as matching the selection. For instance, a resource in the VLO may be classified as pertaining to the language "French", country "Cameroon", and resource types "Audio" and "Text". One means by which a user might discover this resource is by selecting *{country: 'Cameroon'}*; this will not only reduce the search results to items pertaining to this specific country but will also restrict the values shown in other facets, such as language, to values that occur within the remaining search results. By presenting these values in order of occurrence along with the number of matching items, a user can quickly gain an understanding of a specific "landscape" of available resources. For instance, the VLO might prominently display filter options such as the languages Gyele, Wuzlam, Bafia, Vute, and Kwasio after this one particular selection within the country facet (see Figure 8).

The above illustrates the possibilities of resource exploration. As is common for this type of interface, the VLO combines the faceted browser approach with a "free" search option, allowing users to enter search terms or a more complex query, which is then applied to all the available items, optionally in conjunction with one or more facet selections. In earlier versions, the VLO very prominently showed the facets and their values, with a relatively small search box and a list of titles of search results only to the side. This design made it easy to "observe" the landscape, but wasn't very well suited for browsing through individual resource descriptions or carrying out more targeted searches. In a later version (Goosen and Eckart 2014), the design and functionality of the VLO was adapted to be more like that of faceted browser interfaces commonly applied in, for example, library

4 The VLO is publicly accessible at https://vlo.clarin.eu.

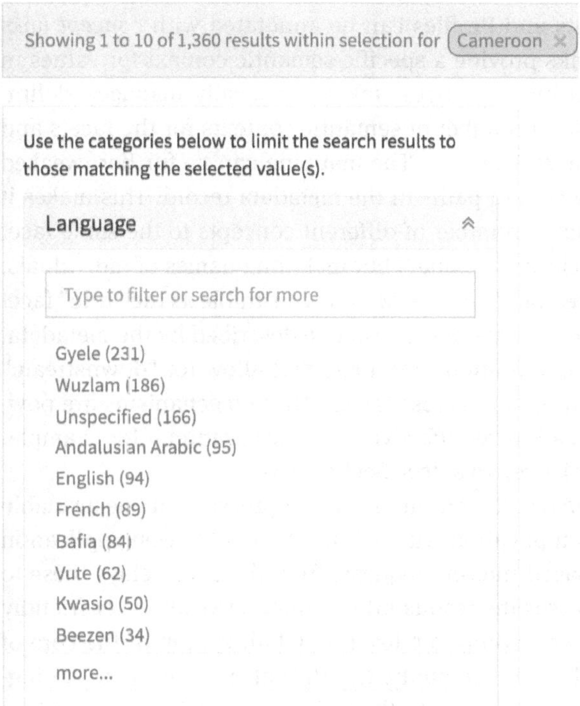

Figure 8: An example of available values being displayed for a single facet (screenshot from the VLO).

catalogues and online shops, with more space allocated for search results with additional details and a prominent free text search box.

The VLO as an application is at the end the metadata distribution and processing pipeline described in Section 3.5. Every time new or updated metadata has been gathered by the harvester, all available metadata is *processed* for *indexation* by the so-called *VLO importer. Processing* here means extracting, post-processing, and normalizing information from the metadata records, while *indexation* refers to the ingestion of the processed data into a dedicated data store that is optimized for search and retrieval – for this, the current version of the VLO uses Apache Solr (The Apache Software Foundation, 2021). While the indexing software is an "off-the-shelf" product, the processing that precedes it is highly specific to CMDI and, in particular, takes advantage of the semantic interoperability features of Component Metadata.

The process of extracting facet values from CMDI records by the VLO importer is based on a *concept-facet mapping* mechanism. As described in Section 3.2, definitions of CMDI Components and Profiles can be annotated with *concept links* at different levels. These links provide a specific semantic context for values in metadata records. The VLO import process takes a centrally managed definition as input, which specifies a number of semantic contexts for the facets and other fields that exist in the VLO's index. The mapping can be further tweaked by including or blacklisting certain paths in the metadata record. This makes it possible to, for instance, map a number of different concepts to the same facet "title" (for instance, also including "name") but including names of individuals, institutions, or titles of related publications, which is desirable as the "title" facet should only contain the title or name of the resource described by the metadata. The VLO contains additional definitions and logic that allow for "downstream" processing and mapping within and across facets. These mechanisms are powerful and flexible enough to allow for effective post-hoc curation – for example, value harmonization and noise removal (see Section 3.6).

The indexed information resulting from the import process is made available to end users through a web application. The publicly accessible web application takes search and/or facet-based filtering requests from the user, relays these to the Solr backend, and processes the results into an interactive and user-friendly "view" on the metadata at an appropriate level of detail. On top of the core of search and discovery enabling functionality, the VLO also serves as a "springboard" for further processing of metadata through other services provided by CLARIN and others. At time of writing, it integrates two essential CLARIN services: the Language Resource Switchboard (Zinn and Dima 2022), and the Virtual Collection Registry (Elbers 2017). These services and the broader CLARIN services "tapestry" is discussed in more detail in de Jong et al. (2022).

5.2 Modelling, authoring, and editing

When it comes to the *creation* of CMDI, a number of distinctions can be identified. A primary distinction is that between, on the one hand, what is generally referred to in the context of CMDI as *modelling*, and on the other hand, the creation of metadata records, or *authoring*. "Modelling" refers to the definition of CMD Components and Profiles. For the end user, this can exclusively be done through the Component Registry and its built-in component editor. As this has already been discussed in detail in Section 3.3, for the remainder of this section we will focus on the creation of metadata records.

Metadata records can have a variety of origins. They may be "primary" records, that is, created as such by a metadata author with or without assistance from dedicated software for metadata creation. They may also be "secondary", that is, a reflection of information that was obtained from one or more primary sources. Such a primary source may be a database, for which export logic is available that is capable of generating a metadata record with values from the database; it may also be a metadata record that is compliant with a different standard, in which case logic and/or mapping definitions are used to convert the original record into the target format. Both the primary and secondary type of origin can be found among the CMDI records that are harvested at regular intervals by CLARIN.

The CCSL and the CMDI toolkit make it possible to know the valid structure and all constraints in the context of a specific profile, and to verify the syntactic validity of a given CMDI record in terms of the profile definition. Metadata authors who have the skills and willingness to work with XML technology can therefore use their preferred generic tools and applications to produce CMDI instances. However, it was recognized at an early stage that there is a need for convenient and reliable means to create CMDI records for users with limited technical skills as well. A number of solutions addressing this need were introduced in the first few years after the introduction of CMDI. At a very early stage, Arbil (Withers 2012; Defina 2014), a desktop application originally designed as an editor for the IMDI metadata format, was extended to provide general support for CMDI as well, by which we mean that CMDI records based on any Profile could be opened, edited, and exported using the application. A few years later, the web-based editor ProFormA (Dima et al. 2012) was introduced. It builds heavily on existing XML-centred standards and tools, and was designed in a modular fashion as a set of web services, so as to allow for easy integration into, for instance, third party repository systems. In contrast to Arbil, it had to be customized for the use of specific Profiles, and therefore the end user could not load or edit arbitrary metadata records using ProFormA. Both Arbil and ProFormA are currently no longer maintained or supported.

In the following years, two new editors were introduced. CMDI-Maker (CLASS – Cologne Language Archive Services 2018) is a browser-based editor that is designed to be easy to use and to keep working in offline situations (e.g., for data elicitation in a field work context). Like ProFormA, its use is limited to a predefined set of Profiles. COMEDI (Lyse, Meurer, and De Smedt 2015) is also a web-based editor; while lacking support for offline usage, it can deal with arbitrary Profiles and is arguably the most powerful and feature-rich editor currently under active maintenance.

All of the editors mentioned above support CMDI 1.1; however there is currently no production-ready editor that (also) supports CMDI 1.2. A new version of COMEDI is planned, which will have several enhancements including support for CMDI 1.2, but it is not yet available at the time of writing. The same applies to CLARIAH CMDI Forms (Zeeman and Windhouwer 2018), which is currently under development and will also offer a web-based solution for creating and editing

CMDI. By design, it supports any CMD Profile and aims to exploit several of the features introduced in CMDI 1.2, including cues for tools and automatic values. As a unique feature, it promises to provide a solution for "tweaking" any profile by means of an additional, external definition that acts as a functional "overlay" that can, for instance, define additional labels, validation conditions, cues, and value derivation rules. Integration into third party environments such as repositories is foreseen.

There also exists a variety of complete or partial solutions that cannot properly be classified as editors but nevertheless offer a means of creating CMDI compliant metadata without requiring specialized skills. Many of the metadata repositories used within the wider CLARIN infrastructure have some kind of form-based metadata creation and/or editing possibilities. In those cases, metadata properties are generally stored in a database or some repository-specific format that is not specific to CMDI, but the repository system will allow users and aggregators to retrieve a CMDI-compliant representation of the metadata. An example of a somewhat different approach towards CMDI generation is Coala (Kisler et al. 2016). It works on the basis of a specifically defined set of tabular data structures. Users can upload their compliant data files to a conversion service, which will then produce CMDI renderings of the same data.

With the availability of a number of conversion solutions, users can of course also create metadata in a supported other format using the applicable tools and methods for that format, and then, where required by the infrastructure, offer the conversion output instead of the original. As mentioned in Section 3.5, CLARIN can harvest a number of other formats, and carries out the necessary conversion to CMDI on its side.

5.3 Repositories

CLARIN centres store their valuable language resources in a safe and sustainable way. In general, it means that they are managed by means of a dedicated repository system. Such systems generally allow the description of the stored resources with metadata; however, the broadly available generic repository systems did not support CMDI. Additionally, centres were and are free to choose the repository system that meets their needs. So various solutions for supporting CMDI in repositories came into existence. As the MPI for psycholinguistics was, to a large extent, the birthplace of CMDI, it was also the first to support CMDI. Their repository system, LAT (Wittenburg, Skiba, and Trilsbeek 2005), had been built around IMDI (Broeder and Wittenburg 2006; MPI 2020) but the institute enabled their OAI-PMH endpoint to also provide this metadata converted into CMDI. With the growth of CMDI the repository became "hybrid", that is, supporting both IMDI and CMDI at the point of ingestion. More recently LAT was replaced by FLAT (Trilsbeek and Windhouwer 2016), which is based on Fedora (DuraSpace 2021), a generic repository system, and is completely built around CMDI. Fedora has been used by many other centres as well, especially in Germany during the first CLARIN-D project when many repositories were set up.

At LINDAT in Czechia, they decided to base their repository on DSpace (DuraSpace 2021). Like the MPI, LINDAT also extended the OAI-PMH endpoint with support for providing CMDI by converting DSpace's internal metadata model. The resulting LINDAT DSpace, which includes many more tweaks to tailor DSpace for use by CLARIN centres, was later rebranded as CLARIN DSpace (Mišutka 2016). This repository setup has become a popular choice among centres who have newly joined CLARIN and wish to store and provide resources with metadata.

CLARIN B-centres register their choice of repository system in the Centre Registry (Dima et al. 2012). At time of writing, Fedora and DSpace are numbers 1 and 2, with 9 and 8 mentions, respectively. The long tail is formed by custom builds, META-SHARE and the generic version control system Git. The META-SHARE repository was built as part of the META-SHARE project (Piperidis 2012). They adopted a component-based approach and created several profiles and components matching their metadata model in the Component Registry and made it possible to harvest the metadata as CMDI from the repository's OAI-PMH endpoint.

6 Challenges and future for CMDI

By its nature, the Component Metadata Infrastructure is one that needs some degree of continual maintenance, perhaps even more so than is the case for more "rigid" metadata frameworks. Its foremost strength – flexibility – is also a weakness in that the CMDI landscape can become polluted and fragmented relatively easily. However, we believe that by directing attention to the right aspects – both technical and community-related – the ecosystem can remain sufficiently clean and healthy that it does not require more than a sustainable amount of ongoing attention and maintenance.

One of the main lessons learned over the years is that users want and need guidance. In the first few years of CMDI, the community was quite small, and shared visions and "unwritten guidelines" made for relatively low entropy; but when more and larger communities started using CMDI, a varied landscape of practices, conventions, and vocabularies took shape. Due to the proliferation observed in the Component Registry, it became harder for modellers to choose fitting Components and for metadata authors to know which Profile to use for their records. Moreover, unsupervised reuse also meant that quality issues could easily arise and propagate. Although several available solutions for metadata curation have been discussed, there is a practical limit to the extent to which these can be applied, and it is more effective and efficient to address issues at the root. Therefore, a number of more recent, centrally coordinated efforts have been aimed at mitigating these issues; these include support for component lifecycle in CMDI 1.2 and the Component Registry and the publication of a *CMDI best practices guide*.

A still-ongoing activity is the development of a set of *Core Components* and recommended Profiles based on these components (CLARIN ERIC 2021b). The objective is to present the Core Components as the default choice for metadata modellers and authors. These can be considered an implementation of CMDI best practices. They also provide an opportunity to "push" Components and Profiles that maximally encourage FAIR (Wilkinson, Dumontier, and Mons 2016) metadata through the inclusion of mandatory or recommended metadata properties pertaining to findability, accessibility, interoperability, and reusability aspects, such as identifiers for all referenceable entities and licensing information, and the use of FAIR vocabularies for value domains. During and after the development of the Core Components, they will also be tested and optimized for discoverability and presentation in CLARIN's core services, such as the VLO. At the same time, Core Components can receive dedicated attention on the exploitation side (e.g., in the VLO). By supporting newly introduced conventions and harnessing the additional information provided by linked FAIR vocabularies, search and discoverability can be improved. In a similar way, Core Components can also serve as a pivot for alignment between editors, and editing features can be built on top of these to improve the experience of the metadata author.

There are also potential improvements that require changes at a more technically fundamental level (i.e., the specification of CMDI, the core toolkit) but also conventions with respect to the representation of metadata. The following are few potential additions or changes to the CMDI framework that can realistically be applied in a minor update:

1. Support for foreign namespaces in metadata records would make CMDI more extensible and enable ways of achieving interoperability with other standards.
2. Multilinguality in metadata could be better supported than it currently is.
3. A default solution for provenance metadata is currently lacking.
4. There is no standard way of specifying a license for a metadata record.

While XML was the dominant exchange format in the years the work on CMDI started, the dominant format nowadays is JSON and especially the linked data variant JSON-LD. As the CMD metamodel (Figure 1) is oblivious to the representation format, CCSL can be converted in a schema language other than XSD, and concept links can function as predicates, a pilot was undertaken to convert the CMD profiles and components to RDFS and the harvested records into RDF (Windhouwer, Indarto, and Broeder 2017). This conversion worked reasonably well but also revealed that the existence of the XML-inspired feature of attributes leads to problems and a counterintuitive mapping into RDF. In a future version of CMDI, the support for attributes might be dropped or at least discouraged to enable an easier alignment with the Linked Data cloud. Next to the CCR, Schema.org (Guha, Brickley, and Macbeth 2016) could function as a stable source for concept links, making the step to Linked Data even easier.

Other metadata schemes have arisen alongside CMDI, for example, DCAT (Albertoni et al. 2020) and DataCite (DataCite 2021). Two possible strategies exist for CMDI to cooperate with them:

1. create matching components and profiles, as was done for, e.g., IMDI and TEI Header in the past;
2. use the Core Components currently being created to map to or from.

Although metadata is in general already open, CMDI can assist centres in making their metadata and resources (more) FAIR. Once more, the new Core Components play an important role there, for instance by stressing the need to make explicit the license under which resources are available. Another area where the FAIR properties of CMDI are being strengthened is in vocabularies, for example, by making it easier to reuse existing vocabularies and thus discouraging the need to create new proprietary vocabularies. FAIR Digital Objects (FAIRDO Forum Steering Committee 2021) are the next concepts being hashed out and core CMDI developers are involved to take CMDI into this next phase of making resources findable, accessible, interoperable, and reusable for the scientific community.

7 Conclusion

This chapter has shown how CMDI has served the CLARIN community well in the last decade. Hardened by real world usage it has become reliable, versatile, and stable. The statistics in Section 4 show that the extent of CMDI in the form of providers and records has grown over the years, supported by research data repositories and metadata editors. With the creation of the Component Metadata Infrastructure, CLARIN has thus added a versatile metadata ecosystem to its infrastructure. It has been able to incorporate the already existing LRT metadata landscape when it came to life, and adapt well to this changing landscape while it matured. With core components and FAIR vocabularies in the pipeline, CMDI is ready to take on new challenges to optimally situate the CLARIN community and its resources within the continuously expanding global metadata network of research objects.

Bibliography

Albertoni, Riccardo, David Browning, Simon Cox, Alejandra Gonzalez Beltran, Andrea Perego & Peter Winstanley. 2020. *Data Catalog Vocabulary (DCAT) – Version 2.* W3C. https://www.w3.org/TR/vocab-dcat-2/ (accessed 27 March 2022).

Bird, Steven & Gary Simons. 2003. Extending Dublin Core metadata to support the description and discovery of language resources. *Computers and the Humanities* 37 (4). 375–388.

Broeder, Daan, Thierry Declerck, Erhard Hinrichs, Stelios Piperidis, Laurent Romary, Nicoletta Calzolari & Peter Wittenburg. 2008. Foundation of a component-based flexible registry for language resources and technology. *International Conference on Language Resources and Evaluation (LREC)* 6: 1433–1436.

Broeder, Daan, Marc Kemps-Snijders, Dieter Van Uytvanck, Menzo Windhouwer, Peter Withers, Peter Wittenburg & Claus Zinn. 2010. A data category registry- and component-based metadata framework. *International Conference on Language Resources and Evaluation (LREC)* 7: 43–47.

Broeder, Daan, Oliver Schonefeld, Thorsten Trippel, Dieter Van Uytvanck & Witt, Andreas. 2011. A pragmatic approach to XML interoperability: The Component Metadata Infrastructure (CMDI. *Balisage: The Markup Conference* 7. https://doi.org/10.4242/BalisageVol7.Broeder01.

Broeder, Daan, Dieter Van Uytvanck, Menzo Windhouwer, Maria Gavrilidou & Thorsten Trippel. 2012. Standardizing a component metadata infrastructure. *International Conference on Language Resources and Evaluation (LREC)* 8: 1387–1340.

Broeder, Daan & Peter Wittenburg. 2006. The IMDI metadata framework, its current application and future direction. *International Journal of Metadata, Semantics and Ontologies* 1 (2). 119–132.

Bruce, Thomas R. & Diane I. Hillmann. 2004. The continuum of metadata quality: Defining, expressing, exploiting. In Diane I. Hillmann & Elaine L. Westbrooks (eds.), *Metadata in practice*, 238–256. Chicago: American Library Association.

Brugman, Hennie. 2017. CLAVAS: A CLARIN vocabulary and alignment service. In Jan Odijk & Arjen van Hessen (eds.), *CLARIN in the Low Countries*, 61–70. London: Ubiquity Press.

Brugman, Hennie & Mark Lindeman. 2012. Publishing and exploiting vocabularies using the OpenSKOS. *Describing Language Resources with Metadata Workshop*. Istanbul, 22 May.

Bruseker, George, Martin Doerr & Maria Theodoriou. 2017. *Report on the common semantic framework (D5.1)*. Parthenos. https://doi.org/10.5281/zenodo.2668433 (accessed 27 March 2022)

Chiarcos, Christian, Christian Fäth & Frank Abromeit. 2020. Annotation interoperability for the post-ISOCat era. *Language Resources and Evaluation Conference (LREC)* 12: 5668–5677.

CLARIN CMDI and Metadata Curation Task Forces. 2019. *CLARIN's CMDI Best Practices Guide*. CLARIN ERIC: https://www.clarin.eu/content/cmdi-best-practices-guide (accessed 14 September 2021).

CLARIN CMDI Task Force. 2014. *CMDI 1.2 changes – executive summary*. CLARIN ERIC. https://office.clarin.eu/v/CE-2014-0318-CMDI_1_2-executive_summary.pdf (accessed 27 March 2022).

CLARIN CMDI Task Force. 2016. *CMDI 1.2 specification*. CLARIN ERIC. https://office.clarin.eu/v/CE-2016-0880-CMDI_12_specification.pdf (accessed 27 March 2022).

CLARIN ERIC. 2021a. *Centre Registry*. CLARIN Centre Registry – Centres: https://centres.clarin.eu/ (accessed 14 September 2021).

CLARIN ERIC. 2021b. *Core Components for CLARIN Metadata*. R Core components for CLARIN metadata: https://clarin-eric.github.io/cmdi-core-components/ (accessed 14 September 2021).

CLARIN ERIC. 2021c. *Link Checker*. https://github.com/clarin-eric/linkchecker (accessed 14 September 2021).

CLASS – Cologne Language Archive Services. 2018. *CMDI-Maker*. http://cmdi-maker.uni-koeln.de (accessed 27 March 2022).

DataCite. 2021. *Welcome to DataCite*. https://datacite.org/ (accessed 14 September 2021).

DCMI. 2021. *Dublin Core Metadata Initiative*. https://dublincore.org/ (accessed 14 September 2021).

Defina, Rebecca. 2014. Arbil: Free tool for creating, editing, and searching metadata. *Language Documentation & Conservation 8*: 307–314.

Dima, Emanuel, Erhard Hinrichs, Marie Hinrichs, Alexander Kislev, Thorsten Trippel & Thomas Zastrow. 2012. Integration of WebLicht into the CLARIN infrastructure. In *Service-oriented Architectures (SOAs) for the Humanities: Solutions and Impacts, Joint CLARIN-D/DARIAH Workshop at Digital Humanities Conference*, 17–23.

Dima, Emanuel, Erhard Hinrichs, Christina Hoppermann, Thorsten Trippel & Claus Zinn. 2012. A metadata editor to support the description of linguistic resources. *International Conference on Language Resources and Evaluation (LREC)* 8: 1061–1066.

Doerr, Martin, Stefan Gradmann, Steffen Hennicke, Antoine Isaac, Carlo Meghini & Herbert van der Sompel. 2010. The Europeana Data Model (EDM). *World Library and Information Congress: 76th IFLA general conference and assembly*. https://www.ifla.org/past-wlic/2010/149-doerr-en.pdf (accessed 27 March 2022).

DuraSpace. 2021. *DSpace – A Turnkey Institutional Repository Application*. https://duraspace.org/dspace/ (accessed 14 September 2021).

DuraSpace. 2021. *Fedora – The Flexible, Modular, Open-Source Repository Platform*. https://duraspace.org/fedora/ (accessed 14 September 2021)

Ďurčo, Matej & Menzo Windhouwer. 2013. Semantic mapping in CLARIN Component Metadata. In Emmanouel Garoufallou & Jane Greenberg (eds.), *Metadata and Semantics Research Conference*, 163–168. Berlin: Springer.

Ďurčo, Matej & Menzo Windhouwer. 2014. The CMD cloud. *International Conference on Language Resources and Evaluation (LREC)* 9: 687–690.

Ďurčo, Matej, Matteo Lorenzini & Go Sugimoto. 2017. Something will be connected: Semantic mapping from CMDI to Parthenos entities. In Maciej Piasecki (ed.), *Selected papers from the CLARIN Annual Conference 2017* (Linköping Electronic Conference Proceedings 147), 25–35. Linköping: Linköping University Electronic Press.

Elbers, W. 2017. *Virtual Collection Registry v2.* CLARIN ERIC. https://collections.clarin.eu/ (accessed 27 March 2022).

FAIRDO Forum Steering Committee. 2021. *Fair Digital Objects Forum.* https://fairdo.org/ (accessed 14 September 2021).

Giordano, R. 1995. The TEI header and the documentation of electronic texts. In Nancy Ide & Jean Véronis (eds.), *Text Encoding Initiative*, 75–84. Dordrecht: Springer.

Goosen, Twan. 2017. *Bridging the Europeana and CLARIN infrastructures.* https://www.clarin.eu/blog/bridging-europeana-and-clarin-infrastructures (accessed 27 March 2022).

Goosen, Twan & Eckart, T. 2014. Virtual language observatory 3.0: What's new. *CLARIN Annual Conference.* Soesterberg, 23–25 October.

Goosen, Twan, Menzo Windhouwer, Oddrun Ohren, Axel Herold, Thomas Eckard, Matej Ďurčo, Oliver Schonefeld. 2014. CMDI 1.2: Improvements in the CLARIN Component Metadata Infrastructure. In Jan Odijk (ed.), *Selected papers from the CLARIN Annual Conference 2014* (Linköping Electronic Conference Proceedings 116), 36–53. Linköping: Linköping University Electronic Press.

Guenther, Rebecca S. 2003. MODS: The metadata object description schema. *Portal: Libraries and the Academy* 3 (1). 137–150.

Guha, Ramanathan, Dan Brickley & Steve Macbeth. 2016. Schema. org: Evolution of structured data on the web. *Communications of the ACM, 59* (2), 44–51.

Hansen, Dorte Haltrup, Lene Offersgaard & Sussi Olsen. 2014. Using TEI, CMDI and ISOcat in CLARIN-DK. *International Conference on Language Resources and Evaluation (LREC)* 9: 613–618.

Jong, Franciska de, Darja Fišer, Francesca Frontini, Dieter Van Uytvanck & Andreas Witt. 2022. Language matters: The European research infrastructure CLARIN, today and tomorrow. In Darja Fišer & Andreas Witt (eds.), *CLARIN. The infrastructure for language resources.* Berlin: De Gruyter.

Kemps-Snijders, Marc, Menzo Windhouwer, Peter Wittenburg & Sue Ellen Wright. 2009. ISOcat: Remodeling metadata for language resources. *International Journal of Metadata, Semantics and Ontologies* 4 (4). 261–276.

Kisler, Thomas, Uwe D.Reichel, Florian Schiel, Christoph Draxler, Bernhard Jackl & Nina Pörner. 2016. BAS speech science web services: An update of current developments. *International Conference on Language Resources and Evaluation (LREC)* 10: 3880–3885.

Lyse, Gunn Inger, Paul Meurer & Koenraad De Smedt. 2015. COMEDI: A component metadata editor. In Jan Odijk (ed.), *Selected papers from the CLARIN Annual Conference 2014* (Linköping Electronic Conference Proceedings 116), 82–98. Linköping: Linköping University Electronic Press.

MacWhinney, B. 2021. *Tools for analyzing talk. Part 1: The CHAT transcription format.* https://talkbank.org/manuals/CHAT.pdf (accessed 27 March 2022).

Mišutka, Jozef. 2016. LINDAT/CLARIN DSpace Repository. *CLARIN workshop "DSpace digital repository".* Prague, 8–10 November.

MPI. 2020. *IMDI Metadata information.* The Language Archive: https://www.mpi.nl/IMDI/ (accessed 14 September 2021).

Neumann, Jenna & Jan Brase. 2014. DataCite and DOI names for research data. *Journal of Computer-Aided Molecular Design* 28 (10). 1035–1041.

OAI. 2015. *The Open Archives Initiative Protocol for Metadata Harvesting.* https://www.openarchives.org/OAI/openarchivesprotocol.html (accessed 14 September 2021).

OLAC. 2011. *OLAC: Open Language Archives Community*. http://www.language-archives.org/ (accessed 14 September 2021).

Ostojic, Davor, Go Sugimoto & Matej Ďurčo. 2016. Curation module in action-preliminary findings on VLO metadata quality. *CLARIN Annual Conference*. Aix-en-Provence, 26–28 October.

Piperidis, Stelios. 2012. The META-SHARE language resources sharing infrastructure: Principles, challenges, Solutions. *International Conference on Language Resources and Evaluation* 8: 36–42.

Schuurman, Ineke, Menzo Windhouwer, Oddrun Ohren & Daniel Zeman. 2015. CLARIN Concept Registry: The new semantic registry. In Konraed De Smedt (ed.), *Selected papers from the CLARIN Annual Conference 2015* (Linköping Electronic Conference Proceedings 123), 62–70. Linköping: Linköping University Electronic Press.

SIL. 2021. *ISO 639-3 |*. https://iso639-3.sil.org/ (accessed 14 September 2021).

Straňák, Pavel, Ondřej Košarko & Jozef Mišutka. 2019. CLARIN-DSpace repository at LINDAT/CLARIN. *Grey Literature and Repositories*. https://repozitar.techlib.cz/record/1430/files/Stranak_Kosarko_Misutka_fulltext.pdf (accessed 27 March 2022).

Suominen, Osma, Henri Ylikotila, Sini Pessala, Mikko Lappalainen, Matias Frosterus, Jouni Tuominen, Thomas Baker, Caterina Caracciolo & Armin Retterath. 2015. *Publishing SKOS vocabularies with Skosmos*. https://skosmos.org/publishing-skos-vocabularies-with-skosmos.pdf (accessed 27 March 2022).

TC37, Language resource management. 2015. *Component metadata infrastructure (CMDI) – Part 1: The Component metadata model*. ISO. https://www.iso.org/standard/37336.html (accessed 27 March 2022).

TC37, Language resource management. 2019. *Component metadata infrastructure (CMDI) – Part 2: Component metadata specification language*. ISO. https://www.iso.org/standard/64579.html (accessed 27 March 2022).

TC37, Terminology and other language and content resources. 2009. *Specification of data categories and management of a data category registry for language resources*. ISO. https://www.iso.org/standard/37243.html (accessed 27 March 2022).

TEI Consortium. 2021. *Text encoding initiative*. https://tei-c.org/ (accessed 14 September 2021).

The Apache Software Foundation. 2021. *Apache Solr*. https://solr.apache.org/ (accessed 14 September 2021).

Trilsbeek, Paul & Menzo Windhouwer. 2016. FLAT: A CLARIN-compatible repository solution based on Fedora Commons. *CLARIN Annual Conference*. Aix-en-Provence, 26–28 October.

Trippel, Thorsten, Daan Broeder, Matej Ďurčo & Oddrun Ohren. 2014. Towards automatic quality assessment of component metadata. *International Conference on Language Resources and Evaluation (LREC)* 9: 3851–3856.

Van Uytvanck, Dieter, Herman Stehouwer & Lari Lampen. 2012. Semantic metadata mapping in practice: The virtual language observatory. *International Conference on Language Resources and Evaluation (LREC)* 8: 1029–1034.

Van Uytvanck, Dieter, Claus Zinn, Daan Broeder, Peter Wittenburg & Mariano Gardellini. 2010. Virtual language observatory: The portal to the language resources and technology universe. *International Conference on Language Resources and Evaluation (LREC)* 7: 900–903.

Váradi, Tamás, Steven Krauwer, Peter Wittenburg, Martin Wynne & Kimmo Koskenniemi. 2008. CLARIN: Common language resources and technology infrastructure. *International Conference on Language Resources and Evaluation* 6: 1244–1248.

Vardigan, Mary. 2014. The DDI matures: 1997 to the present. *IASSIST Quarterly* 37 (1). 45–50.

W3C. 2008, November 26. *Extensible markup language (XML) 1.0*, 5th edn. World Wide Web Consortium (W3C): https://www.w3.org/TR/2008/REC-xml-20081126/#attdecls (accessed 14 September 2021).

W3C. 2021. *XSLT cover page*. World Wide Web Consortium (W3C): https://www.w3.org/TR/xslt/ (accessed 14 September 2021).

Warburton, Kara & Sue Ellen Wright. 2020. Data category repository for language resources. In Antonio Parejo-Lora, María Blume, Barbara C. Lust & Christian Chiarcos, *Development of Linguistic Linked Open Data Resources for Collaborative Data-Intensive Research in the Language Sciences*, 69–88. Cambridge, MA: MIT Press.

Wilkinson, Mark D., Michel Dumontier & Barend Mons. 2016. The FAIR guiding principles for scientific data management and stewardship. *Scientific Data* 3 (160018). https://doi.org/10.1038/sdata.2016.18.

Windhouwer, Menzo. 2012. RELcat: A relation registry for ISOcat data categories. *International Conference on Language Resources and Evaluation (LREC)* 8: 3661–3664.

Windhouwer, Menzo, Twan Goosen, Jozef Misutka, Dieter Van Uytvanck & Daan Broeder. 2016. Flexible Community-driven metadata with the component metadata infrastructure. *Digital Humanities*. Kraków, 11–16 July.

Windhouwer, Menzo, Eko Indarto & Daan Broeder. 2017. CMD2RDF: Building a bridge from CLARIN to linked open data. In Jan Odijk & Arjen van Hessen (eds.), *CLARIN in the Low Countries*, 95–103. London: Ubiquity Press.

Withers, Peter. 2012. Metadata management with Arbil. *International Conference on Language Resources and Evaluation.*

Wittenburg, Peter, Romuald Skiba & Paul Trilsbeek. 2005. The language archive at the MPI: Contents, tools, and technologies. *Language Archives Newsletter* 5: 7–9.

Wright, Sue Ellen, Menzo Windhouwer, Ineke Schuurman & Daan Broeder. 2014. Segueing from a data category registry to a data concept registry. *International Conference on Terminology and Knowledge Engineering*. Berlin, 14 June.

Zeeman, Robert & Menzo Windhouwer. 2018. Tweak your CMDI forms to the max. *CLARIN Annual Conference.* Pisa, 8–10 October.

Zinn, Claus. 2016. The CLARIN language resource switchboard. *CLARIN Annual Conference.* Aix-en-Provence, 26–28 October.

Zinn, Claus & Emanuel Dima. 2022. The CLARIN Language Resource Switchboard: Current state, impact, and future roadmap. In Darja Fišer & Andreas Witt (eds.), *CLARIN. The infrastructure for language resources*. Berlin: De Gruyter.

Martina Trognitz, Matej Ďurčo, and Karlheinz Mörth

Text Technology for the Digital Humanities

Maximizing Impact in a Diverse Field of Disciplines

Abstract: This chapter presents the Austrian experience of building CLARIN-related infrastructures and services and describes its impact on the wider humanities research community. We will focus on the activities of the Austrian Centre for Digital Humanities and Cultural Heritage at the Austrian Academy of Sciences (ACDH-CH), a centre of expertise which now supports projects in a broad range of humanities disciplines. Part of ACDH-CH's services are concerned with research data preservation in the long-term repository ARCHE, which will be elaborated on here, as will a set of text-technological and semantic services. Furthermore, the crucial role of knowledge sharing measures for the increased adoption of DH methods is described and Austrian contributions and cooperation in the context of building European research infrastructures for the humanities are highlighted.

Keywords: Austria, data preservation, knowledge sharing, national consortium, text technology, semantic services

1 Introduction

Over the years, CLARIN has evolved into a lively biotope of national communities which have taken on different forms in indvidual countries (see Hajič et al. 2022 and Petrauskaitė et al. 2022 in this volume). In our contribution, we aim to share the Austrian experience on building CLARIN-related infrastructures and services and to describe their impact on the wider humanities research community. We will elaborate on the special case of the Austrian Centre for Digital Humanities and Cultural Heritage at the Austrian Academy of Sciences (ACDH-CH) as an example of a central competence centre in the country, which has been firmly rooted in

Acknowledgments: The rapid ascent of the ACDH-CH relied to a large extent on the substantial five-year start-up funding obtained from the Austrian National Endowment for Research, Technology and Development.

Martina Trognitz, Matej Ďurčo, and Karlheinz Mörth, Austrian Centre for Digital Humanities and Cultural Heritage, Austrian Academy of Sciences, Wien, Austria, e-mails: martina.trognitz@oeaw.ac.at, matej.durco@oeaw.ac.at, karlheinz.moerth@oeaw.ac.at

https://doi.org/10.1515/9783110767377-009

the European research infrastructures CLARIN and DARIAH and has been supporting projects in such diverse fields as religious studies, art history, literature studies, oriental studies, history, archaeology, numismatics, musicology, and archival studies. The ACDH-CH, as a local hub for the deployment of technical as well as social infrastructures, has been acting as the coordinating institution for CLARIN in Austria, with a strong focus on developing adequate digital research concepts and methods, technological frameworks and data models for researchers and scholars in the humanities. Special attention will be given to the data repository ARCHE as the flagship data service in the ACDH-CH's portfolio, which also includes a set of text technology and semantic services. The description of ACDH-CH's role in international cooperations will conclude this contribution.

The notion of text technology, as used in this contribution, has grown out of many years of practical work at the boundary between modern information technology and a range of text-oriented humanities disciplines, such as the various philologies, literary studies, or history, which were successively applied to other less text-oriented humanities disciplines like musicology, religious studies, or numismatics. To put it differently, in the light of the ongoing digitization efforts in all research areas, text technology constitutes an increasingly important methodological base that is being employed in more and more humanities disciplines. An increasingly important part constitutes semantic tasks, like entity extraction and linking, as well as curating controlled vocabularies and semantic resources, which plays an important role in following the open paradigms and the propagation of linked data.

This chapter is structured as follows: first, the general setup of the Austrian consortium CLARIAH-AT is described, including its composition and activities. Then the position and activities of the Austrian Centre for Digital Humanities and Cultural Heritage as a central hub of expertise in DH in Austria are accounted for, detailing the broad range of services for the DH community and its strong ties with and contributions to the development of European research infrastructures.

2 CLARIN + DARIAH in Austria = CLARIAH-AT

Austria was a founding member of both "Common Language Resources and Technology" (CLARIN, 2012) and "Digital Research Infrastructure for the Arts and Humanities" (DARIAH, 2014) (digital humanities austria 2022), the main representatives of the humanities among the European research infrastructure consortia. Austrian activities that ultimately led to the participation in these consortia can be traced back as far as 2009 (Ďurčo and Mörth 2014: p. 14). In 2013, a three-year project to establish the platform and network *digital humanities austria* (dha) further fuelled the interweaving of the two research infrastructures in Austria, which by 2014 were already referred to as CLARIN-DARIAH.AT (Ďurčo and Mörth 2014).

The intertwining of and the many overlaps between the activity areas of and the involved actors behind CLARIN and DARIAH in Austria (Mayer 2020: pp. 36–38) finally led to a merge of CLARIN and DARIAH into the joint initiative CLARIAH-AT, which was formalized as a consortium in 2019. The name CLARIAH-AT was established with the "DH-Austria-Strategie" published in 2015 (Alram et al. 2015). The merging of the two research infrastructures on a national level has found imitators across Europe.

The CLARIAH-AT consortium brings together key institutional actors, acts as a central hub for Austrian DH activities, and represents the link to the wider international context. Partners of the consortium include the Austrian Academy of Sciences, the Austrian National Library, the Universities of Graz, Innsbruck, Klagenfurt, Salzburg, Vienna and the Danube University Krems. The cooperation inside the group ensures maximum synergy and efficiency and is meant to maximize the impact in the Austrian digital humanities research communities.

In the early years, the research disciplines involved in the activities that developed into the present CLARIAH-AT consortium were very much oriented towards language processing in speech and text. The disciplines included linguistics, artificial intelligence, translation studies and oriental studies (Wissik and Budin 2010). With a growing digital humanities research community, the range of disciplines widened, as illustrated, for example, by the topics at the Digital Humanities Austria conference in 2015 (dha2015), where the GLAM sector was also already present (Hannesschläger 2016).

CLARIAH-AT is mainly concerned with strategic planning and coordination of the activities of its national partners. The activities are well aligned with those of CLARIN and DARIAH and largely complement them. Furthermore, CLARIAH-AT represents the community's interests with regards to the ministry and other stakeholders. An important achievement in this role was the strategic paper "DH-Austria-Strategie" (Alram et al. 2015), which was co-authored by representatives of the main partner institutions and coordinated by the ÖAW. This document formulates seven guiding principles, each of them with a number of concrete measures. The "DH-Austria-Strategie" serves as a roadmap for the DH community in Austria.

In May 2021, an update of the strategy in the new paper "Digital Humanities Austria Strategy 2021+. 4 Guidelines for Digital Humanities in Austria" (CLARIAH-AT Konsortium 2021, digital humanities austria 2022) was released after a commenting period by CLARIAH-AT. It encompasses the following areas: (1) research infrastructures and networks – especially broadening the collaboration with memory institutions; (2) research data – further development of infrastructures for preservation and publication of research data in line with the FAIR Data Principles; (3) digital methods and tools; and (4) education, training, and knowledge sharing activities that accompany the other areas and ensure knowledge sharing and dissemination of results, new tools, and methods. The action plan is congruent with the overarching international activities of CLARIN and DARIAH.

Members of CLARIAH-AT are actively involved in DARIAH Working groups (ELDAH, DH Course Registry, dariahTeach, Thesaurus Maintenance, and Guidelines and Standards – GiST) as well as in CLARIN groups and committees (User Involvement Group, CLIC – CLARIN Legal Issues Committee, (see Kamocki, Kelli and Lindén 2022 in this volume), Standards Committee, and SCCTC – Standing Committee of CLARIN Technical Centres).

On the national level, numerous innovative digital projects could be conducted thanks to the go!digital programme, with three calls in 2014, 2016, and 2018.[1] The programme was organized by the Austrian Academy of Sciences, financed by funds from the Academy and the Austrian National Endowment for Research, Technology, and Development. A key requirement for funded projects was to be aligned with the activities of CLARIN and DARIAH initiatives. The go!digital initiative was also designed as an incentive for participation of young researchers. In the three rounds a total of 30 projects was selected by international experts. The funded projects were characterized by a particularly high degree of methodological innovation and had a considerable impact on the Austrian research landscape. Furthermore, another 25 active or recently completed projects have been funded by CLARIAH-AT (digital humanities austria 2022). The actors of CLARIAH-AT and the wider Austrian digital humanities community are brought together via the network known as "digital humanities austria" (dha).[2] The network organizes conferences for the local community, offers a mailing list and hosts a digital humanities bibliography. An invaluable resource hosted by dha is the database of Austrian digital humanities projects and online resources.[3] The project list was significantly updated in 2021 when the dha conference was held as a Twitter conference,[4] and currently features over 100 projects. This resource gives an excellent insight into current digital humanities research in Austria.

Austria is a part of CLARIN's distributed network of centres, with two CLARIN B-Centres (the Austrian Centre for Digital Humanities and Cultural Heritage – A

1 https://www.oeaw.ac.at/en/foerderungen/foerderprogramme/subsites/godigital
2 https://digital-humanities.at/
3 https://digital-humanities.at/en/dha/projects
4 https://digital-humanities.at/en/dha/s-news/digitaldhaustria-dh-schaukasten-and-twitter-event

Resource Centre for the HumanitiEs at the Austrian Academy of Sciences[5] and the ZIM Centre for Information Modelling at the University of Graz[6]), and two K-Centres (the CLARIN Knowledge Center for Terminology Resources and Translation Corpora, University of Vienna[7] and the Phonogrammarchiv – Institute for Audiovisual Research and Documentation – at the Austrian Academy of Sciences[8]). The history of CLARIN Centres in Austria goes back to 2014 with the CLARIN Centre Vienna (CCV), which began as a repository for digital language resources created in Austria run by the ACDH-OeAW.

3 The Austrian Centre for Digital Humanities and Cultural Heritage (ACDH-CH)

The Austrian Centre for Digital Humanities and Cultural Heritage (ACDH-CH) at the Austrian Academy of Sciences furnishes an excellent example of an institution that developed from text- and language-focused research activities to a broader scope defined by the canon of the digital humanities. The initial focus on language resources broadened into more general digital humanities and data-centric approaches, ultimately extending into the archival and cultural heritage sector.

3.1 Becoming ACDH-CH

In the years from about 2009 until 2014, the CLARIN- and DARIAH-related activities of the Austrian Academy of Sciences were bundled in a working group of the Institute for Corpus Linguistics and Text Technology (ICLTT). The Academy, with its numerous humanities institutes, had a growing need for dedicated capacities and expertise in digital methodolgies for the humanities. The ICLTT working group, already engaged in and connected to the initiatives on the European level, led the efforts to work out a corresponding concept for the Academy. In 2015, this working group became the nucleus of the newly founded "Austrian Centre for Digital Humanities" (ACDH) of the Austrian Academy of Sciences, which in subsequent years has grown into a central hub for many infrastructural activities

5 https://centres.clarin.eu/centre/45
6 https://centres.clarin.eu/centre/65
7 https://centres.clarin.eu/centre/55
8 https://centres.clarin.eu/centre/41

in the humanities at the Academy and in Austria. The ACDH was installed as a research institute with the declared intention of fostering humanities research by applying digital methods and tools to a wide range of academic fields after the Academy had taken over from the University of Vienna as the Austrian coordinating instance in the CLARIN and DARIAH infrastructures in 2014.

In 2020, having existed for five years, the institute was restructured into three main task areas: Infrastructure and Services, Digital Humanities Research (DH), and Cultural Heritage Research (CH). With the reorganization, relevant research groups originally part of other Academy units were integrated into the institute. Since the restructuring, the institute has been operating under the name "Austrian Centre for Digital Humanities and Cultural Heritage" (ACDH-CH).

The new structure of the institute was meant to bring together two key areas of the Austrian Academy of Sciences: basic research in long-term projects with a focus on the preservation of cultural heritage, and research on methodological and theoretical aspects of documentation, processing, and visualization in the digital humanities. Within the ACDH-CH, the DH and CH research pillars are expected to increasingly cross-fertilize each other, and thus contribute to the development of joint endeavours on the rich treasure of Europe's cultural memory.

In recent years, the infrastructure and service unit has been developing a growing portfolio of services: running a repository for digital resources, hosting and publishing data, developing software, and thus contributing to a network of specialized knowledge centres across Europe offering advice and guidance to various research communities.

The teams at the DH research pillar have been working on research questions with an emphasis on digital editing and text modelling as well as digital knowledge representation. Research projects have been built around questions of the representation, modelling, and analysis of digital text, not only in terms of language, but also in terms of content. Research activities have been situated at the crossroads between well-established encoding methods from digital edition practice (TEI) and the Semantic Web. Digital prosopography has come to play an important part in a number of these projects. Among other tasks, the teams apply semantic tools and Artificial Intelligence (AI) on food images derived from Europeana in order to enhance access to and analysis of cultural data (ChIA[9]), analyse historical language as an expression of human culture (in the Austrian Baroque Corpus[10] as well as the Wien[n]erisches Diarium,[11] which covers over 300 issues

9 https://chia.acdh.oeaw.ac.at/
10 https://abacus.acdh.oeaw.ac.at/
11 https://digitarium.acdh.oeaw.ac.at/

of the oldest daily news journal still published) and engage in the European Time Machine project.

The CH pillar of the ACDH-CH mainly pursues long-term encyclopedic and lexicographic undertakings of the Academy dealing with language, music, literature, and biographies with a special emphasis on the Austrian context. In contrast to the infrastructure and DH sectors, where methodological innovation has played an inherently important role, the focus in CH projects has been primarily laid on content creation, like for example lexicographic data (WBÖ – Dictionary of Bavarian Dialects in Austria[12]), prosopographic knowledge (ÖBL – Austrian Biographical Lexicon[13]) and reference works (The Austrian Encyclopedia of Music – OEML[14]).

3.2 ACDH-CH's activities

The developments in research methodologies and the increased employment of digital methods to address research questions in recent years has created a fast-growing community in various disciplines with an increased demand for digital services. Given the high degree of diversity of requirements, the considerable heterogeneity of data such services deal with, and the limited availability of ready-made solutions, the general approach on the technical side was that of research-driven exploration and experimentation in combination with continuous technology scouting. Over the years, these efforts have lead to the gradual build-up of a robust and broad portfolio of technology stacks and services. Web applications, research software, and tools are all built with reusability in mind, to enable their application beyond single projects. All of the institute's development work is open source licensed. The institute's account on GitHub currently features 303 code repositories.[15] Selected examples are detailed below in the section 3.2.2.

The overall strategy of ACDH-CH is guided by two main principles: the fundamental interconnectedness of infrastructure development and research, and the need for knowledge sharing via a wide range of channels to make the infrastructure accessible and usable for humanities scholars. A number of factors influence the work oriented towards these principles. While the institute has managed to bring

12 https://www.oeaw.ac.at/acdh/projects/wboe-dictionary-of-bavarian-dialects-in-austria
13 http://www.biographien.ac.at/oebl
14 https://www.musiklexikon.ac.at
15 https://github.com/acdh-oeaw

together an efficient team with a broad range of expertise, made up of experts who often combine a humanities and technical background in one person, the communication of the importance of hybrid career paths and the accommodation of dedicated positions like "research software engineers" or "data analysts" has remained a challenge in the conservative academic contexts that the Academy represents.

Building on the methodological and theoretical paradigms of the digital humanities, the dichotomy of service or technology on the one side and research on the other is to be productively dissolved through cross-fertilization between technology and humanities research questions and methods. Through the application of new technologies, the methodological inventory of the humanities is fine-tuned and expanded, while at the same time technical solutions, standards, and best practices are further developed. In this process, the infrastructural work and technological expertise oscillates between testing innovative approaches and providing technologically sound and stable solutions. The technical or infrastructural component is not merely a service that fulfills the wishes and needs of researchers, but also acts as an inspiration and source of innovation in its own right. In this way technology provides important impulses for the methodological sharpening and further development of research methodology that lead to the generation of new ideas and approaches.

An indispensable prerequisite for this approach of close entanglement in research-driven technological development are the principles of Open Science, not only open access to research results, but also open data for research data, open source for the software developed and used, and open methods for new methodological approaches. In addition, the FAIR Data Principles (Wilkinson et al. 2016) as well as the "DH-Austria-Strategie" (Alram et al. 2015) have determined ACDH-CH's strategic orientation to a large extent.

In our experience, efficient knowledge transfer and continuous educative measures have to accompany the development and provision of methods and tools in order to ensure their uptake by the researchers. The existence of institutions with digital humanities know-how, and in particular the human experts, constitutes an integral part of the development of digital humanities methods and infrastructures.

Measures for knowledge transfer can be dedicated training events focusing on specific tools or methods, presentations on symposia, engagement with the broader public, or even intensive individual consulting for researchers and research groups. Over the past five years, the ACDH-CH has designed its own series of events, and has participated in numerous workshops and conferences making use of a varied range of presentation formats. Theoretical and practical knowledge has been communicated to researchers and experts as well as to young researchers and the interested public. In addition, reports and information were disseminated via various print and online channels. Details can be found below in the section 3.2.3.

Individual consulting services for researchers and potential cooperation partners are offered via the ACDH-CH Helpdesk. Consulting has grown into a central tool of service delivery and provides researchers with information and assistance on the topics of digital methods, data management, standards, and legal issues. Ideally, one-on-one meetings with research groups will already have been initiated during the project's proposal phase in order to sound out respective needs, present implementation options, and fathom out relevant technologies and best practices, and thereby also set the course – as early as possible – for an efficient and sustainable technical realization that is in line with the technical infrastructure of the ACDH-CH. Early consultation not only supports researchers during the project preparation phase, but also ensures at an early stage that the technologies and standards to be employed are already in line with best practices in the different research communities.

Researchers are also supported in regards to systematic and efficient research data management, which is not only one of the main concerns of the ACDH-CH, but is also a requirement in the guidelines of national (FWF 2022) and international (European Commission 2022) funding bodies. Crucial to data management in projects is a data management plan that clearly outlines the various data types and their handling throughout the whole lifecycle of the project, including creation, processing, archiving, and publication.

3.2.1 Data preservation with ARCHE

The long-term availability of digital (research) data is another core service of the ACDH-CH. It is also one of the most important prerequisites for conducting DH research in conformity with recognized principles such as Open Science (openscienceASAP 2022, Open Knowledge Foundation 2022) and FAIR data (Wilkinson et al. 2016) and the general rules of good scientific practice (European Science Foundation and ALLEA 2011, Deutsche Forschungsgemeinschaft 2019). Long-term preservation and dissemination of research data not only enable data publication, permanent referenceability, and sustainable reusability, but also the reproducibility of research results.

With the launch of ARCHE (A Resource Centre for the Humanities) in 2017, a service offering digital long-term archiving for the Austrian humanities community was realized by the ACDH-CH. The genesis of ARCHE is described here, and we also cast a spotlight on recent developments.

The digital archive ARCHE[16] serves as an example of how a system initially dedicated to text and language resources was opened and adapted for wider humanities research. ARCHE is operated by the ACDH-CH and is the successor of the first official CLARIN centre in Austria, CLARIN Centre Vienna / Language Resources Portal (CCV/LRP), which was in operation from 2013 until 2017. The CCV/LRP specialized in digital language resources like digital dictionaries, recorded interviews with transcriptions, and language corpora. Its mission was to provide depositing services for and easy and sustainable access to digital language resources in Austria. Its replacement by ARCHE marked the shift towards a repository now available to researchers in all humanities disciplines, with a correspondingly wider range of data types that now includes images, texts, structured and tabular data, audio recordings, videos, 3D models, geographic information and more. Some of these data types can be quite large with regard to their file size and some digital methods lead to a large amount of files. Both factors influenced the design of the repository system and the accompanying workflows.

In contrast to many Austrian repositories that focus on written research output like articles, ARCHE is one of the few repositories in Austria that accepts research data (Trognitz 2021). In 2017, ARCHE became the first of now three repositories in Austria to be certified with the Core Trust Seal (ARCHE 2018). Of these three certified repositories – ARCHE, GAMS and AUSSDA – only the first two accept and host data from the humanities. Both ARCHE and GAMS are also certified as a CLARIN Centre B. GAMS, the Graz Humanities Asset Management System, has been developed and operated for several years at the Centre for Information Modelling at the Karl Franzens University Graz. This OAIS-compliant system is based on Fedora Commons 3 and builds on a largely XML-based content strategy and numerous system-inherent functionalities for the management and publication of digital data.[17]

ARCHE's content strategy is file based with extensive accompanying metadata. To enhance sustainability, the use of open access and open data policies is promoted, including the application of the FAIR Data Principles (Wilkinson et al. 2016) to provide Findable, Accessible, Interoperable and Reusable data and metadata. Furthermore, principles of the Semantic Web and Linked Open Data are applied for metadata management in ARCHE (Trognitz and Ďurčo 2018).

Every resource and collection in ARCHE needs to be described with ARCHE's custom metadata schema. The modelling of this schema faced challenges related to the heterogeneity of data from the wide range of humanities disciplines and

16 https://arche.acdh.oeaw.ac.at
17 https://informationsmodellierung.uni-graz.at/en/research/gams/

the aim of supporting multiple metadata schemas such as the Component Metadata of CLARIN (CMDI) (Broeder et al. 2012, see Windhouwer and Goosen 2022 in this volume), Dublin Core (DCMI Usage Board 2020), DataCite (DataCite 2021) and others (Trognitz and Ďurčo 2018). The current version 3.x of the metadata schema contains 16 main classes, 91 datatype properties, and 39 object properties to describe data collections, their files, and their related entities, such as contributors involved.[18] Additional metadata in a dedicated XML-based format for a resource or for the physical object related to a collection or resource can be stored as an additional resource and linked to the respective entities.

The technical background of ARCHE was initially based on Fedora Commons 4 (Trognitz and Ďurčo 2018). But with the increase of metadata and data, both in numbers and in file size, the design flaws of Fedora Commons 4 had an impact on the stability and performance of the application and even on the consistency of the data. Since the development of work-arounds for the deficiencies was getting out of hand, we had serious technical shortcomings related to metadata management, and none of the available open source repository software solutions provided what we were looking for, in 2020 we decided to develop a software solution from scratch tailored to our requirements: the ARCHE Suite.[19]

The ARCHE Suite relies on the use of proven stable and reliable technologies, particularly PHP and PostgreSQL, and a more economical use of technical resources. Its design was focused on reusability, both in terms of reusing existing libraries and modules and in terms of reusability by others. The latter is achieved by open-source availability, an extensive and growing documentation,[20] a dockerized environment, and easy configurability. The entire code, including the extensive documentation, underwent an external reviewing process before its initial release in 2020. The ARCHE Suite now provides a solid foundation for ARCHE, even for increasingly large data collections.

A unique feature of the ARCHE Suite is that it is metadata agnostic, that is, it does not enforce any particular metadata schema. The only requirement is the metadata is expressed in RDF, which enables compliancy with the Linked Open Data (LOD) principles (Berners-Lee 2010) with five levels (stars) of compliance. The suite has only one built-in metadata consistency check for foreign keys, but more checks can be introduced by implementing custom plug-ins, which can bind to certain events, such as before or after metadata creation, using the language-agnostic Advanced Message Queuing Protocol (AMQP[21]), with bindings to all major

18 https://github.com/acdh-oeaw/arche-schema
19 https://github.com/orgs/acdh-oeaw/projects/2
20 https://acdh-oeaw.github.io/arche-docs/
21 https://www.amqp.org/

programming languages. This flexible yet powerful plug-in system also allows for custom metadata enrichment and synchronization with external services. One service shipped with the ARCHE Suite is the OAI-PMH service, which converts metadata into various XML-based formats via a flexible templating system. For linguistic content ARCHE provides CMDI for the Virtual Language Observatory by CLARIN and for selected cultural heritage content metadata is serialized to the European Data Model (EDM) for Kulturpool, the Austrian aggregator for Europeana. Further output formats are being prepared and will be available in 2022. One will serve the data model of the research infrastructure for archaeology, ARIADNEplus. Another will map the ARCHE schema to the dha-ontology,[22] which represents the first step of a joint effort by the Austrian initiative CLARIAH-AT to develop a national aggregating catalogue within the project DiTAH.[23]

Another key feature of the ARCHE Suite and ARCHE is the use of so-called *dissemination services*, that is, applications and services that present and deliver specific data types in various presentation forms and formats. Typical examples are the conversion of TEI documents into HTML pages,[24] the online preview of a 3D model via the web-based 3D viewer 3DHOP,[25] or providing images in different sizes and formats via a dedicated IIIF server.[26] These dissemination services allow users to preview the digital objects in ARCHE online and developers can integrate the objects in ARCHE directly into their own web applications by using the endpoints provided by the dissemination services. In fact, a dedicated dissemination service allows the user to pass on individual resources or a set of resources to the Virtual Collection Registry (VCR) of CLARIN, thus allowing for reusing stored resources with resources from other repositories. The mechanism behind the dissemination services, which relies on calling stand-alone services with raw data as a parameter, is compatible with the way the CLARIN Language Resources Switchboard (LRS) works. Thus, configuration efforts are minimized and resources in ARCHE conforming to TEI can already be passed to the LRS.

It is important to understand that a repository like ARCHE is not just a piece of technology, but very much the human curation and interaction that is needed in order to meet high quality standards. Over the last few years, the ARCHE team has worked intensively on documentation, workflows, and policies that aim to

22 https://github.com/KONDE-AT/dha-ontology

23 https://www.ditah.at/

24 Example: https://id.acdh.oeaw.ac.at/daacda/bomber__917.xml click on *Custom TEI to HTML transformation*

25 Example: http://hdl.handle.net/21.11115/0000-000C-22F6-8, click on *3D viewer.*

26 Example: http://hdl.handle.net/21.11115/0000-000C-5037-C, click on *View image* or *IIIF Endpoint*

make internal processes more efficient, support the researchers, and attain a high level of transparency of procedures. These efforts have been accompanied by outreach activities, workshops, and presentations detailing the deposition process in ARCHE in particular, and highlighting the importance of data preservation and management in general.

3.2.2 Text technologies and semantic services

As previously described, the roots of the ACDH-CH go back to the Institute for Corpus Linguistics and Text Technology (ICLTT). Its mission was corpus linguistic and text technological research that included tasks such as development and annotation of text corpora, lexicographical documentation, and fostering the use of standards such as TEI (ICLTT 2013). The methods that are applied to fulfill these tasks are not tied to data from a specific research discipline, which means that data from such diverse disciplines as art history, musicology, oriental studies, history, or archaeology can be processed directly with adjustments to the workflows.

In digital humanities research, often a textual source stands at the beginning of a research question and requires digitization for automated processing and analysis. The sources may come in the form of a clay tablet, a stone inscription, a historic manuscript, a printed newspaper archive, a handwritten postcard convolute, or a set of audio recordings.

On the path from the analogue to the digital object, a number of technologies must be applied to make the original source usable in a digital research environment. Automated processes like optical character recognition (OCR) or handwritten text recognition (HTR) or more manual tasks like transcription or double-keying are among the first processing steps, often followed by basic morphological and syntactic analysis tasks such as lemmatization, POS tagging or shallow parsing.

Once the object is digitized, the content can be semantically analysed with methods like named entity recognition (NER), information and relation extraction, or entity linking. With a growing size of digital datasets and sufficiently clean data, machine learning tasks like classification, clustering, or sentiment analysis can be applied.

There is a growing range of proven tools for each of these tasks. Therefore, the ACDH-CH's general strategy in this area is primarily to simplify the use of the existing tools, adapt them for specific applications, and integrate them into more complex workflows. These workflows are often characterized by a combination of quantitative and qualitative methods that pair automatic preprocessing steps with digitally supported intervention by experts.

One of the currently most popular NLP frameworks, Python-based spaCy,[27] offers a wide range of pre-built resources, like pre-trained models for numerous languages, specialized components for different NLP tasks, or pre-built pipelines. It has largely replaced traditional tools such as Stanford OpenNLP, treetagger, or Python NLTK and is now used in all projects at the ACDH-CH that have a NLP component.

After the initial digitization and before analysis, texts often require tokenization. While most NLP toolkits have integrated tokenizers for "plain text", the tokenization of XML/TEI documents while still preserving their structure is a complex task and is not natively supported by any NLP toolkit. Therefore, the specialized application xtx[28] was developed at the ACDH-CH for this task.

A small, but still very useful application is ABBR,[29] used as a storage and curation platform to collaboratively maintain abbreviations found in any kind of texts. Those curated abbreviations are exposed through an API so that they can be reused by other projects. This is especially useful as a helper utility for the tokenization task, where unrecognized abbreviations produce erroneous sentence boundaries.

After tokenization, digital texts can be further annotated and enriched. At the ACDH-CH, TEI is the preferred format for text-based and annotated resources. But many NLP toolkits, like spaCy, usually expect plain text without interweaved annotations as input. To overcome this discrepancy and, more importantly, to convert the result of the automatic annotation process back into a TEI-compliant structure, the experimental application spacyapp[30] was developed. It provides a simple user interface and a web service to add linguistic annotations to TEI-encoded files. Users can upload files, which in the background are then sent through several processing steps, tools – among them the aforementioned xtx – and corresponding interfaces, until the enriched result is returned, preserving the existing TEI annotation. As part of this development, a Python library for working with TEI data in spaCy was created and released open source.[31]

Adding linguistic annotations to TEI-compliant digital documents or curating such annotations can also be done with the tokenEditor.[32] This is a web application based on the idea of the table-like data structure traditionally used in corpus linguistics, in which the text is decomposed to one token per line and extended

27 https://spacy.io/
28 https://xtx.acdh.oeaw.ac.at
29 https://abbr.acdh.oeaw.ac.at/
30 https://spacyapp.acdh.oeaw.ac.at/
31 https://github.com/acdh-oeaw/acdh-spacytei
32 https://clarin.oeaw.ac.at/tokenEditor/

by additional annotation levels as columns. This makes the tokenEditor particularly suitable for checking and correcting word classes and lemma information. The tool is integrated with the federated identity infrastructure of CLARIN, which allows users to log in via their academic user accounts.

Manual high quality training data is the crucial factor for the quality of machine learning models. At the same time, their creation is very time-consuming and costly. Therefore, it is important to ensure that training data, once created, can be reused as easily as possible. For this purpose, a platform was developed in the NERDPool project to publish and easily reuse training data for Named Entity Recognition.[33] Another tool used at the ACDH-CH to support manual creation of training data is the web-based application Prodigy. It integrates with spaCy and allows users to generate production-ready models with a small training set. Although Prodigy at the ACDH-CH is primarily used for annotating named entities, it is very flexible and configurable for a wider range of annotation tasks that include text classification, POS tagging, parsing, or even image annotation.

Entity linking goes one step further than named entity recognition, by resolving the lexical reference in the text against a semantic reference resource such as dbpedia or Geonames, or the German National Library's Gemeinsame Normdatei. For this purpose, the service enrich[34] is provided, which is based on the Apache Stanbol[35] framework featuring a RESTful API for entity lookup. Named entity recognition of mentions of persons, places, and other entities, their automatic identification and, if possible, automatic linking to established reference resources, has gained importance in the processing of digital humanities data.

All these existing or self-developed tools form a diverse suite of tools for digital processing of texts in a continuum from text resources to more structured relational data and further to Linked Open Data (LOD). A logical complement to these processing tasks is the management and handling of semantic LOD resources. Next to a number of triplestores with project-specific datasets expressed in RDF, the ACDH-CH hosts the Vocabs service,[36] a platform for publication and management of controlled vocabularies, based on the software SKOSMOS,[37] implementing the SKOS data model.[38] Controlled vocabularies are key to semantic interoperability between heterogeneous data.

---

33 https://github.com/acdh-oeaw/nerdpool, https://nerdpool.acdh-dev.oeaw.ac.at/
34 https://enrich.acdh.oeaw.ac.at/
35 http://stanbol.apache.org/
36 https://vocabs.dariah.eu
37 http://skosmos.org/
38 http://www.w3.org/TR/skos-reference

A particularly advanced example of integration of text and semantic technologies is APIS – Austrian Prosopographical Information System, a framework for managing prosopographical data, that is, information about persons and their relations to other persons, places and institutions. It was originally developed in the Austrian Prosopographical Information System project (2015–2020), dealing with approximately 18,000 biographies of the "Österreichisches Biographisches Lexikon 1815–1950" (Austrian Biographical Dictionary 1815–1950), one of the most visible long-term projects of the Austrian Academy of Sciences. In this project the encyclopedic entries, which previously only existed as continuous text, were recorded in structured form and enriched with links interconnecting persons, places, institutions, and events using semantic technologies and automatic methods of named entity recognition, relation extraction, and entity linking. Although APIS was a stand-alone project, both the methods of text analysis and the application for managing the structured data have become integral parts of the ACDH-CH's portfolio of core services and are used and further developed in a variety of thematically similar projects with a prosopographical focus.

3.2.3 Training, outreach, and knowledge sharing

The importance of educational measures flanking the build-up of innovative infrastructures has been gaining more and more attention. Using new technologies usually requires prior knowledge and specialist know-how. This is why effective social infrastructures accompanying technical infrastructures have become a key factor in driving the digital transformation. The highly dynamic developments, a considerable time lag in the development of curricula, and limited resources in the university sector has further added urgency to the issue. It is essential not only to create the infrastructure, but also to empower the target groups to use it.

As one measure to react to the dichotomy of technological and social infrastructures, a specialized ACDH-CH working group, acting under the title of ERICs and Education, has been focusing on the question of knowledge transfer from the infrastructure specialists into the wider research communities. Special concerns of their work have been data awareness, data stewardship, open research paradigms, the FAIR principles, standards relevant to DH, legal frameworks for research in the humanities, and work with cultural heritage. The group aims to develop a comprehensive set of educational measures, ranging from the creation and provision of relevant materials to outreach and dissemination activities.

Among other things, the group has been working on the development of tools to facilitate the availability and production of digital teaching materials. The main incentive behind this activity has been to make practice-oriented DH knowledge and methodological skills, which were presented in the manifold lectures, workshops, internships, and other elements, permanently available by documenting the events and creating accompanying digitally available material that remains available in the long run to be re-used later on other occasions and teaching activities. One experimental application that is currently being created is the continuation of an in-house project, the ACDH-HowTo-Blogs. The working group targets groups inside the CLARIAH-AT consortium as well as the wider DH community. As is the case with many ACDH-CH endeavours, they have been striving to embed their activities in larger European frameworks; in this particular case the developments are undertaken jointly with the DARIAH Campus[39] endeavour. The intention is to first produce locally relevant material and then to push this to the European level.

In addition to collecting and curating existing resources, relevant new teaching materials will also be created in a targeted manner, which will be achieved primarily through the "Training" work package of the project "Digital Transformation of the Austrian Humanities" (DiTAH).[40] Interactive tutorials about repositories (e.g., ARCHE), metadata, data management, copyright issues, annotations, and NLP, as well as on Semantic Web and Linked Open Data, will be developed by colleagues and experts in the fields.

The ACDH-CH has also been offering various knowledge sharing event types, like lectures, the so-called Tool Galleries and internships. The lectures serve primarily to connect the local research communities with international DH experts, provide information about their research, and present the latest developments in the field. The Tool Galleries provide practical knowledge through hands-on training on specific DH tools. Both lectures and tool galleries have been offered for several years now, attracting a lot of interest and participation, and some have been planned and organized in close cooperation with universities. They are not meant to be full-fledged courses or parts thereof but rather to complement existing programmes by filling in temporary gaps arising through the dynamicity of developments, turning the spotlight on selected methodological topics.

It is planned to feed materials created in these contexts into the aforementioned HowTo-blogs. An interesting development over the past two years, with all events being held virtually, has been the extension of the target groups, with increasingly large audiences from abroad.

An important initiative aimed at reaching out to the next generations of researchers is the ACDH-CH internship programme, which has been running for

39 https://campus.dariah.eu/
40 https://www.ditah.at/

several years now. It is targeted at prospective young humanities scholars and programmers and systematically familiarizes them with the innovative approaches and methods employed in digital humanities. Interns are invited to participate in a real-world research environment and thus gain experience in working with innovative technologies. Many of the students' interests are language and text-oriented and here they learn for the first time about infrastructures such as CLARIN and DARIAH.

3.3 Creating impact through research cooperations

Through the years, the embedding and involvement of the ACDH-CH and its predecessors in the European research infrastructure consortia CLARIN and DARIAH have represented a central pillar and a permanent international social and technical framework for the infrastructural activities of the institute. The institute's activities have been conceived and implemented in the context of and in close coordination with activities of the CLARIN and DARIAH research infrastructures at the wider European level. Indeed, weaving the network between international and local developments, acting as a broker and centre of expertise ensuring the flow of information and ideas between European and local stakeholders has been at the core of ACDH-CH's mission.

Correspondingly, the ACDH-CH team has intensively engaged in numerous committees at the European level of these research infrastructures, for instance in the DARIAH working groups Ethical and Legal Issues (ELDAH), Guidelines and Standards (GiST), and Thesaurus Maintenance or in the CLARIN Standards Committee, the Standing Committee for CLARIN Technical Centers, and the CLARIN Legal Issues Committee.

Among numerous contributions to the central infrastructures, we would like to highlight the early participation in the development of CLARIN's Component Metadata Infrastructure and the Federated Content Search activities, the Vocabulary Repository for publication of controlled vocabularies, as well as the CLARIN Curation Dashboard, which offers important feedback to data providers regarding the quality of their metadata and is described in more detail further below. Furthermore, the DH Course Registry,[41] a curated platform that provides an overview of the growing range of teaching activities in the field of digital humanities worldwide (see Wissik, Wessels and Fischer 2022 in this volume), was developed

41 https://dhcr.clarin-dariah.eu/

and is hosted and coordinated by the ACDH-CH as a first joint project of CLARIN and DARIAH (Wissik et al. 2020, Schmeer and Wissik 2019).

Another major mode of collaboration are infrastructural EU projects where research infrastructures play an ever-increasing role in pulling together EU-wide consortia out of the pool of established partners and offer a stable base for harmonizing technological developments. Over the years, the ACDH-CH has contributed to numerous projects, mainly: CLARIN-PLUS,[42] HaS-DARIAH,[43] dariahTeach,[44] Parthenos,[45] ARIADNE and ARIADNEplus,[46] ELEXIS,[47] SSHOC,[48] and most recently InTaVia[49] and CLS INFRA.

All of these activities have created a considerable source of expertise which has in recent years translated into a large number of local and international cooperations. The many cooperative projects have in turn contributed to the spread of know-how into and within the research community. These efforts align perfectly with numerous activities on the EU level, the build-up of EOSC, the FAIRification of data and the focus on training, promising synergetic flourishing exchange of ideas, and sharing of efforts between the numerous stakeholders in Austria and international initiatives to continue in the coming years.

3.3.1 SSHOC

In the research infrastructure cluster project SSHOC (Social Sciences and Humanities Open Cloud, 2019–2022),[50] the major social sciences and humanities consortia (CESSDA, CLARIN, DARIAH, ESS, SHARE) are collaborating with over 30 other partners to implement the idea of the European Open Science Cloud (EOSC) for these disciplines. In line with the general idea of EOSC as a "system of systems", that is, a federated, distributed agglomeration of subsystems, SSHOC aims to integrate a variety of existing components and data from the participating partners, focusing on interoperability and reuse.

42 https://www.clarin.eu/content/clarin-stronger-ever-clarin-plus-project-outcomes
43 http://has.dariah.eu/
44 http://dariah.eu/teach
45 http://www.parthenos-project.eu/
46 https://ariadne-infrastructure.eu/
47 https://elex.is/
48 https://sshoc.eu/
49 https://intavia.eu/
50 https://sshopencloud.eu/

The ACDH-CH is involved in three work packages: “WP 3 Lifting Technologies and Services into the SSH Cloud”, “WP 6 Fostering Communities, Empowering Users and Building Expertise” and “WP 7 Creating the SSH Open Marketplace”.

The participation in WP 7 continues and culminates the long-standing activities of the institute in metadata aggregation, metadata quality assurance, controlled vocabularies, and resource discovery at the European level. In WP 7, the ACDH-CH is responsible for the implementation of the SSHOC Marketplace,[51] a discovery platform for resources, tools, and methods in the social sciences and humanities domain. This platform is one of the strategic goals of DARIAH-EU. The system design lays emphasis on curation and quality of information, contextualization of data, that is, capturing relations between items, and engaging the community.

Additionally, the tasks of the ACDH-CH in WP6, concerned with creating and inventorying existing training materials, align perfectly with the institute's emphasis on knowledge transfer, training, and outreach. One milestone within this task was the creation of a catalogue of training materials and sources relevant to the SSH domain, which is now available as the training toolkit[52] (Ďurčo, Illmayer and Barbot 2019).

In WP 3, led by CLARIN, the ACDH-CH team contributes to tasks revolving around interoperability and service integration. The team is developing a conversion hub, a catalogue of services and solutions for converting metadata between various formats. Another topic in WP 3 towards fostering interoperability is the integration of existing well-established services. This specifically addresses the Language Resources Switchboard (see Zinn and Dima 2022 in this volume) and the Virtual Collection Registry. As described in the section 3.2.1, the ARCHE repository has been successfully integrated with both services.

3.3.2 CLARIN Curation Dashboard and Link Checker

The ACDH-CH has been involved in the CLARIN metadata activities (CMDI: Common Metadata Infrastructure; ISO 24622-1:2015) [see Windhouwer and Goosen 2022 in this volume] for many years with a focus on curation and quality assurance. A major long-standing contribution by the ACDH-CH to the CLARIN

51 https://marketplace.sshoc.eu/
52 https://training-toolkit.sshoc.eu/

infrastructure in this regard is the Curation Dashboard,[53] formerly known as the Curation Module. It is an application aimed at supporting CMDI metadata authors and curators to evaluate and consequently enhance the quality of metadata for language resources (King et al. 2015, Ostojic, Sugimoto and Ďurčo 2017).

The Curation Dashboard allows users to analyse individual CMDI profiles, individual CMDI records, as well as entire metadata collections with regard to their quality, based on a set of assessment criteria, like facet coverage, validity of links, or descriptive completeness. The Curation Dashboard is used by the repository providers of CLARIN centres all over Europe and especially by the Centre Assessment Committee when evaluating CLARIN centres. A special functionality of the Curation Dashboard is the automated control of the validity of references to resources in the metadata, which was a long-standing desideratum of the CMDI developer community. This component, dubbed LinkChecker, continuously processes the over 1 million metadata records available as part of the Virtual Language Observatory in the background and checks over 6 million links contained within. The results are made available in the statistical analyses of individual collections. They are also fed back into the VLO to provide users with a priori information about the quality and availability of the catalogued research data.

4 Conclusion

In this contribution we described how work and research at the ACDH-CH have accordingly been characterized by a clear shift from language-related services for linguistics to a much broader scope in which text technology is being put to use in a wide array of different domains. Examples included the digital long-term preservation service ARCHE and the evolution of text technology and semantic services offered by the ACDH-CH.

We have also shown the crucial role that knowledge transfer and "social infrastructures" have come to play in the process of introducing new technologies and methods and how the intensified communication and numerous collaborations with partners at universities and other research institutions nationally and internationally have fuelled the evolution of the ACDH-CH into a knowledge hub, on the one hand drawing on the wide-ranging collaborative network as a source of knowledge, new methodological approaches, and innovative technologies, and on the other feeding into this evergrowing network.

53 https://curation.clarin.eu/

European research infrastructures like CLARIN and DARIAH have provided a reliable framework that allows local activities to be coordinated internationally. They also provide a fertile ground for cross-border collaborations. The ACDH-CH has been acting as a pivot, mediating on several levels – both vertically between researchers and technology providers like data centres or e-infrastructures, and horizontally as a national and international collaborator, bringing researchers with similar or complementary interests into contact. These processes have always been seen as fundamentally transdisciplinary in nature establishing not only new networks of researchers active in different disciplines but also as a stepping stone from which to reach out to parts of society not directly involved with research, such as the educational sector or the interested public.

In alignment with broader developments in the digital humanities community, we discern two major tendencies for the institute to move along in the foreseeable future: text technology is more and more growing into a mature set of methods being applied in a wide range of humanities disciplines. As language and text constitute a broad common denominator in many tasks and research questions, not only in the narrower field of the digital humanities, these methods have started to spill over into more and more fields of research, fundamentally changing the ways research is being done.

Another important observation is the fact that semantic technologies have become an integral part of the methodological canon of text technology, representing the bridge from unstructured to structured data. As such, they appear to be a perfect match for a range of traditional humanities disciplines with their deep rootedness in the doctrine of meaning and understanding, and with their concept-based hermeneutical approaches which have posed and will pose particular challenges to many issues of modelling in the digital world.

Bibliography

Alram, Michael, Christoph Benda, Matej Ďurčo, Karlheinz Mörth, Sibylle Wentker, Tanja Wissik & Gerhard Budin. 2015. *DH-AUSTRIA-STRATEGIE: Sieben Leitlinien für die Zukunft der digitalen Geisteswissenschaften in Österreich*. https://doi.org/10.1553/dh-austria-strategie-2015s1.

ARCHE. 2018. *CoreTrustSeal certification 2017–2019*. https://www.coretrustseal.org/wp-content/uploads/2018/03/ARCHE.pdf (4 April, 2022).

Berners-Lee, Tim. 2010. *Linked Data*. https://www.w3.org/DesignIssues/LinkedData.html (4 April, 2022).

Broeder, Daan, Menzo Windhouwer, Dieter Van Uytvanck, Twan Goosen & Thorsten Trippel. 2012. CMDI: a component metadata infrastructure. In Victoria Arranz, Daan Broeder, Bertrand Gaiffe, Maria Gavrilidou, Monica Monachini & Thorsten Trippel (eds.),

Proceedings of the workshop describing language resources with metadata: towards flexibility and interoperability in the documentation of language resources. LREC 2012, may 22, 2012, Istanbul, Turkey. 1–4. Paris: European Language Resources Association. https://nbn-resolving.org/urn:nbn:de:bsz:mh39-108677 (4 April, 2022).

CLARIAH-AT Konsortium. 2021. *Digital Humanities Austria Strategie 2021+: 4 leitlinien für digital humanities in österreich.* http://gams.uni-graz.at/o:clariah.dha-strategie-2021 (4 April, 2022).

DataCite. 2021. *DataCite Metadata Schema.* https://schema.datacite.org/ (4 April, 2022). DCMI Usage Board. 2020. *DCMI Metadata Terms.* https://www.dublincore.org/specifications/dublin-core/dcmi-terms/ (4 April, 2022).

Deutsche Forschungsgemeinschaft. 2019. *Guidelines for safeguarding good research practice.* Available in German and in English. Deutsche Forschungsgemeinschaft. https://doi.org/10.5281/zenodo.3923602.

digital humanities austria. 2022. *CLARIAH-AT.* https:// digital-humanities.at/en/dha/clariah-at (4 April, 2022).

Ďurčo, Matej, Klaus Illmayer & Laure Barbot. 2019. *Inventory of existing learning materials.* D6.7. https://doi.org/10.5281/zenodo.3596003.

Ďurčo, Matej & Karlheinz Mörth. 2014. CLARIN-DARIAH.AT – Weaving the network. In *9th Language Technologies Conference, 14–18. Ljubljana, Slovenia: Information Society – IS 2014.* http://nl.ijs.si/isjt14/proceedings/isjt2014_02.pdf (4 April, 2022). European Commission. 2022. *Data management.* https://ec.europa.eu/research/participants/docs/h2020-funding-guide/cross-cutting-issues/open-access-data-management/data-management_en.htm (4 April, 2022).

European Science Foundation & ALLEA. 2011. *The European code of conduct for research integrity.* https://www.allea.org/wp-content/uploads/2015/07/Code_Conduct_ResearchIntegrity.pdf (4 April, 2022).

FWF. 2022. *Open Access für Forschungsdaten.* https://www.fwf.ac.at/de/forschungsfoerderung/open-access-policy/open-access-fuer-forschungsdaten/ (4 April, 2022).

Hajič, Jan, Eva Hajičová, Barbora Hladká, Jozef Mišutka, Ondřej Košarko & Pavel Straňák. 2022. LINDAT/CLARIAH-CZ: Where we are and where we go. In Darja Fišer & Andreas Witt (eds.), *CLARIN. The infrastructure for language resources.* Berlin: De Gruyter.

Hannesschläger, Vanessa. 2016. *DHA2015 Conference Report.* https://www.oeaw.ac.at/acdh/events/event-detail/dha2015-conference-report/ (4 April, 2022).

ICLTT. 2013. *Institute for Corpus Linguistics and Text Technology.* https://www.oeaw.ac. at/fileadmin/nfg/PH_13_ICLTT.pdf (4 April, 2022).

Kamocki, Paweł, Aleksei Kelli & Krister Lindén. 2022. The CLARIN Committee for Legal and Ethical Issues and the Normative Layer of the CLARIN infrastructure. In Darja Fišer & Andreas Witt (eds.), *CLARIN. The infrastructure for language resources.* Berlin: De Gruyter.

King, Margaret, Davor Ostojic, Matej Ďurčo & Go Sugimoto. 2015. Variability of the facet values in the VLO – a case for metadata curation. In Koenraad De Smedt (ed.), *Selected papers from the CLARIN annual conference 2015, october 14–16, 2015, Wroclaw, Poland* (Linköping Electronic Conference Proceedings 123), 25–44. Linköping: Linköping University Electronic Press. http://www.ep.liu.se/ecp/123/003/ecp15123003. pdf (4 April, 2022).

Mayer, Katja. 2020. *Digital Humanities in Österreich: Ergebnisse der Studie "Exploratives Mapping", Dezember 2019.* Zentrum Soziale Innovation. https://doi.org/10.22163/fteval.2020.473.

Open Knowledge Foundation. 2022. *Open Definition 2.1: Defining Open in Open Data, Open Content and Open Knowledge*. https://opendefinition.org/od/2.1/en/ (4 April, 2022).

openscienceASAP. 2022. *Was ist Open Science?* http://openscienceasap.org/open-science/ (4 April, 2022).

Ostojic, Davor, Go Sugimoto & Matej Ďurčo. 2017. The curation module and statistical analysis on VLO metadata quality. In Lars Borin (ed.), *Selected papers from the CLARIN annual conference 2016, Aix-en-Provence, 26–28 October 2016* (Linköping Electronic Conference Proceedings 136), 90–101. Linköping: Linköping University Electronic Press. http://www.ep.liu.se/ecp/136/007/ecp17136007.pdf (4 April, 2022).

Petrauskaitė, Rūta, Darius Amilevičius, Virginijus Dadurkevičius, Tomas Krilavičius, Gailius Raškinis, Andrius Utka & Jurgita Vaičenonienė. 2022. CLARIN-LT: Home for Lithuanian language resources. In Darja Fišer & Andreas Witt (eds.), *CLARIN. The infrastructure for language resources*. Berlin: De Gruyter.

Schmeer, Hendrik & Tanja Wissik. 2019. Data about DH training and education: The API for the DH course registry and its use cases. In *DARIAH annual event 2019: humanities data: Book of abstracts*, 71–73. https://dariah-ae-2019.sciencesconf.org/data/pages/ AE2019_BookOfAbstracts_1.pdf (4 April, 2022).

Trognitz, Martina. 2021. Saving us from the Digital Dark Age: The Austrian perspective. *Internet Archaeology* 58. https://doi.org/10.11141/ia.58.2.

Trognitz, Martina & Matej Ďurčo. 2018. One schema to rule them all: The inner workings of the digital archive ARCHE. *Mitteilungen der Vereinigung Österreichischer Bibliothekarinnen und Bibliothekare* 71(1). 217–231. https://doi.org/10.31263/voebm.v71i1.1979.

Wilkinson, Mark D., Michel Dumontier, IJsbrand Jan Aalbersberg, Gabrielle Appleton, Myles Axton, Arie Baak, Niklas Blomberg, Jan-Willem Boiten, Luiz Bonino da Silva Santos, Philip E. Bourne, Jildau Bouwman, Anthony J. Brookes, Tim Clark, Mercè Crosas, Ingrid Dillo, Olivier Dumon, Scott Edmunds, Chris T. Evelo, Richard Finkers, Alejandra Gonzalez-Beltran, Alasdair J.G. Gray, Paul Groth, Carole Goble, Jeffrey S. Grethe, Jaap Heringa, Peter A.C 't Hoen, Rob Hooft, Tobias Kuhn, Ruben Kok, Joost Kok, Scott J. Lusher, Maryann E. Martone, Albert Mons, Abel L. Packer, Bengt Pers- son, Philippe Rocca-Serra, Marco Roos, Rene van Schaik, Susanna-Assunta Sansone, Erik Schultes, Thierry Sengstag, Ted Slater, George Strawn, Morris A. Swertz, Mark Thompson, Johan van der Lei, Erik van Mulligen, Jan Velterop, Andra Waagmeester, Peter Wittenburg, Katherine Wolstencroft, Jun Zhao & Barend Mons. 2016. The FAIR guiding principles for scientific data management and stewardship. *Scientific Data* 3(1). https://doi.org/10.1038/sdata.2016.18.

Windhouwer, Menzo & Twan Goosen. 2022. Component Metadata Infrastructure. In Darja Fišer & Andreas Witt (eds.), *CLARIN. The infrastructure for language resources*. Berlin: De Gruyter.

Wissik, Tanja & Gerhard Budin. 2010. *CLARIN-AT – Project Report: Erhebung Sprachres sourcen und Sprachtechnologien in Österreich*.

Wissik, Tanja, Jennifer Edmond, Frank Fischer, Franciska de Jong, Stefania Scagliola, ScharnhorstAndrea, Hendrik Schmeer, Walter Scholger & Leon Wessels. 2020. Teaching digital humanities around the world: An infrastructural approach to a community-driven DH course registry. *Library Tribune* 40(6). 1–27.

Wissik, Tanja, Leon Wessels & Frank Fischer. 2022. The DH Course Registry: A piece of the puzzle in CLARIN's technical as well as knowledge infrastructure. In Darja Fišer & Andreas Witt (eds.), *CLARIN. The infrastructure for language resources.* Berlin: De Gruyter.

Zinn, Claus & Emanuel Dima. 2022. The CLARIN Language Resource Switchboard: Current state, impact, and future roadmap. In Darja Fišer & Andreas Witt (eds.), *CLARIN. The infrastructure for language resources.* Berlin: De Gruyter.

Gisle Andersen and Peder Gammeltoft

The Role of CLARIN in Advancing Terminology: The Case of *Termportalen* – the National Terminology Portal for Norway

Abstract: This contribution describes a CLARIN use case which is of particular benefit for the purposes of language standardization, language policy, and higher education, namely the efforts to develop *Termportalen* ('the terminology portal') in Norway. This resource is the result of coordinated work which has been ongoing since even before the inception of the CLARIN ERIC but which has gained enormously from its establishment. Originally initiated at NHH Norwegian School of Economics, this effort now involves the entire "ecosystem" of stakeholders, from language resource owners, field experts, terminologists, language technologists and computer scientists, administrative and managerial staff, to several private and public actors and governmental authorities who use this infrastructure as a repository for terminology resources.

Keywords: terminology, language for specific purposes (LSP), translation, multilingual resources, termbase

1 Introduction

The systematic development of terminology is key to achieving official language policy goals. Accessible bi-/multilingual terminological resources, in the form of simple term lists or structured terminology bases, are essential for pedagogical success in scientific subjects as well as publication, dissemination, and popularization of research. Terminological language resources are also valuable for the purposes of language technology, semantic modelling, and machine translation (see e.g., Cabré 1999, 2003; Temmerman 2000).

Standardization and harmonization of work in terminology is extremely important in order to ensure the interoperability and reusability of language resources. Importantly, harmonization does not entail a terminological straitjacket in which

Gisle Andersen, NHH Norwegian School of Economics, Bergen, Norway,
e-mail: gisle.andersen@nhh.no
Peder Gammeltoft, University of Bergen, Bergen, Norway,
e-mail: peder.gammeltoft@uib.no

https://doi.org/10.1515/9783110767377-010

scientists must agree on a specific term to designate a particular concept, but it does entail the utilization of commonly agreed practices for structuring and annotating scientific terms and concepts. Key to achieving such goals are the ISO TC37, TBX, and SKOS standards, among others.

In the context of the pan-European CLARIN research infrastructure, an array of lexical and terminological resources have been made accessible for a wide range of purposes and in many languages.[1] In this chapter, we will zoom in on a particular Norwegian use case, namely the portfolio of terminological resources made accessible in the CLARIN infrastructure via the CLARINO Bergen Centre (see also Rauset et al. 2022).[2] We also describe the tools and methods that have been developed to make terminology available for scientists, terminologists, and end users in the infrastructure Termportalen ('the terminology portal'; see also Andersen and Kristiansen 2013, 2015; Andersen, Gammeltoft, and Gundersen 2021).[3]

The remainder of this chapter is structured as follows: we first describe both the historical and scientific context of this effort (Sections 1.1–1.2), including policy decisions and governmental white papers that have argued in favour of a renewed prioritization of terminology in Norway. In Section 2, we account for international standards and best practices that lay the premises for the work on Termportalen. Section 3 gives an overview of tools and procedures that have been developed in the project, thanks in great part to funding from CLARINO via the Research Council of Norway. These include the search facility, conversion tools, and end user interface. Collectively, we argue, these resources have made life easier for a wide range of end users of terminology, including language policymakers, translators, field experts/scientists, and students, and they are thus of great societal significance. In this section, we also review briefly some legal aspects relating to IPR. Finally, in Section 4, we outline our plans for future work.

1.1 Historical context: Language policy and funding

Norwegian terminology work has its roots in the years preceding WWII but has been through some stormy weather, especially in the last few decades, and the effort to develop Termportalen in the context of CLARIN represents a major revitalization of this line of work.

1 https://www.clarin.eu/resource-families/lexical-resources-glossaries
2 https://clarino.uib.no/ and https://repo.clarino.uib.no/xmlui/
3 https://term.uib.no/

In the last few decades, the Norwegian language debate has shifted from a concern with the relation between and relative importance of the two written varieties to a less dogmatic and ideology-based climate. The outside pressure from English on the vocabulary has become the main focus of attention, and the threat of domain loss is perceived as real in some knowledge fields. Establishing and advocating the use of Norwegian terminology has been part of official language policy and a central aim for the Language Council since its establishment in 1951. The body called Rådet for teknisk terminologi was founded as a member organization in 1956 and later reorganized as a trust. This cooperated closely with Standards Norway, the official standardization body, and with the Language Council, and it was operative until its liquidation in 2001 (Myking 2005, 2006). Another key institution, Norsk termbank, started as a project at the University of Bergen in 1979 and developed substantial terminological resources for a range of scientific fields. The oil industry in particular saw the value of developing Norwegian terminology, and its largest player, the state-owned company Statoil (now Equinor), worked in close cooperation with the term bank to achieve this. However, this largely project-funded organization began to decline and eventually met its end in the late 1990s. Since 2000, systematic terminology work has been carried out within key organizations such as Standards Norway (technical domains), Norges Bank (the central bank, economics), and the EEA Secretariat of the Foreign Secretary (EU/EEA legal terminology). Notwithstanding these continuous efforts, the last decade has seen what could be characterized as revival of terminology work in Norway. Strategies to counter domain loss have been put in place through the adoption of language policy documents and the establishment of a terminology secretariat within the Language Council. Through legislation, the responsibility for terminology development has been placed firmly in higher education institutions. In 2020, a governmental white paper prepared the ground for new legislation on language. This made academia's responsibility to develop Norwegian terminology for scientific domains more explicit.

The launch of the pan-European CLARIN ERIC in 2012 gave an opportunity to secure a permanent digital home for a wide range of language resources in the Norwegian context, among them terminological resources. The first instantiation of the national project, CLARINO, was aimed at collecting resources and establishing a national infrastructure (Rauset et al. 2022). A separate work package was devoted to Terminology Integration. This project was successful in collecting and consolidating a range of existing terminological resources and initiating the development of some new ones, as described in Section 3. The second national project, CLARINO+, started in 2020 and aims at further developing and increasing the resource base as well as adding value through fruitful combination of various resources.

A major breakthrough for terminology came in 2020, when the Terminology Portal secured permanent funding via governmental legislation. This came about thanks to relentless efforts by the Language Council, its Advisory group for terminology, and the Termportalen project group, as well as individual stakeholders with an interest in terminology. For the first time, Norway will have legislation fully aimed at regulating its official language policy. The law *Lov om språk (Språklova)* 'Language Act' was ratified by the Storting (parliament) on 8 April 2021. With this new legislation, the Norwegian government assigns a key role for Termportalen as a national infrastructure for terminology:

> Regjeringa meiner at Termportalen kan bli eit viktig verktøy som vil bidra til at universiteta og høgskulane oppfyller dei pliktene dei har etter universitets- og høgskulelova § 1–7 og i dei språkpolitiske retningslinjene for kvar institusjon. I tillegg vil Termportalen bidra til at vi når den overordna målsetjinga i framlegget til språklov om å sikre norsk som eit samfunnsberande språk. Prop. 108 L (2019–2020) *Lov om språk (språklova)*
>
> (Governmental white paper: 72)[4]

> [The Government considers the Terminology Portal an important tool that will enable the universities and university colleges to fulfil their legal requirements according to the Universities Law § 1–7 and the language policies of each institution. In addition, the Terminology Portal will contribute to reaching the overall objective of securing the role of Norwegian as a fully functional language in all domains of society.]

Given this priority, and in order to meet its language policy goals, the Norwegian Government decided to grant permanent funding to Termportalen in late 2020. Originally a project-funded effort initiated by the Norwegian School of Economics (NHH), the long-term repository and operations and future development of the portal will hosted by *Språksamlingane* (the Language Collections) at the University of Bergen Library.

1.2 Scientific context: Terminological resources in CLARIN and beyond

Terminology as a scientific discipline is three-tiered, and each tier relates to a main element of resource production. One of these is inventory, that is, the actual terminological content of domain-specific expressions and concepts that the user is confronted with and makes use of. The second tier concerns the practical aspect on the production of terminological content. The third tier constitutes

4 Prop. 108 L (2019–2020) *Lov om språk (språklova)*; https://www.regjeringen.no/no/dokumenter/prop.-108-l-20192020/id2701451/.

the science of terminology, specifically research into terminological practice, the development of terminological methodology and strategies for harmonization. As such, terminology is based both on practice (production) and on research, which drives the creation of terminological content (Draxler et al. 2022).

A central aspect of terminology is that it is highly domain-specific, as well as typically (but not exclusively) multilingual in scope, and with a strong data-linguistic component. In particular, the multilingual side of terminology has been seen as a means of addressing the dangers of domain losses in specific knowledge domains, as described in Section 1.1. This is certainly true for Norwegian, but also for several other languages, as is evident from terminological resources in CLARIN. Here, the terminological resources are situated under the family lexical resources, mainly nested within glossaries,[5] albeit related but not expressly domain-specific resources also occur in the lexical resource of wordlists.[6]

The terminological resources in the CLARIN glossaries lexical resource are generally divided into monolingual resources and multilingual resources. Interestingly, monolingual terminology consists mainly of dialectal glossaries or onomastic resources relating to place names, family names, and place-name elements. Monolingual terminology resources proper seemingly only exist for domain dominant languages, such as English in the areas of biodiversity,[7] and medical[8] terminology, as well as Greek knowledge bases for Ancient Greek dramaturgy[9] and xenophobia.[10]

The multilingual term glossaries and bases are more often bilingual than multilingual, and virtually always count English as one of the languages. This is probably owing to the above attempt at avoiding domain loss to English by less dominant languages. Among the multilingual terminology resources are also three Norwegian-language resources: the English for Business termbase,[11] the UHR Termbase for higher education institutions (see Section 3.1),[12] and the Norwegian biodiversity terminology database.[13] Apart from the first resource, they all have entries in both official written languages, Norwegian Bokmål and Norwegian Nynorsk, thus writing themselves into the current official language policy.[14]

5 https://www.clarin.eu/resource-families/lexical-resources-glossaries
6 https://www.clarin.eu/resource-families/lexical-resources-wordlists
7 http://hdl.handle.net/21.11115/0000-000B-D395-E
8 http://hdl.handle.net/21.11115/0000-000B-D37A-E
9 http://hdl.grnet.gr/11500/IONION-0000-0000-2510-4
10 https://inventory.clarin.gr/resources/search/?q=xenophobia
11 http://hdl.handle.net/11509/116
12 http://hdl.handle.net/11509/122
13 http://hdl.handle.net/11509/115
14 https://www.sprakradet.no/localfiles/12399/ifip2005.doc

At present, the Norwegian terminology resources in CLARIN consists of a subset of the resources that are under development in the Terminology portal. A set of updated termbases will be made accessible in the CLARIN repository before the end of the ongoing project, known as CLARINO+. Among these are Marine Evertebrates,[15] Norwegian–German legal Terminology,[16] the initial version of the Maritime Dictionary (*Maritim ordbok*, see Section 3.1),[17] and Bergen municipality's interpreters' termbase (*Tolketjenestens termbase*; see Section 3.1).[18] Of these, the first and last resources feature only Norwegian Bokmål, whereas the second and third include terms with both Norwegian Bokmål and Norwegian Nynorsk. All Norwegian termbases are to be considered scientific bases, apart from Bergen municipality's interpreters' termbase. This termbase is purely practice-oriented and contains only two of the three tiers that defines terminology as a scientific discipline.

In addition to the CLARIN and CLARINO resources, Norway has, as mentioned in Section 1.1, resources such as the termbases Snorre, Standards Norway (technical domains), the EU-termbase by the EEA Secretariat of the Foreign Secretary (EU/EEA legal terminology), and the Term-wiki by the Norwegian Language Council, as well as 140 other national terminological resources.[19]

2 Methods and standards for term data collection and dissemination

Standardization and harmonization of work in terminology is extremely important in order to ensure the interoperability and reusability of language resources. Importantly, harmonization does not entail a terminological straitjacket in which scientists must agree on a specific term to designate a particular concept, but it does entail the utilization of commonly agreed practices for structuring and annotating scientific terms and concepts. Among the standards that are key to achieving this goal are the ISO TC37, TBX, and SKOS standards, described in the sections that follow.

15 https://repo.clarino.uib.no/xmlui/handle/11509/117
16 https://repo.clarino.uib.no/xmlui/handle/11509/120
17 https://repo.clarino.uib.no/xmlui/handle/11509/119
18 https://repo.clarino.uib.no/xmlui/handle/11509/121
19 https://www.sprakradet.no/Sprakarbeid/Terminologi/termlister-og-termbaser#norske

2.1 Ensuring interoperability: The TBX and SKOS standards

To ensure interoperability between different termbases in the structure and exchange with external terminology producers and consumers, Termportalen uses two national versions of the terminology exchange formats, TBX and SKOS, namely TBX-AP-NO[20] and SKOS-AP-NO.[21] TBX is the primary exchange format in the CLARIN and CLARINO frameworks, whereas SKOS is the main exchange format in data communication in Termportalen. In the following, the two exchange formats will be outlined.

TBX, or TermBase eXchange, is the international standard for representing and exchanging information from termbases; it is compliant with the Terminology Markup Framework (ISO 16642:2003) and Unicode-encoded. TBX is an open-source XML-based terminology exchange format, designed to make terminology databases easier and safer with regard to maintenance, distribution, and use. Since the standard is open source, any termbase may be accessed via any software to access, display, update, process, or migrate the resource. The TBX standard was first published in 2008. It was developed by the Localization Industry Standards Association (LISA), and the International Organization for Standardization (ISO) as ISO 30042:2008, under the Management of Terminology Resources Technical Committee, ISO/TC 37/SC 3.[22] The TBX standard is currently on its third version and published as ISO 30042:2019.[23]

One major advantage of TBX is that it ensures interoperability and thus technical accuracy, even across multiple projects. The other major advantage is that TBX can be used to distribute terminology by software for authoring, translation, or quality control. TBX defines a family of formats that share a common structure and a limited range of information types, and the main purpose of the exchange format is to ensure that data can be used in different software applications.

The other exchange format used by Termportalen is SKOS, or Simple Knowledge Organization System.[24] SKOS is a W3C recommendation designed for representation of thesauri, classification schemes, taxonomies, subject-heading systems, or any other type of structured controlled vocabulary built upon RDF and RDFS. The main objective of the standard is to enable easy publication and distribution as linked data. Termportalen is currently available as a Sparql end-

20 https://data.norge.no/specification/tbx-ap-no/
21 https://data.norge.no/specification/skos-ap-no-begrep/
22 https://www.iso.org/committee/48136.html
23 https://www.iso.org/standard/62510.html
24 https://www.w3.org/2009/08/skos-reference/skos.html

point API in the SKOS-format, which also acts as the interchange layer between backend and frontend.

SKOS is a common W3C data model for sharing and linking knowledge organization systems via the Semantic Web. SKOS is a small vocabulary (meta-model) for the most central classes and the properties of concepts. To use SKOS as a language of representation in concept descriptions, the vocabulary must be expanded with other vocabularies. This standard complements SKOS with the following vocabulary:

- Dublin Core Terms (DCT) supplements with general properties related to documentation;
- Data Catalog Vocabulary (DCAT) supplements with general properties related to datasets;
- SKOS extension for labels (SKOS-XL) supplements with properties related to terms;
- SKOS extension for representing statistical classifications (XKOS) supplements with properties related to relationships; and
- Norwegian-specific SKOS extensions.

SKOS uses the Resource Description Framework (RDF) to represent knowledge organization systems in a standardized way. Encoding RDF allows the structured information to be passed between computer applications in an interoperable way. RDF also allows for distributed use of knowledge organization systems as decentralized metadata applications, thus adding value to metadata harvested from multiple sources. The SKOS semantic vocabulary is an OWL class based on concepts, objects, and events, and is intended to provide ways to declare relationships between concepts within a concept scheme.

2.2 Procedures for data conversion

All the CLARINO terminology resources are stored in the ISO-certified TBX standard, whereas Termportalen adheres to the W3C SKOS-standard. Both standards are considered well suited for terminological and technical language purposes. They represent two different outsets and areas of application. To put it simply, SKOS is based on web semantic technology and linked data, whereas TBX is developed in a terminological and linguistics environment. Either standard is compatible with the other, for example, by means of conversion applications, such as those given in the W3C guidelines in for conversion from TBX to SKOS/

RDF[25] (albeit for the earlier TBX standard), as well as in the Norwegian management standards for terminological resources from The Norwegian Digitalisation Agency (Digdir).[26]

Converting between the two is straightforward and the additional costs of converting between two standards are minimal. Termportalen has a functioning system set up for conversion between the two standards based on available online conversion tools, such as on Github,[27] and of the above mentioned guidelines and management standards. In addition, Termportalen has also set up a conversion system for conversion of termbases from Excel.

2.3 Domain-modelling and harmonization

In Section 3, we describe in some detail a few of the specific terminology projects that have utilized the tools developed in Termportalen as a means for making terminology accessible for editing and dissemination. Common to all terminology resources is that *scientific domain* must be specified for each term base and terminological entry. Some resources cover a wide range of domains, for example, the NOT Terminology Base (the oil sector, medicine, etc.) and the RTT base (a variety of technical fields). Other resources are much narrower, such as the resource *Marine evertebrater*, which covers all concepts of a discrete domain, namely the totality of marine evertebrates that are part of the marine fauna in Norwegian coastal areas and waterways, and the UHR-base, which exclusively contains terminology for the higher education sector (see Section 3.1). Yet other resources cover a set of connected domains that pertain to a restricted area of use but involve different sciences. This is the case for the termbase *Maritim ordbok*, which covers all maritime areas including fauna, flora, marine industries, tools and equipment, and so on. Consequently, the termbases that are integrated in Termportalen differ greatly with regard to their degree of complexity and their coverage and representation of concepts in various domains.

One observation that was made early in the project when traversing masses of terminological data from various sources was that different practices had been followed with regard to the labelling and granularity of domain specification. In fact, some resources were rather messy in how domain information was listed. As a representative example of this, see Figure 1.

25 https://www.w3.org/2015/09/bpmlod-reports/multilingual-terminologies/

26 https://www.digdir.no/digitale-felleslosninger/forvaltningsstandarder-maskinell-tilgjengeliggjoring-av-begrepsbeskrivelser/1684

27 https://github.com/cimiano/tbx2rdf

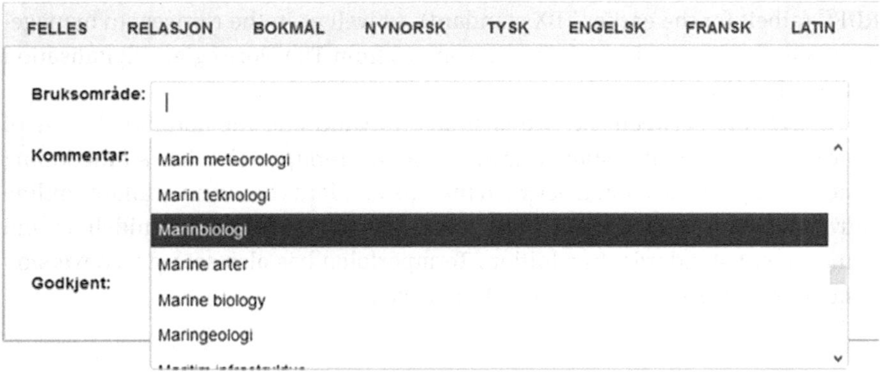

Figure 1: Maritime subdomains pre-harmonization.

The dropdown menu contains two entries, *Marinbiologi* and *Marine biology*, showing that both English and Norwegian labels were used in the data with reference to the same domain. For reasons of practicality and interoperability, and given the language-political context of the project, a decision was made to standardize – where possible – domain designations in accordance with the labels used in the Norwegian version of the Dewey Decimal Classification system.[28] In some cases, more customized domain designations were needed to reflect the contents of a database. This applies, for instance, to the UHR base, whose entire content was labelled as *Studie- og forskningsadministrativ terminologi* ('Terminology for research and higher education'). The process of domain harmonization and developing a national standard for denoting scientific subjects is not completed but is a prioritized task in the project in the months ahead.

3 Integration and dissemination of terminology resources

In this section, we describe our concrete work with terminological data and various operations and tools that have been developed and applied. The computational tools developed in the project include conversion tools between different formats, an editing module, and an end user interface with advanced and simplified search facilities. In the sections below, we report on resource development as

28 See https://bibliotekutvikling.no/kunnskapsorganisering/kunnskapsorganisering/norsk-webdewey/ and https://deweysearchno.pansoft.de/webdeweysearch/index.html.

technical descriptions and via screen shots that visualize the functionality of the infrastructure. We also briefly survey some of the tools for semi-automatic term extraction that have been developed and utilized in the project (Section 3.3).

3.1 Pilot projects: The UHR termbase, *Maritim ordbok* and *Tolketjenestens termbase*

The infrastructure for terminology is meant to secure a permanent home for a wide variety of resources. Some of these have been considerably enhanced during the establishment phase of the CLARINO/CLARINO+ projects, with the addition of new concepts to the database and revision of existing ones. In this section, we zoom in on three such projects.

Universitets og høyskolerådet (UHR) – Universities Norway – is the governmental body with the responsibility to "to promote the quality, coordination and the division of work in the higher education sector, nationally and internationally", describing itself as "an interest organization for accredited institutions, pursuant to the Norwegian Act relating to universities and university colleges, 1 April 2005" (Regulations for Universities Norway).[29] For a long time it has prioritized standardization of terminology used in the sector, and the UHR termbase has existed since before the launch of the CLARINO project. UHR has nominated a Terminology Group with official representatives from the faculty and staff of most institutions in higher education (bar private institutions), which is responsible for developing and making public terminology relevant for administration of higher education and research. This resource was previously available in the form of a flat, alphabetical term list from a web page hosted by UHR. As part of the project, its content was completely overhauled by a terminologist. Furthermore, a substantial backlog of terminology that had been decided by the term group but not included in the old term list was incorporated, along with the addition of more recent terminology decisions. Revisions were made using the Termportalen editing module (Section 3.3). As a result, the UHR termbase is fully updated as of spring 2021.[30] A sample entry is seen in Figure 2.

The figure shows the terminological entry for *eksamen* 'exam' and links to all other entries containing this form (e.g., *eksamen fra videregående opplæring* 'upper secondary education examination'; see Section 3.3 for further details). The UHR termbase contains some 1,870 concepts with terms and synonyms in Nor-

29 https://www.uhr.no/en/about-uhr/regulations-and-strategy/regulations-for-universities-norway-uhr/

30 See and http://termbase.uhr.no/, see also https://www.uhr.no/ressurser/uhrs-termbase/.

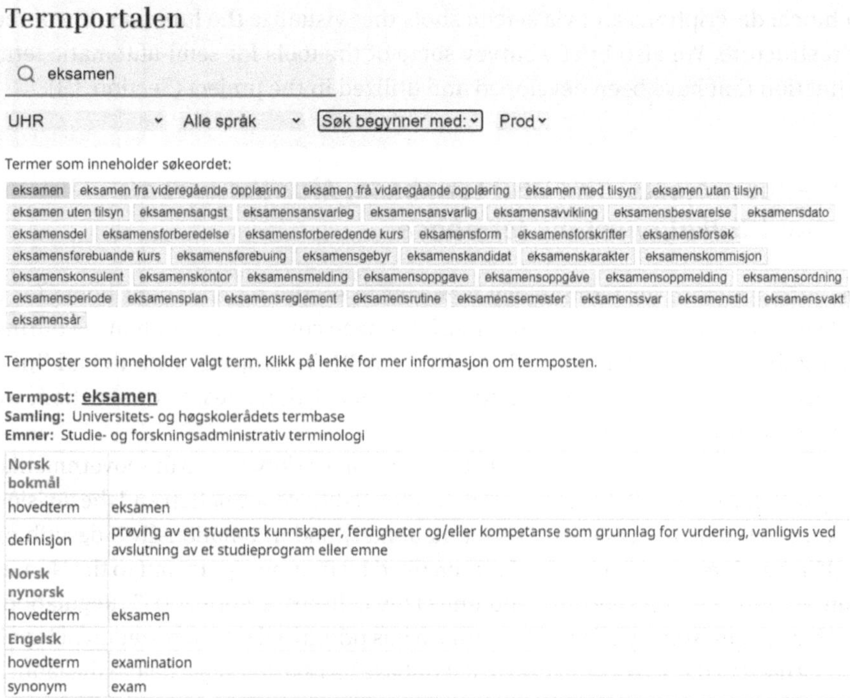

Figure 2: Snapshot of the UHR termbase.

wegian Bokmål and Nynorsk and English. This is considered a valuable resource for the entire sector, ensuring harmonization of terminology across institutions for concepts relating to study administration, admission, examination, mobility, publication, and so on.

Representing an entirely different discipline, *Maritim ordbok* ('Maritime Dictionary') is a project aimed at collecting, consolidating and making available a critical mass of terminology in maritime domains. This project was initiated in 2005 by a group representing NHH, *Havforskningsinstituttet* ('The Norwegian Institute of Marine Research'), and translation professionals (see Andersen 2022 for a more detailed account). Despite being a significant maritime nation, Norway has lacked a unified terminology resource covering this sector. The target domain of the project thus encompasses all concepts pertaining to maritime domains. These include biological and cultural concepts both above and below the sea surface, such as marine species and natural resources, industries and infrastructures, landforms and waterways. In addition to concepts pertaining to the sea, the resource also includes species and geoformations pertaining to freshwater. A survey of the top-level domains of *Maritim ordbok* is shown in Figure 3.

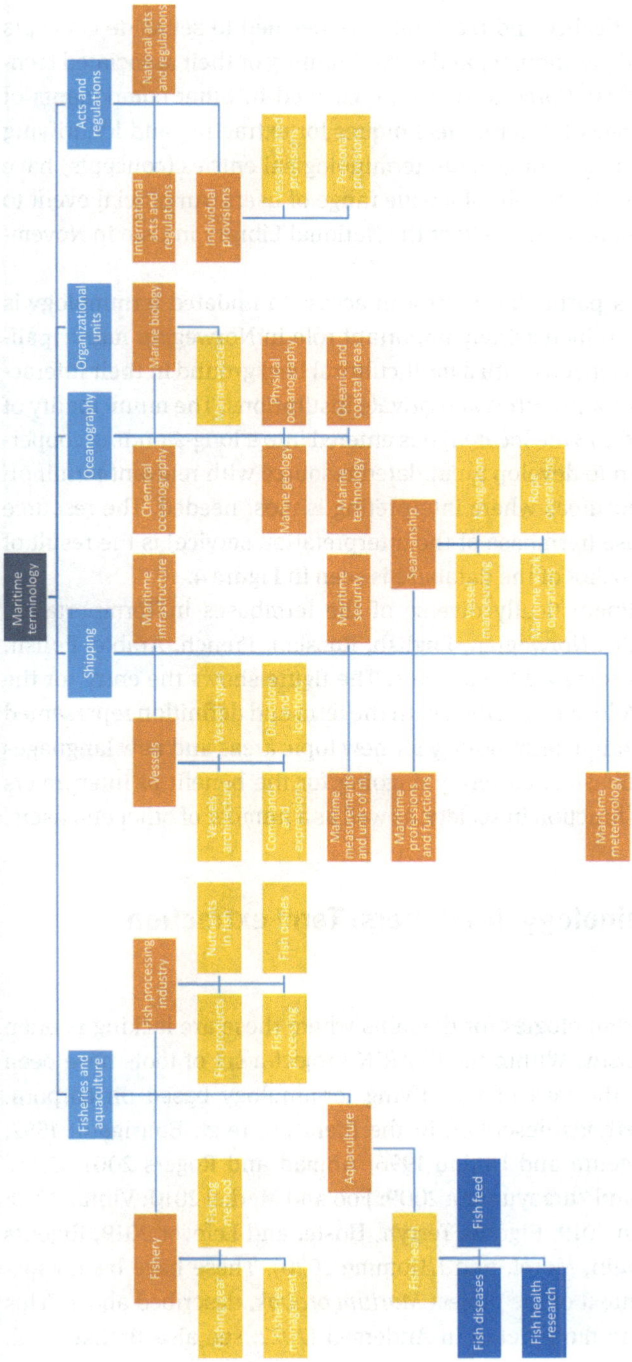

Figure 3: Survey of top-level domains covered in *Maritim ordbok*.

For reasons of practicality and feasibility, we decided to set aside concepts pertaining to the oil and gas industry and subsea mining or their associated technologies (subsea robotics). Some of these are covered in other components of Termportalen. Via a range of different techniques for extracting and identifying terminology (see Section 3.2) some 2,800 terminological entries (concepts) have been made available for the benefit of a wide range of users. An official event to launch this national resource was held at the National Library in Oslo in November 2019.

A user group with a particular interest in access to updated terminology is interpreters, who play an increasingly important role in Norwegian municipalities, offering services to citizens with a multicultural background in their interactions with various public authorities and private institutions. The municipality of Bergen (where NHH and UiB are located) has entered into a long-standing cooperation with Termportalen to develop an updated resource with relevant terminology for the various topic areas where interpreting is most needed. The resource Tolketjenestens termbase (termbase of the interpretation service) is the result of this cooperation. A snapshot of the database is seen in Figure 4.

This is the most linguistically diverse of the termbases in Termportalen, and at present it contains Norwegian, English, Russian, French, Arabic, Polish, and Somali and covers some 2,200 concepts. The figure shows the entry for the concept *alderspensjon* 'old age pension', with the term and definition represented in Arabic. The task of adding terminology for new topic areas and new languages in Tolketjenestens termbase is currently ongoing for the benefit of interpreters who fulfil an important function in society, as well as a number of other end users.

3.2 Tools for terminology developers: Term extraction procedures

The development of terminologies for domains where these are lacking is often time-consuming and costly. Within the CLARIN project a set of tools have been developed to alleviate the task of identifying terminology based on corpora, in accordance with methods described in the literature (e.g., Bourigault 1992; Ahmad et al. 1992; Kageura and Umino 1996; Ahmad and Rogers 2001; Cabré et al. 2001; Nazarenko and Zargayuouna 2009; Foo and Merkel 2010; Vintar 2010; Kageura and Marshman 2019; Rigouts Terryn, Hoste, and Lefever 2019; Rigouts Terryn et al. 2020; Drouin, Morel, and L'Homme 2020). These have been especially helpful in the context of the project *Maritim ordbok*, described above. This work is accounted for in more detail in Andersen (2022; see also Brekke et al.

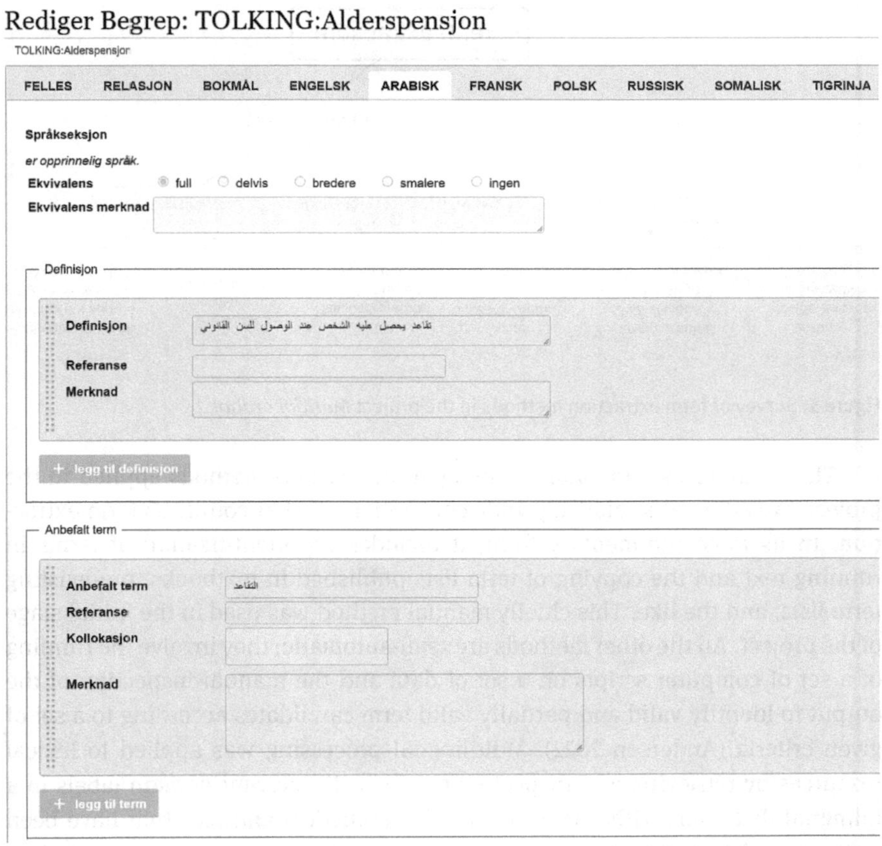

Figure 4: Snapshot of Tolketjenestens termbase (editing module).

2006; Andersen 2008, regarding similar term extraction efforts for Norwegian). As the tools and methods are generic and aimed at application in future projects, a brief account of this work is given here.

With a limited budget for corpus compilation and manual term extraction, the goal was to obtain a maximally wide range of language resources and to exploit these with a view to charting the inventory of term candidates in technical and scientific fields relevant to the maritime sector. Further, we aimed at developing, using, and reusing a range of computational tools and methods in order to identify term candidates in a largely technology-driven and bottom-up fashion. Given the language resources available to the project, both monolingual and multilingual data processing was applied, and the extraction was based on either pre-existing or purpose-built corpora and both specialized and general-purpose language resources. A survey of the methods used is given in Figure 5.

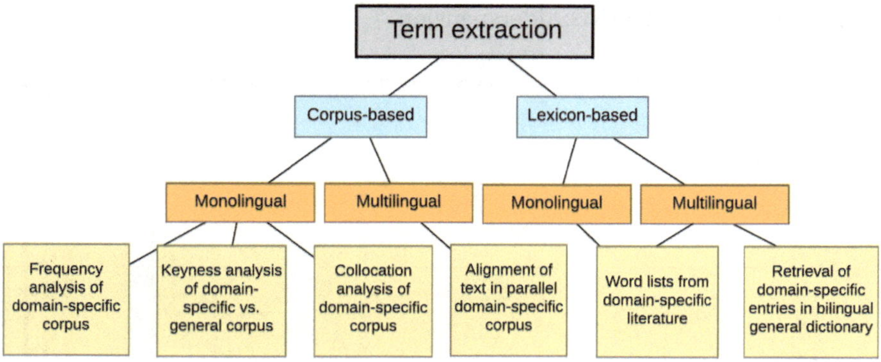

Figure 5: Survey of term extraction methods in the project *Maritim ordbok.*

The figure gives a taxonomic survey of the various methods applied in the project. We adopted a relatively wide conception of what counts as term extraction. In its most rudimentary form, it includes the identification of terms in running text and the copying of term lists published in textbooks, pre-existing term lists, and the like. This chiefly manual method was used in the initial stage of the project. All the other methods are semi-automatic; they involve the running of a set of computer scripts on a set of data and the manual inspection of the output to identify valid and partially valid term candidates according to a set of given criteria (Andersen 2022). Multilingual processing was applied to lexical resources by retrieving and inspecting entries with relevant domain labels in a bilingual dictionary. Other methods involve statistical analyses that have been well attested in corpus linguistics and natural language processing, including analysis of *n-gram frequency* of a domain-specific corpus, *keyness analysis* of the same corpus matched against the large Norwegian Newspaper Corpus (Andersen and Hofland 2012) and *collocation analysis* of the domain-specific corpus (à la Lyse and Andersen 2012). It also includes experiments with term extraction from a purpose-built domain-specific corpus of translated texts from international safety regulations for shipping.

Using these various methods, it was possible to extract a large amount of term candidates for subsequent manual checking and integration into the *Maritim ordbok* termbase, and a multitude of formally distinguishable terms were identified as relevant designations of individual concepts in the domain. Single-word terms are constituted as simplex words (*torsk* 'cod'), compounds (*torskeyngel* 'cod spawn'), or derived forms (*akklimatisering* 'acclimatization'). Multi-word candidates are constituted, for instance, as adjective + noun combinations (*signifikant bølgehøyde* 'significant wave height'), as (e.g., English-based) noun + noun combinations (*Alaska pollock*), or as longer, usually nominal phrases (*lukkede anlegg i sjø* 'closed sea-based facilities'). Although by far outnumbered by concepts constituted as noun phrases, other word classes also emerge via the applied methods, such as verbs (*låre* 'lower'), adverbs (*akter* 'abaft'), and prepositions (*aktenfor* 'abaft'). The overall result of the term extraction venture is that the various methods differ somewhat in their *pre hoc* work-intensity, precision/recall, and need for post-editing, but all have the potential to be reused in future projects involving other domains and language resources.

3.3 Tools for termbase developers: The editing module

Termportalen consists of two main tools, namely an editing module and a search interface. We will look closer at the editing module here, whereas the search interface will be presented in Section 3.4 below. Termportalen is based on web semantic data principles and modelled on the SKOS-AP-NO specification. Access to Termportalen data is communicated via Sparql endpoint API, both for external use and internally in Termportalen between the editing module, its dataset, and the search interface.

As mentioned in Section 1.2, the editing module in Termportalen is based on the Language Council's Termwiki, which was developed for their terminological resources. Both modules build on the open-source MediaWiki software, although Termportalen uses a more recent extension, the Semantic MediaWiki (SMW), to comply with the SKOS exchange format. SMW is a free, open-source extension to MediaWiki, which enables the storing and querying of data within a wiki's pages, making it a powerful and flexible knowledge management system.

All data housed in an SMW environment may easily be exported or published via the Semantic Web, allowing other systems to use this data seamlessly. The advantages of using SMW are that it is easily scalable, stable, and powerful, allowing for powerful yet simple annotation and reuse of the content inside a wiki. In addition, the Semantic MediaWiki adds database-like structuring and querying capabilities on top of an existing wiki, without requiring users to develop or adhere to a rigid database schema when authoring content. Because of the wiki layout, even people who are not accustomed with logic or ontologies can easily use the SMW.

Access to the editing module in Termportalen is granted through login, and uses the MediaWiki system of user right granting, where persons or groups can be assigned specific rights, such as editing access to certain datasets but not others. This is crucial in order to make sure that editing is not done on terms and datasets unintentionally, outside the control of the datasets' copyright holders.

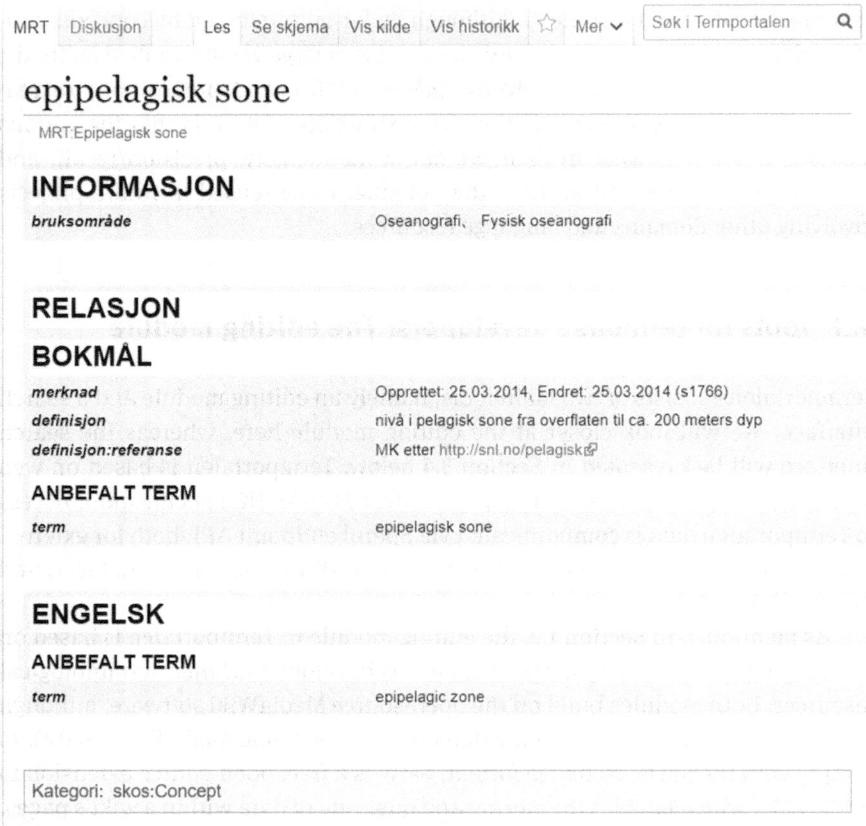

Figure 6: The editing module in Termportalen.

Once inside the editing module, it is possible to search for a term or look up a term through one of the termbases. The SMW architecture enables term results in the form of "terminological concepts", a result page ("Les") giving an overview of the actual terminological concept, its various terms, the domain, definitions, and source references; see Figure 6. It is also possible via the tabs on the top bar to view the editing scheme ("Se skjema"), the source code ("Vis kilde"), and what changes the concept has undergone ("Vis historikk").

Concept editing is very scalable and adaptable to any kind of termbase at any level of detail, and editing forms may be customized accordingly. Editing takes place under the tab "Se skjema" in predefined forms, for domain, relations, and languages.

Every language defined in a termbase will have its own editing form, where the specific information pertaining to the language in question and sources for

Figure 7: Editing concepts in Termportalen.

term use is entered and stored See Figure 7. The first tabs ("Felles" and "Relasjon") are used to define the domain of the concept and to state any relations of the term to other terms, be they generic, associative, or partitive, or, more specifically, superordinate or subordinate concepts. For each language, it is possible to give a definition of the concept, state references, and write remarks concerning the concept. Each concept may have a number of terms associated with it, such as *preferred term*, *synonym*, *not advised*, and *abbreviation*. Each associated term may also be given its own comments and source references, and so on.

As can be seen in Figure 8, nothing is deleted or overwritten in the Semantic MediaWiki system. Any change made to a concept is stored and logged under the tab "Vis historikk". It is possible to undo changes in certain circumstances and with proper user rights.

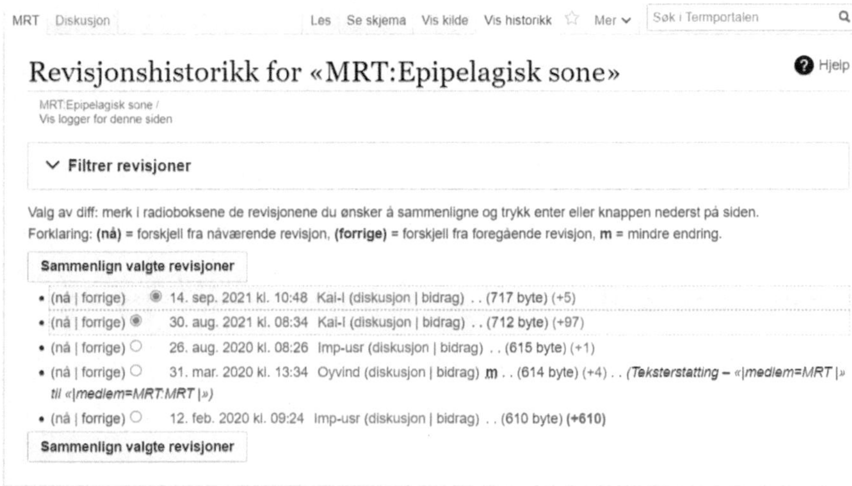

Figure 8: Display of revision history in Termportalen.

3.4 Tools for end users: The search interface

The Termportalen frontend, or search interface, is a free-to-use, open access portal, which communicates with the editing module (see Section 3.3) and its datasets through a Sparql endpoint API.[31] The search interface is built with Vue.js, which is a lightweight, open-source frontend JavaScript framework for building user interfaces and single-page applications.[32] Thanks to its components, its incrementally adaptable architecture, and lightweight nature, Vue.js has turned out to be suitable for this project, as well as other projects under the umbrella of the Language Collections (*Språksamlingane ved UiB*).[33]

From the user perspective, the search interface is designed to be both as intuitive and as adaptable as possible. It features a continuously updateable search field, which may be both used to query into all database concept terms in an open search and scaled to make specific queries within individual termbases or languages, including where in a concept term the search expression should find matches.

31 https://www.w3.org/TR/sparql11-query/
32 https://vuejs.org/
33 https://www.uib.no/ub/102215/innhaldet-i-spr%C3%A5ksamlingane

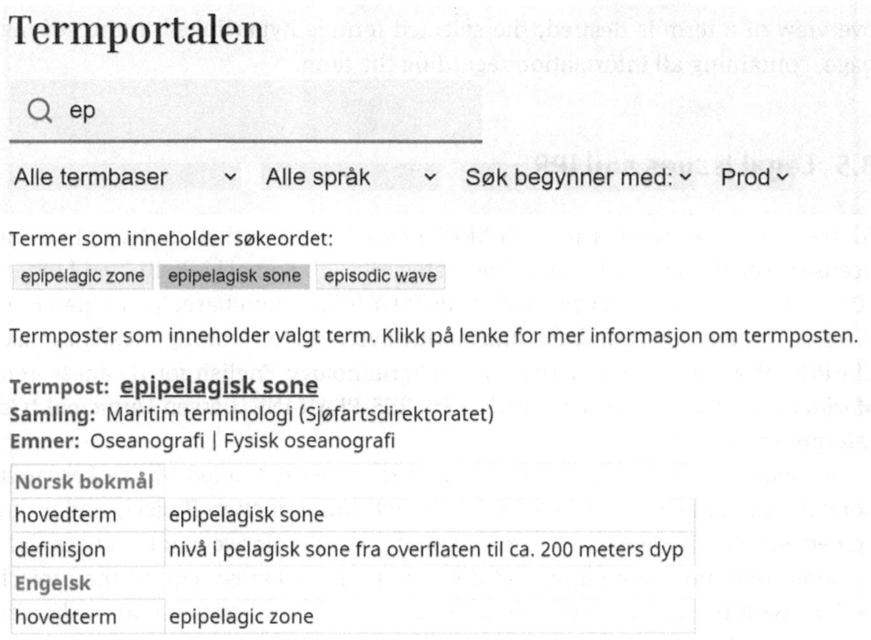

Figure 9: The end user interface for Termportalen.

The standard mode is a wide search in all term bases ("Alle termbaser"), all languages ("Alle språk"), and a search from the beginning of a term ("Søk begynner med"). This search will find any term beginning with the expression typed into the search box. Individual search suggestions are visible immediately under the search panel. Each suggestion may be selected for further investigation.

Specialized searches can be scaled infinitely through the combination of termbases, languages, and position of match one chooses from the drop-down menus below the search field. Any filtering on termbases and languages will restrict search results accordingly. An expression typed into the search box may be restricted to the start of a term, part of a term, or the full term. An additional search match type inspired by elastic search is also being tested for usability.

A query result may be obtained by writing the full expression or by writing part of it and then selecting the relevant expression among the search suggestions below the search panel. The result is both shown in the result panel as well as being highlighted as a search suggestion (shown in green in Figure 9).

The result panel shows the selected term ("Termpost"), the termbase ("Samling"), and domain ("Emner") as the top-level result, in keeping with terminological principles. This is followed by an overview of the term, its term status, definition, and equivalent terms in other languages. If a more detailed overview of a term is desired, the selected term is hyperlinked to the editing page, containing all information regarding the term.

3.5 Legal issues and IPR

All the Norwegian termbases in CLARINO have been reposited under individual licenses. The licenses fall under three categories (cf. Kamocki, Kelli, and Lindén 2022), ranging from open use CLARIN_PUB-BY (UHR's termbase, Norwegian Biodiversity Terminology Database, and Marine Evertebrates), through academic use CLARIN_ACA (Norwegian-German Legal Terminology English for Business and *Maritim ordbok*), to restricted use CLARIN_RES-PLAN-INF (Bergen Municipality's Interpreters' Termbase).

Development relating to Termportalen is currently funded by the Research Council of Norway in the CLARINO+ Research Infrastructure Project, under the agreement that the Bergen University Library and the Norwegian Language Collections continue maintaining and developing the resource beyond the project period. With the elevation of Termportalen to a national resource for technical language and terminology (see Sections 1.1 and 4), it is necessary to investigate if the new status of Termportalen affects the current agreement and if an addendum or replacement is needed. Any legal issues relating to API exchange between Termportalen and external resources (cf. Section 4 below), as well as authentication regulations must be considered also.

Once Termportalen is fully developed, issues such as accreditation of termbase publishers and contributors will have been addressed. However, this is not yet fully implemented.

4 Conclusions and future work

In addition to the possible addenda or replacements of licences necessitated by the transfer of resources to UiB's Language Collections, mentioned above, other more technical tasks are equally imminent. As is clear from our discussion above, several terminological resources are being further developed, and new TBX versions of all databases will be made accessible in the pan-European CLARIN ERIC as part of the deliverables of the ongoing national CLARINO+ project. Other suggestions for future work are implementing improved techniques for displaying concept relations and new routines for user authentication and authorization.

As mentioned in Section 1.1 above, the recently adopted *Lov om språk* (the Language Law) for Norway sets out a new direction for Termportalen:

> Termportalen kan derfor bli ein nasjonal infrastruktur for å sikre vidareutviklinga av norsk fagspråk og terminologi. Prop. 108 L (2019–2020) *Lov om språk (språklova)*
> (Governmental whitepaper: 72; see footnote 4)
>
> [Therefore, Termportalen can become a national infrastructure to ensure the ongoing development of Norwegian technical language and terminology.]

To elevate Termportalen to a national resource of the scale envisaged by the Language Law whitepaper, it is necessary to think of it as both a termbase host as well as a connecting hub for terminological and technical language resources. As there are already well over 140 terminological resources in Norway (see Section 1.2), it is not practically possible to host all existing resources, even if Termportalen is technically scaled for it. It is necessary to factor in that many of these resources have been developed at considerable cost for the commissioning companies or interest organizations, and a strong sense of ownership over some of the resources is still felt.

What is possible, however, is to focus on termbase inter-communication via API. This is developed for Termportalen and operationable through a SKOS exchange format Sparql endpoint API (see Section 3.2). The API allows for a two-way communication between Termportalen and external resources. This means that external resources can use and display existing Termportalen termbases under the conditions stated in the CLARINO repository agreement for each termbase. It also means that we can display external resources directly in Termportalen, with the external resources remaining entirely autonomous in terms of storage, maintenance, and development. This will ensure a quicker path for Termportalen to become the truly national resource envisaged by the Language Law governmental whitepaper (and, indeed, by us!).

It is also possible to envisage a hybrid situation where a resource remains hosted externally, but where the editing module of Termportalen is used to augment, edit, and maintain the resource. Such a scenario requires additional upgrading of the API so that it can also handle editing.

With the elevation of Termportalen from a local project to a national portal for terminology and scientific and technical vocabulary, procedures for user authentication must be reconsidered and strengthened. Some of the prospective users and technical language experts will be connected to external resources and parts of the authentication will probably need to be administered externally. These, therefore, are among the many tasks that lie ahead.

Bibliography

Ahmad, Khurshid, Andrea E. Davies, Heather Fulford & Margaret Rogers. 1992. What is a term? The semi-automatic extraction of terms from text. In Mary Snell-Hornby, Franz Pöchhacker & Klaus Kaindl (eds.), *Translation studies: An interdiscipline*, 267–278. Amsterdam: John Benjamins. https://doi.org/10.1075/btl.2.33ahm.

Ahmad, Khurshid & Margaret A. Rogers. 2001. Corpus linguistics and terminology extraction. In Sue-Ellen Wright & Gerhard Budin (eds.), *Handbook of terminology management: Volume 2*, 725–760. Amsterdam: John Benjamins. https://doi.org/10.1075/z.htm2.28ahm.

Andersen, Gisle. 2008. Quantifying domain-specificity: The occurrence of financial terms in a general corpus. *SYNAPS* 21. 37–52.

Andersen, Gisle. 2022. Utilising heterogeneous language resources for term extraction in maritime domains. *Terminology* 28 (1). 1–36.

Andersen, Gisle, Peder Gammeltoft & Kjetil Gundersen. 2021. Termportalen – fra forprosjekt til fast finansiering [The terminology Portal: From pilot project to permanent funding]. *Nordterm* 22. 65–76. http://www.nordterm.net/wiki/sv/index.php/Nordterm_22

Andersen, Gisle & Knut Hofland. 2012. Building a large corpus based on newspapers from the web. In Gisle Andersen (ed.), *Exploring newspaper language: Using the web to create and investigate a large corpus of modern Norwegian*, 1–28. Amsterdam: John Benjamins. https://doi.org/10.1075/scl.49.01and.

Andersen, Gisle & Marita Kristiansen. 2013. Towards a national portal for Norwegian terminology in the CLARINO project. *Terminologen* 2. 188–189.

Andersen, Gisle & Marita Kristiansen. 2015. Termportalen som infrastruktur for terminologi i Norge [The Terminology Portal as infrastructure for terminology in Norway]. *Terminologen* 5. 53–60.

Bourigault, Didier. 1992. Surface grammatical analysis for the extraction of terminological noun phrases. In *COLING '92: Proceedings of the 14th International Conference on Computational Linguistics*, 977–981. Nantes: ICC.

Brekke, Magnar, Kai Innselset, Marita Kristiansen & Kari Øvsthus. 2006. KB-N: Automatic term extraction from a knowledge-bank of economics. *International Conference on Langauge Resources and Evaluation* 5. 1912–1915.

Cabré, M. Teresa. 1999. *Terminology: Theory, methods and applications*. Amsterdam: John Benjamins. https://doi.org/10.1075/tlrp.1.

Cabré, M. Teresa. 2003. Theories of terminology: Their description, prescription and explanation. *Terminology* 9 (2). 163–199. https://doi.org/10.1075/term.9.2.03cab.

Cabré, M. Teresa, María Estopa, Rosa Bagot & Jordi Palatresi. 2001. Automatic term detection: A review of current systems. In Didier Bourigault, Christian Jacquemin & Marie-Claude L'Homme (eds.), *Recent advances in computational terminology*, 53–88. Amsterdam: John Benjamins. https://doi.org/10.1075/nlp.2.04cab.

Draxler, Christoph, Alexander Geyken, Erhard Hinrichs, Annette Klosa-Kückelhaus, Elke Teich & Thorsten Trippel. 2022. How to connect language resources and infrastructures, and communities. In Darja Fišer & Andreas Witt (eds.), *CLARIN. The infrastructure for language resources*. Berlin: De Gruyter.

Drouin, Patrick, Jean-Benoît Morel & Marie-Claude L'Homme. 2020. Automatic term extraction from newspaper corpora: Making the most of specificity and common features. In Béatrice

Daille, Kyo Kageura & Ayla Rigouts Terryn (eds.), *Proceedings of the LREC 2020 6th International Workshop on Computational Terminology (COMPUTERM 2020)*, 1–7. Paris: ELRA.

Foo, Jody & Magnus Merkel. 2010. Computer aided term bank creation and standardization: Building standardized term banks through automated term extraction and advanced editing tools. In Marcel Thelen and Frieda Steurs (eds.), *Terminology in everyday life*, 163–180. Amsterdam: John Benjamins. https://doi.org/10.1075/tlrp.13.12foo.

Kageura, Kyo & Elizabeth Marshman. 2019. Terminology extraction and management. In Minako O'Hagan, (ed.), *The Routledge handbook of translation and technology*, 61–77. New York: Routledge. https://doi.org/10.4324/9781315311258-4.

Kageura, Kyo & Bin Umino. 1996. Methods of automatic term recognition. *Terminology*. 3 (2). 259–289.

Kamocki, Paweł, Aleksei Kelli & Krister Lindén. 2022. The CLARIN Committee for Legal and Ethical Issues and the Normative Layer of the CLARIN infrastructure. In Darja Fišer & Andreas Witt (eds.), *CLARIN. The infrastructure for language resources*. Berlin: De Gruyter.

Lyse, Gunn Inger & Gisle Andersen. 2012. Collocations and statistical analysis of n-grams. In Gisle Andersen (ed.), *Exploring newspaper language: Using the web to create and investigate a large corpus of modern Norwegian*, 79–110. Amsterdam: John Benjamins. https://doi.org/10.1075/scl.49.05lys.

Myking, Johan. 2005. Terminologi i Noreg – historisk oversyn [Terminology in Norway – an historical survey]. In Jan Hoel (ed.), *Hvem tar ansvaret for fagterminologien?*, 2–15. Oslo: Språkrådet.

Myking, Johan. 2006. Nyare terminologiarbeid i Noreg [Recent terminology work in Norway]. *Språknytt* 2006 (2). 13–18.

Nazarenko, Adeline & Haifa Zargayouna. 2009. Evaluating term extraction. *International Conference on Recent Advances in Natural Language Processing (RANLP'09), Sep 2009, Borovets, Bulgaria*, 299–304. https://hal.archives-ouvertes.fr/hal-00517090/ (24 November 2021).

Rauset, Margunn, Gyri Smørdal Losnegaard, Helge Dyvik, Paul Meurer, Rune Kyrkjebø & Koenraad De Smedt. 2022. Words, words! Resources and tools for lexicography at the CLARINO Bergen Centre. In Darja Fišer & Andreas Witt (eds.), *CLARIN. The infrastructure for language resources*. Berlin: De Gruyter.

Rigouts Terryn, Ayla, Patrick Drouin, Veronique Hoste & Els Lefever. 2020. TermEval 2020: Shared task on automatic term extraction using the annotated corpora for term extraction research (ACTER) dataset. In Béatrice Daille, Kyo Kageura & Ayla Rigouts Terryn (eds.), *Proceedings of the LREC 2020 6th International Workshop on Computational Terminology (COMPUTERM 2020)*, 85–94. Paris: ELRA.

Rigouts Terryn, Ayla, Veronique Hoste & Els Lefever. 2019. In no uncertain terms: A dataset for monolingual and multilingual automatic term extraction from comparable corpora. *Language Resources and Evaluation* 54 (2). 385–418. https://doi.org/10.1007/s10579-019-09453-9.

Temmerman, Rita. 2000. *Towards new ways of terminology description*. Amsterdam: John Benjamins. https://doi.org/10.1075/tlrp.3.

Vintar, Špela. 2010. Bilingual term recognition revisited. *Terminology* 16 (2). 141–158. https://doi.org/10.1075/term.16.2.01vin.

Christoph Draxler, Alexander Geyken, Erhard Hinrichs,
Annette Klosa-Kückelhaus, Elke Teich, and Thorsten Trippel

How to Connect Language Resources, Infrastructures, and Communities

Abstract: This chapter will present lessons learned from CLARIN-D, the German CLARIN national consortium. Members of the CLARIN-D communities and of the CLARIN-D consortium have been engaged in innovative, data-driven, and community-based research, using language resources and tools in the humanities and neighbouring disciplines. We will present different use cases and users' stories that demonstrate the innovative research potential of large digital corpora and lexical resources for the study of language change and variation, for language documentation, for literary studies, and for the social sciences. We will emphasize the added value of making language resources and tools available in the CLARIN distributed research infrastructure and will discuss legal and ethical issues that need to be addressed in the use of such an infrastructure. Innovative technical solutions for accessing digital materials still under copyright and for data mining such materials will be presented. We will outline the need for close interaction with communities of interest in the areas of curriculum development, data management, and training the next generation of

Acknowledgments: The work reported here was funded by the Federal Ministry of Education and Research, Germany (BMBF) and the home institutions of the authors within various projects and funding programmes, especially in the CLARIN-D and CLARIAH-DE contexts. It also involves work within affiliated projects supported by other funders such as the Ministry of Science, Research and Art of the Federal State of Baden-Württemberg (MWK), and the German Research Foudation (DFG), and projects funded by the European Commission involving the institutions of the authors.

Christoph Draxler, Ludwig-Maximilians-Universität München, Institut für Phonetik, Munich, Germany, e-mail: draxler@phonetik.uni-muenchen.de
Alexander Geyken, Berlin-Brandenburgische Akademie der Wissenschaften, Berlin, Germany, e-mail: geyken@bbaw.de
Erhard Hinrichs, University of Tübingen, Tübingen, Germany, e-mail: erhard.hinrichs@uni-tuebingen.de
Annette Klosa-Kückelhaus, Leibniz Institut für Deutsche Sprache, Mannheim, Germany, e-mail: klosa@ids-mannheim.de
Elke Teich, Saarland University, Saarbrücken, Germany, e-mail: e.teich@mx.uni-saarland.de
Thorsten Trippel, University of Tübingen, Tübingen, Germany; Leibniz Institut für Deutsche Sprache, Mannheim, Germany, e-mail: thorsten.trippel@uni-tuebingen.de

https://doi.org/10.1515/9783110767377-011

digital humanities scholars. The importance of community-supported standards for encoding language resources and the practice of community-based quality control for digital research data will be presented as a crucial step toward the provisioning of high quality research data. The chapter will conclude with a discussion of important directions for innovative research and for supporting infrastructure development over the next decade and beyond.

Keywords: CLARIN-D, research infrastructure, humanities, user communities, use cases

1 Introduction

The availability of digital research data of various kinds has led to new research paradigms and innovative research results in many fields of science, including the humanities, the social sciences, and related disciplines. Findability of research data, easy access to such data, interoperability among research data, and the reuse of data have become important desiderata. These requirements have been summarized in the FAIR principles (see Wilkinson et al. 2016) and more recently in the additional CARE principles (see Carroll et al. 2021).

Language data play a key role in this digital turn since unstructured textual data account for up to 80% of all digital data (see ESFRI Roadmap 2018: 108). Given the enormous and ever-increasing volume of digital data, text and data mining techniques in combination with sophisticated data analysis and data visualization tools have become an indispensable part of data-driven research. More generally, these demands have led to the development of research data infrastructures that couple data resources with such analysis tools and a rich portfolio of other services that facilitate uptake of digital research methods by a growing number of researchers.

1.1 The digital turn

In the humanities and social sciences, research is increasingly based on empirically collected data, especially in the Digital Humanities (DH), sometimes also referred to as eHumanities. While in early DH projects, a main concern was the (retro-) digitization of data (see, e.g., Presner 2010), more recent work is based on large stocks of digitized material feeding into working environments to create, manage, and deal with digital knowledge. This new way of dealing with data results in innovative questions that lead to prototypical computer-assisted approaches to analysis in the digital humanities (see also Schaal and Kath 2014).

The development of legacy – "born analogue" – and data already digitally archived from the beginning – "born digital" – does not constitute a discrete differentiation, but rather forms a continuum. The extremes here are analogue data at one end of the spectrum, with data that is available on paper accessible only in restricted facilities, and fully interoperable, interlinked, and reusable data at the other end. The latter is often referred to as FAIR, as mentioned above, indicating data that is Findable, Accessible, Interoperable, and Reusable.

The availability of data on the continuum between legacy and born digital data opens up new methodological approaches or entirely new scientific questions. These questions go hand in hand with discussions on the "digital turn" (see, e.g., Berry 2011; Baum and Stäcker 2015). Domain-related research infrastructures take up these methods and have the task of supporting research in all phases – in data research, the digital provision of data, the linking of data to form virtual collections, the analysis of data with the aid of interoperable software tools. It also includes the storage and archiving of the resulting research data. Originally often installed on the personal computing devices of researchers, more and more tools are becoming available with web interfaces (see, e.g., Gomes et al. 2022). The web based infrastructure allows complex querying of data, including data that is distributed at different institutions. Users apply the tools without having to install them, work collaboratively, and unknowingly benefit from hardware and service scalability due to the operation of service providers.

To achieve transparency in an opaque server-side processing of research data, the interaction and discussion between applying researchers and service providers becomes an indispensable requirement. This interaction is needed on both sides, on the side of the users and on the side of the research infrastructures. The researchers need the interaction to understand the limits and capabilities of the infrastructure to assess the results provided in the process. The infrastructure providers on the other side need the discourse to understand the requirements and research questions to adjust the services as needed. The discussion requires Research Data Management (RDM) services and consultation. Here the users receive the support they need to efficiently provide their own results according to the FAIR principles without the overhead costs of having to provide the services themselves. A helpdesk for specific questions helps researchers to work with the tools and find the expert knowledge they might require for their specific questions. This process may result in consulting requirements to adjust the infrastructure services or to find appropriate methods available for a given research question. Often the first point of contact between young researchers and services provided by the infrastructures is in the context of academic teaching or at conferences and workshops run by professional associations. This contact allows the infrastructures to connect to the researchers who will use the services and create new datasets that may be made available for reuse by other researchers with the help of the infrastructure providers.

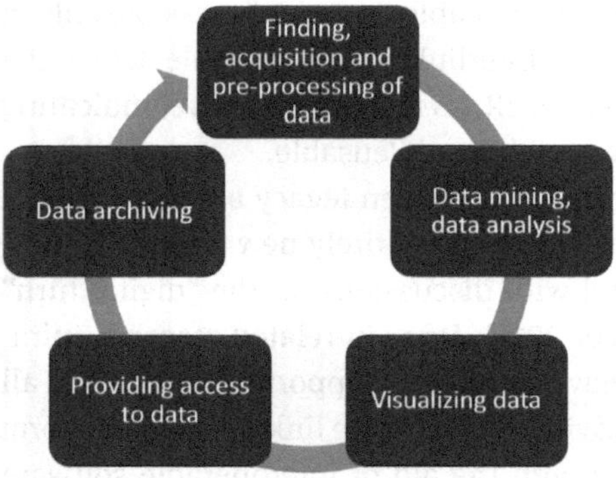

Figure 1: Illustration of the Research Data Lifecycle as a continuous process of data reuse and re-analysis, as often practised in the humanities.

1.2 Research Data Infrastructures (RDI) by researchers for researchers

Data is created at all stages of the research data lifecycle, from (1) finding, acquisition, and pre-processing data for reuse or creating new primary data, to (2) analysing data, including through data mining, (3) visualizing data, (4) making data available for review, and finally (5) archiving data.

Figure 1 illustrates the research data life cycle, which is used in different variants in many disciplines. What they have in common is that the entire process is viewed from the research perspective. However, some of the phases require cooperation with research infrastructure providers, for example, long-term archiving, which individual researchers can hardly be expected to do. Infrastructures are also useful for other tasks along the research data lifecycle, be it the provision of inventory data, tools for converting or searching and analysing data, virtual research environments, computing capacity, or the like. The research-driven data processing using infrastructures requires a continuous dialogue between data providers and data users – which can in some cases hardly be distinguished – and research infrastructures. In the case of CLARIN, a research infrastructure initiative was even created by and for researchers, along with national nodes. The present chapter originates from participants in the German part of CLARIN.[1] Researchers joined forces to provide a sustainable infrastructure for their reference data and tools. Through sharing and collaboration they started to provide their data and services according to FAIR principles even before this term was coined, opening their data and services also for researchers, with an initiative that is open to new contributions and developments.

1.3 Use cases to extend the portfolio of Research Data Infrastructures

The dialogue between users of a research infrastructure (RI) and researchers providing the RI is needed to extend the portfolio of services and data. Though the researchers providing the RI also contribute to new developments based on their own research interests, new impulses can efficiently result from researchers not originally part of this development. This dialogue becomes transparent by providing uses cases.

Via use cases, the infrastructures demonstrate their existing abilities and options with data that is provided. Users of the infrastructure, on the other hand, also describe additional functionalities and required datasets by drafting a use case that fits their research interest. Hence, use cases are an effective means of extending the portfolio of research data and associated tools and for improving the usability of research data infrastructures. These use cases allow us to describe how research infrastructures can be used for new research topics, for new datasets, with new technologies, and for illustrating research questions in academic education.[2]

In the next section we will provide examples of the continuous enhancement and use of the research infrastructure, as illustrated by use cases.

1 Other national partners in CLARIN contributing to this volume are South Africa with Hennelly et al. 2022, Portugal with Silva et al. 2022, Czech Republic with Hajič et al. 2022, Lithuania with Petrauskaitė et al. 2022, and Austria with Trognitz, Ďurčo, and Mörth 2022.

2 More use cases for data and services are also included in this volume, for example in Silva et al. 2022 on diachronic Portuguese corpora; Lindahl and Rødven-Eide 2022 on Swedish corpora; Hoeksema, de Glopper, and van Noord 2022 on investigating secondary school writing; Pozzo et al. 2022 on aligning Chinese translations of Kant; Kučera 2022 on using NLP tools in psychological research; Fridlund et al. 2022 on cross-lingual text mining.

2 Development of the infrastructure by user-driven use cases

We established the need for infrastructures and user communities to interact. This interaction makes sure that new developments in the infrastructure are made available to the communities and the communities provide impulses for new developments as needed. To illustrate the interaction we draw on a number of use cases. We distinguish three classes of uses cases:

- addressing emerging research topics driven by public discourse;
- application of new technologies;
- new, faster more precise answers to established research questions;
- integration of new research data and developing community-methods for maintaining and improving research data quality.

In the remainder of this section, we will provide examples for each. These examples illustrate the interaction of user communities and infrastructure providers, which was key to answering the research questions.

2.1 Addressing emerging research topics driven by public discourse

Public discourse can lead to new research questions, for which an answer should be provided as part of this discussion. These questions may result from natural phenomena or long-term developments in society.

An example of natural phenomena influencing public discourse is the Covid-19 pandemic, which appeared in public media in 2020. Besides research in the life sciences and so forth, it also initiated research with regards to language change and language use, addressing the pandemic from a lexicographic perspective. An almost real-time investigation requires the availability of data and tools provided by a research infrastructure.

An example of long-term developments in society driving research topics is based on an intensive and long-lasting discussion rooted in emancipation and striving for non-discriminatory communication strategies. Here, the investigation of gender-neutral forms and their influence on pronunciation provides a new perspective on research on language change. Again, the tools and data for investigating such a research question can reuse data and tools developed for other purposes, provided by research infrastructures.

Interactions between infrastructures and scholarly users dealing with this type of question are characterized by their embeddedness in current events, but not necessarily by new methods and technologies. Though some new resources may be added, these questions are addressed with existing tools and often with existing resources.

2.1.1 Addressing the pandemic with lexicography

In 2020, the Covid-19 pandemic changed the world on a large scale; it also affected lexicographic work, as new words and phrases or new meanings of established words emerged on a daily basis and medical as well as epidemiological terminology became part of the general language. This is why early on in the pandemic, the *Digital Dictionary of the German Language* (DWDS)[3] compiled a thematic glossary with approximately 300 entries, containing medical terms (e.g., *Triage* 'triage', *Tröpfcheninfektion* 'droplet infection'), older lexemes with high current relevance in the public discourse on the pandemic (e.g., *Mundschutz* 'face mask', *Kontaktsperre* 'contact ban'), and neologisms (e.g., *Coronaparty* 'party during the Covid-19 pandemic defying rules of social distancing').[4] Existing entries were updated and new entries compiled based on corpus evidence to document the current changes in the German lexicon promptly. The thematic glossary presents the entries in an alphabetical list with (mostly) only the definition(s), but links them to the complete entry for each lexeme in the dictionary itself (with corpus citations, information on frequency, etc.).

The *Neologismenwörterbuch*[5] chose a different approach. This dictionary focuses on German neologisms from the three decades 1991–2000, 2001–2010, and 2011–2020. Starting in April 2020, it presents Covid-19 neologisms (new words, phrases, and meanings) in a continually updated list containing (as of March 2021) roughly 1,300 entries.[6] The meaning of each word or phrase is explained and at least one corpus citation is given. Not all words and phrases have yet been lexicographically described

3 See https://www.dwds.de/.
4 See https://www.dwds.de/themenglossar/Corona. Later in 2020, a thematic glossary on the US election campaign and one with Christmas words were published, see https://www.dwds.de/themenglossar/US-Wahl-2020 and https://www.dwds.de/themenglossar/Weihnachten, respectively.
5 See https://www.owid.de/docs/neo/start.jsp; more information on this portal can be found in Engelberg, Klosa-Kückelhaus, and Müller-Spitzer 2020; for dictionary portals in general see Engelberg and Müller-Spitzer 2013.
6 See https://www.owid.de/docs/neo/listen/corona.jsp.

in full, as neologisms are usually monitored for some years[7] before being accepted into the dictionary as part of the general language. Many of the Covid-19 neologisms will probably disappear at some point (e.g., many synonyms for grown-out haircuts due to periods of lock-down throughout the pandemic, such as *Coronafrisur*, *Coronamatte*, *Coronamähne*, *Lockdownfrisur*, *Lockdownlocken*, etc.). Thus, the *Neologismenwörterbuch* list is a snapshot of the current extension of the lexicon, based on evidence from online press and social media. One corpus-linguistic tool used to find candidates for the list is the *cOWIDplus Viewer* (cf. Section 2); information in the entries is also based on data from *Deutsches Referenzkorpus – DeReKo*.[8]

2.1.2 Exploring language change: The pronunciation of gender-neutral forms

With the ongoing debate about equal rights, non-discriminatory communication is part of public discourse. Currently, there is an ongoing discussion about gender neutrality in language in many countries. In German, the traditional male form to collectively refer to groups of people, for example, *Bäcker*, includes both male and female members, but with a perceived bias towards the male sex/gender.[9] New forms to express gender neutrality in German first appeared in written language in newspapers, social media, and job descriptions, for instance, a capital 'I' inside a word as in *BäckerIn*, or an asterisk or an underscore, as in *Bäcker*in* or *Bäcker_in*.

In a class for students in the master's programme, three students (two studying phonetics, one studying Ancient Greek) decided to explore how these gender neutral forms are spoken. Their hypothesis: gender-neutral forms are spoken with a perceivably lengthened final /I/ vowel. A quick check via general-purpose search engines and in CLARIN's virtual language observatory did not return matching resources. Thus, the students decided to record their own corpus, compute a phonetic segmentation which contains both the sound label (in the IPA alphabet) and their duration, run their analyses, and create a speech database to be added to a CLARIN-D repository for others to work with.[10]

---

7 A list of all words or phrases currently monitored by the dictionary project has been published online since 2019, see https://www.owid.de/docs/neo/listen/monitor.jsp.

8 For the use of a diachronic corpus to detect language change (such as lexical or semantic change) see Pettersson and Borin 2022.

9 For some interesting thoughts on the topic see, for example, https://www.nzz.ch/feuilleton/gendern-genus-und-sexus-sind-eng-miteinander-verbunden-ld.1578299.

10 This database is now available in the BAS repository: http://hdl.handle.net/11022/1009-0000-0003-FF39-F.

For the recordings, the students collected sentences from the German newspaper *taz, die tageszeitung*, edited them for readability, and generated both a gender-neutral and a non-gendered version of each sentence. The sentences were then read by 18 speakers in the studio of the phonetics institute in Munich, using the SpeechRecorder software (Draxler and Jänsch 2004).

The orthographic transcription was generated by listening to the audio files and manual modification of the prompt text to create a verbatim transcript, including filled pauses, self-repairs, and deviations from the prompt text. The result of these steps was a collection of more than 600 pairs of audio and text files.

A first look at the transcripts showed an unexpected phenomenon: for the production of gender neutral forms, speakers deviate from the given prompt in roughly 26% of the recordings. They expand the given form by adding its complement, either with or without a junctor, or they substitute the given form with the male form (see Table 1). Apparently, some speakers try to *avoid* the gender-neutral forms – the reasons are unknown.

Table 1: Avoidance strategies for sentences with a gender neutral form, for instance, *BäckerInnen.*

Type	Example	%
elliptical expansion	*Bäcker Bäckerinnen*	15.9%
complete expansion	*Bäcker und Bäckerinnen*	6.8%
substitution by male form	*Bäcker*	4.3%
other		2.0%

To generate a phonetic segmentation, that is a time-aligned annotation with the duration of words and individual speech sounds, the WebMAUS service (Kisler, Schiel, and Sloetjes 2012) was used. The students uploaded the file pairs to the CLARIN-D server via the graphical interface, selected standard German as the input language, IPA symbols as the output character set, and the Praat TextGrid file format (Boersma 2001). After a few minutes, the service displayed the segmentation in the Emu WebApp viewer (Winkelmann and Raess 2014), and the resulting files were downloaded to the local computer – this would have taken weeks if done manually.

The TextGrid files were converted to a tabular format and imported into a relational database system to be accessed from the statistics package R.

A statistical analysis of the duration of the final /I/ vowel showed both that the median duration was higher and the variation greater for gender neutral forms (see Figure 2 (b)). A plausible interpretation is that speakers produce gender neutral forms differently, but that there is not yet a consensus on how they should be produced.

The paper was successfully submitted to a phonetics conference (Slavik, Cronenberg, and Draxler 2018). A reviewer noted that this work describes one of the rare cases where orthography leads the way in sound change – a thrilling experience for students, made possible by CLARIN tools.

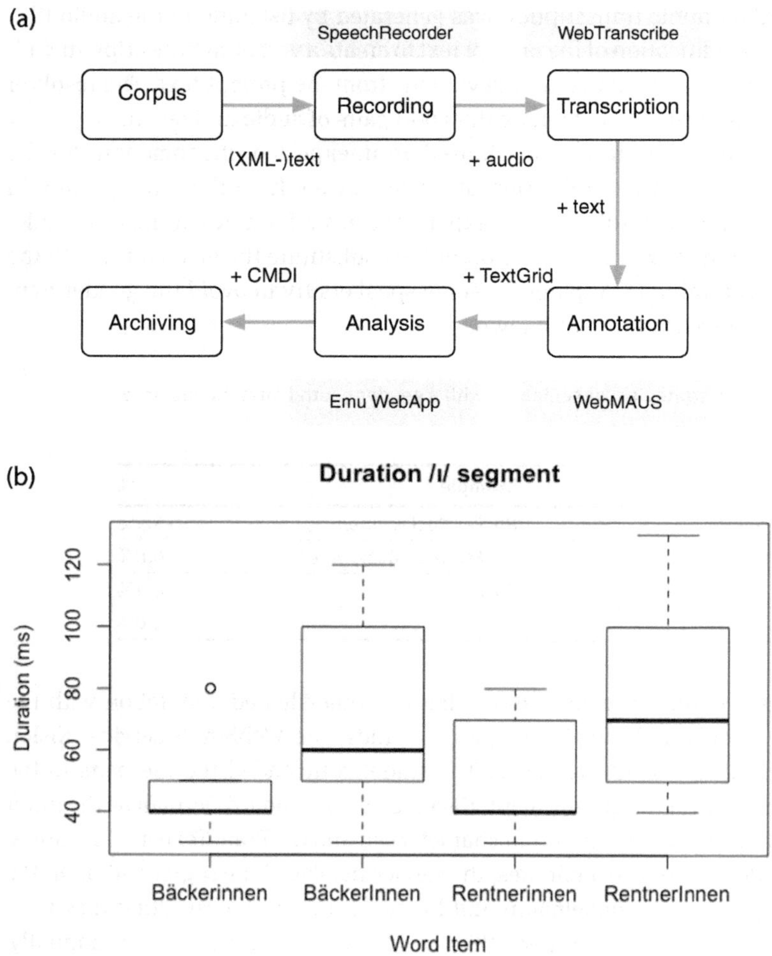

Figure 2: (a) Block diagram of the workflow with CLARIN tools (grey) and data types. (b) Duration of the final /I/ vowel in the gender-neutral and non-gendered forms of *Bäckerinnen* and *Rentnerinnen*.

Within a semester, the students were thus able to record, annotate, analyse, and publish a speech database, and to present their findings at an international phonetics conference. Since then, similar student projects, where all aspects of data collection, curation, and analysis are performed, have run every year, with topics as varied as the analysis of what makes a voice agreeable or interviews with immigrants on their life in Germany.

2.2 Application of new technologies

Research infrastructures need to constantly monitor the emergence of new research paradigms, research methods, innovative technologies, and new types of research data, in order to be able to serve the research needs of their community of interest well. Such responsiveness among research infrastructures is crucial for junior researchers and for more senior researchers who have progressed further in their careers. Doctoral and postdoctoral researchers are often major contributors to paradigm shifts and benefit directly from research infrastructures that offer novel research data and tools that directly serve their research goals. More advanced researchers can also benefit from such research data and tools – not only for their own research, but as extremely valuable resources for their teaching duties.

With the exponential growth in the availability of digital data (see Section 1.1), many scientific disciplines have experienced an empirical turn in their research paradigms and methods. Consequently, machine learning and other data-driven techniques now play a major role not only in computer science and in fields such as computational linguistics, but in a broader range of disciplines, including the (digital) humanities, which are based on data exploration and data analysis. In recent years, neural methods of machine learning have become particularly influential. These methods rely heavily on the distributional profiles of words that can be induced from very large corpora and that can be embedded into high-dimensional vector spaces. The resulting representations are therefore commonly referred to as *word embeddings*.

2.2.1 Advancing interoperability and reusability of word embeddings

With the support of CLARIN-D and under the guidance of Daniël de Kok, researchers at various stages of their careers at Tübingen University have advanced the interoperability of data formats for word embeddings, integrated neural tools into the annotation tool WebLicht, and developed an evaluation environment for assessing the data quality provided by deep learning tools for NLP. The Finalfusion tool which allows the use of a common data format for different word embeddings is described in de

Kok et al. (2020). Since the literature on deep learning implies that the amount of data is growing fast, it is timely and significant to offer a common data format that supports the interoperability and reuse of these formats. Finalfusion offers a data format that subsumes embeddings with character n-grams, quantized embedding storage, and memory mapping. Finalfusion also includes tools for training new embeddings, conversion tools (that map legacy formats into the final fusion format), and a code base for different programming languages, including Rust, Python, C, and C++. It is distributed with a set of new annotation tools and tool pipelines for Dutch and German, which are collectively referred to as the *sticker-2* tools. These tools provide high-quality annotations for both languages: lemmatization, part-of-speech tagging, and morphology at word level, and syntactic dependencies at sentence level. These tools can be used from within virtual research environments (VRE).

A Virtual Research Environment that integrates web services for processing language is provided by CLARIN-D. The Web-Based Linguistic Chaining Tool (WebLicht, M. Hinrichs, Zastrow, and E. Hinrichs 2010) provides a number of different tools for various languages for automatically annotating and analysing texts. WebLicht is productively used in academic education and research.

2.2.2 Enhancing virtual research environments

With the technical options of virtual research environments, tool suites for natural language processing (NLP) can be made available via web interfaces in a Service Oriented Architecture (SOA). These technologies enable scholars from various disciplines to utilize such tools for their own research without having to install them on their own computers or without requiring prior knowledge in programming. With WebLicht (M. Hinrichs, Zastrow, and E. Hinrichs 2010; Dima et al. 2012) such a research environment has been developed in CLARIN-D and has been widely used by humanities scholars in Germany and other CLARIN countries. WebLicht helps users to automatically annotate their reseach data. For this purpose, WebLicht provides a user with a selection of available NLP tools appropriate for a given language and a specific annotation task. Novice users can apply predefined tool chains, while experienced users can customize their own annotation workflows and select from a suite of available tools.

The WebLicht architecture has been designed with an open and scalable system architecture that allows for easy integration of additional annotation tools, as they become available. Given the fast-moving developments in deep learning and the improvements to be gained in annotation quality, researchers in CLARIN-D started to investigate how such neural annotation tools could be made available in WebLicht. In a disciplinary working group of CLARIN-D, they discussed options and developed a neural part-of-speech tagger, to increase the performance of existing taggers. The result was sticker2, which is a sequence labeller. Trained for German and Dutch and capable of outperforming state of the art HMM taggers, sticker2 is a production ready multi-task sequence-labeller, lemmatizer, and dependency parser (de Kok, Falk, and Pütz 2020) which is itself used for further research (de Kok and Pütz 2020).

Another recent enhancement of the CLARIN infrastructure is offered by the virtual language environment *Language Resource Switchboard* (Zinn 2018). This tool suggests suitable tools available for a given dataset that a user wants to reuse for their own research. From these suggestions, the user can start the process directly with the data they have provided, including WebLicht, but also other tools such as Voyant (Sinclair and Rockwell 2016). With such a low, data-based entry threshold to the virtual language environments, the infrastructures provide easy access for all users, independently of their technical background.

Figure 3 illustrates the result of uploading an English-language PDF file to the Language Resource Switchboard. For this example, we uploaded an earlier version of this article as a PDF into the Switchboard. By dropping the file onto the

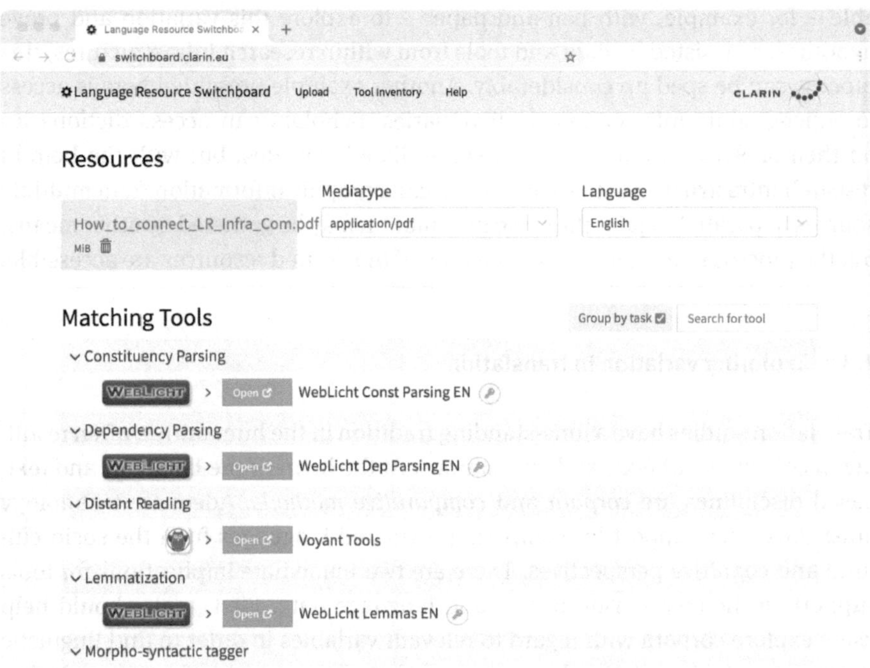

Figure 3: Result of uploading an English-language PDF file to the Language Resource Switchboard.

web page of the Switchboard, the Switchboard identifies the media type (here: PDF), and the language. Both can be adjusted manually if needed. The Switchboard then shows applicable tools: the first tools shown are various parsers and a tool for distant reading. Other tools are also presented but not shown due to the size of the browser window. By clicking on the respective "Open" button, the user directly invokes the tool. A dedicated section on the Switchboard is included in Zinn and Dima (2022).

2.3 New, faster, more precise answers to established research questions

Independent of benefits for the infrastructure and for new research, another aspect of this cooperation is in working with established research questions. These are typical questions that are used in teaching but also occur in other research processes. One example is the variation in translations, which is explored in translation studies. With detailed analysis of translated works researchers are able – for example, with pen and paper – to explore this variation and prove hypotheses. Assisted by data and tools from within research infrastructures, this process can be sped up considerably. Another example presented here is access to lexicographic information in dictionaries. Scholars can access dictionaries on their shelves or, more recently, via affiliated websites, but with the help of research infrastructures they can access lexicographic information from multiple sources in parallel. Again, the same information may be gathered by other means, but the process is accelerated considerably if the desired resources are accessible.

2.3.1 Exploring variation in translation

Translation studies have a long-standing tradition in the humanities, often resulting in collections of texts and translations. At the heart of the language and text-based disciplines are *corpora* and *comparative methods*. Adequate technology must thus offer support for comparing texts and languages from the socio-cultural and cognitive perspectives. There are two immediate implications for tools supporting the comparison of text and language data. First, tools should help users explore corpora with regard to relevant variables in order to find linguistic features in which variation becomes manifest. For example, if we observe that sermons in the 17th century tend to use a lot of 1st person plural pronouns, is that a *distinctive* feature of sermons in that time period? Second, tools should enable users to extract linguistic features from corpora that then undergo quantitative and qualitative analysis. For example, is the use of passive constructions in academic text a *significant* feature? What are the *contexts of use* of the passive in academic text?

We illustrate here how we use a combination of two tools that are part of the CLARIN-D portfolio to show students how to find distinctive features by comparing two corpora and further exploring their usage context, both quantitatively and qualitatively. For the first step, we implemented a dedicated visualization tool that highlights distinctive words in two (or more) corpora under comparison (Fankhauser, Knappen, and Teich 2014). For the second step, a sophisticated concordance tool provides the means for quantitative and qualitative analysis (Evert and the CWB Development Team 2019).

This concrete example is taken from translation studies, where we are interested in the linguistic differences between (simultaneous) interpreting and translation (see example in Figure 4), but any question of intralingual variation can be approached in the same way. The underlying corpora are the EuroParl-UdS (translation) and the EPIC-UdS (interpreting) (Karakanta, Vela, and Teich 2018), both of which are available at the Saarbrücken CLARIN-D centre.[11]

The underlying models are uni-gram models. The word cloud not only encodes relative frequency (item colour) but also distinctivness of words (item size). The measure underlying distinctivness is relative entropy (here, Kullback-Leibler Divergence [KLD]). KLD measures the number of bits needed for encoding when the underlying model is non-optimal. In the example shown in Figure 4, we model interpreting based on translation and vice versa. The items with the greatest distinctiveness for interpreting are the hesitation markers 'euh' and 'hum' (which are also high frequency items) and the 1st person plural 'we'. These clearly mark online, spoken production. For translation, by contrast, the most distinctive items are 'this', 'we' and 'that' ('that' is the most frequent among the three but slightly less distinctive). Note that it is not surprising that the most distinctive items are grammatical words (pronouns, deictic elements), since grammatical use is a marker of mode and style. In contrast, lexical items (mostly in blue shades) are in lower frequency bands and are not very distinctive.

From the visual representation (shown in Figure 4) of corpora under comparison, we can enter the Corpus Query Processor (CQP; Evert and the CWB Development Team 2019), simply by clicking on a word. CQP runs as a web application at the Saarbrücken CLARIN-D centre and is accessible upon registration.[12] For

11 http://hdl.handle.net/21.11119/0000-0000-D5EE-4.
12 http://corpora.clarin-d.uni-saarland.de/cqpweb/.

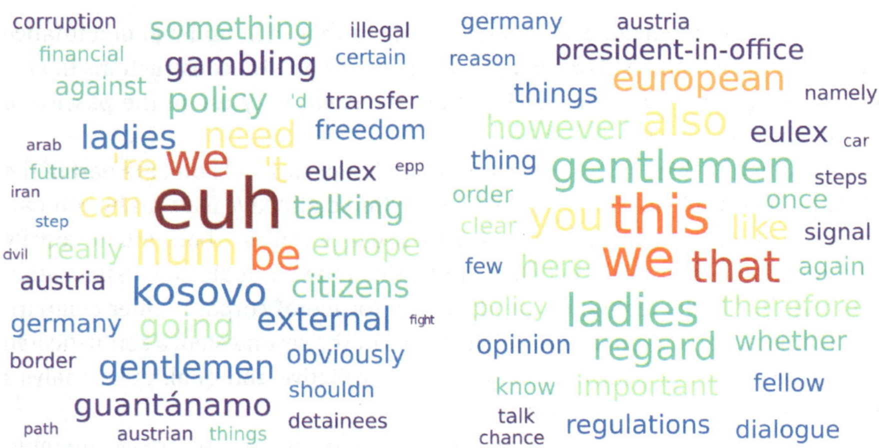

Figure 4: Variation in translation mode in target language English from source language German: interpreting (left), translation (right). Item colour: relative frequency (red=high, blue=low), item size: degree of distinctiveness, $p < 0.5$.

the given example, we are now interested in the context of the hesitation marker 'euh' as a highly distinctive item for simultaneous interpreting. Querying 'euh' in CQP provides detailed information on its surrounding context as well as number of occurrences and distribution in the corpus (see Figure 5). If the corpus is part-of-speech (POS) annotated, for better generalization we can inspect the context at POS level. Interestingly, for 'euh' we observe that it primarily occurs in the context of proper nouns as well as common nouns. This is an interesting descriptive result that provides a good basis for hypothesis building regarding the specific processing difficulties in simultaneous interpreting: nouns, and proper nouns in particular, are generally considered high entropy items and can therefore be expected to incur a high processing cost. This cost may be particularly high in interpreting. To test this, further analysis would be needed.

The kind of exploration and analysis shown in this example provides a typical agenda for a one-week course at a summer school, and we taught it many times at the European Summer University (ESU).[13] In our experience, students at all levels are extremely grateful to be offered an exploratory perspective on corpus comparison that can be easily combined with familiar tools such as concordances for more hypothesis-driven analysis. Exploration of potentially interesting and relevant features prior to qualitative and quantitative analysis lowers the initial

13 https://esu.culintec.de/, https://esu.fdhl.info/

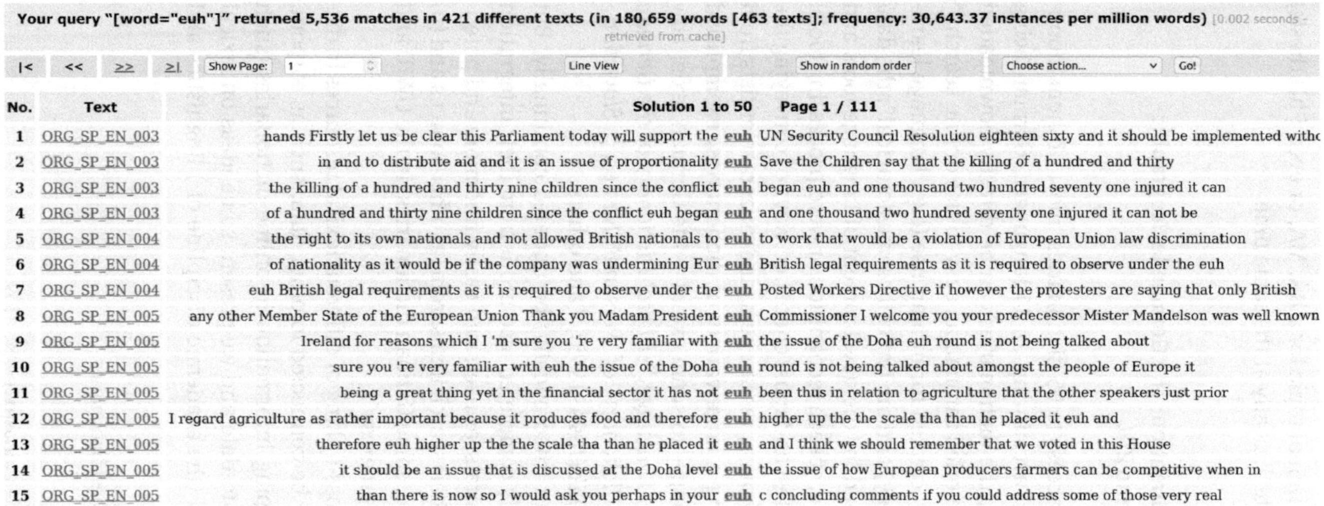

Figure 5: CQP concordance for ‘euh’ in interpreting corpus EPIC-UdS.

threshold for coming up with an original topic for a BA, MA, or even PhD thesis, which may feasibly be carried out technically at the same time.

2.3.2 Access to lexicographic information: The German lexicographic-lexicological portals *OWID* and *ZDL*

The CLARIN infrastructure offers access to 95 dictionaries, most of them monolingual, others bi- or multilingual, accounting for 14 languages, German being one. In the vast majority of cases, the dictionaries can be directly downloaded from the national repositories or queried through an easy-to-use online search.[14] While dictionaries "were primarily created for human use (e.g., language learning/teaching, translation, lexicology) and are typically semasiological", the data collected in dictionaries is now used for the development of language tools and technology of all kinds, for example, speech recognition or word processing tools. Thus, CLARIN offers one of the oldest and most cherished ways of conveying the meaning and usage of words to scholars, researchers, and citizen-scientists from very different backgrounds, linking a large variety of dictionaries, exemplified here by language resources covering – to some extent – the German lexis: *Low German Loanwords in the Estonian Language*,[15] *Digital Dictionary of the German Language (DWDS)*,[16] *Rendering Dictionary of Personal Names*,[17] *Slovenian–German Dictionary of Maks Pleteršnik (1894–1895)*,[18] and others.

All online reference works can (theoretically) be updated continually. But those dictionaries that are officially completed also profit from their integration into lexicographic-lexicological portals, as users can easily find more and potentially more recent information on their search items from (a) other sources and (b) from corpus data.[19]As shown above, some German dictionaries (in the OWID and ZDL portals) are indeed "works in progress".

In this chapter, we describe cross-linking of different lexical resources in dictionary portals and how they may be connected to other data, such as corpora. We discuss the challenges of keeping information in online dictionaries (such as a dictionary of neologisms) up-to-date and we present some ideas on lexical resources as connections between (the academic discipline of) linguistics and

14 https://www.clarin.eu/resource-families/dictionaries
15 See http://www.eki.ee/dict/asl/.
16 See https://www.dwds.de/.
17 See https://www.letonika.lv/groups/default.aspx?g=2&r=1109.
18 See https://www.fran.si/136/maks-pletersnik-slovensko-nemski-slovar.
19 For one example in the Norwegian context, see Rauset et al. 2022.

the language community. As an example, the *Online-Wortschatz-Informationssystem Deutsch (OWID)*,[20] a dictionary portal developed at the Leibniz-Institute for the German Language (IDS), Mannheim,[21] one of the CLARIN-D centres,[22] is introduced. One of the dictionaries in OWID is the *Neologismenwörterbuch*. This dictionary is also one of the online resources presented in a dictionary portal of the *Zentrum für digitale Lexikographie der deutschen Sprache (ZDL)*,[23] containing information on the German lexicon from its beginnings to the present day, hosted at the Berlin-Brandenburg Academy of Sciences and Humanities, another of the CLARIN-D centres.

The OWID dictionary portal offers (as of March 2021) access to 10 different lexicographic resources comprising, for example, a paronym dictionary[24] documenting easily confusable expressions in their current public usage, a dictionary on German proverbs and slogans, the revised edition of *Deutsches Fremdwörterbuch*[25] explaining the origin and meaning of today's learned everyday language, the *Neologismenwörterbuch* and others. OWID contains retro-digitized online dictionaries as well as dictionaries that were developed directly for online publication. Besides completed dictionaries, there are some that are constantly worked on and are published dynamically (e.g., the *Paronymwörterbuch*), and there are diachronic (e.g., *Deutsches Fremdwörterbuch*) as well as synchronic dictionaries (e.g., *Neologismenwörterbuch*). All dictionary content can be accessed by search functions on two levels: the level of the portal and the level of an individual dictionary, thus addressing two different user needs (searching for one word in any dictionary, cf. Figure 6, or restricting the search to one specific dictionary).

In addition, appropriate advanced searches for each dictionary in the portal are developed using diverse technologies. All dictionaries in OWID are based on extensive empirical, mostly corpus-derived, linguistic data and are products of scholarly lexicography resulting from lexicological-lexicographic and metalexicographic research. They are not only innovative in choosing specific parts of German vocabulary as dictionary matter, but also in developing new types of lexicographic information by consistently linking between lexicographic information and corpus data, and in presenting information to users in new ways that have been adapted to each dictionary type. Although most of them focus on specific areas of vocabulary and not the general language, exploring them in the OWID

20 See https://www.owid.de/.
21 See https://www1.ids-mannheim.de/.
22 See https://www.clarin-d.net/de/aufbereiten/clarin-zentrum-finden.
23 See https://www.zdl.org/.
24 See https://www.owid.de/parowb/.
25 See https://www.owid.de/wb/dfwb/start.html.

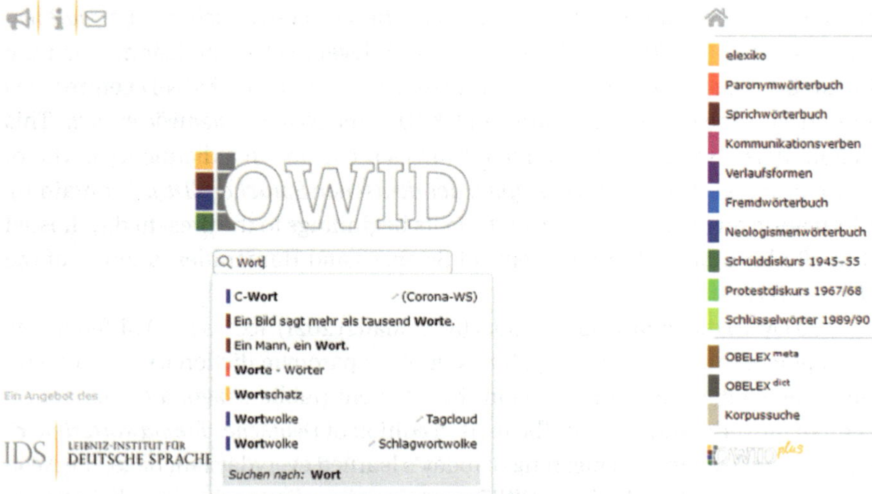

Figure 6: Search for *Wort* in OWID with results from five different dictionaries.

portal offers end users fascinating insights into the German vocabulary. In addition, the experimental platform *OWIDplus*[26] was established at IDS, containing a variety of lexicological-lexicographical data in mono- and multilingual interactive applications, for example, a *Lexical Explorer*[27] for corpus data on spoken German, browsable log file statistics of six Wiktionary language editions,[28] or the *cOWIDplus Viewer*[29] in which frequency curves of the use of word forms during the Covid-19 pandemic in 13 German online media are visualized. As of 2021, work is being done on a common faceted search option that will connect the resources in OWID and OWIDplus. In addition, OWID offers an easy-to-use corpus query interface with *DeReKo – Deutsches Referenzkorpus* of IDS.[30]

The dictionary portal of ZDL gives access to six dictionaries: the first and second edition of the diachronic general language dictionary *Deutsches Wörterbuch.*[31], the diachronic general language dictionary of Swiss German *Schweiz-*

26 See https://www.owid.de/plus/index.html.
27 See https://www.owid.de/lexex/.
28 See https://www.owid.de/plus/wikivi2015/index.html.
29 See https://www.owid.de/plus/cowidplusviewer2020/.
30 See https://www1.ids-mannheim.de/kl/projekte/korpora.html.
31 See information on https://www.dwds.de/d/wb-1dwb and https://www.dwds.de/d/wb-2dwb. *Deutsches Wörterbuch* in both editions was retro-digitized in collaboration with the Trier Centre for Digital Humanities and the Göttingen Academy of Sciences and Humanities. The Trier Centre for Digital Humanities is part of the CLARIAH-DE initiative, where CLARIN-D and DARIAH-DE are

erisches Idiotikon,[32] the new diachronic dictionary focused on central lexemes of politics and society *Wortgeschichte digital*,[33] the synchronic general language dictionary *Digitales Wörterbuch der deutschen Sprache (DWDS)*,[34] and the synchronic *Neologismenwörterbuch* of IDS. *Schweizerisches Idiotikon*, *DWDS*, *Wortgeschichte digital* and *Neologismenwörterbuch* are continually updated, while work on the first as well as the second edition of *Deutsches Wörterbuch* is now completed. Any search in ZDL generates a search result page where extracts from each dictionary containing the lemma are shown (cf. Figure 7). When clicking on the links "Vollständigen Artikel im . . . lesen" ('Read full entry in . . .') or "Detailansicht . . ." ('Detailed view of . . .'), users leave the ZDL portal and access the lexicographic or lexicological content of separate web pages.

In addition, users are shown a word frequency curve created from corpus queries in *Deutsches Textarchiv*[35] and the DWDS corpora[36] and a word cloud with typical collocates of the lemma generated from the DWDS corpora, thus cross-linking content from dictionaries and corpora successfully. ZDL also offers access to DeReKo – Deutsches Referenzkorpus at IDS as well as the diachronic language tool DiaCollo,[37] where information on the diachronic development of collocational behaviour can be obtained. Overall, both portals presented here facilitate the search for information on meaning and usage of words and phrases, as they offer easy access to different sources (dictionaries, lexicological interactive applications, visualizations of corpus data and corpora).

Dictionaries and lexicographic-lexicological portals address primarily human users. They serve as a link between research on words and its documentation and speakers of natural language. Data in dictionaries or lexicological information systems is based on corpus evidence and utilizes what corpus linguistics and language technologies have to offer. Users contribute to the compilation of language resources as well, either directly (e.g., by filling out feedback forms, such as the form to suggest a new word to the editors in the *Neologismenwörterbuch*[38]) or indirectly (e.g., when dictionaries use log-file analysis to find out which words are looked up most often; see de Schryver, Wolfer, and Lew 2019 and Wolfer et al. 2014).

combined in one network for research infrastructure: see https://dig-hum.de/forschung/projekt/clariah-de.

32 See https://www.idiotikon.ch/.

33 See information on https://adw-goe.de/forschung/weitere-forschungsprojekte/wortgeschichte-digital-teilprojekt-im-zdl/.

34 See https://www.dwds.de/.

35 See https://www.deutschestextarchiv.de/.

36 See https://www.dwds.de/r.

37 See https://clarin-d.net/de/kollokationsanalyse-in-diachroner-perspektive.

38 See https://www.owid.de/wb/neo/mail.html.

Figure 7: Result page of search for *Wort* in ZDL with results in three dictionaries and corpus-based additional information.

Lexicography and lexicological research are a perfect example for illustrating manifold connections: between different dictionaries and other lexical sources in portals, using infrastructure such as provided in the CLARIN framework; between lexicographers or lexicological researchers on one side and corpus linguists and language technology on the other, such as found in the CLARIN network; and finally between linguistic research (in its widest sense) and the language community.

2.3.3 The German Text Archive: An active archive for historical data in CLARIN

The *German Text Archive* (DTA), located at the Centre for Language at the Berlin-Brandenburg Academy of Sciences and Humanities (BBAW), was funded by the German Research Foundation (DFG) from 2007 to 2016 and now forms an essential component of the research data infrastructure of the German part of CLARIN. In this section, the DTA is presented as a web-based research platform for the creation and curation of corpus texts as well as for corpus analysis.

The aim of the DTA has been to create a basic stock of German-language texts spanning all disciplines and genres for the period ca. 1600–1900. The text selection was based on an extensive bibliography, annotated and supplemented by members of the BBAW Academy. From this, the DTA project group compiled a text corpus balanced according to text types and disciplines, which serves as the basis for a reference corpus on the development of New High German. In order to reflect the historical state of the language as accurately as possible, the first editions of the works were generally used as a basis for digitization. The DTA core corpus compiled according to these criteria is continuously being expanded. It currently comprises about 1,500 works with a volume of about 120 million words. In addition, there are another nearly 4,000 works (about 100 million tokens) that have been curated together with external projects for the DTA platform (as of April 2021); most of them via the DTAQ quality assurance platform (see below).

The basis for the DTA is a structured format that was developed from the multitude of different texts it contains in order to be usable for as many contexts as possible. This so-called DTA Base Format (DTABf), in addition to serving as an interchange format for different corpora, ensures interoperability for use cases as diverse as corpus display, full-text search, and text mining. The DTABf is a true subset of the TEI's text document encoding guidelines: the TEI's tagset has been reduced in terms of available elements and attributes and specified in terms of attribute values (Haaf, Geyken, and Wiegand 2015; Geyken, Haaf, and Wiegand 2012). The DTABf annotation scheme for historical prints (and other document classes such as newspapers and manuscripts, cf. Haaf and Thomas 2015), together with extensive documentation and a Schematron rule set, forms the basis for XML markup of all works in the DTA. With the help of conversion tools, numerous other formats can be automatically generated from DTABf documents for further processing with linguistic tools, for search engine indexes, for presentation of the texts (e.g., reading versions for various media), and for export (e.g., to citation environments, graph databases, or in the CLARIN context for WebLicht). The further development of the DTABf guidelines[39] is ensured by a steering group.[40]

For the quality assurance of the full texts and the structural data, a web-based platform was developed (DTA Quality Assurance, DTAQ[41]), which allows the distributed proofreading and correction of texts. For this purpose, flexible options for text import from different formats and a text-image view were created, and an editor was integrated into the platform, with which texts can be edited without the need for additional software to be installed. At the end of the correction process, the work is published on the DTA website, where it is accessible via a text-image view and linked to various analysis tools (see below). DTAQ includes a user management system that provides multiple levels of access and annotation options for different user groups through roles and permissions. Users of DTAQ register with a personalized account on the platform and can specify various types of expertise (expertise in literary or linguistic history, knowledge of foreign languages, expertise in transcribing mathematical formulas, etc.). This makes it possible to specifically address other users with the help of the ticket system when in doubt or when using difficult text passages, and thus to work collaboratively on the documents. In addition, this makes it easy to work in a team, as certain types of errors can be specifically assigned to individual users. Personalization also makes it possible to save the user's own preferences with regard to the DTAQ display for each account, including the optimal text and image width or the preferred text view, among others. As of June 2021, more than 2,000 users have been active on DTAQ; some have commented on text errors and others have curated entire works via the platform.

Another key element of DTA is its collection of analysis tools. CAB (Cascaded Analysis Broker; cf. Jurish 2012), a tool for normalizing historical spellings, provides a spelling-tolerant full-text search across all texts in the DTA. In addition, with the integration of GermaNet (Hamp and Feldweg 1997; Henrich and E. Hinrichs 2010), a lexical resource that groups nouns, verbs, and adjectives into SynSets according to similarity of meaning, full-text search by semantic categories is also made possible. Furthermore, a number of lexicometric analysis tools are available, including the visualization of diachronic collocations (Jurish and Nieländer 2019), and a quantitative text analysis based on the Voyant tools.[42]

---

39 See https://www.deutschestextarchiv.de/doku/basisformat/leitlinien.html.

40 See https://www.deutschestextarchiv.de/doku/basisformat/steuerungsgruppe.html.

41 See https://www.deutschestextarchiv.de/dtaq/.

42 See https://voyant-tools.org/.

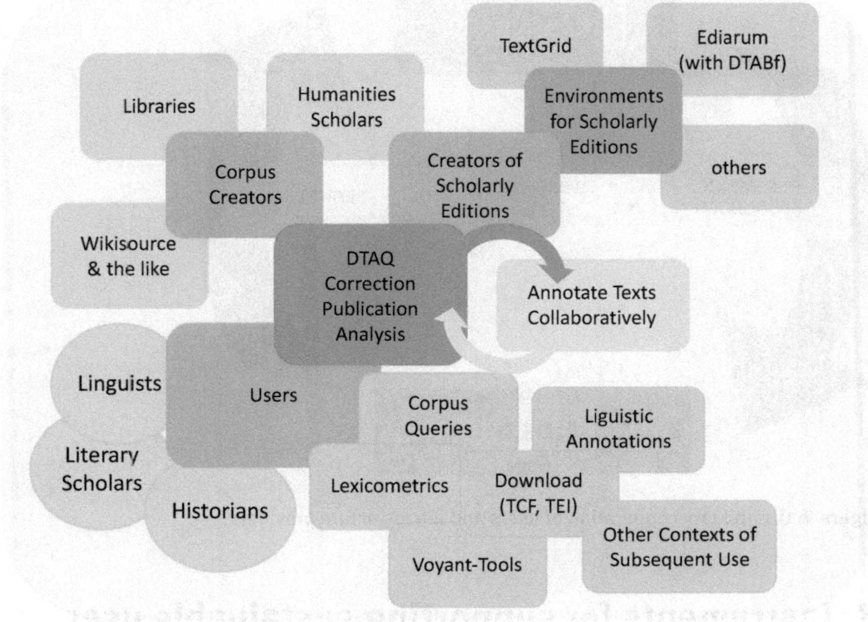

Figure 8: DTA as a research, publication, and analysis platform.

All texts of the DTA are under an open Creative Commons (CC)[43] license and can thus be easily reused as a complete set in scientific contexts.[44] Furthermore, due to the interoperability ensured by the encoding in DTABf, all texts of the DTA can be easily converted into different formats.

Figure 8 summarizes the various components, at the centre of which is DTAQ as a proofreading, publication, and analysis platform. On one side are the various corpus producers (humanities and social scientists, libraries, and non-academic initiatives such as Wikisource); on the other side are edition environments and producers of editions. The "classic" use of DTAQ consists of collaborative annotation of texts. All DTA texts can be corrected and annotated at any time, and the continually updated version can be exported from the platform. The fourth and final component is analysis, with the aforementioned CAB and GermaNet tools for linguistic annotation, the various analysis tools, and the export formats for flexible reuse in other contexts.

43 See https://creativecommons.org/.

44 See https://deutschestextarchiv.de/download.

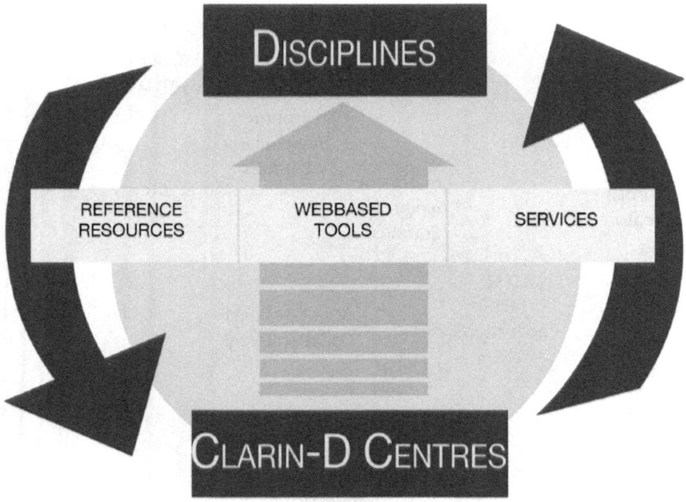

Figure 9: Disciplinary cooperation of users and infrastructure providers.

3 Instruments for supporting sustainable user involvement

In the development of the CLARIN infrastructure, we see large benefits on both sides from a strong cooperation between users of a research infrastructure and infrastructure providers, as illustrated by Figure 9. We have shown how the developments have already cross-fertilized in the past and have led to a significant improvement on the research side and to an enhancement of the offerings. In addition to the fact that the offerings were initially developed very much in line with the research background of those who also provided the offerings to others, further measures were established in CLARIN-D to ensure collaboration. In this section, we present some of the measures that we have taken to foster this collaboration, namely:

- discipline-specific working groups
- curation projects
- tools for collaboration on resources
- training[45] and consulting activities.

45 Hennelly et al. 2022 describe the motivation and processes for training in South Africa.

Discipline-specific working groups were created to integrate disciplinary needs in the infrastructure and to encourage feedback to service providers. For scholars using the infrastructure, the working groups also established a channel to spread information about the availability and use of the infrastructure. Chaired by distinguished scholars in the field, around 200 researchers from Germany, with varying backgrounds in the humanities and social sciences, met in eight discipline-specific working groups, supported by travel grants and with administrative support from CLARIN-D. These working groups included disciplines such as German philology, other philologies, linguistic fieldwork, anthropology, language typology, human speech processing (including psycho-linguistics, speech technology and other modalities), applied linguistics and computational linguistics, content analysis in social sciences, and history. The groups met on a regular basis, reviewing the infrastructure, services, and available datasets. They also devised application scenarios, projects, and uses of the infrastructure and presented at academic conferences and workshops. In the process of applying scenarios, they detected usability issues, gaps in the infrastructure, and valuable add-ons to the infrastructure. The discipline-specific working groups also establish a bridge to professional associations. With their publications, conferences, and workshops, these associations provide another point of contact between infrastructure providers and the research community.

Curation projects in CLARIN-D are measures within the infrastructure to help close the detected gaps and integrate valuable add-ons. Supported by the infrastructure, the discipline-specific working groups decided on priorities, such as the preparation and depositing of legacy data, or the development of new tools. For this, each discipline-specific working group received a budget and an infrastructural partner with which to work on curating data resources or tools.

The activities of the discipline-specific working groups, curation projects, and technical tools for collaboration are complemented by established outreach activities, including workshops and tutorials, summer school courses, consulting services, and a helpdesk. Each of these activities disseminates the infrastructure's resources and provides a low access threshold for scholars at all stages of their academic career.

One example for supporting training activities is the European Summer University in Leipzig, Germany. This established summer school is used by CLARIN-D to disseminate tools, services, and other resources by training individuals to use them. The classes are based on the requirements and feedback of participants. For example, users pointed to the need for training on low-level query methods for CLARIN data, the application of tools and services for specific research questions, applying and evaluating NLP technologies in the humanities, and analysing language data for humanities scholars. Together with other classes on data management, legal and ethical questions, metadata modelling, and so on, CLARIN offered a wide spectrum of infrastructure-related training to young researchers.

4 Conclusion

In this chapter we have illustrated that the integration of language resources infrastructures and communities is beneficial both for the communities and for the services provided by the infrastructures. The German national project CLARIN-D established strong bonds with the research community through discipline-specific working groups, curation projects that were prioritized by the discipline-specific working groups, training, and dissemination activities. With this strong connection between the community and the infrastructure, researchers achieved results when addressing emerging research questions, confirmed research hypotheses faster and with more precision, and developed new methods, contributing to new research paradigms. The cooperation between users and infrastructure providers thus contributed to the success story of CLARIN in Germany.

Bibliography

Baum, Constanze & Thomas Stäcker. 2015. Methoden – Theorien – Projekte. In Constanze Baum & Thomas Stäcker (eds.), *Grenzen und Möglichkeiten der Digital Humanities: Sonderband der Zeitschrift für digitale Geisteswissenschaften*, 4–12. https://doi.org/DOI10.17175/sb001_023.

Berry, David M. 2011. The computational turn: Thinking about the digital humanities. *Cultural Machine* 12. 1–22.

Boersma, Paul. 2001. Praat, a system for doing phonetics by computer. *Glot International* 5(9/10). 341–345.

Carroll, Stephanie Russo, Edit Herczog, Maui Hudson, Keith Russell & Shelley Stall. 2021. Operationalizing the CARE and FAIR Principles for indigenous data futures. *Scientific Data* 8(1). 108. https://doi.org/10.1038/s41597-021-00892-0.

Dima, Emanuel, Erhard Hinrichs, Marie Hinrichs, Alexander Kislev, Thorsten Trippel & Thomas Zastrow. 2012. Integration of WebLicht into the CLARIN infrastructure. In *Service-oriented architectures (soas) for the humanities: Solutions and impacts joint clarin-d/dariah workshop at digital humanities conference 2012*, 17–23. http://clarin-d.de/images/workshops/proceedingssoasforthehumanities.pdf.

Draxler, Christoph & Klaus Jänsch. 2004. SpeechRecorder – a universal platform independent multi-channel audio recording software. In *International Conference on Language*

Resources and Evaluation (LREC) 4, 559–562. European Language Resources Association (ELRA). http://www.lrec-conf.org/proceedings/lrec2004/summaries/242.htm.

Engelberg, Stefan, Annette Klosa-Kückelhaus & Carolin Müller-Spitzer. 2020. Internet lexicography at the Leibniz-institute for the German language. *K Lexical News* 28. 54–77. http://nbn-resolving.de/urn:nbn:de:bsz:mh39-99953.

Engelberg, Stefan & Carolin Müller-Spitzer. 2013. Dictionary portals. In Rufus Hjalmar Gouws, Ulrich Heid, Wolfgang Schweickard & Herbert Ernst Wiegand (eds.), *Dictionaries. An international encyclopedia of lexicography: Supplementary volume: Recent developments with focus on electronic and computational lexicography*, 1023–1035. Berlin: De Gruyter Mouton. https://doi.org/doi:10.1515/9783110238136.

European Strategy Forum on Research Infrastructures (ESFRI). 2018. *Strategy report on research infrastructures: Roadmap 2018*. Report. http://roadmap2018.esfri.eu/media/1060/esfri-roadmap-2018.pdf.

Evert, Stefan & the CWB Development Team. 2019. The IMS Open Corpus Work Bench (cwb), CQP query language tutorial (CWB version 3.4.16). http://cwb.sourceforge.net/files/CQP_Tutorial.pdf.

Fankhauser, Peter, Jörg Knappen & Elke Teich. 2014. Exploring and visualizing variation in language resources. In *International Conference on Language Resources and Evaluation (LREC) 9*, 4125–4128. Reykjavik: European Language Resources Association (ELRA). http://www.lrec-conf.org/proceedings/lrec2014/pdf/185_Paper.pdf.

Fridlund, Mats, Daniel Brodén, Tommi Jauhiainen, Leena Malkki, Leif-Jöran Olsson & Lars Borin. 2022. Trawling and trolling for terrorists in the digital Gulf of Bothnia: Cross-lingual text mining for the emergence of terrorism in Swedish and Finnish newspapers, 1780—1926. In Darja Fišer & Andreas Witt (eds.), *CLARIN. The infrastructure for language resources*, 1780–1926. Berlin: De Gruyter.

Geyken, Alexander, Susanne Haaf & Frank Wiegand. 2012. The DTA 'base format'. A TEI-subset for the compilation of interoperable corpora. In Jeremy Jancsary (ed.), *11th conference on natural language processing (KONVENS), lthist 2012 workshop* (Scientific Series of the ÖGAI 4), 383–391. Vienna: Österreichische Gesellschaft für Artificial Intelligence.

Gomes, Luís, Ruben Branco, João Silva & António Branco. 2022. Open and inclusive language processing: Language processing services by PORTULAN to meet the widest needs of CLARIN users. In Darja Fišer & Andreas Witt (eds.), *CLARIN. The infrastructure for language resources*. Berlin: De Gruyter.

Haaf, Susanne, Alexander Geyken & Frank Wiegand. 2015. The DTA " Base Format": A TEI subset for the compilation of a large reference corpus of printed text from multiple sources. *Journal of the Text Encoding Initiative* 8. https://doi.org/10.4000/jtei.1114.

Haaf, Susanne & Christian Thomas. 2015. Enabling the encoding of manuscripts within the DTABf: Extension and modularization of the format. *Journal of the Text Encoding Initiative* 10. https://doi.org/10.4000/jtei.1650.

Hajič, Jan, Eva Hajičová, Barbora Hladká, Jozef Mišutka, Ondřej Košarko & Pavel Straňák. 2022. LINDAT/CLARIAH-CZ: Where we are and where we go. In Darja Fišer & Andreas Witt (eds.), *CLARIN. The infrastructure for language resources*. Berlin: De Gruyter.

Hamp, Birgit & Helmut Feldweg. 1997. GermaNet – A lexical-semantic net for German. In Piek Vossen, Geert Adriaens, Nicoletta Calzolari, Antonio Sanfilippo & Yorick Wilks (eds.), *Proceedings of the ACL workshop automatic information extraction and building of lexical semantic resources for NLP applications*, 9–15. Somerset, NJ: Association for Computational Linguistics.

Hennelly, Martin, Langa Khumalo, Juan Steyn & Menno van Zaanen. 2022. Training of digital language resources skills in South Africa. In Darja Fišer & Andreas Witt (eds.), *CLARIN. The infrastructure for language resources*. Berlin: De Gruyter.
Henrich, Verena & Erhard Hinrichs. 2010. GernEdiT – the GermaNet editing tool. In *International conference on language resources and evaluation (LREC) 7*, 2228–2235. Valletta: European Language Resources Association (ELRA). http://www.lrec-conf.org/proceedings/lrec2010/pdf/264_Paper.pdf.
Hinrichs, Marie, Thomas Zastrow & Erhard Hinrichs. 2010. WebLicht: Web-based LRT Services in a Distributed eScience Infrastructure. In N. Calzolari (ed.), *International Conference on Language Resources and Evaluation (LREC) 7*, 489–493.
Hoeksema, Jack, Kees de Glopper & Gertjan van Noord. 2022. Syntactic profiles in secondary school writing using PaQu and SPOD. In Darja Fišer & Andreas Witt (eds.), *CLARIN. The infrastructure for language resources*. Berlin: De Gruyter.
Jurish, Bryan. 2012. *Finite-state canonicalization techniques for historical German*. (completed 2011, published 2012). Universität Potsdam dissertation. http://opus.kobv.de/ubp/volltexte/2012/5578/.
Jurish, Bryan & Maret Nieländer. 2019. Using DiaCollo for historical research. In *CLARIN annual conference 2019 (Leipzig, Germany, 30 September – 2 October, 2019)*. https://www.clarin.eu/clarin-annual-conference-2019-abstracts#L.
Karakanta, Alina, Mihaela Vela & Elke Teich. 2018. Europarl-UdS: Preserving metadata from parliamentary debates. In Darja Fišer, Maria Eskevich & Franciska de Jong (eds.), *ParlaCLARIN@LREC2018, at International Conference on Language Resources and Evaluation (LREC) 11*. Miyazaki: European Language Resources Association (ELRA). https://www.clarin.eu/sites/default/files/ParlaCLARIN_Session2_2.2.EuroParl-UdS_Alina-Karakanta_LREC2018.pdf.
Kisler, Thomas, Florian Schiel & Han Sloetjes. 2012. Signal processing via web services: The use case WebMAUS. In Erhard Hinrichs, Heike Neuroth & Peter Wittenburg (eds.), *Workshop on service-oriented architectures (SOAs) for the huamnities: solutions and impacts at digital humanities 2012*, 30–34. Hamburg: Universität Hamburg. https://www.mpi.nl/publications/item_1850150.
Kok, Daniël de, Neele Falk & Tobias Pütz. 2020. Sticker2: A neural syntax annotator for Dutch and German. In Constanza Navarretta & Maria Eskevich (eds.), *Proceedings of the CLARIN annual conference 2020*, 27–31. https://office.clarin.eu/v/CE-2020-1738-CLARIN2020_ConferenceProceedings.pdf.
Kok, Daniël de, Sebastian Pütz, Eric Schill & Erhard Hinrichs. 2020. Finalfusion: Fusing all your embeddings into one format. In *Knowledge, language, models: Volume in honor of Prof. Galia Angelova*, 57–73. Shoumen: INCOMA Ltd.
Kok, Daniël de & Tobias Pütz. 2020. Self-distillation for German and Dutch dependency parsing. *Computational Linguistics in the Netherlands Journal* 10. 91–107. https://www.clinjournal.org/clinj/article/view/106.
Kučera, Dalibor. 2022. Application of CLARIN linguistic tools in psychological research. In Darja Fišer & Andreas Witt (eds.), *CLARIN. The infrastructure for language resources*. Berlin: De Gruyter.
Lindahl, Anna & Stian Rødven-Eide. 2022. Argumentative language resources at Språkbanken text. In Darja Fišer & Andreas Witt (eds.), *CLARIN. The infrastructure for language resources*. Berlin: De Gruyter.

Petrauskaitė, Rūta, Darius Amilevičius, Virginijus Dadurkevičius, Tomas Krilavičius, Gailius Raškinis, Andrius Utka & Jurgita Vaičenoniene. 2022. CLARIN-LT: Home for Lithuanian language resources. In Darja Fišer & Andreas Witt (eds.), *CLARIN. The infrastructure for language resources*. Berlin: De Gruyter.
Pettersson, Eva & Lars Borin. 2022. Swedish Diachronic Corpus. In Darja Fišer & Andreas Witt (eds.), *CLARIN. The infrastructure for language resources*. Berlin: De Gruyter.
Pozzo, Riccardo, Timon Gatta, Hansmichael Hohenegger, Jonas Kuhn, Axel Pichler, Marco Turchi & Josef van Genabith. 2022. Aligning Immanuel Kant's work and its translations. In Darja Fišer & Andreas Witt (eds.), *CLARIN. The infrastructure for language resources*. Berlin: De Gruyter.
Presner, Todd. 2010. Digital humanities 2.0: A report on knowledge. In Melissa Bailar (ed.), *Emerging disciplines: Shaping new fields of scholarly inquiry in and beyond the humanities*. Online: OpenStax CNX. http://cnx.org/contents/2742bb37-7c47-4bee-bb34-0f35bda760f3@6.
Rauset, Margunn, Gyri Smørdal Losnegaard, Helge Dyvik, Paul Meurer, Rune Kyrkjebø & Koenraad De Smedt. 2022. Words, words! Resources and tools for lexicography at the CLARINO Bergen centre. In Darja Fišer & Andreas Witt (eds.), *CLARIN. The infrastructure for language resources*. Berlin: De Gruyter.
Schaal, Gary S. & Roxana Kath. 2014. Zeit für einen Paradigmenwechsel in der politischen Theorie? In André Brodocz, Dietrich Herrmann, Rainer Schmidt, Daniel Schulz & Julia Schulze Wessel (eds.), *Die Verfassung des Politischen: Festschrift für Hans Vorländer*, 331–350. Wiesbaden: Springer Fachmedien Wiesbaden. https://doi.org/10.1007/978-3-658-04784-9_20.
Schryver, Gilles-Maurice de, Sascha Wolfer & Robert Lew. 2019. The relationship between dictionary look-up frequency and corpus frequency revisited: A log-file analysis of a decade of user interaction with a Swahili-English dictionary. *GEMA Online Journal of Language Studies* 19(4). 1–27. https://doi.org/10.17576/gema-2019-1904-01.
Silva, João, Sara Grilo, Márcia Bolrinha, Rodrigo Santos, Luís Gomes, António Branco & Rui Vaz. 2022. Where do I belong in six centuries of literature? Datasets and AI-based tools for Portuguese literary documents made possible and available by PORTULAN CLARIN. In Darja Fišer & Andreas Witt (eds.), *CLARIN. The infrastructure for language resources*. Berlin: De Gruyter.
Sinclair, Stéfan & Geoffrey Rockwell. 2016. *Voyant Tools*. http://voyant-tools.org/.
Slavik, Korbinian, Johanna Cronenberg & Christoph Draxler. 2018. A study on the pro-nunciation of gender-neutral nouns in German. In Malte Belz, Christine Mooshammer, Susanne Fuchs, Stefanie Jannedy, Oksana Rasskazova & Marzena Żygis (eds.), *Proceedings of the conference on phonetics & phonology in german-speaking countries (P&P 13)*, 185–188. Berlin: Leibniz-Zentrum Allgemeine Sprachwissenschaft & Humboldt-Universität.
https://doi.org/http://dx.doi.org/10.18452/18805.
Trognitz, Martina, Matej Ďurčo & Karlheinz Mörth. 2022. Text technology for the digital humanities: Maximizing impact in a diverse field of disciplines. In Darja Fišer & Andreas Witt (eds.), *CLARIN. The infrastructure for language resources*. Berlin: De Gruyter.
Wilkinson, Mark D., Michel Dumontier, IJsbrand Jan Aalbersberg, Gabrielle Appleton, Myles Axton, Arie Baak, Niklas Blomberg, Jan-Willem Boiten, Luiz Bonino da Silva Santos, Philip E. Bourne, Jildau Bouwman, Anthony J. Brookes, Tim Clark, Mercè Crosas, Ingrid Dillo,

Olivier Dumon, Scott Edmunds, Chris T. Evelo, Richard Finkers, Alejandra Gonzalez-Beltran, Alasdair J.G. Gray, Paul Groth, Carole Goble, Jeffrey S. Grethe, Jaap Heringa, Peter A.C. 't Hoen, Rob Hooft, Tobias Kuhn, Ruben Kok, Joost Kok, Scott J. Lusher, Maryann E. Martone, Albert Mons, Abel L. Packer, Bengt Persson, Philippe Rocca-Serra, Marco Roos, Rene van Schaik, Susanna-Assunta Sansone, Erik Schultes, Thierry Sengstag, Ted Slater, George Strawn, Morris A. Swertz, Mark Thompson, Johan van der Lei, Erik van Mulligen, Jan Velterop, Andra Waagmeester, Peter Wittenburg, Katherine Wolstencroft, Jun Zhao & Barend Mons. 2016. The FAIR guiding principles for scientific data management and stewardship. *Scientific data* 3. https://doi.org/https://doi.org/10.1038/sdata.2016.18.

Winkelmann, Raphael & Georg Raess. 2014. Introducing a web application for labeling, visualizing speech and correcting derived speech signals. In Nicoletta Calzolari (Conference Chair), Khalid Choukri, Thierry Declerck, Hrafn Loftsson, Bente Maegaard, Joseph Mariani, Asuncion Moreno, Jan Odijk & Stelios Piperidis (eds.), *International Conference on Language Resources and Evaluation (LREC) 9*, 4129–4133. Reykjavik: European Language Resources Association (ELRA).

Wolfer, Sascha, Alexander Koplenig, Peter Meyer & Carolin Müller-Spitzer. 2014. Dictionary users do look up frequent and socially relevant words. Two log file analyses. In Andrea Abel, Chiara Vettori & Natascia Ralli (eds.), *Proceedings of the XVI Euralex International Congress, Bolzano/Bozen, 15.-19.07.2014*, 281–290. Bozen: Institute for Specialised Communication & Multilingualism. http://nbn-resolving.de/urn:nbn:de:bsz:mh39-31125.

Zinn, Claus. 2018. The language resource switchboard. *Computational Linguistics* 44(4). 631–639. https://doi.org/10.1162/coli_a_00329.

Zinn, Claus & Emanuel Dima. 2022. The CLARIN Language Resource Switchboard: Current state, impact, and future roadmap. In Darja Fišer & Andreas Witt (eds.), *CLARIN. The infrastructure for language resources*. Berlin: De Gruyter.

Piotr Bański* and Hanna Hedeland

Standards in CLARIN

Abstract: This chapter looks at a fragment of the ongoing work of the CLARIN Standards Committee (CSC) on producing a shared set of recommendations on standards, formats, and related best practices supported by the CLARIN infrastructure and its participating centres. What might at first glance seem to be a straightforward goal has over the years proven to be rather complex, reflecting the robustness and heterogeneity of the emerging distributed digital research infrastructure and the various disciplines and research traditions of the language-based humanities that it serves and represents, and therefore part of the chapter reviews the various initiatives and proposals that strove to produce helpful standards-related guidance. The focus turns next to a subtask initiated in late 2019, its scope narrowed to one of the core activities and responsibilities of CLARIN backbone centres, namely the provision of data deposition services. Centres are obligated to publish their recommendations concerning the repertoire of data formats that are best suited for their research profiles. We look at how this requirement has been met by the particular centres and suggest that having centres maintain their information in the Standards Information System (SIS) is the way to improve on the current state of affairs.

Keywords: standards, formats, CSC, SIS, data deposition

1 Introduction

This chapter looks at the ongoing work of the CLARIN Standards Committee (CSC) on producing a shared set of recommendations on standards, formats, and related best practices supported by the CLARIN infrastructure and its participating centres.

Acknowledgment: We are grateful to the members of the CLARIN Standards Committee for their participation in the process that resulted in publishing the re-vamped Standards Information System, and for their support and sharing ideas on how it can be made better. Very special thanks are due to Eliza Margaretha Illig, the main coder of the SIS, for her enthusiastic and professional participation in the project. Hanna Hedeland's work was funded by the BMBF-project QUEST (16QK09D) at the Leibniz-Institut für Deutsche Sprache.

***Corresponding author: Piotr Bański,** Leibniz-Institut für Deutsche Sprache, Mannheim, Germany, e-mail: banski(at)ids-mannheim.de
Hanna Hedeland, Berlin-Brandenburgische Akademie der Wissenschaften, Berlin, Germany, e-mail: hedeland@bbaw.de

https://doi.org/10.1515/9783110767377-012

What might at first glance seem to be a straightforward task has over the years proven to be rather complex, reflecting the robustness and heterogeneity of the emerging distributed digital research infrastructure and the various disciplines and research traditions of the language-based humanities that it serves and represents.

In late 2019, the CSC decided to reduce the initial scope of the task in order to make it both manageable and immediately relevant to the current needs of the CLARIN community. The focus was therefore narrowed to one of the core activities of CLARIN centres, namely data deposition services, and stress was placed on a measurable requirement concerning the so-called B-centres, namely the publication of each centre's recommendations concerning the repertoire of data formats that are best suited for deposition at that particular centre. While it is more restricted than the original goal, and thus more tangible, this smaller task requires a careful balance between the top-down across-the-board demands of a modern distributed research infrastructure, and the bottom-up expression of the research orientation of the particular nodes in the network, that is, the individual centres. It also requires the formation of an inventory of formats and ways of evaluating them for appropriateness as shared recommendations. Another goal that must be met in order to address the task is that of ensuring sustainability and ease of maintenance of the proposed solutions, while at the same time ensuring that these solutions will become a useful tool – for the CLARIN staff, both in the centre-assessment process and as a source of developer-oriented detailed information on data formats, and also for the users of CLARIN who wish to deposit data, to assist them in the task of identifying centres that best suit their needs. The emerging system, in the next step, will serve the larger goal of gathering information on the major relevant standards used across CLARIN, as well as other related research infrastructures.

In the remainder of this section, we first define the scope of the present chapter, and then outline its structure.

1.1 Scope

For the purpose of this chapter, we differentiate between

(a) standards, which are the result of a formalized standardization process and are published by a standardization body, such as ISO, W3C, OASIS or others;

(b) (data) formats, which may be a serialization of a standard, but where the only requirement is a reliable specification or schema;[1] and

1 For an interesting discussion of several possible definitions of the somewhat narrower term 'file format', in the context of sustainability assessments, see, among others, (Pennock, Wheatley, and May, 2014).

(c) best (or good) practices, which are formats and *de facto* standards that are generally accepted as the (or *a*) recommended solution for a particular method or context, considering both the usage of, and the tool support for, the given format, as well as its features.

Given the complex nature of the task of defining a shared set of recommendations, the space and time restrictions of this publication, and the fact that the work of the CSC is far from finished, we narrow the focus of the present chapter to data formats. Our special attention here is on the implementation of a flexible and maintainable solution based on reliable transparent workflows for revisions and quality control to ensure that CLARIN is able to respond appropriately to relevant future development within and beyond the infrastructure.

Furthermore, we focus entirely on CLARIN, to the exclusion of other projects or research infrastructures. Due to our own backgrounds and the composition and activities of the CLARIN Standards Committee, our perspective will inevitable also be somewhat tied to the German consortium, CLARIN-D.

1.2 Structure

In what follows, we first sketch the theoretical and institutional background for the activity of the CSC (Section 2), and after that, we look at the history of the struggle to flesh out standards-related guidelines for CLARIN researchers and users (Section 3). In Section 4, we present the formal factors that influence the task at hand, and in Section 5, we show how the CSC has addressed it, culminating in the re-emerging Standards Information System. We finish with a summary and indication of directions for the next steps.

2 Background

Within CLARIN's designated communities, there exist, on the one hand, users whose work results in the development of new standards and formats that are later adopted by others, and, on the other hand, users who are unable to make a suitable choice from existing standards and formats for their own research project. The extreme variation in data literacy often accompanies methodological differences, and additional dimensions are introduced due to different linguistic modalities, research areas, and traditions. This heterogeneity results in a plethora of standards, formats, and localized best practices in use within CLARIN and associated institutions. In order to handle such a situation, an infrastructure would need highly specific expertise in an increasing number of areas. Fortunately, each centre joining the CLARIN project contributes substantial and often innovative expertise based on their own research and the needs of their designated communities. While this is undoubtedly one of the strengths of a distributed infrastructure, it also implies that centres may have differing views on both their own and their users' needs when it comes to shared recommendations and other kinds of support in matters concerning standards and formats. And that calls for solutions that respect and embrace heterogeneity without confusing it with arbitrariness. Some established formats exist alongside very similar – possibly more modern – formats, due to minor yet crucial differences in expressiveness, superior tool support or local habits, and so on, and in many cases this can only be recognized with highly specific expertise within the relevant area. Therefore, any centralized or otherwise non-representative decision-making process in producing a set of shared recommendations on standards and formats will inevitably fail to receive the necessary support from the partners – and users – of CLARIN.

In this section, we first look at how CLARIN deals with the heterogeneity that is implied by its structure (Section 2.1), and then, in Section 2.2, we present requirements concerning data and services that are generally accepted across modern research infrastructures and that act as a top-down framework that prevents heterogeneity from becoming chaos.

2.1 Heterogeneity and interoperability

While CLARIN as a whole benefits from the expertise of individual centres, the converse is also true: interconnected CLARIN centres also benefit from being part of the infrastructure, both as institutions and with regard to what they can offer to their users. Certified CLARIN B-centres accepting digital resources can ensure long-term archiving by their own means, but can also be supported by other CLARIN centres, should one centre run into funding problems or even be forced to shut down completely. The common infrastructure also includes services that a single centre could never provide, such as the Virtual Language Observatory (VLO)[2] (Windhouwer and Goosen, 2022), the Federated Content Search (FCS)[3] (Schonefeld et al., 2014; Olsson, 2017), and the Language Resource Switchboard[4]

2 https://vlo.clarin.eu/
3 https://contentsearch.clarin.eu/
4 https://switchboard.clarin.eu/

(Zinn and Dima, 2022). Services on a national level, for example, the German WebLicht web service orchestration platform (Hinrichs, Hinrichs, and Zastrow, 2010), the LINDAT/CLARIAH-CZ web services (Hajič et al., 2022) or the PORTULAN Workbench (Gomes et al., 2022), can also aggregate the efforts of several centres or institutions and become discoverable beyond the national context through the CLARIN infrastructure.

In these cases, CLARIN has shaped its own best practices: for example, centres are required to provide metadata in the CMDI format (Broeder et al.,2012; Goosen et al., 2015; Windhouwer and Goosen, 2022) for the resource portal VLO, and although the FCS uses generic standards such as the query protocol Search/Retrieve via URL (SRU)[5] and the Contextual Query Language (CQL)[6] to enable searching in collections across the infrastructure, centres also comply with additional CLARIN FCS specifications for querying language resources on various levels. The development of such common CLARIN-specific practices and procedures has been achieved by the respective task forces of the Standing Committee for CLARIN Technical Centres (SCCTC). In contrast with services like the VLO and the FCS, for which centres provide resources and users interact with controlled GUIs, the situation is much more challenging when users are allowed to interact directly with services such as WebLicht or the Language Resource Switchboard using their own data, which comes in various formats, or when users are generally looking for tools and services to implement their data creation and analysis workflows.

CLARIN cannot and should not support all conceivable formats, but rather a well-defined subset[7] including *de facto* standards and formats relevant to the respective disciplinary and data communities (cf. Cooper and Springer, 2019). One of the first steps in specifying any measure of CLARIN-wide guidelines is therefore not only to review what these formats are, but also to make clear why certain formats should not be supported by CLARIN, even though some centres might still need to accept them.[8] This is a way of gently pointing users towards formats that comply with the current data quality requirements (see Section 2.2), thereby avoiding immense data curation costs.

---

5 https://www.loc.gov/standards/sru/

6 https://www.loc.gov/standards/sru/cql/

7 A more comprehensive, fine-grained approach to categorizing format impact, defining several levels of interoperability based on the status of formats ranging from internationally recognized or *de facto* standards and best practices, via formats and standards that are only regionally relevant or discipline-specific, to less prioritized and more rarely used formats, is outlined in Odijk (2016).

8 Depending on the research profile and target data, this is indeed the case in some centres, where the value of the donated data outweighs up-translation costs, cf. Thomas and Wiegand (2015).

To arrive at transparent, widely acknowledged recommendations reflecting the situation in individual CLARIN centres and their designated communities, a crucial requirement is to understand the functions and roles of the various formats in the research process and as parts of complex resources. When assessing individual formats, it is just as crucial to differentiate between, on the one hand, aspects that reflect research traditions or theories, which become visible through data modelling decisions, and, on the other hand, aspects that are not defined by, or relevant for, the research process, but nevertheless vary across formats. An example of the latter would be various ways of modelling alignment between a recording and a transcript that are not directly relevant from the perspective of researchers using their customary tools and formats, as opposed to different options for annotation structure and schemes that directly affect the way in which research questions and analyses can be expressed (cf. Schmidt, 2011). Such a task is by no means trivial. The expertise and experience accumulated within CLARIN offers a unique opportunity to arrive at the appropriate solutions and to provide researchers with the information they need to create better data. Accumulating detailed and qualified information on recommended and used formats, and appropriately exposing and visualizing that information for the purposes of querying and comparison, makes it possible to move forward and enhance interoperability across the infrastructure.

2.2 Quality criteria for data formats

When it comes to research data, quality criteria go beyond assessing generic format sustainability, although the latter is always required as a baseline. For this generic type of sustainability assessment, several organisations provide information, guidelines, and metrics (see Section 5.2 for examples). Even if, until recently, the criteria for basic research data quality and best practices were not entirely clear, today the FAIR principles, which require data to be findable, accessible, interoperable, and reusable (Wilkinson et al., 2016), have become common ground among initiatives related to research data management. At the same time, the idea of machine-actionable data with a well-defined semantic model promoted with these principles is new to most of the humanities, and maybe even out of reach according to some (RDA FAIR Data Maturity Model Working Group, 2020, 10).[9]

9 "[D]ata coming from humanities fields, especially from outside of Digital humanities, will often not be expressed in a machine understandable knowledge representation (RDF, SKOS or LOD) by nature but instead, it is often expressed in natural language, even if encoded using machine readable methods (e.g., TEI). Therefore, it becomes quite clear that the indicator treating machine-

Many formats traditionally used in the Humanities, for example, formatted text documents, are indeed not even reliably machine-readable or processable. Due to their nature as domain-independent, high-level principles, the FAIR principles do not offer direct guidance on actual formats. The idea is that they serve as the basis of an implementation process for a specific discipline and/or context.

Implementation of the FAIR principles within the CLARIN infrastructure has come a long way (de Jong et al., 2018, 2020), and the technical and administrative means are in place to guarantee that resources in certified CLARIN B-centres are findable and accessible. Thanks to advanced solutions for metadata, PIDs (Persistent Identifiers), and AAI (Authentication and Authorization Infrastructure), these first two aspects of FAIR, which are not directly related to the resources themselves, are already fulfilled. However, when it comes to the requirements that the data should be interoperable and reusable, the technical infrastructure used for the safeguarding and distribution of research data is not in a position to fulfill these, as they to a large extent depend on characteristics of the deposited data itself. While many CLARIN resources are undoubtedly among the FAIRest of their kind, there is still work to be done to ensure interoperability that goes beyond format conversion and syntax. In order to enhance data interoperability and reusability, resources need to be understandable to both humans and machines. Therefore, the semantics of data formats and the schemes and conventions used within these formats have to be taken into consideration. Established "domain-relevant community standards" (Principle R1.3, Wilkinson et al., 2016) for data and metadata are still lacking, for example, in the area of (Linguistic) Linked (Open) Data (cf. Chiarcos, Fäth, and Abromeit, 2020). The technical and methodological expertise of CLARIN together with the expertise and needs of its users from various research and data communities will allow for a successful evaluation and further development of relevant data formats based on the FAIR principles.

3 Evolving standards recommendations in CLARIN

This section briefly outlines the context and results of previous initiatives that led to the approach described in the present chapter. One has to bear in mind that the concept of a distributed digital research infrastructure for the language-based humanities is novel in its nature, and both technical and governance solutions

understandable knowledge representation will be less relevant according to the Humanities." (RDA FAIR Data Maturity Model Working Group, 2020, 10) have been emerging over the years and are still being developed in a natural process of maturation. Still, the need for a common set of recommendations concerning standards to be used in CLARIN was already obvious in the preparatory phase of the project. This resulted in several takes on the issue and eventually several sets of recommendations, differing in their structure, granularity, outreach and authority, although all of them seem to have made a single assumption about such a list: namely that it can be established centrally and that it can be effectively imposed on the centres and users in a top-down fashion.

At the beginning of the CLARIN project, research data deposits were not common. With the increasing digitalization and datafication of society in general, awareness of topics related to research data management, and funders' requirements to deposit data for scientific reuse whenever possible, a cultural change was initiated, and is still very much in progress. And with the increased amount of data available, the focus has turned from building technical solutions for the "F" and "A" in FAIR to the data itself, that is, to the "I" and the "R", and questions of data quality (RfII, 2020). As certain centres experienced an increase in deposits, it became clear that these experiences must be continuously integrated into the corresponding recommendations – and that, conversely, these recommendations must be available to users who are interested in creating or depositing resources complying with current good practice.

In 2015, someone looking for CLARIN recommendations on standards and formats would face a number of partly contradictory sources (an extensive list of the documents and other sources that punctuated the project timeline can be found in Annex A to this chapter). In the German use case, the CLARIN-D Data Management Wizard was based on incomplete sources and therefore also omitted formats accepted by several German centres. The "User manual for CLARIN-D" referenced from the wizard referenced in turn the "Standards for LRT" document from 2009 with different information. At the same time, on the CLARIN website, there was information on some centres' format preferences on the "Standards and formats" page, but also another list of standards in a FAQ titled "What standards are recommended by CLARIN?". Around 2012, the CLARIN-D centre at the IDS also provided the CLARIN Standards Guidance (a predecessor of the SIS, to which we turn in Section 5), which was technically advanced, interactive, and user-friendly, but based on incomplete and by then already somewhat outdated information. In 2013, the German funder DFG published a set of recommendations on technical aspects of the creation of language corpora, which was partly based on the (work leading to the) document CLARIN-D5C-3. The latter was not publicly available, and that also applies to the English translation of the DFG recommendations created later in 2015. There were also internal sources; in particular, the CLARIN document "Relevant data formats" (Van Uytvanck, 2014) describes exactly what steps needed to be taken in order to arrive at a list of relevant formats for CLARIN and even references a spreadsheet (Annex A, 8.) with an initial list of formats and columns for information on their purpose and CLARIN-wide (top-down) level of recommendation. The document also makes clear the benefits that such an aggregated list would bring to several areas of the infrastructure, but the initiative was sadly not followed up. At their meeting at the annual conference in Wrocław, in late 2015, the Standards Committee decided to undertake the task of producing an up-to-date list in a bottom-up manner.

In our stall at the Bazaar of the CLARIN Annual Conference 2018 (Hedeland and Bański, 2018), an attempt was made to gather information directly from centre staff about their current practices and general preferences in recommending or discouraging formats. The discussions showed that the task was not only a matter of logistics and endurance in eliciting the information. Some centres rejected the idea of recommendations altogether, arguing that format-related preferences were something to be decided not by an infrastructure, but by individual researchers in accordance with their needs, and that attempts to regularize them might limit freedom of research. Recall that CLARIN serves very different users, highly skilled computer linguists as well as non-tech conversation analysts who are simply trying to comply with the funders' newest requirements. In both cases, standardization can only be implemented by abstracting away the theory-ladenness of research data formats and only applying recommendations to those aspects that are not affected. It also should be stressed that a list of supported formats will never imply that individual CLARIN centres should not accept additional FAIR-compliant data formats, or legacy data in discouraged formats. Guidance is, however, necessary for researchers who need support in creating high quality FAIR research data and to enhance interoperability within the CLARIN infrastructure.

4 Format recommendations: Assessment conditions and metrics

The backbone of CLARIN is composed of B-centres (service-providing centres; see Wittenburg et al. (2020) for more details), one of the primary roles of which is ensuring the longevity and curation of data that users may deposit with them. This section looks at how the relevant obligations of B-centres are specified in the certification requirements, fulfilled by centres, and used as one of the performance metrics of CLARIN.

4.1 Format-related assessment requirements

The assessment and certification of CLARIN centres is handled by the CLARIN Assessment Committee (CAC), and part of that process requires that centres are certified with the CoreTrustSeal (https://www.coretrustseal.org/, CTS for short).

As Wittenburg et al. (2020, 3) state in their CLARIN centre description, "Centres need to have a proper and clearly specified repository system and participate in a quality assessment procedure as proposed by the CoreTrustSeal." Wittenburg et al. (2019, 1), in a checklist document for centres that are candidates for type B, strengthen this requirement by stating that "[t]he centre cannot be certified as a B-centre until the CoreTrustSeal assessment has been successfully concluded (...) The application for the CoreTrustSeal, or proof that the CoreTrustSeal has been awarded, has to be provided."

The CTS requirements concerning formats, listed in the "Extended Guidance" document (CoreTrustSeal Standards and Certification Board, 2019), Section 8: "Requirements/Appraisal", are as follows:

> For this Requirement, responses should include evidence related to the following questions:
> (...)
> – Does the repository publish a list of preferred formats?
> – Are checks in place to ensure that data producers adhere to the preferred formats?
> – What is the approach towards data that are deposited in non-preferred formats?
> (...)

Of these questions, it is the first one that we focus on in the present chapter. In the remainder of this section, we look at how centres have addressed the requirement to publish lists of preferred formats, show how the degree of fulfillment was measured, and list features desirable in a system designed to assist in aggregating and visualizing the relevant information, while minimizing the effort needed to keep it current.

4.2 Addressing format-related assessment requirements

The CTS and thus B-centre-assessment requirements reviewed above provide a reasonably clear and measurable framework for centres to fit in. A KPI (Key Performance Indicator) has been established that measures the "percentage of centres offering repository services that have published an overview of formats that can be processed in their repository" (Maegaard and Wessels, 2019).

In theory, due to the assessment process, this KPI should be close to 100%, potentially deviating from the maximum only in the case of non-B-centres that allow for data deposition but are not regulated by the CTS, or, marginally, in the case of B-centres that are in the process of reassessment.

In practice, centres have adopted various strategies to address the CTS requirements: some centres have indeed published lists of recommended formats,[10] with their own subdivisions and varying granularity, and various ways to indicate their interest in receiving various formats, while other centres, possibly as an expression of their readiness to accept any data in nearly any format, have directed users towards the previously announced CLARIN top-down recommendations, most notably the "LRT standards" document.[11]

Another factor, pointed out to us in personal communication by Dieter Van Uytvanck, is that the above-mentioned requirement for B-centres to provide deposition services has acquired a fuzzy interpretation that sometimes invokes "internal deposition" as a way to satisfy the assessment procedure. We do not take a stance here on the formal status of such an approach, merely noting it as another factor that influences centres' willingness to publish information about recommended formats.

In 2019, the CSC decided to focus on data-deposition format recommendations as a first step towards developing a list of standards recommendations in CLARIN that would be more modern and easier to maintain than the existing standards recommendations (see Annex A for a hopefully complete list). That decision led to the welcome consequence that the KPI rose from 33% reported in 2018 and 2019 to 46% in the following year.[12]

It has to be borne in mind that, for some colleagues responsible for addressing the CTS requirements, the issue is tied to freedom of research or the need to collect rare and valuable data at all costs. We believe that such an attitude is a natural consequence of the quasi-Platonic assumption that there exists a central

10 These centres can be found listed at https://www.clarin.eu/content/standards-and-formats.

11 These centres can be found listed at https://github.com/clarin-eric/standards/issues/14. A strong impetus towards recommending the "LRT standards" document came as a result of the precious initiative by LINDAT colleagues that unifies the information for data depositors and provides a FAQ that directs the reader to the "LRT standards" document. Current work on the SIS promises a replacement of that link with a centre-specific link to the recommendations (see Section 5.3 for an example).

12 The measurement reported to us is probably not perfect, because it does not take into account newly certified centres; what is important, however, is a significant rise in the percentage of centres publishing their own format recommendations; we are told by Dieter Van Uytvanck (personal communication) that a new round of KPI measurements is in progress at the time of writing.

top-down format recommendations list (even if the list is yet to be codified), and that format recommendations have an absolute, binary nature, not allowing for any form of gradation. We also believe that such an assumption should be eliminated and replaced with a more satisfactory system. The features of such a system are enumerated below:

1. There should be a way for a centre to publish format recommendations suited to and reflecting its own research profile, in such a way
   a. that the decision and the act of publishing can take place relatively quickly and painlessly,
   b. that the resulting collection can be updated quickly and straightforwardly.
2. These recommendations should ideally be structurally uniform across the board, to form a reliable basis that would enable users to select a centre for data deposition.
3. A new centre should be able to use a template, rather than devise yet another list.
4. Centres should not be tempted to "just link" to a single set of top-down recommendations, because those will rarely match a research profile (and are never meant to match a single profile).
5. The format taxonomy should be comparable (preferably, shared), and should ideally be able to also provide additional information (about comparable formats as well as about the standards documents that define many formats).
6. The results should be visualized in a way that allows one to glean extra information from the aggregation of the recommendations (e.g., about the most and least popular formats).

The following section shows that the upgraded Standards Information System meets the above description.

5 Standards Information System: Goals and description

The solution described in this chapter has arisen out of several sources: the general tension in the CLARIN community reflected in the Wrocław declaration of 2015, the stalled CLARIN Standards Guidance project and, more recently, discussions within the Standards Committee and the relevant part of the CLARIN KPI-related research.

Out of the above-mentioned factors, two have already been at least briefly touched upon in the preceding sections: the community tension (Section 3) and the KPI-related research (Section 4). CLARIN Standards Guidance (Stührenberg, Werthmann, and Witt, 2012) was an early project meant to consolidate the repertoire of standards advocated by CLARIN (in a top-down fashion, by marking some of them as “recommended by CLARIN”). Despite being well-designed, based on modern XML and Semantic Web technology, and featuring useful visualizations, it became stalled due to the amount of work that its maintenance by a small team would involve, and effectively made the list of “previous standards collections” that is the subject of Annex A, with an outdated fragment of it quoted until recently at one of the clarin.eu pages as yet another set of recommendations.

The KPI-related research within CLARIN has been described by Maegaard and Krauwer (2018) and Maegaard and Wessels (2019). A part of that research relevant to the beginnings of the present-day SIS concerns the indicator “Collection of standards and mappings” (Maegaard and Krauwer, 2018), with the accompanying measure defined as “Percentage of centres offering repository services that have published an overview of formats that can be processed in their repository”, and gave the Standards Committee an opportunity to focus more narrowly on an issue that promised to be both practical and useful, and to constitute a seed for further work on the far-reaching goal of the CSC.

The last of the factors that contributed to the rebirth of the Standards Guidance as the Standards Information System is work of the CSC after 2015, punctuated by Bański (2018), a white paper circulated among the members of the CSC and other interested colleagues that contained ideas that were further polished into the current proposal, among them a crude function-based division of formats and a version of levels of recommendation, encoded as a parameter matrix.

The present section looks at the CSC research concerning the relevant KPI, then moves on to outline the concept and content of functional domains and levels of recommendation, finally focusing on the current SIS and on how it addresses the various needs outlined in Section 4.2 and elsewhere.

5.1 Data collection

The data that formed the initial core of the work of the CSC after mid-2019 was collected by Dieter Van Uytvanck in a spreadsheet designed to measure the format-related KPI and at the same time to check how popular certain formats were among the CLARIN centres. The spreadsheet consisted initially of format names (of varying granularity) and collected data from the initial seven centres that published their requirements concerning deposition formats (Bański, Hedeland, and Van Uytvanck, 2019). In the course of 2019 and 2020, the spreadsheet was extended thanks to the efforts of the CSC members, finally embracing all those centres (whether of the B-status or not) that offered deposition services, expanding the number of format names and gathering them into format families (in many ways preceding the functional domains that are the topic of Section 5.2.1). Popularity of the particular formats was measured by indicating a "1" in cells where the format name row and the centre name column met, and then by calculating the number of occurrences of "1", with results relativized to a particular format family, so that text annotation formats would not compete with audio encoding formats. The results of these stages of the CSC work can be found in the early, internal, releases at https://www.clarin.eu/content/standards; a glimpse is also provided in CLARIN Standards Committee (2020).

While the initial work on the KPI spreadsheet was fruitful and moved the KPI to another level within a year, with the members of the CSC ensuring that many B-centres in their spheres of influence published their recommendations, it also became clear that the system of counting only "1"s for an occurrence of a format name in a format list was far from satisfactory, as it did not take into consideration domains of application of the given format, or the level of support that the given centre assigned to it. This inadequacy was eventually addressed by formulating a list of functional domains (Section 5.2.1) and encoding three levels of recommendation (Section 5.2.2), and in a longer perspective, by abandoning the KPI spreadsheet as insufficiently expressive and focusing on the Standards Information System as the locus for information on format recommendations as well as the tool for gathering that information from centres as a way to enable them to satisfy the assessment requirements in a comparable and sustainable way (Section 5.3).

5.2 Design of format recommendations

The transition to the relaunched Standards Information System required the definition of both a data model for more elaborate format descriptions than the ones in the KPI spreadsheet and a schema for adequately modelled format recommendations. In order to be accepted as a reasonable alternative to existing practices, format recommendations in the Standards Information System have to be at least as expressive as those currently provided by centres. On the other hand, to encourage the contribution of information, brevity and simplicity are crucial, especially regarding descriptions of additional formats. The CSC decided to focus on those formats that CLARIN is particularly suited to provide the relevant information about. This way, it is possible to avoid information gathering and management in parallel with existing generic initiatives such as the Sustainability of Digital Formats Website[13] of the Library of Congress, the U.S. National Archives and Records Administration (NARA) Digital Preservation Framework,[14] or PRONOM[15] of the U.K. National Archives. These initiatives already provide comprehensive and detailed information on most widely used formats, including assessments of their sustainability – and they also use persistent format identifiers that can be referenced from less detailed descriptions in the Standards Information System. Apart from the more generic orientation of the format registries and assessments of these examples in comparison with the intended purpose of the Standards Information System, the former focus mainly on long-term preservation and sustainability of the formats, while for CLARIN, the aspect of interoperability within the technical infrastructure in its current state is also important. Format recommendations provided by centres also differ from format assessments in the sense that centres do not need to provide any explanations for their recommendations and preferences. For these reasons, it has been decided initially to restrict the data models of the Standards Information System compared to the detailed format descriptions available elsewhere, and to only incorporate the information currently required for the task at hand.

5.2.1 Functional domains

The CLARIN centres that published white lists of formats or format recommendations most often used content-oriented categories for the sake of structural clarity and in order to provide guidance for users. That was not fully adequate for two reasons: firstly, no uniform categorization was adopted across centres, and, secondly, it was often assumed that categorization was a secondary projection of the nature of the particular formats and thus merely grouped them into "families" of a sort. This is also the approach in the Summary Guide to Preferred Formats[16] by The Dutch Digital Heritage Network (NDE),[17] based on the PRONOM and NARA Digital Preservation Framework information, where archives and data centres in the Netherlands list their preferred formats. If format sustainability is the only requirement, that is a sensible approach, but when the range of *functions* of data used by CLARIN centres is taken into consideration, it becomes clear

13 https://www.loc.gov/preservation/digital/formats/
14 https://www.archives.gov/preservation/electronic-records/digital-preservation-risk
15 https://www.nationalarchives.gov.uk/PRONOM/
16 https://www.wegwijzervoorkeursformaten.nl/index.php/Summary_Guide_to_Prefered_Formats
17 https://netwerkdigitaalerfgoed.nl/

that the relationship between formats and functional domains must be many-to-many, because very often a single format can be (and is) used for more than one purpose. One common example is PDF/A, which is a highly recommended format for long-term archiving of, for instance, unstructured resource documentation such as annotation guidelines or a corpus manual, or for digitized scans of original texts. It is, however, seldom a recommended format for the resource itself, for example, for text annotations or audiovisual annotations. No common set of categories describing these functions has been in use in CLARIN, although a Resource and Technology Taxonomy including this type of information was drafted already in the preparation phase (Wittenburg et al., 2008); the current status of this draft or its impact on CLARIN centres remain unclear.

While the CLARIN Standards Committee was extending the KPI spreadsheet, the initial workaround was to focus solely on a single purpose: the use of formats for linguistic research data in the narrowest sense, such as text and annotations, while ignoring other format recommendations. The wish to reflect the greater and more complex picture, however, soon led to the development of a set of functional domains reflecting the relevant data types in CLARIN repositories. The initial set was based on the results of a survey of several repositories holding various types of resources, which was carried out in the project QUEST[18] at the IDS, complemented with the expertise and experience of the members of the CLARIN Standards Committee.

The proposed functional domains overlap with the draft taxonomy of Wittenburg et al. (2008) to a large extent, as would be expected from two descriptions of the same area. However, The Resource and Technology Taxonomy also includes some abstract categories such as Object, Situation and Session, which are not relevant to the format-oriented CLARIN Standards Information System. The taxonomy differentiates between speech (audio) and multimodal (video) resources, both of which belong to the functional domain Audiovisual Source Data, but it does not differentiate between annotations referring to audio or video resources on the one hand, and those referring to text on the other; in the SIS, these annotations are considered to represent different functional domains. Furthermore, in contrast to the taxonomy, the functional domains proposed here consider transcripts to be a subtype of annotation.

The currently identified set of functional domains is listed in Annex B. In the remainder of this section, some less obvious choices and categories are briefly explained. A fundamental assumption that has to be borne in mind is that the purpose behind using functional domains is not so much for them to constitute

18 https://www.slm.uni-hamburg.de/en/ifuu/forschung/forschungsprojekte/quest.html

a complete knowledge resource or ontology concerning data types or functions in the language-oriented humanities, but rather to allow the Standards Committee to elicit relevant information about standards and formats in use within the CLARIN infrastructure. The original set of domains is thus a first version that might be refined and extended according to additional requirements established through the actual use of the SIS. For each functional domain, there will most likely always exist a set of recommended formats – there are valid reasons why a single uniform exchange or standard format has not yet replaced all others – especially given that several formats already have a strong geographic or discipline-based support.

In the area of (structured) resource documentation, a distinction is drawn between the three categories: "Contextual Information", "Catalogue Metadata", and "Metadata". This distinction is not used explicitly in all centres, and the aim in providing three categories is to find out more about which highly related formats are used for which exact purposes. The reason for singling out information on texts or communicative events and authors or participants as "Contextual Information" is that this information (a) is highly dependent on the research question at hand, and can therefore never be standardized with regard to the elements and values used, and (b) can contain too much potentially sensitive information to be in the public domain. In CLARIN, the standard metadata format is CMDI (cf. Section 2.1), but one of the main aims of CMDI is the harmonization and standardization of metadata within a centre (and partly within CLARIN), and another is the public availability of the metadata records for harvesting. It is therefore expected that centres use, or at least handle, additional formats for richer and potentially non-public information. Furthermore, in addition to CMDI, which is required within CLARIN, many centres also provide reduced sets of metadata for resource discoverability in contexts other than the VLO, with Dublin Core[19] being the typical example of "Catalogue Metadata". This metadata only contains very basic discoverability information required for being listed in generic catalogues or portals for archives or research data centres of various types.

Other categories in the set are very broad, for instance, the category "Tool support", including all kinds of formats related to tools and services. While there are undoubtedly conceptual differences between a tagset, a language model, and a settings file including tier formatting information, for the purpose of gathering information on formats, further subcategories seem unnecessary, at least in the

19 https://www.dublincore.org/

initial stage. Likewise, the category "Language Description" might need further refinement depending on the insights during the upcoming survey period.

5.2.2 Level of recommendation

Apart from grouping formats into functional categories, another issue reflected in format white lists and recommendations was the varied means of expressing the extent to which a centre would be ready to accept particular kinds of data and data formats. Centres are willing to go to varying measures in order to ensure data deposition. Some kinds of data are too valuable not to invest the centre's resources in conversion and curation. In most cases, the centre needs to conserve its resources and expects the donor to take care of the easy details, such as the format. For this reason, the centre's interest is not merely binary – "interested" vs. "not interested" – but rather (apart from cases where the data in question is extremely valuable), the scale is minimally composed of three values: recommended, acceptable (can be up-converted with relatively little effort), and deprecated (effectively discouraged – the cost of up-conversion from that format may outweigh the value of the data by far). Note that the very fact that each centre's recommendations may easily differ in this regard, due to traditions of supporting certain formats or local research communities, speaks against an attempt to formulate any sort of specific top-down format recommendations.

How strictly centres need to control incoming deposits depends on the intended further processing. Some centres distribute data sets more or less as they were deposited, with additional standardized metadata added in the deposition process, while other centres want to make sure that all deposited resources comply with requirements at various levels, in order for them to be further enriched, visualized, and/or integrated into a local search engine. The question of whether or not to accept data in non-compliant formats and possibly curate it can be answered by assessing the data value, which is difficult to operationalize, and the curation cost, which is often very hard to estimate for inconsistent and/or legacy data sets. On the other hand, if a repository offers data sets with highly varying characteristics, it becomes very difficult for people wanting to reuse resources to determine which reuse scenarios would be possible for an individual resource. One solution, described in Hedeland (2021), would be to formally define different levels of data maturity, in order to describe linguistic resources as being curated and structured to a certain extent. This would allow depositors to comply with requirements suitable for their research project and users to know what to expect from individual data sets.

5.2.3 Granularity

Another aspect of the design of format recommendations is the amount of detail in the description or the point of discrimination between (sub)types of formats, which also varies greatly in the documents and lists published by CLARIN centres. This question is often related to whether centres process and possibly curate deposited data in order to integrate it into services such as platforms for querying or visualization, since the technical workflows are often designed for specific formats, not for generic formats such as XML[20] or TEI (TEI Consortium, 2021). The same is true for tools and services provided via the infrastructure, and this practical relevance of specific format descriptions became visible in the development of the CLARIN-D WebLicht web service orchestration platform at the German CLARIN centre EKUT (cf. Section 2.1). Since WebLicht uses its own internal format, TCF,[21] various German centres provided converters from their preferred formats to TCF. Users would then upload their data to WebLicht and a suitable converter would be suggested on the basis of the media type. However, it soon turned out that the IANA media type for TEI data (application/tei+xml) was not sufficient to differentiate between, for example, the DTA Base Format for printed texts (DTABf, Haaf, Geyken, and Wiegand, 2015) used at the German CLARIN centre BBAW and the TEI-based ISO 62462:2016 "Transcription of spoken language" (ISO/TC 37/SC 4, 2016) used at the German CLARIN centres HZSK and IDS. Since the respective converters provided by the BBAW and the HZSK were specific to their preferred TEI variants, users' requests for conversion from more or less random TEI customizations to TCF would often fail.

Apart from the two variants of the TEI mentioned above, several other well-documented TEI-based formats are used within CLARIN. These are either tailored to specific research areas, such as Parla-CLARIN (Erjavec et al., 2022) for parliamentary data, CMC-core (Beißwenger and Lüngen, 2020) for computer mediated communication data, or MENOTA (Haugen, 2019) for Nordic medieval texts, or they are locally used variants such as the I5 format (Lüngen and Sperberg-McQueen, 2012) of the IDS centre in Germany, the TEIP5DKCLARIN (Asmussen, 2015) of the Danish consortium, or the TEITOK system (Janssen, 2021) now hosted by the LINDAT centre. These formats are not interchangeable and though they can all be described as "TEI", such a generic description is often insufficient. For the WebLicht use case, a solution was suggested based on required and optional parameters added to the IANA media type by analogy to, for instance,

20 https://www.w3.org/TR/xml/
21 https://weblicht.sfs.uni-tuebingen.de/weblichtwiki/index.php/The_TCF_Format

charset for text files (cf. Schmidt, Hedeland, and Jettka, 2017). The parameter "format-variant" was successfully used within WebLicht, and it is a good example of how standardization should follow community practice: at the time of writing, this parameter is not yet part of any official standard for the relevant IANA media types, and any initiative to make it officially recognized must wait until the practice is sufficiently well established within the community.

Similar cases of related but different formats can be found in the CoNLL[22] family and for other TSV-based (tool) formats, which means that this is not a TEI-related problem, but a more general one. And when considering audio and video data with varying codecs, as well as quality-related parameters specified in the recommendations published by CLARIN centres and other organizations, it becomes clear that also for this kind of non-textual data, media type labels are often insufficient for the purpose of an adequate format identification. The PRONOM initiative of The National Archives and the Sustainability of Digital Formats Website of the Library of Congress (cf. Section 5.2) have both found ways of dealing with this very issue. The PRONOM PUID Scheme specification (Brown, 2006, 5), which explains the minting and use of persistent unique identifiers for formats, stresses the importance of granularity decisions and describes how the system differentiates at a fine-grained level:

> The granularity at which separate formats are identified is a crucial feature of the scheme. The PUID identifies formats at the most specific possible level of granularity. For example, the eXtensible Markup Language (XML) is a format which exists in a number of different versions (currently 1.0 and the forthcoming 1.1).

On the other hand, for other features, such as the image compression algorithms of the TIFF 6.0 format (Adobe Developers Association, 1992), no individual PUIDs are issued. In comparison, the Library of Congress issues an ID to the TIFF 6.0 format[23] and also for individual subtypes according to the various compression algorithms. In the context of digital language resources, source data quality is crucial, which was also reflected in the existing recommendations by parameters such as sampling rate and bit depth for audio recordings. Figure 3 shows how this information, encoded as comments in the SIS, discriminates between two entries with different levels of recommendation for the format "WAVE" by the IDS centre. At the time of writing, there is no final solution to these questions for the SIS,

---

22 CoNLL formats have been born in the context of shared tasks of the SIGNLL Conference on Computational Natural Language Learning https://www.conll.org/. The most popular of them is CoNLL-U (https://universaldependencies.org/format.html), with a template for extensions; versions of CoNLL-U addressing word lattices and anaphora resolution have also been proposed.
23 https://www.loc.gov/preservation/digital/formats/fdd/fdd000022.shtml

but as in the case of the functional domains (cf. Section 5.2.1), the CSC intends to base decisions regarding granularity of format descriptions on the practical use by service providers and users of the infrastructure.

5.3 Standards Information System: Data model

Figure 1 below presents the addition of format recommendation information to the (simplified) data model of the earlier version of the SIS. What can be seen in the diagram is that formats, while in most cases defined by published standards, are a class of their own, with information that is in many cases independent from standards, such as the recommended file extension or the recommended MIME type – information items that have proven to be of use to CLARIN developers.

For the purpose of aggregating and visualizing deposition format recommendations, we consider a single instance of recommendation as a qualified link between a triple: {Format, Domain, Centre}, where the former two are combined in what is basically a Cartesian product dubbed "Relativized format" – that is, a format that realizes a function described by the given domain. For example, the following recommendation: {FLAC, Audiovisual Source Language Data, IDS}, qualified as "acceptable", expresses the fact that the IDS declares it will accept depositions in the FLAC format for data belonging to the domain "Audiovisual Source Language Data".[24]

5.4 Workflows for format recommendations

Several workflows have been considered for creating and maintaining format recommendations, depending on what the subparts of the system were assumed to be – for example, while the KPI (Google) spreadsheet was still the locus of format-related information, users of the published system were expected to interact with the spreadsheet via Google Forms. That required third-party add-ons for Google Forms and a lot of data manipulation within the spreadsheet in order to populate the Forms adequately, as well as a non-trivial XML transformation from Forms into the SIS, for visualization. In June 2021, the CSC decided to abandon the KPI spreadsheet and to make the SIS the basis for user workflows. The workflow that is currently envisioned is described below, taking advantage of predefined templates for each depositing centre and of the fact that many formats are already

24 See e.g. https://standards.clarin.eu/sis/views/view-format.xq?id=fFLAC for an implementation.

described within the system. Note that, at this point, the existing format recommendations announced by centres on their home pages must be additionally interpreted in order to be converted into the qualified {Format, Domain, Centre} triples. This in turn means that centre representatives should approach the initial information presented by the SIS with an eye to modifying it to make sure that it fully reflects the given centre's stance. Naturally, the workflow is designed to be applied iteratively, whenever the given centre decides to adjust its recommendations. New centres can also apply it by reusing recommendations from other centres and editing them appropriately.

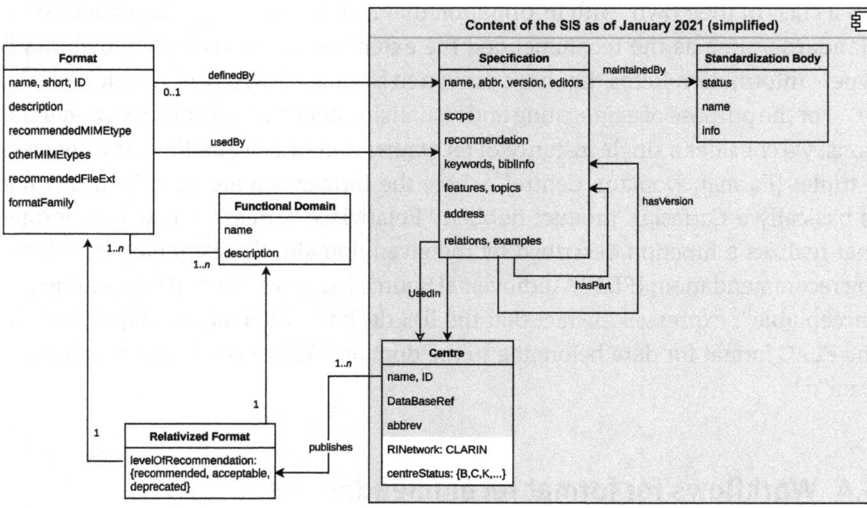

Figure 1: Simplified data model of the SIS; the original parts on bluish background.

The example centre representative (assume that the centre is IDS Mannheim) should start by checking the recommendations encoded for their centre at https://standards.clarin.eu/sis/, either by opening the menu item "Format recommendations" and selecting "IDS" in the first drop-down menu to filter the results, or by opening the IDS-related section from the menu item "Centres". The next step is to verify that the recommendations are correct and complete, and the SIS assists with this by making it possible to sort the data by any column. Figure 2 shows an example screenshot of the filtered sorted recommendations screen, while Figure 3 is a fragment of centre-specific information screen, where additional comments are also shown.

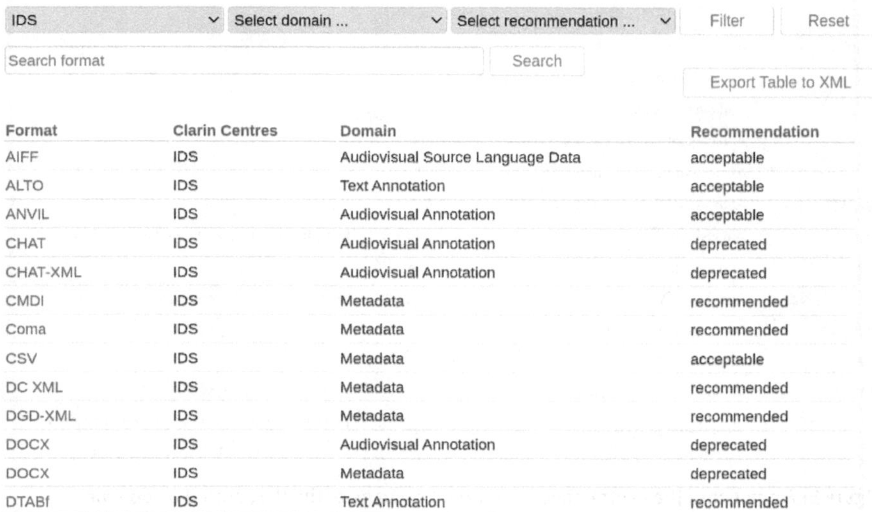

Format	Clarin Centres	Domain	Recommendation
AIFF	IDS	Audiovisual Source Language Data	acceptable
ALTO	IDS	Text Annotation	acceptable
ANVIL	IDS	Audiovisual Annotation	acceptable
CHAT	IDS	Audiovisual Annotation	deprecated
CHAT-XML	IDS	Audiovisual Annotation	deprecated
CMDI	IDS	Metadata	recommended
Coma	IDS	Metadata	recommended
CSV	IDS	Metadata	acceptable
DC XML	IDS	Metadata	recommended
DGD-XML	IDS	Metadata	recommended
DOCX	IDS	Audiovisual Annotation	deprecated
DOCX	IDS	Metadata	deprecated
DTABf	IDS	Text Annotation	recommended

Figure 2: Example screenshot of format recommendations in the SIS (v. 2.2.0), filtered for "IDS" and sorted alphabetically by format names.

After the potential filtering, recommendations can be exported as XML, to yield a listing similar to the example fragment shown in Figure 4.

This is an editable file that can be modified or extended as necessary, and afterwards submitted to the SIS via GitHub: either by means of a pull request from a forked repository, or by opening the relevant document in the browser and pasting the new content, thus creating a new commit.[25] The commit will be checked for well-formedness and content errors, and eventually uploaded to the live instance of the SIS. If the file is edited with XML-aware software, the underlying schema restricts the options for functional domains and recommendations (they are presented as drop-down lists with glosses for each option).

25 The document relevant for this example resides at https://github.com/clarin-eric/standards/blob/master/SIS/clarin/data/recommendations/IDS-recommendation.xml.

TEISpoken	Audiovisual Annotation	recommended	
plainText	Audiovisual Annotation	deprecated	
Transana	Audiovisual Annotation	deprecated	
TRS	Audiovisual Annotation	acceptable	
AIFF	Audiovisual Source Language Data	acceptable	
FLAC	Audiovisual Source Language Data	acceptable	
M2J ⊕	Audiovisual Source Language Data	acceptable	
MP3	Audiovisual Source Language Data	deprecated	lossy formats should be avoided if possible
MP4	Audiovisual Source Language Data	acceptable	
MPEG-4 AVC	Audiovisual Source Language Data	recommended	25 fps, 1920×1080, constant bit rate
MPEG-1	Audiovisual Source Language Data	acceptable	
MPEG-2	Audiovisual Source Language Data	acceptable	
WAVE	Audiovisual Source Language Data	recommended	PCM-WAV, 48 kHz, 16 bit
WAVE	Audiovisual Source Language Data	acceptable	PCM-WAV with non-recommended parameters (not 48 kHz, 16 bit)

Figure 3: Fragment of the centre-specific information page of the IDS, sorted by domain names, showing example comments that differentiate between seemingly conflicting recommendations.

The live system is cross-linked to predefined GitHub "tickets", which are a way of communicating to the developers and users that something can be added, extended, or fixed. An example of that is shown in Figure 3, where the format "M2J" does not yet have a corresponding information page and the "+" sign indicates that clicking on it will open a GitHub ticket.

6 Summary and outlook

The present chapter provides a glimpse of the work of the CLARIN Standards Committee and locates it within the context of the evolution and maturation of a distributed research infrastructure that needs to establish balance between, on the one hand, the top-down requirements of uniformity and, on the other, the bottom-up tension that stems from freedom of research and the complexity of the target fields of interest. Such a balance contributes to ensuring a satisfactory measure of interoperability among the growing network, and a uniform basis for outreach.

The current picture is one in which a top-down frame of general research principles (FAIR and others) is set over a predefined information structure, which the individual centres can fill in by using shared (and open-ended) taxonomies, in fulfilment of the assessment criteria, but also in order to communicate their profile in practical and uniform terms, both to other centres and to outside users.

Expanding the existing information and adding new centres is simple and transparent, with the contributions guaranteed to be attributable and under version control.

```
<format id="fWave">
   <domain>Audiovisual Source Language Data</domain>
   <level>recommended</level>
   <comment>PCM-WAV, 48 kHz, 16 bit</comment>
</format>
<format id="fWave">
   <domain>Audiovisual Source Language Data</domain>
   <level>acceptable</level>
   <comment>PCM-WAV with non-recommended parameters (not 48 kHz, 16 bit)</comment>
</format>
<format id="fPDFA">
   <domain>Documentation</domain>
   <level>recommended</level>
</format>
<format id="fTextPlain">
   <domain>Documentation</domain>
   <level>recommended</level>
</format>
<format id="fCMDI">
   <domain>Metadata</domain>
   <level>recommended</level>
</format>
```

Figure 4: XML representation of a fragment of format recommendations.

The nearest future for the CSC will consist in ironing out any wrinkles in how the system and the envisioned maintenance workflow function, adding more visualization options, and, in the next step, in looking at the part of the SIS that addresses standards in order to make it as useful in practical terms as the format-related part promises to be. Apart from CLARIN-internal dissemination of information and documentation on the SIS, integration with existing generic initiatives by the Library of Congress and The National Archives (cf. Section 5.2) and the more recently developed FAIRsharing platform[26] is also being considered in order to reach out to users and research infrastructures beyond CLARIN. Furthermore, the SIS could also become valuable as a sound knowledge basis for initiatives targeting interoperability, such as the SSHOC Conversion Hub.[27]

26 https://fairsharing.org/standards/
27 https://conversion-hub.sshopencloud.eu/

Annex A: Major standards-related recommendations in the history of CLARIN

These are standards guidelines that have been circulated as semi- or fully official in the history of CLARIN. This list is most probably incomplete and the ordering is not generally meant to indicate the level of influence or importance, except for the first item, which is important because it was a product of a task force of specialists, and because (as such) it received a lot of attention, and is referenced in many of the other items listed here.

1. *Standards for LRT*, a 2009 document provided on the CLARIN website (at the standards recommendations page, https://www.clarin.eu/content/standard-recommendations) – the most recent version comes from March 2009. This is a relevant document because it is commonly referenced, and because it has been prepared by a committee of experts and representatives of several projects.
2. CLARIN preparatory phase deliverable *D5.C-3: Interoperability and Standards*, edited by Erhard Hinrichs and Iris Vogel. 2010. https://office.clarin.eu/pp/D5C-3.pdf. This document was created in the D-Spin preparatory phase for CLARIN-D and later became the basis for the DFG recommendations for technical and software aspects of corpus creation (cf. 12 in this list).
3. *Standards and Formats*, an overview of recommended CLARIN standards on the CLARIN website: https://www.clarin.eu/content/standards-and-formats
4. *Overview of standard related resources in CLARIN centres*, compiled by Maik Stührenberg in 2014 with input from the CSC: https://trac.clarin.eu/attachment/wiki/StandardsCommittee/Overview_of_Standard-related_resources-2014-08-26-TLA_DK_PL.docx (restricted access).
5. *CLARIN standards guidance* (later renamed *Standards Information System* and deposited at GitHub) hosted at the IDS; see Section 5 of the present chapter.
6. *What standards are recommended by CLARIN?* is a CLARIN website FAQ item: https://www.clarin.eu/faq/what-standards-are-recommended-clarin.
7. *CE-2014-0421 "Relevant data formats"* (https://www.clarin.eu/sites/default/files/CE-2104-0421-relevant-formats.pdf).
8. *"CE-2014-0421-relevant-formats"* (an internal spreadsheet accompanying CE-2014-0421).
9. *DMPTY*, the (experimental) CLARIN-D data management plan wizard (Trippel and Zinn (2015), https://www.clarin-d.net/en/preparation/data-management-plan) refers to the CLARIN-D User guide (cf. 11.) and provides a short (outdated) list of formats.

10. *Format Registry*, a collection of format recommendations mainly resulting from a recent (2015) survey on formats accepted by German CLARIN centres: https://trac.clarin.eu/wiki/FormatRegistry (restricted access).
11. *CLARIN user guide* (in German and English; the former appears to be no longer available in full) https://media.dwds.de/clarin/userguide/text/ (since 2012, but the most recent version is from 2019). An alternative link is: https://www.clarin-d.net/en/language-resources-and-services/user-guide.
12. *DFG Handreichung: Empfehlungen zu datentechnischen Standards und Tools bei der Erhebung von Sprachkorpora*, 2nd edition, 2019 (hosted at the DFG website: http://www.dfg.de/download/pdf/foerderung/grundlagen_dfg_foerderung/informationen_fachwissenschaften/geisteswissenschaften/standards_sprachkorpora.pdf; there is an unofficial English translation (of the 1st edition) in preparation: Recommendations for Technical Standards and Tools for Building Language Corpora).
13. *Adoption and implementation of standards*, a CLARIN-Plus document authored by Claus Povlsen and Lene Offersgaard (CLARINPLUS-D5.3-7): https://office.clarin.eu/v/CE-2016-0879-CLARINPLUS-D5_3-7-Standards.pdf (referencing the SIS but indirectly also the LRT Standards document).
14. CLARIN Short Guides:
    a. *Standards for text encoding* (May 2009): https://www.clarin.eu/sites/default/files/standards-text-CLARIN-ShortGuide.pdf
    b. *Standards and best practices* (Feb 2009): https://www.clarin.eu/sites/default/files/standards-CLARIN-ShortGuide.pdf
    c. *Web services interoperability* (Feb 2010): https://www.clarin.eu/sites/default/files/ws_interop-CLARIN-ShortGuide.pdf
15. *Interoperability* webpage at https://www.clarin.eu/content/interoperability (maintained by the Interoperability Task Force).

Annex B: Functional domains for deposition formats

This section lists the functional domains that correspond to the most common use scenarios to which data deposited at CLARIN centres may be put; see Section 5.2.1 for the motivation behind some of the choices. The current list is to be found at https://standards.clarin.eu/sis/views/list-domains.xq.

Annotation

- **Audiovisual Annotation**
  Annotations of audiovisual sources, usually including a basic rendering of the spoken content (transcription) and sometimes further annotation.
- **Image Annotation**
  Annotations of image sources.
- **Text Annotation**
  Annotations of textual sources/written text, with the original text included or as stand-off.

Data/resource description

- **Metadata**
  Comprehensive structured information including descriptive, structural, and administrative metadata.
- **Catalogue Metadata**
  Basic structured information for discoverability and general description, to be openly provided for harvesting.
- **Contextual Information**
  Structured information on the communicative event or text and its creators (i.e. participants or authors) relevant for analysis.
- **Documentation**
  Unstructured documentation of the resource and its parts, such as corpus or annotation guidelines.

Databases

- **Language Description**
  Structured or unstructured descriptions of linguistic varieties or phenomena, typological databases, etc.
- **Lexical Resource**
  Structured (item-based) resources for lexical and/or conceptual information on units of language (e.g., wordlists, lexicons, WordNets, etc.)
- **Geodata**
  Information on geographic locations.
- **Statistical Data**
  Data from surveys and tests in numeric formats.

Source data

- **Audiovisual Source Language Data**
  Audio or video recordings providing spoken/multimodal or signed language data for research purposes.
- **Image Source Language Data**
  Digitized images of analogue sources of written language data for research purposes (e.g., facsimiles, scans of handwriting, photos of inscriptions).
- **Textual Source Language Data**
  Written unstructured/plain text or originally structured text (e.g., HTML) without linguistic or other mark-up added for research purposes.
- **Contextual Data**
  Images (photos or drawings) or documents relevant to the communicative event or text but not part of the source language data.

Uncategorized

- **Tool support**
  Tool-related formats required for specific functionality of the tool or reliable reuse of resources (e.g., tagsets, annotation schemes, vocabularies, language models, parameter files, and other specifications or settings)
- **Other**
  Functions not covered by the other domains.

Bibliography

Adobe Developers Association. 1992. TIFF revision 6.0. Technical report, Adobe Systems Incorporated. https://www.awaresystems.be/imaging/tiff/specification/TIFF6.pdf (accessed May 3, 2022).

Asmussen, Jørg. 2015. Text formatting. what an annotated text should look like. Technical report, DK-CLARIN WP 2.1. https://info.clarin.dk/clarin-dk-infrastrukturen/vejledninger/text-format.pdf (accessed May 3, 2022).

Bański, Piotr. 2018. Towards unified CLARIN recommendations for the use of standards: a pilot study on "text formats" (CE-2021-1931), Version 0.2, 2018-05-10. Technical report, CLARIN ERIC. https://hdl.handle.net/11372/DOC-164 (accessed May 3, 2022).

Bański, Piotr, Hanna Hedeland & Dieter Van Uytvanck. 2019. Unified list of standards: next steps forward. Poster presented at the Bazaar, CLARIN Annual Conference 2019, Leipzig, Germany, 30 September-2 October. https://www.clarin.eu/sites/default/files/clarin2019_bazaar_csc.pdf (accessed May 3, 2022).

Beißwenger, Michael & Harald Lüngen. 2020. CMC-core: a schema for the representation of CMC corpora in TEI. *Corpus* 20. https://doi.org/https://doi.org/10.4000/corpus.4553

Broeder, Daan, Menzo Windhouwer, Dieter Van Uytvanck, Thorsten Trippel & Twan Goosen. 2012. CMDI: a component metadata infrastructure. In *Proceedings of LREC-workshop "describing LRs with metadata: Towards flexibility and interoperability in the documentation of LR"*, 1–4. ELRA. http://www.lrec-conf.org/proceedings/lrec2012/workshops/11.LREC2012MetadataProceedings.pdf (accessed May 3, 2022).

Brown, Adrian. 2006. Digital preservation technical paper 2: The PRONOM unique identifier scheme: A scheme of persistent unique identifiers for representation information (DPTP-02). Digital PreservationTechnical Paper 2, The National Archives. https://www.nationalarchives.gov.uk/aboutapps/pronom/pdf/pronom_unique_identifier_scheme.pdf (accessed May 3, 2022).

Chiarcos, Christian, Christian Fäth & Frank Abromeit. 2020. Annotation interoperability for the Post-ISOCat era. In *International conference on language resources and evaluation (lrec) 12*, 5668–5677. https://aclanthology.org/2020.lrec-1.696.pdf (accessed May 3, 2022).

CLARIN Standards Committee. 2020. Pursuing the elusive KPI: Filling the gaps in centre self-published standards-related information. Presentation given at the CLARIN Annual Conference, in September 2020. https://www.clarin.eu/sites/default/files/Clarin2020_bazaar_CSC_Core_1.pdf (accessed May 3, 2022).

Cooper, Danielle & Rebecca Springer. 2019. Data communities: A new model for supporting STEM data sharing [issue brief]. *DigitalCommons@University of Nebraska – Lincoln.* https://digitalcommons.unl.edu/scholcom/109 (accessed May 3, 2022).

CoreTrustSeal Standards and Certification Board. 2019. CoreTrustSeal trustworthy data repositories requirements 2020–2022. https://doi.org/10.5281/zenodo.3638211

Erjavec, Tomaž, Maciej Ogrodniczuk, Petya Osenova, Nikola Ljubešić, Kiril Simov, Andrej Pančur, Michał Rudolf, Matyáš Kopp, Starkaður Barkarson, Steinþór Steingrímsson, Çağrı Çöltekin, Jesse de Does, Katrien Depuydt, Tommaso Agnoloni, Giulia Venturi, María Calzada Pérez, Luciana D. de Macedo, Costanza Navarretta, Giancarlo Luxardo, Matthew Coole, Paul Rayson, Vaidas Morkevičius, Tomas Krilavičius, Roberts Dar´gis, Orsolya Ring, Ruben van Heusden, Maarten Marx & Darja Fišer. 2022. The ParlaMint corpora of parliamentary proceedings. *Language Resources and Evaluation* https://doi.org/10.1007/s10579-021-09574-0

Gomes, Luís, Ruben Branco, João Silva & António Branco. 2022. Open and inclusive language processing: Language processing services by PORTULAN to meet the widest needs of CLARIN users. In Darja Fišer & Andreas Witt (eds.), *CLARIN. The infrastructure for language resources.* Berlin: deGruyter.

Goosen, Twan, Menzo Windhouwer, Oddrun Ohren, Axel Herold, Thomas Eckart, Matej Ďurčo & Oliver Schonefeld. 2015. CMDI 1.2: Improvements in the CLARIN Component Metadata Infrastructure. In *Selected papers from the CLARIN 2014 conference, October 24–25, 2014, Soesterberg, the Netherlands*, 36–53. https://ep.liu.se/ecp/116/004/ecp15116004.pdf (accessed May 3, 2022).

Haaf, Susanne, Alexander Geyken & Frank Wiegand. 2015. The DTA "base format": A TEI subset for the compilation of a large reference corpus of printed text from multiple sources. *Journal of the Text Encoding Initiative* 8. https://doi.org/10.4000/jtei.1114

Hajič, Jan, Eva Hajičová, Barbora Hladká, Jozef Mišutka, Ondřej Košarko & Pavel Straňák. 2022. LINDAT/CLARIAH-CZ: Where we are and where we go. In Darja Fišer & Andreas Witt (eds.), *CLARIN. The infrastructure for language resources.* Berlin: deGruyter.

Haugen, Odd Einar, (ed.). 2019. *The Menota handbook: Guidelines for the electronic encoding of medieval Nordic primary sources. Version 3.0*. Bergen: Medieval Nordic Text Archive. http://www.menota.org/handbook.xml (accessed May 3, 2022).
Hedeland, Hanna. 2021. Towards comprehensive definitions of data quality for audiovisual annotated language resources. In *Selected papers from the CLARIN Annual Conference 2020, online, 5–7 October 2020*, 93–103. https://doi.org/10.3384/ecp18011
Hedeland, Hanna & Piotr Bański. 2018. Towards CLARIN recommended formats: a bottom-up approach. poster presented at the Bazaar, CLARIN Annual Conference 2018, Pisa, Italy, 8–10 October. https://www.clarin.eu/sites/default/files/CLARIN2018_Bazaar_Hedeland_Banski.pdf (accessed May 3, 2022).
Hinrichs, Erhard W., Marie Hinrichs & Thomas Zastrow. 2010. WebLicht: Web-Based LRT Services for German. In *Proceedings of the ACL 2010 System Demonstrations*, 25–29. USA: Association for Computational Linguistics. http://www.aclweb.org/anthology/P10-4005 (accessed May 3, 2022).
ISO/TC 37/SC 4. 2016. ISO 24624:2016 Language resource management – Transcription of spoken language. http://www.iso.org/iso/catalogue_detail.htm?csnumber=37338 (accessed May 3, 2022).
Janssen, Maarten. 2021. A corpus with wavesurfer and TEI: Speech and video in TEITOK. In *Text, speech, and dialogue*, 261–268. Cham: Springer International.
Jong, Franciska de, Bente Maegaard, Darja Fišer, Dieter Van Uytvanck & Andreas Witt. 2020. Interoperability in an infrastructure enabling multidisciplinary research: The case of CLARIN. In *International conference on language resources and evaluation (lrec) 12*, 3406–3413. https://aclanthology.org/2020.lrec-1.417 (accessed May 3, 2022).
Jong, Franciska de, Bente Maegaard, Koenraad De Smedt, Darja Fišer & Dieter Van Uytvanck. 2018. CLARIN: Towards FAIR and responsible data science using language resources. In *International conference on language resources and evaluation (lrec) 11*, 3259–3264. http://hdl.handle.net/1874/364776 (accessed May 3, 2022).
Lüngen, Harald & C. Michael Sperberg-McQueen. 2012. A TEI P5 document grammar for the IDS text model. *Journal of the Text Encoding Initiative* 3. https://doi.org/10.4000/jtei.508
Maegaard, Bente & Steven Krauwer. 2018. Key performance indicators for CLARIN ERIC (CE-2018-1266), Version 2, 2018-11-07. Technical report, CLARIN ERIC.
Maegaard, Bente & Leon Wessels. 2019. Measuring CLARIN's key performance indicators (CE-2019-1515), version 1.4, 2019-09-24. Technical report, CLARIN ERIC. Draft.
Odijk, Jan. 2016. Towards Interoperability in CLARIN (CE-2016-0845),Version 1, 2016-08-25. techreport Version 1, 2016-08-25, CLARIN ERIC. https://office.clarin.eu/v/CE-2016-0845-towards-interoperability.pdf (accessed May 3, 2022), draft, Distribution NCF.
Olsson, Leif-Jöran. 2017. Federated content search engine v2 (software), CLARINPLUS-D2.9 (CE-2017-1035), 2017-06-09. techreport, CLARIN PLUS. https://office.clarin.eu/v/CE-2017-1035-CLARINPLUS-D2_9.pdf (accessed May 3, 2022), distribution Public.
Pennock, Maureen, Paul Wheatley & Peter May. 2014. Sustainability assessments at the British Library: Formats, frameworks and findings. In *Proceedings of the 11th International Conference on Digital Preservation, iPRES 2014, Melbourne, Australia, October 6–10, 2014*, 141–148. https://doi.org/11353/10.378694
RDA FAIR Data Maturity Model Working Group. 2020. FAIR data maturity model. specification and guidelines (1.0). techreport, RDA. https://doi.org/10.15497/rda00050

RfII. 2020. The data quality challenge. recommendations for sustainable research in the digital turn. http://www.rfii.de/?p=4203 (accessed May 3, 2022).
Schmidt, Thomas. 2011. A TEI-based approach to standardising spoken language transcription. *Journal of the Text Encoding Initiative* 1, 1–28. https://doi.org/10.4000/jtei.142
Schmidt, Thomas, Hanna Hedeland & Daniel Jettka. 2017. Conversion and annotation web services for spoken language data in CLARIN. In *Selected papers from the CLARIN Annual Conference 2016, Aix-en-Provence, 26–28 october 2016*, 113–130. http://www.ep.liu.se/ecp/136/009/ecp17136009.pdf (accessed May 3, 2022).
Schonefeld, Oliver, Thomas Eckart, Thomas Kisler, Christoph Draxler, Kai Zimmer, Matej Ďurčo, Yana Panchenko, Hanna Hedeland, Andre Blessing & Olha Shkaravska. 2014. CLARIN federated content search (CLARIN-FCS) – core specification (CE-2014-0316), version 1.0, 2014-04-07. techreport, CLARIN ERIC. https://svn.clarin.eu/FederatedSearch/docs/CLARIN_FCS_Specification_Core_1_0.docx (accessed May 3, 2022), draft for approval by SCCTC, Distribution SCCTC.
Stührenberg, Maik, Antonina Werthmann & Andreas Witt. 2012. Guidance through the standards jungle for linguistic resources. In *Proceedings of the LREC-12 workshop on collaborative resource development and delivery. Istanbul, Turkey, May 2012*, 9–13. European Language Resources Association (ELRA). https://ids-pub.bsz-bw.de/frontdoor/deliver/index/docId/4494/file/Stuehrenberg_Werthmann_Witt_Guidance_through_the_standards_jungle_2012.pdf (accessed May 3, 2022).
TEI Consortium. 2021. TEI P5: Guidelines for electronic text encoding and interchange. Technical Report 4.3.0, TEI Consortium. http://www.tei-c.org/Guidelines/P5/ (accessed May 3, 2022).
Thomas, Christian & Frank Wiegand. 2015. Making great work even better: Appraisal and digital curation of widely dispersed electronic textual resources (c. 15th–19th cent.) in CLARIN-D. In *Historical corpora. challenges and perspectives*. Tübingen: Narr. https://www.deutschestextarchiv.de/files/Thomas-Wiegand-2015_Making-Great-Work-Even-Better_CLIP-5_2018-07-05.pdf (accessed May 3, 2022).
Trippel, Thorsten & Claus Zinn. 2015. DMPTY – a wizard for generating data management plans. In *Selected papers from the CLARIN Annual Conference 2015, October 14–16, 2015, Wroclaw, Poland*, 71–78. Linköping: Linköping University Electronic Press. https://ep.liu.se/en/conference-article.aspx?series=ecp&issue=123&Article_No=6 (accessed May 3, 2022).
Van Uytvanck, Dieter. 2014. Relevant data formats (CE-2014-0421), Version 1, 2014-10-17. Technical report, CLARIN ERIC. https://www.clarin.eu/sites/default/files/CE-2104-0421-relevant-formats.pdf (accessed May 3, 2022), draft, Distribution SCCTC.
Wilkinson, Mark D., Michel Dumontier, IJsbrand Jan Aalbersberg, Gabrielle Appleton, Myles Axton, Arie Baak, Niklas Blomberg, Jan-Willem Boiten, Luiz Bonino da Silva Santos, Philip E. Bourne, Jildau Bouwman, Anthony J. Brookes, Tim Clark, Mercè Crosas, Ingrid Dillo, Olivier Dumon, Scott Edmunds, Chris T. Evelo, Richard Finkers, Alejandra Gonzalez-Beltran, Alasdair J. G. Gray, Paul Groth, Carole Goble, Jeffrey S. Grethe, Jaap Heringa, Peter A. C. 't Hoen, Rob Hooft, Tobias Kuhn, Ruben Kok, Joost Kok, Scott J. Lusher, Maryann E. Martone, Albert Mons, Abel L. Packer, Bengt Persson, Philippe Rocca-Serra, Marco Roos, Rene van Schaik, Susanna-Assunta Sansone, Erik Schultes, Thierry Sengstag, Ted Slater, George Strawn, Morris A. Swertz, Mark Thompson, Johan van der Lei, Erik van Mulligen, Jan Velterop, Andra Waagmeester, Peter Wittenburg, Katherine Wolstencroft, Jun Zhao & Barend Mons. 2016. The FAIR guiding principles for scientific data management and stewardship. *Scientific Data* 3, 160018–. https://doi.org/10.1038/sdata.2016.18

Windhouwer, Menzo & Twan Goosen. 2022. Component Metadata Infrastructure. In Darja Fišer & Andreas Witt (eds.), *CLARIN. The infrastructure for language resources.* Berlin: deGruyter.

Wittenburg, Peter, Daan Broeder, Bertrand Gaiffe, Maria Gavrilidou, Erhard Hinrichs, Lothar Lemnitzer, Dieter Van Uytvanck & Andreas Witt. 2008. Metadata Infrastructure for Language Resources and Technology, (CLARIN-2008-5), D2.4, Version 5. Technical report, CLARIN. https://www.clarin.eu/sites/default/files/wg2-4-metadata-doc-v5.pdf (accessed May 3, 2022).

Wittenburg, Peter, Dieter Van Uytvanck, Thomas Zastrow & Lene Offersgaard. 2020. CLARIN centre types (CE-2012-0037), version 0.8, 2020-02-18. techreport Version 0.8, 2020-02-18, CLARIN ERIC. http://hdl.handle.net/11372/DOC-77 (accessed May 3, 2022), for approval by SCCTC, Distribution SCCTC, CAC, BoD.

Wittenburg, Peter, Dieter Van Uytvanck, Thomas Zastrow, Pavel Straňák, Daan Broeder, Florian Schiel, Volker Boehlke, Uwe Reichel & Lene Offersgaard. 2019. CLARIN B centre checklist (CE-2013-0095), version 7.3.1, 2019-09-30. Technical report, CLARIN ERIC. http://hdl.handle.net/11372/DOC-78 (accessed May 3, 2022).

Zinn, Claus & Emanuel Dima. 2022. The CLARIN Language Resource Switchboard: Current state, impact, and future roadmap. In Darja Fišer & Andreas Witt (eds.), *CLARIN. The infrastructure for language resources.* Berlin: deGruyter.

Part III: **Knowledge Infrastructure**

Jakob Lenardič and Darja Fišer

The CLARIN Resource and Tool Families

Abstract: This chapter presents the CLARIN Resource and Tool Families initiative, whose aim is to offer researchers from Digital Humanities, Social Sciences, and Human Language Technologies aggregated, user-friendly overviews of the tools and resources available through the CLARIN infrastructure, including a unified, human-readable presentation of their metadata. The initiative also raises awareness of the importance of good and harmonzed metadata documentation, thus supporting other core CLARIN services like the Virtual Language Observatory and the CLARIN Language Resource Switchboard in relation to findability and (re)usability.

Keywords: CLARIN Infrastructure, curation, metadata, corpora, Digital Humanities, Social Sciences, Language Processing Tools

1 Introduction

The CLARIN Resource and Tool Families (henceforth CRF) initiative provides manually curated overviews of prominent language resources and technologies (LRTs) deposited in CLARIN repositories.[1] CRF was launched in 2018 (Fišer, Lenardič, and Erjavec 2018) and at the time consisted of four corpus families – corpora of parliamentary proceedings, computer-mediated communication (CMC), newspaper articles, and parallel texts. Since then, it has become one of the flagship initiatives of User Involvement in CLARIN ERIC and now comprises 12 corpus families (incl. L2-learner, historical, spoken, manually curated, literary, academic, reference, and multimodal corpora), 5 families of lexical resources

1 https://www.clarin.eu/resource-families

Acknowledgments: The work described in this paper was funded by the Slovenian Research Agency research programme P6-0436: *Digital Humanities: resources, tools and methods* (2022–2027) and the DARIAH-SI and CLARIN ERIC (the Resource Families Project) research infrastructures.

Jakob Lenardič, Faculty of Arts, University of Ljubljana; Jožef Stefan Institute, Ljubljana, Slovenia, e-mail: jakob.lenardic@ff.uni-lj.si
Darja Fišer, Institute of Contemporary History, Ljubljana; Faculty of Arts, University of Ljubljana; Jožef Stefan Institute, Ljubljana, Slovenia, e-mail: darja.fiser@inz.si

https://doi.org/10.1515/9783110767377-013

(lexica, dictionaries, conceptual resources, glossaries, and wordlists), and 4 families of language tools (tools for normalization, tools for named entity recognition, part-of-speech taggers and lemmatizers, and tools for sentiment analysis), which together amount to more than a thousand manually curated LRTs.[2]

The aim of CRF is twofold. On the one hand, it offers researchers from Digital Humanities, Social Sciences and Human Language Technologies aggregated, user-friendly overviews of LRTs of similar kinds available through the CLARIN infrastructure, including a unified, human-readable presentation of their metadata. On the other hand, this initiative aims to raise awareness of the importance of good and harmonized metadata documentation, and thus support other core CLARIN services primarily in relation to findability and (re)usability. As a result, the visibility of the LRTs and the CLARIN infrastructure in general has been enhanced well beyond its core community, additional existing LRTs have been incorporated, and new ones have even been developed.

This chapter is structured as follows. In Section 2, we discuss the aims of CRF in relation to the rest of the CLARIN infrastructure. In Section 3, we present the resource families. In Section 4, we present the tool families. Section 5 discusses the curatorial aspect of CRF. Section 6 concludes the chapter.

2 The background and aim(s) of CRF

One of the long-term goals of large-scale project-independent research infrastructures such as CLARIN ERIC is to ensure continued and open access to digital language resources and tools, as well as the on-going maintenance and improvement of the infrastructure itself (McGillivray et al. 2020: 18). As noted by Pustejovsky et al. (2017: 20), a major issue in the field of Human Language Technologies is the risk of fragmentation, which is characterized by the absence of standard practices and a lack of (re)usable tools and resources. In order to circumvent such infrastructural fragmentation, CLARIN strives to meet the requirements of the so-called FAIR Guiding Principles for scientific data management and stewardship (Wilkinson

2 The individual resource and tool families are generally also top-ranked Google results for searches that include associated keywords. Furthermore, monthly Google Analytics for the clarin.eu domain show that apart from the main landing site, the most visited webpages are consistently CRF subpages. This initiative is thus increasingly becoming a prominent entry point through which researchers or the developers of LRTs discover the CLARIN infrastructure.

et al. 2016), of which there are four – findability, accessibility, interoperability, and reusability.[3]

The four FAIR principles are facilitated through various endeavours. As CLARIN is a distributed infrastructure whose tools and resources are made accessible through certified repositories hosted by national consortia, findability is facilitated by the so-called Virtual Language Observatory (VLO, Van Uytvanck, Stehouwer, and Lampen 2012; Goosen and Eckart 2014), which automatically harvests the metadata from the repositories and thereby provides a catalogue of all the available tools and resources. The repositories contribute to accessibility through their user-oriented design, which among others includes support for persistent identification, authorship attribution, versioning, and crucially through the employment of the CMDI metadata schema (Broeder et al. 2021; Windouwer and Goosen 2022), which ensures interoperability between the distributed repositories by allowing them to "instantiate the vocabulary [of CMDI] to suit their particular needs" (McCrae et al. 2015: 40). Interoperability is furthermore achieved through services like the CLARIN Language Resource Switchboard (Zinn 2018; Zinn and Dima 2022),[4] which is integrated with the VLO and bridges the gap between CLARIN resources and tools by automatically identifying tools that can be used to process the resources harvested by the VLO from the CLARIN repositories. In this way, CLARIN is contributing towards an Open Research Infrastructure (De Smedt et al. 2018), whose goal is effective knowledge dissemination both within and beyond computational linguistics (Schroeder 2007).

However, one of main challenges of infrastructures where resources and tools are scattered across several repositories is that full harmonization of the metadata is difficult to implement, partly because of different approaches to repository administration. Even though the tools and resources findable through the VLO are curated by their individual contributors who deposit them in the national repositories, limited integration has been achieved between them, so their metadata descriptions differ both in size and in detail (Cimiano et al. 2020: 265). This hinders the users' ability to effectively search for specific tools and resources and then to (re)use them in their research (Cimiano et al. 2020: 263), as potentially valuable resources and tools whose metadata documentation lacks detail in comparison to others belonging to the same family can have a significantly lower rate of recall in services like the VLO.

3 CLARIN also has a Standards Committee, which maintains and promotes the adoption of standards across the infrastructure; see Banski and Hedeland (2022) for an introduction to the Committee.

4 https://switchboard.clarin.eu/

The main aim of CRF is thus to support other core services of the CLARIN infrastructure like the VLO by accounting for such gaps related to findability (and by extension accessibility) and metadata harmonization (and by extension reusability). Findability is enhanced by collating the resource and tools under their most common typological characteristic, which is the type or organization of the primary data in the case of the corpora and lexical resources (e.g., corpora of newspapers vs. corpora of parliamentary proceedings vs. parallel corpora vs. dictionaries vs. morphological lexica) and functionality in the case of tools (e.g., tools for named entity recognition vs. tools for part-of-speech tagging). This is crucial because the VLO does not afford faceted search across such typological characteristics, and making basic search queries like *parliament* corpora* leads to the aforementioned problems in recall, where many of the parliamentary corpora collated in the resource family are not trivially findable this way (see Fišer and Lenardič 2018 for a use case on this particular findability problem).

On the other hand, this initiative facilitates metadata harmonization by providing a unified description of each of the tools and resources that is also tailored to the unique technical features of each of the families, as well as their qualitative characteristics, particularly those aspects "that users need to know about [tools and] resources to help them decide whether [they] match their needs" (McCrae et al. 2015: 42). Although the CLARIN repositories generally ensure a detailed description of the tools in terms of the sheer number of CMDI-metadata components included in the particular tool or resource profile, it is often the case that certain metadata are lacking or are too general from a qualitative perspective. For instance, in the case of spoken-language corpora that consist of audio recordings where the target language in which the interview takes place differs from the metalanguage of the annotation, the two languages are often listed together under the same generic language component, even though this is otherwise a crucial distinction for researchers working with such multimodal materials (Burke et al. 2021). Additionally, often a basic metadata category is listed at various levels of granularity for the same resource family; for instance, the size of certain corpora is given only in tokens, while for others it is only in sentences, which hinders the cross-comparability of the resources. It is therefore the aim of CRF to be particularly mindful of such metadata gaps and disharmony, and to make sure that metadata documentation is such that it is valuable not only to developers but also for the researchers that will (re)use the tools and resources.

3 The resource families

3.1 Presentation

Figure 1 exemplifies how corpora and lexical resources are documented in CRF on the basis of the L2-learner Tisus Corpus (Volodina et al. 2016).[5] Structural metadata include size, linguistic annotation and license, while qualitative characteristics are described in the free text-description field next to the listed language. In terms of size, CRF specifies as detailed a description as possible, which aside from word/token size usually also includes the number of sentences and, in the case of speech corpora, utterance number. In many of the CLARIN repositories (especially those that are DSpace-based, see Smith et al. 2003), linguistic annotation is not spelled out under a separate metadata component (often the information is missing in the repositories and can be obtained only in repository-external documentation, such as publications describing the tool), so CRF seeks to bridge this metadata gap by spelling out the annotation levels explicitly and by also separately listing linguistic annotation (part-of-speech tagging, lemmatization, syntactic parsing, etc.) from extra-linguistic information, which is often resource family specific – in the case of the Tisus Corpus, for instance, this latter type of annotation corresponds to the markup of language proficiency levels according to the CERIF schema. In repositories, it is often difficult to determine whether a corpus is unannotated or if the annotation information is simply missing (without of course downloading/accessing the corpus itself) because of the lack of the dedicated metadata component, so we also explicitly spell out if the resource is unannotated, as is the case of many of the literary corpora.

The free-text field primarily focuses on a qualitative description that takes into account those features that are important for humanities and social sciences researchers (i.e., temporal period, geographic coverage, text types, text sources, the most important domain-specific characteristics such as age and L1 of participants in the case of learner corpora). Lastly, we also provide links to relevant publications describing the resource, as well as hyperlinks for download and/or online access locations such as search interfaces, while specifying the CLARIN centre in which the resource is deposited.

5 https://spraakbanken.gu.se/eng/resource/tisus

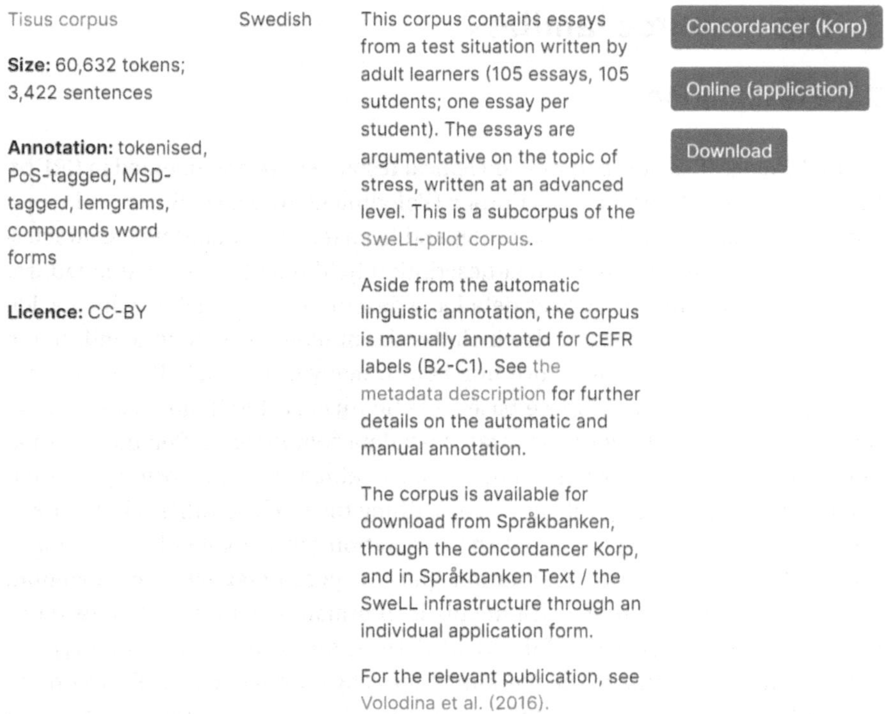

Tisus corpus **Size:** 60,632 tokens; 3,422 sentences **Annotation:** tokenised, PoS-tagged, MSD-tagged, lemgrams, compounds word forms **Licence:** CC-BY	Swedish	This corpus contains essays from a test situation written by adult learners (105 essays, 105 sutdents; one essay per student). The essays are argumentative on the topic of stress, written at an advanced level. This is a subcorpus of the SweLL-pilot corpus. Aside from the automatic linguistic annotation, the corpus is manually annotated for CEFR labels (B2-C1). See the metadata description for further details on the automatic and manual annotation. The corpus is available for download from Språkbanken, through the concordancer Korp, and in Språkbanken Text / the SweLL infrastructure through an individual application form. For the relevant publication, see Volodina et al. (2016).	Concordancer (Korp) Online (application) Download

Figure 1: The Tisus Corpus listed in the L2-learner corpus family.

3.2 Accessibility

It is worth noting that the vast majority of the corpora in CRF are available either for download, typically from one of the approximately 20 CLARIN B-certified repositories,[6] or for online browsing through dedicated or CLARIN-related concordancers. Of interest for Digital Humanities and Social Sciences researchers without a technical background are especially the online searchable corpora, almost half of which are available through CLARIN-developed online search environments that are usually integrated with the repository where the corpus is deposited.

The most prominently featured concordancers across the 12 corpus families are Korp and KonText. Korp was originally developed at the Swedish Language Bank of the Swedish CLARIN consortium in 2012 (Borin, Forsberg, and Roxendal 2012) and has since then been adopted by the Estonian CLARIN consortium and

6 See the full list of the repositories here: https://www.clarin.eu/content/certified-centres.

all the other Nordic consortia (Laak et al. 2019), while the concordancer KonText was originally developed for the purposes of the Czech National Corpus (Machálek 2014). KonText is used for browsing the corpora of the Slovenian CLARIN.SI and the Czech LINDAT repositories,[7] and is currently being tested for integration with the Polish CLARIN-PL repository (Machálek 2020: 7008). Both KonText and Korp provide powerful search capabilities, such as a CQL editor with a user-friendly selection of individual morphosyntactic tags, the storage of query history, and several modules for the visualisation of results (Machálek 2020: 7004–7005).

Furthermore, KonText stands out among query systems in that it is also tailored to both spoken corpora and syntactically annotated corpora. For spoken corpora in CRF, such as ORAL2013: Balanced Corpus of Informal Spoken Czech (Benešová, Křen, and Waclawičová 2016), KonText provides a concordance view where the transcriptions are aligned with the audio recordings, as well as the means to visualise the "dialogues in [the corpus] with a clear indication of speaker turns and overlaps" (Machálek 2020: 7005). For syntactically annotated corpora, such as the 2.3 version of the multilingual Universal Dependencies treebanks (Nivre et al. 2018), KonText can visualise the concordance lines in the form of Prague Dependency Treebank-like syntax trees (Machálek 2020).[8] Such query options make KonText especially well suited for syntacticians and researchers of spoken language.

3.3 Language

The majority of the corpora and lexical resources in CRF are monolingual. For the corpora, the most represented language is German, which likely reflects the fact that the German CLARIN consortium has by far the greatest number of B-certified data-providing centres (i.e., 7 in total, whereas there is typically 1 data-providing centre per country). The most common language for the monolingual lexical resources is Estonian, which reflects a high number of monolingual Estonian dictionaries offered through the collection of the Center of Estonian Language Resources.[9] While the most common languages among the monolingual resources are languages spoken in CLARIN countries, the less commonly featured languages include Welsh (e.g., The National Corpus of Contemporary Welsh, Knight 2020), Uralic languages such as Saami and Veps (e.g., North Saami Literature Corpus, Vuolab 2007),

7 See Hajič et al. (2022) for a comprehensive introduction to LINDAT.
8 https://ufal.mff.cuni.cz/pdt3.0
9 https://vlo.clarin.eu/search?1&fq=collection:Center+of+Estonian+Language+Resources

dead languages like Latin (e.g., The LatinISE corpus, McGillivray 2020), and extinct languages like Old Norse (e.g., The Saga Corpus, Helgadóttir and Barkarson 2020).

For multilingual resources, there are several parallel corpora deposited in the Greek CLARIN:EL consortium that offer data in more than 50 languages, with the parallel corpus Tatoeba (Tiedemann 2015) containing translated sentences in 117 languages. Apart from parallel corpora, the Universal Dependencies collection, which is likely the largest collection of syntactically annotated corpora (i.e., treebanks) in the world, covers 112 languages in its current (i.e., 2.9 as of November 2021) version (see Zeman et al. 2021).

3.4 The families

3.4.1 Academic corpora

Corpora of academic texts contain scholarly writing, which includes research papers, essays and abstracts published in academic journals, conference proceedings, and edited volumes, as well as theses written by students at the undergraduate and graduate levels, and scientific monographs. Research-wise, academic corpora are particularly interesting for the study of pragmatic topics in functional linguistics, such as the use of hedging devices and other communication strategies (Hyland 1998) and the stylistic and idiomatic features of the academic register (Simpson and Mendis 2003).

Roughly half of the CRF academic corpora are collections of journal articles, either from a specific field, such as the Czech Sociological Review corpus (Hladik 2018), or from a multitude of disciplines, such as the Greek OROSSIMO Corpus (ILSP 2015), which contains texts in computer science, law, astronomy, linguistics, etc. The other CRF academic corpora consist of students' theses, such as the Corpus of Academic Slovene KAS (Erjavec et al. 2019), which contains BA, MA, and PhD theses.

3.4.2 Computer-mediated communication corpora

Computer-mediated communication (CMC) constitutes public and private communication online, such as posts on blogs, forums, comments on online news sites, social media and networking sites such as Twitter and Facebook, mobile phone applications such as WhatsApp, e-mail and chat rooms. Because corpora that compile computer-mediated communication often include very informal styles of writing, they are interesting for a wide range of research fields (Vandekerckhove et al. 2019), such as sociology (Androutsopoulos 2006), computer-mediated discourse analysis (Herring 2001), and political science, where Twitter, for instance, is nowadays one of the main online platforms used for communication and promotion by political parties (Praet et al. 2018).

The CMC corpora in this family are almost exclusively monolingual, such as SoNaR New Media (INT 2013), which is a 35-million-word corpus of Tweets, chat messages and SMSs in Dutch. The only multilingual CMC corpus is the DiDi Corpus of South Tyrolean CMC, which consists of Facebook posts by South Tyrolean Facebook users communicating in English, German, Italian, and Ladino. One of the unique annotation layers of CMC corpora is word normalization, as "orthographic mistakes are ubiquitous" (Proisl et al. 2020: 6142) in such communication, while emoticons are typically annotated as a separate part-of-speech category, which is crucial from the perspective of the sentiment analysis of CMC (Hogenboom et al. 2013).

3.4.3 Historical corpora

According to Curzan (2009: 1091), historical corpora are important resources for diachronic linguistics as their data "capture stages of linguistic development over time" and are therefore "used to test modern theories about variation and change", both in functional and formal approaches. Such corpora are also important for sociohistorical approaches, as they allow researchers to examine the relationships between historical speech communities and their language use (Archer and Culpeper 2003).

The historical corpora in this family cover time periods ranging from ancient history to the 20th century. The corpus with the oldest data is the Open Richly Annotated Cuneiform Corpus (Jauhiainen, Sahala, and Alstola 2019), which includes the cuneiform scripts of extinct languages like Sumerian, Akkadian, and Hittite. In the case of widely spoken languages like English and German, there exist corpora for each of the main stages of linguistic development, such as the York-Helsinki Parsed Corpus of Old English Poetry (Oxford Text Archive 2001) for Old English, the Helsinki corpus of English texts (Oxford Text Archive 1991) for Old and Middle English, and The Old Bailey Corpus (Huber, Nissel, and Puga 2016) for early and late Modern English.

3.4.4 L2-Learner corpora

L2-learner corpora play a crucial role in second language research and pedagogy, allowing for a systematic study of how a learner of a second language acquires the new language on the lexical and syntactic levels, and how this process is influenced by his or her native language (Granger 2009). Almost half of the L2-learner corpora in this family belong to the SLABank Collection,[10] which is a component of TalkBank (MacWhinney 2007) dedicated to providing resources for the cross-linguistic study of second language acquisition and learning.

A special characteristic of this family is the markup of errors and the prosodic features of the learners (Granger 2003). For instance, the Langman Corpus (Langman 1998) from SLABank, which contains interviews with learners of Hungarian with Chinese as their first language, has error codes assigned to certain prosodic phenomena such as the non-standard repetition of words. Aside from written and spoken corpora, this family also includes multimodal corpora, which together with the annotation of speech phenomena also include the annotation of nonverbal behaviours (e.g., eye gaze, gesture).

3.4.5 Lexical resources

There are five major subtypes of lexical resources in the CLARIN infrastructure – lexica, dictionaries, concept-based resources, glossaries, and wordlists.

Lexica are primarily used in NLP applications. They typically contain an extensive lexical inventory with specific linguistic information, such as morphosyntactic features, verb valency, and sentiment. Examples of this lexical-family subtype include the Database of Modern Icelandic Inflections (Bjarnadóttir 2019), the Czech–English valency lexicon CzEngVallex (Urešová et al. 2015), and the LiLaH Emotion Lexicon of Croatian, Dutch and Slovene (Daelemans et al. 2020).

Dictionaries are primarily created for human use (e.g., language learning/teaching, translation, lexicology) and are typically semasiological (Santos and Costa 2015), which means that they are organized around words and contain information on their meanings, definitions, pronunciation, and so forth. The CRF dictionaries mostly account for combinations of languages spoken in CLARIN-member countries, such as the Lithuanian–Latvian–Latgalian Dictionary (Leikuma et al. 2013). There is also a rich inventory of dictionaries for dialectal variants of Modern Arabic provided by the Austrian CLARIN consortium; for instance, the Digital Dictionary of Damascus Arabic (Mörth, Procházka, and Ramos 2011).

Concept-based resources include onomasiological lexical resources (see Fernández-Domínguez 2019) such as wordnets (e.g., Ancient Greek Wordnet, Boschetti, Del Gratta, and Diakoff 2016), framenets (e.g., Finnish FrameNet, Uni-

---

10 https://slabank.talkbank.org

versity of Helsinki 2019), thesauri (e.g., Thesaurus of Modern Slovene, Krek et al. 2018) and ontologies (e.g., Ontology for the Area of Nanoscience and Nanotechnology for Brazilian Portuguese, Kasama 2012). Such resources are typically interlinked with paradigmatic semantic relations such as hypernymy and hyponymy.

Glossaries are specialized dictionaries that contain domain-specific terminology and/or expressions (e.g., Time-Sensitive Inventory of Medical Terminology, Thompson 2015), while wordlists are lexical resources which only provide alphabetical or frequency-based lexical inventories (e.g., Frequency List of Written Finnish Word Forms, Institute for the Languages of Finland 2011).

3.4.6 Literary corpora

Literary corpora comprise poetry and fictional prose texts, such as novels, short stories, and plays. For research, they are especially well suited for a quantitative and qualitative approach to comparative literary analysis, within or across different genres and historical periods. From the interdisciplinary perspective, literary corpora bridge the gap between corpus linguistics and literary stylistics, as literary concepts such as symbolism and the speech/thought representation of literary characters can be studied through quantitative phenomena such as collocations, n-grams, and keywords (Mahlberg 2007: 219–220).

The CRF literary corpora bring together the collected works of a single author (or even a single work) or are representative of a specific literary period. Examples of single-author corpora include the parallel MULTEXT-East "1984" Annotated Corpus 4.0 (Erjavec et al. 2010), which contains linguistically annotated translations of George Orwell's *Nineteen Eighty-Four* in 11 languages aside from the English original, and the Johannes V. Jensen Corpus (Iversen 2011), which contains the collected work of the titular Danish modernist and Nobel Laureate, while multi-author literary corpora include the historical York-Helsinki Parsed Corpus of Old English poetry (Oxford Text Archive 2001) and Classics of Finnish Literature, Kielipankki Version (The Language Bank of Finland 2016), among many others.

3.4.7 Manually annotated corpora

Manually annotated corpora are collections of texts containing manually validated or manually assigned linguistic information, such as morphosyntactic tags, lemmas, syntactic parses, and named entities. These corpora can be used to train new language annotation tools as well as to test the accuracy of existing ones.

In addition to the corpora with manual part-of-speech tags and lemmas, there are more than 30 syntactically annotated corpora (that is, treebanks) in which the syntactic dependency relations between words or tokens are also manually annotated or checked; an example is the FicTree corpus (Jelínek, Hnátková, and Skoumalová 2017), which is a treebank of Czech fiction whose dependency annotations follow the Prague Dependency Treebank schema (see Hajič et al. 2018 for the latest, consolidated, version), which is one of the most common framework for dependency parsing in CRF, second only to the aforementioned Universal Dependencies (Zeman et al. 2021).

Other annotation layers in this family include named entity recognition (e.g., Czech Named Entity Corpus, Ševčíková et al. 2014) and sentiment analysis (e.g., NoReC: The Norwegian Review Corpus, Velldal et al. 2017).

3.4.8 Multimodal corpora

Multimodal corpora are data collections used to study how two or more modalities interface with one another in human communication. In this sense, multimodal corpora are collections of video and speech recordings accompanied with transcriptions and gesture annotations, although multimodal corpora of textual data supplemented with images exist as well. Such corpora can be used for "the exploration of a range of lexical, prosodic and gestural features of conversation, and for investigations of the ways in which these features interact in real, everyday speech" (Abuczki and Ghazaleh 2013: 88).

Most of the multimodal corpora in this family are video-audio corpora; for instance, the Multimodal and Multiparty Corpus of Text Comprehension Interactions (Koutsombogera 2015), which contains fine-grained annotations of facial expressions, i.e., gaze, head, eye, eyebrows and mouth movement, and the Italian PoliModal Corpus (Trotta 2019), which aside from facial expressions also contains annotations of body movement. On the other hand, examples of the fewer text-image corpora include Hindi Visual Genome (Parida and Bojar 2019), which contains short English segments (captions) from the Visual Genome database[11] along with associated images and translations into Hindi, and the Finnish Multimodal Corpus of Tourist Brochures (Hiippala 2014).

11 https://visualgenome.org/

3.4.9 Newspaper corpora

Collections of newspapers in digital form are a rich source of information for researchers in a number of disciplines in the Digital Humanities and Social Sciences and are especially valuable for synchronic as well as diachronic studies, ranging from history (Huistra and Mellink 2016) and media studies (Bednarek 2006; Partington 2010) to lexicography, for which newspapers are a rich source of neologisms and other lexical phenomena (Falk, Bernhard, and Gérard 2014).

While most CRF newspaper corpora feature relatively contemporary newspaper data, such as the SYN2013PUB corpus (Čermák et al. 2006), which includes articles from Czech newspapers published between 2005 and 2009, several newspaper corpora are historical in scope, such as the Korp-browsable Swedish corpora Kvinnornas Tidning,[12] Morgonbris,[13] and Rösträtt för Kvinnor,[14] all of which contain articles published between 1904 and 1925.

3.4.10 Parallel corpora

Parallel corpora play a two-fold role when it comes to their application. In the context of Digital Humanities, they are central to translation studies, as they provide an empirical basis for studying the general linguistic properties of translated texts from a comparative perspective as well as help develop translator competence, often acting as substitutes for conventional dictionaries (Doval and Nieto 2019). In relation to computational linguistics, parallel corpora serve as training data for statistical machine translation systems.

A unique structural feature of parallel corpora that facilitates such research and developmental endeavours is alignment, which is most typically at the sentence level. Examples of sentence-aligned corpora include the bidirectional Czech–English Parallel Corpus (Bojar et al. 2011) and HindEnCorp (Bojar et al. 2014), which contains English news texts and their translations into Hindi. A smaller number of corpora, such as the Czech–English Manual Word Alignment (Mareček 2016) corpus, are also aligned at the word level.

12 https://spraakbanken.gu.se/eng/resource/ub-kvt-kvt
13 https://spraakbanken.gu.se/eng/resource/ub-kvt-morgonbris
14 https://spraakbanken.gu.se/eng/resource/ub-kvt-rostratt

3.4.11 Parliamentary corpora

Parliamentary corpora are a very important multidisciplinary language resource that can be approached from many research perspectives, including not only political science (Van Dijk 2010), but also sociology (Cheng 2015), history (Pančur and Šorn 2016), and applicative approaches to linguistics such as critical discourse analysis (Hirst et al. 2014).

This resource family mostly includes monolingual corpora of the transcriptions of national parliament debates in CLARIN member countries, generally from the 1990s onwards. Examples of such corpora are the Danish Parliament Corpus 2009–2017 (Hansen and Navarretta 2021), which is a 41 million-word corpus of Danish debates between 2009 and 2017, and Talk of Norway (Lapponi and Søyland 2016), which is a 64 million-token corpus of Norwegian debates between 1998 and 2016. Among the multilingual parliamentary corpora, one of the most noteworthy resources is ParlaMint (Erjavec et al. 2021), which is actually the result of an on-going inter-consortium collaboration that has so far produced a collection of comparable corpora containing parliamentary debates between 2015 and 2020 in 16 languages, with the sessions in the corpora being marked as belonging to the COVID-19 period (after October 2019) or to the period before (Erjavec et al. 2022). The ParlaMint corpora are also richly linguistically annotated – apart from PoS-tagging and lemmatization they also exhibit syntactic parsing using the Universal Dependencies schema (de Marneffe et al. 2021).

Apart from linguistic annotation, such corpora typically contain extensive extra-linguistic metadata about the MPs, such as name, gender, age, role, title and party affiliation (Hansen, Navarretta, and Offersgaard 2018), which is crucial for researching the sociopolitical context and for determining the diachronic development of such discourse that is reflected through language use in the debates, as in the language of female vs. male MPs (Fišer and Pahor de Maiti 2020).

3.4.12 Reference corpora

According to Leech (2002), a "reference corpus is designed to provide comprehensive information about the language [. . .] It has to be a general corpus of wide coverage of the language, and hopefully it will be treated by its user community as some kind of 'standard' for the language." Reference corpora thus contrast with specialized corpus families (e.g., parliamentary corpora, CMC-corpora) in that they are comprehensive with respect to genre inclusion, typically sampling a diverse set of primarily written genres.

This family boasts several gigaword corpora – that is, corpora that contain at least 1 billion tokens and are thus much larger in size than the average corpus, which has usually between 1 and 100 million tokens in CRF. The German reference corpus DeReKo (Institute for the German Language 2021) contains 50.6 billion tokens and is the largest reference corpus for any language in the world. Other gigaword corpora in this family include the National Corpus of Polish (Przepiórkowski 2011) with 1.6 billion tokens, the Estonian National Corpus (Institute of the Estonian Language 2019) with 1.5 billion tokens, the Icelandic Gigaword Corpus (Steingrímsson, Barkarson, and Rögnvaldsson 2019) with 1.5 billion tokens, and the Slovenian Gigafida 2.0 (Krek et al. 2019) corpus with 1.3 billion tokens.

3.4.13 Spoken-language corpora

Corpora of spoken language contain transcriptions of spontaneous or planned speech, such as broadcast news or elicited narratives and dialogues. They are often aligned with the accompanying recordings. As the audio recordings are often transcribed both orthographically and phonemically, such corpora are an invaluable resource for various kinds of linguistic research, such as phonology, conversational analysis, and dialectology. The corpora are also carefully sampled and rich in sociodemographic metadata.

Aside from general-purpose "reference" spoken corpora like the Icelandic Spoken Language Corpus[15] and the Slovenian Spoken corpus Gos 1.0 (Zwitter Vitez et al. 2021), which contain speech samples from a multitude of sources (e.g., radio and TV shows, school lessons, private conversations, business meetings), there are also several dialectal corpora in this family, such as the Czech DIALEKT v1: Dialectal Corpus with Multi-Tier Transcription (Goláňová et al. 2017), as well as corpora of speech elicited in very specific contexts, such as the BAS Alcohol Language Corpus (BAS 2016).

4 The tool families

4.1 Presentation

Figure 2 exemplifies how tools are documented in CRF on the basis of the Czech-English named-entity recognizer NameTag (Straka and Straková 2014a). As has

15 https://clarin.is/en/resources/spoken/

already been observed by Odijk (2019), the majority of the current CMDI profiles used for describing software in CLARIN repositories lack metadata components that are otherwise crucial for and unique to software, such as tool functionality and the subcomponents of the tool's input or output, such as the types of named entity categories recognized by a tool like NameTag. The CRF initiative seeks to fill this gap by explicitly specifying the tool-intrinstic metadata components, such as the platform on which the software can be run and the functionality of the tool, as certain tools are part of larger toolchains that perform additional tasks. We furthermore try to provide an exhaustive list with possible cross-references for structural features that are unique to the family, which in the case of named entity recognizers are the categories of named entities taken into account. For availability, we also distinguish the fact that different components of a tool, such as the downloadable software, can have different license conditions compared to other components such as a possible online interface or the language models.[16]

NameTag **Functionality:** NER **Platform:** Linux, Windows, OS X **Licence:** MPL 2.0 (software), CC BY-NC-SA (models)	Czech, English	NameTag is an open-source tool that recognizes different NER categories per language model. For Czech, it recognizes a complex hierarchy of categories. The English model, which is trained on CoNLL-2003 NER annotations (Sang and De Meulder 2003), distinguishes the following four NER classes: person, organisation, location and miscellaneous. The trained model for Czech is available for through LINDAT: Czech Models (CNEC) for NameTag. A user manual is also available. **Availability:** download, online service, web API **CLARIN Centre:** LINDAT **NER categories:** per model, see above **Publication:** Straková, Straka and Hajič (2013)

Figure 2: The NameTag named entity recognizer listed in the Tool families.

16 For a discussion of licenses and other legal aspects of the CLARIN infrastructure, see Kamocki, Kelli, and Lindén (2022).

4.2 Accessibility

It is worth noting that, in contrast to the resources, many of the tools that are listed in the B-certified repositories are not downloadable from there, but rather through external platforms that are tailored to software such as GitHub (see, for instance, MorphoDiTa: Morphological Dictionary and Tagger, Straka and Straková 2014b). Most of the tools available for on-the-fly online use are accessible through dedicated web services or through the aforementioned CLARIN Language Resource Switchboard (Zinn 2018).[17] Tools that are integrated with the Switchboard mostly belong to the family of part-of-speech taggers and lemmatizers, such as the CLARIN-PL morphological analyser Morfeusz (Woliński and Lenart 2016) and several PoS-taggers that are part of WebLicht (CLARIN-D/SfS-Uni. Tübingen 2012), and to the named entity recognizers family, such as the CLARIN-PL tools Liner2[18] and Nerf.[19]

4.3 Language

The vast majority of tools have a monolingual scope. The most frequent language of the monolingual tools is Polish, while the second most frequent language is Bantu, which technically refers to the Bantu languages spoken in South Africa, such as Swahili, Zulu, and Shona. Most of these tools for Bantu languages are lemmatizers developed by the SADiLaR South African CLARIN consortium, such as a set of PoS taggers (Puttkammer and Schlemmer 2018). All of these tools are for download and made available online as part of NCHLT Text Web Services (Puttkammer et al. 2018).[20]

On the other hand, the tools with the largest multilingual scope include Sparv (Borin et al. 2016),[21] which is the corpus annotation pipeline of the Swedish CLARIN Consortium used for processing corpora made available through Korp (see also Section 3.2) and has pre-trained models for 20 languages; the Turku Neural Parser Pipeline,[22] which has pre-trained models for more than 50 languages (Kanerva et al. 2018); as well as tools made available through the WebLicht environment (CLARIN-D/SfS-Uni. Tübingen 2012).

17 https://switchboard.clarin.eu/
18 https://github.com/CLARIN-PL/Liner2
19 http://hackage.haskell.org/package/nerf
20 https://hlt.nwu.ac.za/
21 https://spraakbanken.gu.se/sparv/
22 https://turkunlp.org/Turku-neural-parser-pipeline/

4.4 The families

4.4.1 Named entity recognizers

Named entity recognition is a language processing task which identifies mentions of various named entities and classifies them into predetermined categories, such as person names, organisations, locations, date/time, monetary values, and so forth. Named entity recognizers can be used as stand-alone tools for information extraction as well as in NLP applications like text summarization and question answering (Li et al. 2020).

While all the CRF named entity recognizers classify named entities based on the three basic categories of person, organization, and location, several tools recognize a complex, nested hierarchy of categories – for instance, the Czech model for the NameTag tool (Straka and Straková 2014a) recognizes a total of 42 fine-grained classes of named entities grouped together under seven super-classes (numbers, geographic items, institutions, media names, artefact names, personal names, and time expressions; Straková, Straka, and Hajič 2013: 69), where for instance the personal name class consists of subtypes such as first name, religious/mythological personas, surnames, and second names.

4.4.2 Part-of-speech taggers and lemmatizers

Part-of-speech tagging is the automatic text annotation process in which words or tokens are assigned part of speech tags, which typically correspond to the main syntactic categories in a language (e.g., noun, verb) and often to subtypes of a particular syntactic category which are distinguished by morphosyntactic features (e.g., number, tense). Lemmatization is the process by which inflected forms of a lexeme are grouped together under a base dictionary form. Part-of-speech tagging and lemmatization are crucial steps of linguistic pre-processing.

Almost half of the tools in this family have multiple functionalities – for instance, the IceNLP Natural Language Processing toolkit (Loftsson 2019) and UDPipe (Straka and Straková 2016) both perform syntactic parsing in addition to part-of-speech tagging and lemmatization, while Frog (van den Bosch et al. 2020) also performs named entity recognition, phrase chunking, and syntactic parsing.

4.4.3 Sentiment analysers

Sentiment analysis refers to the method of determining the sentiment of a particular sentence (or potentially other grammatical construction) by assigning it a ternary ("positive", "neutral", "negative") or scalar value. Sentiment analysis is thus a text analysis method used to identify people's opinions and attitudes within a text (Liu 2012: 1153). In terms of applicability, sentiment analysis is widely used in domains like social media or customer reviews, where the user's voice is expressed.

A state-of-the-art CLARIN sentiment analyser is MultiEmo,[23] which is trained on a benchmark collection of customer reviews in 11 languages (Kocoń, Miłkowski, and Kanclerz 2021), among which are German, Russian, Japanese, and Polish. MultiEmo can be used (both as a downloadable application or online) to mark sentiment at the sentence, paragraph and text levels according to four values (positive, ambivalent, neutral, negative). It is also noteworthy that two tools in this family perform sentiment analysis on a sub-sentential level, i.e., they add sentiment labels to phrasal constituents in syntactic trees (e.g., OptaHopper, Żak and Skuczyńska 2018).

4.4.4 Text normalizers

Text normalization is the process of transforming parts of a text into a single canonical form. It represents one of the key stages of linguistic processing for texts in which spelling variation abounds or deviates from the contemporary norm, as in historical documents (Bollmann, Petran, and Dipper 2011) or on social media (Clark and Araki 2011). After text normalization, standard tools for all further stages of text processing can be used. Another important advantage of text normalization is improved search (Ntoulas, Stamou, and Tzagarakis 2001) which can be performed by querying a single, standard variant that takes into account all its spelling variants, be it historical, dialectal, colloquial or slang.

As text normalization is a crucial pre-processing step in the case of non-standard language data, most CRF normalizers are part of larger toolchains performing additional functionalities. An example of such a toolchain is the Nederlab Pipeline,[24] which uses the FoLia-wordtranslate[25] tool to normalize historical

23 http://ws.clarin-pl.eu/multiemo
24 https://github.com/proycon/nederlab-pipeline
25 https://github.com/LanguageMachines/foliautils

Dutch data, after which step it can invoke other annotation tools such as the Frog tagger to further annotate the historical texts with part-of-speech tags, lemmas, named entities, and dependency parses (Brugman et al. 2016).

5 The next steps for CRF

CRF has proven itself to be a highly visible initiative appreciated by a broad spectrum of CLARIN users. The families presented in the previous section therefore warrant continued upkeep, which is why one of the key aims of CRF is to work towards harmonized metadata curation. This means providing a uniform and comprehensive presentation of structural metadata such as size and license as well as describing the domain-specific qualitative characteristics of each family.

CRF leads an on-going curatorial activity that is a collaborative effort involving the help of national CLARIN representatives, mainly members of the User Involvement Committee and administrators of the national CLARIN repositories where the tools and resources are hosted. We have established a ticket system on GitHub where for each of the families described in the previous sections we provide a list of issues hindering metadata harmonization, such as missing information of size, annotation, and license.[26] The issues are listed as GitHub tickets assigned to the CLARIN centres that host the tool and resource. We periodically ask the relevant repository representatives to consult the tickets and provide information on the missing items, which has so far turned out to be a successful endeavour that has resulted in the solving of many metadata gaps and inconsistencies. As discussed in Section 2, one of the main issues of distributed infrastructures is that metadata provision is uneven because each repository has different standards for curating their deposits, so CRF attempts to overcome this by helping the administrators of the distributed repositories to curate metadata in a unified way, by ensuring that the metadata problems identified and listed on GitHub are consistent across all families.

In the future, CRF is going to focus on the development and implementation of preventive measures which will minimize the number of metadata issues for newly deposited resources and tools. To this end, we are currently drafting a best practice guide for new deposits, which will encourage authors to provide information on crucial metadata that otherwise is not required by the submission process itself, as in the case of DSpace-based repositories, whose depositing system does not explicitly prompt users to describe the annotation of a resource in contrast to, for example, the size and license. The best-practice guide will also

26 https://github.com/clarin-eric/resource-families-issues/issues

add specific guidelines for describing the qualitative characteristics of a tool or resource. We are also going to organize an online training session for designated reviewers from each CLARIN centre where the best practice guide and suggestions for reviewing new deposits are going to be be presented and discussed.

Furthermore, CLARIN ERIC has set up an on-going funding opportunity for small projects that can contribute to CRF,[27] where envisaged activities include extending existing families by developing additional resources and tools that will support comparative research, as well as the consolidation of a resource family through comprehensive metadata curation and harmonization. A very successful example of a CLARIN-funded project whose aim is to create a harmonized set of multilingual resources is ParlaMint (Erjavec et al. 2022), in which a collection of richly annotated parliamentary corpora is being developed. Here, harmonization is achieved by encoding already existing national parliamentary corpora as well as by creating new ones using a single corpus encoding schema, that is, the Parla-CLARIN TEI recommendation,[28] which is becoming a de-facto standard for encoding national parliamentary corpora and specifically aims for cross-parliamentary comparability (Erjavec et al. 2022: 24).

6 Conclusion

This chapter has presented CLARIN Resource and Tools Family, a User Involvement initiative which seeks to supplement the CLARIN technical infrastructure by providing manually curated overviews of language resources and tools aimed at researchers in the Digital Humanities and Social Sciences. We have first presented the main aim of this initiative, which is the fact that it seeks to address those gaps in metadata provision which arise due to the distributed nature of the CLARIN infrastructure. In this respect, we try to ensure that resources and tools are described as uniformly as possible when it comes to their basic structural metadata (for instance, size and license/general availability conditions) while at the same time ensure that resource and tool documentation also presents qualitative characteristics that are domain specific and of importance for (re)use by researchers in Digital Humanities and Social Sciences. We have then discussed the resource and tool families, where we have shown how the listings of resources and tools are concretely presented in this initiative, discussed some of the salient characteristics in relation to language and accessibility and then

27 https://www.clarin.eu/content/clarin-resource-families-project-funding
28 https://clarin-eric.github.io/parla-clarin

presented each resource and tool family in turn, discussing their importance for Digital Humanities and Social Sciences research, presenting unique characteristics in relation to both linguistic annotation and domain-specific extra-linguistic markup, and exemplifying prominent tools and resources for each family. Finally, we have discussed how this initiative facilitates curation of the distributed tools and resources, which is done in two ways: on the one hand, through a collaborative inter-consortium approach that involves direct cooperation with repository administrations and on the other, through the recently established CLARIN Resource and Tool Families project funding opportunity, which among other activities envisages comprehensive metadata curation and harmonization.

In terms of general User Involvement outreach, the CLARIN Resource and Tool Families are very much appreciated by the wider research community, which is for instance shown by the increasing number of non-CLARIN-affiliated authors who ask us to feature their tools and resources on the relevant webpages. For future work, we plan to continue the curation of the CLARIN Resource and Tool Families and to work on adopting preventive measures such as a best-practice guide on overcoming common metadata issues in new deposits, as well as expand the initiative with new overviews, thereby incorporating new research communities, such as scholars working with sign languages and speech disorders, as well as medical and legal texts.

Bibliography

Abuczki, Ágnes & Esfandiari Baiat Ghazaleh. 2013. An overview of multimodal corpora, annotation tools and schemes. *Argumentum* 9: 86–98.

Androutsopoulos, Jannis. 2006. Introduction: Sociolinguistics and computer-mediated communication. *Journal of Sociolinguistics* 10 (4): 419–438.

Archer, Dawn & Jonathan Culpeper. 2003. Sociopragmatic annotation: New directions and possibilities in historical corpus linguistics. In A. Wilson, P. Wilson & A.M. McEnery (eds.), *Corpus linguistics by the lune: A festschrift for Geoffrey Leech*. Frankfurst/Main: Peter Lang.

Banski, Piotr & Hanna Hedeland. 2022. Standards in CLARIN. In Darja Fišer & Andreas Witt (eds.), *CLARIN. The infrastructure for language resources*. Berlin: De Gruyter.

BAS. 2016. BAS Alcohol Language Corpus. Bavarian Archive for Speech Signals, Ludwig-Maximilians-Universität München. http://hdl.handle.net/11022/1009-0000-0001-88E5-3.

Bednarek, Monika. 2006. *Evaluation in media discourse: Analysis of a newspaper corpus*. A&C Black.

Benešová, Lucie, Michal Křen & Martina Waclawičová. 2016. ORAL2013: balanced corpus of informal spoken Czech (transcriptions). LINDAT/CLARIAH-CZ digital library at the Institute of Formal and Applied Linguistics (ÚFAL), Faculty of Mathematics and Physics, Charles University. http://hdl.handle.net/11234/1-1847.

Bjarnadóttir, Kristín. 2019. The Database of Modern Icelandic Inflection (DMII). CLARIN-IS. http://hdl.handle.net/20.500.12537/5.

Bojar, Ondřej, Vojtěch Diatka, Pavel Straňák, Aleš Tamchyna & Daniel Zeman. 2014. HindEnCorp 0.5. LINDAT/CLARIAH-CZ digital library at the Institute of Formal and Applied Linguistics (ÚFAL), Faculty of Mathematics and Physics, Charles University. http://hdl.handle.net/11858/00-097C-0000-0023-625F-0.

Bojar, Ondřej, Zdeněk Žabokrtský, Ondřej Dušek, Petra Galuščáková, Martin Majliš, David Mareček, Jiří Maršík, Michal Novák, Martin Popel & Aleš Tamchyna. 2011. Czech- English Parallel Corpus 1.0 (CzEng 1.0). LINDAT/CLARIAH-CZ digital library at the Institute of Formal and Applied Linguistics (ÚFAL), Faculty of Mathematics and Physics, Charles University. http://hdl.handle.net/11234/1-1458.

Bollmann, Marcel, Florian Petran & Stefanie Dipper. 2011. Rule-based normalization of historical texts. *Proceedings of the workshop on language technologies for digital humanities and cultural heritage*, 34–42.

Borin, Lars, Markus Forsberg, Martin Hammarstedt, Dan Rosén, Roland Schäfer & Anne Schumacher. 2016. Sparv: Språkbanken's corpus annotation pipeline infrastructure. *The sixth Swedish language technology conference (SLTC), Umeå University*, 17–18.

Borin, Lars, Markus Forsberg & Johan Roxendal. 2012. Korp – the corpus infrastructure of språkbanken. *International conference on language resources and evaluation (LREC)* 8, 474–478.

Bosch, Antal van den, Bertjan Busser, Sander Canisius & Walter Daelemans. 2020. Frog. Instituut voor de Nederlandse Taal. http://hdl.handle. net/10032/198143d2010 e74ae17d4223dfc00e2a8.

Boschetti, Federico, Riccardo Del Gratta & Harry Diakoff. 2016. Open Ancient Greek WordNet 0.5. ILC-CNR for CLARIN-IT repository hosted at Institute for Computational Linguistics "A. Zampolli", National Research Council, in Pisa. http://hdl.handle.net/20.500.11752/ILC-56

Broeder, Daan, Menzo Windhouwer, Dieter Van Uytvanck, Twan Goosen & Thorsten Trippel. 2021. CMDI: a Component metadata infrastructure. *International conference on language resources and evaluation (LREC)* 8, 1–4.

Brugman, Hennie, Martin Reynaert, Nicoline van der Sijs, René van Stipriaan, Erik Tjong Kim Sang & Antal van den Bosch. 2016. Nederlab: Towards a single portal and research environment for diachronic dutch text corpora. *International conference on language resources and evaluation (LREC)* 10, 1277–1281.

Burke, Mary, Oksana L. Zavalina, Mark Edward Phillips & Shobhana Chelliah. 2021. Organization of knowledge and information in digital archives of language materials. *Journal of Library Metadata* 20 (4): 185–217. http://doi.org/10.1080/19386389.2020.1908651.

Čermák, František, Jaroslava Hlaváčová, Milena Hnátková, Tomáš Jelínek, Jan Kocek, Marie Kopřivová, Michal Křen, Renata Novotná, Vladimír Petkevič, Věra Schmiedtová, Hana Skoumalová, Johanka Spoustová, Michal Šulc & Zdeněk Velíšek. 2006. SYN2006PUB: Corpus of Czech newspapers. LINDAT/CLARIAH-CZ digital library at the Institute of Formal and Applied Linguistics (ÚFAL), Faculty of Mathematics and Physics, Charles University. http://hdl.handle.net/11858/00-097C-0000-0023-1358-3.

Cheng, Jennifer E. 2015. Islamophobia, muslimophobia or racism? parliamentary discourses on islam and muslims in debates on the minaret ban in switzerland. *Discourse & Society* 26 (5): 562–586.

Cimiano, Philipp, Christian Chiarcos, John P. McCrae & Jorge Garcia. 2020. *Linguistic Linked Data: Representation, Generation and Applications*. Cham, Switzerland: Springer.

CLARIN-D/SfS-Uni. Tübingen. 2012. WebLicht: Web-Based Linguistic Chaining Tool. https://weblicht.sfs.uni-tuebingen.de/.

Clark, Eleanor & Kenji Araki. 2011. Text normalization in social media: progress, problems and applications for a pre-processing system of casual English. *Procedia – Social and Behavioral Sciences* 27: 2–11.

Curzan, Anne. 2009. Historical corpus linguistics and evidence of language change. In Anke Lüdeling & Merja Kytö (eds.), *Corpus linguistics*, 1091–1109. De Gruyter. https: //doi.org/10.1515/9783110213881.2.1091.

Daelemans, Walter, Darja Fišer, Jasmin Franza, Denis Kranjčić, Jens Lemmens, Nikola Ljubešić, Ilia Markov & Damjan Popič. 2020. The LiLaH Emotion Lexicon of Croatian, Dutch and Slovene. Slovenian language resource repository CLARIN.SI. http://hdl.handle.net/11356/1318.

De Smedt, Koenraad, Franciska de Jong, Bente Maegaard, Darja Fiser & Dieter Van Uytvanck. 2018. Towards an open science infrastructure for the digital humanities: The case of CLARIN. In Eetu Mäkelä, Mikko Tolonen & Jouni Tuominen (eds.), *Digital humanities in the Nordic countries conference (DHN)* 3, 139–151.

Dijk, Teun A. van. 2010. Political identities in parliamentary debates. In Cornelia Ilie (ed.), *European parliaments under scrutiny: Discourse strategies and interaction practices*, 29–56. Amsterdam: John Benjamins.

Doval, Irene & Maria Teresa Sanchez Nieto. 2019. *Parallel corpora for contrastive and translation studies: New resources and applications*. John Benjamins Publishing Company.

Erjavec, Tomaž, Ana-Maria Barbu, Ivan Derzhanski, Ludmila Dimitrova, Radovan Garabík, Nancy Ide, Heiki-Jaan Kaalep, Natalia Kotsyba, Cvetana Krstev, Csaba Oravecz, Vladimír Petkevič, Greg Priest-Dorman, Behrang QasemiZadeh, Adam Radziszewski, Kiril Simov, Dan Tufiş & Katerina Zdravkova. 2010. MULTEXT-East "1984" annotated corpus 4.0. Slovenian language resource repository CLARIN.SI. http://hdl.handle.net/11356/1043.

Erjavec, Tomaž, Darja Fišer, Nikola Ljubešić, Marko Ferme, Mladen Borovič, Borko Boškovič, Milan Ojsteršek & Goran Hrovat. 2019. Corpus of Academic Slovene KAS 1.0. Slovenian language resource repository CLARIN.SI. http://hdl.handle.net/11356/1244.

Erjavec, Tomaž, Maciej Ogrodniczuk, Petya Osenova, Nikola Ljubešić, Kiril Simov, Vladislava Grigorova, Michał Rudolf, Andrej Pančur, Matyáš Kopp, Starkaður Barkarson, Steinhór Steingrímsson, Henk van der Pol, Griet Depoorter, Jesse de Does, Bart Jongejan, Dorte Haltrup Hansen, Costanza Navarretta, María Calzada Pérez, Luciana D. de Macedo et al. 2021. Linguistically annotated multilingual comparable corpora of parliamentary debates ParlaMint.ana 2.1. Slovenian language resource repository CLARIN.SI. http://hdl.handle.net/11356/1431.

Erjavec, Tomaž, Maciej Ogrodniczuk, Petya Osenova, Nikola Ljubešić, Kiril Simov, Andrej Pančur, Michał Rudolf, Matyáš Kopp, Starkaður Barkarson, Steinþór Steingrímsson, Çağri Çöltekin, Jesse de Does, Katrien Depuydt, Tommaso Agnoloni, Giulia Venturi, María Calzada Pérez, Luciana D. de Macedo, Costanza Navarretta, Giancarlo Luxardo, Matthew Coole et al. 2022. The ParlaMint corpora of parliamentary proceedings. *Language Resources and Evaluation*, p. 34.

Falk, Ingrid, Delphine Bernhard & Christophe Gérard. 2014. From non word to new word: Automatically identifying neologisms in french newspapers. *International conference on language resources and evaluation (LREC)* 9.

Fernández-Domínguez, Jesús. 2019. The onomasiological approach. In Mark Aronoff (ed.), *Oxford research encyclopedia of linguistics*. http://doi.org/10.1093/acrefore/9780199384655.013.579.

Fišer, Darja & Kristina Pahor de Maiti. 2020. Voices of the parliament. *Modern Languages Open* 1: 46.

Fišer, Darja & Jakob Lenardič. 2018. CLARIN corpora for parliamentary discourse research. In Darja Fišer, Maria Eskevich & Franciska de Jong (eds.), *ParlaCLARIN: Creating and using parliamentary corpora*, 2–7. http://lrec-conf.org/workshops/lrec2018/W2/pdf/book_of_proceedings.pdf (accessed 28 March 2022).

Fišer, Darja, Jakob Lenardič & Tomaž Erjavec. 2018. CLARIN's key resource families. *International conference on language resources and evaluation (LREC)* 11, 1320–1325.

Goláňová, Hana, M. Waclawičová, Z. Komrsková, D. Lukeš, M. Kopřivová & Poukarová. 2017. DIALEKT: Nářeční Korpus. Czech National Corpus. http://www.korpus.cz/.

Goosen, Twan & Thomas Eckart. 2014. Virtual language observatory 3.0: What's new. *Proceedings of the CLARIN annual conference, Oesterberg, 24–25 october, 2014*.

Granger, Sylviane. 2003. Error-tagged learner corpora and call: A promising synergy. *CALICO Journal* 20 (3): 465–480.

Granger, Sylviane. 2009. The contribution of learner corpora to second language acquisition and foreign language teaching. *Corpora and Language Teaching* 33: 13–32.

Hajič, Jan, Eduard Bejček, Alevtina Bémová, Eva Buráňová, Eva Hajičová, Jiří Havelka, Petr Homola, Jiří Kárník, Václava Kettnerová, Natalia Klyueva, Veronika Kolářová, Lucie Kučová, Markéta Lopatková, Marie Mikulová, Jiří Mírovský, Anna Nedoluzhko, Petr Pajas, Jarmila Panevová et al. 2018. Prague Dependency Treebank 3.5. LINDAT/CLARIAH-CZ digital library at the Institute of Formal and Applied Linguistics (ÚFAL), Faculty of Mathematics and Physics, Charles University. http://hdl.handle.net/11234/1-2621.

Hajič, Jan, Eva Hajičová, Barbora Hladká, Jozef Mišutka, Ondřej Košarko & Pavel Straňák. 2022. LINDAT/CLARIAH-CZ: Where we are and where we go. In Darja Fišer & Andreas Witt (eds.), *CLARIN. The infrastructure for language resources*. Berlin: De Gruyter.

Hansen, Dorte Haltrup & Costanza Navarretta. 2021. The Danish Parliament Corpus 2009–2017, v2, w. subject annotation. CLARIN-DK-UCPH Centre Repository. http: //hdl.handle.net/20.500.12115/44.

Hansen, Dorte Haltrup, Costanza Navarretta & Lene Offersgaard. 2018. A pilot gender study of the Danish parliament corpus. *International conference on language resources and evaluation (LREC* 11*)*, 67–72.

Helgadóttir, Sigrún & Starkaður Barkarson. 2020. The Saga Corpus. CLARIN-IS. http: //hdl.handle.net/20.500.12537/32.

Herring, Susan C. 2001. Computer-mediated discourse. *The handbook of discourse analysis*, 612. Wiley Online Library.

Hiippala, Tuomo. 2014. A Multimodal Corpus of Tourist Brochures Produced by the City of Helsinki, Finland (1967–2008). The Language Bank of Finland. http://urn.fi/urn:nbn:fi:lb-2015030301.

Hirst, Graeme, Vanessa Wei Feng, Christopher Cochrane & Nona Naderi. 2014. Argumentation, ideology, and issue framing in parliamentary discourse. In Elena Cabrio, Serena Villata & Adam Z. Wyne (eds.), *Proceedings of the workshop on frontiers and connections between argumentation theory and natural language processing, forlì-cesena, italy, july 21–25, 2014*.

Hladik, Radim. 2018. Czech Sociological Review 1993-2016. LINDAT/CLARIAH-CZ digital library at the Institute of Formal and Applied Linguistics (ÚFAL), Faculty of Mathematics and Physics, Charles University. http://hdl.handle.net/11372/LRT-2703.

Hogenboom, Alexander, Daniella Bal, Flavius Frasincar, Malissa Bal, Franciska de Jong & Uzay Kaymak. 2013. Exploiting emoticons in sentiment analysis. *Proceedings of the 28th annual acm symposium on applied computing*, 703–710. New York: Association for Computing Machinery.

Huber, Magnus, Magnus Nissel & Karin Puga. 2016. Old Bailey Corpus 2.0. CLARIN-D. http://hdl.handle.net/11858/00-246C-0000-0023-8CFB-2.

Huistra, Hieke & Bram Mellink. 2016. Phrasing history: Selecting sources in digital repositories. *Historical Methods: A Journal of Quantitative and Interdisciplinary History* 49 (4): 220–229.

Hyland, Ken. 1998. Boosting, hedging and the negotiation of academic knowledge. *Text & Talk* 18 (3): 349–382.

ILSP. 2015. OROSSIMO Corpus. CLARIN:EL. http://hdl.handle.net/11500/ATHENA-0000-0000-2410-5.

Institute for the German Language. 2021. Deutsches Referenzkorpus / Archiv der Korpora geschriebener Gegenwartssprache 2021-I (Release vom 02.02.2021). https://www.ids-mannheim.de/digspra/kl/projekte/korpora (accessed 28 March 2022).

Institute for the Languages of Finland. 2011. Frequency List of Written Finnish Word Forms. Language Bank of Finland. http://urn.fi/urn:nbn:fi:lb-20140730146.

Institute of the Estonian Language. 2019. Estonian National Corpus. CELR, Metashare distribution. http://hdl.handle.net/10.15155/3-00-0000-0000-0000-08489L.

INT. 2013. SoNaR New Media Corpus (Version 1.0). Dutch Language Institute. http: //hdl.handle.net/10032/tm-a2-k3.

Iversen, Stefan. 2011. Johannes V. Jensen Corpus. CLARIN-DK-UCPH Centre Repository. http://hdl.handle.net/20.500.12115/20.

Jauhiainen, Heidi, Aleksi Sahala & Tero Alstola. 2019. Open Richly Annotated Cuneiform Corpus, Korp Version, May 2019. The Language Bank of Finland. http://urn.fi/urn:nbn:fi:lb-2019060601.

Jelínek, Tomáš, Milena Hnátková & Hana Skoumalová. 2017. FicTree 1.0. LINDAT/CLARIAH-CZ digital library at the Institute of Formal and Applied Linguistics (ÚFAL), Faculty of Mathematics and Physics, Charles University. http://hdl.handle.net/11234/1-2517.

Kamocki, Paweł, Aleksei Kelli & Krister Lindén. 2022. The CLARIN Committee for Legal and Ethical issues and the Normative Layer of the CLARIN infrastructure. In Darja Fišer & Andreas Witt (eds.), *CLARIN. The infrastructure for language resources*. Berlin: De Gruyter.

Kanerva, Jenna, Filip Ginter, Niko Miekka, Akseli Leino & Tapio Salakoski. 2018. Turku neural parser pipeline: An end-to-end system for the conll 2018 shared task. *Proceedings of the conll 2018 shared task: Multilingual parsing from raw text to universal dependencies*, 133–142. Association for Computational Linguistics.

Kasama, Deni Yuso. 2012. Ontology for the Area of Nanoscience and Nanotechnology. PORTULAN CLARIN. https://hdl.handle.net/21.11129/0000-000B-D318-C.

Knight, Dawn. 2020. CorCenCC: Corpws Cenedlaethol Cymraeg Cyfoes – the National Corpus of Contemporary Welsh. Oxford Text Archive. http://hdl.handle.net/20.500.12024/2564.

Kocoń, Jan, Piotr Miłkowski & Kamil Kanclerz. 2021. MultiEmo: Multilingual, Multilevel, Multidomain Sentiment Analysis Corpus of Consumer Reviews. CLARIN-PL digital repository. http://hdl.handle.net/11321/798.

Koutsombogera, Maria. 2015. Multimodal and Multiparty Corpus of Text Comprehension Interactions. CLARIN:EL. http://hdl.grnet.gr/11500/ATHENA-0000-0000-2546-8.

Krek, Simon, Tomaž Erjavec, Andraž Repar, Jaka Čibej, Špela Arhar Holdt, Polona Gantar, Iztok Kosem, Marko Robnik-Šikonja, Nikola Ljubešić, Kaja Dobrovoljc, Cyprian Laskowski, Miha Grčar, Peter Holozan, Simon Šuster, Vojko Gorjanc, Marko Stabej & Nataša Logar. 2019. Corpus of Written Standard Slovene Gigafida 2.0. CJVT/CLARIN.SI. http://hdl.handle.net/11356/1320.

Krek, Simon, Cyprian Laskowski, Marko Robnik-Šikonja, Iztok Kosem, Špela Arhar Holdt, Polona Gantar, Jaka Čibej, Vojko Gorjanc, Bojan Klemenc & Kaja Dobrovoljc. 2018. Thesaurus of Modern Slovene 1.0. Slovenian language resource repository CLARIN.SI. http://hdl.handle.net/11356/1166.

Laak, Marin, Kaarel Veskis, Olga Gerassimenko, Neeme Kahusk & Kadri Vider. 2019. Literary studies meet corpus linguistics: Estonian pilot project of private letters in korp. *Digital humanities in the Nordic countries conference (DHN)* 4, 283–294.

Langman, Juliet. 1998. Langman Corpus. TalkBank. http://hdl.handle.net/10.21415/T5C027.

Lapponi, Emanuele & Martin G. Søyland. 2016. Talk of Norway. Common Language Resources and Technology Infrastructure Norway (CLARINO) Bergen Repository. http://hdl.handle.net/11509/123.

Leech, Geoffrey. 2002. The importance of reference corpora. *Hizkuntza-corpusak. Oraina etageroa*, pp. 1–10.

Leikuma, Lidija, Liga Bernane, Jurs Cibuls, Alvydas Butkus, Violeta Butkiene, Kristina Vaisvalavičiene & Ilze Sperga. 2013. The Lithuanian–Latvian–Latgalian Dictionary. CLARIN-LV digital library at IMCS, University of Latvia. http://hdl.handle.net/20.500.12574/52.

Li, Jing, Aixin Sun, Jianglei Han & Chenliang Li. 2020. A survey on deep learning for named entity recognition. *IEEE Transactions on Knowledge and Data Engineering* 34 (1): 50–70.

Liu, Bing. 2012. *Sentiment analysis and opinion mining*. Morgan & Claypool Publishers.

Loftsson, Hrafn. 2019. IceNLP Natural Language Processing toolkit. CLARIN-IS. http: //hdl.handle.net/20.500.12537/8.

Machálek, Tomáš. 2020. KonText: Advanced and flexible corpus query interface. *International conference on language resources and evaluation (LREC)* 12, 7003–7008.

Machálek, Tomáš. 2014. KonText – Corpus Query Interface. Czech National Corpus. http://kontext.korpus.cz.

MacWhinney, Brian. 2007. The talkbank project. In Joan C. Beal, Karen P. Corrigan & Hermann L. Moisl (eds.), *Creating and digitizing language corpora*, 163–180. Springer.

Mahlberg, Michaela. 2007. Corpus stylistics: Bridging the gap between linguistic and literary studies. *Text, Discourse and Corpora: Theory and Analysis* 8: 219–246.

Mareček, David. 2016. Czech–English Manual Word Alignment. LINDAT/CLARIAH-CZ digital library at the Institute of Formal and Applied Linguistics (ÚFAL), Faculty of Mathematics and Physics, Charles University. http://hdl.handle.net/11234/1-1804.

Marneffe, Marie-Catherine de, Christopher D. Manning, Joakim Nivre & Daniel Zeman. 2021. Universal dependencies. *Computational linguistics* 47 (2): 255–308.

McCrae, John P., Philipp Cimiano, Luca Matteis, Roberto Navigli, Victor Rodriguez Doncel, Daniel Vila-Suero, Jorge Garcia, Andrejs Abele, Gabriela Vulcu & Paul Buitelaar. 2015. Reconciling heterogeneous descriptions of language resources. *Proceedings of the 4th workshop on linked data in linguistics*, 39–48. Beijing: Association for Computational Linguistics.

McGillivray, Barbara. 2020. LatinISE corpus (version 4). LINDAT/CLARIAH-CZ digital library at the Institute of Formal and Applied Linguistics (ÚFAL), Faculty of Mathematics and Physics, Charles University. http://hdl.handle.net/11372/LRT-3170.

McGillivray, Barbara, Beatrice Alex, Sarah Ames, Guyda Armstrong, David Beavan, Arianna Ciula, Giovanni Colavizza, James Cummings, David De Roure, Adam Farquhar, Simon Hengchen, Anouk Lang, James Loxley, Eirini Goudarouli, Federico Nanni, Andrea Nini, Julianne Nyhan, Nicola Osborne, Thierry Poibeau, Mia Ridge, Sonia Ranade, James Smithies, Melissa Terras, Andreas Vlachidis & Pip Willcox. 2020. The challenges and prospects of the intersection of humanities and data science: A white paper from The Alan Turing Institute. http://doi.org/10.6084/m9.figshare.12732164.

Mörth, Karlheinz, Stephan Procházka & Carmen Berlinches Ramos. 2011. A Machine-Readable Dictionary of Damascus Arabic. ARCHE. https://hdl.handle.net/11022/0000-0007-C093-9.

Nivre, Joakim, Mitchell Abrams, Željko Agić, Lars Ahrenberg, Lene Antonsen, Katya Aplonova, Maria Jesus Aranzabe, Gashaw Arutie, Masayuki Asahara, Luma Ateyah, Mohammed Attia, Aitziber Atutxa, Liesbeth Augustinus, Elena Badmaeva, Miguel Ballesteros, Esha Banerjee, Sebastian Bank, Verginica Barbu Mititelu, Victoria Basmov, John Bauer, Sandra Bellato et al. 2018. Universal Dependencies 2.3. LINDAT/CLARIAH-CZ digital library at the Institute of Formal and Applied Linguistics (ÚFAL), Faculty of Mathematics and Physics, Charles University. http: //hdl.handle.net/11234/1-2895.

Ntoulas, Alexandros, Sofia Stamou & Manolis Tzagarakis. 2001. Using a WWW search engine to evaluate normalization performance for a highly inflectional language. *Association computational linguistics 39th annual meeting (companion volume)*, 31–36. Toulouse: Association for Computational Linguistics.

Odijk, Jan. 2019. Discovering software resources in CLARIN. *Selected papers from the CLARIN conference, Pisa, 8–10 october, 2018*, Linköping Electronic Conference Proceedings 159, 121–132. Linköping University Electronic Press, Linköpings universitet.

Oxford Text Archive. 1991. Helsinki Corpus of English Texts. Oxford Text Archive. http://hdl.handle.net/20.500.12024/1477.

Oxford Text Archive. 2001. The York-Helsinki Parsed Corpus of Old English poetry (YCOEP). Oxford Text Archive. http://hdl.handle.net/20.500.12024/2425.

Pančur, Andrej & Mojca Šorn. 2016. Smart big data: Use of Slovenian parliamentary papers in digital history. *Contributions to Contemporary History* 56 (3): 130–146.

Parida, Shantipriya & Ondřej Bojar. 2019. Hindi Visual Genome 1.0. LINDAT/CLARIAH-CZ digital library at the Institute of Formal and Applied Linguistics (ÚFAL), Faculty of Mathematics and Physics, Charles University. http://hdl.handle.net/11234/1-2997.

Partington, Alan. 2010. Modern diachronic corpus-assisted discourse studies (md-cads) on uk newspapers: An overview of the project. *Corpora* 5 (2): 83–108.

Praet, Stiene, Walter Daelemans, Tim Kreutz, Peter Van Aelst, Stefaan Walgrave & David Martens. 2018. Issue communication by political parties on Twitter. Paper presented at *Data Science, Journalism and Media*, August 20, 2018.

Proisl, Thomas, Natalie Dykes, Philipp Heinrich, Besim Kabashi, Andreas Blombach & Stefan Evert. 2020. EmpiriST corpus 2.0: Adding manual normalization, lemmatization and semantic tagging to a german web and cmc corpus. *International conference on language resources and evaluation (LREC)* 12, 6142–6148.

Przepiórkowski, Adam. 2011. National Corpus of Polish. LINDAT/CLARIAH-CZ digital library at the Institute of Formal and Applied Linguistics (ÚFAL), Faculty of Mathematics and Physics, Charles University. http://hdl.handle.net/11372/LRT-676.

Pustejovsky, James, Marc Verhagen, Nancy Ide & Keith Suderman. 2017. Enhancing access to media collections and archives using computational linguistic tools. In Thierry Declerck &

Sandra Kübler (eds.), *Proceedings of the workshop on corpora in the digital humanities (CDH 2017), Bloomington, IN, USA, january 19, 2017*, Volume 1786, 19–28. CEUR-WS.org.

Puttkammer, Martin, Roald Eiselen, Justin Hocking & Frederik Koen. 2018. Nlp web services for resource-scarce languages. In Iryna Gurevych & Yusuke Miyao (eds.), *Proceedings of the 56th annual meeting of the association for computational linguistics – system demonstrations*, 43–49. Stroudsberg, PA: Association of Computational Linguistics.

Puttkammer, Martin & Martin Schlemmer. 2018. NCHLT Part of Speech Taggers. SADiLaR. https://hdl.handle.net/20.500.12185/323.

Santos, Claudia & Rute Costa. 2015. Domain specificity. In Hendrik J. Kockaert & Frieda Steurs (eds.), *Handbook of terminology*, Volume 1, 153–179. Amsterdam: John Benjamins.

Schroeder, Ralph. 2007. e-research infrastructures and open science: Towards a new system of knowledge production? *Prometheus* 25 (1): 1–17. http://doi.org/10.1080/08109020601172860.

Simpson, Rita & Dushyanthi Mendis. 2003. A corpus-based study of idioms in academic speech. *TESOL Quarterly* 37 (3): 419–441.

Smith, MacKenzie, Mary Barton, Mick Bass, Margret Branschofsky, Greg McClellan, Dave Stuve, Robert Tansley & Julie Harford Walker. 2003. DSpace: An open source dynamic digital repository. *D-Lib Magazine* 9, no. 1. http://doi.org/10.1045/january2003-smith.

Steingrímsson, Steinþór, Starkaður Barkarson & Eiríkur Rögnvaldsson. 2019. The Icelandic Gigaword Corpus. CLARIN-IS. http://hdl.handle.net/20.500.12537/15.

Straka, Milan & Jana Straková. 2014a. NameTag. LINDAT/CLARIAH-CZ digital library at the Institute of Formal and Applied Linguistics (ÚFAL), Faculty of Mathematics and Physics, Charles University. http://hdl.handle.net/11858/00-097C-0000-0023-43CE-E.

Straka, Milan & Jana Straková. 2014b. MorphoDiTa: Morphological Dictionary and Tagger. LINDAT/CLARIAH-CZ digital library at the Institute of Formal and Applied Linguistics (ÚFAL), Faculty of Mathematics and Physics, Charles University. http://hdl.handle.net/11858/00-097C-0000-0023-43CD-0.

Straka, Milan & Jana Straková. 2016. UDPipe. LINDAT/CLARIAH-CZ digital library at the Institute of Formal and Applied Linguistics (ÚFAL), Faculty of Mathematics and Physics, Charles University. http://hdl.handle.net/11234/1-1702.

Straková, Jana, Milan Straka & Jan Hajič. 2013. A new state-of-the-art czech named entity recognizer. In Ivan Habernal & Václav Matoušek (eds.), *Text, speech and dialogue*, 68–75. Springer, Berlin.

The Language Bank of Finland. 2016. Classics of Finnish Literature, Kielipankki Version. The Language Bank of Finland. http://urn.fi/urn:nbn:fi:lb-20140730186.

Thompson, Paul. 2015. Time-sensitive Inventory of Medical terminology. PORTULAN CLARIN. https://hdl.handle.net/21.11129/0000-000B-D37A-E.

Tiedemann, Jörg. 2015. Tatoeba. CLARIN:EL. http://hdl.grnet.gr/11500/ATHENA-0000-0000-2589-C.

Trotta, Daniela. 2019. PoliModal Corpus. ILC-CNR for CLARIN-IT repository hosted at Institute for Computational Linguistics "A. Zampolli", National Research Council, in Pisa. http://hdl.handle.net/20.500.11752/OPEN-534.

University of Helsinki. 2019. Finnish FrameNet. The Language Bank of Finland. http://urn.fi/urn:nbn:fi:lb-2019040201.

Urešová, Zdenka, Eva Fučíková, Jan Hajič & Jana Šindlerová. 2015. CzEngVallex. LINDAT/CLARIAH-CZ digital library at the Institute of Formal and Applied Linguistics (ÚFAL), Faculty of Mathematics and Physics, Charles University. http://hdl.handle.net/11234/1-1512.

Vandekerckhove, Reinhild, Lisa Hilte, Darja Fišer & Walter Daelemans. 2019. Computer-mediated communication (cmc) and social media corpora: Introduction. *European Journal of Applied Linguistics* 7 (2): 157–162.

Van Uytvanck, Dieter, Herman Stehouwer & Lari Lampen. 2012. Semantic metadata mapping in practice: the virtual language observatory. *International conference on language resources and evaluation (LREC)* 8, 1029–1034.

Velldal, Erik, Lilja Øvrelid, Eivind Alexander Bergem, Cathrine Stadsnes, Samia Touileb & Fredrik Jørgensen. 2017. NoReC: The Norwegian Review Corpus. Common Language Resources and Technology Infrastructure Norway (CLARINO) Bergen Repository. http://hdl.handle.net/11509/124.

Volodina, Elena, Ildikó Pilán, Ingegerd Enström, Lorena Llozhi, Peter Lundkvist, Gunlög Sundberg & Monica Sandell. 2016. Swell on the rise: Swedish learner language corpus for european reference level studies. *International conference on language resources and evaluation (LREC)* 10, 206–212.

Vuolab, Kerttu. 2007. North Saami Corpus (Literature) (UHLCS). The Language Bank of Finland. http://urn.fi/urn:nbn:fi:lb-2014032620.

Wilkinson, Mark D., Michel Dumontier, IJsbrand Jan Aalbersberg, Gabrielle Appleton, Myles Axton, Arie Baak, Niklas Blomberg, Jan-Willem Boiten, Luiz Bonino da Silva Santos, Philip E. Bourne, Jildau Bouwman, Anthony J. Brookes et al. 2016. The fair guiding principles for scientific data management and stewardship. *Scientific Data*, vol. 3. http://doi.org/10.1038/sdata.2016.18.

Windouwer, Menzo & Twan Goosen. 2022. Component Metadata Infrastructure. In Darja Fišer & Andreas Witt (eds.), *Clarin. The infrastructure for language resources*. Berlin: De Gruyter.

Woliński, Marcin & Michał Lenart. 2016. Morfeusz 2. CLARIN-PL digital repository. http://hdl.handle.net/11321/257.

Żak, Paulina & Beata Skuczyńska. 2018. OptaHopper: phrase-level sentiment with opinion targets. CLARIN-PL digital repository. http://hdl.handle.net/11321/584.

Zeman, Daniel, Joakim Nivre, Mitchell Abrams, Elia Ackermann, Noëmi Aepli, Hamid Aghaei, Željko Agić, Amir Ahmadi, Lars Ahrenberg, Chika Kennedy Ajede, Gabrielė Aleksandravičiūtė, Ika Alfina, Lene Antonsen, Katya Aplonova, Angelina Aquino, Carolina Aragon, Maria Jesus Aranzabe, Bilge Nas Arıcan, Ĥórunn Arnardóttir, Gashaw Arutie et al. 2021. Universal Dependencies 2.9. LINDAT/CLARIAH-CZ digital library at the Institute of Formal and Applied Linguistics (ÚFAL), Faculty of Mathematics and Physics, Charles University. http://hdl.handle.net/11234/1-4611.

Zinn, Claus. 2018. The language resource switchboard. *Computational Linguistics* 44 (4): 631–639. http://doi.org/10.1162/coli_a_00329.

Zinn, Claus & Emanuel Dima. 2022. The CLARIN Language Resource Switchboard. In Darja Fišer & Andreas Witt (eds.), *CLARIN. The infrastructure for language resources*. Berlin: De Gruyter.

Zwitter Vitez, Ana, Jana Zemljarič Miklavčič, Simon Krek, Marko Stabej & Tomaž Erjavec. 2021. Spoken corpus Gos 1.1. Slovenian language resource repository CLARIN.SI. http://hdl.handle.net/11356/1438.

Ševčíková, Magda, Zdeněk Žabokrtský, Jana Straková & Milan Straka. 2014. Czech Named Entity Corpus 2.0. LINDAT/CLARIAH-CZ digital library at the Institute of Formal and Applied Linguistics (ÚFAL), Faculty of Mathematics and Physics, Charles University. http://hdl.handle.net/11858/00-097C-0000-0023-1B22-8.

Henk van den Heuvel, Nelleke Oostdijk, Caroline Rowland, and Paul Trilsbeek

The CLARIN Knowledge Centre for Atypical Communication Expertise

Abstract: In this chapter we introduce the CLARIN Knowledge Centre for Atypical Communication Expertise. The mission of ACE is to support researchers engaged in languages which pose particular challenges for analysis; for this, we use the umbrella term "atypical communication". This includes language use by second-language learners, people with language disorders or those suffering from language disabilities, and languages that pose unique challenges for analysis, such as sign languages and languages spoken in a multilingual context. The chapter presents details about the collaborations and outreach of the centre, the services offered, and a number of showcases for its activities.

Keywords: knowledge centre, atypical communication, sensitive data, data sharing solutions

1 Introduction

Over the past years the European Research Infrastructure for Language Resources and Technology (CLARIN; see clarin.eu) has taken shape (Hinrichs and Krauwer 2014; de Jong et al. 2018; Krauwer and Maegaard 2022). The infrastructure is directed towards researchers in the humanities and social sciences. It provides users with access to distributed data and tools through a single sign-on online environment (de Jong 2019). Apart from its technical infrastructure and accompa-

Acknowledgements: This publication was supported by CLARIN ERIC, and by the SSHOC Project (Grant Agreement 823782 under H2020).

Henk van den Heuvel, CLS/CLST, Radboud University, Nijmegen, the Netherlands, e-mail: henk.vandenheuvel@ru.nl
Nelleke Oostdijk, CLS/CLST, Radboud University, Nijmegen, the Netherlands, e-mail: nelleke.oostdijk@ru.nl
Caroline Rowland, Donders Institute for Brain, Cognition & Behaviour, Nijmegen & The Language Archive, MPI for Psycholinguistics, Nijmegen, the Netherlands, e-mail: caroline.rowland@mpi.nl
Paul Trilsbeek, The Language Archive, MPI for Psycholinguistics, Nijmegen, the Netherlands, e-mail: paul.trilsbeek@mpi.nl

https://doi.org/10.1515/9783110767377-014

nying protocols, CLARIN has been investing in what is referred to as the Knowledge Sharing Infrastructure (KSI).[1] The goal of the KSI is to share knowledge and expertise about the technical infrastructure, the way it operates, and how it can be used, between all stakeholders – from resource and technology providers to end users. In the CLARIN networked organizational structure, the Knowledge (K-)Centres play a central role in this. K-centres advise on issues pertaining to data collection and data management, provide information regarding available resources and services, where to find them, and how to access them, and provide support for various methodologies and applications. K-centres can also offer training courses in their respective fields of expertise.

At present there are over 20 certified K-centres.[2] One of the later additions is the K-centre for Atypical Communication Expertise[3] (ACE for short) which has been established at the Centre for Language and Speech Technology (CLST) at Radboud University.[4] The mission of ACE is to support researchers engaged in languages which pose particular challenges for analysis; for this, we use the umbrella term "atypical communication". This includes language use by second-language learners, people with language disorders or those suffering from language disabilities, and languages that pose unique challenges for analysis, such as sign languages and languages spoken in a multilingual context. It involves multiple modalities (text, speech, sign, gesture) and encompasses different developmental stages. The target audience for ACE includes linguists, psychologists, neuroscientists, computer scientists, speech and language therapists, and education specialists. A recent overview publication about the centre can be found in van den Heuvel, Oostdijk et al. (2020). This chapter is an extension of this publication, elaborating on latest developments.

In Section 2 we will address the collaborations in which the ACE centre is engaged. In Section 3 we highlight the services offered by the centre. Section 4 presents a number of resources as showcases for our work. In Section 5 we illustrate the potential of collaboration in making resources accessible via two CLARIN data centres. Finally, in Section 6 our outreach strategies are outlined.

1 https://www.clarin.eu/content/knowledge-infrastructure
2 https://www.clarin.eu/content/knowledge-centres
3 https://ace.ruhosting.nl/
4 https://www.ru.nl/clst/

2 Collaboration

Within Radboud University the Knowledge centre has CLST[5] as its core but it also has close links to researchers and research groups within the Centre for Language Studies,[6] with ample expertise in the fields of language acquisition,[7] language learning and therapy,[8] and sign language.[9]

Within CLARIN,[10] CLST has the status of C-centre and as such provides metadata to the infrastructure and enables access to tools and web applications through the Federated Identity services that CLARIN offers.

For hosting data and corpora for atypical communication and making these accessible in a FAIR manner, CLST has established a close collaboration with The Language Archive (TLA). TLA is situated at the Max Planck Institute for Psycholinguistics (MPI) in Nijmegen. As a CLARIN B-centre[11] the goal of TLA is to provide a unique record of how people around the world use language in everyday life. They focus on collecting spoken and signed language materials in audio and video form along with transcriptions, analyses, annotations, and other types of relevant material such as photos and accompanying notes. TLA offers storage of sensitive data (speech, audio, and transcripts) and supports the CMDI[12] metadata framework (see also Windhouwer and Goosen 2022). TLA also supports strong authentication procedures, layered access to data, and persistent identification.

For corpora of speech from people with language disorders the ACE centre works closely together with the DELAD initiative.[13] DELAD stands for Database Enterprise for Language And speech Disorders.[14] DELAD is an initiative for sharing corpora of speech of individuals with communication disorders (CSD) among researchers. This is done in a way that is compliant with EU's General Data Protection Regulation (GDPR),[15] at secure repositories in the CLARIN infrastructure (see also Kamocki, Kelli, and Lindén 2022). DELAD organizes workshops focusing on

---

5 https://www.ru.nl/clst/ and https://www.ru.nl/cls/our-research/research-groups/language-speech-technology/

6 https://www.ru.nl/cls/

7 https://www.ru.nl/cls/our-research/research-groups/first-language-acquisition/

8 https://www.ru.nl/cls/our-research/research-groups/language-speech-learning-therapy/

9 https://www.ru.nl/cls/our-research/research-groups/sign-language-linguistics/

10 https://www.clarin.eu/content/clarin-centres;
http://roadmap2018.esfri.eu/projects-and-landmarks/browse-the-catalogue/clarin-eric/

11 https://tla.mpi.nl/resources/

12 https://www.clarin.eu/content/component-metadata

13 http://delad.net/

14 It is also Swedish for "shared".

15 https://eur-lex.europa.eu/legal-content/EN/TXT/PDF/?uri=CELEX:32016R0679

how such corpora can be made shareable with other researchers. (For more information, see Lee et al. 2021). For CSD in particular, DELAD fosters a close collaboration through the ACE centre with CMU's TalkBank / Clinical banks.[16] Our collaboration allows for data to be registered at TalkBank and metadata and landing pages to be obtained at the TalkBank website, whereas the storage of data and the authentication of access to the "raw" data (typically audio and video data) is handled at TLA. Examples of such collaboration are presented in Section 5.

For granting access to sensitive data, the ACE centre is also involved in the SSHOC project,[17] in which one of the tasks is devoted to making an inventory of systems and technologies suitable for conduct research on sensitive data, such as video and audio recordings from data subjects with, for example, speech pathologies. This is relevant for offering various ways of accessing sensitive data stored at central repositories, where they can be downloaded, or at shielded repositories, where they can only be remotely accessed. It is essential for the latter option of remote secure access that the data does not leave a safeguarded place. A user cannot download the data but has to access a secure network where analysis of the data can take place, typically using tools available within the secure network. The user can only download analysis results, which may be subject to inspection by the network or data provider. In this way data leakage is avoided, as well as data corruption. This makes exploration of this type of access very relevant for the sensitive data the ACE centre is often dealing with. In Section 3 we will further address the challenges that the General Data Protection Regulation (GDPR) poses in sharing this type of sensitive data.

In 2021 a new collaboration in the area of sign language was set up with other CLARIN K-centres. This happened on the occasion of a K-centre meeting organized by CLARIN in late 2020. In this meeting it was concluded that eight K-centres were involved in the data collection and research on sign language. As a follow-up, these eight K-centres virtually convened a couple of times in 2021. In these meetings they exchanged information regarding the research topics and infrastructure area in which they were active. Further, the resources of each centre, as offered through CLARIN, were included in their websites, and this was the basis of further ideas for collaboration and proposals for funding. In 2021 this resulted in a Resource Family project for Sign Languages, funded by CLARIN-ERIC[18] and carried out by four of the K-centres specializing in sign languages, and supported by all (see also Lenardič and Fišer 2022). This project will be completed in 2022.

16 https://talkbank.org/
17 https://sshopencloud.eu/
18 https://www.clarin.eu/resource-families

3 Services offered

The mission of the ACE centre is to support researchers engaged in languages which pose particular challenges for collection, annotation and analysis, storage and sharing. This includes language use by second-language learners, people with language disorders or those suffering from language disabilities, and languages that pose unique challenges for analysis, such as sign languages and languages spoken in a multilingual context. It often involves multiple modalities (text, speech, sign, gesture) and encompasses different developmental stages.

Researchers working with these types of data face two particular challenges. First, such data often come with unique privacy and ethical challenges, and researchers need to take particular care to follow the strict rules and procedural requirements imposed by ethical committees and by governments or other relevant organizations. In the European Union, this includes the GDPR (see, for example, van den Heuvel, Kelli et al. 2020). At all stages appropriate measures must be in place to gain informed consent and to prevent unwanted disclosure.

For example, children and people with severe learning disabilities may not be able to give informed consent themselves for data collection and sharing, but rely on consent given by an advocate. In these cases, researchers may not wish to share data widely but to restrict access to registered users, even if the advocate has given consent for sharing (for example to restrict access those who have agreed in writing to keep the participants' identity anonymous and use the data only for academic purposes). With particularly sensitive data, or data in which participants have not given consent for sharing, the original non-anonymized data may need to remain stored in a dark archive, not to be copied or distributed in any form. Resource owners and users thus often need advice about how they can preserve sensitive data in a safe manner, from the point where the raw data came into existence up to the moment where the data and information obtained from it are shared with others.

Moreover, atypical communication data poses unique challenges when it comes to choosing tools and methods for annotation and analysis. Guidelines and tools that have been developed for "standard" data are often inappropriate or require adaptation. Researchers require information about the availability of relevant tools and guidelines such as those presented in Crasborn (2015).

The ACE centre provides the information and advice needed to meet these challenges in three ways. First, it provides advice on data collection and data management. This includes general advice available on the website about relevant issues (for instance, examples of GDPR-compliant consent forms), a helpdesk for specific questions, and individually tailored consultancy for larger projects. For example, the procedure of gaining consent for data collection, analysis, and sharing often requires particular attention when the data itself is very sensitive (for example, videotaped conversations with children with learning disabilities). In these cases, the procedure for gaining informed consent often requires carefully managed conversations as well as participant information sheets and consent forms written in clear, plain language. This ensures that the person giving consent is made fully aware of how the data may be shared and reused, and the manner in which it is kept secure and confidential. Such well-designed procedures not only protect the participants but also maximize the opportunity for data sharing since participants are often more willing to allow data sharing when they understand the conditions under which their data will be stored, protected, and reused.

Second, the ACE centre provides information about the methods and tools available for processing and using the data, and advice about which might best fit particular use cases. For example, the ELAN tool developed by the Language Archive team (ELAN 2020) is particularly well suited to the annotation of sign language data, since it is designed for use with video data, and has a flexible tier system that means that researchers can capture simultaneous face, hand, body, eye, and mouth movements (see for example, the corpus of Dutch Sign Language hosted at The Language Archive here[19]). For projects focussed on the acoustic properties of speech, the PRAAT annotation system may be more appropriate (Boersma and Weenink 2021), since it provides a suite of powerful tools for speech analysis, synthesis, manipulation, and labelling. For projects that require detailed morphosyntactic analysis, the CHILDES CLAN system (MacWhinney 2000) may be more suitable, since it contains an automatic morphosyntactic tagger for a number of languages (see, for example, the VALID collection of data on language impairments in Dutch here[20]). Note that many annotation systems are interoperable, meaning that one could, for example, annotate speech and gesture in ELAN and then convert the file to CLAN format for morphosyntactic tagging.

Third, the ACE centre provides advice on secure long-term data storage, including options for data sharing and the reuse of data. This includes technical assistance for designing, creating, annotating, formatting, and meta-dating, which is crucial because it can be very difficult to interpret, and navigate, unlabelled or badly labelled data collections. For this, the partnership with the archiving experts at The Language Archive is particularly useful. For example, TLA hosts

19 https://archive.mpi.nl/tla/islandora/object/tla%3A1839_00_0000_0000_0004_DF8E_6
20 https://archive.mpi.nl/tla/islandora/object/tla%3A1839_00_8C315BC1_AD5E_4348_9A79_A41FE3DE1150

on its website a number of screencasts providing advice about how to create data collections that are labelled and structured in such a way that it facilitates their reuse by other researchers, as well as a detailed deposit manual.[21] For researchers who are not collecting new data themselves but wish to reuse data, the ACE centre also provides information about where to find relevant corpora and datasets.

4 A collection of showcases

The website of ACE presents a number of showcases. We have already alluded to rich corpora of speech from children and adults with language disorders collected in the VALID project (Klatter et al. 2014) and stored at TLA. Within VALID, four existing digital datasets were curated in order to make them available for scientific research in CLARIN-compatible format. The datasets included are:

- SLI RU-Kentalis database, containing around 40 hours of audio and 150,000 transcribed words;
- Bilingual Deaf Children RU-Kentalis database, containing around 9 hours of video and 19,500 transcribed words;
- ADHD and SLI Corpus UvA database, containing around 26 hours of video and 23,000 transcribed words;
- Deaf Adults RU database, containing results of a writing task in ScriptLog format.

More information about these datasets can be found at VALID's web page,[22] which also contains a link to the persistent identifier of the curated datasets at TLA.[23]

Another showcase is the P-MoLL dataset,[24] which is accessible to all registered users of TLA. The project P-MoLL (Modalität von Lernervarietäten im Längsschnitt) was led by Prof. Norbert Dittmar at the Free University in Berlin from 1987 to 1992. It dealt with the study of the acquisition of modality in German as a second language by untutored adult immigrants with Polish or Italian as their native language. The longitudinal data collection covers about two and a half years of the learners' acquisition process. It contains their oral speech production from different elicitation tasks and free conversations with native speak-

21 https://archive.mpi.nl/forums/c/tla/archiving-info/9

22 https://validdata.org/clarin-project/datasets/

23 https://hdl.handle.net/1839/00-8C315BC1-AD5E-4348-9A79-A41FE3DE1150

24 https://hdl.handle.net/1839/00-0000-0000-0000-4EAB-A

ers and consists of approximately 100 hours of audio, 16 hours of video, and 520,000 transcribed words (Dittmar et al. 1990).

Another example of a well-documented dataset on second-language learning is the LESLLA corpus. LESLLA stands for Literacy Education and Second Language Learning for Adults.[25] The corpus contains speech data of 15 low-educated learners of Dutch as a second language. All of them are women; eight are Turkish, seven Moroccan. (Turks and Moroccans are the two largest immigrant groups in the Netherlands.) At the time of the recordings, they were between 22 and 45 years old. Participants had to carry out five tasks, which all involved spoken language but varied from strictly controlled to semi-spontaneous. In total, the corpus contains around 30 hours of audio and about 180,000 transcribed words. An extensive description of the curated corpus can be found in Sanders, van de Craats et al. (2014). This corpus is also accessible at TLA.[26]

The LeaP (Learning Prosody in a Foreign Language) corpus[27] (Gut 2012) was collected with the goal of studying the acquisition of prosody by non-native speakers of German and English. The German and English parts of the corpus contain audio recordings of 62 and 50 different speakers, respectively, with a wide variety of native languages. The audio recordings (over 12 hours in total) have been transcribed and annotated by hand, resulting in approximately 72,000 transcribed and annotated words. Part-of-speech tagging and lemmatization were carried out automatically. A detailed description of the corpus can be found in the manual that is included.

The Dutch Bilingual Database[28] (Muysken et al. 2008) is another rather substantial collection of data fitting within the scope of ACE and hosted at TLA. It results from a number of projects and research programmes that were directed at investigating multilingualism and comprises data originating from Dutch, Sranan, Sarnami, Papiamentu, Arabic, Berber, and Turkish speakers. In total, it contains over 500 hours of audio recordings, 10 hours of video recordings, and approximately 615,000 transcribed words. It is accessible to any academic user.

Further, TLA also hosts a wealth of sign language corpora. Many of these are carefully annotated using the ELAN annotation software.[29] The Corpus NGT (Nederlandse Gebarentaal / Dutch Sign Language;[30,31] see Crasborn and Zwitser-

25 https://www.leslla.org/
26 https://hdl.handle.net/1839/00-37EBCC6D-04A5-4598-88E2-E0F390D5FCE1
27 https://hdl.handle.net/1839/00-0000-0000-000A-3D5E-1
28 https://hdl.handle.net/1839/00-0000-0000-0001-4AF0-7
29 https://tla.mpi.nl/tools/tla-tools/elan/
30 https://hdl.handle.net/1839/00-0000-0000-0004-DF8E-6
31 https://www.ru.nl/corpusngtuk/

lood 2008; Crasborn, Zwitserlood, and Ros 2008) is a highly systematically collected dataset of 92 signers of Dutch Sign Language. It contains over 72 hours of dialogues recorded on video from different angles, using a variety of tasks and genres. A significant part of the recordings has been manually annotated using ELAN, with approximately 200,000 annotation tokens in the latest version. Most of the corpus is freely accessible.

Note that many of the language datasets that come under the scope of the ACE centre are not datasets of atypical communication systems. For example, sign languages are not atypical forms of communication. They are mature, complex languages that evolved spontaneously in deaf communities in the same way that spoken languages evolved in hearing communities. However, the collection, analysis, and storage of sign language data poses particular challenges that are often not addressed by standard systems and tools. Thus, the ACE centre also provides resources to support researchers working with sign languages.

5 Exploiting collaborative potential

In this section we address corpora that are made accessible by exploiting the potential of the collaborations in the ACE centre. In Section 2 we mentioned our collaboration with CMU's TalkBank. As a use case for the curation of a dataset, registering it at the TalkBank and storing the primary data (only) at TLA, we processed the Polish Cued Speech Corpus of Hearing-Impaired Children. The corpus contains legacy data of 20 hearing impaired children aged between 8 and 12 years (11 girls and 9 boys) and was kindly provided by Anita Trochimyuk-Lorenc and Katarzyna Klessa from the University of Warsaw (Institute of Applied Polish Studies). The corpus is described in Trochymiuk (2003, 2005). The curation of this dataset involved the creation of CMDI metadata records as well as the creation of a script for normalizing filenames and for converting the text files into CHAT format – including the required metadata headers that could partially be derived from the filenames. A landing page for this collection has been created at TalkBank.[32] The CHAT transcripts have been added to the TalkBank database, and the Handle persistent identifier for the collection containing the audio files in The Language Archive[33] has been added to the landing page, such that users will be able to download them there. Thus, we have created a situation where the corpus can be found via the TalkBank (which is a popular repository for research-

32 https://phonbank.talkbank.org/access/Clinical/PCSC.html
33 https://hdl.handle.net/1839/77ea572d-f4c4-48d8-b67b-956f946b59c5

ers of second-language acquisition and special language impairments) whereas the sensitive audio data is on European servers with the appropriate protection measures and licensing arrangements.

Since the structures and systems of the TalkBank and TLA repositories differ quite significantly, a script was created to extract specific file types from collections in the Fedora Commons repository system at TLA and to put those into a structure that can be easily ingested into the TalkBank repository. The script also transforms TLA's metadata into TalkBank metadata, which is relatively straightforward as both are based on the IMDI[34] metadata schema.

A second use case is the archiving of a collection of materials related to the Arezzo neuropsychiatric hospital. This collection consists of recordings and transcripts of interviews by historian Anna Maria Bruzzone with patients of the hospital in the 1970s, as well as a diary written by a patient with schizophrenia from the same hospital. Many of the interviews have been published (Bruzzone 2021). However, the corresponding audio recordings are currently not accessible through an archive. While most patients have passed away now and therefore may technically not be protected under the GDPR, the recordings should be handled with care and with consideration for the patients' relatives. The archiving of this collection is still in the early stages, where the researchers from the University of Siena, which inherited the collection, are determining which parts can be shared anonymously and which parts need more restricted access policies (Nodari, Calamai, and van den Heuvel 2021). A dynamic process is foreseen in which material flagged as not accessible can be released once the required consent is obtained. Moreover, Calamai and colleagues are preparing a fine-grained metadata profile for these recordings, which will be an important additional feature of this collection. As with the Polish Cued Speech Corpus of Hearing-Impaired Children, we will create a landing page at TalkBank and store derived data such as transcriptions there, whereas the original audio recordings will be stored on the servers of the TLA.

6 Reaching out

The target audience for the ACE centre encompasses anyone working with datasets that pose particular challenges for research on language and communication. The audience thus includes linguists, psychologists, neuroscientists, computer scientists, speech and language therapists, and education specialists. The ACE centre provides online resources via its website, a helpdesk for specific ques-

34 https://tla.mpi.nl/imdi-metadata/

tions, and a bespoke consultancy service for researchers who need more individualized advice.

The focus of ACE's outreach programme is its website, https://ace.ruhosting.nl/, where all information is made available, including links to relevant resources hosted on other sites, such as The Language Archive and TalkBank. However, its services are publicized in a variety of other ways. Its launch in December 2019 was announced via a press release published on both the Radboud University and Max Planck Institute websites. Centre personnel are now disseminating further information and advice via invited presentations and at workshops, as well as via webinars and screencasts published on the website (see Draxler et al. 2022).

A first workshop was held as a webinar and was organized under the auspices of the SSHOC project, due to its close links with a task about secure access to sensitive data in that project. The webinar was held on 14 October 2020 with the title *Sharing Datasets of Pathological Speech*.[35] In this webinar the following topics were addressed:

- progress achieved by the DELAD initiative for sharing corpora of speech disorders (CSD) and the role of the ACE centre;
- GDPR and the ethics of special category data relevant for collecting and sharing CSD;
- how storing and sharing CSD is arranged in a GDPR-compliant way at the Language Archive of the Max Plank Institute for Psycholinguistics and the collaboration with the TalkBank at CMU;
- infrastructure requirements for secure remote access to sensitive research data with diverse legal (for example, social media terms of service), ethical (for instance, children as subjects), and technical (typically audio and video) challenges, and assessment of several existing platforms;
- the CAVA audio-visual human communication archive project – a digital video repository to support the work of the international human communication research community, which enhances the discoverability and reusability of expensively created specialist video content;
- the curation and disclosure of pathological speech corpora: how CSD can be found through one organization and made accessible through another; this includes a demonstration using the example of the Polish Cued Speech Corpus of Hearing-Impaired Children, as discussed above.

35 https://www.sshopencloud.eu/sshoc-webinar-sharing-datasets-pathological-speech

The webinar has been recorded and published on YouTube.[36] The slides are available on Zenodo.[37] A report in the form of webinar notes is available via the Social Sciences and Humanities Open Cloud.[38]

On 27 and 28 January 2021 DELAD organized a workshop entitled *How to Share Your Data in a GDPR-Compliant Way.* In this workshop, a number of researchers presented the corpora they collected and the research carried out with them. The central question here was how the data were or could be shared with other researchers. Further presentations addressed:

- the potential of the ACE centre for hosting CSD of DELAD members;
- exchanging deeper insights on Data Protection Impact Assessments (DPIAs), including role play;
- presenting and discussing voice conversion as a means to pseudonymize speech.

The DPIA and role play was led by a member of CLARIN's Committee for Legal and IPR issues (CLIC).[39] A report on the workshop was published by CLARIN[40] and all materials are available via Zenodo.[41] An educational version of the DPIA role play was recorded, published, and presented at the CLARIN Annual Conference 2021.[42]

The ACE centre was also featured at the TOK day in Nijmegen in December, 2021 (the annual meeting of the TaalOntwikkeling van Kinderen network of researchers and speech and language therapists from the Netherlands and Belgium). Printed materials such as posters, leaflets, and a one-page briefing document will be created ready for dissemination when in-person events resume after the Covid-19 pandemic.

36 https://www.youtube.com/watch?v=qjTJ4ZxzfvI
37 https://zenodo.org/record/4081602#.X42YC9Azba8
38 https://www.sshopencloud.eu/news/webinar-notes-sharing-datasets-pathological-speech
39 The roleplay can be found at https://sites.google.com/rug.nl/privacy-in-research/cases
40 https://www.clarin.eu/blog/outcomes-fifth-delad-workshop
41 https://zenodo.org/record/4560478#.YEeAEJ1Ki71
42 All materials can be found via this link: https://delad.ruhosting.nl/wordpress/dpia-role-play-with-video/

Bibliography

Broersma, Paul & David Weenink. 2021. *Praat: doing phonetics by computer* [Computer program]. Version 6.1.41. http://www.praat.org/ (accessed 25 March 2021).

Bruzzone, Anna Maria. 2021. *Ci chiamavano matti. Voci dal manicomio (1968–1977)*. Milan: Il Saggiatore.

Crasborn, Onno 2015. Transcription and notation methods. In Eleni Orfanidou, Bencie Woll, & Gary Morgan (eds.), *Research methods in sign language studies: A practical guide*, 74–88. Chichester: John Wiley & Sons.

Crasborn, Onno & Inge Zwitserlood. 2008. The Corpus NGT: An online corpus for professionals and laymen. In Onno Crasborn, Thomas Hanke, Eleni Efthimiou, Inge Zwitserlood & Ernst Thoutenhoofd (eds.), *Proceedings of the 3rd Workshop on the Representation and Processing of Sign Languages: Construction and exploitation of sign language corpora*, 44–49. Paris: ELRA.

Crasborn, Onno, Inge Zwitserlood & Johan Ros. 2008. The Corpus NGT. A digital open access corpus of movies and annotations of sign language of the Netherlands. Centre for Language Studies, Radboud Universiteit Nijmegen. ISLRN175-346-174-413-3.https://hdl.handle.net/hdl:1839/00-0000-0000-0004-DF8E-6

Dittmar, Norbert, Astrid Reich, Romuald Skiba, Magdalena Schumacher & Heiner Terborg. 1990. Die Erlernung modaler Konzepte des Deutschen durch erwachsene polnische Migranten: Eine empirische Längsschnittstudie. *Informationen Deutsch als Fremdsprache: Info DaF* 17 (2). 125–172.

Dittmar, Norbert, Astrid Reich, Romuald Skiba, Magdalena Schumacher & Heiner Terborg. 2002. The P-MoLL Corpus. https://hdl.handle.net/1839/00-0000-0000-0000-4EAB-A

Draxler, Christoph, Alexander Geyken, Erhard Hinrichs, Annette Klosa-Kückelhaus, Elke Teich & Thorsten Trippel. 2022. How to connect language resources, infrastructures, and communities. In Darja Fišer & Andreas Witt (eds.), *CLARIN. The infrastructure for language resources*. Berlin: deGruyter.

ELAN (Version 6.0) [Computer software]. 2020. Nijmegen: Max Planck Institute for Psycholinguistics, The Language Archive. Retrieved from https://archive.mpi.nl/tla/elan

Emmerik. Joanne van. 2014. Deaf Adults RU Database. ISLRN 944-022-313-325-3. https://hdl.handle.net/1839/00-97AF29EA-877D-422A-BAF7-25FA269351A6

Gut, Ulrike. 2009. LeaP Corpus. https://hdl.handle.net/1839/00-0000-0000-000A-3D5E-1

Gut, Ulrike. 2012. The LeaP corpus. A multilingual corpus of spoken learner German and learner English. In Thomas Schmidt and Kai Wörner (eds.), *Multilingual corpora and multilingual corpus analysis*, 3–23. Amsterdam: John Benjamins.

Heuvel, Henk van den, Nelleke Oostdijk, Caroline Rowland & Paul Trilsbeek. 2020. The CLARIN knowledge centre for atypical communication expertise. *International Conference on Language Resources and Evaluation (LREC)* 12. 3312–3316.

Heuvel, Henk van den, Aleksei Kelli, Katarzyna Klessa & Satu Salaasti. 2020. Corpora of disordered speech in the light of the GDPR: Two use cases from the DELAD initiative. *International Conference on Language Resources and Evaluation (LREC)* 12. 3317–3321.

Hinrichs, Erhard & Steven Krauwer. 2014. The CLARIN research infrastructure: Resources and tools for ehumanities scholars. *International Conference on Language Resources and Evaluation (LREC)* 9. 1525–1531.

Jong, Franciska de. 2019. CLARIN: Infrastructural support for impact through the study of language as social and cultural data. In Bente Maegaard, Riccardo Pozzo, Alberto Melloni and Matthew Woollard (eds). *Stay tuned to the future: Impact of the research infrastructures for social sciences and humanities* (Lessico intellettuale Europeo 128), 121–129. Rome: Leo Olschki.

Jong, Franciska de, Bente Maegaard, Koenraad De Smedt, Darja Fišer & Dieter Van Uytvanck. 2018. CLARIN: Towards FAIR and responsible data science using language resources. *International Conference on Language Resources and Evaluation (LREC)* 11. 3259–3264.

Kamocki, Paweł, Aleksei Kelli & Krister Lindén. 2022. The CLARIN Committee for Legal and Ethical Issues and the Normative Layer of the CLARIN infrastructure. In Darja Fišer & Andreas Witt (eds.), *CLARIN. The infrastructure for language resources*. Berlin: deGruyter.

Klatter, Jetske, Roeland van Hout, Henk van den Heuvel, Paula Fikkert, Anne Baker, Jan de Jong, Frank Wijnen, Eric Sanders & Paul Trilsbeek. 2014. Vulnerability in acquisition, language impairments in Dutch: Creating a VALID data archive. *International Conference on Language Resources and Evaluation (LREC)* 9. 356–364

Kolen, Esther. 2014. Bilingual Deaf Children RU-Kentalis Database. ISLRN 941-351-623-486-4. https://hdl.handle.net/1839/00-F6BC06C4-B2AD-4ED8-8527-AB81F4EF4E8F

Krauwer, Steven & Bente Maegaard. 2022. CLARIN – how it started. In Darja Fišer & Andreas Witt (eds.), *CLARIN. The infrastructure for language resources*. Berlin: deGruyter.

Lee, Alice, Nicola Bessell, Henk van den Heuvel, Satu Saalasti, Katarzyna Klessa, Nicole Müller & Martin J. Ball. 2021. The latest development of the DELAD project for sharing corpora of disordered speech. *Clinical Linguistics & Phonetics*. https://doi.org/10.1080/02699206.2021.1913514

Lenardič, Jakob & Darja Fišer. 2022. The CLARIN Resource and Tool Families. In Darja Fišer & Andreas Witt (eds.), *CLARIN. The infrastructure for language resources*. Berlin: deGruyter.

Lorenc, Anita. 2019. Polish Cued Speech Corpus of Hearing-Impaired Children. https://hdl.handle.net/1839/77ea572d-f4c4-48d8-b67b-956f946b59c5

MacWhinney, Brian. 2000. *The CHILDES Project: Tools for analyzing talk*, 3rd edn. Mahwah, NJ: Lawrence Erlbaum Associates.

Made, Annika van der. 2014. SLI RU-Kentalis Database. ISLRN 541-534-411-504-6. https://hdl.handle.net/1839/00-712802F3-C245-4EF0-BE9D-D09714DEDE67

Muysken, Pieter, et al. 2008. Dutch Bilingual Database. https://hdl.handle.net/1839/00-0000-0000-0001-4AF0-7

Nodari, Rosalba, Silvia Calamai & Henk van den Heuvel. 2021. Less is more when FAIR. The Minimum Level of Description in Pathological Oral and Written Data. In Monica Monachini & Maria Eskevich (eds.), *CLARIN Annual Conference Proceedings, 2021*, 166–171. Virtual edition.

Parigger, Esther. 2014. ADHD and SLI Corpus UvA database. ISLRN 456-360-189-350-0. https://hdl.handle.net/1839/00-2766F32F-4305-4F13-A02C-F4A8F5216425

Sanders, Eric, Ineke van de Craats & Vanja de Lint. 2014. The curated Dutch LESLLA corpus. https://hdl.handle.net/1839/00-37EBCC6D-04A5-4598-88E2-E0F390D5FCE1

Trochymiuk, Anita. 2003. Voiced realisations of plosives in word initial position by hearing impaired children: Acoustic phonetics analysis. In Katharina Böttger, Sabine Dönninghaus & Robert Marzari (eds.), *Die Welt der Slaven*. Vol. 16 (Beiträge der Europäischen Slavistischen Linguistic 6). 111–123. Munich: Sagner.

Trochymiuk Anita. 2005. Realization of the voiced-voiceless contrast by hearing impaired children. *Studia Phonetica Posnaniensia* 7. 75–96.

Sanders, Eric, Ineke van de Craats & Vanja de Lint. 2014. The Dutch LESLLA corpus. *International Conference on Language Resources and Evaluation (LREC)* 9. 2715–2718.

Windhouwer, Menzo & Twan Goosen. 2022. Component Metadata Infrastructure. In Darja Fišer & Andreas Witt (eds.), *CLARIN. The infrastructure for language resources*. Berlin: deGruyter.

Tanja Wissik, Leon Wessels, and Frank Fischer

The DH Course Registry: A Piece of the Puzzle in CLARIN's Technical and Knowledge Infrastructure

Abstract: This chapter presents the Digital Humanities Course Registry (DHCR) as part of CLARIN's Technical and Knowledge Infrastructure. The DHCR is an initiative started to provide an overview of the growing number of training activities in the field of Digital Humanities around the world. The goal of the registry, which is run jointly with DARIAH, is to collect information on the rich offerings of different courses with the help of the community and to delineate an up-to-date picture of the teaching and training opportunities in the field. First, we will introduce the DHCR, its goals, genesis, and main features. Then we will elaborate on the DHCR's position within CLARIN's Technical Infrastructure and how it helps to address CLARIN's agenda and strategic goals in terms of Technical Infrastructure, Open Science, and especially the FAIR Principles. Particular attention will be paid to the results of a cross-national hackathon using data and metadata from the DHCR. Furthermore, we will examine the position of the DHCR within CLARIN's Knowledge Infrastructure, which includes training and education.

Keywords: Training and Education, DH Course Registry, community-driven platform, API, Knowledge Infrastructure

1 Introduction to the DHCR

It is part of the grassroots history of the Digital Humanities (DH) that the first courses, workshops, and hackathons had to be organized outside established academic teaching formats because there was simply no place for them in the curriculum of higher education yet. Since information on offered courses was scattered across the internet, it soon became difficult to keep sight of the overall picture.

Tanja Wissik, Austrian Academy of Sciences, Vienna, Austria, e-mail: tanja.wissik@oeaw.ac.at
Leon Wessels, CLARIN ERIC and Utrecht University, Utrecht, the Netherlands, e-mail: leon@clarin.eu
Frank Fischer, Freie Universität Berlin, EXC 2020 Temporal Communities, Berlin, Germany, e-mail: fr.fischer@fu-berlin.de

https://doi.org/10.1515/9783110767377-015

To increase visibility, the Digital Humanities Course Registry (DHCR), originally a German initiative, was founded. As early as 2011, Manfred Thaller and Patrick Sahle published a list of courses related to digital methods in the Humanities (Sahle, Puhle, and Rau 2011). Gradually, this community-driven information collection has been internationalized and supplemented by an interactive map of Europe (and eventually, since 2018, a world map) showing the various locations of institutions offering DH-relevant courses (Figure 1).

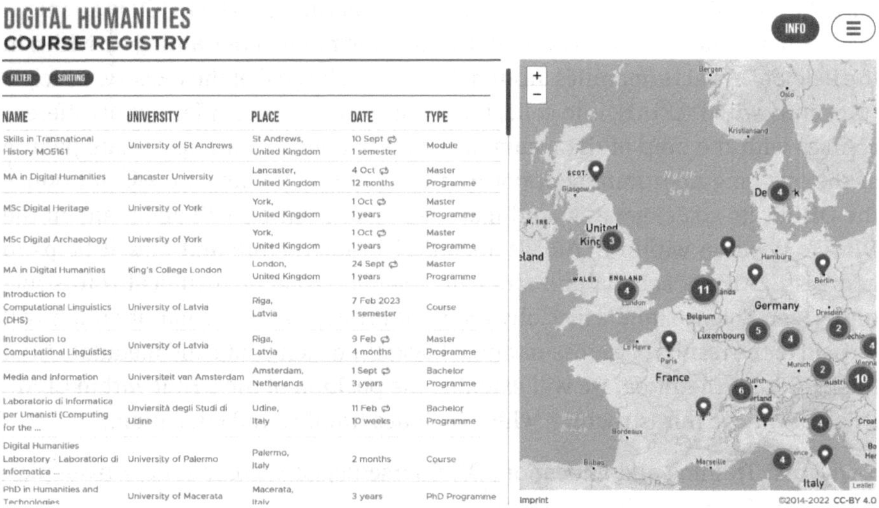

Figure 1: DH Course Registry list and map view.

The revamp of the frontend in 2019 also included a technical change, the introduction of the API (Application Programming Interface), which is the prerequisite for a truly community-driven initiative and for versatile access to the data.

Many DH courses are now firmly established at universities and other institutions (for specific examples of courses and training events from South Africa and Lithuania, see Hennelly et al. (2022) and Petrauskaitė et al. (2022)). The formats covered include Bachelor, Master, and PhD courses with different focuses, as well as summer schools and workshop series. Courses can be held in-person or online and have to be recurring to be featured in the registry. We are especially targeting the following groups with the DHCR (cf. Wissik, Edmond, Fischer, et al. 2020):

- students (who want to join a university programme in Digital Humanities or related fields or want to find an opportunity for student exchange);
- lecturers (who wish to promote their teaching activities);

- programme administrators (who wish to promote and facilitate student and staff exchanges);
- researchers (who are interested in the proliferation of DH education);
- decision makers (who need quantitative evidence to drive funding for DH activities).

Since 2016, the DHCR has been jointly operated by the two infrastructures CLARIN and DARIAH. This solution guarantees the necessary stability, as it is a big challenge to keep a globally active and growing community-driven initiative like this alive, both technically and socially. This cannot be mastered by temporary research or infrastructure projects with a national or regional scope. Data curation within the DHCR follows a community-driven approach. The DARIAH working group "DH Course Registry" plays a key role,[1] taking care of the coordination, user administration and technical maintenance of the registry. Lecturers can upload their own courses, but there is also a group of national moderators mainly responsible for content maintenance and consistency; they are joined by volunteers from the CLARIN and DARIAH communities. For each country represented in the course registry, a national moderator is appointed (sometimes more than one for bigger countries) to monitor, curate, and update the database entries. To support this, the system also sends notifications – for example, when a new course has been submitted or when information is out of date – whereupon the owner of a record (the course maintainer) can be contacted to update an entry. Course metadata is collected in English. The TaDiRAH taxonomy, another DH community-driven project, is also used (Borek et al. 2016). Its integration makes it possible to search the course data for specific activities, objects, and techniques. The proof of the relevance and success of the course register is, of course, in its use and up-to-dateness. As of April 2021, the DH Course Registry contains 234 active courses and programmes in 29 countries. The collaborative collection of information is valuable both for individuals seeking to find or promote DH training opportunities and for those seeking to understand the evolution of DH over time and on an international scale. The rich data contained in the DHCR is now also explorable through an open API, a facility that makes the inherent knowledge of the database more accessible, as the following chapters will show. The remainder of this chapter is structured as follows: in Section 2 we will elaborate on the position of the DHCR within CLARIN's Technical Infrastructure and on how the DHCR addresses CLARIN's strategic goals, again in terms of Technical Infrastructure. In Section 3 we will discuss how the DHCR aligns with CLARIN's Knowledge Infrastructure.

1 See https://www.dariah.eu/activities/working-groups/dh-course-registry/

2 DHCR as part of CLARIN's Technical Infrastructure

Since 2016 the DH Course Registry, as a joint initiative from the research infrastructures CLARIN and DARIAH, has been part of the CLARIN ecosystem and Technical Infrastructure. CLARIN's mission is to create and maintain an infrastructure to support the sharing, use, and sustainable availability of language data and tools for research in the humanities and social sciences (SSH) (cf. de Jong et al. 2020). Over the last few years, CLARIN has fulfilled its mission by creating "a sound and robust technical basis to enable the sharing and reuse of language data and tools across institutional, disciplinary and international borders" (CLARIN ERIC Strategy 2021–2023). Part of the CLARIN strategic goals in terms of Technical Infrastructure are the FAIR Principles (findability, accessibility, interoperability, and reusability) and the initiative "CLARIN for Programmers". In this section we will elaborate on the position of the DHCR within CLARIN's Technical Infrastructure and on how the DHCR addresses CLARIN's strategic goals in terms of technical infrastructure. Furthermore, we will discuss how various initiatives (e.g., provision of an API and organization of hackathons) contribute to the fact that the DHCR is not only a community-driven initiative when it comes to data collection, as described in Section 1, but also when it comes to data use and functionality improvement.

2.1 Open Science and FAIR Principles

One of the strategic goals of CLARIN in terms of Technical Infrastructure is to support the Open Science and FAIR Principles agenda. CLARIN has taken a leading role in the Open Science and FAIR agendas (cf. Rossi et al. 2020) as an early adopter of the FAIR Principles (de Jong et al. 2018). For example, all the design decisions of all data services are guided by the FAIR Principles (CLARIN ERIC Strategy 2021–2023, de Jong et al. 2018). Furthermore, CLARIN has a well-defined access policy and policies for data protection, as well as a template for Terms of Service (cf. Rossi et al. 2020).

Regarding two of the principles – interoperability and reusability – APIs can play an important role. APIs are services that allow direct and structured access to data, without having to download entire data sets. In Section 2.3 we describe the API of the DH Course Registry and illustrate how it contributes to the Open Science and FAIR agenda and the CLARIN ERIC Strategy.

2.2 "CLARIN for Programmers"

Another strategic goal in terms of Technical Infrastructure is to disseminate Natural Language Processing services more prominently to programming scientists, for example, with well-documented application programming interfaces and example snippets in popular development environments (CLARIN ERIC Strategy 2021–2023). In order to reach this goal, the initiative "CLARIN for Programmers" was created. As a study by Edmond and Garnett (2015) found that researchers "only cared about the data, and had no specific opinions about how that data was accessed and no particular need for some of the special functionality an API could offer", it makes sense to promote APIs especially to programmers or programming scientists. We will show in Sections 2.4 and 2.5 how, for example, the ACDH-CH virtual hackathon series – a CLARIAH-AT initiative[2] – and its outcomes helped to support the CLARIN ERIC Strategy in relation to the Open Data agenda (Hannesschläger and Wissik 2020) and in terms of "CLARIN for Programmers". In addition, it helped to improve the infrastructure.

2.3 DHCR API

Until 2019 the course data in the DH Course Registry – e.g., name of the course, name of the institution offering the course (see also Figure 2 for the data model) – was only accessible via the search interface and it was not possible to download the data. In addition, only recent data was visible on the platform; the historical records were hidden in the backend and not publicly accessible. The solution to this problem was the implementation of an Application Programming Interface (API) in the framework of the DH Course Registry Sustain Project.[3] As noted by Tasovac et al. (2016), APIs have the potential to be "powerful, practical building blocks of digital humanities infrastructures. On the technical level, they let heterogeneous agents dynamically access and reuse the same sets of data and standardized workflows. On the social level, they help overcome the problem of 'shy

2 CLARIAH-AT is the national counterpart of CLARIN and DARIAH in Austria. See https://digital-humanities.at/en/dha/clariah-at

3 Within the DHCR Sustain Project (https://www.oeaw.ac.at/acdh/projects/dhcr-sustain/), funded within the DARIAH Theme funding call 2018/2019, the API and its documentation was improved. The general technical development work and maintenance was funded by PARTHENOS (H2020 Grant Agreement n. 654119) and CLARIN-ERIC. The API can be accessed here https://dhcr.clarin-dariah.eu/api/v1/ and the documentation is available here https://app.swaggerhub.com/apis/hashmich/DHCR-API/1.2

data', i.e., data you can 'meet in public places but you can't take home with you' (Cooper 2010)." The DH Course Registry provides a public JSON data API for data export, custom analysis visualizations, and so on. Since one of the main purposes is the export of data, the following explains the data model behind the DH Course Registry, which revolves around courses as key entities (Figure 2). All metadata related to the courses can be grouped into two types of metadata: metadata related to the course content (education type, education parent type, language, modality, recurrence, disciplines, objects, and techniques) and metadata related to the provider of the courses (institutions, cities, countries). For education types, we have elaborated our own classification: Bachelor Programme, Master Programme, Research Master, and PhD Programme as whole degree programmes offered at higher education institutions; modules and courses as part of degree programmes; and summer schools and continuous education as education activities outside of degree programmes (cf. Wissik, Edmond, Fischer, et al. 2020). For modalities, we have online or on-site training activities and for recurrence, there is the choice between training activities that occur once (e.g., a specific course that is only offered for one semester) or training activities that are recurring, such as Bachelor Programmes.

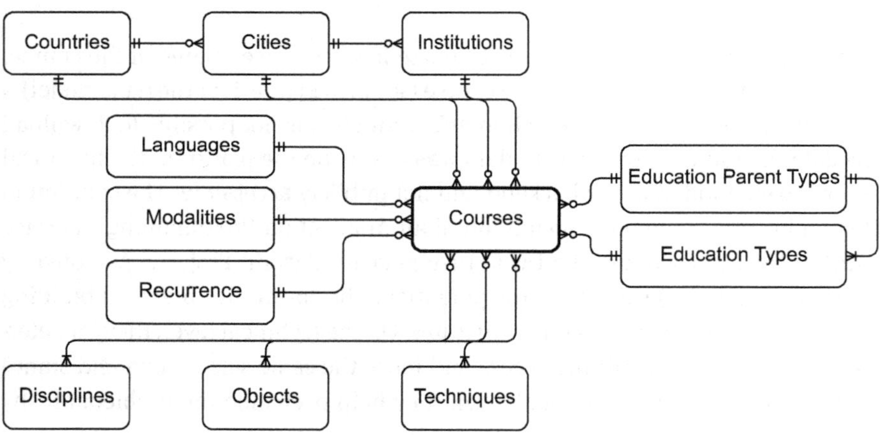

Figure 2: DH Course Registry Data Model (Adapted from Wissik, Edmond, Fischer, et al. 2020).

The entities, objects, and techniques come from the TaDiRAH Taxonomy (Borek et al. 2016) and the disciplines are based on the disciplinary categorization as applied by the Dutch Scientific Council for Academic Research (NWO) or NARCIS (Safradin and de Jong 2017), respectively, but have been modified and enriched based on the needs of the growing DH Course Registry (cf. Wissik, Edmond, Fischer, et al. 2020). Figure 2 shows the data model of the DH Course Registry.

2.4 ACDH-CH Virtual Hackathon Series

The Open Data movement is not only gaining momentum in the context of the Digital Humanities, but also in other research areas. As we saw in Section 2.1, CLARIN ERIC supports the Open Science agenda and FAIR Principles, and the same can be said for the Austrian manifestation of CLARIN and DARIAH, CLARIAH-AT. One of the fundamental concepts and principles of Open Science is Open Data. Therefore, in early 2019, CLARIAH-AT funded an initiative launched by the Austrian Centre for Digital Humanities and Cultural Heritage (ACDH-CH) of the Austrian Academy of Sciences: a virtual hackathon series to promote Open data. These virtual hackathons focused on different Open Data sets that are publicly available online, and the tasks to be performed on these data included the creation of open-source code. Typically, hackathons take place on-site, where participants have to solve tasks within a short period of time. This requires programmers to be flexible, available, and willing to travel. A virtual hackathon, on the other hand, offers people around the globe the opportunity to participate and contribute without having to travel. Moreover, by setting a longer timeframe (in this case two to four weeks, depending on the hack), people with fixed time schedules could also participate. Therefore, our approach enabled a much larger and more diverse community to participate while also promoting the benefits of Open Data (cf. Hannesschläger and Wissik 2020). In the virtual hackathon series, the ACDH-CH organized four hacks over the course of 2019 and 2020. In 2020 the chosen data set was the data and metadata from the DH Course Registry, not only to promote Open Data but also to point programming scientists in the direction of the API. The task for the DH Course Registry hack was to develop a creative way of visualizing data and metadata about teaching activities. It was possible to visualize the data itself or the results of statistical analysis with the data. Participants were free to choose the visualization method, except for the map-based visualization, as this visualization is already implemented in the official DH Course Registry.[4] The best contributions were selected by an international jury. The judging criteria were creativity and innovation, accessibility, reusability, and reproducibility, as well as elegance (cf. Hannesschläger and Wissik 2020). The winners received cash prizes and were published on GitHub[5] and shared via Twitter. In the following, we will present the outcomes of the ACDH-CH Hackathon and discuss how they contributed to the improvement of the DHCR.

4 https://github.com/acdh-oeaw/ACDHchHackathon2020/blob/master/README.md
5 https://github.com/acdh-oeaw/ACDHchHackathon2020/blob/master/results.md

2.5 Outcomes of the ACDH-CH Hackathon

Since for the virtual hackathon task there were no strict requirements, it is not surprising that the winning projects[6] took very different approaches. The Notlef Project by Philip Allfrey was the only submission that worked only with the data provided via the DH Course Registry API. The DH Education Knowledge Map project by Marta Palandri and Raphael Mitsch enriched the DH Course Registry data with Wikipedia data. The ACDH-2020 project by Francesca Giovannetti, Ivan Heibi, and Bruno Sartini used the DH Course Registry data as starting point and enriched it with DH-related publication data from Crossref and Microsoft Academic. And the CORIANDER (COurse RegIstry stAtistics aNd aDditional matERial) project by Martina Trognitz and Lukas Gehrig enriched the DH Course Registry data with data from a Zotero bibliography, which also used the TaDiRAH taxonomy. In the following, we will describe the ACDH-CH Hackathon outcomes and the winning projects in more detail.

The CORIANDER project (Tognitz and Gehrig 2020) added further functionalities to the DH Course Registry in order to visually explore the metadata categories disciplines, TaDiRAH objects, and TaDiRAH techniques further; in the original platform these are only used as filter options. It is browser-based, using HTML, CSS, and JavaScript as well as common JavaScript libraries for visualization. Python3 is used for data processing. The prototype application[7] has two main visualization modes for the data, organized by courses or keywords. In the course view, the courses can be explored by keywords (i.e., discipline, TaDiRAH objects and TaDiRAH techniques, countries and years) which are then visualized in a bar chart. For each individual course, additional literature (from Zotero and Wikidata) is accessed by clicking on the respective course. In the keyword mode, the co-occurrence of keywords can be explored (see Figure 3).

In the DH Education Knowledge Map project (Palandri and Mitsch 2020), the DH Course Registry Data was not seen as a "set amount of information but a starting point for the creation of a web of knowledge that can help us make unexpected connections" (Palandri 2020). For this purpose, a layer of wikification was added on top of the given data set via Wikipedia's API. The application was developed with Dash, a Python framework for building web analytic applications. The DH Education Knowledge map is divided into four panels, presenting the courses as a table and a scatterplot, and the Wikipedia information in the form of a graph with an accompanying paragraph from Wiki about the selected node from the

6 All the winning projects, their description and their evaluation can be found on the following GitHub page https://github.com/acdh-oeaw/ACDHchHackathon2020/blob/master/results.md

7 The prototype application can be accessed here https://bellerophons-pegasus.github.io/CORIANDER/index.html

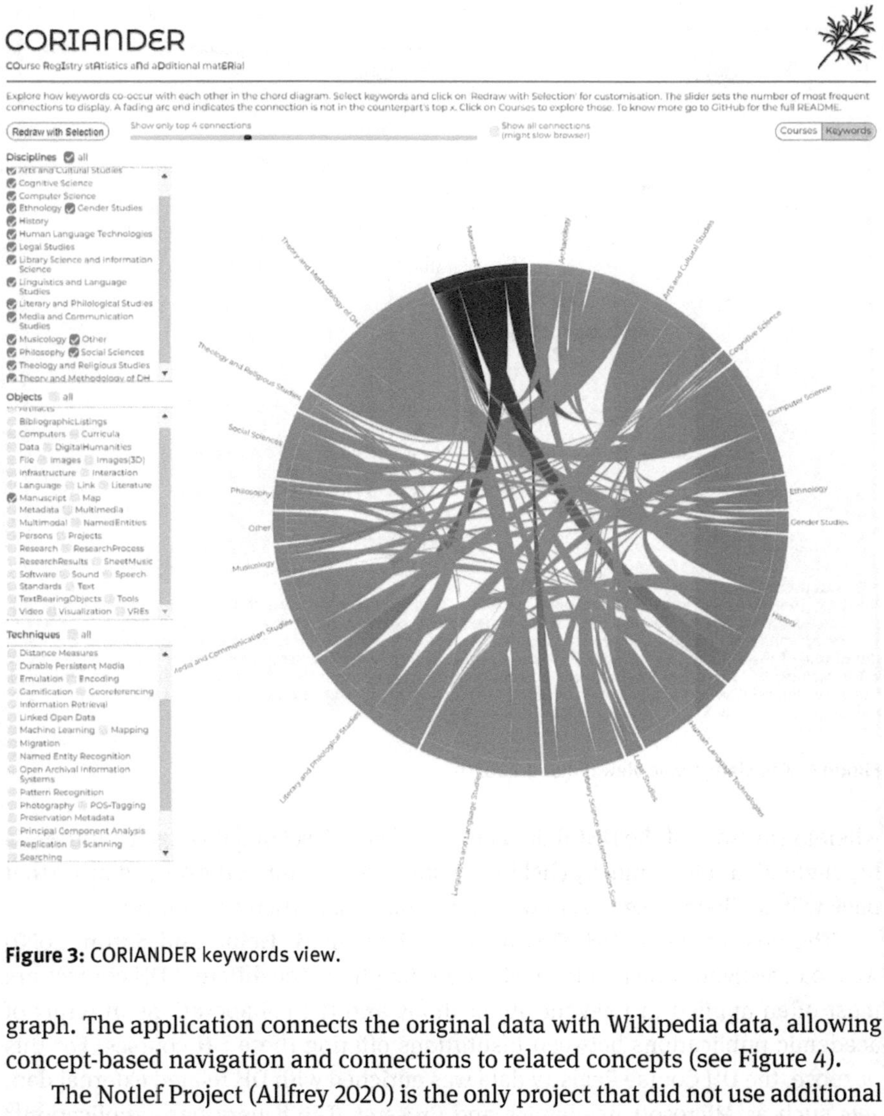

Figure 3: CORIANDER keywords view.

graph. The application connects the original data with Wikipedia data, allowing concept-based navigation and connections to related concepts (see Figure 4).

The Notlef Project (Allfrey 2020) is the only project that did not use additional external data resources to enrich the given DH Course Registry data set. The design for the Notlef visualization, as stated by the developer, was inspired by the 2009 Feltron Annual Report,[8] written by Nicholas Felton and implemented as an Angular 9 app. The Notlef app[9] consists of two pages – courses and places (see Figure 5) –

8 http://feltron.com/info.html

9 The app can be accessed here: https://notlef-dhcr.web.app/overview

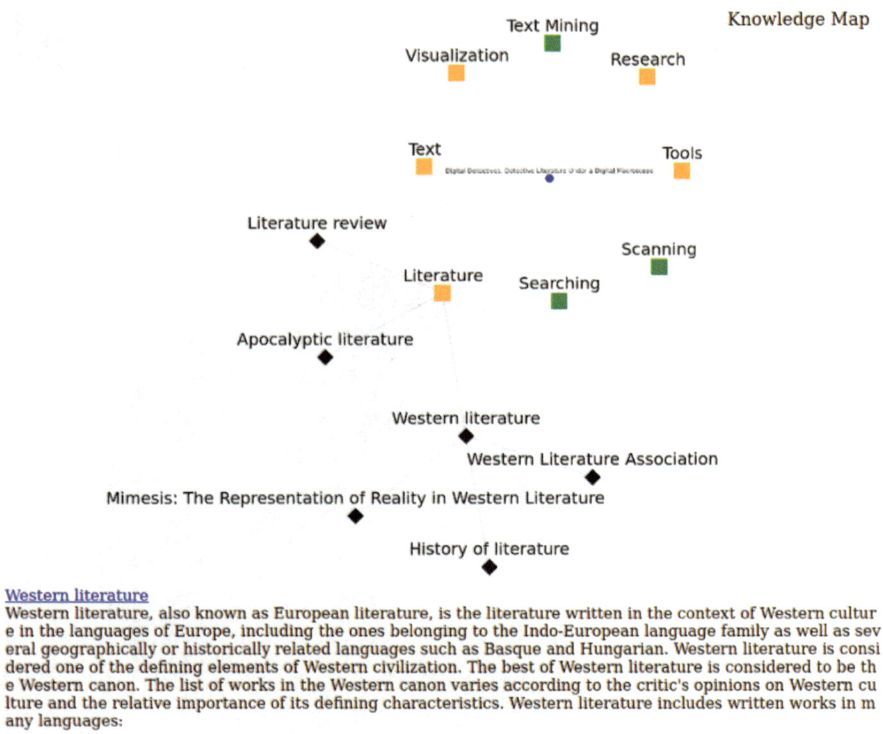

Figure 4: Knowledge Map view (Palandri 2020).

wherein statistics of the DHCR data are visualized. A set of data (e.g., countries) is highlighted in colour and, by clicking on one of these values, the other data on that page will be filtered (e.g., to show information for a particular country).

The goal of the ACDH-2020 project (Giovannetti, Heibi, and Sartini 2020) was to investigate which of the techniques taught by the different DH courses are most often applied in relevant publications and the collaborations in terms of academic publications between institutions offering these DH courses. For this purpose, the DH Course Registry data was enriched with DH related external data sets such as Microsoft Academics and Crossref. The jQuery base application[10] contains two different types of visualization: bar charts and networks (Figure 6). In the network visualization, the institutions are the nodes, and by clicking on the nodes the user can access information about the courses taught by these institutions and the publications associated with these institutions.

10 The app can be accessed here: https://br0ast.github.io/ACDH-2020/

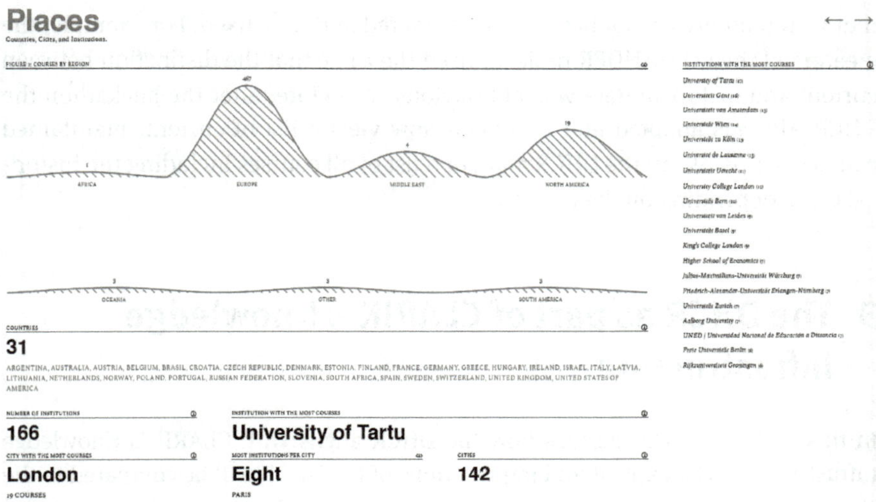

Figure 5: Places view mode in the Notlef app.

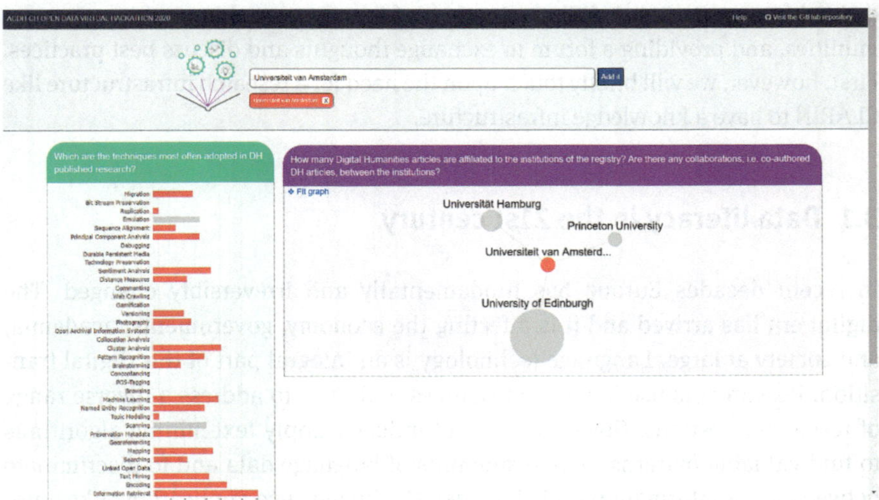

Figure 6: Network visualization publication collaboration for the search term "University of Amsterdam" in the ACDH-CH app.

The winning hackathon projects are a demonstration of what the community can do with the collected DHCR data if it is easily available through an API. The creators of these projects not only presented inspiring examples of how the data could be visualized and enriched and which questions could be answered with the data and visualization, but also addressed issues with the DHCR API that would otherwise not have been discovered and thus fixed. For example, the creators of the CORIANDER project raised the issue that the distinction between current and historical data was not obvious. Therefore, after the hackathon the DHCR API was adapted and users can now view a list of current, maintained courses (as visible on the DHCR map) or a list of all courses including the historical ones, depending on the use case.

3 The DHCR as part of CLARIN's Knowledge Infrastructure

In this section we will discuss how the DHCR aligns with CLARIN's Knowledge Infrastructure. The explicit and implicit aims of the DHCR will be compared to the strategic objectives of the overall Knowledge Infrastructure as expressed in several strategic documents. Over the years the DHCR has become an essential instrument of CLARIN's Knowledge Infrastructure. The elements of its contribution can be divided into gathering and disseminating information, reaching out to user communities, and providing a forum to exchange thoughts and discuss best practices. First, however, we will briefly touch upon the need for a research infrastructure like CLARIN to have a knowledge infrastructure.

3.1 Data literacy in the 21st century

In recent decades Europe has fundamentally and irreversibly changed. The digital era has arrived and it is affecting the economy, governments, academia, and society at large. Language technology is an integral part of this digital transition. Researchers use language resources and tools to address a diverse range of research questions. Governments and industry apply text-mining algorithms to find valuable patterns in large amounts of language data and to discriminate between valid information and "fake news". Citizens use applications like automatic speech recognition, machine translation, and autocomplete on a daily basis (CLARIN ERIC Strategy 2021–2023). In addition to a myriad of opportunities, however, the digital era comes with a number of challenges. Data and algorithms can and have been used as "weapons of math destruction", leading to, for instance, unwanted gender- and ethnicity-based discrimination and injustice (O'Neil 2017). Overcoming these difficulties requires increased levels of computational know-how.

The advance of the data economy has led to a growing need to train data professionals and to increase data literacy among citizens. Data literacy here is used according to Prado and Marzal's definition: the ability to "access, interpret, critically assess, manage, handle and ethically use data" (Prado and Marzal 2013: 126). The European Commission has acknowledged this view in its European Strategy for Data. According to this strategy, data analysis is among the most critical of skills shortages, resulting in about 500,000 unfilled positions in the EU. The EC believes that, if Europe's shortage in data professionals and lack of data literacy is not properly addressed, it will "affect the EU's capacity to master the challenges of the data economy and society" (European Commission 2020).

The digital era is affecting the academic world as well. Data-driven research methods allow researchers to address research questions that were previously considered too big to answer. Numerous authors have called upon linguists, historians, literary scientists, and other humanities scholars to adopt these new research methods (Borgman 2009; Guldi and Armitage 2014: 88–116; McGillivray et al. 2020). The emerging field of humanities scholars that have applied data-driven methods in their research and teaching is commonly known as the Digital Humanities. However, as stated in the Digital Humanities Manifesto, the Digital Humanities "is not a unified field but an array of convergent practices" (Schnapp et al. 2009). Some humanities disciplines have embraced the digital turn with more enthusiasm than others. Jenset and McGillivray, for example, note that corpus-based quantitative methods for historical linguistics have not gone mainstream. According to their diagnosis, there is a "chasm" dividing the early adopters from the majority of users. Jenset and McGillivray suggest this chasm is caused by, among other factors, a lack of training opportunities and educational practices (Jenset and McGillivray 2017: 22–25).

European Research Infrastructure Consortia (ERICs) such as CLARIN play an important role in increasing data literacy and advocating responsible data use among new generations of researchers, data professionals, and more generally among citizens. As such, ERICs enable researchers to apply data-driven methods, support EU countries to improve their position in the global economy, and to empower citizens to safely and efficiently interact with everyday technology (ERIC Forum 2020). Within CLARIN, increasing data literacy is one of the main objectives of what is called the Knowledge Infrastructure. The Knowledge Infrastructure serves as the "glue" for the various communities engaged with CLARIN and is the structure that aims to secure a continuous transfer of knowledge (CLARIN ERIC Strategy 2021–2023). It encapsulates a range of initiatives, including the DHCR. In what follows, we will outline three branches of activities that are part of the Knowledge Infrastructure and highlight the strategic role of the DHCR.

3.2 Disseminating information

CLARIN is a distributed research infrastructure. It consists of dozens of nodes spread across Europe and to a growing extent across the world. Making sure that researchers, teachers, citizen-scientists, commercial partners, policy makers, journalists, and other players involved can find the information they need, is one of the key objectives of the Knowledge Infrastructure. To achieve this goal, CLARIN has established a network of Knowledge Centres (abbreviated as K-centres). These K-centres offer information services, such as a help desk, online courses, best-practice documents, and guidance in gaining access to and using data and tools. Each K-centre has its own field of expertise, which could be an individual language, a type of language modality, a linguistic topic, a form of language processing, a type of data, or a generic method or issue.[11]

Much like CLARIN, the Digital Humanities are also characterized by their distributed nature. Researchers and teachers who apply and critically reflect on DH methods in their research and teaching, can be found in many humanities departments across the world. Though there are common platforms for them to exchange information – notably DH conferences organized at the national, supranational, and global level – information provided about DH courses is mostly limited to institutional catalogues. The DHCR offers an online platform with structured basic information about DH courses taught in and beyond Europe and with links to more detailed information. One of its strengths is that the DHCR centralizes information about a distributed field, while keeping its diverse nature intact. Consequently, the DHCR is specifically mentioned in the CLARIN ERIC Strategy 2021–2023 as an information platform for training opportunities (CLARIN ERIC Strategy 2021–2023).

3.3 Reaching out

Gathering and publishing information, however, is not enough. One cannot expect users to find the information they are looking for without actively promoting the available overviews. To increase awareness about the resources, tools, and services offered by CLARIN, a number of instruments are in place to actively reach out to existing and new communities of use. Both CLARIN ERIC and national CLARIN consortia organize User Involvement events to inform potential users about how they might benefit from the CLARIN infrastructure. In addition,

11 See https://www.clarin.eu/content/knowledge-centres

there is a programme of CLARIN Ambassadors, who present CLARIN at scientific conferences and events.[12]

Another way of reaching out is to integrate CLARIN in existing structures. In 2019 CLARIN's Knowledge Infrastructure Committee organized a workshop on teaching CLARIN at universities. Prior to the workshop, participants were asked to complete a survey on the integration of CLARIN in university curricula. The results show that out of 22 participating CLARIN member and observer countries, CLARIN was integrated into courses taught at 31 different universities in 20 different countries. These courses are attended by nearly 6,000 students each year (Fišer and Krauwer 2019). To further encourage lecturers to integrate CLARIN within their courses, CLARIN has been involved in the development of teaching and training material. Currently these and other materials are being brought together and put in the spotlight through an initiative called the CLARIN Training Suite. This Training Suite will be enriched with material resulting from a continuous call for contributions.[13]

The DHCR is a virtual platform connecting students, teachers, and policy makers on a global scale and allowing them to exchange valuable information. Since Marshall McLuhan coined the term "global village" in the early 1960s (McLuhan 1962), the world has become ever more interconnected. As a result, spending a semester or more abroad, previously considered a luxury reserved for the upper class, has become increasingly mainstream. Though the COVID-19 pandemic temporarily limited opportunities for student exchanges, the overall trend shows that over the last few decades the number of internationally mobile students has been steadily growing (UNESCO Science Report 2015). Countless students spend part of their education abroad, selecting courses that best fit their needs and learning more about the world's cultural diversity along the way. The DHCR displays how the various areas of expertise within the Digital Humanities are distributed over Europe and to an increasing extent over the world, allowing those interested in the intersection of culture and the digital to find the courses they seek.

To make the DHCR's target groups aware of the platform, the DHCR has been presented at various DH conferences worldwide and in articles published in scientific journals (Wessels, Gheldof, and Wissik 2019; Wissik, Edmond, Fischer, et al. 2020; Wissik, Schmeer, Fischer, et al. 2020). On a more informal level, promotional material, including professionally designed postcards, has been distributed at numerous events. More recently the outreach strategy has been explicated in a dissemination plan. As part of this plan, among other initiatives, the DHCR has

12 See https://www.clarin.eu/content/clarin-ambassadors-programme
13 See https://www.clarin.eu/content/call-contributions-clarin-training-suite

started its own Instagram account in September 2020.[14] Through this social platform the DHCR will be promoted among target groups that do not regularly attend conferences and other formal academic events, in particular students (Woldrich, Strnadl, and Wissik 2020). Those interested can also sign up to receive updates related to newly published DH courses (e.g., in a particular country).[15]

3.4 Providing a forum

The final branch of activities discussed here is to provide a forum for researchers, teachers, and other users to exchange thoughts and discuss best practices. CLARIN facilitates such a forum by organizing online and physical events and making funding available through calls for proposals for workshops. As part of these calls, among others a series of workshops on oral history have been organized. Researchers interested in oral history archives and speech technology specialists gathered to discuss the challenges of using digitized oral history records. These workshops resulted in the development of a "chain" of tools to make oral history archives machine actionable.[16] Another instrument to connect users is the Mobility Grant. It is designed to fund short-term stays at a CLARIN node, used for sharing technical expertise and strengthen collaborations.[17]

As of 2020 the CLARIN Annual Conference has a dedicated session for teachers to present and discuss how they have integrated CLARIN in their courses. This session is titled CLARIN in the Classroom. During the CLARIN Annual Conference 2020, 11 showcases were presented, demonstrating the use of specific corpora, tools, and services. These showcases display the breadth and depth of CLARIN's integration in the university curricula. In addition to these showcases, the UPSKILLS project was presented, which had just been accepted for funding through the Erasmus+ programme. This project aims to better prepare linguistics and language students pursuing a career in research or industry, by identifying and tackling the gaps in digital skills taught at universities. As one of the project partners, it is part of CLARIN's role to integrate research infrastructures into teaching.[18]

The DHCR is a community-driven initiative. The national moderators involved are not just responsible for curating courses uploaded in the DHCR, but also func-

14 See https://www.instagram.com/dhcourseregistry/
15 See https://dhcr.clarin-dariah.eu/subscriptions/add
16 See https://oralhistory.eu/
17 See https://www.clarin.eu/content/clarin-mobility-grants
18 See https://www.clarin.eu/content/factsheet-clarin-upskills

tion as a sounding board for the DHCR's central management. By default, each national moderator is invited to participate in meetings of the DHCR Working Group. This Working Group is part of the DARIAH infrastructure. It assembles at least once a year to discuss progress and future improvements of the DHCR. As such, the DHCR Working Group functions as a forum to discuss initiatives of research infrastructures related to teaching and training.

4 Conclusion

In this chapter we have presented the DHCR as part of CLARIN's ecosystem. We have introduced the DHCR, its genesis, main features, and goals, and have elaborated on the DHCR's position within CLARIN's Technical and Knowledge Infrastructures. We have shown that the DHCR is a true community-driven initiative, both on side of the data providers, that is, lecturers and programme directors who submit the course metadata, and the national moderators, who curate the data and on side of the data users. With the implementation of the DHCR API, the registry has opened up its treasure trove of data and contributed to CLARIN's ecosystem in terms of Open Science and FAIR Principles and in terms of "CLARIN for Programmers". The several dissemination activities such as virtual hackathons, screencasts, and social media campaigns have helped to reach out to the different user communities. In addition, the events (co-)organized by CLARIN and/or the DH Course Registry and the DHCR Working Group, in which the DHCR is embedded, provide a forum to discuss research infrastructure initiatives related to DH teaching and training, since education and training are important for research infrastructures to train the future generations of researchers in data literacy in the digital era.

Bibliography

Allfrey, Philip. 2020. *Notlef*. GitHub Repository. https://github.com/philipallfrey/notlef (accessed 14 April 2021).

Borek, Luise, Quinn Dombrowski, Jody Perkins & Christof Schöch. 2016. TaDiRAH: A case study in pragmatic classification. *Digital Humanities Quarterly* 10 (1). http://www.digitalhumanities.org/dhq/vol/10/1/000235/000235.html (accessed 14 April 2021).

Borgman, Christine L. 2009. The digital future is now: A call to action for the humanities. *Digital Humanities Quarterly* 3 (4). http://www.digitalhumanities.org/dhq/vol/3/4/000077/000077.html (accessed 14 April 2021).

Cimiano, Philipp, Chiarcos, Christian, McCrae, John P. & Jorge Gracia. 2020. *Linguistic linked data: Representation, generation and applications*. Berlin: Springer.
CLARIN ERIC Strategy 2021–2023. CLARIN ERIC https://www.clarin.eu/content/vision-and-strategy (accessed 14 April 2021).
Common Language Resources and Technology Infrastructure. Strategy 2021–2023 at a glance. https://office.clarin.eu/v/CE-2020-1709-CLARIN-Strategy-Summary-2021-2023-twopager.pdf (accessed 14 April 2021).
Cooper, D. (2010). When nice people won't share: Shy data, web APIs, and beyond, *Second International Conference on Global Interoperability for Language Resources (ICGL 2010)*, n.p.
Dissemination Strategy (1/2). *Reaching out: Dissemination strategy and planning for the DH Course Registry Project*. Internal report.
Edmond, Jennifer, Frank Fischer, Laurent Romary & Toma Tasovac. 2020. Springing the floor for a different kind of dance: Building DARIAH as a twenty-first-century research infrastructure for the arts and humanities. In Jennifer Edmond (ed.), *Digital technology and the practices of humanities research*, 207–234. Cambridge: Open Book Publishers. https://doi.org/10.11647/OBP.0192.09.
Edmond, Jennifer & Vicky Garnett. 2015. APIs and researchers: The emperor's new clothes? *International Journal of Digital Curation* 10 (1). 287–297.
ERIC Forum. 2020. The ERIC Community and Horizon Europe mission areas, June 2020. https://www.eric-forum.eu/wp-content/uploads/2020/06/ERIC-Forum_Horizon-Europe-Missions_Position-Paper.pdf (accessed 14 April 2021).
European Commission. 2020. A European strategy for data, COM/2020/66 final. https://eur-lex.europa.eu/legal-content/EN/TXT/?uri=CELEX%3A52020DC0066 (accessed 14 April 2021).
Fišer, Darja & Steven Krauwer. 2019. *Report on the survey for the CLARIN@Universities Workshop*. Internal report.
Giovannetti, Francesca, Ivan Heibi & Bruno Sartini. (2020). ACDH-2020. GitHub Repository. https://github.com/br0ast/ACDH-2020 (accessed 14 April 2021).
Guldi, Jo & David Armitage. 2014. *The history manifesto*. Cambridge: Cambridge University Press.
Hannesschläger, Vanessa & Tanja Wissik. 2020. *Opening up open data: Strategies and success stories*. Abstracts of the DH2020. https://dh2020.adho.org/wp-content/uploads/2020/07/112_OpeningupOpenDataStrategiessuccessstories.html (accessed 14 April 2021).
Hennelly, Martin, Langa Khumalo, Juan Steyn & Menno van Zaanen. 2022. Training of digital language resources skills in South Africa. In Darja Fišer & Andreas Witt (eds.), *CLARIN. The infrastructure for language resources*. Berlin: deGruyter.
Jenset, Gard B. & Barbara McGillivray. 2017. *Quantitative historical linguistics: A corpus framework*. Oxford: Oxford University Press.
Jong, Franciska de, Bente Maegaard, Koenraad De Smedt, Darja Fišer & Dieter Van Uytvanck. 2018. CLARIN: Towards FAIR and responsible data science using language resources. *Proceedings of the International Conference on Language Resources and Evaluation (LREC)* 11. 3259–3264.
Jong, Franciska de, Bente Maegaard, Darja Fišer, Dieter Van Uytvanck & Andreas Witt. 2020. Interoperability in an infrastructure enabling multidisciplinary research: The case of CLARIN. *Proceedings of the International Conference on Language Resources and Evaluation (LREC)* 12. 3406–3413.

McGillivray, Barbara, Beatrice Alex, Sarah Ames, Guyda Armstrong, David Beavan, Arianna Ciula, Giovanni Colavizza, James Cummings, David De Roure, Adam Farquhar, Simon Hengchen, Anouk Lang, James Loxley, Eirini Goudarouli, Federico Nanni, Andrea Nini, Julianne Nyhan, Nicola Osborne, Thierry Poibeau, Mia Ridge, Sonia Ranade, James Smithies, Melissa Terras, Andreas Vlachidis & Pip Willcox. 2020. The challenges and prospects of the intersection of humanities and data science: A white paper from The Alan Turing Institute. https://ndownloader.figshare.com/files/24463460 (accessed 14 April 2021).

McLuhan, Marshall, 1962. *The Gutenberg galaxy: The making of typographic man*. Toronto: University of Toronto Press.

O'Neil, Cathy. 2017. *Weapons of math destruction: How Big Data increases inequality and threatens democracy*. London: Penguin.

Palandri, Marta. 2020. DH Education Knowledge Map – creating knowledge maps via hypertext. Blog post. https://medium.com/@marta.p/dh-education-knowledge-map-creating-knowledge-webs-via-hypertext-cfb6cc094c17 (accessed 23 March 2021).

Palandri, Marta & Raphael Mitsch. 2020. DH Education Knowledge Map – creating knowledge maps via hypertext. GitHub Repository. https://github.com/rmitsch/dh-knowledge-map (accessed 14 April 2021).

Petrauskaitė, Rūta, Darius Amilevičius, Virginijus Dadurkevičius, Tomas Krilavičius, Gailius Raškinis, Andrius Utka & Jurgita Vaičenonienė. 2022. CLARIN-LT: Home for Lithuanian language resources. In Darja Fišer & Andreas Witt (eds.), *CLARIN. The infrastructure for language resources*. Berlin: deGruyter.

Prado, Javier Calzada & Miguel Ángel Marzal. 2013. Incorporating data literacy into information literacy programs: Core competencies and contents. *Libri* 63 (2) 123–134.

Rossi, Giorgio, Jelena Angelis, Filipa Borrego, Joy Davidson, Elena Hoffert, Richard Wade & Patricia Postigo McLaughlin (eds.). 2020. Supporting the transformative impact of research infrastructures on European research. Report of the high-level expert group to assess the progress of ESFRI and other world class research infrastructures towards implementation and long-term sustainability. European Commission. https://ec.europa.eu/info/sites/info/files/research_and_innovation/strategy_on_research_and_innovation/documents/ec_rtd_transformative-impact-ris-on-euro-research.pdf (accessed 14 April 2021).

Safradin, Barbara & Franciska de Jong. 2017. CLARIN-PLUS D5.2 Operational course and education material registry. https://office.clarin.eu/v/CE-2017-0986-CLARINPLUS-D5_2.pdf (accessed 14 April 2021).

Sahle, Patrick, Johanna Puhle & Lisa Rau. 2011. Digitale Geisteswisschenschaften. https://dig-hum.de/sites/dig-hum.de/files/cceh_broschuereweb.pdf (accessed 14 April 2021).

Schnapp, Jeffrey, Peter Lunenfeld & Todd Presner. 2009. The digital humanities manifesto 2.0. https://www.digitalmanifesto.net/manifestos/17/ (accessed 14 April 2021).

Tasovac, Toma, Adrien Barbaresi, Thibault Clérice, Jennifer Edmond, Natalie Ermolaev, Vicky Garnett & Clifford Wulfman. 2016. APIs in digital humanities: The infrastructural turn. Digital Humanities 2016, Kraków, Poland, 11–16 July. 93–96. https://hal.archives-ouvertes.fr/hal-01348706/document

Tognitz, Martina & Gehrig, Lukas. 2020. CORIANDER. GitHub Repository. https://github.com/bellerophons-pegasus/CORIANDER (accessed 14 April 2021).

UNESCO Science Report. 2015. Towards 2030. https://unesdoc.unesco.org/ark:/48223/pf0000235406 (accessed 14 April 2021).

Wessels, Leon, Tom Gheldof & Tanja Wissik. 2019. The DH Course Registry: An international platform for finding and promoting DH courses. Poster presented at the DH Benelux Conference 2019, University of Liège, 11–13 September.
Wilkinson, Mark D., Michel Dumontier, IJsbrand Jan Aalbersberg, Gabrielle Appleton, Myles Axton, Arie Baak, Niklas Blomberg, Jan-Willem Boiten, Luiz Bonino da Silva Santos, Philip E. Bourne, Jildau Bouwman, Anthony J. Brookes, Tim Clark, Mercè Crosas, Ingrid Dillo, Olivier Dumon, Scott Edmunds, Chris T. Evelo, Richard Finkers, Alejandra Gonzalez-Beltran, Alasdair J.G. Gray, Paul Groth, Carole Goble, Jeffrey S. Grethe, Jaap Heringa, Peter A.C 't Hoen, Rob Hooft, Tobias Kuhn, Ruben Kok, Joost Kok, Scott J. Lusher, Maryann E. Martone, Albert Mons, Abel L. Packer, Bengt Persson, Philippe Rocca-Serra, Marco Roos, Rene van Schaik, Susanna-Assunta Sansone, Erik Schultes, Thierry Sengstag, Ted Slater, George Strawn, Morris A. Swertz, Mark Thompson, Johan van der Lei, Erik van Mulligen, Jan Velterop, Andra Waagmeester, Peter Wittenburg, Katherine Wolstencroft, Jun Zhao & Barend Mons. 2016. The fair guiding principles for scientific data management and stewardship. *Scientific Data* 3. 160018. https://doi.org/10.1038/sdata.2016.18.
Wissik, Tanja, Jennifer Edmond, Frank Fischer, Franciska de Jong, Stefania Scagliola, Andrea Scharnhorst, Hendrik Schmeer, Walter Scholger & Leon Wessels. 2020. Teaching digital humanities around the world: An infrastructural approach to a community-driven DH Course Registry. *Library Tribune* (6). 1–27.
Wissik, Tanja, Hendrik Schmeer, Frank Fischer, Franciska de Jong, Walter Scholger & Leon Wessels. 2020. DH teaching activities as a resource for research: Accessing the DH Course Registry data via an API. Poster presented at the DH Conference 2020, virtual.
Woldrich, Anna, Katharina Strnadl & Tanja Wissik. 2020. *Deliverable: Digital Humanities Course Registry. Dissemination Strategy*. Unpublished project deliverable.

Martin Hennelly, Langa Khumalo, Juan Steyn, and Menno van Zaanen

Training of Digital Language Resources Skills in South Africa

Abstract: South Africa recognizes eleven official languages, although more languages are spoken in the country. Most of these languages are considered under-resourced: there is only a limited set of computational resources available. This includes linguistic data collections as well as computational linguistic tools. This scarcity of resources limits the computational linguistic and more applied (e.g., digital humanities) work on these languages. However, in South Africa there is currently also a lack of people who know how to use these resources.

The South African Centre for Digital Language Resources (SADiLaR) is a government-funded research infrastructure that aims to tackle both problems. First, it runs a digitization programme, which develops new digital language resources. This programme digitizes analogue linguistic data collections, but also develops new computational linguistic tools. Second, a digital humanities programme aims to build research capacity in the field of digital humanities. This is done through training events, among other initiatives, which have recently been clustered in the SADiLaR-run "Escalator project". Escalator aims to develop a community of practice in the field of digital humanities. By taking a comprehensive approach to training events with follow-ups, combined with the development of a Champions Initiative programme consisting of the training of experts, Escalator aims to make it easier for researchers to transition into more computational types of research in the humanities and social sciences.

This chapter will provide a historical overview of the field of natural language processing and digital humanities in South Africa. In particular, it will focus on the development of computational linguistic resources and their application. Additionally, an overview of activities in this area performed by SADiLaR will be

Martin Hennelly, South African Centre for Digital Language Resources, North-West University, Potchefstroom, South Africa, e-mail: martin.hennelly@nwu.ac.za
Langa Khumalo, South African Centre for Digital Language Resources, North-West University, Potchefstroom, South Africa, e-mail: langa.khumalo@nwu.ac.za
Juan Steyn, South African Centre for Digital Language Resources, North-West University, Potchefstroom, South Africa, e-mail: juan.steyn@nwu.ac.za
Menno van Zaanen, South African Centre for Digital Language Resources, North-West University, Potchefstroom, South Africa, e-mail: menno.vanzaanen@nwu.ac.za

https://doi.org/10.1515/9783110767377-016

provided, illustrating information sharing with language communities as well as researchers.

Keywords: linguistic resources, South Africa, digital humanities, training, digital championship programme

1 Introduction

The South African Centre for Digital Language Resources (SADiLaR) is a research infrastructure that is government-funded through the SARIR (South African Research Infrastructure Roadmap) programme. "The SARIR initiative is a high-level strategic and systemic intervention to provide research infrastructure across the entire public research system, building on existing capabilities and strengths, and drawing on future needs" (SARIR: 6).

SADiLaR runs two programmes: *digitization* and *digital humanities*. The digitization programme deals with the creation of digital language resources for all of the eleven official South African languages. Within this programme, data collections of different modalities are developed, including text, audio, and multi-modal collections. The resources may stem from the digitization of analogue resources, but digitally born resources are also collected and made available through SADiLaR's repository. In addition to digital language data collections, natural language processing tools for the different languages are developed and made available within this programme.

In this chapter, we will mainly focus on the digital humanities programme. The field of digital humanities in South Africa is currently still in its infancy. Even though many researchers from the fields of humanities and social sciences are interested in digital humanities, they often do not really know where to start learning more about digital tools and methodologies. This has led to a paucity of research in the field of computational linguistics and digital humanities in South Africa, which in turn has compounded the scarcity of resources both in terms of expertise in these areas and the sophisticated linguistic and digital resources with which to carry out scientific research in computational linguistics and digital humanities. As a result, this again severely limits the research performed in the fields of computational linguistics and digital humanities as well as the development of necessary computational linguistic resources, as researchers with access to linguistic data are not actively developing digitized resources (in particular for the South African languages for which limited resources are available).

To resolve these circular limitations, SADiLaR emphasizes training of researchers as well as creating awareness about the field of digital humanities. This is done internally by providing direct training to eleven researchers, one for each of the official languages, who are located at SADiLaR's hub, but also externally, where different training events have been (and still are) organized. These events are often presented by SADiLaR's researchers. The impact of these training events, however, has been limited, although they have received positive feedback. To enlarge the visibility and impact of SADiLaR, language celebration events have been organized, which emphasize the importance of the South African languages in the country. Furthermore, the new national Escalator project will provide a more structured and incremental way of training interested researchers. A specific focus will be placed on researchers from historically disadvantaged universities in the country.

Here, we provide an overview of the initial state of affairs related to computational linguistics and digital humanities in South Africa and describe the activities organized by SADiLaR to improve this situation. The hope is that lessons can be learned from our experiences, which may be particularly useful for researchers and organizations from countries in a similar situation. Additionally, we hope that readers may provide feedback or become involved in SADiLaR's activities, further boosting the fields of computational linguistics and digital humanities in South Africa specifically and in Africa more generally.

This chapter is structured, essentially, in chronological order. It starts with a description of the field of digital humanities before the start of SADiLaR. Next, we describe a range of activities organized and implemented by SADiLaR to provide information and training in the fields of computational linguistics and digital humanities. Three phases can be identified: first, we provide an overview of the training events, which relate to mostly ad hoc tutorials and workshops organized by the Centre. Second, we describe the SADiLaR-organized language celebrations, which comprise of large events that emphasize the importance of each of the eleven official South African languages and create awareness about SADiLaR as a research infrastructure as well as the fields of digital humanities and computational linguistics. Third, we provide information on the Escalator project, which is currently on-going. This project aims to provide a more structured approach to training in computational linguistic and digital humanities tools and research methodologies with the ultimate aim of developing a community of practice. We also discuss the digital infrastructure developed and made available by SADiLaR.

2 Initial state of digital humanities in South Africa

When describing the start of digital humanities, one often refers to Father Roberto Busa, who pioneered work in the area of computational linguistic and literary analysis after the Second World War, for instance by analysing the work of Saint Thomas Aquinas (Sula and Hill 2019). However, one may argue that Ada Lovelace (1815–1852) had already published on the topic (Green 2001). She is often recognized as the first computer programmer, working alongside Charles Babbage, who developed the Analytical Engine. This computer was never fully built, but Ada Lovelace published an algorithm that could compute Bernoulli numbers. There is, however, also some controversy around Lovelace's influence on programming (Bromley 1982). Then again, she wrote:

> [The Analytical Engine] might act upon other things besides number, were objects found whose mutual fundamental relations could be expressed by those of the abstract science of operations, and which should be also susceptible of adaptations to the action of the operating notation and mechanism of the engine... Supposing, for instance, that the fundamental relations of pitched sounds in the science of harmony and of musical composition were susceptible of such expression and adaptations, the engine might compose elaborate and scientific pieces of music of any degree of complexity or extent.

This hypothetical indicates that she realized that computers could be used for other modalities besides numbers only (Hooper 2012).

Digital humanities developed into a research area several years later, which can be seen from the establishment of several publications and organizations, such as the *Computers and the Humanities Journal* (1966), the Association for Literary and Linguistic Computing (1973), the Association for Computers and the Humanities (1978), and the Society for Digital Humanities (1986). In 2005, several digital humanities associations decided to join forces, which led to the formation of the Alliance of Digital Humanities Associations, abbreviated as ADHO.

2.1 Digitization in South Africa

In South Africa, the field of digital humanities, or working digitally in the humanities, became active a bit later. For instance, the South African History Online (SAHO)[1] organization was founded in 1998. Around that time, other digital humanities activities also started around the country. For instance, at the University of Cape Town, one can find the Humanitec Digital showcase;[2] University of KwaZulu-Natal hosted the Digital Innovation South Africa;[3] and the International Library

1 https://www.sahistory.org.za/
2 https://digitalcollections.lib.uct.ac.za/humanitec/
3 https://disa.ukzn.ac.za/

of African Music[4] at Rhodes University started digitizing material through the ILAM digitization project. As may be clear from these examples, the initial work in the field of digital humanities in South Africa was performed in the area of archives, which strive to digitize their materials and make them available online.

Soon after the beginning of the new millennium, however, the field of computational linguistics or human language technologies became more active as well. For instance, in 2004, the Centre for Text Technology (CTexT), hosted at the North-West University, was founded, but other universities, including University of South Africa, University of Pretoria, and Stellenbosch University had active research groups working on computational linguistics. Additionally, the then Meraka Institute, part of the Council for Scientific and Industrial Research (CSIR), a scientific research and development organization, had an active research group.

In 2011, an audit of the South African digitization initiatives was performed (Grover, van Huyssteen, and Pretorius 2011a, 2011b), which indicated the need for the establishment of a national heritage repository, as well as the necessity of training on digitization (for instance, for librarians and archivists). Following various academic interactions with government since 2002, a cabinet decision gave rise to the establishment of the National Centre for Human Language Technology (NCHLT) in 2009, which in 2012 became the Resource Management Agency (RMA). The RMA was regarded as a four-year project. Through commissioned projects and its own research, the RMA, which was unique in Africa, has rendered impressive results in the acquisition, enhancement, and distribution of (South African) language resources and software tools. These resources and tools have found their way to various research and development projects worldwide.

At the end of the RMA funding cycle, it was clear that it was essential to continue activities in order to build the computational linguistic domain as well as consolidate efforts towards a sustainable single home for language resources in the country. It was seen to be strategically important to maintain and grow the activities of the RMA by incorporating it in a new centre (i.e., SADiLaR) that would play a major role in the centre's digitization programme. This is part of a grand challenge, which is to be addressed by the establishment of this new centre and pertains not only to the development of the languages per se, but also to their functional use, inter alia, through the implementation of technologies to foster effective multilingual communication and social cohesion in South Africa and among its citizens. To illustrate the need for continued work in this area, in 2018, a follow-up audit was performed (Moors et al. 2018; Wilken et al. 2018), which

4 https://www.ru.ac.za/ilam/

showed that more language resources for the different South African languages are available, but that there are still gaps and more work should be done.

2.2 Digital humanities in South Africa

Around 2014, specific digital humanities activities started. For instance, the University of Pretoria organized a symposium entitled "DH and representations of self"; Durban University of Technology handed out the "best digital humanities tool" award; and one of the first national workshops in digital humanities was hosted by the North-West University. At that event, a steering committee was established to develop the ground work for the establishment of a Southern African Digital Humanities Association. During the second national Digital Humanities Workshop, again hosted at North-West University, a collective decision was made to establish the Digital Humanities Association of Southern Africa (DHASA)[5] in 2016, which later joined the umbrella digital humanities organization ADHO in 2017 as an observer and was then fully accepted in 2018 as a constituent organization within the ADHO.

Around the same time, the South African Centre for Digital Language Resources (SADiLaR)[6] was announced (in 2016). This research infrastructure falls under the South African Research Infrastructure Roadmap (SARIR), which is funded by the South African Department of Science and Innovation. SADiLaR is a country-wide organization consisting of several nodes, including the Centre for Text Technology (CTexT) located at North-West University, focusing on the development of text technologies; the department of African Languages at the University of Pretoria, which is the digitization node; the department of African Languages at the University of South Africa, dealing with African Wordnet project and multilingual linguistic terminology; the department of General Linguistics at Stellenbosch University, which hosts the child language development node; the inter-institutional centre for language development and assessment (ICELDA), which is a collaboration between several institutes dealing with language development and language assessment; and CSIR's HLT research group, which serves as SADiLaR's speech node. SADiLaR also incorporates the resources that were available through the previously noted RMA.

The parallel developments in the area of computational linguistics (e.g., RMA) and digital humanities (e.g., DHASA) have led to the realization of the strategic

5 https://digitalhumanities.org.za/
6 https://www.sadilar.org/

importance of the South African Centre for Digital Language Resources (SADiLaR). This becomes even more relevant as new methodological approaches towards research and development in the domains of humanities and social sciences pose new challenges to researchers. It is therefore strategically important to assist South African researchers not only in gaining access to large corpora of authentic digital data and applicable software tools, but also to acquire skills related to the use of such data in order to render high quality research outputs nationally and internationally. This is furthermore an attempt to incubate the field of digital humanities in the South African context with benefits to society, academia, industry, and government.

Since its inception, SADiLaR has organized several events to highlight the availability of digital language resources for the South African languages and to show the applicability of these resources. These events have several aims:

1. to illustrate the already available resources;
2. to provide examples of what research can be done with the tools and data collections that are available;
3. to emphasize the importance of the availability of these resources;
4. to ask people to contribute to the collection of resources by submitting new or existing digital language collections;
5. to illustrate how one can perform research in the field of digital humanities using the language resources.

In the following sections, we will first provide information on the initial training events organized by SADiLaR, followed by a description of language celebrations, which were organized for each of the official languages. Experiences and lessons learned from the organization of these events have led to the start of the Escalator project, which aims to provide a more structured and sustainable training programme and to develop communities of practice in the area of digital humanities across South Africa. We will also provide an overview of the digital infrastructure made available through SADiLaR.

3 Training events: Engaging academia

At the inauguration of SADiLaR, the centre aimed to hire eleven researchers, each with a background in one of the eleven official South African languages. Having researchers in all official languages ensured that all languages were equally supported. The researchers all had a background in linguistics or literature in their respective languages, but they did not have extensive experience in the field of computational linguistics or digital humanities. This was mainly due to the fact that only a limited number of university curricula contained courses related to computational linguistics or the use of computational tools in the humanities.

To resolve the lack of computational (linguistic) skills of the researchers, they each had to learn how to use and get practical experience with at least two computational tools. This task had several aims. First, it allowed the researchers to experience using computational tools themselves. Becoming familiar with the capabilities of these tools allowed them to incorporate them directly into their own research, allowing them to continue their research given their background, but gradually moving more into the digital domain. Second, investigating the possibilities of multiple computational tools leads to greater insight into the possibilities of computational linguistic tools more generally. This not only leads to knowledge of the learned tools, but places these tools in a larger context. The underlying idea is that this will lead to a change in the attitude towards how research can be done, where computational research methodologies are considered in addition to the more qualitative approaches that were taught in the researchers' previous studies. Finally, the experience, knowledge, and skills the researchers obtained by learning how to use the different computational tools allowed them to teach others to learn to use these tools as well. Partnering with the Carpentries,[7] an international organization that teaches foundational coding and data science skills to researchers worldwide, also assisted in the development of researchers to understand concepts of open science better, as well as providing a practical introduction to base-level programming skills.

In order to share the usefulness of the different digital tools with the wider academic community in South Africa, training and awareness events were organized. At these events, researchers as well as other subject experts would present their knowledge on specific tools and work towards contextualizing computational approaches for the benefit of participants who were generally very new to digital approaches in the humanities. These training events had several advantages. First, by teaching participants at the training events, the possibilities of computational (linguistic) tools were promoted more widely. Most participants had not worked with such tools before. Training events can be requested through the SADiLaR website and a range of topics are available (although training events on additional topics can be made available in discussion with SADiLaR). In particular, several training events are provided that discuss tools that enable analyses of corpora (such as the Voyant tools,[8] the Autshumato machine translation

7 https://carpentries.org/
8 http://voyant-tools.org/

system,[9] or CATMA[10]) but courses on digital humanities, corpus creation, and linguistic text processing tools, and Carpentries courses (Data, Software, and Library Carpentries), which treat more general computational skills, are also available.

Second, the researchers prepared some of the training sessions and taught at these sessions themselves. Not only did this deepen their knowledge of the different tools (as the participants sometimes had questions that required further investigation), it also allowed the researchers to provide examples using material in their own respective languages. This made it easier for the participants in the training events to relate the functionality of the tools to their own work.

Finally, as the training events were hosted at different universities throughout the country, a wide geographical range of communities was reached. For example, training events have been hosted at Durban University of Technology (Durban, KwaZulu-Natal) which hosted several students and researchers from universities in the region, North-West University (Potchefstroom, Mahikeng, North-West, and Vanderbijlpark, Gauteng), Tshwane University of Technology, University of Pretoria (Pretoria, Gauteng), University of the Witwatersrand (Johannesburg, Gauteng), University of Cape Town and Stellenbosch University (Cape Town and Stellenbosch, Western Cape), and Rhodes University (Grahamstown, Eastern Cape).

Even though the training events were well received, they had only limited impact in the sense that each event had around 30 participants. On the one hand, this allowed for personal interaction between the presenters and the participants, yielding high-quality knowledge transfer. However, on the other hand, as can be imagined, the overall impact on the entire group of researchers interested in digital humanities was limited. To resolve this, several larger events were organized by the researchers. For each language, a dedicated language celebration was held, which will be discussed in the next section.

Analysing the training initiatives at this moment in time, we identified two key lessons. First, it is essential to collaborate with individuals and organizations that share similar aims. In this case, for instance, the collaboration with the Carpentries is essential. This allows for the use, reuse, and extension of broader (existing) networks. Access to such networks can jump-start of one's own activities, in contrast to the cold start that such activities would normally entail. Second, the success of training events will be limited if the training events take place in isolation. This isolation has two aspects: training events without follow-up and training events without a community to support participants afterwards.

9 https://mt.nwu.ac.za/
10 https://catma.de/

4 Language celebrations: Connecting with language communities

To increase the visibility and impact of SADiLaR, events were organized that included a much larger participant base compared to the training events discussed in the previous section. The reasoning behind this choice of event is that South Africa views multilingualism as an asset, which means that one cannot work on language technologies and digital humanities in isolation without engaging with the different language communities.

Multilingualism is explicitly articulated in the South African constitution (Republic of South Africa 1996), which has been lauded as one of the most progressive in the world. Multilingualism can afford the country a way to foster social cohesion, break down barriers, and improve access to social, economic, and academic activities.

The constitution recognizes eleven official languages, namely, Afrikaans, English, Sesotho, Sesotho sa Leboa, Setswana, Siswati, Tshivenda, Xitsonga, isiNdebele, isiXhosa, and isiZulu. While the government, through the constitution, has expressed a commitment to elevate the status and advance the use of the hitherto under-resourced languages, English and Afrikaans remain the most resourced of these languages, with English clearly the dominant language in terms of resources because of its global currency. The other languages remain largely under-resourced.

It is clear in our view that language is an important medium through which human beings generate, organize, and disseminate all forms of knowledge. The organization and transmission of all forms of knowledge are facilitated through language. Education, which is part of structured citizenship training, and intellectual development, is conducted through language using various discourses (Mchombo 2017).

It is our submission that access to epistemologies from kindergarten to higher education must be through the languages that the learners are most familiar with. In order for this to happen, all eleven official languages must be developed sufficiently in order to be used in all spheres of life, and must have resources that enable their use in learning and teaching. The introduction and use of African languages in all areas of life affirms them, allows them to grow, and in the process empowers the users to confidently deploy them in knowledge generation, production, and dissemination.

The establishment of SADiLaR as a research infrastructure aims in part to develop and promote all eleven official languages so that they are capable of expressing all forms of knowledge, and to drive their use and function in research and development, education, social transformation, trade, and economic and scientific development. In its recently developed strategic plan, which is derived from its national mandate, SADiLaR identifies the following objectives. First, it aims to stimulate and advance the scholarship of digital humanities throughout South African higher education. This is done, among others, through the Escalator project (see Section 5); second, to open up new frontiers of research in the humanities and social sciences in general; third, to provide digital language resources and tools for the development of a wide range of language technology applications (e.g., in the fields of health services, education, social services, and business); and finally, to document the nature and use of local African languages, including cultural heritage practices as part of a living archive (e.g., enabled through language laboratories or language hubs).

To quote the South African Human Rights Commission Report on Transformation at Public Universities in South Africa (South African Human Rights Commission and others 2016: 12):

> In recognition of the reality that language continues to be a barrier to access and success in higher education (both in the sense that African and other languages have not been developed as academic/scientific languages and the majority of students entering higher education are not proficient in English and Afrikaans) the Language Policy for Higher Education emphasized that language and access to language skills is critical to ensure the right of individuals to realize their full potential to participate in and contribute to the social, cultural, intellectual, economic and political life of South African society[.]

SADiLaR's work is in part a response to this national and constitutional imperative that all the official languages of the country have parity of esteem.

In a similar vein, the United Nations declared 2019 as the International Year of Indigenous Languages (IY2019).[11] One of the cited reasons for this declaration was to foster a link between language, development, peace, and reconciliation. Furthermore, it aimed to create conditions for knowledge sharing and dissemination of good practices.

As part of its celebrations of the UNESCO's IY2019, SADiLaR celebrated the eleven official languages by assigning each language a specific month of the year (as shown in Figure 1). This was done by hosting collaborative events at various universities in South Africa. Each celebration event was unique and offered mother tongue speakers, academics, language specialists, and the general public a unique opportunity to share ideas on the status and role of their language in education, economy, and in all spheres of life. These celebrations created a national awareness of the culture and rich indigenous knowledge that is inherently part of these languages. It also offered a platform for all stakeholders to discuss and created

11 https://en.iyil2019.org/

synergistic relations for the future development of these languages, and furthermore to create and make available language resources in the form of grammars, lexicons, human language technologies, and other multi-modal digital resources.

Figure 1: SADiLaR's language celebration calendar.

SADiLaR's language celebrations were in sync with the objectives of UNESCO's IY2019, which led SADiLaR to report on these activities at the Language Technology For All conference[12] that closed UNESCO's IY2019. The celebrations also affirmed the ideals of multilingualism that are expressed in the constitution. While the goal to achieve parity between the eleven official languages is still a long way off, the commitment to develop resources for all official languages (with a special focus on the under-resourced languages) has been articulated and is being driven through the research infrastructure.

An important lesson learned through these multilingual language celebrations is that it is important not to loose sight of who the end users and beneficiar-

12 https://lt4all.org/

ies of the language technologies would be. In the words of South African president Cyril Ramaphosa: “Language is an integral part of the identity of a people. It is at the heart of who they are, of their culture, of how they define themselves, and the most important legacy they pass to their children” (Ramaphosa 2019).

Though well received, the language celebrations required large amounts of preparations and, thus cannot be organized too frequently. The language celebrations are also less focused on training of digital language resources, although they do increase the visibility of the language communities and illustrate the reason why research into different aspects of the language is important and relevant.

5 Conceptualization of the Escalator project

The experiences of the training events and the larger scale language celebrations showed that specific areas needed to be strengthened to maximize the effect of SADiLaR on the academic and language communities, as well as in South Africa as a whole (and potentially beyond).

The language celebrations showed that there is a need for additional support for the language communities in the country. The celebrations brought together people from a wide range of backgrounds, although they did not directly increase the research in the area of computational linguistics and digital humanities in the country.

In contrast, the training events that were organized were more directly focused on training researchers and students on the use of digital language resources. However, even though several events were organized and positive feedback was received, several limitations still remain.

First, the training events were ad hoc in the sense that they were organized mainly on the basis of requests from the universities or active outreach from SADiLaR. This also meant that no explicit follow-up events (that built on the knowledge of the previous training events) were planned.

Second, the content of the training events were still relatively generic, not explicitly focusing on the South African context. Even though examples using some of the South African languages were provided, the training material was still mostly focused on English.

Third, the impact of the training events is unclear. Limited evaluation of the immediate or long-term impact was performed. This means that it is unclear whether the participants in the training events actually use the tools that were presented or whether they incorporate the use of these tools in the educational programme.

Finally, and this is probably the most important limitation of the training events, participants did not have access to additional help after the training event. Even though they were welcome to contact the researchers who provided the training, there was no structural network that the participants could go to when they ran into problems using the tools, or to ask questions afterwards.

To resolve these issues, SADiLaR is currently developing and systematically rolling out a novel programme, Escalator, in an agile way. This programme aims to provide a more structured approach. It is not just a collection of training events, but should be seen as a programme that aims to develop an inclusive and active community of practice in the field of digital humanities and computational social sciences in South Africa (and potentially beyond in the future).

The main part of the programme currently consists of an overarching digital Champions Initiative, which is open to all universities and research councils in South Africa. The core of this Champions Initiative is a mentorship programme, which consists of multiple tracks designed to mentor and connect researchers, support staff, and students to existing and new networks with the aim of building connected communities of practice.

Currently, the Champions Initiative consists of six tracks:

Explorer This track aims to grow awareness of fundamental concepts of digital scholarship. It consists mainly of short videos and content to introduce the computational environment to participants. This track launched at the end of May 2021.

Embarker In the Embarker track, participants are able to learn about the vast landscape of digital scholarship and start applying it to their own work in a more traditional way by taking part in multi-week courses.

Enhancer The Enhancer track allows participants to learn more advanced digital skills by applying them in a hands-on way projects in the fields of humanities or social sciences.

Enabler The Enabler track focuses on supporting people in (academic) institutions, to help them grow digital humanities and computational social science communities in their own environments.

Educator This track will assist educators, trainers, and content developers to develop and share their skills in creating open educational resources that can be used not only in their respective educational settings, but also as part of the digital Champions Initiative.

Empower The Empower track specifically aims to highlight and build the community of women using digital and computational skills in South Africa and further afield.

The main reason for revisiting SADiLaR's training approach is to tackle the challenges identified earlier in this section. First, Escalator replaces the ad hoc nature of training events by structuring training tracks where participants can grow and progress from a novice explorer of the computational field to an active contributing member of a community. Second, training and awareness events that lack local context are being expanded and specialized to include South African examples and applications by localizing course content or developing content specifically fit for purpose. Third, impact measurement is built into the programme itself, requiring active reporting (internally within SADiLaR) on how the Escalator programme is progressing. Finally, as Escalator has a focus on building communities of practice, by active mentoring within the designated tracks, the Escalator programme aims to address the lack of follow-up by connecting the tracks' participants and hence building networks in their domain.

To learn from previous experiences in developing mentorship programmes, a mentorship indaba was organized.[13] During this event, multiple existing mentorship programmes shared their successes and challenges with each other. The event illustrated the value of learning from what is already available and building on it or using existing opportunities. The Escalator is still refining the detail of its own mentorship programme. However, using broader collaborations, participants in the Escalator programme can already be connected to existing programmes, allowing participants to be introduced to working in an interdisciplinary way within the open science domain. In line with the notions of open science, all resources developed within the Escalator programme are available through Open Access to allow for reuse.

6 Digital infrastructure

The focus of the previous sections has been on the development of the human participation in the area of digital humanities. However, this endeavour is pointless if no computational tools and resources are available to perform this type of research. As mentioned in Section 2.1, several resources exist, but need to be made accessible. For this purpose, SADiLaR has developed implementations

13 https://escalator.sadilar.org/post/2021/05/2021-05-03-mentorship-indaba/

for digital infrastructures for web, repository, and application services allowing access to the resources for the eleven official South African languages.

The digital infrastructure had several requirements:

1. delivery of a repository service for the distribution of data collections, tools, and other knowledge;
2. (data) archiving functionality;
3. delivery of web services;
4. delivery of online tools through portal or services.

The different requirements are partially related. We will discuss the repository and its infrastructure first. Next, we discuss the web service and the related tools that are made accessible through the web service.

The infrastructure of the data repository needs to support all digital resources, including speech, text, and multi-modal data collections. This is a core requirement to enable downstream research in the area of digital humanities, academic and literary research, and the development of core computational tools for text processing and speech processing for the different languages. Development of the speech and text processing tools typically requires collections of speech and text data that represent samples from all of South Africa's official languages. Note that SADiLaR has a diverse approach to data acquisition, including funding of corpora development especially suited for text and speech processing and digital humanities, acquisition of content oriented to language preservation and documentation, and acquisition of corpora derived from academic research on various levels.

On a practical level, the core data repository infrastructure is virtualized within an environment up to operating system level by an external supplier. The external supplier manages the virtualization environment and network environment including security and firewall functionality. The infrastructure is backed up daily in line with standard industry practice for recovery of data in a disaster recovery scenario. This core infrastructure comprises six virtual servers.

The requirements of the base operating system software were: fully functional integration of core operating system services, availability of standard tool chains, proven performance, low costing of acquisition and ownership, and commercial performance levels. For this, the CentOS 7 Linux distribution is used. On top of the operating system, a core application environment has been built, focusing on performance, compatibility with standard software, capability, and cost of ownership and maintenance considerations.

The core repository uses DSpace, which is an open-source repository management system used in thousands of instances worldwide. It supports customization of the front end, so SADiLaR can apply its own look and feel. The submission process flow is made available online so that contributors can submit resources and metadata online as candidates for inclusion in the repository. Metadata entry is automatically validated for compliance to the requirements. The submissions are validated and promoted to the repository if they meet the quality requirements.

The repository data collections can be made available at several levels of access. They can be made available as open for download by anyone, without access control, for controlled access with limited distribution to the academic community in general, or for even more strongly controlled access in which an application process for information access is in force. Access control is implemented by a standard Shibboleth implementation with SADiLaR as the Service Provider and in combination with SAFIRE[14] as South Africa's national identity management federation and TENET[15] as South Africa's national education environment service provider.

The DSpace repository is designed to integrate into the wider domain infrastructure delivered by CLARIN[16] and CLARIN member organizations. Some aspects of the implementation are mandatory in compliance with CLARIN standards, with the intent to deliver interoperability to drive the uptake of resource contribution and consumption of resources. These include identity management, metadata standards, and searching of metadata.

Governance of the data and the repository is documented in a set of policy documents. In general, the intention is to drive uptake in submission and consumption of resources, drive standardization of data formats and metadata to enable use of toolchains and develop products and services, and protect data and people by assuring appropriate data management.

The repository and other services are made available through a webserver, which is based on Joomla. It is implemented for all human interaction to deliver information content and a front end for the repository. The services/application environment uses Apache Tomcat for the application execution environment, PostgresDB as the database environment, and Apache httpd as the webserver.

This combined environment has proven reliable and meets the needs of the core service of the repository web server, and basic portal and service applications. The limitation of the environment, however, starts to show when multiple applications are integrated with a single server, which produces increasing conflict between multiple applications in the file system, database, and other dependencies. As the SADiLaR application suite has grown, the limitations of the environment have become apparent and transition to a containerized environ-

14 https://safire.ac.za/
15 https://www.tenet.ac.za/
16 https://www.clarin.eu/

ment is planned. Note that all servers have an equivalent test instance to support development prior to production release.

The available (web) applications are implemented from standard open source code, from code developed by partner organizations, or industry collaborations. Additionally, SADiLaR has also sponsored development of applications for text and speech processing in the main. Through the website, currently, a corpus portal, the NCHLT text services, Autshumato machine translation services, the Voyant tools, and ZulMorph, a morphological analyser for isiZulu, are currently made available.

To summarize, the base implementation of virtualized hardware, open-source operating system, and core applications of the web server, repository, and web applications has delivered an introductory level of integration into the CLARIN infrastructure, which meets the current needs of the research community in South Africa and globally.

7 Conclusion

The phrase "build it and they will come" is often used when embarking on novel initiatives. At SADiLaR, we can attest that this is not true, at least not entirely. Simply having a research infrastructure that offers tools and resources does not guarantee uptake by academics, industry, and the broader community, even when training events are organized. This experience seems to mirror that of the broader CLARIN enterprise as can be seen through initiatives such as CLARIN in the Classroom, which aims to accelerate the integration of CLARIN resources in university curricula.

The training events organized by SADiLaR can be considered successful in the sense that they were well attended and showed that there is an interest (from researchers in the fields of humanities and social sciences) in learning more on computational resources and research methodologies. However, due to their size, these events have had limited impact. It is unclear in how far participants actively use the learned skills and whether they teach these skills in their classrooms.

Whereas the training events were small in scale, SADiLaR's language celebration events targeted the (much larger) general language communities. During these events the individual official South African languages were celebrated in their widest sense. These events were very well received and showed that each of the languages has an active community associated with it. However, these events did not lead to an increased activity in the field of computational linguistics and digital humanities for the languages.

Realizing that both types of events have their uses, the Escalator project aims to bring together the best of both worlds: supporting researchers interested in working in the field of digital humanities, especially linked to the South African languages, while at the same time building a large community of practice (or several connected, smaller communities of practice), which allow for the sharing of information and collaboration. In practical terms, Escalator realizes that researchers have their own needs, which translates to the different tracks within the digital Champions Initiative mentorship programme. This allows people to be introduced to the field of digital humanities, build on their existing knowledge and skills, and grow to be digital champions in the field of digital humanities.

Though SADiLaR has come far since its inception, the question of whether the research infrastructure will have a lasting impact depends on how broad the research infrastructure can enable the uptake of computational approaches to become in the fields of humanities and social sciences. The lessons learned during the startup phase of the project, in particular the experiences of the training events and the language celebrations, but also the practical experiences of setting up the required digital infrastructure, have been valuable. We believe that the development and roll-out of the Escalator project, in particular the digital Champions Initiative programme will lead to the establishment of communities of practice around a plethora of research topics and domains in the humanities and social sciences, truly leading towards an active field of digital humanities in South Africa.

Bibliography

Bromley, Allan G. 1982. Charles Babbage's analytical engine, 1838. *Annals of the History of Computing* 4 (3), 196–217.

Green, Christopher D. 2001. Charles Babbage, the analytical engine, and the possibility of a 19th-century cognitive science. In Christopher D. Green, Marlene Shore & Thomas Teo (eds.), *The transformation of psychology: Influences of 19th-century philosophy, technology, and natural science*, 133–152. Washington, DC: American Psychological Association.

Grover, Aditi Sharma, Gerhard B. van Huyssteen & Marthinus W. Pretorius. 2011a. The South African human language technology audit. *Language Resources and Evaluation* 45 (3), 271–288.

Grover, Aditi Sharma, Gerhard B. van Huyssteen & Marthinus W. Pretorius. 2011b. A technology audit: The state of human language technologies (HLT) R&D in South Africa. In Dundar F. Kocaoglu, Timothy R. Anderson & Tugrul U. Daim (eds.), *Proceedings of PICMET'11: Technology management in the energy smart world (PICMET)*, 1693–1706, Portland, OR: IEEE.

Hooper, Rowan. 2012. Ada Lovelace: My brain is more than merely mortal. *New Scientist* 216 (2886), 29.

Mchombo, Sam. 2017. Politics of language choice in African education: The case of Kenya and Malawi. *International Relations and Diplomacy Journal* 5 (4), 181–204.

Moors, Carmen, Ilana Wilken, Karen Calteaux & Tebogo Gumede. 2018. Human language technology audit 2018: Analysing the development trends in resource availability in all South African languages. In *Proceedings of the annual conference of the South African institute of computer scientists and information technologists*, 296–304. New York: Association for Computing Machinery.

Ramaphosa, Cyril. 2019. Keynote address for National Human Rights Day. George Thabe Sports Ground, Sharpeville. https://www.thepresidency.gov.za/speeches/keynote-address-president-cyril-ramaphosa-occasion-national-human-rights-day-george-thabe (accessed 10 May 2022).

Republic of South Africa. 1996. *Constitution of the Republic of South Africa*. Pretoria: Department of Justice.

SARIR. 2016. *South African Research Infrastructure Roadmap*. Pretoria: Department of Science and Technology.

South African Human Rights Commission and others. 2016. *Transformation at public universities in South Africa, SAHRC Report*. Cape Town: South African Human Rights Commission.

Sula, Chris Alen & Heather V. Hill. 2019. The early history of digital humanities: An analysis of computers and the humanities (1966–2004) and literary and linguistic computing (1986–2004). *Digital Scholarship in the Humanities* 34 (Supplement_1), i190–i206.

Wilken, Ilana, Tebogo Gumede, Carmen Moors & Karen Calteaux. 2018. Human language technology audit 2018: Design considerations and methodology. In *International conference on intelligent and innovative computing applications (iconic)*, 553–559, Plaine Magnien, Mauritius: IEEE.

Nikola Ljubešić*, Tomaž Erjavec, Maja Miličević Petrović, and Tanja Samardžić

Together We Are Stronger: Bootstrapping Language Technology Infrastructure for South Slavic Languages with CLARIN.SI

Abstract: In this chapter we describe the recent developments in language technology infrastructure building for three South Slavic languages – Slovenian, Croatian, and Serbian. These developments are primarily the result of intense coordination between different projects. Our experience shows that the infrastructure for language technologies can be significantly improved even in countries with a less favourable socio-economic situation, such as Croatia and Serbia, where insufficient organizational capacity and funding are available for a standard, top-down development. We suggest that such countries can adopt a bottom-up approach in which even minor, personal, or topically marginal projects are coordinated within the emerging community. Furthermore, such bottom-up environments can benefit from coordination with other similar environments, in our case in Croatia or Serbia. We further propose that bottom-up approaches can profit from coordination with top-down environments in neighbouring and/or culturally close countries, Slovenia in our case, with both sides experiencing a positive impact. We illustrate the synergistic effect of these different types of collaboration and coordination on the examples of textual data harvesting, manual data annotation, language tool development, and general infrastructure building. We wrap up with the most recent development – a CLARIN knowledge centre for South Slavic languages, where the collaborative methodology is expanded to all South Slavic languages. We close the chapter with a set of suggestions and good practices for researchers and language communities in a similar position to the ones discussed in this chapter.

Keywords: South-Slavic languages, collaborative LT infrastructure development, CLARIN Knowledge Centre

***Corresponding author: Nikola Ljubešić,** Dept. of Knowledge Technologies, Jožef Stefan Institute, Ljubljana, Slovenia, e-mail: nikola.ljubesic@ijs.si

Tomaž Erjavec, Dept. of Knowledge Technologies, Jožef Stefan Institute, Ljubljana, Slovenia, e-mail: tomaz.erjavec@ijs.si

Maja Miličević Petrović, Dept. of Interpreting and Translation, University of Bologna, Bologna, Italy, e-mail: maja.milicevic2@unibo.it

Tanja Samardžić, University of Zürich, Zürich, Switzerland, e-mail: tanja.samardzic@uzh.ch

https://doi.org/10.1515/9783110767377-017

1 Introduction

Slovenian, Croatian, and Serbian have a lot in common. They are not only linguistically closely related, but also share a complex history in and out of former Yugoslavia. However, the countries in which they are currently spoken differ substantially in the approach to infrastructure building for language technologies: while an open infrastructure is continuously being developed in Slovenia, such an infrastructure is for the most part still missing in Croatia[1] and Serbia. In this chapter, we describe the efforts of a group of researchers to start a collaboration on language technology infrastructure building for Croatian and Serbian from 2012 onward. We also recount the collaboration between these bootstrapping efforts and the well-developed Slovenian infrastructure CLARIN.SI (founded in 2013, part of CLARIN ERIC since 2015), which has yielded an added value for all three parties involved.

To capture the cross-country differences, we propose a distinction between *top-down* and *bottom-up* infrastructure building approaches. We consider any approach to scientific infrastructure building that is based on strategic national documents and well funded to be top-down. Where there is a lack of an overall strategy and of the necessary funding (which mostly go hand in hand), we refer to the efforts to bootstrap at least parts of an infrastructure as bottom-up. Given that infrastructure building is a complex and non-monolithic process, our position is that no single case can be strictly defined as top-down or bottom-up, but that most infrastructure building processes can be considered to predominantly belong to one or the other type. In the case of infrastructure building for Slovenian, Croatian, and Serbian, we consider Slovenian to mostly follow the top-down paradigm, while Croatian and Serbian predominantly rely on the bottom-up approach.

We also propose a preliminary explanation for why a country and a language take the top-down or the bottom-up approach, based on socio-economic factors such as GDP per capita[2] and R&D expenditure. While we do not claim that the same kind of explanation is appropriate for all contexts, we do believe that this is a suitable systematization of the course of infrastructure building taken in the three countries we are interested in.

---

1 Croatia became a member of CLARIN ERIC in 2018, but the infrastructure building process is still in an early phase.

2 There have already been attempts at explaining the level of technical maturity of a language through the GDP of its speakers, as was the case with the GLP (Gross Language Product) in (Hammarström 2009).

The remainder of this chapter is structured as follows. We first give a very brief introduction to what is the currently dominant paradigm in language technology development, namely machine learning. We continue with an outline of the linguistic, socio-economic, and technological context of the collaborations we discuss. We then move on to present two projects, dedicated respectively to Croatian and Serbian (ReLDI) and to Slovenian (JANES), whose separate and joint efforts led to major improvements in the quality and availability of language technologies for South Slavic languages. A CLARIN knowledge centre (CLASSLA) established as a follow-up initiative that also involves Bulgarian and Macedonian is subsequently described. We conclude the chapter with some practical remarks that can be taken as a set of guidelines for researchers working on resource-poor languages and/or in unsupportive environments.

A timeline visualization of the main projects described in this chapter is given in Figure 1.

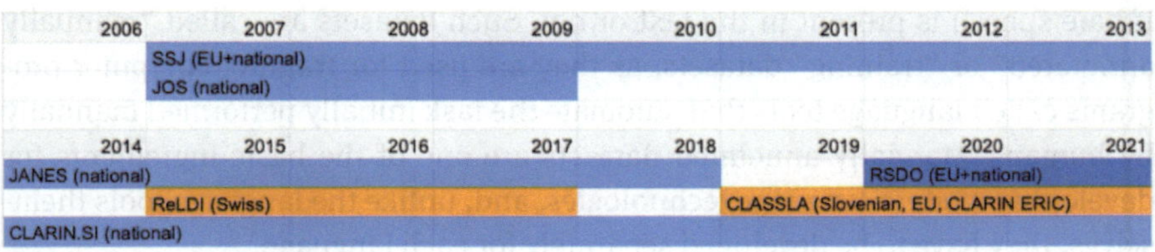

Figure 1: The timeline of the main projects described in this chapter. Blue indicates Slovenian (top-down) projects, while orange is used to mark bottom-up initiatives. The type of funding is given in parentheses.

The content of this chapter is related to (Hennelly et al. 2022), who discuss the development of digital language resources skills in South Africa, and also portray the historical development of language technologies in the area. The chapter by (Lindén et al. 2022) describes the collection of spoken data in Finland via an online platform, and is also related to this chapter in terms of identifying elegant technological solutions for collecting large quantities of language data, and taking into account the language variation present in an area.

2 Machine learning as the backbone of current language technologies

Language technologies can be simply defined as computer programs that can process language input into some desired (language) output (Tadić 2003). Some examples of language technologies are machine translation systems (accepting input in one language and producing the output in another), speech-to-text systems (accepting recorded speech as input and producing textual output), text normalization (accepting user-generated textual content and producing standardized text on output), or hate speech identification (accepting a text as input and producing a label that indicates whether hate speech is present in the text).

Since the mid-1990s, the dominant paradigm in developing language technologies has been machine learning. This paradigm allows computers to solve language-related problems (machine translation, text normalization, hate speech detection, etc.) by learning from examples, i.e., from instances in which the task at hand has already been solved by humans. For text normalization such examples would be sentences of non-standard, user-generated text paired with a manually normalized version of the same sentences. For hate speech detection such data would be a set of texts complete with manually assigned labels that show if hate speech is present in the text or not. Such datasets are called "manually annotated" or "training" datasets, as they are used for training computer programs called language tools that automate the task initially performed manually by humans. Manually annotated datasets are one of the basic ingredients for developing modern language technologies, and, unlike the language tools themselves, they have to be developed separately for each language.

The production of manually annotated datasets is a costly and complex process if such data are not created as a side-product of a regular human activity, for example, translation of texts. For the most part, the process requires multiple steps: (1) a detailed definition of the problem in the form of annotation guidelines; (2) the training of human annotators; (3) the annotation itself; and (4) the resolution of annotation disagreements. To complicate matters further, this process is not linear, but rather iterative, for instance, disagreements between annotators mostly point to issues either in the annotator training or in the definition of the problem itself. Given the complex, labour-intensive, and costly set-up of annotation campaigns, the possibility of reducing the complexity and/or costs of annotation campaigns through joint efforts of multiple teams or projects is highly attractive, yet difficult to implement in practice.

An important feature of machine learning is the capacity to generalize from training data, which enables language tools to process previously unseen data. This feature is also very useful in settings where similar languages are to be processed. Specifically, language tools, trained on one language, are capable of processing another, similar language, where the quality of this processing depends, inter alia, on the language similarity, the processing task, and the amount and quality of the training data.

3 Setting the scene: The case of South Slavic

In order to provide some background on the synergistic potential of collaborative development of language technology infrastructures for South Slavic languages, we first briefly introduce the language group and the three languages for which the synergy has been exploited the most – Slovenian, Croatian, and Serbian. Next, we outline a basic socio-economic context and describe the language technology infrastructure developments in the last decade in the countries where the three languages are spoken.

3.1 The South Slavic language group

One of three branches of the Slavic languages (along with East and West Slavic), the South Slavic language group is itself divided in branches: a western branch that comprises Slovenian, Croatian, Bosnian, Serbian, and Montenegrin, and an eastern branch composed of Macedonian and Bulgarian (Stanojčić and Popović 2008). Both are rather unique in terms of linguistic and sociolinguistic properties. The eastern branch is somewhat of a linguistic outlier among Slavic languages in general, having a definite article but no nominal cases or infinitive verb forms (Ivić 1985). The western branch is particularly well-known for the complex sociolinguistic situation surrounding the languages that used to be part of Serbo-Croatian, which underwent gradual separation and have been developing as separate standards from the 1990's onward.

Despite now being independent standard languages, Croatian, Bosnian, Serbian, and Montenegrin remain highly mutually intelligible, reflecting the fact that standard Serbo-Croatian was based on a single dialect (called Shtokavian, from the question word *što* 'what'). Such a high level of mutual intelligibility does not exist among any other pairs of standard South Slavic languages. However, when dialectal variation is taken into account, it is easily observed that the South Slavic group forms a continuum spanning from Slovenia at the north-west to Bulgaria at the south-east (see e.g., Ivić 1985). In fact, the Kajkavian dialect (from another version of 'what', *kaj*), spoken in densely populated north-western Croatia, is closer to standard Slovenian than to standard Croatian (Kapović 2017), while Torlak vernaculars spoken in eastern Serbia are closer to Macedonian and Bulgarian than to Serbian (Ivić 1985). The continuum is also reflected in alphabet choices, with Slovenian and Croatian using only the Latin script, Bosnian, Serbian, and Montenegrin both Latin and Cyrillic, and Macedonian and Bulgarian only the Cyrillic script.

The synergistic efforts described in this chapter were in part made possible by the dialectal continuum and the ensuing similarities between South Slavic languages. Our focus is on language technology developments for three languages of the western branch, namely Slovenian, Croatian, and Serbian. As outlined above, standard Slovenian is the most distinct of the three, while Croatian and Serbian are fully mutually intelligible (albeit with some phonetic, lexical, and morphosyntactic differences). Croatian and Serbian thus provide particularly rich opportunities for joint language technology developments, with technologies developed for one language often being applicable to the other, but Slovenian is sufficiently close to also take part in the collaborative efforts.

3.2 The state of infrastructure for language technologies in Slovenia, Croatia and Serbia

From 1918 to 1991, Slovenia, Croatia and Serbia were parts of the same country (initially the Kingdom of Serbs, Croats, and Slovenes, and then Yugoslavia) and their scientific development was to some extent coordinated, although differences in the socio-economic status were present throughout the whole period. For instance, in 1988 the GDP index (which averaged to 100 for Yugoslavia as a whole) was 198 for Slovenia, 125 for Croatia and 89 for Serbia and Montenegro (Stiperski and Lončar 2008). After the break-up of Yugoslavia, Croatia and Serbia were heavily affected by the Yugoslav wars, while for Slovenia this was the case to a much lesser extent. The conflicts of the 1990s deepened the economic divide even more. In 2005, years after the conflicts, the previously introduced GDP index in Slovenia amounted to 313, in Croatia it was 152, while in Serbia and Montenegro it was only 59 (Stiperski and Lončar 2008). A similar divide is still visible today, with the 2019 GDP per capita (in euros) being 21,260 in Slovenia, 13,480 in Croatia, and 5,890 in Serbia.[3] A similar divide is visible in the expenditure on research and development in 2018, with Slovenia spending 1.94% of its GDP on R&D, while the figure for Croatia is 0.97% and for Serbia 0.92%.

The differences in socio-economic factors also follow the level of Euro-Atlantic integration, with Slovenia being a member of the European Union since 2007, Croatia joining in 2013, and Serbia being at present a candidate state. This kind of integration has been particularly important in terms of funding for research infrastructure developments.

3 https://ec.europa.eu/eurostat/databrowser/view/sdg_08_10/default/table?lang=en, data for 2021.

And indeed, the development of language technology infrastructure in the three countries roughly matches their overall socio-economic and political situation depicted above. In Slovenia, there have been continuous developments since the national project "Linguistic annotation of Slovene language: methods and resources"[4] (2007–2010) and the EU structural funds project "Communication in Slovene" (2007–2013), followed by Slovenia setting up its CLARIN.SI infrastructure in 2013, with a repository of language resources and tools. Currently ongoing is the project "Development of Slovenian in a digital environment" (2020–2022),[5] which is funded with EUR 4 million through the Slovenian Ministry of Culture and the European Regional Development Fund. These projects were both supported and followed by development of strategic documents and bodies on the national level, the most prominent being the Resolution on the National Programme for Language Policy (2013), the Action Plan for Language Infrastructure (2015), and the Council for Monitoring the Development of Language Resources and Technologies (2017).[6]

In Croatia and Serbia there have been very few top-down efforts and no wide-reaching national projects aimed at building a language technology infrastructure. Academic institutions and societies for language technologies (established in both countries) did participate in some relevant projects and language technology developments, but not comparable in magnitude to the ones in Slovenia. Croatia has in addition become a CLARIN ERIC member in 2018, but the infrastructure building is still in its early days. Moreover, the transfer potential between Croatian and Serbian, enabled by their great linguistic similarity, was not at all exploited and no joint projects were realized, with the exception of the MULTEXT-East project (Erjavec 2012) (1995–1997), which produced, inter alia, unrelated morphosyntactic specifications and resources for Croatian and Serbian. In fact, the lack of joint efforts in developing language technologies is a consequence of a complicated language history, with opposing and intertwined tendencies towards unification and diversification (Ljubešić, Miličević Petrović, and Samardžić 2018).

This is why a largely bottom-up approach had to be taken for both languages, with researchers personally dedicating themselves to develop basic language technologies, frequently within projects that were in fact focused on different, more specific topics. A good example is the development of the largest training dataset for basic processing of Croatian, which started as a personal side-pro-

4 http://nl.ijs.si/jos/index-en.html
5 https://slovenscina.eu/
6 http://www.efnil.org/projects/lle/slovenia/slovenia

ject, was improved through projects on unrelated topics of machine translation and text input assistant development, and finally received some focused attention in the ReLDI project that is described in more detail in Section 4.1. Such a development, although strenuous for the researchers involved, ensured that both Croatian and Serbian are today present in the Universal Dependencies project,[7] an open community effort with nearly 200 treebanks in over 100 languages with consistent syntactic annotation, and can be processed through the many annotation pipelines developed on the basis of these treebanks, such as Stanza (Qi et al. 2020), UDPipe (Straka and Straková 2017) or SpaCy.[8]

4 ReLDI, JANES, and CLARIN.SI: Moving forward together

In this section we present examples of bottom-up infrastructure development (the ReLDI project), examples of top-down developments (the JANES project), as well as the collaboration of bottom-up and top-down activities through collaboration of the ReLDI and the JANES project, with the support of the CLARIN.SI infrastructure.

4.1 Bottom-up infrastructures for Croatian and Serbian: The ReLDI project

The Swiss-funded institutional partnership Regional Linguistic Data Initiative – ReLDI[9] – had as one of its primary objectives the coordination of bottom-up infrastructure developments for Serbian and Croatian, two mutually intelligible languages with shared linguistic history, but with little prior history of joint language technology development.

We showcase the ReLDI project as a good example of bottom-up infrastructure development via international funding in a situation in which socio-economic reasons do not allow for top-down developments. We reiterate here why we consider the ReLDI project to be a bottom-up initiative in building language technology infrastructure for Croatian and Serbian: due to a lack of strategic

7 https://universaldependencies.org/
8 https://spacy.io
9 https://reldi.spur.uzh.ch

documents and national funding for infrastructure building in both countries, younger generation researchers aware of the need for a language technology infrastructure had to apply for international funding to start a collaborative cross-border process of infrastructure building for both languages. The partners in the project were the University of Zürich, the University of Belgrade, and the University of Zagreb.

4.1.1 How it all started

An initiative for a collaboration between younger generation researchers from Croatia and Serbia on joint development of language technologies for the two languages first occurred at the outskirts of the LREC 2012 conference in Istanbul, where they decided to apply for a bilateral Croatian-Serbian project that would provide them with some basic funding for meetings, and a formal framework for joint work. However, following major organizational issues, the call for projects was cancelled and the proposal was not even evaluated. The same researchers then applied to a call for the Swiss-funded SCOPES programme, aimed at strengthening scientific cooperation between Eastern Europe and Switzerland. The submitted ReLDI project proposal was positively evaluated, enabling researchers to start coordinating the development of language technologies, with substantial financial support for activities other than travelling and networking.

4.1.2 Early efforts in Croatia

Prior to these coordination efforts, bottom-up data collection projects were already underway in Croatia, in the form of building large web corpora. Since there was full awareness of the lack of open language technologies for Serbian as well, and given the simplicity of extending the collection process to highly similar languages, while building the second version of the Croatian web corpus, a web corpus of Serbian and Bosnian was also built, with minimal additional efforts (Ljubešić and Klubička 2014). Similarly, while crawling parallel data from the Southeast European Times website, which used to publish news in languages of South-Eastern Europe, parallel data in Serbian, Croatian, and Bosnian were collected. The Southeast European Times (SETimes) parallel corpus kick-started research on discriminating between similar languages (Tiedemann and Ljubešić 2012), as well as the VarDial evaluation campaigns on natural language processing for similar languages, dialects and varieties (Zampieri et al. 2014; Chakravarthi et al. 2021).

In parallel with these data collection efforts, basic open language technologies for the Croatian language, based on manually annotated data and machine learning algorithms, also started to emerge (Agić, Ljubešić, and Merkler 2013; Agić and Ljubešić 2015). This provided additional motivation for setting up a Croatian–Serbian collaboration and for transferring to Serbian the resource and tool development methodology, as well as the data themselves, given the relatedness of the two languages. The key dataset behind these first open language technologies for Croatian was based on a portion of the SETimes Croatian corpus, which was manually annotated for part-of-speech information, lemmas, syntactic dependencies, and named entities, resulting in the SETimes.HR dataset (Agić, Ljubešić, and Merkler 2013). The entire endeavour was a side-project with no dedicated funding, but it represented the turning point in the future development of language technologies for Croatian. The annotation of the dataset was performed by one annotator only and without quality assurance in the form of double annotations or annotation curation, primarily due to the very limited resources available. However, this set of limited activities did not just result in the first freely available tagger and lemmatizer for the Croatian language, but in similar tools for Serbian as well, as a Serbian test set, constructed along the SETimes.HR dataset, showed that Croatian models performed reasonably well on Serbian too (Agić, Ljubešić, and Merkler 2013).

4.1.3 Main activities and results

The ReLDI project focused primarily on two tasks: joint development of language technologies for Croatian and Serbian, and training sessions in using these technologies for linguistic research.

As part of the language technology building, the first freely available manually annotated dataset for Serbian, SETimes.SR, was constructed (Batanović, Ljubešić, and Samardžić 2018), an obvious result of know-how transfer from Croatian (the SETimes.HR dataset) to Serbian. In addition to transferring the know-how in manually annotated dataset development for basic linguistic processing, the already-developed language technologies for Croatian proved to be highly useful for pre-annotating Serbian data, which cut the production costs of the Serbian dataset significantly. Inside the ReLDI project, the SETimes.HR dataset was also expanded to the hr500k dataset (Ljubešić et al. 2016), more than five times the size of the original SETimes.HR dataset (taking its ssj500k Slovenian dataset equivalent (Krek et al. 2019) as motivation and an example of good practice). Both datasets were much more carefully annotated than their predecessor SETimes.HR, and improvements on these datasets have since been turned into an ongoing process. Simultaneously, both languages were also added to the Universal Dependencies project[10] (Agić and Ljubešić 2015; Samardžić et al. 2017), which put Croatian and Serbian on the map of the modern language technology world.

Together with the development of manually annotated datasets for basic technologies, the recently finished inflectional lexicon of Croatian, hrLex (Ljubešić 2019a), built in a semi-automatic process (Ljubešić et al. 2015, 2016) inside the Abu-MaTran FP7 machine translation project, was used as a basis for building a comparable inflectional lexicon of Serbian, srLex (Ljubešić 2019b). With this coordinated effort, a 100,000-lexeme inflectional lexicon of Serbian was built for a fraction of the cost of building an inflectional lexicon of a highly-inflected language.

All the resources developed inside the ReLDI project were deposited in the Slovenian CLARIN.SI repository,[11] the nearest point that enabled high-quality long-term depositing of language resources for Croatian and Serbian.

4.2 Top-down infrastructure for Slovenian: The JANES project

The Slovenian national project JANES – *Jezikoslovna analiza nestandardne slovenščine* (Linguistic Analysis of Nonstandard Slovene) (Fišer, Ljubešić, and Erjavec 2020) had as one of its main goals the development of basic language technologies for Slovenian user-generated content. The project was run by the Faculty of Arts from the University of Ljubljana, and the Jožef Stefan Institute, also located in Ljubljana. This project was a logical continuation of top-down infrastructure building for the Slovenian language, given that basic language technologies for processing standard Slovenian had already been developed (Erjavec et al. 2010; Holdt, Kosem, and Berginc 2012), but were not fully suitable for user-generated online language. Previous research had shown that language technologies developed for standard language fail on non-standard variants, and that the most effective way forward is to build manually annotated datasets for non-standard variants that would enable an efficient adaptation of language technologies (Gimpel et al. 2011).

The three main outputs of the JANES projects were: (1) the JANES corpus, (2) the JANES manually annotated datasets, which were the basis for (3) the JANES toolchain, used for linguistically annotating the JANES corpus, the

10 https://universaldependencies.org
11 https://www.clarin.si/repository/xmlui/

most important resource to date for research into non-standard Slovenian. We describe these three components in the following subsections.

4.2.1 The JANES corpus

To produce the JANES corpus, three main sources were used: (1) Twitter (with a very good API for content harvesting); (2) web pages with a significant amount of user-generated content, i.e., newspapers with comments, blogs and fora; and (3) Wikipedia talk and discussion pages. The first two sources proved to be the richest in terms of non-standard features.

For the collection of data from Twitter, a simple dedicated tool was built, TweetCat (Ljubešić, Fišer, and Erjavec 2014), which enables continuous collection of tweets written in a low-density language. TweetCat requires only seed words (very frequent words specific of a language), to start the data collection process. Given the simplicity of extending the procedure to other languages, the decision was made to collect, in parallel with Slovenian tweets, Twitter posts in Croatian and Serbian. This was the starting point of a future collaboration and parallel infrastructure building for user-generated-content technologies for the two additional South Slavic languages described in Section 4.3.

As opposed to the Twitter collection procedure, scraping content from web pages proved to be highly site-dependent, as each web platform requires a specific tool to be built. What is more, the tool has a limited lifetime as any modifications in the web page layout break it. For that reason, harvesting of similar sources written in other languages was not even considered. Finally, while harvesting Wikipedia pages is simple, the analyses of the data showed them to be of limited informativeness for non-standard language features, so no harvesting of additional languages was performed.

4.2.2 The JANES manual data annotation

As discussed in Sections 2 and 4.2, to develop language technology tools that are able to process user-generated content, it was necessary to produce manually annotated datasets that would serve as their training data. The types of processing that were of most interest were (1) text standardness prediction, (2) text normalization, (3) part-of-speech and morphosyntactic tagging, (4) lemmatization, and (5) named entity recognition. A very basic example of a sentence with these annotation layers is given in Table 1.

Table 1: An example sentence of low orthographic and linguistical standardness, with manual token-level annotation of normalization, part-of-speech tagging, lemmatization, and named entity recognition.

Token	Normalized	Part-of-speech	Morphosyntax	Lemma	NER
ja	ja	PART	Q	ja	O
jst	jaz	PRON	Pp1-sn	jaz	O
sm	sem	AUX	Va-r1s-n	biti	O
poa	pa	CCONJ	Cc	pa	O
slisau	slišal	VERB	Vmbp-sm	slišati	O
da	da	SCONJ	Cs	da	O
je	je	AUX	Va-r3s-n	biti	O
CLARIN.SI	CLARIN.SI	PROPN	Npmsn	CLARIN.SI	B-ORG
top	top	ADJ	Agpmsnn	top	O
...	...	PUNCT	Z	...	O

The standardness level annotation was performed at the (short) text level (tweet, comment) and it indicated the degree of orthographic standardness (punctuation usage, character repetitions, etc.) and linguistic standardness (use of non-standard word forms). Identifying non-standard texts in an automatic manner was important for two reasons: (1) it was crucial that manually annotated datasets over-represent non-standard content, as this content is hard to process with standard technologies; and (2) having non-standardness information available in the whole JANES corpus enables researchers to focus on those parts of the corpora that contain non-standard features. Manually annotating and then automating the annotation of these two variables on the entire JANES corpus was crucial for the project given that, perhaps unexpectedly, most of user-generated content closely follows the norm.

The two main manually annotated datasets produced in the project were Janes-Norm (Erjavec et al. 2016) and Janes-Tag (Erjavec et al. 2019). In Janes-Norm (185,000 tokens in size), each word was manually assigned a standardized spelling. While the process of standardizing words might seem straightforward, it proved to be the most challenging of all the manual annotation campaigns in the project. This was mostly due to a large number of borderline cases (e.g., what is the normalized form of a word without a standard equivalent?), where problems had to be discovered first, a solution then agreed upon, and finally added to the annotation guidelines. Once the annotation guidelines were prepared, annotator training followed. The second dataset, Janes-Tag (Erjavec et al. 2019) (75,000 tokens), is a subset of Janes-Norm that was manually annotated at the levels of part-of-speech, lemma, and named entity.

Overall, these annotation campaigns were by far among the most complex to be performed by the research team, mostly due to a lack of standards for linguistic analysis of user-generated content. The opportunity to transfer the accumulated knowledge to other languages thus became very appealing.

4.2.3 The JANES toolchain

The tools developed inside the JANES project correspond for the most part to the levels of annotation described in the previous subsection. The first tool to be developed was the text standardness predictor which, given a text, returns two continuous values – one encoding orthographic standardness, the other linguistic standardness.

The remaining tools in the JANES toolchain consist of a text normalizer (Ljubešić et al. 2016),[12] part-of-speech tagger, lemmatizer, and named entity recognizer (Ljubešić, Erjavec, and Fišer 2017).[13] Given that all the developed tools were based on the machine learning paradigm, in order to adapt them for other languages, only manually annotated data in the specific languages were required, making the already considered possibility of constructing annotated datasets for other languages even more interesting.

All the three main deliverables of the JANES project were deposited and made available to the research community via the CLARIN.SI infrastructure.

The JANES project is a good example showing that almost any top-down infrastructure building activity carries a significant potential for extending the impact of that activity to other languages. While collecting data for the language of primary interest, data in related languages was collected as well, with minimal additional effort. During the manual annotation of a part of the collected data, to automate the annotation of the remaining data collection via machine learning, the significant potential for transfer of annotation guidelines and the annotation methodology to other languages was observed. Finally, a machine-learning-based toolchain was developed, which requires only the manually annotated data in the other languages to automate the annotation of these languages.

12 https://github.com/clarinsi/csmtiser
13 https://github.com/clarinsi/janes-tagger

4.3 Bottom-up *and* top-down: JANES + ReLDI = more than the sum

Thanks to the time overlap (as seen in Figure 1) and good personal relationships, ReLDI and JANES collaborated closely on extending the language technology infrastructure for user-generated-content processing from Slovenian to Croatian and Serbian. This is a great example of collaboration between a top-down language technology development environment (Slovenia), and two bottom-up environments (Croatia and Serbia), serving both sides involved. It is important to note that none of the developments described in this section would have been possible without the many preceding activities described in the previous sections.

4.3.1 How it all started

Unlike the unsuccessful application for a bilateral project between Croatia and Serbia, which produced the ReLDI partnership as a direct consequence, researchers from Slovenia and Serbia did receive a bilateral project grant with limited funding, primarily aimed at funding joint meetings. Given that this funding was obtained around the beginning of the JANES project, when the collection of Croatian and Serbian Twitter data via the TweetCat tool was already underway, and the initial manual annotation campaigns for text standardness in Slovenian have already been performed, the focus in the bilateral project was on producing Twitter datasets manually annotated with standardness level for Croatian and Serbian.

Aside from producing datasets manually annotated for standardness, developing training tools, and applying standardness labels over the full Twitter collections for Croatian and Serbian, this bilateral project also included a series of comparative studies on the three languages performed on the issue of standardness of user-generated content (Fišer et al. 2015; Miličević and Ljubešić 2016; Miličević, Ljubešić, and Fišer 2017). These studies were of great use in future activities on preparing training datasets for user-generated content processing in Croatian and Serbian. Specifically, they showed that, while the amount of non-standard elements in user-generated content was already low in Slovenian, in Croatian it was even lower, with non-standardness in Serbian being mostly encoded through lexical choices only, rather than through non-standard grammatical forms present in the two other languages.

4.3.2 JANES EXPRESS

The JANES project put a lot of emphasis on dissemination. One of the related activities in the project was the JANES EXPRESS series of lectures for students and fellow researchers in corpus and computational linguistics, which were organized in Ljubljana (Slovenia), Zagreb (Croatia) and Belgrade (Serbia). The lectures were organized in collaboration with the ReLDI project and they were meant to communicate the guidelines for the manual annotation of corpora for user-generated content processing, and to provide an introduction to the annotation platform WebAnno,[14] an offering of the CLARIN.SI infrastructure, used for annotating the Janes-Norm and Janes-Tag datasets. In addition to communicating with potential annotators and the interested public, the goal of the meetings was also to adapt the guidelines to the specificities of Croatian and Serbian, so more focused activities were performed with the annotators for both languages at the outskirts of the JANES EXPRESS events.

Once the JANES annotation procedure was communicated to Croatian and Serbian colleagues via JANES EXPRESS, and the annotation guidelines were (moderately) adapted, manual annotation on the Croatian and Serbian data excerpts, sampled in a manner comparable to Slovenian data for the Janes-Tag dataset, was performed as part of the ReLDI project activities. The CLARIN.SI infrastructure offered technological support for the WebAnno platform, and the JANES project offered advice on linguistic issues arising during the annotation process. The results of this collaboration are the ReLDI-NormTagNER-hr manually annotated dataset of non-standard Croatian (Ljubešić et al. 2019a), 89,000 tokens in size, and the ReLDI-NormTagNER-sr manually annotated dataset of non-standard Serbian (Ljubešić et al. 2019b), composed of 92,000 tokens.

Our rough estimate is that the time and energy invested in setting up annotation guidelines for the two additional languages was lowered to one fifth of the effort that was required for the original Slovenian dataset. In addition to the annotation guidelines being obtained for a minor fraction of the effort, the comparability of the annotation schemas was ensured, which is an important added value for the usage of the three datasets. The cost of the manual annotation itself were also moderately lower for Croatian and Serbian than was the case for the Slovenian dataset. In particular, during the Slovenian annotation campaign, pilot campaigns were necessary to test-run the annotation process and improve the annotation guidelines and the annotator training. No such pilots were necessary during the development of the Croatian and Serbian datasets.

14 https://webanno.github.io/webanno/

4.3.3 Joint technology development

The JANES project made a significant impact on the Croatian and Serbian language technology infrastructure by ensuring the production of manually annotated datasets of user-generated-content for a fraction of the overall price. In return, the ReLDI project developed a CRF-based tagger, named reldi-tagger,[15] which also included models for Slovenian (Ljubešić and Erjavec 2016). This tagger achieved not only new state-of-the-art results on part-of-speech tagging and lemmatization of Croatian and Serbian (Ljubešić et al. 2016), but also on Slovenian (Ljubešić and Erjavec 2016), regardless of the intensive language technology developments in Slovenia. The reldi-tagger tool was primarily built for processing of standard language, therefore an adaptation to the requirements of non-standard language was performed as part of the JANES project. The main modification was the usage of Brown clusters – a predecessor of the now omnipresent word embeddings. These activities resulted in the janes-tagger (Ljubešić, Erjavec, and Fišer 2017),[16] which was equipped not just with a model for tagging and lemmatizing non-standard Slovenian, but also non-standard Croatian and non-standard Serbian. This was possible primarily due to the comparable manually annotated datasets described above.

These developments show how the well-resourced, top-down infrastructure for Slovenian managed to profit from the two bottom-up infrastructures in the realm of technology development. Because of the collaboration between the JANES and the ReLDI teams, the top-down infrastructure obtained a new state-of-the-art tool for processing standard and non-standard language from the two bottom-up infrastructures. The two bottom-up infrastructures did not need to invest any additional resources to be of use to the Slovenian infrastructure because of (1) the relatedness of the three languages, and (2) the high capacity for technology reuse under the machine learning paradigm.

5 Scaling up and ensuring long-term impact: The CLASSLA knowledge centre

Given the successful collaboration between the JANES and the ReLDI projects and the CLARIN.SI infrastructure on building the language technology infrastructure

15 https://github.com/clarinsi/reldi-tagger
16 https://github.com/clarinsi/janes-tagger

for processing user-generated content for the three South Slavic languages, and also the success of the ReLDI project in coordinating the development of language technologies for the standard language, an idea emerged to institutionalize this paradigm for future collaborative language technology development.

Two possibilities were considered: (1) keeping the language focus on the Western South Slavic branch, i.e., continuing working on Slovenian, Croatian and Serbian (and, as much as resources allow, Bosnian and Montenegrin); or (2) expanding the collaboration to the Eastern South Slavic branch, namely Macedonian and Bulgarian. The decision was made to embrace the latter option, for the following reasons: (1) while Slovenian and Croatian use only the Latin alphabet, Serbian is a two-script language, being in that respect close to the eastern branch which uses the Cyrillic script only; (2) the Macedonian language has significant similarities to both Serbian and Bulgarian; (3) Macedonian is a heavily under-resourced language that would significantly benefit from such collaboration and, finally; (4) colleagues from the Bulgarian CLADA-BG infrastructure were enthusiastic about such a collaboration.

Following this idea, the CLARIN Knowledge Centre for South Slavic Languages (CLASSLA)[17] was born. The knowledge centre received official status in March 2019 and thereby became part of the CLARIN ERIC infrastructure. It is currently jointly led by the Slovenian CLARIN.SI and the Bulgarian CLADA-BG infrastructures. The main components of the knowledge centre are an e-mail-based helpdesk, frequently asked questions documents for all the mentioned languages, the CLARIN.SI concordancers (which are being expanded with various South Slavic corpora), and the CLARIN.SI repository, which already contains many resources and tools for various South Slavic languages. The main planned activities for the CLASSLA knowledge centre are – similar to the ReLDI project – to coordinate development of additional language technologies, but also to jointly build and serve a user base of the developing infrastructure.

As part of the CLARIN.SI infrastructure and the RSDO project (2020–2022), both aimed at enhancing the Slovenian language technology infrastructure, the CLASSLA linguistic processing pipeline[18] was produced. Its aim was to become the new state-of-the-art tool for basic linguistic processing, primarily of Slovenian, by exploiting the newer neural technologies (Ljubešić and Dobrovoljc 2019). Thanks to previous collaboration and the existence of comparable datasets for Croatian and Serbian, the CLASSLA pipeline covered both standard and non-standard Slovenian, Croatian, and Serbian from the very start.

17 https://www.clarin.si/info/k-centre/
18 https://pypi.org/project/classla/

As part of the collaboration inside the CLASSLA knowledge centre, the Bulgarian CLADA-BG infrastructure prepared the required data for training the CLASSLA pipeline for Bulgarian as well. The Bulgarian data enabled the training of a full stack of tools for the standard language. Manually annotated training data for user-generated content in Bulgarian are not yet available.

Another successful collaboration inside the CLASSLA knowledge centre was on the development of basic linguistic processing for the Macedonian language, namely tokenization, part-of-speech and morphosyntactic tagging, and lemmatization. For this to happen, a manually annotated dataset had to be produced, which was made possible through two developments: (1) a dataset of Macedonian suitable for training language technologies had been, starting with the MULTEXT-East project, continuously developed in a bottom-up approach for more than a decade, receiving recently a push from the CLASSLA knowledge centre to become usable for the CLASSLA pipeline; and (2) a large crawl of the Macedonian web was performed by the CLASSLA knowledge centre to enable the learning of good word embeddings (Ljubešić 2020), a crucial ingredient of any modern language technology. Thanks to these coordination efforts, the CLASSLA pipeline is now able to process Macedonian on a basic tokenizer-tagger-lemmatizer level, making it the go-to tool for the processing of Macedonian.[19]

Other successful collaborations of the CLASSLA knowledge centre concern the construction and publication of the first two corpora of the Montenegrin language, namely the English-Montenegrin parallel corpus (Božović et al. 2018)[20] and the Montenegrin web corpus (Ljubešić and Erjavec 2021),[21] as well as the preparation of Wikipedia corpora of all South Slavic languages, processed and presented in a uniform way, to be updated on a yearly basis (Ljubešić et al. 2021; Markoski et al. 2021).[22]

Many future collaborative activities are planned. One is the production of methodologically comparable monitor web corpora of all South Slavic languages, an activity planned inside the MaCoCu project,[23] focusing on enhancing machine translation for less-resourced languages. Another very timely development are open speech technologies and the significant impact CLASSLA would have if it managed to produce spoken corpora for South Slavic languages with available

19 The only tool previously freely downloadable for basic linguistic processing of Macedonian was BTagger (Aepli, von Waldenfels, and Samardžić 2014).

20 https://www.clarin.si/noske/run.cgi/corp_info?corpname=opusmonte_cnr&struct_attr_stats=1

21 https://www.clarin.si/noske/run.cgi/corp_info?corpname=mewac&struct_attr_stats=1

22 https://github.com/clarinsi/classla-wikipedia

23 https://macocu.eu

transcriptions. A strong source candidate for such a resource are parliamentary proceedings. Transcripts of parliamentary speeches in three South Slavic languages – Slovenian, Croatian and Bulgarian – have recently been processed with the CLASSLA pipeline with minimum overhead, inside the CLARIN ERIC-funded ParlaMint project (Erjavec et al. 2021).[24] A transcript-to-speech-aligned resource of just a few tens of hours could be all one needs to train basic speech-to-text systems[25] given the recent developments in pre-trained models for speech (Baevski et al. 2020). Having at least a basic speech-to-text system would start opening the ever-growing collection of spoken language recordings to researchers who nowadays still focus, mostly due to technical constraints and accessibility issues, primarily on written language.

6 An experiential "how-to" for other languages

In this section we share some insights and best practices for researchers and communities who find themselves in positions similar to those of the three languages we work on. The insights and advice focus on three topics: (1) general infrastructure building, (2) building language technology infrastructure, and (3) funding bottom-up infrastructure building.

6.1 General infrastructure building

Building an infrastructure top-down should not be considered "easy", as it requires the highest possible level of dedication by researchers, who need to push for the strategic documents to be drafted and accepted on the national level, for funding to be ensured, for projects to be successfully run, and so on. It is also crucial to consider in advance whether such top-down developments are feasible at all, and, depending on one's estimate, the choice between a top-down and a bottom-up road should be made as early as possible. For example, there are rather evident socio-economic and political reasons behind the lack of more top-down developments in open language technology infrastructures in Croatia and

24 https://www.clarin.eu/content/parlamint-towards-comparable-parliamentary-corpora

25 While finalizing this chapter, we have released such a system for Croatian (https://huggingface.co/classla/wav2vec2-xls-r-parlaspeech-hr), with the release of a two-thousand-hour ASR training dataset pending. The released dataset will be the first openly available ASR dataset for Croatian or Serbian.

Serbia, and waiting for a top-down approach to happen would not have made much sense in these countries.

Building an infrastructure in a bottom-up fashion is a very laborious endeavour, with fewer results than is the case with the top-down approach, but this is the only option available in most countries of a lower socio-economic standing. We also wish to stress here that it is not only the funding that is required for an infrastructure to be built top-down, but an overall high research and public administration capacity as well, which tends to go hand in hand with finances.

If one needs to rely on bottom-up infrastructure building, the best remedy is to ensure continuous coordination of efforts between researchers ready to take on specific tasks, even if this coordination is established through less official channels. Individual researchers investing all their efforts in their own solutions are highly unlikely to produce any tangible results.[26]

Regardless of whether two bottom-up infrastructures start to coordinate their efforts, or a bottom-up and a top-down infrastructure work together, benefits are to be expected for both sides.

6.2 Language technology infrastructure building

While performing language data collection, APIs and data dumps should be considered first, as their harvesting tends to be much simpler than any sort of web scraping. Moreover, data collection projects based on APIs and dumps can often be easily expanded to additional domains or languages with almost no extra effort.

Today's language technologies are based on machine learning algorithms that require manually annotated datasets. Building good quality datasets of this type is a very costly and complex process. Once an annotation campaign focused on a specific language problem starts, it is highly advisable to set the annotation goal as wide as possible, covering – if possible – additional domains or languages. This is because a comparable annotation result on another domain or language can be achieved with a fraction of resources that would be required for a full annotation campaign on that domain or language.

The technologies based on machine learning do require manually annotated datasets, but not much more than that. This opens up the space for training

26 Coordination is a crucial ingredient for top-down infrastructure building as well. However, in top-down environments coordination tends to be present from the beginning and tends to be a key ingredient behind the very existence of a top-down infrastructure.

developed technologies for multiple languages if comparable training data are available.

Technology is becoming ever more available, and our advice is that most energy, especially for bottom-up infrastructure building, should be invested in the production of manually annotated datasets. Once high-quality manually annotated data are available, it is quite easy to train different tools on that data. On top of that, machine-learning-based technology is nowadays developing at an unprecedented pace and the best bet for making an infrastructure future-proof is to invest in high-quality manually-annotated data. While we are still improving, and heavily using the CLASSLA pipeline, it is obvious that BERT-like pre-trained language models will be production-ready in the very near future. The code base for this new paradigm will be developed by large infrastructures and companies, and smart small infrastructures, especially the bottom-up ones, will be waiting in the wings with high-quality training data, ready for when the technology ripens and is easily offered to the users of the infrastructure.

6.3 Funding bottom-up infrastructure building

On the question of funding and running infrastructures, the situation is rather simple for the infrastructures being built top-down – these mostly receive significant national funding and have the necessary organizational capacity. For those infrastructures that have to be built bottom-up, we suggest the following.

International funding is much preferred, as national funding can be very hard to obtain, which is likely one of the reasons for the specific infrastructure not being built top-down in the first place. The Croatian and Serbian bottom-up infrastructure efforts were mostly supported by international funding.

Collaboration with other infrastructures-to-be that are in a similar bottom-up situation is highly advisable on the financial level as well. Any funding is much more likely to be obtained with joint forces. The good example are Croatian and Serbian joint efforts in obtaining funding.

There is no such thing as bad or too little funding. Work on the Croatian and Serbian user-generated content infrastructure was started on a project that only received a few thousand euros in funding.

It is worth coordinating efforts with top-down infrastructures as well, as this type of coordination effort might bring you by far the most return. Do not feel like you are exploiting someone: the other side will benefit from the collaboration as well, just as the Slovenian infrastructure has benefited from working on Croatian and Serbian.

Most activities need to be performed in an iterative manner. This is often the case even for top-down approaches, and when the funding is lacking, and conditions are far from optimal, the probability of obtaining a major single-run result is rather low. The Croatian standard-language training dataset came to its current size through three expansions and many more quality improvement iterations, another one being performed as we write.

Performing linguistic research alongside infrastructure building activities will inform these activities enormously. Research infrastructure building is full of pitfalls and identifying them early on is crucial. In our case, the user-generated-content infrastructure building profited enormously from the early observation that most data in this type of content is actually standard. This seemingly simple observation significantly changed the direction of the infrastructure development for all three languages.

7 Conclusion

This chapter has described the rather different roads to language technology development taken by three South Slavic languages. While the development in Slovenia has been predominantly top-down, relying on strategic documents and targeted funding, the developments in Croatia and Serbia have been rather bottom-up and most results have been achieved via smaller projects not formally embedded in any wider-scope strategy of infrastructure building. We have also shown the benefits of two types of collaboration between infrastructures(-to-be). The first type is between two bottom-up initiatives, for Croatian and Serbian, that was mostly driven by international funding, breaking the vicious circle related to the lack of national strategy, political will and funding for infrastructure building. The second type of collaboration, between top-down and bottom-up infrastructures, was illustrated on the collaboration between JANES and ReLDI projects. These two types of collaboration, together with CLARIN.SI as an overarching institutional framework, resulted in a crucial aggregation of resources and competences, which can now be streamed towards efficient future joint developments. The direction for scaling up these future developments is set by the recent establishment of the CLASSLA CLARIN knowledge centre.

We hope that this contribution will motivate further research in infrastructure development methodology in general, and especially on the coordination of infrastructure developments for related languages. We hope even more that it will enhance the practice of coordinating infrastructure developments, especially in the case of communities and languages that lack the socio-economic support necessary for the development of a top-down language technology infrastructure. The types of coordination that we have described in this chapter are, in our opinion, the best chance communities and languages have to kick-start an infrastructure development and ensure the functioning of a language in the digital age.

Acknowledgment: The results presented in this work have been funded by the Swiss National Science Foundation grant IZ74Z0_160501 (ReLDI), the European Union Seventh Framework Programme FP7/2007–2013 under grant agreement PIAP-GA-2012-324414 (Abu-MaTran), the Slovenian Research Agency within the national basic research project "Resources, Tools and Methods for the Research of Nonstandard Internet Slovene" (J6-6842, 2014–2017), and the Slovenian research infrastructure CLARIN.SI.

The authors also acknowledge the financial support from the Slovenian Research Agency (research core funding No. P6-0411 Language resources and technologies for Slovene language), from the European Union's Rights, Equality and Citizenship Programme (2014–2020) project IMSyPP (Innovative Monitoring Systems and Prevention Policies of Online Hate Speech, grant no. 875263), the Slovenian Research Agency and the Flemish Research Foundation bilateral research project LiLaH (The linguistic landscape of hate speech on social media, grant no. ARRS-N6-0099 and FWO-G070619N), and the Slovenian Research Agency and the Serbian Ministry of Education bilateral project "The Construction of Corpora and Lexica of Non-standard Serbian and Slovenian" (BI-RS/14-15-068).

Bibliography

Aepli, Noëmi, Ruprecht von Waldenfels & Tanja Samardžić. 2014. Part-of-speech tag disambiguation by cross-linguistic majority vote. *Proceedings of the first workshop on applying NLP tools to similar languages, varieties and dialects*, 76–84. Dublin, Ireland: Association for Computational Linguistics and Dublin City University.

Agić, Željko & Nikola Ljubešić. 2015. Universal Dependencies for Croatian (that work for Serbian, too). *The 5th workshop on Balto-Slavic natural language processing*, 1–8. Hissar, Bulgaria: INCOMA Ltd. Shoumen, BULGARIA.

Agić, Željko, Nikola Ljubešić & Danijela Merkler. 2013. Lemmatization and morphosyntactic tagging of Croatian and Serbian. *Proceedings of the 4th biennial international workshop on Balto-Slavic natural language processing*, 48–57. Sofia, Bulgaria: Association for Computational Linguistics.

Baevski, Alexei, Henry Zhou, Abdelrahman Mohamed & Michael Auli. 2020. wav2vec 2.0: A framework for self-supervised learning of speech representations. *arXiv preprint arXiv:2006.11477*.

Batanović, Vuk, Nikola Ljubešić & Tanja Samardžić. 2018. SETimes.SR – a reference training corpus of Serbian. *Proceedings of the Conference on Language Technologies & Digital Humanities 2018 (JT-DH 2018)*, 11–17. Ljubljana: Ljubljana University Press.

Božović, Petar, Tomaž Erjavec, Jörg Tiedemann, Nikola Ljubešić, Vojko Gorjanc et al. 2018. Opus-MontenegrinSubs 1.0: First electronic corpus of the Montenegrin language. *Proceedings of the Conference on Language Technologies & Digital Humanities 2018* (JT-DH 2018), 24–28. Ljubljana: Ljubljana University Press.

Chakravarthi, Bharathi Raja, Mihaela Gaman, Radu Tudor Ionescu, Heidi Jauhiainen, Tommi Jauhiainen, Krister Lindén, Nikola Ljubešić, Niko Partanen, Ruba Priyadharshini, Christoph Purschke et al. 2021. Findings of the VarDial Evaluation Campaign 2021. *Proceedings of the 8th VarDial Workshop on NLP for Similar Languages, Varieties and Dialects*, 1–11. Kiyv, Ukraine: Association for Computational Linguistics.

Erjavec, Tomaž. 2012. MULTEXT-East: morphosyntactic resources for Central and Eastern European languages. *Language Resources and Evaluation* 46 (1): 131–142.

Erjavec, Tomaž, Darja Fišer, Simon Krek & Nina Ledinek. 2010. The JOS Linguistically Tagged Corpus of Slovene. *Proceedings of the Seventh International Conference on Language Resources and Evaluation (LREC'10)*. Valletta, Malta: European Language Resources Association (ELRA).

Erjavec, Tomaž, Darja Fišer, Jaka Čibej & Špela Arhar Holdt. 2016. CMC training corpus Janes-Norm 1.2. Slovenian language resource repository CLARIN.SI.

Erjavec, Tomaž, Darja Fišer, Jaka Čibej, Špela Arhar Holdt, Nikola Ljubešić, Katja Zupan & Kaja Dobrovoljc. 2019. CMC training corpus Janes-Tag 2.1. Slovenian language resource repository CLARIN.SI.

Erjavec, Tomaž, Maciej Ogrodniczuk, Petya Osenova, Nikola Ljubešić, Kiril Simov, Vladislava Grigorova, Michał Rudolf, Andrej Pančur, Matyáš Kopp, Starkaður Barkarson, Steinhór Steingrímsson, Henk van der Pol, Griet Depoorter, Jesse de Does, Bart Jongejan, Dorte Haltrup Hansen, Costanza Navarretta, María Calzada Pérez, Luciana D. de Macedo, Ruben van Heusden & M. 2021. Linguistically annotated multilingual comparable corpora of parliamentary debates ParlaMint.ana 2.0. Slovenian language resource repository CLARIN.SI.

Fišer, Darja, Tomaž Erjavec, Nikola Ljubešić & Maja Miličević. 2015. Comparing the nonstandard language of Slovene, Croatian and Serbian tweets. *Simpozij Obdobja* 34: 225–231.

Fišer, Darja, Nikola Ljubešić & Tomaž Erjavec. 2020. The Janes project: language resources and tools for Slovene user generated content. *Language resources and evaluation* 54 (1): 223–246.

Gimpel, Kevin, Nathan Schneider, Brendan O'Connor, Dipanjan Das, Daniel Mills, Jacob Eisenstein, Michael Heilman, Dani Yogatama, Jeffrey Flanigan & Noah A. Smith. 2011. Part-of-speech tagging for Twitter: Annotation, features, and experiments. *Proceedings of the 49th annual meeting of the association for computational linguistics: Human language technologies*, 42–47. Portland, Oregon, USA: Association for Computational Linguistics.

Hammarström, Harald. 2009. Unsupervised Learning of Morphology and the Languages of the World. PhD dissertation, University of Gothenburg.

Hennelly, Martin, Langa Khumalo, Juan Steyn & Menno van Zaanen. 2022. Training of digital language resources skills in South Africa. In Darja Fišer & Andreas Witt (eds.), *CLARIN. The infrastructure for language resources*. Berlin: De Gruyter.

Holdt, Špela Arhar, Iztok Kosem & Nataša Logar Berginc. 2012. Izdelava korpusa Gigafida in njegovega spletnega vmesnika. *Proceedings of Eighth Language Technologies Conference IS-LTC*, Volume 12.

Ivić, Pavle. 1985. *Dijalektologija srpskohrvatskog jezika. Uvod i štokavsko narečje*. 2nd edition. Novi Sad: Matica srpska.
Kapović, Mate. 2017. The position of kajkavian in the South Slavic dialect continuum in light of old accentual isoglosses. *Zeitschrift für Slawistik* 62 (4): 606–620.
Krek, Simon, Kaja Dobrovoljc, Tomaž Erjavec, Sara Može, Nina Ledinek, Nanika Holz, Katja Zupan, Polona Gantar, Taja Kuzman, Jaka Čibej, Špela Arhar Holdt, Teja Kavčič, Iza Škrjanec, Dafne Marko, Lucija Jezeršek & Anja Zajc. 2019. Training corpus ssj500k 2.2. Slovenian language resource repository CLARIN.SI.
Lindén, Krister, Tommi Jauhiainen, Mietta Lennes, Mikko Kurimo, Aleksi Rossi, Tommi Kurki & Olli Pitkänen. 2022. Donate Speech: Collecting and sharing a large-scale speech database for Social Sciences, Humanities and Artificial Intelligence research and innovation. In Darja Fišer & Andreas Witt (eds.), *CLARIN. The infrastructure for language resources*. Berlin: De Gruyter.
Ljubešić, Nikola. 2019a. Inflectional lexicon hrLex 1.3. Slovenian language resource repository CLARIN.SI.
Ljubešić, Nikola. 2019b. Inflectional lexicon srLex 1.3. Slovenian language resource repository CLARIN.SI.
Ljubešić, Nikola. 2020. Word embeddings CLARIN.SI-embed.mk 0.1. Slovenian language resource repository CLARIN.SI.
Ljubešić, Nikola & Kaja Dobrovoljc. 2019. What does neural bring? Analysing improvements in morphosyntactic annotation and lemmatisation of Slovenian, Croatian and Serbian. *Proceedings of the 7th Workshop on Balto-Slavic Natural Language Processing*, 29–34. Florence, Italy: Association for Computational Linguistics.
Ljubešić, Nikola & Tomaž Erjavec. 2016. Corpus vs. lexicon supervision in morphosyntactic tagging: the case of Slovene. *Proceedings of the tenth international conference on language resources and evaluation (LREC'16)*, 1527–1531. Portorož, Slovenia: European Language Resources Association (ELRA).
Ljubešić, Nikola & Tomaž Erjavec. 2021. Montenegrin web corpus meWaC 1.0. Slovenian language resource repository CLARIN.SI.
Ljubešić, Nikola, Tomaž Erjavec, Vuk Batanović, Maja Miličević & Tanja Samardžić. 2019a. Croatian Twitter training corpus ReLDI-NormTagNER-hr 2.1. Slovenian language resource repository CLARIN.SI.
Ljubešić, Nikola, Tomaž Erjavec, Vuk Batanović, Maja Miličević & Tanja Samardžić. 2019b. Serbian Twitter training corpus ReLDI-NormTagNER-sr 2.1. Slovenian language resource repository CLARIN.SI.
Ljubešić, Nikola, Tomaž Erjavec & Darja Fišer. 2017. Adapting a state-of-the-art tagger for South Slavic languages to non-standard text. *Proceedings of the 6th workshop on Balto-Slavic natural language processing*, 60–68. Valencia, Spain: Association for Computational Linguistics.
Ljubešić, Nikola, Miquel Espla-Gomis, Filip Klubička & Nives Mikelić Preradović. 2015. Predicting inflectional paradigms and lemmata of unknown words for semi-automatic expansion of morphological lexicons. *Proceedings of the International Conference Recent Advances in Natural Language Processing*, 379–387. Hissar, Bulgaria: INCOMA Ltd. Shoumen, BULGARIA.
Ljubešić, Nikola, Darja Fišer & Tomaž Erjavec. 2014. TweetCaT: a tool for building Twitter corpora of smaller languages. *Proceedings of LREC*, 2279–2283. Reykjavik, Iceland: European Language Resources Association (ELRA).

Ljubešić, Nikola & Filip Klubička. 2014. {bs, hr, sr} WaC – Web corpora of Bosnian, Croatian and Serbian. *Proceedings of the 9th Web as Corpus Workshop (WaC-9)*, 29–35. Gothenburg, Sweden: Association for Computational Linguistics.

Ljubešić, Nikola, Filip Klubička, Željko Agić & Ivo-Pavao Jazbec. 2016. New inflectional lexicons and training corpora for improved morphosyntactic annotation of Croatian and Serbian. *Proceedings of the Tenth International Conference on Language Resources and Evaluation (LREC'16)*, 4264–4270. Portorož, Slovenia: European Language Resources Association (ELRA).

Ljubešić, Nikola, Filip Markoski, Elena Markoska & Tomaž Erjavec. 2021. Comparable corpora of South-Slavic Wikipedias CLASSLA-Wikipedia 1.0. Slovenian language resource repository CLARIN.SI.

Ljubešić, Nikola, Katja Zupan, Darja Fišer & Tomaž Erjavec. 2016. Normalising Slovene data: historical texts vs. user-generated content. *Proceedings of the 13th Conference on Natural Language Processing (KONVENS 2016)*, Volume 16, 146–155.

Ljubešić, Nikola, Maja Miličević Petrović & Tanja Samardžić. 2018. Borders and boundaries in Bosnian, Croatian, Montenegrin and Serbian: Twitter data to the rescue. *Journal of Linguistic Geography* 6 (2): 100–124.

Markoski, Filip, Elena Markoska, Nikola Ljubešić, Eftim Zdravevski & Ljupco Kocarev. 2021. Cultural topic modelling over novel Wikipedia corpora for South-Slavic languages. *Proceedings of the international conference on recent advances in natural language processing (ranlp 2021)*, 910–917. Held Online: INCOMA Ltd.

Miličević, Maja & Nikola Ljubešić. 2016. Tviterasi, tviteraši or twitteraši? Producing and analysing a normalised dataset of Croatian and Serbian tweets. *Slovenščina 2.0: empirical, applied and interdisciplinary research* 4 (2): 156–188.

Miličević, Maja, Nikola Ljubešić & Darja Fišer. 2017. Birds of a feather don't quite tweet together: An analysis of spelling variation in Slovene, Croatian and Serbian Twitterese. In Darja Fišer & Michael Beißwenger (eds.), *Investigating Computer-Mediated Communication: Corpus-based Approaches to Language in the Digital World*, 14–43. Ljubljana: Ljubljana University Press.

Qi, Peng, Yuhao Zhang, Yuhui Zhang, Jason Bolton & Christopher D Manning. 2020. Stanza: A python natural language processing toolkit for many human languages. *arXiv preprint arXiv:2003.07082.*

Samardžić, Tanja, Mirjana Starović, Željko Agić & Nikola Ljubešić. 2017. Universal Dependencies for Serbian in comparison with Croatian and other Slavic languages. *Proceedings of the 6th workshop on Balto-Slavic natural language processing*, 39–44. Valencia, Spain: Association for Computational Linguistics.

Stanojčić, Živojin & Ljubomir Popović. 2008. *Gramatika srpskog jezika za gimnazije i srednje škole*. 11th. Belgrade: Zavod za udžbenike i nastavna sredstva.

Stiperski, Zoran & Jelena Lončar. 2008. Changes in levels of economic development among the states formed in the area of former Yugoslavia. *Hrvatski geografski glasnik* 70 (2): 5–32.

Straka, Milan & Jana Straková. 2017. Tokenizing, PoS tagging, lemmatizing and parsing UD 2.0 with UDPipe. *Proceedings of the CoNLL 2017 Shared Task: Multilingual Parsing from Raw Text to Universal Dependencies*, 88–99. Vancouver, Canada: Association for Computational Linguistics.

Tadić, M. 2003. *Jezične tehnologije i hrvatski jezik*. Zagreb: Ex libris.

Tiedemann, Jörg & Nikola Ljubešić. 2012. Efficient discrimination between closely related languages. *Proceedings of COLING 2012*, 2619–2634. Mumbai, India: The COLING 2012 Organizing Committee.

Zampieri, Marcos, Liling Tan, Nikola Ljubešić & Jörg Tiedemann. 2014. A report on the DSL shared task 2014. *Proceedings of the first workshop on applying NLP tools to similar languages, varieties and dialects*, 58–67. Dublin, Ireland: Association for Computational Linguistics and Dublin City University.

Paweł Kamocki, Aleksei Kelli, and Krister Lindén

The CLARIN Committee for Legal and Ethical Issues and the Normative Layer of the CLARIN Infrastructure

Ville Oksanen, in Memoriam (26 December 1976– 23 November 2014)

Abstract: The normative layer of CLARIN is, alongside the organizational and technical layers, an essential part of the infrastructure. It consists of the regulatory framework (statutory law, case law, authoritative guidelines, etc.), the contractual framework (licenses, terms of service, etc.), and ethical norms. Navigating the normative layer requires expertise, experience, and qualified effort. In order to advise the Board of Directors, a standing committee dedicated to legal and ethical issues, the CLIC, was created. Since its establishment in 2012, the CLIC has made considerable efforts to provide not only the BoD but also the general public with information and guidance. It has published many articles (both in proceedings of CLARIN conferences and in its own White Paper Series) and developed several LegalTech tools. It also runs a Legal Information Platform, where accessible information on various issues affecting language resources can be found.

Keywords: CLIC, copyright, license, ethics

1 Introduction

CLARIN, just like any research infrastructure (and most infrastructures for that matter), is a shared (or *common*) resource: instead of being privately owned, it is managed by a community for the benefit of all its members, and sometimes even of the general public. Experience teaches us that in the case of shared resources, the ideal of peaceful and sustainable exploitation is particularly diffi-

Paweł Kamocki, Leibniz-Institut für Deutsche Sprache, Mannheim, Germany, e-mail: kamocki@ids-mannheim.de
Aleksei Kelli, University of Tartu, Tartu, Estonia, e-mail: aleksei.kelli@ut.ee
Krister Lindén, University of Helsinki, Helsinki, Finland, e-mail: krister.linden@helsinki.fi

https://doi.org/10.1515/9783110767377-018

cult to achieve in practice. Hardin (1968) argued that such resources are doomed to fail. To illustrate the inevitable "tragedy of the commons" (overpopulation and the resulting depletion of natural resources), Hardin quoted the example from a little-known 19th-century pamphlet (Lloyd 1980) of an overgrazed common pasture: by making an economically justifiable decision to increase the number of their cattle, individual herders cause damage to the community. This theory was criticized (if not disproven) by a 2009 Nobel prize laureate, Elinor Ostrom, who formulated a list of design principles for sustainable self-organized governance of common resources. All these principles circle around clear, effective, and enforceable community rules regulating the use of the resource (e.g., mechanisms for exclusion of non-participants, sanctions for violations, and mechanisms of conflict resolution).

Both Hardin's and Ostrom focused on natural resources, many of which are indeed in imminent danger of over-exploitation; some could argue that there is no such danger for digital and intellectual resources, which do not depreciate with use, and which can be identically reproduced at little to no cost. However, deterioration is also a menace for shared digital resources. Wikipedia, probably the most successful digital commons so far, can be quoted as an example. Wikipedia owes its success partly to its large community respecting some fundamental principles (e.g., neutrality, freedom, mutual respect) summarized in the Five Pillars, and partly to the use of "copyleft" licenses, mostly CC BY-SA, which require that any modifications be released under the same license – a condition that can, if necessary, be enforced in court. It is easy to imagine that without either of these elements, Wikipedia could quickly fork into a privately-owned commercial product, or become useless due to low quality of its content (caused by e.g., overuse of editing rights), or simply be deserted by its users and gradually forgotten. The same can happen to a digital infrastructure like CLARIN.

In addition to this, CLARIN also faces another challenge which relates to the restricted use of language resources affected by third-party rights (intellectual property and personal data protection); we can call it "the tragedy of the anticommons". In the literature, the tragedy of the anticommons is explained as follows: "The anticommons thesis is that simple: when too many people own pieces of one thing, nobody can use it. Usually, private ownership creates wealth. But too much ownership has the opposite effect – it leads to resource underuse in an anticommons" (Heller 2013: 7). It has been suggested that "Fixing anticommons tragedy is a key challenge for our time" (Heller 2013: 6).

Fortunately, efforts are continuously being made to guarantee the sustainability of CLARIN and to protect it from the tragedies of both the commons and the anticommons. These efforts take many forms: updating the technical side of the infrastructure to keep it state-of-the-art, carefully defining long-term strategic goals, or building a strong community. But no such effort would be sufficient without the legal and normative frameworks of the infrastructure, which are needed to address the use restrictions of language data and support the dissemination of language resources.

It has been argued that law and legal norms on their own are never sufficient; despite burglary being a criminal offence punishable by imprisonment, people still lock their homes, and many are willing to invest in state-of-the-art locks and alarm systems. But the reverse is also true: no lock and no alarm system would be useful if burglary was not punished by law, and burglars could spend hours in broad daylight trying to work around them. The legal (or ethical) rule comes first, and the technical and organizational solutions that safeguard it or put it into action come second. It is therefore fair to say that without the Normative Layer, neither the technical nor the organizational structure of CLARIN would exist.

This chapter is structured as follows: Section 2 introduces and defines the notion of the Normative Layer of CLARIN, which consists of three components: the Regulatory Framework, the Contractual Framework, and Ethical Norms. Section 3 presents the CLARIN Committee for Legal and Ethical Issues (CLIC), its history, structure, missions, and tasks. Section 4 then discusses the CLIC's actions related to the Regulatory Framework, and Section 5 those related to the Contractual Framework.

2 The normative layer of CLARIN

Legal norms (i.e., to put it simply, state-enforceable rules meant to regulate people's behaviour) that regulate the functioning of CLARIN can stem from external (objective) or internal (subjective) sources. We will refer to the norms stemming from the former as the Regulatory Framework, and to the latter as the Contractual Framework. These two frameworks form what we jointly refer to as the Normative Layer.

2.1 The regulatory framework

The most important part of the Regulatory Framework is statutory law, that is, acts passed by legislative bodies such as national parliaments (for national law) or by EU institutions (for EU law). From the perspective of CLARIN, the main legal challenges can be divided into two groups: intellectual property (chiefly copyright and related rights) and personal data protection. Indeed, language data potentially contains copyright-protected content (written or oral works), subject matter of related rights (performances, parts of phonograms, and databases), or personal data. These fields of law are harmonized at EU level. Therefore, the most important legal acts for CLARIN include, for example, several copyright directives, the Database Directive, the Open Data Directive, or the General Data Protection Regulation (GDPR), as well as a plethora of associated national laws in every CLARIN member country. In addition to this, the Regulation 723/2009 on the community legal framework for a European Research Infrastructure Consortium (ERIC) is fundamental for the functioning of CLARIN ERIC; this Regulation was the basis for the European Commission's Decision of 29 February 2012, setting up the CLARIN ERIC consortium.

Another objective source of legal norms (i.e., another part of the Regulatory Framework) are court decisions, especially those emanating from the highest courts, which often – *de facto* or *de jure*, depending on the legal system – also apply beyond the facts of a specific case and provide a binding interpretation of statutes or even fill some grey areas in statutory law. For CLARIN as an entity, the most important court decisions are undeniably those emanating from the Court of Justice of the European Union (CJEU).

Finally, some highly authoritative guidelines, although not binding *de jure*, can also be regarded as an objective source of legal norms, and therefore part of the Regulatory Framework. This is especially the case of guidelines emanating from the European Data Protection Board (EDPB) and its direct predecessor, the Article 29 Data Protection Working Party. The EDPB is an independent advisory body made up of representatives of Data Protection Authorities from every Member State of the European Economic Area. Its guidelines are very likely to be followed by national courts and administrative bodies and provide a *de facto* binding interpretation of the GDPR.

The Regulatory Framework form a "legal exoskeleton", independent of CLARIN ERIC's will – that is, it cannot be altered by the sole decision of CLARIN bodies and they cannot opt out of it. Instead, it needs to be integrated and navigated in the decision-making process, as well as in the day-to-day functioning of the infrastructure. However, a powerful actor like CLARIN ERIC should not adopt a completely passive attitude toward the regulatory framework; it can also try to actively influence its future shape by participating in public consultations or by lobbying efforts.

The practical impact of the Regulatory Framework (in this case, the GDPR) on the compilation of language data is amply illustrated by Lindén et al. (2022).

2.2 The contractual framework

Unlike the Regulatory Framework, the Contractual Framework is internal to CLARIN, and CLARIN bodies can exercise proactive (i.e., not retroactive) control over it.

A part of this "legal endoskeleton" discussed in this chapter consists of contracts related to the everyday functioning of the CLARIN infrastructure, that is, contracts between CLARIN centres and providers of resources or tools (DELAs, Deposition License Agreements), and between CLARIN centres and end-users (EULAs, End-User License Agreements (for every user of a given resource) and ToS, Terms of Service (for all users of a repository).

In the spirit of Open Science and according to the FAIR principles, providers are encouraged to make their resources and tools open (i.e., available to anyone and for any purpose). This is best accomplished using standardized public licenses such as Creative Commons Attribution (CC BY) 4.0 (for datasets), or the General Public License (GPL) 3.0 (for software). Such licenses can be analysed as offers from the rights holder to the general public (hence the name "public license"); the actual contract is formed when a member of the public accepts the offer simply by using the content. In this model, there is no middleman (such as a distributor). To respond to the growing need of the community, public licenses are also incorporated in the CLARIN Contractual Framework, as parts of DELAs and EULAs.

Since these internal rules need to comply with the Regulatory Framework (or, to continue with the skeleton metaphor, the endoskeleton cannot extend beyond the exoskeleton), they need to be regularly revised and updated to adapt to the changes in the latter.

The practical impact of the Contractual Framework on the CLARIN infrastructure is illustrated, for example, by Hajič et al. (2022).

2.3 The role of ethical norms

Ethical norms are also part of the Normative Framework. Although they are not as such enforceable by the State, they indirectly shape both the Regulatory and the Contractual frameworks.

There seems to be no fixed content in ethics, as it changes very significantly, even over short periods of time. To an extent, the scientific community has developed its own ethical codes (Merton 1942).

3 The CLARIN Committee for Legal and Ethical Issues

As highlighted in the previous section, the Normative Layer of the CLARIN infrastructure is quite complex. Navigating thousands of pages of legal acts, court decisions, guidelines, and standard contracts requires considerable expertise. In order to advise the Board of Directors, the CLARIN Committee for Legal and Ethical Issues (hereinafter: the CLIC) was created.

3.1 History

The CLIC was formally established in 2012, during the first CLARIN Annual Conference in Sofia, Bulgaria (25–28 October 2012). However, even before that the CLIC existed informally (as the CLARIN Legal Issues Committee, hence the acronym). In its early days, Ville Oksanen and Krister Lindén from the University of Helsinki played the key role in the development of the CLIC.

Ville Oksanen (26 December 1976–23 November 2014) was a Finnish civic activist and lawyer known as a defender of civil rights and the freedom of expression, as well as a social debater. He defended his doctoral dissertation on digital copyright in 2008. In 2014, he was employed as a researcher at the Department of Computer Science at Aalto University. He was one of the founders of the Electronic Frontier Finland association and served as its president from 2004 to 2005, and was its vice-president at the time of his death. He wrote blogs for several computer magazines, and from a political point of view, Oksanen was a member of the Liberal Coalition Party. He was the Vice-Chairman of the Coalition Youth and was a deputy member of the Coalition Party Board from 1999 to 2000.

Research Director Krister Lindén, PhD in Language Technology and national coordinator of FIN-CLARIN, has a background in business, where he received hands-on training in legal issues as the first CEO of Lingsoft while negotiating with WordPerfect, Xerox, and Microsoft on including spellchecking and grammar-checking technology for all the Scandinavian languages and German in their products. He was the first chair of CLIC (2012–2015).

Erik Ketzan, a legal scholar from the Institute for the German Language in Mannheim, was the first co-chair. Since the very beginning it has been a tradition that the chair and co-chair are a language researcher and a legal scholar.

In 2016, Aleksei Kelli, professor of law from the University of Tartu in Estonia, took over as chair of the CLIC. Penny Labropoulou from Athena/ILSP served as co-chair.

In 2021, Paweł Kamocki, legal expert from the Institute for the German Language in Mannheim, holding both a PhD in law and a master's degree in linguistics, became chair of the CLIC. It is worth noting that he was among the original members of the CLIC when it was established in 2012, underpinning the CLIC's activities. Vanessa Hannesschläger, a digital humanities researcher from the Austrian Academy of Sciences, became co-chair.

3.2 Structure

The CLIC members are experts appointed by national consortia for two years, with a possible prolongation (Article 2 of the CLIC Bylaws). Every consortium is invited to appoint an expert, but there is no obligation to do so; as a result, several consortia are regretfully not represented in the CLIC. There is also a possibility for a consortium to appoint more than one expert – for example, Germany has always appointed two or three experts – however, only one expert per consortium (a "core member") has the right to vote. There is no formal requirement for appointed experts to be affiliated with a CLARIN centre. CLARIN observers ("emerging consortia") can appoint experts upon invitation from the Board of Directors. The Board of Directors can also appoint additional experts, or invite related initiatives to appoint representatives, but none of these powers have been used so far. The CLIC Chair can invite external experts to participate in CLIC meetings (without granting them membership). Members of the Board of Directors can also attend meetings of the CLIC. Traditionally, one of the Directors is delegated to serve as liaison between the Board and the Committee.

There are no formal requirements as to the level of expertise of CLIC experts, or as to their training. Despite this, the absence of candidates with legal training seems to be one possible reason why some CLARIN consortia are not represented in the CLIC. It should be emphasized that the CLIC is not a traditional legal "department" providing legal assistance but it is rather a legal competency centre interdisciplinarily integrating domains of legal and language research. Therefore, researchers whose background is not in law are also needed and valuable members. In practice, most CLIC members have long-standing experience in handling legal issues, acquired through management of language resources and tools. Some members of the CLIC are trained lawyers with experience in academia or in administration. The number of trained lawyers seems to have slowly but steadily increased since the establishment of the Committee, which is a very positive tendency, given the nature of the CLIC's missions. The CLIC is not intended to become a group composed exclusively of members with legal training, as this could move it far from the reality of language research and technology.

The CLIC Chair and Vice-Chair are appointed by the Board of Directors after consultation with the Committee, for two years. In practice, the Committee recommends the candidates in a vote, and the Board follows the recommendation. The same Chair and Vice-Chair can be appointed for more than one consecutive term; the bylaws do not limit the number of consecutive terms, but the practice seems to have limited it to two.

The CLIC meets at least once a year (often during the CLARIN Annual Conference). In practice, the Committee meets at least on a quarterly basis, and most of the meetings are virtual. Meetings are called by the Chair; at least three members of the CLIC may ask the Chair to call a meeting. Traditionally, CLIC meetings are open to non-members – physical meetings during the CLARIN Annual Conference can be attended by anyone, and the virtual meetings are announced on the CLARIN legal mailing list.

So far, the CLIC members have always been able to reach consensus on all debated matters, and there has been no need to vote. However, according to the by-laws, where consensus cannot be reached, the Committee should make decisions by simple majority vote, with casting vote held by the Chair.

Besides formal meetings, members of the CLIC are in regular contact via e-mail, usually in smaller groups, working on articles, updates of the CLIC materials or various other tasks. Apart from such informal subgroups, there is also a possibility to create formal subcommittees of at least three members, with the obligation to report on their activities to the Chair every year. Due to the relatively small and manageable size of the CLIC, and the fact that the Chair or Vice-Chair participate in every activity of the Committee, so far there has been no need to establish a formal subcommittee.

Neither membership nor chairmanship of the CLIC are remunerated, but they can be listed as contributions from national consortia to the CLARIN ERIC.

3.3 Mission and tasks

The main mission of the CLIC, as per Article 1 of its by-laws, is to "advise the Board of Directors on all issues related to [Intellectual Property], privacy and data protection and ethical matters, as well as legal issues related to access and dissemination policies and their implementation". This mission is particularly important if one takes into consideration the fact that the legal portfolio (unlike some other portfolios, like User Involvement, which is attributed to a member of the Board of Directors and a thematic committee) has never been expressly attributed to any member of the Board of Directors, therefore it can be assumed that it falls within the many competences of the Executive Director, who is likely to need advice on legal matters. The scope of this mission is limited (for example, legal issues related to the establishment of new national consortia, or contractual relations between consortium partners, are not included), yet still very broad.

Firstly, it covers advice on all questions (also those unrelated to language resources) related to any form of intellectual property including, but not limited to, copyright, the *sui generis* database right, but also trade secrets, patents, and trademarks – areas that today remain underexplored by the CLIC and the language community in general, but which potentially may become important for the whole infrastructure.

Secondly, all questions related to privacy and data protection are also within the scope of the CLIC's mission. The distinction between privacy and data protection is fully justified, as privacy laws are not limited to data protection (privacy claims can be based on, e.g., tort law, criminal law, or specific grounds, such as Article 9 of the Napoleonic Code and the numerous legal norms that it inspired), and conversely data protection (i.e., a legal framework stemming mostly from the GDPR and the ePrivacy Directive) does not only apply to the private sphere of individuals' life.

Thirdly, the CLIC also advises the Board on all legal issues "related to access and dissemination policies and their implementation". Therefore, when it comes to policies concerning access to and dissemination of language resources and tools, the CLIC is also competent to advise the BoD on issues that go beyond intellectual property, privacy and data protection, and include for example, contract law, administrative law (such as reuse of public sector information) and even criminal law (e.g., hate speech in language resources).

Fourthly, advice on "ethical matters" of all sorts is also within the scope of the CLIC's mission. This should be interpreted as analysing compliance with commonly recognized norms of general and scientific ethics. Purely ethical issues are rarely debated within the CLIC, as it seems that they are better handled at the national or even institutional level.

In order to fulfil its mission, CLIC by-laws attribute the following tasks to the Committee:

- to prepare and publish analyses;
- to organize and participate in competency-building events;
- to collect, consolidate and prepare for publication in a single place various documents ("findings and recommendations") related to CLARIN activities;
- to maintain and adapt a set of licenses;
- to develop and implement procedures for the discussion and adoption of new recommendations for dealing with legal and ethical issues;
- to liaise closely with the Standing Committee for CLARIN Technical Centres;

- to ensure harmonization of legal and ethical policies between CLARIN ERIC and related initiatives;
- to publish and promote legal and ethical policies adopted by CLARIN;
- to follow the ongoing debates on legal and ethical issues at EU and national level, and to report on this to the BoD;
- to make an annual workplan; and
- to advise the Board of Directors in all legal and ethical issues [within the scope of its Mission].

3.4 Communication channels

The CLIC's tasks require regular communication within the Committee, as well as with other CLARIN bodies and the general public.

The most important communication channel within the CLIC are meetings – as stated above, there is one face-to-face meeting per year (unless, of course, travelling is made impossible, as it was during the Covid-19 pandemic), which is collocated with the CLARIN Annual Conference. The remaining meetings are virtual, using online communication technology. In between meetings, CLIC members usually work in smaller, task-oriented groups which communicate via e-mail or, occasionally, by videoconference.

The CLIC also communicates with the Board of Directors and the National Coordinators' Forum. The Board appoints a liaison who participates in CLIC's meetings. Once a year, the CLIC chair reports to the National Coordinator's Forum during one of their meetings. Communication with other CLARIN standing committees is less formalized; it normally takes place by e-mail (usually between chairs and/or co-chairs), but exceptionally also during face-to-face meetings.

The CLIC's primary channel for communicating with the general public is its dedicated webpage on the CLARIN ERIC's website,[1] administrated by the CLARIN Office. It contains an up-to-date list of CLIC members, a description of its mission and tasks, links to the description of the CLARIN licensing framework, the Legal Information Platform, the latest CLIC White Paper, as well as the address of the legal mailing list.

The Legal Information Platform is part of the CLARIN website administered directly by the CLIC. It contains detailed explanations on copyright and related rights, licensing and data protection, written by Paweł Kamocki and Erik Ketzan

1 https://www.clarin.eu/governance/legal-issues-committee

specifically with the CLARIN audience in mind. The platform also features a legal bibliography and links to useful online resources.

The mailing list legal@lists.clarin.eu is accessible to anyone, and is also used to communicate with all stakeholders within the CLARIN community and beyond. The CLIC also communicates its analyses to the general public via its White Paper Series, openly available online and licensed under the CC BY 4.0 license. The series was launched in 2014 on the initiative of Erik Ketzan, then the CLIC's vice-chair. The idea behind it was to present complex legal issues of fundamental importance for language science and language resources in a comprehensive yet concise form, approachable by language scientists with no legal training. The White Papers are not intended to reflect the official position of CLARIN ERIC, hence they do not use the CLARIN ERIC name or logo. In the future, the Board of Directors may intend to publish official statements on certain legal issues (such as future changes in EU law), in which case it will be the CLIC's role to provide the Board with advice.

On occasion, the CLIC, with financial and organizational assistance from the CLARIN Office, also organizes workshops and other events for other members of the CLARIN community or for the general public.

4 CLIC and the regulatory framework

The EU regulatory framework concerning access to and reuse of language resources, especially for research purposes, has undergone substantial modifications since the establishment of CLARIN ERIC.

In 2012, when the CLIC was officially established, copyright exceptions for research in EU Member States were based on Article 5.3(a) of the Directive 2001/29/CE on Copyright in the Information Society (InfoSoc). This exception, albeit quite broad, covers only non-commercial scientific research and teaching. Moreover, due to its non-mandatory character the exception was implemented very narrowly in most Member States, which made it quite incompatible with modern research practice, especially compared to the relative freedom offered by the fair use doctrine in the United States.

Shortly after the establishment of CLARIN ERIC, the first European countries adopted specific exceptions for text and data mining, still based on the same provision of the InfoSoc Directive, and therefore limited only to non-commercial scientific research. This was the case, for example, in the UK (in 2014), in France (in 2016), and in Germany (in 2017). In 2019, a mandatory exception for text and data mining for scientific research purposes was included in the Directive 2019/970 on

Copyright in the Digital Single Market (DSM). The new exception seems satisfyingly broad in enabling research institutions to copy copyright-protected material for scientific research purposes; however, it does not in itself allow any sharing of the copies (although it can be combined, as in German national law, with the "general" research exception in the InfoSoc Directive, which allows limited sharing), and requires for the copies to be stored with appropriate level of security, which increases the role of specialized research data archives.

The 2019 DSM Directive also introduces other changes that are relevant for language resources, such as, for example, extended collective licensing, or facilitated access to out-of-print works. It had to be implemented in all EU Member States by 7 June 2021.

The adoption of the DSM Directive was not the only important development in the field of copyright law in recent years. For the language community, another noteworthy document is the 2012 Orphan Works Directive (2012/28/EU), allowing for certain uses of some copyright-protected works whose rightsholders cannot be identified or located despite diligent search.

Another branch of EU law that affects language research and that has been thoroughly reformed since the establishment of CLARIN ERIC is data protection law. The General Data Protection Regulation (EU Regulation 2016/679; GDPR), which replaced the 1995 Data Protection Directive (95/26/EC), was adopted in 2016 and entered into application in 2018. Although the GDPR is typically described as a product of an evolution rather than a revolution (indeed, most of the fundamental concepts from the 1995 Directive remain unchanged), it does introduce some important changes for research, emphasizes the importance of accountability and self-assessment (e.g., through records of data processing activities, or through Data Protection Impact Assessments), and substantially increases fines for non-compliance. GDPR-related best practices in research are still crystallizing today, as awareness of data protection issues is growing not only in the research community, but also among research funding organizations.

Besides copyright and data protection, other branches of law are becoming increasingly important for access to and reuse of language data for research purposes. This is the case, for example, with EU rules on the reuse of Public Sector Information (PSI); the 2003 PSI Directive (2003/98/EC) was first amended in 2013 (by the Directive 2013/37/EU), and then replaced by the 2019 Open Data Directive (2019/1024), which also covers research data resulting from public funding. The extended scope of PSI/Open Data regulation created new sources of freely (and legally) reusable language data.

In recent months, the European Commission has been very actively publishing new drafts (e.g., for the Data Governance Act, or the Artificial Intelligence Act) which, when adopted, may have considerable impact on the CLARIN infrastructure. Therefore, the European Union is not at the "end of history" when it comes to legal developments, and there will be no shortage of work for the CLIC in the years to come.

4.1 CLIC's direct participation in the lawmaking process

CLARIN ERIC, a representative of the language research community in the EU, is an important stakeholder in many EU law reforms. As such, it becomes actively involved in stakeholder consultations which are necessary part of a democratic lawmaking process. This involvement requires not only time and qualified effort, but also substantial funds, and therefore it must remain limited. It is also a particularly delicate task, given that CLARIN consortia are financed by national governments which may have conflicting interests and take different positions in negotiations over various law reforms.

One of the earliest and perhaps most prominent examples of such involvement is the participation of Erik Ketzan, then vice-chair of CLARIN ERIC, in the thematic group "Text and Data Mining for Scientific Research Purposes" within Stakeholders Dialogue "Licenses for Europe", organized by the European Commission in 2013.[2] The goal of a long series of meetings (from February to December) was to find rapid, industry-led solutions to facilitate access to online content. Unfortunately, it was only very moderately successful, as most organizations representing the scientific research and open access publishing sectors withdrew from the process due to concerns about its scope, composition, and transparency.[3] CLARIN ERIC was one of the few representatives of the scientific research sector who did not leave the negotiation table until the end. The outcome of the TDM thematic group was a joint statement of commitment by scientific publishers to a roadmap to enable TDM for non-commercial scientific research in the European Union.[4] The roadmap envisioned by publishers was largely license- and subscription-based, and as such it was not widely acclaimed in the scientific research community. The apparent failure of the Stakeholders' Dialogue prompted the EU legislator to adopt a statutory exception for text and data mining for research purposes, which is currently part of the 2019 DSM Directive (Article 3).

Another example of CLARIN ERIC's (and the CLIC's) direct involvement in the lawmaking process is its admission, on the initiative of Ville Oksanen, as a

2 https://digital-strategy.ec.europa.eu/en/library/licences-europe-stakeholder-dialogue
3 https://libereurope.eu/article/stakeholders-representing-the-research-sector-smes-and-open-access-publishers-withdraw-from-licences-for-europe-2/
4 http://ec.europa.eu/newsroom/dae/document.cfm?doc_id=49203

Category C observer (*Other Regional Intergovernmental Organization*, which is a "high" category, given precedence over national governments) at the World Intellectual Property Organization (WIPO). Established in 1967, WIPO is a specialized agency of the United Nations created to protect and promote intellectual property.

Participation in such endeavours is above all an opportunity to establish CLARIN as the representative of the language community in Europe, to accentuate its awareness of legal issues, and to liaise with other stakeholders with similar interests.

4.2 CLIC's research articles and White Papers

Writing research articles is a big part of CLIC's activity. For many years, the CLIC has been submitting a joint article (co-written by several CLIC members on the Chair's initiative) for the CLARIN Annual Conference, which often embraces a comparative approach to various legal issues affecting language science. Most of these articles deal primarily with the Regulatory Framework.

In 2015, an article by Aleksei Kelli, Kadri Vider, and Krister Lindén entitled "The Regulatory and Contractual Framework as an integral part of the CLARIN Infrastructure" (Kelli, Vider, and Lindén 2015) was accepted for the CLARIN conference in Wrocław. General in nature, the article provided a comprehensive overview of the legal framework applicable to language resources and introduced the concept of regulatory and contractual frameworks, which also serve as the backbone of this very chapter.

In 2018, a CLIC paper accepted for the CLARIN Annual Conference in Pisa (Kelli et al. 2019) examined the possibility of processing personal data without consent of the data subject for the development and use of language resources. The paper studied the implementation of research exceptions in various CLARIN countries, as well as the possibility to use alternative grounds (i.e., other than consent) for the processing of personal data for research purposes (such as public interest or legitimate interest).

In 2019, a CLIC paper accepted for the CLARIN Annual Conference in Leipzig (Kelli et al. 2020) explored the degree of legal control that copyright holders and data subjects can exercise over language models derived from "their" data.

CLIC White Paper #3, published in 2018 (Kamocki, Ketzan, and Wildgans 2018), was also devoted to a part of the Regulatory Framework, namely the GDPR. Over 25 pages long, the White Paper contains three parts. The first presents basic terminology and main principles of the Regulation, discusses the rights of data subjects and obligations of data controllers, and summarizes the principles related to cross-border transfers of personal data. The second part analyses research exemptions in the GDPR, while the third presents new opportunities for bottom-up standardization, namely Codes of Conduct and Data Protection Seals. As of November 2021, the CLIC works on an extensive set of around 30 handouts on various GDPR-related issues, which are intended to replace the White Paper.

The idea of a GDPR Code of Conduct, first launched by Kamocki et al. (2018) and likewise discussed in the above-mentioned White Paper, was heavily debated within the CLIC. GDPR Codes of Conduct, regulated in Article 40 of the GDPR, are sets of sector-specific rules intended to contribute to proper application of the GDPR; if a Code of Conduct is approved by a competent supervisory authority, and if an accredited body monitors compliance with the Code, the Code can effectively "supplant" the GDPR for every organization who adheres to it. One could imagine a GDPR Code of Conduct for processing personal data in language resources, monitored by CLARIN, as a mechanism to unify GDPR-related practices in the community, and significantly facilitate cross-border endeavours such as building a pan-European infrastructure for language resources.

However, it emerged from the discussions within the CLIC that such far-reaching measures may not be desirable, given that certain CLARIN centres have already adopted specific data processing policies. It became apparent that many GDPR-related issues remain divisive in Europe: for example, researchers in countries like Germany or Austria are very attached to consent as the legal basis for personal data processing, whereas researchers in other countries, like Finland, rely more on alternative grounds such as public interest. In this context, the CLIC's ambition should be to adopt guidelines in several specific areas of GDPR compliance, such as data anonymization or rights of data subject, rather than opting for an instrument aimed at full unification.

4.3 CLIC's events

In recent years, the CLIC has also organized several events dedicated specifically to informing the language community about the relevant regulatory framework, and discussing legal challenges that language researchers have to face.

A workshop entitled "Hacking the GDPR to Conduct Research with Language Resources in Digital Humanities and Social Sciences", organized by the CLIC, hosted by CLARIN-LT, and supported by the CLARIN ERIC, took place in Vilnius on 7 December 2018.[5] The event, which brought together around 25 participants, featured presentations by several members of the CLIC, as well as invited guests.

5 https://www.clarin.eu/tags/clic

The use cases discussed during the event were focused on such GDPR-related concepts as suitable legal grounds for processing, data anonymization, pseudonymization, storage limitation, and appropriate safeguards.

A CLARIN café on the rights of data subjects in language resources, organized by the CLIC and supported by the TRIPLE project, took place on 30 March 2021.[6] The two-hour event was attended by 50 participants from both the CLARIN community and the private sector. The presentations given by CLIC members discussed not only the content of the rights of data subjects, but also practical aspects of their exercise in the specific context of language resources.

Another CLARIN café organized by the CLIC, this time on Text and Data Mining exceptions in the Directive on Copyright in the Digital Single Market, took place on 28 October 2021. The event attracted 25 participants willing to learn; it will hopefully mark the beginning of a community-wide debate on the impact of the recent EU copyright reform on language resources and language technology.

4.4 LegalTech co-developed by the CLIC and ELDAH

In 2020, three CLIC members (Vanessa Hannesschläger, Paweł Kamocki, and Walter Scholger), who are also members of the DARIAH ELDAH (Ethics and Legality in Digital Arts and Humanities) Working Group, teamed up to create the DARIAH ELDAH Consent Form Wizard.[7] This online tool enables researchers to quickly generate a GDPR-compliant consent form for collecting personal data for research purposes, but which can also be used, for example, for creating mailing lists or organizing academic events. Currently the tool is available in English, German, Italian and Croatian, although there are plans to have it translated to other languages. The launch of the Consent Wizard was an opportunity for the CLIC to liaise more closely with ELDAH, and organize the first joint meeting of both groups in June 2021.

5 CLIC and the contractual framework

The main role of the CLIC with regards to the contractual framework is to host and update the CLARIN license suite. It also prepared guidelines on the use of another popular license suite, Creative Commons 4.0, and two LegalTech tools intended to

6 https://www.clarin.eu/blog/recap-clarin-cafe-rights-data-subjects-language-resources
7 https://consent.dariah.eu/

assist researchers in the choice of an appropriate license for their tools and data. Recently, the CLIC has also started analysing other standard form contracts which govern access to and reuse of large quantities of language data, such as Terms of Service of popular social media services.

5.1 The development of the CLARIN Licensing Framework

At a meeting in Berlin in 2006, a handful of representatives of potential CLARIN members convened to prepare an EC-funded project application for the preparatory phase (PP) of CLARIN ERIC. Ideas were collected on what work package should be included and language technology and language resources were given favourites that every partner candidate was bidding for. However, Prof. Kimmo Koskenniemi from Finland insisted that legal and contractual issues also needed a work package, WP7. As no one else was eager to take on this task, it fell on Finland to carry out this part of the CLARIN PP project. The formation of the CLARIN ERIC statues had a separate work package WP8 and was carried out by Denmark under the direction of Prof. Bente Maegaard.

During the CLARIN preparatory phase project, two significant legal frameworks for the CLARIN operations were drawn up in WP7. The first framework was the CLARIN Service Provider Federation (SPF) which implemented the Single-Sign-On (SSO) principle on a large scale between the CLARIN consortium partners. It was a precursor to EduGain, although EduGain and EduRoam were already being developed at the time. The fact that one could use SSO – i.e., one's own university account and credentials – to sign in to various services was a key driving factor for the design of the second framework designed in WP7 (i.e., the licensing framework).

It was clear that open-source licensing and public licensing like Creative Commons (CC) were to be endorsed by CLARIN and named the PUB licensing category, but at the time CC was still in the process of establishing itself and most data was proprietary or had no clear license, having been painstakingly collected by individual researchers as, for example, manually transcribed and annotated letters, newspaper clips, or interviews, or just individual sentences from such sources. As many researchers had spent years, if not decades, of their life just collecting data, they were reluctant to give up such material to others, but some were willing to share on an individual basis. As mentioned, the datasets collected by researchers were also often personal data based on interviews, so the varying data protection legislations in the EU countries were an additional challenge. A restricted license category named RES was needed for such datasets. The idea was that such resources should only be made available upon individual request and, if containing personal data, only for a limited time.

For political and practical reasons, the CLARIN PP Project Board thought that there should be some benefit to being an accredited researcher who was part of the CLARIN SPF, that is, the fact that a person already was an established researcher with credentials at a university should be recognized when accessing resources provided by CLARIN partners. For this reason, an academic license category was established called ACA. The nature of this category was intended as a public license to a limited public consisting of researchers, but therein lay a conundrum. Who was a legitimate researcher? Should only people from academia count or were people from industry acceptable as well (i.e., should the affiliation or the purpose limit access)? CLARIN opted for the practical solution: organizational status could be checked based on the login credentials. This provided a technological solution to the philosophical problem of restricting the category to academic researchers. Later, this seems to have caught on and will now be enshrined in the text and data mining exception in the DSM Directive, which grants a special status to research organizations, in particular by enabling them to store the copied data for verification purposes.

Both the RES and ACA categories were frowned upon by people from the hard-core Open Access Community, to whom only fully publicly available data was real data. They often had a technological background, where real data is measurement data produced by the research infrastructures themselves through measuring devices, and therefore having no copyright except for a potential *sui generis* database right on the data collection. In social sciences and humanities, interviews and questionnaires may be primary data, for which a license can be determined by the collector, but most data is secondary data, that is, it is used in research for some other purpose than it was originally created for by a human being imbuing it with either copyright or personal data rights.

Initially, the CLARIN categories were intended as metadata, that is, a way to inform the end user about the license to expect when accessing a resource. The idea was that licenses in a particular category had to provide at least a minimum number of rights to the end user, and at most some restrictions to qualify for the category. Originally this was intended only as a checklist to determine the category of the license. This is still visible in the CLARIN License Category Calculator. As Ville Oksanen had also been part of the origins of the Creative Commons (CC) movement, he adapted the CC categories. So as not to infringe on the CC look, it was decided that CLARIN would use a "+" (plus sign) as a connector between the subcategories where CC uses a "-" (hyphen) or a " " (space).

Based on an analysis of the manifold licensing conditions for resources in the Language Bank of Finland, Ville Oksanen devised a few more subcategories in addition to those in CC. With this initial analysis as a basis, the categories and subcategories were tested on a set of more than 800 existing licenses throughout Europe by the CLARIN partners in EU (Oksanen, Lindén, and Westerlund 2010). Based on the response and the clarifying requests, the leading questions currently visible in the category calculator were designed. However, researchers wanted practical advice on how to make new or unpublished resources available, so what were originally only intended as categories and example clauses for classifying existing agreements evolved into ready-made sample contracts called CLARIN license templates. The final stage of the CLARIN licensing category adoption was to include the categories in the VLO as originally intended, using the laundry symbols to offer visual guidance on the openness of a resource. For an example of the use of CLARIN license templates in a repository, see Andersen and Gammeltoft (2022).

The work with the Contractual Framework continues in the CLIC. The majority of CLIC members are involved (see Kelli et al. 2018), and currently there is a preliminary plan to restructure the contractual framework in view of the GDPR.

5.2 CLIC's research articles and guidelines

The Contractual Framework was the subject of several joint CLIC articles. Apart from being discussed in the foundational paper (mentioned in Section 3.3) by Aleksei Kelli, Kadri Vider, and Krister Lindén (2015), it was also thoroughly and critically analysed in an article by Kelli and others (2018), first presented at the 2017 CLARIN Annual Conference in Budapest. The paper, entitled "Implementation of an Open Science Policy in the context of management of CLARIN language resources: a need for changes?", discusses the utility of CLARIN ACA and RES categories, and the possibility of replacing them with other requirements.

Kelli et al. (2021) also discussed some aspects of the Contractual Framework in their paper accepted for the 2020 CLARIN Annual Conference, entitled "CLARIN Contractual Framework for sharing language data: The perspective of personal data protection". The paper provided a preliminary analytical background for redesigning the CLARIN contracts to bring them up to speed with the GDPR.

Finally, a paper by Kamocki et al. (2021) presented at the 2021 CLARIN Annual Conference analysed another aspect of the Contractual Framework affecting language resources, namely the terms and policies of Twitter, an important source of language data. There are plans to extend the scope of this analysis to include other popular social media services in the next CLIC White Paper.

The very first CLIC White Paper (Kamocki and Ketzan 2014) was also dedicated to the contractual framework, namely the Creative Commons 4.0 license suite; it was published in 2014, shortly after the launch of the latest version of Creative Commons licenses. Its intended purpose is to present the CC licenses and their building blocks to language researchers and discuss their utility for licensing language resources.

5.3 LegalTech developed by the CLIC

The first LegalTech tools created by the CLIC were developed to address the complexity of the contractual framework. The CLARIN License Category Calculator categorizes any resource license and aims at extracting an overview of the key licensing conditions, while the Public License Selector specializes in public licenses, guiding the user in choosing the best one for a particular purpose.

The CLARIN License Category Calculator[8] guides a resource depositor when choosing a license category for a language resource. The CLARIN classification system for licenses has been devised for more efficient and transparent management of language resources by providing an at-a-glance overview of the main usage conditions of a language resource. Based on their licenses, language resources compatible with the CLARIN infrastructure can be divided into three main categories: CLARIN PUB, CLARIN ACA, or CLARIN RES. In addition, there are several subcategories based on the most common conditions of use associated with the distribution of language resources. The CLARIN License Category Calculator guides depositors of language resources in selecting the most fitting license category for their resource based on a series of choices they make relating to its contents and intended use(s). CLARIN deposition license agreements (made between resource providers and the CLARIN centres) are available for curating a minimal set of access conditions to include a resource in the CLARIN PUB, ACA, or RES categories. The minimal deposition licenses can be used as checklists if a CLARIN Centre wishes to use its own set of deposition licenses to agree on additional usage conditions with the resource provider.

The Public License Selector[9] was created in 2015 by two CLIC members who also worked together on the EUDAT project: Paweł Kamocki and Pavel Straňák, assisted by software developer Michal Sedlák (Kamocki, Straňák, and Sedlák 2016; see also Hajič et al., 2022). A CLARIN mobility grant was allocated for Kamocki to travel to the Prague CLARIN Centre and finalize the tool. The Public License Selector is intended to assist a researcher in selecting a public license for his or

8 https://www.clarin.eu/content/clarin-license-category-calculator
9 https://github.com/ufal/public-license-selector

her datasets and tools. It covers popular data licenses (such as Creative Commons or Open Data Commons), as well as Free/Open Source Software licenses (GPL, BSD, MIT, Apache, etc.). The user is asked a series of simple, usually "yes/no" questions, with the answers serving to narrow down the available set of compatible licenses. The Public License Selector itself is released under an open license and has been widely reused both within and outside of the CLARIN community.

6 Conclusion

The Normative Layer of CLARIN is, alongside the organizational and the technical layers, an essential part of the infrastructure. It consists of the Regulatory Framework (statutory law, case law, authoritative guidelines, etc.) and the Contractual Framework (licenses, terms of service, etc.), and ethical norms. Navigating the normative layer requires expertise, experience, and qualified effort. In order to advise the Board of Directors, a standing committee dedicated to legal and ethical issues, the CLIC, was created.

Since its establishment in 2012, the CLIC has made considerable efforts to provide not only the BoD but also the general public with information and guidance. It has published many papers (both in proceedings of CLARIN conferences and in its own White Paper Series) and developed several LegalTech tools. It also runs a Legal Information Platform, where accessible information on various issues affecting language resources can be found.

Today, as CLARIN transitions from the development phase to the phase of sustainable functioning, the Normative Layer is changing dynamically, and continuous efforts from the CLIC are still needed to provide the Board of Directors and the whole community with information and guidance.

Bibliography

Andersen, Gisle & Peder Gammeltoft. 2022. The role of CLARIN in advancing work in terminology: The case of Termportalen – the national terminology portal for Norway. In Darja Fišer and Andreas Witt (eds.), *CLARIN. The infrastructure for language resources.* Berlin: De Gruyter.

Hajič, Jan, Eva Hajičová, Barbora Hladká, Jozef Mišutka, Ondřej Košarko & Pavel Straňák. 2022. LINDAT/CLARIAH-CZ: Where we are and where we go. In Darja Fišer and Andreas Witt (eds.), *CLARIN. The infrastructure for language resources.* Berlin: De Gruyter.

Hardin, Garrett. 1968. The tragedy of the commons. *Science* 162 (3859). 1243–1248.

Heller, Michael. 2013. The tragedy of the anticommons: A concise introduction and lexicon. *The Modern Law Review* 76 (1). 6–25. https://scholarship.law.columbia.edu/cgi/viewcontent.cgi?article=2779&context=faculty_scholarship (accessed 17 May 2021).

Kamocki, Paweł, Vanessa Hannesschläger, Esther Hoorn, Aleksei Kelli, Marc Kupietz, Krister Lindén, Andrius Puksas. 2021. Legal Issues Related to the Use of Twitter Data in Language Research. *CLARIN Annual Conference 2021, Proceedings. 27–29 September 2021, Virtual Edition.* Utrecht: CLARIN. 150–153. https://ids-pub.bsz-bw.de/frontdoor/deliver/index/docId/10718/file/Kamocki_Hannesschlaeger_Legal_issues_2021.pdf (accessed 17 May 2022).

Kamocki, Paweł & Erik Ketzan. 2014. *Creative commons and language resources: General issues and what's new in CC 4.0* (CLIC White Paper Series 1). https://www.clarin-d.de/images/legal/CLIC_white_paper_1.pdf (accessed 17 May 2021).

Kamocki, Paweł, Erik Ketzan & Julia Wildgans. 2018. *Language resources and research under the General Data Protection Regulation* (CLIC White Paper Series 3). https://www.clarin.eu/sites/default/files/CLIC_White_Paper_3.pdf (accessed 21 May 2021).

Kamocki, Paweł, Erik Ketzan, Julia Wildgans & Andreas Witt. 2018. Toward a CLARIN data protection code of conduct. *CLARIN Annual Conference 2018, Proceedings. 8–10 October 2018, Pisa, Italy*. Utrecht: CLARIN. 49–52. https://ids-pub.bsz-bw.de/frontdoor/deliver/index/docId/8189/file/Kamocki_Ketzan_Wildgans_Witt_Toward_a_CLARIN_Data_Protection_Code_2018.pdf (accessed 21 May 2021).

Kamocki, Paweł, Pavel Straňák & Michal Sedlák. 2016. The public license selector: Making open licensing easier. *International Conference on Language Resources and Evaluation (LREC)* 10. 2533–2538.

Kelli, Aleksei, Krister Lindén, Kadri Vider, Paweł Kamocki, Ramūnas Birštonas, Silvia Calamai, Penny Labropoulou, Maria Gavrilidou & Pavel Straňák. 2019. Processing personal data without the consent of the data subject for the development and use of language resources. In Inguna Skadin & Maria Eskevich (eds.), *Selected papers from the CLARIN Annual Conference 2018: Pisa, 8–10 October 2018* (Linköping Electronic Conference Proceedings 159), 72–82. Linköping: Linköping University Electronic Press.

Kelli, Aleksei, Krister Lindén, Kadri Vider, Paweł Kamocki, Arvi Tavast, Ramūnas Birštonas, Gaabriel Tavits, Mari Keskküla & Penny Labropoulou. 2021. CLARIN contractual framework for sharing language data: The perspective of personal data protection. In Costanza Navarretta & Maria Eskevich (eds.), *Selected papers from the CLARIN Annual Conference 2020: 5–7 October 2020*, 171–177. Utrecht: CLARIN.

Kelli, Aleksei, Krister Lindén, Kadri Vider, Penny Labropoulou, Erik Ketzan, Paweł Kamocki & Pavel Stranák. 2018. Implementation of an Open Science Policy in the context of management of CLARIN language resources: A need for changes? In *Selected papers from the CLARIN Annual Conference 2017: Budapest, 18–20 September 2017* (Linköping Electronic Conference Proceedings 147), 102–111. Linköping: Linköping University Electronic Press.

Kelli, Aleksei, Arvi Tavast, Krister Lindén, Kadri Vider, Ramūnas Birštonas, Penny Labropoulou, Irene Kull, Gaabriel Tavits, Age Värv, Pavel Stranák & Jan Hajic. 2020. The impact of copyright and personal data laws on the creation and use of models for language technologies. In Kiril Simov & Maria Eskevich (eds.), *Selected papers from the CLARIN Annual Conference 2019* (Linköping Electronic Conference Proceedings 172), 53–65. Linköping: Linköping University Electronic Press. https://ep.liu.se/ecp/159/008/ecp18159008.pdf (accessed 21 May 2021).

Kelli, Aleksei, Kadri Vider & Krister Lindén. 2015. The regulatory and contractual framework as an integral part of the CLARIN infrastructure. In Koenraad De Smedt (ed.), *Selected papers from the CLARIN Annual Conference 2015: October 14–16, 2015, Wroclaw, Poland* (Linköping Electronic Conference Proceedings 123), 13–24. Linköping: Linköping University Electronic Press. https://ep.liu.se/ecp/article.asp?issue=123&article=002 (accessed 17 May 2021).

Lindén, Krister, Tommi Jauhiainen, Mietta Lennes, Mikko Kurimo, Aleksi Rossi, Tommi Kurki & Olli Pitkänen. 2022. Donate Speech: Collecting and sharing a large-scale speech database for Social Sciences, Humanities and Artificial Intelligence research and innovation. In Darja Fišer & Andreas Witt (eds.), *CLARIN. The infrastructure for language resources*. Berlin: De Gruyter.

Lloyd, W. F. 1980. W. F. Lloyd on the checks to population. *Population and Development Review* 6 (3). 473–496. https://doi.org/10.2307/1972412.

Merton, Robert K. 1942. The normative structure of science. In Robert K. Merton (ed.), *The sociology of science: Theoretical and empirical investigations*, 267–278. Chicago: University of Chicago Press.

Oksanen, Ville, Krister Lindén & Hanna Westerlund. 2010. Laundry symbols and license management: Practical considerations for the distribution of LRs based on experiences from CLARIN. LREC 2010, Workshop on Language Resources: From storyboard to sustainability and LR lifecycle management. Valletta, Malta, 23 May 2010. https://helda.helsinki.fi//bitstream/handle/10138/29359/LREC2010.pdf?sequence=2 (accessed 17 May 2021).

Krister Lindén, Tommi Jauhiainen, Mietta Lennes, Mikko Kurimo, Aleksi Rossi, Tommi Kurki, and Olli Pitkänen

Donate Speech

Collecting and Sharing a Large-Scale Speech Database for Social Sciences, Humanities and Artificial Intelligence Research and Innovation

Abstract: The Donate Speech campaign aimed to collect 10,000 hours of ordinary, casual Finnish speech to be used for studying language as well as for developing technology and services that can be readily used in the languages spoken in Finland. In this project, particular attention has been devoted to allowing for both academic and commercial use of the material. Even though this ambitious target currently seems likely to evade us, the Donate Speech campaign has managed to amass an extensive resource of more than 4,000 hours of Finnish colloquial speech comprising more than 220,000 speech recordings by more than 25,000 speakers from all over Finland in just a few months.

Keywords: speech resources, colloquial speech, large-scale data collection, academic and commercial use

Acknowledgements: We are grateful to the Vake Oy (currently Ilmastorahasto) for funding the initial survey and the development of the software platform for speech collection, to the national Finnish Broadcasting Company Yle for developing and advertising the collection campaign in national media, as well as to the Academy of Finland for funding the transcription of a substantial part of the speech data and the development of the framework to distribute the data through FIN-CLARIN and the Language Bank of Finland. In addition, we are grateful to researchers of the Aalto University, the University of Helsinki, and the University of Turku, as well as the staff of Yle and Vake for generously contributing their time to the project.

Krister Lindén, University of Helsinki, Helsinki, Finland, e-mail: krister.linden@helsinki.fi
Tommi Jauhiainen, University of Helsinki, Helsinki, Finland, e-mail: tommi.jauhiainen@helsinki.fi
Mietta Lennes, University of Helsinki, Helsinki, Finland, e-mail: mietta.lennes@helsinki.fi
Mikko Kurimo, Aalto University, Aalto, Finland, e-mail: mikko.kurimo@aalto.fi
Aleksi Rossi, Yle – Finnish Broadcasting Company, Yleisradio, Finland,
e-mail: aleksi.rossi@yle.fi
Tommi Kurki, University of Turku, Turku, Finland, e-mail: tommi.kurki@utu.fi
Olli Pitkänen, 1001 Lakes Oy, Helsinki, Finland, e-mail: olli.pitkanen@1001lakes.com

https://doi.org/10.1515/9783110767377-019

1 Introduction

There are already several commercial systems utilizing AI with Finnish speech recognition in production use, but many more use cases are waiting to be successfully commercialized. To some extent this may be due to the fact that the demand for and supply of language resources do not always align, but the consensus of opinion among experts is that openly available large language resources will further accelerate the development and implementation of various language-based AI applications. Openly available speech processing components make it possible for many different actors wishing to test service ideas to pilot high-level services, while leaving the final decision on what technology to use in the production phase to a later stage. For example, automatic speech recognition (speech-to-text) and speech synthesis (text-to-speech) in Finnish have been available on a few devices and applications for several years (e.g., as speech capabilities in Apple and Google products), but many end-user services require better and more reliable processing support for colloquial Finnish.

A worldwide effort by the Mozilla Common Voice project[1] is ongoing, but their aim is to collect speech that has been read aloud. From previous projects, we know that prompted speech tends to bring people to use standardized and non-colloquial speech, and we specifically wanted everyday spontaneous speech from a large number of speakers.

In the remainder of Section 1, we will describe the process that led to the point where Vake, the Finnish State Development company (currently Ilmastorahasto Oy) was able to make the decision to fund the speech data collection campaign. We also offer a glimpse of the history of the Language Bank of Finland to explain why it was chosen as the distributor of the data, what speech material had previously been collected, why we still decided that we needed to collect new speech material for modern colloquial speech, and how CLARIN has prepared for the distribution of such large personal data collections.

The remainder of this chapter is structured as follows: in Section 2, we get an overview of a similar project (with a purely academic goal) which gave us valuable previous experience. In Section 3, we learn how the Finnish national broadcasting company Yle designed the media campaign to get people to donate speech. In Section 4, we describe the legal framework for collecting the data so that it can be reused by academia and industry alike. In Section 5, we take a look at the technical implementation and where to find the software for the speech collection platform. In Section 6, we overview the data we were able to collect,

1 https://commonvoice.mozilla.org/

and in Sections 7 and 8, we draw some conclusions and acknowledge the funders and the organizations who contributed to the implementation and running of the campaign.

1.1 The need for speech corpora

At the beginning of the 21st century, the efforts and resources of Finnish speech technology and spoken language research were scattered all over Finland and represented by relatively small teams. The USIX – Uusi käyttäjäkeskeinen tietotekniikka [New User-Centric Information Technology] technology programme was launched in 1999 and funded by the Finnish Technology Agency (Tekes, currently Business Finland). The programme, resulting in new projects and cooperation between research teams, boosted research in Finnish speech and language technology. With funding from the Ministry of Education, a survey on the state of the art of speech and spoken language research in Finland was published in 2001 (Toivanen and Miettinen 2001). One of the key findings of the survey was that investments in the availability of digital speech data were required to boost the development of research and technology in Finnish speech processing.

The availability of speech data is a prerequisite for both research in spoken language and the development of speech technological applications, including speech interfaces. The consortium project *Integrated Resources for Speech Technology and Spoken Language Research in Finland (SA-Puhe)*, funded by the Academy of Finland in 2003–2004, aimed to tackle the need for general guidelines and methods for researchers to collaboratively collect, annotate, and share speech corpora. During the project, phoneticians and language researchers at the University of Helsinki worked together with the Laboratory of Acoustics and Audio Signal Processing at Helsinki University of Technology and CSC – IT Center for Science.

The SA-Puhe project made a big effort to address the need for a centralized infrastructure in storing, sharing, and maintaining both speech data and the related annotations for research purposes. The platform was to be built on an object-oriented database system called QuickSig, which had been developed at the Helsinki University of Technology, including some further collaboration with the University of Helsinki, during the 1990s (Karjalainen and Altosaar 1993; Altosaar, Millar, and Vainio 1999). The database system was to provide efficient queries and access via a graphical query formation compiler (Altosaar and Lennes 2005). In order for researchers to be able to contribute, share, and maintain their transcripts and structured annotations for the speech recordings, the first version of a collaborative annotation editor (Puh-Editor) was developed at CSC – IT Center for Science (Grönroos and Miettinen 2004).

Unfortunately, it was not possible to complete the integration of the components of the speech database platform during the funding period. Due to the lack of resources for further development and maintenance, the Puh-Editor software was discontinued after a couple of years in test use, and the database system remained a local development project. During the project, general speech annotation guidelines were developed with the help of the language researcher community (Lennes and Ahjoniemi 2005). These guidelines proved to be useful when the idea of big data for speech processing was revived inspired by recent progress in speech technology due to neural network technology.

The process that led to the launch of the *Donate Speech* campaign began with the meetings of an ad hoc group of companies and public organizations during 2018. In spring 2019, Vake commissioned a preliminary study for the needs of Finnish language resources for artificial intelligence from FIN-CLARIN and the Language Bank of Finland (Kielipankki).[2] The goal was to specify interventions that would enable wide usability of the languages spoken in Finland in various AI applications, beginning with Finnish as the most widely spoken language in Finland. The Language Bank collected opinions and conducted interviews with more than 50 commercial and public organizations in Finland. One of the eight identified development targets was a large corpus of spontaneous colloquial speech, as identified in the study published in October 2019.[3]

FIN-CLARIN, through the Language Bank of Finland, cooperated with the Finnish Broadcasting Company (Yle) and the Finnish State Development Company (Vake Oy, currently Ilmastorahasto Oy) in the Donate Speech campaign (Lahjoita puhetta). Experts from the University of Helsinki, Aalto University, and the University of Turku also participated in the project. Vake assigned the data protection analysis and the drafting of legal documents to 1001 Lakes Oy, and legal counsels from the University of Helsinki and from Yle participated in developing the legal framework of the collection campaign.

2 The FIN-CLARIN consortium (www.helsinki.fi/finclarin) is led by the University of Helsinki and the main service centre of FIN-CLARIN is the Language Bank (www.kielipankki.fi).

3 https://vake.fi/wp-content/uploads/Vaken-suomenkielisen-tekoälyn-kehittämisohjelma-Esiselvitys-2019.pdf

1.2 FIN-CLARIN and the Language Bank of Finland

Since 2009, FIN-CLARIN has been on the national research infrastructures roadmap maintained by the Academy of Finland. The FIN-CLARIN consortium consists of all Finnish universities engaged in linguistic and language technology research,[4] the Institute for the Languages of Finland (Kotus),[5] and CSC – IT Center for Science.[6] FIN-CLARIN maintains the Language Bank of Finland,[7] through which the members of the consortium make available various language resources, both corpora and tools.

From the beginnings of the Language Bank in 1996, the aim has been that both corpora and tools are made available to the research community in the most efficient way possible. Because little attention has been paid to making materials and tools available to companies, many language resources are licensed specifically with a non-commercial restriction. In many cases, copyright or data protection issues have also led to restricted licenses. In FIN-CLARIN, CSC is responsible for the technical maintenance and the University of Helsinki for the acquisition and curating of corpora and tools.

1.3 Potential applications for special needs

Searching speech recordings for content is error-prone, even if word-spotting techniques are available for locating likely speech segments. Another approach is to convert speech into textual transcripts and use existing tools for text analysis. One may wish to count how many recorded telephone calls mention certain issues in a robocall survey. Examples of more complex use cases are various analyses of telephone discussions and their post-processing solutions. Another application is the automatic transliteration of interviews conducted by journalists or researchers. Quickly finding a quote from the speech signal would considerably speed up the verification of the details of such interviews. Improving the searchability of speech recordings also improves the usability of video-recorded debates for later verification, for example, the debates associated with decisions made in the plenary of the Parliament.

---

4 The Aalto University and the universities of Eastern Finland, Helsinki, Jyväskylä, Oulu, Tampere, Turku, and Vaasa.

5 https://www.kotus.fi

6 https://www.csc.fi

7 https://www.kielipankki.fi/language-bank/

Automatic speech recognition (ASR) is frequently needed and used for traditional text dictation, for instance for drafting messages in situations where hands and eyes have other duties. Dictation that adapts to the speech of a single person already works reasonably well in Finnish, for example on mobile devices, especially in conditions where the amount of background noise is low and/or the speaker is close to the microphone.

With improved speech processing, television shows, lectures, and so on can be subtitled automatically, either directly from the original audio or from the dictation of a human subtitler. Special groups such as the hard of hearing would benefit greatly from near-real-time subtitling of speech. Reliably functioning, genre-independent subtitling of Finnish speech would also provide a basis for automatic translation and interpretation, which has innumerable uses in the globalizing world.

Society currently requires a number of digital user skills, such as the utilization of mobile devices. If a user's vision is impaired or their finger dexterity is insufficient for a device, a user may currently be excluded from many services. Often, however, these requirements can be bypassed with a voice-enabled user interface to services in the user's native language. For the elderly and disabled, intelligent applications may complement or even replace personal services and provide an opportunity to live independently while improving the quality of life. On the other hand, if a voice interface exists but works poorly, it creates distrust and the users may avoid using a service. In some cases, such as healthcare services, user interface deficiencies may also pose security risks.

In language learning applications, speech interfaces that adapt to specific users are more useful. Interactional and oral skills are often emphasized in today's society and working life, and they are becoming an increasingly important part of language learning. For immigrants in Finland, having good oral skills in Finnish can be a great advantage in the job market and in building their social networks. A large database of transcribed colloquial speech with known topics is a good reference point, but other types of data are also needed to reliably measure pronunciation features in the speech of individual language learners and to model their speech and communicative activities in real interactional situations.

There are use cases where the speech to be analysed does not need to be presented in textual form but the analysis can be inferred directly from the speech. Such functionalities are, for example, automatic speaker identification or the automated analysis of a user's age, state of alertness, or health. The latter are useful for customizing applications and various services provided to the user, even if the accuracy is less than 100%. Even when such applications do not require the speech to be presented in textual form, they require large training corpora of speech data annotated with personal and health-related features.

1.4 Speech data for commercial use

Transcribing speech into text is a subjective process. A transcript is produced for a particular purpose and it reflects the choices made by an individual annotator. Regardless of the selected transcription system, a written transcript is unable to reflect all features that are relevant to natural interaction and the meaning of speech. These include momentary variations in the production of speech sounds or other noises, as well as longer-term prosodic properties, for example, voice quality, pitch, intensity, speech rate, and pauses. These features contribute not only to the impressions of melody, accents, and rhythm but also to the perceived meanings, intentions, and attitudes that we hear and understand in each other's speech as well as gestures, expressions, gazes, and other activities related to the interaction situation and context. The primary objective for the transcription of the collected Donate Speech data is to provide a phonematically accurate transcription of the sounds in the signal that will later be mapped to standardized speech for searchability and for enabling further language processing research and development.

The construction of secure, privacy-friendly voice user interfaces may in some cases require that the components of an application can be used without the transfer of personal data from one service to another, to a third party, or to another state. These factors argue for the fact that the speech processing components should be openly accessible and open source.

Speech corpora previously distributed by the Language Bank of Finland, such as the "Plenary Sessions of the Parliament of Finland, Downloadable Version 1" containing recordings of Parliamentary Plenary Sessions from 10 September 2008 to 1 July 2016, as well as their transcripts, are licensed CC-BY-NC-ND. Here NC is an abbreviation for *non-commercial*, that is, the materials may not be used for commercial purposes. Renegotiating licenses for this and other similar corpora to allow business use is another way to add commercially usable speech material. While in the case of the Plenary Sessions of the Parliament it may still be possible, it is often not feasible to renegotiate access rights to speech material after it has been collected and licensed. For this reason, it was particularly important to make sure new speech material was collected in a targeted manner, specifically including the possibility of commercial use.

1.5 Legal considerations for sharing data within CLARIN

The legal framework in the EU is intended to provide an interoperable space for various activities. While the legal framework harmonizes many of the activities in other parts of society, the research arena has at times been left for national consideration. This affects the sharing of research data and resources that can be achieved through a research infrastructure like CLARIN as we need to find common legal ground that is applicable to research in all EU countries. In addition, research is not only limited to academia, so to share resources within a country, we often need solutions that apply to industry as well.

The intellectual property aspect of the legal space has been extensively discussed in (Kelli, Lindén, Vider 2016; Kelli, Mets, Vider, et al. 2018; Kelli, Tavast, Lindén, et al. 2019) by members of the CLARIN Legal Issues Committee. CLARIN recommends using Creative Common licenses whenever possible (Oksanen and Lindén 2011). For all datasets, including those that cannot be made openly available, CLARIN offers a legal metadata classification system (Oksanen, Lindén, and Westerlund 2010) to inform the users of potential restrictions that they need to be aware of when accessing a dataset. For datasets that cannot be made openly and publicly available, CLARIN also offers standard license templates for depositing data to be shared through CLARIN Centres (Kelli, Lindén, Vider, et al. 2018). The IPR relevant for sharing research data has been extensively scrutinized by CLARIN over the last ten years, which is documented in Kamocki, Kelli, and Lindén (2022) Section 3.5 of this book, and we are eagerly awaiting new opportunities provided by the EU text and data mining directive (Kelli, Tavast, Lindén, Vider, et al. 2020).

During the last few years, the consequences of EU's General Data Protection Regulation (GDPR) has been widely recognized (Kelli et al. 2021). Some leeway was given to individual EU member countries to implement exceptions for research, and this has led to differing practices for sharing personal data for academic research purposes (Kelli, Lindén, Vider, et al. 2019; Lindén et al. 2020). Resources containing personal data are among the resources that cannot be made available without protective measures, and CLARIN is in the process of updating its license templates to reflect how personal data can still be shared in safe and controlled ways for academic research (Kelli, Lindén, Vider, et al. 2020).

Despite the fact that not all data can be made openly accessible, it is possible to use data to which one has legal access for creating openly accessible language models. For a detailed discussion of this, see Kelli, Tavast, Lindén, Bristonas, et al. (2020). To illustrate how personal data can be collected and shared within the EU, we will present the legal underpinnings of the Donate Speech campaign in Section 4. The campaign involved more than 25,000 citizens in Finland donating more than 220,000 speech samples comprising roughly 4,000 hours of colloquial speech to be used by academia and industry for developing and researching language and AI applications. The fact that the data was collected to be used by industry as well makes it particularly relevant for CLARIN as industry use is regulated by the common EU ground in the GDPR.

2 Earlier speech collections in Finland

In Finland, there are several extensive speech databases previously collected for linguistic research by the Institute for the Languages of Finland, the universities, and memory organizations, but for commercial purposes access to them is limited. In addition, plenty of linguistic research has been done, over a long period, from the perspective of dialectology, sociolinguistics, and interactional linguistics, and there are exceptionally extensive dialectological corpora (most of them representing the regional variation of Finnish in the 1960s and 1970s) and large sociolinguistic corpora representing social variation on the segmental levels of Finnish. However, a new extensive speech database representing large-scale regional and social variation in contemporary Finnish is potentially a valuable new asset also in linguistics. Collecting dialectological and sociolinguistic speech data has typically been done through fieldwork and face-to-face interaction. Due to this aspect, compiling such a database has typically required vast resources of time and funding.

The Donate Speech Campaign is associated, on the one hand, with dialectology and sociolinguistics and their long traditions in obtaining data by doing extensive fieldwork, and on the other hand with phonetics and speech technology, which obtain data in laboratory settings. Both fields are largely empirical in practice. As dialectology and sociolinguistics aim for naturalness, with a focus on conversational speech and representativeness of speakers within communities, phonetics holds the replicability of experiments in high esteem and focuses on speech in laboratory settings (Thomas 2013: 108). In this project, collecting speech data over the internet needed to strike a balance between the two and at the same time take into account the possibilities and limitations of the digital environment.

Collecting speech data over the internet is a faster and more economic method than traditional fieldwork, and it makes it possible to reach a large number of potential participants who would not necessarily otherwise participate. Meanwhile, several questions arise: how can we collect controlled data with elicited tasks that represent speech as naturally or as spontaneously as possible and cover current regional and social variation as widely as possible? How can we obtain a large database that also represents functionally different speech samples (statements, commands, questions, echo questions, etc.)? A dialectologist or sociolinguist seeks ways to grasp the variation of language, and in practice will inevitably face the observer's paradox as Labov (1972: 209) has phrased it: "the aim of linguistic research in the community must be to find out how people talk when they are not being systematically observed; yet we can only obtain these data by systematic observation."

Whether a scholar records an interview or a conversation in which informants are involved or an informant makes a recording alone – in other words, whether the scholar collecting data is present or not – Labov's paradox holds. The same paradox applies to data collection over the internet, especially when the goal of the campaign is not to collect read speech data. When interacting with a computer instead of another human being, how can we overcome the potential distraction that participants are self-consciously aware that they are recorded and, due to this, carefully watch their language use?

2.1 Previous lessons from the Prosovar project

The Donate Speech campaign had a Finnish predecessor that incorporated new methodology and new ways of obtaining speech data over the internet, implementing a crowdsourcing approach. The multidisciplinary project *The Regional and Social Variation of Finnish Prosody* (Prosovar) was conducted by the University of Turku and financed by the Kone foundation (2013–2015; see also Kurki et al. 2014; Nieminen and Kurki 2017). The objectives of this project included (a) the formation of a speech corpus particularly for the study of Finnish prosody and its regional and social variation (The Corpus of Prosodic Variation in Finnish) and (b) the development and testing of a method for data collection and analysis for the study of natural spoken language.

As a complement to old fieldwork for obtaining speech in dialectology and sociolinguistics, a new, partially crowdsourced method for collecting sociolinguistic and sociophonetic data via the internet was developed and tested in the Prosovar project. There was also a precedent for collecting sociolinguistic data on the internet (in particular, Dialect Topography by Professor J. K. Chambers; cf. Chambers 1994), but to our knowledge, Prosovar was one of the first attempts in dialectology, sociolinguistics, and sociophonetics (cf. computational linguistics; e.g., Lane et al. 2010; McGraw 2013) to collect speech data over the internet. The development of data collection methods in Prosovar required a multidisciplinary approach, where dialectological, sociolinguistic, (socio)phonetic, computer science, and Finnish language expertise was needed.

The idea was to motivate non-linguists to participate in data collection by completing recording tasks with a web application created for the Prosovar project. From the beginning of the project, it was crucially important to find ways to attract voluntary participants willing to record their speech samples for linguistic research purposes. The goal of giving public presentations, interviews to newspapers, and campaigning in social media was to arouse public interest. The possibility of listening to anonymous speech samples from other participants and implementing the elements of a game-like design in developing the application were also found to be good ways to attract interest.

Participants were able to make recordings with their personal computers, (Android) tablet computers, and (Android) cellular phones, as long as their device had a microphone and they created a user account. At the same time, this presented a way for them to further participate in the research; as long as they made recordings for the database, they were allowed to listen to randomly selected anonymous voice clips from the database and evaluate them in a folk linguistic manner. For example, a participant was asked to listen to a clip and locate the speaker's dialect on a map, or he/she was asked to describe, using a few adjectives, what the speaker in a clip sounded like. This information was and is possible to investigate from a folk linguistic perspective by analysing the language with regard to respondents and from a computer science perspective by applying dialect recognition techniques (e.g., how humans and computers perceive sounds differently).

Unregistered guest users were only able to listen to a few selected anonymous samples and obtain general information about Finnish colloquial speech and dialect samples in the data obtained so far in the project. In order to access the recording tasks and the "game", in which one listened to short audio clips and tried to locate their speakers, one had to (1) create a user account, (2) accept the conditions and terms of use, and (3) finish at least one recording task in order to access the game. All the data and the background information about the participants were moved to a separate server for privacy and security reasons. By the end of November 2015, there were approximately 1,000 registered users, of whom 395 had made recordings for the project, producing a total of over 9,300 recorded samples.

Inventing and designing suitable elicitation tasks was of crucial importance to the Prosovar project (see also Nieminen and Kurki 2015; Nieminen and Kurki 2017). The objective was to obtain comparable utterances, that is, the same thing in different dialects. In the very first tasks designed for the pilot stage, the participants were just prompted to read out loud the text on a screen; consecutive sentences of the same paragraph one by one, or simply disjointed phrases without any further context. Soon, it became clear that this might lead participants to use standard Finnish and thus obfuscate regional and social variation. The shorter the task and the more time for a participant to react, the more likely it was – at least for some informants – to become notably aware of their own language use; this was not ideal, since the idea was to collect spontaneous verbal reactions and not performances consciously planned to be recorded.

Due to this, tweaks were made to the old tasks and new tasks were designed. For instance, the same phrase was shown in two or three distinct dialects at the same time on a screen and participants were asked to consider how they would express the same phrase in their own way. In another task, a participant was told to list months and weekdays. In addition, tasks with visual, auditory, or audio-visual stimuli were devised. It still seemed that in tasks with textual stimuli, participants paid close attention to their language. Especially if the time to react to a stimulus was unlimited, some participants consciously paid attention to their language use, and as a consequence tended to either exaggerate dialectal forms or strive for perfection speaking in a very standard Finnish manner.

In the end, it was best to have various tasks with different stimuli; in most cases, the task instructions or cues were kept out of the way as much as possible while ensuring decent predictability in what the informant would ultimately say. Thus, the participants were required to react to assignments of various kinds. For instance, there was a task where the participants were shown two pictures with minor differences; their task was to spot the differences and report them verbally. In another task, the participant was shown a map of a fictional town and asked to guide a stranger from one point to another. In some tasks, participants were instructed to speak simultaneously when they saw a stimulus or when they were watching it. For instance, participants were shown a short animated video and, instead of watching it first and then summarizing the plot of the video, they were asked to describe and explain what was happening in the video.

Obtaining functionally different speech samples was one of the most challenging parts in creating the Prosovar database. It was much easier to develop tasks that reached narratives and even declaratives than interrogatives. Some sound samples of tasks in which a participant was asking questions without an actual interlocutor in the scene appeared awkward or unnatural. To mitigate this, tasks were created in which the research group tried to create an illusion of mutual interaction. For instance, there was a setting for social interaction in a marketplace where the participant was instructed to either buy berries from a salesman or to sell berries to a client, while the other party's line was provided by a pre-recorded sound sample on the site. This solution helped to construct a substantially more vivid setting; inevitably, however, it was only slightly reminiscent of actual human interaction. A more functional solution would presumably have been to have two or more participants online simultaneously in the same recording task. In addition to the limited technical resources at the time in the Prosovar project, as well as the risk of data abuse or pestering of other participants prevented the implementation of this collaborative type of task.

Previous experiences in collecting speech data over the internet also showed that sound quality has to be taken into consideration. In the Prosovar project, there was a need to find a balance between catching as many potential participants as possible and setting the system requirements for the devices of potential participants. Overly sophisticated system requirements would have decreased the number of potential users. For the same reason, it was decided that collecting data would be carried out without asking the potential participants to install any application on their device. Because of this, the minimum requirement for a device was basically a microphone (built-in or external). Since the recordings were fully carried out by the participants, it was not possible to control the recording settings. Participants had a varying range of computers with varying quality of sound equipment. The website provided information on how to use the mixer and how to ensure eligible recording conditions, but few participants seem to have made use of them.

This tended to leave the Prosovar research group at the mercy of the web browsers and their plug-ins and add-ons. As a consequence, the quality of speech data was very variable. Still, the majority of the samples were actually of good enough quality as the objective in Prosovar was to study the prosodic features of speech, which are generally more robust than the spectral features.

3 Designing the Donate Speech campaign

This section describes the process that was used to design and launch the Donate Speech campaign. The initial objective of the Donate Speech campaign was to collect data for all languages spoken in Finland. However, the first phase of the campaign focused on Finnish with the objective to obtain 10,000 hours of colloquial Finnish representing the wide variety of ways the Finns currently speak it in everyday settings. The data is intended for linguistic research and development of technology for both academic and commercial purposes. We also describe what kind of meta-information was collected from the participants and how.

The goal of the campaign was not merely to collect a vast amount of any kind of speech, but to reach out to as many different groups of Finnish speakers and to as many individuals as possible. In marketing the campaign to citizens, it was emphasized that all variants of spoken Finnish are welcome, including speech from second-language Finnish learners. However, in order to understand the privacy notice and the instructions, a certain level of language proficiency was required from the speech donors.

In order to strike a balance between the material goals, the technical possibilities, and the resources that were available, design workshops were organized for all interested parties. During these events, general ideas were collected from both industry and academia on the different uses for the collected speech, while most of the planning of the thematic tasks to elicit speech was left to the staff of the national broadcasting company Yle with advice collected from previous efforts like the Prosovar project. Yle was in charge of the public outreach through its radio and TV channels. Yle designed pictures, videos, and texts that were presented to speakers in the web application and the downloadable apps. A number of technical templates were designed to allow the design of themes with various types of content in order to target a desired speaker group.

The workshops to determine potential use cases, target audiences, and required and optional features were conducted in autumn 2019 with key research stakeholders, following up during spring 2020. The workshops were facilitated by the solution developer company Solita and were loosely based on the Design Thinking methodology. Later a series of key features were also tested with quick paper prototypes, and in succession with semi-interactive tools. A multitude of design suggestions were made by professional service designers guided by their experience, and a few crucial ones were also tested in practice.

Key issues and challenges for the design of the user interface were in determining elicitation methods that entice a person to speak freely, gaining the trust of the speaker, making him feel comfortable while also satisfying legal constraints for presenting enough required information in an easy-to-understand format, as well as more technical choices of supported platforms, presentation forms, visual and auditory feedback of the ongoing recording or its quality. After some ideas for themes had been formulated and tested, Yle settled on the fail-safe recurring functions of showing a video, a picture, or some textual content, enticing a person to speak with a single, easy-to-use button for starting and stopping the recording.

There were a number of discussions about whether and how to introduce gamification elements similar to the ones suggested by the Prosovar project, such as telling the user how much he had donated, or elements like scoreboards to compare results and maintain user interest, or social elements like sharing results or collecting teams. Eventually, only the amount of total time donated was included as a gamification element, leaving room for further improvements.

The opening theme *Harjoitellaan ensin* (Let's practice) started by test-driving the recording with the user, and assuring them that mainly AI researchers would use the recordings and reminding them about the privacy notice. The technical platform also presented metadata questions for the user to answer, for example about dialect background (the location of the phone is neither queried nor transmitted), basic demographics like age group, gender, mother tongue, the current county a person lives in or was born in, and their profession and education level. In addition, the technical platform was also collected for statistical purposes.

In the end, Yle developed around 40 rather straightforward themes for stimulating the collecting of speech data. In addition to the opening practice theme, the 12 most popular themes, through which almost half of the data was collected, were: *Rakkain eläimeni* (My dearest pet), *Mistä kodikkuus syntyy?* (What makes a cozy home?), *Tärkeä esineeni* (An important object of mine), *Lempivaate* (My favourite piece of clothing), *Mikä suututtaa?* (What's infuriating?), *Turhat tavarani* (My superfluous things), *Mitä opimme?* (What did we learn?), *Entisajan lemmikit* (Old time pets), *Katson ikkunasta* (While I am looking out the window), *Kuva-arvoitus* (Picture riddle), *Kerro aamiaisesta* (What was your breakfast like?).

As part of the campaign, Yle made comical infomercials with requests to the general public to donate speech. These were broadcast during programme breaks in national radio and TV channels during the summer and autumn of 2020, during the Covid-19 pandemic, with some trailing reruns during spring 2021.

4 Legal aspects

From the beginning, it was clear that the processing of data must be conducted in a legally and ethically sound way. All the central actors in the project – Kielipankki at the University of Helsinki, Vake, and Yle – are public organizations that cannot ignore these aspects.

The speech material donated during the campaign will be stored in the Language Bank of Finland (Kielipankki), coordinated by the University of Helsinki. It was noted that the material may contain subject matter protected by several legal rights (Alen-Savikko and Pitkänen 2016), such as:

- data protection rights (Wrigley, Alen-Savikko, and Pitkänen 2019)
- copyright and neighbouring rights (e.g., the right of the producer of a sound recording, database sui generis right) (Pitkänen 2017)
- patents (Ballardini et al. 2013)
- trademarks (Weckström 2012)
- trade secrets (Schröder 2018).

In particular, the personal data protected by European and national data protection legislation, most notably by the General Data Protection Regulation (GDPR),[8] is considered to be essential from the campaign's viewpoint. The definition of the personal data is very broad and therefore significant parts of the speech material can be considered personal data for various reasons:

- metadata about the speaker, his or her identification, name, etc., can be linked directly to a person.

8 Regulation (EU) 2016/679 of the European Parliament and of the Council of 27 April 2016.

- the recognizable voice of a speaker may also be linked to a person, at least if there is some other information about the speaker available.
- the content of the speech may include personal information, e.g., if the speaker reveals what he was doing with his friends last weekend.

According to the GDPR, it is important, inter alia:
- to define the purpose of the processing of personal data;
- to inform the data subjects about the processing of personal data in a concise, transparent, intelligible, and easily accessible form, using clear and plain language;
- to define a lawful basis to cover data processing, i.e., consent, contract, legal obligation, vital interest, public interest, or legitimate interest;
- to analyse and mitigate the potential risks of personal data processing to individuals.

These requirements were taken very seriously from the beginning.

The speech material can be shared with individual researchers, universities and research organizations or private companies that need it for studying language or artificial intelligence, for developing AI solutions, or for higher education purposes related to the aforementioned areas. During and after the campaign, the privacy practices of the Language Bank of Finland have been developed in accordance with the GDPR.

According to the GDPR, personal data shall be collected for specified, explicit, and legitimate purposes and not further processed in a manner that is incompatible with those purposes.[9] Therefore, it was essential to define the purpose as clearly as possible. In general, it is very difficult to avoid some vagueness when trying to define forthcoming undertakings. However, the following definition is as accurate and comprehensible as it was possible to come up with: "Personal data is processed for the development and research of applications and services that understand and produce speech, as well as for language research and higher education related to these purposes."

According to GDPR Article 6, the processing of personal data is lawful only if and to the extent that at least one of the lawful bases applies:
- consent
- contract
- legal obligation
- vital interest

9 GDPR Article 5(1)(b).

- public interest
- legitimate interest.

In this case, there is no legal obligation or vital interest to collect speech. Public interest could be applicable to scientific research, but it is too restrictive considering that the material should also benefit commercial product development. To use a contract as a legal basis would require that processing is necessary for the performance of a contract to which the data subject is party. That was not the case. In principle, it would have been possible to use consent as the legal basis, but that was considered impractical, because the consent must be specific and the data subjects have the right to withdraw their consents at any time.

Therefore, legitimate interest to collect and process speech to be used for studying language as well as for developing technology and services that can be readily used in the languages spoken in Finland was chosen to be the best basis for the processing of personal data in the campaign. However, it was recognized that if it becomes necessary to also process special categories of personal data, like racial or ethnic origin, political opinions, religious or philosophical beliefs, data concerning health, or data concerning a natural person's sex life or sexual orientation, the explicit consent to the processing of such personal data is needed in accordance with GDPR Article 9. Until then, the controllers strive not to collect and process any personal data in these special categories.

To inform the data subjects (i.e., the individuals who donate their speech to the campaign), two essential documents were drafted:[10]

- A short *information page* including simple conditions of participation. It briefly describes the campaign and the responsible organizations, emphasizes that the donation is completely voluntary, explains that the individual may have copyright or other rights in the speech and he/she will need to assign those rights to the extent necessary, asks not to provide any personal data or intellectual property of others, provides links to the data protection policy and some additional information, and finally asks the person to accept these terms. It should be noted that this is not consent to process personal data as discussed above; rather, the lawful basis is a legitimate interest to process personal data.
- A more comprehensive *data protection policy*, titled "Tietosuoja" (Data Protection). The policy aims to describe, in a comprehensible and clear way, how personal data are processed in the campaign. It gives some basic information on data protection and describes how the donor can remove the donated

10 https://lahjoitapuhetta.fi/

> speech from the campaign. Furthermore, it attempts to fulfil the data subject's right to be informed, as prescribed in the GDPR, Articles 12 and 13. The controllers (University of Helsinki, Yle, and Vake) are identified, their contact information and the contact details of their data protection officers are disclosed, and the controllers' responsibilities specified; the purpose of the processing of personal data is explained, the legitimate interest as the lawful basis of processing is specified and justified, the categories of personal data are listed, the principles to whom the personal data can be transferred are stated, and it is explained for how long the data is stored. The data subject's applicable rights are explained: the right to be informed and to get access to data, the right to request rectification or erasure of personal data or restriction of processing concerning the data subject and to object to processing, and the right to lodge a complaint with a supervisory authority. It is also noted that personal data is not used for automatic decision-making nor for direct marketing.

In order to use legitimate interest as the lawful basis for the processing of personal data, it was necessary to accomplish a balance test to ensure that the legitimate interests are not overridden by the interests or fundamental rights and freedoms of the data subject. The Finnish Data Protection Authority has published a model balance test, which was carefully applied. The model consists of six steps:
1. Is legitimate interest the most appropriate basis for processing?
2. Are the basic requirements (legal, clearly stated, representing a genuine and direct need) met?
3. Is the processing of personal data necessary for pursuing the interest?
4. Does the interest truly override the rights and interests of the data subject?
5. How are additional guarantees for data protection ensured?
6. How is the legality and transparency of the operations demonstrated?

To better understand the risks and possible problems that the processing of personal data may cause to individuals, a careful risk assessment was also performed. After completing all six steps, it seemed clear that a legitimate interest existed, met the legal requirements, and was not overridden by the interests or fundamental rights and freedoms of the data subject.

It was also considered that the risks to the rights and freedoms of natural persons were not very high. However, just to be sure, it was decided, in accordance with GDPR Article 35, to carry out a data protection impact assessment (DPIA) as well. The above-mentioned balance test to ensure that the legitimate interests are not overridden by the interests or fundamental rights and freedoms of the data subject – especially when complemented with a significant risk assessment – is not very different from a data protection impact assessment. Therefore, it was possible to reuse most of the balance test in the DPIA and only complement it as required by the GDPR.

4.1 Data protection impact assessment

A data protection impact assessment (DPIA) was carried out because of possible risks related to the processing of data. In particular, the extensive processing as well as the new technologies and innovation development related to the purpose of processing were taken into account.[11] The University of Helsinki and Yle have data protection officers and they were involved in the data protection impact assessment as required by the GDPR.[12]

In the DPIA, the processing of personal data in the campaign was described in line with the discussion above. The purpose of the processing was described, the controllers and their responsibilities were specified, and the subcontractors were listed. It was explained who may receive the data, and it was noted that they can be located outside the European Union and the European Economic Area. The different phases of the processing were described, and the data that was to be processed, the sources of the data, and the purpose of processing were defined. The assessment of the necessity and proportionality of the processing operations in relation to the purposes was included. An essential part of the DPIA was the listing and the analyses of the recognized risks to the rights and freedoms of data subjects.[13]

The outcome of the DPIA was that the processing does not result in a high risk after the measures taken by the controllers to mitigate the risks. The DPIA will be updated as needed, if for example processing of special categories of personal data becomes necessary.

4.2 Communicating the data to the public

The Language Bank Rights (LBR) is an electronic application system for managing access to language resources. It is based on the Resource Entitlement Management System (REMS) developed by CSC for research data. A solution is being designed for how the LBR REMS will be accessible by private companies as well.

---

11 GDPR Article 35(1).

12 GDPR Article 35(2).

13 GDPR Article 35(7).

The Language Bank of Finland will begin redistributing the speech data when a sufficient amount of material has been donated and when the appropriate rights application process is in place in the beginning of 2022. For academic researchers, the use of the data will be free of charge, like the rest of the services of the Language Bank of Finland. For commercial use, a fee will probably be charged in order to cover handling costs.

5 Technical implementation

Speech for the Donate Speech campaign[14] could be donated via a web browser or mobile app, both of which offered a selection of tasks with light-hearted themes that aimed to inspire and encourage the user to talk about a particular topic. Representatives from both industry and academia developed the general specifications for the app. The software solution development company Solita developed the apps. The software platform has been published as open-source software,[15] allowing other organizations to build their own systems for collecting similar speech material or to enable specialized collection campaigns by researchers, or similar campaigns in other countries.

Technical voice quality is a complicated topic of its own. Having the microphone near the user is imperative, so advising more relaxed use, like leaving the phone on the table, would introduce more echoes and weaker signal. A discussion format with a group of people was also ruled out. There would have been obvious benefits, like the free-flowing, back-and-forth dialogue that characterizes a group discussion but does not exist in a single-speaker situation. However, that would have presented technical challenges rendering it hard to use when everybody should be close to a single microphone, or far away from each other with everyone having his own device to minimize cross-feeds and echoes in the signal. In addition, multiple signals would need to be synchronized in the backend system, or there would be a need to register which phones were co-recording the multi-mic discussion. For this reason, no user testing was conducted on which styles of dialogue triggers would work best for yielding interesting, differing flows of dialogue.

The recordings were kept simple by recording the speech signal in the highest lossless formats possible and accompanying them with metadata about the system, phone type, and version. The metadata therefore allowed for some post-processing

14 https://lahjoitapuhetta.fi/
15 https://github.com/CSCfi/Kielipankki-donatespeech-backend

corrections using, for example, sound equalization according to microphone type. A rudimentary VU-meter to give feedback to the user about an acceptable signal level was considered but not implemented, to conserve battery and diminish the development burden. Based on user testing, the usefulness of this feedback was also in doubt. First, the meter would provide a distraction or most likely be ignored; second, educating the user on how to interpret this additional information would encumber the user interface; and third, the improvement of the signal would not be substantial as the user would mainly move closer to the microphone for some time.

In the end, users were instructed to speak freely in their own environment. A clear signal in a noise-free environment is often preferable, but currently the recordings have a bit more variety as they also contain some noise, such as people in the background or wind in outdoor settings. In any case, according to the user tests, most people did the recording sessions on their own in rather quiet indoor settings. A delayed transmit in the background of locally stored recordings for uploading to the cloud was prepared in case the user did not have a steady internet connection, but it was probably not that important a feature.

The web, Android and iOS were chosen as platforms for smartphones, tablets, and computers with microphones. There was also an associated website informing users about the campaign and Yle published its own articles and campaign site. The apps were released from the Yle account instead of using separate dedicated or campaign-specific accounts to lend trust in an established entity to the campaign.

The solution architecture consisted of multiple frontends on different platforms, backend services and databases to collect data in the cloud, the web hosting, and the analytics. By splitting responsibilities for analytics and backend hosting, the visibility of the legal entities could be limited, so the party driving the campaigns had the option to access usage data to focus the campaign efforts without access to the raw speech donations. The system was developed for monolingual use, but further adaptation and localization to other languages and other themes was kept in mind.

To comply with the GDPR and to enable deletion of contributions, the backend allows easy deletion of user submissions through a long random identifier given to the user at the time of speech donation. There are no other user-specific identifiers in the backend data. One still needs to consider that individual users may be identifiable by their metadata in the case that the participating group is small or a combination of metadata very specific. For example, men of a certain age bracket in a small geographical area with a particular dialect background could potentially result in a tiny group of people both in the collected data and the real world. The technical platform as such does not restrict the collection of overly specific metadata, as the GDPR-compliant processing of data is the responsibility of the controller and the processors when further processing the data or publishing findings in a way that is anonymous.

In spring 2021, the Android and iOS mobile application versions of Donate Speech were submitted to the annual marketing competition GrandOne, for web applications launched during the previous year. The Donate Speech applications won the prestigious first prize[16] in the mobile service category and an honourable mention in the category for best data use. Yle also submitted the Donate Speech campaign to the annual Prix Europa competition for European broadcasters, and in autumn 2021, after a thorough evaluation, the Donate speech campaign won the category of Best European Digital Audio Project 2021[17] in the highly prestigious TV, radio, and online product competition, chosen from among 684 entries from 26 countries. The award recognized a fresh way to conceptualize broadcasting and its output; the new cooperation model between commercial and public service entities and a broadcasting company like Yle; and a great web service accompanied by a light-hearted and humorous campaign.

6 Characteristics of the Donated Speech data

The objective for the Donate Speech campaign was to collect 10,000 hours of speech during half a year of campaigning. That would have meant about obtaining 8.5 seconds from each 10- to 70-year-old person in Finland, or getting 600,000 persons to donate a minute each, or 120,000 persons to donate 5 minutes each. The objective was considered quite a stretch but attainable in an optimal situation.

The campaign collected about 3,500 hours in half a year. The launch on national TV in June 2020 inspired the biggest number of contributions, but as can be seen in Figure 1, the summer of 2020 during the Covid-19 pandemic was quite active. The campaign was able to reach new audiences throughout the autumn but at a considerably slower pace. Towards the end of the campaign, there was a push on regional radio to collect dialects and the last 10% was collected in a week around Christmas 2020. Yle had a campaign page for its campaign events.[18] The campaign had officially ended by New Year 2021, but trailing infomercials

16 https://grandone.fi/kilpailutyo/?entry=lahjoita-puhetta-siivittaeae-suomenkielistae-puheentunnistusta

17 PRIX EUROPA 2021 Winners – PRIX EUROPA (https://www.prixeuropa.eu/news/2021/10/15winners-y4emh).

18 https://yle.fi/aihe/lahjoita-puhetta

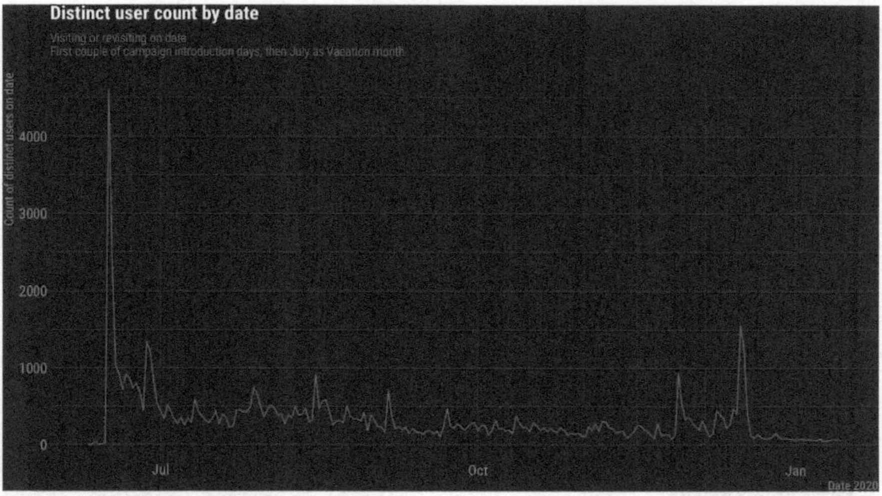

Figure 1: Distinct user count by date.

and reruns were still broadcast during the spring of 2021, resulting in a trickle of additional contributions.

Figure 2 breaks down the speech donations by age group. There are hours of data representing a wide range of age brackets. Perhaps surprisingly, 21- to 30-year-old females, unfazed by the somewhat technical set-up, donated most of the speech. The smallest amount of speech was donated by very young participants (1–10 years old) and very old participants (80 years or more). Two groups to consider for future focus activities are teens around 11–20, and retired people around 71–80. Both have distinctive characteristics from an AI development point of view, speaking with different pitch, vocabulary, pace, breaks, and potentially with interleaving and heavier breathing. One industry partner considers developing AI-powered elderly care systems, and specific modes like talking while lying down would also be useful.

Not everyone provided all the metadata, but among those who provided metadata, we can make some interesting observations. People between 20–60 years old made around three quarters of the donations. More than 70% of the donors were women. As expected, almost half of the donations were from the four regions with the largest Finnish cities: Uusimaa (including Helsinki and Espoo), Pohjois-Pohjanmaa (including Oulu), Varsinais-Suomi (including Turku), and Pirkanmaa (including Tampere), but donations were made from all the regions of Finland and 50 different counties, with 95% of the donors being native speakers. We note that the geographic areas have about the same amount of donations per 100,000 inhabitants, with approximately 60% to 150% deviation from the mean. A considerably larger share of Swedish and Saami minority speakers in some areas probably explains a couple of outliers with smaller contributions. More than two thirds of the data was donated by students, retired persons, teachers, entrepreneurs, experts, and nurses (in descending order of contributor number) with the remainder contributed by more than 30 other professions from diverse areas of society. Approximately 62% had a higher education and 28% a secondary education.

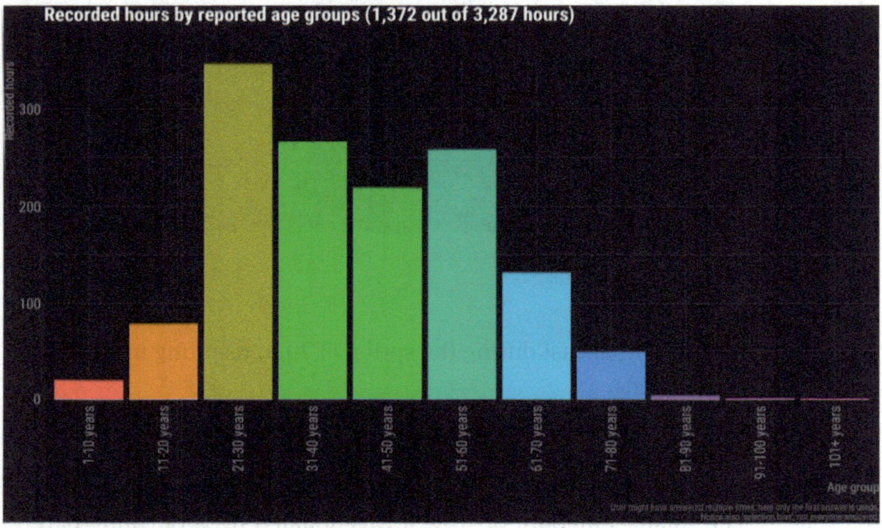

Figure 2: Recorded hours by age group.

Interestingly, the web interface was used by two thirds of the donors, and only 20% used the Android app with the rest using the iPhone app. Close to 90% of the more than 220,000 recordings were between 10 seconds and 3 minutes, with the median length being 30–60 seconds, in the end totalling roughly 4,000 hours.

There are a couple of limitations as to the reliability of these figures. The analytics data consist of a sequence of events of donations and interleaved metadata questions. Some users have not answered all the demographic questions. Other users might have multiple differing answers so the attribution of donation hours per metadata subcategory remains an estimate. In addition, the analytics system missed about 10% of the user events. Still, we believe that the figures paint quite a good initial picture of the success of the campaign.

After 80 hours of an initial random sample of the speech data was quality checked and manually transliterated, the initial impression was quite positive. Small random samples (1, 10, and 80 hours) of manually transcribed data were evaluated by the current automatic speech recognition technology group at Aalto University to assess how accurately this material can be automatically transcribed, what kind of errors occur, and how the accuracy varies according to the conditions and given metadata. The initial impressions were rather positive: the material is on average not harder to recognize than previously recorded conversations at the Aalto University, despite being more diverse in terms of speakers, ages, dialects, and topics, as well as recording devices and conditions.

7 Conclusion

Even though the target of 10,000 hours was ambitious, the Donate Speech campaign has managed to collect an extensive resource of Finnish colloquial speech from a large number of speakers in just a few months. The campaign was implemented by Yle (the National Broadcasting Company of Finland) in cooperation with Ilmastorahasto (former state development company Vake) and the University of Helsinki. The University of Helsinki represented FIN-CLARIN and its service centre Kielipankki (the Language Bank of Finland), through which the FIN-CLARIN members make available various language resources, both corpora and tools.

Society currently requires a number of digital user skills, such as the utilization of mobile devices. If a user's vision is impaired or their finger dexterity is insufficient for a device, a user may currently be excluded from many services. To develop such services, speech data that is also available for commercial purposes was needed. At the beginning of the 21st century, the efforts and resources of Finnish speech technology and spoken language research were scattered all over Finland and represented by relatively small teams or researchers or public bodies. While automatic speech recognition (speech-to-text) and speech synthesis (text-to-speech) in Finnish have been available in a few devices and applications for several years (e.g., as speech capabilities in Apple and Google products), implementing or enhancing many end-user services still requires better and more reliable processing support for colloquial Finnish. To remedy this there was a need for collecting and making available a sizable amount of speech data that could also be used for commercial purposes.

In Finland, there are several extensive speech databases that were previously collected for linguistic research by the Institute for the Languages of Finland, the universities, and memory organizations, but for commercial purposes access to them is limited. Renegotiating licenses for corpora to allow business use is one way to add commercially usable speech material, but it is often not feasible to renegotiate access rights after data has already been collected and licensed.

The Donate Speech campaign had a Finnish predecessor called Prosovar as regards new methodology and new ways of obtaining speech data over the internet, implementing a crowdsourcing approach. The goal of the Donate Speech campaign was not merely to collect a vast amount of any kind of speech, but to reach out to as many different groups of Finnish speakers and to as many individuals as possible. In marketing the campaign to citizens, it was emphasized that all variants of spoken Finnish are welcome, including speech from second-language Finnish learners. However, in order to understand the privacy notice and the instructions, a certain level of language proficiency was required from the speech donors. In order to strike a balance between the material goals, the technical possibilities, and the resources that were available, design workshops were organized for all interested parties.

From the beginning, it was clear that the processing of data must be conducted in a legally and ethically sound way. All the central actors in the project (Kielipankki at the University of Helsinki, Vake, and Yle) are public organizations that cannot ignore these aspects. To better understand the risks and possible problems that the processing of personal data may cause to individuals, a careful risk assessment was also performed. After completing all the six steps of the balance test, it seemed clear that a legitimate interest existed, met the legal requirements, and was not overridden by the interests or fundamental rights and freedoms of the data subject. A data protection impact assessment (DPIA) was carried out because of possible risks related to the processing of data. In particular, the extensive processing as well as the new technologies and innovation development related to the purpose of processing were considered. The Language Bank Rights (LBR) is an electronic application system for managing access to language resources. The Language Bank of Finland will begin redistributing the speech data when a sufficient amount of material has been donated and when the appropriate rights application process is in place in the beginning of 2022.

In the end, Yle developed around 40 rather straightforward themes for stimulating the collecting of speech data. As part of the campaign, Yle made comical infomercials with requests to the general public to donate speech. These were broadcast during programme breaks in national radio and TV channels during the summer and autumn of 2020, during the Covid-19 pandemic, with some trailing reruns during spring 2021. Speech for the Donate Speech campaign (Lahjoita puhetta) could be donated via a web browser or mobile app, both of which offered a selection of tasks with light-hearted themes that aimed to inspire and encourage the user to talk about a particular topic. To comply with the GDPR and to enable deletion of contributions, the backend allows easy deletion of user submissions through a long random identifier given to the user at the time of speech donation.

Not everyone provided all the metadata, but among those who provided metadata, we can make some interesting observations. People between 20 and 60 years old made around three quarters of the donations. More than 70% of the donors were women. As expected, almost half of the donations were from the four regions with the largest Finnish cities: Uusimaa (including Helsinki and Espoo), Pohjois-Pohjanmaa (including Oulu), Varsinais-Suomi (including Turku), and Pirkanmaa (including Tampere), but donations were made from all the regions of Finland – 50 different counties – with 95% of the donors being native speakers. We note that the geographic areas have about the same amount of donations per 100,000 inhabitants, with approximately 60% to 150% deviation from the mean. A considerably larger share of Swedish and Saami minority speakers in some areas probably explains a couple of outliers with smaller contributions. More than two thirds of the data was donated by students, retired persons, teachers, entrepreneurs, experts, and nurses (in descending order of contributor number) with the remainder contributed by more than 30 other professions from diverse areas of society. Approximately 62% had a higher education and 28% a secondary education. Interestingly, two thirds of the donors used the web interface for donating speech, and only 20% used the Android app with the rest using the iPhone app. Close to 90% of the more than 220,000 recordings were between 10 seconds and 3 minutes, with the median length being 30–60 seconds, totalling roughly 4,000 hours.

After 80 hours of an initial random sample of the speech data was quality checked and manually transliterated, the initial impression of the collected data was quite positive. At the time of writing, 1,500 hours of speech has been transliterated, which will allow much more precise training of speaker independent supervised speech recognition, as well as new directions in research in unsupervised or minimally supervised machine learning of speech processing using current neural network technology.

Bibliography

Alen-Savikko, Anette K. & Olli Pitkänen. 2016. Rights and entitlements in information: Proprietary perspectives and beyond. In Tobias Bräutigam & Samuli Miettinen (eds.), *Data protection, privacy and European regulation in the digital age*, 3–33. Helsinki: Forum Iuris.

Altosaar, Toomas & Mietta Lennes. 2005. A graphical query formation compiler for speech database access. In Margit Langemets & Priit Penjam (eds.), *The Second Baltic Conference on Human Language Technologies, Tallinn, Estonia, April 4–5, 2005*, 209–218.

Altosaar, Toomas, Bruce Millar & Martti Vainio. 1999. Relational vs. object-oriented models for representing speech: A comparison using ANDOSL data. In *Proceedings of EUROSPEECH'99, Budapest, Hungary, 5–9 Sept. 1991*, Vol. 2, 915–918.

Ballardini, Rosa Maria, Pamela Lönnqvist, Perttu Virtanen, Nari Lee, Marcus Norrgård & Olli Pitkänen. 2013. The "one-size fits all" European patent system: Challenges in the software context. In Katja Weckström (ed.), *Governing innovation and expression: New regimes, strategies and techniques*, 327–350. Turku: University of Turku.

Chambers, J. K. 1994. An introduction to dialect topography. *English World-Wide* 15 (1). 35–53. https://doi.org/10.1075/eww.15.1.03cha.

Grönroos, Mickel & Manne Miettinen. 2004. Infrastructure for collaborative annotation of speech. *International Conference on Language Resources and Evaluation (LREC)*. 4. 543–546.

Kamocki, Paweł, Aleksei Kelli & Krister Lindén. 2022. The CLARIN Committee for Legal and Ethical Issues and the Normative Layer of the CLARIN infrastructure. In Darja Fišer & Andreas Witt (eds.), *CLARIN. The infrastructure for language resources*. Berlin: deGruyter.

Karjalainen, Matti, and Toomas Altosaar. 1993. An object-oriented database for speech processing. In *Proceedings of Eurospeech 1993*, 183–186. Madrid.

Kelli, Aleksei, Krister Lindén, Kadri Vider, Paweł Kamocki, Ramūnas Birštonas, Silvia Calamai, Penny Labropoulou, Maria Gavrilidou & Pavel Straňák. 2019. Processing personal data without the consent of the data subject for the development and use of language resources. In Inguna Skadin & Maria Eskevich (eds.), *Selected papers from the CLARIN Annual Conference 2018: Pisa, 8–10 October 2018* (Linköping Electronic Conference Proceedings 159), 72–82. Linköping: Linköping University Electronic Press.

Kelli, Aleksei, Krister Lindén, Kadri Vider, Paweł Kamocki, Arvi Tavast, Ramūnas Birštonas, Gaabriel Tavits, Mari Keskküla & Penny Labropoulou. 2020. CLARIN contractual framework for sharing language data: The perspective of personal data protection. In Costanza Navarretta & Maria Eskevich (eds.), *Proceedings of CLARIN Annual Conference 2020. 5–7 October 2020*, online edition, 171–177. Utrecht: CLARIN ERIC.

Kelli, Aleksei, Krister Lindén, Kadri Vider, Paweł Kamocki, Arvi Tavast, Ramūnas Birštonas, Gaabriel Tavits, Mari Keskküla, Penny Labropoulou, Irene Kull, Age Värv, Merle Erikson, Andres Vutt & Silvia Calamai. 2021. Sharing is caring: A legal perspective on sharing language data containing personal data and the division of liability between researchers and research organisations. In Costanza Navarretta & Maria Eskevich (eds.), *Selected Papers from the CLARIN Annual Conference 2020: 5–7 October* (Linköping Electronic Conference Proceedings 180), 129–147. Linköping: Linköping University Electronic Press.

Kelli, Aleksei, Krister Lindén, Kadri Vider, Penny Labropoulou, Erik Ketzan, Pawel Kamocki & Pavel Stranák. 2018. Implementation of an Open Science Policy in the context of management of CLARIN language resources: A need for changes?. In *Selected papers from the CLARIN Annual Conference 2017: Budapest, 18–20 September 2017* (Linköping University Electronic Press 147), 102–111. Linköping: Linköping University Electronic Press

Kelli, Aleksei, Tõnis Mets, Kadri Vider, Age Värv, Lars Jonsson, Krister Lindén & Ramūnas Birštonas. 2018. Challenges of transformation of research data into open data: The perspective of social sciences and humanities. *International Journal of Technology Management & Sustainable Development* 17 (3). 227–251.

Kelli, Aleksei, Arvi Tavast, Krister Lindén, Kadri Vider, Ramūnas Birštonas, Penny Labropoulou, Irene Kull, Gaabriel Tavits & Age Värv. 2019. The extent of legal control over language data: the case of language technologies. In Kiril Simov & Maria Eskevich (eds.), *Proceedings of CLARIN Annual Conference 2019*, 69–74. Utrecht: CLARIN ERIC.

Kelli, Aleksei, Arvi Tavast, Krister Lindén, Ramūnas Bristonas, Penny Labropoulou, Kadri Vider, Irene Kull, Gaabriel Tavits, Age Värv & Vadim Mantrov. 2020. Impact of legal status of data on development of data-intensive products: Example of language technologies. In A. Damberga (ed.), *Legal Science: Functions, Significance and Future in Legal Systems II. Collection of Research Papers in Conjunction with the 7th International Scientific Conference of the Faculty of Law of the University of Latvia*, 383–400. Riga: University of Latvia Press.

Kelli, Aleksei, Arvi Tavast, Krister Lindén, Kadri Vider, Ramūnas Birštonas, Penny Labropoulou, Irene Kull, Gaabriel Tavits, Age Värv, Pavel Straňák & Jan Hajic. 2020. The impact of copyright and personal data laws on the creation and use of models for language technologies. In Kiril Simov & Maria Eskevich (eds.), *Selected Papers from the CLARIN Annual Conference 2019*. (Linköping Electronic Conference Proceedings 172), 53–65. Linköping: Linköping University Electronic Press.

Kelli, Aleksei, Kadri Vider & Krister Lindén. 2016. The regulatory and contractual framework as an integral part of the CLARIN infrastructure. In Koenraad De Smedt (ed.), *Selected papers from the CLARIN Annual Conference 2015: October 14–16, 2015, Wroclaw, Poland* (Linköping Electronic Conference Proceedings 123), 13–24. Linköping: Linköping University Electronic Press.

Kurki, Tommi, Tommi Nieminen, Heini Kallio & Hamid Behravan. 2014. Uusi puhesuomen variaatiota tarkasteleva hanke: Katse kohti prosodisia ilmiöitä [A new project considering variation in spoken Finnish. A view towards prosodical phenomena]. *Sananjalka* 56. 186–195.

Labov, William, 1972. *Sociolinguistic patterns*. Oxford: Blackwell

Lane, Ian, Alex Waibel, Matthias Eck & Kay Rottmann. 2010. Tools for collecting speech corpora via Mechanical-Turk. In Chris Callison-Burch & Mark Dredze (eds.), *Proceedings of the NAACL HLT 2010, Workshop on Creating Speech and Language Data with Amazon's Mechanical Turk*, 184–187. Stroudsberg, PA: ACL.

Lennes, Mietta & Sanna Ahjoniemi. 2005. Puheaineiston annotaatio eli nimikointi (Version 1.01) [Annotating speech data (Version 1.0)]. Zenodo. http://doi.org/10.5281/zenodo.1205453.

Lindén, Krister, Aleksei Kelli & Alexandros Nousias. 2020. A CLARIN Contractual Framework for Sharing Personal Data for Scientific Research. In Kiril Simov & Maria Eskevich (eds.), *Selected papers from the CLARIN Annual Conference 2019* (Linköping Electronic Conference Proceedings 172), 75–84. Linköping: Linköping University Electronic Press.

McGraw, Ian. 2013. Collecting speech from crowds. In Maxine Eskenazi, Gina-Anne Levow, Helen Meng, Gabriel Parent & David Suendermann (eds.), *Crowdsourcing for speech processing: Applications to data collection, transcription and assessment*, 37–71. Chichester: Wiley.

Nieminen, Tommi & Tommi Kurki. 2015. Prosovar-hankkeen väliraportti. Puheaineiston keruusta verkossa sekä havaintoja aineistosta [Collecting speech data on the internet and observations about the data]. In Mona Lehtinen & Unto K. Laine (eds.), *XXIX Fonetiikan päivät, Espoo 20.–21.3.2015, Julkaisut – Papers* (Tiede + Teknologia 7/2015), 29–38. Espoo: Aalto University. http://fp2015.aalto.fi/Fonetiikan_Paivat-2015_Aalto-yliopisto.pdf (accessed 1 March 2022)

Nieminen, Tommi & Tommi Kurki. 2017. Collecting speech data over the internet: Web 2.0 and speech corpora. In *Digital humaniora i Norden / Digital Humanities in the Nordic*

Countries, Göteborg, March 14–16 2017. Book of abstracts, 159–160. Gothenburg: Gothenburg University.
Oksanen, Ville & Krister Lindén. 2011. Open content licenses: How to choose the right one. *NEALT Proceedings Series* 13. 11–18.
Oksanen, Ville, Krister Lindén & Hanna Westerlund. 2010. Laundry symbols and license management: Practical considerations for the distribution of LRs based on experiences from CLARIN. LREC 2010 Workshop on Language Resources: From Storyboard to Sustainability and LR Lifecycle Management. Valletta, Malta, 23 May 2010.
Pitkänen, Olli. 2017. Mitä lähioikeus suojaa? [What does related rights protect?]. *Lakimies* 115 (5). 580–602.
Schröder, Vilhelm. 2018. *Legislative update: Implementation of the Trade Secrets Directive – A new trade secrets act proposed in Finland*. Liikejuridiikka 2018/1.
Toivanen, Juhani & Manne Miettinen. 2001. *Puheentutkimuksen resurssit Suomessa* [Resources for speech research in Finland]. Espoo: CSC.
Thomas, Erik R. 2013. Sociophonetics. In J. K. Chambers & Natalie Schilling (eds.), *The handbook of language variation and change*, 2nd edn., 108–127. Oxford: John Wiley and Sons.
Weckström, Katja. 2012. Trademarks in virtual worlds: Law, outlaws or new in-laws? *Journal of International Commercial Law and Technology* 7 (2). 112–120.
Wrigley, Sam, Anette Alen-Savikko & Olli Pitkänen. 2019. Finding the 'personal' in the industrial internet: Why data protection law still matters. In Rosa Maria Ballardini, Olli Pitkänen & Petri Kuoppamäki (eds.), *Regulating industrial internet through IPR, data protection and competition law*, 235–252. Alphen aan den Rijn: Kluwer Law.

Rūta Petrauskaitė, Darius Amilevičius, Virginijus Dadurkevičius, Tomas Krilavičius, Gailius Raškinis, Andrius Utka, and Jurgita Vaičenonienė

CLARIN-LT: Home for Lithuanian Language Resources

Abstract: CLARIN-LT consortium is one of the leading Lithuanian language research and digital data storage infrastructures. This chapter will present outreach and initiatives performed by or in cooperation with the CLARIN-LT consortium and highlight their most significant outcomes. We will first highlight some of the resources stored in the CLARIN-LT repository and present their usage statistics. Next, we will show a use case of scientific outreach, followed by a success story involving the cooperation of large-scale national projects and CLARIN-LT in the development of IT services for Lithuanian. Finally, we will demonstrate an example of CLARIN content integration in university classes. The initiatives we overview here, although they have different aims and audiences, share one common feature – they all found a home at the CLARIN-LT repository. The presented use cases and success stories performed by or in cooperation with the CLARIN-LT consortium during the relatively short period of time since its establishment in 2015 show that the infrastructure is gaining recognition and is increasingly being addressed by scientific, educational, public, and private communities.

Keywords: CLARIN-LT, Lithuanian language resources and analysis tools, morphologically rich language

1 Introduction

The CLARIN-LT consortium, established in 2015, is one of the leading Lithuanian language research and digital data storage infrastructures. CLARIN-LT was included in the Lithuanian Roadmap for Research Infrastructures (2015),[1] where

1 https://www.lmt.lt/data/public/uploads/2017/10/lmt_kelrodis_en_geras_atvartai.pdf

Rūta Petrauskaitė, Darius Amilevičius, Virginijus Dadurkevičius, Tomas Krilavičius, Gailius Raškinis, Andrius Utka, and Jurgita Vaičenonienė, Vytautas Magnus University, Kaunas, Lithuania, e-mails: ruta.petrauskaite@vdu.lt, darius.amilevicius@vdu.lt, virginijus.dadurkevicius@vdu.lt, tomas.krilavicius@vdu.lt, gailius.raskinis@vdu.lt, andrius.utka@vdu.lt, jurgita.vaicenoniene@vdu.lt

https://doi.org/10.1515/9783110767377-020

it is one of the five infrastructures in the fields of humanities and social sciences. Activities pursued by the consortium are in line with the strategic aims of the CLARIN ERIC infrastructure and answer the societal needs as highlighted in the EU science policy legislation: strengthening science position at the national as well as international levels; contributing to industrial, scientific, educational, technological, and cultural impact via cooperation of academia, public, institutional and private sectors; enhancing international cooperation of researchers and all interested parties (e.g., Leading innovation through EU research;[2] Vignetti 2020: 3).

The national research infrastructure began in 1994, when the *Centre of Computational Linguistics* (CCL) at Vytautas Magnus University was founded. The impetus to start the centre and to compile the first corpora of Lithuanian language was provided by EU concerted actions such as ECI (European Corpus Initiative) and TELRI (Trans-European Language Resources Infrastructure) in the framework of COPERNICUS programme. From the very start, the centre was a repositorium of Lithuanian language resources that was open to the Lithuanian language and computer science research community all over the world resulting in hundreds of corpus-based papers. Dozens of doctoral dissertations in different branches of computer-mediated linguistics have been defended and an interdisciplinary research community was formed around the centre. The spectrum of research topics is so broad, and the publications so numerous, that it is difficult to even keep track of them, which testifies to the centre's considerable impact on the linguistic research of the Lithuanian language. Nevertheless, being a member of CLARIN ERIC opens even wider possibilities, as it allows Lithuanian language data to approach the status of FAIRness.

This chapter aims to present outreach and initiatives performed by or in cooperation with the CLARIN-LT consortium and highlight their most significant outcomes. The remainder of this chapter is structured as follows: firstly, in Section 2, we will present the general overview of CLARIN-LT resources and their usage statistics. In Section 3, we will show a use case of scientific outreach, followed by a success story involving the cooperation of large-scale national projects and CLARIN-LT in the development of IT services for Lithuanian in Section 4. Finally, in Section 5, we will demonstrate an example of CLARIN content integration into university classes.

2 https://europa.eu/european-union/topics/research-innovation_en

2 Public and cultural outreach: Usage statistics of Lithuanian language resources in CLARIN-LT repository

As Vignetti (2020) claims, although it is rather difficult to find a unanimous methodological approach to estimate research infrastructures, there is a general agreement on their main impact areas, specifically, scientific, education, technological and innovation, cultural and science in general. For each impact area, specific indicators can be applied. For example, for the cultural and outreach impact area, the numbers of physical and virtual visitors, the numbers of events, communication and dissemination products and related users, and time spent for virtual visits can be surveyed (Vignetti 2020: 83). Therefore, the usage statistics of Lithuanian language resources and language analysis tools in the CLARIN-LT repository[3] for the period 2016–2021 will further be discussed.

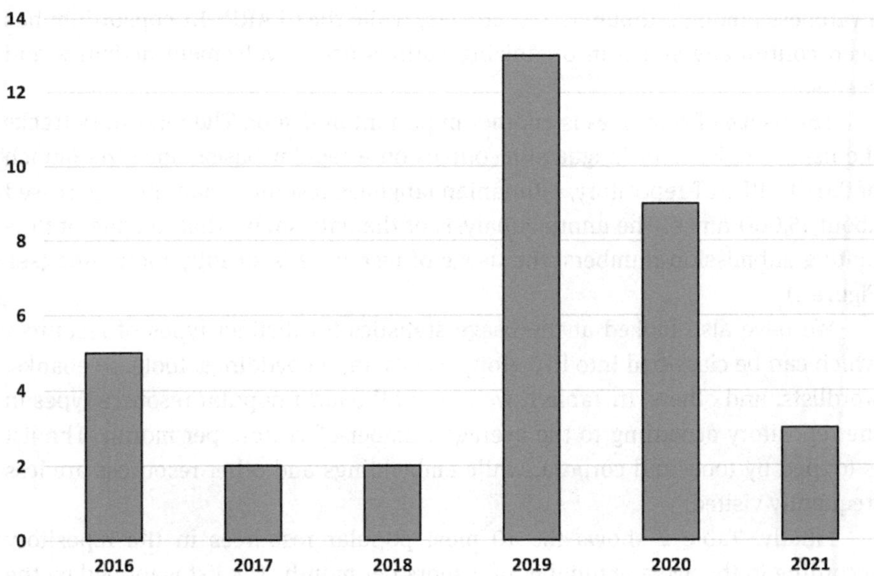

Figure 1: Deposited resources in the CLARIN-LT repository.

3 https://clarin.vdu.lt/xmlui. Accessed 20 March 2022

The Lithuanian language, with only around 4 million speakers globally, is a less-resourced language (also see Hennelly et al. 2022 on the issues of HLT development in lesser-used languages). According to the data of CLARIN Virtual Language Observatory (VLO),[4] the number of resources labelled as "Lithuanian" is 162: of these 36 (22%) reside in the CLARIN-LT repository, while others are distributed around the repositories of other CLARIN centres. Although this is a comparatively small number, the search output features a number of important resources for the Lithuanian language used and valued by the academic community.

The first language resource (namely, Lithuanian Morphologically Annotated Corpus – MATAS) was deposited to the CLARIN-LT repository in October of 2016. During the seven years of the repository's existence, the number of submissions has been fluctuating. It started off slow during the first three years, peaking in 2019, with 13 submitted resources (see Figure 1).

The analysis of the origins of submitted resources suggests that their number correlates with the number of completed projects. We also believe that another factor contributing to submission increase has been the growing data-sharing awareness among Lithuanian researchers, while the CLARIN-LT consortium has been continually active in organizing various user involvement activities and events.

The usage of resources is another important indicator. The repository tracks the usage statistics of language resources on a regular basis: since the launch of the CLARIN-LT repository, Lithuanian language resources have been accessed about 15,000 times. The annual analysis of the data shows that in spite of fluctuating submission numbers, the usage of resources is steadily increasing (see Figure 2).

We have also looked at the usage statistics for distinct types of resources which can be classified into five groups: corpora, embeddings, tools, treebanks, wordlists, and others. In Table 1, we present the most popular resource types in the repository according to the average number of visitors per month. The list is topped by tools and corpora, while embeddings and other resources are less frequently visited.

Finally, Table 2 shows the 10 most popular resources in the repository according to the average number of visitors per month. The list is topped by the Lithuanian Spelling Checker V.1.0.42 for macOS, a practical tool that appeals to Lithuanian users of Macintosh computers. This is due to the fact that Macintosh operating systems lack reliable Lithuanian spell-checking tools.

4 https://vlo.clarin.eu/search?3&q=lithuanian. Accessed 22 March 2022

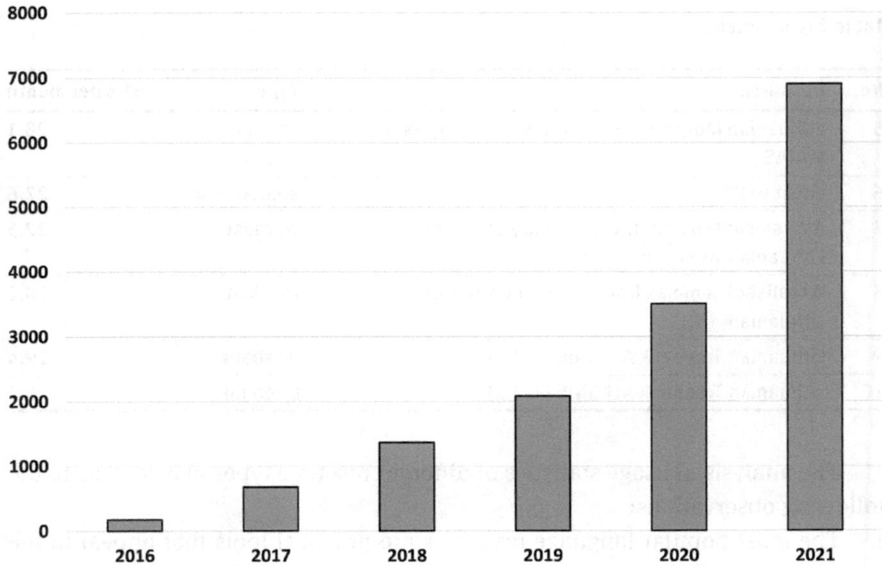

Figure 2: Annual usage statistics of accessed language resources.

Table 1: The most frequently visited resource types in the CLARIN-LT repository.

No.	Type	Number of resources	Visits per month
1	tools	7	155.6
2	corpora	13	99.6
3	wordlists	9	38.8
4	treebanks	2	27.8
5	embeddings	2	22.1
6	other	1	7.0

Table 2: Ten most frequently visited resources.

No.	Resource	Type	Visits per month
1	Lithuanian Spelling Checker V.1.0.42 for macOS	tool	85.6
2	Lithuanian Speech-to-Text Transcriber	tool	68.7
3	Lithuanian Spelling Checker V.1.0.42 for LibreOffice and OpenOffice	tool	31.4
4	Lithuanian Morphologically Annotated Corpus – MATAS v. 1.0	corpus	31.3

Table 2 (continued)

No.	Resource	Type	Visits per month
5	Lithuanian Morphologically Annotated Corpus – MATAS	corpus	28.1
6	LitLat BERT	embeddings	27.6
7	Assessment Data of the Dictionary of Modern Lithuanian versus Joint Corpora	wordlist	22.5
8	Wordlist of Lemmas from the Joint Corpus of Lithuanian	wordlist	20.2
9	Lithuanian Treebank ALKSNIS (v. 2.1)	treebank	19.4
10	Lithuanian Treebank ALKSNIS (v. 3.1)	treebank	16.2

The analysis of usage statistics of different resource types may lead us to the following observations:

1. The most popular language resources are practical tools that appeal to the general public, e.g., Lithuanian Spelling Checker for Macintosh computers, Lithuanian Spelling Checker V.1.0.42 for LibreOffice and OpenOffice, and Lithuanian speech-to-text transcriber (see Section 4 for a use case).
2. The popularity of resources is clearly affected by their usage in university curricula, for example, Lithuanian Morphologically Annotated Corpus – MATAS v. 1.0 and MATAS, as well as ORVELIT v. 3 (see Section 5 for a use case).
3. Although the system has not consistently recorded the number of downloaded resources, the rather substantial number of visits shows that Lithuanian language resources are important not only to the language research community, but also to students, software developers, and the general public.

3 Scientific outreach: CLARIN-LT resources and research

Undoubtedly, the importance of any research infrastructure (RI) correlates with its scientific impact. According to Vignetti (2020), the scientific impact can be evaluated by as many as nine indicators measuring two scientific impact areas: (1) the value of knowledge and its dissemination, and (2) data, information, and communication technology. While some indicators are difficult to track (e.g., the number of scientists that regularly use the RI, the yearly salary of scientists, the time needed to produce/use scientific outputs) other indicators may be registered and assessed more easily (e.g., the number of authors/scientists involved in the

RI, the number of scientific publications, the amount of [FAIR] data content, and the number of users).

The recent report on the CLARIN-LT repository, was conducted in 2019, has shown that there are eight scientists directly involved in the activities of the RI and that more than 30 publications that refer to language resources in the CLARIN-LT repository have been published. Besides this, two-thirds of language resources deposited in the repository are the result of scientific publications, dissertations, or research projects. The research topics are diverse: they range from various areas of NLP and computational linguistics to discourse analysis, translation studies, and lexicography.

3.1 Language resources and lexicography

Nowadays, it would be banal to talk about the importance of corpora and corpus tools for lexicography. Almost from their onset, corpora are *conditio sine qua non* for the compilation of all types of dictionaries. The turning point in the merging of corpus linguistics and lexicography in the 1980s was marked by the appearance of a new type of dictionary that is COBUILD dictionaries. Corpus-based and/or corpus-driven dictionaries thrive on a large amount of data that has to be systematized and used by lexicographers to describe grammatical and collocational behaviour of lexical items. Today, nobody doubts that the so-called corpus revolution enabled lexicographers to better grasp and reflect the authentic usage of language (Rundell & Stock 1992; Krishnamurthy 2008; Hanks 2012). Moreover, corpus-based dictionaries are created faster and more efficiently, and are less prone to errors than dictionaries created without the help of corpora.

There are a number of ways in which corpora and other language resources can support lexicography (see Kilgarriff 2012; Rundell & Kilgarriff 2011). These methods differ as regards the role of the corpus and the types of data derived from it. The most efficient way to exploit a corpus is to take it as a starting point and to continue during different stages of dictionary creation (Kilgarriff 2012). Thus, corpus creation, headword list development based on the frequency list, and analysis of the corpus are used in order to discover the word senses of a lexical item and other lexical units (fixed phrases, phrasal verbs, compounds, etc.) as well as to identify the salient features of each of these lexical units with the help of corpus analysis tools (e.g., Sketch Engine; see Kilgarriff et al. 2004). Corpora come in handy even in the final stages of dictionary creation when providing definitions (or translations) and exemplifying relevant features with material obtained from the corpus (Rundell & Kilgarriff 2011). Such a full-scale cycle of corpus exploitation is typical of dictionaries that are born digital.

As shown in Table 1, corpora and wordlists are the most common resource types in the CLARIN-LT repository. We will now present one of the more recent cases employing these resources, which has significant value for Lithuanian lexicography.

3.2 Use case: An innovative method of updating traditional monolingual dictionaries

Traditional dictionaries that were created before the corpus revolution and only later converted into a digital format can also benefit from modern language resources for their updates. Possibilities range from minimal, that is, using a raw corpus as a source of authentic, albeit random examples of usage, to maximal when usage patterns are derived from annotated corpora with the help of sophisticated tools. Corpora are very important for the overall design of a dictionary: for example, for an update of a headword list. For that purpose, corpus-based frequency lists are used. As few dictionaries in lesser-used languages like Lithuanian are born digital and created from scratch with the help of corpora, traditional digitalized dictionaries prevail. Innovative approaches are needed to help lexicographers to update them, especially when it comes to the lists of headwords. In what follows, such an approach is presented, based on comparison of a large corpus of the Lithuanian language and a digitalized traditional dictionary, which we aim to show is a universal method which can be applied to monolingual dictionaries in other languages.

We present a use case of mapping of a dictionary onto a corpus. The procedure consisted of the following steps: (1) the choice of a dictionary; (2) the choice of a platform that would be able to generate and list all theoretically possible (hypothetical) word forms from the dictionary lemmas; (3) the compilation of a reference corpus as the source of the frequency list of its word forms; (4) a comparison of the dictionary and the corpus-based wordlists; (5) recommendations for lexicographers concerning the update of the list of dictionary headwords with regard to the inclusion and deletion of certain items.

3.2.1 The choice of the dictionary

Although the national lexicographic tradition of monolingual dictionaries of a general type goes back to the beginning of the twentieth century, there are only two monolingual dictionaries of Lithuanian. However, they are quite different: one is an exhaustive, descriptive, and representative *Dictionary of Lithuanian* in 20 volumes with four volumes of postprint additions, whereas another is a one-volume prescriptive *Dictionary of Modern Lithuanian*[5] with seven editions. The latter has been chosen for the analysis, specifically its sixth edition (hence, DML6), published in a digital form on CD in 2006. It is the only edition fully available for its users on CD. It is meant for a wide audience and a diverse readership, mainly as a source of standard Lithuanian with some inclusions from dialects and colloquial language, its examples being derived from a wide range of texts representing all possible functional styles. The dictionary comprises 60,000 entries representing 86,000 common words and 3,000 place names. The disparity in numbers can be explained by the fact that only a fraction of naturally existing lemmas is presented as entry headwords; others are explicitly mentioned within dictionary entries, while some are not mentioned at all. The latter are called implicit lemmas, which can be derived based on regular word formation patterns. In the introduction to the dictionary, they are described as belonging to the regular derivational patterns and therefore assumed to exist "by default" (Dadurkevičius & Petrauskaitė 2020). Since the dictionary is also published in hard copy, it retains concerns about space that determine choice, placement, and presentation of lemmas, especially those of regular derivatives.

3.2.2 The choice of a platform

Hunspell[6] platform has been chosen to generate all the inflected forms which could be theoretically derived from the dictionary lemmas and to provide their morphological information. Although the primary goal of this platform is spell-checking, nevertheless, after substantial modifications it can also be successfully applied to morphological analysis and synthesis (Németh et al. 2004). In Hunspell formalism, the scope of a particular language is represented in two files: affixes (morphological rules) and dictionary (words with references to its rules) (Dadurkevičius 2017). In our case, the Hunspell dictionary was built by obtaining all possible lemmas from DML6 entries (both stated explicitly or implied). There are about 200,000 entries in total. The file of approximately 5,000 morphology rules was used to generate all theoretically possible word forms. The rules were based on the grammar of modern Lithuanian (Dadurkevičius 2017). References from the Hunspell dictionary to the rules were derived based on the

5 *Dabartinės lietuvių kalbos žodynas* [The Dictionary of Modern Lithuanian]. 2006. Edited by Keinys. Sixth edition (third electronic).

6 https://hunspell.github.io/

information provided in DML6 entries. More than 50-million-word forms of DML6 can be generated combining the Hunspell dictionary and its rules. Thus, the tool was made suitable for both spelling and morphological analysis based on DML6 (Dadurkevičius 2017).

3.2.3 Compilation of reference corpus

Three Lithuanian corpora were merged in order to compile a large representative reference corpus: the corpus of Vilnius University, compiled from the Lithuanian internet content from 2014, a legal document corpus, and the Contemporary Corpus of Lithuanian (from the period 1994–2013) of Vytautas Magnus University. The overall size of the Joint Corpus of Lithuanian (hereafter, JCL) is 1,334,845,080 tokens or 4,968,125 types (Dadurkevičius & Petrauskaitė 2020).

Specific approach applied to JCL was that of a non-contextual analysis. This means that each word (or type) was regarded as an individual unit without taking its immediate context into consideration. In practice, the corpus was formatted and analysed as a list of word forms. This approach allowed us to shorten the corpus processing time considerably. The outcome was a list of circa 5 million types of word forms ranging in frequency from a few million occurrences to unique cases.

Prior to any processing, most corpora are lemmatized. A question may arise why in this case a word form instead of a lemma has been chosen as the starting point for the comparison. In other words, why it has been decided to generate all theoretically possible word forms based on the dictionary lemmas instead doing it the other way round (i.e., lemmatizing the corpus). There are a few reasons for this. One of the main reasons comes from the notion of lexical grammar introduced by John Sinclair in corpus linguistics. It is assumed that "each word has a grammar of its own" (Sinclair 2000), and specific word forms combined with contextual partners make up its grammatical pattern. Moreover, some of the word forms can be closely related to specific word senses. Therefore, word forms and not just lemmas are important: they cannot be ignored and neglected, especially in lexicography, while the process of lemmatization may make them oblique. Another reason has to do with the rich inflectional nature of the Lithuanian language. Flections come both from grammatical categories and word formation. Word forms and word formation affixes show a tendency to be lexicalized and to acquire their autonomous meaning. Finally, lexicographic tradition plays a role. In Lithuania, this is based on the prevalence of paradigms, that is regular grammatical and derivational patterns. As such, it tends to overlook syntagmatic approaches, patterns emerging from usage in general and the phenomenon of lexicalization in particular. Therefore, word-form-based comparisons of dictionaries and corpora are much more informative and useful for lexicographers.

3.2.4 Comparison of the dictionary and corpus-based wordlists

The comparison of DML6 and JCL was based on the theoretically derivable word forms of the DML6 and 5 million unique word forms and their counts in JCL. The results of the mapping showed that almost 11% of tokens and 75% of types in JCL are not found in DML6. We filtered out (excluding misspellings, foreign words, proper names, etc.) a list of 254,726 word forms in JCL that are obviously missing in DML6. The DML6 lemmas checked in JCL using their hypothetical word forms and found absent comprised a list of 16,272 items (19%). It can be stated that only 81% of the DML6 lexis was found in JCL, that is in a big and representative dictionary of the present-day Lithuanian language. Thus, almost every fifth lexical item of the DML6 is an outdated, archaic, or dialectal word, or its derivative.

3.2.5 Recommendations for lexicographers

A closer look at the list of DML6 gaps revealed certain groups of lexical items that were absent from the dictionary. One group includes recent borrowings as well as widely used international words having no counterparts in modern Lithuanian. Their absence may be explained by the "division of labour" between the two types of dictionaries: monolingual explanatory and dictionaries of internationalisms. The latter is supposed to take care of loan words. Another reason for loan word omission could be the prescriptive nature of DML6 and a dominant official language policy seeking to diminish the influence of other languages.

Another group in the list of dictionary gaps consists of derivatives with prefixes, suffixes or reflexive particles. Their absence in DML6 can be explained by the lexicographic policy of providing headwords stripped of their numerous word formation morphemes, especially, if they are supposed to have regular word formation patterns devoid of additional semantic features. Nevertheless, derivatives, just like specific grammatical forms of lexical items, acquire new senses and connotations in comparison with their basic lemmas, especially if they are used in specific discourses. Therefore, it would be of paramount importance to look at frequently used word forms and/or derivatives in the corpus for their usage patterns and collocational profiles. That should be done on an individual basis before accepting or refusing derivatives as explicit lemmas of the dictionary. The size of a dictionary entry should not play an important role in the era of digital lexicography.

In general, the linguistic introspection of a lexicographer and his or her decisions remain the most important criteria in the process of dictionary design and update. However, nowadays, decisions should be checked against a large amount of data, especially frequency lists and collocational profiles of word forms, the so-called word sketches obtained from corpora. In this specific case, non-overlapping lists of words and word forms generated from DML6 and JCL, respectively, can be found and used freely in the CLARIN-LT repository together with other resources of lexicographic importance (Dadurkevičius & Petrauskaitė 2020).

4 Technological outreach: CLARIN-LT and Lithuanian language-related projects

An important source of Lithuanian language resources is language-related projects. We may observe a growing tendency to plan the deposits of compiled resources, even in the planning phase of the projects. Two recent projects have deposited a considerable number of resources in CLARIN-LT, namely, PASTOVU, devoted to the automatic identification of Lithuanian multiword expressions[7] (eight language resources), and SEMANTIKA-2[8] (seven language resources). This Section will further describe the existing symbiosis between the CLARIN repository and language-related projects. Some more important tools and resources will be described in greater detail, such as, for example, a Lithuanian speech-to-text transcription service.

During the course of the project SEMANTIKA-2, resources, tools, and public services created during the project SEMANTIKA-1 were further developed. For the development of the tools, deep learning, and other state of the art technologies (Docker, Kafka, web services, and cloud-based infrastructure solutions) were used. Three new cost-free public services (speech-to-text transcription for Lithuanian, text summarization, hate speech detection, and social media aspect-based sentiment analysis) were developed. Moreover, information search and extraction services, language spell-checking, and morphological analysis services were modernized. The following corpora were compiled: the corpus of web news (BIT), the corpus ALKSNIS (v. 3), and the corpus KLASIUS. New spell-checking solutions (public services and services for personal computers using Windows, Linux, and Mac) should also be mentioned. Since the key factors in the successful develop-

7 http://mwe.lt/en_US/
8 https://semantika.lt/

ment of language technologies include the quality, accessibility, and open use of language resources and basic tools, all IT solutions and basic resources were made available to national and international audiences through various channels: CLARIN-LT, GitHub, and the website of the project.

The speech recognition service is a particular success story from the project. At the time of writing, six months have passed since the Lithuanian speech-to-text transcriber tool[9] was released to the public. Copies of this tool have already been implemented at the Lithuanian Parliament, National Radio and Television, Police Department of Lithuania, Vytautas Magnus University, and Kaunas University of Technology, as well as several enterprises that are using them for further development and creation of new products and services. The Hospital of the Lithuanian University of Health Sciences, which is the largest hospital in the Baltic States, is also considering installing this tool. There is an ever-growing number of active users of the web-based service, with approximately 600 daily users. The Lithuanian speech-to-text transcriber received a national award as a "science-based business service of the year, 2020" from the Lithuanian Business Confederation. Lithuanian speech-to-text transcription tool is an important achievement of SEMANTIKA-2 project, providing robust and accurate speech-to-text services and software components free of charge for public use. As the tool is also featured in the CLARIN-LT repository, a more detailed description of this service is provided in the following subsections.

4.1 Lithuanian speech-to-text transcriber

Lithuanian speech-to-text transcriber that was developed during the SEMANTIKA-2 project was made available to the public in two major modes: as a speech-to-text web service and as a speech-to-text software container available for download.

The speech-to-text web service is being used by occasional non-technical users. It allows users to submit and send audio files to the transcription server running in the background. The service supports the most common types of audio files, such as m4a, mp3, and wav. In addition, a user can specify the domain (medicine, law, public administration, unspecified) and provide the number of different speakers (one, two, unknown) heard on the audio file being uploaded. This additional information is exploited by the speech-to-text server to choose an adapted processing scheme. Transcription speed is about 1x real-time. Thus, the

9 https://clarin.vdu.lt/xmlui/handle/20.500.11821/43

user's waiting time depends both on the size of the audio file and on the load of the server at a given time. Once the transcription is finished, transcription results are sent to the user via e-mail. Transcription results consist of a few files that essentially carry the same information but are differently formatted to facilitate different use case scenarios. These formats are plain text file, Web Video Tracks (WebVtt)[10] file, and transcription lattice. Transcription lattice is intended to be used as an input for the text editor that was also developed within the framework of the project SEMANTIKA-2 and that will be described in detail in the next subsection.

The speech-to-text web service limits the maximum size of an uploaded audio file in order to be able to process as many requests as possible with the limited computational infrastructure of the host university. Institutional users, users who need to process lots of audio data without volume limitations, and users who prefer to avoid sending sensitive data over the internet are installing the speech-to-text server on their premises. The Lithuanian speech-to-text transcriber has a flexible modular design and is accompanied by installation scripts for different platforms and demonstration videos. Application programming interface is specified so that institutional users can easily integrate the speech-to-text transcription server with their respective information systems.

4.2 Transcription editor

Editing transcription of an audio file is somewhat different from editing a plain text file. The human editor needs an ability to listen to the audio and to adjust the text on the basis of what he/she is hearing. For this purpose, the speech-to-text transcriber outputs a transcription lattice, which contains the most likely text transcription, feasible alternative transcriptions, and time synchronization anchors which tell the editor when every word is spoken. A specialized web-based single-page editor application was developed to make the transcription editing as easy as possible.

Web-based transcription editor takes a pair of files (original audio file and transcription lattice as received by e-mail) and presents these results for easy editing. The tool distinguishes between different speakers using a special colour scheme, it highlights out-of-vocabulary words, and indicates text segments for which alternative transcription hypotheses have been found.

10 WebVtt: The Web Video Text Tracks Format (2018). w3.org. The World Wide Web Consortium. 10 May 2018.

4.3 Internals of the speech-to-text transcription tool

The speech-to-text transcription tool follows a hybrid automatic speech recognition approach that combines convolutional deep neural networks and finite-state transducers and is based on an open source Kaldi implementation (Povey et al. 2011). The overall structure of this tool is shown in Figure 3.

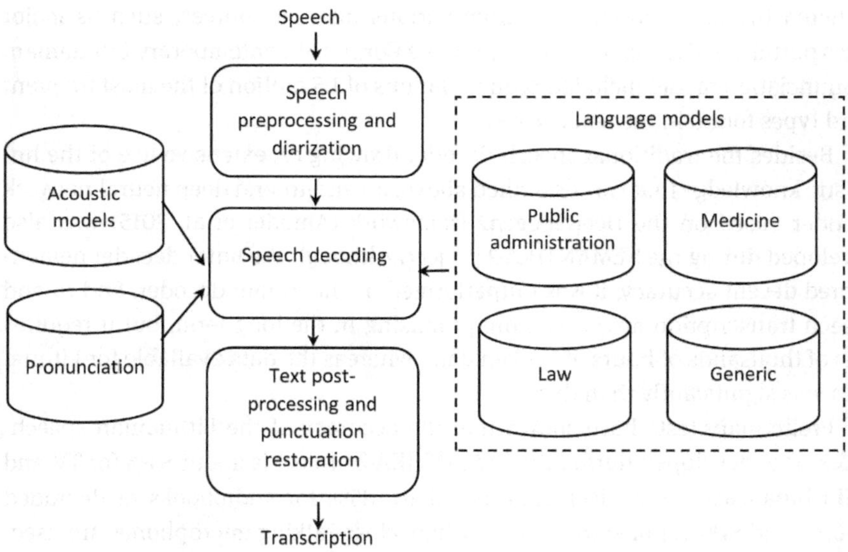

Figure 3: The processing scheme of Lithuanian speech-to-text transcription tool.

Transcription starts by decompressing and converting input files into raw audio data. Thereafter, the diarization procedure based on LIUM SpkDiarization (Rouvier et al. 2013) attempts to recognize who spoke when and splits the audio data into sequences of pause-delimited utterances. Utterances supposedly belonging to the same speaker are collected and subjected to the audio decoding process. The decoder incorporates multiple knowledge sources relating the acoustics, pronunciation, and probable word sequences of Lithuanian. This latter knowledge source is called a Language Model. Lithuanian speech-to-text transcription tool includes four distinct language models adapted to four different application domains: medicine, law, public administration, and non-specialized (generic) model. The decoding results in a network of alternative transcription hypotheses called lattices. Lattices are then rescored by the recurrent neural-network-based language model and the best-rated word sequence is selected. Finally, this word sequence undergoes some post-processing before being returned to the user. The post-processing consists of making decisions about the word capitalization and the placement of punctuation marks. Consecutive numerals are joined to make numbers (e.g., two hundred seventy-four is converted into 274).

Acoustic models were trained on about 300 hours of speech, gathered from a variety of sources: radio and TV broadcasts, audio books, student contributions, recordings available in the CLARIN-LT repository. Language models were trained on a text corpus consisting of about 500 million word tokens. Corpus was mostly gathered through web crawling from various internet sources, such as major news portals. It also included texts from the Corpus of Contemporary Lithuanian. Pronunciation model included pronunciations of 1.5 million of the most frequent word types found in the text corpus.

Besides the traditional speech decoder drawing on extensive use of the linguistic knowledge that was described above, an end-to-end deep neural network decoder based on the DeepSpeech2 framework (Amodei et al. 2015) was also developed during the SEMANTIKA-2 project. Although the latter decoder demonstrated decent accuracy, it was outperformed by the former decoder. End-to-end speech transcription might be more promising in the long term, but it requires tens of thousands of hours of spoken data, whereas the data available for Lithuanian was significantly than this.

Preliminary tests have shown that the accuracy of the Lithuanian speech-to-text tool developed during the SEMANTIKA-2 project is about 83% for TV and radio broadcasts (advertisements included), 85% for audiobooks of degraded quality, and 87% for meeting records where close-talking microphones are used. These estimates seem to be at least as good as the accuracy estimates of other commercial Lithuanian speech-to-text transcription services provided by Tilde (Salimbajevs & Kapočiūtė-Dzikienė 2018), Google,[11] and Trint.[12]

5 Educational outreach: CLARIN resources in university curricula

Lithuanian language resources stored in the CLARIN-LT repository and the Centre of Computational Linguistics are used in a number of language studies-oriented study programmes. For example, corpora, language analysis tools, dictionaries, wordlists, etc., are used in such Vytautas Magnus University BA courses as "Lexicology

11 https://cloud.google.com/speech-to-text/
12 https://trint.com/

and Lexicography of Lithuanian Language", and "Digital Humanities",[13] the MA course "Natural Language Processing", and others. As new resources are being created, their potential spheres of application and accompanying narratives of research or use cases in written and video modes make them quicker and easier to integrate into the university curricula. The inclusion of language resources in teaching content depends on numerous factors such as the aims of the study programme, its relation to the market needs, particular course content and objectives, skills that students have to gain, or the student and lecturer expertise in working with digital data. In this Section, we will demonstrate a case of the application of CLARIN-related content in the course *Contrastive Stylistics*, the framework of which might be adapted in applied linguistics or translation studies-oriented courses with similar goals.

Contrastive Stylistics[14] is an MA-level course in the programme of Applied English Linguistics at Vytautas Magnus University. The course aims to teach students to analyse texts from genre, register, and style perspectives in order to produce, analyse, edit, and translate texts in accordance with their structural and lexico-grammatical patterning in a given language. The programme is strongly oriented towards Translation Studies. The studies of such profiles, according to the Competence Framework of European Master's in Translation (2017)[15] should prepare students in five areas of competence: language and culture, translation, technology, personal and interpersonal, and translation service provision. Language resources and services provided by CLARIN, selected and framed according to the needs of a specific source and target languages, may help to build these competencies.

The expertise and knowledge of students in corpus linguistics, computer-assisted translation or text analysis tools vary as they come from different study backgrounds. Therefore, the course content is adapted each semester according to the needs and expectations of the group. Theoretically and methodologically, the course draws on three pillars: register and genre perspectives in text analysis; corpus-based approach to the analysis of language variation; research on the features of translations. The students are asked to analyse and compare the situational, structural, communicative, and linguistic characteristics of source and target language texts and then evaluate how the translations are similar to or different from the original texts in the target language. The scope of CLARIN related services and resources is very wide and far beyond the limits of one course, which

13 The course of "Digital Humanities" is registered in DH Course Registry (more on the registry see Wissik, Wessels & Fischer 2022).

14 https://www.vdu.lt/lt/study/subject/494/

15 https://ec.europa.eu/info/sites/info/files/emt_competence_fwk_2017_en_web.pdf

is why a framework that would show the students the possibilities of the infrastructure they can exploit in their future investigations and would fit the needs of the course had to be developed. We applied a funnel approach by:

1. introducing the infrastructure and its services in general by showing available demos[16] and navigating the CLARIN ERIC *Language Resources* and *Learn and Exchange* website parts;
2. outlining the knowledge building/sharing (how to do?), data storage/access (where to find?) and reuse/research (what and how to analyse in search of 'why'?) values of the infrastructure;
3. unfolding the building, storage, reuse, and research narrative using an example drawn from one corpus, ORVELIT.[17]

The approach of showing a gradual development of a particular corpus helps to bind the array of information for less experienced users. A comparable corpus ORVELIT v. 3 (approx. four million words) was created for the purpose of representing Lithuanian language variation in original and translated fiction and popular science. The first version of the corpus was compiled and integrated into the curriculum in 2017 and has been made available via the CLARIN-LT repository in raw and morphologically annotated versions since 2020. During the course, the theoretical background (for example, features of fiction from a register perspective), and various questions raised in corpus-based translation studies are introduced. Data extracted from the ORVELIT corpus is used to illustrate the discussion. The students are then asked to brainstorm on the possible research questions and registers that would be interesting for them to explore and create a data management plan. Next, the students download the ORVELIT corpus to try out the basic functions of corpus-analysis tools like the generation and comparison of wordlists, keyword lists, concordances, etc. They then present and discuss their findings on the similarities or differences between original and translated texts, fiction, or popular science.

5.1 Class 1: Generating data management plans

The aim of this class is to show the students the preparatory work that takes place before the actual creation and analysis of any data source, which helps them to

16 See https://www.clarin.eu/blog/clarin-services-european-open-science-cloud

17 Vaičenonienė, Jurgita; Kovalevskaitė, Jolanta; Boizou, Loïc, 2020, ORVELIT v. 3 – A Comparable Corpus of Original and Translated Lithuanian, CLARIN-LT digital library: https://clarin.vdu.lt/xmlui/handle/20.500.11821/40.

better understand the relevance of their project proposals within the context of the field, the actual steps in data collection and creation, and critical evaluation of the data they might want to reuse.

Setting the scene. Theoretical material on corpus creation steps is illustrated by a discussion of the representativeness and balance of the ORVELIT corpus, questioning how various circumstances affect the creation of a corpus, and subsequently the research results. Multiple factors shape translations from English to Lithuanian. Criticism on understanding and researching translations emphasizes their multidimensional nature, simultaneously affected by social, cultural, technological, pragmatic, and cognitive factors (De Sutter & Lefer 2020: 1), political and historical environment, and other variables. In genre and register studies, the importance of identifying the situational characteristics of the studied texts (i.e., participants and relations among them, channel, production circumstances, setting, communicative purposes, and topic) is also given particular attention as this may help students to better understand the patterning of the texts and possible reasons behind certain features (Biber & Conrad 2009: 40–47). The setting and production circumstances of translations may be highly variable. In the ORVELIT corpus, the chronological framework of translations encompasses works written and translated between the second half of the twentieth and the second decade of the twenty-first century; the majority of the texts had language editors, which means that they are a result not of the work of a single translator, but a group of people involved in publishing the work. In some cases, the quantitative data might reflect the patterning of the corpus rather than the features of Lithuanian translations from English. Although the corpus aimed for a balance in terms of size, numbers of texts, genres, author variation, gender, translator variation, publishing house variation, and chronological boundaries, a multitude of other factors might influence the quantitative results. For example, the fiction component of the translations includes more works with first person narration in comparison to original Lithuanian texts, which might result in higher first person pronoun frequency in translations. The different proportions of dialogues and narration in the sub-corpora of originals and translations might also have an effect on the higher or lower numbers of second person pronouns or other parts of speech. As a result of similar discussions, the students come to the conclusion that quantitative data should be supported by qualitative evidence to detect what is typical in translations, rather than what is determined by the composition of the corpus.

Methodology. Next, the students are introduced to existing support for researchers creating their projects – data management plans (DMPs), which help to structure the research proposals and ensure congruence with the data creation standards, including decisions on data collection, storage, backup, selection and preservation, ethical issues, sharing, responsibilities, resources, etc. (see, for example, Trippel & Zinn 2015: 72–73). They are asked to compare two DMPs – one offered by the Research Council of Lithuania[18] and another provided by CLARIN-D[19] – and are asked to simulate the creation of a research proposal. Students choose a particular genre/register they would find interesting to analyse from the perspective of original and translated language or register variation, and search for already existing corpora (in CLARIN's VLO, Resource families) to see if they could reuse the data. Students fill in the template of the tentative language variety study framework provided by (Biber & Conrad 2009: 27):

1. text samples to be used;
2. a summary of situational characteristics important for a register analysis of the chosen variety;
3. specific parts of the texts for the genre study;
4. predictions of linguistic characteristics important in an analysis of (1) linguistic features of the register, (2) textual conventions found in the genre perspective, and (3) language features in the stylistic perspective (adapted from Biber & Conrad 2009: 27).

Activity. The students are asked to choose one of the DMP templates and to generate their own research proposal. Some of the examples chosen as register and genre analysis projects include personal advertisements on online dating websites, online daily horoscope forecasts, theatre reviews, rap lyrics, book cover blurbs, museum labels, magazine editorials, beauty clinic websites, patient information leaflets, and film descriptions. The generated DMPs reveal the developing student attitudes to data search, storage, and reuse issues. For example, in order to answer the DMP question about whether there is any existing data that can be reused, they need to search various online databases and become acquainted with the state of the art in the field. Examples of answers[20] include: "There is no data we can reuse", and "There is existing data on film reviews which we could reuse for our research project". Student knowledge about data sharing possibilities and awareness of related concepts and terminology can be illustrated by the following answers: "The created corpus will be published online for public use for educational and research purposes"; "The data will be stored in the created database that assures long-term access to the members of the project: (CLARIN-LT digital library)"; "The data will be visible and could be downloaded for the

18 https://www.lmt.lt/lt/mokslininku-inicijuoti-projektai/mokslininku-grupiu-projektai/pareiskejams/2532

19 https://www.clarin-d.net/de/aufbereiten/datenmanagementplan-entwickeln

20 Collected during the spring semester of 2021.

specialist of the field to use as a basis for further research". DMPs, the possible corpus, and project creation pitfalls are discussed in class, where students evaluate and give feedback about each other's initiatives. They find it useful to see the input behind the data collection; the activity contributes to the development of their research skills, and their awareness of the possibilities offered by research infrastructures in data creation, storing, sharing, and reuse.

5.2 Class 2: Reusing data to test research questions

In this topic development, students try to use corpus analysis techniques to research questions posed in descriptive translation studies. The classes are structured as follows:

1. Theoretical background: researching translated and original language and features of translations.
2. Illustration: lexical and morphological features of the ORVELIT corpus (Vaičenonienė & Kovalevskaitė 2019).
3. Student activities:
   - download the ORVELIT corpus from the CLARIN-LT repository;
   - go to the CLARIN-UK website and download the corpus analysis software #LancsBox;
   - drawing on the theoretical background and methodological guidelines of corpus-assisted research (Baker et al. 2008), generate research questions;
   - using the basic functions of corpus analysis tools, test research questions;
   - provide feedback.

Setting the scene. According to Toury (1995), "in translation, phenomena pertaining to the make-up of the source text tend to be transferred to the target text" and "tolerance of interference and hence the endurance of its manifestations – tend to increase when translation is carried out from a 'major' or highly prestigious language/culture, especially if the target language/culture is 'minor', or 'weak' in any other sense" (Toury 1995: 278). Eskola (2004) continues that "translations tend to over-represent features that have straightforward translation equivalents which are frequently used in the source language (functioning as some kind of stimuli in the source texts)". Further evidence of interference, seen as a result of cognitive rather than norm-induced processes (see Malmkjær 2011), has been suggested by Tirkkonen-Condit (2004) who proposed the *unique items hypothesis*. Unique items are understood as lexical, phrasal, syntactic, or textual lacunas which may not have direct equivalents in other languages. Tirkkonen-Condit maintains that phenomena existing in the grammatical, lexical, or other patterning of the target language but absent or manifested differently in the source language "do not suggest themselves as translation equivalents as there is no obvious linguistic stimulus for them in the source text" (Tirkkonen-Condit 2004: 177–178). As a result, translations into the target language are more likely to have lower frequencies of these unique items in comparison with the texts originally written in that language.

Methodology. The students are acquainted with the basic terms used in corpus-based and -driven research, as well as freely available corpus analysis and data visualization tools (e.g., AntConc,[21] WordSmith Tools,[22] and available via CLARIN Voyant Tools,[23] LancsBox[24]). Baker et al. (2008) guidelines for corpus-assisted research are provided to help with the workflow of the activity:

1. identify existing topoi via wider reading, reference to other studies;
2. establish research questions/corpus building procedures;
3. corpus analysis of frequencies, clusters, keywords, dispersion, etc. – identify potential sites of interest in the corpus along with possible discourses/topoi/strategies, and relate them to those existing in the literature;
4. qualitative analysis of a smaller, representative set of data (e.g., concordances of certain lexical items or of a particular text or set of texts within the corpus) – identify discourses/topoi/strategies;
5. formulation of new hypotheses or research questions;
6. further corpus analysis based on new hypotheses, identify further discourses/topoi/strategies, etc. (adapted from Baker et al. 2008).

Activity. The students choose to work in small groups or on their own. They learn how to log in the CLARIN repository and download the data, upload it to corpus analysis software, and do the basic searches for instance, generate concordances of a certain lexical item in the original and translated sub-corpora, generate collocation networks, compare keyword lists, compare wordlists and comment on the observed differences and their possible causes, go to concordances for evidence, etc. The students are encouraged to raise various research questions which might help to reveal the interference of English in Lithuanian in the ORVELIT corpus. The unique items hypothesis can be analysed by comparing the manifestation of dual pronouns in translated and original Lithuanian texts. It might be speculated that Lithuanian translations will have lower frequencies

21 https://www.laurenceanthony.net/software/antconc
22 https://wordsmith.org
23 https://voyant-tools.org
24 http://corpora.lancs.ac.uk/lancsbox

of dual pronouns as English does not have the grammatical category of duality. Following this argumentation, the overuse of some pronoun types in translations may be explained by the interference of English in Lithuanian. Other popular questions include preposition variation in originals and translations, vocabulary range differences, diminutive use, expression of formal and informal pronouns, etc. The aim of such activities is not to find explicit answers or to do profound research, but rather to show the means and tools through which research can be done, in case students want to continue developing similar ideas in their research projects and final theses.

6 Conclusions

This chapter has demonstrated several Lithuanian language tools and resources which, though they have different aims and audiences, share one common feature – they all found a home at the CLARIN-LT repository. The presented use cases and success stories, performed by or in cooperation with CLARIN-LT during the relatively short period of time since its establishment in 2015, show that the infrastructure is gaining recognition and is increasingly being addressed by scientific, educational, public, and private communities. In Section 2, it has been shown that the most popular resources in the CLARIN-LT repository are practical tools that appeal to the general public (e.g., spell-checkers and the speech-to-text transcriber). Among the most visited resources are "Lithuanian Morphologically Annotated Corpus – MATAS", "Wordlist of Lemmas from the Joint Corpus of Lithuanian", and "Assessment Data of the Dictionary of Modern Lithuanian versus Joint Corpora", crucial for the development of Lithuanian monolingual dictionaries and lexicography at large. As was shown in Section 4, a number of CLARIN-LT resources and IT solutions produced in the project SEMANTIKA-2 are used in the public sector and private sectors working in the fields of language technologies and AI. In Section 5, we shared our experience of how CLARIN-related content is integrated into the course curriculum to teach students about the tools and resources for the analysis of Lithuanian stored in the national CLARIN centres, and to provide knowledge on services offered by CLARIN in general. Gradual guidance based on a selected corpus creation and research experience helps students to search for open access language resources and their analysis tools on their own; plan individual research projects; gain knowledge of corpus analysis tools; raise questions and conduct small-scale research; and critically report their findings in relation to previous research.

Bibliography

Amodei, Dario, Rishita Anubhai, Eric Battenberg, Carl Case, Jared Casper, Bryan Catanzaro, Jingdong Chen, Mike Chrzanowski, Adam Coates, Greg Diamos, Erich Elsen, Jesse H. Engel, Linxi Fan, Christopher Fougner, Tony Han, Awni Y. Hannun, Billy Jun, Patrick LeGresley, Libby Lin, Sharan Narang, Andrew Y. Ng, Sherjil Ozair, Ryan Prenger, Jonathan Raiman, Sanjeev Satheesh, David Seetapun, Shubho Sengupta, Yi Wang, Zhiqian Wang, Chong Wang, Bo Xiao, Dani Yogatama, Jun Zhan & Zhenyao Zhu. 2015. Deep Speech 2: End-to-end speech recognition in English and Mandarin. *CoRR* abs/1512.02595. http://arxiv.org/abs/1512.02595.

Baker, Paul, Costas Gabrielatos, Majid KhosraviNik, Michał Krzyżanowski, Tony McEnery & Ruth Wodak. 2008. A useful methodological synergy? Combining critical discourse analysis and corpus linguistics to examine discourses of refugees and asylum seekers in the UK press. *Discourse & Society* 19 (3). 273–306. https://doi.org/10.1177/0957926508088962.

Biber, Douglas, & Susan Conrad. 2009. Register, genre, and style. Cambridge & New York: Cambridge University Press.

Dadurkevičius, Virginijus. 2017. Lietuvių kalbos morfologija atvirojo kodo Hunspell platformoje. [Lithuanian morphology in the Hunspell framework], *Bendrinė kalba* 90. 1–15.

Dadurkevičius, Virginijus, & Rūta Petrauskaitė. 2020. Corpus-based methods for assessment of the traditional dictionaries. In Andrius Utka, Jurgita Vaičenonienė, Jolanta Kovalevskaitė, & Danguolė Kalinauskaitė (eds.), *Human language technologies – the Baltic perspective: Proceedings of the 9th international conference, Baltic HLT, Kaunas, Vytautas Magnus University, Lithuania, 22–23 September 2020.* 123–126. Amsterdam: IOS Press.

De Sutter, Gert, & Marie-Aude Lefer. 2020. On the need for a new research agenda for corpus-based translation studies: A multi-methodological, multifactorial and interdisciplinary approach. *Perspective-Studies in Translation Theory and Practice* 28 (1). 1–23. http://dx.doi.org/10.1080/0907676x.2019.1611891.

Eskola, Sari. 2004. Untypical frequencies in translated language: A Corpus-based study on literary corpus of translated and non translated Finnish. In Anna Mauraneen & Pekka Kujamäki (eds.), *Translation universals: Do they exist?*, 83–99. Amsterdam: John Benjamins.

Hanks, Patrick. 2012. The corpus revolution in lexicography. *International Journal of Lexicography* 25 (4). 398–436. https://doi.org/10.1093/ijl/ecs026.

Hennelly, Martin, Langa Khumalo, Juan Steyn & Menno van Zaanen. 2022. Training of digital language resources. Skills in South Africa. In Darja Fišer & Andreas Witt (eds.), *CLARIN. The Infrastructure for Language Resources*. Berlin: De Gruyter.

Kilgarriff, Adam. 2012. Using corpora as data sources for dictionaries. In Howard Jackson (ed.), *The Bloomsbury Companion to Lexicography*, 77–96. London: Bloomsbury. https://doi.org/10.5040/9781472541871.ch-006.

Kilgarriff, Adam, Pavel Rychlý, Pavel Smrž & David Tugwell. 2004. The Sketch Engine. In Geoffrey Williams & Sandra Vessier (eds.), *Proceedings of the eleventh EURALEX Congress*, 105–116. Lorient: Université de Bretagne-Sud.

Krishnamurthy, Ramesh. 2008. Corpus-driven lexicography. *International Journal of Lexicography* 21 (3). 231–242. https://doi.org/10.1093/ijl/ecn028.

Malmkjær, Kirsten. 2011. Translation universals. In Kirsten Malmkjær & Kevin Windle (eds.), *The Oxford handbook of translation studies*. Oxford: Oxford University Press. https://doi.org/10.1093/oxfordhb/9780199239306.013.0007.

Németh, Lászlo, Viktor Trón, Péter Halácsy, Andras Kornai, András Rung & István Szakadát. 2004. Leveraging the open source ispell codebase for minority language analysis. In *First steps in language documentation for minority languages: Computational linguistic tools for morphology, lexicon and corpus compilation. Proceedings of the SALTMIL workshop at LREC*, 56–59.

Povey, Daniel, Arnab Ghoshal, Gilles Boulianne, Lukas Burget, Ondrej Glembek, Nagendra Goel, Mirko Hannemann, Petr Motlicek, Yanmin Qian, Petr Schwarz, Jan Silovsky, Georg Stemmer & Karel Vesely. 2011. The Kaldi speech recognition toolkit. In *IEEE 2011 workshop on automatic speech recognition and understanding*. IEEE Signal Processing Society.

Rouvier, Mickael, Grégor Dupuy, Paul Gay, Elie Khoury, Teva Merlin & Sylvain Meignier. 2013. An open-source state-of-the-art toolbox for broadcast news diarization. In *Proceedings of the Annual Conference of the International Speech Communication Association, INTERSPEECH*, 1477–1481.

Rundell, Michael, & Adam Kilgarriff. 2011. Automating the creation of dictionaries. Where will it all end? In Fanny Meunier, Sylvie De Cock, Gaëtanelle Gilquin & Magali Paquot (eds.), *Studies in Corpus Linguistics*, 45. 257–281. Amsterdam: John Benjamins.

Rundell, Michael, & Penny Stock. 1992. The corpus revolution. *English Today* 8 (4). 45–51. https://doi.org/10.1017/S0266078400006751.

Salimbajevs, Askars, & Jurgita Kapočiūtė-Dzikienė. 2018. General-purpose Lithuanian automatic speech recognition system. In Kadri Muischnek & Kaili Müürisep (eds.), *Human language technologies – the Baltic perspective: proceedings of the 8th international conference, Baltic HLT, Tartu, Estonia, 27–29 September 2018*. Amsterdam: IOS Press, 2018.

Sinclair, John. 2000. Lexical Grammar. *Darbai ir dienos* 24. 191–203.

Tirkkonen-Condit, Sonja. 2004. Unique items: Over- or under-represented in translated language? In Anna Mauraneen & Pekka Kujamäki (eds.), *Translation universals: Do they exist?*, 177–184. Amsterdam: John Benjamins.

Toury, Gideon. 1995. Descriptive translation studies and beyond. Amsterdam: John Benjamins.

Trippel, Thorsten, & Claus Zinn. 2015. DMPTY – A wizard for generating data management plans. In *CLARIN Annual Conference 2015. Linköping Electronic Conference Proceedings*, 71–78.

Vaičenonienė, Jurgita, & Jolanta Kovalevskaitė. 2019. Leksinės ir morfologinės vertimų kalbos ypatybės [Lexical and morphological features of translational Lithuanian]. *Sustainable multilingualism* 14. 208–235. https://doi.org/10.2478/sm-2019-0010.

Vignetti, Silvia. 2020. Designing a research infrastructure with impact in mind. In Hans Peter Beck & Panagiotis Charitos (eds.), *The economics of big science. Science policy reports*. New York: Springer. https://doi.org/10.1007/978-3-030-52391-6_11.

Wissik, Tanja, Leon Wessels & Frank Fischer. 2022. The DH course registry: A piece of the puzzle in CLARIN's technical as well as knowledge infrastructure. In Darja Fišer & Andreas Witt (eds.), *CLARIN. The Infrastructure for Language Resources*. Berlin: De Gruyter.

Margunn Rauset, Gyri Smørdal Losnegaard, Helge Dyvik, Paul Meurer, Rune Kyrkjebø, and Koenraad De Smedt

Words, Words!

Resources and Tools for Lexicography at the CLARINO Bergen Centre

Abstract: The CLARINO Bergen Centre, which provides scholars with access to digital language data and processing services, has in recent years provided substantial services to research and development in lexicography. This chapter describes the interplay between three major lexicography efforts and the centre. Easy access to large corpora in CLARINO and powerful tools for searching and analysing corpus materials help to secure an empirical foundation which far exceeds the lexicographical resources and possibilities available to lexicographers in Norway only a few years ago.

Keywords: CLARINO, lexicography, dictionaries, Norwegian, Bokmål, Nynorsk, corpora, treebanks, written standards

1 Introduction

With funding from the Research Council of Norway and a consortium of institutions, the CLARINO research infrastructure was established in the eponymous CLARINO project, which started in 2012. At present, four technical centres and two knowledge centres embody Norway's in-kind member contribution to CLARIN ERIC. One of these centres is the *CLARINO Bergen Centre*,[1] located at the University of Bergen, in co-operation with the Norwegian School of Economics.

1 https://clarino.uib.no

Acknowledgements: The research infrastructure described in this chapter has been funded in part by the Research Council of Norway under grants 295700 (CLARINO+), 208375 (CLARINO) and 195323 (INESS) and by a consortium of institutions led by the University of Bergen. Revisjonsprosjektet and NO-AH are both fully funded by the Norwegian Government's Department of Culture. The NAOB dictionary project is funded by the Norwegian Government's Department of Culture (about 80%) and by a number of non-profit foundations and funds (about 20%).

Margunn Rauset, Gyri Smørdal Losnegaard, Helge Dyvik, Paul Meurer, Rune Kyrkjebø, and Koenraad De Smedt, University of Bergen, Bergen, Norway, e-mail: clarino@uib.no

https://doi.org/10.1515/9783110767377-021

Like other centres in the CLARIN distributed infrastructure, the CLARINO Bergen Centre provides scholars with access to language resources and tools through a repository and other services (De Smedt et al. 2016).

In recent years, the CLARINO Bergen Centre has started catering to research and development in lexicography in particular. The current chapter describes the interplay between three national lexicography efforts and the centre. Two of these, *Revisjonsprosjektet* and *NO-AH*, are located in Bergen, while the third project, *NAOB*, is governed by the Norwegian Academy for Language and Literature, located in Oslo. They will be described in more detail below.

The current drive in lexicographic activity in Bergen started in 2016, when 15 truckloads of digital and non-digitized language collections, including lexicographical materials and sources, were moved from Oslo to Bergen. With additional national funding, the University of Bergen began to establish itself as a hub for curating and extending these collections under the name *Språksamlingane* ('The Language Collections'). This name refers to the collections of dialects, place names and words that were built and maintained at the University of Oslo from the 19th century. Språksamlingane are based at the University of Bergen Library, steered at the strategic level by a committee led by the Department of Linguistic, Literary and Aesthetic Studies at the University of Bergen, and advised by a national board of experts. The Norwegian terminology portal *Termportalen*, developed with support from CLARINO since 2012, will also be hosted at Språksamlingane (Andersen and Gammeltoft 2022).

The bulk of the material transferred to Bergen consists of about 4 million records on paper cards, a large percentage of which are also digitized, and which have been employed in lexicographical work over the years. The University of Bergen was now faced with the challenge of running and maintaining the lexicographical databases. After the original Oracle system was up and running again, it was decided to reimplement the back-end for Språksamlingane. This is work in progress. A more urgent technical need arose, however, in 2018, when Revisjonsprosjektet got its go-ahead, namely the need for a versatile front-end and user interfaces for searching and revising the lexicographical data.

The technical and professional resources of CLARINO proved decisive for the ability of the University of Bergen to meet this challenge. Among the services provided by the centre, the following in particular provide an important foundation for the work described in this chapter:

1. *Corpuscle* is a corpus management tool providing access to plain text or tagged corpora, including audio and video with transcriptions (Meurer 2012a). It provides a powerful corpus search function based on efficient algorithms (Meurer 2020) and also produces word lists, collocations, and distributions. Its current holdings cover Norwegian and 15 other languages.

2. *INESS* is a treebanking platform providing access to treebanks in LFG, HPSG, dependency and constituency formats (Meurer et al. 2013; Rosén et al. 2012). Available treebanks cover more than a hundred languages and notably include *NorGramBank*, a large treebank for Norwegian, which will be further described below. Closely linked to INESS is the CLARIN Knowledge Centre on Treebanking, which provides expertise on treebanking construction, management, and exploration.

The remainder of this chapter is structured as follows. Section 2 describes NorGramBank as a CLARINO resource for all three lexicographical projects presented in this chapter. Section 3 discusses the relevance of Norwegian language policy for Norwegian lexicography. Section 4 introduces *Revisjonsprosjektet*, aimed at updating the Bokmål and Nynorsk dictionaries. Section 5 discusses work on the Norwegian Dictionary A to H (NO-AH) and Section 6 discusses work on the Norwegian Academy Dictionary (NAOB). The chapter is rounded off by a conclusion in Section 7.

2 NorGramBank: A resource for three lexicographical projects

NorGramBank is a Norwegian treebank, developed in the INESS project (2010–2017) at the University of Bergen (Dyvik et al. 2016) and now curated by CLARINO. It has been constructed through parsing with NorGram, followed by stochastic disambiguation of the parsing results, trained on a manually disambiguated subcorpus. NorGram is a manually written computational grammar for Norwegian within the framework of Lexical Functional Grammar (LFG). By 2017, NorGramBank comprised about 50 million words of analysed text (novels, children's books, non-fiction, newspapers, parliamentary debates, and some other genres). After the addition of more than 3,000 digitized fiction and non-fiction works, as requested by the NAOB project (see Section 6), the corpus now comprises about 160 million words of analysed text. These additional texts were made available to the CLARINO Bergen Centre in OCR-scanned form from the National Library after special permission to use copyrighted works had been obtained from the Norwegian government.

The LFG analyses in NorGramBank provide rich and detailed syntactic information about sentences, as well as some semantic information in the form of predicate-argument structures. The capacity to search for such information and sort the examples according to author, work, and other criteria is valuable for the development of dictionaries. The treebank provides information about the typical syntactic behaviour of a word (the adjectives modifying a noun, the functions of an adjective, the selected prepositions or argument structures of a verb, etc.), and it provides the means to find suitable examples from the literature. Having all this information at one's fingertips is clearly enticing to lexicographers.

Although the treebank query language *INESS Search* has a simple and intuitive syntax (Meurer 2012b), the complexity of the syntactic analyses may still lead to complex query expressions. In order to reduce this problem for the lexicographers, a template-driven "sketch" function has been developed (Rosén et al. 2020). A search template is a parameterized expression allowing the user to provide values for a selection of parameters, such as lemma forms or feature values, without engaging with the full search expression itself, and then run the query. Examples of the use of such templates will be given in the sections on the individual lexicographical projects.

3 Norwegian language policy and its relevance for lexicography

The language policies of Norway have had a clear impact on the development and publication of language resources. Norwegian has two official written standards – Bokmål and Nynorsk. The historical background to this situation is the union between Norway and Denmark, which lasted for 400 years and ended in 1814. Norwegian and Danish are closely related Scandinavian languages and the written language of the union was Danish, with its norm centre in Copenhagen. After Norwegian independence, two paths towards linguistic independence were established during the 19th century.

One path towards a Norwegian written standard, initiated by the poet and linguist Ivar Aasen, was based on the reconstruction of an idealized common ancestor of the most traditional rural dialects, especially in the Western part of the country. This standard, known as Landsmål and later as Nynorsk, had a rich literary development and was officially recognized as being equal with the existing Danish standard as early as 1885. It has later gone through some modernizing reforms.

The other path towards a Norwegian written standard was initiated by the school headmaster Knud Knudsen. It consisted in "Norwegianizing" the spelling and grammar of the existing Danish standard based on educated urban speech or spoken Riksmål, a variety which had its historical origin in a spoken Dano-Norwegian urban koiné that had been in use from the 17th century onwards. The programme was carried through by means of reforms starting in 1907, and the result, known as Riksmål and later as Bokmål, is now the dominant standard, used by about 88% of pupils.

Over the years several language reforms have been undertaken, which have had obvious consequences for lexicography and, more recently, for language technology applications such as spelling correction. A committee, appointed in 1964 with Professor Hans Vogt as its chair, proposed a body to protect and develop the Norwegian language, which resulted in the establishment of *Norsk Språkråd* ('The Language Council of Norway'), now *Språkrådet*.

Several laws ensure the continued use of Nynorsk and Bokmål with equal status. Since 1980, *Mållova* ('The Language Standard Act') regulates the use of the two written standards in the public sector, and all pupils learn Bokmål as well as Nynorsk at school. In 2009, a parliamentary white paper *Mål og meining* ('Language/goal and meaning', an intended ambiguity) aimed at securing the position of Norwegian in a digitizing society and proposed the establishment of the Norwegian Language Bank to provide language resources supporting language technology. The Language Bank is now one of the CLARINO centres. A more recent parliamentary white paper *Humaniora i Norge* ('The Humanities in Norway') acknowledges the important role that CLARINO is playing in language research and technology.

Finally, on 25 March 2021, *Språklova* ('The Language Act') set out an extensive policy to secure the equal status of the two written standards, but also to protect minority languages such as Sami and Norwegian Sign Language.[2] Furthermore, the proposition underlying this law points out the importance of Språksamlingane and of Termportalen, the latter developed through CLARINO. It also mentions the three lexicographical projects described below as important contributions to the Norwegian language. All of this underlines the historical context and the political importance of the current lexicographical work and the role that CLARINO is playing in Norway. The following sections will discuss the three lexicographical projects in some detail.

2 Prop. 108 L (2019–2020) Lov om språk (Språklova), adopted by the Norwegian Parliament on March 25, 2021, based on the following proposal: https://www.regjeringen.no/no/dokumenter/prop.-108-l-20192020/id2701451/.

4 Updating of the Bokmål and Nynorsk dictionaries

Revisjonsprosjektet ('The Updating Project'), is an update of the medium-size dictionaries for modern Bokmål and Nynorsk.[3] One proposal from the above-mentioned Vogt committee was to establish a lexicographical department at the University of Oslo (UiO). Neither Bokmål nor Nynorsk had practical handbook-size dictionaries affordable for regular language users, and compiling such would be the first major task for the new department. The compilation of *Bokmålsordboka* ('the Bokmål dictionary') and *Nynorskordboka* ('the Nynorsk dictionary') in parallel was in itself considered as a tool to build an atmosphere of mutual respect and a recognition of the two written standards with equal official status.

The first printed editions of these dictionaries were published in 1986. One group of lexicographers had been working on *Bokmålsordboka* and another on *Nynorskordboka* since 1974, as a cooperation between the Department of Lexicography at UiO and The Norwegian Language Council. According to the initial plan, both dictionaries should cover modern Bokmål and Nynorsk as used in literature and the media. In addition, they should each have around 600 to 700 pages and 60,000 entries with the same structure and information categories (Kulbrandstad 1976: 8). The editorial staff of *Nynorskordboka* wrote the manuscript of the letters *a–k* and *v*, whereas the editorial staff of *Bokmålsordboka* compiled the entries between *l–u* and *w–å*. They then exchanged manuscripts and thus could benefit from each other's work (Landrø and Wangensteen 1986: v).

Nevertheless, the dictionaries ended up with distinct features and several differences. The most striking difference is that *Nynorskordboka* has around 90,000 entries, whereas *Bokmålsordboka* has 65,000 entries. One reason for this difference is that Bokmål, unlike Nynorsk at the time, already had other comparable dictionary resources. The lexicographers working with *Nynorskordboka* argued that it was important to manifest the close relation between the dialects and written Nynorsk, so they included lemmas documented in use in three Norwegian counties (or two in Northern Norway), even though rarely used in written texts. *Nynorskordboka* thus describes written and oral vocabulary, whereas *Bokmålsordboka* documents written language. *Nynorskordboka* also includes more compound words than *Bokmålsordboka*. On the other hand, the latter contains more loan words from Danish and German (Hovdenak 2014: 234; Worren 1998: 63).

In later editions of both dictionaries, spelling and inflection have been updated according to the official standards. Some new lemmas were added, but most of

3 http://www.uib.no/revisjonsprosjektet

the articles stayed unchanged since the 1986 edition. A thorough content update, based on new material in many genres, was therefore much needed. Whereas the latest printed editions are fairly dated (Hovdenak et al. 2006; Wangensteen 2005), the two dictionaries have also been available as an online edition via a common web interface since 1994.[4] This common portal is extensively used by pupils and the general public, while the app *Ordbøkene* on iOS and Android, available since 2017, has also become quite popular. On average the web page and the app have a combined total of 160,000 hits a day. When users see entries in the online dictionaries in the default side-by-side view, the differences become more noticeable than the lexicographers of the printed editions could foresee. The change of medium makes the need for synchronous updating more visible.

With these editions as a starting point, both dictionaries are being updated in Revisjonsprosjektet, a project carried out from 2018 until 2024 at the University of Bergen, in cooperation with the Language Council of Norway. The project has three main aims. The first goal is to make the dictionaries more similar in structure and coverage, as far as possible. The dictionaries aim to document common language use in the written varieties Bokmål and Nynorsk, and as a principle all entries should be found in both dictionaries if the lemma is used in both varieties. The second goal is to check whether definitions, examples of usage and fixed expressions are in line with present-day language use, defined as the period from the 1970 until today. The third is to supplement the dictionary with new words and meanings that have entered the language (Rauset 2019: 169).

The digital language resources provided by CLARINO are of great help with respect to all three goals. As the project has progressed well by now and the technology has been sufficiently developed, we can report on experiences from our changed lexicographic practice in the remainder of this section.

In 2018, *Corpuscle-Lex* was developed as an extension of the above-mentioned Corpuscle. It is a bespoke online environment for lexicographers in which corpus search and dictionary management are integrated in a single web-based environment, thereby improving the workflow considerably. Corpuscle-Lex provides search in up to 12 online Norwegian corpora simultaneously. With more than 2.8 billion words[5] from a variety of sources and genres, this is the largest corpus collection for Norwegian that lexicographers have ever had available at their fingertips. Simultaneous search in user-selected corpora is enabled thanks to previous work on metadata and search algorithms in CLARINO.

4 Both dictionaries are available online at https://ordbokene.no.

5 Nynorsk comprises 185 million words (6.5%) in this collection and Bokmål 2.65 billion (93.5%).

In addition to corpus search, Corpuscle-Lex has an interface to the existing dictionaries and *Ordbanken* ('the Norwegian Word Bank'). Crucially, it also has a dictionary editing tool in which several dictionaries can be edited side by side. Finally, the system also has a direct communication link to the Language Council, through which normalization issues can be addressed in a very efficient way. The lexicographers at the University of Bergen decide which entries to include, but if in doubt, the Language Council in Oslo has the final say when it comes to how Norwegian words are spelled and inflected.

Work on the dictionary entry *countrymusikk* ('country music') can illustrate various aspects of this lexicographic practice. Figure 1 shows screenshots from the app showing the original entries for this word in both language varieties.

Figure 1: Original entries for *countrymusikk* with a single spelling as shown in the app. The label *bm* is bokmål, *nn* is nynorsk. The explanation is "traditional folk music which originally stems from the southern states in the USA".

The 12 corpora in Corpuscle-Lex document that some language users spontaneously have Norwegianized the spelling of *country* to *køntri*. The search for words matching the regular expression "`countrymusikk.*|køntrimusikk.*`" gives 1,282 hits, 27 (2%) of which are *køntrimusikk*, a form which until recently was not accepted. Furthermore, searching for "`køntri.*`" gives 378 hits, all of them related to the music genre. Based on the results from Corpuscle-Lex, although not great in numbers, the Language Council has defined *køntri* and all of its compounds as a part of the official standard for both Bokmål and Nynorsk. The revised version of the dictionaries therefore includes both *countrymusikk* and *køntrimusikk*, as shown in Figure 2. The lexicographer has also updated the definition and added etymological information and an attested example, based on an authentic example in the concordance, to illustrate a typical use of the lemma.

One of the most frequently used tools in Corpuscle-Lex is the "Word list" (with frequencies) which the lexicographers can generate from a regular expression search in the corpora they consider expedient. The corpus managing tool is very flexible, and based on what they are looking for, the lexicographers include or exclude annotated or unannotated corpora, oral or written corpora, corpora with texts in Bokmål or Nynorsk, corpora with specific genres, and so on. The word list function makes it easy to evaluate whether the existing entries are the most relevant in an updated version of the dictionaries.

country|musikk *m1*, **køntri|musikk** *m1* (av *engelsk country music* 'musikk fra landsbygda')

amerikansk folkemusikk med røtter i irske og britiske sanger og danser; påvirket av blant annet jazz, blues og gospel spille reindyrket countrymusikk

Figure 2: Revised entry for *countrymusikk/køntrimusikk* in *Bokmålsordboka.*

In the old version of the dictionary there were only two entries including the word *country*: *country and western* and *countrymusikk.* However, the word list generated by searching for "country.*" in all 12 corpora in Corpuscle-Lex gives 20,600 hits and 2,004 unique forms, showing that this is a highly productive word in Norwegian. Figure 3 shows the most frequent matches. Based on this word list and on collocations from the corpora, the lexicographer chose to compile two more entries, and the updated dictionaries now have four entries including the word *country*, as shown in Figure 4 from *Nynorskordboka.*

8573	(41,62%)	country
541	(2,63%)	countrymusikk
453	(2,20%)	countrymusikken
393	(1,91%)	countryrock
350	(1,70%)	countryartisten
333	(1,62%)	countryfestival
285	(1,38%)	countrystjernen
255	(1,24%)	countrysangeren
238	(1,16%)	countrymusikkens
226	(1,10%)	country-
219	(1,06%)	countryartist
213	(1,03%)	countryfestivalen
200	(0,97%)	countrysanger
171	(0,83%)	countryelskerne
152	(0,74%)	countryplate

Figure 3: The most frequent of 2,004 words matching "country.*" in Corpuscle-Lex.

The word list is our most efficient tool to identify both neologisms and lemmas that could and maybe should have been included in the dictionaries a long time ago (Lyse 2020: 219). So far, 5,200 new entries have been added to *Bokmålsordboka* and 5,000 to *Nynorskordboka.* Among these are relatively newly imported words in Norwegian, many from the IT domain, such as *backup*, *batch*, *bugg/bøgg* ('bug') and *dokkingstasjon* ('docking station'), along with words referring to new concepts in a Norwegian context, such as *abaya* (a garment), *bilkollektiv* ('car share'), *delingsøkonomi* ('sharing economy'), *designerdop* ('designer drug'), *droneangrep* ('drone strike'), *elsparkesykkel* ('electric scooter') and *koronavirus* ('coronavirus'). Among lemmas with a longer history in Norwegian, but with new dictionary entries, we can find *allmennlege* ('general practitioner'), *alpint* ('alpine skiing'), *badetøy* ('swimwear'), *brukerorientert* ('user-oriented'), *CO_2-utslipp* ('CO_2 emission') and *didjeridu* ('didgeridoo'). Compounds with *atom-* have become a part of everyday speech since the dictionaries first were published in 1986, but there are 10 new compounds in the updated versions, including *atomavfall* ('nuclear waste') and *atomstridshode* ('nuclear warhead').

Figure 4: New and updated entries starting with *country* in *Nynorskordboka*.

All lexicographers in Revisjonsprosjektet are working with both *Bokmålsordboka* and *Nynorskordboka*, and unless the corpora and spelling rules indicate that there are real differences in language use between the two written standards, entries are created or updated in parallel. So far, 5,700 new entries have been compiled in the smaller *Bokmålsordboka* because there were parallel existing entries in *Nynorskordboka*, whereas 2,200 new entries have been compiled in *Nynorskordboka* based on existing entries in *Bokmålsordboka*. The large corpus collection in Corpuscle-Lex and the corpus based methodology in the project makes it easier to identify the differences between the two standards. As a result, the updated selection of entries, both those that are found in only one of the dictionaries and those that are found in both, reflects modern language use to a higher degree than before. Quality is further assured thanks to the interface supporting the sharing of articles with colleagues and with the Language Council of Norway.

Since digital dictionaries allow cross-references to other entries by establishing hyperlinks, attention has been paid to making this process easy and accurate. The word *bildekk (2)*, marked in blue in the updated definition on the right in Figure 5, is such a cross-reference. The process of such linking is exemplified by the editing window for the entry *sommardekk/sumardekk* ('summer tire') in *Nynorskordboka*, shown in Figure 6. The definition contains a word *bildekk* with two meanings in Norwegian ('car deck' or 'car tire'), which motivates a link to the correct meaning in this context. By adding an @ in front of *bildekk* in the definition and choosing the intended meaning *(2)* from a popup menu, an appropriate link is made.

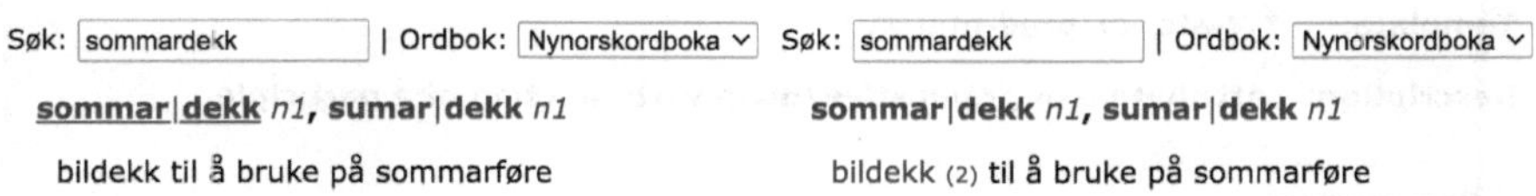

Figure 5: Original (left) and updated (right) entries for *sommardekk/sumardekk* ('summer tire') in *Nynorskordboka*.

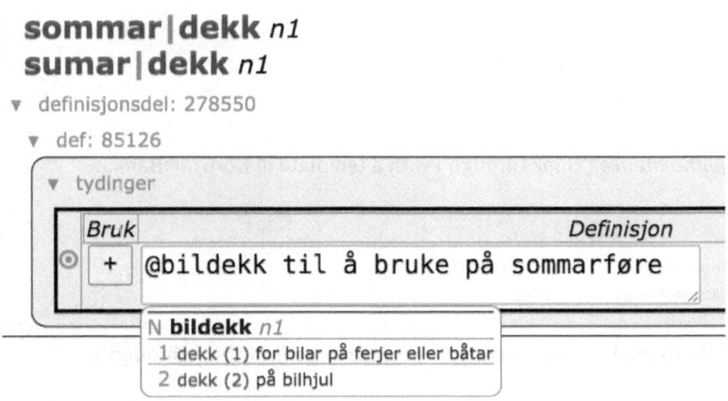

Figure 6: Editing tool showing the linking of the definition of *sommardekk/sumardekk* ('summer tire') in *Nynorskordboka* to the intended meaning (2) of *bildekk* ('car tire').

Another useful resource is NorGramBank, which was introduced in Section 2. In this treebank, one can search for complex syntactic constructions and their frequencies, which is useful for finding typical uses of words in constructions. The lexicographers in Revisjonsprosjektet use templates in NorGramBank to show usage and frequency. The template *V-argframes(@V)* is useful both for finding the most common uses of a verb (valency frames, common prepositions, or particles) and possible reflexive use of the verb. The templates *ADJ-attrib-or-nominal(@ADJ)* and *V-attr-or-pred-ptc(@V)* yield frequencies of adjectival and nominal use of participles, thereby providing empirical grounds for the possible creation of a separate entry for a derived adjective.

As an example, consider the verb *gjennomtenke* ('think through') which had a single entry in *Bokmålsordboka*. With the help of the template *V-attr-or-pred-ptc(@V)*, shown in Figure 7, it was found that the attributive use of the participle *gjennomtenkt* ('well thought out') was higher than its verbal use, cf. the frequencies displayed in Figure 8. Consequently, the entry was split so that a separate entry for the attributive use of *gjennomtenkt* ('well thought out') was established, as shown in Figure 9.

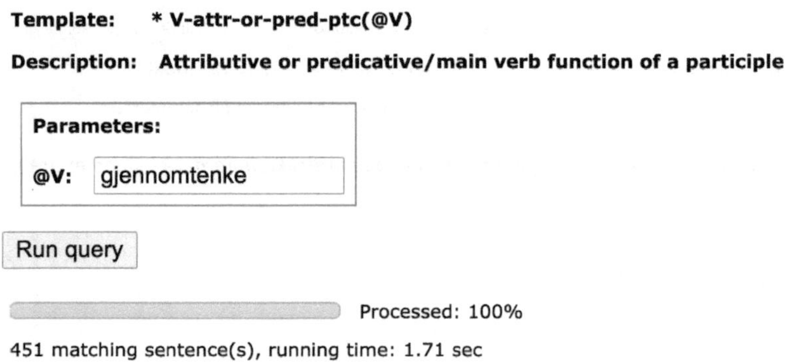

Figure 7: Search for *gjennomtenke* ('think through') with a template in NorGramBank.

Count	#lemma: *atom*	#type: *atom*
334	gjennomtenke	attributive
118	gjennomtenke	main

Figure 8: Frequencies of usage of the past participle of *gjennomtenke* ('think through').

gjennom|tenke *v2*

tenke grundig gjennom argumentene må gjennomtenkes nøye

gjennom|tenkt *a2*

som er tenkt nøye gjennom en gjennomtenkt plan · argumentene var lite gjennomtenkte

Figure 9: Update through separate entries for *gjennomtenke* ('think through') and *gjennomtenkt* ('well thought out').

5 Norwegian Dictionary A to H (NO-AH)

The second project, also at Bergen, is NO-AH, the revision and update of *Norsk Ordbok*,[6] a comprehensive dictionary in twelve volumes with around 330,000 entries, which provides an exhaustive account of the vocabulary of Norwegian dialects and the written language Nynorsk.

Norsk Ordbok (NO) as a lexicographic project started in 1930. Aiming to account for both spoken Norwegian and the then relatively young written language Nynorsk, and building on Ivar Aasen's documentation of the dialects in his dictionary (Aasen 1873), NO would rely on two types of material: citations from the Nynorsk literature and material from the dialects (Vikør 2018: 29). Besides the historical and variational aspects, NO has an emphasis on documentation, including the principle that information about usage, origin, and geography must be linked to source materials. The NO archives and language collections are thus an essential part of the dictionary as a lexical resource. Most of the paper files and archives were digitized in the 1990s by the Unit for Digital Documentation (EDD) at the University of Oslo. EDD also developed the lexicographic monitor corpus *Nynorskkorpuset* (the Nynorsk corpus) as a new empirical basis for NO. These resources were later transferred to Bergen in the context of establishing Språksamlingane. The printed dictionary was finalized under the project Norsk Ordbok 2014, which lasted from 2002 to 2016 with increased funding, more staff, and the digitization of the editorial process. This project also produced a partial digital edition spanning the letters *i* to *å*.

The current project, NO-AH, started in 2019. The main objective is to update the letters *a* to *h*, which is the oldest part of the dictionary, compiled prior to digitization, and thereby complete the digital edition. A second goal is to provide stable and up-to-date resource management. The ambition is to create a dynamic system of interconnected databases, complete with facilities for update and extension. CLARINO is involved in both content update and resource management. New interfaces are being developed in cooperation with CLARINO, with Corpuscle-Lex as an integrated part of the dictionary writing system. NO-AH also benefits from CLARINO services and expertise in activities involving agreements, licensing, and providing standardized metadata descriptions.

Nynorskkorpuset is a valuable source of lexicographic evidence for NO. The current version has more than 100 million words and texts from 1866 onward. Most of these are newer materials: about 85% of the texts were published after 1975 and 75% after 2000. The corpus is extended annually with texts from the publishing company Det Norske Samlaget and other sources. CLARINO assists with

---

6 http://norsk-ordbok.no

rights clearance, the design of licensing agreements, and making the materials searchable on the Corpuscle and Corpuscle-Lex platforms. These provide an easy way to get an overview of the current corpus contents, such as words, lemmas, metadata categories, and grammatical annotation. Inspecting the lemmas in a particular alphabet section facilitates the identification of words that have not been included in the dictionary so far.

The update of NO must account not only for new additions to the vocabulary and the present usage of words, but also for words and senses that may already have become outdated or obsolete. Vikør (2018: 19) describes the documentation in NO of the word *glamour* (Vikør et al. 2002: 321), which has two entries: one for the simplex word and one for the word as part of a compound. There is one example of a compound, *glamour-boy* ('poster boy', 'advertising object'), dating back to 1975. This compound, however, returns zero results in Nynorskkorpuset. Although it seems that the word is no longer in use, the entry will be kept, unchanged, for historical documentation. On the other hand, new compounds with glamour have emerged since 2002. Querying the corpus for words starting with *glamour*, we find that *glamourmodell* ('glamour model') is the most frequent compound. To get a first impression of the development and use of this word, the "Distribution" tool in Corpuscle-Lex can be used to show all occurrences of the lemma relative to year and genre. The resulting overview in Figure 10 shows that the compound appears in corpus texts from 2005 onward, that it seemed to reach a peak around 2008, that it does not occur after 2010, and that it is found mainly in newspapers. There are 23 instances of the lemma in Nynorskkorpuset. Extending the search to the other corpora in Corpuscle-Lex increases the number to 56 instances, limited to the period 2005 to 2011. Although the word is not very frequent in these corpora, it is well-documented in that period. The word *glamourmodell* is thus a candidate for documentation as a compound in NO.

Information from syntactic searches in NorGramBank (described in Section 2) is particularly useful in the lexical description of words with many senses and which occur with high frequency in the sources. NorGramBank allows for targeted queries that can provide evidence for colligations (syntactic collocations). The query template *N-argofverbs(@N)* retrieves information about verbs having a particular noun as its argument 1 or 2. This was used for the noun *bane* ('roadway', 'railway', 'track', 'course', 'bane'). Figure 11 shows the top query results.[7] In the instances where verbs take *bane* as their ARG1 (typically the subject), the verb normally appears after the

7 In this case we have chosen to search in all Norwegian texts, not only Nynorsk. The Nynorsk part of NorGramBank is relatively small, and searching the entire treebank improves the chances of getting enough results to work with. The results should be treated as "seeds" to be followed up by more targeted queries in relevant treebanks.

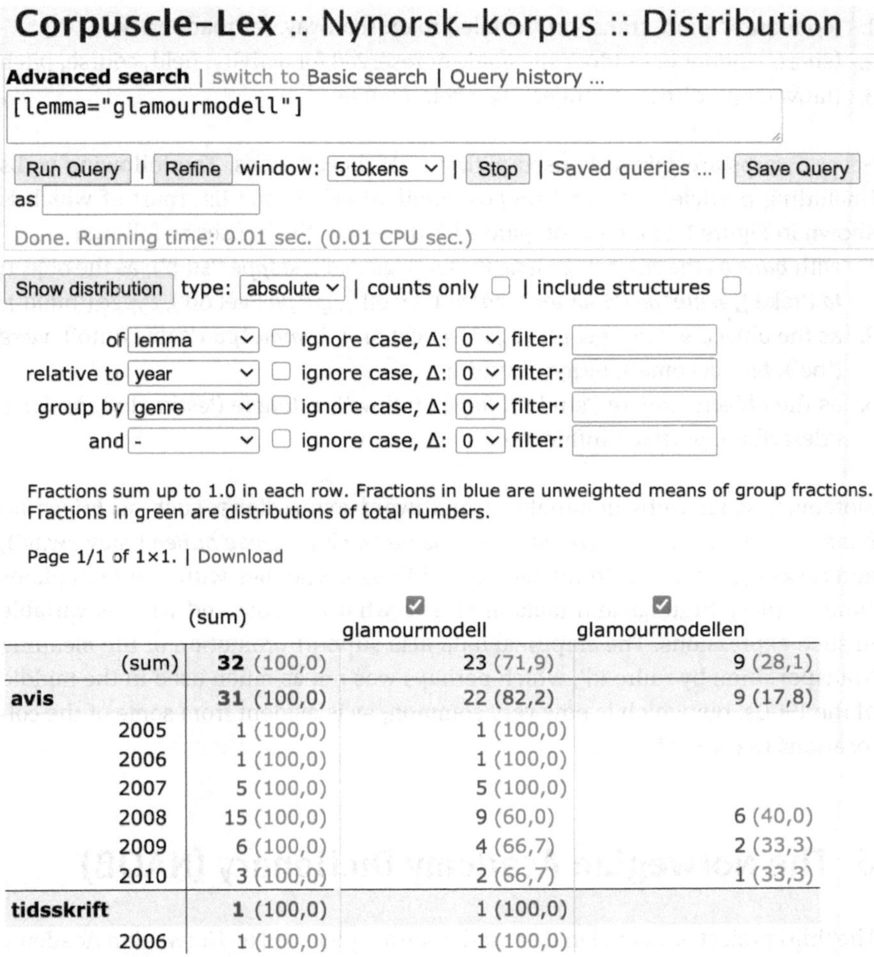

Corpuscle-Lex :: Nynorsk-korpus :: Distribution

Advanced search | switch to Basic search | Query history ...

[lemma="glamourmodell"]

Run Query | Refine window: 5 tokens | Stop | Saved queries ... | Save Query as

Done. Running time: 0.01 sec. (0.01 CPU sec.)

Show distribution type: absolute | counts only | include structures

of lemma ignore case, Δ: 0 filter:
relative to year ignore case, Δ: 0 filter:
group by genre ignore case, Δ: 0 filter:
and - ignore case, Δ: 0 filter:

Fractions sum up to 1.0 in each row. Fractions in blue are unweighted means of group fractions. Fractions in green are distributions of total numbers.

Page 1/1 of 1×1. | Download

	(sum)	glamourmodell	glamourmodellen
(sum)	**32** (100,0)	23 (71,9)	9 (28,1)
avis	**31** (100,0)	22 (82,2)	9 (17,8)
2005	1 (100,0)	1 (100,0)	
2006	1 (100,0)	1 (100,0)	
2007	5 (100,0)	5 (100,0)	
2008	15 (100,0)	9 (60,0)	6 (40,0)
2009	6 (100,0)	4 (66,7)	2 (33,3)
2010	3 (100,0)	2 (66,7)	1 (33,3)
tidsskrift	**1** (100,0)	1 (100,0)	
2006	1 (100,0)	1 (100,0)	

Figure 10: Distribution of the lemma *glamourmodell* ('glamour model') per year and grouped by genre: *avis* ('newspapers') and *tidsskrift* ('magazines').

noun, and therefore is listed in the column to the right ('C-arg1of'). This is the case with the most frequent combination, *bane* + *være* ('be'). Verbs with bane as their ARG2 (normally object) appear in the left column ('A-arg2of'), the verb normally preceding the noun. This is the case with the second most frequent combination, *ha* ('have') + *bane*.

The published NO entry for *bane* (homograph II) has six main senses, as shown in the facsimile in Figure 12. The first three senses (marked with arabic numerals) correspond to the following approximate English counterparts:

1. (communication, transport) levelled road: roadway, railroad, track
2. (sports) indoor or outdoor site made or reserved for activity: field, course, pitch
3. (movement, direction) trajectory, orbit, course

Several verbs are primarily used with one of these senses. The following verbs (including particle verbs and prepositional verbs)[8] in the list (part of which is shown in Figure 11) tend to colligate with the respective senses as follows:

1. with *bane* as the subject: *komme* ('come'), *gå* ('go'), *stoppe* ('stop'); as the object: *ta* ('take'), *vente*på* ('wait for'), *gå*av* ('get off'), *gå*på* ('get on'), *bygge* ('build');
2. as the object: *gå*av* ('get off'), *gå*på* ('get on'), *komme*på* ('come onto'), *være* ('be'), *bli* ('become'), *bygge* ('build');
3. as the object: *studere* ('study'), *følge* ('follow'), *estimere* ('estimate'), *beskrive* ('describe'), *påvirke* ('influence').

Moreover, some verbs dominate in multiword expressions, such as *bringe på bane* ('bring on track'), *være på bane* ('be on track'), *skygge banen* ('stay away'), and *tenke i [. . .] baner* ('think along [. . .] lines'). Searches with other templates support these findings and make it clearer what is stable and what is variable in such expressions. The empirical data also support promotion of the meaning 'transportation by railroad', which perhaps was not as much used in the middle of the 1900s, but which is now very common, as is evident from some of the collocations that were found.

6 The Norwegian Academy Dictionary (NAOB)

The third project is located in Oslo under the auspices of The Norwegian Academy for Language and Literature[9] and consists in the further development of NAOB ('The Norwegian Academy Dictionary'), the most comprehensive dictionary for Bokmål, comprising around 225,000 lemmas with detailed information about semantics and idioms. The descriptions are exemplified with many citations from literature in several genres from a little before 1830 until today.[10] NAOB is freely

8 The * in the example verbal predicates is not the Kleene star, but marks a composition of a verb and a selected preposition.

9 https://www.detnorskeakademi.no

10 Thus it includes about 80 years of literature from the Dano-Norwegian period; see Section 3. In comparison, the Swedish dictionary SAOB describes the period from the 1520s until the time of editing, and the Danish ODS the period from around 1700 until 1955.

Count	#A-arg2of: *value*	#B-noun: *atom*	#C-arg1of: *value*
192		bane	være
109	være	bane	
102	ha	bane	
101	bli	bane	
100		bane	bli
81	følge	bane	
80	komme*på	bane	
78	ta	bane	
47	bygge	bane	
47		bane	gå
42	få	bane	
41		bane	skulle
40		bane	kunne
37		bane	komme
33		bane	ha
32	skygge	bane	
27		bane	ville
27		bane	ligge
27	gå*på	bane	
26	forlate	bane	
25	gå*av	bane	
22	finne	bane	
20		bane	exist
17		bane	måtte
16	beregne	bane	
16	anlegge	bane	
15	lage	bane	
15	nå	bane	
14	gå*ut*på	bane	
13	åpne	bane	
13	gå	bane	

Figure 11: Top frequencies of verb occurrences with *bane* as argument 1 ('C-arg1of') or argument 2 ('A-arg2of').

available online[11] and is not published in book form. On average there are 70,000 searches per day from 30,000 unique users.

NAOB, which came online in 2017 and was officially launched on January 24, 2018, is a product of thorough revision, modernization, and extension of an older

11 http://naob.no

II **bane** m, f [målf m (Va,Hedal,Vestf,Krsand, Li,Vo,Innh), f (Gbr,Hafslo,Selje,Tresfjord); mlty *bane* 'open veg, fritt rom']. **1**) jamna veg. **a**) del av vanleg veg tilskipa for eit sersk slag ferdsle, serl i sms som *køyrebane*. **b**) skjenegang, serl for jarnvegstog; (òg:) jarnvegen som samferdslemiddel el institusjon: *senda* .. (varer) *med eimbåt eller bana* (Åsh.J 112). **c**) overf: *geniet må for at vera geni brjota nye baner og opna nye syn* (Vi.SkrS III,174). **2**) open, avgrensa, planert plass, flate nytta til idrottsøvingar el visse slag arbeid (jfr *fotball-, idrotts-, reipar-, skeise-, skyte-, tråv-bane*): *det var pløgt upp eit skeid elder ein bane på isen* (Vi.SkrS II,14). **3**) (line som syner) veg el lei som ei rørsle går i: *i solsystemet er det tyngdi og svingkrafti som held planetane i banane sine* (EinbuSA 36); jfr *jord-, tanke-bane*. **4**) livsveg: *den akademiske bana krev òg mod i sume høve* (Ra.RR 2) / *etter den siste misslykte freistnaden på å koma inn i ny bane hadde han leti all ting ligge* (H.M.Ves.H 108). **5**) flate på ymse slag reiskapar, såleis **a**) slagflate på hamar o l (Vestf,Verdal; NFL43Nu 24). **b**) slagflate på ambolt (Hafslo, Va). **c**) underflate på høvel; sole (sumst Bratt. LånSn 8). **6**) kvard, (av tyd 'langt stykke papir') i vend *i lange baner* el *banar* i store mengder, ovleg mykje.

Figure 12: Entry II for *bane* in NO (scanned).

dictionary, *Norsk Riksmålsordbok*, a six-volume dictionary whose first volume appeared in 1937. The literary citations, counting more than 300,000 from 6,500 sources at the time of NAOB's launch, are a central part of a documenting dictionary, providing evidence for the semantic and grammatical descriptions in the dictionary entries. An important part of the revision, modernization and extension leading to NAOB has been updating the literary citations with further examples from more modern and more varied literature. This process still goes on within the limits of modest grants, and this is primarily where the CLARINO Bergen Centre and its treebank NorGramBank[12] come in.

As an example we may consider a NorGramBank search template which was used when a dictionary entry turned out to miss a meaning. The verb *utmerke* ('distinguish') is especially common as a reflexive verb *utmerke seg* ('distinguish oneself'). The dictionary only gave examples where this meant to distinguish oneself positively, as shown in Figure 13.

The editors had reasons to assume that the expression can also be used to describe distinguishing oneself in a negative way. Now, the treebank NorGramBank does not allow sorting examples according to word senses, but it may also

12 Cf. Section 2.

2 REFLEKSIVT **utmerke seg** gjøre seg (positivt) bemerket ; skille seg (positivt) ut

SITATER

- *han havde hele dagen sig i legene udmærket* (Henrik Wergeland Samlede Skrifter III 513)
- *[han] udmærker sig [hverken] ved lærdom eller ved nogen synderlig veltalenhed* (Henrik Ibsen Kejser og Galilæer 81 1873)
- *den, der skal være en stor høvding, må udmærke sig på anden måde* (Bjørnstjerne Bjørnson Samlede digter-verker III 150)
- *filmen udmærker sig fra alle andre* (*Stavanger Aftenblad* 05.02.1914/7) | i annonse
- *ingen av dem hadde utmerket sig særlig i kirkens tjeneste* (Sigrid Undset Olav Audunssøn i Hestviken I 55 1925)
- I ADJEKTIVISK PRESENS PARTISIPP *et utmerkende drag hos ham var hans ærlighet* (Nils Collett Vogt *Fra gutt til mann* 315 1932)
- *norske orlogsgaster utmerket seg ... under stjernebanneret* (Trygve Width *Eventyrlyst* 16 1944)
- *det er jevnheten og sikkerheten [i turningen] som utmerker seg hos svenskene* (*Dagbladet* 16.03.1964/10)
- *[skogen] består av høye, bredbladete trær og utmerker seg ellers ved en rikdom på slyngplanter og epifyter* (Christian Valeur *Steffen tar sin del av ansvaret* LBK 2009)

Figure 13: Part of the NAOB entry for the verb *utmerke*, only describing 'distinguishing oneself' in a positive way.

be helpful to sort them according to which words occur in specific syntactic positions around the target word. Specifically, the verb *utmerke seg* typically occurs with a prepositional phrase with *med* ('with') or *ved* ('by'), specifying what something is distinguished by. Examples sorted according to what someone or something is distinguished by (expressed by a verb or a noun) can be found by using the template *V-prepobj(@V,@P)*, which allows the user to specify one or more verbs and one or more prepositions, as shown in Figure 14.

Figure 15 shows a small section of the query output, alphabetically sorted by the prepositional objects. The word *mangel* in the fifth and sixth rows means 'lack', which makes it a likely place to find a negative meaning of the verb. Clicking on the *Ottar Brox* row then displays the relevant examples, as shown in Figure 15. The first of the two examples (meaning 'He will also distinguish himself by lack of consistency in his chosen actions') is suitable and may be selected by clicking on "Copy", which yields information about the example in an XML format, shown in example (1), which can be directly inserted into the NAOB database.

(1)
```
<sitatledd><sitat>Han vil også utmerke seg ved mangel på konsistens i sine
handlingsvalg, og at en ikke kan forutsi hva han vil finne på å gjøre.
</sitat><kilde><forf>Ottar Brox</forf> <verk>Hva skjer i Nord-Norge? :en studie
i norsk utkantpolitikk</verk> <ref>39</ref>

<urn>https://urn.nb.no/URN:NBN:no-nb_digibok_2013071208165</urn></kilde></
sitatledd>
```

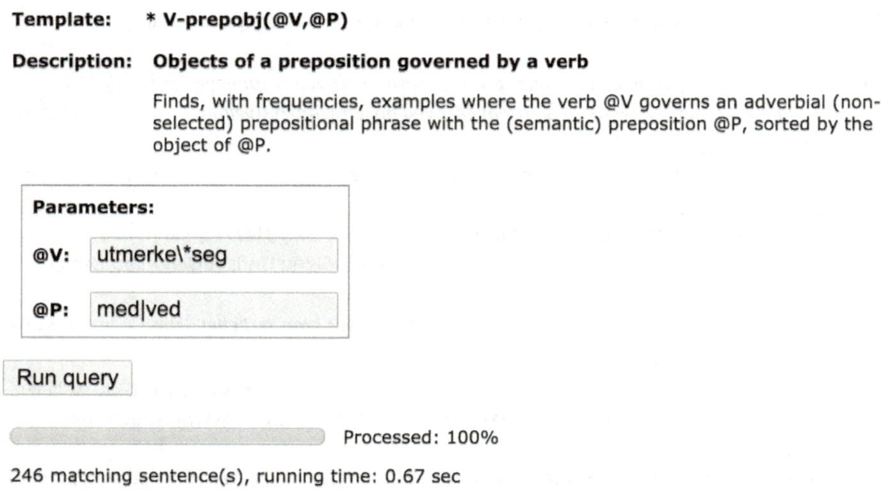

Figure 14: The search template *V-prepobj(@V,@P)* with parameter values filled in by the user.

Using the template to collect examples like this resulted in the extension of the *utmerke* entry in Figure 16, where the Brox quote occurs as the third example. Clicking on the underlined book title in the dictionary entry will bring the user to the relevant scanned page of the book in the National Library, part of which is shown in Figure 17.

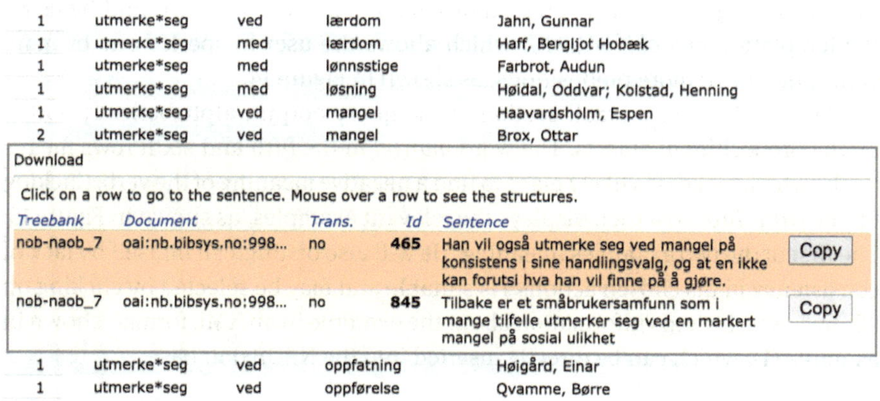

Figure 15: Numbers of matching patterns with authors; examples from the author Ottar Brox are inspected.

2.1 BRUKT MED NEGATIV SPESIFISERING

SITATER

- *et økonomisk geni kan som bekjent på andre områder utmerke seg ved aningsløs tåpelighet* (*Aktuell* 1963/nr. 13/35 Aksel Sandemose)
- *hele 41 av partiets representanter … utmerket seg negativt ved å stemme mot ethvert forslag om forandringer* (*Aftenposten Aften* 09.04.1968/8)
- *han vil … utmerke seg med mangel på konsistens i sine handlingsvalg, og at en ikke kan forutsi hva han vil finne på å gjøre* (Ottar Brox *Hva skjer i Nord-Norge? (1972)* 39)
- *særlig to bombegrupper utmerket seg ved å bombe egne styrker, og det ved flere anledninger* (Olav Farnes *Lege på mange fronter* 128 1987)

Figure 16: Part of the updated NAOB entry for the verb *utmerke*, listing examples of 'distinguishing oneself' in a negative way.

biologi. Reidar Carlsens berømte definisjon av juksa, som «ei lang snor med jarstein og angel i den ene enden og en idiot i den andre», er gått inn i den konvensjonelle visdom om fiskerispørsmål.

Det ser ikke ut til å streife ekspertene at det må være et uholdbart og i alle tilfelle analytisk ufruktbart utgangspunkt at en hel folkegruppe forutsettes å handle stikk i strid med sine egne interesser. Skal vi i det hele tatt forstå menneskelig atferd, må vi forutsette at enkeltindividene i sine handlingsvalg prøver å maksimere sine verdier, og velge alternativer ut fra kalkyler over kostnader og vinningsmuligheter. En viktig del av målsettinga for dette arbeidet er å vise at når f.eks. nordnorske fiskerbønder går imot trålere, så er ikke dette ut fra «konservatisme», «fordommer» eller «negative innstillinger», men ut fra ønsket om å ha det så bra som mulig. Det er like fremmende for deres egne økonomiske interesser å gå imot trålere (slik disse nå introduseres) som det er for industriarbeidere å kreve høyere lønn, eller for bankeiere å kreve høyere renter. Det går an å forstå et en enkelt «idiot» i en populasjon handler i strid med sine egne interesser, vi bygger da også egnete institusjoner for ham. Han vil også utmerke seg ved mangel på konsistens i sine handlingsvalg, og at en ikke kan forutsi hva han vil finne på å gjøre. Men denne måte å betrakte «idioti» på hjelper en ikke til å forstå en hel

39

Figure 17: Excerpt of the scanned page at the National Library of Norway containing the citation from Ottar Brox, accessed from a hyperlink in the updated NAOB entry.

7 Conclusion

Lexicographical work and language technology tools and resources are mutually dependent. On the one hand, a suitable lexicon is paramount for the development of natural language processing applications (Rosén 2014). On the other hand, corpora and related natural language processing tools and resources provide a wealth of information on patterns of lexis (Hasselgård, Ebeling, and Ebeling 2013) and can strongly support lexicographical work, as documented in this chapter.

For three ongoing national lexicographical projects in Norway, the CLARINO Bergen Centre has been providing access to data, tools, and know-how. The update of NO-AH is still in an initial phase, while the other projects are well under way. Although lexicographical resources or applications were not explicitly mentioned in the 2012 project plan that established CLARINO, experience shows that the data, tools and practices in CLARINO are adaptable to the needs of modern lexicography.

Lexicographers are highly dependent on source materials. Corpus resources at the CLARINO Bergen Centre have been made available through the INESS treebanking platform and through the Corpuscle corpus management and search tool. Both systems were further developed to better serve emerging needs. Corpuscle was extended specifically for lexicographical work as the bespoke platform Corpuscle-Lex. To make the advanced search facilities of INESS easier to use and more amenable to the needs of lexicographers, the search interface was adapted and augmented with query templates providing word sketches. Training in Corpuscle-Lex and INESS is given to all new dictionary editors.

Taken together, the infrastructure provides tools and services that simply did not exist before CLARINO, thereby improving a situation with fragmented source materials and unsolved copyright and technical issues. The work carried out within CLARINO with respect to harmonizing data formats and resolving restricted licenses has facilitated and increased the efficiency of the lexicographical work. Easy access to large materials in CLARINO and tools for analysing these data secures an empirical foundation which far exceeds the lexicographical resources and possibilities available only a few years ago. When language resources from Språksamlingane and other sources were included in our current lexicographic practice, best practices from CLARIN were also adopted. CLARIN license agreement templates are employed and if necessary adapted in order to include, deposit, curate, and deploy such resources for academic as well as dictionary development purposes.

The adaptability of the CLARINO infrastructure has been an enabling force for the tight integration of the CLARINO corpus tools with lexicographical editing tools, which makes for an efficient workflow. This would not have been possible without support from the experienced workforce in both Språksamlingane and CLARINO. A strategy must be set out to manage and sustain that combined work force in the future.

Bibliography

Aasen, Ivar. 1873. *Norsk Ordbog med dansk Forklaring [Norwegian dictionary with Danish definitions]*. Christiania: Mallings Boghandel.

Andersen, Gisle & Peder Gammeltoft. 2022. The role of CLARIN in advancing work in terminology: The case of Termportalen – the national terminology portal for Norway. In Darja Fišer & Andreas Witt (eds.), *CLARIN. The infrastructure for language resources*. Berlin: De Gruyter.

De Smedt, Koenraad, Gunn Inger Lyse Samdal, Rune Kyrkjebø, Hemed Ali Hemed Al Ruwehy, Øyvind Liland Gjesdal, Victoria Rosén & Paul Meurer. 2016. The CLARINO Bergen Centre: Development and Deployment. *Linköping Electronic Conference Proceedings* 123: 1–12.

Dyvik, Helge, Paul Meurer, Victoria Rosén, Koenraad De Smedt, Petter Haugereid, Gyri Smørdal Losnegaard, Gunn Inger Lyse & Martha Thunes. 2016. NorGramBank: A 'Deep' Treebank for Norwegian. *LREC Proceedings*, pp. 3555–3562.

Hasselgård, Hilde, Jarle Ebeling & Signe Oksefjell Ebeling. (eds.) 2013. *Corpus perspectives on patterns of lexis*. Studies in Corpus Linguistics no. 57. Amsterdam/Philadelphia: John Benjamins.

Hovdenak, Marit. 2014. Bokmålsordboka og Nynorskordboka gjennom ein generasjon [The Bokmål dictionary and the Nynorsk dictionary spanning a generation]. *Nordiske studier i leksikografi* 12: 229–246.

Hovdenak, Marit, Laurits Killingbergtrø, Arne Lauvhjell, Sigurd Nordlie, Magne Rommetveit & Dagfinn Worren. (eds.) 2006. *Nynorskordboka: definisjons- og rettskrivingsordbok [Nynorsk dictionary: definition and spelling dictionary]*. 4th edn. Oslo: Det Norske Samlaget.

Kulbrandstad, Lars Anders. 1976. Norsk handordbok [Norwegian practical dictionary]. *Språknytt* 2: 7–8.

Landrø, Marit Ingebjørg & Boye Wangensteen. (eds.) 1986. *Bokmålsordboka: definisjons- og rettskrivningsordbok [Bokmål dictionary: definition and spelling dictionary]*. 1st edn. Oslo: Universitetsforlaget.

Lyse, Gunn Inger. 2020. Ut med 'adamsslekt' og inn med 'arveprinsesse'? Leksikografiske metodar i revisjonen av Bokmålsordboka og Nynorskordboka [Throw out 'Adam's kin' and take in 'princess heir'? Lexicographic methods in the revision of the Bokmål dictionary and the Nynorsk dictionary]. *Nordiske Studier i Leksikografi* 15: 215–224.

Meurer, Paul. 2012a. Corpuscle: A new corpus management platform for annotated corpora. In Gisle Andersen (ed.), *Exploring Newspaper Language: Using the web to create and investigate a large corpus of modern Norwegian*, Studies in Corpus Linguistics no. 49, 31–49. Amsterdam/Philadelphia: John Benjamins.

Meurer, Paul. 2012b. INESS-Search: A search system for LFG (and other) treebanks. *The proceedings of the LFG Conference*, pp. 404–421.

Meurer, Paul. 2020. Designing efficient algorithms for querying large corpora. *Oslo Studies in Language* 11 (2): 283–302.

Meurer, Paul, Helge Dyvik, Victoria Rosén, Koenraad De Smedt, Gunn Inger Lyse, Gyri Smørdal Losnegaard & Martha Thunes. 2013. The INESS Treebanking Infrastructure. *Linköping Electronic Conference Proceedings* 85: 453–458.

Rauset, Margunn. 2019. Bokmålsordboka og Nynorskordboka: Einegga, toegga eller siamesiske tvillingar? [The Bokmål dictionary and the Nynorsk dictionary: One-egged, two-egged, or Siamese twins?]. *LexicoNordica* 26: 155–175.

Rosén, Victoria. 2014. Språkteknologiens behov for leksikalsk informasjon [Language technology needs for lexical information]. *Nordiske studier i leksikografi* 12: 13–41.

Rosén, Victoria, Koenraad De Smedt, Paul Meurer & Helge Dyvik. 2012. An Open Infrastructure for Advanced Treebanking. In Jan Hajič, Koenraad De Smedt, Marko Tadić & António Branco (eds.), *META-RESEARCH Workshop on Advanced Treebanking*, 22–29. Paris: ELRA.

Rosén, Victoria, Helge Dyvik, Paul Meurer & Koenraad De Smedt. 2020. Creating and exploring LFG treebanks. *The proceedings of the LFG Conference*, pp. 328–348.

Vikør, Lars S.. 2018. *Inn i Norsk Ordbok: Brukarrettleiing og dokumentasjon [Into the Norwegian Dictionary: User guide and documentation]*. Oslo: Det Norske Samlaget.

Vikør, Lars S., Olaf Almenningen, Reidar Bø, Oddrun Grønvik, Arnbjørg Hageberg, Tor Erik Jenstad, Laurits Killingbergtrø, Magne Myhren, Sigurd Nordlie, Gudrun Dahler Vik & Dagfinn Worren. (eds.) 2002. *Norsk ordbok: Ordbok over det norske folkemålet og det nynorske skriftmålet [Norwegian dictionary: Dictionary of the Norwegian spoken language and the Nynorsk written language]*. Volume 4. Oslo: Det Norske Samlaget.

Wangensteen, Boye. (ed.) 2005. *Bokmålsordboka: definisjons- og rettskrivningsordbok [Bokmål dictionary: definition and spelling dictionary]*. 3rd edn. Oslo: Universitetsforlaget.

Worren, Dagfinn. 1998. Om å avgrense eit ordtilfang: Soga om målføreorda i Nynorskordboka [About delineating a vocabulary: The saga of dialect words in the Nynorsk dictionary]. In Ruth Vatvedt Fjeld & Boye Wangensteen (eds.), *Normer og regler. Festskrift til Dag Gundersen 15. januar 1998*, 59–70. Oslo: Kunnskapsforlaget.

Eva Pettersson* and Lars Borin

Swedish Diachronic Corpus

Abstract: The recently compiled Swedish Diachronic Corpus offers access to a total of approximately 16 billion words, covering texts from the 13th century onwards. The corpus contains 14 main genres, with a number of subgenres, compiled from a wide range of sources, including corpus providers and libraries as well as individual researchers and private citizens. All texts in the corpus follow a consistent format, are extensively annotated with metadata, and freely available for download. We firmly believe that the existence of a Swedish diachronic corpus among the resources offered by CLARIN will open up avenues to new, interesting research questions within humanities research, and be a valuable resource for large-scale studies of the Swedish language throughout history – studies that have previously been impossible to conduct in a thorough and consistent manner. Thanks to its embedding in the CLARIN context it also carries the potential to enable broad historical studies from a comparative European perspective.

Keywords: diachronic corpus, historical corpora, corpus linguistics, digital humanities, language change

1 Introduction

History as an academic discipline is often understood as dealing with that part of our past which coincides with the existence of writing (whatever came before that is normally referred to as *prehistory*). The study of history from various points of view is central to the humanities and social sciences, which are the core research areas supported by the CLARIN research infrastructure. Thus, it is only natural

Acknowledgements: The research reported here has been enabled by the Swedish national research infrastructure SWE-CLARIN, supported (in equal parts) by an infrastructure grant from the Swedish Research Council (Språkbanken & SWE-CLARIN; contract 2017-00626) and by its 10 partner institutions.

***Corresponding author: Eva Pettersson,** Uppsala University, Uppsala, Sweden,
e-mail: eva.pettersson@lingfil.uu.se
Lars Borin, Språkbanken Text, University of Gothenburg, Gothenburg, Sweden,
e-mail: lars.borin@svenska.gu.se

https://doi.org/10.1515/9783110767377-022

that historical corpora figure prominently among the *CLARIN resource families*.[1] For similar reasons, diachronic language resources was one of five thematic activities defined by the Swedish CLARIN consortium in 2019, to be pursued jointly among consortium members in various constellations in order to develop the infrastructure.

This activity – coordinated by the Swedish CLARIN *K-centre for Diachronic Language Resources* (DiaRes)[2] – has consisted mainly in the compilation of the corpus described in this chapter.

Corpora containing comparable texts from several stages of the historical development of a language are a prerequisite for enabling large-scale studies of language change and linguistic phenomena occurring in texts from different time periods. Consequently, diachronic corpora of this kind are a very valuable resource for many disciplines in the humanities and social sciences, including digital humanities, historical linguistics, literature, history, and others.

Although historical language corpora have been compiled for a long time – most notably covering various periods in the history of English (e.g., Biber, Finegan, and Atkinson 1994;Kroch and Taylor 2000; Kroch, Santorini, and Delfs 2004; Taylor et al. 2003), but also other languages[3] – diachronic corpora in the sense intended here are, by and large, a product of the last decade, in which we have seen the creation of the *Corpus of Historical American English* (COHA; Davies 2012), the *Register in Diachronic German Science Corpus* (RIDGES) (Odebrecht et al. 2017), the *Icelandic Parsed Historical Corpus* (IcePaHC) (Rögnvaldsson et al. 2012) and the *BDCamões Collection of Portuguese Literary Documents* (described by Silva et al. (2022) in this volume), to name a few. For Swedish, however, a diachronic corpus has so far been lacking.

This chapter presents the *Swedish Diachronic Corpus*, a freely available resource with a total of approximately 16 billion words, covering Swedish texts from the 13th century onwards. We start by giving a short overview of the conventionally recognised historical stages of Swedish in Section 2, before introducing the methods used and the considerations taken during the compilation of the Swedish Diachronic Corpus, for instance concerning text selection (Section 3). We then move on to describing the structure and contents of the resulting corpus

---

1 For more information about the CLARIN resource families initiative, see Fišer, Lenardič, and Erjavec (2018), where the first batch of resource types is described. Historical corpora have since been included as part of the second batch: https://www.clarin.eu/resource-families.

2 https://sweclarin.se/eng/centers/diares

3 For instance, a collaboration between the Universities in Gothenburg and Lund, Sweden, resulted in several million words of digitized Old and Early Modern Swedish texts, which were made available to researchers in the late 1990s. See https://project2.sol.lu.se/fornsvenska/.

in Section 4, and wrap up by discussing how this resource could be useful to researchers interested in studying the Swedish language over time, from different perspectives. Finally, in Section 6 conclusions are drawn and some ideas for future work are presented.

2 The historical stages of Swedish

To be able to construct a corpus of texts from different time periods throughout the history of Swedish, we need to first define the stages of the Swedish language development. Any sharp division into time periods could be questioned, since languages change gradually. One of the most common ways of describing the Swedish language evolution is outlined in for example Bergman (1995), where the history of the language is divided into five stages: *Runic Swedish* (ca. 800–1225), *Old Swedish* (ca. 1225–1526), *Early Modern Swedish* (ca. 1526–1732), *Late Modern Swedish* (ca. 1732–1900) and *Contemporary Swedish* (1900 onwards).

2.1 Runic Swedish (ca. 800–1225)

As implied by the name “Runic”, the texts from this time period are written using the runic alphabet. It could also be noted that the languages spoken and written in the different parts of Scandinavia during this time period are very similar, and often regarded as dialects of one language, referred to as Old Nordic.[4]

2.2 Old Swedish (ca. 1225–1526)

The Old Swedish period is often defined as starting around 1225; *Västgötalagen* (‘the Westrogothic Law’) is one of the most important documents from this period, as it is written in Latin script (as opposed to Runic Swedish). Old Swedish is characterized by influences from Latin and Greek, due to the establishment of (Catholic) Christianity, and from German, due to trading relations with the Hanseatic League. It also has a considerably more complex morphology than present-day Swedish, with a wider range of inflections for case, gender, and different verb forms.

4 This language is also called Old Norse and Old Scandinavian.

2.3 Early Modern Swedish (ca. 1526–1732)

Following the Old Swedish period, the (Early) Modern Swedish era is generally considered to have started with the publication of a Swedish translation of the New Testament in 1526, commissioned by King Gustav Vasa. This translation was widely disseminated, partly due to the emergence of the printing press, and partly due to a Swedish Church law from 1686, requiring clergymen to ensure that people knew important passages of the bible. This widespread use of one and the same text led to a more standardized orthography.

2.4 Late Modern Swedish (ca. 1732–1900)

The Modern Swedish period is sometimes divided into the Early Modern period and the Late Modern period, where the publication of the first issue of the periodical *Then Swänska Argus* in 1732 marks the beginning of the Late Modern era. Due to its genre, this text has a more informal style of writing than the bible texts.

An important milestone in the linguistic history of Swedish, taking place during the Late Modern period, is the foundation of the Swedish Academy in 1786, contributing to a comprehensive standardization of orthography, which was basically completed by the early 19th century. Many loan words enter the language from French.

2.5 Contemporary Swedish (ca. 1900–)

The Contemporary Swedish period starts around 1900, with two important events influencing the Swedish language: the author August Strindberg's breakthrough novel *Röda rummet* (The Red Room) in 1879, and the spelling reform of 1906, since which the orthography of Swedish has in principle remained unchanged. Other characteristics of the Contemporary Swedish period are the abandonment of plural verb forms, the shift towards a more informal, colloquial language, and English loan words entering the language at a higher rate. These developments belong mainly to the period since the middle of the 20th century, which is often referred to as *Present-Day Swedish*.

3 Compiling the corpus

The corpus compilation work has had both a top-down and a bottom-up aspect, as described by Ljubešić et al. (2022) in this volume. It has been top-down in its conception, as a thematic activity of the Swedish CLARIN consortium, and in most of the activities described below in this section, while the bottom-up element has manifested itself primarily in how the actual content of the corpus – the texts – have become available for inclusion in it (see Section 4).

To secure a high-quality corpus, both content-wise and from a user perspective, three preparatory steps were taken prior to actually compiling the corpus: (i) a survey of existing historical and diachronic corpora for various languages; (ii) a survey of textual resources available for Swedish; and (iii) a user questionnaire.

3.1 Survey of diachronic resources for various languages

As a first step, we conducted a survey of existing historical and diachronic corpora for different languages, with a special focus on the structure and contents of these corpora. The goal of this study was to identify important aspects to be taken into consideration in the development of the Swedish Diachronic Corpus, and how to structure the corpus in order for it to be comparable to other diachronic (and historical) corpora. In this survey, we studied diachronic corpora for Czech, English, Faroese, French, Georgian, German, Hungarian, Icelandic, Portuguese, Slovene, and Spanish. One of the main sources for finding these corpora was the CLARIN Resource Family for Historical Corpora.[5] See pettersson and Borin (2019a) for more details on this survey.

The first thing to note is that these corpora vary considerably in size, ranging from 53,000 words in the *Faroese Parsed Historical Corpus* (FarPaHC), to 400 million words in the *Corpus of Historical American English* (COHA), to many billions of words in the *Google Books Ngram Corpus*. The corpus size is highly dependent not only on available textual resources for the language in question, but also on the level of annotation included in the corpus, and the quality of this annotation. Typically, the smaller corpora in the study are carefully annotated by humans with features such as part-of-speech, lemma, morphological, and syntactic analysis, enabling the user to formulate more advanced search queries with high-quality results. Larger corpora, on the other hand, are crucial for extensive studies of linguistic change over time, but are generally either not annotated

5 https://www.clarin.eu/resource-families/historical-corpora

at all, or (semi-)automatically annotated. From this, we concluded that for the Swedish Diachronic Corpus we want to provide as large a corpus as possible to enable large-scale diachronic studies, with a representative part of this corpus being manually annotated, offering advanced, high-quality search possibilities.

A related consideration is which subcorpora to include, with regard to time periods (granularity) and genres (balance and representativeness). In order for comparisons between time periods to be truly commensurable, the composition of texts from different genres should be as equally distributed over the periods compared as possible. Otherwise, results from studies supposedly investigating language change on the basis of such datasets might indicate differences between genres, rather than differences between certain time periods (unless special methods for comparing datasets of different sizes are incorporated).[6] At the same time, the amount of existing historical texts is limited, especially for certain time periods and genres. Furthermore, some genres do not exist in all time periods, while other genres might prosper during one era, but be far less common during another era. In line with our aim of compiling an open-ended corpus that will grow over time, we therefore include as many texts as we can find in the corpus, especially for the earlier time periods and the less commonly found genres. At a later stage, we aim to create a subset of the corpus that will be more balanced, and better suited to different kinds of comparative studies, as well as develop auxiliary language tools to support such studies.

One example of a well-balanced corpus is COHA, covering the time period 1810–2009. This corpus contains four genres (fiction, popular magazines, newspapers, and non-fiction books), and is divided into decades, with all four genres represented for (nearly) every decade. In the Swedish Diachronic Corpus however, we want to cover a much longer time period, meaning that it might be harder to find texts from the same genre for all time periods included. Newspapers, for example, did not exist in the earliest time periods. One way to overcome this would be to divide the texts into broader domains, such as fiction vs. non-fiction, or try to find one or a few genres that exist for many (if not all) time periods covered, for example, legal texts or church documents. For the corpus to be representative of the language at a given point in time, several other genres should however be included as well, to reflect the actual text production during that period, such as charters and religious legends for earlier stages of the language and newspapers and social media texts to represent present-day text production.

6 Although of course genres, likewise, may not always be stable over time with regard to their linguistic characteristics. Fortunately, a large diachronic corpus such as this one will allow scholars to investigate language change from many different viewpoints simultaneously, which arguably should enhance the reliability of the conclusions.

A very important, yet quite often neglected, aspect of corpus compilation, is the metadata included for each text in the collection, which enables users to select relevant texts for their particular research questions, and to get to know the material from different aspects. For the corpora studied in the survey, information on *title*, *author*, and *publication year* is (almost) always provided (the few exceptions being very old texts, where these features may be unknown). Since historical texts may occur in many versions, metadata for older texts often also state which *edition* the text represents. Other metadata elements included in the corpora are *genre*, *sub-genre*, number of *words/characters/bytes*, *edits* done during transcription (including more formal edits like the representation of characters not included in the Unicode scheme and "correction" of line breaks inside words, etc., as well as more advanced edits, such as spelling standardization), *publisher, editor, transcriber, annotator, volume, issue, language variety* (Early New Modern, etc.), *region* in which the text was produced, *availability* (license etc.), *extent* of the sample (if not the full text), levels of *linguistic annotation*, and *general notes*.

Ideally, it would of course be desirable to include very detailed metadata, to facilitate for the users of the corpus to identify texts of interest to them. However, especially in the case of the oldest texts, even basic information such as author or publication year may be missing or unreliable, meaning that the level of metadata information available may vary greatly between different texts. Thus, for some texts it might only be possible to include limited and less reliable metadata information.

Finally, the format in which the texts, and the metadata associated with them, are stored and made downloadable, needs to be considered. For storage, it is important to use a format suitable not only for storing the actual text, but also for providing metadata information and various levels of linguistic annotation. For download purposes, it could be beneficial to provide a format that the user recognizes from other corpora, so that s/he does not have to learn and understand an entirely unknown format. The most common formats for storage and metadata information in the corpora studied in the survey are:

1. a plaintext format, possibly with headers containing metadata information (using a standardized terminology);
2. a tab-separated format (such as CoNLL) with slots reserved for certain predefined annotation elements;
3. a TEI (XML) format;[7] or

7 Text Encoding Initiative; see https://tei-c.org/.

4. a table listing all the texts and their metadata contents, typically in a spreadsheet format (e.g., xls), or as an HTML table

3.2 Survey of existing Swedish resources

When planning the structure and contents of the Swedish Diachronic Corpus, it was crucial to have an idea of what types and amounts of text are available for different periods of the history of Swedish. In the second step, we therefore surveyed the digital textual resources available (or potentially available) for Swedish, for different time periods and for different genres. What is available, in what format, and what is needed to include the text(s) in the corpus? In this phase, we browsed available corpus repositories, and also reached out to researchers and relevant e-mail lists to inquire about material. In this way, we have managed to strike a good balance between publicly available corpus resources and private collections of texts. See Pettersson and Borin(2019b) for more details.

As could be expected, the volumes of text available[8] increase the closer we get to the present day, with about 4.6 million words for the Old Swedish era, as compared to almost 10.7 billion words for contemporary Swedish, as illustrated in Table 1.

Table 1: Approximate number of words in the text material available for different time periods in the development of the Swedish language. From Pettersson and Borin (2019b).

Time Period	Number of words
Old Swedish	4,641,408
Early Modern Swedish	24,700,328
Late Modern Swedish	1,516,865,748
Contemporary Swedish	10,696,957,453

The survey also shows that there are a number of different types of text available, ranging from more formal laws, governmental texts, and scientific publications to secular prose, song lyrics and newspapers, to informal diaries and letters. Five genres (court records, laws and regulations, religious texts, scientific text, and secular prose) contain texts from all the targeted time periods,

8 "Available" in this context means "available in a more or less directly usable format from the sources listed in this section". Much more material than this could be scraped off the internet, in particular for present-day language.

enabling comparative studies of the same text genre over the whole time span covered by the corpus.

3.3 User questionnaire

To get an idea of the needs and wishes of the primary target users for a Swedish diachronic corpus, we sent out a questionnaire comprising of eight questions to 15 linguists – specialists in Swedish historical linguistics – asking about their experience of working with historical corpora, and which features would be important in order for a Swedish diachronic corpus to be useful for them. In the following, we present the questions and a short summary of some of the answers from the 12 scholars who responded to the questionnaire:

1. Are there any research questions within your field where you think a Swedish diachronic corpus could be useful? If so, how?

All the researchers who answered the questionnaire agree that a Swedish diachronic corpus would be very useful, or even essential, for their research. It is suggested that such a corpus could be used, for example (i) for quantitative hypothesis testing based on qualitative findings; (ii) for contrastive studies between phenomena occurring in several languages or language varieties (such as Swedish in Sweden as opposed to Fenno-Swedish); or (iii) for finding unpredictable patterns in a large and differentiated text material. The specific areas of research mentioned by the participants in the questionnaire as relevant for using a Swedish diachronic corpus are historical morphology (e.g., what stems certain derivative suffixes connect to in different time periods), historical phonology, and historical sociolinguistics, as well as studies on language change (such as lexicalization or semantic change over time), syntax, spelling, word order, word frequencies, stylistics, and variation in texts from different time periods and locations, and in texts written by people with different dialects.

2. Have you previously used any existing diachronic (or historical) corpus, for Swedish or for any other language? If so, which corpus did you use, and what did you think was good with the design and the contents of that corpus? And what could have been done differently to make the corpus more useful to you?

All participants in the survey have experience of using historical corpora in their research, in one way or another. At the same time, several researchers point out that it is often hard to find the relevant texts for their research, since the texts are not gathered in one place, and that the lack of a common corpus format makes it time-consuming to learn new formats and to make comparisons between texts.

Other disadvantages mentioned are the incompleteness of available corpora, the uncertainty about the quality of the transcription and the annotation, and that there is often no way of knowing how much editing the text has undergone as compared to the original. In addition, it is often hard to search in corpora that have been OCR-scanned without manual post-correction, due to bad OCR quality. There is also a need for better graphical user interfaces, such as the one in Korp (Borin, Forsberg, and Roxendal 2012)[9] or CQP (Evert 2019).

As advantageous corpus features, several researchers mention the capability to download texts to process them on their own computer, rather than being limited to a search interface. Moreover, the capability to view a search word (or phrase) in its context, using concordances, is also strongly desired by many users, enabling a quick qualitative assessment of the semantic, collocational, or morphological relevance of the word or phrase in its context. A clear chronological structure of the texts is also vital for being able to select appropriate texts.

3. What time period should be covered by a Swedish diachronic corpus?

The general answer to this question is "as much as possible". All participants agree that the period from Old Swedish (1200s) and onwards should be included. Furthermore, most researchers think that it would be good to include Runic Swedish as well, whereas some argue that it is already available through *Samnordisk runtextdatabas* (Scandinavian Runic-text Database),[10] though this is not linguistically annotated, and that Runic Swedish is a bit too far from Swedish as we know it today to make it useful for conducting comparative studies that include this particular time period.

4. How do you think the corpus should be structured with respect to the time periods covered? Should it for example be divided into decades, 50-year periods or 100-year periods? Or rather periods defined within historical linguistics, such as Old Swedish, Early Modern Swedish, etc.?

The majority of the participants in the questionnaire emphasize that the best thing would be for the user to be able to define his/her own subcorpora, to avoid being stuck with predefined time periods that might not suit particular research questions and interests. However, if the corpus should be divided into predefined time periods, periods based on a certain number of years are generally preferred over linguistically motivated periods, since this yields a more fine-grained division.

9 https://spraakbanken.gu.se/korp/
10 https://www.nordiska.uu.se/forskn/samnord.htm/

5. Are there any particular text types/genres that you think should be included in the corpus?

The general answer to this question is "the more the better", and if large amounts of text are available, it is up to the user to create his/her own balanced subcorpus, if needed. At the same time, one user remarks that it is important that there is some kind of balance in the corpus, so that no particular genre is strongly overrepresented, for example because that particular text type is easier to find. A balance of texts distributed over different time periods is also requested. On the other hand, it is important that the corpus reflects the genre development over time, so that the design of the corpus is not limited to the genres present for the earlier stages of the language.

An interesting observation about this question is that the users are specifically interested in texts that are hard to find, such as informal texts written by "ordinary" people. Particular text types mentioned are letters, diaries, texts written in different dialects, and texts that represent the spoken language in one way or another, for example drama. *Tänkeböckerna* (medieval court records) are also called for.

6. How would you spontaneously interpret the term "Swedish" in the expression "Swedish diachronic corpus"? Should, for example, all texts written within the borders of Sweden (past or present?) be included, regardless of whether they are written in Swedish or, for example, Finnish or Latin? Or should only texts written in Swedish be included? Should the corpus also include texts written in Swedish outside the borders of Sweden, which could then include, for example, texts in Fenno-Swedish or American Swedish?

There is a broad consensus among the researchers that "Swedish" in the context of the Swedish diachronic corpus should be defined as "texts written in the Swedish language", including language varieties such as Fenno-Swedish, American Swedish, and different Swedish dialects. It is, however, pointed out that it could be useful to mark these texts as such, in order for the users to be able to select or deselect specified language varieties.

7. Are there any specific parameters that you would like to be able to search for in the corpus?

Some participants in the questionnaire think that a (word-based and phrase-based) lexical search is enough, stating that the most important factor for their research is to have access to large amounts of text from different time periods, and that they do not trust annotation that has been added automatically, due to annotation errors, especially for older texts. For these researchers, quality is more important than quantity, and there are suggestions that we should only annotate smaller parts of the corpus, but do it manually, or make only a coarse annotation, such as part-of-speech tagging, which has a higher chance of being correct. Alternatively, we could put effort into improving the OCR quality instead, since this is often a troublesome issue.

Most researchers are, however, interested in (automatic) linguistic annotation, which enables them to formulate more advanced search queries. Linguistic annotation types specifically mentioned as interesting are lemmatization and/or truncation of words, morphology, part-of-speech tagging, phrase structures and syntactic categories. Personal names and place names could also be useful in studies of sociolects and geographical location. For semantics, the meaning of the words is important, in order to distinguish between colexified senses.

8. What metadata categories should be included in the corpus

As might be expected, many researchers emphasize that as much metadata as possible is desirable. Features mentioned as particularly interesting are author, year, genre, and geographical location. It is also suggested that it would be good to classify texts as being written in different language varieties, such as Fenno-Swedish, American Swedish, etc., but it might sometimes be hard to make such a classification, due to uncertainty and different opinions on how to classify a specific text in this aspect.

Other metadata elements mentioned are volume, issue, and the name of the editor. For manuscripts that are copies of older texts, the name of the scribe who copied the later manuscript is also important. Even the printer could be of importance, since some printers had their own orthographical norm. For some research questions, the age of the author is relevant, too, and if the text is digitally available as fulltext, there should be a link. Finally, there is a suggestion that we should add a short presentation of the text, to give the user an idea of the contents of the text.

4 Contents of the corpus

Based on the findings from the three preparatory steps described in the previous section, we decided on the structure and contents of a first version of the Swedish Diachronic Corpus. In the following, we describe the principles for inclusion of texts (regarding time periods, genres, and text providers), the format of the corpus, the levels of linguistic annotation, and the metadata elements attached to each text in the corpus.

4.1 Time periods

In the first version of the Swedish Diachronic Corpus, we have chosen to include texts from the 13th century onwards, thus excluding Runic Swedish (see Section 2). The reasons for this are threefold. First, nearly all existing Nordic Runic texts are already accessible through *Samnordisk runtextdatabas* (Scandinavian Runic-text Database),[11] a database containing approximately 6,500 inscriptions, with the texts represented in a transliterated and standardized form, and with a translation in English. This means that researchers working with Runic Swedish may find all texts of interest collected there. Secondly, excluding Runic Swedish means that all texts in the corpus are written using the same alphabet, facilitating comparative studies as well as formatting and annotation issues. Thirdly, the runic inscriptions are quite different content-wise from texts written during other time periods. Starting with Old Swedish, we see text genres that occur in several (or all) time periods, opening up for interesting comparisons and research questions.

At the time of writing, the oldest texts are from the 13th century, and the most recent texts are from 2017. It is, however, worth noticing that the Swedish Diachronic Corpus is designed to be an *open-ended* corpus,[12] meaning that the contents of the corpus are not static, but new texts will be added over time, to extend the breadth and depth of the corpus.

4.2 Genres

Labelling a text as belonging to a certain genre is an important feature in the corpus, enabling the user to select texts according to his/her interest. This labelling task is, however, not always as trivial as it may seem. First of all, how specific should the genre categories be? Should, for example, prayers and hymns be genres of their own, or should these text types simply be categorized as religious texts? This was also commented on by one of the researchers answering the user questionnaire (see Section 3.3), who pointed out that classifying texts as "religious texts" would not be a good idea, since there is quite a difference in text type between religious legends and, for example, prayers.

Secondly, how do we choose a genre when there are several genres that could be considered for a specific text? A hymn, for example, could be labelled either as a religious text or as song lyrics, depending on which characteristics of the text

11 https://www.nordiska.uu.se/forskn/samnord.htm/

12 In other words, a kind of *monitor corpus*, although not entirely prototypical as such.

that are considered most important. Likewise, a medical journal could either be classified as a periodical or as a scientific text.

In the Swedish Diachronic Corpus, we have chosen to classify the texts into a smaller number of main genres, with additional subgenres to account for differences between text types within a specific genre. This way, a religious legend will be grouped with the main genre "religion" and the subgenre "religious prose".

Furthermore, many of the texts included in the Swedish Diachronic Corpus were provided by people or organizations that had already classified the texts as belonging to a certain genre. One example is *Fornsvenska textbanken* (Delsing 2002), containing a collection of machine-readable editions of Old Swedish and Early Modern Swedish texts, covering the time period 1162–1758. These texts are subclassified into seven genres: laws, diplomas and court records, medicine, secular prose, religious prose, verse, and accounts. We have followed their genre classification when including these texts in the Swedish Diachronic Corpus, with some minor changes (such as making "medicine" a subgenre of "scientific text", for example).

The resulting corpus contains 14 main genres, with a number of subgenres, as listed below (subgenres in parentheses):

- Court (court records, parish meetings, judgments)
- Governmental (acts, bills, investigations, memorials, protocols, reports, etc.)
- Informal (diaries, folklore, personal stories)
- Laws and regulations (by-laws, church regulations, laws)
- Letters and charters (letters, charters)
- Lyrics (song lyrics)
- Newspapers
- Political pamphlets
- Periodicals (culture, medicine, politics and economy, popular science, women and society)
- Religious texts (bible texts, hymns, postils, prayers, religious prose)
- Scientific and academic text (agriculture, astrology, humanities, medicine, natural science, protocols, social sciences)
- Secular prose (biographies, children's literature, drama, essays, fiction, folklore, humour, non-fiction, novels, poetry, proverbs, short stories, speeches)
- Student writings (social science)
- User-generated text (blogs, chats, Wikipedia)

Five of the main genres (court records, laws and regulations, religious texts, scientific text, and secular prose) are represented in all the time periods targeted by the corpus, enabling comparative studies of the same text genre over the whole time span.

4.3 Text providers and corpus size

One aim in the corpus compilation process has been to collect texts from many different sources, both from corpus providers and from more private collections. To achieve this, we implemented an approach of both searching on the platforms of known corpus providers and also sending out requests to researchers in the field of historical linguistics, as well as email lists targeted at a digital humanities audience. The result is a collection of texts in the Swedish Diachronic Corpus, retrieved from:

1. **established corpus providers**, such as *Dramawebben* (The Drama Web),[13] *Fornsvenska textbanken* (Delsing 2002), *Litteraturbanken* (Swedish Literature Bank),[14] *Språkbanken Text* (text division of the National Swedish Language Bank),[15] *Project Gutenberg*[16] and *Project Runeberg*;[17]
2. **libraries**, such as *Göteborgs universitetsbibliotek* (Gothenburg University Library),[18] *Kungliga biblioteket* (National Library of Sweden),[19] and *Uppsala universitetsbibliotek* (Uppsala University Library);[20]
3. **archives**, such as *Folklivsarkivet* (the Folklife Archives)[21] and *Riksarkivet* (Swedish National Archives);[22]
4. **local history societies** interested in historical texts, such as *Jämtlands läns fornskriftsällskap*;[23]
5. **research projects**, such as the *Gender and Work* project (Ågren et al. 2011);
6. **individual researchers**, such as Anna Wallberg Gustafsson at Lund University, who has contributed political pamphlets, and Professor Harry Lönnroth at University of Jyväskylä, who has contributed court records;
7. **private citizens**, such as Guno Haskå, volunteer at *Demografisk Databas Södra Sverige* (Demographical Database for Southern Sweden), who has contributed court records.

---

13 https://litteraturbanken.se/dramawebben
14 https://litteraturbanken.se/om/english.html
15 https://spraakbanken.gu.se/
16 https://www.gutenberg.org/
17 http://runeberg.org
18 https://gupea.ub.gu.se/
19 https://www.kb.se/kb-in-english.html
20 https://ub.uu.se/
21 https://www.folklivsarkivet.lu.se/en/
22 https://riksarkivet.se/startpage
23 http://www.fornskrift.se/

In the first version of the corpus, released in 2020, we have limited the texts considered for inclusion to texts that are already digitized. This version of the corpus comprises approximately 16 billion words.

4.4 Format

The format(s) used for corpus storage and user access is of utmost importance for the usefulness of the corpus. Our aim is to be able to provide the corpus in one or more formats that (i) are easy to use and understand; (ii)are standardized and used in other corpora as well; (iii)can hold both metadata information and linguistic annotation in an intuitive and transparent way; and (iv) have the potential to be easily integrated in existing search interfaces, etc. To meet these requirements, we decided on three formats:

1. a plain text format, with a metadata header at the top of each file (see Section 4.6);
2. a tab-separated, CoNLL-U Plus format, with slots reserved for a predefined set of linguistic annotation elements (see Section 4.5) and a metadata header at the top of each file;
3. an XML format (not implemented in the first version of the corpus).

4.5 Annotation

Regarding annotation, we aim to include a wide range of linguistic features for each text. In order not to delay the appearance of the first version of the corpus, released in 2020, we have decided to include only linguistic markup already present in the source text, thus not adding any new annotation. This presents a potential obstacle to harmonization, for example for search and comparison across corpus components. However, most of the texts are, at present, either not annotated at all or annotated with largely compatible part-of-speech tagsets and dependency syntax. In particular, as opposed to English, for example, there are no historical corpora with legacy phrase-structure annotation for Swedish, meaning that aiming to add (minimal) UPOS and UD annotations to all the datasets makes a lot of sense.

For representing the linguistic annotation, we use the tab-separated CoNLL-U Plus format.[24]

24 https://universaldependencies.org/ext-format.html

Table 2: Annotation in the Swedish Diachronic Corpus.

	Name	Description
1	ID	Token index (integer, starting at 1 for each new sentence)
2	SDC:XID	'Native ID' used in the resource (e.g., chapter+verse number used in a bible text)
3	FORM	Word form or punctuation symbol as used by language tools (lower-cased standardized form, possibly in modern spelling)
4	SDC:F_FORM	Form corresponding to the Menota facsimile transcription level
5	SDC:D_FORM	Form corresponding to the Menota diplomatic transcription level
6	SDC:S_FORM	Standardised spelling of a word form (form corresponding to the Menota normalized transcription level)
7	LEMMA	Lemma (base form) of the word, as used in a standard dictionary or in modern spelling
8	UPOS	Coarse-grained part-of-speech tag (from the Universal POS tag set: https://universaldependencies.org/u/pos/index.html)
9	XPOS	Fine-grained part-of-speech tag (including possible named-entity codes for proper nouns)
10	FEATS	Morphosyntactic feature specification
11	HEAD	Syntactic head of the current token (represented by 0 if current token is the root of the sentence, or else by an ID value)
12	DEPREL	Dependency relation to the HEAD
13	DEPS	In the CoNLL-U Plus format, the DEPREL is typically understood to be one of the universal dependency (UD) relations (see https://universaldependencies.org/u/dep/index.html). Some texts may come with dependency analyses already in place reflecting different formats, e.g. that used by PROIEL (Eckhoff et al. 2018). The CoNNL-U DEPS column may then be used to capture this information.
14	MISC	Miscellaneous information not belonging in any of the other columns

Table 2 shows the columns that should be present for each word in a text in the diachronic corpus (where only the token index and the word form columns need to be assigned a value, and unassigned values are represented by an underscore).[25]

25 As per CoNNL-U Plus conventions, project-specific columns are given a namespace prefix ("SDC:").

4.6 Metadata

To enhance searchability and to enable the user to select only the parts of the corpus that are relevant to his/her specific research interests, we have developed a scheme of 42 metadata features, including author, title, date (original date, manuscript date and publication date), genre and subgenre, language variety, printer, digitization method, transcription principles, level of linguistic annotation, source, license, number of words and sentences, and more. What metadata elements to include was decided incrementally. First, a set of initial metadata elements were chosen, based on the elements suggested by the *Text Encoding Initiative*,[26] combined with the authors' own experience of corpus work and corpus use. These were then revised and extended based on input from the user questionnaire (Section 3.3) and the metadata elements suggested by the text providers. Table 3 shows the resulting set of metadata elements present in the Swedish Diachronic Corpus.

Table 3: Metadata elements in the Swedish Diachronic Corpus.

Metadata element	Description
ID	unique ID for referencing this particular text
author	author's name; first name followed by surname
authorBorn	author's date of birth; single year (yyyy) or date (yyyy-mm-dd)
pseudonym	pseudonym used for this text; first name followed by surname
translator	translator's name; first name followed by surname
title	title of the text
subtitle	subtitle of the text
originalTitle	source language title (in case of translations)
manuscriptDate	date of the manuscript on which the digital edition is based; single year (yyyy), specific date (yyyy-mm-dd) or time span
originDate	date of the original manuscript (may be different from the manuscript on which the digital edition is based); single year (yyyy), specific date (yyyy-mm-dd) or time span
retrieveDate	date when the digital edition was accessed (yyyy-mm-dd)
sourceDescription	free text description of the textual content
genre	main genre of the text (e.g., "religion" or "secular prose")
subgenre	subgenre of the text (e.g., 'bible text' or 'poetry')
location	geographical location in which the text was produced

26 https://tei-c.org

Table 3 (continued)

Metadata element	Description
language	ISO 639-3 code for the main language in the text
languageVariety	language variety (e.g., Fenno-Swedish)
codeswitching	ISO 639-3 code(s) for language(s) occurring in the document, in addition to the main language
originalLanguage	ISO 639-3 code for source language (in case of translations)
manuscript	name of the manuscript on which the digital edition is based
manuscriptChapter	manuscript chapter(s) on which the digital edition is based; single chapter or span of chapters
manuscriptPages	manuscript page(s) on which the digital edition is based; single page or page span
printer	name of the printer; first name followed by surname
printedVolume	name or number of volume in which the manuscript is printed
printedIssue	name or number of issue in which the manuscript is printed
printedPages	page(s) in the volume/issue containing the actual text; single page or page span
printedDate	publication date for printed version of the text; single year (yyyy) or date (yyyy-mm-dd)
editor	name of the editor; first name followed by surname
publisher	name of the publisher (person or company)
digitisationMethod	digitization method: manually transcribed, OCR-scanned with manual post-correction, OCR-scanned without manual post-correction, or born-digital
transcriptionPrinciples	transcription principles: diplomatic transcription, standardised spelling, abbreviation expansion, etc.
transcriber	transcriber's name; first name followed by surname
retrievedFrom	URL, organization or person from which the text was retrieved
retrieveFormat	format in which the text was retrieved, e.g., txt, docx, or PDF
annotation	levels of linguistic annotation added to the text
annotationMethod	annotation method: manual, automatic, or semi-automatic
words	number of words in the text
sentences	number of sentences in the text
sentenceOrder	order of the sentences: original or shuffled (due to copyright)
URL	URL reference to digital edition
cite	reference to publication to be cited when using the text
availability	license statement (possibly with URL reference)

4.7 Download and search

An important aspect of the Swedish Diachronic Corpus, is that the user should be able to download and use it, without license restrictions. Hence, all the texts in the corpus are freely accessible and downloadable from the project website.[27] To deal with copyright issues, the order of the sentences has been shuffled in some of the modern texts. This way, researchers may still study phenomena occurring within sentences, even though we are not allowed to share the running text. The metadata element sentenceOrder clearly marks whether the original sentence order is preserved in a text or not, enabling the user to disregard texts with a randomized sentence order.

As seen from Figure 1, the website displays one entry for each main genre. Clicking on a genre displays the subgenres associated with the main genre, along with information on the time period covered, the total number of words, a short readme file, and two download links: one for the plaintext version of the texts and one for the CoNLL-U Plus version (with slots for linguistic annotation; see Section 4.5). It is also possible to sort the columns by genre, time period, or number of words.

For search queries, we intend to integrate the Swedish Diachronic Corpus in Korp,[28] since this search interface contains a majority of the features requested by the users in the user questionnaire (see Section 3.3).

5 Uses and usefulness of the corpus

As is also pointed out by Silva et al. (2022) in this volume (concerning the BDCamões Collection of Portuguese Literary Documents), a diachronic corpus spanning several centuries of text, with a variety of genres and authors, will exhibit a wide range of different orthographic and syntactic traditions, and open up to exciting new areas of research. Furthermore, in the user questionnaire sent out to a number of researchers in Swedish historical linguistics as part of the preparations for compiling the Swedish Diachronic Corpus, we asked (among other things) for their opinions on the usefulness of a Swedish diachronic corpus. As described in Section 3.3, all the researchers who answered the questionnaire agreed that such a corpus would be very useful, or even essential, for their research. Specific areas of research pointed out by the users were:

27 https://cl.lingfil.uu.se/svediakorp/
28 https://spraakbanken.gu.se/korp/

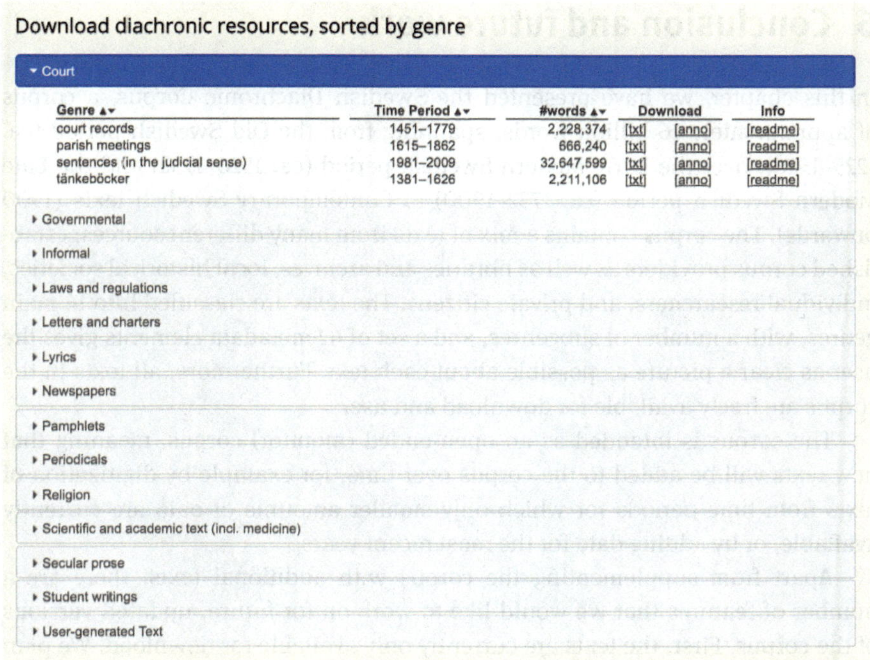

Figure 1: Screenshot from the Swedish Diachronic Corpus project website (https://cl.lingfil.uu.se/svediakorp/).

- quantitative hypothesis testing based on qualitative findings;
- contrastive studies of phenomena occurring in several languages or language varieties (such as Swedish in Sweden as opposed to Fenno-Swedish);
- finding hitherto unstudied patterns in a large and differentiated text material;
- historical morphology (e.g., what stems certain derivational suffixes combine with at different time periods);
- historical phonology and historical sociolinguistics;
- studies of language change (such as lexical or semantic change);
- syntax, spelling, word order, word frequencies, stylistics and variation in texts from different time periods and locations, and in texts written by people with different dialects.

After the release of the first version of the Swedish Diachronic Corpus, in October 2020, it has also been reported that the corpus is used for teaching in courses on the history of the Swedish language, and for developing a BERT language model for named entity recognition in historical Swedish texts.

6 Conclusion and future work

In this chapter, we have presented the Swedish Diachronic Corpus, a corpus of approximately 16 billion words, spanning from the Old Swedish period (ca. 1225–1526), over the Early Modern Swedish period (ca. 1526–1732) and the Late Modern Swedish period (ca. 1732–1900) to Contemporary Swedish texts (1900 onwards). The corpus contains a mix of texts from many different sources; established corpus providers as well as libraries and archives, local historical societies, individual researchers, and private citizens. The texts are classified into 14 main genres, with a number of subgenres, and a set of 42 metadata elements gives the user as clear a picture as possible about each text. Furthermore, all texts in the corpus are freely available for download and use.

The corpus is intended as an open-ended (monitor) corpus, meaning that new texts will be added to the corpus over time, for example by digitization of texts from time periods for which only smaller amounts of data are currently available, or by adding data for the most recent years.

Apart from supplementing the corpus with additional texts, there are a number of features that we would like to work on for future, updated versions of the corpus. First, the texts are currently only available for download. We plan to also offer a search option, by integrating the corpus into the Korp interface.[29] In connection with this, and to broaden the search options, we also intend to add linguistic annotation to more texts in the corpus, including lemma (to enable users to search for a word in all its inflectional forms), part-of-speech, morphology, and syntax. Named entities – identifying names of persons and locations – may also be of interest. In addition, for the older texts (as well as for some of the most recent social media texts), spelling standardization and diachronic linkage of lexical entries would be useful for enabling the user to search for a word regardless of its form in a particular textual material from a particular time in history.

For the download function, we plan to add XML as one of the download formats (something which is also beneficial for the integration into Korp). Furthermore, we want to make it possible for the user to define his/her own time intervals for downloading files, instead of being limited to the zip files currently available on the project website.

Future work also includes defining a sub-corpus within the Swedish Diachronic Corpus, with balanced sets of texts for different time periods, with regard to the amount of text as well as the genres included. In this project, we plan

29 https://spraakbanken.gu.se/korp/

to follow the structure of existing diachronic corpora for other languages, for example the COHA corpus (Davies 2012).

Swedish is one of several closely related Nordic standard languages with long written histories, for all of which digitized historical texts are available to varying extents.[30] An obvious extension of the Swedish Diachronic Corpus would be to include it in a larger Nordic diachronic corpus, where the linguistic closeness of the languages (which increases the further back in time we go) will readily allow, for example, reliable annotation transfer among the languages. For more on this topic, see the contribution by Ljubešić et al. (2022), where a similar scenario is presented for (Western) South Slavic languages, for which the time depth to their common proto-language is about the same as in the case of the Nordic languages.

To sum up, we firmly believe that the existence of a Swedish diachronic corpus among the resources offered by CLARIN will open up avenues to new, interesting research questions within humanities research. It goes without saying that it will be a valuable resource for large-scale studies on the Swedish language throughout history – studies that have previously been impossible to conduct in a thorough and consistent manner – and thanks to its embedding in the CLARIN context it also carries the potential to enable broad historical studies in a comparative European perspective. For instance, the Sweden-Swedish data used in the comparative Swedish-Finnish investigation reported on by Fridlund et al. (2022) is one of the components of the Swedish Diachronic Corpus, viz. the historical newspapers made available by the National Library of Sweden and Språkbanken Text. In the same way that modern corpora have thoroughly re-shaped lexicographic practice (see Petrauskaitė et al. (2022); Rauset et al. (2022)), the Swedish Diachronic Corpus could inform historical dictionary projects such as the large *Swedish Academy Dictionary* (Svenska Akademien 1898–), and complement existing lexicons covering particular historical periods (see, e.g., Adesam et al. 2021).

30 For instance through the *Medieval Nordic Text Archive* (Menota) – https://menota.org/EN_forside.xhtml – or the Old Norse treebanks available through the CLARINO centre INESS: https://clarino.uib.no/iness/treebanks.

Bibliography

Adesam, Yvonne, Peter Andersson Lilja, Lars Borin & Gerlof Bouma. 2021. A lexical resource for computational historical linguistics. In Dana Dannélls, Lars Borin and Karin Friberg Heppin (eds.), *Swedish FrameNet++: Harmonization, integration, method development and natural language processing applications*, 97–121. Amsterdam: John Benjamins.

Ågren, Maria, Rosemarie Fiebranz, Erik Lindberg & Jonas Lindström. 2011. Making verbs count: The research project 'Gender and Work' and its methodology. *Scandinavian Economic History Review* 59 (3). 271–291.

Bergman, Gösta. 1995. *Kortfattad svensk språkhistoria* [A brief history of Swedish]. 5th ed. Stockholm: Prisma Magnum.

Biber, Douglas, Edward Finegan & Dwight Atkinson. 1994. ARCHER and its challenges: Compiling and exploring a representative corpus of historical English registers. In Udo Fries, Gunnel Tottie and Peter Schneider (eds.), *Creating and using English language corpora. Papers from the 14th international conference on English language research on computerized corpora, Zürich 1993*, 1–13. Leiden: Brill.

Borin, Lars, Markus Forsberg & Johan Roxendal. 2012. Korp – the corpus infrastructure of Språkbanken. *International Conference on Language Resources and Evaluation (LREC) 8*, 474–478.

Davies, Mark. 2012. Expanding horizons in historical linguistics with the 400 million word Corpus of Historical American English. *Corpora* 7 (2). 121–157.

Delsing, Lars-Olof. 2002. Fornsvenska textbanken. In Svante Lagman, Stig Örjan Olsson and Viivika Voodla (eds.), *Nordistica tartuensia 7*, 149–156. Tallinn: Pangloss.

Eckhoff, Hanne, Kristin Bech, Gerlof Bouma, Kristine Eide, Dag Haug, Odd Einar Haugen & Marius Jøhndal. 2018. The PROIEL treebank family: A standard for early attestations of Indo-European languages. *Language Resources and Evaluation* 52 (1). 29–65.

Evert, Stefan. 2019. *The IMS Open Corpus Workbench (CWB) – CQP query language tutorial, CWB version 3.4.16*. The CWB Development Team.

Fišer, Darja, Jakob Lenardič & Tomaž Erjavec. 2018. CLARIN's key resource families. *International Conference on Language Resources and Evaluation (LREC) 11*, 1320–1325.

Fridlund, Mats, Daniel Brodén, Tommi Jauhiainen, Leena Malkki, Leif-Jöran Olsson & Lars Borin. 2022. Trawling and trolling for terrorists in the digital Gulf of Bothnia: Crosslingual text mining for the emergence of terrorism in Swedish and Finnish newspapers, 1780–1926. In Darja Fišer and Andreas Witt (eds.), *CLARIN. The infrastructure for language resources*. Berlin: De Gruyter.

Kroch, Anthony, Beatrice Santorini & Lauren Delfs. 2004. Penn-Helsinki Parsed Corpus of Early Modern English (PPCEME). CD-ROM, first edition, release 3.

Kroch, Anthony & Ann Taylor. 2000. The Penn-Helsinki Parsed Corpus of Middle English (PPCME2). CD-ROM, second edition, release 4.

Ljubešić, Nikola, Tomaž Erjavec, Maja Miličević Petrović & Tanja Samardžić. 2022. Together we are stronger: Bootstrapping language technology infrastructure for South Slavic languages with CLARIN.SI. In Darja Fišer and Andreas Witt (eds.), *CLARIN. The infrastructure for language resources*. Berlin: De Gruyter.

Odebrecht, Carolin, Malte Belz, Amir Zeldes, Anke Lüdeling & Thomas Krause. 2017. RIDGES Herbology: Designing a diachronic multi-layer corpus. *Language Resources and Evaluation* 51 (3). 695–725.

Petrauskaitė, Rūta, Darius Amilevičius, Virginijus Dadurkevičius, Tomas Krilavičius, Gailius Raškinis, Andrius Utka & Jurgita Vaičenonienė. 2022. CLARIN-LT: Home for Lithuanian language resources. In Darja Fišer and Andreas Witt (eds.), *CLARIN. The infrastructure for language resources*. Berlin: De Gruyter.

Pettersson, Eva & Lars Borin. 2019a. *Characteristics of diachronic and historical corpora: Features to consider in a Swedish diachronic corpus*. Swe-Clarin Report Series no. SCRS-01-2019. Online: Swe-Clarin.

Pettersson, Eva & Lars Borin. 2019b. *Swedish diachronic texts: Resources and user needs to consider in a Swedish diachronic corpus*. Swe-Clarin Report Series no. SCRS-02-2019. Online: Swe-Clarin.

Rauset, Margunn, Gyri Smørdal Losnegaard, Helge Dyvik, Paul Meurer, Rune Kyrkjebø &Koenraad De Smedt. 2022. Words, words! Resources and tools for lexicography at the CLARINO Bergen Centre. In Darja Fišer and Andreas Witt (eds.), *CLARIN. The infrastructure for language resources*. Berlin: De Gruyter.

Rögnvaldsson, Eiríkur, Anton Karl Ingason, Einar Freyr Sigurðsson & Joel Wallenberg. 2012. The Icelandic Parsed Historical Corpus (IcePaHC). *International Conference on Language Resources and Evaluation (LREC) 8*, 1977–1984.

Silva, João, Sara Grilo, Márcia Bolrinha, Rodrigo Santos, Luís Gomes, António Branco & Rui Vaz. 2022. Where do I belong in six centuries of literature? Datasets and AI-based tools for Portuguese literary documents made possible and available by PORTULAN CLARIN. In Darja Fišer & Andreas Witt (eds.), *CLARIN. The infrastructure for language resources*. Berlin: deGruyter.

Svenska Akademien. 1898–. *Ordbok över svenska språket, utgiven av Svenska Akademien* [Swedish dictionary, published by the Swedish Academy]. Stockholm: Svenska Akademien.

Taylor, Ann, Anthony Warner, Susan Pintzuk & Frank Beths. 2003. The York-Toronto-Helsinki Parsed Corpus of Old English Prose (YCOE). Oxford Text Archive, first edition, http://www-users.york.ac.uk/~lang22/YcoeHome1.htm. Accessed on 2022-03-23.

Part IV: **Research Driven by Infrastructure**

João Silva*, Sara Grilo, Márcia Bolrinha, Rodrigo Santos, Luís Gomes, António Branco, and Rui Vaz

Where do I Belong in Six Centuries of Literature?

Datasets and AI-based Tools for Portuguese Literary Documents made Possible and Available by PORTULAN CLARIN

Abstract: Enhancing the availability of corpora and processing tools for language research is a central endeavour of the CLARIN research infrastructure. In this chapter we report on how PORTULAN CLARIN, with the support of the national institute for the promotion of the Portuguese Language, Camões I.P., has contributed to this effort through the development of BDCamões. This is a collection of Portuguese literary documents suited to a variety of research purposes in the science and technology of the Portuguese language. This collection complements existing corpora by virtue of being composed of complete documents, from various genres and prominent authors, covering a wide time span, and offers an important potential for language science and for the development of language

Acknowledgment: This work was done in collaboration with Camões I.P.

***Corresponding author: João Silva,** PORTULAN CLARIN and University of Lisbon, Departamento de Informática, Faculdade de Ciências de Lisboa, Lisbon, Portugal, e-mail: jsilva@di.fc.ul.pt
Sara Grilo, PORTULAN CLARIN and University of Lisbon, Departamento de Informática, Faculdade de Ciências de Lisboa, Lisbon, Portugal, e-mail: srgrilo@fc.ul.pt
Márcia Bolrinha, PORTULAN CLARIN and University of Lisbon, Departamento de Informática, Faculdade de Ciências de Lisboa, Lisbon, Portugal, e-mail: msbolrinha@fc.ul.pt
Rodrigo Santos, PORTULAN CLARIN and University of Lisbon, Departamento de Informática, Faculdade de Ciências de Lisboa, Lisbon, Portugal, e-mail: rsdsantos@fc.ul.pt
Luís Gomes, PORTULAN CLARIN and University of Lisbon, Departamento de Informática, Faculdade de Ciências de Lisboa, Lisbon, Portugal, e-mail: luis.gomes@di.fc.ul.pt
António Branco, PORTULAN CLARIN and University of Lisbon, Departamento de Informática, Faculdade de Ciências de Lisboa, Lisbon, Portugal, e-mail: antonio.branco@di.fc.ul.pt
Rui Vaz, Camões I.P., Lisbon, Portugal, e-mail: rvaz@camoes.mne.pt

https://doi.org/10.1515/9783110767377-023

technology tools. This chapter also presents and discusses an exemplar case of the exploration of that potential where an automatic authorial style attribution system was developed by resorting to BDCamões.

Keywords: language resources, literary corpora, AI-based language processing tools, language technology, authorial style attribution, Portuguese language

1 Introduction

The oldest document known to have been written in Portuguese (Castro 2015) is "Notícia de Fiadores", a legal text dating back to the 12th century, or 1175 to be precise (Martins 1999). This is also the oldest document written in Portuguese of which a copy is distributed by PORTULAN CLARIN (Branco et al. 2020), and which is included in the CIPM – Corpus Informatizado do Português Medieval (Xavier 2016), a corpus containing texts covering a period from the 12th to the 16th century. The oldest literary document written in Portuguese, in turn, of which a copy is also distributed by PORTULAN CLARIN, and which is included in the same corpus referred to above, is the compilation of love poems "Cantigas d'Amigo", dating back to the 13th century (Cohen 2003).

Legal rules and the rules of love. These are perennial themes for humankind and the two domains that the historical contingency capriciously happened to select for the first documents written in Portuguese that survived until the present day; and that PORTULAN CLARIN is now ensuring that can be read, enjoyed, studied, and preserved, under appropriate and necessary conditions, for future generations.

This aim definitely lies at the heart of the mission of the CLARIN research infrastructure. But CLARIN has been doing far more than just providing help – which is of the utmost importance – to the colleagues who have authored and collected the CIPM corpus, specifically by distributing this corpus through the CLARIN repository so that it can reach the largest possible number of users, readers, and researchers. By means of the Portuguese node PORTULAN CLARIN, the availability of Portuguese literary texts for research has been advanced in two other important directions.

On the one hand, PORTULAN CLARIN complemented the efforts already being made by the authors of the CIPM corpus. With the crucial support of Camões I.P., the national institute for the promotion of the Portuguese language, a new digital collection of literary documents, named BDCamões (Grilo et al. 2020), was developed, covering a historical period starting in the 16th century, precisely where the period covered by the CIPM corpus ended. In its inaugural version,

BDCamões includes close to 4 million words from over 200 complete documents by 83 authors in 14 genres, covering a period from the 16th to the 21st century, and adhering to different orthographic conventions. Importantly, many of the texts in this corpus have also been automatically parsed with state-of-the-art language processing tools. This set of characteristics makes of the new BDCamões corpus an invaluable resource for research in language technology (e.g., authorship attribution, genre classification, etc.) and in language science and digital humanities (e.g., comparative literature, diachronic linguistics, etc.), which is now also being distributed by PORTULAN CLARIN.

On the other hand, on the basis of these corpora, and resorting to Artificial Intelligence techniques based on machine learning with artificial neural networks, PORTULAN CLARIN developed an innovative research instrument for the literary studies of Portuguese. This is an automatic authorial style classification tool that takes as its input an excerpt of text and delivers as its output the indication of the most probable literary writers, from among those represented in BDCamões, who could have authored the input excerpt as a literary text. These achievements by PORTULAN are examples of how CLARIN can accomplish its mission and serve its users in advanced, unheard-of ways, and are examples of initiatives that can be replicated in other languages and literary corpora.

Our goal in this chapter for the volume celebrating the 10th anniversary of CLARIN is thus to expand on the initiatives and results referred to above by describing them in detail, to report on how PORTULAN CLARIN has been undertaking its mission, and to contribute to further spread and improve what CLARIN can do for its users and the advancement of research in the science and technology of language and in Digital Humanities.

The remainder of this chapter is structured as follows: Section 2 describes the BDCamões collection in more detail; Section 3 presents the experiment on authorial style attribution; and Section 4 concludes the chapter.

2 The BDCamões Collection

With close to 4 million words in its 208 documents by 83 authors, the BDCamões Collection of Portuguese Literary Documents possesses a number of characteristics that set it apart from the majority of existing corpora that are primarily aimed at supporting the development of natural language processing tools and applications, typically as training and testing data sets. These characteristics, which make BDCamões an invaluable research resource that complements other related resources (to be more extensively referred to below in Section 2.1), are the following:

- it is composed of complete documents, rather than of fragments or excerpts;
- the texts that form it are of high quality and have been edited carefully, rather than being content that has been automatically or semi-automatically scrapped from web pages;
- it covers a wide time span of six centuries, from the 16th century to the 21st century, rather than being circumscribed by a particular time period;
- it is composed mostly of literary texts, rather than from the more usual, more easily sourced domains of news articles, official documents, social media, legal documents, etc.;
- it includes texts from different genres, such as novels, chronicles, poems, and short stories, among others;
- it contains texts by a number of different authors, in different styles, rather than originating from a single author or adhering to a uniform style;
- its documents have positively identified authors, rather than lacking clear authorship;
- many of its texts are outstanding landmarks of culture expressed in the Portuguese language and/or are of particular historical significance (e.g., the first theatre plays written in Portuguese) or are written by great authors (e.g., Luís de Camões, Eça de Queirós, Fernando Pessoa, Agustina Bessa-Luís, etc.);
- and last but not least, its texts adhere to a range of different orthographic traditions or standards used in Portuguese, *de jure* or *de facto*.

The unique set of characteristics outlined above makes BDCamões a versatile and flexible language resource that is well-suited for a variety of research purposes in the science and technology of the Portuguese language. This is further strengthened by the fact that, alongside the raw text versions of the documents, BDCamões also includes linguistically annotated versions of many of the documents in the collection, with a wide range of linguistic information (cf. Section 2.4), including part-of-speech categories, morphological features, grammatical dependencies, and expressions denoting named entities.

Focusing on the language science applications, this corpus offers a great potential for research in the Digital Humanities and related fields. It makes viable the study of literary works and authors enhanced by computational technology solutions, and thus shows them in a new light that previous methods would not support. For instance, it allows for: the rapid development of (sub-)vocabularies; accurate indexes of words and their occurrence in the context of specific works or authors; comparative studies on different literary schools, different authors or different creative periods within the career of a given author; diachronic studies concerned with the evolution of the Portuguese language; and many other applications.

Focusing, in turn, on the language technology applications, BDCamões can be used to support the development of computational processing tools for authorship analysis, genre classification, grammar checking, orthographic conversion, lexicon construction, etc., on a par of course with the more usual processing tools whose development is also supported by other types of corpora. A concrete example is presented in Section 3, using a case study in which an authorial style attribution system was quickly developed by utilising BDCamões.

2.1 Related corpora

There already exist a few corpora for Portuguese that can be used to support language research and the development of language technology. In the remainder of this section, we contrast BDCamões with some of the more relevant language resources with which it can be closely compared.

- CIPM – Corpus Informatizado do Português Medieval (Xavier 2016) is a corpus of 2,670 texts, totalling 2 million words, from the 12th to the 16th century, comprising several genres, including historical narratives, religious texts, and poetry. It addresses an earlier time span not covered by BDCamões, but lacks coverage from the 16th century onward.
- CTA – Corpus de Textos Antigos contains 29 historiographic texts as well as hagiographic, spiritual, and novelistic texts originally written or translated into Portuguese up to 1525.[1]
- Tycho Brahe – Parsed Corpus of Historical Portuguese (Galves 2018) is a corpus of texts written in Portuguese between the 14th and 19th centuries, with 76 texts from over 50 authors, comprising 3.3 million tokens, which only partly coincide with the texts in BDCamões (an overlap of 6 texts, totalling about 159,000 words). Subsets of Tycho Brahe have been annotated with part-of-speech tags (44 texts) and parsed (27 texts).
- LT Corpus – Corpus de Textos Literários (Généreux, Hendrickx, and Mendes 2012) is a literary corpus containing 70 documents published between the mid-19th century and the 1940s. While similar in design to and complementing BDCamões, it covers a shorter time span, has a smaller variety of genres, fewer authors, and is smaller in size, at about 1.8 million words, which only

1 http://teitok.clul.ul.pt/cta/

partly coincide with the texts in BDCamões (an overlap of 23 texts, totalling about 897,000 words).
- CINTIL – Corpus Internacional do Português (Barreto et al. 2006) is a linguistically interpreted corpus containing 1 million tokens, mostly from anonymised excerpts of news articles but also including some works of fiction, and transcriptions of formal and informal speech. It is annotated with a variety of manually verified linguistic information, including morphological information and part-of-speech tags. Its texts are all from a recent period and it lacks some metadata items, such as information on the author, that would be necessary for some types of studies.

BDCamões, due to its unique characteristics already outlined above, complements these other corpora and opens up new possibilities for research and innovation that were not so amply available before.

2.2 Document gathering

The digital documents that form the BDCamões collection evolved from a set of works collected by Camões I.P., the official national organisation, acting under the indirect administration of the Portuguese Ministry of Foreign Affairs, responsible for promoting the Portuguese language abroad.

The collection campaign undertaken by Camões I.P. covered the conversion of the works into their digital versions in PDF format under appropriate licensing. These documents were deposited in the Digital Library of Camões I.P.[2] – which gives the name to the collection – from where they can be freely retrieved and used under their respective licensing conditions.

The PDF files were either provided in that format already by the editors of the works or produced from digital scans of the pages of the corresponding physical documents. In either case, while the files represent the visual aspect of the original documents (see Figure 1), they cannot be processed as text by language processing tools.

2 https://www.instituto-camoes.pt/en/activity-camoes/online-services/service-desk

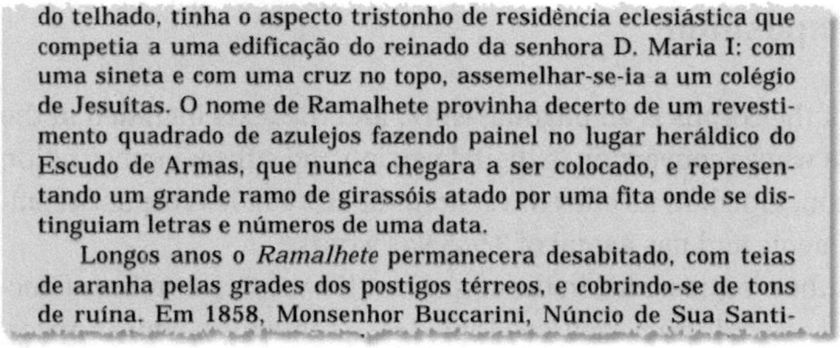

do telhado, tinha o aspecto tristonho de residência eclesiástica que competia a uma edificação do reinado da senhora D. Maria I: com uma sineta e com uma cruz no topo, assemelhar-se-ia a um colégio de Jesuítas. O nome de Ramalhete provinha decerto de um revestimento quadrado de azulejos fazendo painel no lugar heráldico do Escudo de Armas, que nunca chegara a ser colocado, e representando um grande ramo de girassóis atado por uma fita onde se distinguiam letras e números de uma data.

Longos anos o *Ramalhete* permanecera desabitado, com teias de aranha pelas grades dos postigos térreos, e cobrindo-se de tons de ruína. Em 1858, Monsenhor Buccarini, Núncio de Sua Santi-

Figure 1: Snippet of a PDF page from "Os Maias" (background darkened for contrast).

To allow the document to be processed by language processing tools, they were converted by PORTULAN CLARIN into files in plain text format using the command line tool PDFTOTEXT,[3] which extracts any textual content found within a PDF file. This extraction was feasible in the case of the PDF files that were obtained from scanning physical documents because these underwent a process of optical character recognition (OCR) that secured a textual version of the content within the PDF file.

As is to be expected, the OCR process introduces some errors in the transcription, especially for those documents that use uncommon fonts, adhere to old typographic norms, or whose digital scan is of poor quality to begin with. Examples of typical OCR failures are mistaking l (lowercase "L") for I (uppercase "i"), mistaking rn for m, and the transcription of typographic ligatures.

There is no safe heuristic to automatically detect and fix such cases. As such, we performed an exhaustive manual revision of the converted plain text documents and the errors were manually corrected by linguists, taking into account the source PDF version of the documents. Note that the manual correction only addressed the errors introduced by the OCR process. The texts were otherwise transcribed literally, including eventual orthographic errors present in the original edition.

The conversion to plain text is necessarily lossy with regard to some aspects of formatting (e.g., font style, such as italics), hyphenation, and page layout (e.g., headers and footers). For BDCamões, hyphenation was reverted, page headers and page numbering were removed, while the tables of contents (if applicable) and footnote content were preserved. For footnotes, their content is placed at the next available paragraph break after the cue so as not to break the sentence where the footnote is introduced.

3 The PDFTOTEXT tool is part of the XPDF toolkit (http://www.xpdfreader.com).

2.3 Corpus composition

The construction of the corpus is an ongoing work, and the texts included in the collection are those whose conversion to digital version and subsequent curation has already been concluded. In its current version, the BDCamões corpus is composed of 208 documents and has a total of 3,945,943 words.[4]

There are 83 authors represented in the corpus, with a varying number of documents and amount of words from each (see Table 1 for a summary). While a majority of authors – 59 in all – only have one or two documents in the corpus, others are represented more prominently. For instance, Trindade Coelho (1861–1908) has 18 documents in the corpus, making of him the author with the largest number of documents, though not the one with the largest amount of words, as all his works in the corpus are short tales. Júlio Dinis (1839–1871), in turn, is the author with the largest volume of texts in terms of word count, with over 13% of the words in the corpus coming from his 5 works (4 novels and 1 tale).

Table 1: Amount of content per author.

Name	Docs	Words	Name	Docs	Words
Agustina Bessa-Luís	7	378,522	José Luandino Vieira	2	21,089
Alexandre Herculano	8	173,851	José Martins Garcia	1	6,946
Alfredo Margarido	1	9,646	José Régio	1	10,836
Almeida Garrett	4	123,208	José Rodrigues Miguéis	2	17,934
Amadeu Lopes Sabino	1	4,621	Júlio Dantas	2	6,774
Antero de Quental	3	54,211	Júlio Dinis	5	528,249
António Botto	1	2,770	Lídia Jorge	2	13,942
A. Feliciano de Castilho	1	5,385	Luís de Camões	1	146,821
António José da Silva	1	23,877	Luísa Costa Gomes	3	16,248
Aquilino Ribeiro	6	46,295	Luísa Dacosta	1	9,798
Armando Silva Carvalho	1	2,131	Manuel de Arriaga	1	21,686
Augusto Abelaira	1	3,129	M.M. Barbosa du Bocage	7	19,622
Bernardo Gomes Brito	1	8,871	Manuel Teixeira Gomes	5	26,160
Bernardo Santareno	1	8,247	Maria Gabriela Llansol	1	2,373
Brito Camacho	1	4,980	Maria Leonor Buescu	1	32,097
Camilo Castelo Branco	7	177,012	Maria Ondina Braga	1	4,927
Conde de Ficalho	2	5,521	Maria Teresa Horta	1	1,498

4 Here we consider "word" to be any sequence of characters delimited by white space, and the count is obtained by the standard Linux command line tool wc.

Table 1 (continued)

Name	Docs	Words	Name	Docs	Words
Dom F. Manuel de Melo	1	18,591	Maria Velho da Costa	1	1,020
David Mourão-Ferreira	1	5,623	Mário Cláudio	1	578
Eça de Queirós	10	273,011	Mário de Carvalho	5	22,235
Fernando Cabral Martins	2	1,798	Mário de Sá-Carneiro	1	2,218
Fernando Pessoa	1	5,154	Mário Henrique Leiria	1	731
Fernando Venâncio	1	2,855	M. Lemos Júnior	1	6,263
Fernão Lopes	1	36,410	Nun'Álvares Mendonça	1	17,568
Fernão Mendes Pinto	2	19,004	Nuno Júdice	2	3,850
Ferreira de Castro	1	4,347	Oliveira Martins	3	334,693
Fialho D'Almeida	5	92,185	Padre António Vieira	1	12,038
Francisco Maria Bordalo	1	13,395	Pêro Vaz de Caminha	1	9,395
Gil Vicente	6	21,068	Ramalho Ortigão	6	239,252
Gonçalo M. Tavares	3	1,773	Raul Brandão	3	69,207
Hélia Correia	1	2,567	Ruben A.	1	5,878
Jacinto Lucas Pires	1	2,895	Rui de Pina	8	219,031
Jaime Rocha	1	3,801	Sophia de Mello Breyner	1	6,711
J. Osório de Castro	1	8,319	Teófilo Braga	5	227,856
João Braz de Oliveira	1	5,318	Teresa Veiga	1	8,056
João Vaz	1	8,964	Tomaz de Figueiredo	1	4,308
Joaquim Canas Cardim	1	4,443	Tomaz Vieira da Cruz	1	4,224
Joaquim Paço D'Arcos	1	12,521	Trindade Coelho	18	127,166
J.P. Celestino Soares	1	10,218	Venceslau de Moraes	2	43,776
Jorge de Sena	5	37,684	Vergílio Ferreira	2	6,247
José Cardoso Pires	1	6,447	Vitorino Nemésio	4	41,648
José Almada Negreiros	3	14,326			

The corpus covers written texts from several genres, such as tales, novels, chronicles, poems, dramas, and essays, among others, as shown in greater detail in Table 2. Much as we saw regarding authorship, the proportion of documents and words for each genre varies. Tales are the most common genre in terms of the number of documents, accounting for more than 44% of the texts in the corpus, though they only account for 17% of the corpus in terms of words, due to their small size. The much longer novels, though making up only 12% of the documents, account for over 32% of the words in the corpus.

Table 2: Genre distribution in the corpus.

Typology	Docs	Words
tale	92	656,228
chronicle	26	600,018
novel	25	1,290,327
short story	21	295,724
poem	18	296,296
theater play	11	81,589
essay	8	534,515
travel guide	1	6,016
sermon	1	12,038
other	1	6,507
narrative	1	52,715
memoirs	1	17,568
letter	1	9,395
anthology	1	87,007
total	208	3,945,943

In terms of the time span represented, the corpus contains texts from the 16th century to the present day, namely, 7 from the 16th century, 4 from the 17th century, 8 from the 18th century, 84 from the 19th century, 82 from the 20th century, and 23 from the 21st century. As such, this corpus represents different phases of the Portuguese language, including 13 texts from Middle Portuguese (up to the early 16th century) or Classical Portuguese (until the mid-18th century). The remaining texts are in some form of Modern Portuguese (from the mid-18th century onward; or older but in an edition that has been transcribed into those orthographic norm): 21 are written according to the Portuguese orthographic norm of 1911, and 174 according to the norm of 1945.

The various authors, genres, and time periods are not equally represented in the collection, as the goal of BDCamões is to gather and transcribe the documents available in the Digital Library of Camões I.P., making them available for various types of studies. Researchers interested in a particular set of authors, genre, or time period will then be able to take the BDCamões corpus as a resource in which the relevant documents may be found.

2.4 Linguistic annotation and metadata

To broaden the possible uses of BDCamões, a linguistically annotated version of the documents is made available separate from the plain text version. The annotation was automatically obtained using state-of-the-art language processing tools for Portuguese (Branco and Silva 2006). These tools have been developed with Modern Portuguese in mind and, accordingly, the annotation was done only for the subset of documents that were originally written in Modern Portuguese, or which are older but whose edition has been transcribed into that orthographic norm. This annotated subcorpus, BDCamões DependencyBank, contains 195 documents and a total of 4,495,379 tokens.[5]

The resulting linguistic annotation comprises part-of-speech tags (e.g., PREP, ADV, etc.), morphological and inflectional information (lemmas for words from the open categories; gender and number for words from nominal categories; tense, aspect, person, and number for verbs), named entities (in BIO notation, and annotated with their type), syntactic analysis in terms of graphs of grammatical dependencies (e.g., SJ, OBL, M, etc.), and semantic analysis in terms of semantic roles (e.g., ARG1, ARG2, LOC, etc.). The dependency annotation follows the linguistic principles presented in (Branco et al. 2015). Additionally, given the popularity of the so-called Universal Dependencies (de Marneffe et al. 2014) format, BDCamões also provides a second version of the dependency graphs obtained by converting them from their original scheme to Universal Dependencies.

The annotation follows a CoNLL-style format, with one token per line and its linguistic annotation over several tab-separated fields. An excerpt of an annotated sentence may be seen in Figure 2. The 11 columns represent, as follows: (1) raw word form; (2) normalised word form (e.g., after expanding contracted forms); (3) lemma; (4) part-of-speech; (5) morphology and inflection; (6) named entity (BIO notation, with type); (7–8) dependency relation and parent index; (9–10) dependency relation and parent index, in Universal Dependencies; and (11) spacing around the token (e.g., LR indicates the token had spaces to the left and to the right of it in the original sentence).

5 The token count is done after tokenisation, a process that expands contracted forms into multiple tokens and detaches punctuation symbols. As such, the number of tokens far exceeds the number of words.

O	O	_	DA	ms	O	SP	2	DET	2	R
nome	nome	NOME	CN	ms	O	SJ-ARG1	5	NSUBJ	5	LR
de	de	_	PREP	_	O	OBL-ARG1	2	CASE	4	LR
Ramalhete	Ramalhete	_	PNM	_	B-LOC	C	3	POBJ	2	LR
provinha	provinha	PROVIR	V	ii-3s	O	ROOT	0	ROOT	0	LR
decerto	decerto	_	ADV	_	O	M-LOC	5	ADVMOD	5	LR
de	de	_	PREP	_	O	C-ARG2	6	CASE	9	LR
um	um	_	UM	ms	O	SP	9	DET	9	LR
revestimento	revestimento	REVESTIMENTO	CN	ms	O	C	7	DEP	6	LR
quadrado	quadrado	QUADRADO	PPA	ms	O	M-PRED	9	AMOD	9	LR
de	de	_	PREP	_	O	OBL-ARG1	10	CASE	12	LR
azulejos	azulejos	AZULEJO	CN	mp	O	C	11	POBJ	10	LR

................................rest of the sentence omitted................................

Figure 2: Excerpt of an annotated BDCamões document.

Each document is stored in a separate file, associated with the metadata record in XML markup shown in Figure 3. The text itself and, when applicable, the corresponding linguistically annotated data appear in the fields <text> and <annotation>, respectively. The remaining fields in the header contain the title, author, and type (genre) of the work, and information on its publication (the date for the first publication of the work, and the publisher and date of publication for the edition that was transcribed).

```
<document>
  <header>
    <title> ... </title>
    <author> ... </author>
    <type> ... </type>
    <firstPublicationDate> ... </firstPublicationDate>
    <publisher> ... </publisher>
    <publicationDate> ... </publicationDate>
  </header>
  <text> ... </text>
  <annotation> ... </annotation>
</document>
```

Figure 3: XML structure of a document in BDCamões.

2.5 Licensing and distribution

The BDCamões corpus is distributed by the PORTULAN CLARIN Research Infrastructure for the Science and Technology of Language.[6] Due to differences in the licensing conditions regarding document usage, the distribution is split into two parts (cf. Table 3), namely Part I, which includes the documents that are in the public domain; and Part II, which includes the remaining documents. The anno-

6 http://portulanclarin.net

tated sub-corpus BDCamões DependencyBank is part of the distribution of the BDCamões corpus, and additionally, for the convenience of its users, it is also distributed separately, again split into two parts, by PORTULAN CLARIN. The URL handles for these various parts are listed in Table 4.

Table 3: Availability of the documents in BDCamões.

Availability	Docs	Words
public domain (Part I)	127	3,121,986
restricted (Part II)	81	823,957
total	208	3,945,943

Table 4: URL handles for the parts of BDCamões.

BDCamões sub-corpus	Location
plain text – Part I	https://hdl.handle.net/21.11129/0000-000D-F89B-D
plain text – Part II	https://hdl.handle.net/21.11129/0000-000D-F8AB-B
DependencyBank – Part I	https://hdl.handle.net/21.11129/0000-000D-F8AA-C
DependencyBank – Part II	https://hdl.handle.net/21.11129/0000-000D-F8A8-E

The two parts of the corpus are distributed under the most permissive license for each of them. Part I of BDCamões is distributed under the license CC-BY, which requires that when used, the academic authorship of this part of the corpus is acknowledged. Part II has the license CC-BY-NC-ND, which is restricted to research, non-commercial usage, and does not allow the material to be redistributed. The corresponding two parts of the annotated corpus have similar licenses.

3 An experiment on automatic authorial style attribution

BDCamões can be used to support a wide range of research in language technology applications. In this section, we present an experiment where we developed systems for automatic authorial style attribution,[7] with implementations at differ-

7 We have also experimented with assigning an historical period (century) to texts. Apart from the class that is to be learned, nothing else changes in the setup of the experiment, so the system

ent levels of complexity and performance, by resorting to BDCamões and off-the-shelf software. All the systems run over plain text and do not require any kind of linguistic annotation.

Note that the classifiers learn to assign authors to texts given by users, but it would be inaccurate to say that they are performing authorship attribution, as the authors in BDCamões have not, strictly speaking, authored the user-provided texts, unless the user inputs a text from one of those authors. We thus frame the task as authorial style attribution, that is, classifying the given text as being written in the style of a certain author.

3.1 Baseline classifier

For the baseline classifier, we aimed for a system that should be simple to implement, presenting a low barrier to entry for people who may not be well versed in natural language processing or programming, but still achieving competitive performance.

The implementation was done by using scikit-learn (Pedregosa et al. 2011), a Python package for machine learning that strives for accessibility and ease of use. The package comes with functionality for text processing, which makes it straightforward to apply to text-based tasks.

The features used to represent a document are extremely simple and rely solely on the raw text. A document is represented by a bag of character *n*-grams for all *n* in the 2–5 range. That is, a vector with the number of occurrences of every sequence of characters of length 2–5. Such counts would, of course, be large for *n*-grams that are very frequent throughout the corpus and thus not very helpful in terms of discriminating between authors. As such, the values are normalised by the commonly used tf-idf weighting technique, which downplays *n*-grams that occur over many documents and gives greater importance to *n*-grams that are distinctive to a few documents. All these functionalities, i.e., the feature extraction and tf-idf weighting, are provided by scikit-learn.

The classification algorithm is a support vector machine (SVM) with a linear kernel. These are effective even in high dimensional spaces, as in this case,[8] and when there are comparatively few samples. The SVM classifier is provided by scikit-learn. It handles the fact that the task is one with multiple classes, despite

descriptions that follow refer only to assigning authorial style. Results for both tasks are given in Section 3.3.

8 The feature space is the set of character *n*-grams for *n* in the 2–5 range which, for the training set being used (described in Section 3.3), amounts to over 356,000 features.

the SVM being a binary classifier, by automatically recasting the task as multiple one-vs-rest binary classifications.[9]

The feature extraction, training, and evaluation required about a dozen lines of Python code, very similar to those from the "Working with text data" scikit-learn tutorial.[10]

3.2 Neural classifier

Deep neural models have come to the fore as their performance steadily advanced the state of the art in a variety of machine learning tasks and applications. In NLP in particular, the Transformer encoder-decoder architecture of Vaswani et al. (2017) has become a dominant paradigm and the basis for whole families of system architectures.

An encoder-decoder architecture is composed of two parts: the encoder, which maps the input into a compact representation, and the decoder, which takes that compact representation and produces the output. A typical example is found in machine translation, where the encoder maps text in the source language into a compact representation of its meaning and the decoder produces the text in the target language from that representation.

The Transformer makes extensive use of the so-called attention mechanism, which circumvents the requirement to pack the whole input into a single representation – a major bottleneck for previous systems – by allowing the decoder to access (or "pay attention to") the representations of the individual tokens being processed by the encoder.

The descriptions given above of the encoder-decoder architecture and the Transformer are overly simplistic and leave out several details, since an in-depth explanation would be outside the scope of this chapter. We direct the interested reader to (Vaswani et al. 2017).

We have experimented with two neural models, each from a different family, though both are ultimately based on the Transformer. One model is from the BERT (Devlin et al. 2019) family of architectures that take only the encoder part of the Transformer, and the other from the GPT (Radford et al. 2018) family of architectures that take only the decoder part. Both have in common that they are first pre-trained over a large amount of raw text, building up a task-agnostic language

9 In one-vs-rest, for each author A there will be a binary classifier that only outputs whether a given text has been authored by A, with some certainty score. The assigned author is that of the classifier whose prediction has the greatest certainty.

10 https://scikit-learn.org/stable/tutorial/text_analytics/working_with_text_data.html

model which is then extended with an additional layer, the classification head, and fine-tuned on labelled data for the task at hand.

3.2.1 BERT-style

The BERT-style architectures use only an encoder and are pre-trained using some sort of input reconstruction task. For instance, the encoder is given an input sentence where a random token has been masked, and the encoder has to predict what that token is.

The BERT neural model we experiment with is RoBERTa (Liu et al. 2019), a BERT architecture with small adjustments that make it more robust. The model has a vocabulary size of 32,000 subwords,[11] 6 layers and 12 attention heads, for a total of 67.5 million parameters.

The RoBERTa model was pre-trained on a data set of 20 million tokens, 10 million in Portuguese and 10 million in English, from the Oscar corpus (Ortiz Suárez, Sagot, and Romary 2019), an automatically filtered and cleaned subset of the huge (multiple terabytes) Common Crawl corpus. The fact that English text is included in the pre-training of the model may be surprising, given that the classifier is to be used for Portuguese texts only, but similar choices are found in the literature, since the additional pre-training data, even if in a different language, can lead to better performance.[12] For this experiment, we found that adding English pre-training data does indeed help.

After the pre-training phase is finished, the model is fine-tuned on the authorial style attribution task. For this, an extra layer, the classification head, is added to the model. This is a fully connected layer that takes the output of the RoBERTa language model and outputs the author. The weights of this layer, and of the underlying RoBERTa language model, are adjusted during fine-tuning.

---

11 The vocabulary of modern neural architectures is not strictly composed by words. It is instead formed by subwords, which are strings from which words are formed. In this work, a method called byte-pair encoding (Sennrich, Haddow, and Birch 2016) is used.

12 This is likely to hold only if there is a large enough amount of data in the language used to extend the pre-training corpus (English thus being the common choice) and if the languages are not very different from each other.

3.2.2 GPT-style

The GPT-style architectures use only a decoder and are pre-trained using a language modelling task which typically consists of, given a span of tokens, predicting the token that is most likely to follow.

The GPT model we experiment with is GPorTuguese-2.[13] As before, both English and Portuguese texts have been included in the pre-training of the model. The authors took the GPT-2 small model[14] and performed additional pre-training on 1 GB of the Portuguese Wikipedia. It has a vocabulary of 50,257 subwords,[15] 12 layers, and 12 attention heads, for a total of 124.4 million parameters.

Fine-tuning on the authorial style attribution task is done in a similar way to that used on the previous model. The model is extended with an extra layer, the classification head, which is a fully connected layer that takes the output of the language model and outputs the author. The weights of this layer, and of the underlying GPorTuguese-2 language model, are adjusted during fine-tuning.

3.3 Experimental results

The training and testing data set splits are formed by taking, from each document, a randomly chosen 90% of the lines for training and the remaining 10% for testing. Thus, all documents are represented in the training set and in the testing set, in a proportion roughly matching their proportion in the full corpus.[16]

Assigning authorial style and assigning time period (century) are run as separate experiments. For authorial style classification each document is associated with its author (83 classes), and for time period classification each document is associated with the century of its publication (6 classes).

The baseline classifier works at the document level. Each training instance is composed by 90% of the lines of the original document and each testing instance by the remaining 10%. The architectures of the neural classifiers limit the length of the input to 250 words for RoBERTa and 500 words for GPorTuguese-2. As such,

13 https://huggingface.co/pierreguillou/gpt2-small-portuguese

14 GPT-2 (Radford et al. 2019) is the successor to GPT. Much larger than its predecessor, it has 1.5 billion parameters and was pre-trained on 8 million web pages. In this work a much reduced version of it, called GPT-2 small, is used.

15 Like with RoBERTa, byte-pair encoding is used for the vocabulary.

16 Splitting by lines should approximate splitting by words, is easier, and ensures that sentences are not cut short. We have not experimented with balancing the data set as it would require either greatly under-sampling the common classes or greatly over-sampling the rare classes.

instead of working at the document level, the neural classifiers work at the level of the lines in the document. Each line in the training data set, up to the cutoff length, is a training instance. For testing, only the first words in the test instance, up to the cutoff length, are used for classification.

The neural models involve a certain amount of randomness in the process, such as in the initialisation of the weights in the network. To smooth out the variations caused by this, the results for RoBERTa and GPorTuguese-2 are the average of three runs.

Table 5 summarises the results, showing the accuracy and macro-F_1 score[17] of each system on the two tasks. Both neural models outperform the SVM baseline by a large margin and GPorTuguese-2, the larger model, outperforms RoBERTa. This is in line with what has been commonly reported in the literature for various tasks, where deep neural approaches outperform other techniques and where, as long as there is enough data, larger models perform better than smaller models.

Note that GPorTuguese-2 falls behind RoBERTa in terms of macro-F_1 but not in accuracy, for the task of assigning century. A plausible explanation is that GPorTuguese-2 is over-fitting the data, tending more heavily towards the most common classes (the 19th and 20th centuries), a choice that can lead to an inflated accuracy but is penalised by the F_1 metric.

Table 5: Experimental results.

(a) assigning authorial style		
System	**Accuracy**	**Macro-F_1**
baseline	0.7500	0.5367
RoBERTa	0.8448	0.7346
GPorTuguese-2	0.9036	0.8505
(b) assigning century		
System	**Accuracy**	**Macro-F_1**
baseline	0.7644	0.6827
RoBERTa	0.8803	0.8525
GPorTuguese-2	0.8883	0.8370

17 The F_1 is the harmonic mean of precision and recall. Macro-F_1 means that F_1 is calculated for each class and the results averaged, giving equal importance to each class.

3.3.1 A remark on computation time

The neural models clearly outperform the baseline. It is worth noting, though, that the amount of compute they employ is orders of magnitude higher. Each fine-tuning run of RoBERTa takes around 3 hours, while each fine-tuning run of GPorTuguese-2 takes close to 6 hours, and working with these architectures is only feasible with GPU hardware support.[18] A training run of the baseline takes only 2 minutes when assigning authorial style, and 30 seconds when assigning century, and does not require a GPU.

4 Conclusion

This chapter presented how PORTULAN CLARIN, with the support of Camões I.P., has contributed to enhancing the availability of Portuguese literary corpora for research by developing BDCamões, a novel corpus of complete literary texts, from various genres and authors, covering a wide time span.

As mentioned in Section 2.3, the construction of the corpus is an ongoing work and the collection will keep growing as Camões I.P. gathers more texts and converts them into their digital versions.

To showcase an application of BDCamões in the development of language technology tools, we also presented an experiment in authorial style attribution where several systems, at different levels of complexity and performance, were quickly built by using this corpus and off-the-shelf software. This experiment in authorial style attribution was partly intended as an inspiring example of an application of BDCamões in the development of language technology tools.

The GPT-based version of this tool is being integrated into the PORTULAN CLARIN Workbench[19] as the LX-AuthorialStyle online service[20] – see Figure 4 for a screenshot of the current in-development interface. This tool joins a range of

18 We used a single NVidia GeForce RTX 2080 with 12 GB.

19 The PORTULAN CLARIN workbench consists of a number of language processing services based on a large body of research work contributed by different authors and teams, which continues to grow and is acknowledged here: Barreto et al. (2006); Branco et al. (2010); Cruz, Rocha, and Cardoso (2018); Veiga, Candeias, and Perdigão (2011); Branco and Henriques (2003); Branco et al. (2011); Branco and Nunes (2012); Silva et al. (2009); Branco et al. (2014); Rodrigues et al. (2016); Branco and Silva (2006); Rodrigues et al.(2020); Costa and Branco (2012); Santos et al. (2019); Miranda et al. (2011).

20 https://portulanclarin.net/workbench/lx-authorialstyle/

other language processing services that PORTULAN CLARIN makes available to its users, as detailed in Gomes et al. (2022) of this volume.

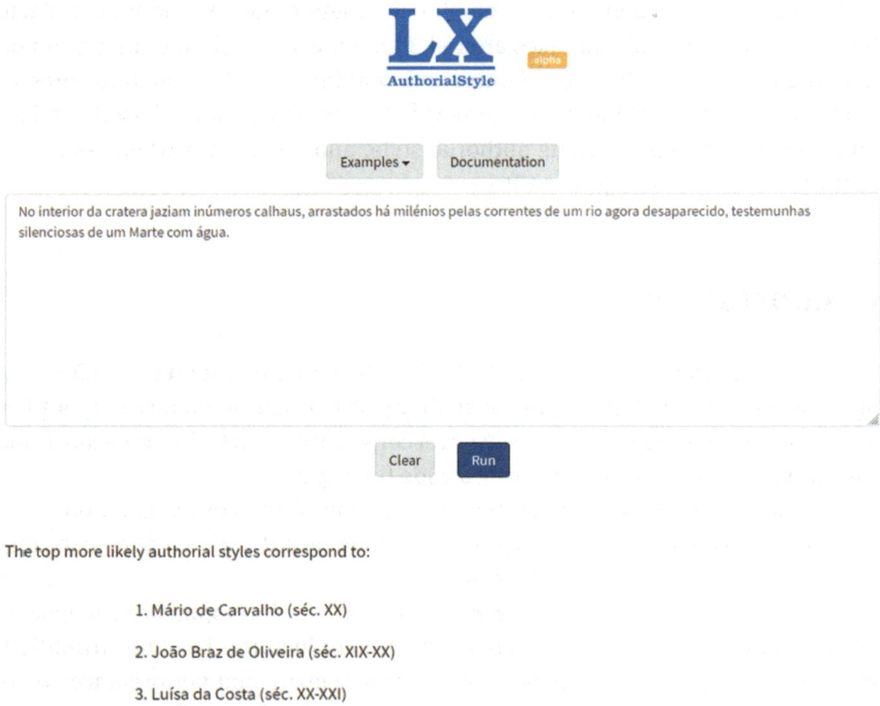

Figure 4: Screenshot of LX-AuthorialStyle service in the PORTULAN CLARIN Workbench.

We plan to extend the experiments presented here, on the task of authorial style attribution, to the different task of authorship verification, by means of which two given texts are checked to ascertain whether they have been authored by the same person, and is not restricted to a pre-defined set of authors. While the task of authorship verification has an important application for Linguistic Forensics, we expect that the current functionality of authorial style attribution now presented, based on a set of well-known, prominent historic Portuguese literary authors, may also be interesting for the general public (e.g., "write a text and find which author you are more similar to", "complete a given text according to the style of an given author", etc.) and contribute to demonstrating the role of the research infrastructure for the advancement of the science and technology of language.

Funding: This work was partially supported by PORTULAN CLARIN – Research Infrastructure for the Science and Technology of Language, funded by Lisboa 2020, Alentejo 2020 and FCT – Fundação para a Ciência e Tecnologia under the grant PINFRA/22117/2016.

Bibliography

Barreto, Florbela, António Branco, Eduardo Ferreira, Amália Mendes, Maria Fernanda Nascimento, Filipe Nunes & João Silva. 2006. Open resources and tools for the shallow processing of Portuguese: The TagShare project. *In Proceedings of the 5th International Conference on Language Resources and Evaluation (LREC)*, 1438–1443.

Branco, António, Sérgio Castro, João Silva & Francisco Costa. 2011. CINTIL DepBank handbook: Design options for the representation of grammatical dependencies. Technical Report DI-FCUL-TR-2011-03, University of Lisbon.

Branco, António, Francisco Costa, João Silva, Sara Silveira, Sérgio Castro, Mariana Avelãs, Clara Pinto & João Graça. 2010. Developing a deep linguistic databank supporting a collection of treebanks: the CINTIL DeepGramBank. *In Proceedings of the 7th International Conference on Language Resources and Evaluation (LREC)*, 1810–1815.

Branco, António & Filipe Nunes. 2012. Verb analysis in a highly inflective language with an MFF algorithm. *In Proceedings of the 11th International Conference on the Computational Processing of Portuguese (PROPOR)*, Lecture Notes in Artificial Intelligence no. 7243, 1–11. Springer.

Branco, António, João Rodrigues, João Silva, Francisco Costa & Rui Vaz. 2014. Assessing automatic text classification for interactive language learning. *In Proceedings of the IEEE International Conference on Information Society (iSociety)*, 72–80.

Branco, António & Tiago Henriques. 2003. Aspects of verbal inflection and lemmatization: Generalizations and algorithms. *In Proceedings of XVIII Annual Meeting of the Portuguese Association of Linguistics (APL)*, 201–210.

Branco, António, Amália Mendes, Paulo Quaresma, Luís Gomes, João Silva & Andrea Teixeira. 2020. Infrastructure for the science and technology of language PORTULAN CLARIN. *In Proceedings of the 1st International Workshop on Language Technology Platforms (IWLTP 2020)*, 1–7.

Branco, António & João Silva. 2006. A suite of shallow processing tools for Portuguese: LX-Suite. *In Proceedings of the 11th European Chapter of the Association for Computational Linguistics (EACL)*, 179–182.

Branco, António, João Silva, Andreia Querido & Rita de Carvalho. 2015. CINTIL DependencyBank PREMIUM handbook: Design options for the representation of grammatical dependencies. Technical Report DI-FCUL-TR-2015-05, University of Lisbon.

Castro, Ivo. 2015. Formação da língua portuguesa. In Eduardo Raposo, Fernanda Bacelar, Antónia Mota, Luísa Segura & Amália Mendes (eds.), *Gramática do português*, 7–13. Fundação Calouste Gulbenkian.

Cohen, Rip. 2003. *500 cantigas d'amigo: Edição crítica / critical edition*. Campo das Letras.

Costa, Francisco & António Branco. 2012. Aspectual type and temporal relation classification. *In Proceedings of the 13th Conference of the European Chapter of the Association for Computational Linguistics (EACL)*, 266–275.
Cruz, André Ferreira, Gil Rocha & Henrique Lopes Cardoso. 2018. Exploring Spanish corpora for Portuguese coreference resolution. *Fifth International Conference on Social Networks Analysis, Management and Security (SNAMS)*, 290–295.
Devlin, Jacob, Ming-Wei Chang, Kenton Lee & Kristina Toutanova. 2019. BERT: Pre-training of deep bidirectional transformers for language understanding. *In Proceedings of the 2019 Conference of the North American Chapter of the Association for Computational Linguistics (NAACL)*, 4171–4186.
Galves, Charlotte. 2018. The Tycho Brahe corpus of historical Portuguese. *Linguistic Variation* 18 (1): 49–73.
Gomes, Luís, Ruben Branco, João Silva & António Branco. 2022. Open and inclusive language processing: Language processing services by PORTULAN to meet the widest needs of CLARIN users. In Darja Fišer & Andreas Witt (eds.), *CLARIN. The Infrastructure for Language Resources*. Berlin: deGruyter.
Grilo, Sara, Márcia Bolrinha, João Silva, Rui Vaz & António Branco. 2020. The BDCamões collection of Portuguese literary documents: a research resource for Digital Humanities and Language Technology. *In Proceedings of the 12th International Conference on Language Resources and Evaluation (LREC)*, 849–854.
Généreux, Michel, Iris Hendrickx & Amália Mendes. 2012. A large Portuguese corpus on-line: cleaning and preprocessing. *In Proceedings of the International Conference on Computational Processing of the Portuguese Language (PROPOR)*, 113–120.
Liu, Yinhan, Myle Ott, Naman Goyal, Jingfei Du, Mandar Joshi, Danqi Chen, Omer Levy, Mike Lewis, Luke Zettlemoyer & Veselin Stoyanov. 2019. RoBERTa: A robustly optimized BERT pretraining approach. *arXiv preprint arXiv:1907.11692*.
Marneffe, Marie-Catherine de, Timothy Dozat, Natalia Silveira, Katri Haverinen, Filip Ginter, Joakim Nivre & Christopher Manning. 2014. Universal Stanford dependencies: A cross-linguistic typology. *In Proceedings of the 9th International Conference on Language Resources and Evaluation (LREC)*, 4585–4592.
Martins, Ana Maria. 1999. Ainda "os mais antigos textos escritos em português": Documentos de 1175 a 1252. In Isabel Hub Faria (ed.), *Lindley Cintra: Homenagem ao Homem, ao Mestre e ao Cidadão*, 491–534. Cosmos.
Miranda, Nuno, Ricardo Raminhos, Pedro Seabra, Joao Sequeira, Teresa Gonçalves & Paulo Quaresma. 2011. Named entity recognition using machine learning techniques. *In Proceedings of the 15th Portuguese Conference on Artificial Intelligence (EPIA)*, 818–831.
Ortiz Suárez, Pedro Javier, Benoî Sagot & Laurent Romary. 2019. Asynchronous pipeline for processing huge corpora on medium to low resource infrastructures. *In Proceedings of the 7th Workshop on the Challenges in the Management of Large Corpora (CMLC-7)*.
Pedregosa, Fabian, Gaël Varoquaux, Alexandre Gramfort, Vincent Michel, Bertrand Thirion, Olivier Grisel, Mathieu Blondel, Peter Prettenhofer, Ron Weiss, Vincent Dubourg, Jake Vanderplas, Alexandre Passos, David Cournapeau, Matthieu Brucher, Matthieu Perrot & Édouard Duchesnay. 2011. Scikit-learn: Machine learning in Python. *Journal of Machine Learning Research* 12: 2825–2830.
Radford, Alec, Karthik Narasimhan, Tim Salimans & Ilya Sutskever. 2018. Improving language understanding by generative pre-training. OpenAI blog. https://openai.com/blog/language-unsupervised/.

Radford, Alec, Jeffrey Wu, Rewon Child, David Luan, Dario Amodei & Ilya Sutskever. 2019. Language models are unsupervised multitask learners. OpenAI blog. https://openai.com/blog/better-language-models/.

Rodrigues, João, Francisco Costa, João Silva & António Branco. 2020. Automatic syllabification of Portuguese. *Revista da Associação Portuguesa de Linguística*, vol. 1.

Rodrigues, João, António Branco, Steven Neale & João Silva. 2016. LX-DSemVectors: Distributional semantics models for the Portuguese language. *In Proceedings of the 12th International Conference on the Computational Processing of Portuguese (PROPOR'16)*, 259–270.

Santos, Rodrigo, João Silva, António Branco & Deyi Xiong. 2019. The direct path may not be the best: Portuguese-Chinese neural machine translation. *In Proceedings of the 19th Portuguese Conference on Artificial Intelligence (EPIA)*, 757–768.

Sennrich, Rico, Barry Haddow & Alexandra Birch. 2016. Neural machine translation of rare words with subword units. *In Proceedings of the 54th Annual Meeting of the Association for Computational Linguistics (ACL)*, 1715–1725.

Silva, João, António Branco, Sérgio Castro & Ruben Reis. 2009. Out-of-the-box robust parsing of Portuguese. *In Proceedings of the International Conference on the Computational Processing of Portuguese (PROPOR)*, 75–85.

Vaswani, Ashish, Noam Shazeer, Niki Parmar, Jakob Uszkoreit, Llion Jones, Aida Gomez, Łukasz Kaiser & Illia Polosukhin. 2017. Attention is all you need. *Advances in Neural Information Processing Systems*, 5998–6008.

Veiga, Arlindo, Sara Candeias & Fernando Perdigão. 2011. Generating a pronunciation dictionary for European Portuguese using a joint-sequence model with embedded stress assignment. *In Proceedings of the 8th Brazilian Symposium in Information and Human Language Technology*.

Xavier, Maria Francisca. 2016. O CIPM – corpus informatizado do português medieval, fonte de um dicionário exaustivo. In Johannes Kabatek (ed.), *Lingüística de corpus y lingüística histórica iberorrománica*, 137–156. De Gruyter.

Eva Hajičová*, Jan Hajič, Barbora Hladká, Jiří Mírovský, Lucie Poláková, Kateřina Rysová, Magdaléna Rysová, Pavel Straňák, Barbora Štěpánková, and Šárka Zikánová

Corpus Annotation as a Feasible and Scientifically Beneficial Task

Abstract: The aim of the present chapter is to demonstrate that a well-designed and theoretically founded corpus annotation contributes significantly to the use of the corpus for testing a linguistic theory and its further development. The data for our analyses come from the Prague Dependency Treebank family, both monolingual Czech and parallel English–Czech, and concern the underlying syntactic level of language description and the annotation of discourse structure. In particular, the case studies concern three research questions, namely (i) the semantic relevance of information structure of the sentence, (ii) the relation between focus sensitive particles and discourse connectives with respect to the semantics of discourse relations, and (iii) the relation between primary and secondary connectives. In the Appendix, some data on measuring inter-annotator agreement are presented and discussed.

Keywords: corpora annotation, inter-annotator agreement, Prague Dependency Treebank, English–Czech parallel data, information structure, focus sensitive particles, discourse connectives

Acknowledgment: Research reported in this chapter was supported by the GACR project "Global Coherence of Czech Texts in the Corpus-Based Perspective" (GA 20-09853S) and by the LINDAT/CLARIAH-CZ project of the Ministry of Education, Youth and Sports of the Czech Republic (LM2018101). It used language resources developed, stored, and distributed by the project LM2018101.

***Corresponding author: Eva Hajičová,** Charles University, Faculty of Mathematics and Physics, Institute of Formal and Applied Linguistics Prague, Czech Republic,
e-mail: hajicova@ufal.mff.cuni.cz
Jan Hajič, Charles University, Prague, Czech Republic, e-mail: hajic@ufal.mff.cuni.cz
Barbora Hladká, Charles University, Prague, Czech Republic, e-mail: hladka@ufal.mff.cuni.cz
Jiří Mírovský, Charles University, Prague, Czech Republic, e-mail: mirovsky@ufal.mff.cuni.cz
Lucie Poláková, Charles University, Prague, Czech Republic, e-mail: polakova@ufal.mff.cuni.cz
Kateřina Rysová, Charles University, Prague, Czech Republic, e-mail: rysova@ufal.mff.cuni.cz
Magdaléna Rysová, Charles University, Prague, Czech Republic,
e-mail: magdalena.rysova@ufal.mff.cuni.cz
Pavel Straňák, Charles University, Prague, Czech Republic, e-mail: stranak@ufal.mff.cuni.cz
Barbora Štěpánková, Charles University, Prague, Czech Republic,
e-mail: stepankova@ufal.mff.cuni.cz
Šárka Zikánová, Charles University, Prague, Czech Republic, e-mail: zikanova@ufal.mff.cuni.cz

https://doi.org/10.1515/9783110767377-024

1 Introduction

The aim of the present chapter is to substantiate our view that corpus annotation on any level of language description, if well designed and theoretically founded, represents an added value to the corpus, and that, in return, it offers a possibility to check the theory and to achieve new observations and theoretical innovations.

The annotation of a corpus is undoubtedly a very difficult and demanding task. Though at present most annotation projects are not fully manual and comprise a pre-annotation phase carried out automatically, the annotation process that would capture also more complicated relations, be they intra- or inter-sentential, necessarily includes a manual part, and as such it is time-consuming and expensive, and also it involves difficulties connected with putting together competent and fully responsible teams of annotators.[1] The latter difficulty may be partially overcome by crowdsourcing but here again the quality of annotations must be thoroughly ensured.

In spite of the above reservations, an annotated corpus, if carefully designed, is a very valuable resource for scientific linguistic studies. It can be used for analyses of single phenomena as well as – using more complex corpora – for research on the interplay of different aspects of language, as we wish to document through several case studies aimed at a linguistic analysis of selected semantic and discourse phenomena.

The remainder of this chapter is structured as follows: in Section 2 we present a brief introduction to the corpora that follow the practice of our annotation-friendly approach, namely the Prague Dependency Treebank (PDT) family and that are available in the LINDAT/CLARIAH-CZ repository (see Hajič et al. 2022).[2] Several case studies resulting from our analysis using the data from this treebank family of corpora, both monolingual Czech and parallel English–Czech, annotated on several levels, are adduced in Section 3.

We have intentionally selected phenomena belonging to the layer of semantic and discourse relations, which have not yet been commonly included into annotation schemes. They are briefly characterized in Section 3.1. One such domain is the information structure of the sentence (its Topic-Focus Articulation, TFA), the annotation of which in our corpora is a component part of the annotation on the underlying syntactico-semantic level (called tectogrammatical). In theoretical linguistics, the relevant discussions concern the issue of the semantic relevance of TFA. We have tested the semantic role of TFA on the data for Czech and English and we present the results in Section 3.2. In Section 3.3 we relate the TFA annotation for

1 One has also to consider the inevitability of annotation mistakes, see Odijk (2022).
2 https://lindat.cz/

a particular class of relations called focalizers with the discourse layer annotation of the so-called discourse connectives, that is, sentence elements that serve for the purpose of the analysis of discourse relations, be they intra- or inter-sentential. The class of discourse connectives is analysed in more detail in Section 3.4, with a special attention paid to the so-called secondary connectives. Besides the information on the corpus data and their analysis, each case study also brings considerations of the impact and consequences of the analysis on the theoretical discussions. Our findings and the contribution of annotated corpora to linguistic theory and to up-to-date methods of natural language processing are summarized in Section 4. Creation of manually annotated text corpora is a complex and resource-demanding task. Ensuring high quality annotations is a crucial issue, which among others involves measuring of inter-annotator agreement. We discuss this topic in the Appendix.

2 Data resources and the annotation scheme

2.1 Data resources

The case studies reported on in the present chapter are carried out using the following data resources: (i) for Czech, the Prague Dependency Treebank – Consolidated 1.0 (PDT-C, Hajič et al. 2020),[3] namely its PDT part with the tectogrammatical annotation containing documents of the total of about 50 thousand sentences annotated, which are also for information structure (Topic-Focus Articulation, TFA) and containing in addition annotation of discourse relations (in a slightly modified style of the Penn Discourse Treebank, Prasad et al. 2008); (ii) for a comparison between Czech and English, the English–Czech parallel corpus Prague Czech–English Dependency Treebank (PCEDT 2.0, Hajič et al. 2012); (iii) for English, the Pennsylvania Discourse TreeBank (PDTB 3.0, Prasad et al. 2019).

The resources under (i) and (ii) are available from the LINDAT/CLARIAH-CZ data repository, both of them under CC-BY-NC-SA licenses, which means they can be freely used for non-commercial research. However, when using the English part of PCEDT there is a necessary additional requirement that the user must own a license for the Penn Treebank 3,[4] because both the text and annotation of Treebank 3 are included in the English part of the PCEDT 2.0 treebank.[5]

---

3 http://hdl.handle.net/11234/1-3185

4 https://catalog.ldc.upenn.edu/LDC99T42

5 In addition, PDT-C is also available to search online, including the relations and examples from this chapter: http://lindat.mff.cuni.cz/services/teitok/pdtc10/index.php.

2.2 The PDT annotation scheme

The PDT annotation scenario is based on the linguistic theory of the Functional Generative Description of Language (FGD) as proposed by Petr Sgall and developed further by his followers (see, e.g., Sgall et al. 1969, Sgall et al. 1986). The description of the language system is conceived of as a multilayered system extending from the lowest, phonological level through the levels of morphology and surface syntax to the highest level of (linguistic) meaning, represented by the underlying syntactic level called tectogrammatical. The representation of the sentence on the two syntactic levels has the form of a dependency syntactic tree, with the verb (Predicate, PRED) being its root. In the surface syntactic tree, the nodes of the tree are labelled with the words (there is a node for each word in the sentence and there are also specific nodes for the punctuation marks) and each word carries an indication of its surface syntactic function in the sentence (such as subject, object, and a kind of adverbial).

The tectogrammatical tree contains only the nodes for the autosemantic lexical units, while the so-called function words (such as auxiliary verbs, prepositions, conjunctions, etc.) are not represented by separate nodes as they are assumed to indicate specific morphological or syntactic features captured within the labels of the autosemantic words. The edges of tectogrammatical trees represent the dependency relations between the governor and its dependent, such as Actor, Patient, Addressee, or some type of temporal, local, or other relations; these labels are called functors. In case of surface deletions, special nodes are established in the tectogrammatical representation and labelled accordingly. The tectogrammatical level conceived as the level of (linguistic) meaning (in the sense that (strictly) synonymous sentences should share their tectogrammatical representation) also comprises the description of the Topic-Focus Articulation (TFA). The primary notion of the TFA description is the notion of contextual boundness, which serves as the basis for the bipartition of the sentence into its Topic and Focus.[6] The nodes of the tectogrammatical tree are ordered from left to right according to the degree of the so-called communicative dynamism they carry; this ordering is a total ordering and leads to the projectivity of the tree.

The annotation scenario of the PDT-family corpora follows the above theoretical approach quite consistently and is illustrated here in Figure 1, using the example of the (rather simplified) tectogrammatical representations of the Czech sentences *Chtěl bych jenom vyměnit velký byt. Pronajímatel však odmítá dát k*

6 It should be noticed that for the time being, the TFA annotation is present only in the PDT part of the PDT-C.

výměně souhlas. [*I would only like to swap a big apartment. But the landlord refuses to give his consent for the exchange.*]. Each node of the tectogrammatical dependency tree is assigned a complex label containing, among other features, one of 67 functors (in our example ACT, PAT, ADDR, RSTR). The label PREC explicitly refers here to the preceding sentence by the expression *však* [*but*] which cannot be linked by a dependency relation to any other element in the sentence structure in which it occurs, and the label CPHR indicates that the given node is a component part of an (idiomatic) phrase (here: *dát souhlas* [*give consent*]). The labels *t*, *c*, and *f* are labels for contextual boundness (*t* for contextually bound non-contrastive, *c* for contextually bound contrastive, and *f* for contextually unbound). There is a label RHEM characterizing the given node (here: *jen* [*only*]) as a representation of a member of a special class of the so-called focalizers (see Section 3.3 below).

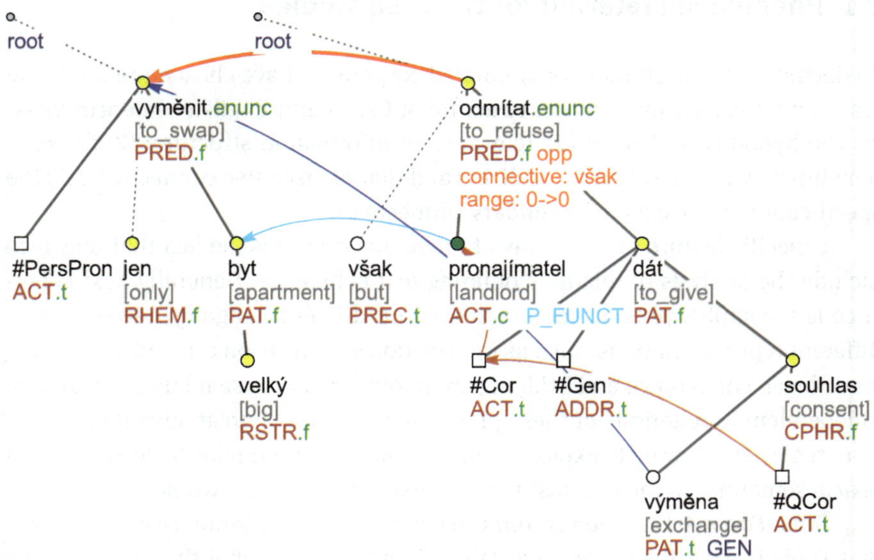

Figure 1: The tectogrammatical representation of sentences: *Chtěl bych jenom vyměnit velký byt. Pronajímatel však odmítá dát k výměně souhlas.* [*I would only like to swap a big apartment. But the landlord refuses to give his consent for the exchange.*].

The PDT scenario also contains an annotation of discourse relations (see Sections 3.3 and 3.4 for details) and of basic coreferential relations; both these kinds of relations are annotated "on" the tectogrammatical trees, which makes it possible to study both the underlying syntactic structure as well as discourse relations in their mutual relationships. The two sentences in Figure 1 are connected by the discourse relation of Opposition, marked in the tree by an orange arrow which is assigned to the discourse connective *však* [*but*]. Furthermore, there are three entity-based relations marked in the Figure: (a) the bridging anaphora between the nodes *byt* [*apartment*] – *pronajímatel* [*landlord*] (bright blue arrow), (b) the textual coreference relation *vyměnit* [*to swap*] – *výměna* [*exchange*] (dark blue arrow), and (c) the chain of grammatical coreference relations *pronajímatel* [*landlord*] – the reconstructed Actor node depending on the verb *dát* [*to give*] – the reconstructed Actor node depending on the word *souhlas* [*consent*] (brown arrows).

3 Case studies

3.1 Phenomena relevant for the case studies

To document the usefulness of annotated corpora we have chosen the following research issues: (1) information structure of Czech and English sentences vis-à-vis the hypothesis of semantic relevance of information structure; (2) the relationship between the class of focalizers and that of discourse connectives; (3) the specification of the class of secondary connectives.

A specific feature of the family of Praguian corpora is the fact that they also include the analysis of relations building text coherence. Generally, text coherence is a complex phenomenon, achieved on different language levels and by different types of relations, such as information structure[7] on the underlying syntactic level, coreference and bridging anaphora, or discourse relations. Mutually independent annotations of these phenomena can be of great advantage to the research: they allow us to explore their interplay and their relation to syntax and lexical semantics in the establishment of text coherence as a whole.

Topic-Focus Articulation is connected with individual sentences: one can say that Topic is what the sentence is "about" and Focus is what the sentence says about its Topic. Nevertheless, the dichotomy of Topic and Focus in each sentence

7 The term *information structure* was originally used by M. A. K. Halliday (see Halliday 1967) and is now used quite commonly to refer to various approaches to this phenomenon. The abundance of terms and approaches was duly observed, for example, by Lambrecht (1996) referring to Levinson's (1983) critical remark. Most of the approaches recognize a basic dichotomy and the terms used are topic–comment, theme–rheme, given–new, background–focus, topic–focus; for a discussion, see also Krifka (2008), In the Praguian approach we subscribe to, as well as in the present chapter, we use the terms Topic and Focus and we reserve the term *information structure* for the linguistic phenomenon as such, rather than its treatment in this or that theoretical framework.

is actually based on the context beyond the sentence boundary, in the previous text. In the Functional Generative Description approach we subscribe to, every autosemantic expression in a sentence (a node in the tectogrammatical tree) is characterized according to its contextual (non-) boundness, independently from its surface position in the sentence and from the syntactic structure. In this way, it is possible to see from the annotation which parts of a sentence are supposed to be deducible from the previous context and which contain the very new information moving the flow of the text forward. Combining this language perspective with other types of annotation (syntactic semantics, syntactic form), many typical language features can be described, such as the characteristic surface position of Topic and Focus, typical syntactic means of topicalization and focalization, or tendencies in the semantics of Topic and Focus.

Another type of text annotation is the analysis of *text coreference*. Within this type of analysis, word chains are labelled so they refer to an identical referent (*a boy – he – Peter – his*). Broader (non-identity) relations between referents are objects of the annotation of *bridging anaphora*, which covers some typical semantic relations between entities (e.g., A WHOLE – A PART, like *a boy – his nose*). These types of the annotation serve as a base, for example, for research on the development of topics in narrative texts.

Besides chains of referents and information structure of sentences, larger text units play a significant role in text coherence, too. They are usually connected by *discourse relations*, that is, relations between discourse arguments (clauses, sentences, clusters of sentences, paragraphs, etc.) carrying specific discourse meaning (e.g., conjunction, generalization, exemplification). The semantics of a discourse relation is often expressed by a discourse connective (e.g., *therefore, the reason is*), but it can be deduced from the context and from other signals in discourse arguments as well (so-called implicit discourse relations). The systematic annotation of discourse relations provides useful data, for example, for research on the differences in the ordering and structuring of thoughts in different text genres (e.g., weather forecast as opposed to reflexive essay). It helps us to see a gradual generation of the structure of a text from small units to large text segments.

Generally, cross-perspective analyses show how the meaning and coherence of the text is built on different language levels. It is very common that research in one language area opens up a set of questions in another one. Thanks to the corpus data and the sophisticated method of multi-level annotation, these questions and hypotheses concerning text coherence can be answered.

3.2 Case study I: The semantic relevance of information structure

3.2.1 Our first case study concerns the fundamental assumption of our approach to the Topic-Focus Articulation, namely the assumption of its semantic relevance (see, e.g., Sgall et al. 1986; Hajičová et al. 1998). One way how to decide on the semantic relevance of a certain linguistic phenomenon is to apply the criterion of synonymy of sentences. Roughly speaking, two sentences are synonymous (in the strict sense) if they share the same meaning. Or, in terms of translation equivalence, translating of a sentence in one language into another language should preserve the meaning of the original sentence, that is, the two sentences should be synonymous. For illustration, two sentences are synonymous (or, in terms of translation, the translation is "correct") if their information structure is the same, leaving other semantically relevant phenomena aside. This is best tested if we take two synonymous sentences in two different languages (one being a translation of the other) and check whether they have the same information structure. If their information structures are not identical then either the translation is not correct or information structure is not semantically relevant. If they are identical, then we can assume that the given phenomenon, information structure in our case, is semantically relevant. We should, of course, keep in mind that when we speak about semantic relevance, this is a relation that occur on the underlying syntactico-semantic level; the given phenomenon, of course, may be expressed in different languages (or even in the same language) by different means of expression in the surface shape of the sentence.

3.2.2 We have tested the hypothesis of semantic relevance of TFA on the example of the appurtenance of local (LOC) and temporal (TWHEN) modifications of verbs (the so-called settings) to the Topic (T) and Focus (F) parts of sentences based on the data from the annotated English–Czech parallel treebank PCEDT.[8] Our data make it possible to compare and evaluate the status of the given modifications from the point of view of TFA, taking into account as well the broader context in which the analysed sentences occur. We have focussed our attention on non-coordinated sentences with (a) node(s) labelled by TWHEN or LOC hanging on the main predicate PRED. With a certain simplification,[9] we assumed that the

8 See Hajičová (2020); a more detailed analysis is presented in Hajičová et al. (2019).

9 This simplification is based on the assumption commonly accepted in studies on information structure both for Czech and for English (see, e.g., Halliday 1967; Sgall et al. 1973; Firbas 1992) that the verb in both languages usually stands on the boundary between Topic and Focus. It is also possible to find some common tendencies in English and Czech concerning the surface word order and prosody, namely the preferred placement of the elements belonging to the Focus at the

borderline between the Topic of the sentence and its Focus is identical with the position of the verb, Topic being placed before the verb and Focus after the verb.

Table 1: The distribution of the position of TWHEN and LOC with respect to PRED.

	TWHEN	LOC
In E. before PRED, in Cz. after PRED	233	67
In E. after PRED, in Cz. before PRED	765	271
Total differences	998	338

We thus had at our disposal total of 42,717 pairs of sentences. In order to study the differences in information structure, we have left aside cases in which the two languages agreed in the position of the given setting, be it in T or in F. We have thus arrived at a total of 1,336 cases of difference (3.12%) relevant for our study, with the distribution given in Table 1.

In order to study the differences in detail, we have randomly chosen 100 sentences for each group with the modification TWHEN and for the group where LOC is positioned after PRED (in English), while we have analysed all the cases of LOC in the preverbal position (in English).

3.2.3 The results of our analysis can be summarized as follows (the parts of sentences relevant for our discussion are underlined and the verb is printed in bold):

(i) First we excluded the cases in which the differences in the linear order in English as compared to Czech are not given by differences in TFA but rather by other factors, mostly grammatically conditioned. The following situations occurred:

(a) in the English sentence, the TWHEN is expressed by a short adverb and is placed immediately after the verb; in Czech, such an adverb is placed before the verb; in both languages, the TWHEN modification should be considered as a part of the Topic:

end of the sentence (so-called *end-focus*), and the placement of the intonation centre on the last element of the Focus. For a systematic account of the relationship between information structure and prosody, see, for example, Steedman (2000).

(1) E.: *In national over-the-counter trading, the company* ***closed*** *yesterday at $23.25 a share, down 25 cents.*
Cz.: *Při celostátním mimoburzovním obchodování společnost včera* ***uzavřela*** *na 23,25.*

(b) in the English sentence, the TWHEN or LOC is expressed by a short adverb and placed at the end of the sentence; the short form of the modification indicates that in the spoken form of the sentence such adverb would not be pronounced with an intonation centre on it and thus it belongs to the Topic; the corresponding Czech equivalent is placed before the verb and as such belongs also to the Topic.

(2) E.: *Democrats* ***had been negotiating*** *with some Republican congressional leaders on a compromise lately.*
Cz.: *V poslední době* ***vyjednávali*** *demokraté s některými čelními republikánskými představiteli Kongresu o kompromisu.*

(3) E.: *Logic* ***plays*** *a minimal role here.*
Cz.: *Logika tady* ***hraje*** *minimální roli.*

(c) If in English the TWHEN or LOC modifications are expressed by a prepositional group or by a dependent clause, their postverbal (or, better to say, final) positions are given by the grammatical rule of so-called end-weight rather than by their appurtenance to the Focus; rather, such modifications belong to the Topic part of the sentence and in Czech they assume the preverbal position.

(4) E.: *The topic never* ***comes up*** *in ozone depletion "establishment" meetings, of which I have attended many.*
Cz.: *Toto téma se na "schvalovacích" schůzích o ozónové díře, kterých jsem navštívil hodně, nikdy* ***neujme***.

(5) E.: *Short-term interest rates* ***rose*** *at the government's regular weekly Treasury-bill auction.*
Cz.: *Na pravidelné týdenní vládní aukci krátkodobých státních obligací* ***vzrostly*** *krátkodobé úrokové míry.*

(d) The word order in the Czech sentence is determined by the tendency in Czech to place the verb in the second position of the sentence, irrespective of its appurtenance to the Topic or to the Focus; this tendency is responsible for the placement of the TWHEN or LOC after the verb in the Czech sentences, whereas while it is placed in the Topic position in English.

(6) E.: *In an interview, Pemberton Hutchinson, president and chief executive,* ***cited*** *several reasons for the improvement: higher employee productivity and "good natural conditions" in the mines, as well as lower costs for materials, administrative overhead and debt interest.*
Cz.: *Prezident a výkonný ředitel Pemberton Hutchinson* ***jmenoval*** *v rozhovoru několik důvodů zlepšení: vyšší produktivitu zaměstnanců a "dobré přírodní podmínky" v dolech, stejně jako nižší cenu materiálu, administrativní režii a úroky z úvěrů.*

(e) In some cases, the word order position of the given modification is determined by the grammatical surface word order rules in Czech or in English (see the position of the subject before the verb in English in examples (7) and (8) with local modifications and (9) with a temporal modification) and the use of a special *there*-construction, likewise due to grammatical surface word order, in (10) and (11).

(7) E.: *A tractor, his only mechanized equipment,* ***stands*** *in front of the pigsty.*
Cz.: *Před prasečím chlívem* ***stojí*** *traktor, jeho jediné mechanizované zařízení.*

(8) E.: *The following issues* ***were*** *recently* ***filed*** *with the Securities and Exchange Commission.*
Cz.: *U Komise pro regulaci prodeje cenných papírů* ***byly*** *v poslední době* ***zaregistrované*** *tyto emise.*

(9) E.: *But losers* ***were spread*** *in a broad range by the end of the session.*
Cz.: Ale koncem burzovního dne ***se rozšířily*** *řady těch, co ztratili.*

(10) E.: *There* ***was*** *no new-issue activity in the derivative market.*
Cz.: *Na trhu odvozených cenných papírů* ***nebyla*** *vyvíjena žádná nová emisní aktivita.*

(11) E.: ***There is,*** *after all, big money in environmentalism.*
Cz.: *V životním prostředí* ***jsou*** *přece jen velké peníze.*

As can be seen from the examples, the tendencies stated above have been observed for both the modification TWHEN and LOC.

(ii) After the elimination of sentences which would seemingly contradict to our thesis on the preservation of information structure in equivalent sentences, but for which a plausible explanation for the difference could be found, we are still faced with a number of examples containing the modifications of time or location, for which such an explanation was difficult to find. In the original English sentence the given modification was in the postverbal position, and in the corresponding Czech counterpart in the preverbal position, see examples (12) through (16); this also occurred the other way round, whereby in the English original the modification was in the preverbal position and in the Czech counterpart the corresponding expression was in the postverbal position; see (17) and (18).

(12) E.: *Coke* ***introduced*** *a caffeine-free sugared cola based on its original formula in 1983.*
Cz.: *Společnost Coke v roce 1983* ***uvedla*** *na trh bezkofeinovou slazenou kolu založenou na původní receptuře.*

(13) E.: *He* ***turned*** *himself in to authorities in New York earlier this year.*
Cz.: *Na začátku tohoto roku se* ***obrátil*** *na úřady v New Yorku.*

(14) E.: *Most stock-market indexes* ***were hitting*** *all-time highs at around the time of the poll.*
Cz.: *V době okolo výzkumu* ***dosahovala*** *většina indexů akciového trhu rekordních výšin.*

(15) E.: *The citation* ***was misstated*** *in Friday's edition.*
Cz.: *V pátečním vydání* ***byla*** *tato citace* ***uvedena*** *chybně.*

(16) E.: *Each* ***has*** *an equal vote at the monthly meetings.*
Cz.: *Na měsíčních schůzích* ***mají*** *všichni stejný hlas.*

(17) E.: *About 20,000 years ago the last ice age* ***ended.***
Cz.: *Poslední doba ledová* ***skončila*** *asi před 20000 lety.*

(18) E.: *Only twice since the 1960s* ***has*** *annual gross domestic product growth here* ***fallen*** *below 5% for two or more consecutive years.*
Cz.: *Roční nárůst hrubého domácího produktu zde* ***spadl*** *pod 5 % během dvou nebo více po sobě jdoucích let pouze dvakrát od šedesátých let.*

Some of these differences can be explained by a possible contrastive understanding of the given modification in the Topic which is comparable to the contrastive interpretation of Focus, be it in Czech, as in (18) or in English, as in (19). Such an explanation might be plausible due to the fact that elements in Focus are, by default, accompanied by a certain shade of contrast.[10]

(19) E.: *But* ***we're . . . going to be*** *in the exact same situation <u>next year</u>.*
Cz.: *Ale <u>příští rok</u>* ***budeme*** *. . . v naprosto stejné situaci.*

Analysing the corpus data we have, of course, considered also a broader context in which the sentences occur. However, even the context sometimes has not helped to decide whether the given modification belongs to the Topic or to the Focus, see, for example, (20) and its preceding context in (21).

(20) E.: *The year* ***was misstated*** *<u>in Friday's editions</u>.*
Cz.: *<u>V pátečním vydání</u>* ***byl*** *rok* ***uveden*** *chybně.*

(21) E.: *QUANTUM CHEMICAL Corp.'s plant in Morris, Ill., is expected to resume production in early 1990.*
Cz.: *Očekává se, že továrna SPOLEČNOSTI QUANTUM CHEMICAL Corp. v Morrisu ve státě Illinois obnoví na počátku roku 1990 svou výrobu.*

3.2.4 Conclusions and summary. The aim of our analysis was to use the annotated data of the English–Czech parallel corpus PCEDT in order to test the plausibility of the hypothesis that information structure of the sentence is semantically relevant. The information we have used involved (i) the (underlying syntactic) dependency relations (underlying sentence structure) of temporal and local modifications of the PREDICATE and (ii) the position of the PREDICATE in this structure. In the discussion of the examples we also took into consideration the position of the modifications concerned in the surface shape of the sentence. Out of a total of 42,717 sentences containing one of the relevant modifications, there were 1,336 sentences which differed in the position of these modifications with respect to the PREDICATE (998 with temporal and 338 with local modifications); these sentences were suspicious for the disagreement in the information structure in English and in Czech. However, after a closer inspection of these suspicious cases we have seen that most of the differences were accounted for differences between the two languages other than information structure (mostly by surface grammatical rules). Nevertheless, even though we have taken also a broader context into consideration, there is a small group of sentences which still

10 For a contrastive interpretation of Focus as a choice of alternatives, cf. Rooth (1985). For the notion and interpretation of contrastive Topic, cf., for example, Büring (2016).

require a more detailed analysis, perhaps from the translation point of view. One has to take into account that in a parallel corpus, only the "source" part of it is original; the other is a translation, which may be influenced by the translator's subjective considerations, or even misunderstandings or mistakes. In any case, the annotation of the data was an extremely useful resource for testing the initial theoretical hypothesis.

3.3 Case study II: Focussing particles and discourse connectives

3.3.1 Focussing particles are a fairly limited set of words emphasizing that part of the sentence that is in their semantic "scope".[11] According to their lexical meaning, they may be categorized into several subclasses. For instance Quirk et al. (1972: 431–438) define (i) restrictive adjuncts, with which what is being communicated is restricted to a part that is focused; these are further divided into two groups: exclusives (*alone, exactly, exclusively, just, merely, only, solely*) and particularizers (*especially, chiefly, largely, mainly, mostly, at least, in particular*); and (ii) additive adjuncts, with which the focused part is an addition (*again, also, even, nor, similarly, too, as well*). In Czech (e.g., Komárek 1979), a further subclass of temporal particles is distinguished (*už* [*already*], *teprve* [*yet*]) (see Nekula 1995: 362).

The specific function of these particles from the point of view of the bipartition of the sentence into theme and rheme (Topic and Focus) was noted first by Firbas (1957), who later called them "rhematizers". A detailed analysis of this function of focalizers is presented, for example, in Hajičová (1995) and Hajičová (2010). Some focalizers (especially *only, too*) have been also studied from the pragmatic and formal semantic point of view as presupposition triggers (Rooth 1992; Krifka 2006).

3.3.2 The analysis of selected focalizers *also*, *only*, *even*, and their Czech counterparts [*také/rovněž/též/zároveň*] for *also*, [*jen/jenom/pouze*] for *only*, and [*dokonce*] for *even*, based on the data from the English–Czech parallel corpus PCEDT (Hajič et al. 2012) indicates that the interpretation of the semantic scope of these particles is highly dependent on the previous context and in several respects these particles have an important influence on the interpretation of discourse relations. Further analyses (e.g., Mladová 2008; Štěpánková 2014) demonstrate that focaliz-

11 Also called focussing adjuncts, rhematizers, focussing adverbials, emphasizing particles, focus sensitive particles, focussing particles, focalizers, etc.

ers have some similar properties to conjunctions, which again indicates their possible effect on discourse relations. These observations have led us to formulate the following research question: In which respects may the selected focalizers be said to function in a discourse as discourse connectives?

3.3.3 For our analysis, we have made use of the following features of the annotated data: (i) underlying syntactic relations captured on the tectogrammatical level of PDT (see above, Section 2.2); on this level, the focalizers are given the functor RHEM and are assigned their position in the tree according to their assumed semantic scope; (ii) discourse relations.

As for discourse relations, the annotation in both of these corpora is based on the Penn Discourse Treebank (PDTB) style. A discourse relation is understood to hold between two Arguments, Arg1 and Arg2, which roughly speaking are segments (adjacent sentences or in some cases between clauses within compound sentences) including a verb as its core. The following types of relations are relevant for our discussion:

(a) Explicit relation – discourse relation expressed by an explicit discourse connective, as in (22); explicit relations manifested by a more complex expression are marked as a separate category (AltLex).
(b) Implicit relation – a certain discourse relation can be inferred but cannot be identified to be expressed by an explicit discourse connective; each Implicit relation is marked with an assumed connective, as in (23).
(c) EntRel – a discourse relation given by a coreference relation between entities that are a part of Arg1 and Arg2, as in (24).
(d) NoRel – no discourse relation between Arg1 and Arg2 can be recognized, as in (25).
(e) Hypophora: a new type of coherence relation for Question–Answer pairs, where one argument (commonly Arg1) expresses a question and the other argument (commonly Arg2) provides an answer. As with EntRel, no explicit or implicit connective is identified and annotated.

(22) *"We've had a few bombs," admits Mr. Peters.* ***<Explicit>*** ***"But*** *by and large this company has only been profitable."*

(23) *The magnitude of the exchange's problems may not become known for some time because of Lloyd's practice of leaving the books open for three years to allow for the settlement of claims.* ***<Implicit=thus>*** *Lloyd's only recently reported its financial results for 1986.*

(24) *This Toronto closed-end fund cut the annual dividend on its Class A common shares to one Canadian cent from 10 Canadian cents.* <**EntRel**> *The fund invests mainly in gold and silver bullion.*

(25) *Mr. Bakker said he was guilty of sin but not fraud.* <**NoRel**> *We can only wonder who will be the next lost soul chosen to be America's Celebrity Convict.*

3.3.4 To find out whether, under which conditions, and in which respects focalizers may function in a discourse as discourse connectives, we have chosen four of the most typical representatives of the class of focalizers, namely the lexical items *also*, *only* (and its semantically related counterpart *just*) and *even.* and subjected them to a more detailed scrutiny.

3.3.4.1 In order to find out whether the focalizer *also* may serve as an indicator of a certain discourse relation, we have focussed our attention on cases with *also* assigned the RHEM functor where no Explicit discourse relation was annotated. There were 60 such cases in the PCEDT corpus, which we have studied in relation to the preceding context. The following tendencies have been identified:

(a) In most cases, the Explicit discourse relation of the type Expansion.Conjunction might be assigned; see (26).

(26) *Yesterday's rise in Nekoosa's share price came on volume of 786,700 shares, four times the daily average. According to Dow Jones Professional Investor Report, options trading in Nekoosa was* ***also*** *heavy, ranking only behind International Business Machines Corp. and UAL in volume on the Chicago Board Options Exchange.*

(b) In only a few cases, could the discourse relation EntRel be assigned based on the coreference relation (between the underlined expressions); see (27).

(27) *State Farm Mutual Automobile Insurance Co., the largest home and auto insurer in California, believes the losses from the earthquake could be somewhat less than $475 million in damages it expects to pay out for claims. – State Farm based in Bloomington, Ind, is* ***also*** *the largest writer of personal-property earthquake insurance in California.*

(c) There were also only a few cases where no relation could be recognized between two adjacent sentences; see (28).

(28) *MCI has made hawks out of the upper echelon of AT&T, said T-2 PaineWebber's Mr. Grubman, who said he expected AT&T to become increasingly aggressive in dealing with longtime nemesis. – Julie Amparano Lopey in Philadelphia* ***also*** *contributed to this article.*

3.3.4.2 As for the particle *only*, we considered only the cases annotated as RHEM for the purpose of our analysis. In particular, we have been interested in cases where *only* depends on PREDICATE and is placed before PREDICATE so that it can be assumed that the whole predicative part of the sentence is in its scope. There were 61 such cases. After a closer inspection of these cases, only in 33 of them was a discourse relation found to hold between the sentence with *only* and the preceding sentence; the rest were sentences without such relations. Most relations were of the Implicit type (19 cases), with only 7 of the Explicit type, 5 of the EntRel type, 1 with NoRel type, and 1 Hypophora. A closer look at the Implicit type has indicated that the presence of the focalizer *only* does contribute to a more detailed specification of the relation Expansion in the sense of a level of detail; see (29).

(29) *The magazine Success, however, was for years lackluster and unfocused.* ***Only*** *recently has it been attractively redesigned and its editorial product improved.*

In case of the Implicit relation of Comparison, the presence of the focalizer *only* contributes to the implication of a contrast; see (30).

(30) *For such products as canned vegetables and athletic shoes, devotion to a single brand was quite low, with fewer than 30% saying they usually buy the same brand.* ***Only*** *for cigarettes, mayonnaise and toothpaste did more than 60% of users say they typically stick with the same brand.*

3.3.4.3 As the semantics of the focalizer *only* is very close to that of the focalizer *just*. we have made a comparative analysis of the occurrences of *just* functioning as RHEM. We have focussed on cases where *just*. RHEM depends on PREDICATE and is placed before it, and where some discourse relation was found between this sentence and the preceding one. There were 48 such cases. It is not surprising that *just* is often (in 16 cases) used to add a specific feature to the interpretation of the relation between the two adjacent sentences; see (31) with the Implicit relation of Comparison and (32) with the Implicit relation of Expansion.

(31) *Consolidation has been long overdue. It was* ***just*** *the culture of the industry that kept it from happening.*

(32) *The move, subject to a definitive agreement, is part of a trend by big-city banks that have been buying up credit-card portfolios to expand their business.* ***Just*** *last month, a Bank of New York subsidiary agreed to buy the credit-card operation of Dreyfus Corp.'s Dreyfus Consumer Bank for $168 million, a transaction that is expected to be completed by the end of the year.*

3.3.4.4 The frequency of the occurrence of the particle *even* (irrespective of its position in the sentence) was analysed as a focalizer only 653 times, a frequency that is much lower than that of the focalizer *also* and a little bit lower than that of the focalizer *only*. However, a more striking fact was that in PDTB 3 *even* does not occur as a pure connective: it occurs only as a part of some multiword complex connectives such as *even if, even though, even as, even when*. We have therefore looked in more detail at the Czech translations of this particle to see if the Czech translations in the given contexts may offer a more varied picture. We have found 19 different Czech equivalents of *even*.RHEM, the most frequent of which was *dokonce* (242 times) and *ještě* (113 times).

Having these data at our disposal, we have decided to investigate whether the occurrence of *even*.RHEM translated as *dokonce* may influence the discourse relations, that is, if it may play the role of a true connective. We have focused our attention on the position of *even*.RHEM before the PREDICATE (in non-coordinated constructions) and translated as *dokonce*, which occurred 98 times. Out of this number, there were 65 cases where a discourse relation to the previous sentence was annotated, 54 of which were marked as Implicit relations (32 of the type Expansion.Conjunction, 14 other types of Expansion, and 8 other Implicit); there were 8 Explicit relations (2 of the type Expansion.Conjuction, 4 Comparison.Concession, 1 Comparison.Contrast, and 1 Temporal.Asynchronous), 2 relations were marked as EntRel and 1 as AltLex. None of the Explicit relations was marked by the focalizer *even*; the connectives were *but* (3), *and* (2), *however, still, even then*.

Looking at the Implicit relations in more detail, we have seen that in most cases marked as Expansion, there was a certain degree of gradation involved; see, for example, (33) of Expansion.Conjunction marked as "in fact". The same is true with the relation annotated as Comparison.Concession and marked as "nevertheless" in (34).

(33) *Rival gangs have turned cities into combat zones.* ***Even*** *suburban Prince George's County, Md., reported last week there have been a record 96 killings there this year, most of them drug-related.*

(34) *But that's for the best horses, with most selling for much less.* ***Even*** *when they move outside their traditional tony circle, racehorse owners still try to capitalize on the elan of the sport.*

Our analysis of the interpretation of discourse relations between pairs of sentences wherein the second contains the focalizer *even* has led to a proposal to introduce into the set of connectives the particle *even* for those relations of Expansion (and perhaps also of Comparison) that can be interpreted as Gradation. It should be noted that the type gradation is not among the types of relations recognized by PDTB 3. Such a solution would comply with the treatment applied in the PDT, namely taking *dokonce* as a connective present in the relation of gradation (73 cases in total).

3.3.4.5 Conclusions and summary. In the present case study, we have reported on our analysis of discourse relations between adjacent sentences (taken as discourse arguments) the second of which (Arg2) contained one of the selected particles *also*, *only*, *just*, or *even* in the (underlying syntactic) function of a focalizer (RHEM). All the analysed focalizers participate in a discourse relation, though the particular function of each focalizer may be different. While *only* and *just* specify the discourse relation in several ways, *also* can be considered an explicit "pure" connective. Focalizer *even*, not considered an explicit connective in the data, may be understood as a connective with the meaning of Gradation. The addition of the Gradation relation to the list of discourse relations is supported by the comparative analysis of the English and Czech data and may serve as an argument how annotated parallel data help to check theoretical assumptions.

3.4 Case study III: Secondary connectives

3.4.1 As already shown, the coherence of the text is ensured not only by focalizers, but also by discourse connectives. Discourse connectives are language means that largely contribute to text cohesion and coherence.[12] Generally, connectives are expressions that have a connecting function in the text and at the same time express semantico-pragmatic relations between two text units.

Discourse connectives may be described from several points of view. Formally (in terms of syntactic behaviour), connectives may be divided into intra- and

12 Higher vs. lower level of cohesion as part of multidimensional analysis is presented in Kučera (2022).

inter-sentential expressions. Intra-sentential connectives operate within compound or complex sentences, as in (35) from PDT, whereas inter-sentential expressions connect individual sentences separated from each other by an end signal, most often a full stop, as in (36) from PDT.

Most connectives allow for both intra- and inter-sentential use. Typically, however, one of these uses outweighs the other. For example, in the case of the connective *ale* [*but*], we find mainly the intra-sentential use. According to the PDT data, the connective *ale* occurs intra-sententially in 73% of occurrences. From this point of view, (35) represents a more typical (i.e., more frequent) use of this connective than (36). For more details, see, for example, Jínová (2012), who analyses typical use of intra- and inter-sentential connectives in Czech.

Intra- and inter-sentential functions are sometimes also distinguished terminologically. Hrbáček (1994) uses the term *junctors* for connective means in a compound sentence, while connective means expressing relations between sentence units after the final punctuation mark are referred to as *connectives*. However, in the discourse annotation in PDT, we use the term *discourse connective* in both cases because the difference between them is only formal. The expression fulfils a connective function in both cases, that is, it always expresses a semantico-pragmatic relation between two text units.

(35) Cz.: *Manželka nepracuje,* ***ale*** *stará se o děti.*
E.: *My wife does not work* ***but*** *she takes care of the children.*

(36) Cz.: *Nyní tito skvěle vycvičení vojáci nemají střechu nad hlavou.* ***Ale*** *zdá se, že není vše ztraceno.*
E.: *Now these perfectly trained soldiers do not have a roof to sleep under.* ***But*** *it seems that not all is lost.*

In terms of semantics, we can divide connectives into several groups. The concept used in the Penn Discourse Treebank (Prasad et al. 2007), which also inspired discourse annotation in PDT, defines four main sense groups of relations: Temporal, Contingency, Comparison, and Expansion. It further divides each of them into smaller subgroups. For example, the Comparison class distinguishes between Contrast, Pragmatic Contrast, and Concession.

Most connectives are polysemic and can express various meanings depending on the context, cf. the Czech connective *když* [*if, when*] in (37) and (38) from PDT. While (37) demonstrates the relation of Condition.Contingency, (38) expresses a Temporal relation, specifically Precedence-Succession.

(37) Cz.: ***Když** je někdo opravdu dobrý, tak si poradí.*
E.: ***If** someone is really good then he will find a way.*

(38) Cz.: ***Když** ho na ulici našli zkrvaveného, zavolali policii.*
E.: ***When** they found him bloodied on the street, they called the police.*

If the different senses of a connective in the original language correspond to different connectives in a foreign language, a parallel corpus such as PCEDT may serve well to distinguish or automatically annotate these meanings. For example, the PCEDT corpus contains 187 occurrences of *když* in the Czech part and *if* in the parallel English part, which indicates a relation of Condition. In contrast, 832 uses of *když* in PCEDT correspond to the English connective *when*, which, on the other hand, indicates a Temporal relation. Pairing a polysemic conjunction with its possible equivalents in a parallel foreign language text can thus serve as a basis for automatic annotation of semantico-pragmatic discourse relations in the text. However, for a precise distinction between the individual types of discourse relations, it is always necessary to make manual checks of such annotation.

Discourse connectives can also be analysed according to the degree of their grammaticalization or lexicalization. From this point of view, we can divide the connectives into primary and secondary (M. Rysová and K. Rysová 2014, 2018). This approach is also captured in the annotation of discourse connectives in PDT.

Primary connectives are grammaticalized expressions (e.g., *but, if, because*), while secondary connectives are not (yet) fully grammaticalized structures (e.g, *for this reason, among other reasons, under this condition*). However, the classes of primary and secondary connectives are not strictly separated. We can rather describe connectives as a scale of expressions with various degrees of grammaticalization.

Primary connectives are usually single-word (e.g., *or, but, however*), rarely multi-word expressions (cf. correlative pairs like *either_or*). They do not fulfil the syntactic function of sentence parts and are uninflected. Secondary connectives, on the other hand, form a relatively heterogeneous group of expressions. They tend to have an unstable lexical form, cf. *for this/that reason*, and can often be used in various morphological variants, such as *for this reason – for these reasons*. Syntactically, they have the function of sentence parts or sentence modifiers, but this function is usually weakened. Secondary discourse connectives (unlike primary) often occur with a lexical modification, for example, *the only/basic/main condition is*, further specifying the meaning of discourse relations.

3.4.2 Annotation of primary and secondary connectives was performed on the entire data of the PDT corpus. Initially, it was carried out in part automatically, followed by a detailed manual annotation. The annotation captures 20,255 primary connectives and 1,161 secondary connectives. This demonstrates that the authors of the texts prefer shorter and more grammaticalized forms of connectives to rather variable multi-word structures. The reason for this may lie in the principle of economy in language (for the theory of language economy, see, e.g., Vicentini 2003). Shorter and lexically stable expressions can help the reader better and faster understand the meaning of the text and comprehend the discourse relations within the text units effectively.

The specific behaviour of connectives may also be fruitfully studied in parallel corpora such as PCEDT. This allows us to examine how the individual connectives are used in different languages, whether the type of connective (primary or secondary) in the original language affects its translation into a foreign language, and so on. It is not unusual that a primary connective in one language has a secondary connective as the direct equivalent in the other language. In this way, we can see which languages tend toward the grammaticalization of connectives more than the others – cf., for example, semantically equivalent connectives *instead* in English, *statdessen* in German and *místo toho* [lit. *instead of this*] in Czech. It is also interesting to observe how the primary and secondary connectives are used in translation practice. We can find cases where the original primary connective was translated as a secondary and vice versa even though a direct equivalent of the given connective does exist in the target language, cf. (39) from PCEDT.

The English source text contains the secondary connective *as a result*. However, the translator used the primary connective *proto* [*therefore*] in Czech to express the discourse relation of reason–result even though there is a formally closer equivalent in the form of a secondary connective – *výsledkem je*.

(39) E.: *But despite more than two years of research showing AZT can relieve dementia and other symptoms in children, the drug still lacks federal approval for use in the youngest patients.* ***As a result****, many youngsters have been unable to obtain the drug and, for the few exceptions, insurance carriers won't cover its cost of $6,400 a year.*
Cz.: *Ačkoli po více než dvou letech výzkumy ukazují, že AZT u dětí zmírňuje demenci a další příznaky, tento lék dosud nebyl schválen federálními úřady pro použití u nejmladších pacientů. Mnoho mladistvých* ***proto*** *nemohlo lék získat a pojišťovny, až na několik výjimek, náklady na tento lék ve výši 6400 dolarů za rok nekryjí.*

Secondary connectives like *výsledkem je* [lit. *the result is*] form a specific group of phrases having the same structure (([(Atr)] noun.instr.) Pred [(AuxCop)]). They contain the core noun in the instrumental case which can optionally be modified by an attribute. The phrase can be followed by a subordinate conjunction (typically *že* [*that*]), cf. examples such as *(hlavním) důvodem je, (že)* [*the (main) reason is (that)*] or *(jedinou) podmínkou je, (že)* [*the (only) condition is (that)*]. These structures are annotated on the entire PDT data within the complex annotation of secondary connectives in Czech.

3.4.3 Based on this annotation, we selected a complete list of these structures that appeared in PDT and we further examined them in the parallel PCEDT corpus. Firstly, we searched for the structures automatically, according to the list. Then we sorted the found occurrences manually and dealt only with cases in which the given structure was used in a connective function.

The occurrences found are Czech translations of the English originals. Our main research questions were: (i) whether the original texts contain a similar connective structure as its translation, that is, a form of a non-grammaticalized secondary connective rather than a grammaticalized primary one; and (ii) whether the structures correspond to each other also lexically (we examined lexical variability of secondary connectives). The results of the analysis are summarized in Tables 2 and 3.[13]

Table 2: PCEDT: Secondary connectives with the structure (([(Atr)] noun.instr.) Pred [(AuxCop)]).

Secondary connective	Occurrences in Czech translation	Secondary connective in E. orig.	Primary connective in E. orig.	No connective in E. orig.
důvodem je [the reason is]	16	16	0	0
výjimkou je [the exception is]	3	2	1	0
příkladem je [an example is]	7	4	1	2
podmínkou je [the condition is]	0	0	0	0
příčinou je [the cause is]	0	0	0	0
účelem je [the aim is]	7	5	0	2
důsledkem je [the consequence is]	5	4	0	1
následkem je [the consequence is]	1	0	0	1
výsledkem je [the result is]	47	44	0	3
In Total	86	75	2	9

Concerning the form of a connective, the results demonstrate that the Czech translations reflect the English originals in the majority of cases (in 75 occurrences out

13 The occurrences in the table cover all possible forms of the verb *být* [*to be*]. We use the phrase in the present simple – *důvodem je* [*the reason is*] – as the basic form.

of 86); see (40) where the Czech secondary connective *výsledkem byl* corresponds to the English secondary connective *as a result.*

(40) E.: *After the trading halt in the S&P 500 pit in Chicago, waves of selling continued to hit stocks themselves on the Big Board, and specialists continued to notch prices down.* ***As a result****, the link between the futures and stock markets ripped apart.*
Cz.: *Po přerušení obchodování v Chicagu se na Newyorské burze akcie obchodovaly ještě živěji a brokeři pokračovali ve snižování jejich cen.* ***Výsledkem byl*** *konec propojení trhu cenných papírů a termínových obchodů.*

The cases where the translator used the secondary connective even though the original text contained the primary connective are rare; see (41).

(41) E.: *Mr. Dell attributed the earnings slide to new product delays,* ***such as*** *a laptop scheduled for September that won't be introduced until early November.*
Cz.: *Společnost Dell pokles výnosů připisuje zpoždění v uvádění nových produktů,* ***příkladem je*** *laptop, který měl být uveden v září, ale bude uveden nejdříve na začátku listopadu.*

Table 3: PCEDT: Secondary connectives with the structure (([(Atr)] noun.instr.) Pred [(AuxCop)]) in Czech and their English semantic equivalents.

Czech translations	Original English connectives
důvodem je [*the reason is*]	*among other reasons. another factor was, that's because the rationale is, the reason is, the situation is caused by*
výjimkou je [*the exception is*]	*an/one exception is, except to*
příkladem je [*an example is*]	*an example is, the example of this is, typical is, such as*
účelem je [*the aim is*]	*intended to, its purpose is, the effect is, the idea is*
důsledkem je [*the consequence is*]	*as a result, the consequence is, [subject] results in*
výsledkem je [*the result is*]	*as a result, causing this, it achieved, resulting in, the result:, the result is, so the results, [subject] would result*

In several cases, the English text with an implicit discourse relation was translated into Czech by an additional secondary connective. It means that there was no primary or secondary connective in the original text, but the translator decided to use an explicit connective in Czech; see (42). Apparently, he/she wanted to clarify the given part of the text and make it easier for the reader to understand.

To clarify the semantico-pragmatic relations within the text is the main function of discourse connectives.

(42) E.: *Faced with a similar situation, Paul Volcker let the dollar soar, (though monetary aggregates also grew so rapidly monetarists issued egg-on-the-face warnings of inflation). But this devastated the U.S. manufacturing sector, laying the seeds of protectionism.*
Cz.: *V podobné situaci nechal Paul Volcker dolar vyletět (ačkoli peněžní agregáty také tak rychle rostly, zveřejnili monetaristé trapná upozornění na inflaci). Ale* ***důsledkem byl*** *ničivý dopad na americký výrobní sektor a počátek protekcionismu.*

Concerning the lexical variability of English original connectives, the analysis demonstrated that these connectives were formed by heterogeneous and lexically rather free expressions. The Czech translations such as *důvodem je* [lit. *the reason is*] corresponded to a scale of English original structures such as *the reason is, the situation is caused by, that's because, another factor was, among other reasons, the rationale is*; see (43).

(43) E.: *John Spencer Churchill, a nephew of the late Sir Winston Churchill, former prime minister of Great Britain, isn't that impressed with most name-droppers he meets.* ***That's because*** *they only drop "mere names," says Mr. Churchill.*
Cz.: *Johnu Spenceru Churchillovi, synovci zesnulého sira Winstona Churchilla, bývalého premiéra Velké Británie, většina vychloubačů slavnými známými, s kterými se setkává, moc neimponuje.* ***Důvodem je, že*** *používají "pouhá jména", říká Churchill.*

The list of various lexical forms of the English original connectives that were translated as a single form in Czech is given in Table 3. The results also demonstrate that the same connective in English was translated into Czech in two forms with a slightly different meaning, cf. *as a result* translated as *důsledkem je* [lit. *the consequence is*] as well as *výsledkem je* [lit. *the result is*].

The results of our analysis have shown that the translators very faithfully preserved the types of a connective from the originals. At the same time, the secondary connectives examined demonstrated a high degree of variability (Czech phrases in translation corresponded to a colourful scale of original English expressions).

Although secondary connectives appear in texts with a significantly lower frequency than primary connectives, they have a substantive function in text coherence. Since they usually contain a core word like *podmínka* [*condition*], *příklad* [*example*] or *příčina* [*cause*], secondary connectives have an ability to directly name the semantico-pragmatic type of a discourse relation and thus to better clarify its meaning.

3.4.4 Conclusions and summary. In the present case study, we analysed the cases where the Czech translators used secondary connectives containing a noun in the instrumental and the verb *být* [*to be*], for example, *důvodem je* [*the reason is*]. Subsequently, we described the structures of the original English connective patterns. The results of our analysis have demonstrated that the secondary connective in the English original also predetermined the occurrence of secondary connective in the Czech translation.

At the same time, we wanted to demonstrate that thanks to the discourse annotation of PDT (with a complete annotation of primary and secondary connectives) and thanks to the PCEDT corpus containing a large amount of parallel data, we can better study connectives in various languages, monitor their similarities and differences and complete the characteristics of the group of connectives as a whole.

4 Conclusion

The aim of the present chapter was to document how a corpus annotated on a theoretically sound scenario may serve not only as a rich resource of data for a complex research but also opens new perspectives and helps to formulate reasonable new research questions. To fulfil this purpose, we have adduced three case studies documenting the relevance of corpus annotation for a verification or further development of a theoretical language description. We have chosen phenomena that are in one way or another related to the semantics of sentence structure and to discourse relations. In particular, the analysis of the English–Czech annotated parallel corpus has confirmed the plausibility of the hypothesis that the information structure of the sentence is semantically relevant. A closer look at four members of the class of the so-called focalizers, namely *also*, *only*, *just*, and *even*, has made it possible to specify in more detail some of the discourse relations identified by discourse connectives and to add the relation of Gradation to the established list of discourse relations. The study of secondary connectives has contributed to the overall specification of the class of discourse connectives as a whole.

All the case studies have been based primarily on the annotated parallel English–Czech corpus PCEDT, which has made a comparative evaluation possible. The work with the parallel corpus has also documented that when working with data from parallel corpora, one has to be very careful in drawing conclusions because only one corpus consists of original texts. The other includes translations, which means that the translator might have been influenced by the shape of the original when making structural choices in the translation.

In addition to authentic language material exemplifying the conclusions drawn, the present chapter contains also statistical data supporting these conclusions. It was the intention of the authors to present a collection of good practice examples in treebanking.

Even though we have focussed our attention on the contribution of annotated data to the study of theoretical issues, we have also put equal importance on the technological track: namely the use of annotated corpora in the language technology development area, where such corpora are used as an input for machine learning methods to train various language analysis tools, such as lemmatizers, morphological analysers, POS taggers, syntactic parsers, semantic role labelling systems, or named entity recognizers and linkers.

In this context, we are grateful to the LINDAT/CLARIAH-CZ (formerly LINDAT/CLARIN) research infrastructure for language resources in the Czech Republic, a node of the CLARIN network following all the CLARIN recommendations and standards, which provides data, tools, and services for experimental as well as theoretical studies such as ours: it would be hard to do such research without the resources created and maintained in the infrastructure, such as the PCEDT corpus, or without efficient search tools, such as Kontext[14] or PML-TQ.[15]

Appendix: Annotation agreement

An important part of any corpus annotation project is the evaluation of the annotation quality and consistency. A standard quality check strategy in corpus development is the inter-annotator agreement measurement (IAA). Depending on the nature of an annotation task, there is a range of appropriate measurements widely used in language resources development. Moreover, in the family of Prague treebanks, a repeatedly applied IAA and its subsequent analysis are the main quality check procedures and an efficient way to improve the annotators' performance

14 https://lindat.cz/en/services#KonText
15 https://lindat.cz/en/services#pmltq

and the resulting resource, as well as, eventually, a way to make the instructions for the annotators more precise and effective.[16]

For Prague annotation projects up to 2015, measuring the IAA was thoroughly described and its outcomes compared to other similar annotation projects in Zikánová et al. (2015: 89ff). Although the numbers themselves are not directly comparable across different tasks, as they originate from different agreement measures[17] and different label sets for classification tasks, they convey two important messages, or, in other words, show two tendencies in language data annotation:

First, similar annotation tasks in terms of language level of description (e.g., morphological level, syntactic level) show similar IAA results across languages and projects, implying that these tasks have a similar degree of difficulty; compare Table 4.

Second, the agreement is very high, in fact close to 100% for morphological annotation (around 98%) and it decreases with the increasing level of language description. It is lower for syntactic annotation tasks and for semantic labelling (ranging from 84% to 92%); compare Table 4. This tendency still prevails if we look at the lower consistency numbers in annotation projects outside the scope of a single sentence, the discourse coherence projects. Here, we cross not only the sentence boundary, but also the area of systematic grammatical rules (langue) and move to the field of, mostly non-systematic, communication strategies and genre preferences. The decreasing IAA figures thus do not refer to a decreasing ability to solve an annotation task, but must be rather interpreted as reflecting the increasing difficulty and complexity of the given task, which brings along some new methodological issues.

In a theoretical study on corpora development, we have previously argued that the higher or lower values of IAA in marking discourse phenomena go hand in hand with analysing (and marking) either surface-present cues such as signals of coherence on the one hand, or annotating "directly the meaning", on the other hand (Poláková 2014). If we annotate forms, "anchors", surface devices such as discourse connectives or pronouns (coreferential ties), the agreement and consistency – given a well-designed annotation scheme and trained annotators – is fair. Once we start annotating meaning, that is, implicit coherence relations or association anaphora (bridging), which are based on our world knowledge and

16 Usually, about 10% of the data is annotated independently by two annotators; subsequently, inconsistencies are measured and studied (and solved by an arbiter). In larger annotation projects, this process is repeated in various stages of the annotations, allowing researchers to study the impact of improved annotation instructions and changes in the annotators' proficiency.

17 Mainly plain percentual accuracy, F1 score as a harmonic mean between precision (P) and recall (R), and Cohen's kappa, which also addresses the role of chance agreement.

inference,[18] the marking is typically quite dependent on the annotator's interpretation. Moreover, often more than one interpretation of a given phenomenon are equally relevant, so there is no one "correct" solution.

Table 4: Overview of a selected number of inter-annotator agreement measurements at different annotation layers. Please note that the numbers represent different measures and cannot be simply compared.

Annotation task	Lang.	Agreement
morphology (5,000 tags)	Czech	97 (%)
morphology (54 tags)	German	98.6 (%)
surface syntax (unlabelled structural annotation)	German	92.4 (%)
surface syntax (labelled structural annotation, 25 phrase types and 45 grammatical functions)	German	88.5 (%)
deep syntax (unlabelled structural annotation)	Czech	91 (%)
deep syntax (assigning the type of dependency, 67 functors)	Czech	84 (%)
Topic–Focus Articulation (assigning contextual boundness, 3 values)	Czech	82 (%)
discourse relations (recognizing a presence of an (explicit) inter-sentential discourse relation)	Czech	83 (F1)
discourse relations (assigning one of 23 types to explicit relations)	Czech	77 (%)
discourse relations (assigning one of 23 types to implicit relations)	Czech	60 (%)
textual coreference (recognizing presence)	Czech	72 (F1)
textual coreference (assigning one of 2 types)	Czech	90 (%)
bridging anaphora (recognizing presence)	Czech	46 (F1)
bridging anaphora (assigning one of 9 types)	Czech	92 (%)
genres of documents (20 genres)	Czech	77 (%)

A pilot study for annotation of implicit relations on a small sample of texts (cca 3 x 35 sentences) was conducted and described in Poláková (2015: 146ff) with deliberately fixed places to annotate the relations (between every sentence pair with no explicit connective link present). It resulted in 49.1% in percentual agreement on the type of semantic relation (25 labels) and 58.2% in a more relaxed measure (23 labels). The most problematic issue proved to be distinguishing between the relations from the Expansion class (conjunction, specification, etc.) on the one hand and between relations based only on coreference on the other.

In a subsequent, larger project of PDiT-EDA annotation in 2019 (Zikánová et al. 2019; Zikánová 2021), where the locus of an implicit relation was defined more

18 Or, more precisely, as Grosz et al. (1995: 208) put it: "an inference load placed upon the hearer".

loosely, the inter-annotator agreement on recognizing the existence of an implicit relation was 0.54 (F1 score) and the simple percentage agreement on semantic types of relations that both annotators agreed on was 57.7% (with 23 labels).

Let us compare the IAA figures for these "marking-of-meaning" tasks. If we take into account as well as the IAA figures for bridging anaphora, there is a difference in results for individual annotation subtasks. While the subtask of finding/identifying the relation in question (0.46–0.54 in a strict F1 score) seems to be the most difficult part to agree on, there is slightly higher agreement in classification tasks, that is, finding the correct label (here: semantic) for a relation identified by both annotators (57%–92% depending on the number of labels to choose from in the particular annotation task).

We have demonstrated that the agreement numbers in annotation projects that go "beyond the sentence boundary" show a decrease, particularly in the relation identification subtask. However, such a drop is only presumable, given the communicative and not strictly systematic nature of the phenomena in question (as opposed to sentential phenomena) and in fact, an agreement above 80% would be a rather suspicious one and point towards possible shortcomings in an annotation scenario. The examples of implicit discourse relations and bridging anaphora demonstrate where the reliability of a corpus analysis comes close to its limits and where individual interpretation plays a role (cf. also Poláková 2014). We see two ways out, and of course they depend on the purpose that the analysis is supposed to serve. Either, based on the experience gained, the existing methodology can be modified or tightened, in which case an increase in agreement can be expected at the cost of possible loss of some relevant information, or we can give up higher agreement but obtain a more detailed analysis, although this will need to be further processed, especially in terms of consistency.

Bibliography

Büring, Daniel. 2016. (Contrastive) topic. In Caroline Féry & Shinichiro Ishihara (eds.), *The Oxford handbook of information structure*. Oxford: Oxford University Press.

Firbas, Jan. 1957. K otázce nezákladových podmětů v současné angličtině [On the nonthematic subjects in English]. In *ČMF* 39, 22–42 and 165–173.

Firbas, Jan. 1992. *Functional sentence perspective in written and spoken communication*. Cambridge: Cambridge University Press.

Grosz, Barbara J., Scott Weinstein & Aravind Joshi. 1995. Centering: a framework for modeling the local coherence of discourse. In *Computational Linguistics* 21 (2), 203–225.

Hajič, Jan, Eduard Bejček, Alevtina Bémová, Eva Buráňová, Eva Fučíková, Eva Hajičová, Jiří Havelka, Jaroslava Hlaváčová, Petr Homola, Pavel Ircing, Jiří Kárník, Václava Kettnerová, Natalia Klyueva, Veronika Kolářová, Lucie Kučová, Markéta Lopatková, David Mareček, Marie

Mikulová, Jiří Mírovský, Anna Nedoluzhko, Michal Novák, Petr Pajas, Jarmila Panevová, Nino Peterek, Lucie Poláková, Martin Popel, Jan Popelka, Jan Rompoltl, Magdaléna Rysová, Jiří Semecký, Petr Sgall, Johanka Spoustová, Milan Straka, Pavel Straňák, Pavlína Synková, Magda Ševčíková, Jana Šindlerová, Jan Štěpánek, Barbora Štěpánková, Josef Toman, Zdeňka Urešová, Barbora Vidová Hladká, Daniel Zeman, Šárka Zikánová & Zdeněk Žabokrtský. 2020. *Prague Dependency Treebank – Consolidated 1.0 (PDT-C 1.0)*. LINDAT/CLARIN digital library, Institute of Formal and Applied Linguistics (ÚFAL), Faculty of Mathematics and Physics, Charles University, http://hdl.handle.net/11234/1-3185.

Hajič, Jan, Eva Hajičová, Barbora Hladká, Jozef Mišutka, Ondřej Košarko & Pavel Straňák. 2022. LINDAT/CLARIAH-CZ: Where We Are And Where We Go. In Darja Fišer & Andreas Witt (eds.), *CLARIN. The infrastructure for language resources*. Berlin: De Gruyter.

Hajič, Jan, Eva Hajičová, Jarmila Panevová, Petr Sgall, Ondřej Bojar, Silvie Cinková, Eva Fučíková, Marie Mikulová, Petr Pajas, Jan Popelka, Jiří Semecký, Jana Šindlerová, Jan Štěpánek, Josef Toman, Zdeňka Urešová & Zdeněk Žabokrtský. 2012. Announcing Prague Czech-English Dependency Treebank 2.0. In *Proceedings of the 8th International Conference on Language Resources and Evaluation*, 3153–3160.

Hajičová, Eva. 1995. Postavení rematizátorů v aktuálním členění věty [Position of rhematizers in the Topic–Focus articulation]. In *Slovo a slovesnost* 56 (4), 241–251.

Hajičová, Eva. 2010. Rhematizers revisited. In *Linguistica Pragensia* 2, 57–70.

Hajičová, Eva. 2020. K otázce tzv. kulisy ve světle paralelního korpusu [On the so-called "setting" through the lens of a parallel corpus.] In *Jak je důležité míti styl*, 155–164. Prague: Nakladatelství Lidové noviny.

Hajičová, Eva, Jiří Mírovský & Kateřina Rysová. 2019. Ordering of adverbials of time and place in grammars and in an annotated English–Czech parallel corpus. In Marie Candito, Kilian Evang, Stephan Oepen & Djamé Seddah (eds.), *Proceedings of the 18th International Workshop on Treebanks and Linguistic Theories (TLT, SyntaxFest 2019)*, 51–60. Association for Computational Linguistics.

Hajičová, Eva, Barbara Partee & Petr Sgall. 1998. *Topic–Focus articulation, tripartite structures, and semantic content*. Dordrecht: Kluwer Academic Publishers.

Halliday, Michael Alexander Kirkwood. 1967. Notes on transitivity and theme in English: Part 1. In *Journal of Linguistics* 3 (1), 37–81.

Hrbáček, Josef. 1994. *Nárys textové syntaxe spisovné češtiny* [Outline of textual syntax of standard Czech]. Prague: Trizonia.

Jínová, Pavlína. 2012. Nejčastější konektivní prostředky kauzálního vztahu v Pražském závislostním korpusu [The most common connective expressions for causal relations in the Prague Dependency Treebank]. In *Studie z aplikované lingvistiky / Studies in Applied Linguistics* 1, 35–52.

Komárek, Miroslav. 1979. K jednomu funkčnímu rozdílu v soustavě partikulí [On one functional difference in the system of particles]. In *Slovo a slovesnost* 40 (2), 139–142.

Krifka, Manfred. 2006. Association with Focus phrases. In Valerie Molnar & Susanne Winkler (eds.), *The Architecture of Focus*, 105–136. New York: Mouton de Gruyter.

Krifka, Manfred. 2008. Basic notions of information structure. In *Acta Linguistica Hungarica* 55 (3–4), 243–276.

Kučera, Dalibor. 2022. Application of CLARIN Linguistic Tools in Psychological Research. In Darja Fišer & Andreas Witt (eds.), *CLARIN. The infrastructure for language resources*. Berlin: De Gruyter.

Lambrecht, Knud. 1996. *Information structure and sentence form: Topic, Focus, and the mental representations of discourse referents*. Cambridge: Cambridge University Press.
Levinson, Stephen C. 1983. *Pragmatics*. Cambridge: Cambridge University Press.
Mladová, Lucie. 2008. K problematice vztahu rematizátorů a textových konektorů [On the relationship of rhematizers and discourse connectives]. In *Čeština doma a ve světě* 16 (3–4), 126–133.
Nekula, Marek. 1995. Částice. [Particles.] In Petr Karlík, Marek Nekula & Zdenka Rusínová (eds.), *Příruční mluvnice češtiny* [Handbook of Czech], 358–367. Prague: Nakladatelství Lidové noviny.
Odijk, Jan. 2022. CLARIN's support for research into the acquisition of lexical properties. In Darja Fišer & Andreas Witt (eds.), *CLARIN. The infrastructure for language resources*. Berlin: De Gruyter.
Poláková, Lucie. 2014. K možnostem korpusového zpracování nadvětných jevů [On the possibilities of a corpus-based approach to discourse phenomena]. In *Naše řeč* 4–5, 241–258.
Poláková, Lucie. 2015. *Discourse relations in Czech*. Prague: Charles University PhD thesis.
Prasad, Rashmi, Nikhil Dinesh, Alan Lee, Eleni Miltsakaki, Livio Robaldo, Aravind Joshi & Bonnie Webber. 2008. The Penn Discourse TreeBank 2.0. In *International Conference on Language Resources and Evaluation (LREC) 6*. 2961–2968.
Prasad, Rashmi, Eleni Miltsakaki, Nikhil Dinesh, Alan Lee & Aravind Joshi. 2007. *The PDTB 2.0 annotation manual*. Philadelphia: University of Pennsylvania.
Prasad, Rashmi, Bonnie Webber, Alan Lee & Aravind Joshi. 2019. *Penn Discourse Treebank Version 3.0*. University of Pennsylvania, Philadelphia. LDC2019T05. Data/Software, Linguistic Data Consortium, https://catalog.ldc.upenn.edu/LDC2019T05.
Quirk, Randolph, Sidney Greenbaum, Geoffrey Leech & Jan Svartvik. 1972. *A grammar of contemporary English*. London: Longman.
Rooth, Mats. 1985. *Association with focus*. Amherst: University of Massachusetts.
Rooth, Mats. 1992. A theory of focus interpretation. In *Natural language semantics* 1 (1), 75–116.
Rysová, Magdaléna & Kateřina Rysová. 2014. The centre and periphery of discourse connectives. In Wirote Aroonmanakun, Prachya Boonkwan & Thepchai Supnithi (eds.), *Proceedings of the 28th Pacific Asia Conference on Language, Information and Computing*, 452–459. Bangkok: Chulalongkorn University.
Rysová, Magdaléna & Kateřina Rysová. 2018. Primary and secondary discourse connectives: constraints and preferences. In *Journal of Pragmatics* 130, 16–32.
Sgall, Petr, Eva Hajičová & Eva Benešová. 1973. *Topic, Focus and generative semantics*. Kronberg Taunus: Scriptor.
Sgall, Petr, Eva Hajičová & Jarmila Panevová. 1986. *The meaning of the sentence and its semantic and pragmatic aspects*. Dordrecht: Reidel / Prague: Academia Company.
Sgall, Petr, Ladislav Nebeský, Alla Goralčíková & Eva Hajičová. 1969. *A functional approach to syntax in generative description of language*. New York: American Elsevier Publishing Company.
Steedman, Mark. 2000. Information structure and the syntax-phonology interface. In *Linguistic inquiry* 31 (4), 649–689.
Štěpánková, Barbora. 2014. *Aktualizátory ve výstavbě textu, zejména z pohledu aktuálního členění* [Focalizers in the structure of text, especially from Topic–Focus articulation perspective]. (Studies in Computational and Theoretical Linguistics). Charles University: ÚFAL.

Vicentini, Alessandra. 2003. The economy principle in language. notes and observations from early modern English grammars. In *Mots, Palabras, Words* 3, 37–57.
Zikánová, Šárka. 2021. *Implicitní diskurzní vztahy v češtině.* [Implicit discourse relations in Czech]. (Studies in Computational and Theoretical Linguistics). Charles University: ÚFAL.
Zikánová, Šárka, Eva Hajičová, Barbora Hladká, Pavlína Jínová, Jiří Mírovský, Anna Nedoluzhko, Lucie Poláková, Kateřina Rysová, Magdaléna Rysová & Jan Václ. 2015. *Discourse and coherence. From the sentence structure to relations in text.* (Studies in Computational and Theoretical Linguistics). Charles University: ÚFAL.
Zikánová, Šárka, Jiří Mírovský & Pavlína Synková. 2019. Explicit and implicit discourse relations in the Prague Discourse Treebank. In Kamil Ekštein (ed.), *Proceedings of the 22nd International Conference on Text, Speech and Dialogue – TSD 2019*, 236–248. Lecture Notes in Computer Science. Cham: Springer.

Silvia Calamai, Duccio Piccardi, Niccolò Pretto, Giovanni Candeo, Maria Francesca Stamuli, and Monica Monachini

Not Just Paper: Enhancement of Archive Cultural Heritage

Abstract: Oral archives and digital technologies have gone hand-in-hand for a very long time. Both sides benefit from this interdisciplinary junction: technology enhances the preservation and diffusion of oral materials, while exploiting them to develop cutting-edge tools for their treatment. This chapter deals with an Italian instantiation of this mutual relationship: the *Archivio Vi.Vo.* project. Offering innovative solutions concerning metadata, audio restoration, description, and access, Archivio Vi.Vo. aims to build an online platform to host the oral archives from Tuscany. The project is powered by CLARIN-IT, which guarantees its compliance with standards and offers resources for data access and discoverability. Archivio Vi.Vo. has not been built from scratch: it is instead a cross-fertilization of previous initiatives and research projects (e.g., the *Gra.fo* project). Moreover, the chapter presents the related, contemporary work of a multidisciplinary group striving to synthesize a Vademecum for future generations of oral

Acknowledgments: The authors would like to express their gratitude to Paola Baroni (ILC-CNR), Claudia Cervini (Florence), Riccardo del Gratta (ILC-CNR), Paquito Forster Bueno (Fiesole), Lucia Geri (Pistoia), Pamela Giorgi (INDIRE), Laura Landini (UNISI), Sabina Magrini (SABTOS), Prospero Marra (UNISI), Cecilia Valentini (UNISI), Susanna Vannocci (Tuscany Region), Diana Marta Toccafondi (Prato), and Giuseppe Versaci (UNISI).

Silvia Calamai, Università degli Studi di Siena, Dipartimento di Filologia e Critica delle Letterature Antiche e Moderne, Arezzo, Italy, e-mail: silvia.calamai@unisi.it
Duccio Piccardi, Università degli Studi di Siena, Dipartimento di Filologia e Critica delle Letterature Antiche e Moderne, Arezzo, Italy / Università degli Studi di Pavia, Pavia, Italy, e-mail: duccio.piccardi@unisi.it
Niccolò Pretto, Università degli Studi di Padova, Padua, Italy / Institute of Computational Linguistics "Antonio Zampolli", CNR, Pisa, Italy, e-mail: niccolo.pretto@dei.unipd.it
Giovanni Candeo, Institute of Computational Linguistics "Antonio Zampolli", CNR, Pisa, Italy, e-mail: giovanni.candeo@ilc.cnr.it
Maria Francesca Stamuli, Ministero della Cultura – Soprintendenza archivistica e bibliografica della Toscana, Firenze, Italy, e-mail: mariafrancesca.stamuli@beniculturali.it
Monica Monachini, Institute of Computational Linguistics "Antonio Zampolli", CNR, Pisa, Italy, e-mail: monica.monachini@ilc.cnr.it

https://doi.org/10.1515/9783110767377-025

archive researchers. Lastly, a brief list of tentative ideas for future developments of the Archivio Vi.Vo. platform will be presented.

Keywords: digital oral archive, research infrastructures, archival heritage, models for digital preservation

1 Introduction

The application of digital technologies to analogue oral archives demonstrates tremendous benefits from the point of view of accessibility, reusability, and cost reduction for their management, as well as cultural and social inclusion. For this reason, researchers of oral archives have always felt the urge to tap into the latest innovations, while at the same time contributing to novel development processes. Almost contemporaneously with the popularization of the first home computers, Quebecker sociologist Nicole Gagnon (1981–1982) reflected on the usefulness of databanks to improve the structure of, and the accessibility to, oral archives. A few years later, at the end of the 1980s, the Alaskan cross-disciplinary Jukebox project – which involved oral historians and information technologists collaborating for what was probably the first time (Schneider 2013: 302) – worked hand-in-hand with Apple to develop a multimedia workstation showcasing digitized oral archives, transcriptions, and photographs, a project described as "a fantastic jump into space age technology" (Lake 1991: 30).

Fast forward to more recent times, and we observe that the relationship between oral archive projects and technology is still sound and fertile, inspiring several research goals, which can be roughly grouped into two categories. On the one hand, working with oral archives may encourage the envisioning of new technologies for the treatment of oral materials (for a general introduction on the programming of language technologies, see Ljubešić et al. 2022). Software concerning speech transcription is a clear example of this. To name a few, the Origins of New Zealand English project, which dealt with the linguistic analysis of a 1,000-hour oral archive covering the whole history of this variety, led to the development of the LaBB-CAT software, a renowned corpus building and annotation tool (Fromont and Hay 2012). Moreover, a project focusing on the disclosing of the historical archive of the Czech Radio encouraged the creation of speech-to-text software for the Czech and Slovak languages (Nouza et al. 2014) and highlighted the potential of oral repositories in the context of under-resourced idioms (see also Hennelly et al. 2022 for the South African context). Of course, linguistics was not the only field benefiting from this cross-disciplinary encounter. For example, in order to enrich the searchability of the ethnomusicological archive of the Parisian Musée de l'Homme, the DIADEMS project invented novel tools for musicological analysis such as, among others, an automatic instrument classifier (Fillon et al. 2014).

On the other hand, oral archive projects adapted existing technologies (and developed new systems) to conceive innovative ways of experiencing sound materials. The INTIMAL project is a recent straightforward instance of this trend. Through the elaboration of an oral archive concerning the narratives from Colombian Women in the diaspora, INTIMAL created embodied systems of relational listening by exploiting, among other tools, motion capture technologies (Alarcón et al. 2019). Oral archives can also be put to use to draw engaging tourist itineraries. In the context of the augmented cultural heritage paradigm, the Italian Gra.fo project (see below, Section 2) conducted an evaluation of the benefits of using the contents of Tuscan oral archives in an augmented reality mobile application based on spatial technologies (Pozzebon, Biliotti, and Calamai 2016).

Indeed, new technologies also lead to new complexities and hurdles for oral archivists. Digitization processes pose various challenges if we are to avoid bad transactions of information and data loss. In addition, the dramatic diffusion potential of web-based archives entails a renewed attention to legal issues, including authorship, ownership, and privacy (see, e.g., Calamai, Ginouvès, and Bertinetto 2016).

In this chapter, a recent Italian contribution to this international cross-fertilization of ideas and methods between oral archivists, linguists and technologists is presented. The remainder of the text is structured as follows. The technological aspects of the *Archivio Vi.Vo.* project, which aims at building a web infrastructure to host Tuscan oral archives while proposing novel solutions concerning metadata, audio restoration, access, and legal issues, are described in detail in Section 3. In this section, we also substantiate how the outcomes of a regional project can be significantly enhanced in the CLARIN context. Archivio Vi.Vo. is introduced by recounting the development of its predecessor, the Gra.fo project (Section 2), and followed by a short presentation of a related Italian initiative: the building of a Vademecum for the next generations of scholars (Section 4). Lastly (in Section 5), we conclude with some ideas for future extensions of the project goals.

2 Before CLARIN-IT: Oral archives in Tuscany

Rather a long tradition characterizes the research on Tuscan oral archives. As early as the 1980s, Giovanni Contini at the Soprintendenza Archivistica e Bibliografica della Toscana started collecting oral and audio-visual archives focused on the economic and manufacturing history of Tuscany. In 1993 the very first Italian handbook dealing with oral archives, their management, and their description came to light (Contini and Martini 1993). In the same period, still in Tuscany, at Siena University, a close cooperation among researchers in anthropology (Pietro Clemente) and linguistics (Luciano Giannelli) yielded seminal works such as Valeria Di Piazza and Dina Mugnaini's *Io so' nata a Santa Lucia: Il racconto autobiografico di una donna toscana tra mondo contadino e società d'oggi* (1988). The transcription of a very long oral narration by an old Tuscan peasant was prefaced by Pietro Clemente in *Autobiografie al magnetofono* (Autobiographies on the tape recorder) and by Luciano Giannelli in *Il testo come documento di lingua: Problemi di rappresentazione* (The text as a linguistic document: Issues of representation), which offered an unparalleled reflection both on the relationship between written text and oral source, and on how to represent vernacular speech on paper, trying to find a balance between authenticity and readability. This experience is still a reference point for scholars dealing with the transcription of oral sources, no matter what field of knowledge they come from.

It is against this background that in 2007 Pietro Clemente edited (with A. Andreini) the first census of Tuscan oral archives and offered a detailed overview of the huge number of audio cassettes, open reel recordings, and VHS tapes scattered around Tuscany (Andreini and Clemente 2007). The census discovered 124 archives (every single archive is described according to a set of metadata), for a total of 82,450 video documents and 32,622 audio documents (Andreini 2007: 64–65). Such meritorious work, albeit somewhat incomplete (since archives collected by linguists were not considered), emphasized several crucial aspects: the huge amount of analogue data, the scattering of archives, and (in the great majority of cases) their inaccessibility. In this context of renewed interest in oral archives, the *Grammo-foni. Le soffitte della voce* (Gra.fo) project emerged.

Gra.fo was a two-year project jointly conducted by the Scuola Normale Superiore, Pisa, and the University of Siena (Regione Toscana PAR FAS 2007-13). Its purposes were as follows: to discover, digitalize, catalogue, and partially transcribe oral documents (e.g., oral biographies, ethno-texts, linguistic questionnaires, and oral literature) collected within the Tuscan territory. Gra.fo thus aimed to provide first-hand documentation of Tuscan speech varieties and Tuscan oral documents from the early 1960s to the present. The project involved different stages, from fostering the level of awareness on the importance of preserving this valuable product of cultural heritage, to contacting the oral recordings' owners and co-signing legal agreements; from collecting, digitizing, and cataloguing the audio materials, to finally implementing a downloadable online catalogue (which provided the opportunity to discover oral texts known, until now, to a very limited number of possible users).

At the beginning of the project, an updated census of Tuscan oral archives was made: already existing censuses (namely Andreini and Clemente 2007; Benedetti 2002; and Barrera, Martini, and Mulè 1993) were used and integrated with information about oral archives collected for linguistic and dialectological research purposes, such as Carta dei Dialetti Italiani, Atlante Lessicale Toscano, and Vocabolario del Fiorentino Contemporaneo. A priority list was defined and the sound archives' owners were directly contacted. The research group met those who accepted the invitation to join the project, in order to collect their archives and sign legal agreements for the temporary borrowing and the dissemination of their materials. In addition, the owners of the archives with no proper bibliography or accompanying material were interviewed so that they could explain the motivation and aims of their research. Indeed, unlike other kinds of materials, oral documents are often obscure objects: usually, the motivation behind them is clear only to the researcher(s) who collected them. Such interviews, called "Tell something about your archive", are crucial as they provide cataloguers with the key for interpreting and describing the archive, and the users with an appropriate guide for understanding it.

Once the audio materials were gathered into the Gra.fo laboratory (at the time hosted in the Linguistic Laboratory of Scuola Normale Superiore), the conservation protocol took place. Open-source software for the preservation and cataloguing of sound archives was developed within the project. Such software allowed the cataloguers to describe both the archives (including their subdivisions) and the single oral documents. During the project, nearly 3,000 hours of speech recordings stemming from around 30 oral archives collected by scholars and amateurs in the Tuscan territory were digitized.

A complex project like Gra.fo required the definition of procedures that do not figure in the available literature. Dealing with extremely heterogeneous archives from different areas, the Gra.fo working group faced a number of critical issues, such as:

- philological issues (i.e., the relationship between the carrier and the document; the proper treatment of documents containing other documents; the discrepancies between the arrangement imposed on to the archive by its owners and the one adopted within Gra.fo);
- legal and ethical issues (i.e., authorship and ownership in oral archives, legal treatment of confidential information).

The project officially ended in 2014, but not all the digitized archives were catalogued; therefore, a subsequent smaller research action was pursued at Siena University (Voci da ascoltare project), with the aim of cataloguing the Carta dei dialetti italiani archive (limited to Tuscan surveys).

In the meantime, in 2015, while researchers were beginning to explore the potential of the Gra.fo materials for linguistic analysis (Calamai and Biliotti 2017), Italy became a member of CLARIN ERIC, and Italian researchers got to know the world of CLARIN better (Monachini and Frontini 2016; Nicolas et al. 2017). Some feasibility studies were conducted in order to verify how the Gra.fo archive could enter the Italian national CLARIN repository (Calamai and Frontini 2016, 2018; Frontini and Calamai 2018). In parallel, an in-depth examination of the legal questions involved in the dissemination of oral archives was carried out by the CLARIN Legal and Ethical Issues committee (Calamai et al. 2018).

3 CLARIN-IT and Archivio Vi.Vo.

The cross-fertilization between the experience gained during the Gra.fo project and a better awareness of the added value provided by the CLARIN infrastructure to the research communities of speech scientists and oral historians gave rise to the Archivio Vi.Vo. project (2019–2021), supported by Regione Toscana, with the aim of building a model and a system for cataloguing, accessing, preserving, and sharing oral archives. The following partners were involved: Università degli Studi di Siena; Soprintendenza Archivistica e Bibliografica della Toscana; Istituto di Linguistica Computazionale "A. Zampolli" del Consiglio Nazionale delle Ricerche (ILC-CNR) and CLARIN-IT; and Unione dei Comuni del Casentino.

Rather than produce the umpteenth project on a specific genre of audio archive, it was decided to concentrate all the team's efforts on building a system designed to be interoperable and compliant with the CLARIN-IT infrastructure, with metadata harmonized and deposited in the CLARIN repository (Monachini and Frontini 2016). Within Archivio Vi.Vo., the presence of Soprintendenza Toscana guarantees the accountability of the project, while CLARIN-IT assures the infrastructure and the compliance with CLARIN standards for long term-preservation and sustainability (Stamuli 2019; Calamai et al. 2021). This latter aspect is far from trivial, if one considers that the Gra.fo archives are no longer accessible via the web and the web portal appears to be unmaintained. In this respect, creating both an infrastructure and a model design for managing oral archives is expected to address a risk which appears to be more common than people know: that is, the fact that the life of a research project – no matter how groundbreaking it might be – is associated with individual working lives, with all the consequences that entails for future reuse of research data (see the sustainability problem discussed in Broeder and Odijk 2022). Accessing and sharing data also opens up legal issues: the Archivio Vi.Vo. project is aiming to provide a legal framework for the reuse of oral archives.

The development of such an infrastructure requires a complex use case for its validation. This is the case of the oral archive of Caterina Bueno (San Domenico di Fiesole, IT, 2 April 1943 – Florence, IT, 16 July 2007), an important Italian folk singer who brought together many folk songs from Tuscany and central Italy that had been orally passed down from one generation to the next, up to the 20th century, when this centuries-old tradition started to vanish (Calamai et al. 2021). The archive was composed of about 500 analogue carriers on magnetic tape (audio open-reel tapes and audio cassettes) and was digitized during the Gra.fo project. The material consists of about 700 hours of very heterogeneous audio recordings (interviews, folk songs, field recordings, concerts, etc.). Their very poor condition and complex archival history make this case study very challenging, providing the opportunity to develop a methodology able to manage complex audio recordings. This case involves open-reel tapes recorded with different speeds and track-head configurations, which are managed by the Archivio Vi.Vo.

The overall infrastructure will exploit the facilities of the Consortium GARR, the Italian Gruppo per l'Armonizzazione delle Reti della Ricerca,[1] the national high-performance network infrastructure that delivers advanced services to the Italian academic and scientific community. The Archivio Vi.Vo. platform is composed of two main parts: a back-office platform for managing, preserving, restoring, and cataloguing oral archives, and an access interface for searching and listening to oral sources. The former is an advanced platform that takes into account the peculiarities of oral sources stored in analogue recordings.

The Archivio Vi.Vo. platform makes two main advances: (a) a new metadata structure, and (b) innovative web interfaces, including advanced functionalities for the restoration and description of audio recordings, typically integrated only into professional desktop applications. The software is designed as a wizard that helps researchers and cataloguers who do not necessarily have specific knowledge in audio restoration. At the time of writing, the metadata structure and main interfaces are already developed and undergoing testing, but not yet integrated in the overall workflow.

1 https://www.garr.it/ (accessed 29 June 2021).

3.1 The Archivio Vi.Vo. model

In what follows, the workflow is briefly presented, with particular attention to the computer processing of the digital constructs that are temporarily created during the analysis. This process aims to link together two main digital constructs, the first of which being the *preservation copy*. This consists of an organized set of data and metadata that groups together all the information represented by the source document, stored and maintained as a digital preservation master (Bressan and Canazza 2013). The degradation process of the original analogue carrier can be slowed down but not stopped. For this reason, these copies are necessary for avoiding the degradation of the carrier (each time it is played back) and accessing the recorded content as soon as the original source is no longer playable or accessible. Therefore, its scope is concerned with long-term preservation. It is the result of the digitization process and is composed of a set of high-quality multimedia files obtained during the digitization process. In the case of open-reel tapes, they are: (a) audio files containing the signal; (b) a set of photos of carrier, container, and (if any) additional documents associated with the audio recordings; and (c) (optional) video of the tape flowing into the reading head of a tape recorder (Pretto et al. 2019).

The other relevant digital construct refers to the content and is the output of an interpretative analysis. The relationship between carrier and content appears to be rather complex and domain-dependent: that is, every discipline dealing with oral sources tends to produce its own taxonomy (Calamai, Biliotti, and Bertinetto 2014; Stamuli 2019). In American oral history tradition, for instance, the content pertaining to the same communicative event, made up of a unit of time and place, is defined as an "intellectual unit". In the cataloguing process, it is fundamental "to distinguish between the physical and the intellectual units, and to keep track of the relationships among the parts" (MacKay 2007: 16). It happens very often that in the same preservation copy (derived by the digitization of a single carrier) more than one communicative event is recorded. For example, in Bueno's archive, we found frequent instances of single carriers containing concerts, field recordings, and music compilations. We thus have to make a distinction between the digital preservation masters and their diverse contents. Conversely, a single event (e.g., an interview) can be recorded in two or even more audio recordings (therefore, stored in multiple preservation copies). The preservation copies and the documents that are created through the analysis of their contents are stored in two distinct archives linked together (the latter being compliant with the hierarchical structure of the General International Standard Archival Description ISAD[G][2]).

Several working phases are envisaged during the creation of the event-based documents from the preservation copies, thus establishing a series of subsidiary digital constructs, such as *group*, *container*, and *clip*. These objects serve the purpose of keeping track of the restoration and description steps needed to circumscribe a document related to a single event. Firstly, our preservation copies may be actually composed of multiple audio files (especially in case of different speed standards: see Pretto et al. 2020). These files are organized into groups, which are specified in the metadata structure of the preservation copies. A very straightforward example of this need is the creation of two separate mono files (one for each channel) during the digitization of a stereo recording. These files need to be grouped in a single set so they can be listened to correctly, as if they were a single audio file. This circumstance must be managed for the correct restoration, analysis, and access of the content. The files that need to be listened to together are part of the same group. At the moment, the configurations managed by the platform are: mono (one channel), stereo (stored either in a single stereo file or two mono files), quadraphonic files (stored either in a single quadraphonic file or four mono files). In other words, the files obtained during the same "reading" of a tape are stored together in a *group*.

Some parts of a group could have digitization errors. In this case, the correct solution is a new digitization of the tape. In some cases, a new digitization cannot be performed, but some digitization errors can be restored in order to at least partially recover the original content. Via an innovative web interface (see Figure 1), the user can divide a group into intervals that can be independently restored. These intervals are named *containers* and can also be composed of a subset of the channels of the group. The restoration features are the change of speed and equalization, following the workflow proposed in Pretto et al. (2021), and the management of the inverted tracks (Bressan et al. 2021). All the containers will be separated into different files and if necessary restored. In the case of multiple digitizations of the same tape at different speeds, some parts can be discarded.

After the restoration phase, each container will be analysed and described by the cataloguer and/or researcher through a description interface (Figure 2). The aim of this step is the detection of parts related to different communicative events (interviews, concerts, etc.). Each part is named *clip* and is divided into a separate audio file. As its name implies, the description interface allows for the

2 https://www.ica.org/en/isadg-general-international-standard-archival-description-second-edition (accessed 19 March 2022).

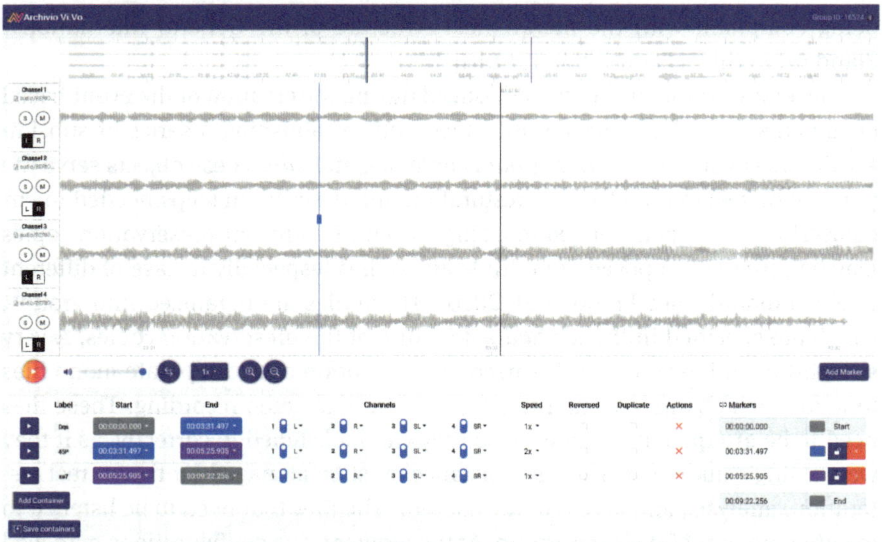

Figure 1: Restoration interface of the Archivio Vi.Vo. platform.

individuation of the clips comprising single content units, and also allows them to be recounted at a fine-grained level of analysis. In this phase, each clip will be described in one or more *segments*. Each segment will be constituted by a time interval and a description of the content, which will be used by researchers to search for an oral document. Unlike containers and clips, the segments will not be separated into different files. In other words, the segments are not separate digital objects, but simple markers of the beginning and the end of a subcategory of events (e.g., the segment of a single song during a concert). The descriptions of the segments compose the *regesto* of each clip. A set of ordered clips will constitute the final document. These event-based documents will be accessible through an interface that will include all the metadata and the ordered list of clips as shown in Figure 3. In the system, the creation of containers, clips, and segments might be skipped in the case of a more straightforward relationship between carrier and content, while the creation of a group is mandatory.

At the moment, the archive consists of 468 *preservation copies* (only a few audio recordings are not included) of 381 audio cassettes and 87 open reel-tapes. There are nearly 600 related oral documents. The goal of the project is to make most of the oral documents available for listening through an access interface open to the public, while the actual download of the files will be behind a federated access barrier or on demand. The documents' metadata will also be accessible via the CLARIN Virtual Language Observatory (VLO; Windhouwer and Goosen 2022).

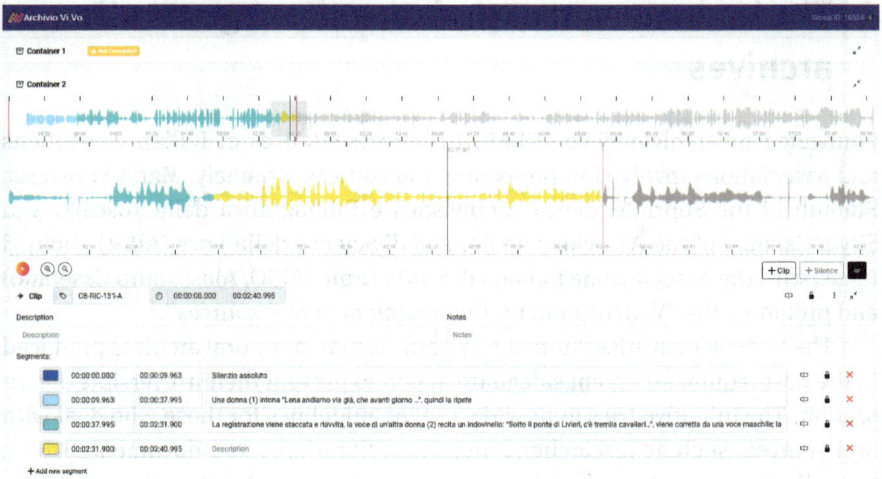

Figure 2: Description interface of the Archivio Vi.Vo. project.

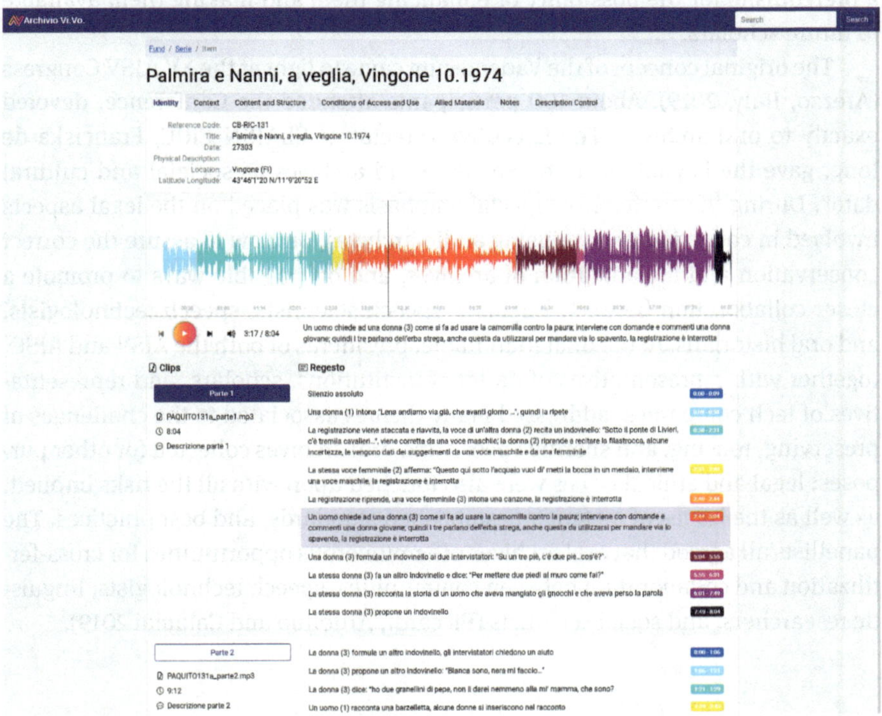

Figure 3: Access interface of the Archivio Vi.Vo. project.

4 The Vademecum experience: Next generation archives

Connected to Archivio Vi.Vo., CLARIN-IT representatives of Italian institutions and associations involved in protecting oral sources – namely, Maria Francesca Stamuli of the Soprintendenza Archivistica e Bibliografica della Toscana and Silvia Calamai of the Associazione Italiana di Scienze della Voce (AISV) – joined forces with the Associazione Italiana di Storia Orale (AISO, Alessandro Casellato) and promoted the "Vademecum for the treatment of oral sources".[3]

The Vademecum arises from the awareness that many oral archives produced in the past require an urgent safeguard action to prevent their irreversible deterioration. The initiative tries to provide a set of guidelines for those who deal with oral sources, such as researchers, archivists, librarians, and documentalists; it also offers conservators of oral archives some basic guidance on how to better carry out their work. The document aims to inform as well as sensitize researchers on the importance of properly creating, archiving, and preserving oral sources, as a prerequisite for the possibility of enhancing them and making them available to future scholars.

The original concept of the Vademecum came to light at the XV AISV Congress (Arezzo, Italy, 2019). About 100 participants attended the Conference, devoted exactly to oral archives. The Executive Director of CLARIN ERIC, Franciska de Jong, gave the keynote lecture "Spoken word archives as societal and cultural data". During the conference, special emphasis was placed on the legal aspects involved in collecting and (re)using audio archives, on how to assure the correct conservation and metadatation of archives, and on possible ways to promote a closer collaboration between linguists, speech scientists, speech technologists, and oral historians. At the final roundtable, presidents of both the AISV and AISO, together with representatives of national institutions, scholars, and representatives of tech companies, addressed many themes associated to the challenges of preserving, reusing, and sharing speech and oral archives collected for other purposes; legal and ethical issues were also touched upon with all the risks implied, as well as the issues of metadata, established standards, and best practices. The panellists all agreed that oral archives offer numerous opportunities for cross-fertilization and collaboration between communities, speech technologists, linguistic researchers, and social scientists (Piccardi, Ardolino and Calamai 2019).

3 http://www.archivi.beniculturali.it/images/pdf_articoli/news/2021/10_ottobre/27_Roma%20MIC/Vademecum_02_11_21.pdf (accessed 19 March 2022).

After the conference, a working group was created in the biennium 2019–2021: after several meetings online and in person a first version of the Vademecum was publicly presented during the UNESCO World Day for Audiovisual Heritage (27 October 2020). On that day, all the documents forming the Vademecum were made available for public review and comment, thus allowing academia, independent researchers, institutions and foundations, and the public at large to contribute to their revision and implementation.

The Vademecum consists of three basic pillars:

- production and description of oral sources (i.e., how to create, describe and make accessible an oral archive);
- conservation of oral archives (i.e., how to best safeguard the oral sources recorded in the past few decades, in consideration of their peculiar fragility);
- enhancement, use, and reuse of oral sources (i.e., the regulatory framework to keep in mind before searching where to deposit oral archives and how to share them).

The document continues and relaunches a tradition of intergenerational and interdisciplinary scientific comparison and exchange of best practices between institutions dealing with oral sources in Italy. Such experience led to the release of an updated version of the Vademecum during the UNESCO World Day of the subsequent year (27 October 2021). In the long and constructive process that resulted in the Vademecum, two relevant aspects deserve attention. Firstly, the plurality and the variety of the people involved in the process: for the very first time, very different stakeholders from different generations (from PhD students to retired scholars) have been working together. Members of the CLARIN-IT consortium, national institutions, and scientific associations have collaborated to offer a valuable manual for different types of users (from independent scholars, to small institutions, to academia). Not only did the writing of the Vademecum envision a public review phase, but several dissemination actions were also planned by the coordinators (Calamai, Casellato, Stamuli), in order to promote the Vademecum among the general public, independent researchers and communities engaged in public history movements (e.g., at Tricase in Puglia, with Liquilab and the Summer School of the History of Folk Tradition), PhD students (e.g., at Pisa University, and the University of Modena and Reggio Emilia), and different scientific communities (e.g., Analisi dell'Interazione e della Mediazione group). The Vademecum was also promoted at a supranational level during a CLARIN Café titled "How Not to Spill Coffee on Your Tapes: Best Practices for Preserving Oral Archives" (24 February 2021, organized as a joint collaboration between CLARIN ERIC and the SSHOC project).

5 Conclusion

In this chapter, we have expounded one of the most recent Italian developments in the long-standing relationship between the management of oral archives and the search for technological innovations: the Archivio Vi.Vo. project. This cross-disciplinary enterprise benefited hugely from the groundwork laid by previous Tuscan research on oral archives, as well as from the involvement and contribution of the Italian CLARIN consortium. Moreover, Archivio Vi.Vo. finds strength in contemporary Italian initiatives that are promoting oral archives to the next generation of researchers through a substantial effort of theoretical systematization and synthesis. Overall, this situation bodes well for the near future: as the Archivio Vi.Vo. project enters its final phases, we are beginning to gather together ideas concerning plausible directions for further developments. This concluding section is dedicated to a sneak peek beyond the current boundaries of Archivio Vi.Vo.

At least three developing areas can be envisaged: (a) user involvement, (b) legal aspects, and (c) technology and computational perspectives. Regarding (a), user involvement (see Draxler et al. 2022 for its importance in CLARIN), in Calamai et al. (2021), we explored the results of a questionnaire distributed through the mailing lists of various Italian research associations. The questionnaire investigated the needs of the potential users of the Archivio Vi.Vo. platform concerning, among other aspects, the searchability functionalities (see Pettersson and Borin 2022 for a similar preparatory inquiry). Our data showed that, overall, the search criterion by dialect/language was the least favoured in terms of perceived frequency of use and usefulness. However, correlation analyses underlined a strong countertrend concerning linguist respondents. Even though this pattern is conceptually unsurprising, it managed to stress the convenience of proposing personalized access options to researchers from different disciplinary backgrounds. Moreover, on a more general level, we are beginning to envision a major divide between the data visualization tools offered to researchers/professional archivists and to the general public. While the former category might be interested, for example, in the inspection of the hierarchical structure of the archive, this information might be regarded as cumbersome by the latter. For this reason, more engaging applications could be developed, such as interactive cartographic overviews of the places where the recordings were actually made. Indeed, georeferencing has always been a staple component of the oral archive/technology relationship (Lake 1991).

As for the legal issues (b), in Marra, Piccardi, and Calamai (2021), we tried to counter excessive risk aversion in the management and diffusion of a web-based oral archive by showing that not all the legal hurdles are equally threatening and that, while universal formulae for legal compliance are a mere chimera, archivists should carefully inspect the nature of their materials and act accordingly. We substantiated this point by looking at our pilot archive: this being the Caterina Bueno collection of ethnomusicological nature, the resulting guidelines were very specific and far from able to cover all the needs of the future users of the Archivio Vi.Vo. platform. We are aware that web tools are being developed to help the research community deal with various legal aspects of data gathering and treatment (e.g., the CLARIN License Category Calculator: see Rodriguez-Doncel and Labropoulou 2015 for discussion; and the DARIAH ELDAH consent form wizard: Hannesschläger, Scholger, and Kuzman Šlogar 2020; for these tools, see also Kamocki, Kelli, and Lindén 2022). Along these lines, we are currently evaluating the feasibility of integrating an interactive legal pipeline in Archivio Vi.Vo., covering a wide range of research scenarios with specific reference to the Italian legal system and its interactions with the GDPR.

A last point concerns the technological perspective (c). In the course of the Archivio Vi.Vo. project, we saw a progressive growth of our knowledge concerning the oral documents contained in our pilot archive, that is, the Caterina Bueno collection. The contributions of researchers with diverse disciplinary backgrounds brought heterogeneous viewpoints to the table, which engendered enriching discussions on data treatment and description. Moreover, through the inspection of related archives and the discovery of new oral documents, we have gradually come to know the original gatherer of the materials better. We argued that this research process might have been of interest for the users of the archive. Collaborative research is a discursive endeavour, and documenting the various steps leading to a result (or to multiple interrelated solutions) promotes transparency and critical thinking. Because of this, we are exploring the idea of implementing versioning in Archivio Vi.Vo. (see e.g., Bürgermeister 2019). Through versioning, an oral archive can become dynamic and capable of recording inside its own structure the academic discussions revolving around its materials. Indeed, versioning is also a great way to improve data citation precision (see Hajič et al. 2022).

Nevertheless, a lot of work will be required in the next few years to include new functionalities and maintain the infrastructure. Preservation is a continuous task that never ends. As the audio recordings need to be continuously moved from one medium to another in order to preserve them, the software requires continuous updates to deal with obsolescence and the advent of new technologies. For example, artificial intelligence promises to deeply impact the oral history field. For this reason, the platform must be ready to include new features for restoring, analysing, retrieving, and reusing oral sources.

Bibliography

Alarcón, Ximena, Lucia Nikolaia Lopez Bojórquez, Olivier Lartillot & Helga Flamtermesky. 2019. From collecting an archive to artistic practice in the INTIMAL project: Lessons learned from listening to a Colombian migrant women's oral history archive. *Acervo. Revista do Arquivo Nacional* 32 (3). 48–63.

Andreini, Alessandro. 2007. Archivi da ascoltare: un primo censimento degli archivi orali in Toscana. In Alessandro Andreini & Pietro Clemente (eds.), *I custodi delle voci. Archivi orali in Toscana: primo censimento*, 51–67. Florence: Regione Toscana.

Andreini, Alessandro & Pietro Clemente (eds.). 2007. *I custodi delle voci. Archivi orali in Toscana: primo censimento*. Florence: Regione Toscana.

Barrera, Giulia, Alfredo Martini & Antonella Mulè (eds.). 1993. *Fonti orali. Censimento degli istituti di conservazione*. Rome: Ministero per i Beni Culturali e Ambientali, Ufficio Centrale per i Beni Archivistici.

Benedetti, Amedeo. 2002. *Gli archivi sonori: fonoteche, nastroteche e biblioteche musicali in Italia*. Genoa: Erga.

Bressan, Federica, Valentina Burini, Edoardo Micheloni, Antonio Rodà, Richard L. Hess & Sergio Canazza. 2021. Reading tapes backwards: A legitimate approach to saving time and money in digitization projects? *Applied Sciences* 11(15). 7092. https://doi.org/10.3390/app11157092.

Bressan, Federica & Sergio Canazza. 2013. A systemic approach to the preservation of audio documents: Methodology and software tools. *Journal of Electrical and Computer Engineering*. https://doi.org/10.1155/2013/489515.

Broeder, Daan & Jan Odijk. 2022. Sustainability and genericity of CLARIN services in the Netherlands. In Darja Fišer & Andreas Witt (eds.), *CLARIN. The infrastructure for language resources*. Berlin: deGruyter.

Bürgermeister, Martina. 2019. Extending Versioning in Collaborative Research. In Roman Blier & Sean M. Winslow (eds.), *Versioning Cultural Objects. Digital Approaches*, 171–190. Norderstedt: Books on Demand.

Calamai, Silvia & Francesca Biliotti. 2017. Archivi orali e migrazione: La costruzione del racconto e il repertorio verbale toscano. *Mnemosyne o la costruzione del senso. Auto/biographie, téléscopie, temporalité. Auto/biography, telescopy, and temporality. Auto/biografia, telescopia, temporalità* 10: 99–116.

Calamai, Silvia, Francesca Biliotti & Pier Marco Bertinetto. 2014. Fuzzy archives: What kind of an object is the documental unit of oral archives?. In Marinos Ioannides, Nadia Magnenat-Thalmann, Eleanor Fink, Roko Žarnić, Alex-Yianing Yen & Ewald Quak (eds.), *Digital Heritage. Progress in Cultural Heritage: Documentation, Preservation, and Protection. EuroMed 2014*. Cham: Springer. https://doi.org/10.1007/978-3-319-13695-0_80.

Calamai, Silvia & Francesca Frontini. 2016. Not quite your usual kind of resource. Gra.fo and the documentation of Oral Archives in CLARIN. In *Proceedings of the CLARIN Annual Conference*. Aix-en-Provence, 26–28 October.

Calamai, Silvia & Francesca Frontini. 2018. FAIR data principles and their application to speech and oral archives. *Journal of New Music Research* 47 (4). 339–354.

Calamai, Silvia, Veronique Ginouvès & Pier Marco Bertinetto. 2016. Sound archives accessibility. In Karol Jan Borowiecki, Neil Forbes & Antonella Fresa (eds.), *Cultural heritage in a changing world*, 37–54. Cham: Springer.

Calamai, Silvia, Chiara Kolletzek, Aleksei Kelli & Francesca Biliotti. 2018. Authorship and copyright ownership in the digital oral archives domain: The Gra.fo digital archive in the CLARIN-IT repository. In Maciej Piasecki (ed.), *Selected papers from the CLARIN Annual Conference 2017: Budapest, 18–20 September 2017* (Linköping Electronic Conference Proceedings 147), 112–127. Linköping: Linköping University Electronic Press.

Calamai, Silvia, Niccolò Pretto, Maria Francesca Stamuli, Duccio Piccardi, Giovanni Candeo, Silvia Bianchi & Monica Monachini, 2021. Community-based survey and oral archive infrastructure in the Archivio Vi.Vo. project. In Costanza Navarretta & Maria Eskevich (eds.), *Selected Papers from the CLARIN Annual Conference 2020* (Linköping Electronic Conference Proceedings 180), 55–64. Linköping: Linköping University Electronic Press.

Contini, Giovanni & Alfredo Martini. 1993. *Verba manent. L'uso delle fonti orali per la storia contemporanea*. Rome: La Nuova Italia Scientifica.

Di Piazza, Valeria & Mugnaini, Dina. 1988. *Io so' nata a Santa Lucia. Il racconto autobiografico di una donna toscana tra mondo contadino e società d'oggi*. Castelfiorentino: Società Storica della Valdelsa.

Draxler, Christoph, Alexander Geyken, Erhard Hinrichs, Annette Klosa-Kückelhaus, Elke Teich & Thorsten Trippel. 2022. How to connect language resources, infrastructures, and communities. In Darja Fišer & Andreas Witt (eds.), *CLARIN. The infrastructure for language resources*. Berlin: deGruyter.

Fillon, Thomas, Joséphine Simonnot, Marie-France Mifune, Stéphanie Khoury, Guillaume Pellerin, Maxime Le Coz, Estelle A. de la Bretèsque, David Doukhan & Dominique Fourer. 2014. Telemeta: An open-source web framework for ethnomusicological audio archives management and automatic analysis. *Proceedings of the 1st International Workshop on Digital Libraries for Musicology (DLfM '14)*. 1–8. New York: ACM.

Fromont, Robert & Jennifer Hay. 2012. LaBB-CAT: An annotation store. *Australasian Language Technology Workshop* 10. 113–117.

Frontini, Francesca & Silvia Calamai. 2018. Speech audio archives and CLARIN metadata. In Amedeo De Dominicis (ed.), *Speech audio archives: Preservation, restoration, annotation aimed at supporting the linguistic analysis*, 11–28. Rome: Bardi.

Gagnon, Nicole. 1981–1982. Objectifs d'un projet d'archives orales. *Oral history Forum d'histoire orale* 5 (1). 39–44.

Hajič, Jan, Eva Hajičová, Barbora Hladká, Jozef Mišutka, Ondřej Košarko & Pavel Straňák. 2022. LINDAT/CLARIAH-CZ: Where we are and where we go. In Darja Fišer & Andreas Witt (eds.), *CLARIN. The infrastructure for language resources*. Berlin: deGruyter.

Hannesschläger, Vanessa, Walter Scholger & Koraljka Kuzman Šlogar. 2020. The DARIAH ELDAH consent form wizard. In *DARIAH Annual Event 2020: Scholarly Primitives Book of abstracts*. 46–47.

Hennelly, Martin, Langa Khumalo, Juan Steyn & Menno van Zaanen. 2022. Training of digital language resources skills in South Africa. In Darja Fišer & Andreas Witt (eds.), *CLARIN. The infrastructure for language resources*. Berlin: deGruyter.

ICA, International Council on Archives. 2000. ISAD(G): General International Standard Archival Description, 2nd edn. Ottawa: https://www.ica.org/sites/default/files/CBPS_2000_Guidelines_ISAD%28G%29_Second-edition_EN.pdf (accessed 30 June 2021).

Lake, Gretchen L. 1991. Project Jukebox: An innovative way to access and preserve oral history records. *Provenance* 9 (1–2). 24–41.

Ljubešić, Nikola, Tomaž Erjavec, Maja Miličević Petrović & Tanja Samardžić. 2022. Together we are stronger: Bootstrapping language technology infrastructure for South Slavic languages with CLARIN.SI. In Darja Fišer & Andreas Witt (eds.), *CLARIN. The infrastructure for language resources*. Berlin: deGruyter.

MacKay, Nancy. 2007. *Curating oral histories. From interview to archive*. Walnut Creek, CA: Left Coast Press.

Kamocki, Paweł, Aleksei Kelli & Krister Lindén. 2022. The CLARIN Committee for Legal and Ethical Issues and the Normative Layer of the CLARIN Infrastructure. In Darja Fišer & Andreas Witt (eds.), *CLARIN. The infrastructure for language resources*. Berlin: deGruyter.

Marra, Prospero, Duccio Piccardi & Silvia Calamai. 2021. Ethnomusicological archives and copyright issues: An Italian case study. In Monica Monachini & Maria Eskevich (eds.), *Proceedings of the CLARIN Annual Conference 2021*. 160–165. Virtual edition. https://office.clarin.eu/v/CE-2021-1923-CLARIN2021_ConferenceProceedings.pdf (accessed 19 March 2022).

Monachini, Monica & Francesca Frontini. 2016. CLARIN, l'infrastruttura europea delle risorse linguistiche per le scienze umane e sociali e il suo network italiano CLARIN-IT. *Italian Journal of Computational Linguistics* 2 (2). 11–30.

Nicolas, Lionel, Alexander König, Monica Monachini, Riccardo Del Gratta, Silvia Calamai, Andrea Abel, Alessandro Enea, Francesca Biliotti, Valeria Quochi & Francesco Vincenzo Stella. 2017. CLARIN-IT: State of affairs, challenges and opportunities. In Maciej Piasecki (ed.), *Selected papers from the CLARIN Annual Conference 2017: Budapest, 18–20 September 2017* (Linköping Electronic Conference Proceedings 147), 1–14. Linköping: Linköping University Electronic Press.

Nouza, Jan, Petr Cerva, Jindrich Zdansky, Karel Blavka, Marek Bohac, Jan Silovsky, Josef Chaloupka, Michaela Kucharova, Ladislav Seps, Jiri Malek & Michal Rott. 2014. Speech-to-text technology to transcribe and disclose 100,000+ hours of bilingual documents from historical Czech and Czechoslovak radio archive. *Proceedings of INTERSPEECH 2014*. 964–968. http://doi.org/10.21437/Interspeech.2014-255.

Pettersson, Eva & Lars Borin. 2022. Swedish Diachronic Corpus. In Darja Fišer & Andreas Witt (eds.), *CLARIN. The infrastructure for language resources*. Berlin: deGruyter.

Piccardi, Duccio, Fabio Ardolino & Silvia Calamai. 2019. (eds.) *Gli archivi sonori al crocevia tra scienze fonetiche, informatica umanistica e patrimonio digitale / Audio archives at the crossroads of speech sciences, digital humanities and digital heritage* (Studi AISV 6). Milan: Officinaventuno. https://www.aisv.it/StudiAISV/2019/vol_6/studiAISV_6.pdf (accessed 19 March 2022).

Pozzebon, Alessandro, Francesca Biliotti & Silvia Calamai. 2016. Places speaking with their own voices. A case study from the Gra.fo Archives. In Marinos Ioannides, Eleanor Fink, Antonia Moropoulou, Monika Hagedorn-Saupe, Antonella Fresa, Gunnar Liestøl, Vlatka Rajcic & Pierre Grussenmeyer (eds.), *Digital heritage. progress in cultural heritage: Documentation, preservation, and protection*, 232–239. Cham: Springer.

Pretto, Niccolò, Carlo Fantozzi, Edoardo Micheloni, Valentina Burini & Sergio Canazza. 2019. Computing methodologies supporting the preservation of electroacoustic music from analog magnetic tape. *Computer Music Journal* 42 (4). 59–74. https://doi.org/10.1162/comj_a_00487.

Pretto, Niccolò, Alessandro Russo, Federica Bressan, Valentina Burini, Antonio Rodà & Sergio Canazza. 2020. Active preservation of analogue audio documents: A summary of the last seven years of digitization at CSC. In Simone Spagnol & Andrea Valle (eds.), *Proceedings of the 17th Sound and Music Computing Conference, SMC20*. 394–398. https://doi.org/10.5281/zenodo.3898905.

Pretto, Niccolò, Nadir Dalla Pozza, Alberto Padoan, Anthony Chmiel, Kurt James Werner, Alessandra Micalizzi, Emery Schubert, Antonio Rodà, Simone Milani & Sergio Canazza. 2021. A workflow and novel digital filters for compensating speed and equalization errors on digitized audio open-reel tapes. *Proceedings of the 16th International Audio Mostly Conference*. 224–231. https://doi.org/10.1145/3478384.3478409.

Rodriguez-Doncel, Victor & Penny Labropoulou. 2015. Digital representation of rights for language resources. In Christian Chiarcos, John Philip McCrae, Petya Osenova, Philipp Cimiano & Nancy Ide (eds.), *Proceedings of the 4th Workshop on Linked Data in Linguistics (LDL-2015)*, 49–58. Stroudsburg: Association for Computational Linguistics.

Schneider, William. 2013. A jukebox full of stories. *Oral Tradition* 28 (2). 299–306.

Stamuli, Maria Francesca. 2019. Fonti orali, documenti e archivi: riflessioni e proposte per la nascita di un "archivio vivo". In Duccio Piccardi, Fabio Ardolino & Silvia Calamai (eds.), *Gli archivi sonori al crocevia tra scienze fonetiche, informatica umanistica e patrimonio digitale / Oral archives at the crossroads of speech sciences, digital humanities and digital heritage* (Studi AISV 6), 95–109. Milan: Officinaventuno.

Windhouwer, Menzo & Twan Goosen. 2022. Component Metadata Infrastructure. In Darja Fišer & Andreas Witt (eds.), *CLARIN. The infrastructure for language resources*. Berlin: De Gruyter.

Anna Lindahl and Stian Rødven-Eide

Argumentative Language Resources at Språkbanken Text

Abstract: Språkbanken Text at the University of Gothenburg is a CLARIN B-centre providing language resources in Swedish, as well as tools to use them, for a wide range of disciplines. In 2017, we began exploring the field of argument mining – the process of automatically identifying and classifying arguments in text – partly aimed at establishing language resources and tools for argument analysis and mining in Swedish.

Keywords: argumentation, language resources, argumentation mining

1 Introduction

Språkbanken Text at the University of Gothenburg is a CLARIN B-centre providing language resources in Swedish, as well as tools to use them, for a wide range of disciplines. In 2017, we began exploring the field of argument mining – the process of automatically identifying and classifying arguments in text – partly aimed at establishing language resources and tools for argument analysis and mining in Swedish. Depending on the context, different definitions of argumentation are applicable. For our resources, we have focused on three ways of approaching argumentation in text:

1. We have devised a set of preliminary guidelines for the annotation of argumentation in text.
2. We have looked at classifying arguments into various types of inference, in accordance with Walton's argument schemes (Walton, Reed, and Macagno 2008).

Acknowledgements: The work presented here has been partly supported by an infrastructure grant to Språkbanken Text, University of Gothenburg, contributing to building and operating a national e-infrastructure funded jointly by the participating institutions and the Swedish Research Council (under contract no. 2017-00626).

Note: The authors contributed equally.

Anna Lindahl, University of Gothenburg, Gothenburg, Sweden, e-mail: anna.lindahl@svenska.gu.se
Stian Rødven-Eide, University of Gothenburg, Gothenburg, Sweden,
e-mail: stian.rodven.eide@svenska.gu.se

https://doi.org/10.1515/9783110767377-026

3. With Inference Anchoring Theory, all rhetorical elements in a dialogue or debate that serve any purpose in argumentation are classified and linked.

Our work on these three approaches is laid out in the remaining sections, which are structured as follows: after an introduction to argumentation in Section 2, we describe our corpora in Section 3, followed by our annotation efforts in Section 4. Finally, we introduce some auxiliary resources in Section 5 that we hope will be beneficial to argument mining.

2 Elements of argumentation

Research on argumentation takes many forms, from Plato's search for universal truth to the pragma-dialectical notion of reasonableness introduced by van Eemeren et al. In this section, we establish a brief overview of argumentation research, with a focus on the models and methods used and discussed by computational linguists.

As for argumentation analysis in general, the model first proposed by Stephen Toulmin in 1958 (2003) represented an important milestone and is still relevant for argument mining today (Lytos et al. 2019). This model marks a shift from the strict absolutism of theoretical arguments to a practical approach, favouring justification over inference. According to Toulmin, every practical argument must consist of at least a claim (what the arguer wishes to convince someone about), grounds (evidence supporting the claim), and a warrant (the reasoning by which the grounds constitutes a valid support for the claim). While Toulmin initially focused on legal arguments, revised editions show how it can be applied to other kinds of debates.

In order to better classify types of argumentation, argumentation schemes allow us to describe structures of inference. Perhaps the best known schemes are the ones presented by Walton (Walton, Reed, and Macagno 2008). Walton presents 60 schemes which are meant to represent the type of argumentation found in everyday reasoning but also schemes present in more specialized domains. Schemes are formalized as seen below, with a minor premise, a major premise, and a conclusion. Each scheme also has a set of critical questions by which the scheme can be weakened or defeated, if the questions can't be answered. The questions can also be used to infer missing premises.

Argument from Position to Know
Major premise: Source *a* is in a position to know about things in a certain subject domain S containing proposition A.
Minor premise: *a* asserts that A (in domain S) is true (false).

Conclusion: A is true (false.)
Critical question 1: Is *a* in a position to know whether A is true (false)?
Critical question 2: Is *a* an honest (trustworthy, reliable) source?
Critical question 3: Did *a* assert that A is true (false)?

A strength of the argumentation schemes is that they often represent defeasible arguments, something which is often present in ordinary argumentation but not in traditional logic argumentation. In artificial intelligence research, argumentation has been introduced as a form of reasoning. Argumentation schemes are proposed to be used both for computational reasoning and as a tool for retrieving and analysing argumentation in speech or texts. For example, if a scheme is identified in a text, the critical questions could be used to infer what information is assumed.

Another important contribution to argument theory was the pragma-dialectical approach heralded by Frans van Eemeren and Rob Grootendorst, starting with their systematic analysis of speech act in argumentative discussions (Eemeren and Grootendorst 2010) and culminating in their book A Systematic Theory of Argumentation in 2003 (Eemeren and Grootendorst 2003). Grounded in pragmatics, this model regards argumentation as a complex form of discourse activity, and aims to describe how argumentation is carried out in practice. In the authors' opinion, speech act theory provides the necessary basis for dealing with dialogue that aims to resolve a difference of opinion. While it is far from trivial to incorporate this approach in argument mining, great strides have been made using several applicable methods, such as inference anchoring theory, which we will describe in Section 4.3.

2.1 Argumentation in natural language processing

As shown in the previous section, there are several aspects of argumentation that can be modelled and studied, and several ways in which this can be done. Argumentation annotated datasets for natural language processing (NLP) purposes reflect this and there are datasets annotated with models from various areas in argumentation theory. (There are also datasets without any clear connection to argumentation theory.) These datasets are often created as training sets, to be used by some kind of machine learning algorithm to learn from. The aim is then to automatically identify and analyse argumentation, in what is called *argumentation mining*. The task of identifying argumentation, and thus the task of modelling it, is often presented in these three steps (Stab and Gurevych 2017; Lippi and Torroni 2016):

1. Component identification;
2. Component classification;
3. Structure identification.

Component identification refers to identifying what is argumentative or not, although this step is often skipped (Ajjour et al. 2017). Component classification refers to which roles these parts are playing in argumentation, for example labelling claims and premises. After labelling components, relations such as attack or support are identified, both within individual arguments and between the arguments. Many studies or datasets do not include all these steps, as it is a complicated task. There are also more complex ways to structure the task (see, for example, Lawrence and Reed 2020). When the components themselves have been identified, some studies have explored further aspects of argumentation: for example Hidey et al. (2017) identified ethos, pathos, or logos in argument components; Park and Cardie (2014) classified components as verified or unverified. In Section 4.1, identifying argumentation schemes is explored.

3 Argumentative corpora

One of Språkbanken Text's central research tools is Korp, a corpus search and browsing tool which provides access to a collection of richly annotated corpora spanning more than 13 billion tokens (Borin, Forsberg, and Roxendal 2012). A more detailed description of Korp can be found in Fridlund et al. (2022).

The corpora we have been working on for the purposes of argumentation mining and analysis are *Anföranden*, annotated and augmented debates from the Swedish parliament Rødven-Eide (2020), as well as a collection of social media texts from two popular Swedish internet forums (Lindahl 2020). In addition, we have analysed annotation of argument schemes in a number of newspaper editorials (Lindahl, Borin, and Rouces 2019).

3.1 Parliamentary debates

During the last 15 years, access to parliamentary data has been greatly improved, especially in Europe following the signing of the Council of Europe Convention on Access to Official Documents in 2009.[1] In large part thanks to the ParlaCLARIN

1 https://www.coe.int/en/web/conventions/full-list/-/conventions/treaty/205

workshops of 2018[2] and 2020,[3] significant corpora of parliamentary debates have been published and enhanced with metadata for research, such as those from the parliaments of Norway (Lapponi et al. 2018), Slovenia (Pančur, Šorn, and Erjavec 2018) and the UK (Nanni et al. 2018), to name but a few.

The Swedish parliament has published digital versions of its minutes for all parliamentary debates from 1971 onward. These files are derived from scans of printed or typed documents and the large amount of HTML formatting present in the files are only for preserving layout; it does not generally segment the text in a way that helps with parsing. Metadata is restricted to document-level information, and as such does not say anything about which speakers participate or which topics are being discussed. Debates from 1993 onwards are, however, also available in a separate dataset, aptly named *anföranden* (meaning parliamentary speeches), where each speech is complemented with appropriate metadata such as speaker, party, topic and speech order. We have processed, enhanced, and augmented this resource in order to improve and simplify research on the debates, through the reduction of noise in the data, the adding of linguistic annotation, and augmenting the resource with a semantic graph, described later in this chapter. Our version of this dataset consists of 325,202 speeches, totalling 122,079,937 tokens.

In Table 1, we show the complete structure of a typical speech document. In our version of the corpus, all properties except for *anförandetext* (speech text) are XML attributes of the speech as a whole. These attributes have been transferred directly from the parliament's data, with the exception of *dok_datum*, which erroneously listed all parliamentary sessions as having taken place at midnight; for this reason, we edited the time stamp in the data, leaving only the dates, which are correct. A more thorough description of the various data can be found in Rødven-Eide (2020).

After processing the documents to fix noisy data, we imported the resulting files into Korp, via the Sparv pipeline. Korp is a tool for searching and exploring corpora (Borin, Forsberg, and Roxendal 2012), while Sparv is the annotation pipeline through which most of the corpora in Korp are processed (Borin et al. 2016). Both of the tools are developed and maintained by Språkbanken Text.

The linguistic annotation provided by Sparv is thorough and multifaceted, ranging from part-of-speech and word sense to compound and dependency anal-

2 https://www.clarin.eu/ParlaCLARIN
3 https://www.clarin.eu/ParlaCLARIN-II

yses. A complete list of the available annotations can be found on the Sparv web page[4] and its user manual.[5] The annotated corpus can be explored with Korp.[6]

Table 1: A typical speech document.

Property	Description
dok_hangar_id	Internal document ID
dok_id	Meeting and speech number
dok_titel	Protocol title
dok_rm	Parliamentary year
dok_nummer	Number of meeting in succession during a year
dok_datum	Date of speech
avsnittsrubrik	Topic title
kammaraktivitet	Type of debate
anforande_id	Unique speech ID
anforande_nummer	Speech number in debate
talare	Speaker name
parti	Speaker party
anforandetext	Full speech text
intressent_id	Speaker's ID
rel_dok_id	Document being debated
replik	Speech type
systemdatum	Date of publishing

3.2 Social media

Our social media dataset is made up of threads from the two Swedish internet forums Flashback and Familjeliv ('Family life'). These forums are among the most popular in Sweden and are rich in debates and argumentation, of varying levels of sophistication. They are thus suitable for studying informal argumentation. The discussions on Familjeliv are often focused on family and relations while Flashback is known for more political topics, but both forums contain a wide range of topics.

Both forums are split up into a set of main sections (19 on Familjeliv, 16 on Flashback) dedicated to different topics, with many subsections in each section. The discussions on these forums are shown in thread structures, where a user

4 https://spraakbanken.gu.se/en/tools/sparv/annotations
5 https://spraakbanken.gu.se/en/tools/sparv/usermanual
6 https://spraakbanken.gu.se/korp/

creates a thread by posting a question or topic and other users reply. The answers are shown in chronological order. The users are able to cite each others' posts, but there is no tree-structure similar to that on, for example, Reddit.[7]

For the annotation, nine threads from these forums were chosen at random but only among the threads which had about 30 posts. As threads on these forums can end up with hundreds of posts, this was done to enable us to annotate a wider range of topics. The most recent threads were considered, which at the time were threads created in Spring 2020. The dataset used for our annotation project has a total of 28,000 tokens. The statistics of this dataset are shown in Table 2.

Table 2: Statistics of the social media dataset.

number of threads	number of posts	number of users	number of tokens	number of cite tokens	total number of tokens
9	266	150	21292	7173	28465

Apart from the annotated social media dataset, most available content posted on Flashback and Familjeliv has been collected in Korp. As much of the content is argumentative in its nature, this data could be used for studies of argumentation in these domains. The data also could be used as a supplement to supervised machine learning or unsupervised machine learning, for argumentation mining or other NLP purposes.

4 Annotating argumentation

Argumentation can be modelled and analysed in several different ways and from different aspects, and there are thus many different ways to annotate it, depending on one's goal and interest. When selecting a model for annotation of argumentation, you want to select a model which is complex enough to capture interesting information but also easy to annotate. You also want a model which a machine can learn from, if the goal is to use the data for machine learning. The choice of model might also depend on the domain. A model which is suitable in a monologic domain, such as editorials or news, might not be a good fit for a more dialogic domain, such as online forums.

When annotating different linguistic phenomena, such as argumentation, it is important to reach as high a degree of inter-annotator agreement (between

7 It would be possible to construct a cite tree, but it can't be seen in the user interface.

as many annotators) as possible. This is to be sure that the annotation is reliable and captures what one seeks to study. There exist several measurements of agreement, such as Cohen's or Krippendorff's, with their respective strengths and weaknesses. Depending the task, certain thresholds are deemed acceptable, although no objective scale exists. The Landis and Koch scale (Landis and Koch 1977) is often referred to in argumentation annotation.

Annotating argumentation is challenging and time-consuming. Reaching high inter-annotator agreement is difficult, especially in unstructured domains such as user-generated content. Efforts in annotating argumentation usually do not reach as high a level of inter-annotator agreement as other tasks in NLP. A reason for this is that whether something is argumentative or not can depend on the context. For example, a statement like "I like cats" could be seen as argumentative or not, depending on which of the following statements precedes it.

1. Which animals do you prefer?
2. We should get a cat.
3. Let's get a dog.

– I like cats

If it follows 1, it could be seen as neutral, while in response to 2 or 3 it could be seen as agreement or disagreement.[8] Argumentation also often relies on implicit assumptions and unstated information. This makes it difficult for annotators to agree, because they might interpret a situation differently, and it is not always clear if there is one correct answer. It also makes it time-consuming to annotate, because the annotators often have to interpret intentions or infer missing information. Annotators might also need training in applying the chosen argumentation model, which can take time.

4.1 Annotating argumentation schemes

Our first argumentation annotation was carried out a corpus of editorials, originally described in Lindahl, Borin, and Rouces (2019). The editorials stem from Swedish newspapers originally collected by Hedquist (1978) in order to study emotive language. They were collected in the period May–September 1973 and consist of 30 editorials from 6 newspapers with about 19,000 words (Lindahl, Borin, and Rouces 2019). The newspapers were together deemed to reflect the views of the parties in the Swedish parliament at the time. The editorials from this

8 Example inspired by a tutorial by Budzynska and Reed (2019).

study are annotated for emotive language, but this was not shown when annotating argumentation.

The corpus was annotated with Walton's argumentation schemes (Walton, Reed, and Macagno 2008), described in Section 2. Out of the 60 schemes described by Walton, 30 were used for the annotation. These schemes were originally presented in Walton (1996). The annotation was carried out by two annotators with a background in linguistics. For instructions, they were given Walton's book describing the schemes. The annotation was done in the annotation tool Araucaria (Reed and Rowe 2004), which has support for annotating the schemes. Using this tool, an annotator annotates arguments by first annotating argument components. A component is a span of text, labelled with the role "conclusion" or "premise".[9] These components are then connected to form an argument, which consists of one conclusion and one or more premises. A component can be reused. For example, it is possible for a premise to be connected to two different conclusions, but the premise will then be considered to be two different occurrences. The argument is then labelled with a scheme. An example of an annotated argument from the editorials is seen below.

Premise: It is already showing in the form of increasing oil and gas prices.
Conclusion: But now energy crisis is not far away.
Scheme: Argument from Sign

The annotation was evaluated on component, argument, and scheme level. The annotators annotated a varying number of components and they also varied in how they connected them to form arguments. Annotator 1 (A1) annotated more arguments and thus more conclusions than annotator 2 (A2) (each argument has only one conclusion) but they annotated about the same number of premises. This could be explained by the way they chose to connect components to arguments, as A1 often constructed arguments consisting of only one premise and a conclusion, and then reused the conclusion but chose another premise. A2 chose instead to construct arguments with several premises.

The annotators mostly used the same four or five schemes, and together they used 22 out of the 30 available schemes. The most popular schemes for both annotators were *Argument from Consequences*, *Argument from Sign* and *Argument from Cause to Effect*. A1 uses *Argument from Evidence to a Hypothesis* the most, while this scheme is used only six times by A2.

Because the annotators were free to use any span of text, the agreement measure was based on how much their annotated spans overlap. Given a certain

9 The distinction between major and minor premise was not made in this annotation.

threshold, two spans were considered to be a match if their overlap was much as or over the threshold. Overlap was calculated as the ratio between the longest common span and the longest of the two spans. Thresholds of 0.9 and 0.5 were used. The agreement was then calculated as seen in (1), where *a1* and *a2* are the number of instances of the component and m the number of matches.

$$(1)\ c = 2 * |m|/(|a_1| + |a_2|)$$

Because a conclusion can be supported by different premises and a premise can support different conclusions, they were compared separately and together. The annotators agreed the most when comparing premises. With a threshold of 0.5, *c* is 0.37 (99 matches) for spans labelled as premises, regardless of whether they are connected to the same conclusion. For conclusions *c* was 0.34, with 92 matching conclusions. Out of these 92 conclusions, 33 share at least one premise. For these premises *c* is 0.71. In the 33 cases where a conclusion and at least one premise matched, the schemes were compared. Four schemes out of these matching conclusions and premises were the same. Comparing only matching conclusions (92), nine schemes were the same. It thus seems that even when annotators agree on how an argument was composed, they did not agree on which scheme was appropriate.

The disagreement between the annotators could be due to several reasons, including the setup of the task and the instructions itself. For example, it might have been better to structure the task so that the annotators first annotated arguments and in a later step annotated only schemes.

Some of the disagreement can be explained by differences in how the annotators structured and composed the arguments. When manually inspecting the annotations, it became clear that there is more than one possible interpretation of how to use the components. For example, below is an example of a premise supporting two different conclusions. It is difficult to say that either one of these should be the "correct" annotation.

Premise: A shift of power will result in us not risking any socialistic experiment during the elected term and instead we can further build on the foundations of the welfare society.
Conclusion A1: Voters should vote for the opposition
Conclusion A2: Do not vote away collaboration!
Scheme A1: Argument from Consequences
Scheme A2: Causal Slippery Slope Argument

Another example of this is shown below, where two different premises support the same conclusion. Again, it is difficult to say whether one is right and the other is wrong. The premises could possibly be used together.

Premise A1: It is already showing in the form of increasing oil and gas prices.
Premise A2: We are not especially used to saving anything in this country.
Conclusion A1 & A2: But now the energy crisis is not far away
Scheme A1: Argument from Sign
Scheme A2: Argument from Cause to Effect

It is not surprising that the annotators have chosen different schemes in the above examples, because different components are involved. In the few cases where they agree on components they mostly do not agree on the schemes. However, as with the components, it is possible that more than one scheme could be suitable in the annotated examples. Below is an example where annotators agreeing on conclusion and premise, but not the scheme.

Premise: It is not unlimited.
Conclusion: It is widely considered necessary to economize energy.
Scheme A1: Argument from Consequences
Scheme A2: Argument From Sign

These two schemes, *Argument from Sign* and *Argument from Consequences*, were among the most frequently used by both annotators. They are quite general and could possibly both be applicable in this case. Another example of scheme disagreement is shown below. These two schemes co-occurred 12 times out of the matching 71 conclusions (0.9 overlap threshold). Again, it is possible that two schemes might be suitable at the same time.

Premise: The high unemployment rate in Sweden is not acceptable from any angle, this must be firmly established.
Conclusion: To create new jobs must be the most important task for now.
Scheme A1: Argument from Consequences
Scheme A2: Argument from Popular Practice

Because of the disagreements between the schemes, the scheme annotation was evaluated by sorting the schemes into three groups. These three groups were originally suggested by Walton as a way to classify the schemes. This increased the agreement a little.

This dataset illustrates the difficulties of evaluating argumentation based solely on agreement between annotators, as there can be many possible interpretations of the arguments presented. It also shows the need for explicit instructions, ensuring that the annotators are coherent as possible.

4.2 Annotation of argumentation in social media

The nine threads of the social media corpus, originally described in Lindahl (2020), were annotated with spans of argumentation. Previous annotations of social media or online forums with labelled argumentation components (Habernal and Gurevych 2017; Rosenthal and McKeown 2012; Morante et al. 2020) have not reached very high levels of agreement. Because of this, the aim of this annotation effort was to investigate if it is possible to reliably annotate argumentative spans, and thus distinguish them from the non-argumentative parts of the text. If successful, these spans could be further annotated with, for example, components in an iterative annotation process. Iterative annotation processes have been previously shown to increase agreement (Miller, Sukhareva, and Gurevych 2019).

The guidelines for the annotation included a definition of argumentation, a set of control questions and tests the annotators could use when annotating. Defining what was to be considered argumentation was a bit of a challenge, as there are different definitions that do not all overlap. The definition we decided upon was inspired by van Eemeren's description of argumentation (Eemeren et al. 2014) and modified by what we found when inspecting the domain. Persuasiveness was also added to the definition, as it is often used as a criteria for argumentation (see, for example, Habernal and Gurevych (2017)). This definition was not intended to capture everything which could be considered argumentation, as this can vary, but rather to describe something which we hoped could be distinguished as argumentation. We thus defined argumentation as follows:

1. A standpoint/stance.
2. This standpoint is expressed with claims, backed by reasons.
3. There is a real or imagined difference of opinion concerning this standpoint, which leads to:
4. The intent to persuade a real or imagined other part about the standpoint.

Together with the definition, the annotators were given three questions:

- Does the poster's text signal that he or she is taking a stance / has a standpoint?
- Does the poster motivate why?
- Do you perceive the poster as trying to persuade someone?

Together with the definition and the questions, two tests were given to the annotators. These tests aimed to guide the annotators, not provide definite answers. The first test asked the annotators to insert "I agree/disagree" in the post. The idea behind this test was to capture if the text expressed any difference of opinion which might not be explicitly stated. If adding "I disagree" did not change how they perceived the text, this was probably the case.

The second test asked the annotators to reformulate the argumentative span as "A because of B". This was to help them clarify what the stance and the motivation for the stance was. Half of the annotators were asked to write this reformulation down in the annotation tool. Examples of the test were included in the guidelines, as exemplified below.

> **I don't agree.** Of course you shouldn't put the dog down! It's a life we are talking about, you can't just throw the dog away when it doesn't suit you anymore. Go to a professional. The dog isn't feeling well. If you can't help the dog you'll have to relocate it.
>
> **Reformulation:** [Do not put the dog down because it has a life which shouldn't be thrown away.]

For the annotation seven annotators were employed, split into two groups. The first group also included one of the authors, resulting in four annotators in each group. All annotators had linguistic experience through either studies or work. The annotation tool WebAnno (Eckart de Castilho et al. 2016) was used. Both groups received the same guidelines and the same threads to annotate. After the first group had annotated, a meeting was held to discuss their experiences. With the second group, a meeting was held before annotation started, in which the guidelines and the annotators' interpretation of them were discussed. The second group was also told to write down their reformulations from the tests with the hope that this would increase agreement.

The annotation results were first compared on token level. The annotators annotated between ca 30–60% of the tokens as argumentation, although one annotator only annotated 10%. The annotators most often annotated one or more sentences in their annotations spans, following sentence boundaries. Because of this sentences instead of spans of text were compared. Most of the annotators included 4–5 sentences on average in their spans, but two of them annotated fewer sentences per span. Even though the annotators varied in how many sentences they included in a span, it was most common to only annotate one span per post. Because of this, post-level agreement was examined.

The inter-annotator agreement is shown in Table 3.[10] As there was no clear difference in agreement between the two groups of annotators, IAA is shown for both groups together. Krippendorff's varied over threads. Unsurprisingly, post-

10 The numbers here are slightly different than previously reported. This is due to a previous error in the calculations, which has been corrected.

level agreement is the highest at 0.51. According to the Landis and Koch scale (Landis and Koch 1977), this is considered moderate agreement. The observed agreement increases if one chooses to look at majority vote (five out of eight annotators agree).

Table 3: IAA for the social media dataset.

Unit	Krippendorff's α	Observed agreement	Observed agr. majority
Token	0.34	31%	74%
Sentence	0.34	31%	75%
Post	0.51	45%	84%

A manual inspection of the disagreements was also made in order to understand why they occurred. Inspection of the reformulations from the second group showed that the annotators had written similar reformulations when they had marked the same spans. Most annotators annotated around 4–5 sentences per argumentation span. In these cases, some of the annotators chose to annotate two spans instead of one, leaving one or more sentences unmarked in between the two spans. This means some annotators has interpreted a particular span of text as parts of the same argumentation, while others have found the same particular span to be to two different distinct argumentation spans, with different standpoints. This difference in argumentation spans has an effect on the sentence and token–level IAA, but not the post–level. This might be the reason why post–level results are the highest out of the three units.

Below is an example of an annotated post, exemplifying the differences in selected spans. Four annotators annotated only the part in bold. One annotator annotated the whole post. Another annotator annotated the first part as one argument, and the second part (the bold part) as another argument. The final annotator also annotated the whole post as two arguments but split the spans at the last sentence.[11]

> I agree. Little children can be bothersome and put a strain on relationships, yes. And to prefer one parent is completely normal, although it is sad, of course. **What has the three year old to be grateful for? That she should be happy and grateful that you 'sacrificed yourself' and moved there to live with them is too complicated and too much to ask of a three-year-old regardless if he/she likes to live with you or not.**

11 One annotator did not annotate the post at all.

These differences highlight the difficulties with annotating argumentation, especially in unstructured domains. All but one annotator agreed this post contained argumentation but not on which parts should be included. In these domains, one standpoint is not always clearly distinguishable from another or they may be implicit. It also not always easy to decide what should be included in the argumentation. These difficulties are probably be the reasons why the annotators chose different spans.

Inspecting what the annotators had marked as annotation, it seemed that when the post authors were very explicit in their standpoints and in their disagreement or agreement, the annotators agreed among themselves. But, when sarcasm or irony was involved, or there was much left unsaid, the annotators disagreed. Thus, when the conditions in the guidelines were explicitly met, the annotators agreed. Examples of this can be seen in the two examples below. They are from the same thread and could be seen having the same message, although the second one is very implicit. In the first post all annotators agreed the post contained argumentation, whereas only three annotators annotated the second example as argumentation.

> So? And how do you think the children are feeling right now? That it's so hard to live with their with their dad that they'd rather refrain from doing it altogether? It doesn't matter that you thought it was boring to not to live with your boyfriend. I agree with the others in this thread that you should stop living together. For the sake of the children. You can't just think of yourself.

> A three-year old should be grateful because you split up his parents? Oh my god! Are you for real?

The annotation of this dataset showed that it is possible to annotate argumentation on post-level but distinguishing the boundaries of the argumentation within a post is more difficult. Further annotations of this dataset would need to consider this. For example, can one ensure that the annotators agree on how to interpret standpoints or should one figure out a way to interpret standpoints even if annotators disagree? Stricter instructions on how to select standpoints might help with this.

4.3 Annotation of argumentation in political debates

A similar approach was used for *anföranden*, where some of the same annotators were tasked with identifying argumentation in the transcript of a single debate. The hope was that we through this would be able to create a gold standard, but first we wanted to see whether the difference in domain and structure made a significant difference to inter-annotator agreement. In contrast to the forum discussions, a parliamentary debate has a relatively formalized and predictable structure. On the other hand, any given entry in a parliamentary debate is usually longer, and may touch upon several points raised in several of the previous entries. Although it is performed orally, a parliamentary speech – especially after having been transcribed – bears characteristics of professionally written argumentation, using carefully constructed formulations, whereas forum discussions often try to emulate spoken language, inserting extra vowels into a word such as "loooong" or including interjections like "*sigh*". Another aspect of parliamentary debates is that their very purpose is to be argumentative. Every speech voices obvious support or opposition to something, and does so in a clearly argumentative way. One could therefore assume that almost everything in a debate is argumentative. From the annotations, we saw that this was, to some extent, a reasonable expectation. A majority of the annotators found 67% of sentences to be argumentation, compared to 30% for the internet forum discussions.

In order to ensure comparability between the annotation efforts on the internet forums and the parliamentary debates, we decided to preserve as much as reasonably possible of the instructions, the main difference being that the examples were changed. However, after noticing that allowing the annotators to mark arbitrary spans as being argumentation somewhat complicated both the argumentation process and the measurement of agreement, we decided to ask annotators to always mark complete sentences in the debates, though spans of more than one sentence were allowed.

Taking all annotators into account, IAA on sentence level was even lower than for the social media dataset, at 0.29 α. Seeing that one of the annotators had marked considerably fewer sentences than the others, we measured IAA among the five other annotators and found it increased to 0.39 α. For the four annotators most in agreement, it rose further to 0.45 α. From this, we can see that the level of agreement was similar to that of the social media annotations.

On the other hand, we saw a major difference with regards to observed agreement among the majority. While we found that all annotators agreed on 25.9% of sentences, again slightly fewer than for the forums, the majority was in agreement of 89%, indicating that it may be easier to agree on argumentation in parliamentary debates, given the right approach. Further analysis of the results of this process is still ongoing, with plans to publish both annotations as well as gold standard evaluation data based on them. An overview of IAA with comparison to the social media dataset is provided in Table 4.

Table 4: IAA comparison on sentence level.

Dataset	α	Observed agreement	Observed agr. majority
Social media	0.34	31%	75% (5 of 8 annotators)
Debates (6 annotators)	0.29	25.9%	89% (4 of 6 annotators)
Debates (5 annotators)	0.39	46.2%	79.5% (4 of 5 annotators)

Another ongoing effort is annotation and analysis of parliamentary debates in accordance with Inference Anchoring Theory (IAT) (Budzynska and Reed 2011). This is a relatively complex method, as it considers all elements of a dialogue or debate that have any purpose in or effect on the argumentation. It is closely related to Rhetorical Structure Theory (Mann and Thompson 1988), but specifically adapted for analysing argumentation. Most importantly, IAT allows for anchoring inference in links between locutions, and not just locutions themselves (Budzynska et al. 2014). As current tools for IAT annotation are designed with the type of dialogue present in radio and TV debates in mind (Janier, Lawrence, and Reed 2014), we found through our initial annotation attempts that the length and complex rhetorical structure of parliamentary debates made them difficult apply in our case. Our project on applying IAT annotation to debates is therefore still ongoing.

5 Auxiliary resources

Due to the complex nature of argumentation, it is not unlikely that various knowledge resources could be helpful for argument mining. We have been working on some resources for this purpose, and as they are general in nature, we hope they will be useful even beyond the task of identifying and classifying arguments.

As a complement to the corpus of parliamentary debates, we published the *Swedish PoliGraph* (Rødven-Eide 2019), a graph of all members of parliament in Sweden. It is, in essence, a semantic database that keeps track of MPs' parliamentary activities, from speeches to responsibilities on commissions and in Governmental roles. One purpose of this graph is to combine it with named entity recognition and resolution, in order to automatically establish the argumentative structure of a given debate. Given the task of mapping a single debate, the procedure would be as follows:

1. Find all speeches with a given *rel_dok_id*.
2. Determine the meeting(s) this was debated in.
3. Establish the chronological order of the speeches during these meetings.

4. Analyse each speech and attempt to determine which previous speech or speeches (if any) was/were addressed or argued against.

For the Swedish PoliGraph, we combined the speech information from *anföranden* with metadata from the MP category, which includes basic biographical information as well as a complete history of their roles in the parliament. Such roles are usually their time working as an MP and commission work, but longer sick leave is also listed here, as well as their substitutes in those cases. In addition to the essential identifiers "name" and "party", links are also created to MPs' Wikidata-IDs and their listed name there, which sometimes provide more detail, as they are stored in the parliament's own database, while simultaneously allowing other data to be pulled from Wikipedia. The structure of the graph is shown in Figure 1.

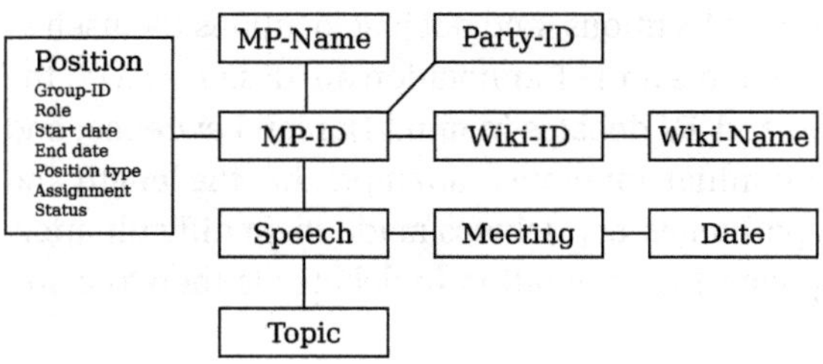

Figure 1: A semantic graph of Swedish MPs and debates.

Roles of MPs are generally described in terms of positions, where each assignment (or leave from that assignment) is stored as a factual predicate with eight arguments:

1. MP-ID
   A unique ID for each MP.
2. Agency code
   An identifying code for the agency. This can be ambiguous, as parties and commissions sometimes use the same identifier.
3. Role
   The MP's role in the agency, e.g., parliamentarian, commission chair, or substitute.
4. From
   Starting date of the position.
5. To
   End date of the position.

6. Type
   The type of position, usually either "kammaruppdrag" for the parliament or "uppdrag" for commission work.
7. Uppdrag
   The info here varies. For commission work and other extraparliamentary duties, it contains the full name of the commission or equivalent. For extended leave, it lists the name of substitutes.
8. Status
   The MP's presence or absence during the given period.

While the Swedish PoliGraph was created for the specific purpose of establishing the structure of parliamentary debates, it was designed to be detailed and flexible enough to be used outside of its planned scope.

Work on named entity recognition has also been initiated, with a number of speeches annotated for six different types of named entities:

1. People, real or fictional
2. Political roles, such as ministerial posts
3. Organizations
4. Locations
5. Works of art and culture, as well as brands
6. Time periods and points in time

These categories, as well as the annotation guidelines were derived from a SWE-CLARIN project that aimed to create a new gold standard for named entity recognition and classification in Swedish (Ahrenberg, Frid, and Olsson 2020). We did, however, choose to remove two of their categories – those pertaining to medical symptoms and treatments – as they were deemed very unlikely to show up in a significant number in the parliamentary debates. On the other hand, we added the category of political roles, in order to capture MPs who were not referred by name. Furthermore, we asked our annotators to designate whether a named person was a member of parliament or not, and whether organizations mentioned were political or not.

We are currently in the process of evaluating the classification methods used by SWE-CLARIN on our data, with the expectation that the Swedish BERT model developed by Kungliga Biblioteket (Malmsten, Börjeson, and Haffenden 2020). We will then proceed to automatically classify the remaining parliamentary debates and release both the manually and the automatically annotated data as a resource.

6 Conclusion

In this chapter we presented our ongoing efforts to create resources for studying argumentation and argumentation mining. As demonstrated here, the annotation of phenomena such as argumentation is complex and challenging. It needs to be carefully thought through, especially the evaluation of such annotations. However, these efforts enable studies from many angles and perspectives. As discussed in Hajičová et al. (2022) in this book, an annotated corpus can both be a resource for linguistic studies and open up new research questions.

The corpora we presented here could be useful for many types of studies aiming to analyse argumentation in the domains covered. Even though the purpose of the annotations have been for use in machine learning, it should be possible to use the annotations for other quantitative studies. For example, are there any specific patterns or words which are more frequent in argumentation than in non-argumentative exchanges? Are there any other patterns to be found, for example between speakers in a debate or users on an online forum?

Much of this chapter has focused on the complexity of argumentation and the disagreement between the annotators. A dataset where annotators disagree might not be the best for machine learning purposes, but it could be used to answer other questions. The disagreements themselves could be studied: are there any patterns to where the annotators agree or disagree? Could one annotator's annotations be easier for a machine learning algorithm to learn compared to the others?

The emergence of the NLP sub-field of argumentation mining has enabled new ways of researching argumentation. This field covers a wide range of possible and envisioned tasks, from argument component identification (Trautmann et al. 2020) to automatic evaluation of arguments or their claims (Sathe et al. 2020). Argumentation mining techniques would also be useful in information retrieval or as teaching aids. But for these tasks to be developed successfully, argumentation annotated corpora from a wide range of domains are essential (Stede and Schneider 2018).

As the annotated parts of the corpora presented here are currently small in size, as is the case for many argumentation corpora due to the challenging nature of the task, their usefulness as machine learning training data is still an open question. In recent years it has been become possible to use smaller amounts of training data due to the introduction of pre-trained language models and the possibility of fine-tuning them, but it still seems that larger amounts of training data is preferred. However, there exists other suggested solutions to the problem of data scarcity in argumentation mining. For example, a small corpus could be suitable for evaluation of unsupervised machine learning methods (Levy et al. 2017) or as a starter for boot-strapping more data (Ein-Dor et al. 2020).

Bibliography

Ahrenberg, Lars, Johan Frid & Leif-Jöran Olsson. 2020. A new resource for Swedish named-entity recognition. SLTC 2020, University of Gothenburg.

Ajjour, Yamen, Wei-Fan Chen, Johannes Kiesel, Henning Wachsmuth & Benno Stein. 2017. Unit segmentation of argumentative texts. *Proceedings of the 4th Workshop on Argument Mining*, 118–128. Copenhagen: Association for Computational Linguistics.

Borin, Lars, Markus Forsberg, Martin Hammarstedt, Dan Rosén, Roland Schäfer & Anne Schumacher. 2016. Sparv: Språkbanken's corpus annotation pipeline infrastructure. *Proceedings of SLTC 2016*. Online: Umeå University.

Borin, Lars, Markus Forsberg & Johan Roxendal. 2012. Korp – the corpus infrastructure of Språkbanken. *International Conference on Language Resources and Evaluation (LREC) 8*, 474–478. Istanbul: European Language Resources Association.

Budzynska, Katarzyna, Mathilde Janier, Chris Reed, Patrick Saint-Dizier, Manfred Stede & Olena Yaskorska. 2014. A model for processing illocutionary structures and argumentation in debates. *International Conference on Language Resources and Evaluation (LREC) 9*, 917–924. Reykjavik: European Language Resources Association.

Budzynska, Katarzyna & Chris Reed. 2011. Whence inference? Technical Report, University of Dundee.

Budzynska, Katarzyna & Chris Reed. 2019. Advances in argument mining. *Proceedings of the 57th annual meeting of the Association for Computational Linguistics: Tutorial abstracts*, 39–42. Stroudsberg, PA: Association for Computational Linguistics.

Eckart de Castilho, Richard, Éva Mújdricza-Maydt, Seid Muhie Yimam, Silvana Hartmann, Iryna Gurevych, Anette Frank & Chris Biemann. 2016. A web-based tool for the integrated annotation of semantic and syntactic structures. In Erhard Hinrichs, Marie Hinrichs and Thorsten Trippel (eds.), *Proceedings of the Workshop on Language Technology Resources and Tools for Digital Humanities (LT4DH)*, 76–84. Osaka: COLING.

Eemeren, Frans H. van, Bart Garssen, Erik C. W. Krabbe, A. Francisca Snoeck Henkemans, Bart Verheij & Jean H. M. Wagemans. 2014. Argumentation theory. *Handbook of argumentation theory*, 1–49. Dordrecht: Springer.

Eemeren, Frans H. van & Rob Grootendorst. 2003. *A systematic theory of argumentation: The pragma-dialectical approach*. Cambridge: Cambridge University Press.

Eemeren, Frans H. van & Rob Grootendorst. 2010. *Speech acts in argumentative discussions*. Reprint 2010. Berlin: De Gruyter Mouton.

Ein-Dor, Liat, Eyal Shnarch, Lena Dankin, Alon Halfon, Benjamin Sznajder, Ariel Gera, Carlos Alzate, Martin Gleize, Leshem Choshen, Yufang Hou et al.. 2020. Corpus wide argument mining – a working solution. *The 34th AAAI Conference on Artificial Intelligence*, 7683–7691. New York: AAAI Press.

Fridlund, Mats, Daniel Brodén, Tommi Jauhiainen, Leena Malkki, Leif-Jöran Olsson & Lars Borin. 2022. Trawling and trolling for terrorists in the digital Gulf of Bothnia: Cross-lingual text mining for the emergence of terrorism in Swedish and Finnish newspapers, 1780-1926. In Darja Fišer & Andreas Witt (eds.), CLARIN. The infrastructure for language resources. Berlin: deGruyter.

Habernal, Ivan & Iryna Gurevych. 2017. Argumentation mining in user-generated web discourse. *Computational Linguistics* 43 (1). 125–179.

Hajičová, Eva, Jan Hajič, Barbora Hladká, Jiří Mírovský, Lucie Poláková, Kateřina Rysová, Magdaléna Rysová, Pavel Straňák, Barbora Štěpánková & Šárka Zikánová. 2022. Corpus annotation as a feasible and scientifically beneficial task. In Darja Fišer & Andreas Witt (eds.), CLARIN. The infrastructure for language resources. Berlin: deGruyter.

Hedquist, Rolf. 1978. *Emotivt språk: En studie i dagstidningars ledare* [Emotive language: A study in newspaper editorials]. Umeå: Umeå University, Dept. of Nordic Languages.

Hidey, Christopher, Elena Musi, Alyssa Hwang, Smaranda Muresan & Kathleen McKeown. 2017. Analyzing the semantic types of claims and premises in an online persuasive forum. In Ivan Habernal, Iryna Gurevych, Kevin Ashley, Claire Cardie, Nancy Green, Diane Litman, Georgios Petasis, Chris Reed, Noam Slonim and Vern Walker (eds.), *Proceedings of the 4th Workshop on Argument Mining*, 11–21. Copenhagen: Association for Computational Linguistics.

Janier, Mathilde, John Lawrence & Chris Reed. 2014. Ova+: an argument analysis interface. In Simon Parsons, Nir Oren, Chris Reed and Federico Cerutti (eds.), *Computational models of argument*, Frontiers in artificial intelligence and applications, 463–464. Amsterdam: IOS Press.

Landis, J. Richard & Gary G. Koch. 1977. The measurement of observer agreement for categorical data. *Biometrics* 33 (1). 159–174.

Lapponi, Emanuele, Martin G. Søyland, Erik Velldal & Stephan Oepen. 2018. The talk of Norway: A richly annotated corpus of the Norwegian parliament, 1998–2016. *Language Resources and Evaluation* 52 (3). 873–893.

Lawrence, John & Chris Reed. 2020. Argument mining: A survey. *Computational Linguistics* 45 (4). 765–818.

Levy, Ran, Shai Gretz, Benjamin Sznajder, Shay Hummel, Ranit Aharonov & Noam Slonim. 2017. Unsupervised corpus–wide claim detection. *Proceedings of the 4th Workshop on Argument Mining*, 79–84. Stroudsberg, PA: Association for Computational Linguistics.

Lindahl, Anna. 2020. Annotating argumentation in Swedish social media. In Elena Cabrio and Serena Villata (eds.), *Proceedings of the 7th Workshop on Argument Mining*, 100–105. Online: Association for Computational Linguistics.

Lindahl, Anna, Lars Borin & Jacobo Rouces. 2019. Towards assessing argumentation annotation – a first step. In Benno Stein and Henning Wachsmuth (eds.), *Proceedings of the 6th Workshop on Argument Mining*. Stroudsberg, PA: Association for Computational Linguistics.

Lippi, Marco & Paolo Torroni. 2016. Argumentation mining: State of the art and emerging trends. *ACM Transactions on Internet Technology (TOIT)* 16 (2). 10.1–10.25.

Lytos, Anastasios, Thomas Lagkas, Panagiotis Sarigiannidis & Kalina Bontcheva. 2019. The evolution of argumentation mining: From models to social media and emerging tools. *Information Processing & Management* 56 (6). 102055.

Malmsten, Martin, Love Börjeson & Chris Haffenden. 2020. Playing with Words at the National Library of Sweden – Making a Swedish BERT. Preprint: https://arxiv.org/abs/2007.01658 (accessed 23 March 2022).

Mann, William C. & Sandra A. Thompson. 1988. Rhetorical structure theory: Toward a functional theory of text organization. *Text & Talk* 8 (3). 243–281.

Miller, Tristan, Maria Sukhareva & Iryna Gurevych. 2019. A streamlined method for sourcing discourse-level argumentation annotations from the crowd. In Jill Burstein, Christy Doran and Thamar Solorio (eds.), *Proceedings of NAACL 2019*, 1790–1796. Stroudsberg, PA: Association for Computational Linguistics.

Morante, Roser, Chantal Van Son, Isa Maks & Piek Vossen. 2020. Annotating perspectives on vaccination. *International Conference on Language Resources and Evaluation (LREC) 12*, 4964–4973. Marseille: European Language Resources Association.

Nanni, Federico, Mahmoud Osman, Yi-Ru Cheng, Simone Paolo Ponzetto & Laura Dietz. 2018. UKParl: A semantified and topically organized corpus of political speeches. In Darja Fišer, Maria Eskevich and Franciska de Jong (eds.), *Proceedings of the LREC 2018 Workshop on Creating and Using Parliamentary Corpora*, 29–32. Miyazaki: European Language Resources Association.

Pančur, Andrej, Mojca Šorn & Tomaž Erjavec. 2018. SlovParl 2.0: The collection of Slovene parliamentary debates from the period of secession. In Darja Fišer, Maria Eskevich and Franciska de Jong (eds.), *Proceedings of the LREC 2018 Workshop on Creating and Using Parliamentary Corpora*, 8–14. Miyazaki: European Language Resources Association.

Park, Joonsuk & Claire Cardie. 2014. Identifying appropriate support for propositions in online user comments. In Nancy Green, Kevin Ashley, Diane Litman, Chris Reed and Vern Walker (eds.), *Proceedings of the 1st workshop on argumentation mining*, 29–38. Stroudsberg, PA: Association for Computational Linguistics.

Reed, Chris & Glenn Rowe. 2004. Araucaria: Software for argument analysis, diagramming and representation. *International Journal on Artificial Intelligence Tools* 13 (04). 961–979.

Rødven-Eide, Stian. 2019. The Swedish PoliGraph: A semantic graph for argument mining of Swedish parliamentary data. In Benno Stein and Henning Wachsmuth (eds.), *Proceedings of the 6th Workshop on Argument Mining*, 52–57. Stroudsberg, PA: Association for Computational Linguistics.

Rødven-Eide, Stian. 2020. Anföranden: Annotated and augmented parliamentary debates from Sweden. In Darja Fišer, Maria Eskevich and Franciska de Jong (eds.), *Proceedings of the 2nd ParlaCLARIN Workshop*, 5–10. Marseille: European Language Resources Association.

Rosenthal, Sara & Kathleen McKeown. 2012. Detecting opinionated claims in online discussions. *2012 IEEE 6th International Conference on Semantic Computing*, 30–37. Palermo: IEEE.

Sathe, Aalok, Salar Ather, Tuan Manh Le, Nathan Perry & Joonsuk Park. 2020. Automated fact-checking of claims from Wikipedia. *International Conference on Language Resources and Evaluation (LREC) 12*, 6874–6882. Marseille: European Language Resources Association.

Stab, Christian & Iryna Gurevych. 2017. Parsing argumentation structures in persuasive essays. *Computational Linguistics* 43 (3). 619–659.

Stede, Manfred & Jodi Schneider. 2018. Argumentation mining. *Synthesis Lectures on Human Language Technologies* 11 (2). 1–191.

Toulmin, Stephen E.. 2003. *The uses of argument*. 2nd edition. Cambridge: Cambridge University Press.

Trautmann, Dietrich, Johannes Daxenberger, Christian Stab, Hinrich Schütze & Iryna Gurevych. 2020. Fine-grained argument unit recognition and classification. *AAAI Conference on Artificial Intelligence* 34 (1). 9048–9056.

Walton, Douglas. 1996. *Argumentation schemes for presumptive reasoning*. Mahwah: Lawrence Erlbaum Associates.

Walton, Douglas, Christopher Reed & Fabrizio Macagno. 2008. *Argumentation schemes*. Cambridge: Cambridge University Press.

Jack Hoeksema, Kees de Glopper, and Gertjan van Noord

Syntactic Profiles in Secondary School Writing Using PaQu and SPOD

Abstract: SPOD is part of the PaQu website created as a CLARIN project. It allows one to generate a syntactic profile of a corpus based on the output of the automatic parser Alpino. It runs a long sequence of queries and provides quantitative information about constituents, sentence types, coordination, length of constituents, and so on. In this chapter, we employ SPOD and the rest of PaQu to analyse a part of the *Schrijfmeterscorpus* of secondary school essays. We use a small subsection of the SPOD output for this purpose, in particular those syntactic properties that correlate most reliably with academically oriented texts. We show that SPOD is able to distinguish, on the basis of these variables, among grades and school types.

Keywords: automatic parsing, writing, query, secondary education

1 Introduction

Online corpora usually do not provide much in the way of syntactic information. Sometimes they allow searches for parts of speech or simple regular expressions, less often they come fully parsed. Even less common is a website that comes with a parser and a query interface. PaQu is such a website, developed as part of the Dutch CLARIN infrastructure, and has turned out to be useful for studying syntactic patterns in corpora (see Bloem 2020; Bouma 2017; Odijk 2015, 2020; Odijk et al. 2017; van der Wouden et al. 2015; van Noord et al. 2020). The website is in Dutch, and can only be used for analysing Dutch corpora. Users with an account can upload their corpus, have it parsed by the Alpino parser (Bouma, van Noord, and Malouf 2001; van Noord 2006) and query it to find out for example how many indirect questions it contains. There is a basic interface window allowing users

Acknowledgements: The development of SPOD has been funded by the Dutch national CLARIN project Common Lab Research Infrastructure for the Arts and Humanities, CLARIAH.

Jack Hoeksema, University of Groningen, Groningen, the Netherlands, e-mail: j.hoeksema@rug.nl
Kees de Glopper, University of Groningen, Groningen, the Netherlands,
e-mail: c.m.de.glopper@rug.nl
Gertjan van Noord, University of Groningen, Groningen, the Netherlands,
e-mail: g.j.m.van.noord@rug.nl

https://doi.org/10.1515/9783110767377-027

to search for combinations between words (for example all adjectives modifying a particular noun, or all nouns modified by a particular adjective). There is also a window in which power users can write Xpath 2.0 queries to search for syntactic patterns. Xpath is a query language for XML.

A new feature of PaQu is SPOD, the Syntactic Profiler of Dutch, which uses a battery of built-in XPath queries to provide an overview of syntactic (and some lexical) properties of the data.[1] The queries make heavy use of dedicated macro's and require knowledge of the underlying Alpino parser. Such queries are difficult to make for non-expert users, even if they are familiar with corpus linguistics, and providing this ready-made query set will help make the PaQu tools more accessible for them. By clicking on the query link, it is possible to open an XPath tab (part of PaQu) to make the query sensitive to corpus metadata. The latter are corpus-specific, and may vary according to the specs and purpose of the corpus. Among the data provided by SPOD are the following:

- basic information concerning the corpus: number of sentences, word (tokens), type/token ratio, mean sentence length, and mean word length;
- part of speech listings: numbers of nouns, verbs, adjectives and so on, including their subcategories, such as number of neuter and common gender nouns, plurals, inflected and noninflected adjectives;
- frequency of four types of main clauses: declarative, wh-questions, yes/no questions, and imperatives;
- frequency and average length of types of subordinate clauses;
- frequency of various subtypes of comparatives;
- frequency of coordinations, subdivided by conjunction word, number of conjuncts, and category of conjuncts;
- frequency and mean length of four phrasal subtypes: NP, PP, AP and AdvP
- frequency of subtypes of PP: attributive, predicative, adverbial, complement;
- frequency of verb clusters of various types;
- information about particle verbs (placement in or outside verb cluster)
- levels of finite clausal embedding;
- topicalization and extraction data;
- parser success (words skipped by the parser, sentences with a partial parsing).

Potential applications for SPOD are manifold. One can extract information about the corpora made available on PaQu, such as the corpus of spoken Dutch, Lassy Small, Basilex, and Wablieft. This can then be used for comparison with a user-provided corpus, uploaded at the PaQu site. A potential application is stylistic

1 SPOD is available via https://www.let.rug.nl/alfa/paqu/spod.

research. There is a fair amount of n-gram based analysis of texts in computational humanities, but PaQu makes syntactic comparisons possible, at the level of individual differences among writers, but also at the level of text types, by comparing, for example, newspaper texts and academic papers, or unprepared spoken language with written genres. See van Noord et al. (2020) for more information on the set-up and main features of SPOD and PaQu. That paper also contains information about the accuracy of the Alpino parser. As with all automatic parsers, accuracy varies with text types, and sometimes manual inspection of the parsed sentences will be necessary to verify results. SPOD normally returns numbers, but it has a built-in option which lists all sentences that were selected from the corpus by a query.

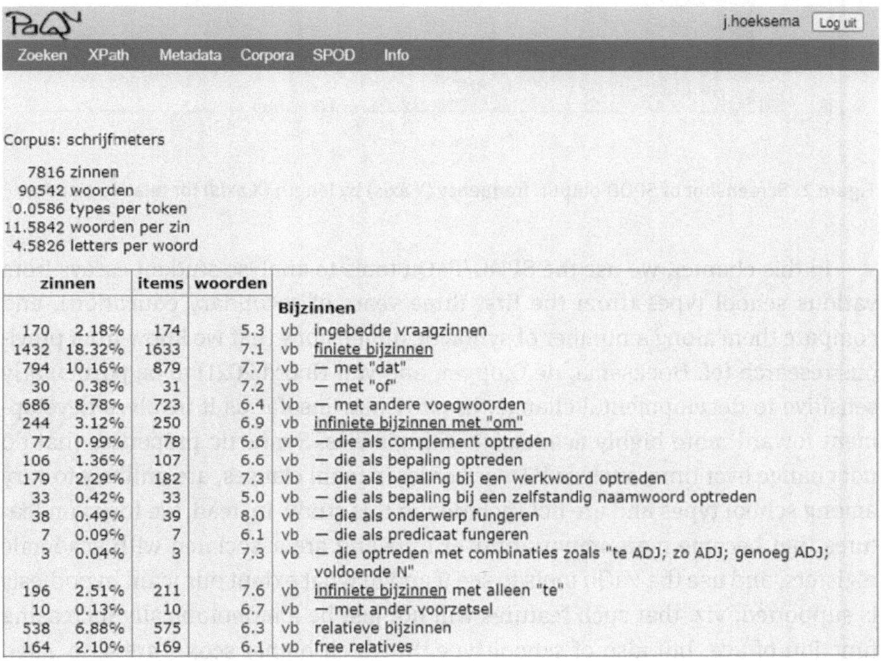

zinnen		items	woorden		
					Bijzinnen
170	2.18%	174	5.3	vb	ingebedde vraagzinnen
1432	18.32%	1633	7.1	vb	finiete bijzinnen
794	10.16%	879	7.7	vb	— met "dat"
30	0.38%	31	7.2	vb	— met "of"
686	8.78%	723	6.4	vb	— met andere voegwoorden
244	3.12%	250	6.9	vb	infiniete bijzinnen met "om"
77	0.99%	78	6.6	vb	— die als complement optreden
106	1.36%	107	6.6	vb	— die als bepaling optreden
179	2.29%	182	7.3	vb	— die als bepaling bij een werkwoord optreden
33	0.42%	33	5.0	vb	— die als bepaling bij een zelfstandig naamwoord optreden
38	0.49%	39	8.0	vb	— die als onderwerp fungeren
7	0.09%	7	6.1	vb	— die als predicaat fungeren
3	0.04%	3	7.3	vb	— die optreden met combinaties zoals "te ADJ; zo ADJ; genoeg ADJ; voldoende N"
196	2.51%	211	7.6	vb	infiniete bijzinnen met alleen "te"
10	0.13%	10	6.7	vb	— met ander voorzetsel
538	6.88%	575	6.3	vb	relatieve bijzinnen
164	2.10%	169	6.1	vb	free relatives

Figure 1: Screenshot of SPOD showing frequency and average length of types of clauses.

The screenshot in Figure 1 illustrates the output for a small part of SPOD. The full output for all variables is too large to show here. As you can see, SPOD, like the rest of PaQu, is in Dutch, and only analyses Dutch texts.

By clicking on one of the elements marked in blue, it is possible to obtain further information: clicking on the number conjures up a graph, showing frequency per unit of length (compare Figure 2), and clicking on *vb*, takes you from SPOD to the XPath window in PaQu where the query is ready to run.

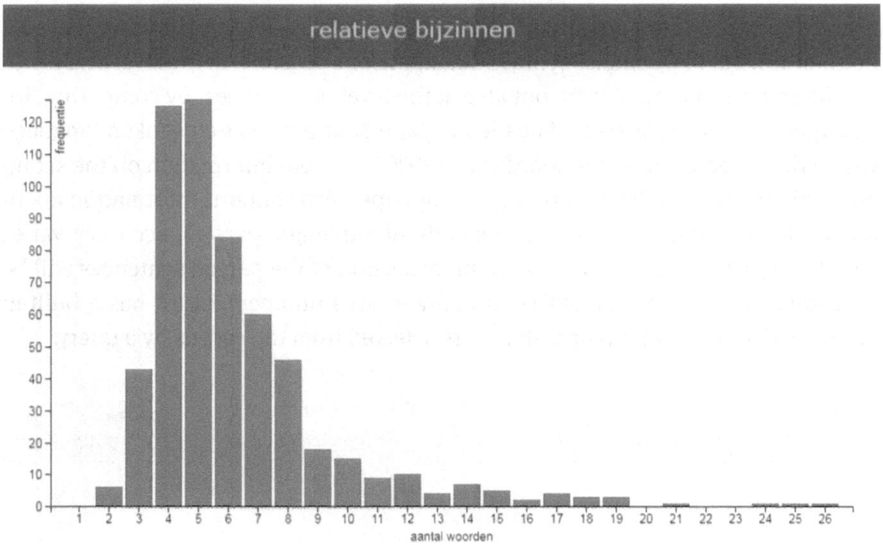

Figure 2: Screenshot of SPOD output: frequency (Y axis) by length (X axis) for relative clauses.

In this chapter, we use the SPOD/PaQu tools to analyse student essays from various school types (from the first three years of secondary education), and compare them along a number of syntactic dimensions that we know from previous research (cf. Hoeksema, de Glopper, and van Noord 2021) to be particularly sensitive to developmental change, in particular insofar as it involves development toward more highly academic writing styles. Syntactic properties that do not change over time, such as V2 word order in main clauses, are unlikely to vary among school types and are not included in this study. Instead, we focus on features that become more important over time and are associated with academic registers, and use the PaQu tools to see if and to what extent our main hypothesis is supported, viz. that such features will not just be a monotonically increasing function of age, but also of school type, in which higher scores are associated with more academically oriented school types.

The chapter is structured as follows: in Section 2, we sketch the Dutch system of secondary education and the various types of schools it consists of, in Section 3 we introduce our corpus, in Section 4 we discuss the variables we selected for this study and in Section 5 we present our main findings. Section 6 discusses these findings. Section 7 contains our conclusions.

2 School types in Dutch secondary education

Unlike primary education, which is uniform for all children attending regular education, Dutch secondary education is divided into pre-vocational secondary education (VMBO, duration four years), senior general secondary education (HAVO, duration five years) and pre-university education (VWO, duration six years).[2] Dutch children are given a secondary school level advice in the last year of primary school, typically at the age of 12.

The gymnasium is a VWO-type school which prepares students for study at the university, and offers them, along with the sciences, humanities and modern languages, classes in Greek and Latin. Atheneum is likewise a preparation for university level study, but without the classical languages.

HAVO students are not directly admitted to universities, but may go on to higher level vocational schools as well as applied universities (called HBO in Dutch, an acronym for higher vocational education). The curriculum consists of modern languages, humanities and sciences.

VMBO TL is a school type which prepares students for midlevel vocational schools (MBO), whereas VMBO BK is a more practically oriented version of the same. Students typically go on to vocational schools for hairdressers, auto mechanics, plumbers, nurses, caterers, as well as various types of office jobs.

3 The corpus

We make use of a 90,000 word corpus of essays, a part of the Schrijfmeterscorpus (cf. de Glopper and Prenger 2013; Pander Maat et al. 2019). This corpus was collected in the academic year 2012–13 by the former Expertise center for Language, Education and Communication (ETOC) at the University of Groningen. The essays in our corpus are based on the same writing assignment for all school types (a letter describing characteristics of the Netherlands for a Swedish girl that will soon join the class) in order to make them fully comparable. A select number of syntactic variables in SPOD will be tracked. Each query associated with one of these variables can be made sensitive to metadata such as school type, or school year (the corpus only covers the first three years of secondary school), by clicking on the *vb* button in the associated line of SPOD, and continuing in the

2 For an overview of the Dutch education system, see https://eacea.ec.europa.eu/national-policies/eurydice/content/netherlands.

Xpath window of PaQu. Table 1 provides an overview of the size of the corpus (in number of sentences) per school type and year.

Table 1: Schrijfmeterscorpus: number of sentences per school type and year.

	gymnasium	atheneum	HAVO	VMBO TL
year 1	562	230	1044	443
year 2	605	391	855	688
year 3	762	529	817	776

Henceforth, we combine the gymnasium and atheneum data into the category VWO. The essays were scored on a number of issues (involving structural properties of the text, such as cohesion, clarity of exposition, and so on) by a panel of experts (three raters per essay, randomly selected from a pool of eight raters). By and large, these scores show differentiation by age and school type. Scores were on a scale from 50 (minimum) to 150 (maximum). The (Cronbach alpha) reliability of the scores was 0.86.

Table 2 contains the average scores and standard deviation for the three school types in our corpus.

Table 2: Schrijfmeterscorpus: scores per school type.

schooltype	average score	S.D.
VMBO TL	98	13.3
HAVO	102	11.5
VWO	112	14.9

From this, we conclude that the overall ranking of essay quality mirrors the ranking of secondary school types in terms of academic rigor. In the remainder of this chapter, we want to see if this ranking is also reflected by differences at the level of sentence structure that are independent of textual qualities such as textual coherence, explicitness of argumentation, and clarity. In a number of cases to be discussed below, we add comparisons to some additional corpora that were available to us, and were parsed and queried by the same PaQu tools. This was done when it was necessary to make a point about the nature of the syntactic variables that were used in this study. They are presented in the next section.

4 Syntactic variables

SPOD allows us to look at a plenitude of syntactic features, not all of which are expected to be of interest for a comparison of school types. Recall that our working hypothesis is that the variables that show continuous development over time from primary school to university level writing will also distinguish texts by secondary school students of the same age, but different school types.

Some of the features identified by Biber and Gray (2010, 2016); Staples et al. (2016) as characteristic of academic writing were studied in Hoeksema, de Glopper, and van Noord (2021), and found to be relevant for analysing the developmental trajectory from early elementary school writing to academic writing. They can be seen as reflecting steady increases in phrasal complexity. The idea that academic texts differ from colloquial speech and writing in sentential complexity as well, in particular in having more subordinate clauses, has been challenged by D. Biber and his associates. They argue, instead, that academic registers abound in complex phrases, in particular elaborate noun phrases, and not in layers upon layers of clausal embedding. In short, they reject earlier accounts of academic writing as being more elaborate than other types of writing, and propose that compactness, or density, is a more apt characterization. However, this finding does not necessarily generalize to the academic registers of languages other than English. In particular, Hoeksema, de Glopper, and van Noord (2021) lists increasing levels of finite embeddings as a developmental trait for Dutch, monotonically rising all the way from elementary school writing to university level and professional academic texts. Given our focus on Dutch, we decided to include sentential complexity among the variables that may characterize differences across school types.

A striking feature about academic registers is their highly nominal character (Heylighen and Dewaele 2002). The nouns-to-verbs ratio is much higher than for fiction, or spoken language. The nominal character of academic texts is further reflected by higher frequencies for ad-nominal modifiers such as attributive adjectives, PPs and relative clauses.

In this chapter we consider the following variables: noun/verb ratio, nominal modifiers, and levels of sentential embedding. One of the features most strongly correlated with academic writing in Biber and Gray (2010, 2016), viz. nouns serving as premodifiers to nouns, is not included here since Dutch does not use nouns in this way. Just to illustrate this point, consider the linguistic term *noun phrase*. Dutch renders it as either an adjective plus noun combination (*nominale woordgroep* 'nominal phrase', or as a compound, written and treated as a single word, for example *substantiefgroep*). One of the developmental variables in Hoeksema, de Glopper, and van Noord (2021), coordination type, is not included in our study either. We intend to study aspects of coordination elsewhere.

5 Main findings

5.1 Noun/verb ratio

In Table 3, we tabulate nouns and verbs for the three school types in our corpus. For the sake of comparison, we also include the pertinent data from the university essay corpus used in Hoeksema, de Glopper, and van Noord (2021), a corpus consisting of four literary novels by Renate Dorrestein, and the corpus of spoken Dutch (CGN – cf. Oostdijk 2002). Note that the score for VWO, the school type preparing for university level higher education, has a lower N/V score than the university corpus, but it should be noted here that we only have data for the first three years of secondary school, and may expect a rising score for the upper level of secondary school, which takes another 3 years.

Table 3: Nouns, verbs, noun/verb ratio.

subcorpus	N	V	N/V
VWO	7848	6206	1.26
HAVO	6646	5294	1.26
VMBO TL	4722	4115	1.15
University	52852	39434	1.34
Dorrestein	50331	57180	0.88
CGN (spoken Dutch)	126199	170538	0.74

An ANOVA with noun/verb ratio as the dependent variable and school type and school year as independent variables yielded no significant results for school year ($F(2, 42) = .006, p = .946$), but school type was significant ($F(2, 419) = 6.33, p = .002$) and there was an interaction effect of school type and school year ($F(4, 419) = 421$, $p = .002$). The differences between HAVO and VMBO and between VWO and VMBO were significant ($p < .05$).

Academic registers have often been referred to as "nouny", cf. for example the findings in Heylighen and Dewaele (2002). Words that typically co-occur with nouns, such as articles and prepositions were found to correlate highly with academic success in Pennebaker et al. (2014). While the latter study is based on English academic prose, we may interpret Table 3 as providing some evidence that the same is true for Dutch. The data from the Dorrestein novels suggest that a high noun/verb ratio is not typical of Dutch literary writing. However, since the study of literary style is not our main concern here, we will not explore this matter in more detail. In the following subsections, we look for differences among the school types in noun modifiers.

5.2 Nominal modifiers

5.2.1 Attributive adjectives

In this subsection, we consider attributive versus predicative use among adjectives. Attributive adjectives modify nouns, predicative adjectives are predicates in copular, resultative, and depictive constructions. These various uses are illustrated for English below:

1. Predicative
   - This towel is dry. [copular]
   - I need to rub myself dry. [resultative]
   - The towels were given to us dry, not wet. [depictive]
2. Attributive
   - Hand me some dry towels, please.

In Dutch, attributive adjectives are inflected (they either end in a schwa or have no ending, see Haeseryn et al. (1997) for some discussion and Stowe et al. (2014) on Belgian-Dutch variation). In Hoeksema, de Glopper, and van Noord (2021) we presented data that show a continuous increase of attributive cases among all occurrences of adjectives from early elementary school to academic level and professional writing of attributive adjectives. We expect to find the same trend both across school years (1, 2, or 3) and school types in our corpus.

In Table 4, we present the PaQu counts for attributive adjectives, adjectives in general and the percentage of attributive adjectives in the Schrijfmeters corpus. The numbers 1, 2, and 3 stand for 1st, 2nd, and 3rd year classes, respectively.

Table 4: Attributive uses among adjectives in three school types.

School type	year	all adjectives	attributive	pct. attr
VMBO TL	1	496	145	29.2
	2	626	157	25.1
	3	861	309	35.9
HAVO	1	1067	377	35.3
	2	838	289	34.5
	3	782	282	36.1
VWO	1	840	307	36.5
	2	1025	378	36.9
	3	1409	569	40.4

An ANOVA with the percentage of attributive cases among adjectives as dependent variable and school type and school year as independent variables yielded no significant effect of school type ($F(2, 418) = 2.42, p = .090$). School year was significant overall ($F(2, 418) = 3.22, p = 0.041$), but the differences between separate years were not. Interaction of school type and school year was not significant ($F(4, 418) = 1.60, p = 0.173$).

5.2.2 Attributive and other PPs

Prepositional phrases come in a variety of uses (Pullum and Huddleston 2002; Haeseryn et al. 1997), both in English and in Dutch. They can be predicates (for example, *to be at peace*), adverbials (*we come in peace*), complements to verbs and adjectives (*to hope for peace, eager for peace*) and attributive (*country at peace*). Both in Dutch and English, attributive PPs are mostly postnominal (though English to a greater extent than Dutch also has prenominal PPs in compound-like combinations such as *under-the-counter sales, out of pocket expenses*. By and large, the trends among prepositional phrases are similar to those noted for adjectives: a rise in attributive cases (see Table 5).

Table 5: Percentage of attributive uses among PPs in three school types.

School type	Year	PP	attr	pct. attr
VMBO	1	411	84	20.44
	2	679	117	17.23
	3	687	161	23.44
HAVO	1	1033	215	20.81
	2	748	174	23.26
	3	798	197	24.69
VWO	1	741	177	23.89
	2	1055	250	23.70
	3	1340	337	25.15

Attributive PPs are among the main factors adding complexity to English noun phrases (cf. Berlage 2014). Rising trends per school year are to be expected, given similar results in Hoeksema, de Glopper, and van Noord (2021). The rising trend per school type from VMBO TL to VWO is a new finding, but in line with our hypothesis that developmental patterns on the road from elementary education to university level writing are reflected in school type diversity as well. However, our findings of increased levels of attributive uses among PPs, though in accordance with Biber and Gray (2010, 2016); Staples et al. (2016) for written varieties of academic English, were not robust enough to be statistically significant.

An ANOVA test with the percentage of PPs that are attributive as the dependent variable and school year and school type as independent variables showed no significant effects. School type is not significant ($F(2, 419) = 2.48$, $p = .085$), nor is school year ($F(2, 419) = 2.22$, $p = .11$). The interaction of schooltype and schoolyear was not significant ($F(4, 419) = 1.35$, $p = .250$). We believe the smallish size of the corpus might be to blame for these non-results.

5.2.3 Relative clauses

In the case of relative clauses, we will not compare attributive with non-attributive cases (free relatives) the way we did in the case of prepositional cases (cf. the preceding subsection), because free relatives are comparatively rare anyway (free and headed relatives differ by a factor of 10 in corpora such as Lassy Small) and in our Schrijfmeters corpus they are mostly part of wh-clefts, which brings with it a host of complications (headed relatives have no comparable role in wh-clefts). Instead, we normalize raw counts by calculating occurrences per 10,000 sentences.

In Table 6, we see a notable increase of relative clauses in VWO essays, no increase in VMBO TL essays, and a weak overall growth in HAVO essays. Somewhat surprising is the relatively high score for VMBO TL in year 1. This might be a statistical fluke, in light of the fact that we have only a small sample for year 1 of VMBO TL (compare Table 1 above). The raw numbers of relative clauses suggest that relative clauses are more common with increasing grades and school levels, but corrected for the number of sentences provided by each student, an ANOVA did not find a significant effect of either school year ($F(2, 419) = .48$, $p = .622$) or school type ($F(2, 419) = 1.856$, $p = .158$), nor did it find a significant interaction effect ($F(4, 419) = 1.962$, $p = .099$). The fact that we are unable to trace this growing importance through school types and grades may be due to the smallish size of the corpus already mentioned in the previous paragraph, in combination with the limited frequency of relative clauses.

Table 6: Relative clauses: absolute and relative frequencies.

School type	Year	Rel cl	per 10K sentences
VMBO TL	1	30	677
	2	47	683
	3	49	631

Table 6 (continued)

School type	Year	Rel cl	per 10K sentences
HAVO	1	62	594
	2	48	561
	3	58	710
VWO	1	47	593
	2	87	873
	3	135	1046

5.3 Finite embedding

A form of structurally complexity that is often associated with written registers is clausal embedding (measured in clauses per sentence, or per T-unit, cf. Hunt 1970). In this subsection we look at finite embeddings only, such as provided by finite complement clauses, relative clauses and adverbial clauses, and compare complex sentences, involving at least one finite clause embedding, with simple sentences. Other conceivable measures, such as number of nodes per syntactic tree (see Sampson 2013), or maximal length of paths from the root of the tree to its leaves, tend to be highly theory-specific, and hence less likely to be of use, especially when results for different parsers are to be compared. SPOD does not include them. However, finite embeddings can be counted in a theory-neutral way. Table 7 contains data from Hoeksema, de Glopper, and van Noord (2021), showing continuous growth of finite embedding from elementary to higher education (note that these data are from different corpora than the ones considered in this chapter).

Table 7: Complex finite clauses in texts by elementary school children (BasiScript), secondary school students (Hofstad corpus), university students and linguists.

Corpus	*FinEmb* = 0	*FinEmb* > 0	*Pct. Finemb* > 0
BasiScript	614815	128187	17.3
Hofstad	17877	10727	37.5
UnivStud	7735	5136	40.1
Linguists	3522	2966	45.7

The (maximal) level of finite embedding (referred to in Table 7 as *Fin Emb*) is a variable running from 0 (no embedding whatever) to 6 or 7 in very complex cases. The Schrijfmeterscorpus does not go beyond level 3. This means that the most complex sentences according to this measure have a finite clause inside another finite clause that is part of yet another finite clause which is part of the main clause. So the measure does not look at the number of clauses in a sentences, but at their hierarchical structure. The following example from the corpus will illustrate this; each square left bracket indicates a further level of embedding:

(1) Dat is een superleuk feest [waarbij er wordt gevierd [dat
That is a superfun feast whereby there gets celebrated that
Sinterklaas (een man uit Spanje) in ons land is [die
St. Nicholas (a man from Spain) in our country is who
onsterfelijk is.]]]
immortal is
"That is a superfun feast which celebrates that Santa Claus (a man from Spain) is in our country who is immortal"

Finite subordination plays a role in various linguistic phenomena, such as long-distance extraction (Ross 1967; Bouma 2017; Schippers and Hoeksema 2021), NEG-raising (Horn 1989; Collins and Postal 2014), long-distance licensing of negative polarity items (Hoeksema 2017) and sequence of tense (Boogaart 1999; Hollebrandse 2000). Consequently, it has been considered one of the core properties of language. While we cannot study these related phenomena in any detail here, we can take a closer look at their common denominator, the presence of finite subordination. Table 8 presents our main findings. Note that we only look at (at least) one level of embedding versus no level of embedding. An ANOVA revealed significant effects of school type ($F(2, 419) = 4.84$, $p = .008$), school year ($F(2, 419) = 17.07$, $p = .000$), and interaction of school type and school year ($F(4, 419) = 3.71$, $p = .006$). For school type there was a significant difference ($p < .05$) between VWO and HAVO.

Table 8: Finite embedding per school type and grade.

School type	Year	*FinEmb* > 0	*FinEmb* = 0	*Pct. Finemb* > 0
VMBO	1	121	502	19.4
	2	234	648	26.5
	3	210	743	22.0
HAVO	1	234	1099	17.6
	2	183	764	19.3
	3	243	720	25.2
VWO	1	182	796	18.6
	2	305	879	25.8
	3	446	1041	30.0

6 Discussion

Our findings bear out the correctness of our hypothesis that variables which show continuous change from elementary school to academic level writing will also differentiate between levels of high school. The degree to which pupils master the demands of academic and professional writing is without doubt important in their academic career, including choice of secondary school level and type of tertiary education. It would therefore be odd if those features which most strongly characterize academic prose were to be randomly scattered across the secondary school essays, rather than clustering around those levels (gymnasium and atheneum) which prepare for university education.

We found that the noun/verb ratio is a reflection of both school type and school year. Higher years and higher school types correspond to a higher noun/verb ratio. Nominal modifiers become relatively more important in higher grades, as we managed to show for attributive adjectives (though not for school types). An increase in attributive prepositional phrase and relative clause usage was also predicted, but could not be established, perhaps owing to the limitations (in size) of the corpus. In Hoeksema, de Glopper, and van Noord (2021) growing amounts of relative clauses were found from elementary school essays all the way to professional academic writing.

Sentential complexity, measured in terms of the percentage of all sentences that involved at least one level of finite embedding, also correlated with higher years and school levels. It is claimed in studies by Biber and his associates that such complexity is not typical of academic prose. The data in Biber and Gray (2010) show that spoken English has more subordinate complement clauses and more adverbial clauses than academic English, and only relative clauses were more prominent in academic than in spoken English. In line with this is a finding of Myhill (2008), a study of writing quality in secondary education, where it was discovered that better writers in that age bracket use significantly less clausal embedding. However, a different conclusion was drawn in Hoeksema, de Glopper, and van Noord (2021) and van Rijt, van den Broek, and Maeyer (2021) for Dutch. While many of the features typical of academic English carry over to Dutch, sentential complexity may well be a factor distinguishing academic English from Dutch, and perhaps, we speculate, from the continental European languages more generally. It should be noted here as well that academic writing styles are not set in stone but may change rapidly, much like any other type of language register, as shown for English by some striking graphs in Biber and Gray (2010). Mean sentence length has declined over time in a variety of English text types, such as fiction and nonfiction (see in particular Rudnicka 2018).

7 Conclusions

PaQu and its new component SPOD make it possible to look at a broad range of syntactic phenomena in automatically parsed corpora in a user-friendly way. Corpora can be uploaded and parsed, in order to be queried by SPOD. In this chapter, we probed the possibilities of this application for analysing syntactic variation in the Schrijfmeterscorpus, a collection of essays from different levels and grades of Dutch secondary education. It was shown for a number of syntactic properties associated with academic writing that the writing of students varies in predicted ways across levels and grades, in particular noun/verb ratio, number of nominal modifiers and the percentage of complex sentences.

The use of noun/verb ratios is not standard in studies of writing proficiency, but might be worthwhile considering for future research. There are studies of noun/verb ratios in the typological literature (for example Polinsky and Magyar 2020), but these are focused on types, not tokens. Languages like Dutch have far more nouns in their lexicon than verbs, but token frequency is more balanced, and sensitive to developmental as well as register variation.

Bibliography

Berlage, Eva. 2014. *Noun phrase complexity in English*. Cambridge: Cambridge University Press.

Biber, Douglas & Bethany Gray. 2010. Challenging stereotypes about academic writing: Complexity, elaboration, explicitness. *Journal of English for Academic Purposes* 9: 2–20.

Biber, Douglas & Bethany Gray. 2016. Phrasal versus clausal discourse styles: A synchronic grammatical description of academic writing contrasted with other registers. In Douglas Biber & Bethany Gray (eds.), *Grammatical complexity in academic English: Linguistic change in writing*, 67–124. Cambridge: Cambridge University Press.

Bloem, Jelke. 2020. Een corpus waar alle constructies in gevonden zouden moeten kunnen worden? Corpusonderzoek met behulp van automatisch gegenereerde syntactische annotatie. *Nederlandse Taalkunde* 25: 39–71.

Boogaart, Ronny. 1999. *Aspect and temporal ordering. A contrastive analysis of Dutch and English*. Utrecht: Netherlands Graduate School of Linguistics.

Bouma, Gosse. 2017. Finding long-distance dependencies in the Lassy corpus. In Hilke Reckman, Lisa Lai-Shen Cheng, Maarten Hijzelendoorn & Rint Sybesma (eds.), *Crossroads semantics: Computation, experiment and grammar*, 39–56. Amsterdam: Benjamins.

Bouma, Gosse, Gertjan van Noord & Robert Malouf. 2001. Alpino: Wide-coverage computational analysis of Dutch. In Walter Daelemans, Khalil Sima'an, Jorn Veenstra & Jakub Zavrel (eds.), *Computational linguistics in the Netherlands 2000*, 45–59. Amsterdam: Rodopi.

Collins, Chris & Paul M. Postal. 2014. *Classical neg raising*. Cambridge, MA: MIT Press.

Glopper, Kees de & Joanneke Prenger. 2013. Schrijfmeters maken. *Zevenentwintigste conferentie onderwijs Nederlands*. Gent: Academia Press.

Haeseryn, Walter, Kirsten Romijn, Guido Geerts, Jaap de Rooij & Maarten van den Toorn. 1997. *Algemene Nederlandse Spraakkunst.* Groningen/Deurne: Martinus Nijhoff and Wolters Plantyn.

Heylighen, Francis & Jean-Marc Dewaele. 2002. Variation in the contextuality of language: An empirical measure. *Foundations of science* 7: 293–340.

Hoeksema, Jack. 2017. Neg-raising and long-distance licensing of negative polarity items. In Debra Ziegeler & Zhiming Bao (eds.), *Negation and contact: With special focus on Singapore English*, 33–61. Amsterdam: John Benjamins.

Hoeksema, Jack, Kees de Glopper & Gertjan van Noord. 2021. The development of syntactic structure in written Dutch. Submitted.

Hollebrandse, Bart. 2000. The acquisition of sequence of tense. Ph.D. diss., University of Massachusetts, Amherst.

Horn, Laurence. 1989. *A natural history of negation*. Chicago: University of Chicago Press.

Hunt, Kellogg. 1970. *Syntactic maturity in school children and adults*. Monographs of the Society of Research in Child Development. Chicago: University of Chicago Press.

Myhill, Debra. 2008. Towards a linguistic model of sentence development in writing. *Language and Education* 22 (5): 271–288.

Noord, Gertjan van. 2006. At Last Parsing Is Now Operational. *Taln 2006 Verbum ex machina, Actes de la 13e Conference sur le Traitement Automatique des Langues Naturelles*, 20–42. Leuven.

Noord, Gertjan van, Jack Hoeksema, Peter Kleiweg & Gosse Bouma. 2020. Spod: Syntactic profiler of Dutch. *Computational Linguistics in the Netherlands Journal* 10: 129–145.

Odijk, Jan. 2015. Linguistic research with PaQu. *Computational Linguistics in the Netherlands Journal* 5: 3–14.

Odijk, Jan. 2020. De verleidingen en gevaren van GrETEL. *Nederlandse Taalkunde* 25 (1): 7–37.

Odijk, Jan, Gertjan van Noord, Peter Kleiweg & Erik Tjong Kim Sang. 2017. The parse and query (PaQu) application. In Jan Odijk & Arjan van Hessen (eds.), *Clarin in the Low Countries*, 281–297. London: Ubiquity Press.

Oostdijk, Nelleke. 2002. The design of the spoken Dutch corpus. *New frontiers of corpus research*, 105–112. Amsterdam: Rodopi.

Pander Maat, Henk, Kay Raaijmakers, Dennis Vermeulen & Kees de Glopper. 2019. Tekst-kenmerken en tekstkwaliteit van leerlingteksten. *Tijdschrift voor Taalbeheersing* 41: 331–361.

Pennebaker, James W., Cindy K. Chung, Joey Frazee, Gary M. Lavergne & David I. Beaver. 2014. When small words foretell academic success: The case of college admissions essays. *PLoS ONE* 9, no. 12.

Polinsky, Maria & Lilla Magyar. 2020. Headedness and the lexicon: The case of verb-to-noun ratios. *Langages* 5: 1–25.

Pullum, Geoffrey K. & Rodney Huddleston. 2002. Prepositions and preposition phrases. In Rodney Huddleston & Geoffrey K. Pullum (eds.), *The Cambridge grammar of the English language*, 597–662. Cambridge: Cambridge University Press.

Rijt, Jimmy van, Brenda van den Broek & Sven De Maeyer. 2021. Syntactic predictors for text quality in Dutch upper-secondary school students' L1 argumentative writing. *Reading and Writing* 34 (2): 449–465.

Ross, John Robert. 1967. Constraints on variables in syntax. Ph.D. diss., MIT, Cambridge, MA.

Rudnicka, Karolina. 2018. Variation of sentence length across time and genre. In Richard J. Whitt (ed.), *Diachronic corpora, genre, and language change*, 220–240. Amsterdam: John Benjamins.

Sampson, Geoffrey. 2013. The structure of children's writing. In Geoffrey Sampson & Anna Babarczy (eds.), *Grammar without grammaticality: Growth and limits of grammatical precision*, 155–171. Berlin: Walter De Gruyter.

Schippers, Ankelien & Jack Hoeksema. 2021. Langeafstandsverplaatsing in het Nederlands, Engels en Duits: de sandwich ontleed. *Nederlandse Taalkunde* 26: 41–78.

Staples, Shelley, Jesse Egbert, Douglas Biber & Bethany Gray. 2016. Academic writing development at the university level: Phrasal and clausal complexity across level of study, discipline, and genre. *Written Communication* 33: 149–183.

Stowe, Laurie, Robert Hartsuiker, Magdalena Devos & Jack Hoeksema. 2014. Measuring variation in perception of acceptability: a magnitude estimation investigation of Netherlands and Belgian Dutch. In Jack Hoeksema & Dicky Gilbers (eds.), *Black book: a Festschrift in honor of Frans Zwarts*, 311–329. Groningen: University of Groningen.

Wouden, Ton van der, Gosse Bouma, Marjo van Koppen, Frank Landsbergen, Jan Odijk & Matje van de Camp. 2015. Enriching a descriptive grammar with treebank queries. In Markus Dickinson, Erhard Hinrichs, Agnieszka Patejuk & Adam Przepiórkowski (eds.), *Proceedings of the fourteenth international workshop on treebanks and linguistic theories (tlt14)*, 13–25. Warszawa: Polish Academy of Sciences.

Jan Odijk

CLARIN's Support for Research into the Acquisition of Lexical Properties

Abstract: Odijk (2011) sketched a research question on the acquisition of lexical properties of words, and illustrated it with some concrete examples, in particular with respect to the lexical properties of the Dutch synonyms *heel*, *erg*, and *zeer* (all meaning 'very'). This work also indicated what the CLARIN infrastructure should offer to make it possible to address this research question. In this contribution I sketch to what extent the CLARIN infrastructure has achieved these requirements and desiderata. The resulting picture is mixed: (1) some have been implemented; (2) some have not been implemented and are still highly desirable; (3) some have not been implemented but turned out to be not so urgent; (4) new requirements and desiderata have arisen in the last 10 years, only some of which have been implemented. In this way, I evaluate the development of the CLARIN infrastructure (mainly its Netherlands part) over the past 10 years, and sketch the requirements and desiderata for the CLARIN infrastructure to address this research question for the next 10 years.

Keywords: text corpus search, treebank search, language acquisition, lexicon search, research infrastructure, CLARIN, CLARIAH

1 Introduction

Odijk (2011) sketched a research question on the acquisition of lexical properties of words, and illustrated it with some concrete examples, in particular with respect to the lexical properties of the Dutch synonyms *heel*, *erg*, and *zeer* (all meaning 'very'). This work also indicated what the CLARIN infrastructure should offer to make it possible to address this research question. Some of this research was actually carried out and reported on at various occasions (inter alia, Odijk

Acknowledgements: I would like to thank colleagues who commented on parts of earlier versions of this chapter, in particular Katrien Depuydt, Jesse de Does, Jan Niestadt, and Vincent Vandeghinste (all from the Institute for the Dutch Language) as well as anonymous reviewers of an earlier version of this chapter.

Jan Odijk, UiL-OTS, Utrecht University, Utrecht, the Netherlands, e-mail: j.odijk@uu.nl

https://doi.org/10.1515/9783110767377-028

2015, 2016, 2020a). When carrying out this research, new requirements and desirable features emerged, some of which were actually implemented.

Though the research question addressed was quite specific, the requirements to address this research question were formulated broadly, so that meeting these requirements enables many other linguistic research questions. Furthermore, the study of the acquisition of a linguistic property by children requires that one knows what the relevant facts of the adult language are, and it requires that one has a theory (model, grammar) of the adult I-language. So this research question also requires facilities to investigate the language of adults. For all of these reasons, it is interesting to investigate to what extent these requirements have actually been met.

In this contribution I sketch to what extent the CLARIN infrastructure has achieved these requirements and desiderata. The resulting picture is mixed: (1) some have been implemented; (2) some have not been implemented and are still highly desirable; (3) some have not been implemented but turned out to be not so urgent; (4) new requirements and desiderata have arisen in the last 10 years, only some of which have been implemented. In this way, I evaluate the development of the CLARIN infrastructure (mainly its Netherlands part) over the past 10 years, and sketch the requirements and desiderata for the CLARIN infrastructure to address this research question for the next 10 years.

I briefly sketch the original research problem in Section 2, introduce the requirements and desiderata derived from this research question in Section 3, and I evaluate their realization in the CLARIN infrastructure in three sections: Section 4 on searching in metadata, Section 5 on searching in lexicons, and Section 6 on searching in annotated corpora. I list new requirements that arose in the past 10 years in Section 7, and conclude this work in Section 8.

2 The research problem

The three Dutch words *heel*, *erg*, and *zeer* are (near-)synonyms meaning 'very', that is (stated informally), they modify a word or phrase that expresses a (gradable) property or state and specify that its modifiee has the property or state it expresses to a high degree. Of these, *heel* can modify adjectival (A) phrases only, while *erg* and *zeer* can modify not only adjectival, but also verbal (V) and adpositional (P) phrases. This is illustrated in example (1).[1]

1 An asterisk is used to mark ill-formed expressions.

(1) a. Hij is daar heel / erg / zeer blij over
he is there very / very / very glad about'
'He is very happy about that'
b. Hij is daar *heel / erg / zeer in zijn sas mee
he is there very / very / very in his lock with
'He is very happy about that'
c. Dat verbaast mij *heel / erg / zeer
That surprises me very / very / very
'That surprises me very much'

In (1a) the adjectival phrase *blij* 'glad' can be modified by each of the three words. In (1b) the (idiomatic) adpositional phrase (PP) *in zijn sas* can be modified by *zeer* and *erg* but not by *heel*. The same holds in (1c) for the verbal phrase *verbaast*.[2] In English, the same holds for the word *very*: it can only modify adjectives.[3] For verbs and prepositional phrases one cannot use *very* but one can use the expression *very much* instead:

(2) a. He is very happy about it
b. He is *very / very much in love with her
c. It surprised me *very / very much

The distinctions illustrated are purely syntactic in nature. The words *heel*, *zeer* and *erg* are synonyms or near-synonyms, and the expressions *blij* and *in zijn sas* are near-synonyms as well, which makes it unlikely that the differences can be derived from semantic properties. It is also not in any way obvious how the differences could follow from universal principles of language or language acquisition.

There are other differences among the words *heel*, *erg*, and *zeer*. If any of these differences is somehow related to the difference under investigation then it must be a difference in which *heel* opposes the other two words *erg* and *zeer*. However, this is not the case (Odijk 2015).

The central problem with regard to these data is now: how do children acquire these properties, in particular that *heel* does **not** take verbs and adpositions as modifiers while *erg* and *zeer* do.

2 Or maybe the whole VP *verbaast mij*.

3 And certain adverbs. I assume that words traditionally assigned the part of speech 'adverb' are either adjectives or (intransitive) adpositions.

3 Requirements

In order to address the research question formulated in Section 2, Odijk (2011) formulated a whole range of requirements that the CLARIN research infrastructure should meet. These requirements concern software and data. We list the requirements for software in Appendix A and the requirements for data in Appendix B.

The software requirements mostly concern options for searching, in metadata and in data. The data requirements list a number of corpora and lexicons that should be accessible and easily searchable.

In this chapter we assess to what extent CLARIN meets these requirements in 2021. We do so in three sections: one on metadata search (Section 4), one on lexicon search (Section 5), and one on corpus search (Section 6).

4 Metadata search

We first consider requirements that relate to search in metadata, as a first step towards identifying relevant data and selecting the ones needed for the research.

4.1 Realized

The requirement "Give me a list of all LRs for the Dutch language" is largely met by CLARIN. A simple query[4] in CLARIN's Virtual Language Observatory[5] yields many results (108,874 on 12 May 2021). This large number of resources is of course too large to inspect fully manually, and doing so would also not be very useful, because over 90,000 of the entries are titles of individual songs from the Dutch song database, as can be seen through this query.[6] The metadata are not at the right level of granularity for our purposes, so we carry out some further filtering. If we in addition select *resource type=corpus* we get a list of 134 corpora, still a long list but one that can be handled by a human. I filter further by selecting all options for modality except *modality=speech* using this query,[7] which leaves

4 https://vlo.clarin.eu/?fqType=languageCode:or&fq=languageCode:code:nld

5 https://vlo.clarin.eu

6 https://vlo.clarin.eu/search?q=liederenbank&fqType=languageCode:or&fq=language Code:code:nld

7 https://vlo.clarin.eu/search?fqType=languageCode:or&fq=languageCode:code:nld&-fqType=resourceClass:or&fq=resourceClass:corpus&fqType=modality:or&fq=modality:writte n&fq=modality:writtenlanguage&fq=modality:spoken

50 corpora. Not all these corpora are relevant for my research, so I would like to select the ones that are and store their description. This is in principle possible by making a virtual collection of the search result, and then removing the corpora that are not relevant from this virtual collection, and I succeeded in saving the query results as a virtual collection.[8]

I had to remove 3 corpora that did not validate. The remaining 47[9] indeed contain corpora that I was looking for, such as the Spoken Dutch Corpus, and the SoNaR corpus, and many others that are potentially relevant (e.g., the Dutch Parallel Corpus, Europarl data), some that are very relevant (e.g., the Basiscript and Basilex Corpora), but also some that are obviously not relevant (e.g., corpora for Middle Dutch). The highly relevant Dutch CHILDES corpora, however, are unfortunately not contained in the search results, because they are not characterized as resourceClass=corpus.

4.2 Not realized

Requirement 2 "What is the size of all Dutch text corpora (in #tokens") has not been realized. This requirement may appear a very simple requirement and easy to realize. It is not completely trivial, because different measures are relevant for different resources and different research purposes, so each researcher who provides data may provide his own metric. Examples of such different metrics are token count, the number of documents, the number of turns taken (in a dialogue), and so on. In addition, many resources have overlap with other resources, or are derivatives of other resources (e.g., the original text of a different resource enriched with linguistic annotations), which complicates the problem considerably. But the main reason why this has not been realized is because there has not been any central coordination for this aspect of the metadata. CLARIN promotes CMDI as the framework for creating metadata (Broeder et al. 2010; Windhouwer and Goosen 2022). CMDI allows researchers to define their own metadata schemata so that there is a lot of flexibility, which was needed in the early years of

8 However, the system works with a web interface, and it shows many of the bad features that are unfortunately common for most web interfaces (for an overview, see Odijk (2018)). For example, one cannot save before all entries are validated (there should be a distinction between saving (possibly with errors) and submitting (with validation). The *Save* button is not in a fixed menu as in a decent interface, but at the bottom of the list of 50 resource descriptions (which keeps one scrolling all the time). And there are many other missing or less fortunate options, which I reported to the developers.

9 Unfortunately, publishing the virtual collection failed, so it is a private collection.

CLARIN because no one had a good overview of what metadata were needed for the available language resources. But there were hardly any minimum requirements on which metadata information must be specified and how it should be specified. As a consequence, when all these metadata were brought together and made accessible via the VLO, the result turned out to be quite messy. This was observed by many, and Odijk (2014) carried out a detailed analysis of the problems and made several suggestions for improvements. The situation has significantly improved since then by the CLARIN CMDI Taskforce,[10] by the CLARIN Curation Task force (Ostojic, Sugimoto, and Ďurčo 2017), by the initiative on the CLARIN resource families[11] (Fišer, Lenardič, and Erjavec 2018; Lenardič and Fišer 2022), and by others, but is still not optimal.

A more complex query such as "Give me a list of all Dutch data that contain children between two and seven years old as speaker" is also not possible at this moment.

A query such as "Give me a list of all Dutch data containing any of the words *heel*, *zeer*, *erg*" is feasible via CLARIN's Federated Content Search (FCS),[12] but too few Dutch corpora currently have endpoints for FCS to make this useful.

5 Lexicon search

The requirement to find words that are closely related to *heel*, *erg* and *zeer*, for example adverbs that function as an intensifier ("booster") and that are synonymous or co-hyponyms of these words can be done via Cornetto (Vossen et al. 2013), for which a completely new search application was developed in CLARIN. For example, this query[13] searches for synonyms and co-hyponyms of the word *heel* as an adverb.

Cornetto includes the RBN dictionary (van der Vliet 2007), so search in RBN is also possible. Search in other dictionaries containing synonym or synonym-like information was therefore not needed (puzzle dictionaries were suggested in (Odijk 2011) as a backup alternative).

10 https://www.clarin.eu/sites/default/files/clarin2019_bazaar_nolda.pdf
11 https://www.clarin.eu/resource-families
12 https://www.clarin.eu/content/federated-content-search-clarin-fcs
13 http://cornetto.clarin.inl.nl/simple_search.xql?type=LE&purpose=S&id=d_r-106880

6 Search in annotated corpora

Many requirements involve search in annotated corpora. Many corpora have been annotated mostly at the token level, that is, linguistic properties are assigned to tokens. In some corpora, utterances have been enriched with syntactic structures. Such annotated corpora are called treebanks.

Many words in natural language are ambiguous, and this is also true of *heel*, *erg*, and *zeer*. In fact, each one is multiply ambiguous. We should be able to search for these words under the intended interpretation. The ambiguity is eliminated or significantly reduced by knowing the syntactic context of these words. Treebanks can be used to achieve this to a high degree, so we should be able to search in treebanks. I started my research using a corpus of CHILDES data in a search application that was created for a completely different research question (COAVA, (Cornips et al. 2016)). This corpus did not contain syntactic structures (it was not a treebank), and if I had based my research solely on this corpus I would have reached wrong conclusions. For details see Odijk (2016: 53). A treebank is required for this research.

A user-friendly treebank search application was developed outside the context of but clearly inspired by CLARIN: LASSY Word Relations Search (Tjong Kim Sang, Bouma, and van Noord 2010). After running for a few years it was not really maintained systematically, was regularly down and there was a real danger that it would disappear. In the context of CLARIN an update of this application was made, resulting in PaQu (Odijk et al. 2017). PaQu has been used extensively for addressing the research question, and it was especially suited for this because it has special provisions for searching for word relations, a crucial property for investigating the modification potential of words and its acquisition.

In the context of the cooperation between the Netherlands and Flanders on CLARIN, a new treebank search application was developed with query-by-example as its main distinguishing feature: GrETEL (Augustinus, Vandeghinste, and Eynde 2012; Augustinus et al. 2017). This application has also been used a lot for this and other research, and several improved versions of the application have been created (e.g., Odijk, van der Klis, and Spoel 2018).

These applications offer a number of treebanks for search, but they also allow a user to upload the user's own corpus, which is then parsed resulting in a treebank, which is then available for search. This feature has turned out to be very useful, and it made it possible to turn data for which no treebank existed into a treebank. It thus also enabled searching in treebanks derived from CHILDES corpora (which was one of the requirements), and a treebank for the Dutch CHILDES corpora was made generally available in PaQu.

Queries such as

1. find me sentences containing occurrences of the lemma *erg* of any part of speech (POS) which acts as a modifier to another word of any POS;
2. for each child, give a list of pairs (session, age) of the child;
3. for each child, give me #sessions by period, where period is e.g., every month, week, half year, year;
4. for child and each session, give #occurrences of *zeer, heel, erg*;

can be carried out. Others, which require more advanced aggregation of data currently cannot be carried out when using the applications mentioned:

1. for each child give me the list of new words uttered by period;
2. for child and each session, give #occurrences of *zeer, heel, erg*, by period;
3. give me utterances containing occurrences of *zeer, erg, heel* uttered by the child before any adult used any of these words;
4. give me #occurrences of *heel* uttered by the parent before the child utters it (idem for *zeer, erg*, etc.);

These have to be carried out by exporting the search results and do the analysis with different software. Exporting search results is possible, though there are severe limitations due to IPR. Therefore it is necessary to be able to carry out such queries and analyses inside the application.

For token-annotated corpora several search applications have been created, in particular the OpenSoNaR application (van de Camp, Reynaert, and Oostdijk 2017; de Does, Niestadt, and Depuydt 2017), which not only gives access to the 550 million token SoNaR corpus (Oostdijk et al. 2013) but also to the Spoken Dutch Corpus (CGN, (Oostdijk et al. 2002)), including its audio. And several search applications have been made available outside the context of but in close collaboration with CLARIN. These include search applications for modern Dutch (e.g., CHN (Contemporary Dutch Corpus)), but also for historical varieties of Dutch (e.g., Corpus Gysseling, Nederlab (Brouwer, Brugman, and Kemps-Snijders 2016; Brugman et al. 2016))

We discuss the current status of some other requirements:

- All annotated corpora contain errors. This is true not only for automatically annotated corpora but also for manually annotated corpora. None of the search applications have systematic provisions for reporting such errors. Reporting such errors so far goes via e-mail, which is not an ideal situation.
- Support for batch processing of queries is explicitly supported by OpenSoNaR. In PaQu and GrETEL one can achieve similar results by a combination of alter-

natives in a single query, made easier by using macros, in combination with the options for analysing the search results.

- All search applications can combine metadata and content search, but each does it in a different way, and all have limitations.
- In OpenSoNaR and the treebank applications one can formulate queries such as:
  1. give absolute and relative frequencies of *heel/hele/erg/erge/zeer* as adj by text genre, and speaker/participants education level, and by corpus;
  2. idem but for the word + the following POS-tag;
  3. idem but in the fully parsed part of CGN and in LASSY + the POS-tag of the modifiee head;
- To my knowledge, the requirements in (9) of Appendix A, i.e that new data created by enriching existing data is dealt with fully automatically in a fully CLARIN-compatible way has not been realized anywhere within the Netherlands and perhaps not even in Europe.
- Concerning the requirement (10) of Appendix A, i.e. maximizing the use of restricted vocabularies with well-defined semantics, a lot of work has been done on it, but in my view it is still insufficient to ensure true interoperability. The systems to store the vocabularies and their semantics changed over time (initially ISOCAT, since 2015 the CLARIN Concept Registry, and a new change is immanent). They usually had other uses by other communities as well, which often complicated things, and none of these systems had their concepts organized in such a way that it was easier to reuse existing ones than creating new ones. This topic is too broad to deal with properly here, so I will leave it at these general remarks.

7 New requirements

During our research, we found that we need many new features of the treebank query applications. Many of these were described in Odijk (2020b).

All annotated corpora contain errors. If one wants to draw reliable conclusions on the basis of corpus data, one has to assess the quality of the annotations in the corpus. In most cases a full manual evaluation is not feasible since the amount of data is too large. In those cases one can evaluate a representative sample of the data. But the treebank search applications should support selecting such representative samples. Currently PaQu offers some support for this (only via the word relations interface), but it is lacking in GrETEL and OpenSoNaR.

One technique that is especially effective for investigating recall of a search query is to formulate a query that searches for (as small as possible) a superset of the query results. For example, a treebank search for two verbs in a particular syntactic configuration can be generalized to a search for two verbs in any syntactic configuration (Bloem 2016). Formulating such a query can be quite difficult (see Odijk 2020b: 32–33). It would be good if the search applications would provide support for this, for example, by automatically suggesting the relevant queries on the basis of the original query.

One should also have the opportunity to annotate utterances in the search results, or specific words or phrases in search results to mark errors in the annotation or add information that is not present in the corpus (e.g., semantic information in a treebank). Ideally one would be supported in this by lookup in or even bootstrapping from external lexical resources (e.g. the CELEX lexicon (Baayen, Piepenbrock, and Gulikers 1996), Cornetto, or the Open Dutch Wordnet (Postma et al. 2016)). And it should of course be possible to use such annotations in the analysis component of the search application. Experiments with combining corpus search with search in external lexical resources have been done under the name "Chaining Search" (Dekker, Fanee, and de Does 2019), but the results of these experiments have not been integrated in any of the search applications.

Extensions of the analysis components (even the most advanced one, that found in GrETEL) are also desirable. The analysis component of GrETEL enables a user to combine arbitrary attributes of nodes that match with node descriptions in the query and metadata in a pivot table. But one should also be able to include computed relations between nodes, such as "node1 precedes / follows/ contains / overlaps with node2", "node1 is adjacent to node2", or "node1 and node2 are in a projective / non-projective grammatical relation",[14] as well as user definable ranges of numerical and date values.[15] Ideally, for advanced users a full database query language with functionality comparable to that of SQL would be provided,[16] but currently that is certainly not the case.[17]

An important feature of an analysis component is that one can easily get from an aggregate (e.g., the frequency of the combination of a token property, a node property and/or a metadata property) to the actual examples on which this is based. This feature has been implemented very well and is efficient in PaQu and

14 That is, informally stated: the relation between two nodes is projective if there are no crossing branches in a phrase structure tree over the surface string.

15 A limited number of these is actually possible, but not in a very user-friendly way.

16 The XQuery language would be the natural candidate for PaQu and GrETEL.

17 Such functionality is offered by the Prague Mark-up Language Treebank Query (PMLTQ) system, https://lindat.mff.cuni.cz/services/pmltq/#!/home.

in OpenSoNaR, but it has more limitations and is very inefficient in GrETEL 4. Other search applications (e.g., Nederlab) have only very limited options here.

It is often necessary to execute one and the same query at multiple occasions or by different researchers. However, it is currently not possible to store queries in the application so that they can be reused, though this is clearly a desirable feature. Our experiences with facilities to store queries in other applications (e.g., in SHEBANQ[18]), taught us that it is also necessary to carefully organize the storage of queries in order to make them easily findable for reuse: a simple list of stored queries is not enough because this list tends to get quite large very soon.

We also found several times that we wanted to compare results of two queries. It is therefore desirable if results of queries can be stored and set-like operations (union, difference, intersection) can be applied to stored queries, as e.g. MIMORE offers (Barbiers et al. 2016).

Some problems are caused by the nature of the syntactic structures in the treebanks for Dutch (Odijk et al. 2017: Section 23.3). One problem with the *de facto* standard treebank format is that single words that form a phrase on their own are not dominated by a phrase node: so in *de man sliep* 'the man slept' there is a node labeled NP for the phrase *de man*, but in *Jan sliep* 'Jan slept' there is no node labeled NP for the (single-word) phrase *Jan*. This complicates almost all queries, as also observed by Van Eynde, Augustinus, and Vandeghinste (2016: 106–107). It is clearly desirable that for each treebank a version in which there are nodes for all single word phrases is made available. This is not difficult to achieve since the relevant information to construct these phrasal nodes is present in the treebanks.

A second problem concerns so-called index-nodes. If a word or phrase has multiple functions in an utterance, the syntactic structure for this utterance contains multiple nodes for it: apart from the node that one expects (which we will call the antecedent), one or more nodes may occur that contain only an index and a grammatical relation as properties and that are coindexed with the antecedent. Other properties of their antecedent are not present at this node. It is very difficult to define queries in Xpath to obtain all properties of the antecedent of an index node.[19] It is desirable to provide a version of the treebanks in which such index nodes are replaced by a copy of their antecedents. This feature actually has recently been implemented in PaQu,[20] but it is not available in GrETEL.

Finally, it should be possible for a user to share corpora uploaded by him/her with a group of selectable users. Currently, some applications either keep

18 See https://shebanq.ancient-data.org/hebrew/queries.

19 See the DACT Cookbook, Section Antecedents of co-indexed nodes for an implementation of inclusion of indexed nodes in Xpath.

20 https://paqu.let.rug.nl:8068/info.html#expanded

an uploaded corpus private to the user, or make it openly available to all users. This is a problem because a user does not want to bother everybody with his/her uploaded corpora (e.g., in an experimental phase), and because a user may want to share the data only with a small group of collaborators during the initial phase of a research project.

8 Conclusions

I sketched to what extent the CLARIN infrastructure has achieved requirements and desiderata put forward by Odijk (2011) on the basis of a research question. The resulting picture is mixed: (1) some have been implemented; (2) some have not been implemented and are still highly desirable; (3) some have not been implemented but turned out to be not so urgent; (4) new requirements and desiderata have arisen in the last 10 years, only some of which have been implemented. In this way, I evaluated the development of the CLARIN infrastructure (mainly its Netherlands part) over the past 10 years, and gave a sketch of the requirements and desiderata for the CLARIN infrastructure to address this research question (and many others) in the next 10 years. It is my hope that these new requirements and desiderata will be taken up in future projects both at the ERIC level (where appropriate) and at the national level.

Appendix A: Software requirements

1. Give me a list of all LRs for the Dutch language.
2. What is the size of all Dutch text corpora (in #tokens)?
3. Give me a list of all Dutch data that contain children between two and seven years old as speaker.
4. Give me a list of all Dutch data containing any of the words *heel*, *zeer*, *erg*.
5. Find words that are closely related to *heel*, *erg*, and *zeer*, e.g., adverbs that function as an intensifier ("booster") and that are synonymous or co-hyponyms. A recursive search for synonyms is therefore desirable, limited by a maximum depth (since otherwise there is no guarantee the process will finish), and for each found synonym the level of depth at which it was found. The search engine should be clever enough to determine that this kind of information can be found in (certain) dictionaries, but not, e.g., in text or speech corpora, preferably without having to search through all these data (e.g. based on metadata, or based on a classification of types of resources).

6. As with many words in natural language, each of the three words is multiply ambiguous, so we should be able to search for these words under the intended interpretation.
7. Treebanks can achieve this to a high degree, so we should be able to search in treebanks.
   (a) Queries such as:
      i. Find me sentences containing occurrences of the lemma *erg* of any POS which acts as a modifier to another word of any POS.
      ii. For each child, give list of pairs session + age of the child
      iii. For each child, give me #sessions by period, where period is e.g., every month, week, half year, year.
      iv. For each child give me the list of new words uttered by period.
      v. For child and each session, give #occurrences of *zeer, heel, erg*.
      vi. Idem, by period.
      vii. Give me utterances containing occurrences of *zeer, erg, heel* uttered by the child before any adult used any of these words.
      viii. Give me #occurrences of *heel* uttered by the parent before the child utters it (idem for *zeer, erg,* etc.).
   (b) Treebanks contain errors. I would like to report the errors I found in the treebank in a systematic manner (so provisions for that should be available).
   (c) Batch processing of queries should be supported, or there should be a simple way of issuing the same query for different lexical items without too much manual work. (e.g., a map function that applies a query to each item in a list of lexical items, and yields a list of query results per lexical item).
   (d) Some simple queries use a mix of metadata and content search, and the content search is on multiple tiers, so that should be possible in the search engine
   (e) In the CHILDES corpus, we again run into the problem of the ambiguity of the words. So perhaps I would like to parse these corpora (or at least the parts where adults speak),
8. POS-tagged corpora such as CGN and SoNaR can also be useful and are usually larger than treebanks. We would like to be able to formulate queries such as:
   (a) Give absolute and relative frequencies of *heel/hele/erg/erge/zeer* as adj by text genre, and speaker/participants education level, and by corpus.
   (b) Idem but for the word + the following POS-tag.
   (c) Idem but in the fully parsed part of CGN and in LASSY + the POS-tag of the modifiee head.

9. Of course, the found and newly created data
   - should be stored in a supported format;
   - with automatically generated metadata;
   - with automatically generated provenance data;
   - using data categories mapped to or from ISOCAT;
   - for which PIDs are provided;
   - stored on a server of a CLARIN-centre;
   - so that they can become proper resources on their own;
   - and are visible, accessible and interpretable as part of enriched publications
10. Even simple and well-definable data categories at the time allowed any string as value. These should be defined in a very strict manner, at least by specifying a regular expression for the values they can take. If any string can be filled in, no search engine can do anything with it that makes sense.

Appendix B: Data requirements

1. Dutch EuroWordnet (in 2011 it was only available as a download via ELRA M0016).
2. Or Cornetto (in 2011 available as a download via the Dutch HLT-Agency).
3. Ordinary dictionaries containing synonyms (e.g., Van Dale dictionaries, perhaps RBN).
4. Puzzle dictionaries with synonym information.
5. Relevant data can be found in the CHILDES system (part of TalkBank), with 7 corpora for Dutch, but of course with their own data formats (CHAT) and tools (CLAN).
6. Spoken Dutch Corpus.
7. SoNaR Corpus.

Bibliography

Augustinus, Liesbeth, Vincent Vandeghinste & Frank Van Eynde. 2012. Example-based treebank querying. In Nicoletta Calzolari, Khalid Choukri, Thierry Declerck, Mehmet Uğur Doğan, Bente Maegaard, Joseph Mariani, Asunción Moreno, Jan Odijk & Stelios Piperidis (eds.), *Proceedings of the eighth international conference on language resources and evaluation (LREC 2012)*. Istanbul, Turkey: European Language Resources Association (ELRA).

Augustinus, Liesbeth, Vincent Vandeghinste, Ineke Schuurman & Frank Van Eynde. 2017. Gretel: A tool for example-based treebank mining. In Jan Odijk & Arjan van Hessen (eds.), *CLARIN in the low countries*, 269–280. London, UK: Ubiquity. DOI: http://dx.doi.org/10.5334/bbi.22. License: CC-BY 4.0.

Baayen, R H., R Piepenbrock & L. Gulikers. 1996. *Celex2*. Philadelphia: Linguistic Data Consortium. LDC96L14: https://catalog.ldc.upenn.edu/LDC96L14.

Barbiers, Sjef, Marjo van Koppen, Hans Bennis & Norbert Corver. 2016. MIcrocomparative MOrphosyntactic REsearch (MIMORE): Mapping partial grammars of Flemish, Brabantish and Dutch. *Lingua* 178: 5 – 31. Linguistic Research in the CLARIN Infrastructure.

Bloem, Jelke. 2016. Evaluating automatically annotated treebanks for linguistic research. *Proceedings of the 4th workshop on challenges in the management of large corpora (CMLC-4)*, 8–14. Portorož, Slovenia: European Language Resources Association (ELRA).

Broeder, D., M. Kemps-Snijders, D. Van Uytvanck, M. Windhouwer, P. Withers, P. Wittenburg & C. Zinn. 2010. A data category registry- and component-based metadata framework. In N. Calzolari, B. Maegaard, J. Mariani, J. Odijk, K. Choukri, S. Piperidis, M. Rosner & D. Tapias (eds.), *Proceedings of the seventh international conference on language resources and evaluation (LREC 2010)*, 43–47. Valetta, Malta: European Language Resources Association (ELRA).

Brouwer, Matthijs, Hennie Brugman & Marc Kemps-Snijders. 2016. A Solr/Lucene based multi tier annotation search solution. *Selected papers from the CLARIN annual conference 2016, 26–28 October, Aix-en-Provence*, 29–37. Linköping, Sweden: Linköping University Electronic Press.

Brugman, Hennie, Martin Reynaert, Nicoline van der Sijs, René van Stipriaan, Erik Tjong Kim Sang & Antal van den Bosch. 2016. Nederlab: Towards a single portal and research environment for diachronic Dutch text corpora. In Nicoletta Calzolari, Khalid Choukri, Thierry Declerck, Sara Goggi, Marko Grobelnik, Bente Maegaard, Joseph Mariani, Helene Mazo, Asuncion Moreno, Jan Odijk & Stelios Piperidis (eds.), *Proceedings of the tenth international conference on language resources and evaluation (LREC 2016)*. Paris, France: European Language Resources Association (ELRA).

Camp, Matje van de, Martin Reynaert & Nelleke Oostdijk. 2017. WhiteLab 2.0: A web interface for corpus exploitation. In Jan Odijk & Arjan van Hessen (eds.), *CLARIN in the low countries*, 231–243. London, UK: Ubiquity. DOI: http://dx.doi.org/10.5334/bbi.19. License: CC-BY 4.0.

Cornips, Leonie, Jos Swanenberg, Wilbert Heeringa & Folkert de Vriend. 2016. The relationship between first language acquisition and dialect variation: Linking resources from distinct disciplines in a CLARIN-NL project. *Lingua* 178: 32 – 45. Linguistic Research in the CLARIN Infrastructure.

Dekker, Peter, Mathieu Fanee & Jesse de Does. 2019. CLARIAH chaining search: A platform for combined exploitation of multiple linguistic resources. In K. Simov & M. Eskevich (eds.), *Proceedings of CLARIN annual conference 2019*, Theory and Applications of Natural Language Processing, 24–27. CLARIN.

Does, J. de, J. Niestadt & K. Depuydt. 2017. Creating research environments with BlackLab. In Jan Odijk & Arjan van Hessen (eds.), *CLARIN in the low countries*, 245–257. London, UK: Ubiquity. DOI: http://dx.doi.org/10.5334/bbi.20. License: CC-BY 4.0.

Fišer, Darja, Jakob Lenardič & Tomaž Erjavec. 2018. CLARIN's Key Resource Families. In Nicoletta Calzolari, Khalid Choukri, Christopher Cieri, Thierry Declerck, Sara Goggi, Koiti Hasida, Hitoshi Isahara, Bente Maegaard, Joseph Mariani, Hélène Mazo, Asuncion Moreno, Jan Odijk, Stelios Piperidis & Takenobu Tokunaga (eds.), *Proceedings of the eleventh*

international conference on language resources and evaluation (LREC 2018). Miyazaki, Japan: European Language Resources Association (ELRA).
Lenardič, Jakob & Darja Fišer. 2022. The CLARIN Resource and Tool Families. In Darja Fišer & Andreas Witt (eds.), *CLARIN. The infrastructure for language resources.* Berlin: De Gruyter.
Odijk, Jan. 2011. User scenario search. internal CLARIN-NL document, http://www.clarin.nl/sites/default/files/User %20scenario%20Serach%20110413.docx, last accessed 2022-03-25.
Odijk, Jan. 2014. Discovering resources in CLARIN: Problems and suggestions for solutions. unpublished article, Utrecht University. http://dspace.library.uu.nl/handle/1874/303788.
Odijk, Jan. 2015. Linguistic research with PaQu. *Computational Linguistics in the Netherlands Journal* 5 (December): 3–14.
Odijk, Jan. 2016. A Use case for Linguistic Research on Dutch with CLARIN. In Koenraad De Smedt (ed.), *Selected papers from the CLARIN annual conference 2015, October 14–16, 2015, Wroclaw, Poland*, Linköping Electronic Conference Proceedings no. 123, 45–61. CLARIN, Linköping, Sweden: Linköping University Electronic Press. http://www.ep.liu.se/ecp/article.asp?issue=123&article=004, http://dspace.library.uu.nl/handle/1874/339492.
Odijk, Jan. 2018. Why I do not like web interfaces for data entry. Utrecht University, https://dspace.library.uu.nl/handle/1874/375225.
Odijk, Jan. 2020a. CLARIN-supported research on modification potential in Dutch first language acquisition. *Selected papers from the CLARIN annual conference 2019*, Volume 172 of *Linköping Electronic Conference Proceedings*, 94–107. Linköping, Sweden: Linköping University Press.
Odijk, Jan. 2020b. De verleidingen en gevaren van GrETEL. *Nederlandse Taalkunde* 25 (1): 7–38.
Odijk, Jan, Martijn van der Klis & Sheean Spoel. 2018. Extensions to the GrETEL treebank query application. *Proceedings of the 16th international workshop on treebanks and linguistic theories (tlt16)*, 46–55. Prague, Czech Republic. http://aclweb.org/anthology/W/W17/W17-7608.pdf.
Odijk, Jan, Gertjan van Noord, Peter Kleiweg & Erik Tjong Kim Sang. 2017. The parse and query (PaQu) application. In Jan Odijk & Arjan van Hessen (eds.), *CLARIN in the low countries*, 281–297. London, UK: Ubiquity. DOI: http://dx.doi.org/10.5334/bbi.23. License: CC-BY 4.0.
Oostdijk, N., M. Reynaert, V. Hoste & I. Schuurman. 2013. The construction of a 500 million word reference corpus of contemporary written Dutch. In Peter Spyns & Jan Odijk (eds.), *Essential speech and language technology for dutch: Results by the STEVIN-programme*, 219–247. Berlin: Springer. http://link.springer.com/book/10.1007/978-3-642-30910-6/page/1.
Oostdijk, Nelleke, Wim Goedertier, Frank Van Eynde, Lou Boves, Jean-Pierre Martens, Michael Moortgat & Harald Baayen. 2002. Experiences from the Spoken Dutch Corpus project. *Proceedings of the third international conference on language resources and evaluation (LREC-2002)*, 340–347. Las Palmas: ELRA.
Ostojic, Davor, Go Sugimoto & Matej Ďurčo. 2017. The Curation Module and Statistical Analysis on VLO Metadata Quality. In Lars Borin (ed.), *Selected papers from the CLARIN annual conference 2016, Aix-en-Provence, 26–28 October 2016*, Linköping Electronic Conference Proceedings no. 136, 90–101. CLARIN, Linköping, Sweden: Linköping University Electronic Press. https://ep.liu.se/ecp/article.asp?issue=136&article=007&volume=0#.

Postma, Marten, Emiel van Miltenburg, Roxane Segers, Anneleen Schoen & Piek Vossen. 2016. Open Dutch WordNet. *Proceedings of the eighth global WordNet conference*. Bucharest, Romania.

Tjong Kim Sang, Erik, Gosse Bouma & Gertjan van Noord. 2010. LASSY for beginners. Presentation at CLIN 2010, Utrecht, http://ifarm.nl/erikt/talks/clin2010.pdf, last accessed 2022-03-25.

Van Eynde, Frank, Liesbeth Augustinus & Vincent Vandeghinste. 2016. Number agreement in copular constructions: A treebank-based investigation. *Lingua* 178: 104 – 126. Linguistic Research in the CLARIN Infrastructure.

Vliet, H.D. van der. 2007. The referentiebestand Nederlands as a multi-purpose lexical database. *International Journal of Lexicography* 20 (3): 239–257.

Vossen, Piek, Isa Maks, Roxanne Segers, Hennie van der Vliet, Marie-Francine Moens, Katja Hofmann, Erik Tjong Kim Sang & Maarten de Rijke. 2013. Cornetto: a lexical semantic database for Dutch. In Peter Spyns & Jan Odijk (eds.), *Essential speech and language technology for dutch, results by the STEVIN-programme*, Theory and Applications of Natural Language Processing, 165–184. Berlin Heidelberg: Springer.

Windhouwer, Menzo & Twan Goosen. 2022. Component Metadata Infrastructure. In Darja Fišer & Andreas Witt (eds.), *CLARIN. The infrastructure for language resources.* Berlin: De Gruyter.

Riccardo Pozzo*, Timon Gatta, Hansmichael Hohenegger, Jonas Kuhn, Axel Pichler, Marco Turchi, and Josef van Genabith

Aligning Immanuel Kant's Work and its Translations

Abstract: This chapter discusses using CLARIN to edit Kant's work and to consider how to align it with its translations, with special attention to Chinese. *Kangde* 康德 is the two-character phonetic loan that renders Kant's name in Chinese. We have chosen *Kangde* 康德 as the name for our vision to express the challenge of setting up the new edition of the *Druckschriften* and their Chinese translation in the form of aligned corpora, thus opening up the way to further alignments with versions in other languages. From a philosophical-historical and cultural-political perspective, the chapter presents the idea of aligning two parallel corpora of around 1,580,000 German words and the corresponding characters in Chinese. The project is curiosity-driven and lays the foundations for investigating Kant's philosophy and discussing it in a global context, a long-term effort that relies on the synergies among philosophy, computational linguistics, machine learning, translation studies, and China studies. The idea of the alignment is to offer unrivalled material for historical-philosophical investigations and serve as a viable infrastructure to be scaled up to other languages. To date, few aligned corpora exist that connect German and Chinese philosophical texts. The tools are not statistically implemented. As suggested by Franco Moretti's notion of distant reading, experimentation on meaningful patterns in philosophical corpora is a step towards making new machine learning technologies usable for tackling issues in the humanities. Looking forward, we focus on the assumption that philosophers ought to explore new technologies to rethink conventional ways of interpreting texts in the humanities.

***Corresponding author: Riccardo Pozzo**, Department of History, Humanities and Society, Tor Vergata University of Rome, Rome, Italy, e-mail: riccardo.pozzo@uniroma2.it
Timon Gatta, DSPFS, Tor Vergata University of Rome, Rome, Italy, e-mail: timon.gatta@uniroma2.it
Hansmichael Hohenegger, Italian Institute of Germanic Studies, Rome, Italy, e-mail: hohenegger@studigermanici.it
Jonas Kuhn, IMS, University of Stuttgart, Stuttgart, Germany, e-mail: jonas.kuhn@ims.uni-stuttgart.de
Axel Pichler, IMS, University of Stuttgart, Stuttgart, Germany, e-mail: axel.pichler@ts.uni-stuttgart.de
Marco Turchi, ICT, Bruno Kessler Foundation, Povo-Trento, Italy, e-mail: turchi@fbk.eu
Josef van Genabith, MLT, German Research Center for Artificial Intelligence, Saarbrücken, Germany, e-mail: josef.van_genabith@dfki.de

https://doi.org/10.1515/9783110767377-029

Keywords: China studies, contemporary Chinese, corpus linguistics, critical editions, digital humanities, history of philosophy, intercultural philosophy, Immanuel Kant, multilingual philosophical corpora, translation studies

1 Introduction

Let us start with a thought experiment. Imagine a first-generation diaspora youth (*huaqiao* 华侨) who studies philosophy at a European university. At a certain point, she might be expected to read Kant's *Grounding of the Metaphysics of Morals*, first translated into the language of the country she lives in – for Europe's official languages are as many as 24 (Schlüter and Hohenegger 2020) – then in the German original and the English rendering, say, of Mary Gregor. Let us assume that through the library of her university or one of the e-corpora, she finds access to the same text in Chinese, say, in the fourth volume of Li Qiuling's 李秋零 (2003–2019) translation. At this point, she might be able to start a discussion on Kant in her Chinese-speaking environment (Wen Haiming 2012). In turn, fellow students would appropriate the fourth-century BC philosopher of human nature Mengzi 孟子, through the references indicated by her. In the end, by referring Kant's German to texts in Chinese, English, and possibly other languages, our imaginary classroom might start thinking together on batches of multilingual concepts. Eventually, they would come to grasp some key tenets of global significance on the autonomy of human nature (Tu Weiming 2010). This is something philosophers today might want to take advantage of (Pozzo 2020a: 57).

This chapter is about a corpus construction project (see Hajičová et al. 2022). It is based on our experience when using the constellation of resources offered by CLARIN to edit Kant's work and consider how to align it with its translations, with special attention to Chinese. The results of the corpus construction are yet to come. However, thinking of the multilingual dialogues that are to take place in the coming years – first and foremost, the 25th World Congress of Philosophy of Rome in 2024 – what we wish to offer here is the unfolding of a vision, spelling out the single stages of a procedure to follow. The challenge is of setting up in the form of aligned corpora the new edition of the *Druckschriften* and their complete Chinese translation (Li Qiuling 2003–2019), thus opening the way to further alignments such as with the Cambridge Edition of the works of Immanuel Kant (Guyer and Wood 1992–2016), the Russian translations coordinated by the Institute of Philosophy of the Russian Academy of Sciences (Tuschling and Motroshilowa 1994–2020), and many other translation endeavours (Schlüter and Hohenegger 2020). However, because few aligned corpora connect German and Chinese, we remain focused on Kant in Chinese.

This chapter aims to reach out to social sciences and humanities (SSH) scholars who are not used to combining resources with metadata in order to analyse and enrich them with linguistic tools, as well as to scholars of non-SSH disciplines, more generally, those researchers who "are not just consumers of data and tools, but also providers" (Maegaard Bente, Van Uytvanck, and Krauwer 2017: 5–6) who are encouraged to share their data and tools with others, thus enhancing familiarity with approaches that allow the communities of CLARIN users to benefit from text corpora for philosophical research in multilingual and multicultural contexts (see Draxler et al. 2022). After describing the state of the art, the remainder of this chapter is about editing Kant's re-established polygraphy for systematic comparison of translations and analysing the evolution of contemporary Chinese philosophical terminology in relation to Kant's work.

2 State of the art

Information technology is revolutionizing how we approach texts and practice philosophical inquiry. The vision of *Kangde* is about transformative effects on methodologies in the history of philosophy. In this context, we argue that the time is ripe for a paradigm shift from thinking of texts to thinking of corpora, which is an issue that connects with hard, theoretical questions such as how to conceive of philosophical works within the infosphere (Blair et al. 2011; Floridi 2019; Romele 2020; Pozzo 2021). Philosophers have always been strenuous advocates of the close reading of texts and champions of the centrality of text. However, they have also been among the first to seize the opportunity to profit from the distant reading of corpora for the history of ideas, the history of scientific terminology, the translation of philosophical texts, and the translation of studies (Gregory et al. 1967). "Distant reading," says Franco Moretti, "is a condition of knowledge," for it allows one "to focus on units that are much smaller or much larger than the text: devices, themes, tropes – or genres and systems." (Moretti 2013: 48–49) Texts that are findable, accessible, interoperable, and reusable (FAIR) are expected to engage readers in the coming years, while the fact that only a few recent translations of philosophical works are available via open-access on the internet ought to quickly become an issue of the past (Schäfer and Serres 2016).

Advances in technology enable the history of philosophy to exercise an influence beyond its narrowly understood disciplinary borders, to reach scholars of different disciplines worldwide and far into the future. However, individual scholars continue to lag behind and remain somewhat ill-equipped to deal with the challenges of the digital transformation we face in our globalized era. As Timothy Williamson (1998) has said, philosophy is a science, but not a natural science (mathematics is another example of a non-natural science; it is, rather, a language of rigorous demonstration). At its best, philosophy strives to be as systematic, rigorous, precise, accurate, critical, and evidence-based as its questions permit and to use the best methods available to answer them. We are only beginning to become aware that digital rights management is a key enabling technology. Considering current trends towards a *data-driven history of philosophy* as a branch of both philosophy and digital humanities (Betti et al. 2019), our point is that the future of the history of philosophy urgently depends on finding ways to bring about radical enhancements of the way we edit, store, annotate, access, and translate corpora.

When we propose to look into *corpora talking to each other*, we are aware of the objection that a corpus does not talk – only human beings who are reading and understanding texts that belong to a corpus can talk. The anthropomorphism is charming. However, it must not cover up crucial details in the act of encoding, which links the texts supposedly in *conversation*, namely the embedding of assumptions and implicit interpretations that make talking possible, but which also prejudice it. Users must understand what annotation entails, the discipline it imposes, the caution it requires of anyone using the results, and the amount of critical work on text analysis, concept modelling, so-called machine learning, and so on (see Lenardič and Fišer 2022). The case for extensive application of CLARIN corpora and tools on this scale is the occasion to consider their potentialities together with their heuristically stimulating and pragmatically sobering limitations.

One of the most dynamic projects in the construction of parallel text corpora of modern languages and the development of reliable tools for alignment and morphosyntactic annotation of words is InterCorp (Bozzi 2015: 37).[1] The necessity and added value of providing easy access to complex, highly structured philosophical content through corpora that talk to each other have been highlighted in the literature (Pozzo 2016). The aim is to break new ground for knowledge organization systems that produce synergies while optimizing crosswalks for future translation projects involving Chinese, eventually to be applied to other languages (Pozzo 2020b).

An interesting precedent is the ERC-AdG-2009 project led by Cristina D'Ancona, "Greek into Arabic: Philosophical concepts and linguistic bridges" (G2A) which aligns passages from Plotinus's *Enneads* with their ninth-century Arabic translation in the text known as *Theologia Aristotelis*. From the point of view of sociolinguistics, of particular interest are the sentences from the original text that would have been difficult to understand for those who lived and were formed in a different cultural environment and who, moreover, were dedicated to conveying

1 https://ucnk.ff.cuni.cz/cs/

ideas, philosophical concepts, moral, and religious principles from one culture to another (Bozzi 2015). The idea of *Kangde* goes beyond the G2A in four ways. First, the extent of Kant's complete *Druckschriften* is far larger than the individual passages of Plotinus. Second, *Kangde* is meant to develop a research interface with functionalities for parallel view and search, and interfaces to other research tools and networks, which is planned to offer a wider spectrum of functions than the G2A Web App (a resource offered by ILC CNR, leading institution of CLARIN-IT and host of the ILC4CLARIN B centre).[2] Third, the access being tied to validated contemporary translations (starting with Chinese and potentially extended to other languages) the interface is expected to be used by philosophers in the years to come for new multilingual investigations, with a different impact from that of a scholarly discussion of a manuscript tradition. Fourth, the tackling of contemporary Chinese contributes to a living language's morphological and syntactic enrichment, while G2A is about ancient Greek and Arabic, which are dead languages.

We find an analogous endeavour in the project to translate the *Corpus Iuris Iustinianeum* into Chinese (*Luoma fa* 罗马法), which has made considerable progress in China studies. Not only have 16 volumes been published so far (Schipani 1994–2001, 2001–2021; see Colangelo 2015), but most importantly, Chinese terms have been charged with new, more precise meanings. However, the *Luoma fa* 罗马法 does not offer users any interface. Instead, it remains in published volumes on paper, which means it is not open to annotation and represents only an initial stage of implementing the alignment of translations among corpora. As regards philosophical terms, Timon Gatta has pointed to the *linguistic-lexical development of contemporary Chinese*, which the gradual introduction of Western philosophical production, especially through published translations, has enriched with new terms: the main issue here is "to adequately conform the new discipline [of philosophy] to East Asia's millennial philosophical speculations about religion, moral habits, political and social behavior." (Gatta 2020: 193, 194)

The methodology and tools are appropriate to achieve the objectives of a parallel consideration of Kantian texts in German and Chinese insofar as it is based on tools such as vocabularies, ontologies, concordances, frequencies – more generally, on the analysis of texts and corpora, which integrates quantitative and formal methods into the portfolio of methods in the history of philosophy and intellectual history. Generally, we take up the *text-corpus method*, which derives a set of abstract rules that govern a natural language from texts in that language, and explores how it relates to others (Baker 1993). We also take up

2 https://g2a.ilc.cnr.it/Teologia_Wapp/Home.xhtml

approaches from science and technology studies with regard to research infrastructures-based innovation. The scientific approach is empirical, it is about presenting Kant's writings in a digital edition and operationalize his terminology for corpus linguistic questions.

Using the CLARIN resource families fully enhances the fruitful interaction among the history of philosophy, computational linguistics, machine learning, translation studies, and China studies. To achieve this truly interdisciplinary vision, we aim to integrate the methodologies of five different fields, thereby pursuing a disruptive overarching approach. Methodology and tools are understood to play an enabling role. First and foremost, however, the group that advances *Kangde* relies on the methodology of the history of concepts in its global extension (Betti and van den Berg 2016; Pichler et al. 2020; Pozzo 2021). What is more, the group takes advantage of achievements that have proven to be particularly effective for the advancement of the history of philosophy from a global perspective, such as the English-French *Vocabulaire de Philosophie* (INIST 2018, a CLARIN lexicon),[3] the *Lessico Intellettuale Europeo* (Gregory et al. 1967–2022), and the *Key Concepts in Chinese Thought and Culture* (Wang Lin and Han Zhen 2015–2021).

3 Edition

Due to the celebrations of the tercentenary of Kant's birth, the history of the editions of the work is expected to reach a turning point in 2024 when the Berlin-Brandenburgische Akademie der Wissenschaften (BBAW) and the De Gruyter publishing house will present the new complete edition of the published writings, that is volumes 1–9 of the Kant Academy Edition (BBAW 2022–2024; see Gerhardt 2007; BKGE 2016).

Before going into alignment issues, we are aware we need first to open up Kant's re-established polygraphy for systematic text analysis of conceptual networks, which is now feasible, for the current (and new) Kant Academy Edition – thanks to the efforts of the De Gruyter publishing house – has been reset as proprietary HTML files and offers rich material for experimenting with reflected text analytics and machine learning (BBAW 2022–2024). The editions sponsored by the BBAW started with the *Aristotelis Opera* edition of Immanuel Bekker in the nineteenth century (continued by Olof Gigon in the twentieth century), which was followed by – among others – the editions of Gottfried Wilhelm Leibniz and Wilhelm von Humboldt. In 1894, Wilhelm Dilthey initiated the Kant Academy Edition to

3 https://www.ortolang.fr/market/terminologies/philosophie/v1.1

provide reliable and complete texts for scholars and students. At Dilthey's time, the Kant-Kommission (in the predecessor of the BBAW) asked the editors to iron out most orthographic and syntactic variants. Since Kant's orthographical habits – so argued the editors of the first volume of the *Druckschriften*, which appeared in 1902 – are neither systematic nor consequential, the Kant-Kommission thought it better not disturb most readers with obsolete forms (BBAW 1968: 1.513). Hence, Kant's works from 1747 onward were rewritten using orthography and punctuation of Kant's works after the *Kritik der reinen Vernunft*, with the result that Kant's polygraphy was lost.

For this reason, the first move by the editors of Kant's *Neuedition* was to submit queries to CLARIN's historical corpora in order to check Kant's polygraphy and see whether variants were in use at the time. Hansmichael Hohenegger and Riccardo Pozzo have found numerous examples of Kant's polygraphy (BBAW 2022–2024). Let us just mention the many cases of oscillating orthography such as *ascendat/adscendat*, *caussa/causa*, *Cirkul/Cirkel*, *drücken/drucken*, *excentum/exemptum*, *exsistentia/existentia*, *Heerde/Herde*, *kömmt/kommt*, *promptus/promtus*, *siehet/sieht*, *soepenumero/saepenumero*, *sumptum/sumtum* (BBAW 1968: 1.514–516). The old Academy edition accounts neither for oscillations in the use of *v* and *u* as in *vniuersalitas/universalitas*, nor in the use of *ſ* and *s* as in *vniuerſalitas*. Also interesting is Kant's consistent usage of *quum* for causality and of *cum* for togetherness, which marks a grammatical difference, although it does not belong to Classical Latin. Finally, the old Academy edition irons out most capitalizations that Kant evidently used to stress the term's meaning as a *terminus technicus*, as was pointed out previously by Johann Joachim Lange (1734: 372; see Hohenegger 2020). Concerning editorial decision making on reading a word as a typo or leaving it in the text on its own account, today it has become indispensable to use CLARIN's historical corpora, such as the LatinISE corpus[4] and the Deutsches Textarchiv (1600–1900),[5] as well as, obviously, the DWDS (*Digitales Wörterbuch der deutschen Sprache*),[6] and among its tools the DTA-CAB (Deutsches Text-Archiv Cascade Analysis Broker).[7]

---

4 https://lindat.mff.cuni.cz/repository/xmlui/handle/11372/LRT-3170

5 https://clarin.bbaw.de:8088/fedora/objects/dta:3503/datastreams/cmdi/content?asOfDateTime=2019-09-30T09:20:47.158Z

6 https://www.dwds.de

7 https://kaskade.dwds.de/~moocow/software/DTA-CAB/

4 Alignment

Being a user of CLARIN means having access to a whole intangible network of knowledge with specific areas of expertise.[8] Moreover, the alignment itself is meant to use many of the CLARIN resource families, especially the parallel corpora insofar as they serve as training data for statistical machine translation systems. Parallel corpora make up the largest CLARIN resource family and are central to translation studies and contrastive linguistics. Many of them are accessible through easy-to-use concordancers that considerably facilitate the study of interlinguistic phenomena. CLARIN provides access to 86 parallel corpora, the majority of which are available for download from national repositories and through concordancers such as Korp, Corpuscle, and KonText. CLARIN offers access to 47 bilingual corpora, mostly containing European language pairs but also non-European languages such as Hindi, Tamil, and Vietnamese. 39 corpora are multilingual, five of which contain texts in more than 50 languages. Almost half of the corpora are sentence-aligned, which allows for easy comparative research.[9] While overviewing the corpora that are already part of the CLARIN resources families, one cannot help seeing the amount of work still to be done for Chinese, which is present, for example, in MultiUN (Multilingual U.N. Parallel Text 2000–2009).[10]

The corpora alignment of the German *Urtext* with its Chinese translation will be carried out on the Kant Online platform. The platform is currently under construction.[11] Kant Online takes the *Kant-Lexikon* (Willaschek at al. 2015) as its nomenclature. The endeavour consists, in no small part, in the extraction of terminology. The study of terminology is indispensable for a non-arbitrary translation but also for producing non-arbitrary dictionaries. Hence, we should reconsider the possibility of a dictionary with nomenclatures of different granularity: from basic to very fine. To name an analogous undertaking, one can look at the Nietzsche Online platform (Nietzsche Online 2011), which provides access to the complete edition of Friedrich Nietzsche's work by Giorgio Colli and Mazzino Montinari together with almost all publications published by De Gruyter on Nietzsche. In addition to about 70 volumes of the Nietzsche edition, the platform offers access to monographs and reference works such as the *Nietzsche-Wörterbuch* (van Tongeren, Schank & Siemens 2004) and all issues of the *Nietzsche-Studien*: all in all, more than 110,000 book pages. The platform offers significantly

8 https://office.clarin.eu/v/CE-2017-1093-ValueProposition-update2020.pdf
9 https://www.clarin.eu/resource-families/parallel-corpora
10 http://www.euromatrixplus.net/multi-un/
11 https://www.degruyter.com

more than the sum of its printed content. A philological apparatus that justifies critical choices between variants and historical-critical explanations that provide information about the content and context of the corpus makes it possible to combine the reconstructed text with a textual universe (Pozzo 2014). It should be noted that the Kant Online platform is expected to go beyond Nietzsche Online by providing advanced access and more processing tools for philosophical and linguistic research. Besides this, the interface offers datasets in several formats available to download for future research ventures, tools, and networks. Indeed, the German-to-Chinese interface on Kant Online is meant to be focused on bilingual corpora, which are not considered in Nietzsche Online. Finally, it is constructed for annotation around an adaptation of traditional concept analysis to computational methods, designed by digital humanities scholars to enable a *computational history of ideas* (Betti and van den Berg 2016).

Annotating Kant has been undertaken with increasing regularity over more than 50 years alongside the progress of computational linguistics. The start was given by the *Allgemeiner Kantindex* (Martin 1967; Roser and Mohrs 1992), which gives Kant's words in non-inflected form and is currently preserved within the *Korpora.org* platform.[12] A giant leap forward was achieved by Tullio Gregory et al. (1967–2022) and Norbert Hinske (1982–2019), respectively, with the *Lessico Intellettuale Europeo* (which since its inception used a markup language very similar to TEI and now uses TEI) and the *Kant-Index* (built on TUSTEP), which granted access to Kant's writings in lemmatized form with metadata and semantic annotations that are interoperable with regard to multilingualism (i.e., Kant's use of Greek, Latin, German, and French). The next giant leap forward is expected to be achieved by recontextualizing Kant within multilingual philosophical corpora around computational concept modelling. Once humanities scholars have agreed to study a corpus, such as the ones envisaged by *Kangde*, they first identify appropriate levels and categories of analysis; they then perform annotations on a subsample of the corpus that acts as reference data, which become the basis for "machine learning experiments with candidate model classes, including additional tools or data resources" (Kuhn 2020: 76).

The nine volumes of Kant's printed works, with their 1,580,000 words, offer material for a full lemmatization and a formidable basis for reflected text analytics. Starting from an *Urtext* of German lemmata, it is possible to create an induced network of concepts through which to pursue empirically verifiable hypotheses on meaning shifts over the centuries. Restoring Kant's *Urtext* requires the closest attention for annotation so that the surface text does not lose anything of the orig-

12 https://korpora.zim.uni-duisburg-essen.de/kant/

inal richness while accounting for historical usages, with deeper layers that offer standardized tokens for horizontal investigation. Methods for theory- and data-driven corpus analysis enable scholars to formulate hypotheses regarding systematic patterns in the distribution of specific concepts in a corpus and test them empirically (Kuhn 2020). For example, one might try to verify a presumed tendency for a school of thinking to translate the term *A* as *A'* in the context of debate *X*, but as *A*" in other contexts. This is what happened with the first translation of some passages into French (in 1788, i.e., at the very end of the Enlightenment) from Kant's *Kritik der reinen Vernunft* (published in 1781 and again in 1787), when the word *Vernunft* was rendered as *raison* in some contexts and as *entendement* in others (Müller and Pozzo 1988). In this perspective, Chinese offers a particularly challenging state of the art. Some sinologists – one thinks first and foremost of Marcel Granet (1968: 7) – have maintained that the difficulty of mutual understanding between Western and Chinese cultures might lie in the impossibility of Chinese to express logically defined and precisely circumscribed concepts that are necessary for philosophical arguments. However, current understandable and faithful Chinese translations of many Western philosophical works – and the translation of Kant's work by Li Qiuling 李秋零 (2003–2019) is certainly one – show that this assumption is incorrect and biased by cultural preconceptions. This is where the idea of *Kangde* reveals its added value insofar as it provides computational concept modelling of Kant's terminology referred to a validated Chinese translation.

5 Western Grammar in Contemporary Chinese

This enterprise is about creating a multilingual textual database knowledge extraction program for enabling context-guided lexical analysis in the form of an *open-ended knowledge-based architecture* that provides users with access to datasets while including the corpus in the LLOD cloud.[13] For instance, in the cultural exchange between China and the West, the history of philosophy can play a significant role, notwithstanding the difficulties of engaging with the mutual textual legacy. We are talking of momentous cultural exchanges that raise awareness of the need for a culturally sensitive approach to different traditions, including challenges related to cultural and religious diversity.

Tradi, *perpoliri*, and *transferre* are terms that express Cicero's commitment to bringing over philosophical texts from Greece to Rome. They are the foundation

13 https://linguistic-lod.org

pillars of the *translatio studiorum* from Greek to Latin, which lasted for centuries. *Transferre* and *translatio* lie at the root of neosemic creativity: under certain conditions, writes Quintilian, "necesse sit transferre aut circumire" (*De institutione oratoria* XII, 10, 34). Tullio Gregory (2012: 6) has suggested one could inscribe in the hendiadys *transferre aut circumire* the history of all problems related to translating. Boethius was well aware of this, and so too was Cassiodorus in the sixth century AD, that is, in the decades that saw the rise and the fall in the Latin West of that final renaissance of Hellenism, which marked the sunset of the ancient world.

In contrast with Western languages, Chinese does not allow free use of any Greek or Latin etymology. The long and arduous process of defining a Chinese philosophical lexicon undertaken during the last decades of the nineteenth and the first half of the twentieth century is not a mere linguistic issue. It also involves issues of political and social acceptance of the influence of the West over China, its culture, and its way of thinking. This process did not only consist in introducing philosophy into China as a new branch of knowledge and making it acceptable to and consistent with the intellectual sensibility of the ruling class, while introducing new terms for new ideas (Pozzo 2018). The main issue was to adequately conform the new discipline of philosophy to East Asia's millennial religions, moral habits, political, and social behaviors (Gatta 2020).

As regards Kant studies in China, the Chinese Kant Society was established at Peking University in June 2019, as the final stage of a confrontation with Kant's works that has pervaded the entire twentieth century, and at the center of which was the philosopher Mou Zongsan 牟宗三, a leading figure of contemporary neo-Confucianism (Heubel 2016; Gatta 2022). Since Chinese scholars began to actively study and research Western culture at the beginning of the twentieth century, Kant was perceived as a challenge in systematic and lexical fields. These two fields were interconnected, so that different lexical renditions have helped Chinese scholars adapt and domesticate Kant's theories using words rooted in China's literary and philosophical traditions. The introduction, translation, and adaptation of Kant's philosophy in China have greatly influenced modern Chinese philosophy and have had a key role in the formation and standardization of a modern Chinese philosophical vocabulary.

Interestingly, we have started reflecting on *Kangde* due to the impact the alignment of corpora can have on the development of the so-called *Western Grammar in Contemporary Chinese-Xiandai hanyu ouhua yufa* 现代汉语欧化语法 (Masini 2009: 648–650; Gatta 2022: 8), which has been proven to produce not only terminological enrichment but also significant modifications – both morphological and syntactic – of Chinese grammar. Translation corpora such as those studied for *Kangde* provide an ample repertoire of translation strategies

(Zanettin 2014). The alignment itself can be tied to the existing anchor points: in the paratext, these are the pages of the original editions and the lines of the old (and new) Kant Academy Edition; and in the text, the pericopes, and the periods. For this purpose, we can use unsupervised sentence aligners for symmetrical and asymmetrical parallel corpora.

From the point of view of translation theory, *Kangde* is about encoding a source language (German) through the translational language (machine-operated) to a target language (Chinese) to be decoded. The reverse process is a feasible possibility. We know of two types of translation universals (Mauranen 2007): one shapes the process from the source to the target text (S-universals), while the other (T-universals) compares translations to other target-language texts. The distinctive features of translational language can be identified by comparing translations with similar native texts, thus throwing new light on the translation process and helping to uncover translation patterns, or what William Frawley (1984) has called the *third code of translation*. The most precious added value of the *Kangde* idea lies in facilitating access to validated translations of complex texts. To this purpose, orientation among CLARIN corpora, lexica, and tools includes the Sheffield Corpus of Chinese Annotation (of the Oxford Text Archive),[14] GATE (General Architecture for Text Engineering),[15] and the BilingBank (of TalkBank).[16] *Kangde* ought to empower Chinese readers (and, indeed, Western readers) with automatically generated references for words, whose translation and definition they might otherwise have to look for in glossaries or vocabularies, "because graphically the term would not contain any clue as to its meaning" (Gatta 2020: 201; see Fan Bingqing 1926).

Translating Western philosophy into Chinese is a complex phenomenon involving the linguistic-lexical development of contemporary Chinese through the gradual introduction of Western philosophical production, especially through published translations (Masini 1993). For example, Timon Gatta has presented a selection of exemplary concepts that attest to the formative process of China's philosophical lexicography (Fan Bingqing 1926). Western philosophical terms have reached standardized translations in Chinese through similar, yet not identical paths of explicitation, simplification, normalization, sanitization, and levelling out. Think, for instance, of the long history that has led to establishing the current Chinese terms for logic-*luoji* 逻辑, metaphysics-*xing er shang xue* 形而上学, and aesthetics-*meixue* 美学 (Kurtz 2011; Gatta 2020).

---

14 https://ota.bodleian.ox.ac.uk/repository/xmlui/handle/20.500.12024/2481#
15 https://gate.ac.uk
16 https://biling.talkbank.org

Translating Kant into Chinese offers a striking visualization of a *third code in motion* by means of increasingly successful adaptations of translated language to native language. As Timon Gatta has explained, the lexical renderings (phonetic loans or semantic loans) of Western concepts that Chinese translators have experimented with over the centuries were, initially, hardly capable of adequately expressing the richness of meanings and nuances of the original language. Given the difficulty in the Chinese language of embracing words from other languages, however, translators have been forced, step by step, to look for one- or two-character words that recall the original meaning of the foreign term, often with results that are anything but satisfactory (Gatta 2020: 200–201). For example, if the rendering of intellect-*Verstand-zhixing* 知性, has been established in all translations of Kant's three *Critiques* over the past 50 years (Gatta 2021: 95), the rendering of phenomenon-*Phänomen/Erscheinung-xianxiang* 现象 tells a different story, for it was seemingly established very early but underwent recent oscillations with, for example, Li Qiuling 李秋零 (2003–2019) who established a character that includes the meaning of appearing, of showing itself (Gatta 2021: 312). The few dozen cases in which Kant uses *Phänomen/Erscheinung* actually mean a 'surprising case' in the context of the antinomic nature of the higher faculties complicate the translation but help refine the terminological analysis (Hohenegger 2020: 346–349). This effect is even more pronounced in the case of the translations of transcendental-*transzendental-xianyan* 先验, which sparked a debate in Japan and China during the first decades of the last century, so that, even now, one finds different opinions about it (Gatta 2022: 177–191).

6 Forward look

Philosophy requires critical editions and hermeneutics for text interpretation, while translation studies require attention to history and trust (Rizzi, Lang & Rym 2019). A translation "is always an interpretation, as shown by the connection of terms with the synonymic values *interpretari*, *vertere*, and *transferre*" (Gregory 2012: 4). From this perspective, the ground-breaking element of our vision lies in letting *corpora talk to each other*, and not simply individuals born in different parts of the world. Corpora are constituted according to the type of the text, the theme to be translated, and the target language. They are search-accessible complete collections of traditions of texts, with corresponding dictionaries, thesauri, and reference works. They are instrumental in engaging with traditions in innovative ways.

This chapter shows how *corpora alignment provides further steps towards enhancing data-driven philosophical translation* (Frawley 1984; Mauranen 2007; McEnery and Xiao 2007; Xiao and Yue 2008; Xiao, Lianzhen & Yue 2010; Zanettin 2014; Pozzo 2016). *Kangde* belongs to the long history of traditional translation techniques and theories that go back to Latin translations of Greek. The questions that ought to be posed reflect the vast differences in culture, which have to be bridged between European philosophy, as represented by Kant, and traditional Chinese thought, which cannot be described as philosophical in the Western sense.

All translations are likely to show specific linguistic characteristics simply by virtue of being translations – characteristics that are caused in and by the process of translation. The effect of the source language on the translation is strong enough to make the translated language perceptibly different from the target native language. Consequently, translational language (*Translationese*) is at best a particular unrepresentative variant of the target language (McEnery and Xiao 2007). Translational language entails the elimination of ambiguities regarding the choice of one word over another and has four core patterns of lexical use: a relatively lower proportion of lexical words over function words, a relatively higher proportion of high-frequency words over low-frequency words, a relatively more significant repetition of the most frequent words, and a smaller vocabulary (Xiao, Lianzhen & Yue 2010). Centuries before machine translation, famous historical examples of token-to-token translations include William of Moerbeke's translations of philosophical, medical, and scientific texts from Greek into Latin, in particular, of many works by Aristotle, which he did at the request of Aquinas between 1253 and 1286. William's translations were literal (*de verbo in verbo*), faithful to the spirit of Aristotle, and without elegance, that is, without any attempt at diminishing the impact of both his rudimentary command of Greek and of the primitiveness of medieval Latin philosophical terminology, which shows that the embedding on which machine translation is based existed long before machines. While William of Moerbeke's Aristotle are texts written in what we call today translational language, the translations of Plato from Greek into Latin by Marsilius Ficinus between 1462 and 1484 represent a famous example of a literary translation that is quite close to the native target language. We recall William and Marsilius to make it clear where the challenge lies. Machine translation of philosophical texts today produces, at best, William's of Moerbeke translational language, while the idea of *Kangde* is to boost machine translation until it pushes the third code so as to mould the translation into the native language, that is, to make it as close as possible to the results achieved by Ficinus. It is important to note that the alignment of two or more philosophical corpora will add substantial numbers of datasets to enable machine translation, training, and data development. Today, the role of machine translation in assisting with the translation of literary texts shows both limitations and potential benefits. A key challenge in literary translation is preserving the meaning (as in other domains such as technical translation) and the reading experience, which means that a literary translator must carefully select from possible options (Toral and Way 2015, 2018).

A close study of the Chinese translation of Kant's writings is useful in gauging the reception of Kant's thinking within the limitations of Chinese semantics. The value of the aligned corpora is also useful for the study of the mechanics of translations into very different linguistic environments, which could eventually be instrumental for computer-based translations. The great challenge remains the *protection of datasets under intellectual property rights* (IPR). Our idea is to tackle this challenge from the very beginning because, thanks to an administrative system that manages inclusion and consultation rights, we wish to settle IPR issues of the German and the Chinese texts for making them open access for users in an editorial setting that fully exploits both government-sponsored research (BBAW) and the efforts of two prestigious publishing houses (De Gruyter in Berlin and China Renmin Press in Beijing). The envisioned interface is meant to connect German and Chinese texts first. It is structured, however, to be scaled up to other languages. On top of boosting Kantian philosophical reception in China, straight from German into Chinese, *Kangde* aims to reach out to communities of practices that receive and confer datasets and tools to research infrastructures such as CLARIN. *The challenge of the sustainability of the Kangde endeavour can be effectively tackled by conferring datasets to CLARIN while reusing its corpora, lexica, and tools.* As Martin Wynne has made clear, CLARIN is "keen to deal with all non-European languages, including major world languages such as Arabic, Chinese, Russian, Japanese, etc."[17]

7 Conclusion

Wrapping up, this chapter lays out some interesting use cases of corpora, corpus linguistics, computational linguistics, natural language processing, and their contribution to digital humanities. It suggests approaches that impact humanities research through digital media, artificial intelligence, data mining, and machine learning. In connection with the CLARIN resource families, the chapter fosters the adoption of FAIR data standards, which

17 https://www.clarin.eu/blog/users-clarin-who-are-they

> stimulates the reuse and repurposing of available research data, thereby enabling scholars in the SSH – including the DH – to increase their productivity and open new research venues in and across disciplines that address one or more of the multiple societal roles of language: as a carrier of cultural content and information, both synchronically and diachronically, as a reflection of scientific and instrumental knowledge, as an instrument for human communication, as one of the central components of the identity of individual groups, cultures, or nations, as an instrument for human expression, as an object for study and preservation. (ESFRI 2018: 213)

All things considered, then, this chapter engages research agendas that "illustrate the added value of well-supported access to the wealth of data types that are available for multiple languages are the research initiatives for the study of migration patterns, intellectual history, language variation across period and region, dynamics in mental health conditions, customer opinions and parliamentary discourse, just to name a few" (de Jong 2019: 123).

We are looking forward to fruitful cooperation between CLARIN and Chinese-speaking infrastructures, for our project is about *cultural innovation* (Pozzo et al. 2020) in very concrete terms. Philosophy is, in fact, one of the core SSH disciplines, for which widespread use of language data is central to many key methods. Last but not least, we will discuss the *Kangde* vision at two events of global impact planned for the year 2024, which will focus on the tercentenary of Kant's birth: the 14th International Kant Congress in Bonn and the 25th World Congress of Philosophy in Rome.

Bibliography

Baker, Mona. 1993. Corpus linguistics and translation studies: Implications and applications. In Mona Baker, Gill Francis & Elena Tognini-Bonelli (eds.). *Text and Technology*, 232–252. Philadelphia & Amsterdam: Benjamins.

BBAW: Berlin-Brandenburgische Akademie der Wissenschaften (ed.). 1968. *Kants Werke: Akademie Textausgabe*. 9 vols. Berlin: De Gruyter.

BBAW: Berlin-Brandenburgische Akademie der Wissenschafte (ed.). 2022–2024. *Immanuel Kant, Gesammelte Schriften. Abteilung 1 – Neuedition*. 9 vols. Berlin: De Gruyter.

Betti, Arianna & Hein van den Berg, 2016. Towards a computational history of ideas. *CEUR Workshop Proceedings* 1681.

Betti, Arianna, Hein van den Berg, Yvette Ortwijn & Caspar Treijtel. 2019. History of Philosophy in Ones and Zeros. In Eugen Fischer & Mark Curtis (eds.), *Methodological Advances in Experimental Philosophy*, 295–332. London: Bloomsbury.

BKGE: Bundesinstitut für Kultur und Geschichte der Deutschen im östlichen Europa. 2016. *300 Jahre Immanuel Kant: Der Weg ins Jubiläum*. Oldenburg: BKGE.

Blair, Ann, Paul Duguid, Anja-Silvia Goeing & Anthony Grafton (eds.). 2011. *Information: A historical companion*. Princeton: Princeton University Press.

Bourdieu, Pierre. 2002. Les conditions sociales de la circulation internationale des idées. *Actes de la recherche en sciences sociales* 145. 5–9.
Bozzi, Andrea. 2015. Greek into Arabic: A research infrastructure based on computational models to annotate and query historical and philosophical digital texts. In Andrea Bozzi (ed.), *Digital texts, translations, lexicons in a multi-modular web application: Methods and samples*, 27–42. Florence: Olschki.
Colangelo, Lara. 2015. L'introduzione del diritto romano in Cina: Evoluzione storica e recenti sviluppi relativi alla traduzione e produzione di testi e all'insegnamento. *Roma e America: Diritto romano comune* 36. 175–210.
Draxler, Christoph, Alexander Geyken, Erhard Hinrichs, Annette Klosa-Kückelhaus, Elke Teich & Thorsten Trippel. 2022. How to connect language resources, infrastructures, and communities. In Darja Fišer & Andreas Witt (eds.), *CLARIN: The infrastructure for language resources*. Berlin: De Gruyter.
ESFRI. 2018. *Roadmap 2018: Strategy report on research infrastructures*. Milan: ESFRI.
Fan Bingqing 樊炳清. 1926. *Zhexue cidian* 《哲學辭典》 [Philosophical Dictionary]. Beijing: Business Press 商务印书馆.
Floridi, Luciano. 2019. *The Logic of information*. Oxford: Oxford University Press.
Frawley, William. 1984. *Translation: Literary, linguistic, and philosophical perspectives*. Wilmington: University of Delaware Press.
Gatta, Timon. 2020. The translation of western philosophical terms in Chinese: The case studies of Logic, Metaphysics and Aesthetics. In Marina Miranda (ed.), *Dal Medio all'Estremo Oriente 2: Studi del dottorato di ricerca in Civiltà dell'Asia e dell'Africa*, 193–219. Rome: Carocci.
Gatta, Timon, 2022. *Lo sviluppo del lessico filosofico nel cinese moderno*. Florence: Olschki.
Gerhardt, Volker. 2007. Erschließung und Sicherung des kulturellen Erbes: Zur Aktualität des Forschungsprogramms der Akademien. In Annette Sell (ed.), *Editionen: Wandel und Wirkung*, 3–9. Tübingen: Niemeyer.
Granet, Marcel. 1968. *La pensée chinoise*. Paris: Albin Michel.
Gregory, Tullio. 2012. Translatio Studiorum. In Marco Sgarbi (ed.), *Translatio Studiorum: Ancient, medieval and modern bearers of intellectual history*, 1–21. Leiden: Brill.
Gregory, Tullio, Antonio Lamarra, Cesare Pasini & Riccardo Pozzo (eds.). 1967–2022. *Lessico intellettuale europeo*. 129 vols. Florence: Olschki.
Guyer, Paul & Allen B. Wood (eds.). 1992–2016. *Cambridge Edition of the Works of Immanuel Kant*. 16 vols. Cambridge: Cambridge University Press.
Hajičová, Eva, Jan Hajič, Barbora Hladká, Jiří Mírovský, Lucie Poláková, Kateřina Rysová, Magdaléna Rysová, Pavel Straňák, Barbora Štěpánková & Šárka Zikánová. 2022. Corpus annotation as a feasible and scientifically beneficial task. In Darja Fišer & Andreas Witt (eds.), *CLARIN: The infrastructure for language resources*. Berlin: De Gruyter.
Heubel, Fabian. 2016. *Chinesische Gegenwartsphilosophie: Zur Einführung*. Hamburg: Junius.
Hinske, Norbert (ed.). 1982–2019. *Kant-Index*. 55 vols. Stuttgart-Bad Cannstatt: Frommann-Holzboog.
Hohenegger, Hansmichael. 2020. Philologie und Übersetzung: Technische Ausdrücke in Kants philosophischer Sprache. In Gisela Schlüter & Hansmichael Hohenegger (eds.), *Kants Schriften in Übersetzungen, Archiv für Begriffsgeschichte Sonderheft 15*, 337–366. Hamburg: Meiner.

Institut de lu2019information scientifique et technique-CNRS UPS76 (INIST). (2018. *Vocabulaire de philosophie* [Terminologie]. ORTOLANG (Open Resources and TOols for LANGuage) – www.ortolang.fr, v1.1, https://hdl.handle.net/11403/philosophie/v1.1.
Jong, Franziska de. 2019. CLARIN: Infrastructural support for impact through the study of language as social and cultural data. In Bente Maegaard, Riccardo Pozzo, Alberto Melloni & Matthew Woolard (eds.), *Stay Tuned to the Future: Impact of Research Infrastructures for Social Sciences and Humanities*, 121–129. Florence: Olschki.
Kuhn, Jonas. 2020. Computational text analysis within the humanities. In Nils Reiter, Axel Pichler & Jonas Kuhn (eds.), *Reflektierte algorithmische Textanalyse*, 61–106. Berlin: De Gruyter.
Kurtz, Joachim. 2011. *The discovery of Chinese logic: Genealogy of a twentieth-century discourse*. Leiden: Brill.
Lange, Johann Joachim. 1734. *Verbesserte und Erleichterte Lateinische* Grammatica. Halle: Waisenhaus.
Lenardič, Jakob & Darja Fišer. 2022. The CLARIN Resources and Tool Families. In Darja Fišer & Andreas Witt (eds.), *CLARIN: The infrastructure for language resources*. Berlin: De Gruyter.
Li Qiuling 李秋零 (ed.). 2003–2019. *Kangde zhuzuo quanji* 《康 康德著作全集》集 *Di yi jie* 第一节 [The Complete Works of Immanuel Kant: Section 1]. 9 vols. Beijing: China Renmin Press 中国人民大学出版社.
Maegaard, Bente, Dieter Van Uytvanck & Steven Krauwer. 2017. *CLARIN Value Proposition*. Utrecht: CLARIN ERIC.
Martin, Gottfried. 1967. *Allgemeiner Kantindex zu Kants gesammelten Schriften*, ed. Dieter Krallmann. Berlin: De Gruyter.
Masini, Federico. 1993. *The formation of modern Chinese Lexicon and its evolution toward a national language: The period from 1840 to 1898*. Berkeley: Project on Linguistic Analysis.
Masini, Federico. 2009. La riforma della lingua. In Guido Samarani & Maurizio Scarpari (eds.), *La Cina*, vol. III, *Verso la modernità*, 621–662. Turin: Einaudi.
Mauranen, Anna. 2007. Universal tendencies in translation. In Margaret Rogers & Gunilla Anderman (eds.), *Incorporating corpora: The linguist and the translator*, 32–48. Clevedon: Multilingual Matters.
McEnery, Tony & Richard Xiao. 2007. Parallel and comparable corpora: What is happening? In Margaret Rogers & Gunilla Anderman (eds.), *Incorporating Corpora: The Linguist and the Translator*, 18–31. Clevedon: Multilingual Matters
Moretti, Franco. 2013. *Distant Reading*. London: Verso.
Müller, Gerhard & Riccardo Pozzo. 1988. Charles Bonnet: Bonnet critico di Kant: Due *Cahiers* ginevrini del 1788. *Rivista di storia della filosofia* 43 (1). 131–64.
Nietzsche Online (NO). 2011. https://doi.org/10.1515/nietzsche.
Palmquist, Stephen. 1995. *A complete index to Kemp Smith's translation of Immanuel Kant's Critique of Pure Reason*. Oxford: Oxford University Computing Services. http://staffweb.hkbu.edu.hk/ppp/indx/toc.html.
Pichler, Axel, André Blessing, Nils Reiter & Mirco Schönfeld. 2020. Algorithmische Mikrolektüre philosophischer Texte. In Nils Reiter, Axel Pichler & Jonas Kuhn (eds.), *Reflektierte algorithmische Textanalyse*, 327–372. Berlin: De Gruyter.
Pozzo, Riccardo. 2014. "*Nietzsche Online*: A critical appraisal." *Lexicon Philosophicum* 2. 337–341.

Pozzo, Riccardo. 2016. Corpora that talk to each other. In Suwanna Satha-Anand, Kanit Sirichan & Lowell Skar (eds.). *Proceedings of the international symposium: Philosophies in dialogue: Bridging the great philosophical divides: 26–28 March 2015*, 235–245. Bangkok: Chulalongkorn University.

Pozzo, Riccardo. 2018. 《主主旨演讲: 东西方哲学: 创新，反思与包容: 章含舟》– Zhuzhi yanjiang: Dongxi fang zhexue: Chuangxin, fansi yu baorong: Zhanghanzhou – Keynote address: East-west philosophy: Innovation, reflection, and inclusion. In Li Nian 李念 (ed.), 在这里, 中国哲学与世界相遇: 24 位世界哲学家访谈录 *Zai zheli, Zhongguo zhexue yu Shijie Xiangyu: 24wei Shijie Zhexuejia Fangtanlu – Interviews of 24 philosophers all over the world (Chinese edition)*, 379–387. Beijing: China Renmin Press 中国人民大学出版社.

Pozzo, Riccardo. 2020a. Bilingualism and multilingualism in Chinese and Western philosophy. 中国学第八辑 *China Studies Quarterly* 8. 56–67.

Pozzo, Riccardo. 2020b. Blick nach vorn: Kant-Übersetzungen und Korpora. In Gisela Schlüter & Hansmichael Hohenegger (eds.), *Kants Schriften in Übersetzungen*, *Archiv für Begriffsgeschichte Sonderheft 15*, 323–334. Hamburg: Meiner.

Pozzo, Riccardo. 2021. *History of Philosophy and the Reflective Society*. Berlin: De Gruyter. https://doi.org/10.1515/9783110709292.

Pozzo, Riccardo, Andrea Filippetti, Mario Paolucci & Vania Virgili. 2020. What does cultural innovation stand for? Dimensions, processes, and outcomes of a new innovation category. *Science and Public Policy* 47 (3). 425–436. https://doi.org/10.1093/scipol/scaa023.

Rizzi, Andrea, Birgit Lang & Anthony Rym. 2019. *What is translation history?* London: Palgrave.

Romele, Alberto. 2020. *Digital hermeneutics: Philosophical investigations in new media and technologies*. London: Routledge.

Roser, Andreas & Thomas Mohrs. 1992. *Kant-Konkordanz zu den Werken Immanuel Kants*. 10 vols. Hildesheim: Olms.

Schäfer, Valérie, and Alexander Serres. 2016. *Histories of the Internet and the Web*. Bern: Infoclio. https://doi.org/10.13098/infoclio.ch-lb-0006.

Schipani, Sandro (ed.). 1994–2001. *Corporis Iuris Civilis Fragmenta Selecta-Luoma fa yu xiandai minfa* 罗马法与现代民法. 6 vols. Rome-Beijing: Sapienza-Consiglio Nazionale delle Ricerche-Zhongguo Zhengfa Daxue 中国政法大学.

Schipani, Sandro (ed.). 2001–2021. *Corporis Iuris Civilis Digesta-Luoma fa yu xiandai minfa* 罗马法与现代民法. 20 vols. Rome-Beijing: Sapienza-Consiglio Nazionale delle Ricerche-Zhongguo Zhengfa Daxue 中国政法大学.

Schlüter, Gisela & Hansmichael Hohenegger (eds.). 2020. *Kants Schriften in Übersetzungen. Archiv für Begriffsgeschichte: Sonderheft 15*. Hamburg: Meiner.

Shanghai Times Press. 2010. *Jinxiandai Hanyu ciyuan* 《近现代汉语辞源》 [Dictionary of Contemporary Chinese]. Shanghai: Shanghai Times Press 上海辞书出版社.

Tongeren, Paul van, Gerd Schank & Herman Siemens (eds.). 2004. *Nietzsche Worterbuch*. Berlin: De Gruyter.

Toral, Antonio & Andy Way. 2015. Machine-assisted translation of literary text: A case study. *Translation Spaces* 4 (2). 240–267. https://doi.org/10.1075/ts.4.2.04tor.

Toral, Antonio & Andy Way. 2018. What level of quality can neural machine translation attain on literary text? https://doi.org/10.48550/arXiv.1801.04962.

Tu Weiming 杜維明. 2010. *The global significance of concrete humanity: Essays on the Confucian discourse in cultural China.* New Delhi: New Delhi Centre for Studies in Civilizations.

Tuschling, Burkhard & Nelly Motroshilowa (eds.). 1994–2020. *Immanuel Kant: Werke: Zweisprachige deutsch-russische Ausgabe*. 6 vols. Moskow: RAS Institute of Philosophy.
Xiao, Richard & Ming Yue 名月. 2009. Using corpora in translation studies: The state of the art. In Paul Baker (ed.), *Contemporary approaches to corpus linguistics*, 237–262. London: Continuum.
Xiao, Richard, He Lianzhen 何莲珍 & Ming Yue 名月. 2010. In pursuit of the third code: Using the ZJU Corpus of Translational Chinese in translation studies. *Using Corpora in Contrastive and Translation Studies* 2010. 182–214.
Wang Lin 王琳 & Han Zhen 韩震 (eds.). 2015–2021. *Key Concepts in Chinese Thought and Culture*, 6 vols. Beijing: Foreign Language Teaching and Research Press 外语教学与研究出版社 and 6 vols. Singapore: Palgrave-Macmillan.
Wen Haiming 温海明. 2012. *Chinese Philosophy*. Cambridge: Cambridge University Press.
Willaschek, Marcus, Jürgen Stolzenberg, Georg Mohr & Stefano Bacin (eds.). 2015. *Kant-Lexikon*. 3 vols. Berlin: De Gruyter.
Williamson, Timothy. 1998. *The philosophy of philosophy*. London: Wiley.
Zanettin, Federico. 2014. Corpora in translation. In Juliane House (ed.), *Translation: A Multidisciplinary Approach*, 178–199. London: Palgrave-MacMillan.

Dalibor Kučera

Application of CLARIN Linguistic Tools in Psychological Research

Abstract: The chapter deals with the topic of psychological research based on the analysis and interpretation of verbal communication using methods of computational linguistics and natural language processing. In the text, we present two psychological-linguistic studies focused on the description of relationships between verbal communication (its form and content) and social/personality characteristics of the communicating person. The chapter aims to acquaint the reader with the possibilities of utilization of the CLARIN Linguistic Tools in current psychological research and to give examples of available methodological solutions and good practice.

Keywords: psychological research, verbal communication, quantitative analysis, personality markers, CLARIN

1 Introduction

The relationship between verbal communication and the personality of the communicating person (speaker/writer) is not new: as Sanford famously wrote, "Language is a vehicle of personality" (1942). As such, it has attracted the attention of both laymen and researchers. The way people use words as a marker of social and personality processes has been considered by many psychologists, linguists, anthropologists, and philosophers (Hamilton 1957), and it has been scientifically studied since the beginning of the 20th century (for example, Freud 1901). More than 100 years later, the relationships between specific communication patterns and a person's interpersonal and intrapersonal functioning have been established in a large number of studies focused on, for instance, authorship attribution (Matoušková 2013; Canter and Youngs 2009), specific linguistic markers of gender (for example, Sboev et al. 2016), emotionality (for example, Brewer and Gardner 1996), relationships (for example, Newman et al. 2008), temperament (for example, Schwartz et al. 2013; Mairesse et al. 2007; Kučera 2020), or pathological characteristics (for example, Havigerová et al. 2019). The studies are generally

Dalibor Kučera, Department of Psychology, Faculty of Education, University of West Bohemia, Plzeň, Czech Republic, e-mail: dkucera@kps.zcu.cz

https://doi.org/10.1515/9783110767377-030

focused on finding specific markers in the text (linguistic variables, for example, text features, semantic variables, patterns, and so forth) that refer to specific psychological variables, identified mostly through methods of psychological diagnostics (for example, tests, questionnaires, observational data, and so forth).

The aim of this chapter is to provide the reader with a basic overview of this area of research, to describe its methods, and to bring documentation and results of the original psychological-linguistic study conducted in the Czech Republic. For the linguistic element, we used techniques and services provided within the CLARIN knowledge infrastructure. In terms of its content, the chapter relates to several sections of this book: for example, chapters focused on the use of text technology (see Trognitz, Ďurčo, and Mörth 2022), the analysis of authorial texts (see Pozzo et al. 2022), or media communication analysis (see Fridlund et al. 2022). The remainder of this chapter is structured as follows: we first discuss the psychology of language use background (presenting the basic theoretical and empirical background), then Czech psychological-linguistic research, specifically the CPACT and PS Projects (presenting the original CPACT and PS studies, their design, methods, and results), before summarizing the studies from the perspective of further research in the Conclusion.

2 Psychology of language use

To place this chapter in a broader scientific framework, we use the term *psychology of language use* to define the view of language and speech as mediators of information about the nature and structure of the human mind and related processes (see Harley 2014; Pennebaker, Mehl, and Niederhoffer 2003). Indicators (manifestations) of these processes in human behaviour – in this case in verbal behaviour – are referred to as *personality markers* (Scherer and Giles 1979; Mairesse et al. 2007) and cover both the interpersonal and intrapersonal layers of language use (Holtgraves 2014; Tausczik and Pennebaker 2010). The methods and procedures that are the key to research are based primarily on linguistic and psychological methodology. One of the most common approaches to systematic text description is content analysis, which focuses on the analysis of explicit communication content (Berelson 1952). In terms of quantitative processing of the communication material, the natural language processing method (NLP) is used.

If we focus on the topic from the perspective of personality research, numerous studies confirmed the relationship between a text and the personality characteristics of the communicator. Barbara (1958: 69) specified the relation between the use of universal and negative quantifiers (for example, "each", "all", "nothing") and the character of the author (opinionated, biased, rigid). Knapp et al. (1974) demonstrated the relation between lying and the lack of words expressing ownership, first person singular words, and words related to exclusion (for example, "but", "except for", "without"). Rodriguez, Holleran, and Mehl (2010) demonstrated a correlation between the frequency of verbs used in the past tense and the intensity of depression. Chen & Vazsonyi (2013) revealed that languages that grammatically associate the future and the present foster future-oriented behaviour. Rude et al. (2004) found a correlation between higher levels of depression and the use of the singular pronoun "I" of the first person associated with the lack of singular pronouns of the second and third person. J. Pennebaker et al. (cf. Esposito et al. 2010) repeatedly documented that neuroticism is characterized by the more frequent use of the first person singular and of negative emotional words (Pennebaker and Stone 2003). Stepikhov and Loukina (2014: 110) analysed the relation between the length of sentences in four different text types (description, narrative, commentary, and control text) and personality type, finding that 18% of variability is explained by FFPQ scales unemotionality vs. emotionality and practicality vs. playfulness. This means who people who are less emotional and who score more on the openness scale structure texts into longer sentences. Another research project by Canadian authors Kwantes, Derbentseva, Lam, Vartanian, and Marmurek (2016) worked with five text types (scenarios) that were analysed using latent semantic analysis (LSA). They found that for three of the Big Five personality traits, there was a reliable relationship between a person's psychological scores and how closely his/her essay's semantic content was to the related trait vector (ibid.).

An essential shift towards the usage of the English psychological language analysis was the development of *LIWC software* (Linguistic Inquiry and Word Count; Pennebaker et al. 2007) in the mid-1990s. The LIWC application relies on an internal dictionary which defines which words should be counted in the target text files. The calculation procedure has been continuously optimized for more than 20 years of its existence (see LIWC2015; Pennebaker et al. 2015). The dictionary was translated into numerous languages (for example, Bjekić et al. 2012; see below) and it provides relatively clear and understandable data in numerous linguistic and psychological categories. The application of LIWC has become to some extent a "gold standard" for psychological-linguistic analyses (see Kučera and Haviger 2019). It should also be noted that this word counting technique is intentionally somewhat naive, that is, "it makes naive assumptions about the meaning of words (that they are grouped within pre-set categories and that every occurrence of a word in a category is equivalent) in order to model constructs effectively and intuitively" (see Kennedy et al. 2021).

In present-day studies, *machine learning methods* (artificial neural networks or artificial intelligence, AI) are employed in psychology research with increasing frequency. These methods allow us to expand the spectrum of observed variables and, at the same time, effectively predict their relationships. However, its disadvantage is the problematic interpretation of the analytical processes performed, that is, the so-called black-box problem (Castelvecchi 2016). For example, it is possible to train AI on a large number of texts so that it can effectively recognize the specific characteristics of speakers (and then, for example, allow the AI to predict them), but it is difficult to get clearer information on what procedures and variables are involved in the process (cf. Zednik 2019). AI is thus a more promising method for predicting relationships than for explaining them (Yarkoni and Westfall 2017). Due to the nature of our research, we will therefore pay attention to methods that are more transparent in terms of the analysis process and providing traditional empirical outputs.

In current research, the question of the *discriminativeness* (stability) of verbal communication also often arises. While we focus on one type of text only (for example, a specific genre of interviews or texts from social networks), it is difficult to determine the impact of subjective factors (for example, personal idiolect) and objective factors (for example, situational context) on language variability (Shoda and Mischel 1994; Cvrček et al. 2020). On the other hand, a substantial influence of the communication context has been repeatedly described both at the general level of language use (for example, Chen and Bond 2010) and at the level of specific linguistic features (for example, Newman et al. 2008; Ireland and Mehl 2014; Kučera 2020).

Another question relating to the *cross-linguistic perspective* of the research is the generalizability of personality and social markers cross-culturally. So far, current psychological processing of cross-language variation has been based predominantly on word counting methods such as the above mentioned LIWC (Pennebaker et al. 2015), which covers 11 world languages (see Lazarević et al. 2020). However, the development and adaptation of a dictionary is very time consuming, since it requires alterations in the software itself, and its outputs are still afflicted by several issues (for example, problems with homonyms or segmentation; Bjekić et al. 2014; Lazarević et al. 2020). Additionally, numerous studies pointed out that linguistic features are not used randomly and in isolation (for example, Labov 1966, Biber 1995), that is, that features have different functions in different situations and serve different communicative purposes and the use of one linguistic feature triggers the use of another with a similar function. Therefore, instead of relying on isolated words, a complex linguistic analysis needs to be based on combinations of features (for example, dimensions) which represent prominent communicative functions.

Although there are studies available in, for example, Chinese, Arabic, Spanish, Dutch, French, German, Italian, or Turkish, the vast majority of research has been conducted in English only. It should be noted that the number of studies focusing on Slavic languages is still negligible (for example, Bjekić et al. 2012; Sboev et al. 2016; Sikos et al. 2014; Litvinova et al. 2017; Kučera et al. 2018) limiting the opportunity for analytic comparison (see, for example, Panicheva, Ledovaya, and Bogolyubova 2016; Kartelj, Filipović, and Milutinović 2012; Kučera 2020). However, from a research perspective, Slavic languages show an evident potential for cross-linguistic comparison with commonly studied Germanic languages. Being part of the same Indo-European language family, they share the general properties of language structure with English, but at the same time, they also show numerous typological differences (Sussex and Cubberley, 2006). Czech (as a West Slavic language) is a highly interesting language for this type of research as it exhibits a high degree of inflection (which goes hand in hand with abundant morphological variation), productive derivation patterns (cf. scarcity of diminutives in English in comparison to their abundance in Czech), loose word order (as opposed to fixed order in English) (Hornová 2003) and a sociolinguistic situation bordering on diglossia (for example, Bermel 2014). Such features may be very relevant when studying the way a speaker makes use of verbal communication, and they can provide a more complex understanding of its psychological basis.

3 Czech psychological-linguistic research: CPACT and PS projects

In this part of the text, we focus on two original Czech projects based on the application of NLP methods in personality research. We present two key studies that were part of the projects "Text specifics in relation to the communicator" and "Communicator's personality characteristics in the context of language traits". These studies were carried out in 2020 (Kučera 2020) and they work with two research samples, CPACT (N = 200) and PS (N = 1887) (see the description below). The source of textual data was based on four types of research texts (elicited texts of approximately 180 to 200 words, based on the assigned scenarios) that were processed by the NLP describing their lexical-semantic, morphological, and stylistic linguistic features in the form of 47 linguistic variables. The analysis was carried out by the CNC K-centre (Czech CLARIN Knowledge Centre for Corpus Linguistics, operated by the Czech National Corpus), resulting in linguistic variables that formed a basis for our study. As psychological measures, the Big Five Inventory (BFI-44/BFI-10) and Interpersonal Adjective Scales (IAS/IAS-32) tests were used as a source of information about the personality of the communicator. The tests were administered in two variants – speaker self-assessment (self-report) and assessment by another person (so called "judge", that is, other-report), providing 13 psychological variables in each variant.

The *CPACT project* (Computational Psycholinguistic Analysis of Czech Text, CSF/GAČR nr. 16-19087S) was a pioneering project in the area of verbal communication and psychological analysis in the Czech context (Kučera et al. 2018). The research was carried out in 2016–2018 and was carried out with a research sample that represents the Czech population according to data from the Czech Statistical Office (CSU n.d.) in categories (quotas) of gender, age, and education. The sample consisted of 100 pairs of participants in a close personal relationship (that is, N = 200). During the one-day research sessions, the participants provided their personal information, wrote four written texts with different content, and completed a series of psychological tests. Materials were obtained in a controlled environment, according to a predetermined scenario (see below), and an electronic interface was used to collect all materials (see Kučera et al. 2018). Within the CPACT research, we published many statistically robust relationships between linguistic features and the Big Five dimensions, depression, dominance, but also gender divergences and differences in the manifestation of personality markers across different types of texts (see, for example, Kučera 2020; Kučera, Haviger, and Havigerová 2020; Havigerová et al. 2019; Kučera and Haviger 2019; Kučera et al. 2018; Kučera 2017).

The *PS project* (PoznejSe, meaning "KnowYourself") is an informal follow-up of the CPACT project (running from 2018). As part of the studies presented in this chapter, we will work with data collection from 2018–2020. Data collection took place through the open web interface Poznejse.cz, where each participant (visitor) could anonymously complete a set of personality questionnaires, to write a short text, and obtain an automatically generated interpretation of his/her results subsequently. The PS project aimed to gather research evidence on the variability of personal assessment of participants by different judges (assessors of their choice, other-reporters) and, at the same time, to verify the relationships between the specifics of the elicited written text (its linguistic features) and the personality of its author. Therefore, it is a two-module research design, while the second module is essential for the analyses described in this chapter. A detailed description of the project is available in the book of Kučera (2020).

Within the projects, several studies and goals were set. Two goals are key to this chapter:

1. To describe the linguistic specifics of the research texts (linguistic features) and their relationship to the communicators in terms of their social classification.
2. To identify the relationships between linguistic characteristics and personality characteristics of a communicator.

Within the first study, we will focus on a detailed description of research texts and on whether speakers belonging to a certain social group (social category determined based on the gender and age) share similar usage of linguistic features. Within the second study, we will look for relationships between personality characteristics (scores of two psychological questionnaires in self-report and other-report variants) and linguistic features of the text.

3.1 Method

3.1.1 Sample

Both research samples are described in detail in Table 1. In terms of demographic descriptors, the CPACT sample shows the highest representativeness, which respects the demographic distribution of the Czech population. Its disadvantage is its smaller size (N = 200). Although the sample is larger in the PS project, it shows a disproportionate representation of women, university-educated people, and especially participants aged 18–24. It can be noted that such a skewed distribution is relatively common in social science research, which usually works with non-random sampling. Some groups of respondents (for example, categories of men aged 35+ with primary or secondary education) are significantly underrepresented, while others (for example, university students) dominate the sample. In addition, research generally attracts those participants across all demographic categories that share certain characteristics. In terms of personality characteristics, for example, a higher rate of extraversion or a lower rate of neuroticism is often mentioned (Lönnqvist et al. 2007; Almeida et al. 2008). Within our studies we try to reduce these risks (especially the effects of the sampling error; see Clark et al. 2021), for instance, by a separate analysis in both datasets and emphasizing the consensual nature of results.

Table 1: Research samples description.

Samples	CPACT			PS			
	S	O	%	S	%	O	%
N	200	200	100	552	100	1335	100
Men	100	100	50	183	33	459	34
Women	100	100	50	369	67	876	66
E: Primary	36	36	18	63	11	223	17
E: Secondary	128	128	64	285	52	764	57
E: University	36	36	18	204	37	348	26

Table 1 (continued)

Samples	CPACT			PS			
	S	O	%	S	%	O	%
A: 18–24	26	26	13	283	51	877	66
A: 25–34	34	34	17	120	22	188	14
A: 35–55	67	67	34	120	22	212	16
A: 55+	73	73	37	29	5	58	4
Texts per person	4			1			
Total texts	800			552			

Note. S = self-reporters, O = other-reporters; E = education level; % = sample percentage; A = age (years).

3.1.2 Material and procedure

Text material

The relationship between linguistic features and personality characteristics depend to a large extent on the *type of text* being analysed. To find more distinct relationships, it is preferable to work with categorized data, that is, to group together texts that exhibit situational and content similarities. Within our study, we asked participants to write different elicited texts, fictitious letters each with an overall length of 180–200 words. This minimum text length is based on the prediction of the usual text length and the length needed to perform efficient language analyses (see Kučera 2020). All texts were typed on a computer using a pre-defined electronic interface on the same day. Participants in the CPACT project followed four scenarios: a Cover Letter (TXT1), a Letter from a Vacation (TXT2), a Complaint (TXT3) and a Letter of Apology (TXT4). The sequence of the texts was selected randomly during the day. Participants in the PS project wrote only one text, a Letter from Vacation (TXT2).

- Cover Letter (TXT1): "You have found a job offer that captivated your interest and you really aspire to be hired for this particular position. Therefore, you are going to write a letter to the company's director as a response to his/her offer, to try to persuade the director that you are the right candidate for this position."
- Letter from a Vacation (TXT2): "You are enjoying your time on an amazing vacation. Everything is going well, as expected, and you fully indulge in some popular activities. Therefore, you have decided to write a letter to your friend and convince him/her to come over and enjoy this perfect time with you."

- Complaint (TXT3): “Until recently, you were living contentedly in your apartment (or your house); you wanted for nothing. Nevertheless, recently, issues have arisen that have made your happy home more like a hellish home. Although you originally strived to sort out these issues in a gentle way, your efforts did not make any difference. Therefore, you decided to write an official letter of complaint to the respective authorities.”
- Letter of Apology (TXT4): “You have done something that substantially harmed your relationship with a person you were very close to for a long time. You promised something that you did not fulfil. You feel sorry and you know that you made a mistake. Because you do not want to lose this person, you have decided to write a letter of apology to him/her.”

The choice of scenarios reflected the results and the experiences reported of the participants in the previous data collection within the pilot research (see Kučera et al. 2018). Furthermore, there was an assumption that all four texts would contain obvious linguistic discrepancies; a Letter from Vacation and Letter of Apology (TXT2 and TXT4) can be written in colloquial or common Czech, but the text of the Cover Letter or letter of Complaint (TXT1 and TXT3) is likely to be official and use more correct and formal language. The interpersonal context of the texts also differs; whereas TXT2 and TXT3 are based on relatively equal relations between communicational partners or a certain dominance of the author who is proactive, TXT1 and TXT4 are based on an unequal relationship between the author and the recipient or some level of submissiveness of the author who needs to reveal or defend himself. It is also possible to divide the texts by the expected affiliative content, where TXT2 and TXT4 will most likely include a higher rate of emotional investment by the author, compared to other types of text. Due to the capability and accessibility of the electronic interface, only one text scenario (TXT2) was used in the PS project. The choice of this text type was based on the results of previous research, which pointed to a higher diagnostic potential of this text type (see ibid.).

Linguistic variables

For psychological-linguistic research, it is crucial to interrelate relevant psychological variables with relevant *linguistic variables*. Defining appropriate psychological variables is usually not a major challenge (since the assessment methods are relatively well established in psychology; see below). The definition and selection of suitable linguistic variables is a much more demanding task, especially with respect to their factual psychological meaningfulness. Unfortunately, in a majority of studies we encounter rather artificially defined sets of basic grammatical categories (for example, Yarkoni 2010; Lee et al. 2007; Boyd and Pennebaker 2015; Kučera et al. 2018; Yeomans 2021), instead of more psychologically elaborate linguistic variables.

In the two studies we present here, we thus used a combination of (1) the basic set of linguistic variables (that is, variables that most often occur in psychological studies based on English language) and (2) a set of variables that have not been more widely applied in psychology. The first category is represented by lexical-semantic and morphological features, and the second category by stylistic features. The key linguistic methods we will work with are based on the tools and services provided by the CNC K-centre (see above) and UTKL FF UK (Institute of Theoretical and Computational Linguistics of the Charles University).

The *lexical-semantic analysis* consists of determining the frequency of occurrence of emotionally loaded words from the SENS lexicon, that is, *Dictionary of Emotionally Loaded Words*. The lexicon was created by adjusting the Czech SubLex 1.0 dictionary (Veselovská and Bojar 2013), performed by the UTKL FF UK. The adjustment consisted of deleting 94 words without a sufficient emotional load. SENS comprises 928 words (lemmas) altogether, annotated by a positive, negative, or undetermined emotional load. All three categories are processed in terms of values of the relative frequency occurrence (that is, the ratio of the given category to the number of words in the text).

Morphological analysis is focused on the description of 26 linguistic features, grammatical categories. These features were chosen mainly on the basis of their comprehensibility and the possibility of a subsequent cross-linguistic comparison with English research (see above). All texts obtained were processed using PMA applications (Prague Morphological Analysis; Jelínek 2018; Hajič 2001). These applications represent an advanced Czech alternative to the LIWC (see the comparison in Kučera and Haviger 2019). The outcome of this process is the allocation of morphological tags to every lexical unit of the text with an average of 95% accuracy and, in the case of detection of various linguistic variables (for example, part of speech), as high as 99.5% accuracy (Skoumalová 2011). In this study, we used such linguistic categories that show high compatibility with the English LIWC, that is, the grammatical categories of Part of speech, Person, Tense, Degree, and Negation. These categories were processed in terms of the values of their relative frequency in the text.

The third type of linguistic analysis, which we will work on in our studies, is stylistic analysis, represented by *multidimensional analysis* (MDA). The aim of this complex analysis is to interpret the variability of a text based on more complex characteristics of the text (dimensions). The model is based on the concept of the American linguist Douglas Biber (1991) in English, other variants of MDA were developed for other languages subsequently (including Czech; Cvrček et al. 2020).

In constructing the MDA, Biber assumed that the variability of the language is not random, but that it has a certain function, most often related to the communication situation, that is, that the extratextual characteristics directly affect the intra-textual characteristics. This non-randomness has also been pointed out by numerous sociolinguistic studies (for example, Labov 1966). Manifestation of variability (according to Biber 1991) involves the use of linguistic features from various levels (phonology, morphology, lexicon, syntax, pragmatics, and so forth), so it is also related to the types of analyses that we have presented earlier. By grouping linguistic features into categories according to how they occur together in similar texts (genres), basic dimensions can be defined, by which the texts can be broadly stylistically characterized (for example, in terms of a specific communication situation and register, or in terms of expectations of certain language features associated with the situation).

With the help of MDA, each of our texts was described in eight basic dimensions, that is, factors GLS1–GLS8 (generalized weighted least squares). The dimensions of the MDA text are as follows (Cvrček et al. 2020):

1. dynamic (+) vs. static (–);
2. spontaneous (+) vs. prepared (–);
3. higher (+) vs. lower (–) level of cohesion;
4. polythematic (+) vs. monothematic (–);
5. higher (+) vs. lower (–) amount of addressee coding;
6. general (+) vs. particular (–);
7. prospective (+) vs. retrospective (–);
8. attitudinal (+) vs. factual (–).

Using the MDA within the Koditex corpus (that is, synchronous representative reference corpus, which contains 9 million words without punctuation; see Cvrček and Richterová 2020), 10 CNC (Czech National Corpus) registers were defined by the clustering method (that is, groups of texts that share language characteristics and which serve as additional classifications to genres). These *CNC registers* cover the whole spectrum of Czech-language texts (spoken, web, and written; Cvrček et al. 2020). The categorization of a text in the register was processed automatically based on the linguistic features that appear in the text. The CNK registries were divided into two groups – static and dynamic registers (see classification of registers in Cvrček and Richterová 2020).

In the following studies, we will therefore work with the definition of a specific text using these eight dimensions (GLS1–GLS8) and with variables related to the distance of text from the CNK registers (RD: register distances). Table 2 provides an overview of all 47 linguistic variables.

Table 2: List of linguistic variables.

Category	Linguistic feature	Example	Abbreviation
Lexical-semantic*	Emotionally charged word – ambivalent	*velmi, velice, vážený*	Em2.ˣ
	Emotionally charged word – positive	*ráda, dobrý, děkuji*	Em2.+
	Emotionally charged word – negative	*mrzí, problém*	Em2.-
Morphological*	Part of speech – noun	*den, práce*	POS–N
	Part of speech – adjective	*ráda, dobrý*	POS–A
	Part of speech – pronoun	*se, to, mi*	POS–P
	Part of speech – numeral	*pár, dva, několik*	POS–C
	Part of speech – verb	*jsem, mám, vím*	POS–V
	Part of speech – adverb	*tu, tak, už*	POS–D
	Part of speech – preposition	*na, v, s*	POS–R
	Part of speech – conjunction	*a, že, i*	POS–J
	Part of speech – particles	*ahoj, opravdu, asi*	POS–T
	Part of speech – interjection	*pa, fajn, hele*	POS–I
	Punctuation	*, . !*	POS–Z
	Unknown word	*cz, jobs, XY*	POS–X
	First person	*jsem, mi, mám*	Per–1
	The second person	*ti, jsi, Vás*	Per–2
	Third person	*je, mrzí, jejich*	Per–3
	Number – singular	*mé, jeho, tvůj*	Num–S
	Number – plural	*naše, vaší, jejich*	Num–P
	Future time	*budu, pojedeme*	Ten–F
	Present tense	*jsem, mám, vím*	Ten–P
	Past tense	*byla, chtěl, zaujala*	Ten–R
	First degree (positive)	*dobrý, vážený*	Deg–1
	Second degree (comparative)	*dále, víc, lepší*	Deg–2
	Third degree (superlative)	*nejlepší, nejdříve*	Deg–3
	Form is not negated (affirmative)	*jsem, den, mám*	Neg–A
	Form is negated (negative)	*není, nevím, nepříjemné*	Neg–N
	Verbal negation	*není, nemá, nedá*	Vneg
Stylistic			
Dimensions	Dynamic (+) vs. Static (–)		GLS1
	Spontaneous (+) vs. Prepared (–)		GLS2
	Higher (+) vs. Lower (–) level of cohesion		GLS3
	Polythematic (+) vs. Monothematic (–)		GLS4
	Higher (+) vs. lower (–) amount of addressee coding		GLS5

Table 2 (continued)

Category	Linguistic feature	Example	Abbreviation
	General (+) vs. Particular (–)		GLS6
	Prospective (+) vs. Retrospective (–)		GLS7
	Attitudinal (+) vs. Factual (–)		GLS8
Register distances	Analysis: static monothematic		RD_1_ANA
	Popularization: static polythematic general		RD_2_POP
	Question answering: dynamic without addressee coding		RD_3_ANK
	Conversation: dynamic spontaneous		RD_4_KONV
	Commentary: dynamic attitudinal		RD_5_KOM
	Journalism: static mixed		RD_6_ZURN
	Screenplay: dynamic with addressee coding		RD_7_SCEN
	Facts: static polythematic particular		RD_8_FAK
	Narration: dynamic retrospective		RD_9_NAR
	Argumentation: static cohesive		RD_10_ARG

* The values are represented in relative frequency (relative to total number of words).

Personality measures

A set of two psychological tests was used to describe the personality of the speakers – Big Five Inventory (BFI) and Interpersonal Adjective Scales (IAS) questionnaires. The models on which they are based (five-factor model in BFI and circumplex model in IAS) are widely used in psychology and generally known; moreover, their structure follows lexical research describing personality using words that occur in natural language (Wiggins 1995). The complementarity of both models and the benefits of their parallel use are also mentioned (Trapnell and Wiggins 1990; McCrae and Costa 1989). Both questionnaires offer, thanks to a simple formulation of the test items, an easy transfer to the other-report variant and their length makes successful administration feasible.

Big Five Inventory (BFI; John, Naumann, and Soto 2008) is focused on five basic personality traits – extraversion (E), neuroticism (N), openness to experience (O), agreeableness (A), and conscientiousness (C). Two test versions were used for the study, the full version BFI-44 from the CPACT project and the short version BFI-10 from the PS project. BFI-44 consists of 44 items, BFI-10 of 10 items. Items take the form of adjectives used for character descriptions. Participants answer using a five-point scale (Likert-type scale: disagree strongly, disagree a little, neither agree nor disagree, agree a little, agree strongly). The psychometric properties of the BFI test are presented in detail in Kučera (2020).

Interpersonal Adjective Scales (IAS; Wiggins 1979) is a test based on a circumplex model of interpersonal behaviour, which is known, for example, from the

Interpersonal Check List test (Leary 1958). The standard version of IAS (Wiggins 1995) uses 64 items (adjectives), participants answered using an eight-point scale. The test describes the dimensions: Assured-Dominant (PA), Arrogant-Calculating (BC), Cold-hearted (DE), Aloof-Introverted (FG), Unassured-Submissive (HI), Unassuming-Ingenuous (JK), Warm-Agreeable (LM), Gregarious-Extraverted (NO). The Czech version of the questionnaire has been used in the 64-item variant in the CPACT research (see Kučera et al. 2018), the short version of IAS-32 (which contains half the number of items) in the PS research. Psychometric properties of the IAS test are presented in detail in Kučera (2020).

An overview of the psychological tests, the personality characteristics measured and the number of test items is shown in Table 3.

Table 3: Personality measures – BFI-44, BFI-10, IAS-64, and IAS-32 tests.

Test / scale	Description	Number of items (versions)	
BFI		BFI-10	BFI-44
E	Extraversion	2	8
N	Neuroticism	2	8
O	Openness to experience	2	10
P	Agreeableness	2	9
S	Conscientiousness	2	9
IAS		IAS-64	IAS-32
PA	Assured-Dominant	4	8
BC	Arrogant-Calculating	4	8
DE	Cold-hearted	4	8
FG	Aloof-Introverted	4	8
HI	Unassured-Submissive	4	8
JK	Unassuming-Ingenuous	4	8
LM	Warm-Agreeable	4	8
NO	Gregarious-Extraverted	4	8

3.2 Results

3.2.1 Text description

In the following text, we provide a basic linguistic description of the TXT1–TXT4 texts, that is, frequency/occurrence of linguistic features in the texts, degree of their similarity with the 10 CNC registers, and position of the texts within the dimensions of the MDA, including a comparison with selected genres of the Koditex. This descriptive part is very important, since a more specific definition of elicited texts (their comparison with texts created in natural environments) allows us to assume a higher ecological validity of subsequent psychological studies.

The first description of research texts includes *descriptive statistics of the average frequency* of each linguistic feature within a given text. The descriptives indicate (for full report see Kučera 2020: 75–76) that all texts (TXT1–TXT4) show relatively different characteristics, but PS_TXT2 (TXT2 text type in the PS project) is very similar to the text CPACT_TXT2 (TXT2 text type in the CPACT project). It should be mentioned that even in terms of other linguistic variables not included in this study (see Kučera et al. 2018), both texts (PS_TXT2 and CPACT _TXT2) are highly comparable, even identical from a descriptive point of view. We also find a higher similarity within the texts TXT1 and TXT3 (Cover letter and Complaint).

When we compare the research texts with 10 basic registers of the CNC, a high similarity between the PS_TXT2 and CPACT_TXT2 texts is also evident. Both types of texts are closest to the Commentary register (dynamic attitudinal register). TXT1 and TXT3 are both very similar, closest to the Argumentation (static cohesive text) and the Journalism register (static mixed text). For TXT4, the closest is the Commentary register (less significantly than for TXT2). It is clear from this type of analysis that the text types TXT1/3, TXT2, and TXT4 form three different groups, at least in terms of their intratextual classification. A graphical overview of the descriptives is given in Figure 1.

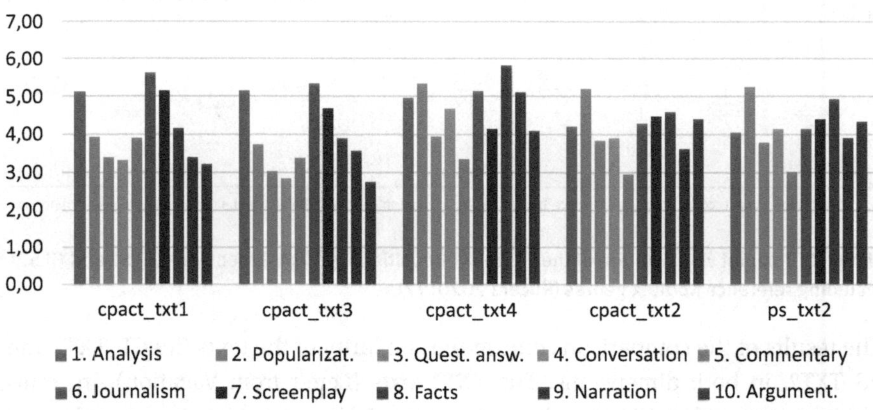

Figure 1: Distance of research texts TXT1–TXT4 from the definition of 10 CNC registers (lower value = higher agreement with the given register; Cvrček et al. 2020) (Kučera 2020: 76).

The second set of descriptions is focused on the *position of the research texts in the dimensions* (factors GLS1–GLS8) of the MDA. We supplement this description with a comparison with the *definition of five genres*, that is, text types from the Koditex corpus, selected from a total of 45 genres. The selection of these four genres is based on a study by Cvrček, Komrsková and Lukeš (2018), which underlines their linguistic relation with research texts. One genre (spo-int-inf) was chosen as a complementary one (as reference) – unlike the others, it covers a modality of spoken communication. Genres selected for the dimensional comparison are thus spo-int-inf (spoken, interactive, informal conversation), web-mul-fcb (internet, multidirectional; Facebook statuses), web-uni-blo (internet, one-way communication; blogs), web-uni-wik (internet, one-way communication; Wikipedia) and wri-pri-cor (written, private; letters). Figure 2 shows the representation of texts' positions in two MDA dimensions (GLS1 and GLS2). Full report is available in Kučera (2020: 77–79).

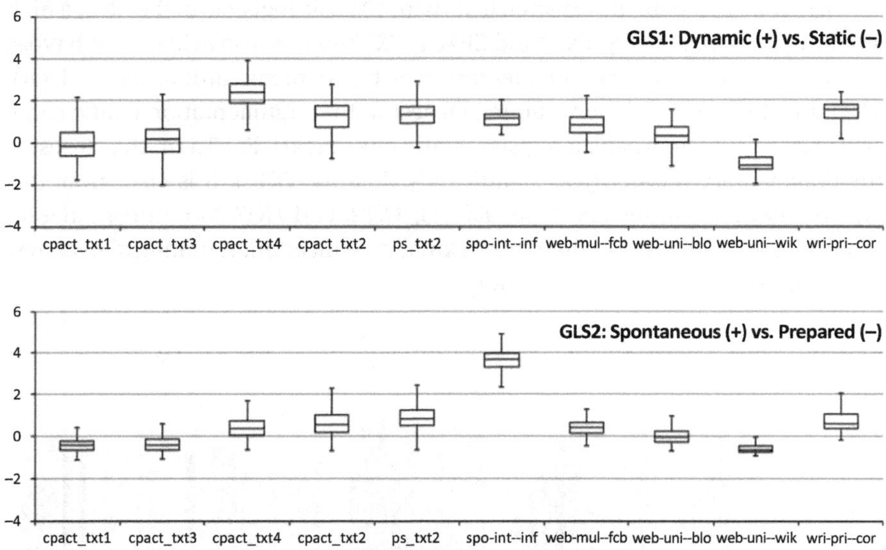

Figure 2: Box-plot visualization of the TXT1–TXT4 positions in MDA dimensions (GLS1 and GLS2) including reference Koditex genres (Kučera 2020: 77).

The results of the comparison confirm the similarity of the texts CPACT_TXT2 and PS_TXT2, in both dimensions. The TXT2 texts (Letter from Vacation), in terms of higher dynamics (GLS1) and spontaneity (GLS2), are similar to the register of correspondence (wri-pri-cor). If we focus on other texts, the highest multidimensional agreement can be found in the texts TXT1 (Cover letter) and TXT3 (Complaint). Both are closest to the genres of Internet communication, namely blogs and Wikipedia articles (web-uni-blo/wik). TXT4 (Letter of Apology) is a specific, very dynamic text type, even in comparison with, for example, fiction (wri-fic). The most distinguishable difference across the texts is visible between TXT1/TXT3 vs. TXT2 (CPACT_TXT2/PS_TXT2) and TXT4.

To sum up, the implementation of research texts in the research shows *the expected ecological validity* – their linguistic profile corresponds to the given scenarios, communication situations, and the purpose of communication. The research participants (speakers) clearly respected the scenarios and created texts that in their parameters correspond to natural language communication. Whereas the Koditex Corpus and CPACT/PS research are completely independent projects, the research texts have no direct equivalents in the registers and genres of the corpus – that is, they incorporate several genres and registers (sub-registers).

3.2.2 Text specifics in relation to the communicator

The first research study focuses on the specifics of the research texts in relation to the social (demographic) category of the speakers. Numerous social science studies pay attention to those linguistic features that do not relate primarily to psychological characteristics, but to, for instance, the gender and age of the authors. In this study, we will thus focus on these socio-categorical descriptors. We created groups, two in the gender category and four in the age category (see Table 1). Subsequently, we determined the relationship of socio-categorical variables to specific linguistic features through descriptive statistics, analysis of variance, and correlation analysis. Let us add that the comparison of four age groups (cohorts) is based on a cross-sectional model, not a longitudinal model, which may affect the generalizability of our results, for example, through a risk of interindividual differences (see, for example, Ferjenčík 2008).

To compare the representation of 47 linguistic features (lexical-semantic, morphological, and stylistic features) in research texts in terms of the speakers' gender, that is, when comparing a group of women and a group of men, we use the nonparametric Mann-Whitney U Test, while for significant differences we also determine the effect size (in Cohen's d; Cohen 1988). We analyse the texts separately (five text types, that is, CPACT_TXT1 – CPACT_TXT4 and PS_TXT2) and aggregately (aggregated text consisting of all four texts from the CPACT dataset, that is, CPACT_TXT1–TXT4).

When comparing the frequency of specific linguistic features *between groups of women and men*, no significant differences were found for all types of text (although in the case of some features the correspondence across texts is high). Complete results of analysis of the relationship between the linguistic features and the gender of the speakers are given in the publication of Kučera (2020: 81–82). To identify features that are related to the speaker's gender, the so-called gender markers, it is desirable for a feature to manifest consensually across types of text (that is, a feature is predominant in either men or women) and the differences between groups to be significant. The closest to these criterions is a frequency of verbs (POS–V), which is higher in women's texts. The only type of text where the result is not significant is PS_TXT2 (but only slightly above the set level α; $p = 0.058$). For aggregated data (CPACT_TXT1–TXT4), the result shows a high significance ($p = 0.0004$). Another feature is the GLS1 dimension (dynamic/static), which indicates a higher dynamism of the text in women (significant for separate texts CPACT_TXT2, CACT_TXT3, CPACT_TXT4 and aggregated CPACT_TXT1–TXT4, non-significant for the other two texts).

In the case of the texts CPACT_TXT2 and PS_TXT2, which both show very similar linguistic parameters (see above), a concurrent significant result occurs only in the category of first-person use (Per–1; women use more) and negation (Neg–N; men use more). However, negation is also a feature in which there are contradictory findings in all research texts – while in TXT2 men use negation more, in TXT3 and TXT4, on the contrary, the proportion of negation is higher in women. It is also worth noting that when comparing all the differences (even nonsignificant ones) between men and women, there are 26 similar results in the CPACT_TXT2 and PS_TXT2 texts, but in 11 features the signs of the effect are opposite. Let us add that the magnitudes of all observed effects are considered small (see Cohen's d; Cohen 1988).

When determining the relationship between the linguistic features and the *age of the speakers* (based on their classification in predefined age categories), we use the calculation of Spearman's rank-order correlation (ρ – rho). The non-parametric test was chosen with respect to the distribution of data that does not meet the criteria of normality. As in the previous case, none of the features show a significant relationship across all types of texts, however, the representation of some features shows comparable parameters. The features that show the most apparent relationships with the age of the speaker are prepositions (POS-R; with age, their representation increases) and the distance from the register analysis (RD_1_ANA).

Among the potential markers of age, we could also include those linguistic features that are more expressed in certain types of text. These features are, for example, the frequency of nouns (POS-N; older speakers use significantly more; but not in formal texts TXT1 and TXT3), the frequency of affirmations (Neg–A; older speakers use significantly more forms without the negative prefix *no-*; but not in TXT1 and TXT3), positively emotionally charged words (Em2. +; older people use more; but not in TXT1 and TXT3), the dynamic/static dimension (GLS1; younger speaker texts are more dynamic; but not in TXT1 and TXT3), and the spontaneous/prepared dimension (GLS2; younger speaker texts are significantly more spontaneous; but not in TXT1 and TXT3).

If we focus on the degree of convergence of the results between CPACT_TXT2 and PS_TXT2, we find the same direction of correlations across linguistic features in 38 cases (out of 47 monitored features), significant convergence in 14 cases, and only in one case (GLS3) a significant result in the opposite direction. The correlation values found are considered low to medium (CPACT_TXT4) (see Cohen 1988; De Vaus 2002). The complete results of the analysis of the relationship between the linguistic characteristics and the age of the speakers are given in the publication of Kučera (2020: 83–84).

We can sum up that the *gender and age of a speaker are not reflected in the same features in all types of texts*. The most reliable indicators of gender (that is, gender markers in text) can be considered more frequent use of verbs (POS–V), higher dynamism of the text (GLS1) and more frequent use of the first person (Per–1; in TXT2 texts) in the group of women. As the age marker could be considered, the more frequent use of prepositions (POS–R) and in informal types of texts TXT2 and TXT4 also the frequency of nouns (POS–N), affirmatives (Neg–A) and overall static character and preparedness of the text (GLS1 and GLS2) – all more frequent in older speakers.

For completeness, we add that the presented results are valid only for the texts and groups of speakers involved in this study. It is possible that, by, for instance, dividing the speakers into other groups (for example, a combination of older women, young men, and so forth), by choosing a different design (for example, longitudinal model), by adding other linguistic variables (for example, combination of features or indexes), the gender/age markers could be better captured.

3.2.3 Personality markers in text

The second study is dedicated to the description of the relationships between linguistic traits in research texts (TXT1–TXT4) and personality characteristics of speakers (texts' authors). The study works with linguistic features that cover lexical (lexical-semantic), morphological, and stylistic levels of communication. When defining personality characteristics, we draw from the results of the BFI (Big Five Inventory) and IAS (Interpersonal Adjective Scales) tests, both in the self-report (S) and other-report (O) variants. We process the data similarly to in the previous subchapter, that is, we process six types of text – four from the CPACT dataset (CPACT_TXT1–CPACT_TXT4), an aggregated text consisting of all four texts (CPACT_TXT1–TXT4), and one from the PS dataset (PS_TXT2). In terms of statistical processing, we use Spearman correlations (ρ, rho; with respect to the criteria of distribution normality) with a set level $\alpha = 0.05$. The results will also be supplemented with result of statistical correction (Benjamini-Hochberg FDR and Bonferonni FWER; Benjamini and Hochberg 1995; Šidák 1967). While in the PS project the number of judges (O) varied between 0 and 34 per speaker (assessed person, S) (see Table 1), we work with an average score of judges (O), that is, if two or more judges describe a person assessed (S). No adjustments were made to the CPACT dataset, where there was always one judge per person assessed.

The results of the analyses give the highest number of uncorrected significant correlations ($p < 0.05$, rho > 0.1) in the text of PS_TXT2 (164 relationships), CPACT_TXT4 (119 relationships) and CPACT_TXT2 (110 relationships), and the lowest number in the aggregated text CPACT_TXT1–TXT4 (16 relationships). After the FDR correction, we find 62 correlations, since the PS_TXT2 text completely dominates in the number of relationships found, as well as variables related to the self-report (S) (see Table 4).

Table 4: Number of relationships found between linguistic features and personality characteristics (Spearman correlation ρ, no gender differentiation).

Text Type	N	NR*	NR (FDR)**	NR S*	NR S (FDR)**	NR O*	NR O (FDR)**
CPACT_TXT1	200	93	0	35	0	58	0
CPACT_TXT3	200	81	0	48	0	33	0
CPACT_TXT4	200	119	10	67	9	52	1
CPACT_TXT2	200	110	1	54	0	56	1
PS_TXT2	552	164	51	100	43	64	8
CPACT_T1–T4	800	16	0	9	0	7	0
Total		583	62	313	52	270	10

* NR = Number of relationships found (number of correlations); $p < 0.05$, rho > 0.1
** sign. αFDR = 0.05 (Benjamini-Hochberg, adjusted p-value < 0.05)

In corrected (FDR) relations we find a convergence (agreement) between the texts CPACT_TXT4 and PS_TXT2, namely, a negative correlation between GLS1 (static/dynamic) and BFI–S_S (self-reported conscientiousness), and a negative correlation between RD_2_POP (popularization register) and BFI–S_S (see Kučera 2020: 98–99). From these relationships, we can conjecture that the texts of speakers who describe themselves as more conscientious show less dynamism and are closer to the register of popularization. There is also a potentially interesting relationship between POS–N and BFI–S, that is, the frequency of nouns positively correlates with conscientiousness. In further analyses, in which we assess the numbers and the level of convergences of relationships across different types of texts (significant, but not statistically corrected), we identify a number of findings (see Kučera 2020, Appendix 8). Their numbers are for both variants of personality questionnaires (S and O).

For a concise presentation of the results, we use three more variables: The variable "P–T", that is, the number of significant relations within a text type ($p < 0.05$ and $rho > 0.1$; without correction), the dichotomous variable "Sh", which expresses the convergence of correlations, that is, agreement in the direction of correlations (+/–) across texts, and the variable "Sh_S / O", which points to the same convergence for both variants of the evaluation (S and O). For example, if a relationship is significant within two types of text, CPACT_TXT2 and CPACT_TXT4, it will be set as P–T = 2. If the direction of the correlation (even nonsignificant) coincides between all six types of texts, it will be set as the value of the convergence Sh = 1. If a positive correlation was also found between, for example, POS-N (nouns) and the characteristic BFI-S_O (other-reported conscientiousness) was also found in the variant BFI-S_S (self-reported conscientiousness), within all types of text, the value would be Sh_S/O = 1.

The personality characteristic with the most apparent relationship to linguistic features is clearly conscientiousness (BFI–S), both in variant S and O. In the variant BFI–S_S, we find n(P–T) = 33 relationships with linguistic features, while in 12 characteristics there is a strong convergence in the direction of correlation between texts, that is, n(Sh) = 12. In the variant BFI–S_O, we find n(P–T) = 31 relationships and n(Sh) = 16 matches in all texts. In terms of linguistic features, as markers of personality characteristics, the largest number of relationships, n(P–T) = 15 (out of a total of 26 personality characteristics), was found for verb frequency (POS–V), plural (Num–P) and affirmatives (Neg–A). A summary of the analyses is given in Table 5.

Table 5: Summary of the relationships between linguistic features and personality characteristics (PC) ($p < 0.05$, $rho > 0.1$). Comparison of all types of text and aggregated text, without gender differentiation of speakers.

Pers. Char.	Ling. feature	CP_T1	CP_T3	CP_T4	CP_T2	PS_T2	CP_T1–4	P–T	Sh	Sh_S/O
BFI–S_O	POS–N	+	+	+	+	(+)	+*	5	1	1
BFI–S_S	POS–N	(+)	+	+	+	+*	(+)	4	1	1
BFI–S_O	Neg–A	+	(+)	+	+	+	+	5	1	1
BFI–S_O	GLS2	–	(–)	–	–	–	–	5	1	0
BFI–S_O	GLS7	–	–	–	(–)	(–)	–	4	1	1
BFI–S_O	GLS1	–	–	–*	(–)	(–)	(–)	3	1	1
BFI–S_S	RD_8_FAK	(+)	(–)	–	–	–*	–	4	0	0
BFI–S_S	POS–R	(+)	(+)	(+)	+	+*	+	3	1	1
BFI–S_O	POS–T	(–)	(–)	–	(–)	–	–	3	1	1
IAS–JK_S	POS–Z	–	–	(–)	–	(+)	–	4	0	0

Table 5 (continued)

Pers. Char.	Ling. feature	CP_T1	CP_T3	CP_T4	CP_T2	PS_T2	CP_T1–4	P–T	Sh	Sh_S/O
IAS–JK_S	GLS7	–	–	–	(–)	(–)	–	4	1	0
IAS–BC_S	RD_1_ANA	(+)	(+)	+	+	+	+	4	1	1
IAS–BC_S	GLS2	(+)	(+)	+	+	+	(+)	3	1	1
IAS–HI_S	POS–N	(–)	–	(–)	–	–*	(–)	3	1	0
IAS–HI_S	POS–V	(+)	+	+	(+)	+*	(+)	3	1	1
BFI–N_S	GLS1	(+)	+	+	(+)	+*	(+)	3	1	1
BFI–N_O	Deg–1	–	–	(–)	(–)	–	(–)	3	1	1

Note. + = sign. positive correlation, – = sign. negative correlation; (+) / (–) = non-sign. positive/negative; P–T = number of significant relations within one text type; Sh = correlation convergence (agreement in the direction of correlations +/– across texts); Sh_S/O = convergence across both variants of assessment (S/O); CPACT_TXT1 (CP_T1, n = 200), CPACT_TXT3 (CP_T3, n = 200), CPACT_TXT4 (CP_T4, n = 200), CPACT_TXT2 (CP_T2, n = 200), PS_TXT2 (PS_T2, n = 552), CPACT_T1 – T4 (CP_T1-4, n = 800).

* sign. αFDR = 0.05 (Benjamini-Hochberg)

As mentioned above, the personality characteristic that dominates the overview is undoubtedly conscientiousness (BFI–S), both in the S (self-report) and O (other-report) variants. This characteristic is associated with a higher frequency of nouns (POS–N), affirmatives (Neg–A), and prepositions (POS–R), and conversely with a lower proportion of particles (POS–T). Conscientious speaker texts are less spontaneous (GLS2), more retrospective (GLS7), and more static (GLS1). The texts of the speakers, who describe themselves as more unassuming and ingenuous (IAS–JK_S), are also rather retrospective (GLS7). Speakers who describe themselves as more arrogant and calculating (IAS–BC_S) write more spontaneous texts (GLS2) and diverge from the register of analysis (static monothematic text; RD_1_ANA). Speakers who describe themselves as unassured and submissive (IAS–HI_S) use fewer nouns (POS–N) but more verbs (POS–V). Speakers who show a higher score in emotional lability (BFI–N) write more dynamic texts (GLS1) and use less positivity (that is, first-degree adjectives and adverbs, Deg–1). All these relationships are significantly present within a minimum of three types of text and usually show the same parameters across all types of text and in both variants of assessment (S and O).

To summarize the results, we present the most relevant findings. In research texts, *it is possible to identify markers of personality characteristics*. Specific relationships between linguistic features and personality characteristics, both for men and women, which show statistically corrected significance (αFDR = 0.05), reach average values of correlations rho = 0.18 (ranged 0.13 – 0.31), that is, they explain about 3% variance in the texts. It should be mentioned that if we provide further analyses (see Kučera 2020), the correlations for the sample of women reach an average value of rho = 0.26 (ranging 0.18–0.44), that is, they explain about 7% of the variance, and in men, the average value of rho = 0.22 (ranging 0.18–0.42), that is, they are explaining about 5% variance. It is therefore clear that the personality characteristics of the speaker contribute to the linguistic variability only to a lesser extent.

The most versatile personality markers, such as noun frequency (POS–N) and dynamic/static dimension (GLS1), relate primarily to personality characteristics conscientiousness (BFI–S), unassured-submissiveness (IAS–HI) and neuroticism (BFI–N). The relationships between linguistic features and personality characteristics depend to a large extent on the type of text analysed and on the specifics of the speaker. To find salient relationships, it is therefore necessary to work with data that are categorized, for example, to group texts that show similar parameters (for example, are of same or similar register) and to group speakers into categories that meaningfully cover their shared properties (for example, in terms of socio-categorical descriptors).

4 Conclusion

The chapter deals with the analysis and interpretation of verbal communication through psychological and linguistic quantitative methods, that is, the psychology of language use. Its objective was to familiarize the reader with the relationships that can be found between verbal communication (linguistic characteristics of written text) and the personality characteristics of the communicator (results of psychological tests).

In the first study, Text Specifics in Relation to the Communicator, our objective was to describe the relationships between a speaker's social category and selected linguistic features. The Mann-Whitney U test was used to calculate differences between groups of men and women and the Spearman correlation to calculate relationships between features and the age of the speakers. Within these analyses, numerous relationships were found (see above). However, none of these relationships was significant in all types of research texts and the values of the effects were most often considered small. The strongest indicators (markers) of the speaker's gender could be considered to be the most frequent use of verbs (POS–V) and the higher dynamism (GLS1) of the text in women. As indicators (markers) of age, for example, a more frequent use of prepositions (POS-P) could be found in informal texts from older speakers. Within single text types, we can support the results of English studies related to more frequent use of verbs and first person in women (Biber 1991; Newman et al. 2008; Pennebaker and Stone 2003; Argamon et al. 2007; Mehl and Pennebaker 2003) and more frequent use of third person, present tense, and negation (also in women; Schwartz et al. 2013). In terms of age markers, we can support the results of a higher frequency of words with a positive emotional charge in older people (Pennebaker and Stone 2003) as well as a higher proportion of affirmations and adverbs (Schwartz et al. 2013). However, the degree of agreement with the results of these studies largely depends on which texts were analysed and to what extent they are comparable with our research texts.

If we summarize the first study, we can state that in many respects it shows relatively surprising results. Undoubtedly, the most important is the confirmation of the above-mentioned influence of the type of text (genre, register) on the occurrence of linguistic features as gender and age linguistic markers. At the same time, these markers generally explain only a small part of the overall language variability.

The second goal was to identify the relationships between linguistic features and speaker's personality characteristics, covering both self-report and other-report personality measures. The results have shown numerous significant and statistically corrected relationships within single text types, although none of those relationships have been found for all text types after statistical correction. The most important relationships are given in Table 5.

In terms of statistically corrected results (FDR), we can present, for instance, that informal texts of speakers who describe themselves as more conscientious (BFI–S) show less dynamism (GLS1) and are closer to the popularization register (RD_2_POP). From the point of view of more consensual results (between-text correlation convergency), the relationships between linguistic features and conscientiousness (BFI–S) predominated – texts of conscientious speakers are less spontaneous (GLS2), more retrospective (GLS7), and less dynamic (GLS1). In terms of other relationships found, we can support the results of English research, which highlights the relationships between conscientiousness and a higher proportion of affirmatives (Pennebaker and King 1999; Yarkoni 2010; Schwartz et al. 2013), prepositions and conjunctions (Schwartz et al. 2013), and relationships between higher frequency of negations in speakers with a lower agreeableness score, and a lower frequency of nouns in emotionally unstable speakers (Kim and Klinger 2018). Other significant relationships of personality characteristics with linguistic features, quite often mentioned in English research (for example, the use of first person or pronouns), were not widely supported in our study.

In connection with these findings, we should discuss the issue of cross-linguistic comparability in more detail. Regarding a lower number of relationships found in accordance with foreign research, a logical explanation could cover, for example, different parameters of research samples, intercultural differences, methodological flaws, or distortions resulting from inappropriate publication practices (so-called publication bias; see Francis 2012). However, we could mention at least three other aspects that undoubtedly affect the comparability of the results on a cross-cultural basis.

The first aspect is the influence of the type of text. As we pointed out in our studies, personality markers do not manifest in the same way in all types of texts; in contrast, they vary in communication contexts. Recent research works primarily with texts obtained in an online environment, such as statuses, tweets, or blogs (see Tadesse et al. 2018), which are specific on numerous relational and linguistic levels. Thus, it could be assumed that if we do not compare comparable texts, we cannot identify a broader agreement across research (and not only at the cross-linguistic level).

Another aspect that could be related to the variables we use, in particular, the linguistic features. The variables with which numerous studies work were often determined by a simple availability of their definitions or ad hoc (see, for example, Pennebaker 2013). After all, we also used a set of such linguistic features in the study (part of speech, number, and so forth), which were based primarily on a technical feasibility of quantitative linguistic analysis, and which are often referred to in foreign studies. Many authors try to compensate this deficit in the repertoire and meaningfulness of variables and employ, for instance, combinations of linguistic features (for example, "pronouns + first person + singular"; see Kacewicz et al. 2014; Kučera et al. 2018) or linguistic-psychological indexes (for example, Readiness to action index, Aggressiveness index, and so forth; see Sboev et al. 2016; Litvinova et al. 2017). The results of such studies often show not only a higher number of relationships found, but also their wider comparability in a cross-linguistic perspective (see, for example, Havigerová, Haviger, and Franková 2018; Havigerová et al. 2019). Let us add that in our study, about half of the significant relationships between personality characteristics and linguistic features (after FDR correction) were connected to those traits that were not based on simple grammatical descriptors but on the stylistic definition of dimensional or register parameters of the text.

The third aspect related to the cross-linguistic level of research is the diversity of languages as such (see the first section of this chapter). If we consider the diversity, it would be possible to explain why some "favoured" personality markers in English studies, such as pronouns, do not play such an important role in Czech language studies. In this context, it is therefore necessary to emphasize further development and internationalization of cross-psychological-linguistic studies, and international infrastructures and frameworks can be of great help in this regard (see Pozzo et al. 2022).

The Czech language does not offer sufficient background for major psychological-linguistic research (owing to its limited personnel, publishing, technical, and financial capacities) and needs to be bridged to international cross-linguistic studies. Moreover, it is possible to assume that a number of important relationships between personality and text would result only from contrasting (confrontation) findings across different languages (for example, Mach and Machová 1974; Karlík et al. 2016). As in intercultural psychology, it is often pointed out that personality traits are functionally comparable across cultures (for example, Allik and McCrae 2002; McCrae et al. 2004), it is thus necessary to examine to what extent a similar hypothesis can be valid for the relations of personality and linguistic features (cf. Peabody and De Raad 2002; Saucier, Hampson, and Goldberg 2000). However, if the replicability and sufficient comparability of the studies are not ensured, such efforts are difficult to implement. If we were to consider what solution would be appropriate here, one of the ways to increase comparability is to co-analyse linguistically more related languages, for instance, other Slavic languages in the case of the Czech language. At the level of language comparison, such a topic is also addressed by Fridlund et al. (2022), which uses word picture analysis between Swedish and Finnish.

To summarize our study, we can consider that that the use of analytical tools that allow the analysis of various languages, such as the applications and services of the CLARIN (European Research Infrastructure for Language Resources and Technology[1]) and the LINDAT/CLARIAH-CZ projects,[2] are very beneficial for psychological research. As for the linguistic tools, we can also recommend, for example, the UDPipe framework[3] available for cross-linguistic tokenization, tagging, and lemmatization of texts, or the InterCorp framework,[4] which consists of a parallel synchronous corpus for different languages. The accessibility of these applications, infrastructures, as well as the long-term availability of digital research data (see Trognitz, Ďurčo, and Mörth 2022), are key to the implementation and further development of psychology of language use methods.

1 www.clarin.eu
2 www.lindat.cz
3 universaldependencies.org
4 www.intercorp.korpus.cz

Bibliography

Allik, Jüri & Robert R. McCrae. 2002. A five-factor theory perspective. In Robert R. McCrae & Jüri Allik (eds.), *The Five-Factor Model of Personality across Cultures*, 303–322. Boston: Springer.

Almeida, L., A. Falcao, M. Vaz-da-Silva, R. Coelho, A. Albino-Teixeira & P. Soares-da-Silva. 2008. Personality characteristics of volunteers in phase 1 studies and likelihood of reporting adverse events. *International Journal of Clinical Pharmacology and Therapeutics* 46 (7). 340–348.

Argamon, S., Koppel, M., Pennebaker, J. W., & Schler, J. (2007). Mining the blogosphere: Age, gender and the varieties of self-expression. *First Monday*. http://firstmonday.org/ojs/index.php/fm/article/view/2003/1878 (accessed 18 September 2021).

Barbara, Dominick A. 1958. *Your speech reveals your personality*. Springfield, IL: Charles C. Thomas.

Benjamini, Yoav & Yosef Hochberg. 1995. Controlling the false discovery rate: A practical and powerful approach to multiple testing. *Journal of the Royal Statistical Society: Series B (Methodological)* 57 (1). 289–300.

Berelson, Bernard. 1952. *Content analysis in communication research*. Glencoe, IL: Free Press.

Bermel, Neil. 2014. Czech diglossia: Dismantling or dissolution? In Judit Árokay, Jadranka Gvozdanović & Darja Miyajima (eds.), *Divided languages? Diglossia, translation, and the rise of modernity in Japan, China, and the Slavic world*, 21–37. Cham: Springer.

Biber, Douglas. 1991. *Variation across speech and writing*. Cambridge: Cambridge University Press.

Biber, Douglas. 1995. *Dimensions of register variation: A cross-linguistic comparison*. Cambridge: Cambridge University Press.

Bjekić, Jovana, Ljiljana B. Lazarević, Milica Erić, Elena Stojimirović & Teodora DJokić. 2012. Development of Serbian dictionary for automatic text analysis (LIWCser). *Psihološka Istraživanja* 15 (1). 85–110.

Bjekić, Jovana, Ljiljana B. Lazarević, Marko Živanović & Goran Knežević. 2014. Psychometric evaluation of the Serbian Dictionary for automatic text analysis – LIWCser. *Psihologija* 47 (1). 5–32.

Boyd, Ryan L. & James W. Pennebaker. 2015. A way with words: Using language for psychological science in the modern era. In Claudiu V. Dimofte, Curtis P. Haugtvedt & Richard F. Yalch (eds.), *Consumer Psychology in a Social Media World*, 250–264. New York: Routledge.

Brewer, Marilynn B. & Wendi Gardner. 1996. Who is this "we"? Levels of collective identity and self representations. *Journal of Personality and Social Psychology* 71 (1). 83–93.

Canter, David V. & Donna Youngs. 2009. *Investigative psychology: Offender profiling and the analysis of criminal action*. Chichester: John Wiley & Sons.

Castelvecchi, Davide. 2016. Can we open the black box of AI? *Nature News* 538 (7623). 20–23.

Chen, Sylvia Xiaohua & Michael Harris Bond. 2010. Two languages, two personalities? Examining language effects on the expression of personality in a bilingual context. *Personality and Social Psychology Bulletin* 36 (11). 1514–1528.

Chen, Pan & Alexander T. Vazsonyi. 2013 Future Orientation, School Contexts, and Problem Behaviors: A Multilevel Study. *Journal of Youth and Adolescence, 42*, 67–81.

Clark, Tom, Liam Foster, Luke Sloan & Alan Bryman. 2021. *Bryman's social research methods*, 6th edn. New York: Oxford University Press.

Cohen, Jacob. 1988. *Statistical power analysis for the behavioral sciences*, 2nd edn. Hillsdale, NJ: Lawrence Erlbaum.

ČSU. n.d. Věkové složení obyvatelstva – 2015. Věkové složení obyvatelstva – 2015. https://www.czso.cz/csu/czso/vekove-slozeni-obyvatelstva (accessed 18 September 2021).

Cvrček, Václav, Zuzana Komrsková & David Lukeš. 2018. Rozsah Registrové Variability Textů [Scope of register variability of texts]. In Kučera, Dalibor, Jana Marie Havigerová, Jiří Haviger, Václav Cvrček, Tomáš Urbánek, Tomáš Jelínek, David Lukeš & Zuzana Komrsková, *Výzkum CPACT: Komputační Psycholingvistická Analyza Českého Textu [CPACT Research: Computational Psycholinguistic Analysis of Czech Text]*, 153–172. České Budějovice: Pedagogická Fakulta Jihočeské Univerzity v Českých Budějovicích.

Cvrček, Václav, Zuzana Laubeová, David Lukeš, Petra Poukarová, Anna Řehořková & Adrian Jan Zasina. 2020. Author and register as sources of variation: A corpus-based study using elicited texts. *International Journal of Corpus Linguistics* 25 (4). 461–488.

Cvrček, Václav & Olga Richterová. 2020. Cnk:Koditex – Příručka ČNK. 2020. https://wiki.korpus.cz/doku.php?id=cnk:koditex&rev=1541085311 (accessed 18 September 2021).

Esposito, Anna, Nick Campbell, Carl Vogel, Amir Hussain & Anton Nijholt. 2010. *Development of multimodal interfaces: Active listening and synchrony: Second COST 2102 International Training School, Dublin, Ireland, March 23–27, 2009, revised selected papers* (Lecture Notes in Computer Science 5967). Berlin: Springer.

Ferjenčík, Ján. 2008. *Úvod do metodologie psychologického výzkumu: Jak zkoumat lidskou duši* [Introduction to psychological research methodology]. Prague: Portal.

Francis, Gregory. 2012. Publication Bias and the Failure of Replication in Experimental Psychology. *Psychonomic Bulletin & Review* 19 (6). 975–991.

Freud, Sigmund, James Strachey & Anna Freud. 1978. *The standard edition of the complete psychological works of Sigmund Freud, vol. VI: Psychopathology of everyday life (1901)*. Hogarth Press: Institute of Psycho-Analysis.

Fridlund, Mats, Daniel Brodén, Tommi Jauhiainen, Leena Malkki, Leif-Jöran Olsson & Lars Borin. 2022. Trawling and trolling for terrorists in the digital Gulf of Bothnia: Cross-lingual text mining for the emergence of terrorism in Swedish and Finnish newspapers, 1780–1926. In Darja Fišer & Andreas Witt (eds.), *CLARIN. The infrastructure for language resources*. Berlin: De Gruyter.

Hajič, Jan. 2001. *Disambiguation of rich inflection: Computational morphology of Czech, Svazek I*. Prague: Univerzita Karlova, Nakladatelství Karolinum.

Hamilton, Robert V. 1957. A Psycholinguistic analysis of some interpretive processes of three basic personality types. *The Journal of Social Psychology, 46* (2), 153–177.

Harley, Trevor A. 2013. *The psychology of language: From data to theory*. Hove & New York: Psychology Press.

Havigerová, Jana M., Jiří Haviger, & Justýna Franková (2018). Odraz osobnosti v textu – projevy deprese [Reflection of personality in the text – manifestations of depression]. In Dalibor Kučera et al. *Výzkum CPACT: Komputační psycholingvistická analýza českého textu*. České Budějovice: Faculty of Education, University of South Bohemia (201–243).

Havigerová, Jana M., Jiří Haviger, Dalibor Kučera & Petra Hoffmannová. 2019. Text-based detection of the risk of depression. *Frontiers in Psychology* 10: 513. https://doi.org/10.3389/fpsyg.2019.00513

Holtgraves, Thomas. 2011. Text messaging, personality, and the social context. *Journal of Research in Personality* 45 (1). 92–99.
Holtgraves, Thomas M. 2014. Languages and social psychology. In Thomas M. Holtgraves (ed.), *Oxford handbook of language and social psychology*, 1–10. Oxford: Oxford University Press.
Hornová, Libuše. 2003. *Referenční slovník gramatických termínů* [Reference dictionary of grammatical terms]. Olumouc: Univerzita Palackého.
Ireland, Molly E. & Matthias R. Mehl. 2014. Natural language use as a marker. In Thomas M. Holtgraves (ed.), *The Oxford handbook of language and social psychology*, 201–237. Oxford: Oxford University Press.
Jelínek, Tomáš. 2008. Nové značkování v Českém Národním Korpusu. *Naše řeč* 91 (1). 13–20.
Jelínek, Tomáš. 2018. Současná východiska komputační lingvistiky a její aplikace. In Kučera, Dalibor, Jana Marie Havigerová, Jiří Haviger, Václav Cvrček, Tomáš Urbánek, Tomáš Jelínek, David Lukeš & Zuzana Komrsková, *Výzkum CPACT: Komputační psycholingvistická analýza českého textu* [CPACT Research: Computational Psycholinguistic Analysis of Czech Text], 16–18. České Budějovice: Faculty of Education, University of South Bohemia.
John, Oliver P., Laura P. Naumann & Christopher J. Soto. 2008. Paradigm shift to the integrative big five trait taxonomy: History, measurement, and conceptual issues. In Oliver P. John, Richard W. Robins & Lawrence A. Pervin (eds.), *Handbook of personality: Theory and research*, 3rd edn., 114–158. New York: Guilford.
Kacewicz, Ewa, James W. Pennebaker, Matthew Davis, Moongee Jeon & Arthur C. Graesser. 2014. Pronoun use reflects standings in social hierarchies. *Journal of Language and Social Psychology* 33 (2). 125–143.
Karlík, Petr, Marek Nekula, Jana Pleskalová, Jarmila Bachmannová, Jan Balhar, Aleš Bičan, Lenka Bičanová, Jana Bílková, Petr Biskup & Ondřej Bláha. 2016. *Nový Encyklopedický Slovník Češtiny* [New Encyclopedic Dictionary of Czech]. Nakladatelství Lidové noviny.
Kartelj, Aleksandar, Vladimir Filipović & Veljko Milutinović. 2012. Novel approaches to automated personality classification: Ideas and their potentials. In *2012 Proceedings of the 35th International Convention MIPRO*, 1017–1022. Opatija: IEEE.
Kennedy, Brendan, Ashwini Ashokkumar, Ryan L. Boyd & Morteza Dehghani. 2021. Text analysis for psychology: Methods, principles, and practices. http://doi.org/10.31234/osf.io/h2b8t
Kim, Evgeny & Roman Klinger. 2018. *A survey on sentiment and emotion analysis for computational literary studies*. arXiv preprint. ttps://doi.org/10.48550/arXiv.1808.03137.
Knapp, Mark L., Hart, Roderick P. & Harry S. Dennis. 1974. An exploration of deception as a communication construct. *Human Communication Res., 1*, 15–29.
Kučera, Dalibor. 2017. Computational Psycholinguistic Analysis of Czech Text and the CPACT Research. In ISC SGEM (Eds.), 4th International Multidisciplinary Scientific Conference on Social Sciences and Arts SGEM 2017: Science & Society Conference Proceedings (pp. 77–84). Albena, Bulgaria: ISC SGEM. https://doi.org/10.5593/sgemsocial2017/32/s11.010
Kučera, Dalibor. 2020. *Osobnostní Markery v Textu* [Personality Markers in Text]. České Budějovice: Faculty of Education, University of South Bohemia.
Kučera, Dalibor & Jiří Haviger. 2019. Analysis of formal characteristics of text in the CPACT research: Enhancing the LIWC linguistic processing for the Czech language. *Journal of Advanced Research in Social Sciences and Humanities* 4 (2). https://doi.org/10.26500/JARSSH-04-2019-0203.

Kučera, Dalibor, Jiří Haviger & Jana M. Havigerová. 2020. Personality and text: Quantitative psycholinguistic analysis of a stylistically differentiated Czech text. *Psychological Studies* 65 (3). 336–348.
Kučera, Dalibor, Jana Marie Havigerová, Jiří Haviger, Václav Cvrček, Tomáš Urbánek, Tomáš Jelínek, David Lukeš & Zuzana Komrsková. 2018. *Výzkum CPACT: Komputační psycholingvistická analýza českého textu* [CPACT Research: Computational psycholinguistic analysis of Czech text]. České Budějovice: Faculty of Education, University of South Bohemia.
Kwantes, Peter J., Natalia Derbentseva, Quan Lam, Oshin Vartanian & Harvey H. C. Marmurek. 2016. Assessing the big five personality traits with latent semantic analysis. *Personality and Individual Differences* 102. 229–233.
Labov, William. 1966. The linguistic variable as a structural unit. *Washington Linguistics Review* 3. 4–22.
Lazarević, Ljiljana B., Jovana Bjekić, Marko Živanović & Goran Knežević. 2020. Ambulatory assessment of language use: Evidence on the temporal stability of electronically activated recorder and stream of consciousness data. *Behavior Research Methods* 52 (5). 1817–1835.
Leary, Timothy. 1958. Interpersonal diagnosis of personality. *American Journal of Physical Medicine & Rehabilitation* 37 (6). 331.
Lee, Chang H., Kyungil Kim, Young Seok Seo & Cindy K. Chung. 2007. The relations between personality and language use. *The Journal of General Psychology* 134 (4). 405–413.
Litvinova, Olga, Pavel Seredin, Tatiana Litvinova & John Lyell. 2017. Deception detection in Russian texts. In Florian Kunneman, Uxoa Iñurrieta, John C. Camilleri, Mariona Coll Ardanuy (eds.), *Proceedings of the Student Research Workshop at the 15th Conference of the European Chapter of the Association for Computational Linguistics*, 43–52. Stroudsburg, PA: Association for Computational Linguistics.
Lönnqvist, Jan-Erik, Sampo Paunonen, Markku Verkasalo, Sointu Leikas, Annamari Tuulio-Henriksson & Jouko Lönnqvist. 2007. Personality characteristics of research volunteers. *European Journal of Personality: Published for the European Association of Personality Psychology* 21 (8). 1017–1030.
Mach, Vladimír & Svatava Machová. 1974. Kontrastivní výzkum: Pokračování konfrontačních metod české lingvistiky [Contrastive research: the continuation of confrontational methods in Czech linguistics]. *Slovo a Slovesnost* 35 (1). 43–48.
Mairesse, François, Marilyn A. Walker, Matthias R. Mehl & Roger K. Moore. 2007. Using linguistic cues for the automatic recognition of personality in conversation and text. *Journal of Artificial Intelligence Research* 30. 457–500.
Matoušková, Ingrid. 2013. *Aplikovaná forenzní psychologie* [Applied Forensic Psychology]. Prague: Grada Publishing.
McCrae, Robert R., Paul T. Costa Jr, Thomas A. Martin, Valery E. Oryol, Alexey A. Rukavishnikov, Ivan G. Senin, Martina Hřebíčková & Tomáš Urbánek. 2004. Consensual validation of personality traits across cultures. *Journal of Research in Personality* 38 (2). 179–201.
McCrae, Robert R. & Paul T. Costa. 1989. The structure of interpersonal traits: Wiggins's circumplex and the five-factor model. *Journal of Personality and Social Psychology* 56 (4). 586–595.
Mehl, Matthias R. & James W. Pennebaker. 2003. The sounds of social life: A psychometric analysis of students' daily social environments and natural conversations. *Journal of Personality and Social Psychology* 84 (4). 857–870.

Newman, Matthew L., Carla J. Groom, Lori D. Handelman & James W. Pennebaker. 2008. Gender differences in language use: An analysis of 14,000 text samples. *Discourse Processes* 45 (3). 211–236.

Panicheva, Polina, Yanina Ledovaya & Olga Bogolyubova. 2016. Lexical, morphological and semantic correlates of the dark triad personality traits in Russian Facebook texts. In Andrey Filchenkov, Lidia Pivovarova & Jan Žižka (eds.), *2016 IEEE Artificial Intelligence and Natural Language Conference (AINL)*, 1–8. St. Petersburg: IEEE.

Peabody, Dean & Boele De Raad. 2002. The substantive nature of psycholexical personality factors: A comparison across languages. *Journal of Personality and Social Psychology* 83 (4). 983–997.

Pennebaker, James W. 2013. *The secret life of pronouns: What our words say about us*. New York: Bloomsbury Press.

Pennebaker, James W., Roger J. Booth, Boyd, Ryan. L. & Martha E. Francis. 2015. Linguistic Inquiry and Word Count: LIWC2015. Austin, TX: Pennebaker Conglomerates (www.LIWC.net).

Pennebaker, James W., Cindy Chung, Molly Ireland, Amy Gonzales & Roger Booth. 2007. *The development and psychometric properties of LIWC2007*. Austin: University of Texas.

Pennebaker, James W. & Laura A. King. 1999. Linguistic styles: Language use as an individual difference. Journal of Personality and Social Psychology, 77, 1296–1312.

Pennebaker, James W., Mehl, Matthias R. & Kate G. Niederhoffer. 2003. Psychological aspects of natural language use: Our words, our selves. *Annual review of psychology, 54* (1), 547–577.

Pennebaker, James W. & Lori D. Stone. 2003. Words of wisdom: Language use over the lifespan. *Journal of Personality & Social Psychology, 85*, 291–301.

Petkevič, Vladimír. n.d. Matematická Lingvistika'. Nový Encyklopedický Slovník Češtiny [Mathematical Linguistics'. New Encyclopedic Dictionary of Czech]. https://www.czechency.org/slovnik/MATEMATICK%C3%81%20LINGVISTIKA (accessed 18 September 2021).

Pozzo, Riccardo, Timon Gatta, Hansmichael Hohenegger, Jonas Kuhn, Axel Pichler, Marco Turchi & Josef van Genabith. 2022. Aligning Immanuel Kant's work and its translations. In Darja Fišer & Andreas Witt (eds.), *CLARIN. The infrastructure for language resources*. Berlin: De Gruyter.

Rodriguez, Aubrey J., Holleran, Shannon E. & Matthias R. Mehl. 2010. Reading between the lines: the lay assessment of subclinical depression from written self-descriptions. *Journal of Personality, 78*, 575–597.

Rodriguez-Puente, Paula. 2014. *Current research in applied linguistics: Issues on language and cognition*. Edited by Teresa Fanego, Evelyn Gandon-Chapela, Sara Maria Riveiro-Outeiral & Maria Luisa Roca-Varela (unabridged edition). Newcastle Upon Tyne: Cambridge Scholars Publishing.

Rude, Stephanie S., Gortner, Eva M., & James W. Pennebaker. 2004. Language use of depressed and depression-vulnerable college students. Cognition & Emotion, 18(8), 1121–1133.

Sanford, Fillmore H. 1942. Speech and personality. *Psychological Bulletin 39* (10). 811–845

Saucier, Gerald, Hampson, Sarah E. & Lewis R. Goldberg. 2000. Cross-language studies of lexical personality factors. *Advances in personality psychology, 1*, 1–36.

Sboev, Alexander, Litvinova, Tatiana, Gudovskikh, Dmitry, Rybka, Roman & Ivan Moloshnikov. 2016. Machine learning models of text categorization by author gender using topic-independent features. *Procedia Computer Science, 101*, 135–142.

Scherer, Klaus R & Howard Giles. 1979. *Social markers in speech*. Cambridge, UK & New York; Paris: Cambridge University Press; Éditions de la Maison des sciences de l'homme.
Schwartz, H. Andrew, Eichstaedt, Johannes C., Kern, Margaret L., Dziurzynski, Kern,Lukasz, Ramones, Stephanie M., Agrawal, Megha & Lyle H. Ungar. 2013. Personality, gender, and age in the language of social media: The open-vocabulary approach. *PloS one, 8* (9): e73791.
Shoda, Yuichi, Mischel, Walter & Jack C. Wright. 1994. Intraindividual stability in the organization and patterning of behavior: Incorporating psychological situations into the idiographic analysis of personality. Journal of personality and social psychology, 67(4), 674.
Sikos, Jennifer, David, Peter, Habash, Nizar, & Reem Faraj. 2014. Authorship analysis of Inspire Magazine through stylometric and psychological features. 2014 IEEE Joint Intelligence and Security Informatics Conference.
Skoumalová, Hana. 2011. Porovnání úspěšnosti tagování korpusu [Comparison of corpus tagging success rates]. In Vladimír Petkevič and Alexandr Rosen, editors, Korpusová lingvistika Praha 2011. 3 Gramatika a značkování korpusů, 16, Studie z korpusové lingvistiky (199–207). Praha: Nakladatelství Lidové noviny/Ústav Českého národního korpusu.
Stepikhov, Anton & Anastassia Loukina. 2014. Annotation and personality: Individual differences in sentence boundary detection. In: Ronzhin A., Potapova R., Delic V. (Eds.) *Speech and Computer. SPECOM 2014*. Lecture Notes in Computer Science, vol 8773. Cham: Springer.
Sussex, Roland, & Paul Cubberley. 2006. *The slavic languages*. Cambridge University Press.
Šidák, Zbyněk. 1967. Rectangular confidence regions for the means of multivariate normal distributions. *Journal of the American Statistical Association* 62 (318). 626–633. https://doi.org/10.1080/01621459.1967.10482935.
Tadesse, Michael M., Lin, Hongfei, Xu, Bo, & Lianf Yang. 2018. Personality predictions based on user behavior on the facebook social media platform. *IEEE Access, 6*, 61959–61969.
Tausczik, Yla R. & James W. Pennebaker. 2010. The psychological meaning of words: LIWC and computerized text analysis methods. *Journal of Language and Social Psychology* 29 (1): 24–54. https://doi.org/10.1177/0261927X09351676.
Trapnell, Paul D. & Jerry S. Wiggins. 1990. Extension of the interpersonal adjective scales to include the big five dimensions of personality. *Journal of Personality and Social Psychology* 59 (4). 781–790. https://doi.org/10.1037/0022-3514.59.4.781.
Trognitz, Martina, Matej Ďurčo & Karlheinz Mörth. 2022. Text technology for the digital humanities: Maximizing impact in a diverse field of disciplines. In Darja Fišer & Andreas Witt (eds.), *CLARIN. The infrastructure for language resources*. Berlin: De Gruyter.
Vaus, David de. 2002. *Analyzing social science data: 50 Key problems in data analysis*. London: Sage.
Veselovská, Kateřina & Ondřej Bojar. 2013. Czech SubLex 1.0. http://ufal.mff.cuni.cz/seance. https://lindat.mff.cuni.cz/repository/xmlui/handle/11858/00-097C-0000-0022-FF60-B.
Wiggins, Jerry S. 1979. A psychological taxonomy of trait-descriptive terms: The interpersonal domain. *Journal of Personality and Social Psychology* 37 (3). 395–412. https://doi.org/10.1037/0022-3514.37.3.395.
Wiggins, Jerry S. & Inc Psychological Assessment Resources. 1995. *IAS, Interpersonal adjective scales: Professional manual*. Odessa, FL: Psychological Assessment Resources.

Yarkoni, Tal. 2010. Personality in 100,000 words: A large-scale analysis of personality and word use among bloggers. *Journal of Research in Personality* 44 (3). 363–373. https://doi.org/10.1016/j.jrp.2010.04.001.
Yarkoni, Tal & Jacob Westfall. 2017. Choosing prediction over explanation in psychology: Lessons from machine learning. *Perspectives on Psychological Science: A Journal of the Association for Psychological Science* 12 (6). 1100–1122. https://doi.org/10.1177/1745691617693393.
Yeomans, Michael. 2021. A concrete example of construct construction in natural language. *Organizational Behavior and Human Decision Processes* 162. 81–94. https://doi.org/10.1016/j.obhdp.2020.10.008.
Zednik, Carlos. 2019. Solving the black box problem: A normative framework for explainable artificial intelligence. *ArXiv:1903.04361 [Cs]*, July. https://doi.org/10.48550/arXiv.1903.04361.

Mats Fridlund*, Daniel Brodén, Tommi Jauhiainen,
Leena Malkki, Leif-Jöran Olsson, and Lars Borin

Trawling and Trolling for Terrorists in the Digital Gulf of Bothnia

Cross-lingual Text Mining for the Emergence of Terrorism in Swedish and Finnish Newspapers, 1780–1926

Abstract: In pursuing the historical emergence of the discourse on terrorism, this study trawls the "digital Gulf of Bothnia" in the form of a corpus of combined Swedish and Finnish digitized newspaper texts. Through a cross-lingual exploration of the uses of the concept of terrorism in historical Swedish and Finnish news, we examine meanings anchored in the two culturally close but still decidedly different national political contexts. The study is an outcome of an integrative interdisciplinary effort

Note: This chapter uses the following notational conventions for source-language data. Source-language expressions are set in italics accompanied by English glosses in single quotes (also used when a gloss is repeated without the source-language expression): *hirmutyö* 'atrocity'. Furthermore, English expressions in single quotes are used to refer to the central concepts under discussion, for example, 'terrorism'. Some source-language material passages are provided as historical arguments rather than linguistic examples. Translations of such passages – made by the chapter's authors – are rendered in double quotes.

Acknowledgements: This work has been partly supported by an infrastructure grant to Språkbanken Text and Centre for Digital Humanities, University of Gothenburg, to contribute in building and operating a national e-infrastructure funded jointly by the participating institutions and the Swedish Research Council (under contract no. 2017-00626).

***Corresponding author: Mats Fridlund,** Centre for Digital Humanities, Department of Literature, History of Ideas and Religion, University of Gothenburg, Gothenburg, Sweden, e-mail: mats.fridlund@lir.gu.se
Daniel Brodén, Centre for Digital Humanities, Department of Literature, History of Ideas and Religion, University of Gothenburg, Gothenburg, Sweden, e-mail: daniel.broden@lir.gu.se
Tommi Jauhiainen, Department of Digital Humanities, University of Helsinki, Helsinki, Finland, e-mail: tommi.jauhiainen@helsinki.fi
Leena Malkki, Centre for European Studies, University of Helsinki, Helsinki, Finland, e-mail: leena.malkki@helsinki.fi
Leif-Jöran Olsson, Språkbanken Text, Department of Swedish, Multilingualism, Language Technology, University of Gothenburg, Gothenburg, Sweden, e-mail: leif-joran.olsson@svenska.gu.se
Lars Borin, Språkbanken Text, Department of Swedish, Multilingualism, Language Technology, University of Gothenburg, Gothenburg, Sweden, e-mail: lars.borin@svenska.gu.se

https://doi.org/10.1515/9783110767377-031

by Swe-Clarin, using resources accessible through the CLARIN infrastructure to enrich scholarship in the humanities. The capabilities of the corpus tool Korp enable us to affirm prior research on the conceptual history of terrorism, but also to suggest a complex and diverse picture of the connotations of terrorism, both as state and sub-state violence up until the 20th century. At the same time, the study allows us to explore the potentials of cross-lingual text mining for historical analysis of national online newspaper corpora provided by Swe-Clarin and FIN-CLARIN.

Keywords: history of terrorism, digital history, Korp, comparative corpus studies

1 Introduction

The development of large-scale digitization initiatives (LSDIs) and language technology (LT) infrastructures has contributed significantly to opening up historical big data for research, allowing scholars to pursue large-scale research questions and explore past phenomena by "trawling" through massive amounts of text. (Weller 2013; Graham, Milligan, and Weingart 2016; Paju, Oiva, and Fridlund 2020). However, critical commentators such as Tahmasebi et al. (2019) argue that many such projects are deficient, being strongly biased either towards data science or humanities, and thus lacking in either technical and linguistic proficiency for utilizing the potential of big data text analysis or appropriate humanistic domain knowledge to evaluate whether the results are pertinent.

The present study is part of an integrative interdisciplinary initiative to overcome such limitations launched by the Swedish CLARIN node (Swe-Clarin: sweclarin.se), which includes pilot projects where researchers in natural language processing collaborate closely with humanities scholars to explore the broad research potential of LT-based e-science tools (see Viklund and Borin 2016; Karsvall and Borin 2018). The chapter builds and expands on two preliminary studies coordinated by Swe-Clarin that used text mining of Swedish-language newspaper corpora from the late 18th to the early 20th century to explore the historical emergence and evolution of terrorism (Fridlund et al. 2019, 2020). This study deepens these earlier efforts through a cross-lingual investigation of Swedish and Finnish newspaper discourse, involving researchers from Sweden and Finland. A key point is the mutually beneficial outcome of the interdisciplinary collaboration: while the terrorism scholars produce a complex historical analysis of the results from the LT resources, the humanistic research questions provide a cross-lingual use case for the data analysts.

This chapter proceeds by discussing the LT tools and the Swedish- and Finnish-language newspaper corpora we have used to approach and trawl through the historical newspaper discourses on terrorism. Following that, the chapter turns to the analysis of the attributions of terrorism in our dataset. This is the longest section, as it concerns the exploration of a range of attributions of both state terrorism and sub-state terrorism that are explored through a combination of distant and close reading. The distant reading discussion is, to some extent, centered around attributions of nationality, which proved to be a particularly significant factor. After a comprehensive exploration, we turn to a case study using close readings of the emergence of domestic attributions of terrorism in Finland in the early 20th century. Here, we abandon non-selective trawling in favour of directed "trolling", or precision searches, to catch specific uses of the term related to different contexts from those in Russia, which influenced its early uses. We conclude by emphasizing our more significant findings and also make some reflections on the potentials of evaluative historical studies based on cross-lingual text corpora.

2 Computing the history of terrorisms

The first known uses of 'terrorism' as an exclusive description of violent state practices (Erlenbusch 2015) is from the French Revolution's Reign of Terror in 1794. The traditional scholarly view is that the later so-called sub-state terrorism, or "rebel" terrorism, which today is primarily associated with the concept, was first introduced as a tactic by Russian social revolutionaries in the late 1870s (sometimes referred to as "the Russian method") which had already spread to Western Europe, Asia, and America during the 19th century, and reached the rest of the world in the early 20th century (Ker 1917; Law 2009; Miller 2013; Sageman 2017). Notably, this historical picture has essentially been based on close reading of primary and secondary textual sources. Only rarely have researchers examined the emergence of new forms of terrorism through a quantitative approach, including newspaper text mining (cf. Ditrych 2011, 2014; Jensen 2018). However, combining historical, theoretical, and technical expertise, the present study performs both distant reading and close reading analysis of the development of the historical discourse on terrorism in Swedish and Finnish newspapers.

A central component of the research presented in this chapter is *conceptual history*, a field of inquiry which by necessity must grapple with the vexed questions of the nature of concepts and their relationship to the words that express them (Ifversen 2011). As a concrete illustration of this issue, Princeton WordNet (PWN; Fellbaum 1998), a lexical resource for English heavily used in all kinds of text-processing and text-understanding applications, makes a distinction between concepts (called *synsets*), words, and word senses. Almost half – or close to 54,000 –

of the PWN synsets consist of more than one word sense and consequently find expression in more than one way in texts. On average, such senses belong to almost three synsets each. While concepts are not words, scholars of conceptual history have arguably tended to downplay this distinction, investigating the use of particular words as a stand-in for the concepts these words (purportedly) express. A concern that tends to emerge and which is not typically addressed in disciplines that mainly rely on close reading and "thick description", however, is that of typicality or representativeness: how is a posited concept typically expressed – in the way suggested by the researcher's "pre-empirical" intuition or by some other means? In our case, the combination of, on the one hand, distant reading and, on the other, close reading and abduction on the basis of individual instances embedded in rich contexts provides a way of working through this problem.

2.1 Purpose and aims

The main aim of the study is to evaluate the established hypothesis that the modern meaning of terrorism as sub-state political violence did not emerge outside the revolutionary context of Russia until the 20th century (see Fridlund 2018; Jensen 2018). Also included in this aim is the assessment of how the original meaning of state terrorism persisted as an integral historical part of the concept of terrorism.

Sweden and Finland provide a pertinent combination of historical contexts for exploring the development of the discourse on terrorism. Notably, the two countries share a common history – Finland was a part of Sweden from medieval times until 1809 and still retains Swedish as one of its two official languages (about 5% of the Finnish population have Swedish as their mother tongue and a significant number of Finns are bilingual). At the same time, the national conditions have been different when it comes to political violence. Sweden, like many other Western European countries, experienced few instances of terrorism during the period in focus (one bombing and one shooting 1908–1909). However, Finland, following a war in 1809, was incorporated into the Russian Empire as a Grand Duchy (1809–1917), bringing the country closer to the Russian political culture and its revolutionary and terroristic contexts. In fact, Finland suffered a domestic terrorist campaign 1904–1907 in one of the earliest examples of sub-state terrorism (Kujala 1992; Fridlund and Sallamaa 2016; Jensen 2018). In this sense, a dual focus on Sweden and Finland provides deep and different historical horizons on the phenomenon of terrorism.

To trace the development of the discourse on terrorism in Sweden and Finland during the period in focus, our study mainly pursues two research questions: (1) what attributions of terrorism were made in the two countries; (2) to what extent did the "original" meanings of terrorism persist and other meanings emerge? This encompasses an interest in the historical political events and practices that terrorism has been associated with in the Swedish and Finnish contexts.

3 LT-driven trawling in shared waters

To pursue the historical emergence on terrorism, our study maps the meanings associated with terrorism in Swedish and Finnish newspapers from the late 18th century to the early 20th century. To use a familiar metaphor for text mining in digital humanities, our study "trawls" (see Tangherlini and Leonard 2013) through the vast and deep "digital Gulf of Bothnia" of digitized historical Swedish and Finnish newspapers. This gulf is the Baltic Sea's northernmost part, consisting of Swedish and Finnish territorial waters and a shared body of water in between (which before 1809 was domestic Swedish waters); see Figure 1. Similarly, the body of texts we trawl through for occurrences of words (such as 'terrorism' or 'terrorists') consists of uniquely domestic Swedish and Finnish news as well as shared "transnational" news published in newspapers in both countries. The specific resources we use for trawling are the corpus search tool Korp and historical Swedish- and Finnish-language newspaper corpora provided by the National Swedish Language Bank (Nationella språkbanken) and the Language Bank of Finland (Kielipankki/Språkbanken).

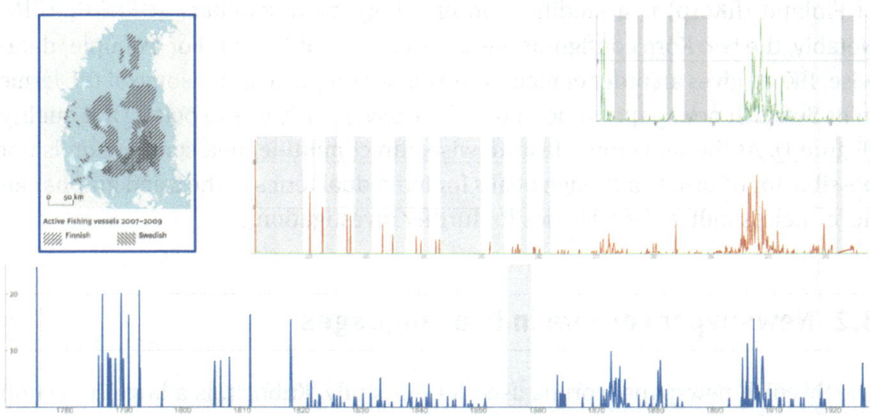

Figure 1: Gulf of Bothnia with partly overlapping Swedish and Finnish fishing waters. From Backer and Frias (2013:52). Courtesy of the Helsinki Commission. Trend graphs showing hits in Swedish and Finnish corpora for *terrorist/terrorism* for seKorp 1780–1926 (bottom), fiKorpSV 1805–1925 (middle) and *terroristi/terrorismi* for fiKorpFI 1880–1925 (top).

3.1 Korp for Swedish and Finnish

Korp (Borin, Forsberg, and Roxendal 2012) is a sophisticated corpus search tool with modular design and an online search interface that, although designed to fulfill the research needs of linguists, has proven useful in addressing humanities research questions.

Its interface allows searches and queries based on automatic linguistic annotations with structured result presentations: a *contextual hit list* or *KWIC* (keyword in context); *statistical data* of keyword occurrences in sub-corpora allowing creation of *trend graphs* plotting relative frequencies over time for text words, lemmas (dictionary headwords), or other linguistic items; a so-called *word picture* presenting statistically prominent fillers of selected syntactic dependency relations of a keyword, for instance typical subjects and objects of a verb, and nominal premodifiers (e.g., adjectives) and post-modifiers (prepositional phrases or main verbs of relative clauses); see Figure 2. The word picture can be used as a topical map to guide users to closer readings of the corpus. Korp also supports navigation between the statistics, trend-graph, and word picture views, and the KWIC view allows close reading of individual hits in their newspaper article context.

The original Swedish version of Korp (from now on seKorp) is developed and maintained by Språkbanken Text (the Swedish Language Bank's Text Division), a national language technology infrastructure development center and the coordinating node of Swe-Clarin, while the Korp implementation in the Language Bank of Finland (fiKorp) is a modification of seKorp by researchers at FIN-CLARIN. Notably, the two Korp configurations are somewhat different. For example, data-wise, fiKorp gives an order of magnitude higher frequencies for some of the terms in its Swedish newspaper subcorpora (fiKorpSV), partly due to better OCR quality (Figure 1). At the same time, feature-wise, direct multi-lemma comparison is not possible for fiKorpSV, although peaks for individual terms in the trend graphs can nevertheless indicate tendencies for further investigation.

3.2 Newspaper corpora in two languages

The Swedish newspaper corpus used for our study, Kubhist, is a large collection of historical newspapers of Sweden from the late 18th to the early 20th century digitized by the National Library of Sweden, containing about 5.5 billion words

(Adesam, Dannélls, and Tahmasebi 2019).[1] While Kubhist is smaller than, for example, the Google Books dataset, it distinguishes itself from many historical newspaper LSDIs such as impresso, Europeana, and NewsEye in being linguistically annotated on several levels (lexical, morphological, lexical-semantic, syntactic, named entities, etc.). The annotation tools also draw on high-quality lexical resources (historical and modern), which compensates for its smaller size, relatively speaking (Borin and Johansson 2014; Tahmasebi et al. 2015; Adesam, Dannélls, and Tahmasebi 2019).

One notable omission in Kubhist, in the context of this study, is that it does not include any newspapers from the Swedish region of Finland. However, the Finnish Newspaper and Periodical Corpus of the National Library of Finland (NLF),[2] includes newspapers of Finland both in Finnish (NLF 2011a) and Swedish (NLF 2011b) from the period chosen. As Finland was a part of the Swedish realm until 1809, Swedish was for a long time the dominant written language in Finland, even during the Russian reign 1809–1917 (although its influence waned during the 20th century). The current version of the corpus includes 5.2 billion words in Finnish and 3.5 billion words in Swedish. Like Kubhist, the Finnish corpus is not complete for any given period of time, as the NLF digitization effort has not been comprehensive.[3]

It should be noted that the period for analysis, 1780–1926, is chosen for both historical and pragmatic reasons with regard to the corpora used. While Kubhist covers the years 1749–1926, the corpus is complete from 1780, that is, about ten years before the French Revolution, which "birthed" the concept of terrorism, providing us with a baseline against which to trace its development. Kubhist also ends in 1926 due to copyright restrictions, effectively limiting the analysis to the period chosen.

---

1 Kubhist also forms one of the major components of the Swedish Diachronic Corpus, a Swe-Clarin initiative described elsewhere in this volume (Pettersson and Borin 2022).

2 http://urn.fi/urn:nbn:fi:lb-201405276

3 For example, the largest Finnish language newspaper *Helsingin Sanomat* is missing issues from 1913 onwards and the Swedish language newspaper *Helsingfors Tidningar* is missing at least 1,218 issues from 1860–1864. However, a significantly expanded version of the corpus, including many of the missing issues, is currently under construction. Preliminary figures indicate that the number of Finnish publications in the corpus will increase by c. 740,000 and the number of Swedish publications by c. 120,000. See http://urn.fi/urn:nbn:fi:lb-202009152, which has a link to the list of new issues in all languages.

4 Reading emergent forms of terrorism

To reach and capture the wide context of terrorism during the period 1780–1926, we formulated Korp queries combining the search terms *terrorist/terroristi* (for 1780–1926 there were 259, 1,364, and 2,629 hits in the Swedish, Finnish-Swedish, and Finnish corpora respectively) and *terrorism/terrorismi* (570, 2,361, and 1,633 hits). Figure 1 (see above) shows the three graphs for *terrorist/terrorism* in seKorp (bottom/blue) 1780–1926 and fiKorpSV (middle/red) 1805–1925 and for *terroristi/terrorismi* in fiKorpFI (top/green) 1880–1925 (there were no hits in the Finnish-Swedish corpus before 1805 or after 1925 and in the Finnish corpus before 1880 and after 1925). In Figure 3, the left column shows the graph for 'terrorist' from bottom to top from seKorp (red) 1780–1926, fiKorpSV (blue) 1805–1925, and fiKorpFI (green) 1880–1925, which have similar profile shapes.

It is important to note the difficulty in generalizing about how common different terrorism/terrorist attributions were, based on the *quantity* of these and other hits, due to the fact that a high number of attributions might refer to multiple descriptions of one specific event in different newspapers. The reuse of near identical news texts in different newspapers (often without attributing the original source) was also a common and accepted practice (Salmi et al. 2013). Thus, what is most relevant in the following is not the quantity of occurrences of a certain attribution, but the qualitative *existence* of such an attribution to terrorism.

One should also note that when 'terrorism' is used in the material to designate certain activities, it is often not clear how violent or lethal these were. As Claudia Verhoeven writes, the verb *terrorise* "suggests the use, power, and violence of the *word*, not the act: 'to terrorize' means to force or provoke certain actions via threats and intimidation, but does not automatically imply physical violence" (Verhoeven 2004: 18). Consequently, it may be difficult to distinguish the type and the "quality" of the terror that the various attributions of 'terrorism' refer to.

4.1 Word picture analysis and terrorism in contexts

The use of Korp's "word picture" function enables a comparison between Swedish and Finnish newspapers, while uneven as it is not activated in the Swedish-language part (fiKorpSV) of the fiKorp NLF newspaper and periodical collection (there are plans to eventually extend this functionality to all fiKorp corpora). Moreover, word pictures are only activated for searches in the collections's Finnish language part when using the "simple search" function, which does not make it possible to distinguish between newspapers and periodicals. The multitude of Finnish-language word forms in word pictures also makes it more difficult to interpret the results, compared to similar Swedish-language word pictures. For example, the Swedish word for 'Russian', *rysk* (adj),[4] corresponds to more than 50 different words in the Finnish *terroristi* word picture. Many of these words include slight OCR errors, which makes using automated methods difficult, such as the form *venäläiset* in modern Finnish – nominative plural of the adjective *venäläinen* 'Russian' – which is found in the following two erroneous forms on the top 44 list as attributes for the word *terroristi*: *menäläiset* and *roenäläifet*, in addition to the older spellings *wenäläiset* and *Wenäläiset*.

Nevertheless, to compare the Swedish and Finnish contexts, we used the results from the seKorp word pictures and manually scanned the 3,725 concordances for *terrorist* and *terrorism* in the fiKorpSV KWIC view for significant pre- and post-modifiers, including nationalities, locations, and gender. As another form of analysis, we performed close readings in the KWIC view of seKorp and fiKorp, selectively reading the digitized newspaper articles where the hits occurred. While this strategy potentially missed out on some uniquely Finnish uses of terms that Finnish-Swedish word pictures might have revealed, it arguably strengthened the comparative aspect to a feasible level.

Through the word picture function, we were able to examine national or ethnic attributes given to *terrorism* and *terrorist* and to determine that the dominant terrorism-related *national context* in Swedish and Finnish newspapers, as expected, is 'Russian' with 15 hits (*rysk*) in seKorp and some 200 (*venäjän*) in fiKorpFI. Additionally, 25 other terrorist nationalities were identified, although it is difficult to determine how prominent these actually were, due to the limited number of hits.

The seKorp word pictures attributed 8 nationalities (Russian, Chinese, Finnish, French, German, Hungarian, Irish, and Polish) with Chinese as the only unique seKorp attribution (see Figure 2). KWIC readings of fiKorpSV resulted in 23 nationalities (Russian, American, Armenian, Baltic, Bengali, Bulgarian, Czechian, Croatian, Finnish, French, German, Grusinian [Georgian], Hungarian, Indian, Irish, Italian, Latvian, Polish, Prussian, Romanian, Spanish, Vatican, Wallachian) of which 11 were unique (American, Baltic, Bengali, Croatian, Czechian, Grusinian, Latvian, Prussian, Romanian, Vatican, Wallachian) and several were also subjects of the Russian empire. The Finnish-language newspapers attributed 14 nationalities (Russian, Argentinian, Armenian, South African, Bulgarian, Estonian, Greek, Indian, Irish, Livonian [Estonian], Polish, Serbian, Spanish, Turkish) of which 4 were unique (Argentinian, Greek, Serbian, Turkish) and 3 were connected to the Ottoman empire. In total, 27 nationalities were attributed to terrorism in our dataset (17 uniquely attributed in newspapers of one of the three language contexts).

4 Also *ryss* (noun), but not in this context.

4.2 Broadening of regime terrorism

The neglect of state or regime terrorism "as a subject for systematic and sustained research" is said to be a "perennial criticism" of terrorism studies (Jackson 2008: 377), and even more so the lack of historical studies (for an exception, see Miller 2013). However, through our data-driven approach, we were able to follow the discursive trajectory of state terrorism and to determine that in both Sweden and Finland terrorism remained strongly associated with political violence and repression perpetrated by regimes at least up until the early 20th century.

Word picture attributive modifiers, such as 'monarchical', 'oligarchic', 'dictatorial', 'military', 'official', 'statist', and 'government/al' (*hallitus/hallinnollinen*) terrorism, clearly show that regimes were held to be agents of terrorism during the period. However, notably, our KWIC readings of these results showed that some attributes, such as 'ministerial' and 'autocratic' terrorism, referred to what may be called "soft" regime terrorism, involving intimidation, harassment, or repression but rarely physical violence. This could be taken as an indication that the meanings of 'terrorism' were widening during the period so that at times they took on metaphorical meanings, as when used in a Swedish political context to describe a statist 'inquisitorial' terrorism or when Finnish temperance advocates were criticized for their allegedly fanatic actions which were labelled 'sobriety terrorism'.

Our analysis of terrorism's national-ethnic attributions shows that the concept of 'terrorism' was used both for *state* regime terrorism and *sub-state* rebel terrorism during the period in focus. For example, the frequent 'Russian' attributions point toward Russian regime terrorism as well as the revolutionary rebel terrorism campaigns of the 1880s and early 1900s.

That state terrorism remained a significant part of the discourse is further indicated by the nations and regions associated with *terrorism* and *terrorist* in Korp's word pictures (for terrorists 'in France' see Figure 2). The findings contain many national forms of state terrorism during the period 1848–1867. The 'German' terrorism found in seKorp refers to activities by a Prussian army in 1848 in the occupied Danish Duchy Schleswig-Holstein. Similarly, the 'Hungarian' and 'Polish' terrorisms are connected to war and occupation following the failed 1849 Hungarian revolution, where an occupying Austrian regime in 1850 was accused of terrorism, as was a temporary rebel regime 1863 in Russian Poland. Such regime terrorism in contested regions, domestic or occupied, accounts for several other regional attributions, such as Armenian, Baltic, Czechian, Finnish, Grusinian, Indian, Latvian, Romanian, Svecoman, and Wallachian terrorism, many of these nationalities belonging to European and Asian empires and the Russian empire in particular, consolidating the significance of the Russian context in the development of the terrorism discourse.

Pre-modifier		terrorist	Post-modifier	
1. rysk	15		1. tillfredstälde	2
2. ifrig	4		2. från minskov	2
3. utsjmigna	2		3. 5kte	2
4. kvionlige	2		4. afiossade	2
5. håktade	2		5. iått	2
6. fîterlomne	2		6. voro	2
7. frigifna	2		7. i hufvudstaden	2
8. verklig	4		8. hos Antonia	1
9. finsk	3		9. samhällsställning	1
10.revolutionär	2		10.till grad	1
11.werkliga	2		11.i åker	1
12.kvinnlig	2		12.vara	2
13.kvinnlig²	2		13.polisman	1
14.wore	2		14.skola²	2
15.sjålf	2		15.uppträda	1
16.absolutistisk	1		16.orsak	1
17.ka	2		17.döda	1
18.namnkunnig	1		18.för dag	1
19.dödsdömd	1		19.tro	1
20.ung	2		20.skola	1
21.utpräglad	1		21.i del	1
22.industriell	1		22.i Frankrike	1
23.irländsk	1		23.stad	1
24.bekant	1		24.i Petersburg	1
25.sjelfva	2		25.ha	1
26.monarkisk	1			
27.kinesisk	1			
28.farlig	1			
29.framstående	1			
30.riktig	1			
31.militär	1			

Pre-Modifier		terroristi	Post-Modifier	
1. Wenäjän	56		1. kiihoittunut	2
2. venäläinen	33		2. suunnitella	3
3. Venäjä	17		3. ilmi	3
4. vangita	10		4. lva	5
5. Venäläinen	8		5. tietää	4
6. toimia	10		6. roaati	2
7. tukialainen	7		7. mies	4
8. wangituilta	3		8. paeta	2
9. wenäläistä	4		9. Gershunista	1
10.wenäläiset	5		10.w2nä	1
11.usea	12		11.murhayrilytsiä	1
12.taantumuksellinen	4		12.unkaavat	1
13.menäläiset	4		13.TiflisiSsii	1
14.kokenut	4		14.teiifiiuät	1
15.salaperäinen	5		15.Lausannesta	1
16.paeta	4		16.luomutlamista	1
17.lysymylsenalaisten	2		17.pontenmmmin	1
18.uhkafimat	2		18.Sötiten	1
19.roenäläifet	3		19.Vlmerifaiin	1
20.keksiä	4		20.pehmeänahkainenimpi	1
21.turwaa	2		21.tuonnttamaksi	1
22.vallankumouksellinen	4		22.Harloloin	1
23.kumouksellinen	3		23.karjoittaneet	1
24.salainen	4		24.ponteroammin	1
25.juutalainen	4		25.meretlla	1
26.vaarallinen	3		26.fuljetuttaa	1
27.ryhtyä	3		27.toiiiieciipaimeet	1
28.menäläistcn	2		28.paustaistelijllt	1
29.määrällinen	3		29.i>li	1
30.wenäläinen	3		30.Jnnmac-ja	1
31.Puola	3		31.jiumnittefeuat	1
32.merraten	2		32.Luttichissä	1
33.näläisten	2		33.poliisitirehtööri	1
34.Wenäjän	2		34.-tomnenfon	1
35.Wenäläiset	2		35.suumutteleiuat	1
36.monarkistinen	2		36.VmgtttaeSfa	1
37.oiva	4		37.tnaifj	1
38.paha	4		38.oliwat	3
39.joukko	4		39.mastaan	3
40.Indian	2		40.pääkaupunki	2

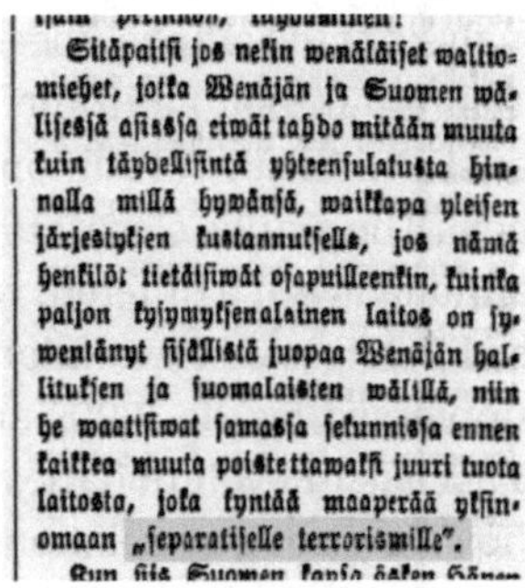
Sitäpaitsi jos nekin wenäläiset waltio-
miehet, jotka Wenäjän ja Suomen wä-
lisessä asiassa eiwät tahdo mitään muuta
kuin täydellisintä yhteensulatusta hin-
nalla millä hywänsä, waikkapa yleisen
järjestyksen kustannuksella, jos nämä
henkilöt tietäisiwät osapuilleenkin, kuinka
paljon kysymyksenalainen laitos on sy-
wentänyt sisällistä juopaa Wenäjän hal-
lituksen ja suomalaisten wälillä, niin
he waatisiwat samassa sekunnissa ennen
kaikkea muuta poistettawaksi juuri tuota
laitosta, joka synnyttää maaperää yksin-
omaan „separatiselle terrorismille".

Figure 2: Distant and close readings of terrorists and terrorism in context. Word picture in seKorp and fiKorpFI showing pre- and post-modifiers for *terrorist* (left) and *terroristi*. Finnish editorial warning about 'separatist terrorism' in *Vaasa* (12 September 1905). From *digi.kansalliskirjasto.fi*.

4.3 Diversification of rebel terrorism

It took time, however, for the phenomenon of sub-state or rebel terrorism, to acquire a wider meaning beyond the Russian political context. This broadening of the 'terrorism' concept to include national sub-state political militants other than Russians, as well as violent anarchists and anti-imperial revolutionaries, can be studied by comparing and contrasting occurrences of 'terrorists' in our dataset with closely associated terms for sub-state actors traditionally regarded as among the period's prominent practitioners of political violence.

The most prominent such political militants were *anarkist/anarkisti* 'anarchist' (3,028, 20,837, and 22,481 hits), *nihilist/nihilisti* (1,660, 3,113, and 3,148 hits) ('nihilists' and 'nihilism' were up until the 1890s often used as synonyms for Russian social revolutionaries and their ideologies), and *revolutionär/vallankumouksellinen* 'revolutionary' (noun: 1,285, 9,618, and 0 hits) (the fiKorpFI count is zero for 'revolutionary' due to incorrect part of speech tagging in the corpus; all the *vallankumouksellinen* nouns are tagged as adjectives).

Figure 3 shows in its right column a 'terrorist' trend graph and trend graphs for the other political militants for the period 1848–1920, which covers numerous turbulent events, including the European political upheaval of 1848 and the emergence of Russian sub-state proto-terrorism from 1866 (Verhoeven 2009). The analysis of the graphs' specific details is secondary to that of their relative shapes. From top to bottom in the right column are the fiKorpSV trend graphs for 'terrorist', 'nihilist', 'revolutionary', and 'anarchist', showing co-occurrences among them. The graphs closest to the 'terrorist' profile are 'nihilist' for the 1880s bump (although with a different relative scale) and 'revolutionary' for the 1905 peak of the First Russian Revolution. This makes sense, as the Russian nihilists had been suppressed by the 1890s and were from 1902 replaced by activists of the Party of Socialist-Revolutionaries (SRs). However, the 'terrorist' and 'anarchist' profiles show no strong correlations, indicating that terrorism was at this point not yet understood to also include anarchism.

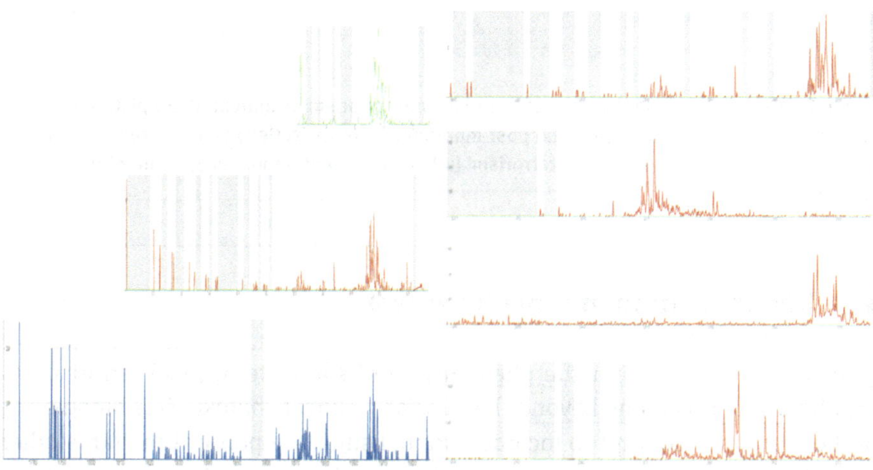

Figure 3: Political militants trend graphs. Left column: *terrorist* for seKorp 1780–1926 (bottom), fiKorpSV 1805–1925 (middle), and *terroristi* for fiKorpFI 1880–1925 (top). Right column (from top): 'terrorist', 'nihilist', 'revolutionary', and 'anarchist' from fiKorpSV for 1848–1920.

A closer reading of the modifiers referring to the classical examples of rebel terrorism in the material reveals that the 'revolutionary', 'nihilistic', and 'socialistic' terrorisms exclusively referred to non-state terrorism, with the exception of 'revolutionary terrorism', which at times also connoted the French Revolution's Reign of Terror and 19th-century French fears of the return of terroristic regimes.

Probably the earliest example before 1900 of non-Russian rebel 'terrorists' are the Fenians. Irish Fenian terrorism appears to a very limited extent (1882–1889) in the material, in reference to local Irish agrarian terrorism in the form of boycotts and murders of English settler farmers ('agrarian murder') and also an urban terrorist campaign with assassinations and bombings (with the agrarian murders as a spin-off). However, these mentions are rare (further discussed in Section 4.4).

Nevertheless, at the beginning of the 1900s other forms of anti-imperial terrorism decidedly entered the terrorism discourse, as evidenced through a spectrum of new nationalities modifiers. One of its earliest manifestations is a Macedonian "band of terrorists, known as the band of dynamitards" that fought Turkish authorities in 1903, using explosives to "gain Europe's attention" (*Åbo Tidning* 1903-10-01). From 1905 'terrorism' became used in relation to both non-socialist and socialist Finnish terrorists, with the 'non-socialist' terrorism referred to as "the budding terrorism in Finland" (1905-08-14) (which receives an in-depth analysis in Section 5). This was followed in 1907 by reports on arrested "Armenian terrorists" in Odessa.

It is noteworthy that among the manifestations of anti-imperial terrorism in the fiKorp material, several are tied to the Russian empire, such as 'Baltic' (1906), 'Latvian' (1907), and 'Grusinian' (1912), although other empires and imperial regions such as Persia, Poland, and Turkey also figure. Also at this time, anti-imperial terrorism appears in East Asia in our dataset. First in 1909 in seKorp and fiKorp descriptions of "Indian terrorists" who renewed their secretive activities and later in 1916 in a unique seKorp mentioning of a female "Chinese terrorist", who took part in the 1911 Xihai Revolution (*Kalmar* 1916-07-15). This woman – a non-Russian, non-socialist revolutionary – indicates how the rise of anti-imperialism contributed to the widening of the notion of sub-state terrorism beyond the Russian context.

4.4 The absent terrorists

For rebel terrorism, an intriguing finding is the contexts in which the word 'terrorism' was *not* used. Several 19th century events frequently described as "terrorism" in historical research do in fact not show up in our word pictures. For example, spectacular terrorist deeds by anarchists in Europe and the USA, as well as anti-imperial separatists in Europe and Asia during the 19th century, were not found to be directly associated with terrorism, neither in Swedish or the Finnish newspapers – attacks which are nowadays seen as constituting parts of a major phase in the history of terrorism, as when David Rapoport writes about "systematic Anarchist efforts to put atrocities in the service of revolution" during "the anarchist wave of rebel terror" (Rapoport 2003: 38). While nihilist terrorists figure prominently in our dataset, there are very few examples of attributions of 'terrorism' to anarchistic activities or, as already discussed above, Fenian activities, which are held to be two of the other major forms of terrorism during the 19th century.

In the case of anarchism, there is only one instance of anarchist terrorism attribution in our dataset in the form of an 1884 article published in two Finnish-Swedish newspapers, reporting that Vienna had been put under a state of siege to make the population safe against "the anarchists' terrorism". Besides that, no other instances of anarchist terrorism appear in the material (although an article in 1880 warns about "anarchic" terrorism in Ireland).

At the same time, we can observe how the terms 'terrorism' and 'terrorist' gradually acquire new meanings and there are indications from 1906 that 'terrorism' became more firmly associated with 'anarchism'. This comes out explicitly, for example, when a Finnish newspaper explains that 'terrorism' and 'anarchism' "are two different concepts", although they "are difficult for a layman to distinguish from each other" (*Nuori Suomi* 1906-02-02). Thus, from then on a more ideologically inclusive 'terrorism' concept is emerging. In 1909, we find that 'terrorism's' history is, so to speak, retrospectively revised accordingly, when an article states that Russian terrorists in the 1890s "had committed anarchist propaganda acts" (*Suomalainen Kansa* 1909-07-13) and in 1910 it was said that 'anarchism' in "everyday speech" had acquired the meaning of perpetrators "of atrocities [*hirmutöiden*]" (*Ilkka* 1910-05-07). By 1912 the conversion appears to have become established, when the famous anarchist tactic of "propaganda by deed" is merged with terrorism, as when militant anarchists were described by *Helsingin Sanomat* as "those 'propaganda by deed' terrorists" (1912-12-10).

5 Trolling for new terrorisms in Finland

To examine how the meanings of 'terrorism' started to broaden outside of the immediate Russian context, we in the following limit our attention to the emergence of the discourse on Finnish terrorism. Here, we leave the indiscriminate trawling "readsearch" method in favour of precision "trolling" (cf. "angling" readsearch in Fridlund 2020) to carefully catch specific emerging meanings in the Finnish context. Thus, we use targeted searches to find Finnish 'terrorism' and 'terrorists' without Finnish pre- or post-modifiers, and also include journals and clandestine newspapers in the fiKorp searches (which were excluded earlier for more equal cross-lingual analysis).

In our searches, references to 'Finnish terrorism' occur in two periods: 1905–1911 and in 1918, the latter referring to Finnish socialists who started the Finnish Civil War in the newly independent state. Our analysis will focus on the discourse during the first period, in order to explore the context of how 'terrorism' came to denote a more ideologically inclusive rebel terrorism closer to the contemporary kind.

5.1 Emergence of restorative and separatist terrorism

From 1899 to 1905, the Russian Grand Duchy of Finland suffered a Russification campaign with increased repression and decrease of its political autonomy. Subsequently, an increasingly violent resistance campaign developed and when the general governor Nikolay Bobrikov was killed by the Finnish nobleman Eugen Schauman in 1904, the duchy had its first act of rebel terrorism. In the assassination's immediate aftermath, no newspapers in our dataset characterized it as 'terrorism'. However, soon afterwards it was interpreted as a sign that Russian rebel terrorism had been appropriated by Finnish nationalists. Yet, the motivations of the Finns were different than the Russian precursors. Schauman's terrorism was not socialist or revolutionary, but "restorative". While directed against the oppressive Russian regime, its foremost aim was not separatism but to restore Finland's earlier autonomy within the empire (Fridlund and Sallamaa 2016: 41; Jensen 2018).

In November 1904, the (non-socialist) Finnish Active Resistance Party (FAM) was founded; modelled on the Russian SR Party, it included a terrorist Combat Organization. Although the Russian tactic and novel institutional form of rebel terrorism thus had arrived, the use of the term 'terrorism' emerged only after a second assassination in February 1905, when FAM sympathizer Lennart Hohenthal shot the Finnish Chancellor of Justice Eliel Soisalon-Soininen.

The official police report in May 1905 did not explicitly call the killing 'terrorism', but it is clear it was viewed as such. According to our results, Finnish newspapers now begun to describe the Soisalon-Soininen killing and similar Finnish acts of political violence in terms of terrorism. According to *Helsingin Sanomat*, the official police report stated that those actively protesting against Russification had incited others to "terrorism and violent acts" (1905-05-05). Although 'terrorism' had rarely been used earlier in relation to similar acts of Finnish political violence, these newspaper accounts basically created a historical narrative about Finnish terrorism, retrospectively.

In *Helsingin Sanomat*, the Soisalon-Soininen assassination was described as born out of previous years-long harassments of Finnish politicians who complied with the Russian regime, especially by Finns close to the Finnish Swedish-language underground journal *Fria Ord*. The journal had revealed "its terrorist purposes by its defamatory accusations and writing in a threatening way", inciting "violence and hatred against officials and supporting revolutionary social democracy, anarchism and terrorism", and by reprinting "defences of murder by Russian terrorists etc., the resistance men have tried to prepare the ground in Finland for such actions" (1905-05-05). The use of the word 'terrorism' was not entirely new in this context, as Finnish supporters of concessions to the Russian oppression had on some earlier occasions used it in reference to threats expressed by their opponents.

The Finnish-nationalist politician Yrjö Sakari Yrjö-Koskinen, a common target of the resistance's harassment and hatred, had already used it in such a way in 1900, in his *Open Letter to my Friends*, where he, as quoted in the police report, accused the resistance of fomenting terrorism, as according to him there had been public and veiled attempts "to implement general terrorism which in my view cannot produce anything but destruction". Even though it is not clear what Yrjö-Koskinen exactly meant by terrorism, the police report on the Soisalon-Soininen killing commended him for daring to "call its actions by their right name: *terrorismi ja hirmuwalta* ['terrorism and reign of terror']" (*Helsingin Sanomat*, 1905-05-05).

Thus, the emergence of Finnish terrorism became framed as a reaction to Russian regime terrorism. The *Karjala* newspaper somewhat later stated that "[w] ith the Russian system, also the concomitant terrorism has been brought to our state's government". Furthermore, Finland was deemed "vulnerable to horrors of terrorism – terrorism that grows and grows", while the Russian regime had tried but failed "to set official terrorism against terrorism" (*Karjala*, 1905-07-23). A similar argument was put forward two months later in an editorial published in several newspapers during the Hohenthal trial. It warned unification-minded "Russian statesmen" that if they knew how much the Gendarmerie military security force in Finland had "deepened the chasm between the Russian government and Finns, then they would immediately demand the abolishment of this institution which only creates a breeding ground for 'separatist terrorism"' (see Figure 2). This referred to the actions of Hohenthal, who had been an informer for the Gendarmerie (*Vaasa* 1905-09-12).

Consequently, these findings show that the meaning of 'terrorism' had by this time become associated with both specifically Finnish strivings as well as a new general motivation. Through this new explicit connection between separatism and terrorism crafted by commentators in the Finnish press, the understanding of rebel terrorism, from then on, was widened from the Russian socialist or revolutionary terrorism to also include anti-imperial separatism. Other parts of the world soon followed, such as when an Indian nationalist in 1907 pointed to "the Russian method" as the most likely one to drive the British out of India (Ker 1917:107).

5.2 Rebel terrorism in the shadow of Russian repression

This new conceptualization of (Finnish) terrorism can also be seen in Sweden, where one of its earliest appearances is almost literally in the actual geographic Gulf of Bothnia. In 1905, the *Kalmar* newspaper reported that a skipper in Northern Finland had found an abandoned shipment of weapons on a rocky islet close to the Swedish border, which might be connected to the "Finnish terrorism, a child of Bobrikoff and [Russian Minister of the Interior] Plehve, [which] has long striven for association with its Russian kind" (1905-09-18). The statement was later followed by a mentioning in a later article of "the more and more growing crowd of Finnish terrorists" (*Kalmar* 1905-10-25).

The Russification campaign and its 'Years of Oppression' (*sortovuodet*) ended in November 1905 with the Finnish offshoot of the First Russian Revolution, sometimes described as the Finnish Revolution. From now on, the 'terrorism' designation was repeatedly used in the Finnish context. The Constitutionalists party was occasionally accused of 'terrorism' tendencies in their ranks (meaning FAM sympathizers) (see for example, *Uusimaa* 1905-11-10 and *Vaasa* 1905-11-25). In 1906, we can even see that Finnish terrorists were mentioned in a positive, or at least not pejorative way, when a newspaper stated that "[o]ur terrorists during *sortovuodet*, as misguided as their actions could sometimes be, were using violent means to fight for a legal societal system and against its oppressors and destroyers" (*Karjala* 1906-10-28). In 1907 FAM's programme for the first time in public defined Finnish independence and thus separatism as an objective.

However, Russian oppression returned in 1908 and lasted until Finland's independence in 1917. Although the terrorist campaign did not recommence, in 1911 a journal warned about terrorist attacks from below: "Before Bobrikov, no-one in Finland accepted terrorism as a method of liberation struggle and criticized also the Russians for using it. When the oppression by Russians continued, Finns also started to realize that violence from above also produces violence from below and that an unavoidable companion of an oppressive government is terror" (*Keski-Suomen Sanomat*, 1911-09-15). This could, then and now, be read as showing an acceptance of separatism as an ideal and of terrorism as a legitimate tactic against Russian oppression.

In other words, from our results it seems that the cultural-political closeness to the Russian regime and the Russian revolutionary context heavily factored into the development of the discourse on Finnish rebel terrorism – both when it comes to how Finnish nationalists' and separatists' activities were cultivated against the background of the political violence of the Russian revolutionaries and the representatives of the Russian regime, and also how the new Finnish deeds of political violence were framed and evaluated.

6 Conclusions

This study has demonstrated the considerable opportunities for historical analysis afforded by distant reading of national online newspaper corpora through the

Korp interface. A crucial part of the investigation has been the integrative interdisciplinary collaboration between Swedish and Finnish researchers in the history of terrorism and natural language processing, which enabled a complex comparative and contrastive analysis of the historical discourse on terrorism based on both distant and close reading. As we have seen in this chapter, the LT-based automatic linguistic annotations offered by Korp – notably lemmatization and dependency parsing, which enable its "word picture" functionality – together with its sophisticated search abilities add considerable value to this kind of investigation, enabling broad trawling as well as targeted trolling.

As expected, our findings strengthen the earlier hypothesis within history of terrorism that the modern meaning of sub-state terrorism was not widely established in the 19th century. The study also further contributes to the understanding of the historical emergence of terrorism in Europe in at least three ways. Firstly, our results support the supposition that terrorism remained associated with state terror and the Russian context for a long time, but also indicate a great diversity in state character attributions for the later period of the 19th century, as manifested by its presence in a number of national contexts. Secondly, another important finding is the rare occurrence during the 19th century of attributions of terrorism to anarchist and Fenian militants that otherwise figure prominently in the contemporary academic discourse on 19th century terrorism. Although we are not the first to note this, we present new quantitative findings that support this supposition and indicate how such groupings were only in the early 1900s incorporated into the concept of terrorism specifically. Thirdly, we provide a singular exposition of the broadening of terrorism to previously analytically neglected national contexts of anti-colonial separatist terrorism. In this, by turning from trawling to trolling in the form of specifically targeted search methodologies, our investigation yielded detailed novel insights into the domestication of rebel terrorism in Finland. These results indicate that closeness to both the Russian regime and Russian rebels factored into how terrorism in Finland became used specifically in reference to perceived nationalist and separatist activities.

It seems safe to assume that the use of LT resources could contribute further to research on the history of terrorism. Concerning future research, there are now LT methods – for example, topic modelling and (neural) word embedding models – which allow for studies of a fuller range of linguistic expressions of given concepts in vast volumes of text, even in the absence of resources such as Princeton WordNet, which in any case are available only for a few languages.[5] There is a

5 In order to be useful for purposes such as the one described here, the vocabulary coverage of such a lexical resource should arguably correspond to a full-sized reference dictionary of a

large wordnet for Finnish (Lindén and Niemi 2014), but not for Swedish, although there are other similar lexical resources for Swedish (see Dannélls, Borin, and Friberg Heppin 2021). When dealing with texts in their entirety rather than words in isolation, in order to see the full picture we should also take into account such linguistic devices as *coreference* – that is when *this phenomenon*, *version*, and *it* all can refer to *terrorism*.

Importantly in our context, the LT methods also apply in multilingual settings, which would allow us to look for word usage correspondences across languages (Ruder, Vulić, and Søgaard 2019). Through wider trawling, one may build a more comprehensive and complex picture of the meanings of terrorism during the 19th and 20th century, and one could go deeper through trolling of terrorism-related nouns such as *attentat* and *dynamitard*, or through the use of diachronic word embeddings to trace conceptual changes in terms over time.

A final given extension of our investigation would be to investigate later periods as well as to seek out the emergence of terrorism in other "discursive transnational bodies of water", including the wider Baltic, Atlantic, and Pacific contexts.

Bibliography

Adesam, Yvonne, Dana Dannélls & Nina Tahmasebi. 2019. Exploring the quality of the digital historical newspaper archive KubHist. *Digital Humanities in the Nordic Countries Conference (DHN) 4*, 9–17.

Backer, Hermanni & Manuel Frias (eds.). 2013. *Planning the Bothnian Sea – key findings of the Plan Bothnia project. Digital edition*. Turku: Finepress Turku.

Borin, Lars, Markus Forsberg & Johan Roxendal. 2012. Korp – the corpus infrastructure of Språkbanken. *International Conference on Language Resources and Evaluation (LREC) 8*, 474–478.

Borin, Lars & Richard Johansson. 2014. Kulturomik: Att spana efter språkliga och kulturella förändringar i digitala textarkiv. Blog Historia i en digital värld.

language, say a minimum of 50,000 entries (Princeton WordNet has more than 150,000 entries). Against this background, lists such as that found at http://globalwordnet.org/resources/wordnets-in-the-world/ are somewhat deceptive. First, many of the 78 links to wordnets provided there are dead. Further, no (easily retrievable) statistics are given even for those wordnets which can be accessed. A fair picture of the state of the art can be gleaned from the Open Multilingual Wordnet page http://compling.hss.ntu.edu.sg/omw/, where data on wordnets for 150 languages are provided, that is about 2% of the world's languages. From this information we can calculate that the average number of words (lemmas) in these 150 wordnets is 10,780, but in true Zipfian fashion the median is much lower: 1,429. A size of 50,000 words is attained only at the 95th percentile, that is, about 8 of these wordnets fulfil the requirement.

Dannélls, Dana, Lars Borin & Karin Friberg Heppin (eds.). 2021. *Swedish FrameNet++: Harmonization, integration, method development and natural language processing applications*. Amsterdam: John Benjamins.
Ditrych, Ondřej. 2011. A genealogy of terrorism in states' discourse. Ph.D. diss., Prague: Charles University.
Ditrych, Ondřej. 2014. *Tracing the discourses of terrorism: Identity, genealogy and the state*. Basingstoke: Palgrave Macmillan.
Erlenbusch, Verena. 2015. Terrorism and revolutionary violence: The emergence of terrorism in the French revolution. *Critical Studies on Terrorism* 8 (2). 193–210.
Fellbaum, Christiane (ed.). 1998. *WordNet: An electronic lexical database*. Cambridge: MIT Press.
Fridlund, Mats. 2018. Digital history 1.5: Historical research between domesticated and paradigmatic digital methods. HumLab Seminar Series, Umeå University, 18 May 2018. https://web.archive.org/web/20190331123529/http://stream.humlab.umu.se/?streamName=digital_history_1_5.
Fridlund, Mats. 2020. Digital history 1.5: A middle way between normal and paradigmatic digital historical research. In Mats Fridlund, Petri Paju and Mila Oiva (eds.), *Digital histories: emergent approaches within the new digital history*, 69–87. Helsinki: Helsinki University Press.
Fridlund, Mats, Daniel Brodén, Leif-Jöran Olsson & Lars Borin. 2020. Trawling the Gulf of Bothnia of news: A big data analysis of the emergence of terrorism in Swedish and Finnish newspapers, 1780–1926. In Costanza Navarretta and Maria Eskevich (eds.), *Selected Papers from the CLARIN Annual Conference 2020, Virtual Edition*, 61–65. (Linköping Electronic Conference Proceedings 180).
Fridlund, Mats, Leif-Jöran Olsson, Daniel Brodén & Lars Borin. 2019. Trawling for terrorists: A big data analysis of conceptual meanings and contexts in Swedish newspapers, 1780–1926. In Melvin Wevers, Mohammed Hasanuzzaman, Gaël Dias, Marten Düring and Adam Jatowt (eds.), *The 5th International Workshop on Computational History (HistoInformatics 2019)*, 30–39.
Fridlund, Mats & Daniel Sallamaa. 2016. Radikale Mittel, gemäßigte Ziele: Repression und Widerstand im Großfürstentum Finnland. *Osteuropa* 66 (4). 35–47.
Graham, Shawn, Ian Milligan & Scott Weingart. 2016. *Exploring big historical data: The historian's macroscope*. London: Imperial College Press.
Ifversen, Jan. 2011. About key concepts and how to study them. *Contributions to the History of Concepts* 6 (1). 65–88.
Jackson, Richard. 2008. The ghosts of state terror: Knowledge, politics and terrorism studies. *Critical Studies on Terrorism* 1 (3). 377–392.
Jensen, Richard Bach. 2018. The 1904 assassination of governor general Bobrikov: Tyrannicide, anarchism, and the expanding scope of "terrorism". *Terrorism and Political Violence* 30 (5). 828–843.
Karsvall, Olof & Lars Borin. 2018. SDHK meets NER: Linking place names with medieval charters and historical maps. *Digital Humanities in the Nordic Countries Conference (DHN) 3*, 38–50.
Ker, James Campbell. 1917. *Political trouble in India*. Calcutta: Superintendent Government Printing, India.
Kujala, Antti. 1992. Finnish radicals and the Russian revolutionary movement, 1899–1907. *Revolutionary Russia* 5 (2). 172–192.
Law, Randall D. 2009. *Terrorism: A history*. Cambridge: Polity Press.

Lindén, Krister & Jyrki Niemi. 2014. Is it possible to create a very large wordnet in 100 days? An evaluation. *Language Resources and Evaluation* 48 (2). 191–201.

Miller, Martin A. 2013. *The foundations of modern terrorism: State, society and the dynamics of political violence*. Cambridge: Cambridge University Press.

NLF. 2011a. The Finnish Sub-corpus of the Newspaper and Periodical Corpus of the National Library of Finland, Kielipankki Version.

NLF. 2011b. The Swedish Sub-corpus of the Newspaper and Periodical Corpus of the National Library of Finland, Kielipankki Version.

Paju, Petri, Mila Oiva & Mats Fridlund. 2020. Digital and distant histories: Emergent approaches within the new digital history. In Mats Fridlund, Petri Paju and Mila Oiva (eds.), *Digital histories: Emergent approaches within the new digital history*, 3–18. Helsinki: Helsinki University Press.

Pettersson, Eva & Lars Borin. 2022. Swedish Diachronic Corpus. In Darja Fišer and Andreas Witt (eds.), *CLARIN. The infrastructure for language resources.* Berlin: De Gruyter.

Rapoport, David C.. 2003. The four waves of rebel terror and September 11. In Charles W. Kegley Jr. (ed.), *The new global terrorism: Characteristics, causes, controls*, 36–52. Upper Saddle River: Prentice Hall.

Ruder, Sebastian, Ivan Vulić & Anders Søgaard. 2019. A survey of cross-lingual word embedding models. *Journal of Artificial Intelligence Research* 65: 569–631.

Sageman, Marc. 2017. *Turning to political violence: The emergence of terrorism*. Philadelphia: University of Pennsylvania Press.

Salmi, Hannu, Petri Paju, Heli Rantala, Asko Nivala, Aleksi Vesanto & Filip Ginter. 2013. The reuse of texts in Finnish newspapers and journals, 1771–1920: A digital humanities perspective. *Historical Methods: A Journal of Quantitative and Interdisciplinary History* 54 (1). 14–28.

Tahmasebi, Nina, Lars Borin, Gabriele Capannini, Devdatt Dubhashi, Peter Exner, Markus Forsberg, Gerhard Gossen, Fredrik Johansson, Richard Johansson, Mikael Kågebäck, Olof Mogren, Pierre Nugues & Thomas Risse. 2015. Visions and open challenges for a knowledge-based culturomics. *International Journal on Digital Libraries* 15 (2–4). 169–187.

Tahmasebi, Nina, Niklas Hagen, Daniel Brodén & Mats Malm. 2019. A convergence of methodologies: Notes on data-intensive humanities research. *Digital Humanities in the Nordic Countries Conference (DHN)* 4, 437–449.

Tangherlini, Timothy R. & Peter Leonard. 2013. Trawling in the Sea of the Great Unread: Sub-corpus topic modeling and Humanities research. *Poetics* 41 (6). 725–749.

Verhoeven, Claudia. 2004. April 4, 1866: The Karakozov Case and the Making of Revolutionary Terrorism. Ph.D. diss., University of California, Los Angeles.

Verhoeven, Claudia. 2009. *The odd man Karakozov: Imperial Russia, modernity, and the birth of terrorism*. Ithaca: Cornell University Press.

Viklund, Jon & Lars Borin. 2016. How can big data help us study rhetorical history? In Koenraad De Smedt (ed.), *Selected Papers from the CLARIN Annual Conference, October 14–16, 2015, Wroclaw, Poland*, 79–93. (Linköping Electronic Conference Proceedings 123).

Weller, Toni (ed.). 2013. *History in the digital age*. London: Routledge.

Index

https://doi.org/10.1515/9783110767377-032